New International Fourth Edition

ABBREVIATIONS
DICTIONARY

New International Fourth Edition

ABBREVIATIONS DICTIONARY

Abbreviations
Acronyms
Anonyms
Contractions
Initials and Nicknames
Short Forms and Slang Shortcuts
Signs and Symbols

by Ralph De Sola

**American Elsevier
Publishing Company, Inc.**

New York   London   Amsterdam

AMERICAN ELSEVIER PUBLISHING COMPANY, INC.
52 Vanderbilt Avenue, New York, N.Y. 10017

ELSEVIER PUBLISHING COMPANY
335 Jan Van Galenstraat, P.O. Box 211
Amsterdam, The Netherlands

International Standard Book Number 0-444-00139-5
Library of Congress Card Number 73-7687

Library of Congress Cataloging in Publication Data

De Sola, Ralph, 1908–
    Abbreviations dictionary.
    1. Abbreviations, English.   2. Acronyms.
3. Signs and symbols.   I. Title.
PE1693.D4   1974   423'.1   73-7687
ISBN 0-444-00139-5

Manufactured in the United States of America

Contents

Preface

Contemporary conversation, as well as modern printed communication, is filled with undefined bits of jargon. Abbreviations, acronyms, conversational shortcuts, geographical equivalents, and specialized terms occupy some 25 percent of the mass of words heard or overheard. Anyone from another industry or profession or walk of life will be almost completely baffled if subjected to such talk and to such writing. The pace of modern life has accelerated the appearance of new communicative forms to such an extent that it was impossible to include in this edition many last-minute entries, some of which are: **Exxon** (formerly Esso); **FEO,** Federal Energy Office; **Mipu,** *Mikropunkt* (German—microdot) —World War II's masterpiece of espionage technique; **ppv,** people-powered vehicle; **System ABC,** System of Automation of Bibliography through Computerization.

For this reason this new international fourth edition contains many items not usually found in such reference works. All this material would not be germane to such a dictionary were it not that such terms serve as cultural abbreviations in contemporary conversation. Reference librarians and school teachers assure me that such definitions are necessary and add much to this new edition.

Numerous entries, definitions of abbreviations, acronyms and other short forms in this greatly expanded new international fourth edition of *Abbreviations Dictionary* appear as a result of generous contributions and suggestions made by many friends and associates. To all of them, my sincere thanks and appreciation.

Many critics of previous editions graciously lent their support to this new volume by providing fresh material, by suggesting new sources of information, and by donating their support in many practical ways. Both George F. Drake of Santa Barbara and Edward J. Reid of Stromberg DatagraphiX in San Diego contributed their entire collection of short forms. Martin J. Lendzian, also of San Diego, once again gave freely of his knowledge and loaned valuable reference material for use in this edition. Many new entries were contributed by Paul Whitlock of San Diego. K.G. Brown and Michael J. Sadoski both made many worthwhile suggestions, provided needed material and made several important corrections in the manuscript. Also, my thanks to James Denning of Cobalt, Ontario and Howard Sherkin of Toronto, for their many new entries.

Reference librarians continued to provide encouragement and help in compiling short forms. Many on the staff of the San Diego Public Library were helpful, including Mary Allely, Michael J. Archuleta, Patricia Darling, Anna

Martinez, Dalton Degitz, David Galt, Max Gozesky, Helen Johnson, Matt Katka, Anne Koran, Margret Queen, Ed Rouen, Lloyd Wisdom, Vere Wolf, and others. At Mesa College, aid was received from Warren Heyer, Jeanne Newhouse, and their many student assistants in the library.

Dorothy, my wife and companion, aided in so many ways to help make what will hopefully be the most comprehensive volume of its kind ever to be published. She deserves a great deal of thanks for her unrelenting efforts.

Readers and researchers owe much to the entire staff of American Elsevier and their printer for their fine efforts and cooperation in producing the new international fourth edition of the *Abbreviations Dictionary*. To them my gratitude and much deserved credit.

Ralph De Sola
San Diego, California

Introduction

Definitions of Terms

abbreviations abridged contractions such as acdt: accident; AEC: Atomic Energy Commission; NASA: National Aeronautics and Space Administration.

acronyms words formed from letters in a series of related words such as ABLE: Activity Balance Line Evaluation; AGREE: Advisory Group on Reliability of Electronic Equipment; DYNAMO: Dynamic Action Management Operations.

anonyms attempts of authors to enjoy anonymity while maintaining their identity by such devices as the capitalized diphthong AE standing for Aeon, pen name of George William Russell.

contractions words shortened by dropping non-pronounced letters which are indicated by apostrophes as in can't: can not; li'l: little; doesn't: does not; and let's: let us.

initials FDR: Franklin Delano Roosevelt; HST: Harry S. Truman; JFK: John Fitzgerald Kennedy; LBJ: Lyndon Baines Johnson; initials of all American Presidents are included as well as initials of other noted personalities.

nicknames Al: Alfred; Bea: Beatrice; Hal: Harold; Ike: Dwight David Eisenhower; Isaac.

short forms amps: amperes; Olds: Oldsmobile; pots.: potentiometers.

sign $ & ¢ —dollars and cents.

slang shortcuts B-girl: bar girl; C-note: $100 bill; 1-G: $1000.

symbols Al: aluminum; Pt: platinum; Rx: prescription; recipe.

Editors—Teachers—Writers

Editors, teachers, and writers will perform a splendid service for readers if they insist that abbreviations and acronyms be defined the first time they are used. The old argument, "everyone knows what that stands for," no longer is true. Many abbreviations stand for at least ten different things. Many acronyms, also, stand for several different things.

The style of writing abbreviations and acronyms requires the attention of editors, teachers, and writers. They should be unwilling to let things get out of hand to the point that a paragraph comes cluttered with unexplained capital-letter combinations. Technical literature will become almost impossible to read if the permissive trend continues wherein all abbreviations and acronyms appear in solid capital letters and without benefit of preliminary definition.

Throughout this *Abbreviations Dictionary* an attempt is made to follow the rules of English grammar. Capital letters are reserved for proper nouns. Lowercase letters are used for common nouns. However, when custom has become so strong that correctly written short forms are not recognized quickly, their more common equivalents are added parenthetically: icbm (ICBM): intercontinental ballistic missile.

Explanations

If readers and researchers did not continue to find themselves engulfed and ensnared in the modern abracadabra of abbreviations and acronyms, in the bewildering bafflegab and gobbledygook of corporationese, initialese, officialese, pentagonese, politicalese, and technicalese, there would be no need to provide this new international fourth edition of the *Abbreviations Dictionary*.

Because so many creators of abbreviations and coiners of acronyms fail to define their shortcuts the first time they use them, and because so many who use them also fail to define these things, it becomes increasingly difficult to understand what people are saying or writing when their sayings and writings are filled with abbreviations, acronyms, anonyms, contractions, initials, nicknames, pseudonyms, short forms, signs, slang shortcuts, and symbols created for their own convenience, without regard for their ability to create communicative and easily understood statements.

Daily speech, newspapers, magazines, books, and signs along the airways, highways, railways, and waterways reveal the universality of these shortcuts to communication and the growing tendency to use and devise more and more of them. This appears to be done in response to the rapid development of technological civilization. But witness the confusion compounded when someone without a knowledge of Spanish turns on the C tap in a shower bath in Acapulco, Buenos Aires, or Madrid. Hot water steams out instead of cold. North is N in most languages of western civilization, but west can be W or O or even V.

Abbreviations of every sort cover contemporary civilization like a deep and ever-deepening snowdrift, concealing the main features of the landscape; leaving the beholder mystified and perplexed by the overwhelming obscurity imposed by these letter and number combinations. Usually these shortcuts to communication are created without reference to the niceties of typography, the requirements of official and logical regulations, or even the rules of grammar. Most appear without definitions. More and more appear each year. And more and more duplicate already existing abbreviations standing for other things. The letter a, for example, stands for more than twenty-five different things. Capital A stands for more than thirty different things. And so it goes throughout the alphabet, with many varied combinations of letters and numbers, signs and symbols.

Arrangement

Everything in this book is arranged in alphabetical and numerical order. Particles, prepositions, and the ampersand (&) are ignored in the arrangement. For example, U of P is alphabetized as UP; A & M and IT & T are placed as if they were AM and ITT. The singular and plural and tense of words do not alter the general sense of the abbreviation defined.

Golden Rule

"When in doubt, spell it out," insisted Ralph Bayless when he was chief engineer of all General Dynamics engineering organizations of Convair. He urged all to define abbreviations the first time they were used.

If, for example, a Gulf Missile Range is being described, and the term *GMR* will be used again and again, the text should begin something like this:

> The Gulf Missile Range (GMR) affords facilities for national defense and space exploration. GMR personnel are active in all phases of aerospace research, development, and engineering. GMR headquarters are in Mobile.

Common sense rules about abbreviations are most often ignored. Therefore it is necessary to repeat that short words like Maine, Ohio, Samoa, etc., should not be abbreviated, although their unofficial abbreviations exist and are shown in this book. Similarly it is best to avoid the truncation of words spelling other words when abbreviated: cat.: catalog; king.: kingdom; man.: management.

Because this is a reference dictionary there are many duplications. Airlines have two and three-letter designations. The same is true of many place names. Many items are included so it will not be necessary for readers to try to guess what the abbreviations are intended to mean. Many unauthorized abbreviations are included for the same reason—to help readers find their way through the alphabet soup.

Capitalization

Capitalization of abbreviations, according to Department of Defense Military Standard 12-B (Mil-Std 12-B), must follow the rules of English grammar. All proper nouns are capitalized. All common nouns are written in lowercase letters. Units of weight, measure, and velocity, such as lb, kg, in., cc., mm, rpm, and the like, appear in lowercase to avoid confusion with other letter combinations they resemble.

Many military establishments and offices use full capitals for everything because message machines are provided only with capital letters. That is why many engineering drawings supplied the armed forces contain all abbreviations in capital letters. It is also true many draftsmen are afraid small letters will fill up, especially *a's, b's, d's, e's, g's, o's,* and the like. Therefore they also like to use capital letters. In text, however, 1500 RPM presents a typographical blob, as compared to the more sophisticated 1500 rpm.

At first loran was LORAN. As people became used to it, it became Loran. Today it is loran. The same is true of other combinations. The trend is to capitalize only those letters standing for proper nouns, running all common nouns in lowercase. Nevertheless, for the sake of readers and researchers, some incorrectly rendered abbreviations appear in this book. Many people have a marked tendency to capitalize everything they think is important. If this tendency is unchecked, confusion follows. All abbreviations and acronyms look alike. So follow the commonsense rules of good grammar and correct usage.

Chemical element symbols, however, have the first letter capitalized: Au (gold), Zn (zinc), etc. The second letter of a chemical symbol always appears in lowercase.

Exceptions

The singular, plural, and tense of the words abbreviated do not alter abbreviations except in a few instances, such as fig.: figure; figs.: figures; lb: pound; lbs: pounds; no.: number; nos: numbers; p: page; pp: pages; S: Saint; *SS: Saints.*

However, readers should be aware the International (*SI*) System of Measurements calls for the abolition of all pluralized abbreviations. Hence in. stands for inch or inches, lb for pound or pounds, oz for ounce or ounces. This system will probably gain widespread approval.

Documentary abbreviations are rendered as follows: FARs (Failure Analysis Reports) or IRs (Inspector's Reports) or RARs (Reliability Action Reports). In the singular they appear as FAR, IR, RAR.

Italics

Items from Latin and other non-English languages, as well as titles of books and periodicals, are usually set in italic type. Many physical symbols are also set in italics to differentiate them from other letter combinations they resemble.

Punctuation

Short forms are devised to save time and space and to overcome the necessity of repeating long words and phrases. All punctuation is avoided in modern practice unless the form is taken from Latin or there is some conventional use demanding punctuation, as in the case of academic degrees and a few governmental designations. U.S.A. is the country; USA is the army. D.C. is the District of Columbia; DC is direct currenct when used as a noun. Cash on delivery is not cod but c.o.d. Similarly, fig., figs. and no. require periods to keep readers from thinking they may be words instead of abbreviations for figure, figures, and number. Again, when in doubt, spell it out.

Signs and Symbols

Frequently used signs and symbols are in the back of this dictionary. Many are found on typewriters (&: ampersand—the *and* sign; *: asterisk; ¢: cent; $: dollar; %: percent).

Symbols include the chemical elements (Al: aluminum; Au: gold—from the Latin *aurum*; C: carbon; Sn: tin—from the Latin *stannum*). All are listed in the alphabetical section without special definition to indicate they are not abbreviations but symbols. The chemical elements are also grouped together in the back of this dictionary.

Airlines use two-letters symbols for convenience in baggage handling, ticketing, and scheduling operations. Thus American Airlines is AA, Delta Air Lines is DL, National Airlines is NA, Pan American World Airways is PA, United Air Lines is UA. All airlines are shown in these two-letter code symbols as well as in other multiletter combinations. Railroads and steamship lines are included in the alphabetical sections.

Naval craft are designated by many arbitrary symbols. All available are shown.

This is the short and the long of it.

—Shakespeare

A

a: abbreviation; absent; acceleration in feet per second; account; acre; adjective; adult; aerial; afternoon; altitude intercept; amateur; ampere; annealing; anthracite; arc; are (unit of metric land measure); area; argent; at; atmosphere; audit; auditor; automatic; available; aviation; aviator; axis; azure; distance from leading edge to aerodynamic center

a′: all (contraction); a minute (angle); a prime

a″: second (angle); a doubleprime

a‴: a triple-prime

a: *am, an, an der* (German-on the, at the); angle of attack; *annus* (Latin-year); attenuation constant (symbol)

A: absolute; absolute temperature; academy; acid; acoustic source; actual weight of an aircraft; aircraft; airman; Alaska Steamship Company; Alcoa Steamship Company; Alfacode for A; ambassador; America; American; Americanization; Americanize; Amos, The Book of; amphibian; Anchor Line; anode; anterior; April; argon; Army; artillery; aspect ratio; astragal; Atlantic; atomic weight; attack; August; Austria (auto plaque); chemical activity; first van der Waals constant; Fraunhofer line due to oxygen; linear acceleration; mean sound absorption coefficient; total acidity

A-1 air personnel officer; excellent; first class; first rate; *Lloyd's Register* symbol indicating a vessel's equipment is first rate; personnel section of an air force staff; skyraider single-engine general-purpose attack aircraft flown from aircraft carriers; top quality; tops; very best

A-I: (motion pictures) for general patronage

Alc: Airman, first class

A2: aortic second sound

A-2: air intelligence officer; almost A-1 in quality; intelligence section of an air force staff; just short of being the best

A-II: (motion pictures) for adults and adolescents only

A-3 air operations and training officer; operations and training section of an air force staff; Skywarrior twin-engine turbojet tactical all-weather attack aircraft operating from aircraft carriers; training and operations

A-III: (motion pictures) for adults only

A-4 air material and supply officer; material and supply section of an air force staff; Skyhawk single-engine turbojet attack aircraft operating from aircraft carriers; supply and materiel

A-IV: (motion pictures) for adults with reservations

A-5 planning; supersonic twin-engine turbojet all-weather attack aircraft operating from aircraft carriers

A-6 communications

A-6A: Intruder twin-engine turbojet long-range carrier-based low-altitude attack aircraft

A: *abajo* (Spanish—down); *abasso* (Italian—down); *alas* (Finnish—down); *albus* (Latin—white); arrival; *arrivare* (Italian—arrival); arrive; *arrive* (French—arrival); *auf* (German—up); *aus* (German—out); *avbeta* (Swedish—departure)

Å: angstrom unit

Å: *aas* (Dano-Norwegian—hills)

aa: acting appointment; adjectives; always afloat; approximate absolute; armature accelerator; author's alteration

aa(AA): achievement age; antiaircraft

aa: equal parts

a-a: air-to-air

AA: absolute alcohol; absolute altitude; achievement age; Addicts Anonymous; Administrative Assistant; Aerolineas Argentinas (Argentine Airlines); Airman Apprentice; Alcoholics Anonymous; Aluminum (Company of) America; American Airlines; American Association; Ann Arbor (railroad); Ansett Airways; antiaircraft; Appropriate Authority; arithmetic average; Arlington Annex; Asian-African; Athletic Association; author's alteration(s); Automobile Association; Aviation Annex; *Aviatsionnaya Armiya* (Russian—Air Army)

AA: *Air Almanac; Astronautica Acta* (journal of the International Astronautical Federation)

A.A.: Associate in Accounting; Associate in Arts

aaa: acute anxiety attack; amalgam

aa & a: armor, armament, and ammunition

Aaa: Alaska (government style is to spell it out—there is no official abbreviation)

AAA: Agricultural Adjustment Administration; Agricultural Aircraft Association; Alaska (unofficial abbreviation—government style recommends name be spelled out); All American Aviation; Allegheny Airlines (3-letter coding); Allied Artists of America; American Academy of Advertising; American Academy of Allergy; American Accordionists Association; American Accounting Association; American Airship Association; American Antarctic Association; American Anthropological Association; American Arbitration Association; American Association of Anatomists; American Astronomers Association; American Australian Association; American Automobile Association; antiaircraft artillery; Antique Airplane Association; Appraisers Association of America; Archives of American Art; Army Audit Agency; Associated Agents of America; Association of Attenders and Alumni (Hague Academy of International Law); Association of Average Adjusters

AAAA: American Association for the Advancement of Atheism; American Association of Advertising Agencies; Army Aviation Association of America; Associated Actors and Artistes of America

AAAB: American Association of Architectural Bibliographers

AAAC: American Association for the Advancement of Criminology; Antiaircraft Artillery Command

AAACE: American Association of Agricultural College Editors

AAAD: American Athletic Association for the Deaf

AAAE: American Association of Airport Executives

AAA (AFL-CIO): Actors and Artistes of America

AAAEE: American Afro-Asian Educational Exchange

A.A. Ag.: Associate of Arts in Agriculture

AAAI: Affiliated Advertising Agencies International

AAAIMH: American Association for the Abolition of Involuntary Mental Hospitalization

AAAIP: Advanced Army Aircraft Instrumentation Program

AAAIS: Antiaircraft Artillery Information Service; Antiaircraft Artillery Intelligence Service

aaal: abolish all abortion laws

AAAL: American Academy of Arts and Letters

AAAM: American Association of Aircraft Manufacturers; American Association for Automotive Medicine

AAAN: American Academy of Applied Nutrition

AAAOC: Antiaircraft Artillery Operation Center

AAAR: Association for the Advancement of Aging Research

AAARC: Antiaircraft Artillery Reception Center

AAAS: American Academy of Arts and Sciences; American Academy of Asian Studies; American Association for the Advancement of Science

A.A.A.S.: Associate in Arts and Science

AAASS: American Association for the Advancement of Slavic Studies

AAASUSS: Association of Administrative Assistants and Secretaries to United States Senators

AAAUS: Association of Average Adjusters of the United States

AAB: Aircraft Accident Board; American Association of Bioanalysts; Army Air Base; Army Artillery Board; Association of Applied Biologists

AABB: American Association of Blood Banks

AABC: American Amateur Baseball Congress; Association for the Advancement of Blind Children

AABD: Aid to the Aged, Blind, or Disabled

AABEVM: Association of American Boards of Examiners in Veterinary Medicine

AABGA: American Association of Botanical Gardens and Arboretums

AABI: Antilles Air Boats Incorporated

AABL: Associated Australian Banks of London

AABM: Association of American Battery Manufacturers

AABPDF: Allied Association of Bleachers, Printers, Dyers, and Finishers

AABT: Association for the Advancement of the Behavioral Therapies

AABTM: American Association of Baggage Traffic Managers

aaby: as amended by

aac: automatic aperture control; average annual cost

AAC: Aeronautical Advisory Council; Aeronautical Approach Chart; Aircraft Armament Change; Alaskan Air Command; All-American Canal (serving California and Baja California); Alumnae Advisory Center; American Academy of Criminalistics; American Alpine Club; American Alumni Council; American Association of Criminology; American Cement Corporation (stock exchange symbol); Antiaircraft Command; Army Air Corps; Association of American Choruses; Association of American Colleges; Automotive Advertisers Council

A.A.C: *anno ante Christum* (Latin—year before Christ)—same as before Christ

AACA: Antique Automobile Club of America; Automotive Air Conditioning Association

AACAP: Association of American Colleges Arts Program

AACB: Aeronautics and Astronautics Coordinating Board

AACBC: American Association of College Baseball Coaches

AACBP: American Academy of Crown and Bridge Prosthodontics

aacc: all-attitude control capability; automatic approach control complex

AACC: American Association of Cereal Chemists; American Association of Clinical Chemists; American Association for Contamination Control; American Association of Credit Counselors; American Automatic Control Council; Association for the Aid of Crippled Children

AACCLA: Association of American Chambers of Commerce in Latin America

AACCP: American Association of Colleges of Chiropody-Podiatry

AACE: American Association of Cost Engineers

AACFT: Army Aircraft

AACHS: Afro-American Cultural and Historical Society

AACI: American Association for Conservation Information; Association of Americans and Canadians in Israel

AACJC: American Association of Community and Junior Colleges

AACM: American Academy of Compensation Medicine

AACO: American Association of Certified Orthoptists; Assault Airlift Control Office(r)

AACOBS: Australian Advisory Council on Bibliographical Services

AACOMS: Army Area Communications System

AACP: American Academy for Cerebral Palsy; American Academy for Child Psychiatry; American Association of Colleges of Podiatry; American Association of Commercial Publications; American Association of Convention Planners; American Association of Correctional Psychologists

AACPR: American Association for Cleft Palate Rehabilitation

AACR: American Association for Cancer Research

AACRAO: American Association of Collegiate Registrars and Admissions Officers

AACS: Airborne Astrographic Camera System; Airways and Air Communications Service; Army Airways Communications System

AACSA: Anglo-American Corporation of South Africa

AACSB: American Association of Collegiate Schools of Business

AACSL: American Association for the Comparative Study of Law

AACSM: Airways and Air Communications Service Manual

AACT: American Association of Commodity Traders

AACTE: American Association of Colleges for Teacher Education

AACUBO: American Association of College and University Business Officers

aad (AAD): alloxazine adenine dinucleotide

AAD: Aircraft Assignment Directive; American Academy of Dentists; American Academy of Dermatology; Army Air Defense

AADA: Advanced Air Depot Area; American Academy of Dramatic Arts; Army Air Defense Area

AADC: Army Air Defense Command(er)

AADCP: Army Air Defense Command Post

AADE: American Association of Dental Editors; American Association of Dental Examiners

AADIS: Army Air Defense Information Service

AADLA: Art and Antique Dealers League of America

AADM: American Academy of Dental Medicine

AADN: American Association of Doctors' Nurses

AADOO: Army Air Defense Operations Office(r)

AADPA: American Academy of Dental Practice Administration

AADS: Advanced Army Defense System; American Association of Dental Schools; American Association of Dermatology and Syphilology; Army Air Defense System

AAE: American Association of Endodontists; American Association of Engineers; Army Aviation Engineers

AAEA: American Agricultural Editors Association

AAEC: Association of American Editorial Cartoonists; Australian Atomic Energy Commission

A.Ae.E.: Associate in Aeronautical Engineering

AAEE: American Academy of Environmental Engineers; American Association of Economic Entomologists

AAEH: Association to Advance Ethical Hypnosis

AAEKNE: American Association of Elementary-Kindergarten-Nursery Educators

AAEP: American Association of Equine Practitioners

AAES: Australian Army Education Service

AAEW: Atlantic Airborne Early Warning

a-a-f: acetic-alcohol-formalin (fixing fluid)

AAF: American Advertising Federation; American Air Filter (company); American Architectural Foundation; American Astronautical Federation; Army Air Field; Army and Air Force; Army Air Forces

A.A. Fair: Erle Stanley Gardner

AAFB: Auxiliary Air Force Base

aafc (AAFC): antiaircraft fire control

AAFC: Air Accounting and Finance Center; Army Air Forces Center; Army Air Force Classification Center; Association of Advertising Film Companies

AAFCE: Allied Air Force, Central Europe

AAFCO: Association of American Feed Control Officials; Association of American Fertilizer Control Officials

AAFCWF: Army and Air Force Central Welfare Fund; Army and Air Force Civilian Welfare Fund

AAFE: American Association of Feed Exporters

AAFEC: Army Air Forces Engineering Command

AAFEMPS: Army and Air Force Exchange and Motion Picture Service

AAFES: Army and Air Force Exchange Service

AAFIS: Army Air Forces Intelligence School

AAFM: American Association of Feed Microscopists

AAFMC: Army Air Forces Materiel Center

AAFMPS: Army and Air Force Motion Picture Service

AAFNE: Allied Air Force, Northern Europe

AAFNS: Army Air Forces Navigation School

AAFOIC: Army Air Forces Officer in Charge

AAFPS: Army and Air Force Pilot School; Army and Air Force Postal Service

AAFRS: American Academy of Facial Plastic and Reconstructive Surgery

AAFS: American Association of Foot Specialists; American Academy of Forensic Sciences

AAFSE: Allied Air Force, Southern Europe

AAFSS: Advanced Aerial Fire Support System

AAFSW: Association of American Foreign Service Women

AAFTS: Army Air Forces Technical School

AAFWB: Army and Air Force Wage Board

AAG: Air Adjutant General; Association of American Geographers

AAGC: American Association of Gifted Children

AAGFO: American Academy of Gold Foil Operators

AAGp: Aeromedical Airlift Group (USAF)

AAGP: American Academy of General Practice

A. Agr.: Associate in Agriculture

A.Agri.: Associate in Agriculture

AAGR: Air-to-Air Gunnery Range

AAGS: All-American Gladiolus Selections

AAGUS: American Association of Genito-Urinary Surgeons

AAH: American Academy of Homiletics

aaha: awaiting action of higher authority

AAHA: American Animal Hospital Association; American Association of Homes for the Aging; American Association of Hospital Accountants

AAHC: American Association of Hospital Consultants

AAHD: American Academy of the History of Dentistry

AAHDC: American Association of Hospital Dental Chiefs

AAHE: American Association for Higher Education; American Association of Housing Educators

A.A.H.E.: Associate in Arts in Home Economics

AAHM: American Association for the History of Medicine; Association of Architectural Hardware Manufacturers

AAHP: American Association for Hospital Planning; American Association of Hospital Podiatrists; American Association for Humanistic Psychology

AAHPA: American Association of Hospital Purchasing Agents

AAHPER: American Association for Health, Physical Education, and Recreation

AAHPhA: American Animal Health Pharmaceutical Association

AAHQ: Allied Air Headquarters

AAHS: American Aviation Historical Society

aai: air-to-air identification; angle-of-approach indicator

AAI: African-American Institute; Afro-American Institute; Agricultural Ammonia Institute;

Akron Art Institute; Alfred Adler Institute; Allied Armies in Italy (World War II); American Association of Immunologists

AAIA: Association of American Indian Affairs

AAIAN: Association for the Advancement of Instruction about Alcohol and Narcotics

AAIB: American Association of Instructors of the Blind

AAIC: Allied Air Intelligence Center

AAICD: American Association of Imported Car Dealers

AAID: American Academy of Implant Dentures; American Association of Industrial Dentists

AAIE: American Association of Industrial Editors; American Association of Industrial Engineers

AAII: Association for the Advancement of Invention and Innovation

AAIM: American Association of Industrial Management

AAIN: American Association of Industrial Nurses

AAIPS: American Association of Industrial Physicians and Surgeons

AAIT: American Association of Inhalation Therapists

AAJ: Arab Airways, Jerusalem; Axel Axelson Johnson (Johnson Line)

AAJC: American Association of Junior Colleges

AAJE: American Association for Jewish Education

AAJR: American Academy for Jewish Research

AAJS: American Association for Jesuit Scientists

AAJSA: American Association of Journalism School Administrators

AAK: Alfred A. Knopf

aal: anterior axillary line

AAL: American Airlines; Ames Aeronautical Laboratory; Arctic Aeromedical Laboratory; Australian Air League

AA de L: Academia Argentina de Letras (Argentine Academy of Letters)

AALA: American Auto Laundry Association; American Automotive Leasing Association

AALC: African-American Labor Center (AFL-CIO)

AALD: Australian Army Legal Department

AALL: American Association of Law Libraries

aalmg (AALMG): antiaircraft light machine gun

AALPA: Association of Auctioneers and Landed Property Agents

AALPP: American Association for Legal and Political Philosophy

AALS: American Association of Language Specialists; Association of American Law Schools; Association of American Library Schools

AALT: American Association of Library Trustees

AALU: Association for Advanced Life Underwriting

aam (AAM): air-to-air missile

AAM: American Association of Microbiology; American Association of Museums; Australian Air Mission

AAMA: American Academy of Medical Administrators; American Apparel Manufacturers Association; American Association of Medical Assistants; Architectural Aluminum Manufacturers Association

AAMBP: Association of American Medical Book Publishers

AAMC: American Association of Marriage Counselors; American Association of Medical Clinics; Army Air Materiel Command; Association of American Medical Colleges; Australian Army Medical Corps

AAMCH: American Association for Maternal and Child Health

AAMD: American Association on Mental Deficiency; Association of Art Museum Directors

AAMES: American Association for Middle East Studies

AAMF: American Association of Music Festivals

aamg (AAMG): antiaircraft machine gun

AAMGA: American Association of Managing General Agents

AAMI: American Association of Machinery Importers; Association for the Advancement of Medical Instrumentation; Association of Allergists for Mycological Investigation

AAMIH: American Association for Maternal and Infant Health

AAML: Arctic Aeromedical Laboratory

AAMMC: American Association of Medical Milk Commissions

AAMP: American Academy of Maxillofacial Prosthetics

AAMR: American Academy on Mental Retardation

AAMRL: American Association of Medical Record Librarians

AAMS: American Air Mail Society

AAMSW: American Association of Medical Social Workers

AAMU: Army Advanced Marksmanship Unit

AAMVA: American Association of Motor Vehicle Administrators

AAMW: Association of Advertising Men and Women

AAMWS: Australian Army Medical Women's Service

AAN: American Academy of Neurology; American Academy of Nutrition; American Association of Neuropathologists; American Association of Nurserymen

AANA: American Association of Nurse Anesthetists

AANR: American Association of Newspaper Representatives

AANS: American Association of Neurological Surgery

AANSW: Archives Authority of New South Wales

aao: amino-acid oxidase

aaO: *am angeführten Ort* (German—in the place cited); *an anderen Orten* (German—elsewhere; in the place cited)

AAO: Academy of Applied Osteopathy; American Academy of Optometry; American Association of Orthodontists

AAO: *Abastumanskaya Astrofizicheskaya Observatoriya* (Russian—Abastumani Astrophysical Observatory)

AAOA: Ambulance Association of America

AAOC: American Association of Osteopathic Colleges; Antiaircraft Operations Center

AAOD: Army Aviation Operating Detachment

AAODC: American Association of Oilwell Drilling Contractors

AAOG: American Association of Obstetricians and Gynecologists

AAOGAS: American Association of Obstetricians, Gynecologists, and Abdominal Surgeons

AAOM: American Academy of Occupational Medicine; American Academy of Oral Medicine

AAOME: American Association of Osteopathic Medical Examiners

AAONMS: Ancient Arabic Order of Nobles of the Mystic Shrine

AAO & O: American Academy of Ophthalmology and Otolaryngology

AAOP: American Academy of Oral Pathology; Antiaircraft Observation Post

AAOPB: American Association of

Pathologists and Bacteriologists
AAOPS: American Association of Oral and Plastic Surgeons
AAOR: American Academy of Oral Roentgenology
AAOS: American Academy of Orthopaedic Surgery
AAP: Academy of American Poets; Allied Administrative Publication; American Academy of Pediatrics; American Academy of Periodontology; Association for the Advancement of Psychoanalysis; Association for the Advancement of Psychotherapy; Association of American Physicians; Association of Applied Psychoanalysis; Australian Associated Press
AAPA: American Amateur Press Association; American Association of Physical Anthropologists; American Association of Port Authorities
AAPB: American Association of Pathologists and Bacteriologists
AAPC: All-African Peoples' Conference
AAPCC: American Association of Poison Control Centers; American Association of Psychiatric Clinics for Children
AAPCM: Association of American Playing Card Manufacturers
AAPCO: Association of American Pesticide Control Officials
AAPD: American Academy of Physiologic Dentistry
AAPE: American Academy of Physical Education
AAPG: American Association of Petroleum Geologists
AAPH: American Association of Professional Hypnologists
AAPHD: American Association of Public Health Dentists
AAPHP: American Association of Public Health Physicians
AAPIU: Allied Aerial Photographic Interpretation Unit
AAPL: Afro-American Policemen's League; American Artists Professional League; American Association of Petroleum Landmen
aapm: amphiapomict
AAPMR: American Academy of Physical Medicine and Rehabilitation
AAPO: All-African Peoples' Organization
AAPOR: American Association for Public Opinion Research
AAPRM: American Association of Passenger Rate Men
AAPS: American Association of Plastic Surgeons; American As-

sociation for the Promotion of Science; Association for Ambulatory Pediatric Services; Association of American Physicians and Surgeons
AAPSE: American Association of Professors in Sanitary Engineering
AAPSS: American Academy of Political and Social Sciences
AAPT: American Association of Physics Teachers; Association of Asphalt Paving Technologists
AAPTO: American Association of Passenger Traffic Officers
aar: after action report; against all risks; average annual rainfall
Aar: Aarhus
AAR: Aircraft Accident Record; Aircraft Accident Report; American Academy in Rome; Army Area Representative; Association of American Railroads; Automotive Affiliated Representatives
AARC: Ann Arbor Railroad Company
AARD: American Academy of Restorative Dentistry
AARDCO: Association of American Railroad Dining Car Officers
aarg: *aargang* (Dano-Norwegian or Swedish—yearbook)
Aarh: Aarhus
AARL: Advanced Applications and Research Laboratory
aarp: annual advance retainer pay
AARP: American Association of Retired Persons
AARPS: Air-Augmented Rocket-Propulsion System
AARR: Ann Arbor Railroad
AARRC: Army Aircraft Requirements Review Committee
AARS: American Association of Railroad Superintendents; American Association of Railway Surgeons; Army Aircraft Repair Ship; Army Amateur Radio System
AART: American Association for Rehabilitation Therapy
AARTA: American Association of Railroad Ticket Agents
aarv: aerial armored reconnaissance vehicle
AARWBA: American Auto Racing Writers and Broadcasters Association
aas: advanced antenna system
AA's: author's alterations
AAS: Aircraft Airworthiness Section; All-America Selections; American Amaryllis Society; American Antiquarian Society; American Astronautical Society;

American Astronomical Society; Army Air Service; Army Attache System; Arnold Air Society; Association for Asian Studies; Australian Academy of Science
A.A.S.: Associate in Applied Science
AASA: American Association of School Administrators
AASB: American Association of Small Business
AASC: Allied Air Support Command
aascm: awaiting action summary court martial
AASCO: Association of American Seed Control Officials
aasd: antiaircraft self-destroying
AASDJ: American Association of Schools and Departments of Journalism
AASE: American Academy of Sanitary Engineers; Association for Applied Solar Energy
AASEC: American Association of Sex Educators and Counselors
AASF: Advanced Air Striking Force
AASFE: American Association of Sunday and Feature Editors
AASG: Association of American State Geologists
AAS & GP: American Association of Soap and Glycerin Producers
AASHO: American Association of State Highway Officials
AASI: Advertising Agency Service Interchange; American Academy for Scientific Interrogation
aasl: antiaircraft searchlight
AASL: American Association of School Librarians; American Association of State Librarians
A & ASL: American & Australian Steamship Line
AASLH: American Association for State and Local History
AASM: Association of American Steel Manufacturers
AASND: American Association for the Study of Neoplastic Diseases
AASO: Association of American Ship Owners
AASP: American Association for Social Psychiatry
AASPA: American Association of School Personnel Administrators
AASPRC: American Association of Sheriff's Posses and Riding Clubs
aasr: airport and airways surveillance radar
AASR: Ancient and Accepted Scottish Rite
AASRI: Arctic and Antarctic Scien-

tific Research Institute

AASS: Afro-American Students Society; American Association for Social Security

AAST: American Association for the Surgery of Trauma

AASU: Afro-American Student Union

AASWA: American Association for the Study of World Affairs

AASWI: American Aid Society for the West Indies

aat: after acid treatment

aat (AAT): alpha-1 antitrypsin

AAT: Achievement Anxiety Test

AATA: Anglo-American Tourist Association

AATB: Advanced Amphibious Training Base

AATC: Anti-Aircraft Training Center; Army Aviation Test Command

AATCC: American Association of Textile Chemists and Colorists

AATCLC: American Association of Teachers of Chinese Language and Culture

AATEA: American Association of Teacher Educators in Agriculture

AATF: American Association of Teachers of French

AATG: American Association of Teachers of German

AATI: American Association of Teachers of Italian

AATM: American Academy of Tropical Medicine

AATOE: American Association of Theatre Organ Enthusiasts

AATP: American Academy of Tuberculosis Physicians

AATPA: American Association of Traveling Passenger Agents

AATRACEN: Anti-Aircraft Training Center

AATRIS: Army Air Traffic Regulation and Identification System

AATS: American Academy of Teachers of Singing; American Association of Theological Schools; American Association for Thoracic Surgery

AATSEEL: American Association of Teachers of Slavic and East European Languages

AATSP: American Association of Teachers of Spanish and Portuguese

AATT: American Association for Textile Technology

AAT & TC: Anti-Aircraft Training and Test Center

AATU: Association of Air Transport Unions

AATUF: All-African Trade Union Federation

AAU: Administrative Area Unit; Al-Azhar University; Amateur Athletic Union; Association of American Universities

AAUN: American Association for the United Nations

AAUP: American Association of University Presses; American Association of University Professors

AAUTI: American Association of University Teachers of Insurance

AAUUS: Amateur Athletic Union of the U.S.

AAUW: American Association of University Women

aav: airborne assault vehicle

AAV: Antiaircraft Volunteer

AAVA: American Association of Veterinary Anatomists

AAVB: American Association of Veterinary Bacteriologists

AAVC: Australian Army Veterinary Corps

AAVCS: Automatic Aircraft Vectoring Control System

aavd: automatic alternate voice/data

AAVMC: Association of American Veterinary Medical Colleges

Aavn: Army aviation

AAVN: American Association of Veterinary Nutritionists

AAVP: American Association of Veterinary Pathologists

AAVRO: American Association of Variable Star Observers

AAVRPHS: American Association of Vital Records and Public Health Statistics

AAVS: American Anti-Vivisection Society

AAVSO: American Association of Variable Star Observers

AAW: Advertising Association of the West; Anti-Air Warfare

AAWA: American Automatic Weapons Association

AAWB: American Association of Workers for the Blind

AAWC: Australian Advisory War Council

AAWD: Association of American Women Dentists

AAWg: Aeromedical Airlift Wing (USAF)

AAWPI: Association of American Wood Pulp Importers

AAWU: Amateur Athletic Western Union

AAXICO: American Air Export and Import Company

AAYM: American Association of Youth Museums

AAZPA: American Association of Zoological Parks and Aquariums

ab: abscess; abortion; about; adapter booster; afterburner; airbrake; anchor bolt; antibody; asthmatic bronchitis; axiobuccal

ab: *abril* (Spanish—April)

a/b (A/B): airborne

a & b: applejack and benedictine; assault and battery

aB: *auf Bestellung* (German—on order)

Ab: abnormal; alabamine

AB: able-bodied seaman; Aid to the Blind; Air Base; Arnold Bernstein (steamship line); Assembly Bill

A-B: Allen-Bradley; Ambrose Bierce; Anton Bruckner

A.B.: *artium baccalureus* (Latin—Bachelor of Arts)

A/B: Aid to the Blind; Airman Basic

A/B: *Aktiebolag* (Swedish—limited company)

ab-a: abampere

ABA: American Badminton Association; American Bakers Association; American Bandmasters Association; American Bankers Association; American Bar Association; American Bell Association; American Berkshire Association; American Booksellers Association; American Bowhunters Association; American Brazilian Association; American Buddhist Association; Annual Budget Authorization

ABAA: Antiquarian Booksellers Association of America

abac: a basic coursewriter

ABAC: Abraham Baldwin Agricultural College

ABACUS: Air Battle Analysis Center Utility System; Autonetics Business and Control United Systems

abad: (Indian or Persian suffix—dwelling; town, as in Ahmadabad, Bahramabad, Hyderabad)

ABAD: Air Battle Analysis Division

ABAG: Association of Bay Area Governments (San Francisco)

ABAI: American Boiler and Affiliated Industries

abamp: absolute ampere (10 amperes)

aband: abandoned

abandt: abandonment

ABAS: American Board of Abdominal Surgeons

abat: abattoir

ABATU: Advance Base Air Task Unit; Advance Base Aviation

Abb 9 ABF

Training Unit
Abb: Abbess; Abbey; Abbot
Abb: *Abbildung* (German—illustration)
Abb.: *abbas* (Latin—abbot)
ABB: Akron & Barberton Belt (railroad)
ABBA: American Blind Bowling Association; American Board of Bio-Analysis; American Brahman Breeders Association
ABBB: Association of Better Business Bureaus
ABBF: Association of Bronze and Brass Founders
Abbild: *Abbildungen* (German—illustrations)
ABBMM: Association of British Brush Machinery Manufacturers
abbr: abbreviate; abbreviated; abbreviation
ABBRA: American Boat Builders and Repairers Association
abbrev: *abbreviatura* (Italian—abbreviation)
abbreviaz: *abbreviazione* (Italian—abbreviation)
abbrev(s): abbreviation(s)
Abby: Abigail
abc: abcedarius (alphabet primer); advanced biomedical capsule (ABC); alphabet; atomic, biological, chemical; alum, blood, and charcoal; automatic bass compensation; automatic base control; automatic brightness control
ABC: Aerated Bread Company; Alcohol Beverage Control; American Bowling Congress; American Brass Company; American, British, Canadian; American Broadcasting Company; Argentina, Brazil, Chile; atomic, biological, chemical (warfare); Audit Bureau of Circulation; Australian Broadcasting Commission; Australian Broadcasting Corporation; Automotive Booster Clubs
ABC: (Madrid's daily newspaper)
AB & C: Atlanta, Birmingham and Coast (railroad)
ABC³: Airborne Battlefield Command and Control Center
ABCA: American-British-Canadian-Australian; Antique Bottle Collectors Association; Army Bureau of Current Affairs
ABC-ASP: American-British-Canadian—Army Standardization Program
abcb: air-blast circuit breaker
ABCB: American Bottlers of Carbonated Beverages; Australian

Broadcasting Control Board
ABCC: Association of British Chambers of Commerce; Atomic Bomb Casualty Commission
ABCCC: Airborne Battlefield Command and Control Center
ABC—Clio: American Bibliographical Center—Clio Press (Santa Barbara, California)
ABCCTC: Advanced Base Combat Communication Training Center
abcd: airway (opened), breathing (restored), circulation (restored), definitive (therapy); atomic, biological, chemical, and damage (control); awaiting bad conduct discharge
ABCD: Accelerated Business Collection and Delivery (of mail); Action for Boston Community Development; Advanced Base Construction Depot; America, Britain, China, Dutch East Indies (ABCD Powers during World War II); American Society of Bookplate Collectors and Designers
A-B-C-Dieren: German musical exercises wherein names of notes replace words
ABCFM: American Board of Commissioners for Foreign Missions
ABCH: American Board of Clinical Hypnosis
ABC Islands: Aruba, Bonaire, Curaçao (Netherlands Antilles)
ABCM: Association of British Chemical Manufacturers; Aviation Chief Boatswain's Mate
ABCMR: Army Board for Correction of Military Records
abcoulomb: absolute coulomb (10 coulombs)
ABCP: Association of Blind Chartered Physiotherapists
ABC Powers: Argentina, Brazil, Chile
ABCR: Association for Beautiful Colorado Roads
ABCRS: American Board of Colon and Rectal Surgery
ABCS: American Board on Counseling Services
ABCSP: American-British-Canadian Standardization Program
ABC Std: American-British-Canadian Standard(s)
abcw (ABC or ABCW): atomic chemical, biological warfare
ABCW: American Bakery and Confectionery Workers
abd: abdicated; abdomen; abdominal; abduction; abductor; average body dose (radiation)
ABD: Abadan, Iran (airport); Ad-

vanced Base Depot; Advanced Base Dock; American Board of Dermatology
ABD: *Association Belge de Documentation* (Belgian Documentation Association)
A.B.D.: All But Dissertation (doctoral lacking)
ABDA: American-British-Dutch-Australian (forces in World War II)
ABDACOM: Advanced Base Depot Area Command; American-British-Dutch-Australian Command (World War II)
abdc: after bottom dead center
abde: airport bird-detection equipment
ABDI: Administrative Board of the Dress Industry
abdl: automatic binary data link
abdom: abdomen; abdominal
ABDPH: American Board of Dental Public Health
Abdr: *Abdruck* (German—copy, printing)
abd's: all but their dissertations (Ph.D. candidates)
ABDSP: Anza-Borrego Desert State Park (California)
abe: airborne bombing evaluation; augmented ballast expulsion
Abe: Abraham
ABE: Airborne Bombing Evaluation; Allentown-Bethlehem-Easton, Pennsylvania (airport)
ABEA: American Broncho-Esophagological Association
ABEC: Annular Bearing Engineers Committee
ABEM: *Association Belge pour l'Etude, l'Essais, et l'Emploi des Materiaux* (Belgian Association for the Study, Testing, and Use of Materials)
ABEP: Adult Basic Education Program
ABEPP: American Board of Examiners in Professional Psychology
aber: aberration
Aber: Aberdeen; Aberdonian
Aberc: Abercrombie; Abercrombian
abes: aerospace business environment simulator
abets: airborne beacon electronic test set
ab ex.: *ab extra* (Latin—from outside)
ABEX: American Brake Shoe Company
Abf: *Abfahrt* (German—departure)
ABF: Aircraft Battle Force; American Bar Foundation; American Beekeeping Federation; As-

sociated British Foods

abfarad: absolute farad (10⅔ farads)

ABFLO: Association of Bedding and Furniture Law Officials

ABFM: American Board of Foreign Missions

ab'ft: abaft (toward the stern)

abg: axiobuccogingival

Abg: Abgeordnete (German —Member of Parliament)

ABG: Air Base Group; American Ship Building Company (stock exchange symbol)

abgk: abgekürzt (German—abbreviated)

ABGP: Air Base Group

abh: alpha-benzene-hexachloride

Abh: Abhandlungen (German —transactions, treatises)

abhenry: absolute henry (10⁻⁹ henries)

ABHP: American Board of Health Physics

abi: assignment of beneficial interest

ABI: American Butter Institute; Associazione Bibliotecari Italiani (Association of Italian Librarians); Authorized Break of Inspection

ABI: Advance Book Information

Abie: Abraham

ABIM: American Board of Internal Medicine; American Board of International Missions

ab in.: ab intra (Latin—from within)

ab init.: ab initio (Latin—from the beginning)

ABJS: Association of Bone and Joint Surgeons

Abk: Abkürzung (German—abbreviation)

ABK: American Brake Shoe (stock exchange symbol)

Abkürz: Abkürzungen (German—abbreviations)

abl: ablative; axiobuccolingual

Abl: Atlas basic language (data processing)

Abl: Abríl (Spanish—April)

ABL: Alameda Belt Line (railroad); Allegheny Ballistic Laboratory; Animated Biological Laboratories (NASA); Aquatic Biological Laboratory; Automated Biological Laboratory

ABLA: Amateur Bicycle League of America; American Business Law Association

ablat: ablative

ABLE: Action for Better Law Enforcement; Activity Balance Line Evaluation; Agricultural-Biological Literature Evaluation

ABLM: American Board of Legal Medicine

ABLS: Association of British Library Schools; Atlas Biomedical Literature System

A.B.L.S.: Bachelor of Arts in Library Science

abm: automated batch mixing

ABM (ABM): antiballistic missile

Abm: Abraham

ABM: Advance Bill of Material; Aviation Boatswain's Mate

A.B.M.: Associate in Business Management

AB de M: Academia Brasileira de Musica

ABMA: American Boiler Manufacturers Association; American Brush Manufacturers Association; Army Ballistic Missile Agency

ABMAC: Association of British Manufacturers of Agricultural Chemicals

ABMC: American Battle Monuments Commission

ABMD: Air Ballistics Missile Division

ABMEWS: Antiballistic Missile Early Warning System

ABMIS: Airborne Anti-Ballistic Missile Intercept System

ABMPM: Association of British Manufacturers of Printing Machinery

ABMRF: American Business Men's Research Foundation

ABMS: American Bureau of Metal Statistics

ABMU: American Baptist Missionary Union

abn: airborne

Abn: Aberdeen

ABN: American Bank Note (stock exchange symbol)

ABNCO: American Bank Note Company

ABNE: Association for the Benefit of Non-contract Employees

abni: available but not installed

ABNINF: Airborne Infantry

ABNM: American Board of National Missions

abnor: abnormal

ABNPHSBM: Advisory Board on National Parks, Historic Sites, Buildings, and Monuments

ABNS: American Board of Neurological Surgery

abo: aboriginal; aborigine

ABO: American Board of Ophthalmology; American Board of Opticianry; American Board of Orthodontics; American Board of Otolaryngology; Association of Buying Offices

ABOG: American Board of Obstetrics and Gynecology

abohm: absolute ohm (10⁻⁹ ohms)

A-bomb: atomic bomb; (underground slang—cigarette containing hashish or marijuana plus heroin or opium)

abon: abonné (French—subscriber)

abonn: abonnement (French—subscription)

ABOPS: Association of Business Officers of Preparatory Schools

abos: aborigines

ABOS: American Board of Oral Surgery; American Board of Orthopedic Surgery

abp: arterial blood pressure

Abp: Archbishop

ABP: American Board of Pathology; American Board of Pediatrics; American Board of Pedodontics; American Board of Peridontology; American Board of Prosthodontics; American Business Press

ABPA: Advanced Base Personnel Administration

ABPC: American Book Publishers Council

ABPD: American Board of Pediatric Dermatology

ABPG: Advanced Base Proving Ground

ABPI: Association of the British Pharmaceutical Industry

ABPM: American Board of Preventive Medicine

ABPMR: American Board of Physical Medicine and Rehabilitation

ABPN: American Board of Psychiatry and Neurology

ABPO: Advanced Base Personnel Officer

ABPS: American Board of Plastic Surgery

ABPU: Advanced Base Personnel Unit

ABPVM: Association of British Plywood and Veneer Manufacturers

ABQ: Albuquerque, New Mexico (airport)

abr: abridge; abridgment

abr: abril (Portuguese or Spanish —April)

Abr: Abraham

ABR: American Board of Radiology; American Commercial Barge Line (stock exchange symbol); Real Aerovias Brasil (Brazilian airline symbol)

ABR: American Bankruptcy Reports

Abra: Abraham

abracadabra: *abbreviations and*

related acronyms associated with defense, astronautics business, and radio-electronics (acronym devised by the Office of Public Relations of Raytheon in an effort to abolish acronyms)

abras: abrasions

ABRB: Advanced Base Receiving Barracks

A & B R C: Antofagasta and Bolivia Railway Company

ABRD: Advanced Base Repair Depot; Advanced Base Reshipment Depot; American Bill of Rights Day (association)

ABRES: Advanced Ballistic Re-Entry System

abrev: abreviation (French—abreviation); abreviatura(s) [Spanish—abbreviation(s)]

abrew: abrewiacja (Polish—abbreviation)

ABRO: Animal Breeding Research Organization

ABRSM: Association Board of the Royal Schools of Music

abrsv: abrasive

abr sw: airbrake switch

abs: abalones; absent; absolute; abson; abstrene; acrylonitrile-butadiene-styrene (ABS) resin(s); air-break switch; alkyl benzene sulfonate

abs: aux bons soins de (French—in care of)

Abs: Absatz (German—paragraph); Absender (German—sender)

ABS: Air Base Squadron; American Begonia Society; American Berlioz Society; American Bible Society; American Board of Surgery; American Boxwood Society; American Brake Shoe; American Bureau of Shipping

ABSA: African Boy Scouts Association; Association of British Secretaries in America

abs alt: absolute altitude

absap: airborne search and attack plotter

ABSC: American Brake and Screw Company

Abschn: Abschnitt (German—chapter, paragraph)

absd: advanced base sectional dock

ABSD: Advanced Base Supply Depot

abse. rec: absente rec (Latin—in the absence of the accused)

abs. feb.: absente febre (Latin—in the absence of fever)

ABSIE: American Broadcasting Station in Europe (World War II)

ABSMA: American Bleached Shellac Manufacturers Association

absol: absolute

ABSP: Aid to the Potentially Self-supporting Blind

abst jdg: abstract of judgment

abstr: abstract

ABSW: Association of British Science Writers

abs z: absolute zero (—273 degrees centigrade)

abt: about; abundant

Abt: Abteilung (German—part)

ABT: Abbott Laboratories (stock exchange symbol); American Ballet Theater

ABTA: Association of British Travel Agents

ABTF: Airborne Task Force

ABTICS: Abstract and Book Title Index Card Service (Iron and Steel Institute)

ABTTA: American Bridge, Tunnel, and Turnpike Association

ABTU: Advanced Base Torpedo Unit; Advanced Base Training Unit; Air Bombers Training Unit

ABTUC: All-Burma Trade Union Congress

ABU: Alliance Biblique Universelle (Universal Biblical Alliance)

A. Bus.: Associate in Business

abut: abutment

abv: above

abvolt: absolute volt (10^{-8} volts)

abw: anterior bite wing

Abw: Abwehr (German—defense)

ABWA: American Bottled Water Association; American Business Writing Association; Associated Business Writers of America

ABWG: Air Base Wing

abwik: assault and battery with intent to kill

ABWRC: Army Biological Warfare Research Center

ABY: Albany, Georgia (airport)

ABYA: Association of British Yacht Agents

ABYC: American Boat and Yacht Council

ac: absolute ceiling; aerodynamic center; air cool; anticorrosive; arithmetic computation (test); asbestos cement; auxiliary console

a-c: alternating-current (when used as an adjective—a-c transformer)

a/c: account; account current; aircraft

a.c.: ante cibos (Latin—before meals)

a C: avanti Cristo (Italian—before Christ)

Ac: actinium; altocumulus

AC: Adelbert College; Adelphi College; Aden Colony; Adrian College; aerodynamic center (symbol); Air Canada; Alabama College; Albion College; Albright College; Allegheny College; Alliance College; Alma College; alternating current (when used as a noun—220 volts AC); Alverno College; Amarillo College; Ambulance Corps; Amherst College; Anderson College; Andrew College; Annhurst College; anodal contraction or closure; Antioch College; Aquinas College; Arcadia College; Arithmetic Computation (test); Arkansas College; Armstrong College; Asbury College; Ashland College; Assumption College; Athens College; Athletic Club; Augusta College; Augustana College; Aurora College; Austin College; Averett College; Azusa College

AC: Atlanta Constitution

A.C.: année courante (French —current year)

A-C: Allis-Chalmers

A/C: Air Commodore; aircraft; Aviation Cadet

A/1C: Airman First Class

A/2C: Airman Second Class

A²C²: see AACC

A/3C: Airman Third Class

ac a: acetic acid

Aca: Acapulco (inhabitants —Acapulqueños)

ACA: Acapulco, Mexico (airport); Aircraft Castings Association; American Camping Association; American Canoe Association; American Carnivals Association; American Casting Association; American Cat Association; American Cemetery Association; American Chiropractic Association; American Civic Association; American College of Allergists; American College of Anesthesiologists; American College of Apothecaries; American Communications Association; American Composers Alliance; American Congregational Association; Americans for Constitutional Action; American Correctional Association; American Cryptogram Association; American Crystallographic Association; Arts Council of America; Arts Council of Australia; Assembly Constitutional Amendment; Associated Chiropodists of America; Association of Correctional Administrators

ACAA: Agricultural Conservation

and Adjustment Administration

ACAB: Army Contract Adjustment Board

ACAC: Allied Container Advisory Committee; Association of College Admission Counsellors

acad: academic; academician; academy

Acad: Acadia; Academy

ACAD: American Conference of Academic Deans

Acad b-a: Académie des beaux arts (Academy of Fine Arts)

Acad fran: Académie française (French Academy)

Acad ins b-l: Académie des inscriptions et belles-lettres (Academy of Inscriptions and Literature)

Acad Med: Academy of Medicine

Acad Mus: Academy of Music

Acad sci: Académie des sciences (Academy of Science)

Acad Sci: Academy of Science

Acad Sin: Academia Sinica (Chinese Academy of Science)

Acad St Cec: Academia di Santa Cecilia, Rome

Acad U: Acadia University

ACAF: Amphibious Corps, Atlantic Fleet

ACAN: Army Command and Administrative Network

ACAnes: American College of Anesthetists

a. cant.: after cant frames

Acanth: Acanthocephala

Acap: Acapulco

ACAP: Army Contract Appeals Panel

ACAPA: American Concrete Agricultural Pipe Association

a capp: *a cappella* (Italian—in chapel style, without musical accompaniment)

ACAS: Association of Casualty Accounts and Statisticians

AC/AS: Assistant Chief of Air Staff

ACAST: Advisory Committee on Applications of Science and Technology (UNESCO)

acb: air circuit breaker; asbestos cement board

ACB: Advertising Checking Bureau; Airman Classification Battery; Army Classification Battery; Association Canadienne des Bibliothèques (Canadian Library Association); Association of Customers' Brokers; Association of the Customs Bar

ACBA: Academy of Comic Book Artists

ACB of A: Associated Credit Bureaus of America

ACBB: American Council for Better Broadcasts

ACBL: American Commercial Barge Line; American Contract Bridge League

acbm: atomic cesium beam maser

ACBM: Associated Corset and Brassiere Manufacturers; Aviation Chief Boatswain's Mate

ACBs: Associated Credit Bureaus

ACBS: Accrediting Commission for Business Schools

ACBWS: Automatic Chemical Biological Warning System

acc: account; altocumulus castellatus (clouds); anodal closing contraction; astronomical great circle course (ACC); automatic chroma circuit (tv)

ACC: Accra, Ghana (airport); Adirondack Community College; Administrative Committee on Coordination; Air Center Commander; Air Control Center; Air Coordinating Committee; Allied Control Commission; Allied Control Council; American College of Cardiology; American Concert Choir; American Conference of Cantors; American Craftsmen's Council; Army Chemical Center; Army Cooperation Command; Association of Choral Conductors; Auburn Community College

A-C-C: Appleton-Century-Crofts

ACCA: Aeronautical Chamber of Commerce of America; American Clinical and Climatological Association; American College of Clinic Administrators; American Cotton Cooperative Association; Art Collectors Club of America

acc & aud: accountant and auditor

ACCC: Alternate Command and Control Center

ACCCE: Association of Consulting Chemists and Chemical Engineers

ACCCF: American Concert Choir and Choral Foundation

AC & CCI: American Coke and Coal Chemicals Institute

acce: acceptance

ACCE: American Chamber of Commerce Executives

accel: accelerate

accel: *accelerando* (Italian—accelerating)

ACCELS: Automated-Circuit Card -Etching Layout System

access: accessory

ACCESS: Automatic Computer-Controlled Electronic Scanning System

ACCF: American Committee for Cultural Freedom; Association

of Community College Facilities

ACCFA: Agricultural Credit Cooperative Finance Administration

ACCHAN: Allied Command Channel (NATO)

acci: accidental injury

ACCI: American Cottage Cheese Institute

accid: accident(al)

ACCION: Americans for Community Cooperation in Other Nations

ACCL: American Council of Commercial Laboratories

ACCM: American College of Clinic Managers

ACCN: Associated Court and Commercial Newspapers

acco: *accompagnamento* (Italian—accompaniment)

accom: accommodation

accomp: accomplish

ACCP: American College of Chest Physicians

ACCR: American Council on Chiropractic Roentgenography

ACCRA: American Chamber of Commerce Researchers Association

accrd int: accrued interest

accred: accredited

ACCS: Automated Calibration Control System

acct: account; accountant; accounting

ACCTU: All-Union Central Council of Trade Unions (USSR)

accum: accumulate

accur: *accuratissime* (Latin—most accurately)

accus: accusative

accw: alternating current continuous wave

accy: accessory

acd: absolute cardiac dullness; accord; accordion; acid-citratedextrose

ACD: Administrative Commitment Document; Allied Chemical Corporation (stock exchange symbol); American Choral Directors; American College of Dentists

ACDA: American Choral Directors Association; Arms Control and Disarmament Agency; Aviation Combat Development Agency

a-c/d-c: alternating current/direct current; (underground slang —bisexual person engaging in heterosexual and homosexual intercourse)

a-c/d-c's: bisexuals; persons responding to both sexes

acdt: accident

acdu: active duty

acdutra: active duty for training
ACDUTRA: Active Duty Reserve Army
ace.: acetic; adrenal cortical extract; aerospace control environment; air crash equipment; alcohol-chloroform-ether (anesthetic mixture); attitude control electronics; automatic checkout equipment; automatic circuit exchange
ACE: Allied Command, Europe; American Cinema Editors; American Council on Education; American Hard Rubber Company (trademark); Army Corps of Engineers; Aviation Construction Engineers
ACEA: Air Line Communication Employees Association
ACEAA: Advisory Committee on Electrical Appliances and Accessories
ACEC: Army Communications and Electronic Command; Ateliers de Constructions Électriques de Charleroi (Electrical Construction Workshops of Charleroi—Belgium)
A.C. Ed.: Associate in Commercial Education
ACEF: Asian Cultural Exchange Foundation; Association of Commodity Exchange Firms
ACEI: Association for Childhood Education International
ACEJ: American Council on Education for Journalism
ACEL: Air Crew Equipment Laboratory
ACELF: Association Canadienne des Educateurs de Langue Française
ACEM: Aviation Chief Electrician's Mate
ACEN: Assembly of Captive European Nations
ACEORP: Automotive and Construction Equipment Overhaul and Repair Plant
ACEP: American Council for Émigrés in the Professions
ACEPD: Automotive and Construction Equipment Parts Depot
ACER: Australian Council for Educational Research
ACERP: Advanced Communications-Electronics Requirements Plan
aces: automatic control evaluation simulator
ACES: Americans for the Competitive Enterprise System; Association for Counselor Education and Supervision
ACESA: Australian Commonwealth Engineering Standards Association
ace-s/c: acceptance checkout equipment—spacecraft
acet: acetone
acetl: acetylene
ACEUR: Allied Command, Europe
ACEWR: American Committee for European Worker's Relief
acf: accessory clinical findings
ACF: Alternate Communications Facility; American Car & Foundry; American Checker Federation; American Chess Foundation; American Choral Foundation; American Culinary Federation; Association of Consulting Foresters
ACF: *Académie Canadienne Française* (French-Canadian Academy)
ACFA: American Cat Fanciers Association; Association of Commercial Finance Attorneys
ACFC: Aviation Chief Fire Controlman
ACFEA: Air Carrier Flight Engineers Association
ACFEL: Arctic Construction and Frost Effects Laboratory (Greenland)
ACFL: Atlantic Coast Football League
ACFM: Association of Canadian Fire Marshals
ACFN: American Committee for Flags of Necessity
ACFO: American College of Foot Orthopedics
ACFR: Advisory Committee of the Federal Register; Advisory Council on Federal Reports; American College of Foot Roentgenologists
ACFS: American College of Foot Surgeons
acft: aircraft
ACFT: Aircraft Flying Training
acftc: aircraft carrier
acg: automatic caution guard; automatic control gear
ACG: Airborne Coordinating Group; Air Cargo Express (symbol); Airline Carriers of Goods; American College of Gastroenterology; American Council on Germany; Association for Corporate Growth
ACGA: American Cranberry Growers' Association
ACGB: Arts Council of Great Britain
ACGBI: Automobile Club of Great Britain and Ireland
ACGD: Association for Corporate Growth and Diversification
ACGF: American Child Guidance Foundation
ACGIH: American Conference of Governmental Industrial Hygienists
ACGM: Aircraft Carriers General Memorandum
ACGP: Army Career Group
ACGPOMS: American College of General Practitioners in Osteopathic Medicine and Surgery
ACGS: American Council on German Studies
ACGSq: Aerial Cartographic and Geodetic Squadron (USAF)
ACHA: American Catholic Historical Association; American College Health Association; American College of Hospital Administrators
AC & HBR: Algoma Central and Hudson Bay Railway
ACHE: Alabama Commission on Higher Education
achiev: achievement
ach index: arm (girth), chest (depth), hip (width) index (of nutrition)
ACHNHP: Appomattox Court House National Historical Park
ACHR: American Council of Human Rights
achrom: achromatism
ACHS: Association of College Honor Societies
aci: airborne-controlled interception; automatic car identification
aci: *assure contre l'incendie* (French—insured against fire)
ACI: Air Cargo Incorporated; Air Combat Information; Air Combat Intelligence; Alliance Coopérative Internationale (International Cooperative Alliance); Alloy Casting Institute; American Carpet Institute; American Concrete Institute; American Cryogenics Incorporated
ACIA: Associated Cooperage Industries of America
ACIAA: Australian Commercial and Industrial Artists' Association
ACIAS: American Council of Industrial Arts Supervisors
ACIASAO: American Council of Industrial Arts State Association Officers
ACIATE: American Council of Industrial Arts Teacher Education
acic: acicular
ACIC: Aeronautical Chart and Information Center; Allied Captured Intelligence Center; Aux-

iliary Combat Information Center

acid.: acidosis

ACIID: A Critical Insight Into Israel's Dilemmas

ACIL: American Council of Independent Laboratories

acim: axis-crossing interval meter

ACIM: American Committee on Italian Migration

ACIO: Air Combat Intelligence Office(r)

ACIPCO: American Cast Iron Pipe Company

ACIR: Advisory Committee on Intergovernmental Relations; Automotive Crash Injury Research

AC/IREF: American Chapter—International Real Estate Federation

ACIS: American Committee for Irish Studies

acit: air-cannon impact tester

ACIWLP: American Committee for International Wild Life Protection

ACJ: American Council for Judaism

ack: acknowledge; acknowledgment

ACK: accidentally killed; Armstrong Cork (stock exchange symbol)

ack-ack: antiaircraft

Ack Ack: Aluminum Company of America (stock exchange nickname)

ackt: acknowledgment

acl: air-cushion landing; allowable cabin load

ACL: American Classical League; Association of Cinema Laboratories; Atlantic Coast Line (railroad); Aviation Circular Letter

ACLA: American Comparative Literature Association; American Cotton Linter Association; American Association Life Association; Anti-Communist League of America

ACLAM: American College of Laboratory Animal Medicine

AClant: Allied Command, Atlantic

ACLC: Air Cadet League of Canada

acld: aircooled

ACLD: Association for Children with Learning Disabilities

aclg: air-cushion landing gear

ACLM: American College of Legal Medicine

ACLP: Association of Contact Lens Practitioners

acls: automatic carrier landing system

ACLS: American Council of Learned Societies; Automatic Carrier Landing System

ACLU: American Civil Liberties Union; American College of Life Underwriters

aclv: accrued leave

acm: anatomy-covering material; anatomy-covering memo; asbestos-covered metal

ACM: Air Chief Marshal; Air Commerce Manual; Air Court-Martial; American Campaign Medal; Association for Computing Machinery; auxiliary mine layer (3-letter symbol); Aviation Chief Metalsmith

ACMA: Acidproof Cement Manufacturers Association; Air Carrier Mechanics Association; Alumina Ceramic Manufacturers Association; American Certified Morticians Associations; American Circus Memorial Association; American Comedy Museum Association; American Cutlery Manufacturers Association

acme.: attitude control and maneuvering electronics

ACME: Advisory Council on Medical Education; Association of Consulting Management Engineers

ACMET: Advisory Council on Middle East Trade

ACMF: Air Crops Medical Forces; Allied Central Mediterranean Forces; American Corn Millers' Federation; Australian Commonwealth Military Forces

ACMI: American Cotton Manufacturers Institute

ACMM: Aviation Chief Machinist's Mate

acmp: accompany

ACMP: Amateur Chamber Music Players

ACMRR: Advisory Committee on Marine Resources Research (FAO)

acmru: audio commercial-message repeating unit

ACMS: Advanced Configuration Management System; Army Command Management System

ACMT: American College of Medical Technologists

acn: all concerned notified; assignment control number; automatic celestial navigation (ACN)

ACN: American Chain & Cable (stock exchange symbol); American College of Neuropsychiatrists; American Council on NATO: Authorized Code

Number

A.C.N.: *Ante Christum Natum* (Latin—before the birth of Christ)

ACNA: Advisory Council on Naval Affairs; Arctic Institute of North America

ACNB: Australian Commonwealth Naval Board

ACNE: Alaskans Concerned for Neglected Environments

ACNHA: American College of Nursing Home Administrators

ACNO: Assistant Chief of Naval Operations

ACNOT: Assistant Chief of Naval Operations—Transportation

ACNS: American Council for Nationalities Service; Associated Correspondents News Service

ACNY: Advertising Club of New York

aco: anodal closing odor

a co: *a cargo* (Spanish—against)

ACO: Administrative Contracting Officer; Air Congo (Leopoldville—Republic of the Congo); American Academy of Optometry

ACOFO: American College of Foot Orthopedists

acog (ACOG): aircraft on ground

ACOG: American College of Obstetricians and Gynecologists

ACOHA: American College of Osteopathic Hospital Administrators

ACOI: American College of Osteopathic Internists

ACOM: Aviation Chief Ordnanceman

ACOOG: American College of Osteopathic Obstetricians and Gynecologists

ACOP: American College of Osteopathic Pediatricians

ACORN: Associative Content Retrieval Network

ACOS: American College of Osteopathic Surgeons

acous: acoustics

acp: auxiliary control panel

a & cp: anchors and chains proved

ACP: Agricultural Conservation Program; Air Control Point; Airline Carriers of Passengers; Allied Communications Publications; American College of Pharmacists; American College of Physicians; Anti-Comintern Pact; Associated Collegiate Press; Association of Clinical Pathologists; Association of Correctional Psychologists

ACPA: Affiliated Chiropodists-Podiatrists of America; American Capon Producers Association; American Cleft Palate Association; American College Personnel Association; American Concrete Paving Association; American Concrete Pipe Association

A-CPA: Asbestos-Cement Products Association

ACPAE: Association of Certified Public Accounts Examiners

a/c pay: accounts payable

ACPC: American College of Probate Counsel; American Council of Parent Cooperatives

ACPD: Army Control Program Directive

ACPE: American Council on Pharmaceutical Education

ACPF: Amphibious Corps, Pacific Fleet

ACPFB: American Committee for Protection of Foreign Born

ACPIC: American Council for Private International Communications

acpm: attitude-control propulsion motor(s)

ACPM: American Congress for Preventive Medicine

ACPRA: American College Public Relations Association

ACPS: American Coalition of Patriotic Societies

ACPSAHMWA: American Commission for the Protection and Salvage of Artistic and Historical Monuments in War Areas

acpt: accept

acpu: auxiliary computer power unit

acq: acquire; acquittal

ACQT: Aviation Cadet Qualifying Test

acquis: acquisition(s)

acr: advanced capabilities radar; aerial combat reconnaissance; airfiled-controlled radar; anti-constipation regimen

ACR: Advisory Commission on the Realm; Aircraft Contral Room; Allied Commission on Reparations; American Academy in Rome; American College of Radiology

AC & R: American Cable and Radio (corp)

ACRA: American Collegiate Retailing Association

ACRB: Aero-Club Royal de Belgique (Royal Belgian Aero Club); Army Council of Review Boards

ACRC: Air Compressor Research Council

acrd: accrued

ACRE: Automatic Checkout and Readiness Equipment

a/c rec: accounts receivable

acre ft: acre foot

ACRES: Airborne Communication Relay Station

acrg: acreage

ACRI: Air Conditioning and Refrigeration Institute; American Cocoa Research Institute

ACRL: Association of College and Research Libraries

ACRM: Aviation Chief Radioman

acro: acrobat(ic); acrophobe; acrophobia

acron: acronym (word formed from initials or letters in a series of words, such as ACE—American Council of Education)

ACRR: American Council on Race Relations

ACRS: Advisory Committee on Reactor Safeguards

ACRT: Aviation Chief Radio Technician

ACRW: American Council of Railroad Women

acs: alternating current synchronous; anodal closing sound

Ac of S: Academy of Sciences (USSR)

ACS: Airline Charter Service; Alaskan Communications System; American Camellia Society; American Cancer Society; American Carnation Society; American Ceramic Society; American Chemical Society; American College of Surgeons; American Colonization Society; American Crystal Sugar (company); Armament Control System; Assistant Chief of Staff; Association of Clinical Scientists

A.C.S.: Associate in Commercial Science

AC/S: Assistant Chief of Staff

ACSA: American Cotton Shippers Association; Association of Collegiate Schools of Architecture

ACSC: Air Carrier Service Corporation; Air Command and Staff College; American Council on Schools and Colleges; Association of Casualty and Surety Companies; Australian Coastal Shipping Commission

ACSCP: Association of California State College Professors

ACSDO: Air Carrier Safety District Office(r)

ACSEA: Air Command—Southeast Asia

ACSF: Attack Carrier Striking Force

ACSI: Assistant Chief of Staff for Intelligence

ACSIL: Admiralty Centre for Scientific Information and Liaison (United Kingdom)

ACSI-MATIC: Assistant Chief of Staff—Intelligence (automatic processing system for large-scale intelligence information)

ACSM: American Congress of Surveying and Mapping

ACSMA: American Cloak and Suit Manufacturers Association

ACSN: Association of Collegiate Schools of Nursing

ACSOC: Acoustical Society of America

ACSP: Advisory Council on Scientific Policy (United Kingdom)

ACSPA: Australian Council of Salaried and Professional Associations

A/cs Pay: Accounts Payable

acsr: aluminum cable, steel reinforced

A/cs Rec: Accounts Receivable

ACSS: Air Command and Staff School; American Cheviot Sheep Society; Army Chief of Support Services

ACSSAVO: Association of Chief State School Audio-Visual Officers

ACSSN: Association of Colleges and Secondary Schools for Negroes

ACSSRB: Administrative Center of Social Security for Rhine Boatmen

acst: acoustic; acoustical; acoustics

ACST: Army Clerical Speed Test

acst plas: acoustical plaster

acst t: acoustical tile

act: acting; action; active; actor; actress; actuate; actuating

ACT: Air Control Team; American College Testing (program); American Conservatory Theatre; Associated Community Theaters; Association of Classroom Teachers; Australian Capital Territory; Aviation Classification Test

a cta: a cuenta (Spanish—on account)

ACTA: Aircoach Transport Association; American Community Theatre Association

ACTB: Aircrew Classification Test Battery

ACTC: Air Commerce Type Certificate

act. ct: actual count

ACTFL: American Council on the Teaching of Foreign Languages

actg: acting

ACTG: Advance Carrier Training

Group

acth (ACTH): adrenocorticotrophic hormone

act/ic: active—in commission

ACTION: American Council To Improve Our Neighborhoods

ACTION: (not an acronym but the current fusion of U.S. government youth agencies such as the Peace Corps and VISTA)

act/is: active—in service

ACTIV: Army Concept Team in Vietnam

ACTL: American College of Trial Lawyers

ACTM: Association of Cotton Textile Merchants of New York

ACTMC: Army Clothing, Textile, and Material Center

actnt: accountant

acto: automatic computing transfer oscillator

act/oc: active—out of commission

actol: air-cushion takeoff and landing

ACTOR: Askania cine-theodolite optical-tracking range

act/os: active—out of service

actp (ACTP): adrenocorticotrophic polypeptide

ACTR: Air Corps Technical Report

Acts: The Acts of the Apostles

ACTS: Acoustic Control and Telemetry System; Air Corps Tactical School; Airline Computer Tracing System (for identifying and returning lost luggage or other objects); Automatic Computer Telex System

ACTT: America's Christmas Train and Trucks (collects clothing, food, medical supplies, and toys for the people of South Vietnam)

ACTU: Association of Catholic Trade Unionists; Australian Council of Trade Unions

actv: activate

act. val: actual value

act. wt: actual weight

acu: address control unit

ACU: American Church Union; American Congregational Union; American Conservation Union; American Cycling Union; Association of College Unions; Association of Commonwealth Universities; Autocycle Union

ACUCM: Association of College and University Concert Managers

ACUE: American Committee of United Europe

ACUHO: Association of College and University Housing Officers

ACUNY: Associated Colleges of Upper New York

ACUP: Association of College and University Printers

ACUS: Administrative Conference of the United States; Atlantic Council of the United States

acv: actual cash value; air-cushion vehicle

ACV: air-cushion vehicle; auxiliary aircraft carrier or tender (3-letter symbol)

ACVAFS: American Council of Voluntary Agencies for Foreign Service

ACVC: American Council of Venture Clubs

ACVP: American College of Veterinary Pathologists

acw: aircraft control and warning; alternating continuous waves; automatic car wash

ACW: Air Control and Warning (system); Aircraftwoman; American Chain of Warehouses

AC & W: Air Communications and Weather (naval group)

ACWA: Amalgamated Clothing Workers of America

ACWAI: Automatic Car Wash Association International

ACWC: Advisory Committee on Weather Control

ACWF: Army Central Welfare Fund

ACWL: Army Chemical Warfare Laboratory

ACWO: Aircraft Control and Warning Officer

ACWRON: Aircraft Control and Warning Squadron

ACWRRE: American Cargo War Risk Reinsurance Exchange

ACWS: Aircraft Control and Warning System

AC & WS: Aircraft Control and Warning Station(s)

ACY: Akron, Canton & Youngstown (railroad); American Cyanamid Company (stock exchange symbol); Atlantic City, New Jersey (airport)

AC & Y: Akron, Canton & Youngstown (railroad)

ad: active duty; a drink; a drug (addict); advertisement; advertising; aerodynamic decelerator; after drain; air dreied; airdrome; area drain; average deviation

a/d: altitude/depth; analog-to-digital

a & d (A & D): accounting and disbursing

a d: *a droit* (French—to the right)

a.d.: *auris dexter* (Latin—right ear)

ad 2 vlc.: *ad duas vices* (Latin—for two doses; for two times)

a D: *ausser Dienst* (German

—retired)

Ad: Adam

AD: Aden Airways; Air Defense; Air Depot; Air Division; Airdrome; Airframe Design (division); Airworthiness Directive; Appellate Division; Assembly District; Astia Document; Atlantic & Danville (railroad); *Aviatsionnaya Diviziya* (Russian—Aviation Division); destroyer tender (naval symbol)

A-D: Albrecht Dürer; Antonin Dvořák

A/D: Air Depot

A & D: Atlantic & Danville (railroad)

AD: *Acción Democratica* (Spanish—Democratic Action Party)—Venezuela's democratic movement begun by Romulo Betancourt

A.D.: *Anno Domini* (Latin—in the Year of our Lord)

ada: action data automation; actuarial data assembly; average daily attendance; average deviation adjustment

ada: *adalah* (Arabic—equity; justice)

ADA: Air Defense Area; American Dairy Association; American Dehydrators Assocation; American Dental Association; American Dermatological Association; American Diabetes Association; American Dietetic Association; Americans for Democratic Action; Atomic Development Authority; Automobile Dealers Association

ADAA: American Dental Assistants Association; Art Dealers Association of America

adac: automatic direct analog computer

ADAC: *Allgemeiner Deutscher Automobilclub* (The German Automobile Club)

adacx: automatic data acquisition and computer complex

adad: air defense artillery director

Adag: *adagio* (Italian—slowly and expressively)

adaline: adaptive linear neuron

adam: adamantine; advanced data management; air deflection and modulation; automatic distance and angle measurement

ADAM: Agriculture Department Automated Manpower

adaml: advise by airmail

adamm (ADAMM): area defense anti-missile missile

adandac: administrative and accounting purposes

ADAOD: Air Defense Artillery Operations Detachment

ADAOO: Air Defense Artillery Operations Office(r)

adap: adapted

ADAP: Airport Development Aid Program (FAA)

ADAPS: Automatic Display and Plotting System

ADAPSO: Association of Data Processing Service Organizations

adapt.: adaption of automatically-programmed tools

adapticom: adaptive communication

ADAPTS: Air-Deliverable Anti-Pollution Transfer System (USCG)

adar: advanced development array radar; analog-to-digital-to-analog recording

ADAR: Air Defense Area

ADAS: Action Data Automation System; Agricultural Development Advisory Service

ADASC: Auto Dismantlers Association of Southern California (often called ADA)

ada(si): (Turkish—island)

adat: automatic data accumulation and transfer

adaval: advise availability

A-day: assault day

ADB: Apollo Data Bank (NASA); Asian Development Bank; Atlantic Development Board (Canada)

ADB: Australian Dictionary of Biography

A.D.B.: Bachelor of Domestic Arts

ADBC: American Defenders of Bataan and Corregidor

ADBM: Association of Dry Battery Manufacturers

adc: active duty commitment; adopted child; advance delivery of correspondence

ADC: Aerophysics Development Corporation; Agricultural Development Council; Aide-de-Camp; Aid to Dependent Children; Air Defense Command; Air Development Center Air Diffusion Council; Alaska Defense Command; American Distilling Company; American Dock Company; Aviation Development Council

adcad: airways data collection and distribution

ADCC: Air Defense Control Center

ADCI: American Die Casting Institute

ADCO: American Dredging Company

ADCOC: Area Damage Control Center

ADCOM: Administrative Command

adcon: advise or issue instructions to all concerned; analog-to-digital computer

ADCONSEN: (with the) advice of consent of the Senate (of the United States)

ADCOP: Area Damage Control Party

adc's: analog-to-digital converters

ADCSP: Advanced Defense Communications Satellite Program

ADCT: Art Director's Club—Toronto

ad curtain: advertisement curtain (theater)

add.: addendum (Latin—addition)

add.: airborne digital decoder

ad & d: accidental death and dismemberment (insurance)

ADD: Addis Ababa, Ethiopia (airport); Aerospace Defense Division; Aviastiia Dalnego Deistviia (Russian—Long-Range Bombing Force)

ADDA: Air Defense Defended Area

addar: automatic digital data acquisition and recording

ADDAS: Automatic Digital Data Assembly System

ADDC: Air Defense Direction Center

ADDL: Anti-Digit Dialing League

Add-Can: Addicts-Canada

ADDDS: Automatic Direct Distance Dialing System

adder.: automatic-digital data-error recorder

Addie: Ada; Adela; Adelaide; Adelina; Adeline

ADDP: Air Defense Defended Point

ADDS: Apollo Document Descriptions Standards (NASA); Automatic Data Digitizing System; Automatic Direct Distance Dialing System

addsd: addressed

addu: additional duty

ade: automated drafting equipment

ADE: Animal Disease Eradication (Department of Agriculture division)

ADEA: American Driver Education Association

Adeen: Aberdeen(shire)

ad effect.: ad effectum (Latin—until effective)

Adel: Adelaide; Adelochorda

ADELA: Atlantic Community Development Group for Latin America

ADEP: Air Depot

adept.: automatic data extractor and plotting table

ADEPT: Agricultural and Dairy Educational Political Trust

a des: a destra [Italian—at (to) the right]

ADES: Automatic Digital Encoding System

adf: after deducting freight; air direction finder; automatic direction finder

Adf: Adolf

ADF: Air Defense Force; Air Development Force; Army Distaff Foundation

adfc: adiabatic film cooling

ADFC: Air Defense Filter Center

ADFI: American Dog Feed Institute

ad fin.: ad finem (Latin—to the end)

ADFL: Association of Departments of Foreign Languages

ADFOR: Adriatic Force Force

ADFS: American Dentists for Foreign Service

ADFSC: Automatic Data Field Systems Command

adg: axiodistogingival

ADG: degaussing vessel (3-letter symbol)

ADGA: American Dairy Goat Association

ADGB: Air Defence of Great Britain

A & D G C: Alliance and Dublin Consumers Gas Company

adge: air-defense ground environment

ad grat. acid.: ad gratam acidatem (Latin—to a pleasing acidity)

ADGRU: Advisory Group

adh: adhesive; antidiuretic hormone

ADH: Academy of Dentistry for the Handicapped

ADHA: American Dental Hygienists Association

adhca: advise this headquarters of complete action

adhib: adhibeatur (Latin—administer)

ad hoc: (Latin—for this special purpose)

adi: adiabat(ic); air defense intercept; air defense interceptor; alien declared intention; antidetonation injection; attitude direction indicator; automatic direction indicator

ADI: Acoustical Door Institute; Air Defense Interceptor; Air Distribution Institute; American Documentation Institute

ADIC: American Dental Interfraternity Council

adil (ADIL): air defense identification line

ad inf: ad infinitum (Latin—to

infinity)

ad init.: *ad initium* (Latin—at the beginning)

ad int.: *ad interim* (Latin—in the interim; meanwhile)

Ad Intel Cen: Advanced Intelligence Center

ADIOS: Automatic Digital Input-Output System

adipu: advise whether individual may be properly used in your installation

ADIS: Air Defense Integrated System; Automatic Data Interchange System

adit: analog digital integrating translator

ADiv: Air Division

ADIZ: Air Defense Identification Zone

adj: adjective; adjoint; adjust

Adj: Adjutant

Adj.A.: Adjunct in Arts

Adj Gen: Adjutant General

adl: activities of daily living; automatic data link(ing)

ADL: Adelaide, Australia (airport); Admiral Corporation (stock exchange symbol); Anti-Defamation League (B'nai B'rith); Arthur D. Little (corporation); Authorized Data List; Automatic Data Link(ing)

ADLA: Art Directors' (club) Los Angeles

Adlai: Adlai Stevenson II

ad lib.: *ad libitum* (Latin—at one's pleasure)

ADLO: Air Defense Liaison Office(r)

ad loc.: *ad locum* (Latin—at this passage or place)

ADLOG: Advance Logistical Command

ADLP: Australian Democratic Labour Party

ADLS: Air Dispatch Letter Service

ADLTDE: Association of Dark Leaf Tobacco Dealers and Exporters

adm: air defense missile; atomic demolition munition; average daily membership

Adm: Admiral; Admiralty

ADM: Affiliated Dress Manufacturers; Air Defense Missile; American Drug Manufacturers (association)

adma: automatic drafting machine

ADMA: Aircraft Distributors and Manufacturers Association; American Drug Manufacturers Association; Aviation Distributors and Manufacturers Association

Adm Cen: Administration Center;

Administrative Center; Admiralty Center

Adm Co: Admiralty Court

ADMI: American Dry Milk Institute

admin: administration; administrative; administrator

AdminInstr: Administrative Instructions

AdminO: Administrative Order(s)

ADMIRAL: Automatic and Dynamic Monitor with Immediate Relocation, Allocation, and Loading (system)

admire.: automatic diagnostic maintenance information retrieval

ADMIRES: Automatic Diagnostic Maintenance Information Retrieval System

admix: administratrix

adml: average daily member load

Adml: Admiral; Admiralty

admn: administration

admón: *administración* (Spanish —administration)

Admor: *Administrador* (Spanish —Administrator)

ad mov.: *ad moveatur* (Latin—let it be moved); apply

admr: administrator

adms: administrator

ADMSC: Automatic Digital Message Switching Centers (DoD)

ADMSLBN: Air Defense Missile Battalion (USA)

admx: administratrix

Adn: Aden

ADN: Accession Designation Number; Allgemeiner Deutscher Nachrichtendienst (General German News Service); Ashley, Drew & Northern (railroad)

ADNAC: Air Defense of the North American Continent

ad naus.: *ad nauseam* (Latin—boring to the point of nausea)

ado: advanced development objective; axiodistoclusal

Ado: *adagio* (Italian—slowly and expressively)

ADO: Air Defense Officer

ADOBE: Atmospheric Dispersion of Beryllium (program)

ADOC: Air Defense Operations Center

ADOGA: American Dehydrated Onion and Garlic Association

adoit: automatically-directed outgoing intertoll trunk (Bell)

ADONIS: Automatic Digital On-Line Instruments System

adop: adoption

adot: automatically-directed outbound trunk (Bell)

adp: adenosine diphosphate; air-

borne data processor; ammonium dihydrogen phosphate; automatic data processing

ADP: Academy of Denture Prosthetics; Air Defense Position; Airport Development Program; Animal Disease and Parasite (Research Division—Department of Agriculture); Automatic Data Processing

ADPB: Australian Dairy Produce Board

ADPC: Automatic Data Processing Center

adpe: automatic data processing equipment

adpl: average daily patient load

adplan: advancement planning; advertising planning

adpo: aircraft depot

ad pond. om.: *ad pondus omnium* (Latin—to the whole weight)

ADPS: Automatic Data Processing System(s)

ADPSO: Association of Data Processing Service Organizations

adpt: adapter

adr: address; asset depreciation range

adr: *address* (Swedish—address); *addresse* (Dano-Norwegian —address)

Adr: *Adresse* (German—address)

Adr: Adrian; Adriatic

ADR: Accepted Dental Remedies; Aircraft Direction Room

ADRA: Animal Diseases Research Association

adrac: automatic digital recording and control

ADRB: Army Disability Review Board; Army Discharge Review Board

ADRDE: Air Defense Research and Development Establishment

adren: adrenal; adrenalin

ADRI: Angkatan Darat Republik Indonesia (Indonesian Army)

ADRIS: Automatic Dead Reckoning Instrument Systems

adrm: airdrome

ADROBN: Airdrome Battalion

ADRS: Analog-to-Digital Data Recording System

adrt: analog data recording transcriber

adr tel: *addresse telegraphique* (French—telegraphic address)

ads: advertisements; area, date, subject; autograph document signed; automatic door seal

ADS: Académie des Sciences (Academy of Science); Aerial Delivery System; Air Defense Sector; American Daffodil Society; American Dahlia Society; American Denture Society; American Dialect Society; American Dental Service; Association of Diesel Specialists

ADSA: American Dairy Science Association; American Dental Society of Anesthesiology; Atomic Defense Support Agency

ad. saec.: ad saeculum (Latin—to the century)

ADSAS: Air-Derived Separation Assurance System

adsc: average daily service charge (in hospitals)

ADSC: Advanced Section Communication Zone; Automatic Data Service Center

adscom: advanced shipboard communications

ad sec.: ad sectam [(Latin—at [Latin suit of (legal)]

AdSec: Advanced Section

adshpdat: advise shipping data

ADSID: Air Defense Systems Integration Division

ADSL: Assembly Department Shortage List

ADSM: American Defense Service Medal

ADSMO: Air Defense Systems Management Office

ADSN: Accounting and Disbursing Station Number

ADSOC: Administrative Support Operations Center

adss: analysis of digitized seismic signals

ADSS: Aircraft Damage Sensing System; Australian Defense Scientific Service

ADST: Atlantic Daylight Saving Time

adstadis: advise status and/or disposition

adstkoh: advise stock on hand

ADSUP: Automatic Data Systems Uniform Practice(s)

adt: any damn thing (abbreviation for a placebo); automatic damage template; average daily dose

adT: an demselben Tage (German—the same day)

ADT: American District Telegraph; Applied Drilling Technology; Atlantic Daylight Time

ADTA: American Dental Trade Association

ADTC: Armament Development Test Center (USAF)

adtech: advanced decoy technology

ADTIC: Arctic, Desert, Tropic Information Center

ADTSEA: American Driver Traffic Safety Education Association

adtu: automatic digital test unit; auxiliary data translator unit

ad 2 vic.: ad duas vices (Latin—for two doses)

adu: acceleration-deceleration unit; accumulation-distribution unit

ADU: Aircraft Delivery Unit

adult.: adulterant; adulterate; adulteration

ad us.: ad usum (Latin—according to custom)

adv: advance; adverb

adv.: adversum (Latin—adversely; (Latin—adversely; against)

a/dv: arterio/deep venous (injection)

Adv.: Adventist; Adviser

ad val.: ad valorem (Latin—according to value)

adv chgs: advance charges

advdisc: advance discontinuance of allotment

adven: adventure; adventurer

advert: advertising

adv frt: advance freight

Adv Intel Cen: Advanced Intelligence Center

ad virus: adenovirus

ADVISE: Area Denial Visual Identification Security Equipment

advl: adverbial

advon: advanced echelon; advanced operations unit

adv pmt: advance payment

adv poss: adverse possession

advst: advance stoppage

advt: advertise; advertisement; advertiser; advertising

adw: assault (with) deadly weapon

ADW: Air Defense Warning

ADWA: Atlantic Deeper Waterways Association

ADWC: Air Defense Weapons Center (USAF)

ADWKP: Air Defense Warning Key Point

adx: automatic data exchange

ADX: Adams Express Company (stock exchange symbol)

Adyg: Adygey

Adzh: Adzhar

ae: above the elbow; account executive; aircraft equipment; air escape; almost everywhere

ae.: aetatis (Latin—aged; at the age of)

a & e: aerospace and electronic; armaments and electronics

AE: Agricultural Engineering (Department of Agriculture research division); Airborne Equipment (naval division); Air Explorer; Aktiebolaget Atomenergi (Swedish Atomic Energy Corporation); ammunition ship (naval

symbol); Automatic Electric

A-E: Adam and Eve; Astro-Eugenics

AE: Aeon (pen name of George William Russell

AÉ: *Atomnaya Énergiya* (Russian—Atomic Energy)

AE: *American Ephemeris*

A.E.: Aeronautical Engineer; Agricultural Engineer; Architectural Engineer; Associate in Education; Associate in Engineering

A & E: Agricultural and Engineering; Architectural and Engineering

A & E: *Adolphus and Ellis*

AEA: Actors' Equity Association; Adult Education Association; American Economic Association; American Education Association; American Enterprise Association; American Export Airlines; Airtists Equity Association; Atomic Energy Authority; Automotive Electric Association

AEAA: *Asociación de Escritores y Artistas Americanos* (Association of American Writers and Artists)

AEAO: Airborne Emergency Actions Officer

AEAs: American Entertainers Abroad

AEAUSA: Adult Education Association of the United States of America

AEB: Area Electricity Board

aec: altitude engine control

AEC: Aeronautical Research Council; Agricultural Economics (division of Department of Agriculture); Aircraft Radio Corporation; Airworthiness Examination Committee; Alaska Engineering Commission (Alaska Railroad); Aluminum Extruders Council; American Engineering Council; Army Education Center; Army Educational Center; Army Educational Corps; Army Electronics Command (formerly Signal Corps); Atlantic & East Carolina (railroad); Atlas Educational Center; Atomic Energy Commission

A & EC: Atlantic & East Carolina (railroad)

AEC-A: Atomic Energy Commission—Albuquerque Operations Office

AEC-AI: Atomic Energy Commission—Argonne, Illinois

AEC-ANM: Atomic Energy Commission—Albuquerque, New

Mexico
AEC-ASC: Atomic Energy Commission—Aiken, South Carolina
AECB: Atomic Energy Control Board (Canada)
AEC-BC: Atomic Energy Commission—Berkeley, California
AECC: Aeromedical Evacuation Control Center
AEC-CC: Atomic Energy Commission—Canoga Park, California
AEC-FOA: Atomic Energy Commission—Fernal Office Area, Cincinnati, Ohio
AEC-HW: Atomic Energy Commission—Hanford, Washington
AECI: African Explosives and Chemical Industries
AEC-II: Atomic Energy Commission—Idaho Falls, Idaho
AECL: Atomic Energy of Canada, Limited
AEC-LN: Atomic Energy Commission—Las Vegas, Nevada
AEC-LOC: Atomic Energy Commission—Lockland Aircraft Reactors Operations, Cincinnati, Ohio
AECM: Albert Einstein College of Medicine
AECP: Airman Education and Commissioning Program
AEC-NY: Atomic Energy Commission—New York Operations Office
AECOM: Army Electronic Command
AEC-OR: Atomic Energy Commission—Oak Ridge Operations Office
AEC-OT: Atomic Energy Commission—Oak Ridge, Tennessee
aecp: altitude engine control panel
AECP: Airman Education and Commissioning Program
AEC-PP: Atomic Energy Commission—Pittsburgh, Pennsylvania
AEC-PR: Atomic Energy Commission—Pittsburgh Naval Reactors Operations Office
AEC-RW: Atomic Energy Commission—Richland, Washington
AECT: Association for Educational Communications and Technology
AEC-UN: Atomic Energy Commission—Upton, L.I., N.Y.
aed (AED): automatic engineering design
AED: Associated Equipment Distributors; Association of Electronic Distributors
A.Ed.: Associate in Education
A.E.D.: *artium elegantium doctor* (Latin—Doctor of Fine Arts)
AEDB: Apollo Engineering Development Board

AEDC: Arnold Engineering Development Center
AEDD: Air Engineering Development Division
AEDO: Aircraft Engineering District Office
AED-RCA: Astro-Electronics Division-RCA
AEDS: Association of Educational Data Systems; Atomic Energy Detection System
aee: absolute essential equipment; absolutely essential equipment
Ae.E.: Aeronautical Engineer
AEE: Atomic Energy Establishment
A.E.E.: Associate in Engineering
AEEC: Airlines Electronic Engineering Committee
AEEL: Aeronautical Electronic and Electrical Laboratory
AEEN: Agence Européenne pour l'Energie Nucleaire (European Agency for Atomic Energy)
AEET: Atomic Energy Establishment, Trombay (India)
AEF: Advertising Educational Foundation; Aerospace Education Foundation; Aircraft Engineering Foundation; Allied Expeditionary Force; American Economic Foundation; American European Foundation; American Expeditionary Force; Americans for Economic Freedom; Artists Equity Fund; Aviation Engineer(ing) Force
A-effect: alienation effect
AEFORT: American-European Friends of ORT (Organization for Rehabilitation through Training)
AEFR: Aurora, Elgin & Fox River (railroad)
aeg: active element group(ing); air encephalogram(s)
aeg.: *aeger* (Latin—sick)
Aeg: Aegean
AEG: Allgemeine Elektrizitäts Gesellschaft (General Electric Company)
AEGIMRDA: Army Engineer Geodesy, Intelligence and Mapping Research and Development Agency
AEGp: Aeromedical Evacuation Group (USAF)
AEHA: Army Environmental Health Agency
AEHL: Army Environmental Health Laboratory
AEI: Air Express International; American Express International; Annual Efficiency Index; Associated Electrical Industries;

Association des Écoles Internationales
AEIB: Association for Education in International Business
AEIC: Association of Edison Illuminating Companies
AEIL: American Export Isbrandtsen Lines
A.E.I.O.U.: *Austria Erit In Orbe Ultima* (Latin—Austria will be the world's last survivor)—ancient acrostic of House of Hapsburg
AEIPPR: American Enterprise Institute for Public Policy Research
AEJ: Association for Education in Journalism
aek: all-electric kitchen
ael: audit error list
AEL: Aeronautical Engine Laboratory; Aircraft Engine Laboratory; American Electronic Laboratories; American Emigrants League; Americanism Education League; Animal Education League; Automation Engineering Laboratory
AELE: Americans for Effective Law Enforcement
AELTC: All England Lawn Tennis Club
AEM: Advance Engineering Memorandum; Aircraft and Engine Mechanic; American Meter Company (stock exchange symbol); Association of Electronic Manufacturers; Aviation Electrician's Mate
AE & MP: Ambassador Extraordinary and Minister Plenipotentiary
AEMS: American Engineering Model Society
AEMSA: Army Electronics Material Support Agency
aen: advance evaluation note
aen.: *aeneus* (Latin—made of bronze or copper)
Aen.: *Aeneid* (Virgil's epic poem)
A.En.: Associate in English
A.Eng.: Associate in Engineering
AEO: Air Engineer(ing) Office(r); Appeal Examining Office(r)
AEOB: Advanced Engine Overhaul Base
Aeol: Aeolian; Aeolic
AEOO: Aeromedical Evacuation Operations Officer
aeop: amend existing orders pertaining to
aep: accrued expenditure paid
AEP: Addo Elephant Park (South Africa); Adult Education Program; American Electric Power
AEP: *Agence Européene de*

Productivité (French—European Production Agency)

AE & P: Ambassador Extraordinary and Plenipotentiary

AEPC: Appalachian Electric Power Company

AEPCO: American Elsevier Publishing Company

AEPEM: Association of Electronic Parts and Equipment Manufacturers

AEPG: Army Electronic Proving Ground

AEPI: American Educational Publishers Institute

AEPS: American Electroplaters Society

aer: auditory-evoked response

AER: Abbreviated Effectiveness Report; Aeronautical Engineering Report; Airman Effectiveness Report; Army Emergency Relief; Association for Education by Radio; Association Européenne pour l'Étude du Probleme des Refugies (European Association for the Study of the Refugee Problem)

aera: aeration

AERA: American Educational Research Association; American Engine Rebuilders Association

AERB: Army Education Requirements Board

AERC: Association of Executive Recruiting Consultants

aercab: advanced escape/rescue capability; advanced aircrew escape/rescue capability

AERDL: Army Electronics Research and Development Laboratory

AERE: Atomic Energy Research Establishment

AERI: Automotive Exhaust Research Institute

AERNO: Aeronautical Equipment Reference Number

aero: aerographer; aeronautical; aeronautics

AERO: Association of Electronic Reserve Officers

aerobee: aerojet/bumblebee (naval missile)

aerodyn: aerodynamics

Aero E: Aeronautical Engineer

Aer Of: Aerological Officer

AEROFLOT: Aero Flotilla (Soviet Air Lines)

aerol: aerological

aeromed: aeromedical

aeron: aeronautical

AERONAVES: Aeronaves de México

AERONORTE: Empresa de Transportes Aereos Norte do Brasil

(North Brazil Airways)

Aero O/Y: Finnair (Finnish Airlines)

aerosp: aerospace

aerospace: aeronautics + space

aerospacecom: aerospace communication(s)

aerotel: airplane hotel (hangar)

Aerovias "Q": Aerovias Cubana (Cuban Airlines)

AERS: Atlantic Estuarine Research Society

AERT: Association for Education by Radio-Television

Aes: Aesop (Greek fabulist)

Aes: (Latin—bronze or copper)—used by numismatists to denote bronze or copper coins or coins of such colors

AES: Aerospace Electrical Society; Agricultural Estimates (division of Department of Agriculture); Agricultural Experiment Station; Aircraft Electrical Society; Airways Engineering Society; American Electrochemical Society; American Electroencephalographic Society; American Electroplaters Society; American Entomological Society; American Epidemiological Society; American Epilepsy Society; American Equilibration Society; American Ethnological Society; American Eugenics Society; Apollo Extension System; Army Exchange Service; Atlantic Estuarine Society; Audio Engineering Society

AESBOW: Association of Engineers and Scientists of the Bureau of Weapons (USN)

AESC: American Engineering Standards Committee

AESE: Association of Earth Science Editors

AESHS: Alfred E. Smith High School

AESOP: Artificial Earth Satellite Observation Program Program; Automated Engineering and Scientific Optimization Program (NASA)

AESq: Aeromedical Evacuation Squadron (USAF)

AESQ: Air Explorer Squadron

aet.: aetatis (Latin—at or of the age of)

AET: Aerlinte Eireann Teoranta (Irish Airlines)

A.E.T.: Associate in Electrical Technology; Associate in Electronic Technology

AETA: American Educational Theatre Association

AETE: Aerospace Engineering Test

Establishment (Canada)

AETFAT: Association pour l'Étude Taxonomique de la Flore d'Afrique Tropicale (Association for the Taxonomic Study of African Tropical Flora)

AETM: Aviation Electronic Technician's Mate

AETR: Advanced Engineering Test Reactor

AETS: Association for the Education of Teachers in Science

aeu: accrued expenditure unpaid

AEU: Amalgamated Engineering Union; American Ethical Union

aev (AEV): aerothermodynamic elastic vehicle

aevac: air evacuation

AEW: Airborne Early Warning

AEW & C: Airborne Early Warning and Control

AEWES: Army Engineers Waterways Experiment Station

AEWRON: Airborne Early Warning Squadron

AEWS: Advanced Earth Satellite Weapon System (USAF); Aircraft Early Warning System (DoD)

aex: automatic electronic exchange (facilitating telephony)

AExO: Assistant Experimental Officer

af: ale firkin; audio fidelity (AF)

af: afgang (Danish—departure); *anno futuro* (Italian—next year)

a-f: anti-foam; audio-frequency

a & f (A & F): accounting and finance

Af: Africa; Afrikaans; African(s); Académie française (French Academy)

AF: Africa(n); Air Force; air freight; Anglo-French; Armored Force; Aviation Photographer's Mate; provision stores ship (2-letter symbol)

A & F: Agriculture and Forestry (Senate Committee)

AFA: Aerophilatelic Federation of the Americas; Air Force Association; Alien Firearms Act; American Finance Association; American Foundrymen's Association; American Freedom Association; Association of Federal Appraisers

A.F.A.: Associate in Fine Arts

AF of A: Advertising Federation of America

AFAA: Adult Film Association of America; Automatic Fire Alarm Association

AFAAEC: Air Force Academy and Aircrew Examining Center

AFAC: Air Force Armament Center; American Fisheries Advisory Committee
AFADO: Association of Food and Drug Officials
AFAFC: Air Force Accounting and Finance Center
AFAG: Airforce Advisory Group
AFAITC: Armed Forces Air Intelligence Training Center
AFAL: Air Force Avionics Laboratory
AF & AM: Ancient Free and Accepted Masons
Af-Am(s): Afro-American(s)
AFAPL: Air Force Aero-Propulsion Laboratory
AFAR: Azores Fixed Acoustic Range (NATO)
AFAS: Air Force Aid Society
AFASE: Association for Applied Solar Energy
AFA-SEF: Air Force Association—Space Education Foundation
AFAUD: Air Force Auditor General
afb: acid-fast bacillus; antifriction bearing
afb: afbeelding (Dutch—illustration)
AFB: Air Force Base; American Farm Bureau; American Foundation for the Blind
AFBF: American Farm Bureau Federation
AFBMA: Antifriction Bearing Manufacturers Association
AFBNM: Agate Fossil Beds National Monument (Nebraska)
AFBS: American and Foreign Bible Society
AFBSD: Air Force Ballistic Systems Division
afc: automatic frequency control
AFC: Air Force Cross; American Football Conference; Apollo Flight Control (NASA); Area Forecast Center; Australian Flying Corps
AFCAL: Association Français de Calcul
AFCC: Air Force Communications Center
AFCCB: Air Force Configuration Control Board
AFCCDD: Air Force Command and Control Development Division
AFCCP: Air Force Component Command Post
AFCD: Air Force Cryptologic Depot
AFCEA: Armed Forces Communications and Electronics Association

AFCent: Allied Forces, Central Europe
AFCI: American Foot Care Institute
AFCM: Air Force Commendation Medal
AFCMA: Aluminum Foil Container Manufacturers Association
AFCMD: Air Force Contract Management Division
AFCMO: Air Force Contract Management Office
AFCN: American Friends of the Captive Nations
afco: automatic fuel cutoff
AFCO: Air Force Contracting Officer
AF Compt: Air Force Comptroller
AFCON: Air Force Controlled (units)
AFCOS: Armed Forces Courier Service
AFCR: American Federation for Clinical Research
AFCRC: Air Force Cambridge Research Center
AFCRL: Air Force Cambridge Research Laboratories
AFCS: Active Federal Commissioned Service; Adaptive Flight Control System; Air Force Communications Service; Automatic Flight Control System
AFCSL: Air Force Communications Security Letter
AFCSM: Air Force Communications Security Manual
AFCSP: Air Force Communications Security Pamphlet
AFCWF: Air Force Civilian Welfare Fund
afd: accelerated freeze drying
afd: afdeling (Dano-Norwegian or Dutch—part)
AFD: Air Force Depot; Association of Food Distributors; Association of Footwear Distributors; mobile floating drydock (naval symbol)
AFDAP: Air Force Directorate of Advanced Technology
AFDATACOM: Air Force Data Communications System
AFDB: African Development Bank; Air Force Decorations Board; large auxiliary floating drydock (naval symbol)
AFDC: Aid to Families with Dependent Children
AFDCB: Armed Forces Disciplinary Control Board
AFDCMI: Air Force Policy on Disclosure of Classified Military Information
AFDCUF: Aid to Families with Dependent Children of Unem-

ployed Fathers
AFDE: American Fund for Dental Education
AFDEA: American Funeral Directors and Embalmers Association
AFDL: small auxiliary floating drydock (naval symbol)
AFDM: medium auxiliary floating drydock (naval symbol)
AFDO: Air Force Duty Officer; Association of Food and Drug Officials
AFDOA: Armed Forces Dental Officers Association
AFDOUS: Association of Food and Drug Officials of the United States
AFDP: Air Force Development Plan
AFDRB: Air Force Disability Review Board; Air Force Discharge Review Board
AFDRD: Air Force Director of Research and Development
AFDRQ: Air Force Director of Requirements
AFE: Administración de Ferrocarriles del Estado (State Railway Administration of Uruguay)
AFEA: American Farm Economic Association; American Film Export Association
AFEB: Armed Forces Epidemiological Board
AFELIS: Air Force Engineering and Logistics Information System
AFEM: Armed Forces Expeditionary Medal
AFEMS: Air Force Equipment Management System
AFERB: Air Force Educational Requirements Board
AFES: Air Force Exchange Service; American Far Eastern Society; Armed Forces Examining Stations
AFETR: Air Force Eastern Test Range (see ETR)
AFEX: Air Forces Europe Exchange
aff: affairs
AFF: Army Field Forces
AFFA: Air Freight Forwarders Association
AFFC: Air Force Finance Center
AFFDL: Air Force Flight Dynamics Laboratory
AFFE: Air Force Far East; Allied Forces Far East; Army Forces Far East
affet: affettuoso (Italian—tenderly; with pathos)
AFFFA: American Forged Fitting and Flange Association
AFFI: American Frozen Food Insti-

tute
affil: affiliated
AFFJ: American Fund for Free Jurists
AFFLC: Air Force Film Library Center
affores: afforestation
affret: *affrettando* (Italian—speeding the tempo)
AFFS: American Federation of Film Societies
afft: affidavit
AFFTC: Air Force Flight Test Center; Air Force Flying Training Command
afg: analog function generator
afg: *afgang* (Danish—departure)
Afg: Afghan; afghani (currency); Afghanistan; Afghans
AFGC: American Forage and Grassland Council
AFGCM: Air Force Good Conduct Medal
AFGE: American Federation of Government Employees
Afghan: Afghanistan
AFGIS: Aeiral Free Gunnery Instruction School
AFGM: American Federation of Grain Millers
AFGU: Aerial Free Gunnery Unit
AFGW: American Flint Glass Workers
AFGWC: Air Force Global Weather Central
AFH: Air Force Hospital; American Foundation for Homeopathy; Associated Federated Hotels
AFHC: Air Force Headquarters Command
AFHF: Air Force Historical Foundation; American Foot Health Foundation
AFHQ: Air Force Headquarters, Allied Forces Headquarters; Armed Forces Headquarters
AFHW: American Federation of Hosiery Workers
AFI: Air Filter Institute; American Film Institute; American Filter Institute; American Friends of Israel; Armed Forces Institute; Atlantic Refining Company (stock exchange symbol)
AFIA: American Foreign Insurance Association
AFIC: Air Force Intelligence Center
AFICCS: Air Force Interim Command and Control System
AFICE: Air Forces—Iceland
AFIED: Armed Forces Information and Education Division
AFII: American Federation of International Institutes

AFINE: *Association Française pour l'Industrie Nucleaire d'Equipment* (French Association for the Nuclear Equipment Industry)
AFINS: Airways Flight Inspector
AFIP: Air Force Intelligence Publication; Armed Forces Information Program; Armed Forces Institute of Pathology
AFIPS: American Federation of Information Processing Societies
AFIR: Air Force Installation Representative
afirm: affirmative
AFIRO: Air Force Installations Representative Officer
AFIS: Armed Forces Information School
afism: aluminum-free inorganic suspended material
AFISR: Air Force Industrial Security Regulations
AFIT: Air Force Institute of Technology
AFITAE: *Association Française d'Ingenieurs et Techniciens de l'Aeronautique et de l'Espace* (French Association of Aeronautical and Aerospace Engineers and Technicians)
AFJKT: Air Force Job-Knowledge Test
afk: *afkorting* (Dutch—abbreviation)
afl: abstract family of languages; anti-fatty liver
afl: *aflevering* (Dutch—part)
AFL: Aeroflot (Soviet Air Lines); Air Force Letter; American Federation of Labor; American Football League; Applied Fisheries Laboratory (University of Washington); Association for Family Living
AFLA: Amateur Fencers League of America; American Foreign Law Association; Asian Federation of Library Associations
AFLAT: Air Force Language Aptitude Test
AFLC: Air Force Logistics Command
AFL-CIO: American Federation of Labor and Congress of Industrial Organizations
afld: airfield
AFLP: American Farmer Labor Party; Armed Forces Language Program
AFLS: Air Force Library Service
AFLSA: Air Force Longevity Service Award
afm: antifriction metal
AFM: Air Force Manual; Air Force Medal; Air Force Museum;

American Federation of Musicians; Associated Fur Manufacturers
AFMA: Armed Forces Mangement Association
AFMA: *Air Force Manual of Abbreviations*
AFMBT: Artificial Flower Manufacturers Board of Trade
AFMDC: Air Force Missile Development Center
AFME: American Friends of the Middle East
AFMEC: African Methodist Episcopal Church
AFMed: Allied Forces, Mediterranean
AFMF: Air Fleet Marine Force
AFMH: American Foundation for Mental Hygiene
AFML: Air Force Materials Laboratory; Armed Forces Medical Library
AFMMFO: Air Force Medical Materiel Field Office
afmo: *afectísimo* (Spanish—most affectionate)
AFMPA: Armed Forces Medical Publication Agency
afmr: antiferromagnetic resonance
AFMR: American Foundation for Mangement Research; Armed Forces Master Records
AFMS: Air Force Medical Service; American Federation of Minerological Societies
AFMSC: Air Force Medical Specialist Corps
AFMTC: Air Force Missile Test Center
AFMVOP: Air Force Motor Vehicle Operator Test
AFN: Afrique du Nord (French North Africa); Air Force Finance Center; American Forces Network; Armed Forces Network
AF of N: Alaska Federation of Natives
AFNA: Air Force with Navy
AFNB: Armed Forces News Bureau
AFNC: Air Force Nurse Corps
AFNE: Allied Forces, Northern Europe
AFNOR: Association Française de Normalisation (French Standards Association)
AFNorth: Allied Forces, Northern Europe
AFO: Accounting and Finance Office(r); Airports Field Office; Atlantic Fleet Organization
AFOAR: Air Force Office for Aerospace Research
AFOAS: Air Force Office of Aerospace Sciences

AFOAT: Air Force Office for Atomic Energy
AFOB: American Foundation for Overseas Blind
AFOC: Air Force Operations Center
AFOECP: Air Force Officer Education and Commissioning Program
AFOIC: Air Force Officer in Charge
AFOQT: Air Force Officer Qualifying Test
AFORG: Air Force Overseas Replacement Group
a fort: a fortiori (Italian—with greater force)
AFOSI: Air Force Office of Special Investigations
AFOSR: Air Force Office of Scientific Research
AFOUA: Air Force Outstanding Unit Award
AFP: Agence France-Presse (successor to Havas); Air Force Pamphlet; Alternate Flight Plan; Annual Funding Program; Armed Forces Police; Authority for Purchase
afpa: automatic flow process analysis
AFPA: Aquarama and Fairmount Park Aquarium; Australian Fire Protection Association
AFPAO: Air Force Property Accountable Office(r)
AFPB: Air Force Personnel Board
AFPC: Air Force Personnel Council; Air Force Procurement Circular; American Food for Peace Council; Armed Forces Policy Council
AFPCB: Armed Forces Pest Control Board
AFPD: Armed Forces Police Detachment
AFPE: American Foundation for Pharmaceutical Education; American Foundation for Political Education
AFPH: American Federation of the Physically Handicapped
AFPI: Air Force Procurement Instructions; American Forest Products Industries
AFPP: Air Force Procurement Procedures
AFPPA: American Federation of Poultry Producers Associations
AFPR: Air Force Plant Representative
AFPRO: Action for Food Production; Air Force Plant Representatives's Office
AFPs: American Freeway Patrol cars (American Oil Company's

free service to motorists in trouble on freeways)
AFPS: Armed Forces Press Service
AFPT: Air Force Personnel Test
AFPTRC: Air Force Personnel and Training Research Center
AFPU: Air Force Postal Unit
AFQ: Association Forestière Québecoise (Quebec Forestry Service)
AFQA: Air Force Quality Assurance
AFQC: Air Force Quality Control
AFQT: Armed Forces Qualification Test
afr: airframe
Afr: Africa; African; Africans; Afrikaans (South African Dutch)
A Fr: Algerian franc
AFR: Air Force Regulation(s); Air Force Reserve
afra: average freight rate assessment
AFRA: American Farm Research Association; American Federation of Television and Radio Artists
A-frame: capital-A-shaped support frame
AFRASEC: Afro-Asian Organization for Economic Cooperation
Afrasia: Africa + Asia
AFRB: Air Force Retiring Board
AFRBA: Armed Forces Relief and Benefit Association
AFRBSG: Air Force Reserve Base Support Group
AFRC: Air Force Records Center
AFRCE: Air Force Regional Civil Engineer
AFRCSTC: Air Force Reserve Combat Support Training Center
AFRD: Air Force Research Division; Air Force Reserve Division; Association of Fund-Raising Directors
AFRes: Air Force Reserve
AFRESM: Armed Forces Reserve Medal
AFRESNAVSQ: Air Force Reserve Navigation Squadron
AFRFI: American Friends of Religious Freedom in Israel
AFRI: Applied Forest Research Institute
Afro: prefix meaning African or Black
AFROTC: Air Force Reserve Officers Training Corps
AFRPL: Air Force Rocket Propulsion Laboratory
AFRR: Air Force Reserve Region
AFRRG: Air Force Reserve Recovery Group
AFRRI: Armed Forces Radiobiology Research Institute

AFRS: Air Force Reserve Sector; Armed Forces Radio Service
AFRTS: Armed Forces Radio-Television Service
AFRVN: Air Force of the Republic of Viet Nam
afs: aforesaid ; atomic fluorescence spectroscopy
afs: afsender (Danish—sender)
AFS: Air Force Specialty; Air Force Station; Air Force Supply; Airline Feed System; Airways Facilities Shop; Alaska Ferry Service; American Feline Society; American Fern Society; American Field Service; American Fisheries Society; American Folklore Society; American Foundrymen's Society; American Fuchsia Society; Aviation Facilities Service
AFSA: Air Force Sergeants Association; American Flight Strips Association; American Foreign Service Association; Armed Forces Security Agency
AFSAB: Air Force Science Advisory Board
AFSAW: Air Force Special Activities Wing
AFSBO: American Federation of Small Business Organizations
AFSC: Air Force Service Command; Air Force Specialty Code; Air Force Supply Catalog; Air Force Systems Command; American Federation of Soroptimist Clubs; American Friends Service Committee; Armed Forces Staff College
AFSCC: Air Force Special Communications Center; Armed Forces Supply Control Center
AFSCF: Air Force Satellite Control Facility
AFSCM: Air Force Systems Command Manual
AFSCME: American Federation of State, County, and Municipal Employees
afsd: aforesaid
AFSec: Air Force Section
AFSF: Air Force Stock Fund
AFSMAAG: Air Force Section—Military Advisory Group
AFSN: Air Force Serial Number; Air Force Service Number; Air Force Stock Number
AFSouth: Allied Forces, Southern Europe
AFSS: Air Force Service Statement
AFSSD: Air Force Space Systems Division
AFSSO: Air Force Special Security

Office
AFSTC: Air Force Space Test Center
AFSUB: Army Air Forces Anti-Submarine Command
AFSWA: Armed Forces Special Weapons Agency
AFSWC: Air Force Special Weapons Center
AFSWP: Armed Forces Special Weapons Project
aft: after; afternoon; at, near, or toward the rear; automatic fine tuning
Aft: Aftenposten (Evening Post —Oslo)
AFT: Air Freight Terminal; American Federation of Teachers; Annual Field Training (USA)
AFTA: Atlantic Free Trade Area
AFTAC: Air Force Technical Applications Center
AFT (AFL-CIO): American Federation of Teachers
AFTB: Air Force Test Base
AFTC: Airborne Flight Training Command; American Fair Trade Council; American Fox Terrier Club; American Free Trade Clubs
AFTE: American Federation of Technical Engineers
AFTF: Air Force Task Force
AFTLI: Association of Feeling Truth and Living It
AFTM: American Foundation for Tropical Medicine
aftn: afternoon
AFTN: Aeronautical Fixed Telecommunications Network
AFTO: Air Force Technical Order
AFTOSB: Air Force Technical Order Standardization Board
AFTR: American Federal Tax Reports
AFTRA: American Federation of Television and Radio Artists
AFTRC: Air Force Training Command
AFTTH: Air Force Technical Training Headquarters
AFU: Advanced Flying Units; American Fraternal Union; Assault Fire Unit (U.S. Army)
AFUS: Air Force of the United States; Armed Forces of the United States
afv: armored fighting vehicle; armored force vehicle
AFVA: Air Force Visual Aid
AFvg: Anglo-French variable geometry
AFVN: Armed Forces Vietnam Network
AFW: Association for Family Welfare

AFWA: Air Force with Army
AFWETS: Air Force Weapons Effectiveness Testing System
AFWL: Air Force Weapons Laboratory; Armed Forces Writers League
AFWN: Air Force with Navy
AFWOFS: Air Force Weather Observing and Forecasting System
AFWR: Atlantic Fleet Weapons Range
AFWST: Armed Forces Women's Selection Test
AFWTR: Air Force Western Test Range (see WTR)
ag: armor grating; atrial gallop; axiogingival
a g: a gauche (French— to the left)
a-g: air-to-ground; anti-gas
a/g: air-to-ground
Ag: argentum (Latin—silver)
AG: Adjutant General; Aeronautical Standards Group; Air Group; Aktiengesellschaft (German —Joint stock company); Allegheny Ludlum Steel (stock exchange symbol); Artists Guild; Attorney General; Auditor General; escort research vessel (naval symbol); miscellaneous autiliary vessels (naval symbol); sonar research ship (naval symbol); technical research ship (naval symbol)
AG: Arkansas Gazette; Astronomische Gesellschaft
a/g/a: air-to-ground-to-air
aga: accelerated growth area
AGA: Abrasive Grain Association; Adjutants General Association; Alabama Gas (symbol); American Gas Association; American Gastroenterological Association; American Gastroscopic Association; American Genetic Association; American Glassware Association; American Goiter Association; American Gold Association
AGAC: American Guild of Authors and Composers
agacs: automatic ground-air-communication system
AGAFBO: Atlantic and Gulf American Flag Berth Operators
AGARD: Advisory Group for Aeronautical Research and Development (NATO)
agave.: automatic gimballed antenna vectoring equipment
agb: any good brand
AGB: Audits of Great Britain (television survey); icebreaker (3-letter symbol)
AGBAD: Alexander Graham Bell Association for the Deaf

agc: automatic gain control
AGC: Adjutant General's Corps; Aerojet-General Corporation; American Grassland Council; amphibious force flagship (naval symbol); Armed Guard Center; Associated General Contractors; astronomical great circle (course)
agca: automatic ground control approach
AGCA: Associated General Contractors of America
agcl: automatic ground-controlled landing
AGCM: Army Good Conduct Medal
AGCMWA: Amon G. Carter Museum of Western Art
AGCRSP: Army Gas-Cooled Reactor Systems Program
AGCT: Army General Classification Test
AGCTS: Armed Guard Center Training School
Ag-Cu al: silver-copper alloy (new U.S. coin facing)
agcy: agency
AGD: Academy of General Dentistry; Adjutant General's Department; American Gage Design; Auditor General's Department
AGDA: American Gasoline Dealers Association; American Gun Dealers Association
AGDE: escort research ship (naval symbol)
Ag. Dei: Agnus Dei (Latin—Lamb of God)
Ag Dept: Agriculture Department
AGDS: American Gage Design Standard
age. (AGE): aerospace ground equipment; automatic guidance electronics
Age: The Age (Melbourne)
Ag.E.: Agricultural Engineer
AGE: Amarillo Grain Exchange
A.G.E.: Associate in General Education
AGEC: Army General Equipment Command
AGED: Advisory Group on Electronic Devices
AGEH: hydrofoil research ship (naval symbol)
AGEHR: American Guild of English Handbell Ringers
ageocp: aerospace ground equipment out of commission for parts
AGEP: Advisory Group on Electronic Parts
AGER: environmental research ship (naval symbol)
agerd: aerospace ground-equipment requirements data

AGERS: Auxiliary General Electronics Research Ship(s)

AG & ES: American Gas & Electric System

AGET: Advisory Group on Electronic Tubes

AGF: Army Ground Forces; miscellaneous command ship (naval symbol)

AGFA: Aktiengesellschaft für Anilinfabrikation (Corporation for Aniline Manufacture)

AGFRTS: Air and Ground Forces Resources and Technical Staff (U.S. Army)

AGFSRS: Aircraft Ground Fire Suppression and Rescue System (DoD)

agg: aggregate

aggie: agriculture

Aggie: Agatha; Agnes

aggies: agate playing marbles; students of agricultural colleges or schools

aggr: aggregate

AGGR: Air-to-Ground Gunnery Range

aggred. feb.: *aggrediente febre* (Latin—while fever is developing)

AGGS: American Good Government Society

agi: adjusted gross income

AGI: American Geographical Institute; American Geological Institute; Annual General Inspection

AGIC: Air-Ground Information Center

AGIFORS: Airlines Group of International Federation of Operations Research Societies

agil: airborne general illumination light

AGILE: Autonetics General Information Learning Equipment

agit.: *agitatum* (Latin—shaken)

agit-prop: agitation and propaganda

agit. vas.: *agitato vase* (Latin—shaking the vessel)

agl: above ground level; airborne gun laying

AGL: lighthouse tender (3-letter symbol)

AGLC: Air-to-Ground Liaison Code

aglm: agglomerate

AGLS: Association of General and Liberal Studies

A-glue: airplane glue

agm (AGM): air-to-ground missile

AGM: American Guild of Music; missile range instrumentation ship (naval symbol)

AGMA: American Gear Manufacturers Association; Athletic

Goods Manufacturers Association

AGMA (AFL-CIO): American Guild of Musical Artists

AGMR: major communications relay ship (naval symbol)

agn: again; agnomen

Agn: Augustin

AGN: Aerojet-General Nucleonics

agnos: agnostic; agnosticism

AGO: Adjutant General's Office; Air Gunnery Officer; American Guild of Organists; Attorney General's Office; Attorney General's Opinion

AGOR: Auxiliary General Oceanographic Research (vessel)

AGP: Academy of General Practice; Adjutant General's Pool; Army Ground Pool; motor torpedo boat tender (naval symbol)

AGPA: American Group Psychotherapy Association

agpe: angle plate

agpi: automatic ground position indicator

agr: agree(ment); agricultural; agriculture

a/g ratio: albumin-globulin ratio

Agra U: Agra University

AGREE: Advisory Group on Reliability of Electronic Equipment

AGRF: American Geriatric Research Foundation

agri: agricultural; agriculturalist; agriculture; agriculturist

agribusiness: agricultural business (large-scale farming)

Agric E: Agricultural Engineer

Agricola: George Bauer

agro: aggravation; agrobiological; agrobiologist; agrobiology; agrologic; agrological; agronomical; agronomics; agronomist; agronomy; etc.

agrogeol: agrogeology

agron: agronomy

agros: agrostology

ags: agencies

Ags: Aguascalientes (inhabitants —Hidrocalidos)

AGS: Aircraft General Standards; Alabama Great Southern (railroad); Allied Geographic Section; American Gem Society; American Geographical Society; American Geriatrics Society; American Goat Society; American Gynecological Society; Army General Staff; Army Guard School; surveying ship (naval symbol)

A.G.S.: Associate in General Studies

agst: against

agt: agent; agreement

AGT: Art Gallery of Toronto; Association of Geology Teachers

AGTE: Association of Group Travel Executives

agto: *agosto* (Portuguese and Spanish—August)

AGU: American Geophysical Union

Agu Cur: Agulhas Current

Aguila y Serpiente: (Spanish—eagle and serpent)—creatures on Mexico's coat of arms

agv: aniline gentian violet

AGVA: American Guild of Variety Artists

agw: allowable gross takeoff weight

AGWI: American Gulf and West Indies (steamship line)

agz: actual ground zero

ah: after hatch; alter heading; antihalation

a-h: ampere-hour

a & h: accident and health; alive and healthy

Ah: ampere-hour; hyperopic astigmatism

AH: Airfield Heliport; Alfred Holt's Blue Funnel Line (house flag and funnel mark); Allis Chalmers (stock exchange symbol); Animal Husbandry (division of Department of Agriculture); Army Hospital; hospital ship (naval symbol)

A-H: American-Hawaiian Line; Arrow-Hart & Hegeman Electric Company

A.H.: *Anno Hebraico* (Latin—in the Hebrew Year)

A & H: Arm and Hammer (trade mark)

AHA: Adirondack Historical Association; American Hardboard Association; American Heart Association; American Hereford Association; American Historical Association; American Hospital Association; American Hotel Association; American Humane Association; American Humanist Association; American Hypnotherapy Association; Association of Handicapped Artists; Association for Humane Abortion

AHAM: Association of Home Appliance Manufacturers

AHAUS: Amateur Hockey Association of the U.S.

AHC: Academy of Hospital Counselors; American Hardware Corporation; American Hockey Coaches; American Horticultural Council; American Hospital Corps; Army Hospital Corps

AHCEI: American Histadrut Cultural Exchange Institute
ahd: ahead; airhead; aired head
AHD: American Heritage Dictionary
A-H DT: Alaska-Hawaii Daylight Time
AHE: Association for Higher Education
A.H.E.: Associate in Home Economics
AHEA: American Home Economics Association
A-head: acid head (underground slang—LSD addict)
AHEL: Army Human Engineering Laboratory (USA)
AHEM: Association of Hydraulic Equipment Manufacturers
AHEPA: American Hellenic Educational Progressive Association
AHES: American Humane Education Society
ahf: anti-hemophilic factor
AHF: American Health Foundation; American Heritage Foundation; American Hobby Federation; American Hungarian Foundation; Associated Health Foundation
AHF: American Hospital Formulary
ahg: antihemolytic globulin; antihuman globulin
AHG: American Housing Guild
AHHS: Alexander Hamilton High School
AHI: American Health Institute; American Honey Institute; American Hospital Institute
AHIL: Association of Hospital and Institution Libraries
AHIS: American Hull Insurance Syndicate
a.h.l.: *ad hunc locum* (Latin—at this place)
AHL: Alaska Historical Library; American Hockey League; Associated Humber Lines
AHLMA: American Home Laundry Manufacturers Association
ahm: ampere-hour meter
Ahm: Ahmadabad; Arnhem
ahma: advanced hypersonic manned aircraft
AHMA: American Hardware Manufacturers Association; American Hemisphere Marine Agencies; American Hotel and Motel Association
AHMC: Association of Hospital Management Committees
AHMI: Appalachian Hardwood Manufacturers Incorporated
AHMS: American Home Missionary Society

AHN: Assistant Head Nurse
AHNA: Accredited Home Newspapers of America
ahp: air horsepower
AHP: Assistant House Physician; Association for Humanistic Psychology
AHPC: American Heritage Publishing Company
AHPR: Academy of Hospital Public Relations
ahps: auxiliary hydraulic power supply
AHQ: Air Headquarters; Allied Headquarters; Army Headquarters
ahr: acceptable hazard rate
AHR: Association for Health Records
AHRGB: Association of Hotels and Restaurants of Great Britain
AHS: Aerospace High School; American Harp Society; American Hearing Society; American Helicopter Society; American Hibiscus Society; American Horticultural Society; American Hospital Supply (stock exchange symbol); American Humane Society; American Hypnodontic Society; Assistant House Surgeon; Aviation High School; Aviation Historical Society
AHSA: American Hampshire Sheep Association; American Horse Shows Association; Art, Historical, and Scientific Association
AHSB: Authority Health and Safety Branch
AHSC: American Hospital Supply Company
ahse: assembly, handling, and shipping equipment
ahsr: air height-surveillance radar
AHSS: Association of Home Study Schools
A-H ST: Alaska-Hawaii Standard Time
AHT: Animal Health Trust
a.h.v.: *ad hunc vocem* (Latin—at this word)
AHV: Altos Hornos de Vizcaya
AHWG: Ad Hoc Working Group (USA)
ai: airborne intercept; anti-icing; articulation index; artificial insemination
a.i.: *ad interim* (Latin—in the interim)
a & i: abstracting and indexing
AI: Aaland Islands; Admiralty Islands; Air India; Air Inspector; Air Installation(s); Airways Inspector; Alianza Interamericana (Inter-American Alliance); American Institute; Arc-

tic Institute; Army Intelligence; Astrologers International
A/I: Aptitude Index
A & I: Arts and Industries
aia: ain't it awful
AIA: Aerospace Industries Association; American Institute of Accountants; American Institute of Aeronautics; American Institute of Architects; Archeological Institute of America; Arctic Institute of America; Association Internationale d'Allergologie
AIAA: Aerospace Industries Association of America; American Institute of Aeronautics and Astronautics
AIAC: Air Industries Association of Canada
AIAE: Association of Institutes of Automobile Engineers
AIAESD: American International Association for Economic and Social Development (AIA)
AIAOS: Academic Instructor and Allied Officer School
AIAP: Ardmore Industrial Air Park
AIAS: Australian Institute of Agriculture and Science
AIB: American Institute of Baking; American Institute of Banking
AIB: Association des Industries de Belgique (Association of Belgian Industries)
AIBA: American Industrial Bankers Association
AIBS: American Institute of Biological Sciences
aic (AIC): aircraft in commission
AIC: Advanced Intelligence Center; Allied Intelligence Center; Allied Intelligence Committee; American Institute of Chemists; American Institution of Cooperation; Ammunition Identification Code; Arab Information Center; Army Industrial College; Army Intelligence Center; Art Information Center; Art Institute of Chicago
AICA: Association Internationale des Critiques d'Art (International Association of Art Critics)
aicbm (AICBM): anti-intercontinental ballistic missile
AICC: All-India Congress Committee
AICCC: American Institute of Child Care Centers
AICE: American Institute of Chemical Engineers; American Institute of Consulting Engineers
AI-CE: Atomic International—Combustion Engineering
AICF: America-Israel Cultural

Foundation

AIChE (preferred abbreviation): American Institute of Chemical Engineers

AICMA: Association Internationale des Constructeurs de Matériel Aéronautique

AICO: American Insulator Corporation

AICPA: American Institute of Certified Public Accountants

AICS: Air Induction Control System; American Institute of Ceylonese Studies

aid.: acute infectious disease; artificial insemination donor; avalanche injection diode

AID: Agency for International Development; Airline Interline Development; American Institute of Decorators; American Instructors of the Deaf; Army Information Digest; Army Intelligence Department; Artificial Insemination Donor; Association for International Development

AID: Acronyms and Initialisms Dictionary

A & ID: Acquisition and Improvement District

aida: attention-interest-desire-action (marketing formula); automatic instrumented diving assembly; automobile information data advertising

AIDA: Associated Independent Dairies of America

AIDD: American Institute of Design and Drafting

aide.: airborne insertion display equipment; aircraft installation diagnostic equipment

AIDIS: Asociación Interamericana de Ingenería Sanitaria (Inter-American Association of Sanitary Engineering)

AIDS: Abstracts Information Dissemination System; Automatic Inventory Dispatching System

AI & DSC: Army Information and Data System Command

AIEA: Agence Internationale de l'Energie Atomique (International Atomic Energy Agency)

AIECF: American Indian and Eskimo Cultural Foundation

A.I.Ed.: Associate in Industrial Education

AIEE: American Institute of Electrical Engineers

AIEF: Association Internationale des Études Françaises (International Association for French Studies)

AIEST: Association Internationale d'Experts Scientifiques du Tourisme (International Association of Scientific Experts in Tourism)

AIF: Air Intelligence Force; American Institute of France; Amphibian Imperial Forces; Army Industrial Fund; Atomic International Forum; Australian Imperial Forces

AIFCS: Airborne Interception Fire-Control System

AIFD: Alaska Institute for Fisheries Development

AIFLD: American Institute for Free Labor Development

AIFM: Association Internationale des Femmes Médecins (International Association of Women Doctors)

AIFT: American Institute for Foreign Trade

AIFTA: Anglo-Irish Free Trade Area

aig: all inertial guidance

AIG: Adjutant Inspector General; Association Internationale de Géodésia (International Geodesy Association)

AIGA: American Institute of Graphic Arts

aih: artificial insemination by husband

AIH: American Institute of Homeopathy; Aspen Institute of the Humanities

aiha: autoimmune hemolytic anemias

AIHA: American Industrial Hygiene Association

AIHED: American Institute for Human Engineering and Development

AIHS: American Irish Historical Society; Association Internationale d'Hydrologie Scientifique (International Association of Scientific Hydrology)

AIHSC: Auto Industry Highway Safety Committee

AII: Air India International

AIIA: Association of International Insurance Agents

AIIC: Army Imagery Intelligence Corps

AIID: American Institute of Interior Designers

AIIE: American Institute of Industrial Engineers

AIIMS: All-India Institute of Medical Sciences

AIKD: American Institute of Kitchen Dealers

ail.: aileron

AIL: Aeronautical Instruments Laboratory; Airborne Instruments Laboratory; Air Intelligence

Liaison; American Institute of Laundering; American Israeli Lighthouse; Art Institute of Light; Aviation Instrument Laboratory

AILA: American Institute of Landscape Architects

AILAS: Automatic Instrument Landing Approach System

AILS: Advanced Integrated Landing System

aim.: aerotriangulation (by observation of) independent models; air intercept missile; air-isolated monolithic (circuit)

AIM: Academy Introduction Mission (USCG); American Indian Movement; American Institute of Management; American Institute of Musicology; Army Installation Management; Association for the Integration of Management; Australian Institute of Management

AIM: Abstracts of Instructional Material

aima: as interest may appear

AIMA: All-India Management Association

AIMBW: American Institute of Men's and Boy's Wear

AIMES: Association of Interns and Medical Students

AIMF: American International Music Fund

AIMH: Academy of International Military History

AIMILO: Army/Industrial Material Information Liaison Office(s)

AIML: All-India Muslim League

AIMME: American Institute of Mining and Metallurgical Engineers

AIMMPE: American Institute of Mining, Metallurgical, and Petroleum Engineers

aimo: air mold; audibly-instructed manufacturing operations

aimp: air intercept missile package

AIMS: Advanced Intercontinental Missile System; Air Traffic Control Radar Beacon / Identification Friend or Foe / Mark XII / System; American Institute for Marxist Studies; American Institute for Mathematical Statistics; American Institute for Mental Studies; Association for International Medical Study; Automated Industrial Management System

AIMU: American Institute of Marine Underwriters

AIN: American Institute of Nutrition

AINA: Arctic Institute of North

America
AINEC: All-India Newspaper Editors' Conference
AINS: Assateague Island National Seashore (Maryland and Virginia)
ain't: ungrammatical contraction—am not, are not, has not, have not, is not
AINWR: Aleutian Islands National Wildlife Refuge (Alaska)
aio: activity-interest-option (marketing factor scores)
Aio: Aioi
AIO: Air Installation Office; Americans for Indian Opportunity; Arecibo Ionospheric Observatory
aip: accident insurance policy
AIP: Aeronautical Information Publication; Aerovias Panama (Panamanian airline); American Independent Party; American Institute of Planners; American Institute of Physics; American Institute for Psychoanalysis
AIPA: American Indian Press Association
AIPC: Association Internationale des Ponts et Charpentes (International Association of Bridges and Scaffolds); Association Internationale de Prophylaxie de la Cécité (International Association for the Prevention of Blindness)
AIPCEE: Association des Industries du Poisson de la Communauté Economique Européenne (Association of Fishing Industries of the European Economic Community)
AIPCN: Association Internationale Permanente des Congrès de Navigation (International Association of the Permanent Congress of Navigation)
AIPCR: Association Internationale Permanente des Congrès de la Route (International Association of the Permanent Congress of Routes)
AIPE: American Institute of Park Executives; American Institute of Plant Engineers
AIPG: American Institute of Professional Geologists
AIPLU: American Institute for Property and Liability Underwriters
AIPO: American Institute of Public Opinion
AIPR: American Institute of Pacific Relations
AIPS: Automatic Indexing and Proofreading System
AI & Q: Animal Inspection and

Quarantine
air.: average injection rate
AIR: Action for Industrial Recycling; Air Control Products; All-India Radio; American Institute of Refrigeration; American Institute of Research; Army Intelligence Reserve
AIRA: Air Attaché
AIRB: Alabama Inspection and Rating Bureau; Arkansas Inspection and Rating Bureau
airbm (AIRBM): anti-intermediate-range ballistic missile
AIRCAL: Air California
Air Can: Air Canada (formerly Trans-Canada Air Lines)
Air Cav: Airmobile Cavalry
Air Cdr: Air Commander
AIRCENT: Allied Air Forces, Central Europe
AIRCEY: Air Ceylon
Air Cmdre: Air Commodore
AIRCO: Air Reduction Chemical Company
AIRCOM: Air Force Communication Complex
AIRCOMNET: Air Communications Network
AIREA: American Institute of Real Estate Appraisers
AiRepDn: Aircraft Repair Division
airew: airborne infrared early warning
AIRH: Association Internationale des Recherches Hydrauliques (International Association of Hydraulic Research)
air hp: air horsepower
AIRI: Atomic Industry Research Institute
AIRIMP: ATC/IATA (q.q.v.) reservations interline message procedures
Air Jam: Air Jamaica
AIRL: Aeronautical Icing Research Laboratory
Air LO: Air Liaison Officer
AIRLORDS: Airlines Load Optimization Recording and Display System
Air Mad: Air Madagascar
airmada: airplane armada
AirNorth: Allied Air Forces, Northern Europe
Air NZ: Air New Zealand
AIROPNET: Air Operational Network
AIRS: Airline Interline Reservations System
AIRSouth: Allied Air Forces, Southern Europe
airsurance: air insurance
airvan: airmobile van
AIRWORK: Airwork Atlantic Limited

AIRX: American Industrial Radium and X-Ray Society
ais (AIS or Lunik III): automatic interplanetary station
AIS: Aeronautical Information Service; Air Intelligence Service; American Iris Society; American Israeli Shipping (Zim Lines); Army Intelligence School; Association Internationale de la Savonnerie et de la Detergence (International Association of Soaps and Detergents); Association Internationale de Sociologie (International Sociology Association); Association of Iron and Steel
AI & S: Army Intelligence and Security
aisa: analytical isoelectrofocusing scanning apparatus
AISC: American Institute of Steel Construction
AISE: Association of Iron and Steel Engineers
AISI: American Iron and Steel Institute
AISM: Association Internationale des Sociétés de Microbiologie (International Assocation of Microbiology Societies)
AISS: Association Internationale de la Science du Sol (International Solar Science Association)
ait: auto-ignition temperature
AiT: Anjuman-i-Tarikh (Historical Society of Afghanistan)
AIT: Académie Internationale du Tourisme (International Academy of Tourism); American Technology Institute; Army Intelligence Translator; Automatic Information Test
AITA: Air Industries and Transport Association
AITC: American Institute of Timber Construction
AITI: Aero Industries Technical Institute
aiu: abort interface unit; advanced instrumentation unit
AIU: Alliance Israelite Universelle (Universal Israelite Alliance)
aiv: accelerated inverse voltage
AIV: Association Internationale de Volcanologie (International Association of Vulcanology)
AIVAF: American-Israeli Vocal Arts Foundation
aiw: auroral intrasonic wave
AIW: Atlantic Intracoastal Waterway (Cape Cod to Florida Bay)
AIWM: American Institute of Weights and Measures
Aix: Aix-en-Provence
aj: ankle jerk; antijamming

aj: *a jini* (Czech—and others)
AJ: *American Jurisprudence; Architects Journal;* Air Jordan; Alma & Jonquieres (railroad); Andrew Jackson; Andrew Johnson; Associate Justice
A.J.: Associate in Journalism
AJA: American Jewish Archives
A-JA: Anglo-Jewish Association
ajai: antijamming anti-interference
AJAs: Americans of Japanese Ancestry
AJASS: African Jazz Art Society Studios
AJAZ: American Jewish Alternatives to Zionism
AJC: Altus Junior College; American Jewish Committee; American Jewish Congress; Anderson Junior College
A de JC: *Antes de Jesucristo* (Spanish—before Jesus Christ)
AJCC: Alternate Joint Communications Center
AJCSA: All Japan Cotton Spinners Association
AJHS: American Jewish Historical Society; Andrew Jackson High School
AJLAC: American Jewish League Against Communism
AJNHS: Andrew Johnson National Historic Site (Greeneville, Tennessee)
AJPA: American Jewish Press Association
AJRC: American Junior Red Cross
AJS: *American Journal of Sociology*
ak: above the knee (amputation); ass kisser (underground slang)
a k: *alter kocker* (Yiddish colloquialism—old man)
AK: Alaska Coastal—Ellis Airlines; cargo ship (2-letter naval designation)
AK: *Avtomat Kalasnikov* (Russian —submachine gun)
a k a: also known as
AKA: Associated Klans of America; cargo vessel, attack (3-letter coding)
Akad: Akademie (German —Academy)
Akad Nauk: Akademiya Nauk (USSR Academy of Sciences)
AKAG: Albright-Knox Art Gallery
ak amp: above-the-knee amputation
AKBS: Advanced Kinematic Bombing System
AKC: American Kennel Club; Associate King's College
AKL: Algemene Kunstzijde Unie (Artist's Union); Auckland, New Zealand (airport)

AKN: King Salmon, Alaska (airport)
Akr: Akron
AKR: vehicle cargo ship (naval symbol)
AKS: general stores issue ship (3-letter symbol)
Akt: *Aktiebolag* (Swedish—limited company)
Akt Ges: *Aktiengesellschaft* (German—corporation or joint stock company)
Aktieb: *Aktiebolag* (Swedish—limited company)
Akties: *Aktieselskab* (Swedish—joint stock company)
AKV: cargo ships and aircraft ferries (3-letter symbol)
Al: accommodation ladder; air lock; alcohol; alias; all lengths; annual leave; autograph letter
a l: *apres livraison* (French—after delivery)
aL: assumed latitude
AL: Alan; Albert; Albin; Alden; Alex(ander); Alf; Alfred; Allan; Allen; Alley; Allied; Alton; aluminum; aluminum; Alva; Alvah; Alvin; Alvina; Alyn
Alo: Alonso
AL: Abraham Lincoln; Accession List(s); Acoustics Laboratory; Aeronautical Laboratory; Air Liaison; Aircraft Laboratory; Aircraft Logistics; Allegheny Airlines; Aluminium Limited; aluminum (machine shop symbol); América Latina (Spanish —Latin America); American League; American League of Professional Baseball Clubs; American Legion; Angkatan Laut (Indonesian—Naval Forces); Anglo-Latin; Annual Lease; Annual Leave; Architectural League; Assumed Latitude; Astronomical League; Aviation Electronicsman
A-L: Allegheny-Ludlum; Anglo-Latin
A.L.: *Anno Lucis* (Latin—in the Year of Light)
A/L: airlift
ala: alanine; axiolabial
Ala: Alabama; Alabamian
ALA: Amalgamated Lithographers of America; American Landscape Architects; American Laryngological Association; American Latvian Association; American Legion Auxiliary; American Liberal Association; American Library Association; Assembly of the Librarians of the Americas; Authors League of America

A.L.A.: Associate in Liberal Arts
alaar: air-launched air-recoverable rocket
ALABEL: American Library Association Board of Education for Librarianship
alabol: algorithmic and business-oriented language
ALACP: American League to Abolish Capital Punishment
Al Ahr: *Al Ahram* (Arabic—The Pyramids)—Cairo's daily paper
ALA (I): Amalgamated Lithographers of America (Independent)
alal: axiolabiolingual
ALALC: Asociación Latinoamericana de Libre Comercio (Latin American Free Trade Association)
alarm.: automatic light aircraft readiness monitor
Alas: Alaska; Alaskan; (unauthorized abbreviation)
Alas Cur: Alaska Current
Alas DST: Alaskan Daylight Saving Time
Alasia: Australasia
Alas ST: Alaskan Standard Time (150th meridian west of Greenwich; however, Alaskans use four time zones: 120, 135, 150, and 165 degrees west of Greenwich)
a la v: *a la vista* (Spanish—at sight; payable upon presentation)
Alb: Albania; Albanian; Albany; Albert; Alberta; Albertan; Albion; Albalasserdam
ALBA: American Lawn Bowling Association; American Leather Belting Association
Albac: Albacete
Alban: Albania; Albanian
ALBE: Air League of the British Empire
Alberto Moravia: (pseudonym —Alberto Pincherle)
Alberto Savinio: (pseudonym —Andrea de Chirico)
albm (ALBM): air-launched ballistic missile
Alb Mus: Albany Museum (Grahamstown, South Africa)
Albn: Albanian
Albq: Albuquerque
Albr: Albrecht
Albturist: Albanian Tourism
albus: all bureaus (naval coding)
alc: alcohol; avian leukosis complex; axiolinguocervical
a l c: *a la carte* (French—on the menu)
ALC: Alabama Central (railroad); Associated Lutheran Charities
ALCA: American Leather Chemists Association; Associated Land-

scape Contractors of America

ALCAC: Airlines Communications Administrative Council

AlCan: Alaska-Canada (as in AlCan Highway)

ALCC: Airborne Launch-Control Center

Alc^de: *Alcalde* (Spanish—justice of the peace; mayor)

alch: approach-light contact height

alchem: alchemy

ALCO: American Lava Corporation

ALCOA: Aluminum Company of America

alcohol: ethyl alcohol (C₂H₅OH)

alcon: all concerned

ALCOP: Alternate Command Post

alcr: aluminum crown (dental)

ald: aldolase; a later date

Ald: Aldabra; Alderman; Aldermanic

ALDA: Air Line Dispatchers Association

aldehyde: al(cohol) dehy(rogenated)—dehydrogenated (oxidized) alcohol

aldep: automated layout design program

aldo: aldosterone

aldp: automatic language-data processing

ALDS: Apollo Launch-Data System

ALEA: Airline Employees Association

alec: algebraic components and coefficients

Alej°: Alejandro

ALERT: Automatic Linguistic Extraction and Retrieval Technique

ALESCO: American Library and Educational Service Company

Aleut: Aleutian; Aleutian Islands

Aleut Cur: Aleutian Current

Alex: Alexander; Alexandra; Alexandria

Alexander Serafimovich: Alexander Serafimovich Popov

Alexandrian Century: the 4th century before the Christian era when Alexander of Macedonia conquered Egypt, Persia, and India as well as encouraging Greek philosophers and poets—the 300s

alf: automatic letter facer

alf: (Swedish—river)

Alf: Alfonso; Alfred

ALF: American Life Foundation

Alfa: code for letter A

ALFA: Anonima Lombarda Fabbrica Automobili

Alfo: Alfonso

ALFORD: Appalachian Laboratory for Occupational Respiratory Diseases

alft: airlift

alg: algae; algal; algebra; algebraic; allergic; allergical; allergy; along; alongside; antilymphocyte globulin (ALG)

Alg: Algeria

ALG: Air Algérie; Algiers, Algeria (airport)

Algie: Algernon

alglyn: aluminum glycinate

algol: algebraically oriented language (algorithmic international language)

ALGU: Association of Land Grant Colleges and Universities

Alh: Alhambra

ALHS: Abraham Lincoln High School

ali.: *alibi* (Latin—elswhere)

ALI: American Law Institute

ALIA: Royal Jordanian Airlines

Alic: Alicante

alice (ALICE): automatic laundering instrument control equipment

Alice: Allis-Chalmers Manufacturing Company (stock exchange slang)

ALICS: Advanced Logistics Information and Control System (USAF)

alien.: alienist

align.: alignment

alim (ALIM): air-launched interceptor missile

ALIMDA: Association of Life Insurance Medical Directors of America

ALIS: Advanced Life Information System

alit: automatic line insulation tester

ALITALIA: Italian International Airline

A.Litt.: Associate in Letters

aljak: aluminum-jacketed coaxial cable

ALJC: Alice Lloyd Junior College

alk: alkali

alki: alcohol; homeless alcoholic

all.: above lower limit; acute lymphocytic leukemia; allergy

al.l.: *alia lectio* (Latin—a different reading)

All: Alloa

ALL: Admiralty Lines Limited

allcat: all critical atmospheric turbulence (programs)

All 8va: *all'ottava* (Italian—in the octave)

Alld: Allahabad

Allem: *Allemagne* (French—Germany)

allergol: allergologic(al)

Allison: Allison Division, General Motors

ALLNAVSTAS: All Naval Stations

allo: allonym

Allo: *allegro* (Italian—lively, quickly)

alloc: allocate; allocation

allp: audiolingual language programming

ALLS: Apollo Lunar Logistic Support

All's Well: *All's Well That Ends Well*

Alltto: *allegretto* (Italian—lively but less so than *allegro*)

alm.: alarm

Alm: Almería

ALM: Antilliaanse Luchtvaart Maatschappij (Dutch Antillean Airlines)

A & LM: Arkansas & Louisiana-Missouri (railroad)

ALMA: Aircraft Locknut Manufacturers Association

ALMAJCOM: All Major Commands

ALMC: Army Logistic Mangement Center

ALMS: Analytic Language Manipulation System

alnico: aluminum, nickel, copper (magnet alloy also containing iron and cobalt)

alnmt: alignment

ALNP: Abraham Lincoln National Park

ALNZ: Air League of New Zealand

alo: axiolinguoclusal

ALO: Air Liaison Office(r); Allied Liaison Office(r); Aloha Airlines; Amalgamated Lace Operatives; American Liaison Office(r); Army Liaison Office(r)

ALOA: Amalgamated Lace Operatives of America; Amalgamated Lithographers of America; Assembly of Librarians of the Americas; Associated Locksmiths of America

aloc: air lines of communication; allocation

ALOC: Air Line of Communication

ALOHA: Aloha Airlines

ALOE: A Lady Of England —pseudonym of Charlotte Maria Tucker

alor: advanced lunar orbital rendezvous

alot: allotment

alotm: allotment

ALOTS: Airborne Lightweight Optical Tracking System

alp.: anterior lobe (of) pituitary; assembly language program (data processing); autocode list processing

Alp: Alphen

ALP: Air Liaison Party; Allied Liaison and Protocol; Ambulance Loading Post; American Labor Party; Australian Labour Party; Automated Learning Process; Automated Library Program

ALP: *Agence Lao Presse* (French —Lao Press Agency)

ALPA: Air Line Pilots' Association

ALPAC: Automatic Language Processing Advisory Committee (National Research Council)

alpak: algebra package

ALPCA: Auto License Plate Collectors Association

Alph: Alphonse

alpha: alphabetical

alphameric: alphanumeric and alphabetic-numeric

alphametic: alphabet arithmetic

alphanumeric: alphabetical-numerical

ALPHAS: Automatic Literature Processing, Handling, and Analysis System

ALPO: Association of Lunar and Planetary Observers

ALPS: advanced Linear Programming System

alr.: *aliter* (Latin—otherwise)

ALR: *American Law Reports*

ALRA: Abortion Law Reform Association

alri: airborne long-range input

ALRI: Angkatan Laut Republik Indonesia (Indonesian Navy)

ALROS: American Laryngological; Rhinological, and Otological Society

ALRTF: Army Long-Range Technological Forecast

als: autograph letter signed

ALS: Alton & Southern (railroad); American Littoral Society; Approach Light System

A.L.S.: Associate of the Linnean Society

ALSA: American Law Student Association

ALSAA: Americans of Lebanese-Syrian Ancestry for America

alsam (ALSAM): air-launched surface-attack missile

ALSC: American Lumber Standards Committee

ALSCP: Appalachian Land Stabilization and Conservation Program

Al seg: *al segno* (Italian—return to the sign :S: and play to end or finale)

alsep (ALSEP): apollo lunar surface experiments package

ALSO: Alex Lindsay String Orchestra (New Zealand)

alsor: air-launch sounding rocket

alss: airline system simulator

ALSS: Apollo Logistics Support System

ALST: Alaska Standard Time

alt: alternator; altimeter; altitude

Alt: alternating (light)

ALT: Aer Lingus (Irish Air Lines)

Alta: Alberta

ALTA: American Land Title Association; American Library Trustee Association; Association of Local Transport Airlines

altac: algebraic translator and compiler

altair (ALTAIR): ARPA (*q.v.*) long-range tracking and instrumentation radar

altan: alternate alerting network

alt. dieb.: *alternis diebus* (Latin—alternate days)

Alt Fl: alternating flashing (light)

Alt F Fl: alternating fixed and flashing (light)

Alt F Gp Fl: alternating fixed and group flashing (light)

Alt Gp Occ: alternating group occulting (light)

Alt Gr Fl: alternating group flashing (light)

alt. hor.: *alternis horis* (Latin—at alternate hours

altm: altimeter

alt. noc.: *alternis noctibus* (Latin—on alternate nights)

Alt Occ: alternating occulting (light)

altran: algebraic translator

ALTS: Advanced Lunar Transportation System

alt set.: altimeter setting

ALTUC: All-India Trade Union Congress

alt udk: *alt udkomne* (Dano-Norwegian—all published)

alu (ALU): arithmetic and logic unit

alue: admissible linear unbiased estimator

alum.: alumna; alumnae; alumni; alumnus

alv: alveolar

älv: (Swedish—river)

alv. adstrict.: *alvo adstricto* (Latin—bowels being constipated)

alv. deject.: *alvi dejectiones* (Latin—intestinal discharges)

Alvº: Alvaro

alvx: alveolectomy

alw: allowance; arch-loop whorl

Alweg: Axel Lennert Wenner-Gren (Swedish industrialist's name applied to monorailroad systems)

ALWL: Army Limited War Laboratory

Alx: Alexandria

aly: alloy

Aly: Alley

am.: aircooled motor; ammeter; amplitude modulation

a.m.: *ante meridiem* (Latin—before noon)

a & m: agricultural and mechanical; ancient and modern; architectural and mechanical; archy and mehitabel

a M (a/M): *am Main* (German—on the Main River)

Am: Amazonas; America; American; americium; myopic astigmatism (symbol)

AM: Academy of Management; Aeronaves de México (Mexican Airlines); Air Marshal; Air Medal; Air Ministry; Almacenes Maritimos; Alpes Maritimes (Maritime Alps); amplitude modulation; angular momentum; Aviation Medicine; Aviation Structural Mechanic; large minesweeper (naval symbol); metric angle (symbol)

A.M.: Air Mail

A.M.: *artium magister* (Latin—Master of Arts); *Ave Maria* (Latin—Hail Mary)

A-M: Addressograph-Multigraph; Alpes-Maritimes

A & M: Agricultural and Mechanical; Agricultural and Mechanical College of Texas

A of M: Academy of Music

a/m²: amperes per square meter

ama: against medical advice

amª: *amiga* (Spanish—female friend)

AMA: Academy of Model Aeronautics; Acoustical Materials Association; Aerospace Medical Association; Agricultural Marketing Administration; Aircraft Manufacturers Association; Air Matériel Area; Amarillo, Texas (airport); Amateur Trapshooting Association; Ambulance Manufacturers Association; American Machinery Association; American Management Association; American Maritime Association; American Marketing Association; American Medical Association; American Ministerial Association; American Monument Association; American Motel Association; American Motorcycle Association; American Municipal Association; Arena Managers Association; Automobile Manufacturers Association

A & MA: Advertising and Marketing Association

AMAA: Adhesives Manufacturers Association of America; Army Mutual Aid Association; Association of Medical Advertising Agencies

AMACUS: Automated Microfilm Aperture Card Updating System

Amad: Amadeus

AMAE: American Museum of Atomic Energy

AMAERF: American Medical Association Education and Research Foundation

amal: amalgam; amalgamate; amalgamation

AMAL: Aero-Medical Acceleration Laboratory; American Medical Acceleration Laboratory

amalg: amalgamated

AMARS: Air Mobile Aircraft Refueling System; Automatic Message Address Routing System

AMAS: American Military Assistance Staff

amat: amateur

AMATC: Air Materiel Armament Test Center

amatol: ammonia + toluene (explosive)

A-matter: advance matter (written in advance of a newspaper story)

AMAUS: Aero Medical Association of the United States

AMAX: American Metal Climax

amb: amber; ambient; ambulance

Amb: Ambassador

AMB: Airways Modernization Board

AMBAC: American Bosch Arma Corporation

Amb Brdg: Ambassador Bridge (Detroit—Windsor)

ambel: ambiguity eliminator

Amb Ex: Ambassador Extraordinary

Amb Ex/Plen: Ambassador Extraordinary and Plenipotentiary

ambig: ambiguity; ambiguous

ambish: ambition

ambit: algebraic manipulation by identity translation

ambl: ambulatory

Amb Lib: Ambrosian Library (Milan)

Ambridge: American Bridge (company)

AMBRL: Army Medical Biomechanical Research Laboratory

Ambrosian: Ambrosian Library (Milan)

ambt: ambulant

ambul: ambulation; ambulatory

amc: automatic mixture control

AMc: coastal minesweeper (3-letter naval symbol)

AMC: Aerospace Manufacturers Council; Air Mail Center; Air Materiel Command; Aircraft Manufacturers Council; American Maritime Cases; American Mining Congress; American Mission to the Chinese; American Motors Corporation; Animal Medical Center; Appalachian Mountain Club; Army Materiel Command; Army Medical Center; Army Medical Corps; Army Missile Command; Army Mobility Command; Army Munitions Command; Association of Management Consultants

AMCA: Air Moving and Conditioning Association; American Mosquito Control Association

AMC-ASC: Air Materiel Command—Aeronautical Systems Center

amcbh: auxiliary machine casing bulkhead

AMC & BW: Amalgamated Meat Cutters and Butcher Workmen

AMCEA: Advertising Media Credit Executives Association

AMCL: African Metals Corporation Limited

AMCM: Air Materiel Command Manual

AMCMFO: Air Materiel Command Missile Field Office

AMCO: American Manufacturing Company

AMCOA: AiResearch Manufacturing Company of Arizona

AMCOM: American Stock Exchange Communications

Am Con: American Consul(ate)

AMCR: Air Materiel Command Regulation

AMCS: Airborne Missile Control System; Association of Military Colleges and Schools

AMCSA: Army Materiel Command Support Activity

AMCSOF: Army Combat Surveillance Office

am. cur.: amicus curiae (Latin—a friend at court)

amd: air movement designator

AMD: Aerospace Medical Division; Air Movement Data; Army Medical Department

AMD: Aerospace Material Document

AMDA: Airlines Medical Directors Association

a.m. D.g.: ad majorem Dei gloriam (Latin—to the greater glory of God)—also A.M.D.G.

AMDI: Associazione Medici Dentisti Italiani (Association of Italian Medical Dentists)

AmdlEvac: aeromedical evacuation

Amdoc: American Doctors (organization)

AMDS: Association of Military Dental Surgeons

amdt: amendment

ame: angle-measuring equipment

AME: African Methodist Episcopal

A.M.E.: Advanced Master of Education

AMEC: Airframe Manufacturing Equipment Committee

amecd: antimechanized

AMedD: Army Medical Department

AMedS: Army Medical Service

AMEG: Association for Measurement and Evaluation in Guidance

AMEL: Aero Medical Equipment Laboratory

amelior: amelioration

Am Elsevier: American Elsevier Publishing Company

Am Emb: American Ambassador; American Embassy

AMEMIC: Association of Mill and Elevator Mutual Insurance Companies

amend.: amendment(s)

Am Engr: American Engineer

Amer: America; American

AMERADC: Army Mobility Equipment Research and Development Center

AMERICAL: Americans in New Caledonia (Army division)

American Century: the 20th century marked by invention and industrial activity, highest standard of living for the most people, discovery of the North Pole, landing of men on the moon, victory in two world wars, devotion to the democratic ideal—the 1900s

Amerind: American + Indian (American Indian or Eskimo)

Amer Men Sci: American Men of Science

Amer Std: American Standard

Amer Trauma Soc: American Trauma Society

AMeS: American Meteorological Society

AMES: Association of Marine Engineering Schools

AMETA: Army Management Engineering Training Agency

AMETS: Artillery Meteorological System

Amex: American Stock Exchange

AMEX: Agencia Mexicana de Noticias (Mexican News Agency)

Amexco: American Express Company

AMEZ: African Methodist Episcopal Zion

AMEZC: African Methodist Episcopal Zionist Church

amf (AMF): airmail facility

AMF: Air Materiel Force; American Machine and Foundry; Arctic Marine Freighters; Australian Marine Force

AMF(A): Allied Mobile Force (Air) —NATO

AMFGC: Association of Midwest Fish and Game Commissioners

AMFIE: Association of Mutual Fire Insurance Engineers

AMFIS: Automatic Microfilm Information System

AMF(L): Allied Mobile Force (Land)—NATO

am/fm: amplitude modulation/frequency modulation

amg: automatic magnetic guidance; axiomesiogingival

AMG: Aircraft Machine Gunner; Albertus Magnus Guild; Allied Military Government

AMGNY: Associated Musicians of Greater New York

AMGOT: Allied Military Government

Amh: Amharic

AMHA: American Motor Hotel Association

AMHIS: American Marine Hull Insurance Syndicate

AMHS: American Material Handling Society

AMHT: Automated Multiphasic Health Testing

ami: advanced manned interceptor; air mileage indicator

AMI: Advanced Manned Interceptor; American Meat Institute; American Military Institute; American Museum of Immigration; American Mushroom Institute; Association of Medical Illustrators

AMIA: American Metal Importers Association

AMIADB: Army Member—Inter-American Defense Board

AMIC: Aerospace Materials Information Center

AMICA: Automobile Mutual Insurance Company of America

AMICI: Association Mondiale des Interprètes de Conférences International

AMICO: American Measuring Instrument Company

AMICOM: Army Missile Command

AMIGOS: Americans Interested In Giving Others a Start

AMILO: Army-Industry Materiel Information Liaison Office

AMIN: Advertising and Marketing International Network

Am Ind: American Indian

AMINOIL: American Independent Oil (company)

AMIS: Aircraft Movement Information Section

Am Jour Sci: *American Journal of Science*

aml (AML): amplitude-modulated link

AML: Aeromedical Laboratory; American Mail Line

AMLC: Aerospace Medical Laboratory (USAF)

Am Lib Dir: *American Library Directory*

amm: ammunition; anti-missile missile

AMM: Air Mining Mission; Amman, Jordan (airport); Anti-Missile Missile; Associated Millinery Men; Association Medicale Mondiale (World Medical Association); Aviation Machinist's Mate

AM & M: Applied Mathematics and Mechanics

AMMA: American Museum of Marine Archeology

Am Mach: *American Machinist*

ammeter: ampere + meter (current-measuring instrument)

AMMI: American Merchant Marine Institute

AMMIS: Aircraft Maintenance Manpower Information System (USAF)

AMMLA: American Merchant Marine Library Association

ammo: ammunition

Ammo: American Motors (stock exchange slang)

Ammon: Ammonite

ammonia water: ammonium hydroxide (NH_4OH)

amn: airman

AMNH: American Museum of Natural History

amnip: adaptive man-machine no-narithmetic information processing

AmnM: Airman's Medal

am⁰: *amigo* (Spanish—male friend)

amo (AMO): air mail only; alternant molecular orbit

AMO: Advance Material Order; Aircraft Materiel Officer; Air Ministry Order; American Motors (stock exchange symbol)

amob: automatic meteorological oceanographic buoy

AMOCO: American Oil Company

amor: amorphous

AMORC: Ancient Mystic Order Rosae Crucis (Rosicrucian Order)

AMOS: Automatic Meteorological Observation Station

amp: ampere; amplitude; ampule

amp (AMP): adenosine monophosphate (hormonal chemical)

AMP: Air Mail Pioneers; American Museum of Photography; Army Mine Planter; Aurora Memorial Park (Philippines); Aviation Modernization Program

AMPAC: American Medical Political Action Committee

AMPAS: Academy of Motion Picture Arts and Sciences

AMPCO: Associated Missile Products Corporation

ampersand: and per se and; & by itself is and—name for *and* sign (&)

AMPFTA: American Military Precision Flying Teams Association

amph: amphibian; amphibious; amphimict

Amph: Amphibia

AMPH: Association of Management in Public Health

amphet: amphetamine (stimulant)

amphetamine: alphamethylpenethylamine

amphets: amphetamines (narcotics often causing death; colloquially known as ''speed'')

amphib: amphibia(n); amphibious

amp hr: ampere hour

AMPI: Associated Music Publishers, Incorporated

Ampico: American Piano Company

ampl: amplifier

ampl: *ampliata* (Italian—enlarged)

ampr: advanced multipurpose radar; automatic manifold pressure regulator

AMPR: Aeronautical Manufacturers Planning Report; Airframe Manufacturers Planning Report

amps: amperes; ampules

AMPS: Accrued Military Pay System; American Metered Postage Society; Army Mine Planter Service; Army Motion Picture Service; Associated Music Publishers; Automatic Message Processing System

AMPTP: Association of Motion Picture and Television Producers

amp-turns: ampere-turns

AMR: Advanced Material Request; Airman Military Record; American Airlines (stock exchange symbol); Atlantic Missile Range

A.M.R.: Master of Arts in Research

AMRA: Army Materials Research

Agency

AMRAC: Anti-Missile Research Advisory Council

AMRC: Advanced Metals Research Corporation; Army Mathematics Research Center; Automotive Market Research Council

AMRCA: American Miniature Racing Car Association

AMR & DL: Air Mobility Research and Development Laboratory (USA)

AM & RF: African Medical and Research Foundation

AMRL: Aerospace Medical Research Laboratories; Army Medical Research Laboratory

AMRNL: Army Medical Research and Nutrition Laboratory

amrpd: applied manufacturing research and process development

AMRS: American Moral Reform Society

AMs: auxiliary motor minesweeper

AMS: Administration Management Society; Aeronautical Material Specification; Agricultural Marketing Service; American Mathematical Society; American Meteor Society; American Meteorological Society; American Microscopical Society; American Mineral Spirits; American Museum of Safety; American Musicological Society; Army Map Service; Army Medical Service; Association of Messenger Services; Association of Museum Stores

amsa (AMSA): advanced manned strategic aircraft

AMSA: American Metal Stamping Association

amsam: anti-missile surface-to-air-missile

Am Sam: American Samoa

AMSC: Army Medical Specialist Corps

AMSCO: American Mineral Spirits Company; American Sterilizer Company

amsl: above mean sea level

AMSMH: Association of Medical Superintendents of Mental Hospital

AMSOC: American Miscellaneous Society

AMSP: Army Master Study Program

AMSq: Avionics Maintenance Squadron (USAF)

AMSS: Advanced Meteorological Sounding System

Amst: Amsterdam

AMSUS: Association of Military Surgeons of the United States

amt: amount

AMT: Academy of Medicine, Toronto, Canada; Aerial Mail Terminal; American Medical Technologists; Astrograph Mean Time

A.M.T.: Associate in Mechanical Technology; Associate in Medical Technology; Master of Arts —Teaching

amta: airborne moving target attack

amtank: amphibious tank

AMTC: Airframe Manufacturing Tooling Committee

AMTCL: Association for Machine Translation and Computational Linguistics

Am Tel & Tel: American Telephone and Telegraph

amti: airborne moving target indicator

Amtorg: Amerikanskaya Torgovlya (Russian-American Trading Company)

amtrac: amphibious tractor

AMTPI: Associate Member of the Town Planning Institute (UK)

Amtrak: (American railroad tracks)—the National Railway Passenger Corporation

amtran: automatic mathematical translator

amt(s): amphetamine(s)

amu: air mileage unit; air mission unit; astronaut maneuvering unit; atomic mass unit

AMU: Alaska Methodist University; American Malacological Union; American Marksmanship Unit; Army Marksmanship Unit; Associated Midwestern Universities; Association of Marine Underwriters

AMURT: Anada Marga Universal Relief Team (India)

amv: alfalca-mosaic virus; avian myeloblastitis virus

AMVERS: Automated Merchant Vessel Reporting System

AMVETS: American Veterans of World War II and Korea

AMW: Association of Married Women

AMWA: American Medical Women's Association

AMWM: Association of Manufacturers of Woodworking Machinery

amy: amytal (barbiturate depressant and sedative)

Amy: Amelia; Amoy, China

an.: airman; anode; annual

an': and

a/n: acidic and neutral

An: Annam; Annamese

A$_n$: normal atmosphere

AN: Acid Number; Aerodynamic Note; Air Force-Navy; Airmail Notice; Air Navigation; Air Navigator; Air Reduction (stock exchange symbol); Anglo-Norman; Apalachicola Northern (railroad); Army-Navy; net laying vessel (naval symbol)

A.N.: Associate in Nursing

AN-22: Antonov 22 (Soviet super transport plane)

Ana: Anita

ANA: Air Force-Navy Aeronautical; All Nippon Airways; American Nature Association; American Neurological Association; American Newspaper Association; American Numismatic Association; American Nurses' Association; Army-Navy Aeronautical; Asociación Nacional Automovilista (National Automobile Association); Association of National Advertisers; Australian National Airways

ANAAS: Australian and New Zealand Association for the Advancement of Science

anacom: analog computer

anaesth: anaesthesia; anaesthetic(s); anaesthesiologist; anaesthesiology

ANAF: Army, Navy, Air Force

anal.: analogy; analysis; analytical

anal. psychol: analytical psychology

analyt: analytical

ANARC: Association of North American Radio Clubs

anarch: anarchist; anarchism; anarchy

ANARE: Australian National Antarctic Research Expeditions

anat: anatomical; anatomist; anatomy

Anatole France: Jacques Anatole François Thibault

Anatolia: Asia Minor

anatran: analog translator

anav: area navigation

ANB: Army-Navy-British Standard

anbs (ANBS): armed nuclear bombardment satellite

ANB & TC: American National Bank and Trust Company

anc: all numbers calling; ancient

Anc: Ancona

ANC: Air Force-Navy-Civil; American News Company; Arlington National Cemetery; Army and Navy Civil Committee on Aircraft; Army Nurse Corps

ANCA: Allied Naval Communications Agency; American National Cattlemen's Association

ANCAP: Administración Nacional

de Combustibles Alcohol y Portland
ANCAR: Australian National Committee for Antarctic Research
anch: anchorage
ANCO: Andersen-Collingwood (tanker service)
ancr: aircraft not combat ready
ANCs: African National Congress members
ANCS: American Numerical Control Society
ANCXF: Allied Naval Commander Expeditionary Force
And: Andalucía; Andaman Islands
AND: Army-Navy Design
ANDB: Air Navigation Development Board
Andno: *andantino* (Italian—slower than *andante*)
Ando: Andorra; Andorran
Andrea del Sarto: Andrea Domenico d'Agnolo di Francesco
Andre Maurois: Emile Salomon Wilhelm Herzog
andro: androsterone
Andte: *andante* (Italian—of moderate speed)
Andy: Andrew
anec: anecdotal; anecdote(s)
ANEDA: *Association Nationale d'Etudes pour la Documentation Automatique* (National Association for Automatic Documentation Studies)
anes: anesthesia; anesthesiologist; anesthesiology; anesthetician; anesthetic(s)
anesthesiol: anesthesiology
an. ex: anode excitation
anf: anchored filament; antinuclear factor(s)
ANF: American Nurses' Foundation; Atlantic Nuclear Force (NATO)
anfe (ANFE): aircraft not fully equipped
anfo: ammonium nitrate + fuel oil (explosive)
ang: angle; angular
ang: *angaende* (Danish, Norwegian, Swedish—concerning)
Ang: Angel (phonograph records); Anglo-; Angola
ANG: Air Force-Navy-Army Guided Missiles; Air National Guard; American Newspaper Guild; Australian New Guinea
ANGAU: Australian New Guinea Administrative Unit
Ångfart: *Ångfartygas* (Swedish—steamship company)
Angie: Angela; Angelina; Angeline
angiol: angiology
Angl: Anglican
ANGLICO: Air and Naval Gunfire

Liaison Company
Anglo(s): Anglo-Saxon(s)
Angola: Portuguese West Africa
Ang-Sax: Anglo-Saxon
ANGUS: Air National Guard of the United States
anh: anhydrite; anhydrous
Anh: *Anhang* (German—appendix)
ANHA: American Nursing Home Association
anhed: anhedral
anhic: anhydritic
ANHS: Adams National Historic Site
anhyd: anhydrous
ani: automatic number identification
ANI: Agencia Nacional de Informaciones (Uruguayan press service); Army-Navy-Industry
A & NI: Andaman and Nicobar Islands
ANIB: Australian News and Information Bureau
ANICO: American National Insurance Company
anil: aniline
aniline: phenyl amine
anim: animal; animate; animism
anim: *animato* (Italian—animated)
ANIM: Association of Nuclear Instrument Manufacturers
ANIP: Army-Navy Instrumentation Program
ank: *ankomen* (Dutch—arrival); *ankomst* (Danish—arrival); *ankunft* (German—arrival)
Ank: Ankara
ANK: Ankara, Turkey (airport)
anl: annoyance level (aircraft noise); automatic noise limiter
ANL: Argonne National Laboratory; Australian National Line; net-laying ship (naval symbol)
ANLCA: Alaska Native Land Claims Act (helping even quarter-blooded Alaskan Aleuts, Eskimos, and Indians)
anld: annealed
an. lt: anchor light
anlys: analysis
anm: *anmaerkning* (Danish, Norwegian, Swedish—footnote, note, remark, observation)
Anm: *Anmerkung* (German—footnote; note)
ANMCC: Alternate National Military Command Center
ann: announce(ment); announcer; annual(ly); annuity; annunciator
Ann: Anastasia; Angela; Angelina; Angeline; Anita; Anna; Annabelle; Anne; Annelida; Annetta; Annette; Annie; Antoinette
Ann: *Annalen* (German—annals); *Annales* (French—annals); *Annali* (Italian—annals)

Anna: Annabella; Annapolis, Maryland; Annette
ANNA: Army, Navy, NASA, Air Force
Anna Seghers: (pseudonym—Netty Radvanyi)
Anng: Annapolis graduate
anniv.: *anniversarium* (Latin—anniversary)
annot: annotated; annotation
Ann Rept: Annual Report
annu: annual; annuale; annuario
annul.: annulment
ANO: Air Navigation Office; Anti-Narcotics Office
anod: anodize
Anon.: *anonymous* (Latin—nameless)
anorm: aircraft not operationally ready—maintenance
anors: aircraft not operationally ready—supplies
anot: annotate
anov: analysis of variance
anova: analysis of variance
anp: aircraft nuclear propulsion
ANP: Aberdare National Park (Kenya); Acadia National Park (Maine); Aircraft Nuclear-propulsion Program; Aircraft Nuclear Propulsion; Akan National Park (Japan); Albert National Park (Zaire); Angkor National Park (Cambodia); Arusha National Park (Tanzania); Associated Negro Press; Awash National Park (Ethiopia)
ANP: *Administración Nacional de Puertos* (Colombia's National Administration of Ports); *Algemeen Nederlandsch Persbureau* (Netherlands Press Bureau)
ANPA: American Newspaper Publishers Association
ANPO: Aircraft Nuclear Propulsion Office
anpod: antenna-positioning device
ANPP: Aircraft Nuclear Propulsion Program
ANPPF: Aircraft Nuclear Power Plant Facility
ANPS: American Nail Producers Society
anpt: aeronautical national taper pipe threads
ANR: American Newspaper Representatives; Antwerp, Belgium (airport)
ANR: *Asociación Nacional Republicana* (Spanish—National Republican Association)—Paraguay's Colorado Party
ANRA: Amistad National Recreation Area (Texas); Arbuckle National Recreation Area (Ok-

lahoma)

anrac: aids navigation radio control

ANRC: American National Red Cross; Animal Nutrition Research Council; Australian National Research Council

ANRT: *Association Nationale de la Recherche Technique* (National Association of Technical Research)

ans: answer; answered; answering; autograph note signed; autonomic nervous system

Ans: Anselm; Anselmo

ANS: Agencia Noticiosa Saporiti (Argentine press service); American Name Society; American Nuclear Society; American Numismatic Society; American Nutrition Society; Army Newspaper Service; Army News Service; Army Nursing Service

ansa: aminonapthosulfonic acid; automatic new structure alert

ANSA: *Agenzia Nazionale Stampa Associata* (Italian—National Press Association Agency)

ansam (ANSAM): antimissile surface-to-air missile

ANSETT: Ansett Airways

ANSETT-ANA: Ansett Australian National Airways

ANSI: American National Standards Institute

ANSIC: Aerospace Nuclear Safety Information Center

ANSP: Academy of Natural Sciences of Philadelphia

answ (ANSW): antinuclear submarine warfare

ant.: antenna(s); anterior; anticipated; antilog; antilogarithm; antiquarian; antique; antiquities; antiquity; antonym

ant.: *antico* (Italian—antique); *antiporta* (Italian—half-title)

Ant: Antigua; Antillea—West Indian Federation; Antillean; Antilles; Antwerp

ANT: Australian Northern Territory

ANTA: American National Theater and Academy; Australian National Travel Association

antag: antagonistic

Antarc: Antarctic; Antarctica

Antarc O: Antarctic Ocean

Ant & Cl: *Antony and Cleopatra*

Ant Cur: Antilles Current

antec: annual technical conference

ANTELCO: Administración Nacional de Telecomunicaciones (Paraguayan National Telecommunication Administration)

antennafier: antenna + radiofrequency amplifier

antennamitter: antenna + transmit-

ter

antennaverter: antenna + converter

Antf: Antofagasta

Ant f: Antillean florin (guilder)

anthol: anthological(ly); anthologist; anthologize; anthology

Anthony Hope: nom de plume of Sir Anthony Hope Hawkins

anthro: anthropogeography; anthropological; anthropologist; anthropology; anthropometry; anthropomorphism; anthropophagy

anthrop: anthropology

anthropom: anthropometry

antifreeze: grain or methyl alcohol (CH_3OH) mixture

antilog: antilogarithm

Anthy: Anthony

antichlor: anti + chlorine; antichloristic

antidis: antidisestablishmentarianism

antimag: antimagnetic

antipol: antipollutant; antipollution

antiq: antiquarian; antique; antiquities; antiquity

antiquar: antiquarian

Ant⁰: Antonio

anton: antonym

antu: alpha-naphthyl-thiourea (rat poison)

ANU: St. John's, Antigua; Australia National University

ANWG: Apollo Navigation Working Group (NASA)

ANWR: Agassiz National Wildlife Refuge (Minnesota); Aransas NWR (Texas); Arrowhead NWR (North Dakota); Audubon NWR (North Dakota)

anx: annex

ANZ: Air New Zealand

ANZAAS: Australian and New Zealand Association for the Advancement of Science

ANZAC: Australia and New Zealand Army Corps

ANZAM: Australia, New Zealand, and Malaysia (defense pact)

ANZUS: Australia, New Zealand, United States (mutual security pact)

ao: access opening; anti-oxidant; area of operations (AO)

a/o (A/O): account of

a O (a/O): *an der Oder* (German—on the Oder River)

AO: Administration Office; Airdrome Office(r); American Optical (company); Arkansas & Ozarks (railroad); Autonomous Oblast; Aviation Ordnanceman; fleet tanker (2-letter naval designation)

AO: *Ahonim Ortaklik* (Turkish —joint stock company)

aoa: at or above

AoA: Administration on Aging (HEW)

AOA: American Oceanology Association; American Optometric Association; American Ordnance Association; American Orthopaedic Association; American Orthopsychiatric Association; American Osteopathic Association; American Overseas Airlines; American Overseas Association

AOAC: Association of Official Agricultural Chemists

AOAD: Army Ordnance Arsenal District

aob: at or below

AOB: Advanced Operational Base

AO-BIRMDis: Army Ordnance —Birmingham District

AOBMO: Army Ordnance Ballistic Missile Office (USA)

AO-BOSTDis: Army Ordnance— Boston District

AOBs: Antediluvian Order of Buffaloes

AOBSR: Air Observer

AoC: Architect of the Capitol (D.C.)

AOC: Air Officer Commanding; Air Operations Center; Airport Operators Council; American Optical Company (stock exchange symbol); American Orthoptic Council; Arabian Oil Company; Army Ordnance Corps; Aviation Officer Candidate

AOCA: American Osteopathic College of Anesthesiologists

AO-CHIDis: Army Ordnance— Chicago District

AOCI: Airport Operators Council International

AO-CLEVDis: Army Ordnance— Cleveland District

aocm (AOCM): aircraft out of commission for maintenance

AOCO: Atomic Ordnance Cataloging Office

aocp (AOCP): aircraft out of commission for parts

AOCs: American Olympic Committee members

AOCS: American Oil Chemists' Society

aod: as-of-date

AOD: Air Officer of the Day

AODs: Ancient Order of Druids

AODS: All Ordnance Destruct System

aoe: airborne operational equipment; auditing order error

AoE: Aerodrome of Entry
AOEHI: American Organization for the Education of the Hearing Impaired
AOEM: Automotive Original Equipment Manufacturers
AOF: Afrique Occidentale Française (French West Africa); Ancient Order of Foresters
aog (AOG): aircraft on ground
AOG: Atlantic Oceanographic Group; gasoline tanker (3-letter symbol)
AOGM: Army of Occupation of Germany Medal
AOH: Ancient Order of Hibernians
aoi: angle of incidence
aok: all okay; everything in good order
AOL: American-Oriental Lines; Atlantic Oceanography Laboratories
AO-LADis: Army Ordnance—Los Angeles District
aolo: advanced orbit laboratory operations
AOM: Army of Occupation Medal
AOMAA: Apartment Owners and Managers Association of America
AOMC: Army Ordnance Missile Command
AOMSA: Army Ordnance Missile Support Agency
AO-NYDis: Army Ordnance—New York District
aoo: anodal opening odor
AOO: American Oceanic Organization
AOP: Association of Osteopathic Publications
AOPA: Aircraft Owners and Pilots Association
AO-PHILDis: Army Ordnance—Philadelphia District
ao Prof: *auszerordentlicher Professor* (German—associate professor)
AOPU: Asian Oceanic Postal Union (China, Korea, Philippines, Thailand)
aoq: average outgoing quality
aoql: average outgoing quality limit
aor: angle of reflection; aorist
AOR: Army Operational Research; auxiliary oil replenishment (USN)
AORB: Aviation Operational Research Branch
AORG: Army Operational Research Group (United Kingdom)
AORL: Apollo Orbital Research Laboratory
AORN: Association of Operating Room Nurses
AOrPA: American Orthopsychia-

tric Association
AORT: Association of Operating Room Technicians
aos: acquisition of signal; add or subtract; angle of sight; anodal opening sound
AOS: American Opera Society; American Ophthalmological Society; American Orchid Society; American Oriental Society; American Otological Society
AOSC: Association of Oilwell Servicing Contractors
AOSE: American Order of Stationary Engineers
AOSO: Advanced Orbiting Solar Observatory
aosp: automatic operating and scheduling program
AOSPS: American Otorhinologic Society for Plastic Surgery
AOSs: Ancient Order of Shepherds
AO-STLDis: Army Ordnance—St. Louis District
Aot: Askania optical tracker
AOT: Alameda-Oakland Tunnel; Association of Occupational Therapists
AOTA: American Occupational Therapy Association
AotOS: Admiral of the Ocean Sea (U.S. Merchant Marine award recalling title of Christopher Columbus)
AOtS: American Otological Society
aou: apparent oxygen utilization
AOU: American Ornithologists' Union
AOUW: Ancient Order of United Workmen
AOW: Articles of War
ap: access panel; aerial port; aiming point; airplane; armor piercing; as prescribed; author's proof; Welsh prefix meaning son of
ap: *anno passato* (Italian—last year)
ap.: *apud* (Latin—according to)
a.p.: *ante prandium* (Latin—before a meal)
a/p: after perpendicular; air port (porthole); angle point; authority to pay; authority to purchase; autopilot
a & p: apogee and perigee (apex and antapex); auscultation and percussion
a$_p$: geomagnetic index
Ap.: *Apostolus* (Latin—Apostle)
AP: Air Police; Airport; Air Publication; American President Lines; Associated Press; Aviation Pilot; personnel transport (naval symbol)
AP: *Acción Popular* (Spanish—Popular Action); *Arbeiderpar-*

tiet (Norwegian—Labor Party —*Det Norske Arbeiderpartiet* (The Norwegian Labor Party); *Atlanska Plovidba* (Russian—Atlantic Press); *Aviapolk* (Russian—Air Regiment)
A.P.: *à protester* (French—to be protested later)
A-P: American Plan (includes meals)
A/P: allied papers; authority to pay
A & P: Great Atlantic & Pacific Tea Company
A y P: Almonester y Pontalba (initials on cast-iron grillework of first apartment building in America—Pontalba Apartments in French Quarter of New Orleans)
apa: axial pressure angle
APA: Aerovias Panama Airways; Agricultural Publishers Association; American Patients Association; American Pharmaceutical Association; American Philological Association; American Philosophical Association; American Photoengravers Association; American Physiotherapy Association; American Pilots Association; American Podiatry Association; American Poultry Association; American Press Association; American Protective Association; American Psychiatric Association; American Psychoanalytical Association; American Psychological Association; American Psychotherapy Association; American Pulpwood Association; Animation Producers Association; Anti-Papal Association; transport attack vessel (naval symbol)
APA: *Austria Presse Agentur* (German—Austrian Press Agency)
apache: analog programming and checking
APACHE: Application Package for Chemical Engineers
apacs: adaptive planning and control sequence (marketing)
APADS: Automatic Programmer and Data System
APAE: Association of Public Address Engineers
APAG: Atlantic Political Advisory Group (NATO)
APAL: American Puerto-Rican Action League
AP & AM: Adler Planetarium and Astronomical Museum
apar: apparatus
APAR: Automatic Programming and Recording
a-part: alpha particle(s)

APAS: Automatic Performance Analysis System
APATS: Antenna Pattern Test System (USA)
APB: barracks ship, self-propelled (3-letter symbol)
APB: All-Points Bulletin
APBA: American Power Boat Association; Associated Press Broadcasters Association
apc: acoustical plaster ceiling; all-purpose capsule (aspirin, phenacetin, caffeine); armor piercing capped; automatic phase control
a/p c: autopilot capsule
APc: coastal transport (3-letter symbol)
APC: Aeronautical Planning Chart; Aerospace Primus Club; American Parents Committee; American Philatelic Congress; Area Positive Control; Arkansas Polytechnic College; Armored Personnel Carrier; Army Petroleum Center; Army Policy Council; Association of Private Camps; Association of Pulp Consumers
APCA: Air Pollution Control Association; American Petroleum Credit Association; American Planning and Civic Association
APCB: Air Pollution Control Board
APCD: Air Pollution Control District
apche: automatic programmed checkout equipment
apci: armor-piercing capped with incendiary
apcit: armor-piercing capped incendiary with tracer
APCM: Asiatic-Pacific Campaign Medal
APCO: Air Pollution Control Office; Alabama Power Company
APCS: Air Photographic and Charting Service
apct: armor-piercing capped with tracer
a/p ctl: autopilot control
apd: aiming point determination
APD: Air Pollution Division (U.S. Dept Agriculture); Air Procurement District; high-speed troop transport (3-letter naval symbol)
APDC: Albany Port District Commission
APDF: Asian-Pacific Dental Federation
APdS: American Pediatric Society
APDSMS: Advanced Point Defense Surface Missile System
APDUSA: African People's Democratic Union of Southern Africa
APE: aerial port of embarkation

A.P.E.: Air Pollution Engineer
Apeco: American Photocopy Equipment Company
apers: antipersonnel
apex.: advance-purchase excursion (airline fare); assembler and process executive
APEX: Advance-Purchase Excursion (Plan)—pay 90 days ahead of excursion flight
apf: acidproof floor; animal protein factor
APF: American Progress Foundation; Association of Pacific Fisheries; Association of Protestant Faiths
APFA: American Pipe Fittings Association
APFC: Asia-Pacific Forestry Commission
APFRI: American Physical Fitness Research Institute
Apg: Appingedam
APG: Aberdeen Proving Ground; Air Proving Ground; American Pewter Guild; Army Planning Group; Army Proving Ground; Australian Proving Ground
APGA: American Personnel and Guidance Association
APGC: Air Proving Ground Center
apgcu: autopilot ground control unit
APG/HEL: Aberdeen Proving Ground—Human Engineering Laboratory
APG/OBDC: Aberdeen Proving Ground—Ordnance Bomb Disposal Center
APGOEF: Air Proving Ground —Eglin, Florida
aph: anterior pituitary hormone
APH: transport fitted for evacuation of wounded (3-letter symbol)
A.P.H.: A(lan) P(atrick) Herbert
APHA: American Public Health Association
APHB: American Printing House for the Blind
APHI: Association of Public Health Inspectors
APHIS: Animal and Plant Health Inspection Service
aphro(s): aphrodisiac(s)
APHS: Arizona Pioneer Historical Society
api: air position indicator; armor-piercing incendiary tracer
API: Alabama Polytechnic Institute; American Paper Institute; American Petroleum Institute; American Potash Institute; American Press Institute; armor-piercing incendiary; Association Phonétique Internationale (International Phonetic Association)
APIC: Apollo Parts Information

Center; Army Photo Interpretation Center
APICP: Association for the Promotion of the International Circulation of the Press
APICS: American Production and Inventory Control Society
APICSC: Atlantic-Pacific Interoceanic Canal Study Commission
apicult: apiculture
APID: Army Photo Interpretation Detachment
A-pill: abortion pill
APIM: Association Professionelle Internationale des Medecins (International Professional Association of Physicians)
APIN: Atlas Propulsion Information Notice
apipocc: appropriating property in possession of (a) common carrier
APJ: American Power Jet (company)
apl (APL): anterior pituitary-like hormone
a/pl: armorplate
Apl: Appledore
APL: Air Provost Marshal; Akron Public Library; Albany Public Library; Albuquerque Public Library; American Pioneer Line; American President Lines; Applied Physics Laboratory; Assembly Parts List; Augusta Public Library; barracks ship (naval symbol)
A-PL: All-Purpose Linotype
APLA: American Patent Law Association; Armenian Progressive League of America; Atlantic Provinces Library Association
APLC: Automated Parking Lot Control
APLE: Association of Public Lighting Engineers
APLS: American Plant Life Society
apm: apomict; associative principle for multiplication
apm (APM): antipersonnel missile
APM: Academy of Physical Medicine; Association for Psychoanalytic Medicine
apma: advance payment of mileage authorized
APMA: Absorbent Paper Manufacturers Association; Automatic Phonograph Manufacturers Association
APMAC: A.P. Møller Associated Concerns
APMC: Academy of Psychologists in Marital Counseling
a/p mcu: autopilot monitor and control unit

APME: Associated Press Managing Editors (Association)

apmi: area precipitation measurement indicator

APMR: Association for Physical and Mental Rehabilitation

APMT: Antenna Pattern Measuring Test (USA)

APN: *American Practical Navigator*

APNP: Arthur's Pass National Park (South Island, New Zealand)

apo: apogee

APO: Accountable Property Office(r); Advanced Post Office; Air Force (Army) Post Office; American Potash & Chemical (stock exchange symbol); Animal Procurement Office(r); Area Patrol Office(r); Area Petroleum Office(r); Association of Physical Oceanographers

apob: airplane observation

Apoc: Apocalypse; Apocrypha; Apocryphal

APOC: Army Point of Contact

APOD: Aerial Port of Debarkation

APOE: Aerial Port of Embarkation

Apollyon: The Devil

apos: apostrophe

APOS: Advanced Polar Orbiting Satellite

Apostle of Peace: Bertrand Russell

Apostles: Apostle Islands (off northern Wisconsin in Lake Superior)

apota: automatic positioning of telemetering antenna

apotek: *apoteket* (Danish—apothecary)—drugstore

apoth: apothecaries' (weight); apothecary

A-powered: atomic-powered

app: apparatus; apparel; apparent; appeal; appelate; appendage; appended; appendix; apperception; appetite; appetizer; applause; applied; appointed; apprehended; apprentice; approach; appropriate; appropriation; approval; approve; approximate

App: Appellate; Lucius Appuleius

App: *Apparat* (German—apparatus)

App.: *Apostoli* (Latin—Apostles)

APP: Air Parcel Post; Algonquin Provincial Park (Ontario); *Alianza Para Progreso* (Spanish—Alliance for Progress); Army Procurement Procedure; Association of Professional Photogrammetrists

APPA: American Pulp and Paper Association

appar: apparatus

APPC: Advance Procurement Plan-ning Council

appd: approved

appellat: appellative

appi: advanced planning procurement information

appl: applicable; application; applied

APPL: Advance Procurement Planning List(s)

appmt: appointment

appn: appropriation

a/p poi: autopilot positioning indicator

appr: approval; approve; approved

APPR: Army power package reactor

appren: apprentice

approx: approximate(ly)

apps: appendixes

appt: appoint; appointment

apptd: appointed

appx: appendix

apr: annual percentage rate; apprentice

Apr: April

Apr: *Aprel* (Russian—April)

APR: Airman Performance Report; Air Pictorial Service; Air Priority Raging; Annual Progress Reports; Association of Petroleum Re-Refiners; Association of Publishers' Representatives

APRA: Aircraft Resources Production Agency

APRA: *Alianza Popular Revolucionaria Americana* (Spanish—Popular American Revolutionary Alliance)—Peru's Aprista Party of Haya de la Torre

APRC: Army Physical Review Council

APRDC: Army Polar Research and Development Center

APRE: Air Procurement Region—Europe

après JC: *après Jesus Christ* (French—after the birth of Jesus Christ; A.D.)

APRF: Army Pulse Radiation Facility

APRFE: Air Procurement Region—Far East

APri: air priority

APRL: American Prosthetic Research Laboratory

Aprmay: April and May

APRO: Aerial Phenomena Research Organization; Army Personnel Research Office

AprS: American Proctologic Society

APRS: Association of Professional Recording Studios

aprt: airport

APRTA: Associated Press Radio and Television Association

aprthd: *Apartheid* (Afrikaans—apartness)—pronounced *a-parth-ate*—racial segregation enforced by many South African whites and now advocated by Black militants in the United States

aprx: approximately

aps: accessory power supply; adenosine phosphosulfate; autograph postcard signed; auxiliary power supply; auxiliary propulsion system

APS: Academy of Political Science; Adenosine Phosphosulfate; American Metal Products (stock exchange symbol); American Pediatric Society; American Pheasant Society; American Philatelic Society; American Philosophical Society; American Physical Society; American Physiological Society; American Phytopathological Society; American Plant Selections; American Poinsettia Society; American Polar Society; American Proctologic Society; American Prosthodontic Society; American Psychosomatic Society; Army Pilot School; Army Postal Service; Association of Photo Sensitizers; submarine transport (naval symbol)

APS: *Algerie Presse Service* (French—Algerian Press Service)

APSA: Aerolíneas Peruanas, South America; American Political Science Association; Associate of the Photographic Society of America

A & PSA: Aden and Protectorate of South Arabia

APsaA: American Psychoanalytic Association

APSB: Aid to the Potentially Self-supporting Blind

APSF: Alfred P. Sloan Foundation

APSq: Aerial Port Squadron

APSS: Association for the Psychophysiological Study of Sleep

APsychoA: American Psychoanalytic Association

APsychosomS: American Psychosomatic Society

APsychpthA: American Psychopathological Association

apt.: alum-precipitated toxoid; apartment; armor-piercing with tracer; automatically-programmed tool(s); automatic picture transmission

apt: *apartadero* (Spanish—platform)

APT: Advanced Passenger Train; Automotive Professional Training; Airman Proficiency Test; Automatic Picture Transmission

APTA: American Physical Therapy Association; American Pioneer Trails Association; American Platform Tennis Association

APTC: Allied Printing Trades Council

Aptdo: apartado (Spanish—post office box)

apth: apthong (a silent letter like the *p* in pneumatic)

apto: aluminum plastic tearoff (container cover)

apt(s): apartment(s)

APTs: Advanced Passenger Trains

APTS: Automatic Picture Transmission System

APTU: African Postal and Telecommunications Union

apu: auxiliary power unit

APU: Army Postal Unit

APV: Avenida Presidente Vargas, Rio de Janeiro, Brazil

apw: architectural projected window

APW: Accelerated Public Works; American Prisoner of War

APWA: American Public Welfare Association; American Public Works Association

APWU: American Postal Workers Union

apx: appendix

aq: accomplishment quotient; achievement quotient; any quantity; aqueous

aq.: aqua (Latin—water)

a-q: aircraft quality

AQ: achievement quotient; aviation fire-control technician (USAF symbol); Schreiner Aerocontractors (Hague)

AQ: Australian Quarterly

AQAB: Air Quality Advisory Board

aq. astr.: aqua adstricta (Latin—ice)

aq. bull.: aqua bulliens (Latin—boiling water)

aq. com.: aqua communis (Latin—ordinary water)

AQCR: Air Quality Control Region (EPA)

aq. dest.: aqua destillata (Latin—distilled water)

aqdm: air quality display model

AQE: Airman Qualifying Examination

aq. ferv.: aqua fervens (Latin—hot water)

aq. fluv.: aqua fluvii (Latin—river water)

aq. font.: aqua fontana (Latin—spring water)

aql: acceptable qualifying levels; acceptable quality level; approved quality level

aq. mar.: aqua marina (Latin—sea water)

aq. ment. pip.: aqua menthae piperitae (Latin—peppermint water)

aq. niv.: aqua nivalis (Latin—snow water)

aq. pluv.: aqua pluvialis (Latin—rain water)

aq. pur.: aqua pura (Latin—pure water)

AQREC: Army Quartermaster Research and Engineering Command

aq. reg.: (Latin—royal water) hydrochloric and nitric acid

AQT: Applicant Qualification Test

aq. tep.: aqua tepida (Latin—tepid water)

aqua.: aquaria; aquarium; aquatic

aquacult: aquaculture

aqua fortis: (Latin—strong water) nitric acid

aquar: aquarium

Aquar: Aquarius

aqua regia: (Latin—royal water) hydrochloric and nitric acid

aque: aqueduct

ar: achievement ratio; acid resisting; active resistance; alarm reaction; all rail; all risks; allocated reserve; analytical reagent; aromatic; arrival; artificial respiration; aspect ratio

ar: avis de reception (French —return receipt)

a/r: all risks; armed robbery; at the rate of

a & r: approved and removed; assault and robbery

a/R: *am Rhein* (German—on the Rhine River)

Ar: Arab; Arabia; Arabian; Arabic; Aragon; argon; Aries; aryl

AR: Aberdeen & Rockfish (railroad); Administrative Ruling; Aerodynamic Report; Aerolineas Argentinas (Argentine Airlines); Aeronautical Radionavigation; Airman Recruit; Airship Rigger; Amendment Request; American Smelting & Refining (stock exchange Symbol); Annual Report; Army Regulation(s); Army Reserve; repair ship (naval symbol)

AR: Aller et Retour (French —roundtrip); *Andata-Ritorno* (Italian—roundtrip)

A.R.: *Anno Regni* (Latin—In the Year of the Reign of)

A/R: *Aksjerederi* (Norwegian—shipping company)

A & R: assembly and repair

ara: assigned responsible agency (DoD)

ara ara(ARA): aerial rocket artillery

Ara: Argentina

ARA: Aerospace Research Association; American Railway Association; American Rationalist Association; American Relief Association; American Rental Association; American Republics Area; American Rheumatism Association; Arcade & Attica (railroad); Area Redevelopment Administration; Armada República Argentina (Argentine Navy); Artists' Representatives Association; Automatic Retailers of America

A.R.A.: Associate of the Royal Academy

ARA (AFL-CIO): American Radio Association

Arab.: Arabia; Arabian; Arabic

ARAC: Aerospace Research Applications Center

arach: arachnology

Arach: Arachnida

arad: airborne radar and doppler

ARADCOM: Army Defense Command

aral: automatic record analysis language

Aram: Aramaic

ARAM: Association of Railroad Advertising Managers

Aramco: Arabian-American Oil Company

aras: ascending reticular activating system

araucanos: (Latin American nickname—Chileans or *chilenos*) —sobriquet recalls the liberty-loving Araucanian Indians who were never conquered by the Spaniards

arb: arbitrary; arbitration

arb: arbeid(er) [Dano-Norwegian —work(s)]

Arb: Arbroath

ARB: Accident Records Bureau (NYC Police Dept.); Air Registration Board; Air Research Bureau; Armored Rifle Battalion; Army Rearming Base; Army Retiring Board; ASTIA Report Bibliography; battle damage repair ship (naval symbol)

ARBA: American Railway Bridge and Building Association; American Road Builders Association; Associated Retail Bakers of America

arb & aw: arbitration and award

ARBED: Aciéries Réunies de Burbach-Eich-Dudelange

ARBM: Association of Radio Battery Manufacturers
arbor.: arboriculture
ARBs: Air Resources Boards (pollution-control agencies)
arbtrn: arbitration
arbtror: arbitrator
arc.: arcade; auto-refrigerated cascade
arc: arco (Italian—bow, indicating end of *pizzicato* passages)
Arc: Arachon; Arcade; Archaic; Arctic
ARC: Agricultural Relations Council; Agricultural Research Council; Aircraft Radio Corporation; Air Reserve Center; Air Rescue Center; Airworthiness Requirements Committee; American Red Cross; Ames Research Center (NASA); Appalachian Regional Commission; Armada República de Colombia (Colombian Navy); Asian Research Center (Harvard); Association of Retail Confectioners; Association of Rehabilitation Centers; Atlantic Research Corporation; Atomedic Research Center; cable laying or repair ship (naval symbol)
ARCA: Associate of the Royal College of Art
Arc Arch: Arctic Archipelago (Canadian Arctic)
ARCAS: Automatic Radar Chain Acquisition System
Arc Cur: Arctic Current
arce: amphibious river-crossing equipment
ARCen: Air Reserve Center
arch.: archaic; archipelago; architect(s); architectural; architecture
Arch-Bish: Archbishop
Archd: Archdeacon; Archduke
Arch de Cln: Archipelago de Colón
Arch E: Architectural Engineer
archeo: archeological; archeologist; archeology
Archeoz: Archeozoic
archi: archival; archive; archivist
ARCHI: asociacion de Radiodifusoras de Chile (Association of Chilean Broadcasters)
Archie: Archibald
archip: archipelago
archv: archive
ARCI: American Railway Car Institute
Arclos: Army Close support
ARCM: Associate of the Royal College of Music
Arc O: Arctic Ocean Command
ARCO: Associate of the Royal

College of Organists; Atlantic Richfield Company
ARCom: Army Research
ARCON: Advanced Research Consultants
ARCOV: Army Combat Operations Vietnam
arcp: air refueling control point
ARCR: Arthritis and Rheumatism Council for Research
ARCRL: Agricultural Research Council Radiobiological Laboratory
ARCS: Air Resupply and Communication Service
A.R.C.S.: Associate of the Royal College of Science; Associate of the Royal College of Surgeons
ARCSA: Aviation Requirements for the Combat Structure of the Army
arct: air refueling control time
arc/w: arcweld
ard: acute respiratory disease
ar & d: aeronautical research and development; air research and development
Ard: Ardrossan
ARD: Arbeitsgemeinschaft Rundfunkanstalten Deutschland (German National Broadcasting); Accelerated Rural Development; Air Reserve District; American Research and Development (corporation); Army Renegotiation Division; Association of Research Directors; auxiliary floating dock (naval)
AR & D: air research and development
ARDA: Advanced Reactor Development Associates; American Railway Development Association
ARDC: Aberdeen Research and Development Center; Air Research and Development Command; American Racing Drivers Club
ARDCM: Air Research and Development Command Manual
ARDCO: Applied Research and Development Company
ARDE: Armament Research and Development Establishment (Ministry of Supply)
ARDG: Army Research and Development Group (USA)
ARDG(E): Army Research and Development Group (Europe)
ARDG(FE): Army Research and Development Group (Far East)
ARDIS: Army Research and Development Information System
ARDM: medium auxiliary repair drydock (naval symbol)

ard's: analog recording dynamic analyzers
are. (ARE): air reactor experiment
ARE: Association for Research and Enlightenment
A.R.E.: Associate in Religious Education
AREA: Aerovias Ecuatorianas (Ecuadorian Airways); American Railway Engineering Association; American Recreational Equipment Association; Army Reactor Experimental Area; Association of Records Executives & Administrators
AREC: Amateur Radio Emergency Corps
AREFS: Air Refueling Squadron
ARENA: Aliança Renovadora Nacional (Portuguese—National Renovating Alliance)—political party in Brazil
aren't: are not
ARENTS: ARPA Environmental Test Satellite
AREUEA: American Real Estate and Urban Economics Association
ARF: Advertising Research Foundation; African Research Foundation; Air Reserve Force(s); American Radio Forum; American Rationalist Federation; American Rehabilitation Foundation; American Retail Foundation; American Rose Foundation; Armour Research Foundation; Arthritis and Rheumatism Foundation
ARFA: Allied Radio Frequency Agency
ARFCOS: Armed Forces Courier Service
ARFDC: Atomic Reactor and Fuel Development Corporation
arfor: area forecast
ARFPC: Air Reserve Forces Policy Committee
arg: argent; argot; argument; argumentation; argumentative; argumentator (a controversialist); argus; arresting; arresting gear
arg: argang (Dano-Norwegian —yearbook); argol (mongolian—dried camel or cattle dung fuel)
arga: appliance, range, adjust (data processing)
Arg: Argentina; Argentinian
ARG: Aerolineas Argentinas; repair ship, internal combustion engine
ARGCA: American Rice Growers Cooperative Association
Argen: Argentine; Argentinian
argus: advanced research on groups

under stress

ARGUS: Automatic Routine Generating and Updating System

Argyll: Argyllshire

a/Rh: *am Rhein* (German—on the Rhine)

ARH: heavy-hull repair ship (3-letter symbol)

Ari: Aristotle

ARI: Air-Conditioning and Refrigeration Institute; Aluminum Research Institute; American Reciprocal Insurers; American Refractories Institute; American Russian Institute

ARIANA: Ariana Afghan Airlines

ARIB: Asphalt Roofing Industry Bureau

ARIBA: Associate of the Royal Institute of British Architects

ARIC: Associate of the Royal Institute of Chemistry

ARICRSU: American Russian Institute for Cultural Relations with the Soviet Union

ARIEM: Army Research Institute of Environmental Medicine

ARIES: Advanced Radar Information Evaluation System

ARINC: Aeronautical Radio Incorporated

arip: automatic rocket impact predictor

aris (ARIS): advanced range instrumentation ships

ARIS: Advanced Research Instrument System; Aircraft Research Instrumentation System

ARIST: *Annual Review of Information Science and Technology*

Arista: high-school honor society

aristocat(s): aristocratic cat(s)

aristo(s): aristocrat(s)

ARISTOTLE: Annual Review and Information Symposium on the Technology of Training, Learning, and Education (DoD)

A.R.I.T.: American Registered Inhalation Therapist

arith: arithmetic

Ariz: Arizona; Arizonian

Ark: Arkansas; Arkansan

ARKIA: Israel Inland Airlines

Arkie: migratory farm worker or sharecropper from Arkansas

arl: acceptable reliability level; air run landing

ARL: Aeromedical Research Laboratory; Aeronautical Research Laboratory; Aerospace Research Laboratory; American Reefer Line; American Republics Line; American Roque League; Anesthesia Research Laboratories; Applied Research Laboratory (Johns Hopkins University); As-

sociation of Research Libraries; landing craft repair ship (3-letter naval symbol)

ARLD: Army Logistics Research and Development

ARLIS: Arctic Research Laboratory Island (USN)

ArLO: Army Liaison Officer

ARLO: Art Reference Libraries of Ohio

arm.: anti-radar missile (ARM); anti-radiation missile; armature; arming

Arm: Armagh; Armenia(n)

Ar.M.: Architecturae Magister (Master of Architecture)

ARMA: American Bosch Arma Corporation

a & r man: artist and repertory man (recording)

armd: armored

armet: area forecast (given in metric system)

armgrd: armed guard

ARMI: American Rack Merchandisers Institute; American Research Merchandising Institute; Army Resources Management Institute

ARMM: Association of Reproduction Materials Manufacturers

ARMMA: American Railway Master Mechanics' Association

ARMMS: Automated Reliability and Maintainability Measurement System

AR/MONP: Ayers Rock/Mount Olga National Park (Northern Territory, Australia)

armpl: armorplate

armr: armorer

ARMS: Advanced Receiver Model System; Aerial Radiological Measuring Survey; Amateur Radio Mobile Society

arm-saf: arm-safe (switch)

armt: armament

ARMU: Associated Rocky Mountain Universities

a Rn: *am Rhein* (German—on the Rhine)

Arn: Arnold

ARN: Stockholm, Sweden (Arlanda Airport)

ArNa: Army with Navy

arng: arrange

ARNG: Army National Guard

ARNMD: Association for Research in Nervous and Mental Disease

Arnold Bennett: Enoch Arnold Bennett

aro: after receipt of order; airborne range only

ARO: Air Radio Office(r); Applied Research Objective; Army Research Office; Army Routine

Order; Asian Regional Organization; Association for Research in Ophthalmology; Association of Roentgenological Organizations

arod: airborne range and orbit determination

ARO-FE: Army Research Office—Far East

arom: aromatic

AR-ONP: Ayers Rock-Olgas National Park (Australia)

arp: airborne radar platform; airport reference point; alternator research package; (cartoonist's symbol—dog's bark)

ARP: Advanced Research Project(s); Aeronautical Recommended Practice(s); Air Raid Precautions; American Registry of Pathologists; Ammunition Refilling Point; Area Redevelopment Program; Association for Realistic Philosophy; Australian Reptile Park (New South Wales)

ARP: *Anti-Revolutionaire Partij* (Dutch—Anti-Revolutionary Party)

ARPA: Advanced Research Projects Agency

ARPAS: Air Reserve Pay and Allowance System

ARPAT: Advanced Research Projects Agency Terminal (defense system)

ARPC: Air Reserve Personnel Center

arpd (ARPD): applied research planning document

Arpo: *arpeggio* (Italian—producing the tones in a chord successively rather than simultaneously)

ARPS: Associate of the Royal Photographic Society

ARPT: American Registry of Physical Therapists

arr: airborne radio receiver; arrestor; arrival; arrive; arriving

Arr: *arrondissement* (French—district)

ARR: Air Regional Representative; Air Reserve Record(s); Army Retail Requirements

ARRC: Air Reserve Records Center; Associate of the Royal Red Cross

ARRF: Automatic Recording and Reduction Facility

ARRGp: Aerospace Rescue and Recovery Group (USAF)

ARRL: American Radio Relay League

arr n: arrival notice

arrowhead: symbol used to indicate direction

ARRS: Aerospace Rescue and Recovery Service; American Roentgen Ray Society

ARRSq: Aerospace Rescue and Recovery Squadron (USAF)

ARRT: American Registry of Radiologic Technologists

ARRTC: Aerospace Rescue and Recovery Training Center (USAF)

ARRWg: Aerospace Rescue and Recovery Wing (USAF)

ars: aerospace research satellite; arsenal; asbestos roof shingles

ARs: Action Requests

ARS: Aerospace Research Satellite; Agricultural Research Service; Airail Service (monorail); Air Rescue Service; American Records Society; American Recreation Society; American Repair Society; American Rescue Service; American Rhododendron Society; American Rocket Society; American Rose Society; Army Relief Society; salvage ship (naval symbol)

ARSA: Associate of the Royal School of Art

ARSC: Association of Recorded Sound Collections

arsen: arsenal

ARSH: Associate of the Royal Society for the Promotion of Health

ARSM: Associate of the Royal School of Mines

ARSP: Aerospace Research Support Program

arsr: air route surveillance radar

ARST: salvage craft tender (naval symbol)

ARSTRAC: Army Strike Command

ARSV: armored reconnaissance scout vehicle (USA)

art.: airborne radiation thermometer; article; artifact; artificial; artillery; artisan; artist; artistic; artistry

art⁰: *artículo* (Spanish—article)

Art: Arthur; Arturo

Art: *Artikel* (German—article)

ART: Accredited Record Technician; Air Reserve Technician; Arithmetic Reading Test; Arithmetic Reasoning Test; Aviation Radio Technician

ARTA: Association of Retail Travel Agents

artac: advanced reconnaissance and target acquisition capabilities

ARTC: Air Route Traffic Control

ARTCC: Air Route Traffic Control Center

Art C-Part: articles of co-partner ship

ARTE: Admiralty Reactor Test Establishment

Artemus Ward: (pseudonym —Charles Farrar Browne)

Arth: Arthropoda; Arthur; Arthurian

Artigas: José Gervasio Artigas —defender of Uruguayan independence after leading Gaucho revolt against Spanish misrule

art. insem: artificial insemination

arto: air run takeoff

ARTOC: Army Tactical Operational Control; Army Tactical Operations Central

ARTP: Army Rocket Transportation System

artrac: advanced range testing, reporting, and control

artron(s): artificial neuron(s)

arts.: articles

ARTS: Advanced Radar Traffic Control System; Automatic Radar Traffic Control System

artu: automatic range tracking unit

arty: artillery

aru: analog remote unit; audio response unit

Aru: Aruba

ARU: Air Reserve Unit; American Railway Union

arv (ARV): aeroballistic reentry vehicle

Arv: *Arvoisa* (Finnish—esteemed)

ARV: aircraft engine overhaul and structural repair ship; American Revised Version

ARVA: aircraft repair ship for aircraft (4-letter designation)

ARVE: aircraft repair ship for engines (4-letter designation)

ARVH: aircraft repair ship —helicopter (naval symbol)

ARVN: Army of the Republic of Vietnam

ARVSG: Air Reserve Volunteer Support Group

arw: attitude reaction wheel

ARW: Air Raid Warden; Air Raid Warning

ARWA: American Right-of-Way Association

ARWC: Army War College

as.: airscoop; air-to-surface missile; alloy steel; antiseptic; asymmetric

a-s: ascendance-submission

a/s: airspeed; antisubmarine

a.s.: *auris sinistra* (Latin—left ear)

a/s: *aux soins de* (French—in care of)

As: altostratus; arsenic; Asia; Asian; Asiatic; astigmatism; aunicles; Australia(n)

AS: Abilene & Southern (railroad);

Academy of Science(s); Aeronautical Standard(s); air-to-surface missile; Air Service; Air Speed; Air Staff; Air Station; Airports Service; Air Surveillance; Alaska Airlines; Anglo-Saxon; antisubmarine; Apprentice Seaman; Army Security; Army Staff; submarine tender (naval symbol)

A.S.: Antonius Stradivarius (initials usually accompanied by a Maltese cross, both enclosed in a double circle)

A/S: alongside (barge, cargo carrier, lighter)

AS: *Anonim Sirket* (Turkish—joint stock company); *Aviaeskadra* (Russian—air squadron)

A/S: *Aksjeselskap* (Norwegian—limited company); *Aktieselskab* (Danish—joint stock company)

A & S: Alton & Southern (railroad)

A de S: Académie des Sciences

asa: acetylsalicylic acid (aspirin); antistatic additive

asa: (Norwegian or Swedish—hill)

ASA: Acoustical Society of America; Actuarial Society of America; Aerovias Sud Americana (South American Airways); African Studies Association; Alaska Airlines; Aluminum Siding Association; Amateur Softball Association; Amateur Swimming Association; American Scientific Affiliation; American Shorthorn Association; American Sightseeing Association; American Society for Abrasives; American Society for Aesthetics; American Society of Agronomy; American Society of Anesthesiologists; American Society of Appraisers; American Society of Auctioneers; American Sociological Association; American Sociometric Association; American South African Line; American Soybean Association; American Standards Association; American Statistical Association; American Stockyards Association; American Studies Association; American Sunbathing Association; American Surgical Association; Anthroposophical Society of America; Army Seal of Approval; Army Security Agency; Assistant Secretary of the Army; Associated Stenotypists of America; Association of Southeast Asia; Atomic Security Agency; Aviation Supply Annex

A of SA (ASA): Association of

Southeast Asia

ASAA: Amateur Softball Association of America; Armenian Students Association of America

ASAC: American Society for African Culture; American Society of Agricultural Consultants; Army Study Advisory Committee

ASAE: American Society of Agricultural Engineers

AS of AF: Assistant Secretary of the Air Force

ASAH: American Society of Association Historians

Asahi: (Japanese—Morning Sun) —Japan's leading daily newspaper

ASAM: American Society for Abrasive Methods

ASAN: Adriatica Società per Azioni di Navigazione

ASAnes: American Society of Anesthesiologists

ASAO: Association for Social Anthropology in Oceania

asap: as soon as possible

ASAP: Airlines of South Australia; antisubmarine attack plotter

ASAPS: Anti-Slavery and Aborigines Protection Society

ASARCO: American Smelting and Refining Company

ASAS: American Society of Abdominal Surgery; American Society of Animal Science; Army Security Agency School

asb: aircraft safety beacon; asbestos

as & b: aloin, strychnine, and belladonna (pills)

ASB: Administration and Storage Building; Aircraft Safety Beacon; Air Safety Board; Air Staff Board; American Society of Bacteriologists

asb c: asbestos covered

ASBC: American Society of Biological Chemists

ASBC: American Standard Building Code

ASBCA: Armed Services Board of Contract Appeals

ASBD: Advanced Sea-Based Deterrent Program

ASBDA: American School Band Directors Association

ASBE: American Society of Bakery Engineers

asb & i: aloin, strychnine, belladonna, and ipecac

asbl: assemble

ASBPA: American Shore and Beach Preservation Association

ASBPE: American Society of Business Press Editors

‹ **asc:** automatic switching center; auxiliary switch closed

as & c: aerospace surveillance and control

Asc: Ascidian

ASC: Adelaide Steamship Company; Aeronautical Systems Center; Air Service Command; Air Support Command; Air Support Control; Air Systems Command; Alabama State College; Alaska Steamship Company; Albany State College; American Security Council; American Silk Council; American Society of Cinematographers; American Society of Criminology; American Society of Cytology; Arizona State College; Arkansas State College; Army Service Corps; Army Subsistence Center; Asian Socialist Conference; Associated Sandblasting Contractors

A & SC: Adhesive and Sealant Council

asca: automatic science citation alerting

ASCA: American Senior Citizens Association; American Speech Correction Association

ASCAA: Automobile Seat Cover Association of America

ASCAC: Antisubmarine Contact Analysis Center

ASCAP: American Society of Composers, Authors, and Publishers

ASCAT: Antisubmarine Contact Analysis Team

ASCATS: Apollo Simulation Checkout and Training System

ASCC: Adams State College of Colorado; Air Standardization Coordinating Committee; American Society for the Control of Cancer; Army Strategic Communications Command; Association of Senior Citizens Clubs

ASCD: Association for Supervision and Curriculum Development

ASCE: American Society of Civil Engineers

ASCET: American Society of Certified Engineering Technicians

ASCHAL: American Society of Corporate Historians, Archivists, and Librarians

ASCHE: American Society of Chemical Engineers

ASCI: American Society for Clinical Investigation

ASCII: American Standard Code for Information Interchange

ASCMA: American Sprocket Chain Manufacturers Association

ASCN: American Society of Clinical Nutrition

asco: automatic sustainer cutoff

Asco: Automatic Switch Company

ASCom: Army Service Command

ascore: automatic shipboard checkout and readiness equipment

ASCP: American Society of Clinical Pathologists; American Society of Consulting Pharmacists; American Society of Consulting Planners

ASCRO: Active Service Career for Reserve Officers

ASCS: Agricultural Stabilization and Conservation Service; Automatic Stabilization and Control System

ASCU: Association of State Colleges and Universities

ASD: Aeronautical Systems Division; Army Shipping Document; Artillery Spotting Division; Assistant Secretary of Defense; Association of Steel Distributors; Aviation Supply Depot

ASDA: American Safe Deposit Association; American Seafood Distributors Association; American Stamp Dealers Association; Asbestos and Danville (railroad); Association of Structural Draftsmen of America; Atomic and Space Development Authority

ASDAE: Association of Seventh-Day Adventists Educators

AsDB: Asian Development Bank

ASDC: Aeronomy and Space Data Center (NOAA)

asde: aircraft surface detection equipment

ASDF: Air Self-Defense Force (Japanese Air Force)

ASDG: Aircraft Storage and Disposition Group

asdi: automatic selective dissemination of information

ASDIC: Anti-Submarine Detection Investigation Committee (British sonar, named for this wartime committee)

ASDIRS: Army Study Documentation and Information Retrieval System

asdr: airport surface-detection radar

ASDR: American Society of Dental Radiographers

A/S D/S: Akties Dampskibsselskab (Danish—steamship company, limited)

ase: airborne search equipment

ASE: Amalgamated Society of Engineers; American Society of Enologists; American Steel Equipment; American Stock Exchange; Association of Science Education

ASEA: Allmänna Svenska Elektriska Aktiebolaget; American Society of Engineers and Architects

ASEAN: Association of Southeast Asian Nations

ASEB: Aeronautics and Space Engineering Board

ASEC: All Saints' Episcopal College; American Standard Elevator Code

ASECA: Association for Education and Cultural Advancement (South Africa)

ASECS: American Society for Eighteenth-Century Studies

ASEE: American Society of Electrical Engineers; American Society for Engineering Education

ASEP: American Society for Experimental Pathology

ASESA: Armed Services Electro-Standards Agency

ASESB: Armed Services Explosives Safety Board

ASESS: Aerospace Environment Simulation System

ASETC: Armed Services Electron Tube Committee

asf: additional selection factor; amperes per square foot

ASF: Advisory Support Force; Aircraft Services Facility; Alaskan Sea Frontier; American Scandinavian Foundation; American Schizophrenia Foundation; Ammunition Storage Facility; Army Service Forces; Army Stock Fund; Association of State Foresters; Automotive Safety Foundation

ASFA: American Steel Foundrymen's Association

ASFC: Atlantic Salt Fish Commission (Canada)

ASFE: American Society For Aesthetics

ASFEC: Arab States Fundamental Education Center

asfir: active swept-frequency interferometer radar

ASFMRA: American Society of Farm Managers and Rural Appraisers

asfts: airborne systems functional test stand

asfx: assembly fixture

asg: assignment

ASG: Aeronautical Standards Group (Air Force and Navy); American Saint Gobain (glass); American Society of Genetics

ASGB: Aeronautical Society of Great Britain

ASGBI: Association of Surgeons of Great Britain and Ireland

asgd: assigned

asgmt: assignment

asgn: assign; assignment

ASGp: Aeronautical Standards Group (USAF)

ASGS: American Scientific Glassblowers Society

ash.: airship; armature shunt

Ash: Asahi Shimbun (leading Japanese newspaper)

As H: hyperopic astigmatism

ASH: Action on Smoking and Health; American Society of Hematology; Ashland Oil and Refining (stock exchange symbol)

A-S-H: Allen-Sherman-Hoff

ASHA: American School Health Association; American Social Health Association; American Social Hygiene Association; American Speech and Hearing Association

ASHACE: American Society of Heating and Air-Conditioning Engineers

ASHC: All-States Hobby Club

ASHE: American Society of Hospital Engineers

ASHG: American Society of Human Genetics

ASHH: American Society for the Hard of Hearing

ASHI: Association for the Study of Human Infertility

Ashken: Ashkenazim (Hebrew —Jews of central and northern Europe)

Ash Mus: Ashmolean Museum

ashp: airship

ASHP: American Society of Hospital Pharmacists

ASHRAE: American Society of Heating, Refrigerating, and Air-Conditioning Engineers

ASHS: American Society for Horticultural Science

asi: airspeed indicator

ASI: Advanced Scientific Instruments; Aero-Space Institute; Aerospace Studies Institute; Africa Service Institute; Air Society International; Amended Shipping Instruction(s); American Specifications Institute; American Swedish Institute

ASIA: Army Signal Intelligence Agency

ASIC: Air Service Information Circular

ASIDIC: Association of Scientific Information Dissemination Centers

ASIF: Airlift Service Industrial Fund

ASI & H: American Society of

Ichthyologists and Herpetologists

ASII: American Science Information Institute

a sin: a sinistra [Italian—at (to) the left]

ASIRC: Aquatic Sciences Information Retrieval Center (U of RI)

ASIS: Abort-Sensing Implementation System; American Society for Information Science; ammunition stores issue ship (naval designator)

ASIWPCA: Association of State and Interstate Water Pollution Control Administrators

ask.: amplitude shift keying

ASK: Association for Social Knowledge

ASKA: Automatic System for Kinematic Analysis

ASKS: Automatic Station-Keeping System

ASKT: American Society of Knitting Technologists

asl: abandon ship ladder; above sea level

ASL: American Association of State Libraries; American Scantic Line; American Shuffleboard Leagues

A-S L: Abelard-Schuman Limited

ASLA: American Society of Landscape Architects

ASLB: Atomic Safety and Licensing Board (AEC)

ASLE: American Society of Lubrication Engineers

ASLH: American Society for Legal History

ASLIB: Association of Special Libraries and Information Bureaus

ASLNY: Art Students League of New York

aslo: assembly layout

ASLO: American Society of Limnology and Oceanography

ASLP: Association of Special Libraries in the Philippines

ASLRA: American Short Line Railroad Association

aslt: assault

aslv: assurance sur la vie (French —life insurance)

asm: air-to-surface missile; assembly

As M: myopic astigmatism

ASM: Air-to-Surface Missile; American Society of Mammalogists; American Society for Metals; American Society for Microbiology; Antarctic Service Medal

ASMA: Aerospace Medical Association; American Society of Music Arrangers

rut

AUBC: Association of Universities of the British Commonwealth

AUBTW: Amalgamated Union of Building Trade Workers

auc: average unit cost

a.u.c.: *ab urbe condita* (Latin—from the founding of the city; usually refers to Rome)

AUC: Aberystwyth University College

AU of C: American University of Cairo

AUCA: American Unitarian Christian Association

AUCC: Association of Universities and Colleges of Canada

Auck: Auckland

AUCOA: Association of United Contractors of America

AUCSRLFRVWAM: All-Union Central Scientific Research Laboratory for the Restoration of Valuable Works of Art in Museums

auct: auction(eer)

auct: *auctorum* (Latin—of authors)

AUCTU: All-Union Council of Trade Unions

aud: audible; audit; audition; auditor; auditorium

audar: autodyne detection and ranging

Aud*ᵃ*: *audiencia* (Spanish—court of justice; hearing)

aud disb: auditor disbursements

Aud Gen: Auditor General

Aud Gen Nav: Auditor General of the Navy

Audie: Audry

audio: audiofrequency; audiogenic; audiogram; audiology; audiometer; audiometry; audiophile; audiovisual; audiovisual aids; etc.

audiol: audiology

audiovis: audiovisual; audiovisual aids

audre: audio response; automatic digit recognizer

AUEC: Association of University Evening Colleges

Aufdr: *Aufdrucke* (German—imprint)

Aufl: *Auflage* (German—edition)

AUFS: American Universities Field Staff

AUFUSAF: Army Unit for United States Air Force

aug: augment; augmentation; augmentative

Aug: August; Augusta; Augustan

Augember: August and September

Augie: August; Augustine; Augustus

augm: *augmente* (French—augmented)

AUI: Associated Universities Incorporated

auj: *aujourd'hui* (French—today)

Auk: Auckland

aul: above upper limit

AUL: Aberdeen University Library; Air University Library

AULC: American University Language Center

AULLA: Australasian Universities Language and Literature Association

aum (AUM): air-to-underwater missile

aum: *aumentado* (Spanish—augmented)

a. u. n.: *abseque ulla nota* (Latin—without annotation)

AUNT: Alliance for Undesirable but Necessary Tasks

auntie.: automatic unit for national taxation and insurance (UK)

AUP: Australian United Press

AUPG: American University Publishers Group

aur: auricle; auricular; auricularis; aurum

AUR: Association of University Radiologists

AURA: Association of Universities for Research in Astronomy

Aurelian Century: the 100s—reigr of Roman emperor-philosopher Marcus Aurelius—the 2nd century

AURI: Angkatan Udara Republik Indonesia (Indonesian Air Force)

Aus: Austin

AUS: Army of the United States; Austin, Texas (airport)

AUSA: Association of the United States Army

Ausg: *Ausgabe* (German—edition)

AUSLFL: All-Union State Library of Foreign Literature (Moscow)

aur fib: auricular fibrillation

auric: auricular

Aus: Austin; Austria; Austrian

AUSS: Association of University Summer Sessions

Aussie(s): Australian(s)

Aust: Australia; Australian

Aust Cur: Australian Current

austen: austenitic

austral: (Spanish—southern)

Austral: Australian

Australas: Australasian

aut: *autore* (Italian—author)

AUT: American Union Transport; Association of University Teachers

AUTEC: Atlantic Underwater Test Evaluation Center

auth: authentic; authenticate; authenticity; author; authority; au-

thorization; authorize(d)

Auth: Authority

authab: authorized abbreviation (USAF)

Author of the Declaration of Independence: Thomas Jefferson

Auth Ver: Authorized Version

auto.: automobile; automatic; automotive

autocade: automobile parade

autodin: automatic digital network

autodoc: automatic documentation

autog: autograph

auto. lean: automatic lean

autom: automobile; automotive

automap: automatic machining program

automast: automatic mathematical analysis and symbolic translation

automation: automation action; automatic operation

automtn: automation

auton: autonomous; autonomy

autonet: automatic network

autop: automatic pistol; autopsy

AUTOPIC: Automatic Personal Identification Code

autopilot: automatic pilot

autopistol: automatic pistol

autoprompt: automatic programming of machine tools

AUTOPSY: Automatic Operating System (IBM)

auto. recl: automatic reclosing

auto. rich: automatic rich

autorotic(s): automobile neurotic(s)

autos: automobiles; automatics

autosate: automatic data systems analysis technique

autoscript: automated system for composing, revising, illustrating, and typesetting

auto s & cv: automatic stop and check valve

AUTOSERVCEN: Automated Service Center

autosevcom: automatic secure voice communications

autospot: automatic system for positioning tolls

autostatis: automatic statewide auto theft inquiry

autostrad: automated system for transportation data

autosyn: automatically synchronous

autotran: automatic translation

autovon: automatic voice network

autran: automatic target-recognition analysis

AUU: Association of Urban Universities

auv: armored utility vehicle

auw: airframe unit weight

AUWE: Admiralty Underwater

Weapons Establishment
aux: auxiliary
aux m: auxiliary machinery
AUXOPS: Auxiliary Operational Members (USCG)
auxrc: auxiliary recording control
av: arteriovenous; aviator; avoirdupois
a-v: atriventricular; audio-visual
av: *avril* (French—April)
a v: *a vista* (Italian—at sight)
a/v *(A/V): ad valorem* (Latin—as valued)
Av: Aves; Avian; Avila(n)
Av: *avenida* (Portuguese or Spanish—avenue)
AV: American Viewpoint; Antonio Vivaldi; arteriovenous; audiovisual; Authorized Version; large seaplane tender (naval symbol)
A. V.: *Anno Vixit* [Latin—he (she) lived (a given number of) years]
ava: arteriovenous anastomosis
AVA: Aerodynamische Versuchsanstalt; American Vocational Association; Audio-Visual Aids
aval: availability; available
avb: *avbeta* (Swedish—departure)
AVB: advanced aviation base ship (naval symbol)
avbl: armored vehicle bridge launcher
avc: allantoid vaginal cream; automatic volume control
AVC: American Veterans Committee; Antelope Valley College; Association of Vitamin Chemists; Audio-Visual Center
AvCad: Aviation Cadet
AVCS: Advanced Videcon Camera Systems; Assistant Vice Chief of Staff
avd: automatic voice data; automatic voltage digitizer
avd: *avdeling* (Dano-Norwegian —part; section)
AvD: Automobil Club von Deutschland (German Automobile Club)
AVD: Army Veterinary Department; high-speed seaplane tender (3-letter naval symbol)
Avda: *Avenida* (Spanish—Avenue)
AVDA: American Venereal Disease Association
AVDO: Aerospace Vehicle Distribution Office(r)
avdp: avoirdupois
ave: automatic volume expansion
Ave: Avenue
avec: amplitude vibration exciter control
AVEM: Association of Vacuum Equipment Manufacturers
AVENSA: Aerovias Venezolanas (Venezuelan Airlines)

avf: azimuthally varying field
avfr: available for reassignment
avg: average
Avg: *Avgust* (Russian—August)
avgas: aviation gasoline
Avh: *Avhandlinger* (Swedish —transactions
avi: airborne vehicle identification; aviation
AVI: American Virgin Islands; Association Universelle d'Aviculture Scientifique (Universal Association of Scientific Aviculture)
Aviaco: Aviación y Comercio (Spanish airline)
AVIANCA: Aerovias Nacionales de Colombia (National Airlines of Colombia)
AVIATECA: Empresa Guatemalteca de Aviación (Guatemalan Aviation Enterprise)
AVID: Audio-Visual Instruction Department
avigation: aircraft navigation
avionics: aviation and astronautics electronics
AVISCO: American Viscose Corporation
AVISPA: Aerovias Interamericanas de Panamá (Interamerican Airways of Panama)
av JC: *avant Jésus Christ* (French —before Jesus Christ; B.C.)
avl: angle versus length
av l: average length
AVL: Asheville, North Carolina (airport)
Av Labs: Aviation Laboratories (USA)
avlm: anti-vehicle land mine
avlub: aviation lubricant
avm: automatic voting machine
AVM: guided-missile ship (naval symbol)
AVMA: American Veterinary Medical Association
AVMF: *Aviatsiya Voenno Morskikh Flota* (Russian—Soviet Naval Aviation)
avn: aviation
Avn: Avonmouth
AVN: Air Vietnam
AVNMED: Aviation Medicine (DoD)
avo: ampere-volt-ohm
AVO: Állam Védelmi-Osztály (Hungarian—Hungarian-Secret Soviet Police); avoid verbal orders
Avog: Avogadro
avoid.: airfield vehicle obstacle indication device
avoil: aviation oil
avoir: avoirdupois
avolo: automatic voice link obser-

vation
Avon: Avonmouth (Port of Bristol)
AVP: seaplane tender, small (3-letter symbol); Wilkes-Barre, Pennsylvania (airport)
AVRA: Audio-Visual Research Association
AVRO: A.V. Roe (Ltd)
AVRO: *Algemeene Vereeninging Radio Omroep* (Dutch—General Broadcasting Association)
avs: aerospace vehicle simulation
AVS: American Vacuum Society; Association for Voluntary Sterilization; aviation supply ship (naval symbol)
AVSC: Audio-Visual Support Center (USA)
avst: automated visual-sensitivity test(er)
AVSYCOM: Aviation Systems Command (USA)
avt: audiovisual tutorial
AVT: Adult Vocational Training; auxiliary aircraft transport (naval symbol); Aviation Medicine Technician
avta: automatic vocal transaction analyzer
AVUS: *Automobile Versuchs and Untersuchungs Strecke* (German—Automobile Test Track)
avv: *avvocato* (Italian—advocate) —lawyer
av w: average width
AVX: Avalon Bay, Catalina Island, California (airport)
aw: air-to-water; antiwear
a/w: actual weight; all-water; all-weather
a & w: alive and well
AW: air warning; Air Work, Ltd; American Welding; Articles of War; atomic warfare; atomic weight; automatic weapons(s); distilling ship (naval symbol)
A-W: Addison-Wesley
A & W: Atlantic & Western (railroad)
AWA: Air Warfare Analysis; All-Weather Attack; Aluminum Wares Association; American Warehousemen's Association; American Watch Association; American Waterfowl Association; American Wine Association; American Woman's Association; Association of Women in Architecture; Aviation/Space Writers Association
awac: airborne warning and control
AWACS: Airborne Warning and Control System
AWADS: All-Weather Aerial Delivery System
AWAL: American-West African

Line
awar: area-weighted average resolution
AWARE: Addiction Workers Alerted to Rehabilitation and Education (NYC); Association for Women's Active Return to Education
AWARS: Airborne Weather and Reconnaissance System
awb: air waybill
AWB: Agricultural Wages Board (UK)
AWBA: American World Boxing Association
AWB/CN: Air Waybill or Consignment Note
AWC: Air War College; American Watershed Council; American Wool Council; Anaconda Wire & Cable (stock exchange symbol); Area Wage & Classification (office); Arizona Western College; Army War College; Army Weapons Command
AWCO: Area Wage and Classification Office
awcs: agency-wide coding structure
AWCS: Air Weapons Control System
awd: award
AWD: Air Worthiness Division
AWDA: Automotive Warehouse Distributors Association
awdr: advanced weapon-delivery radar
AWEASVC: Air Weather Service
AWES: Army Waterways Experiment Station
a wf: acceptable work-load factor; adrenal weight factor
AWF: American Wildlife Foundation
AWFS: All-Weather Fighter Squadron
AWG: American Wire Gage
AWH: Association of Western Hospitals
AWI: Animal Welfare Institute
AWIS: Association of Women in Science
AWIU: Allied Workers International Union
AWK: Wake Island (airport)
awl.: absent with leave; artesian well lease
AWLF: African Wildlife Leadership Foundation
AWLS: All-Weather Landing System
awm: automatic washing machine
AWM: Association of Women Mathematicians
awn: awning
AWN: Automated Weather Network

AWngSvc: Air Warning Service
AWO: Accounting Work Order; American Waterways Operators
awol: absent without leave
AWOP: All-Weather Operations Panel
A & WP: Atlanta and West Point (railroad)
AWPA: American Wood Preservers Association
AWPB: American Wood Preservers Bureau
AWPL: Australia-West Pacific Line
awr: adaptive waveform recognition
AWR: Association of Western Railways
AWRA: American Water Resources Association
AWRE: Atomic Weapons Research Establishment
AWRIS: Army War Room Information System
AWRNCO: Aircraft Warning Company (Marines)
AWRT: American Women in Radio and Television
AWS: Aircraft Warning Service; Aircraft Warning System; Air Warning Service; Air Warning Squadron; Air Warning System(s); Air Weather Service; Air Weapon Systems; American War Standards; American Watercolor Society; American Weather Service; American Welding Society; Atlas Weapon System; Attack Warning System; Aviation Weather Service
AWSA: American Water Ski Association
AWSG: Army Work Study Group
AW & ST: *Aviation Week & Space Technology*
awt: advanced waste treatment
AWTE: Association for World Travel Exchange
awu: atomic weight unit
AWU: Aluminum Workers Union
AWWA: American Water Works Association
AWWU: American Watch Workers Union
awy: airway
ax.: axiom(atic); axes; axis
AX: American Air Export & Import Company (stock exchange symbol)
axbt: aircraft-expendable bathythermograph
ax grad: axial gradient
AXO: Assistant Experimental Officer
Axson: Axelson (Swedish—son of Axel)
Ay: Ayala

AY: Allied Youth
AYA: American Yachtsmen's Association
AYC: American Youth Congress
AYD: American Youth for Democracy
ayer: (Malay—water); (Spanish—yesterday)
ayf: anti-yeast factor
AYH: American Youth Hostels
AYI: Academic Year Institute (NSF)
A Y L I: *As You Like It*
Aym: Aymara
AYM: Ancient York Mason; Ancient York Masonry
AYP: Alaska-Yukon Pioneers
Ayr: Ayrshire
az: azure
a Z: aan Zee (Dutch—on sea); *auf Zeit* (German—on account; on credit)
Az: azimuth; Azores; Aztec; Aztecan; azure
Az: Azote (Greek—nitrogen)
AZ: Active Zone; Alitalia (Linee Aeree Italiane)
A to Z: from A to Z; from the beginning to the end; thoroughly covered
AZA: American Zionist Association
azas: adjustable-zero adjustable-span
Azb: Azerbaijan; Axerbaijani; Azerbaijanian
AZC: American Zionist Council
azel: azimuth elevation
AZF: American Zionist Federation
AZGS: Azusa Ground Station
azi: azimuth
Az I: Azores Islands
AZI: American Zinc Institute
Azo: Azores
azon: azimuth only
Azorin: (pseudonym—José Martinez Ruiz)
Azr: Azores
azran: azimuth and range
AZRI: Arid Zone Research Institute
azrock: asbestos rock
azs: automatic zero set
azt: azusa transponder
Azt: Aztec; Aztecan
aztc: azusa transponder coherent
Aztecan and Incan Century: the 1000s—great stone structures still standing in the highlands of Mexico and Peru are mute witnesses to these indigenous American cultures—the 11th century
A-Z Test: Ascheim-Zondek Test (for pregnancy)
azusa: azimuth, speed, altitude

B

b: baby; base; bicuspid; bituminous; black; blue; book; born; brass; breadth; bridge; wing span (symbol)

b: span

b 1: booster 1

b 1 p: booster 1 pitch

b 1 y: booster 1 yaw

b 2: booster 2

b 2 p: booster 2 pitch

b 2 y: booster 2 yaw

B: bacillus; bad; balboa; (Panamanian currency); Baltic; bandwidth; Barber Lines; Baumé; bay; Beatrice (Beatrice Foods) Beech; Belgium (auto plaque); belted; Bendix; benzene; body; Boeing; boils at; bolivar (Venezuelan currency); boliviano (Bolivian currency); bomber; bonded; borderline; boron; Boston; bowels; Bravo—code for letter B; British; Brother; Bruning; Buddhist; Bull Lines; buoyancy; Burroughs; flux density (symbol); Fraunhofer line caused by terrestrial oxygen

B–1: long-range supersonic bomber

B2F: Boeing 720 fan jet airplane

B3F: Boeing 320 fan jet airplane

b4: before

B7F: Boeing 707 fan jet airplane

B-47: Stratojet all-weather strategic medium bomber

B-52: Stratofortress all-weather intercontinental strategic heavy bomber

B-57: Canberra two-place twin-engine turbojet all-weather tactical bomber

B-58: Hustler strategic all-weather supersonic bomber

B-66: Destroyer twin-engine turbojet tactical all-weather light-bombardment aircraft

B/: balboa (Panamanian currency unit = $1.00 U.S.)

B: bajar (Spanish—to descend); *bas* (French—down); *Bay* (Turkish—Mister); brightness (symbol)

B': Ben (Hebrew—son; son of)

ba: base line; blind approach

b/a: backache; billed at; boric acid

b.a.: balneum arenae (Latin—sand bath)

Ba: Baia (Portuguese—Bahia); barium (symbol)

BA: Basic Airman; Bellas Artes (Fine Arts); Berkshire Athenium; Boeing (stock exchange symbol); Boston & Albany (railroad); British Academy; British Admiralty; British Army; British Association (for the Advancement of Science); Buenos Aires; Bureau of Accounts; Bureau of Apprenticeship; Busted Aristocrat (an officer reduced to the ranks)

B-A: Basses-Alpes

B.A.: *Baccalaureus Artium* (Latin—Bachelor of Arts)

B/A: Bank of America; British American (oil company)

B & A: Bangor & Aroostook (railroad); Boston & Albany (raiload)

BA: Biological Abstracts; Bonne Action (French—Good Deed)

B es A: Bachelier des Arts (French—Bachelor of Arts)

Baa: Baal; Baalam

BAA: Brewers Association of America; British Acetylene Association; British Airports Authority; British Archeological Association; British Astronomical Association; Bureau of African Affairs

B.A.A.: Bachelor of Applied Arts

BAAA: British Association of Accountants and Auditors

BAADS: Bangor Air Defense Sector

BAAF: Brigade Airborne Alert Force

baai: (Dutch—bay)

BAAL: Black Academy of Arts and Letters

BAAR: Board for Aviation Accident Research

BAAS: British Association for the Advancement of Science

bab: (Arabic—gate; strait)

Babette: Elizabeth

Bab(s): Barbara

BAB: B.T. Babbitt; Babo (cleanser)

babb: babbit metal

babs: blind approach beacon system

BABS: Babbage Society

BABT: Brotherhood of Associated Book Travelers

Baby: Babylon(ia); Babylonian

Baby Doc: Jean-Claude Duvalier —Haitian president

Babylonian Century: the 6th century before the Christian era when the Babylonians defeated the Israelites, made them captive, and destroyed the temple of Solomon in Jerusalem—the 500s

bac: bacilli; bacillus; bacteria; bacterial; bacteriologist; bacteriology

BAC: Bendix Aviation Corporation; Boeing Airplane Company; British Aircraft Corporation; British Association of Chemists; Bureau of Air Commerce; Business Advisory Council (U.S. Department of Commerce)

BAC: Baile Atha Cliath (Gaelic —Dublin)

BACAIC: Boeing Airplane Company Algebraic Interpretive Computing

BACAL: Butter and Cheese Association Limited

BACAN: British Association for the Control of Aircraft Noise

bac bag: bactine bag (underground slang—plastic bag containing bactine antiseptic sniffed by some school children in imitation of drug-addicted elders) —results often fatal due to suffocation

B.Acc.: Bachelor of Accountancy

BACD: Boeing Airplane Company Design

BACE: Bureau of Agricultural Chemistry and Engineering

bach: bachelor

bach: (German—brook; stream)

Bachelor President: James Buchanan—fifteenth President of the United States

Bach Soc: Bach Society

BACIE: British Association for Commercial and Industrial Education

back.: backwardation

'backs: wetbacks (illegal immigrants from Mexico)

bact: bacteria; bacteriological; bacteriologist; bacteriology; bacterium

bacter: bacteriologist

BACU: Battle Area Control Unit

Bad: Badajoz

BAD: Bantu Administration and Development; Base Air Depot; Berlin Airlift Device; Black, Active, and Determined; British Association of Dermatology
BADA: Base Air Depot Area
BADAS: Binary Automatic Data Annotation System
Baden: Baden-Baden
BADGE: Basic Air Defense Ground Environment
BADGES: Base Air Defense Ground Environment System
BADS: British Association of Dermatology and Syphilology
bae: beacon antenna equipment
BAE: Bureau of Agricultural Economics; Bureau of American Ethnology
B.A.E.: Bachelor of Aeronautical Engineering; Bachelor of Agricultural Engineering; Bachelor of Architectural Engineering; Bachelor of Art Education; Bachelor of Arts in Education
BAE: Buque Armada Ecuatoriana (Ecuadorian Naval Ship)
B.A.Ed.: Bachelor of Arts in Education
B.Ae.E.: Bachelor of Aeronautical Engineering
Ba enem: barium enema
BAEng: Bureau of Agricultural Engineering
baf: baffle
ba & f: budget, accounting, and finance
BAF: British Air Force; Burma Air Force; Burundi Air Force
BAFCom: Basic Armed Forces Communication Plan
bafgab: bafflegab—synonym for gobbledygook, jet-age jargon or officialese sometimes called pentagonese
BAFMA: British and Foreign Maritime Agencies
BAFS: British Academy of Forensic Science
bag.: bagasse; baggage; ballistic attack game; buccoaxiogingival
Bag: Baghdad
B.Ag.: Bachelor of Agriculture
BAGA: British Amateur Gymnastics Association
BAGBI: Booksellers Association of Great Britain and Ireland
B.Ag.E.: Bachelor of Agricultural Engineering
B. Agr.: Bachelor of Agriculture
BAGR: Bureau of Aeronautics General Representative
B.Ag.Sc.: Bachelor of Agricultural Science
Bah: Bahrain

BAH: Bahrain Island, Persian Gulf (airport)
Baha'i: (Abdul) Baha Bahai
bahia: (Spanish—bay)
Bahia: São Salvador de Bahia
Bah Ind: Bahasa Indonesian (national language)
BAHOH: British Association of the Hard of Hearing
bahr: (Arabic—lake; marsh; river; sea)
Ba I: Bahama Islands
BAI: Bureau of Animal Industry
B.A.I.: *Baccalaureus in Arte Ingeniaria* (Latin—Bachelor of Engineering)
bafa: (Portuguese—bay)
BAIC: Bureau of Agricultural and Industrial Chemistry
baid: boolean array identifier
baie: (French—bay; gulf)
BAIE: British Association of Industrial Editors
BAINS: Basic Advanced Integrated Navigation System
bait.: bacterial automated identification technique
baixo: (Portuguese—low; lower)
B.A.J.: Bachelor of Arts in Journalism
baja: (Spanish—lower)
Baja: Baja California (Spanish—Lower California)
Bajan: Barbadan (inhabitant of Barbados)
B.A.Jour.: Bachelor of Arts in Journalism
Bajuns: Barbadans
bak: bakery
bakelite: bormaldehyde formaldehyde plus phenol resin
baking soda: sodium bicarbonate ($NaHCO_3$)
bakke: (Danish—hill)
bal: balance; balcony; baloney
Bal: Baleares
BAL: Baltimore, Maryland (Friendship Airport); Belgian African Line; Bonanza Airlines (3-letter coding); Borneo Airways Ltd.
balance.: basic and logically applied norms—civil engineering
balast: balloon astronomy
Balb: Balboa
balc: balconette; balconied; balcony
Bald: Baldwin
balid: ballistics identification
balkan: (Turkish—mountain range)
ball.: ballast
Ball: Ballerup
ballute: balloon parachute
bally: ballyhoo
balop: balopticon (projector)
B Alp: Basses-Alpes
balpa: balance of payments; ball-

park
BALPA: British Airline Pilot's Association
bals: balsam
bals.: balsamum (Latin—balsam)
B.A.L.S.: Bachelor of Arts in Library Science
Balt: Balthasar; Baltic; Baltimore
balth: balthazar (16-bottle capacity)
Balti: Baltimore (slang)
Balto: Baltimore
Balts: Baltic people (Estonians, Latvians, Lithuanians)
Baluch: Baluchistan
balun: balance-to-unbalance (network)
balute: balloon parachute
bam: broadcasting am
Bam: Bamberger
BAM: broadcasting AM; Brooklyn Academy of Music
'Bama: Alabama
BAMA: British Amsterdam Maritime Agencies
bambi (BAMBI): ballistic missile bombardment interceptor
BAMIRAC: Ballistic Missile Radiation Analysis Center
BAMO: BuAer Material Officer
BAMR: BuAer Maintenance Representative
BAMTM: British Association of Machine Tool Merchants
BAMW: British Association of Meat Wholesalers
Ban: Bantu
BAN: Base Activation Notice; British Association of Neurologists
bana: (Japanese—cape)
bañados: (Spanish—marshes)
Banamex: Banco de México
band: (Persian—mountain range)
Band: Bandung
Banffs: Banffshire
Bang: Bangalore
banir: bombing and navigation inertial reference
bank.: banking
Bank: Bangkok
BANK: International Bank for Reconstruction and Development
banks.: bank holidays (West Indian English)
bank clgs: bank clearings
BANTSA: Bank of American National Trust and Savings Association
B.A. Nurs.: Bachelor of Arts in Nursing
BANWR: Bosque Apache National Wildlife Refuge (New Mexico)
BAO: British-American Oil; British Association of Otolaryngologists
B.A.O.: Bachelor of the Art of Obstetrics; Bachelor of Arts in

Oratory
BAOR: British Army on Rhine
bap: baptism; baptized
b a p: beginning at a point
BAP: Booksellers Association of Philadelphia
B A & P: Butte, Anaconda & Pacific (railroad)
BAPCO: Bahrain Petroleum Company
bape: baseplate
BA Phys Med: British Association of Physical Medicine
BAPL: Bettis Atomic Power Laboratory (AEC)
B.App.Arts: Bachelor of Applied Arts
BAPS: British Association of Paediatric Surgeons; British Association of Plastic Surgeons; Bureau of Air Pollution Sciences
Bapt: Baptist
BAPT: British Association of Physical Training
baq: basic allowance for quarters
BAQ: Barranquilla, Colombia (airport)
bar.: barometer; barometric
Bar: Baroque; Baruch, Book of
B.Ar.: Bachelor of Architecture
BAR: Broadcast Advertisers Reports; Browning automatic rifle; Bureau of Aeronautics Representative
BARA: *Bureau d'Analyse et de Recherche Appliquees* (French —Bureau of Analysis and Applied Research)
barb.: barbarian; barbecue; barber; barbiturate
Barb: Barbados Islands; Barbara
bar-b-q: barbecue
barbs.: barbiturates
Barc: Barcelona
BARC: British Aeronautical Research Committee
B.Arch.: Bachelor of Architecture
B.Arch.E.: Bachelor of Architectural Engineering
Bard of Avon: William Shakespeare
barg(s): bargain(s)
bari: baritone; baritone saxophone
Bari: Bari delle Puglie, Italy
Barme**:** Bartolomé
bari: baritone; baritone saxophone
barn.: bombing and reconnaissance navigation
Barn: Barnard
Barna: Barcelona
Barney: Barnabas; Barnett; Bernard; Bernardino
BARNS: Bombing and Reconnaissance Navigation System
Baroness Orczy: Mrs Montagu Bartstow—author of *The Scarlet*

Pimpernel
Baron Münchausen: Rudolf Erich Raspe who told many tall tales under his own name as well as under the pseudonym of Baron Münchausen—an aristocrat of Göttingen
b & arp: bare and acid resisting paint
barq: barquentine
Barq: Barranquilla
barr: barrister
barra: (Spanish—reef)
Barry: Bernard
BARS: Backup Attitude-Reference System; Ballistic Analysis Research System
BARSTUR: Barding Sands Underwater Test Range
Bart: Baronet
BART: Bay Area Rapid Transit (San Francisco); Brooklyn Army Terminal (New York)
BARTD: Bay Area Rapid Transit District
Bart's: St. Bartholomew's Hospital
barv: beach armored recovery vehicle
bas: basic airspeed; basic allowance for subsistence
Bas: Basilica; Basutoland
BAs: Business Agents (of unions)
BAS: Basic Allowance for Susbsistence; Behavioral Approach Scale; Brazilian-American Society; British Acoustical Society; British Antarctic Survey
B.A.S.: Bachelor of Agricultural Science; Bachelor of Applied Science
B. A. Sc.: Bachelor of Applied Science
BASC: Booth American Shipping Corporation
basc b: bascule bridge
basd: basic active service date
BASEEFA: British Approvals Service for Electrical Equipment in Flammable Atmospheres
BASF: Badische Anilin und Soda Fabrik
basic. (BASIC): battle-area surveillance and integrated communications; beginner's all-purpose symbolic instruction code (computer language)
BASIC: British-American Scientific International Commercial (English)
BASIC: *Biological Abstracts Subjects in Context*
BASICO: Behavior Science Corporation
BASIE: British Association for Commercial and Industrial Education

Bask: Baskir(ia)
BASO: Base Accountable Supply Officer; Bureau of Aeronautics Shipping Order
basops: base operations
basos: basophils
BASR: Bureau of Applied Social Research (Columbia University)
BASRA: British Amateur Scientific Research Association
bass.: bassoon
ba sw: bell-alarm switch
bat.: battery; battle
Bat: Bartholomew
BAT: Blind Approach Training; Boeing Air Transport; Bureau of Apprenticeship and Training
B-A T: British-American Tobacco
BA & T: Bureau of Apprenticeship and Training
batang: (Malayan—river)
BATC: British Amateur Television Club
bat. chg: battery charger; battery charging
BATDIV: battleship division
bate: base activation test equipment
b-a test: blood-alcohol test (used to determine if an automobile driver is under the influence of an intoxicating beverage)
BATFOR: battle force
bath.: best available true heading
batho: bathometer
bathy: bathymeter; bathysphere; bathyscaphe
BATM: British Admiralty Technical Mission
BATRON: battleship squadron
batrop: baratropic
Bat Rou: Baton Rouge
BATS: Business Air Transport Service
batt: batter; batteries; battery
bau: basic assembly unit; British absolute unit (BTU, Btu)
BAUS: British Association of Urological Surgeons
bav: *bon a vue* (French—good at sight)
Bav: Bavaria; Bavarian
BAVA: Bureau of Audio-Visual Aids (NY)
BAVE: Bureau of Audio-Visual Education (Calif)
BAVTE: Bureau of Adult, Vocational, and Technical Education (HEW)
baw: bare aluminum wire
BAWA: British Amateur Wrestling Association
BAWHA: Bide-A-Wee Home Association
bay cand dc: bayonet candelabra double contact
Bayer: *Bayerisch* (German—Ba-

varian)
baz: *bazzana* (Italian—sheepskin)
bb: ball bearing; bank burglar(y); bayonet base (lamp or socket); below bridges; bill book; both bones (fractured); both to blame; bungling bureaucrat; double black; pellet fired from a bb-gun or made for a bb-gun
b-b: black bordered
b/b: bail bond; bottled in bond
b & b: bed and board; bed and breakfast; benedictine and brandy
b or b: brass or bronze (cargo)
bb: *babord* (Swedish—port side)
b de b: *brut de brut* (French—naturally tart champagne or wine)
BB: battleship; B'nai B'rith; Brigitte Bardot; Bureau of the Budget
B.B.: Bernard Berenson
B & B: Brown and Bigelow
B of B: Bureau of the Budget
bba: born before arrival
BBA: Big Brothers of America; British Bankers' Association
B.B.A.: Bachelor of Business Administration
bbb: basic boxed base; bed, breakfast, and bath; blood brain barrier; triple black
BBB: Best Berlin Broadcast; Best British Briar (pipes); Better Business Bureau
BBBC: British Boxing Board of Control
bbc: barrels, boxes, and crates (cargo); bromobenzylcyanide (gas)
BBC: Bank of British Columbia; Beautiful British Columbia; British Broadcasting Corporation
BBCC: Big Bend Community College
BBC dissociation: Braid-Berheim-Charcot dissociation
BBCF: British Bacon Curers' Federation
BBCL: Bermuda Broadcasting Company Limited
bbcw: bare beryllium copper wire
bbdc: before bottom dead center
BB(DCO): Barclays Bank (Dominion, Colonial and Overseas)
BBEA: Brewery and Bottling Engineers Association
bb & em: bed, breakfast, and evening meal
bbf: boron-based fuel
BBF: Biblioteca Benjamin Franklin (Mexico City); Boilermakers, Blacksmiths, Forgers (union)
BBFC: British Board of Film Censors

BBG: Brooklyn Botanic Garden
bb-gun: airgun shooting bb's (ball bearings)
BBHC: Buffalo Bill Historical Center
BBHF: B'nai B'rith Hillel Foundations
BBI: Barbecue Briquet Institute
BBiP: *British Books in Print*
BBIRA: British Baking Industries Research Association
B Bisc: Bay of Biscay
bbj: ball-bearing joint
bbk: breadboard kit
bbl: barrel
BBL: bahia Blanca
BBL: Bangkok Bank Ltd; Big Brothers League
bbl roll: barrel roller
bbls/day: barrels per day
bbm: break-before-make
BBMRA: British Brush Manufacturers Research Association
BBNNR: Braunton Burrows National Nature Reserve (England)
BBNP: Big Bend National Park (Texas)
BBNR: Back Bay National Refuge (Virginia)
Bbo: Bilbao
B-bomb: benzedrine bomb (underground slang—benzedrine inhaler)
B-boy: busboy; mess sergeant
bbp: boxes, barrels, packages (cargo); building block principle
BBP: Beech Bottom Power Company
bbq: barbecue
BBQ: Brooklyn, Bronx, Queens
bbr: balloon-borne radio
BBRR: Brookhaven Beam Research Reactor (AEC)
BBRS: Balloon-Borne Radio System
bbs: ball bearings; barrels of basic sediment; box bark strips
Bb's: British biscuits
BBS: Bermuda Biological Station; Brunei Broadcasting Service
B.B.S.: Bachelor of Business Science
BBSATRA: British Boot, Shoe and Allied Trades Research Association
bbsj: ball-bearing swivel joint
B & B SNC: British and Burmese Steam Navigation Company
BBSR: Bermuda Biological Station for Research
bbs & w: barrels of basic sediment and water
bbt: basal body temperature; bombardment
BBT: Basal Body Temperature
BBTA: British Bureau of Televi-

sion Advertising
BB & TC: Bahamas Broadcasting and Television Commission
bbw: bare brass wire
BBWAA: Baseball Writers' Association of America
bbz: bearing bronze
bc: bad check; base (shield) connection; between centers; binary code; binary counter; birth control; bogus check; bolt circle; bone connection; bottom (dead) center; broadcast control
b/c: bales of cotton; bills for collection; birth control
BC: Before Christ
BC: Bacone College; Baja California; Bakersfield College; Bard College; Barnard College; Barrington College; Barry College; Bates College; Beaver College; Beckley College; Belgian Congo; Belhaven College; Bellarmine College; Belmont College; Beloit College; Benedict College; Bennett College; Bennington College; Berea College; Berry College; Bethany College; Bethel College; Bishop College; Blackburn College; Blinn College; Bliss College; Bloomfield College; Bluefield College; Bluffton College; Bomber Command; Boston College; Bourget College; Bowdoin College; Brandon College; Brenau College; Brentwood College; Brescia College; Brevard College; Briarcliff College; Bridgewater College; British Columbia; Brooklyn College; Bruyere College; Bryant College; Burdett College; Butler College
B.C.: Bachelor of Chemistry; Bachelor of Commerce; Baja California; Before Christ; British Columbia
B-C: Barber-Colman
B & C: Banking and Currency (Senate Committee)
B of C: Bank of Canada; Bureau of the Census
B C: *basso continuo* (Italian—continuous bass background)
bca: best cruise altitude; blood color analyzer
bca: *barrica* (Spanish—cask; keg); *biblioteca* (Portuguese or Spanish—library)
BCA: Battery Control Area; Billiard Congress of America; Blue Cross Association; Boys' Clubs of America; British Caledonian Airways; British Colonial Airlines

B/C of A: British College of Aeronautics

BCAB: Birth Control Advisory Bureau

BCAir: British Commonwealth Air Force

BCAR: British Civil Airworthiness Requirements; British Council for Aid to Refugees

BCAS: British Compressed Air Society

BCAT: Birmingham College of Advanced Technology

bcb: binary code box; broadcast band; button-cell battery

bcbh: boiler casing bulkhead

bcc: beam-coupling coefficient; body-centered cubic

BCC: Battery Control Central; Berkshire Community College; British Communications Corporation; British Crown Colony; Bronx Community College; Bureau Central de Compensation; Burlington Community College

BCCF: British Cast Concrete Federation

BCCG: British Cooperative Clinical Group

BCCO: Base Consolidation Control Office(r)

BCCR: Banco Central de Costa Rica

bccw: bare copper-clad wire

bcd: bad conduct discharge; binary-coded decimal

BCD: Bad Conduct Discharge

BCD: *Business Cycle Developments*

bcdc: binary-coded decimal cunter

BCDC: Bay Conservation and Development Commission (San Francisco)

bcdp: battery control data processor

BCDTA: British Chemical and Dyestuffs Traders' Association

bce: base checkout equipment; bubble chamber experiment; bundle-controlled expansion

BCE: Base Civil Engineer; Before the Christian Era; British Columbia Electric (railroad)

B.C.E.: Bachelor of Civil Engineering; Before the Christian Era

BCEM: Bureau of Community Environmental Management (HEW)

BCER: British Columbia Electric Railway

bcf: bandpass crystal filter; basic control frequency; bulked continuous fiber

BCF: British Columbia Ferries; British Cycling Federation; Bureau of Commercial Fisheries

B Cfa: Baja California

bcg: ballistocardiogram; bidirectional categorical grammar; bucking current generator

BCG: Bacillus Calmette-Guerin (anti-tubercular vaccine)

BCGNM: Black Canyon of the Gunnison National Monument (Colorado)

bch: bunch

B. Ch.: *Baccalaureus Chirurgiae* (Latin—Bachelor of Surgery)

B.Ch.D.: *Baccalaureus Chirurgiae Dentium* (Latin—Bachelor of Dental Surgery)

B. Ch. E.: Bachelor of Chemical Engineering

B.Chem.: Bachelor of Chemistry

Bches-du-R: Bouches-du-Rhône

B. Chir.: Bachelor of Surgery

bci: battery-condition indicator; binary-coded information; broadcast interference

BCIE: Banco Centroamericano de Integración Económica (Central American Bank of Economic Integration)

BCII: Bureau of Criminal Identification and Investigation

BCIRA: British Cotton Industry Research Association

BCIS: Binary Constitution Information Service

BCISC: British Chemical Industrial Safety Council

BCJC: Bay City Junior College

Bck: Buckie

b-c kit: battle-casualty kit; bouillon-cigarette kit (containing bouillon cubes, cigarettes, matches)

bcl: broadcast listener; broom closet

Bcl: Barcelona

BCL: Belfast City Libraries; British Council Library

BCL: *Books for College Libraries*

B.C.L.: Bachelor of Civil Law

BCLA: British Columbia Library Association

BCLS: Bristol City Line of Steamships

bcm: beyond capability of maintenance; binary choice model; business center map

BCM: Boston Conservatory of Music

BCMA: Biscuit and Cracker Manufacturers' Association

BCMD: Boston Contract Management Division

BCMFA: Bowdoin College Museum of Fine Arts

BCMR: Board for Correction of Military Records

bcn: beacon

BCN: Banque Canadienne Nationale (Canadian National Bank); Barcelona, Spain (airport); British Commonwealth of Nations

BCNP: Bryce Canyon National Park (Utah)

BCNRA: Bighorn Canyon National Recreation Area (Montana and Wyoming)

BCO: Baltimore Civic Opera

bcoe: bench checkout equipment

b coef: block coefficient

B. Comm.: Bachelor of Commerce

B.Com.Sc.: Bachelor of Commercial Science

BCP: Bootstrap Commissioning Program (USAF); Budget Change Proposal; Bulgarian Communist Party

B.C.P.: Bachelor of City Planning

BCPIT: British Council for Promotion of International Trade

BCPMA: British Chemical Plant Manufacturers Association

bcps: beam candlepower seconds

bcr: battery control radar

BCR: Bituminous Coal Research

BCRA: British Ceramic Research Institution; British Coke Research Association

BCRC: British Columbia Research Council

BCRUM: British Committee on Radiation Units and Measurements

BCS: British Cardiac Society; British Computer Society; Bureau of Criminal Statistics

B.C.S.: Bachelor of Chemical Science

B & CS: British and Commonwealth Shipping

BCSA: British Constructional Steelwork Association

BCSC: Blue Cross of Southern California

BCSO: British Commonwealth Scientific Office

BCSO (NA): British Commonwealth Scientific Office (North America)

bess: back spotfacer

bcst: broadcast

BCT: Battersea College of Technology; Bristol College of Technology; Brunel College of Technology

BCTC: Buffalo County Teachers College

BCTN: Baja California—Territorio Norte (Northern Territory)

BCTS: Baja California—Territorio Sur (Southern Territory)

BCURA: British Coal Utilization Research Association

bcu's: big closeups

bcw: bare copper wire; buffer control word

BCW: Bakery and Confectionery Workers (union); Bureau of Child Welfare

BCWMA: British Clock and Watch Manufacturers Association

bd: band; bomb disposal; brought down; bundle

b/d: bank draft; barrels per day; bills discounted; brought down

bd: band (Swedish—volume); *bind* (Dano-Norwegian—volume)

Bd: Board

Bd: Band (German—volume)

BD: Birlesik Devletler (Turkish—United States); Bomb Disposal; Bundesrepublik Deutschland (German—Republic of Germany)

B-D: Becton-Dickenson

B.D.: Bachelor of Divinity

B & D: Black & Decker

bda: bomb damage assessment; breakdown acid

Bda: Baroda

BDA: British Dental Association; British Dermatological Association; Hamilton, Bermuda (airport and tracking station—3-letter code symbol)

B.D.A.: Bachelor of Domestic Arts; Bachelor of Dramatic Art

BDAC: Bureau of Drug Abuse Control (Food and Drug Administration)

b & daf: bounded and described as follows

BDART: Battle Damage Assessment and Reporting Team

b'day: (American commercial—bidet)

B-day: Barbarossa Day (German attack on Russia—June 22, 1941)—Barbarossa was code word for this offensive

bdc: bonded double center; bottom dead center

BDC: Boeing Development Center; Bomb Data Center; Book Development Council; Bureau of Domestic Commerce

BD & C: British Dominions and Colonies

bdd: binary-to-decimal decoder

BDDA: British Deaf and Dumb Association

bddi: beading die

bde: brigade

Bde: Bände (German—volumes)

bded: bounded

Bd of Ed: Board of Education

B.Des.: Bachelor of Design

bdf: base detonating fuse

bd ft: board feet

bdg: binding

Bdg: Bridgewater

B de G: Bahía de Guantánamo (Guantanamo Bay)

BDH: British Drug Houses

bdhi: bearing distance heading indicator

bdhsa: bomb director high-speed aircraft

bdi: bearing deviation indicator

BDI: Bureau of Dairy Industry

BDIAC: Batelle Defender Information Analysis Center

BDIC: Batelle Defense Information Center

BDJ: Bund Deutscher Jugend (League of German Youth)

b dk: bridge deck

bdl: bundle

BDL: beach landing lighter (Army); Hartford, Connecticut (Bradley Field)

bdl(s): bundle(s)

bd lt: bow designation light

bdm (BDM): bomber defense missile

BdM: Bund deutscher Mädchen (League of German Girls)

BDMAA: British Direct Mail Advertising Association

bdn: bend down

Bdo: Bodo

BDO: Boom Defense Officer

bdp: breakdown pressure

Bdp: Budapest

BDP: Botswana Democratic Party

BDPA: Bureau of Data Processing and Accounts (Social Security Administration)

BDPEC: Bureau of Disease Prevention and Environmental Control

B en Dr: Bachelier en Droit (French—Bachelor of Laws)

B.Dr.Art: Bachelor of Dramatic Art

bdrm(s): bedroom(s)

bd rts: bond rights

bdry: boundary

bds: boards; bonded double silk; bound in boards; brass divider strip

Bds: Barbados

BDS: Bomb Damage Survey

B.D.S.: Bachelor of Dental Surgery

BDSA: Business and Defense Services Administration

B.D.Sc.: Bachelor of Dental Science

BDSC: Black Diamond Steamship Corporation

bdsd: base detonating, self-destroying

BDST: British Double Summer Time

Bd of Sup: Board of Supervisors

bdt: bidet

bdu: basic display unit

BdU: Befehlshaber der Unterseeboote (German—U-boat Command)

BDU: Bomb Disposal Unit

bdw: buffered distilled water

Bdx: Bordeaux

bdy: boundary

Bdy Mon: boundary monument

BDZ: Borsen-Data Zentrale (German—Stock-exchange Data Center)—computerized stock exchange

bdzr: bulldozer

be.: below the elbow; beveled edge; booster engine

b/e: bill of entry; bill of exchange

b & e: beginning and ending; breaking and entering

Be: Baumé; Belgian; Belgium; beryllium

BE: Board of Education; Bucyrus-Erie

B.E.: Bachelor of Economics; Bachelor of Education; Bachelor of Elocution; Bachelor of Engineering

B-E: Bucyrus-Erie

B & E: Baltimore & Eastern (railroad)

B of E: Bank of England; Board of Education

BE: Berkshire Eagle; Brockhaus Enzyklopädie (German—Brockhaus' Encyclopedia)

Bea: Beatrice; Beatrix

BEA: British East Africa; British Electricity Authority; British European Airways

BEAB: British Electrical Approvals Board (for household appliances)

BEAC: Boeing Engineering Analog Computer; British Export Advisory Committee

BEACON: British European Airways Computer Network

BEAIRA: British Electrical and Allied Industries Research Association

BEAM: Building Equipment Accessories and Materials (Canadian program)

BEAMA: British Electrical and Allied Manufacturers Association

BEAPA: Bureau of East Asian and Pacific Affairs (Dept of State)

bear.: bearing

bearb: bearbeitet (German—revised)

BEAS: British Executive Air Services

Beatles: Beat + Beetles

beat(s): beatnik(s)

Beau & Fl: Francis Beaumont and John Fletcher

beaut: beautiful; beauty
beauts: beauties
Beaux-Arts: École de Beaux-Arts (fine arts academy established in Paris in 1648)
beb: best ever bottled
BEB: Beach Erosion Board
bec: because
BEC: Base Engineering Course; Base Extension Course; Brevard Engineering College; Bureau of Employee's Compensation
BECA: Bureau of Educational and Cultural Affairs (US Department of State)
Bech: Bechstein; Bechuanaland
Bechu: Bechuana (formerly Bechuanaland)
Becky: Rebecca
beco: booster engine cutoff
BECO: Boston Edison Company
BECTO: British Electric Cable Testing Organisation
bed.: bridge-element delay
B. Ed.: Bachelor of Education
BEDA: British Electrical Development Association
Bedaks: Bureau of Drug Abuse Control officers
bed(s): bedroom(s)
Beds: Bedfordshire
BEDT: Brooklyn Eastern District Terminal (railroad)
B.E.E.: Bachelor of Electrical Engineering
beec: binary error-erasure channel
beef.: business-and-engineering-enriched fortran
Bee Gee: British Guiana (now called Guyana)
beet sugar: sucrose
Bee Wee: British West Indian
bef: blunt end first; buffered emitter follower
Bef: *Befehl* (German—command; order)
BEF: Bonus Expeditionary Force; British Expeditionary Force
befm: bending form
beg.: begin; beginning
BEG: Belgrade, Yugoslavia (airport)
begr: *begründet* (German—established)
BEH: Bureau of Education for the Handicapped
behav: behavior; behavioral; behaviorist(ic)
BEHC: Bio-Environmental Health Center
bei: butanol-extractable iodine
BEI: Bridgeport Engineering Institute
BEIA: Board of Education Inspectors' Association
Beibl: *Beiblatt* (German—supple-

ment)
beif: *beifolgend* (German—sent herewith)
Beih: *beihft* (German—supplement)
beil: *beiliegend* (German—enclosed)
Beil: *Beilage* (German—appendix, supplement)
Beitr: *Beitrag* (German—contribution)
bel: below; 10 decibels
bel: (Turkish—pass)
Bel: Belém; Belfast; Belize; Belorussia
BEL: Belém do Pará, Brazil (airport)
belcrk: bellcrank
Bel & Dr: *Bel and the Dragon*
Belém: (Brazil) Amazon River port also known as Belém do Pará; (Portugal) Lisbon suburb
bel ex: *bel example* (French—fine example)—fine copy of a book, engraving, map, etc.
Belg: Belgian; Belgium
Belial: The Devil
Belize: Belize City—principal seaport and old capital of British Honduras; new name of British Honduras assumed upon external independence; *Belice*—Spanish name for Belize used by Central American neighbors
Bell: Bell System (American Telephone and Telegraph and associated companies)
bella: belladonna (drug stimulant whose overdose results in delirium and death)
Bella: Arabella; Isabella
Bellas Artes: *Instituto Nacional de Bellas Artes* (Spanish—National Institute of Fine Arts)—in Mexico City
Belle: Bella; Arabella; Isabella
Belmo: Belmopan
belt: (German—strait)
Belvac: *Societe Belge de Vacuologie et de Vacuotechnique* (Belgian Society for Vacuum Science and Technology)
Bem: *Bemerkung* (German—comment; note; observation)
BEM: British Empire Medal
B.E.M.: Bachelor of Engineering of Mines
BEMA: Business Equipment Manufacturers Association
BEMO: Base Equipment Management Office
bems: bug-eyed monsters (science-fiction jargon)
BEMS: Bakery Equipment Manufacturers Society
ben: (Gaelic—mountain; summit)
Ben: Benedict; Benjamin

BEN: *Bureau d'Etudes nucleaires* (Belgian Bureau of Nuclear Studies)
Ben Cur: Benguela Current
BENDEX: Beneficial Data Exchange (linking Social Security Administration with state welfare agencies)
bene: benzine
Bened: Benedict; Benedictine
benef: beneficiary
Ben Eil: Benedenwindse Eilanden (Dutch—Leeward Islands)
Benelux: economic union of Belgium, Netherlands, and Luxembourg
benev: benevolent
Beng: Bengal; Bengali
Ben-Gurion: (Hebrew—Son of a Lion)—name adopted by David Green
Benj: Benjamin
Benjn: Benjamin
Benjy: Benjamin
Bennie: Benjamin
benny: (underground slang—benzedrine)
Benny: Benjamin
b & ent & pl: breaking and entering and petty larceny
benz: benzedrine; benzine
BEO: Borough Education Office(r)
beoc: battery echelon operating control
B.E.P.: Bachelor of Engineering Physics
BE & P: Bureau of Engraving and Printing
BEPI: Budget Estimates Presentation Instructions
BEPO: British Experimental Pile Operation
bepoc: Burrough's electrographic printer-plotter for ordnance computing
BEPQ: Bureau of Entomology and Plant Quarantine
beqd: bequeathed
beqt: bequest
ber: *berechnet* (German—computed)
Ber: Berlin; Berwickshire
Ber: *Bericht* (German—report)
BER: Berlin, West Germany (Tempelhof airport); Bureau of Economic Regulation
bera: (Dutch—mountain)
Berb: Berber
BERC: Biomedical Engineering Research Corporation; Black Economic Research Center
Berdoo: San Bernardino, California
berg: (Dutch, German, Norwegian, Swedish—hill; mountain)
BERH: Board of Engineers for Rivers and Harbors

Berk: Berkeley
Berks: Berkshire
Berl: Berlin
Berm: Bermuda Islands
Bernie: Bernard
Bern⁰: Bernardo
Bert: Albert; Alberta; Albertina; Bertha; Bertillon (system); Bertram; Bertrand; Cuthbert; Delbert; Elbert; Elberta; Filbert; Gilbert; Herbert; Hilbert; Ibert; Lambert; Norbert; Philbert; Roberta; Wilbert; Zilbert
Bertie: (affectionate nickname—Bertrand Russel —colossus of twentieth-century philosophy)
Berts: Bertillon Measurements
Berw: Berwick
bes: balanced electrolyte solution
bes: besonders (German—especially)
Bes: Bessel's functions
BES: Biological Engineering Society; Bureau of Employment Security
B.E.S.: Bachelor of Engineering Science
BESA: British Engineering Standards Association
BESE: Bureau of Elementary and Secondary Education
BeShT: Baal Shem-Tov (Israel Ben Eliezer)
BESL: British Empire Service League
BESN: British Empire Steam Navigation (company)
BESRL: Behavioral Science Research Laboratory (USA)
Bess: Bessemer; Mrs. Harry S. Truman
BESS: Bank of England Statistical Summary
Bessie: Bethlehem Steel (Wall Street slang); Elizabeth
best: bestellung (German—order)
BEST: Basic Essential Skills Training; Black Efforts for Soul in Television
bet.: best estimate of trajectory; between
Bet: Betsy; Elizabeth
BET: British Electric Traction
BETA: Business Equipment Trade Association
Beth: Bethlehem; Elizabeth
BETHLEHEM: Bethlehem Steel Corporation
betr: betrefend (German—concerning)
Betsy: Elizabeth
Betty: Elizabeth
BEU: British Empire Union
BEUC: Bureau Européen des Unions Consommateurs (Bureau of

European Consumer Unions)
bev: bevel; beverage; billion electron volts
Bev: Beverly
BEW: Board of Economic Warfare
bexec: budget execution
BEY: Beirut, Lebanon (airport)
bez: bezahlt (German—paid); *bezüglich* (German—referring to)
Bez: Bezirk (German—district)
bezw: bezichungsweise beziehungsweise (German—respectively)
bf: back feed; beer firken; before; bold face; both faces; boy friend
b-f: beat-frequency
b/f: black female; brought forward; brown female
b & f: bell and flange
b4: before
BF: Banque de France (Bank of France); Battle Fleet; Battle Force
B.F.: Bachelor of Forestry
B de F: Banque de France (Bank of France); Banco de Fomento (Development Bank of Puerto Rico)
BF: Beogradska Filharmonica (Serbo-Croat—Belgrade Philharmonic)
BFA: Broadcasting Foundation of America
B.F.A.: Bachelor of Fine Arts
BFB: Bureau of Forensic Ballistics
BFBS: British and Foreign Bible Society
BFCF: Bremerton Freight Car Ferry
BFCSD: Brewery, Flour, Cereal, Soft Drink and Distillery (Workers of America)
bfct: boiler feed compound tank
bfcy: beneficiary
BFDC: Bureau of Foreign and Domestic Commerce
bfe: beam-forming electrode
BFEA: Bureau of Far Eastern Affairs (U.S. Department of State)
bfg: brute-force gyro
BFG: B.F. Goodrich
BFHS: Benjamin Franklin High School
BFI: British Film Institute; Business Forms Institute; Seattle, Washington (Boeing Field)
BFIA: British Flour Industry Association
bfl: back focal length
BFL: Barber Fern Line; Belgian Fruit Line; Blue Funnel Line (Holt's)
BFM: Ballet Folklorico de México (Spanish—Folklore Ballet of

Mexico)
BFMA: Business Forms Management Association
BFMIRA: British Food Manufacturing Industries Research Association
BFMP: British Federation of Master Printers
BFN: British Forces Network
bfo: beat-frequency oscillator; blood-forming organs
Bfo: Buffalo
bform: budget formulation
bfp: biological false-positive (reactions); boiler feedpump
BFPA: British Film Producers Association
BFPO: British Field Post Office
BFPPS: Bureau of Foods, Pesticides, and Product Safety (FDA)
bfpv: bona fide purchaser for value
Bfr: Belgische frank (Dutch—Belgian franc)
B Fr: Belgian franc
BFRS: Bio-Feedback Research Society
BFS: Belfast, Northern Ireland (airport); Board of Foreign Scholarships; Bureau of Family Services; Bureau of Federal Supply
B.F.S.: Bachelor of Foreign Service
BFS: Bundesastalt für Flugsicherung (German—Air-Traffic Control Authority)
BFSS: British and Foreign Sailors' Society
bft: bio-feedback training
B.F.T.: Bachelor of Foreign Trade
BFTC: Boeing Flight Test Center
BFUP: Board of Fire Underwriters of the Pacific
BFUSA: Basketball Federation of the United States of America
BFUW: British Federation of University Women
BfV: Bundesamt für verfassungsschutz (German—Federal Office for the Protection of the Constitution)—West German FBI roughly equivalent to Special Branch in Britain
bfw: boiler feedwater
bg: back gear; bluish-green; buccogingival; business girl
b/g: bonded goods
bG: bluish green
Bg: Bengal; Bengalese; Bengali
Bg: Berg (German—mountain)
BG: Benny Goodman; Birmingham Gage; British Guiana
B-G: Bach Gesellschaft; David Ben-Gurion
B & G: Barton and Guestier; buildings and grounds
bga: blue-green algae (virus)

BGA: Better Government Association; British Gliding Association
BGB: Booksellers of Great Britain
bgc: blood group class
BGCC: Bowling Green College of Commerce
B.G.E.: Bachelor of Geological Engineering
BG & E: Baltimore Gas and Electric
B.Gen.Ed.: Bachelor of General Education
BGFE: Boston Grain and Flour Exchange
bgg: booster gas generator
BGGRA: British Gelatine and Glue Research Association
bght: bought
BGI: Bridgetown, Barbados (airport)
BGIRA: British Glass Industry Research Association
B-girl: bar girl
Bgk: Bangkok
bgl: below ground level
BGLA: Business Group for Latin America
bglb: brilliant-green lactose broth
bgl(s): bagel(s); beagle(s); bugle(s)
BGM: Binghamton, New York (airport)
BGMA: British Gear Manufacturers' Association
bgmn: baggageman
Bgn: Bergen
BGN: Board on Geographic Names
BGNR: Barren Grounds Nature Reserve (New South Wales)
bgr: bombing and gunnery range
bgrv (BGRV): boost-glide re-entry veh icle
bgs: bags
bg(s): back gear(s); bag(s)
Bgs: Brightlingsea
BGS: British Geriatrics Society
BGSC: Belfer Graduate School of Science (Yeshiva University); Boise-Griffin Steamship Company
BGSM: Bowman Gray School of Medicine
BGSU: Bowling Green State University
bgt: bought
BGT: Bender Gestalt Test; British Guiana Time
B Gu: British Guiana
BGW: Baghdad, Iraq (airport)
bh: bloody hell (British expletive); boiler house; breast height (4½ feet in U.S.); brinell hardness
Bh: Brinell hardness
BH: Base Hospital; Bath and Hammondsport (railroad); Benjamin Harrison; Bill of Health; Brigade Headquarters; Brinell hard-

ness; British Honduras; magnetization curve (symbol)
B/H: Bill of Health; Bordeaux-Hamburg (range of ports)
B & H: Bell and Howell; Breitkopf and Härtel
B of H: Board of Health
BH: *Bonne Humeur* (French—Good Humor); *Boston Herald*; *Thai bhat(s)—monetary unit(s)*
bha: base helix angle
BHA: British Homeopathic Association; British Honduras Airways
bh ad: broach adapter
B.H.Adm.: Bachelor of Hospital Administration
B'ham: Birmingham
Bharat: Republic of India
BHBNM: Big Hole Battlefield National Monument
B Hbr: boat harbor
BHBS: British Honduras Broadcasting Service
bhc: beaching cradle; benzene hexachloride (BHC)
BHC: Barbers, Hairdressers, Cosmetologists (and Proprietors' Union); Black Hawk College; British High Commissioner
bhd: beachhead; bulkhead
BH$: British Honduras dollar
B of HE: Board of Higher Education
B'head: Birkenhead
B-head: Buddahead (underground slang—Oriental person)
BHEW: Benton Harbor Engineering Works
Bhf: *Bahnhof* (German—station)
bhfx: broach fixture
B H & G: *Better Homes and Gardens*
BHH: Birthplace of Herbert Hoover (West Branch, Iowa)
BHI: British Horological Institute; Bureau Hydrographique Internationale (International Hydrographic Bureau)
bhib: beef-heart infusion broth
BHISSA: Bureau of Health Insurance, Social Security Administration
bhl: biological half-life
Bhm: Birmingham, England
BHM: Birmingham, Alabama (airport)
BHMH: Benjamin Harrison Memorial Home (Indianapolis, Indiana)
Bhn: Bremerhaven; Brinell hardness number
BHNWR: Bombay Hook National Wildlife Refuge (Delaware)
B Hond: British Honduras
bhp: brake horsepower

BHP: Broken Hill Proprietary
bhp hr: brake horsepower hour
bhr: basal heart rate; biotechnology and human research
BHRA: British Hotels and Restaurants Association; British Hydromechanics Research Association
B & HRO: Biotechnology and Human Research Office (NASA)
Bhs: Bohus
BHS: Balboa High School; Boys High School; British Home Stores; British Horse Society; Bureau of Health Services; Burlesque Historical Society; Bushwick High School
B & HS: Bonhomie and Hattiesburg Southern (railroad)
BHSS: Bronx High School of Science
bht (BHT): butylated hydroxytoluene
Bhu: Bhutan
bhw: boiling heavy water
B. Hyg.: Bachelor of Hygiene
bi: background investigation; base ignition; bodily injury; buffer index
b/i: battery inverter
b & i: bankruptcy and insolvency; base and increment
b or i: brass or iron (cargo)
Bi: bismuth (symbol)
BI: Babson Institute; background investigation; Bahama Islands; Bermuda Islands; Braniff International; British India; Brookings Institution; Bureau of Investigation; National Biscuits (stock exchange symbol)
BIA: Bicycle Institute of America; Brazilian International Airlines; Bureau of Indian Affairs; Bureau of Insular Affairs
B I & A: Bureau of Intelligence and Research (US Department of State)
BIAA: Bureau of Inter-American Affairs (US Department of State)
bialy: bialystok (onion-flavored roll)
BIAS: Brooklyn Institute of Arts and Sciences
BIATA: British Independent Air Transport Association
bib.: bottled in bond
bib. (BIB) baby incendiary bomb
bib: *bibliothèque* (French—library)
bib.: *bibe* (Latin—drink)
Bib: Bible; Biblical
BIB: *Berliner Institut für Betriebsführung* (German—Berlin Business Management Institute)
BIBA: Babson Institute of Business

Administration

Bib Apo Vat: Biblioteca Apostolica Vaticana (Vatican Library)

bib b: biblioteksbind (Dano-Norwegian—library binding)

bibl: bibliotec-; bibliotek-; bibliothec-; bibliothek; bibliothèque

biblio: bibliographer; bibliography

bibl mun: bibliothèque municipale (French—city library; public library)

Bib Nac: Biblioteca Nacional (National Library, Madrid—or others so named)

Bib Nat: Bibliothèque Nationale (National Library—Paris)

Bib Naz Cen: Biblioteca Nazionale Centrale (Italian National Central Library—Florence, Naples, Rome, etc. International Business Operations

BIBRA: British Industrial Biological Research Association

Bib Soc Am: Bibliographical Society of America

Bic: Societe Bic (ballpoint pen factory founded by Baron Marcel Bich)

BIC: Barrier Industrial Council; Bureau of International Commerce; Bureau International des Containers (International Bureau of Containers)

bicarb: sodium bicarbonate

bicarbonate (of soda): baking soda; sodium bicarbonate

BICC: British Insulated Callenders Cables

BICEMA: British Internal Combustion Engine Manufacturers Association

BICERA: British Internal Combustion Engine Research Association

BICERI: British Internal Combustion Engine Research Institute

bichloride of mercury: mercuric chloride

BICTA: British Investment Casters' Technical Association

bicv: biconcave

bicx: biconvex

bid. (BID): brought in dead

b.i.d.: bis in die (Latin—twice daily)

Bid: Bideford

BID: Banco Interamericano de Desarrollo (Interamerican Development Bank)

B.I.D.: Bachelor of Industrial Design

B. of I.D.: Bachelor of Interior Design

bidap: bibliographic data processing program

Biddy: Bridget

bidec: binary-to-decimal converter

BIE: Bureau International d'Education (International Bureau of Education); Bureau International des Expositions (International Bureau of Expositions)

B.I.E.: Bachelor of Industrial Engineering

BIEE: British Institute of Electrical Engineers

bien: biennial

BIF: Bombardier's Information File; British Industries Federation

big.: best in group; biological isolation garment

BIG: Beneficial Insurance Group

Big Ben: battleship USS *Franklin*; huge bell attached to clock in Parliament tower, Westminster district of London, named after Sir Benjamin Hall, commissioner of works in 1859 when bell was hung

Big Board: New York City's Stock Exchange

big D: (underground slang—hallucinogen such as diethyltryptamine, dimethyltryptamine, dipropylphyptamine, etc.)

Big-D: Dallas, Texas

Big-E: aircraft carrier USS *Enterprise*

big H: big house (underground slang—penitentiary such as San Quentin or Sing Sing); heroin

big J: big John (underground slang—policeman or other law-enforcement officer)

Big-J: battleship USS *New Jersey*

Big-M: battleship USS *Missouri*

Big Mamie: battleship USS *Massachusetts*

Big N: Vladimir Nabokov

Big-O: attack aircraft carrier USS *Oriskany*

bigs: biological isolation garments

Big Three: Asahi, Mainichi, Yomiuri (Japan's three biggest newspapers)

BII: Biosophical Institute Incorporated

BIIA: British Institute of Industrial Art

Bij: Benjamin

bijv: bijvoorbeeld (Dutch—for example)

bike: bicycle

biki: bikini

bil: billet

b-i-l: brother-in-law

BIL: Billings, Montana (airport); British India Line

bilat: bilateral

bildl: bildeich (German—figuratively)

BILG: Building Industry Libraries Group

bil k: bilge keel

bill: billede (Dano-Norwegian—illustrations)

Bill: William

Billie: William

billion: (American—a thousand million; 10^9); (British—a million million; 10^{12})

Billy: William

Billy Sanders: (pseudonym—Joel Chandler Harris)

Billy the Kid: William Bonney alias William Wright

BILS: British International Law Society

Bim: Barbadan

BIM: British Institute of Management

bimac: bi-stable magnetic core

BIMCAN: British Industrial Measuring and Control Apparatus Manuacturers Association

Bimshire: Barbados

BIMT: Bahama Islands Ministry of Tourism

bin.: binary

BINA: Bureau International des Normes de l'Automobile (International Bureau of Automobile Standards)

binac: high-speed electronic digital computer

bind .: binding

B.Ind.: Bachelor of Industry

B.Ind.Ed.: Bachelor of Industrial Education

Binj: Benjamin

BINM: Buck Island National Monument, St. Croix, Virgin Islands

binocs: binoculars

bins: (Cockney contraction— binoculars)

BINWR: Blackbeard Island National Wildlife Refuge (Georgia)

bio: biographical; biography; biological; biology

BIO: Bedford Institute of Oceanography

BIOA: Bureau of International Organization Affairs (US Department of State)

biochem: biochemistry

biochron: biochronometry

bioclean: biologically clean

biodef: biological defense

biog: biographer; biographical; biography

biol: biological; biologist; biology

Biol Abstr: Biological Abstracts

BIOLWPNSYS: Biological Weapon System (USA)

biomed: biomedical

bionics: biology + electronics

biophys: biophysical; biophysicist; biophysics

bior: business input-output rerun

BIOREP: Biological Attack Report

bios (BIOS): biological satellite

BIOS: Biological Investigations of Space

BIOSIS: Biosciences Information Service of *Biological Abstracts*

biowar: biological warfare

bip: balanced in plane; books in print

Bip: Marcel Marceau

BiP: Books in Print

BIP: British Institute of Physics

BIPAD: Bureau of Independent Publishers and Distributors

bipd: biparting doors

biphet: biphetamine (drug stimulant)

BIPM: Bureau International des Poids et Mesures (International Bureau of Weights and Measures)

BIPO: British Institute of Public Opinion

bipyr: bipyramidal

bir: basic incidence rate

bir: (Arabic—well)

BIR: British Institute of Radiology

BIRD: Banque Internationale pour la Reconstruction et le Développement (International Bank for Reconstruction and Development)

birdie: battery integration and radar display equipment

Birdofredum Sawin: (pseudonym —James Russell Lowell)

BIRE: British Institution of Radio Engineers

B.Ir.Eng.: Bachelor of Irrigation Engineering

birket: (Arabic—pond)

birl: girlish boy (transvestite type of male homosexual)

Birm: Birmingham

BIRMPDis: Birmingham Procurement District (U.S. Army)

BIRS: British Institute of Recorded Sound

birt: bolt installation and removal tool

birthquake: population explosion

bis.: bissextile

Bis: Bismarck

BIS: Bank for International Settlements; Bismarck, North Dakota (airport); Board of Inspection Survey (USN); British Information Service; British Interplanetary Society

BisArch: Bismarck Archipelago

Bisc: Biscayan

BISCO: British Iron and Steel Corporation

bisex: bisexual

BISF: British Iron and Steel Federation

BISFA: British Industrial and Scientific Film Association

Bish: Bishop

bishaw: bicycle rickshaw

Bish Mus: Bishop Museum

BISITS: British Iron and Steel Industry Translation Service (BISRA)

BISL: British Information Service Library

BISN: British India Steam Navigation (company)

BISRA: British Iron and Steel Research Associates

Bister: Bicester

bisw: bisweilen (German —sometimes)

bit.: binary digit

BIT: Bradford Institute of Technology; Bureau International du Travail (International Labor Organization)

BITA: British Industrial Truck Association

BITC: Bahamas International Trust Company

bite.: built-in test equipment

BITE: Base Installation Test Equipment

bitm: bituminous

BITM: Birla Industrial and Technological Museum

bito: burnishing tool

BITO: British Institution of Training Officers

bit(s).: binary digit(s)

Bitter Bierce: Ambrose Bierce

bitum: bituminous

biv: bivouac

BIW: Bath Iron Works; Boston Insulated Wire (and Cable Company)

BIWF: British Israel World Federation

biz: business

BIZ: Bank für Internationalen Zahlungsausgleich (Bank for International Settlements)

bizad: business administration

bizmac: business machine computer

bj: back judge (football); biceps jerk; blow job (fellatio)

b & j: bone and joint

BJ: Benito Juárez; Byron Jackson (Borg-Warner)

B.J.: Bachelor of Journalism

B & J: Burke & James

B of J: Bank of Japan

BJA: Burlap and Jute Association

b/Jan: binding expected in January (for example)

BJC: Baltimore Junior College;

Bismarck Junior College; Boise Junior College; Brevard Junior College

BJCEB: British Joint Communications-Electronics Board

B Jon: Ben Jonson

Bjørn Bjørn: Bjørnstjerne Bjørnson

BJU: Bob Jones University

bk: bank; below the knee; black; book; brake

Bk: berkelium; Brook

B-K: Blaw-Knox

bkbndg: bookbinding

bkbndr: bookbinder

bkcy: bankruptcy

bkd: blackboard

bk di: brake die

bkg: banking; bookkeeping

bkgd: background

bkhs: blockhouse

BKII: Vsesoyuenaya Kommunisticheskaya Partiya (Russian—All-Union Communist Party)

BKK: Bangkok, Thailand (airport)

bklr: black letter

Bklyn: Brooklyn

Bklyn Brdg: Brooklyn Bridge

BKM: Moscow, USSR (Bykovo Airport)

bkn: broken

Bkn: Birkenhead

bkpg: bookkeeping

bkpr: bookkeeper

bkpt: bankrupt

bkr: baker; beaker; breaker

bks: bunks; barracks; books; brakes

BKS: British Kinematograph Society

bk sh: bookshelves

bkt: basket; bracket

bkt(s): basket(s)

bkw: breakwater

bl: bank larceny; billet; blood; blue; bomb line; buccolingual; butt line; buttock line

b/l: basic letter; bill of lading (B/L); blueline blueprint

b & l: ball and lever; business and loan

bl: blad; blank (Dano-Norwegian —leaf, sheet; blank)

Bl: Blatt(er) [German—leaf; leaves; page(s)] *Böluk* (Turkish—company)

BL: Bonanza Airlines

B.L.: Bachelor of Letters

B & L: Bausch & Lomb; Building and Loan (association or bank)

B es L: Bachelier es Lettres (French—Bachelor of Letters)

bl a: blandt andet; blandt andre (Danish—among other things)

Bla: Brasilia

BLA: Black Liberation Army

B.L.A.: Bachelor of Landscape

Architecture; Bachelor of Liberal Arts

BLAC: British Light Aviation Center

black.: blackmail

Black Saturday: Commander's Internal Management Review (held on Saturdays)

blad: blotting pad

B.Land.Arch.: Bachelor of Landscape Architecture

Blast: Blastoidea

BLAST: Black Legal Action for Soul in Television

BLB: Boothby-Lovelace-Bulbulian (oxygen mask)

blc: balance; boundary-layer control

BLC: British Lighting Council

bl cult.: blood culture

bld: blood; blood and lymphatic system; bloody

BLEDCO: Brooklyn Local Economic Development Corporation

bldg: building

bldi: blank die

bldr: builder

BLE: Brotherhood of Locomotive Engineers

B & LE: Bessemer and Lake Erie (railroad)

bleaching powder: calcium hypochlorite

bleu: blind landing experimental unit

BLEU: Belgium-Luxembourg Economic Union

BLF & E: Brotherhood of Locomotive Firemen and Enginemen

BLH: Baldwin-Lima-Hamilton

BLI: Bliss & Laughlin Industries; Buyers Laboratory Incorporated

B.L.I.: Bachelor of Literary Interpretation

Blick: Blickensderfer (portable typewriter popular before World War I)

Blind Poet: John Milton

BLIP: Big Look Improvement Program

B.Litt.: *Baccalaureus Literarum* (Latin—Bachelor of Literature)

bliz: blizzard; blizzardly; blizzardous

blk: black; block; blocking

Blk: Block

blkd: bulkhead

blk lt: black light

blksh: blackish

blksmith: blacksmith

bll: below lower limit

BLM: British Leland Motor (corporation merging Austin, British Motor Holdings, Jaguar, Morris, Riley, Rover, Triumph, Wolseley); Bureau of Land Manage-

ment (General Land Office and Grazing Service)

B.L.M.: Bachelor of Land Management

BLM: *Bonniers Literara Magasin* (Bonnier's Literary Magazine)

BLMRA: British Leather Manufacturers' Research Association

BLMS: Book-Library-Management System

bln: balloon

Bln: Berlin

blnkt: blanket

BLNR: Benton Lake National Refuge (Montana)

BLNWR: Big Lake National Wildlife Refuge (Arkansas); Bitter Lake NWR (New Mexico); Buffalo Lake NWR (Texas)

BLNY: Booksellers League of New York

blo: blower

block.: blockade

Blondin: Charles Emile Gravele—the tightrope walker who crossed Niagara Falls in the mid-nineteenth century

Bloody Mary: Mary I of England (Mary Tudor)

blooper: blunder and error

blou: blouse

blr: boiler; breech-loading rifle

BLR: Ballistic Research Laboratories (USA)

blrmkr: boilermaker

BLROA: British Laryngological, Rhinological, and Otological Association

blrp: boilerplate

bls: bales; barrels; binary light switch; blood sugar

BLS: Brooklyn Law School; Bureau of Labor Statistics

B.L.S.: Bachelor of Library Science; Bachelor of Library Service

BL & SA: Bank of London and South America

blsh: bluish

blt: blood type; built

blstg pwd: blasting powder

blsw: barrels of load salt water

blswd: barrels of load salt water per day

b-l-t: bacon, lettuce, and tomato (sandwich)

BLT: Battalion Landing Team

Bltc: Baltic

bltn(s): built-in(s)

blu: blue

Blubo: *Blut und Boden* (German—blood and soil)

Bluebonnet Bowl: athletic stadium in Houston, Texas

Blue Steel: air-to-surface nuclear missile

bluestone: copper sulfate

blue vitriol: copper sulfate

Blvd: Boulevard

BLW: Baldwin-Lima-Hamilton

BLWA: British Laboratory Ware Association

Bly: Blyth

blz(n): *bladzijde(n)* [(Dutch —page(s)]

Blz: Belize; Belizian

bm: beam; board measure; bowel movement

b/m (B/M): black male; bill of material; brown male; bill of material

bm: *bez mista* (Czech—no place of publication)

b.m.: *balneum maris* (Latin—bath in sea water)

Bm: beam; birthmark; board measure; bowel movement; Burma; Burmese

BM: Banco de México (Bank of Mexico); bench mark; Boatswain's Mate; Boston & Maine (railroad); Brigade Major; British Museum; Brooklyn Museum; Bureau of Medicine; Bureau of Mines; Bureau of the Mint

B.M.: Bachelor of Medicine; Bachelor of Music

B-M: Bolinder-Munktell; Bristol-Myers

B & M: Beaufort & Morehead (railroad); Boston & Maine (railroad)

B de M: Banco de México (Bank of Mexico)

B of M: Bank of Montreal; Bureau of Mines

BM: *Beata Maria* (Latin—Blessed Mary)

BMA: Baltimore Museum of Art; Bible Memory Association; Bicycle Manufacturers' Association; British Medical Association; British Military Authority; Stockholm, Sweden, airport (3-letter code)

B.Mar.E.: Bachelor of Marine Engineering

B.Mar.Eng.: Bachelor of Marine Engineering

BMB: Ballistic Missile Branch (USA); British Metrication Board

BMBW: *Bundesministerium für Bildung und Wissenscaft)*—West German Ministry for Education and Science

bmc: blockhouse monitor console

BMC: Ballistic Missile(s) Center; Ballistic Missiles Committee; British Mountaineering Council; Bryn Mawr College

BMCC: Blue Mountain Community College

BMCS: Ballistic Missile Cost Study; Bureau of Motor Carrier Safety

BMD: Ballistic Missile Defense

BMDMB: Ballistic Missile Defense Missile Battalion (USA)

bmdns: basic mission, design number, and series (aircraft)

bmdr: bombardier

bme: biomedical engineering

BME: Brotherhood of Marine Engineers

B.M.E.: Bachelor of Mechanical Engineering; Bachelor of Mining Engineering; Bachelor of Music Education

BMEC: British Marine Equipment Council

B. Med.: Bachelor of Medicine

B.M.Ed.: Bachelor of Music Education

B.Med.Sc.: Bachelor of Medical Science

BMEL: Barber Middle East Line

bmep: brake mean effective pressure

B.Met.: Bachelor of Metallurgy

B.Met.E.: Bachelor of Metallurgical Engineering

BMEWS: Ballistic Missile Early Warning System

BMFA: Boston Museum of Fine Arts

B.Mgt.Eng.: Bachelor of Management Engineering

BMI: Barley and Malt Institute; Batelle Memorial Institute; Book Manufacturers Institute; Broadcast Music Incorporated; Broadway Memorial Institute

B.Mic.: Bachelor of Microbiology

BMIC: *Bureau of Mines Information Circular*

B.Min.E.: Bachelor of Mining Engineering

BMJ: *British Medical Journal*

BML: Belfast & Moosehead Lake (railroad); Bodega Marine Laboratory (University of California); British Museum Library (London)

B.M.L.: Bachelor of Modern Languages

B & M L : Belfast & Moosehead Lake (railroad)

BMM: Belfast, Mersey and Manchester Steamships

Bmn: Bremen

BMN: British Merchant Navy

BMNH: British Museum (Natural History)

BMNP: Bale Mountains National Park (Ethiopia); Blue Mountains National Park (New South Wales)

BMNT: beginning morning nautical twilight

bmo: business machine operator

BMO: Ballistic Missile Office

bmoc: big man on campus

BMP: Bricklayers, Masons and Plasterers' (Union)

BMPS: British Medical Protection Society; British Musicians Pension Society

bmr: basal metabolic rate; bomber

BMR: Basal Metabolism Rate

BMRB: British Market Research Bureau

BMRR: British Museum Reading Room

BMRS: Ballistic Missile Recovery System

BMs: Black Muslims; Boatswain's Mates

BMS: Boston Museum of Science; British Ministry of Supply; Buffalo Museum of Science; Bureau of Medical Services; Bureau of Medicine and Surgery

B.M.S.: Bachelor of Marine Science; Bachelor of Medical Science

BMSA: British Medical Students' Association

BMSE: Baltic Mercantile and Shipping Exchange

BMSS: British and Midlands Scientific Society

BMT: Basic Military Training; Boston & Maine Transportation (railroad); Brooklyn-Manhattan Transit (subway system)

B.M.T.: Bachelor of Medical Technology

BMTA: Boston Metropolitan Transit Authority

BMTFA: British Malleable Tube Fittings Association

BMTP: *Bureau of Mines Technical Paper*

BMTS: Ballistic Missile Target System

B.Mus.: Bachelor of Music

bmv: bromegrass-mosaic virus

BMW: Bayerische Motoren Werke (Bavarian Motor Works)

BMWE: Brotherhood of Maintenance of Way Employees

bn: battalion

Bn: beacon (daybeacon); bearing (as distinguished from bearing angle)

Bn: *Bayan* (Turkish—Miss; Mrs.)

BN: Braniff; Bureau of Narcotics; Burlington Northern (merger of Chicago, Burlington, and Quincy; Great Northern; Northern Pacific; Spokane, Portland, and Seattle railways)

B.N.: Bachelor of Nursing

B & N: Barnes & Noble; Bauxite & Northern

B of N: Bureau of Narcotics

BNA: Brazil Nut Association; British North America; Bureau of National Affairs; Nashville, Tennessee (airport)

BNA: *Basle Nomina Anatomica* (Basel Anatomical Nomenclature)

B'nai B'rith: *Benai Berith* (Hebrew-Sons of the Covenant)

BNAU: Bulgarian National Agrarian Union

B.Nav.: Bachelor of Navigation

BNB: British North Borneo

BNB: *British National Bibliography*

BNBC: British National Book Centre

BNC: Biblioteca Nacional de Chile; Biblioteca Nacional de Colombia

BNCC: Bay de Noc Community College

BNCF: *Biblioteca Nazionale Centrale Firenzi* (Italian—National Central Library—Florence)

bnchbd: benchboard

BNCM: Bibliothèque Nationale du Consérvatorie de Musique (National Library of the Conservatory of Music—Paris)

BNCOR: British National Committee for Oceanographic Research

BNCS: British Numerical Control Society

BNCSR: British National Committee for Space Research (Royal Society)

b/nd: binding—no date available

BND: *Bundesnachrichtendienst* (German—Federal Intelligence Service)

BNDD: Bureau of Narcotics and Dangerous Drugs

bndy: bindery; boundary

bne: but not exceeding

BNE: Board of National Estimates (CIA); Brisbane, Australia (airport); Buffalo Niagara Electric Corporation

BNEC: British National Export Council; British Nuclear Energy Conference

BNES: British Nuclear Energy Society

BNE & SAA: Bureau of Near Eastern and South Asian Affair (US Department of State)

bnf: bomb nose fuse

Bnf: Banff

BNF: Braniff International Airways

BNF: *British National Formulary*

BNFMRA: British Non-ferrous

Metals Research Association
Bng: Bangor
BNGS: Bomb Navigation Guidance System
bnh: burnish
BNHS: British National Health Service
BNI: Black Nation of Islam
BNIB: British National Insurance Board
BNJ: Bonn, Germany (Cologne-Bonn airport)
BNL: Brookhaven National Laboratory
BNM: Badlands National Monument (South Dakota); Biblioteca Nacional de México (National Library of Mexico—Mexico City)
bno: barrels of new oil; but not over
BNP: Bako National Park (Sarawak); Bahamas NP (West Indies); Banff NP (Alberta); Belair NP (South Australia); Bontebok NP (South Africa)
bnr: burner
BNS: Bathymetric Navigation System; British Nylon Spinners
B.N.S.: Bachelor of Natural Science; Bachelor of Naval Science
B of NS: Bank of Nova Scotia
B.N.Sc.: Bachelor of Nursing Science
BNSM: British National Socialist Movement
Bnt: Burntisland
BNW: Bureau of Naval Weapons
BNWR: Blackwater National Wildlife Refuge (Maryland); Bowdoin National Wildlife Refuge (Montana); Brigantine National Wildlife Refuge (New Jersey)
BNX: British Nuclear Export Executive
BNZ: Bank of New Zealand
bnzn: benzoin
bo: blackout; bowels open
b/o: back order; boiloff; brought over
b & o: belladonna and opium
Bo: Bolivia; Bolivian
BO: Baltimore & Ohio (stock exchange symbol); Base Order; black oil (bunker oil fuel); Board of Ordnance; body odor; box office; branch office; broker's order; Bureau of Ordnance
B & O: Baltimore & Ohio Railroad; Bang & Olufsen
boa.: born on arrival; breakoff altitude
Boa: Balboa, CZ
BOA: Basic Ordering Agreement; British Optical Association; British Orthopedic Association;

British Osteopathic Association; British Overseas Airways (BOAC)
BOAC: British Overseas Airways Corporation
BOAdicea: British Overseas Airways digital information computer for electronic automation
BOADS: Boston Air Defense Sector
BOAT/US: Boat Owners Association of the United States
Bob: Robert
BOB: Bureau of the Budget
Bobby: Robert(a); nickname for a London policeman and so named after Sir Robert Peel who organized the London police force
b-o-b cult: ban-on-bathing cult (hippie subculture)
Bob Dylan: Robert Zimmermann
BOBMA: British Oil Burner Manufacturers Association
bobr: boring bar
boc: back outlet central; blowout coil; body on chassis
Boc: Boccaccio
BOC: Brooklyn Opera Company; Burmah Oil Company
BOCA: Building Officials Conference of America
boca(s): [Spanish—gulf(s); inlet(s); mouth(s)]
bocd: barrels of oil per calendar day
BOCE: Board of Customs and Excise
B & O—C & O: Baltimore and Ohio—Chesapeake and Ohio (merged railroad)
bod: beneficial occupancy date; biochemical oxygen demand; biological oxygen demand; black-out door
bod: *bodega* (Spanish—wineshop); *bodoniana* (Italian—Bodoni-style type)
Bodleian: Oxford University's superb library established in 1445
Bodl Lib: Bodleian Library, Oxford
boe: back outlet eccentric
bof: basic oxygen furnace; binary oxide film
Bog: Bogotá
BOG: Bogotá, Colombia (airport); Boston Opera Group
boggan: toboggan
bogh: *boghandel* (Dano-Norwegian—bookstore; booktrade)
boghaz: (Turkish—strait)
bogie: unidentified aircraft
Bogie: Maxwell Bodenheim; Humphrey Bogart
boh: breakoff height
B O'H: Bernardo O'Higgins
boi: basis of issue; break of inspection

Boi: Boise
BOI: Boise, Idaho (airport)
BOIC: Boarding Officer in Charge
boil.: boiling
bois: (French—woods)—short form for the Bois de Boulogne park, racetrack, and recreation area of Paris
boj: booster jettison
BOK: Book-of-the-Month Club (stock exchange symbol)
Boko: Bohner & Kohle
bol: bollard(s)
bol.: *bolus* (Latin—large pill)
Bol: Bolivia; Bolivian; boliviano
BOLD: Bibliographic On-Line Display (document retrieval system)
bolo(s): bolshevik(s)
bolovac: bolometric voltage and current (voltage measurement)
bols: bolster
BOLSA: Bank of London and South America
bolshie(s): bolshevik(s)
bolsón: (Spanish—depression)
Bolv: Bolivia; Bolivian
bom: business office must
Bom: Bombay
BoM: Bureau of Mines
BOM: Bombay, India (airport)
BOMAP: Barbados Oceanographic and Meteorological Analysis Project
Bomarc: interceptor missile produced by Boeing
BOMARC: Boeing-Michigan Research Center
bomb.: bombardment
Bom Com: Bomber Command
bomst: bombsight
Bon: Bonin Islands
BON: Bonaire, Netherlands West Indies (airport)
bond.: bonding
bone(s): trombone(s)
Bo'ness: Borrowstounness
Boney: Napoleon Bonaparte
bong: (Korean—mountain)
Bon Homme Richard: (French—Good Man Richard)—Benjamin Franklin
Boni: Boniface
BONUS: Benevolent Order of Nurses Under Sedation (an organization existing in the minds of some hospitalized patients)
Boolist: *Booklist and Subscription Books Bulletin*
bop: basic oxygen process(ing); bebop (loud jazz accompanied by nonsensical lyrics); best operating procedure; buy our product (s)
BoPa: *Borgelige Partisaner* (Danish—Middleclass Partisans)—underground resistance against

occupying German forces during World War II

BoPat: Border Patrol

bopd: barrels of oil per day

bops: blowout preventer stack(s)

B. Opt.: Bachelor of Optometry

BOQ: Bachelor Officers' Quarters; Base Officers' Quarters

bor: boring; bowels open regularly

Bor: Borough

BOR: Board of Review; Borg-Warner (stock exchange symbol); Bureau of Outdoor Recreation

boracic acid: boric acid

boram: block-oriented random-access memories

borax: sodium tetraborate

borazon: boron nitrogen compound harder than diamond; boron nitride heated and pressed with a catalyst

boreal: (Spanish—northern)

borg: (Dano-Norwegian or Swedish—castle)

borgo: (Italian—town)

boric acid: H_3BO_3

Boris Pilnyak: (pseudonym—Boris Andreyevich Vogau)

Boris Savinkov: (pseudonym—Vladimir Ropshin)

boro: borough

bos: basic oxygen steel

Bos: Bosphorus; Boston

BoS: Bureau of Ships

BOS: Boston, Massachusetts (airport); British Oil Shipping

bosch: (Dutch—forest; woods)

Boschaps: Boston Symphony Chamber Players

bo'sun: boatswain (pronounced as contracted)

Bosna: (Yugoslav—Bosnia-Herzegovina)

Bos Pops: Boston Pops Orchestra

BOSS: Bioastronautic Orbital Space System

Bost: Boston

BOSTPDis: Boston Procurement District (U.S. Army)

bo's'n: boatswain

Boswash: Boston-to-Washington (city complex)

bot: balance of time (to be served by a convict); botanic; botanical; botanist; botany; bottle; bottled; bottom; bottomed; bottoming

BOT: Board of Trade; Board of Trade unit

bot & can: bottle and can

botel: boat hotel

both.: bombing over the horizon

botmg: bottoming

BOT-ohm: Board of trade ohm

bot(s): bottle(s)

Botswana: Bechuanaland Protectorate

Botticelli: Alessandro dei Filipepi

Bou: Boulogne-sur-Mer

BOU: Boat Operating Unit; British Ornithologists' Union

boul: boulevard

Boul' Mich': (contraction—Boulevard St Michel)—in the student quarter of Paris

bound.: boundaries; boundary

bourg: (French—borough; town)

Bov Eil: *Bovenwindse Eilanden* (Dutch—Windward Islands; Aruba, Bonaire, Curaçao)

bow.: bag of water (amniotic sac); blackout window; born out of wedlock

bo & w: barrels of oil and water

Boy Orator of the Platte: William Jennings Bryan

Boz: Charles Dickens

Bozzy: James Boswell—biographer and friend of Dr Samuel Johnson

bp: bandpass; baptized; beautiful people; before present; below proof; between perpendiculars; bills payable; blood pressure; boiling point

b/p: baking powder; bills payable; blueprint

b & p: bare and painted

bp: Bergstrom Paper Company; *buono per* (Italian—good for)

Bp: Bishop

Bp: *Boerenpartij* (Dutch—Farmers' Party)

BP: Beach Party (amphibious military operation); Beschleunigter Personenzug (German—express train); Board of Parole; British Petroleum; British Pharmacopoeia; British Public; Bureau of Power; Bureau of Prisons; Burns Philp Lines

B.P.: Bachelor of Pharmacy; Bachelor of Philosophy

B-P: Basses-Pyrénées; Bermuda Plan (breakfast only)

B of P: Bureau of Prisons

bpa: broadband power amplifier

BPA: Biological Photographers Association; Bonneville Power Administration; British Pediatric Association; Broadcasters Promotion Association; Brunswick Port Authority; Bureau of Public Assistance; Business Publications Audit (of circulation)

B.P.A.: Bachelor of Professional Arts

BPAA: Bowling Proprietors' Association of America

BPAC: Budget Program Activity Code

BPAO: Branch Public Affairs Office(r)

BPASC: Book Publishers Association of Southern California

bpay: bill(s) payable

BPBD: Bill Posters, Billers and Distributors (Union)

bpc: back-pressure control

BPC: British Pharmaceutical Codex; British Printing Corporation; British Purchasing Commission; Business and Professional Code

BPCF: British Precast Concrete Federation

BPCI: Bulk Packaging and Containerization Institute

bpd: barrels per day; boxes per day

BPD: Bureau of the Public Debt

bpd & a: basic planning data and assumption

BPDC: Berkeley Particle Data Center

BPDP: Brotherhood of Painters, Decorators, and Paperhangers

bpe: bit-plane encoding

B.P.E.: Bachelor of Physical Education

BPE-LCA: Board of Parish Education—Lutheran Church in America

B.Pet.E.: Bachelor of Petroleum Engineering

bpf: bottom pressure fluctuation

bpf: *bon pour francs* (French—good for francs)

BPF: British Polio Fellowship

B$_{pge}$: bearing per gyro compass

bph: barrels per hour; benign prostatic hypertrophy

B. Ph.: Bachelor of Philosophy

B.P.H.: Bachelor of Public Health

B.Pharm.: Bachelor of Pharmacy

B.Phil.: Bachelor of Philosophy

B.Phys.: Bachelor of Physics

BP & HL: Brown Picton and Hornby Libraries (Liverpool)

bpi: bytes per inch

BPI: British Pacific Islands; Brooklyn Polytechnic Institute; Bureau of Public Information

BPICA: Bureau Permanent Internationale des Constructeurs d'Automobiles (Permanent International Bureau of Automobile Manufacturers)

b-pid: book-physical inventory difference

BPISAE: Bureau of Plant Industry, Soils, and Agricultural Engineering

BP & JC FL: Birmingham Public and Jefferson County Free Library

BPKT: Basic Programming Knowledge Test

bpl: birthplace

Bpl: Barnstaple
BPL: Belfast Public Library; Binghamton Public Library; Birmingham Public Library; Boston Public Library; Brass Pounders League; Bridgeport Public Library; Brooklyn Public Library; Buffalo Public Library
bpm: barrels per minute; beats per minute
BPMA: British Photographic Manufacturers Association; British Printing Machinery Association; British Pump Manufacturers Association
BPMF: British Postgraduate Medical Federation
BPMS: Blood Pressure Measuring System
BPO: Base Post Office; Base Procurement Office; Berlin Philharmonic Orchestra; Boston Pops Orchestra; British Post Office; Brooklyn Philharmonia Orchestra; Brooklyn Post Office
BPO: *Berliner Philharmonisches Orchester* (German—Berlin Philharmonic Orchestra)
BPOE: Benevolent and Protective Order of Elks
BPP: Black Panther Party (racists seeking power for black people); Botswana People's Party
BPPMA: British Power Press Manufacturers Association
BPR: Bureau of Public Roads
bprf: bulletproof
bps: bytes per second
bp's: beautiful people
BPS: Border Patrol Sector; Border Patrol Station; Bureau of Product Safety
B$_{psc}$: bearing per standard compass
BPsS: British Psychological Society
B$_{p stg c}$: bearing per steering compass
BPT: British Petroleum Tanker
bptv: battleship propulsion test vehicle
bpu: base production unit
BPU: British Powerboating Union
bpwr: burnable poison water reactor
bq: beauty quotient
BQ: Bachelor's Quarters; Basic Qualification; Basically Qualified (member of USCG Aux)
BQLI: Brooklyn, Queens, Long Island
bque: barque
br: bank rate; bank robber(y); berth; bill of rights; branch; bread (underground slang —money); breath; breeder reactor; brown; builder's risk; butadiene rubber

b/r: bills receivable
b or r: bales or rolls (freight)
br: *bez roku* (Czech—no date; no year)
Br: bearing; branch; bridge; British; bromine; brown (buoy)
BR: Baton Rouge; Brazil (auto plaque); Breeder Reactor; British Railways; British Resident (commissioner); British United Airways; Bureau of Reclamation
B-R: Bas-Rhin; Business Route
B-du-R: Bouches-de-Rhone
B of R: Bureau of Reclamation
bra: brassiere
BRA: Bee Research Association; Boston Redevelopment Authority; Building Renovating Association
BRAC: Brotherhood of Railway and Airline Clerks
brachycephs: brachycephalics (short-skulled people)
Bra Cur: Brazil Current
Brad: Bradford; Bradley
Bradshaw's: *Bradshaw's Railway Guide*
brae: (Scottish—hillside)
Brains of the Confederacy: Judah P. Benjamin—successively attorney general, secretary of war, and secretary of state of the Confederate States of America
bramah: safety lock invented by Joseph Bramah
BRANCHHYDRO: Branch Hydrographic Office
brane: bombing radar navigation equipment
Brangus: 3/8ths Brahman + 5/8ths Angus cattle
bra(s): brassiere(s)
Bras: Brasil; Brasileiro
BRAs: Bosom-Rehabilitation Associates
b-r-a-s-s: breathe, relax, aim, squeeze, shoot (the marksman's acronym)
BRASS: Bottom Reflecting Active Sonar System
BRASTACS: Bradford Scientific, Technical, and Commercial Service
Bravo: code for letter B
braz: brazement; brazier; brazing
Braz: Brazil; Brazilian
Brazza: Brazzaville
Brb: *Borba* (Yugoslav—Struggle) —leading newspaper in Communist-controlled Yugoslavia
BRB: British Railways Board
BRBMA: Ball and Roller Bearing Manufacturers Association
brbzc: brass, bronze, or copper (cargo)
brc: business reply card

BRC: Balcones Research Center (University of Texas); Base Residence Course; Bolivia Railway Company; British Research Council; Brotherhood of Railway Car Men
BRCA: Brotherhood of Railway Carmen of America
Br Col: British Columbia
BRCS: British Red Cross Society
brd: basic retirement date; board; bomb-release distance; broad
BRD: Bundesrepublik Deutschland (Federal Republic of Germany)—West Germany
brdcst: broadcast
Brdw: Broadwood
Bre: Bremen; Bremerhaven
B.R.E.: Bachelor of Religious Education
brec: bills receivable
Breck: Brecknockshire
Brecon: Breconshire (Brecknockshire)
breen: (Norwegian—glacier)
brek: breakfast
BREL: British Rail Engineering Limited
'brella: umbrella
Brem: Bremen; Bremerhafen; Bremerhaven; Bremerton
BREMA: British Radio Equipment Manufacturers Association
Brennero: Brenner Pass
Br'er: Brother
Bres: Breslau
Bret: Brittany; Breton
brev: brevet; breviary; breviate; brevier
brev.: *breviarium* (Latin—abridgement or breviary)
brew.: brewer; brewery; brewing
brf: brief; briefing
BRF: British Road Federation
brg: bearing
BrG: British Guiana
brghd: bridgehead
brghm: brougham (pronounced *broom*)
Brgo Spgs: Borrego Springs
Br Gu: British Guiana
BrH: British Honduras
BRH: Brussels, Belgium (airport); Bureau of Radiological Health
BRHL: British Rail Hovercraft Limited
Br Hon: British Honduras
BRHS: Bay Ridge High School; Betsy Ross High School
Br I: British Isles
BRI: Babson's Reports Incorporated; Banque des Reglements Internationaux (Bank of International Settlements); Biological Research Institute; Brain Research Institute; Building Re-

search Institute; Burlington-Rock Island (railroad)

brig.: brigantine; slang for ship's prison

Brig Gen: Brigadier General

brill: brillante (Italian—brilliant)

Brist: Bristol

Brit: Britain; Britannia; British

Brit: Encyclopaedia Britannica

British Century: the 19th century belongs to the British whose Wellington defeated Napoleon at Waterloo, whose industrial revolution was a pattern for the rest of the world, whose vast colonial empire was the best governed of all known up to the time—the 1800s

brit met: britannia metal (tin, copper, antimony alloy—sometimes bismuth, lead, and zinc)

Brit Mus: British Museum

Brit Pat: British Patent

BritRail: British Railways

Brit—Rail Hover: British Railways Hovercraft

Brit Sam: British Samoa

brk: brick

brklyr: bricklayer

brkmn: brakeman

brkt: bracket

brkwtr: breakwater

brl: bomb-release line

br/l: brown line positive

BRL: Babe Ruth League; Ballistic Research Laboratories; Bible Research Library

brlg: bomb radio longitudinal generator-powered

brlp: burlap

brl sys: barrier ready light system

BRMBR: Bear River Migratory Bird Refuge (Utah)

brn: brown

brng: burning

BRNP: Blue Ridge National Parkway

brnsh: brownish; burnish

Brnx: Bronx

brnz: bronze; bronzing

bro: broach; bronchoscopy; brother

bro: (Dano-Norwegian or Swedish—bridge)

brO: brownish orange

Bro: Brother

broast(ed): broil(ed) + roast(ed)

brok: broker; brokerage

bromo: bromidrosis; bromoform; bromo-seltzer

bromo-seltzer: (bromide + seltzer)

bronc: bronco (Spanish—small half-wild horse)

Bronx Zoo: New York Zoological Gardens (Bronx Park)

bronze: 92% copper, 6% tin, 2% zinc

Bronzino: Agnolo di Cosimo

Bros: brothers

Brose: Ambrose

brotel: brothel + hotel (there are such places)

BROU: Banco de la República Oriental del Uruguay (Bank of the Oriental Republic of Uruguay)

brownulated: granulated brown sugar

brp: bathroom privileges

BRPF: Bertrand Russell Peace Foundation

brph: bronchophony

brPk: brownish pink

BRPL: Baton Rouge Public Library

brpp: basic radio propagation prediction(s)

Br Rys: British Railways

brs: brass

Brs: Bristol

BRS: British Road Services; British Roentgen Society; Brotherhood of Railway Signalmen; Bureau of Railroad Safety; Business Radio Service

BRSA: British Railway Staff Association

BR & SC: Brotherhood of Railway and Steamship Clerks

br sounds: breath sounds

brst: burst

Br std: British standard

brstr: burster

brt: bright

Brt: Brest

BRT: Brotherhood of Railroad Trainmen

BRT: Belgische Radio en Televisie (Belgian Radio and Television); *brutto-Register-Tonnen* (German—registered gross tons)

BR & TC: Bermuda Radio and Television Company

brt fwd: brought forward

Bru: Brunei; Bruno; Brutus

BRU: Brussels, Belgium (National Airport)

Brücke(n): [German—bridge(s)]

B. B.Ru.Eng.: Ru.Eng.: Bachelor of Rural Engineering

Brummagem: Birmingham (colloquial)

Brun: Brunei

brunch(eon): breakfast-lunch(eon)

Bruno Walter: Bruno Walter Schlesinger

Brussels system: universal decimal classification

brut: (French—unadulterated) almost completely tart champagne or wine

Brux: Brussels

BRVMA (BVA): British Radio

Valve Manufacturers' Association

Brw: Barrow

Bry: Barry; Bryant

bryol: bryology

Bryth: Brythonic

brz: bronze

brzg: brazing

bs: bluestone; bomb service; bonded single-silk (insulation); both sides; bullshit

b/s (B/S): bill of sale

b & s: beams and stringers; bell and spigot; boosters and sustainers; brandy and soda

Bs: bolivares (Venezuelan currency); bolivianos (Bolivian currency)

BS: Battle Squadron; Battle Star; Bethlehem Steel; Berlin Sector; Birmingham Southern (railroad); British Standard; Bureau of Ships; Bureau of Standards

B.S.: Bachelor of Science

B & S: Brown and Sharpe; Butterfield and Swire

B de S: Baruch de Spinoza

B es S: Bachelier es Sciences (French—Bachelor of Science)

BSA: Bank Stationers Association; Bibliographical Society of America; Birmingham Small Arms; Blind Service Association; Botanical Society of America; Boy Scouts of America; Boy Scouts Association; British School of Athens; British South Africa; Bruckner Society of America; Bureau of Supplies and Accounts

B.S.A.: Bachelor of Agricultural Science

BSAA: British South American Airways

B.S.A.A.: Bachelor of Science in Applied Arts

BSAC: British South Africa Company; Brotherhood of Shoe and Allied Craftsmen

B.S.Adv.: Bachelor of Science in Advertising

B.S.A.E.: Bachelor of Science in Aeronautical Engineering; Bachelor of Science in Architectural Engineering

B.S.Agr.: Bachelor of Science in Agriculture

BSAP: British South Africa Police

B.S.Arch.: Bachelor of Science in Architecture

B.S.Arch.Eng.: Bachelor of Science in Architectural Engineering

B.S.Art Ed.: Bachelor of Science in Art Education

BSAS: British Ship Adoption So-

ciety
Bsb: Brisbane
BSB: Brasilia, Brazil (airport)
B.S.B.A.: Bachelor of Science in Business Administration
B.S.Bus.: Bachelor of Science in Business
bsc: basic
B. Sc.: Bachelor of Science
BSC: Beltsville Space Center; Bemidji State College; Bethlehem Steel Corporation; Biological Stain Commission; Biomedical Sciences Corporation; Bloomsburg State College; Bluefield State College; Booth Steamship Company; British Society of Cinematographers; British Supply Council
B.S.C.: Bachelor of Science in Commerce
BSCA: Bureau of Security and Consular Affairs (US Department of State)
BSCC: British Society for Clinical Cytology
BSCE: Bank Street College of Education
B.S.C.E.: Bachelor of Science in Civil Engineering
B.S.Ch.: Bachelor of Science in Chemistry
B.S.Chm.: Bachelor of Science in Chemistry
B.Sc.Nurs.: Bachelor of Science in Nursing
B.S.Comm.: Bachelor of Science in Commerce
BSCP: Brotherhood of Sleeping Car Porters
BSCRA: British Steel Castings Research Association
BSCS: Biological Sciences Curriculum Study
bsd: beam-steering device; bit storage density; blast-suppression device; burst-slug detection
BSD: Ballistic Systems Division (USAF); British Space Development
B.S.D.: Bachelor of Science in Design
BSDA: British Spinners and Doublers Association
BSDC: British Space Development Company
B.S.Dent.: Bachelor of Science in Dentistry
B.S.D.H.: Bachelor of Science in Dental Hygiene
bsdl: boresight datum line
bse: base support equipment; breast self-examination (cancer control)
BSE: Base Support Equipment; Birmingham & Southeastern

(railroad); Building Service Employees (Union); Bureau of Steam Engineering
B.S.E.: Bachelor of Sanitary Engineering; Bachelor of Science Education; Bachelor of Science Engineering
B & SE: Birmingham & Southeastern (railroad)
B.S.Ec.: Bachelor of Science in Economics
B.S.Ed.: Bachelor of Science in Education
B.S.E.E.: Bachelor of Science in Electrical Engineering; Bachelor of Science in Electronic Engineering
B.S.El.E.: Bachelor of Science in Electronic Engineering
B.S.Eng.: Bachelor of Science in Engineering
B7D: buyer has seven days to pay (for whatever was bought—usually securities)
bsf: bulk shielding facilities
BSF: Basic Skill Films
B.S.F.: Bachelor of Science in Forestry
bsfc: brake specific fuel consumption
BSFC: Baltic States Freedom Council
B.S.Fin: Bachelor of Science in Finance
BSFL: British Shipping Federation Limited
B.S.For.: Bachelor of Science in Forestry
B.S.F.S.: Bachelor of Science in Foreign Service
BSF & W: Bureau of Sport Fisheries and Wildlife
BSG: British standard gage
bsgdg: *breveté sans garantie du gouvernement* (French—patented without government guarantee)
B.S.G.E.: Bachelor of Science in General Engineering; Bachelor of Science in Geological Engineering
B.S.Gen. Nur.: Bachelor of Science in General Nursing
B.S.Geog.: Bachelor of Science in Geography
B.S.Geol.: Bachelor of Science in Geology
B.S.Geol. Eng.: Bachelor of Science in Geological Engineering
bsh: bushel
B.S.H.A.: Bachelor of Science in Hospital Administration
B.S.H.E.: Bachelor of Science in Home Economics
B.S.H.Eco.: Bachelor of Science in Home Economics

B.S.H.Ed.: Bachelor of Science in Health Education
BSI: British Sailors' Institute; British Standards Institution
BSIA: Better Speech Institute of America
BSIB: Boy Scouts International Bureau
bsic: binary-symmetric independent channel
B.S.I.E.: Bachelor of Science in Industrial Engineering
BSIHE: British Society for International Health Education
B.S. Ind.Art: Bachelor of Science in Industrial Art
B.S.Ind.Chem.: Bachelor of Science in Industrial Chemistry
B.S.Ind.Ed.: Bachelor of Science in Industrial Education
B.S.Ind.Eng.: Bachelor of Science in Industrial Engineering
B.S.I.R.: Bachelor of Science in Industrial Relations
BSIRA: British Scientific Instrument Research Association
BSIs: Baker Street Irregulars
bsj: balanced swivel joint; ball-and-socket joint
B.S.J.: Bachelor of Science in Journalism
B.S.Jr.: Bachelor of Science in Journalism
bsk: basket(s)
bskt: basket
bsl: billet split lens
bs/l: bills of lading
BSL: Barber Steamship Lines; Behavioral Sciences Laboratory; Black Star Line; Blue Sea Line; Blue Star Line; Building Service League; Bull Steamship Lines
B.S.Lab.Rel.: Bachelor of Science in Labor Relations
bslb: ball-and-socket lower bearing
bsl(s): bushel(s)
B.S.L.S.: Bachelor of Science in Library Science; Bachelor of Science in Library Service
bsm: bi-stable multivibrator; bottom sonar marker
BSM: Birmingham School of Music; Bronze Star Medal
BSM: *beso sus manos* (Spanish—I kiss your hands)—respectfully yours
B.S.M.E.: Bachelor of Science in Mechanical Engineering; Bachelor of Science in Mining Engineering; Bachelor of Science in Music Education
B.S.Med.: Bachelor of Science in Medicine
B.S.Med.Rec.: Bachelor of Science in Medical Records
B.S.Med.Rec.Lib.: Bachelor of

Science in Medical Records Librarianship

B.S.Med.Tech.: Bachelor of Science in Medical Technology

B.S.Met.: Bachelor of Science in Metallurgy

B.S.Met. Eng.: Bachelor of Science in Metallurgical Engineering

B.S.Mgt.Sci.: Bachelor of Science in Management Science

B.S.Min: Bachelor of Science in Minerology; Bachelor of Science in Mining

B.S.Min.Eng.: Bachelor of Science in Mining Engineering

BSMMA: British Sugar Machinery Manufacturers Association

bsmt: basement

B.S.Mus.Ed.: Bachelor of Science in Music Education

bsmv: barley-stripe-mosaic virus

bsn: bowel sounds normal

BSN: Baker School of Navigation

B.S.N.: Bachelor of Science in Nursing

BSN: *Bayerische Staatsoper— Nationaltheater* (German—Bavarian State Opera—National Theater—in Munich

B.S.N.A.: Bachelor of Science in Nursing Administration

B.S.Nat.Hist.: Bachelor of Science in Natural History

BSNDT: British Society for Non-Destructive Testing

BSNH: Boston Society of Natural History; Buffalo Society of Natural History

B.S.Nurs.: Bachelor of Science in Nursing

B.S.Nurs.Ed.: Bachelor of Science in Nursing Education

bso: blue stellar objects

BSO: Baltimore Symphony Orchestra; Bamberg Symphony Orchestra; Birmingham Symphony Orchestra; Bombay Symphony Orchestra; Boston Symphony Orchestra; Bournemouth Symphony Orchestra; Budapest Symphony Orchestra

B.S.Occ.Ther.: Bachelor of Science in Occupational Therapy

BSOIW: Bridge, Structural and Ornamental Iron Workers

B.S.Opt.: Bachelor of Science in Optometry

B.S.O.T.: Bachelor of Science in Occupational Therapy

bsp: bromosulphalein

Bsp: British Standard pipe

BSP: Bering Sea Patrol

B-S-P: Bartlett-Snow-Pacific (foundry division)

B.S.P.: Bachelor of Science in Pharmacy

B.S.P.A.: Bachelor of Science in Public Administration

B.S.P.E.: Bachelor of Science in Physical Education

B.S.Per. & Pub. Rel.: Bachelor of Science in Personnel and Public Relations

B.S.Pet.: Bachelor of Science in Petroleum

B.S.Pet.Eng.: Bachelor of Science in Petroleum Engineering

B.S.P.H.: Bachelor of Science in Public Health

B.S.Phar.: Bachelor of Science in Pharmacy

B.S.Pharm.: Bachelor of Science in Pharmacy

B.S.P.H.N.: Bachelor of Science in Public Health Nursing

B.S.Phys.Ed.: Bachelor of Science in Physical Education

B.S.Phys.Edu.: Bachelor of Science in Physical Education

B.S.Phys.Ther.: Bachelor of Science in Physical Therapy

bspl: behavioral science programming language

BSPM: Battlefield Systems Project Management

BSPMA: British Sewage Plant Manufacturers Association

B.S.P.T.: Bachelor of Science in Physical Therapy

bspw: bare silver-plated wire

Bsq: Basque

BSQ: Bachelor Sergeant Quarters

bsr: backspace recorder; balloon-supported rockets (rockoons); basal skin resistance; battle short relay; blue-streak request

Bsr: Basra (Busreh)

BSR: British Society of Rheology

BSRA: British Ship Research Association

BSRC: Biological Serial Record Center

B.S.Rec.: Bachelor of Science in Recreation

B.S.Ret.: Bachelor of Science in Retailing

bsrf: brain stem reticular formation

BSRL: Boeing Scientific Research Laboratories

bss: basic shaft system; beam-steering system

BSS: Bibliothèque Saint-Sulpice (Montreal); British Standard Specification; Bronze Service Star; Bureau of State Services

B.S.S.: Bachelor of Sanitary Science; Bachelor of Science in Secretarial Science; Bachelor of Social Science(s)

B.S.S.A.: Bachelor of Science in Secretarial Administration

B.S.Sc.: Bachelor of Sanitary Science

B.S.Sc.Eng.: Bachelor of Science in Science Engineering

B.S.Sec.Ed.: Bachelor of Science in Secondary Education

B.S.Sec.Sci.: Bachelor of Science in Secretarial Science

BSSG: Biomedical Sciences Support Grant

B.S.Soc.Serv.: Bachelor of Science in Social Service

B.S.Soc.St.: Bachelor of Science in Social Studies

B.S.Soc.Wk.: Bachelor of Science in Social Work

bssp: broadband solid-state preamplifier

BSSR: Bureau of Social Science Research

B.S.S.S.: Bachelor of Science in Secretarial Studies; Bachelor of Science in Social Science

B.S.S.Sc.: Bachelor of Science in Social Science

B.S.Struc.Eng.: Bachelor of Science in Structural Engineering

bssw: bare stainless-steel wire

bst: beam-steering transducer; blood serological test(ing); brief stimulus therapy

b s & t: blood, sweat, and tears

BST: Bering Standard Time; British Summer Time

BSTC: Ball State Teachers College

bstd: bastard

B.S.Text.: Bachelor of Science in Textiles

bst lt: blue stern light

bstr: booster

B.S.Trans.: Bachelor of Science in Transportation

bstrk: bomb service truck

bstr rkt: booster rocket

BSU: Black Students Union; Boat Support Unit

bsub: ball-and-socket upper bearing

B.Sur.: Bachelor of Surgery

bsut: beam-steering ultrasonic transducer

bsv: Boolean simple variable

B.S. Voc. Ag.: Bachelor of Science in Vocational Agriculture

B.S. Voc. Ed.: Bachelor of Science in Vocational Education

bsw: barrels of salt water

bs & w: basic sediment and water

BSW: Boot and Shoe Workers (union); Botanical Society of Washington

bswd: barrels of salt water per day

bt: bathtub; bathythermograph; bent; boat; boat-tail; bombing table; bought

b/t: berth terms (ship chartering)
b & t: bacon and tomato sandwich
Bt: baronet
BT: basic trainer
B of T: Board of Trade
BT: *Berlingske Tidende* (Berling's Times—Copenhagen)
bta: better than average
BTA: Blood Transfusion Association; Board of Tax Appeals; Boston Transportation Authority; Brith Trumpeldor of America; British Travel Association; Brazilian Travel Agency
BTAM: Basic Telecommunications Access Method
BTAO: Bureau of Technical Assistance Operations (UN)
btb: braided tube bundle; bus tie breaker
BTB: Barbados Tourist Board; Belgian Tourist Bureau
BTBA: Blood Transfusion Betterment Association
btc: below threshold change; beryllium thrust chamber
BTC: Bankers Trust Company; Basic Training Center; Bethlehem Transportation Company; Board of Transport Commissioners
B.T.C.: Bachelor of Textile Chemistry
btca: *biblioteca* (Spanish—library)
BTCC: Bloom Township Community College; Board of Transportation Commissioners for Canada; Broome Technical Community College
btd: bomb testing device
BTDB: Bermuda Trade Development Board
btdc: before top dead center
bte: battery terminal equipment; blunt trailing edge; Boltzmann transport equation; bourdon tube element; Brayton turboelectric engine; bulk tape eraser
bté: *breveté* (French—patent)
B.T.E.: Bachelor of Textile Engineering
Btee: Brayton turboelectric engine
btf: barrels of total fluid; bomb tail fuse
btg: ball-tooth gear; battery timing group; beacon trigger generator; burst transmission group
btgj: ball-tooth gear joint
bth: berth
B.Th.: Bachelor of Theology
BT-H: British Thompson-Houston
BTHS: Brooklyn Technical High School
bti: bank-and-turn indicator; bridge-tape isolator
BTI: Bandung Technical Institute

BTIPR: Boyce Thompson Institute for Plant Research
btj: ball-tooth joint
BTJ: *Board of Trade Journals*
btk: buttock
btk l: buttock line
btl: beginning tape label; bottle
BTL: Bell Telephone Laboratories
BTMA: British Typewriter Manufacturers Association
BTME: Babcock Test of Mental Efficiency
btn: button
bto: bombing through overcast
bto: *bruto* (Spanish—gross weight); *bulto* (Spanish—bulk)
BTO: Branch Transportation Officer
bto(s): big time operator(s)
B-town: Bean Town (Boston—sailor's sobriquet)
btp: body temperature and pressure
BTP: Bush Terminal Piers
btps: body temperature and pressure—saturated
btr: bus transfer
BTR: Baton Rouge, Louisiana (airport)
B. Traven: (pen name—Berick Traven Torsvan)
bts: base of terminal service (USAF); Boolean time sequence
btry: battery
BTS: Blood Transfusion Service
BTSB: Bound-to-Stay-Bound Books
bttns: battens
btu (BTU, Btu): British thermal unit
BTU: Board of Trade Unit
BTWHS: Booker T. Washington High School
btwn: between
btx: benzene, toluene, xylene
bu: base unit; builder; bushel
Bu: Bulgaria; Bulgarian; Bureau (United States Navy); butyl
BU: Baker University; Baylor University; Bishop's University; Boston University; Bradley University; Brandeis University; Brown University; Bucknell University; Burma (symbol); Butler University
BUA: British United Airways
BuAer: Bureau of Aeronautics (USN)
BUAF: British United Air Ferries
buc: buccal; buccaneer; buccinator
BUC: Bangor University College
Buchar: Bucharest
Bucht: (German—bay)
buck.: buckram
Bucks: Buckinghamshire
BUCOP: *British Union Catalogue of Periodicals*

bucu: burring cutter
bud.: budget
Bud: Buddha; Buddhism; Buddhist; Buddy; Budweiser
BUD: Budapest, Hungary (airport)
Buda: Budapest
Bud(dy): Brother
budgie(s): budgerigar(s)
BuDocks: Bureau of Yards and Docks (USN)
budr: bromodeoxyuridine
bue: built-up edge
BUE: Buenos Aires, Argentina (Ezeiza airport)
Buen: Buenaventura
Buf: Buffalo (city and port)
BUF: British Union of Fascists; Buffalo, New York (airport)
Buffalo Bill: Colonel William F. Cody
Bug: Bugatti
BUG: Brooklyn Union Gas (company)
Bugd Nyramdakh Mongol Ard Uls: (Mongolian People's Republic)—Outer Mongolia
bugt: (Danish—bay)
BUH: Bucharest, Rumania (airport)
BUIA: British United Island Airways
buic (BUIC): backup interceptor control
BUIC: Bureau (of Naval Personnel) Unit Identification Code (USN)
build.: building
buisys: barrier-up indicating system
bukhta: (Russian—bay)
bukit: (Malayan—hill; mountain)
bul: below upper limit; bulletin
BUL: Bombay University Library
Bulg: Bulgaria; Bulgarian
bull.: *bulla* (Latin—leaden seal; nickname for a papal pronouncement bearing such a seal)
Bull: bulletin
Bull Moose: Theodore Roosevelt—twenty-sixth President of the United States
bull(s): bulletin(s)
buloga: business logistics game
BuMed: Bureau of Medicine and Surgery
Bu M & S: Bureau of Medicine and Surgery (USN)
BUN: blood urea nitrogen
bunwich: bun + sandwich (sandwich made in a bun)
BuOrd: Bureau of Ordnance (USN)
bup: backup plate; bull pup
BUP: British United Press
Bupers: Bureau of Personnel (USN)
bupp: backup plate perforated
bur.: bureau
Bur: Burma; Burmese
BUR: Burbank, California (Lock-

heed Airport)
BuRec: Bureau of Reclamation
Bur Eco Aff: Bureau of Economic Affairs (US Department of State)
Bur Eur Aff: Bureau of European Affairs (US Department of State)
burg: burgess; burgomaster
Burg: Burgos
Burg: (Dutch or German—castle; town)
burger(s): hamburger(s)
Burke's: *Burke's Peerage*
burl.: burlesque
Burlington Route: Chicago, Burlington and Quincy (railroad)
burnu: (Turkish—cape)
buro: bureau
Bur Pub Aff: Bureau of Public Affairs (US Department of State)
Burs: Bursar
bus.: business; omnibus
BuSanda: Bureau of Supplies and Accounts (USN)
BUSARB: British—United States Amateur Rocket Bureau
busbar: omnibus bar
bush.: bushing(s)
BuShips: Bureau of Ships (USN)
Bus Mgr: Business Manager
Busta: Sir Alexander Bustamante
but.: butter; button
BUT: British United Traction
buv: backscatter ultraviolet
buvs: backscatter ultraviolet spectrometer
BuWeps: Bureau of Weapons (USN)
buy.: buyer; buying
buz: buzzer
bv: balanced voltage; bellows valve; blow valve; blood volume; bonnet valve; breviary
bv: *bijvoorbeeld* (Dutch—for example)
b.v.: *balneum vaporis* (Latin —steambath; vapor bath)
B/v: book value
BV: Bureau Veritas (French ship-classification bureau)
BV.: *Beata Virgo* (Latin—Blessed Virgin); *bene vale* (Latin—a good farewell); *bene vixit* (Latin—he lived a good life)
BVA: British Veterinary Association
B.V.A.: Bachelor of Vocational Adjustment; Bachelor of Vocational Agriculture
BVAL: Blackman's Volunteer Army of Liberation
bvbrf: blood vessel of bronchial filament
BVC: Buena Vista College
bvd: beacon video digitizer
BVD: Bradley, Vorhees & Day
BVDs: suits of underwear (derived from BVD)
BVDT: Brief Vestibular Disorientation Test
B.V.E.: Bachelor of Vocational Education
B/ventura: Buenaventura, Colombia
BVG: *Berliner Verkehrs-Betriebe* (German—Berlin Traffic Carrier)—Berlin's transit sytstem
BVI: Better Vision Institute; British Virgin Islands
B.V.M.: Bachelor of Veterinary Medicine; Blessed Virgin Mary
B.V.M.: *Beata Virgo Maria* (Latin—Blessed Virgin Mary)
BVMA: British Valve Manufacturers Association
BVN: Bund der Verfolgten des Nazi Regimes (League of Persons Persecuted by the Nazi Regime)
BVNP: Bolusan Volcano National Park (Luxon, Philippines)
bvo: brominated vegetable oil
bvp: beacon video processor; booster vacuum pump; boundary value problem
BVPS: Beacon Video Processing System; Booster Vacuum Pump System
bvr: balanced valve regulator; black void reactor
BVRO: Base Vehicle Reporting Officer
BVRR: Bureau of Veterans Reemployment Rights
BVRS: Breadboard Visual Reference System
BVS: Best Vested Socialists; Bevier & Southern (railroad)
B.V.S.: Bachelor of Veterinary Science; Bachelor of Veterinary Surgery
bvt: brevet; brevetted
bvw: binary voltage weigher
bw: biological warfare (BW); both ways; braided wire (armor)
b/w: black-and-white
b & w: black and white; bread and water
bw: *bitte wenden* (German —please turn over)
BW: Bendix-Westinghouse; Biological Warfare; Black Watch; Borg-Warner
B-W: Bendix-Westinghouse Automotive Air Brake; Borg-Warner
B & W: Babcock and Wilcox; Barker and Williamson; Burmeister and Wain
BW: *Bitte Wenden* (German —please turn over); *Business Week*
bwa: backward-wave amplifier; bent-wire antenna
BWA: Baseball Writers Association; British West Africa; Building Waterproofers Association
BWAL: Barber West African Line
Bway: Broadway
BWB: British Waterways Board
bwc: basic weight calculator; broadband waveguide oscillator
BWC: British War Cabinet
bwcp: bench welder control panel
bw-cw: biological warfare—chemical warfare
bwd: bacillary white diarrhea; backward; barrels of water per day
BWD: Baldwin Wallace College; British War Cabinet
BWF: Baha'i World Faith
Bwg: Bowling
BWG: Birmingham Wire Gage
bwh: barrels of water per hour
BWI: British West Indies
bwia: better walk if able
BWIA: British West Indian Airways
BWI$: British West Indian dollar
bwk: brickwork; bulwark
bwl: belt work line
BWL: Biological War Laboratory
bwlt : bow light
bwm: barrels of water per minute
BWM: Broom and Whisk Makers (union)
BWMA: British Woodwork Manufacturers Association
BWMB: British Wool Marketing Board
BWN: Brown Company (stock-exchange symbol)
bwo: backward-wave oscillator
bwoc: big woman on campus
bwos: backward-wave oscillator synchronizer
bwot: backward-wave oscillator tube
bwp: ballistic wind plotter
BWP: Basic War Plan
bwpa: backward-wave parametric amplifier
BWPA: British Wood Preserving Association
bwpd: barrels of water per day
bwph: barrels of water per hour
bwr (BWR): boiling-water reactor
BWRA: British Water Research Association; British Welding Research Association
BWRC: Biological Warfare Research Center
BWRWS: Biological Warfare Rapid Warning System (USA)
bws: beveled wood siding
BWS: Bandipur Wildlife Sanctuary (India); Batch Weighing System; Battlefield Weapons System; Beaufort Wind Scale; Biological Weapons System; British

Watercolour Society
BW & S: Boyd, Weir & Sewell
BWSL: Battlefield Weapons Systems Laboratory
bwso: backward wave sweep oscillator
bwt: both-way trunk
BWT: Boeing Wind Tunnel
BWTA: British Women's Temperance Association
BWTP: Bureau of Work-Training Programs
bw-tv: black-and-white television
bwv: back-water valve
BWVA: British War Veterans of America
bx: box
Bx: Beatrix; Brix
BX: Base Exchange (USAF); Bellingham-Seattle Airways (2-letter code)

bx cable: insulated wires within flexible tubing
bxd: boxed
bxk: broadband X-band klystron
bx k: box keel
BXL: Bakelite Xylonite Limited
Bxm: Brixham
bxs: boxes
b-y: bloody
by: (Dano-Norwegian or Swedish—town)
By: Buryat(ic); Byron(ic)
BY: blowing spray
BYC: Brewers Yeast Council
Bye: Byelorussia; Byelorussian
byob: bring your own beer
byod: bring your own drinks
byog: bring your own girl
byp: bypass
Byp: Bypass
bypro(s): by-product(s)

byt: bright young things (British younger set)
BYU: Brigham Young University
Byz: Byzantine
bz: blank when zero; buzzer; (cartoonist's symbol—buzzing; sawing; snoring)
Bz: benzene; benzoyl; Brazil; Brazilian
BZ: Air Congo (Brazzaville, Congo Republic); B'nai Zion
BZ: *Bild Zeitung* (German—Picture Newspaper)
Bza: Bizerta
BZA: Board of Zoning Adjustment
bzfx: brazing fixture
bzw: *beziehungsweise* (German —respectively)
bzz: (cartoonist's symbol—buzzing; sawing; snoring)
bzzz: (same as bzz)

C

c: caudal; cent; centavo; centime; centimeter; child; chord length (symbol); cirrus; conductor; cranial; cube; cubic; cubical; cycle(s); heat capacity per mole (symbol); see; speed of light (symbol)
c: *circa* (Latin—about); cocaine
C: calculated weight (symbol); candle; capacitance; capacitor; Cape; carat; carbon; Cardinal; cargo or transport airplane; cargo vessel; carton; case; cathode; cavalry; celestial; Celsius; Celtic; Centigrade; century; cervical; chairman; Charlie—code for letter C; Chief; Christ(ian); coast; cocaine (drug user's abbreviation); cold; college; colored; combat aircraft; commander; compliance; concentration; consul; control; Convair; copyright; Cosmopolitan Shipping; council; course; Curie's constant; Fraunhofer line characteristic of hydrogen (symbol); hundredweight (symbol); molecular heat (symbol); see (popular phonetic spelling)
C.: carbohydrates (dietary symbol); cocaine; Conservative (political party)
°C: degree Celsius; degree centigrade
C₁: first class

C₂: second class
C₃: third class
C-3: mentally or physically defective (British equivalent of American 4-F)
C³: command, control, communications
C4: Convair 440 airplane
C5: Convair 580 turboprop airplane
C-5A: Lockheed military cargo transport airplane
C¹⁴: radioactive carbon (used in determining age of objects by radioactivity measurement)
C-123: Provider twin-engine assault transport
C-124: Globemaster heavy cargo four-engine transport airplane
C-130: Hercules medium-range cargo and troop transport airplane powered by four turboprop engines
C-133: Cargomaster heavy four-engine turboprop cargo transport airplane
C-140: Jet Star support-type transport aircraft powered by four turbojet engines
C-141: Starlifter large cargo transport airplane powered by four turbojet engines
₡: colón; colones (currency in Costa Rica and El Salvador)
"C": Costa Line
C: absolute coefficient (symbol);

caballeros (Spanish—gentlemen); *caldo* (Italian—hot); *caliente* (Spanish—hot); *calle* (Spanish—street); *chaud*(French —hot); *ciudad* (Spanish—city); cold (on bathroom taps in English-speaking countries only); cross-wind (symbol)
ca: cable; calibrated altitude; capital asset; carbonic anhydrase; caudal; centare; chronological age; civil affairs; civil authorities; clerical aptitude; convening authority; council accepted; croup associated; current assets
ca': calf; call (Scottish contraction)
c/a: capital account; center angle; coated abrasive; current account
c & a: classification and audit
ca.: *circa* (Latin—about); *courant alternatif* (French—alternating current)
Ca: calcium; Canada; Canadian
Ca: *Compagnia* (Italian—company)
Cª: *Compañía* (Spanish—company)
Ca': *Casa* (Venetian—house)
CA: Capital Airlines; Central America; Certificate of Airworthiness; Chargé d'Affaires; Chartered Accountant; Chemical Abstracts; Chief Accountant; Civil Affairs; Coast Artillery; Combat Aircrew; Combat Aircrewman; Commercial Agent; Companhia de Navegação Carregadores

Açoreanos (Azores Line); Compensation Act; Comptroller of the Army; Confederate Army; Consular Agent; Convening Authority; County Attorney; Court of Appeals; Cranial Academy; heavy cruiser (naval symbol)

C.A.: Chartered Accountant

C of A: College of Aeronautics

CA: *corriente alterna* (Spanish—alternating current)

caa: caging amplifier assembly; circular aperture antenna; computer amplifier alarm; crime aboard aircraft

CAA: Canadian Authors' Association; Cantors Assembly of America; Carribbean Atlantic Airlines; Central African Airways; Chester Alan Arthur; Chief of Army Aviation; Civil Aeronautics Administration; Civil Aeronautics Authority; Collectors of American Art; Correctional Administrators Association; Cremation Association of America

CAAA: College Art Association of America; Composers, Authors, and Artists of America

CAAB: California Avocado Advisory Board

CAAC: Civil Aviation Administration of China

CAADRP: Civil Aircraft Airworthiness Data Recording Program (UK)

CAAE: Canadian Association for Adult Education

CAAR: Committee Against Academic Repression

CAARC: Commonwealth Advisory Aeronautical Research Council

CAAs: Community Action Agencies

CAAS: Ceylon Association for the Advancement of Science; Connecticut Academy of Arts and Sciences

CAAT: Canadian Academic Aptitude Test

cab: cabal; cabbage; cabin; cabinet; cable; cabochon; cabriolet; calibration; captured air bubble; cellulose acetate butyrate; taxicab

CAB: Charles A(ustin) Beard; Civil Aeronautics Board; Civil Aeronautics Bulletin; Commonwealth Agricultural Bureau; Contract Appeals Board (Veternas Administration)

CABA: Charge Account Bankers Association

CABAL: Clifford of Chudleigh, Ashley (Lord Shaftesbury), Buckingham (George Villiers),

Arlington (Henry Bennet), Lauderdale (John Maitland)—members of the cabal or secret cabinet of Charles II of England; by coincidence their initials spelled cabal

CABB: Captured Air-Bubble Boat (naval)

CABEI: Central American Bank for Economic Integration

CABM: Commonwealth of Australia Bureau of Meteorology

CABMA: Canadian Association of British Manufacturers and Agencies

CABMS: Chinese-oriented Antiballistic Missile System

cabo: (Portuguese or Spanish —cape)

cabot: cabotage (coastal navigation)

CABRA: Copper and Brass Research Association

cabtmkr: cabinetmaker

Cac: Caceres

CAC: California Aeronautics Commission; Canadian Armoured Corps; Chief of Air Corps; Civil Administration Committee; Civil Administration Commission; Coast Artillery Corps; College Admissions Center; Combat Air Crew; Commander Air Center; Consumer Advisory Council; Continental Air Command; Corrective Action Committee; Corrective Action Commission

CACA: Canadian Agricultural Chemicals Association

CACC: Corrective Action Control Section

CACCE: Council of American Chambers of Commerce in Europe

CACE: California Association for Childhood Education; Chicago Association of Consulting Engineers

CACF: Colombian-American Culture Foundation

cache.: computer-controlled automated cargo-handling envelope

CACHE: Computer Aids for Chemical Engineering Education

CACM: Central American Common Market

CACO: Casualty Assistance Call Office(r)

CaCO3: calcium carbonate (limestone)

cacp: cartridge-actuated compaction press

CACS: California Aqueduct Control System

CACSW: Citizens' Advisory Council on the Status of Women

CACUL: Canadian Association of

College and University Libraries

CAC & W: Continental Aircraft Control and Warning

cad.: cadastral; cadaver; caddie; cadenza; cadet; cadmium; cartridge-activated device; cartridge-actuated device; cash against disbursements; cash against documents; contract award date

cad: *cadenza* (Italian—solo passage near end of a concerto movement)

c-à-d: *c'est-à-dire* (French—that is to say)

Cad: Cádiz; Cadwallader

CAD: Claude Achille Debussy; Combat Air Division (USN); Crown Agents' Department

cada: clear air dot angle

CADA: Centre d'Analyse Documentaire pour l'Archéologie (Document Analysis Center—Archaeology)

CADAN: Centre d'Analyse Documentaire pour Afrique Noir (Document Analysis Center—Africa)

cadc: central air data computer

CADC: Continental Air Defense Command; Corrective Action Data Center

cadco: core and drum corrector

Cad(dy): Cadillac

cadet.: computer-aided design experimental translator

Cadets: Constitutional Democrats (in czarist Russia)

cadf: commutated antenna direction finder

CADF: Central Air Defense Force; Contract Administrative Data File

cadfiss: computation and data flow integrated subsystems

CADIN: Continental Air Defense Integration North

CADIZ: Canadian Air Defense Identification Zone

CADM: CONUS (Continental United States) Air Defense Modernization

'cado(s): avocado(s)

CADO: Central Air Documents Office (USAF); Current Actions Duty Office(r)

Ca' d'Oro: Casa de Oro (Italian —House of Gold)

cadre.: current awareness and document retrieval for engineers

cads.: cellular-absorbed-dose spectrometer

CADS: Central Air Data System (USAF)

Cadwal: Cadwallader

CAE: Canadian Aviation Electronics; Columbia, South Carolina (airport)

CAE: *Cóbrese al Entregar* (Spanish—cash on delivery)

CAEA: California Aviation Education Association; Chartered Auctioneers and Estate Agents

Caern: Caernarvonshire

Caes: Caius Julius Ceasar

CAES: Canadian Agricultural Economics Society; Connecticut Agricultural Experiment Station

caesar: computerized automation by electronic system with automated reservations

Ceasar's Century: the 1st century before the Christian era when he conquered Britain as well as Egypt; he was assassinated in the Roman Senate in the year 44

CAET: Corrective Action Evaluation Team

caf: cafeteria; caffeine; clerical, administrative, and fiscal; cost and freight; cost, assurance, and freight

CAF: Central African Federation; Ceylon Air Force

CAFA: Chicago Academy of Fine Arts

CAFB: Clark Air Force Base

cafetorium: cafeteria-auditorium

caff: caffeine

CAFIT: Computer-Assisted Fault Isolation Test(ing)

cafm: commercial air freight movement

CAFMS: Continental Association of Funeral and Memorial Societies

CAFO: Command Accounting and Finance Office

C Afr Fed: Central African Federation

CAFSC: Control Air Force Specialty Code

CAFU: Civil Aviation Flying Unit

cag: constant altitude glide

CAG: Carrier Air Group; Civil Air Guard; Composers-Authors Guild; Concert Artist Guild; Corrective Action Group; heavy guided-missile cruiser (naval symbol)

CAGA: California Asparagus Growers Association

CAGE: Convicts' Association for a Good Environment

cagel: consolidated aerospace ground equipment list

CAGI: Compressed Air and Gas Institute

Cagliostro: Giuseppe Balsamo

cah: congenital adrenal hyperplasia

CAHS: Comprehensive Automa-

tion of the Hydrometeorological Service

cai: computer-aided instruction; confused artificial insemination

Cai: Cairo

CAI: Computer Applications Incorporated; Configuration Audit Inspection (USA); Culinary Arts Institute

caiop: computer analog input-output

CAIRA: Central Automated Inventory and Referral Activity (USAF)

CAirC: Caribbean Air Command

cairn: (Celtic—rocky headland)

CAIRS: Central Automated Inventory and Referral System (USAF); Computer-Assisted Interactive Resources Scheduling System

CAIS: Canadian Association for Information Science; Central Abstracting and Indexing Service

Caith: Caithness

CAITS: Chemical Agent Indentification Training Set

caj: calked joint

'cajun: Acadian (native of Louisiana)

cak: conical alignment kit; cube alignment kit

CAK: Akron, Ohio (airport)

cal: caliber; calorie; conversational algebraic language

Cal: California (Calif is approved abbreviation); Callao

CAL: China Airlines; Continental Airlines; Conversational Algebraic Language; Cornell Aeronautical Laboratory; Cyprus Airways; Point Arguello (California) tracking station

cala: *calabozo* (Spanish—cell; dungeon; jail)

CALA: Civil Aviation Licensing Act

CALANS: Caribbean and Latin American News Service

calavo: California-grown avocado

calbr: calibration

calc: calculation; calculus

Calc: Calcutta

calcd: calculated

CALCOFI: California Cooperative Oceanic Fishery Investigation

Calc Univ: Calcutta University

CALDA: Canadian Air Line Dispatchers Association

CALDEA: California Driver Education Association

Calder: Cadwalader; Cadwallader

Caled: Caledonia (Scotland); Caledonian (Scotch)

Caled Can: Caledonian Canal

calef.: *calefactus* (Latin—warmed)

calen: calendar; calender

Calex: Calexico (California border city)

Cal Expo: California Exposition (permanent show at Sacramento)

Calhan: Calahan

calib: calibrate; calibration

calibn: calibration

caliche: calcium carbonate crust (or) dust—$CaCO_3$

Caliente: Agua Caliente, Mexico

Calif: California; Californian

CALIF: California

Calif Cur: California Current

Calipuerto: Cali Aeropuerto (Cali, Colombia)

cal$_{IT}$: calorie (International Table calorie)

CALIT: California Institute of Technology (also Caltech or CIT).

CALL: Composite Aeronautical Load List; Counselling at the Local Level (SBA)

calm.: collected algorithms for learning machines

CALM: Citizens Against Legalized Murder; Computer-Assisted Library Mechanization

Calmex: California-Mexico

CALMS: Computer Automatic Line Monitoring System

calo: *calando* (Italian—softer and slower, bit by bit)

calogsim: computer-assisted logistics simulation

calomel: mercurous chloride (Hg_2Cl_2)

CALPA: Canadian Air Line Pilots Association

CALPIRG: California Public Interest Research Group

Cal Poly: California Polytechnic

CALRI: Central Artificial Leather Research Institute

CALSO: California Transport

CalTec: California Institute of Technology

CALTEX: California-Texas Petroleum; Overseas Tankship Corporation

cal$_{th}$: calorie (thermochemical calorie)

Calv: Calvin; Calvinism; Calvinist

Calz: *Calzada* (Spanish—boulevard; highway)

cam.: camber; camouflage; circular area method; commercial air movement

Cam: Camaguey; Cambodia; Cambodian; Cameroons; Campeche; Campechanos

CAM: Civil Aeronautics Manual; Civil Aviation Medicine; Composite Army-Marine; Contract

Air Mail; Contract Audit Manual

cama: centralized automatic message accounting

CAMA: Civil Aerospace Medical Association

camal (CAMAL): continuous airborne missle alert

C'Amalie: Charlotte Amalie

Camb: Cambrian; Cambridge

Cambod: Cambodia; Cambodian

Cambs: Cambridgeshire

CAMEO: Capitol Area Motion Pictures Education Organization (D.C.)

camera.: cooperating agency method for event reporting and analysis

CAMESA: Canadian Military Electronics Standards Agency

CAMI: Civil Aeromedical Institute; Coated Abrasive Manufacturers Institute

CAMMIS: Command Aircraft Maintenance Manpower Information System

camof: camouflage

camp.: cosmopolitan art—modern and personalized

Camp: Campeche (inhabitants —Campechanos

CAMP: Computer Applications of Military Problems; Continuous Air Monitoring Program

campan: campanological; campanologist; campanology

campos: (Portuguese or Spanish —plains

CAMPSA: Compañia Arrendataria del Monopolio de Petroleos

CAMPUS: Comprehensive Analytical Methods for Planning in University Systems

cams.: cybernetic anthropomorphous machines

CAMS: Coastal Antimissile System

CAMSI: Canadian Association of Medical Students and Interns

can.: canal; canalization; canalize; cancel; canceled; cancellation; cansiter; cannon; canon; canopy; canto; canvasback (duck)

Can: Canberra; Caen; Canada; Canadian; Cancer (constellation)

CAN: Canberra, Australia (radio observatory and tracking station); Compagnie Auxiliare de Navigation

CANABRIT: Canadian Navy Joint Staff in Great Britain

Ca Na F: Campaña Nacional Fronterizo (National Frontier Campaign)

CANAIRDEF: Canadian Air Force Defense Command

CANAIRDIV: Canadian Air Force Division

CANAIRHED: Canadian Air Force Headquarters

CANAIRLIFT: Canadian Air Force Transport

CANAIRLON: Canadian Air Force Joint Staff—London, England

CANAIRMAT: Canadian Air Force Material Command

CANAIRNEW: Canadian Air Force—Newfoundland

CANAIRNORWEST: Canadian Air Force—Northwest, Edmonton

CANAIRPEG: Canadian Air Force—Winnipeg

CANAIRTAC: Canadian Air Force Tactical Command

CANAIRTRAIN: Canadian Air Force Training Command

CANAIRVAN: Canadian Air Force—Vancouver

CANAIRWASH: Canadian Air Force Joint Staff—Washington, D.C.

canal: (Portuguese or Spanish—channel)

Canaletto: Antonio Canale

Canar Cur: Canaries Current

CANAS: Canadian Naval Air Station

CANAVAT: Canadian Naval Attaché

CANAVCHARGE: Canadian Naval Officer in Charge

CANAVHED: Canadian Naval Headquarters

CANAVSTORES: Canadian Naval Stores

CANAVUS: Canadian Naval Joint Staff in United States

Canb: Canberra

canc: cancel; canceled; cancellation; cancelling

CANCARAIRGRP: Canadian Carrier Air Group

cand: candelabra; candidate

CANDEP: Canadian Naval Depot

cand sc: candelabra screw

Candu: Canadian deuterium uranium

Candy: Candice

CANDY: Cigarette Advertising Normally Directed to Youth

CANEL: Connecticut Aircraft Nuclear Engine Laboratory (at Middletown)

cane sugar: saccharose or sucrose

CANF: Combined Allied Naval Forces

Can Fr: Canadian French

Can I: Canary Islands

canis: canister

CANLANT: Canadian Atlantic

Can Ltd: Canadair Limited (operating unit of General Dynamics Corporation)

cañon: (Spanish—canyon)

Can Pac: Canadian Pacific

cans.: canvasbacks (ducks)

CAN/SDI: Canadian Selective Dissemination of Information

can't: can not; cannot

cant.: canticum (Latin—canticle or hymn of praise)

Cant: Canterbury; Canton; Cantonese

Cantab.: Cantabrigiensis (Latin—of Cambridge)

CANTAT: Canadian Transatlantic Telephones

cant b: cantilever bridge

Cantinflas: Mario Moreno

cantran: cancel(led) in transmission

cants: cantaloupes

Canuck: Canadian

CANUKUS: Canada—United Kingdom—United States

CANUS: Canada—United States

CANUSE: Canadian-United States Eastern (electric power interconnection)

canv: canvas

Canyon de Chelly: Canyon de Chelly National Monument (cliff-dweller ruins in northern Arizona)

CAO: Central Accounting Office(r); Chief Accounting Office(r); Civil Affairs Office(r); Crimean Astrophysical Observatory (USSR); Cultural Affairs Office(r)

CAOC: Consumers' Association of Canada

CAORE: Canadian Army Operational Research Establishment

CAOSOP: Coordination of Atomic Operations—Standard Operating Procedures

cap.: capacity; capital letter; capsule; caput

'cap: handicap

cap: (French—cape)

Cap: capitol; captain; Charles A. Pearce

CAP: Certificat d'Aptitude Professionnelle (Certificate of Professional Aptitude); Civil Air Patrol; College of American Pathologists; Combat Air Patrol; Community Action Program

CAPA: California Association of Port Authorities

capac: cathodic protection

CAPAC: Composers, Authors, and Publishers Association of Canada

capal: computer-and-photographic-assisted learning

CAPC: Civil Aviation Planning Committee

capche: component automatic programmed checkout equipment

cap com: capsule communicator
CAPE: Classification and Placement Examination; Confederation of American Public Employees
Cape-Cairo: Cape Town-to-Cairo Highway; Cape Town-to-Cairo Railway
capertsim: computer-assisted program evaluation review technique simulation
CAPL: Controlled Assembly Parts List
cap. moll.: capsula mollis (Latin —soft capsule)
Cap^n: Capitán (Spanish—captain)
Cap'n: Captain
capo: [Italian—boss; cape (geog); chief; chief steward; foreman; overseer; ringleader; station master]—*capo*—boss or Cosa Nostra syndicate chief; cape (geog); *capobanda*—bandmaster; *capo cameriere*—chief steward; *capo fabbrica*—factory foreman or overseer; *caporione* —ringleader; *capo stazione*— station master)
CAPPA: Crusher and Portable Plant Association
CAPPS: Council for the Advancement of the Psychological Professions and Sciences
capri: computerized advance personnel requirements and inventory
Capric: Capricorn (constellation)
caps.: capital letters
CAPs: Community Action Programs
CAPS: Clearinghouse on Counselling and Personnel Services; Computer-Aided Pipe Sketching System; Creative Artists Public Service
caps and lower case: capital letters and lower case letters
caps and small caps: upper case capital letters and small capital letters
capsep: capsule separation
Capt: Captain
Capt.: Captain
Captn: old-style English abbreviation—Captain
Car: Carleton; Carlow; Caroline Islands
CAR: Canadian Association of Radiologists; Central African Republic; Chief Airship Rigger; Civil Air Regulation(s); Civil Air Reserve; Comité Agricole Régional (Regional Agricultural Committee); Contract Authorization Request; Corrective Action Request; US Army, Caribbean (area)

CARA: Chinese-American Restaurant Association
Caravaggio, Michelangelo da: Michelangelo Merisio
Caravaggio, Polidoro da: Polidoro Caldara
carb: carbon; carburetor; carburize
CARB: California Air Resources Board
carbecue: car + barbecue (device for melting waste out of junked automobiles)
carbo: carbohydrate
carbolic acid: phenol
carbon dioxide: carbonic acid gas
carbonera: (Spanish—coal mine)
Carbonif: Carboniferous
carbon monoxide: CO
carbontet: carbon tetrachloride
carbopol: carboxpolymethylene
carborundum: silicon carbide (SiC)
carb(s): carburetor(s)
Carcross: Caribou Crossing
card.: cardamom; cardinal
Card: Cardiganshire; Cardinal
CARD: Campaign Against Racial Discrimination; Civil Aeronautics Research and Development; Compact Automatic Retrieval Device (or Display)
CARDA: Continental Airbone Reconnaissance for Damage Assessment (USAF)
cardamap: cardiovascular data analysis by machine processing
CARDE: Canadian Armament Research and Development Establishment
cardiol: cardiology
cardiov: cardiovascular
CARDIV: Carrier Division (naval)
CARDS: Combat Aircraft Recording and Data System
Care: Caretaker
CARE: Cooperative for American Remittances to Everywhere
CARF: Central Altitude Reservation Facility
CARG: Corporate Accountability Research Group (Nader's)
cargotainer: cargo container
CARI: Civil Aeromedical Research Institute
Carib.: Caribbean
CARIBAIR: Caribbean Atlantic Airlines
CARIBCOM: Caribbean Command
Carib Cur: Caribbean Current
CARIBSEAFRON: Caribbean Sea Frontier
CARIC: Contractor All-Risk Incentive Contract (USAF)
CARIFTA: Caribbean Free Trade Association
CARL: Chatfield Applied Research

Laboratories
Carla: Carlotta; Caroline; Karla (as in Karla Marx; etc.)
Carleton Kendrake: Erle Stanley Gardner
Carm: Carmarthenshire
Carmen Silva: (pseudonym—Elisabeth Queen of Romania)
carmrand: civilian application of the results of military research and development
Carnegie Tech: Carnegie Institute of Technology
carnie(s): carnival(s); carnival workers
Caro: Carolina; Caroline
Carolinas: North and South Carolina
Carolines: Caroline Islands
Carolingian Century: the 700s —Charlemagne or Charles the Great reigns as King of the Franks and Emperor of the West as well as being chief patron of learning—the 8th century
carot: centralized automatic recording on trunks (Bell)
carp.: carpenter; carpentry; carpet (ing); computed air-release point; construction of aircraft and related procurement
Carp: Carpathian
CARP: computed air-release point
carp(s): stage carpenter(s)
carr: carrier
Carrie: Carolina; Caroline
cars.: community antenna relay service
CARS: Computer-Aided Routing System
CARTB: Canadian Association of Radio and Television Broadcasters
Carth: Carthage; Carthaginian; Carthusian
Carthaginian Century: the 3rd century before the Christian era when Hannibal crossed the Alps to defeat the Romans—the 200s
cartog: cartographer; cartographic; cartography
cas: calibrated airspeed; casual; casualty; close air support
ca's: combat actions
Cas: Caracas; Casimir; castle
CAs: Consumers Associations; Cooperative Associations
CAS: California Academy of Sciences; Cambrian Airways (symbol); Casualty Actuarial Society; Change Analysis Section; Chemical Abstracts Service; Chicago Academy of Sciences; Chief of Air Staff; Civil Affairs Section; Civil Air Surgeon; Clean(er) Air System; Collision Avoidance System

(aircraft); Commercial Air Service; Contract Administration Services; Courier Air Services; Customs Agency Service

C.A.S.: Certificate of Advanced Studies

CASA: Canadian Automatic Sprinkler Association

CASA: *Construcciones Aeronauticas, SA* (Spain)

Casanova: Giacomo Girolamo

CASB: Cost-Accounting Standards Board

CASC: Council for the Advancement of Small Colleges

cascan: casualty cancelled

cascor: casualty corrected

casdac: computer-aided ship design and construction

CASDO: Computer Applications Support and Development Office (USN)

casdos: computer-assisted detailing of ships

case.: common-access switching equipment; computer-automated support equipment

CASE: Committee on the Atlantic Salmon Emergency; Coordinated Aerospace Supplier Evaluation; Council for the Advancement of Secondary Education

CASEA: Center for the Advanced Study of Educational Administration

CASF: Composite Air Strike Forces

cash.: cashier

Cash: Cassius

CASH: Commission for Administrative Services in Hospitals

CASI: Canadian Aeronautics and Space Institute

casm: cycling air sampling monitor

CASMT: Central Association of Science and Mathematics Teachers

casoff: control and surveillance of friendly forces

CASP: Capability Support Plan; Cape Arago State Park (Oregon); Country Analysis and Strategy Paper (U.S. State Department)

Caspar: Cambridge analog simulator for predicting atomic reactions

Cas Reps: Casualty Reports

Cass: Cassius

CASS: Command Active Sonobuoy System

CASSA: Continental Army Command Automated System Support Agency (USA)

CASSI: Chemical Abstracts Service Source Index

CASSIS: Communication and Social Science Information Service (Canada)

CAST: Center for Application of Sciences and Technology

CAST: *Clearinghouse Announcements in Science and Technology*

CASTE: Collision-Avoidance System Technical Evaluation

CASTS: Canal Safe Transit System

CASW: Council for the Advancement of Science Writing

cat.: carburetor air temperature; catalog; catamaran; catapult; category; caterpillar tractor; clear air turbulence

Cat: Catalan; Catalonia; Catalonian; Caterpillar Tractor; Catherine

CAT: California Achievement Test; Child's Apperception Test; Civil Air Transport; Civilian Actress Technician; Clerical Aptitude Test; Colleges of Advanced Technology; College Ability Test; Commercial Airlift Contract; Control and Assessment Team; Corrective Action Team

catal: catalog; catalogue

Catal: Catalan; Catalonia; Cataluña

cataratas: (Spanish—cataracts; falls)

catawump: catawumpus (catamount; mountain lion)

CATC: Commonwealth Air Transport Council; Continental (Oil), Atlantic (Refining), Tidewater (Oil), and Cities (Service) (combined in mutual drilling)

CATCO: Catalytic Construction Company

cate: comprehensive automatic test equipment

CATE: Current ARDC (Air Research and Development Command) Technical Efforts (program)

catena: (Italian—mountain range)

CATF: Canadian Achievement Test in French

cath: cathedral; catheter

Cath: Catherine; Catholic; Cathedral

Cathay: China

CATHAY: Cathay Pacific Airways

Cathy: Catherine

CATIB: Civil Air Transport Industry Training Board

catk: counterattack

CATM: Canadian Achievement Test in Mathematics

CATRALA: Car and Truck Renting and Leasing Association

CATs: Civic Action Teams

CATS: Civil Affairs Training School (USN); Comprehensive

Analytical Test System; Compute Air-Trans Systems; Computer-Assisted Test Shop; Computer-Automated Test System (AT & T)

catsie: cat's-eye playing marble; polished agate resembling a cat's eye

catt: conveyorized automatic tube tester

cattalo: cattle + buffalo—hybrid

CATTCM: Canadian Achievement Test in Technical and Commercial Mathematics

Catty: Catherine

catv: cabin air temperature valve; cable television; community antenna television

Cau: Caucasian

CAU: Congress of American Unions

cauli: cauliflower

caus: causation; causative

CAUSA: Compañía Aeronautica Uruguay SA

CAUSE: Counselor Advisor University Summer Education

caust: caustic

caustic potash: potassium hydroxide (KOH)

caustic soda: sodium hydroxide (NaOH)

caut: caution

CAUT: Canadian Association of University Teachers

CAUTION: Citizens Against Unnecessary Tax Increases and Other Nonsense (St. Louis citizens)

cav: cavalier; cavalry; cavitation; cavity; continuous airworthiness visit

cavd: completion, arithmetic, vocabulary, directions (test)

caviol: caviology

ca virus: croup-associated virus

CAVN: Compañía Anonima Venezolana de Navegación (Venezuelan Steamship Line)

cavu: ceiling and visibility unlimited

caw: cam-action wheel; channel address word

CAW: Cables and Wireless (company)

CAWA: Canadian-American Women's Association

CAWC: Committee on Air and Water Conservation (American Petroleum Institute)

cawg: coaxial adapter waveguide

CAWM: College of African Wildlife Management

CAWU: Clerical and Administrative Workers' Union

cax: community automatic exchange (telephone)

Cay: Cayenne; Cayman

cayo: (Spanish—cay; key; shoal)

cb: cast brass; catch basin; cement base; center of buoyancy; chemical and biological; circuit breaker; common battery; continuous breakdown

c-b: circuit breaker

c & b: collating and binding

c of b: confirmation of balance

Cb: columbium (symbol); cumulonimbus

CB: Cape Breton (island); Caribair (airline); Caribbean-Atlantic Airlines; Carte Blanche; Cavalry Brigade; Census Bureau; Chief Boilermaker; Children's Bureau; citizen's band (radiofrequency band for short-range two-way communication); Companion of the Bath; compass bearing; confidential book; confidential bulletin; confinement to barracks; Construction Battalions (hence the nickname "seabees"); Consultants Bureau; Control Branch; Counter Battery; Cumulative Bulletin; Currency Bond; large cruiser (naval symbol); William Cullen Bryant

C.B.: *Chirurgiae Baccalaureus* (Latin—Bachelor of Surgery); Companion of the Bath

C-B: (Sir Henry) Campbell-Bannerman

C & B: Clemens and Brenninkmeyer; Cleveland and Buffalo (steamship line)—*Seeandbee*

cba: cost-benefit analysis

CBA: Canadian Booksellers Association; Caribbean Atlantic Airlines; Clydesdale Breeders Association; Community Broadcasters Association; Consumer Bankers Association

CBA: *Chemical-Biological Activities*

CBAA: Canadian Business Aircraft Association

CBAC: *Chemical-Biological Activities*

cbaf: cobalt-base alloy foil

CBAICP: Chemical and Biological Accident and Incident Control Plan (USA)

cbar: counterbore arbor

CBAT: Central Bureau of Astronomical Telegrams

CBB: Chesapeake Bay Bridge (Maryland)

CBBA: Christian Brothers Boys Association

CBBI: Cast Bronze Bearing Institute

CBBII: Council of the Brass and Bronze Ingot Industry

CBBT: Chesapeake Bay Bridge-Tunnel (Maryland to Virginia)

cbc: combined blood count

CBC: Canadian Broadcasting Corporation; Caribbean Broadcasting Company; Ceylon Broadcasting Corporation; Children's Book Council; Columbia Basin Council; Contraband Control; Corset and Brassiere Council; Cyprus Broadcasting Corporation; large tactical-command ship (naval symbol)

cbcc: common bias—common control

CBCII: California Bureau of Criminal Identification and Investigation

CBCMA: Carbonated Beverage Container Manufacturers Association

cbct: circuit board card tester

cbcu: counterbore cutter

cbd: cash before delivery; closed bladder drainage; common bile duct

CBD: Central Business District; Construction Battalion Detachment

CBDNA: College Band Directors National Association

cbe: cesium bombardment engine; chemical binding effect; circuit board extractor; compression bonding encapsulation

CBE: Cheese Bureau of England; Conference of Biological Editors; Council of Basic Education

C.B.E.: Companion of the Order of the British Empire

CBEL: *Cambridge Bibliography of English Literature*

cbf: cerebral blood flow

CBF: Children's Blood Foundation

CBG: Compagnie des Bauxites de Guinée

cbi: complete background investigation

CBI: Cape Breton Island; Carbonated Beverage Institute; Chesapeake Bay Institute; China-Burma-India (theater of war); Coffee Brewing Institute; Confederation of British Industry; Council of Burma Industries

CBI: *Cumulative Book Index*

CB & I: Chicago Bridge and Iron (company)

CBIS: Campus-Based Information System (NSF); Computer-Based Instruction(al) System

cbit (CBIT): contract bulk inclusive tour (travel plan)

cbj: common bulkhead joint

cbk: checkbook

cbl: cable

cb/l: commercial bill of lading

c bl: *carte blanche* (French—white card)—full power to act

CBL: Configuration Breakdown List; Chesapeake Biological Laboratories

cbm: chemical biological munitions; cubic meter(s)

CBMC: Corregidor-Bataan Memorial Commission

cbmu: current bit monitor unit

cbn: chemical, bacteriological, nuclear

CBN: Columbia Carbon Company (stock-exchange symbol)

CBNE: California Bureau of Narcotics Enforcement

CBNM: Custer Battlefield National Monument

Cbo: Colombo

CBO: Conference of Baltic Oceanographers

C-bomb: cobalt bomb

cbore: counterbore

cbp: ceramic beam pentode; constant boiling point

CBP: Centro de Biologia Piscatória (Piscatorial Biological Center—Lisbon)

CBPC: Canadian Book Publishers' Council

CBPO: Consolidated Base Personnel Office

CBQ: Civilian Bachelor Quarters

C B & Q: Chicago, Burlington & Quincy (railroad)

cbr: chemical, biological, radiological

Cbr: Calabar

CBR: Canberra, Australia (airport); Center for Brain Research (University of Rochester)

CBRA: Chemical, Biological, Radiological Agency

CBRE: Chemical, Biological, and Radiological Element

CBRL: Chemical, Biological, and Radiation Laboratories (Ottawa)

cbrn: chemical, biological, radiological, and nuclear

CBRS: Child Behavior Rating Scale

cbrw: chemical, biological, radiological warfare

cbs: chronic brain syndrome; concrete-block stucco

cBs: concerned Black students

CBS: Central Bureau of Statistics (Jerusalem); Columbia Broadcasting System; Currumbin Bird Sanctuary (Queensland)

CBSO: City of Birmingham Symphony Orchestra; City of Bournemouth Symphony Orchestra;

Czechoslovak Broadcasting Symphony Orchestra

cbt: cesium beam tube

CBT: Chicago Board of Trade; Connecticut Bank and Trust (company)

CB & TC: Connecticut Bank & Trust Company

cbts: cesium beam time standard

cbu: cluster bomb unit

CBU: Chicago Board of Underwriters

CBVHS: Clara Barton Vocational High School

cbw: chemical-biological warfare

cby: carboy

cc: camp chair; carbon copy (or copies); centuries; chapters; close control; closing coil; color code; cubic centimeter(s)

Cc: cirrocumulus

Cc.: *Confessores* (Latin—Confessors)

CC: Cabrillo College; Cabrini College; Caldwell College; Calvin College; Calvin Coolidge; Campbell College; Campbellsville College; Campion College; Canisius College; Canterbury College; Carleton College; Carlos Chavez; Carroll College; Carson City; Carthage College; Carver College; Cascade College; Casper College; Catawba College; Centenary College; Central College; Centralia College; Cerritos College; Chaffey College; Chain of Command; Champlain College; change(d) course; Chapman College; Charleston College; Charlotte College; Chatham College; Chicago College; Christian College; chronometer correction; Cincinnati Conservatory; City College; civil commotion; Claremont College; Clark College; Clarke College; Cleary College; Cleveland College; Clowan College; Coalinga College; Coe College; Coffeyville College; Coker College; Colby College; Columbia College; Columbian College; Columbus College; Command Center; Commander-in-Chief; command ship (2-letter symbol); compass course; compound cathartic; Concord College; Concordia College; Connecticut College; Control Center; Converse College; Cornell College; Cost Center; Cottey College; Cottley College; County Councilor; County Courthouse; Cumberland College; Curry College

CC: *corriente continua* (Spanish —direct current)

C & C: Command and Control

C de C (CDC): Canyon de Chelly

C of C: Chamber of Commerce; Circle of Companions; City of County

cca: carrier-controlled approach; cellular cellulose acetate (plastic)

CCA: California Central Airlines; Chief of Civil Affairs; Circuit Court of Appeals; Citizens for Clean Air; Citizens' Councils of America; Comics Code Authority; Committee for Conventional Armaments; Community Concerts Association; Conquest of Cancer Act; Conservative Clubs of America; Consumers Cooperative Association; Container Corporation of America; Continental Control Area; Corduroy Council of America; Cruising Club of America

CCAC: California College of Arts and Crafts

CCAF: Commander-in-Chief—Atlantic Fleet

CCAM: Colby College Art Museum

CCAP: Citizens Crusade Against Poverty

CCAQ: Consultative Committee on Administrative Questions (UN)

CCATS: Communications, Command, and Telemetry Systems

ccb: cubic capacity of bunkers

CCB: command-and-control boat (naval symbol); Configuration Control Board

CCBO: Cape Clear Bird Observatory (Ireland)

ccbv: central circulating blood volume

ccc: central computer complex

CCC: Canadian Chamber of Commerce; Central Control Commission; Chopin Cultural Center; Civilian Conservation Corps; Columbian Carbon Company; Commercial Credit Corporation; Commodity Credit Corporation; Corning Community College; Customs Cooperation Council; Cuyahoga Community College

CC & C: Command Control and Communications (USAF)

CCCA: Classic Car Clubs of America; Conservative Christian Churches of America

CCCB: Component Change Control Board (DoD)

CCCC: Cape Cod Community College

CCCCO: Chicago Coordinating

Council of Community Organizations

CCC Highway: Cleveland-Columbus-Cincinnati Highway

cccl: cathodal closure clonus

CC Co: Commercial Cables Company

CCCP: (Russian transliteration—USSR)—*Soyuz Sovetchikh Sotsialisticheckikh Respublik* (Union of Soviet Socialist Republics)

CCCPS: Chicago College of Chiropody and Pedic Surgery

ccd: charge-coupled device; computer-controlled display; countercurrent distribution

CCD: Center for Curriculum Development; Cost Center Determination

CCDC: Canadian Communicable Disease Center

CCDN: Central Council for District Nursing

CCE: Casa de la Cultura Ecuatoriana (House of Ecuadorian Culture)

CCEBS: Committee for the Collegiate Education of Black Students

CCED: County Council Electoral Division

CCET: Carnegie Commission on Educational Television

CCF: Canadian Commonwealth Federation; Citizens Council Forum; Combined Cadet Force; Common Cold Foundation; Cooperative Commonwealth Federation

CCFC: Citizens Committee for a Free Cuba

ccfe: commercial customer-furnished equipment

ccfm: cryogenic continuous-film memory

ccfr: constant current flux reset

CCG: Choral Conductors Guild; Control Commission of Germany

CCGE: California Council for Geographic Education

ccgt: closed-cycle gas turbine

cch: cubic capacity of holds

Cch: Christchurch, New Zealand

CCH: Chaminade College of Honolulu; Commercial Clearing House

C of CH: Chief of Chaplains

CCHE: California Coordinating Council for Higher Education; Central Council for Health Education; Coordinating Council for Higher Education

cc/hr: cubic centimeters per hour

CCHS: Christopher Columbus

High School

cci: chronic coronary insufficiency; circuit condition indicator; concentric coordinate incident; corrugated, cupped, or indented (cargo)

CCI: Chambre de Commerce Internationale (International Chamber of Commerce); Christians Concerned for Israel; Compactor Company, Incorporated

CCI: *Central Campesina Independiente* (Spanish—Independent Peasant Central)—political party in Mexico

CCIAP: Cooperative Committee on Interstate Air Pollution (New Jersey-New York)

CCIB: Cook County Inspection Bureau

ccig: cold cathode ion gage

CCIL: Commander's Critical Item List (USA)

ccip: continuously computed impact point (USAF)

CCIs: Citizens Committee of Investigation members (investigating assassination of President Kennedy)

CCIS: Command Control Information System

CCITT: Consultative Committee in International Telephone and Telegraph

CCIW: Canada Centre for Inland Waters

CCJC: Chicago City Junior College; Cook County Junior College; Custer County Junior College

CCK: Centre College of Kentucky

cckw: counterclockwise

CCL: Canadian Congress of Labour; Carribbean Cruise Lines

CCl₄: carbon tetrachloride

C-clamp: C-shaped clamp

cclkws: counterclockwise

CCLM: Coordinating Council of Literary Magazines

CCLs: Court of Claims

ccm: cubic centimeter(s); counter-countermeasure(s)

CCM: California College of Medicine

CCMA: Canadian Council of Management Association

ccmc: coincident-current magnetic core

CCMC: College-Conservatory of Music of Cincinnati

ccmd: continuous-current monitoring device

CCMD: Chicago Contract Management District

cc/min: cubic centimeters per minute

CCMR: Central Contract Management Region

CCMS: California College of Mortuary Science; Chicago Chamber Music Society; Committee on the Challenges of Modern Society (NATO)

ccn: communication control number

CCN: Command Control Number; Companhia Colonial de Navegação (Colonial Navigation Company); Contract Change Notice; Contract Change Notification

CCNM: Chaco Canyon National Monument

CCNP : Callao Cave National Park (Luzon, Philippines); Carlsbad Caverns National Park (New Mexico)

CCNS: Cape Cod National Seashore (Massachusetts)

CCNWR: Cross Creeks National Wildlife Refuge (Tennessee)

CCNY: Carnegie Corporation of New York; City College of the City University of New York

cco: current-controlled oscillator

Cco: Curaçao

CCO: Chicago College of Osteopathy; Clandestine Communist Organization; Comprehensive Certificate of Origin

CCOC: Command Control Operations Center (USA)

c conc: cast concrete

CCOS: Cabinet Committee on Opportunity for the Spanish Speaking

ccp: credit card purchase

CCP: Caribbean Conservation Program; Chinese Communist Party; Code of Civil Procedure; Consolidated Cryptologic Program

ccpa: cloud chamber photographic analysis

CCPE: Canadian Council of Professional Engineers

CCPF: Commander-in-Chief— Pacific Fleet

CCPG: Chemical Corps Proving Ground

cc-pill: compound-cathartic pill

CCPL: Corpus Christi Public Library

CCPO: Central Civilian Personnel Office

ccpr: coherent cloud physics radar

CCPR: Central Council of Physical Recreation

ccr: closed-cycle refrigerator; combat crew; command control receiver; complex chemical reaction; computer character recognition; consumable case rocket; control circuit resistance; credit

card reader; cross-channel rejection; crystal can relay; cube corner reflector

CCR: Central Commission for the Navigation of the Rhine; Commission on Civil Rights; Contract Change Request

CCRDC: Chemical Corps Research and Development Command

CCRE: Canadian Council for Research in Education

CCRF: City College Research Foundation

CCR & R: covenants, conditions, restrictions, and reservations

CCRT: Check Collectors Round Table

ccru: complete crew

CCRU: Common Cold Research Unit

ccs: collective call sign; command, control, support (military function)

cc & s: central computer and sequencer

CCS: Cape Cod System; Caracas, Venezuela (Maiquetia Airport); Casualty Clearing Station; Center for Chinese Studies (University of California); Chief Commissary Steward; Church of Christ, Scientist; Combined Chiefs of Staff; Customer Conversion Statistics

CCSB: Credit Card Service Bureau

CCSC: Central Connecticut State College; Central Coordinating Staff, Canada

cc/sec: cubic centimeters per second

ccsep: cement-coated single epoxy

CCSF: City College of San Francisco

CCSL: Communications and Control Systems Laboratory

CCSO: Corpus Christi Symphony Orchestra

CCSS: Charles Camille Saint-Säens; Cleveland-Cliffs Steamship (company)

CCSSO: Council of Chief State School Officers

CCST: Chelsea College of Science and Technology

cct: cathodal closing tetanus; chocolate-coated tablet; controlled cord traction

CCT: Clarkson College of Technology; Combat Control Team; Cumberland College of Tennessee

C & CT: Chemistry and Chemical Technology

CCTC: Chinese Cultural and Trade Center; Columbia County Teachers College

cctep: cement-coated triple epoxy

CC & TI: Community College and Technical Institute

cctks: cubic capacity of tanks

CCTP: Center City Transportation Program

CCTS: Canaveral Council of Technical Societies; Combat Crew Training School

cctv: closed-circuit television

CCTWg: Combat Crew Training Wing (USAF)

ccu: chart comparison unit

CCU: Calcutta, India (airport)

CCUL: California Credit Union League

CCUN: Collegiate Council for the United Nations

CCUS: Chamber of Commerce of the United States

ccv: closed-circuit voltage

ccw: counterclockwise

CCW: Caldwell College for Women

cc wr hdr: canvas-covered wire-rope handrail

ccws: counterclockwise

ccxd: computer-controlled X-ray diffractometer

cd: caesarean delivery; candela; canine distemper; cash discount; center door; certificate of deposit; civil defense; coin dimpler; cold drawn; communicable disease; confidential document; conjugate diameter (pelvic inlet); contagious disease; convulsive disorder; convulsive dose; cord; countdown; curative dose

c-d: countdown

c/d (C/D): carried down (bookkeeping); certificate of deposit

c & d: carpets and drapes; collection and delivery

cdso: median curative dose (abolishing symptoms in 50 percent of all test cases)

cd: cadde (Turkish—street)

Cd: cadmium; caudal

Cd^{115}: radioactive cadmium

Cd: ciudad (Spanish—city)

CD: Canadair turboprop airplane; Civil Defense; coastal defense radar (for surface-vessel detection); communicable disease; Community Development; confidential document; *Corps Diplomatique* (French—Diplomatic Corps); countdown

C.D.: Chancery Division

CD: *Centre Démocrate* (French —Democratic Center)

C $: cordoba (Nicaraguan monetary unit)

C & D: Chemist and Druggist; collection and delivery

C^{2}D^2 (ARDC): Command and

Control Development Division

cda: command and data acquisition

CDA: Canadian Dental Association; Canadian Dietetic Association; Catholic Daughters of America; Compañía Dominicana de Aviación (Dominican Aviation Company); Copper Development Association

CDAE: Civil Defense Adult Education

cdb: caliper disk brake; capacitance decode box; cast double base; central data bank; current data bit

CDB: Caribbean Development Bank; Combat Development Branch

cdba: clearance divers breathing apparatus

CDBA: California Dining and Beverage Association

cdc: calculated date of confinement; call direction code; career development course; command and data-handling console

CDC: Cadaver Disposal Center; California Debris Commission; California Democratic Council; Caribbean Defense Command (er); Center for Disease Control; Certificate of Disposition of Classified Documents; Cesspool Detergent Chemistry; Citizens' Defense Corps; Civil Defense Coordinator; Combat Development Command; Command Destruct Control; Commissioners of the District of Columbia; Communicable Disease Center; Configuration Data Control; Control Data Corporation; Control Distribution Center

cdcm: carbon-dioxide concentration module

CDCR: Center for Documentation and Communication Research; Control Drawing Change Request

CDCS: Civil Defense Countermeasures System; Construction Dollar Control System

cdd: central data display; chart distribution data; coded decimal digit; color data display; command-destruct decoder; computer-directed drawing; cosmic dust detector; cratering demolition device

CDD: Certificate of Disability for Discharge

cddi: computer-directed drawing instrument

CDDP: Canadian Department of Defense Production

cde: carbon dioxide economizer;

contamination-decontamination experiment

CDE: Cornell-Dubilier Electronics

CDEE: Chemical Defense Experimental Establishment

CDEG: Chicago District Electric Generating Corporation

CDEI: Control Data Education Institutes

cdek: computer data entry keyboard

CDEOS: Civil Defense Emergency Operations System

cdf: command decoder film; command decoder filter; confined detonating fuze; constant current fringes

CDF: Community Development Foundation; Congregation for the Doctrine of the Faith; Continental Diamond Fibre

CDFA: California Dried Fruit Association

CDFC: Commonwealth Development Finance Company

CDFGI: Charles Darwin Foundation for the Galapagos Islands

CD film: camouflage detection film

CDFRS: Charles Darwin Foundation Research Station (Academy Bay, Santa Cruz, Galapagos)

CDFSB: Canadian Dairy Foods Service Bureau

cd/ft^2: candela per square foot

CDG: Coder-Decoder Group (USA)

CDGA: California Date Growers Association

CD & GB TC: Chicago, Duluth and Georgian Bay Transit Company

cdh: constant differential height

cdi: course deviation indicator

Cd J: Ciudad Juárez (inhabitants —Juaristas)

cdl: common display logic

CDL: Central Dockyard Laboratory (UK); Citizens for Decent Literature

cd/m^2: candela per square meter

CDM: Consolidated Diamond Mines (South Africa)

cdma: code division multiple access

CDMB: Civil Defense Mobilization Board

CDN: *Chicago Daily News*

CDNRA: Coulee Dam National Recreation Area (Washington)

CDNS: Chicago Daily News Service

CDO: California Disaster Office

cdos: controlled date of separation

cdp: checkout data processor; communications data processor; contract definition phase

CDP: Centralized Data Processing; Certified Data Plan; Critical De-

cision Point
CDPC: California Delinquency Prevention Commission
cd pl: cadmium plate
cdr: command-destruct receiver; composite damage risk (audiometry)
Cdr: Commander
CDR: Countdown Deviation Request
CDRBTE: Canadian Defense Research Board Telecommunication Establishment
Cdre: Commodore
cdrill: center drill
Cdrngtn C: Codrington College
CDRS: Charles Darwin Research Station
cds: cards; cold-drawn steel; single cotton double silk (insulation)
cd's: certificates of deposit
CDS: climatological data sheet; commander destroyer squadron
CDSO: Commonwealth Defense Service Organization
CDSP: *Current Digest of the Soviet Press*
CDSs: Civil Disobedience Squads
CDSS: Compressed Data Storage System
CDST: Central Daylight Saving Time
cdt: command-destruct transmitter; conduct; conductor
CDT: Canadian Department of Transport; Central Daylight Time
Cdte: *Comandante* (Spanish—Commander)
cdts: constant-depth temperature sensor
cdu: cable distribution unit
CDU: Civil Disobedience Unit; coastal defense (radar) unit
CDU: *Christlich-Demokratische Union* (German—Christian Democratic Union)—political party
CDUEP: Civil Defense University Extension Program
cdv: cadaver; *carte de visite* (visiting card, sometimes with photograph)
cdw: chilled drinking water
CDW: Civil Defense Warning
CD & W: Colonial Development and Welfare
c dwr: chest of drawers; chilled drinking water return
cdwt: cordwelt
cdx: control differential transmitter
Cdz: Cádiz
ce: carbon equivalent; center of effort (naval architecture); center entrance; constant error
c-e: communications-electronics

c & e: commission and exchange
c.e.: *curvée extra* (French—special sort)—special quality
Ce: Ceará; cerium; Celyon
CE: Church of England; circular error; compass error; Corps of Engineers; Counselor of Embassy
C-E: communications electronics
C.E.: Civil Engineer
C$_E$: cost effectiveness
C of E: Church of England; Corps of Engineers
CE: *Chemical Engineering*
C.E.: Christian Era; Civil Engineer
cea: circular error average
CEA: Canadian Education Association; College English Association; Commodity Exchange Authority; Conservation Education Association; Council of Economic Advisers
CEA: *Commissariat a l'Energie Atomique* (French—Atomic Energy Commission)
CEAC: Committee for European Airspace Coordination
CEANAR: Commission on Education in Agriculture and National Resources
CEAPD: Central Air Procurement District
CEARC: Computer Education and Applied Research Center
CEAT: Canadian English Achievement Test
ceb: cryogenic expulsive bladder
CEB: Central Electricity Board; Continuing Education Books
CEB: *Comité Électrotechnique Belge* (Belgian Electrotechnical Committee)
cebar: chemical, biological, radiological warfare
Ceb-Vis: Cebu-Visayan
CEC: Central Economic Committee; Ceramic Educational Council; Civil Engineer Corps; Coal Experts Committee; Commodity Exchange Commission; Commonwealth Economic Committee; Commonwealth Edison Company; Communications and Electronics Command; Consolidated Edison Company; Consolidated Electrodynamics Corporation; Consulting Engineers Council; Continental Entry Chart(s); Council for Exceptional Children
Cece: Cecil
CECIL: Compact Electronic Components Inspection Laboratory
CECR: Central European Communication Region (USAF)
CECs: California Ecology Corps-

men
ced: communications-electronics doctrine
c-e-d: carbon-equivalent-difference
c & ed: clothing and equipment development
CED: Committee for Economic Development; Communauté Européenne de Defense (European Defense Community); Communications-Electronics Doctrine (USAF manuals)
CEDA: California Economic Development Agency
CEDA: *Confederación Española de Derechas Autonomas* (Spanish—Spanish Confederation of Autonomous Rights)—rightwing Catholic-fascist party
cedac: central differential analyzer control; cooling effect detection and control
CEDAL: *Centro de Estudios Democráticos de America Latina* (Latin American Center of Democratic Studies)
CEDAM: Conservation, Exploration, Diving, Archeology, Museums (organization)
CEDO: Centre for Educational Development Overseas (UK)
ced's: captured enemy documents
CEE: Communauté Économique Européenne (European Economic Community)
CEEA: Communauté Européenne de l'Énergie Atomique (European Atomic Energy Community)
CEEB: College Entrance Examination Board
CEECC: Consolidated-Edison Energy Control Center
cef: cellular-expansion factor; chicken-embryo fibroblasts
CEF: Canadian Expeditionary Force
ceff: controlled energy flow forming
CEGB: Central Electricity Generating Board
CEHHS: Charles Evans Hughes High School
CEHS: Civilian Employee Health Service
CEI: Cleveland Electric Illuminating Company; Commission Électrotechnique Internationale (International Electrotechnical Commission); Communications-Electronics Instruction
C & EI: Chicago & Eastern Illinois (railroad)
CEIF: Council of European Industrial Federations
cein: contract end-item number
CEIP: Carnegie Endowment for

International Peace; Communications-Electronics Implementation Plan

C-E-I-R: Corporation for Economic and Industrial Research

CEIS: Cost and Economic Information System

cej: cement-enamel junction

cel: celery; celestial; cellar; cellular

c-e-l: carbon-equivalent-liquid

Cel: Celeban; Celebes; Celsius

CEL: Constitutional Educational League; Cryogenics Engineering Laboratory

CELADE: *Centro Latinoamericano de Demografía* (Latin American Demographic Center)

celeb: celebrate; celebration; celebrity

celebs: celebrities

cell.: celluloid

CELL: Continuing Education Learning Laboratory

celli: cellos (violoncellos)

cello: violoncello

cellulose: $(C_6H_{10}O_5)$

celnav: celestial navigation

celt: classified entries in lateral transposition

Celt: Celtic

celtuce: celery-lettuce (lettuce-derived vegetable whose stalks taste like celery)

cem: cement; cement asbestos; cemetery; communication-electronics and meteorological

CEMA: Council for Economic Mutual Assistance; Council for the Encouragement of Music and the Arts; Conveyor Equipment Manufacturers Association

cem ab: cement asbestos board

CEMB: Communications-Electronic-Meteorological Board (USAF)

CEMCO: Continental Electronics Manufacturing Company

cemf: counter-electromotive force

cem fl: cement floor

c-e mix: chloroform-ether mixture

CEMO: Command Equipment Management Office

cem p: cement paint

cem plas: cement plaster

cen: center; central; centralization; centralize

Cen: Cenozoic

CEN: Central Airlines

CENCOMMURGN: Central Communications Region

C of Engrs: Chief of Engineers

CENEUR: Central Europe

CENM: Compañía Española de Navegación Marítima

cens: censor; censorship

cent.: centifugal; century

centen: centennial

centi: 10^{-2}

CENTO: Central Treaty Organization (Great Britain, Iran, Pakistan, Turkey)

central: (French—middle)

centrale: (Italian—middle)

centrex: central exchange

cént(s): céntimo(s), one-hundredth of a peseta

Century of Confusion: the 9th century when the Carolingian empire of Charlemagne disintegrated; European unity dismembered and divided—the 800s

Century of the Exodus: the 13th century before the Christian era when Moses lead the Israelites out of Egypt and across the Red Sea—the 1200s

Century of Saul and David: the 11th century before the Christian era when rule of King Saul was followed by that of King David—the 1000s

ceo: chick embryo origin

CEO: Chief Executive Officer

CEOAS: Corps of Engineers Office of Appalachian Studies (USA)

CEOs: Chief Executive Officers (conglomerate and multinational corporations)

cep: circle of equal probability; circle of error probability

CEP: Color Evaluation Program; Council on Economic Priorities

CEPA: Chicago Educational Publishers Association; Civil Engineering Program Applications; Consumers Education and Protective Association

CEPC: City of Erie Port Commission

CEPE: Central Experimental and Proving Establishment; Corporación Estatal Petrolera Ecuatoriana (Ecuadorian State Petroleum Corporation)

CEPO: Corps of Engineers—Portland, Oregon

CEPS: Commonwealth-Edison Public Service; Cornish Engines Preservation Society

cept(s): concept(s); precept(s)

CEQ: Council on Environmental Quality (appointed by the President of the United States)

cer: ceramic; conditioned emotional response

c & er: combustion and explosives research

CER: Community Educational Resources

CERA/ACCE: Canadian Educational Researchers Association/Association Canadienne des Chercheurs en Education

ceram: ceramic; ceramicist; ceramics

ceramal: ceramic + alloy

CERB: Coastal Engineering Research Board (USA)

cerc: centralized engine-room control

CERC: Coastal Engineering Research Center; Coastal Engineering Research Council

Cer.E.: Ceramic Engineer

CERI: Center for Educational Research and Innovation

CERL: Central Electricity Research Laboratories; Coastal Engineering Research Laboratory

cermet: ceramic - metallic (powders fused to form solid nuclear fuel elements)

CERN: Commission Européenne pour la Recherche Nucléaire (European Commission for Nuclear Research)

CERP: Current Economic Reporting Program

cerro(s): [Spanish—hill(s); mountain(s)]

cert: certificate; certify

certif: certificate(d)

cerv: cervical

ces: central excitatory state; compressor end seal; constant elasticity of substitution

Ces: (German—C-flat)

CEs: Council of Europe members

CES: Closed Ecological System; Commercial Earth Station; Comprehensive Export Schedule; Conference on European Security; Cost-Effectiveness Study; Crew Escape System

CES: *Certificat d'Études Superieures* (French—Advanced Studies Certificate)

CESA: Canadian Engineering Standards Association

CESAR: Capsule Escape and Survival Applied Research

CESAR: *Compagnie d'Études des Stations Air-Route* (French—Company for the Study of Airfields)

CESC: Calcutta Electric Supply Corporation

cesemi: computer evaluation of scanning electron microscopic image

cesi: closed-entry socket insulator

cesk: cable end-sealing kit

CESO-W: Council of Engineers and Scientists Organizations—West

CESP: Centrais Electricas de São Paulo

CESR: Canadian Electronic Sales Representatives

Cess: Cecil

CESS: Council of Engineering Society Secretaries

cet: capsule-elapsed time; controlled environmental test(ing); corrected effective temperature; cumulative elapsed time

CET: Certified Electronic Technician

CETA: Centre d'Études pour la Traduction (Center for the Study of Automatic Translation)

CETAG: Centre d'Études pour la Traduction, Grenoble

CETAP: Centre d'Études pour la Traduction, Paris

CETEC: Consolidated Engineering Technology Corporation

CETEX: Committee on Contamination of Extra-Terrestrial Exploration (NASA)

ceti: communications with extraterrestrial intelligence

CETIS: Centre de Traitement de l'Information Scientifique (Center for Processing Scientific Information)

CETS: Church of England Temperance Society

cev: cryogenic explosive valve

cevat: combined environmental, vibration, acceleration, temperature

cew: circular electric wire

cewrm: communications-electronics war-readiness materiel

cex: charge exchange; civil effects exercise

CEX: Corn Exchange Bank (stock-exchange symbol)

Cey: Ceylon; Singhalese

CEY: Century Electric (stock-exchange symbol)

Ceyl: Ceylon

Cey Rs: Ceylon rupees

cf: calf binding; carried forward; carrier frequency; carry forward; cement floor; center of flotation; center forward; central files; central filing; centrifugal force; communication factor; complement fixation; conception formulation; cost and freight; counterfire; counting fingers; cystic fibrosis

c/f: carried forward

c & f: cost and freight

c-to-f: center-to-face

cf.: *confer* (Latin—compare)

Cf: californium

Cf.: *Confessor* (Latin—Confessor)

CF: Cape Fear (railroad); Chaplain to the Forces; Chief of Finance; Coastal Frontier; Colorado Fuel & Iron (stock-exchange symbol); Conservation Foundation;

Corresponding Fellow

C/F: Contract Formulation

C de F: Collège de France (College of France)

C of F: Chief of Finance

cfa: cowl flap angle; crossed field amplifier

CFA: Chartered Financial Analyst; Colonies Française d'Afrique; Commission of Fine Arts; Community Facilities Administration; Council for Foreign Affairs

C & FA: Cookery and Foods Association

CF & A: Chief of Finance and Accunting (USA)

c factor: cleverness factor

cfae: contractor-furnished aerospace equipment

CFAE: Council for Financial Aid to Education

cfar: constant false alarm rate

CFAT: Carnegie Foundation for the Advancement of Teaching

CFB: Consumer Fraud Bureau

CFBS: Canadian Federation of Biological Societies

cfc: campus-free college; capillary filtration coefficient; colony-forming cells; complex facility console

CFC: Combined Federal Campaign (USA); Consolidated Freight Classification

CFCF: Central Flow Control Facility

cfd: cubic feet per day

CFDTS: Cold-Flow Development Test System (AEC)

cfe: contractor-furnished equipment

cff: critical flicker frequency

Cff: Cardiff

CFF: *Chemin de Fer Federaux* (Swiss Federal Railroad)

cffc: counterflow film cooling

CFG: Camp Fire Girls

cfgd: cubic feet of gas per day

cfgh: cubic feet of gas per hour

cfgm: cubic feet of gas per minute

cfh: cubic feet per hour

CFH: Council on Family Health

CFHQ: Canadian Forces Headquarters

cfi: cost, freight, and insurance

CFI: Canadian Film Institute

CF & I: Colorado Fuel and Iron

CFIA: Center for Independent Action

C-5A: heavy logistics transport airplane

cfl: context-free language

CFL: Carnegie Free Library; Chemins de Fer Luxembourgeois (Luxembourg State Railways)

cflg: counter flashing

cfm: confirm; confirmation;

confirmed; cubic feet per minute; cubic feet per month

CFMC: Consumer-Farmer Milk Cooperative

CFN: Compagnie France-Navigation

cfo: calling for orders; coast for orders

CFO: Complex Facility Operator

cfp: cold frontal passage; contractor-furnished property; cystic fibrosis of the pancreas

CFP: Colonies Française du Pacifique; Compagnie Française des Pétroles

CFPO: Compagnie Française des Phosphates de l'Océanie

cfr: chauffeur

CFR: Code of Federal Regulations; Contact Flight Rules; Coorong Fauna Reserve (South Australia); Council on Foreign Relations

CFRS: Central Fisheries Research Station

cfs: cubic feet per second

CFS: Chemins de Fer Fédéraux Suisses (Swiss Federal Railways)

CFSA: College Food Service Association

CFSR: Commission on Financial Structure and Regulation (White House)

CFSTI: Clearinghouse for Federal Scientific and Technical Information

cft: craft

CFT: Compagnie Française de Télévision

cftb: controlled-flight test bed

CFTH: Compagnie Française Thomson-Houston

cftmn: craftsman

cfts: captive firing test set(s)

cfu: colony-forming units

cfvd: constant-frequency variable dot

cg: center of gravity; centigram; choking gas (phosgene); chorionic gonadotrophin

CG: cargo glider aircraft (DoD symbol); Central of Georgia (railroad); Coast Guard; Commanding General; Connecticut General (Life Insurance Company); guided-missile cruiser (naval symbol)

C of G: Central of Georgia (railway); College of Guam (Agaña)

C G: *cassa grande* (Italian—bass drum)

C de G: *Croix de Guerre:* (French—War Cross)

cga: cargo (proportion of) general average

CGA: Canadian Gas Association; Coast Guard Academy; Coast Guard Auxiliary; Compressed Gas Association; Corcoran Gallery of Art

CGAS: Coast Guard Air Station; Cornell Guggenheim Aviation Safety Center

CGB: Canadian Geographic Board

cgc: ceramic gold coating; critical grid current

CGC: Coast Guard cutter

CGE: *Compagnie Générale d'Electricite* (General Electric Company)

CG&E: Cincinati Gas and Electric Company

CGEL&PB: Consolidated Gas, Electric Light and Power Company of Baltimore

C Gen: Consul General

cgf: chemotaxis-generating factor; coarse-glass frit

CGF: College of Great Falls

CGFA: Columbus Gallery of Fine Arts

cgfp: calcined gross fission product

CGFSA: Consolidated Gold Fields of South Africa

cgg: continuous grinding gage

CGH: São Paulo, Brazil (Congonhas Airport)

C of GH: Cape of Good Hope

CGHB: Cape of Good Hope Bank

CGHSB: Cape of Good Hope Savings Bank

cgi: corrugated galvanized iron; cruise guide indicator

CGI: City and Guilds of London Institute

C-girl: call girl (prostitute); hundred-dollar girl

cgk: grid cathode capacitance

cgl: center-of-gravity locator; continuous-gas laser; controlled ground landing; corrected geomagnetic latitude (CGL)

CGL: Canadian Gulf Line; Central Gulf Lines

CGLI: City and Guilds of London Institute

cg lkr: cleaning gear locker

cgm: centigram(s); ciliated groove to mouth

CGN: Cologne, Germany (airport); nuclear-powered guided-missile cruiser (naval symbol)

CGNM: Casa Grande National Monument

cgo: cargo

Cgo: Chicago

CGO: Committee on Government Operations

CGOU: Coast Guard Oceanographic Unit

cgp: grid plate capacitance

CGP: *Current Geographical Publications*

CGPM: Conference Générale des Poids et Mesures (General Conference of Weights and Measures)

CGPSq: Cartographic and Geodetic Processing Squadron (USAF)

cgr: captured gamma ray; crime on government reservation

CGRA: Canadian Good Roads Association; Chinese Government Radio Administration (Taiwan)

cgs: centimeter gram second

CGS: Canadian Geographical Society; Central Gulf Steamship (corporation); Chief of General Staff; Coast and Geodetic Survey

C & GS: Coast and Geodetic Survey

CGSB: Canadian Government Specifications Board

C & GSC: Command and General Staff College

cgse: centimeter-gram-second electrostatic

cgsfu: ceramic glazed structural facing units

cgsm: centimeter-gram-second-electromagnetic

CGSS: Cryogenic Gas Storage System

CGSSC: Columbia Gas Service Corporation

cgsub: ceramic glazed structural unit base

CGSUS: Council of Graduate Schools in the United States

cgt (CGT): corrected geomagnetic time

CGT: Compagnie Générale Transatlantique (French Line); Confederation Générale du Travail

CGTA: Companie Générale de Transports Aeriens (Air Algeria)

CGTB: Canadian Government Travel Bureau

CGTSF: *Compagnie Générale de Telegraphie San Fils* (French wireless company)

cgu: ceramic glazed units

CGUSCONARC: Commanding General United States Continental Army Command

CGUSFET: Commanding General United States Forces—European Theater

cgv: critical grid voltage

cgvs: ciliated groove to ventral sac

CGW: Chicago Great Western Railway

ch: case harden; chain; change; choke; church; coat hook

c & h: cocaine + heroin; cold and hot

ch.: *chori* (Latin—choruses)

Ch: Chile; Chilean; China; Chinese; choreographer; church

CH: Carnegie Hall; Chicago Helicopter (airways); compass heading; concentration of hydrogen ions in moles per liter (symbol); Switzerland (auto plaque)

C.H.: Companion of Honour

C-H: Cutler-Hammer

CH: *Confederatio Helvetico* (Latin–Swiss Confederation)

CH3COOH: acetic acid

cha: cable-harness analyzer

cha (CHA): cyclohexylamine

Cha: Charles

CHA: Catholic Hospital Association; Chattanooga, Tennessee (airport); Chicago Helicopter Airways; Community Health Association

CHABA: Committee on Hearing and Bio-Acoustics (US Army)

chabak: *chabakano* (Philippine Spanish dialect)

chacom: chain of command

chad: code to handle angular data

CHADS: Chicago Air Defense Sector

CHAFB: Chanute Air Force Base

chai: (Turkish—river)

Chair: Chairman

Chairman Mao: Mao Tse-Tung

chal: challenge

Chald: Chaldean

chalk: calcium carbonate ($CaCO_3$)

cham: chamfer; champion

chamb: chamber

Chamb: Chamberlain

chammy: (English slang—champagne)

champ: champion(ship)

Champ: Beauchamp

champion.: compatible hardware and milestone program for integrating organizational needs

Champion of States Rights: John C. Calhoun—U.S. Senator from South Carolina

CHAMPUS: Civilian Health and Medical Program of the Uniformed Services

chan: channel

Chanc: Chancellor; Chancery

CHANCE: Complete Help and Assistance Necessary for College Education

'change: exchange; produce exchange; stock exchange

CHAOS: Committee for Halting Acronymic Obliteration of Sense

CHAOTIC: Computer-and-Human-Assisted Organization of a Technical Information Center (NBS)

chap.: chapter
Chap: Chaplain
CHAP: Charring Ablation Program (NASA)
chaps.: *chaparajos* (Spanish —open backed leather overall pants worn by cowboys and charros when riding through thorny country)
CHAPS: Children Have A Potential Society; contractor-held Air Force property
char: characteristic
Char: Charter
Char Amal: Charlotte Amalie
Charbray: Charolais-Brahman cattle
charc: charcoal
Charger: Convair multipurpose short takeoff-and-landing airplane
Charl: Charlottenburg
Charles Atlas: Angelo Siciliano
Charles J. Kenney: Erle Stanley Gardner
Charley: Charles
Charlie: Charles; code for letter C
char reac: character reaction (sometimes simply cr)
chars: characters
chart.: *charta* (Latin—paper)
chartul.: *chartula* (Latin—small paper)
chas: chassis
Chas: Charles
chase.: cut holes and sink 'em (navalese acronym for sinking old ammunition cases or obsolescent barges or boats)
Chasn: Charlestown
chat mtg: chattel mortgage
Chauc: Geoffrey Chaucer
chauf: chauffeur
Chb: Cherbourg
Ch.B.: *Chirurgiae Baccalaureus* (Latin—Bachelor of Surgery)
ChBuAer: Chief of the Bureau of Aeronautics
ChBuDocks: Chief of the Bureau of Yards and Docks
ChBuMed: Chief of the Bureau of Medicine and Surgery
ChBuOrd: Chief of the Bureau of Ordnance
ChBuPers: Chief of the Bureau of Naval Personnel
ChBuSanda: Chief of the Bureau of Supplies and Accounts
ChBuShips: Chief of the Bureau of Ships
ChBuWeps: Chief of the Bureau of Weapons
chc: choke coil
CHC: Carnegie Hall Corporation; Chaplain Corps; Checker Motors Corporation (stock-

exchange symbol); Chestnut Hill College; Christchurch, New Zealand (airport); Confederate High Command
ch cab: china cabinet
Chch: Christchurch
CHCL₃: chloroform
CHCMD: Chicago Contract Management District
chd: chaldron
Ch D: Charles Darwin
CHD: Charles Halliwell Duell
Ch d'A: Chargé d'Affaires
chdm: cyclohexanedimethanol
Che: *Chetverg* (Russian—Thursday); Ernesto (Che) Guevara (from Argentina where *Che* is a popular nickname)
Ch. E.: Chemical Engineer
CHE: Chete Game Reserve; Chewore Game Reserve; Chizarira Game Reserve—(all in Rhodesia
C-head: coke head (underground slang—cocaine addict)
CHEAR: Council on Higher Education in the American Republics
chec: checked; checkered
CHEC: Citizens Helping Eliminate Crime
cheesewich: cheese sandwich
Cheka: *Chrezvychainaya Kommissiya po Borbe s Kontrrevolutisiei i Sabotazhem* (Russian—Extraordinary Commission for Combating Counterrevolution and Sabotage)—original Soviet Secret Police founded December 20, 1917 at Lubianka Prison in Moscow (*q.v.*—VOT)
chem: chemical; chemist; chemistry
Chem.E.: Chemical Engineer
chem etch: chemically etched; chemical etching
Chem & Met Eng: *Chemical and Metallurgical Engineering*
chem mill: chemically milled; chemical milling
CHEMTREC: Chemical Transportation Emergency Center
chem war.: chemical warfare
CHEN: *Chail Nashim* (Hebrew-Women's Force of the Israeli Army; *chen* is the Hebrew word for grace
CHEOPS: Chemical Operations System
Ches: Cheshire
chesky: cherry-flavored whiskey
Chet: Chester
Chev(y): Chevrolet
Chey: Cheyenne
chf: congestive heart failure; critical heat flux

Chf: Chief
ch-factor: chutzpah factor (degree of guts or nerve)
CHFC: Carnegie Hero Fund Commission
Chf Engr: Chief Engineer
Chf M Sgt: Chief Master Sergeant
chg: change; charge
Chg: Chittagong
chgd: charged
Chgo: Chicago
chg pl: change plane
chgs: charges
chi: specific magnetic susceptibility
Chi: Chicago
chic: cermet hybrid integrated circuit
Chic: Chicago
Chicano: (diminutive nickname for *Mexicano* used by some Mexican-Americans in Arizona, California, Nevada, New Mexico, and Texas—formerly Mexican territory)
Chick: Chickering
chick(s): chicken(s)
Chicom: Chinese communist
Chicos: Chinese communists
Chidic: Chinese dictionary
Chih: Chihuahua (inhabitants— Chihuahuenses; chihuahua dogs characteristic of this area— chihuahueños)
chil: children('s)
Chil Cur: Chilean Current
child.: computer having intelligent learning and development
Chil$: Chilean peso
Children's Poet: Henry Wadsworth Longfellow
chimponaut: chimpanzee astronaut (primate used in space travel experiments)
chimp(s): chimpanzee(s)
chin.: chinchilla
Chin: China; Chinese
Chinat: Chinese nationalist
Chi Nats: Chinese Nationalists
Chinese Century: the 200s—Chin dynasty rules a reunited China—the 3rd century
Chinese Gordon: British general Charles George Gordon who suppressed the Taiping rebels; later named Gordon Pasha for similar services in the Sudan where he lost his life during the storming of Khartoum by the Mahdi
chinese white: zinc oxide (ZnO)
Chino-Jap: Chino-Japanese
Chinsyn: Chinese-English synthesis-oriented machine translation system
CHIPDis: Chicago Procurement District (US Army)

Chipitt: Chicago-to-Pittsburgh (complex of cities)

Chips: ship's carpenter

CHIPS: Chemical Engineering Information Processing System

chir: chiropody

chiro: chirography; chiropractic; chiropractor

CHIRP: Community Housing Improvement and Revitalization Program

Chis: Chiapas (inhabitants— Chiapanecos)

Chisox: Chicago White Sox (baseball team)

chit: chitty (Hindustani—voucher signed to cover small debts for drinks, food, tobacco, etc.)

Chi-Trib: Chicago Tribune

chix: chickens

Ch J: Chief Justice

CHJM: Carnegie Hall—Jeunesses Musicales

CHJMKHK: Chung-Hua Jen-Min Kung-Ho Kuo (People's Republic of China—communist mainland China whose capital is Peking)

chk: check

chkr: checker

chl: chloroform; confinement at hard labor

CHL: Central Hockey League

Ch Lbr: Chief Librarian

ch-lkr: chiffonier-locker

chlor: chloride; chlorination; chlorine

chloride of lime: bleaching powder

chloro: chloroform; chlorophyll; chloroprene

chloroform: trichlormethane (CHC_3)

chloroprene: synthetic rubber (C_4H_5Cl)

chm: chamber

CHM: Cleveland Health Museum

ch-mir: chiffonier-mirror

CHMK: Chung-Hua Min-Kuo (Republic of China—offshore nationalist China whose capital is Taipei on the island of Formosa or Taiwan)

chmn: chairman

ChMNH: Chicago Museum of Natural History

CHN: College of the Holy Name

C-H-N: carbon-hydrogen-nitrogen

CHNOPS: carbon, hydrogen, nitrogen, oxygen, phosphorus, sulfur (compounds)

chns: chains

CHNSRA: Cape Hatteras National Seashore Recreational Area

Cho: Chosen (Korea)

CHO: carbohydrate (generalized formula)

choc: chocolate

choco: chocolate

chocs: chocolate candies; chocolate drops; chocolates

CHOKE: Care How Others Keep the Environment

chol: cholesterol

CHOP: Change of Operational Control

chor: choral; choreographer; choreographist; choreography; chorus; choruses

Chord: Chordata

C Horn Cur: Cape Horn Current

chortle: chuckle and snort

Chou: Chou (pronounced *Joe*) En-lai

Chou Century: the 18th century before the Christian era when the Chou dynasty began ruling China for the next five centuries— the 700s

chovr: changeover

chow: (Chinese—small town)

Chp: Chepstow

CHP: California Highway Patrol; Chihuahua Pacific (railroad— Ferrocarril de Chihuahua al Pacífico)

chpae: critical human performance and evaluation

CHPP: Cypress Hills Provincial Park (Saskatchewan)

chpx: chickenpox

chq: cheque

CHq: Corps Headquarters

chr: chronic

c hr: candle-hour

CHR: Connecticut Hard Rubber (company)

chrg: charge

Chris: Christian(a); Christopher

CHRIS: Cancer Hazards Ranking and Information System

Christ.: Christian; Christianity; Christmas

Christian Century: the 400s— Christianity affirmed as the official faith by two Roman emperors—the 5th century

Christn: Charleston

chromo(s): chromolithograph(s); chromosome(s)

chron: chronogram; chronograph; chronology; chronometer; chronometry

Chrys: Chrysler

chs: chapters; crime on the high seas

Chs: Chester

CHS: Canadian Hydrographic Service; Charleston, South Carolina (airport); Chicago Historical Society; Childrens Home Society;

Community Health Service (HEW); Cristobal High School; Curtis High School

CHSM: China Service Medal

cht: cylinder head temperature

chtg: charting

CHTNP: Chittagong Hill Tracts National Park (Bangladesh)

Chu: Centigrade heat unit

CHU: Christelijk-Historische Unie (Dutch-Christian Historical Union)—political party

Chubu Nippon Shimbun: (Japanese—Central Japan Newspaper)

Chuck: Charles

Chuey: (Spanish-American nickname—Jesus)

Chung: Chungking

Chunnel: Channel Tunnel (under the English Channel where it will link England and France)

Churchill: Sir Winston Churchill —First Lord of the Admiralty during World War I and just before World War II when he became Great Britain's Prime Minister

'chute: parachute

ch v: check valve

chw: chilled water; cold-and-hot water; constant hot water

CHW: Charleston, West Virginia (airport)

chx: chiro-xylographic

chy: chimney

ci: cast iron; chemotherapeutic index; coefficient of intelligence; color index; compression ignition; contamination index; cost and insurance; counterintelligence

c.i. (C.I.): consular invoice

c/i (C/I): certificate of insurance

c & i: cost and insurance; cowboys and indians

Ci: cirrus; curie (unit of activity in radiation dosimetry)

Ci: cerveau isolé (French—isolated intellect; intellectual)

CI: Carnegie Institute; Channel Islands; Color Index; Combustion Institute; Communist International; Cranberry Institute; Curtis Institute

C & I: Currier and Ives

cia: computer interface adaptor

Cia: Compagnia (Italian—Company); *Companhia* (Portuguese—Company); *Compañía* (Spanish—Company)

Ciac Compañía (Spanish—company)

CIA: Caribbean International Airways; Central Intelligence

Agency; Commerce and Industry Association Institute Conseil International des Archives (International Archival Council); Cotton Insurance Association; Culinary Institute of America

CIAA: Coordinator Inter-American Affairs

CIAC: Career Information and Counseling (USAF)

CIANY: Commerce and Industry Association of New York

CIAO: Congress of Italian-American Organizations

CIAPS: Customer-Integrated Automated Procurement System

CIAS: California Institute of Asian Studies

CIAW: Commission on Intercollegiate Athletics for Women

cib.: cibus (Latin—food)

CIB: Central Intelligence Board; Criminal Intelligence Bureau; Criminal Investigation Bureau

CIB: COBOL Information Bulletin (USAF)

CIBC: Canadian Imperial Bank of Commerce

CIBG: Canadian Infantry Brigade Group

cic: cardio-inhibitor center; cloud in cell

CIC: Cedar Rapids & Iowa City (railroad); Center for Instructional Communications (Syracuse University); Central Inspection Commission; Chemical Institute of Canada; Combat Information Center; Combat Intelligence Center; Combined Intelligence Committee; Comité International de la Conserve (International Canning Committee); Commander-in-Chief; Command Information Center; Committee on Institutional Cooperation; Conseil International des Compositeurs (International Council of Composers); Continental Insurance Companies; Counter-Intelligence Corps; Critical Issues Council; Curaçao Information Center; Customer Identification Code

CICA: Canadian Institute of Chartered Accountants; Council of International Civil Aviation

CICAR: Cooperative Investigations of the Caribbean and Adjacent Regions (UNESCO)

CICP: Committee to Investigate Copyright Problems

CIC's: Change Information Control (numbers)

CICU: Commission for Independent Colleges and Universities

CID: Center for Industrial Development; Central Institute for the Deaf; Centre d'Information et de Documentation (Center for Information and Documentation —Belgium); Change in Design; Commission for International Development; Council for Independent Distribution; Criminal Investigation Department (Scotland Yard); Criminal Investigation Division

CIDA: Canadian International Development Agency

CIDC: Cryogenic Information and Data Section

CIDG: Civil Indigenous Defense Group (Vietnam)

cidi: crimping die

cidnp: chemically induced dynamic nuclear polarization

CIDOC: Centro Intercultural de Documentación (Intercultural Documentation Center)

CIDS: Chemical Information and Data System

cidstat: civil disturbance status (USA reporting activity)

cie: coherent infrared energy

Cie: Compagnie (French—company)

CIE: Chrysler Institute of Engineering; Commission International de l'Eclairage (International Lighting Commission); Coras Iompair Eireann (Irish Transport

C.I.E.: Companion of the Order of the Indian Empire

CIEE: Companion of the Institution of Electrical Engineers

Cie Gle Transatlantique: Compagnie Générale Transatlantique (French Line)

CIEM: Conseil International pour l'Exploration de la Mer (International Commission for the Exploration of the Sea)

CIEN: Comision Interamericana de Ehergia Nuclear (Inter-American Commission for Nuclear Energy)

ciénaga: (Spanish—swamp; marsh)

CIENT: Cambridge and Isle of Ely Naturalist Trust (England)

CIEP: Council on International Economic Policy

CIETA: Centre International d'Étude des Textiles Anciens (International Center for the Study of Antique Textiles)

cif: cost, insurance, and freight

CIF: California Interscholastic Federation; Construction Industry Foundation

CIFC: Council for the Investigation

of Fertility Control

cifci (CIF and C & I): cost, insurance, freight (plus) commission and interest

CIFF: Cannes International Film Festival

cig: cigarette

CIG: Comité International de Géophysique

CIGS: Chief of the Imperial General Staff (Great Britain)

CIGTF: Central Inertial Guidance Test Facility

CII: Chartered Insurance Institute; Coffee Information Institute

CIIB: Consumers Insurance Information Bureau

CIIC: Counter Intelligence Interrogation Center

CIIR: Central Institute for Industrial Research

CIIIA: Soedinennye Shtaty Ameriki (Russian—United States of America)—U.S.A.

cil: current-inhibit logic

CIL: Canadian Industries Limited

C/I/L: Computer/Information/Library Sciences

CILA: Centro Interamericano de Libros Académicos

cim: capital investment model; communication-interface module(s); computer-input microfilm(ing); conductance-increase mechanism; continuous-image microfilm(ing)

CIM: Cleveland Institute of Music; Curtis Institute of Music

C & IM: Chicago & Illinois Midland (railroad)

Cimabue: Cenni di Pepo

CIMBA: Contractor Installation Make-or-Buy Authorization

CIMC: Commander's Internal Management Conference

cimco: card image correction

CIMCO: Congo International Management Corporation

CIME: Council of Industry for Management Education

cimm: constant-impedance mechanical modulation

CIMM: Canadian Institute of Mining and Metallurgy

CIMMS: Civilian Information Manpower Management System (USN)

CIMR: Commander's Internal Management Review

cimu: compatability-integration mockup

Cin: Cincinnati

CIN: Cooperative Information Network (linking libraries by twx)

CIN: Chemical Industry Notes

Cinc: Cincinnati

C-in-C: Commander-in-Chief
CINC: Commander-in-Chief
CINCAFLANT: Commander-in-Chief, Air Force Atlantic Command
CINCAFMED: Commander-in-Chief, Allied Forces Mediterranean
CINCAFSTRIKE: Commander-in-Chief, Air Force Strike Command
CINCAL: Commander-in-Chief, Alaskan Command
CINC ATL FLT: Commander-in-Chief Atlantic Fleet
CINCENT: Commander-in-Chief, Central Europe
Cinci: Cincinnati
CINCLANT: Commander-in-Chief, Atlantic
CINCMEAFSA: Commander-in-Chief, Middle East, Southeast Asia, Africa South of the Sahara
CINCNORAD: Commander-in-Chief, North American Defense Command
CINCNORTH: Commander-in-Chief, Northern Europe
CINCONAD: Commander-in-Chief, Continental Air Defense Command
CINCPAC: Commander-in-Chief, Pacific
CINCPACFLT: Commander-in-Chief Pacific Fleet
CINCSOUTH: Commander-in-Chief, Southern Europe
CINCSTRIKE: Commander-in-Chief, United States Strike Command
CINCUNC: Commander-in-Chief, United Nations Command
CINCUSAFE: Commander-in-Chief, United States Air Forces in Europe
CINCUSAFLANT: Commander in Chief—United States Air Force Atlantic
CINCUSAFSTRIKE: Commander in Chief—United States Air Force Strike
Cincy: Cincinnati
Cindy: Cinderella; Cynthia
cine: cinema; cinematography
cinemactor: cinema actor
cinemactress: cinema actress
CINFAC: Counterinsurgency Information Analysis Center
CINFO: Chief of Information
CINM: Channel Islands National Monument (Southern California)
cinn: cinnabar
Cinn: Cincinnati
cinna: cinnamon
cinnabar: mercuric sufide (HgS)
Cinn Sym Orch: Cincinnati Symphony Orchestra
CINPDis: Cincinnati Procurement District (US Army)
CINS: CENTO Institute of Nuclear Science
CINTA: Compañía Nacional del Turismo (Chilean Airline)
Cinty: Cincinnati
CIO: Commission Internationale d'Optique (International Optical Commission); Congress of Industrial Organizations
CIOMS: Council for the International Organization of Medical Sciences
cip: cast-iron pipe; cipher (zip is derived from this and is a slang shortcut for a cipher or zero—zero)
CIP: Canadian International Paper; Civilian Institution Program; Composite Interface Program; Consolidated Intelligence Program; Cost Improvement Proposal
CIPA: Chartered Institute of Patent Agents; Committee for Independent Political Action
CIPAC: Collaborative International Pesticides Analytical Council (UK)
ciph: cipher
CIPHER: Calculations of Patient and Hospital Education Resources
ciphony: enciphered telephony
CIPL: Canada India Pakistan Line
CIPO: Conseil International pour la Préservation des Oiseaux (International Council for the Preservation of Birds)
CIPRA: Cast-Iron Pipe Research Association
CIPS: Canadian Information Processing Society
cir: circle; circuit; circular
cir.: circa (Latin—about)
cIR: crime on Indian Reservation
Cir: Circle
CIR: Commission on Intergovernmental Relations; Commissioner of Internal Revenue; Cost Information Report; Court of Industrial Relations; Current Industrial Reports
CIRADS: Counter-Insurgency Research and Development System
cir ant.: circular antenna
cir bkr: circuit breaker
circ: circular; circulate; circumference; circumstance
circal: circuit analysis
circle: ancient symbol of annual, eternal, or female principle; Earth symbol if divided into four sectors by an erect cross or if bisected by a horizontal line; Full Moon (sometimes circle contains a cartoon face); Full Moon denoted by solid circle; rain represented by circle with vertical lines; solar corona if circle is divided by a vertical line; Sun if containing a central dot or if periphery contains radiating lines
circltr: circular letter
circum: circumference
Circumv Stz: Circumvesuviana Stazione (Neapolitan railroad station serving Herculaneum, Mt Vesuvius, and Pompeii)
CIRF: Corn Industries Research Foundation
CIRIA: Construction Industry Research and Information Association
CIRIS: Completely Integrated Range-Instrumentation System (NASA)
CIRJP: Commission on International Rules of Judicial Procedure
CIRM: Centro Internazionale Radio-Medico
CIRO: Consolidated Industrial Relations Office
cis: cataloging in source; central inhibitory state
cis (CIS): cataloging in source
ci's: conflict indictors
Cis: (German—C-sharp)
CIS: Catholic Information Society; Center for International Studies (MIT); Central Instructor School; Chartered Institute of Secretaries; Cost Inspection Service; Cranbrook Institute of Science
CISA: Canadian Industrial Safety Association; Council for Independent School Aid
CISAC: Confédération Internationale des Auteurs et Compositeurs (International Federation of Authors and Composers)
Cisco: San Francisco
CISIR: Ceylon Institute of Scientific and Industrial Research
cislun: cislunar; cislunarian; cislunarite
CISR: Center for International Systems Research
Cis(sy): Cecilia
Cist: Cistercian
cit: citation; cited; citizen(ship); citrate
CIT: Calcutta Improvement Trust; California Institute of Technology (Cal Tech); Carnegie Institute of Technology; Case Institute of Technology

cit a: citric acid

CITC: Canadian Institute of Timber Construction

cite.: compression ignition and turbine engine

CITE: Consolidated Index of Translations into English

Citizen Louis Capet: Louis XVI (so named by Thomas Paine before the fall of the Bastille and the king's execution under the guillotine despite Paine's objection as he wished to abolish the office and not the man)

CITL: Canadian Industrial Traffic League

cito disp.: cito dispensetur (Latin —dispense rapidly)

CITP: Civilian Industrial Technology Program

citric acid: $C_6H_8O_7$

citricult: citriculture

città: (Italian—city; town)

CIU: Coopers' International Union

ciudad: (Spanish—city)

CIUS: Conseil International des Unions Scientifiques (International Council of Scientific Unions)

civ: civil; civilian; civilization; civilize

CIV: Commission Internationale du Verre (International Glass Commission)

CivAir NM: Civil Aircraft National Marking(s)

CIW: Carnegie Institute of Washington; Chicago & Illinois Western (railroad)

cj: clip joint; conjectural; construction joint

CJ: Chief Justice

C of J: Court of Justice

CJA: Carpenters and Joiners of America

CJB: Constructors John Brown (British shipbuilders)

CJC: Colby Junior College

CJC: Corpus Juris Canonici (Latin —Code of Canon Law)

CJCA: California Junior College Association

CJCiv: Corpus Juris Civilis (Latin —Code of Civil Law)

CJF: Carlos J. Finley

CJI: Concrete Joint Institute

CJR: Cecil John Rhodes

CJR: Columbia Journalism Review

CJRL: Criminal Justice Reference Library (Austin)

cjs: cotton, jute, or sisal (cargo)

CJS: Canadian Joint Staff; College of Jewish Studies

CJS: Corpus Juris Secundum

CJTF: Commander Joint Task Force

ck: cask; certified kosher; check; coke; cork

ck: *ceekay* (Spanish-American slang —cocaine)

Ck: chalk

CK: cyanogen chloride (poison gas)

C K: Cape Kennedy

ckb: cork base

ckbd: cork board

CKCL: Chicago-Kent College of Law

ckd: completely knocked down

ckf: cork floor

ckfm: checking form

ckga: checking gage

CKIC: Chemical Kinetics Information Center (NBS)

CKMTA: Cape Kennedy Missile Test Area

ck os: countersink other side

ckpt: cockpit

cks: casks; checks

ckt: circuit

CKT: Chung-Kuo Kung-ch'an Tang (Chinese Communist Party)

ckt bd: circuit bozrd

ckt bkr: circuit breaker

ckt cl: circuit closing

ck tp: check templzte

ck ts: countersink this side

ck vlv: check valve

ckw: clockwise

cl: carload; center line; centiliter; class; clearance; climb; close; closure

cl.: classis (Latin—class or collection)

Cl: chlorine; chlorine gas

Cl.: Clericus (Latin—cleric or clergyman)

c/l (C/L): carload lot; cash letter

CL: Capital Airlines; Cooperative League; Critical List; Light cruiser (2-letter naval symbol)

C-L: Canadair Limited (Division of General Dynamics)

C/L: craft loss (insurance)

cla: center line average; communication link analyzer

CLA: Canadian Library Association; Canadian Lumbermen's Association; Catholic Library Association; College Language Association; Connecticut Library Association; Conservative Library Association

CLAA: anti-aircraft light cruiser (4-letter naval symbol)

Clack: Clackmannan(shire)

cl ad: collet adapter

CLAH: Conference of Latin American History

clam (CLAM): chemical low-altitude missile

clamato: clam-and-tomato juice

CLAO: Contact Lens Association of Ophthalmologists

clar: clarification; clarify; clarinet

Clar: Clarence

Clare: Clara; Clarita

Clarin: (pseudonym—Leopoldo Alas y Urena)

clark: combat launch and recovery kit

CLARNICO: Clark, Nichols, and Coombes (confectioners)

clas: classify

c-l-a-s: crowd-lift-actuate-swing (tractor backhoe control)

CLASB: Citizens League Against the Sonic Boom

clasn: classification

clasp. (CLASP): computer liftoff and staging program

CLASP: Client's Lifetime Advisory Service Program; Computer Language for Aeronautics and Space Programming; Computer Launch and Separation Problem

class.: classification

CLASS: Class Action Study and Survey; Close Air-Support System; Closed-Loop Accounting for Store Sales; Computer-based Laboratory for Automated School Systems; Current Literature Alerting Search Service

class A's: class-A narcotics (addictive drugs such as opium and its derivatives)

class B's: class-B narcotics (almost non-addictive drugs such as codeine and nalline)

class M's: class-M narcotics (non-addictive drugs)

class X's: class-X narcotics (drugs containing small amounts of narcotics such as cough syrups with non-narcotic and almost non-addictive codeine)

CLAT: Confederation of Latin American Teachers

clav: clavecin; clavichord; clavicle

claw.: clustered atomic warhead

clayie: playing marble made of clay and often coated with enamel paint

Clb: Caleb

c & lc: capital and lower case letters

CLC: Canadian Labour Congress; Canners League of California; Chiriqui Land Company; Cost of Living Council; task-fleet command cruiser (naval symbol)

CLCB: City of Liverpool College of Building; Committee of London Clearing Banks

CLCMD: Cleveland Contract Management District

CL & Co: Cammell Laird and Company (shipbuilders)

clcr: controlled letter contract reduction

CLCT: City of Liverpool College of Technology

cld: cancelled; cleared; colored; cooled; cost laid down

CLD: Central Library and Documentation

CLDAS: Clinical Laboratory Data Acquisition System

cldwn: cooldown

CLE: Cleveland, Ohio (Hopkins Airport)

Clea: Cleopatra

CLEAN: Committee for Leaving the Environment of America Natural

CLEAR: Center for Lake Erie Area Research; Civic Leaders for Ecological Action and Responsibility; Closed-Loop Evaluation and Reporting (system)

clec: closed-loop ecological cycle

Clem: Clemens; Clement; Clementina; Clementine

Clemte: Clemente

cleo: clear language for expressing orders

Cleo: Cleopatra

CLEP: College-Level Education Program; College-Level Examination Program

CLETS: California Law Enforcement Telecommunication System

Cleve: Cleveland

Cleve Orch: Cleveland Orchestra

CLEVPDis: Cleveland Procurement District (US Army)

CLEW: Chicago Law Enforcement Week

clf: capacitive loss factor

CLF: Church of the Larger Fellowship (Unitarian Universalist)

clg: calling; ceiling; clearing

CLG: light guided-missile cruiser (3-letter symbol)

CLGA: Composers and Lyricists Guild of America

clgsfu: clear glazed structural facing units

clgsub: clear glazed structural unit base

CLGW: Cement, Lime and Gypsum Workers (union)

CLHU: Computation Laboratory of Harvard University

cli: coin-level indicator; cost-of-living index

CLI: Cost-of-Living Index

CLIA: Clinical Laboratory Improvement Act

Cliff: Clifford; Clifton

clim: climatic

climat: climatological; climatologist; climatology

clin: clinic; clinical; clinicial; clinometer

clin path: clinical pathology

clin proc: clinical procedures

Clint: Clinton

clip.: compiler language for information processing

CLIP: Cancel Launch in Progress (USAF); Country Logistics Improvement Program (USAF)

clit: clitoral; clitoridectomy; clitoris

clj: control joint

CLJC: Copiah-Lincoln Junior College

clk: clerk; clock

CLK: hunter-killer cruiser (naval symbol)

clkg: caulking

clkws: clockwise

cll: cholesterol lowering lipid; circuit load logic load logic

CLL: Chief of Legislative Liaison

cllo: *cuartillo* (Spanish—fourth of a real; pint)

c-lm: common-law marriage

CLMA: Cigarette Lighter Manufacturers Association; Contact Lens Manufacturers Association

CLML: *Current List of Medical Literature*

CLMS: Clinical Laboratory Monitoring System

cln: colon

Cln: Colón

clnc: clearance

CLNP: Crater Lake National Park (Oregon)

clnr: cleaner

CLNS: Cape Lookout National Seashore (North Carolina)

clnt: coolant

CLNWR: Crescent Lake National Wildlife Refuge (Nebraska)

clo: closet; cloth; clothing; cod liver oil

Clo: Callao

CLO: Cali, Colombia (Calipuerto Airport); Cornell Laboratory of Ornithology

clora: closed-form ray analysis

clos: closure

clousy: cloudy—lousy (weather)

clp: criminal law and procedure

CLP: Carnegie Library of Pittsburgh

cl pal: cleft pallet

clpr: caliper

clr: clear; clearing; cooler

CLR: Central London Railway; Council on Library Research; Council on Library Resources

clrm: classroom

CLRU: Cambridge Language Research Unit

CLSA: Conservation Law Society of America

CLSC: Chautauqua Literary and Scientific Circle

clsd: closed

clsg: closing

CLSP: Cape Lookout State Park (Oregon)

clsr: closure

clt: communications line terminals

CLT: Charlotte, North Carolina (airport)

CLTA: Chinese Language Teachers Association

cltgl: climatological

cltgr: climatographer

CLU: Chartered Life Underwriter

clurt: come let us reason together (mediator's motto)

CLUS: continental limits United States

CLUSA: Cooperative League of the USA

clv: clevis

Clv: Cleveland

Clw: Collingwood

clwg: clear wire glass

Cly: Clydebank

clz: copper, lead, or zinc (cargo)

cm: centimeter; circular mil; countermortar; mechanic (symbol)

cm (CM): command module

c/m: color modulation (tv); communications multiplexer; control and monitoring

c & m: cocaine-morphine

cm2: square centimeter

cm3: cubic centimeter

cm: *carat metrique* (French—metric carat)

Cm: curium

CM: absolute coefficient of pitching moments (symbol); Clyde-Mallory (steamship line); mine layer (naval symbol)

C-M: Charente-Maritime

C.M.: central meridian

C/M: Curtis/Mathes

C of M: Certificate of Merit

CM4: Comet 4 jet airplane

cma: civil-military affairs

Cma: Camilla

CMA: California Maritime Academy; Canadian Medical Association; Candle Manufacturers Association; Casket Manufacturers Association; Chocolate Manufacturers Association; Cigar Manufacturers Association; Cleveland Metal Abrasive (company); Clothespin Manufacturers of America; Colorado Mining Association; Compañía Mexicana de Aviación (Mexican Aviation Company)—often called Mexicana; Confederate Memorial Association; Court of Military Appeals; Crucible Manufactur-

ers Association
CMAA: Cleveland Musical Arts Association
cmab: clothing maintenance allowance, basic
CMAC: Capital Military Assistance Command
cmai: clothing maintenance allowance, initial
CMAL: Clothing Monetary Allowance List
CMAR: Can't Manage A Rifle
C/marca: Cundinamarca, Colombia
CMAS: Confédération Mondiale des Activités Subaquatiques (World Confederation of Subaquatic Activities); Council for Military Aircraft Standards
CMAT: Canadian Mathematics Achievement Test
CMB: Chase Manhattan Bank; coastal motor boat, Colombo, Ceylon (airport); Combat Manuever Battalion(s); Compagnie Maritime Belge (Royal Belgian Lloyd Line)
CMB: *Cuyas manos beso* (Spanish—whose hands I kiss)— very respectfully yours
CMBI: Caribbean Marine Biological Institute
cmbt: combat
cmc: contact-making clock; coordinated manual control
CMc: coastal mine layer (naval symbol)
CMC: Canadian Music Council; Commandant of the Marine Corps
CMCC: Classified Matter Control Center
cmcr: continuous melting, casting, and rolling
CMCR: Compagnie Maritime des Chargeurs Réunis
cmd: command; common meter double
CMD: California Moderate Democrats; Contract Management District
cmdg: commanding
Cmdr: Commander
Cmdre: Commodore
cmdty: commodity
CME: California Motor Express; Chicago Mercantile Exchange (formerly Chicago Butter and Egg Board); Courtesy Motorboat Examination (U.S. Coast Guard)
CMEA: Council of Mutual Economic Aid
CMERI: Central Mechanical Engineering Research Institute (India)

cmet: coated metal
cmf: calcium-and-magnesium-free
CMF: Commonwealth Military Forces; Composite Medical Facility
CMFNZ: Chamber Music Federation of New Zealand
CMFRI: Central Marine Fisheries Research Institute
cmfsw: calcium-and-magnesium-free seawater
cmg: control-moment gyroscope
CMH: Columbus, Ohio (airport); Congressional Medal of Honor
cmha: confidential, modified handling authorized
CMHA: Canadian Mental Health Association
CMHC: Community Mental Health Center(s)
CMHPA: Cloves Memorial Hall for the Performing Arts (Indianapolis)
CMI: Can Manufacturers Institute; Christian Michelson Institute (for Science and Free Thought —Bergen, Norway); Comité Météorologique Internationale (International Meteorological Committee); Command Maintenance Inspection (US Army); Commission Mixte Internationale (International Mixed Commission for Experience Relative to the Protection of Telecommunication Lines and Underground Cables)
CMI: *Cornell Medical Index*
CMIA: Coal Mining Institute of America; Cultivated Mushroom Institute of America
cmil: circular mil
CMIU: Cigar Makers' International Union
cml: chemical; circuit micrologic; commercial; current mode logic
CML: Container Marine Lines
CMLA: Canadian Music Library Association
CmlC: Chemical Corps
cml def: chemical defense
cmlops: chemical operations
CMLS: Cleveland-Marshall Law School
CM/LSCNP: Cradle Mountain/-Lake Saint Clair National Park (Tasmania)
CMM: Chief Machinist's Mate (USN); Commission for Maritime Meteorology (WMO)
CMMA: Concrete Mixer Manufacturers Association
cmmch: combat Mach change
cmmnd: command(ing)
CMMP: Commodity Management Master Plan

CMMS: Columbia Mental Maturity Scale
cmn: commission
CMN: Common Market Nationals; Common Market Nations
cmnce: commence
CMNH: Cleveland Museum of Natural History
CMNM: Capulin Mountain National Monument; Craters of the Moon National Monument
cmnr: commissioner
cmo: cardiac minute output; computer microfilm output
CMO: Contract Management Office(r)
cmp: corrugated metal pipe; cost of maintaining product
CMP: Catoctin Mountain Park (Maryland); Church Music Publishers; Controlled Materials Plan; Cornell Maritime Press; Corps of Military Police
cmpd: compound; compounded; compounding
cmpld: compiled
cmpnt: component
CMPO: Calcutta Metropolitan Planning Organisation
cmps: centimeters per second
cmpt: component
cmptr: computer
cmr: cerebral metabolic rate; common-mode rejection
CMR: Communications Monitoring Report; Consolidated Mail Room; Contract Management Region
CMRA: Chemical Marketing Research Association
CMRL: Chamber of Mines and Research Laboratories
CMRNWR: Charles M. Russell National Wildlife Range (Montana)
cmrr: common mode rejection ratio
c.m.s.: *cras mane sumendus* (Latin —to be taken tomorrow morning)
CMS: California Museum of Science; Center for Measurement Science (George Washington University); Chicago Medical School; Chief Master Sergeant; Christian Medical Society; Church Missionary Society; College Music Society; Compagnie Maritime de la Seine; Consumers and Marketing Service; Contemporary Music Society
CM & SA: Canning Machinery and Supplies Association
CMSC: Central Missouri State College
CMSgt: Chief Master Sergeant

CMSI: California Museum of Science and Industry

CMS & I: California Museum of Science and Industry

CMSN: China Merchants Steam Navigation (company)

CMSTP & P: Chicago, Milwaukee, St Paul and Pacific (railroad)

cmt: comment

CMT: California Motor Transport; Camden Marine Terminals

CMTA: Chinese Musical and Theatrical Association

CMTC: Citizens Military Training Camp

CMTCU: Communications Message Traffic Control Unit

cmte: committee

CMU: Central Michigan University

C-M U: Carnegie-Mellon University

cmv: cytomegalovirus

CM von W: Carl María von Weber

CMVPB: California Motor Vehicles Pollution Board

CMZ: Compagnie Maritime du Zaire

cn: cannon; coordination number

c/n (C/N): credit note

c.n.: *cras nocte* (Latin—tomorrow night)

Cn: contract number; cumulonimbus

CN: absolute coefficient of yawing moments (aerodynamic symbol); Carl Nielsen; Central Airlines; Chinese Nationalist; Code Napoléon; Commonwealth Nations; compass north; Confederate Navy; cosine of the amplitude (mathematical symbol)

CN: Canadian National-Grand Trunk Railways

C & N: communication and navigation

C-de-N: Côtes-de-Nord

cna: code not allocated

CNA: Canadian Numismatic Association; Center for Naval Analyses (Franklin Institute); Central News Agency (Nationalist China); Central Northern Airways; Chief of Naval Air; Chief of Naval Aviation

CNAA: Council for National Academic Awards

CNAC: China National Aviation Corporation

CNAN: Compagnie Navale Afrique du Nord

CNAS: Civil Navigation Aids System

CNATra: Chief of Naval Air Training

CNAV: Canadian Naval Auxiliary Vessel

CNC: Christopher Newport College

Cncl(r): Council(or)

CNCMH: Canadian National Committee for Mental Hygiene

cncr: concurrent

cnd: conduit

CND: Campaign for Nuclear Disarmament

CND: *Code Names Dictionary*

cn di: combination die

cnds: condensate

CNE: Canadian National Exhibition

cnel: community noise equivalent level

Cnel: Coronel (Spanish—Colonel)

CNEN: Comisión Nacional de Energía Nuclear (National Nuclear Energy Commission)

CNEP: Cable Network Engineering Program (Bell)

CNES: Centre National d'Études Spatiales (National Center for Space Studies)

CNET: Centre National d'Étude des Télécommunications (Telecommunication National Study Center)

CNEXO: Centre pour d'Exploitation des Oceans (Center for the Exploitation of the Oceans)

cnf: confine

CNF: Caribbean National Forest (Puerto Rico)

CNG: Connecticut Natural Gas

CNGA: California Natural Gas Association

CNGB: Chief, National Guard Bureau

CN-GT: Canadian National Railways-Grand Trunk Western

CNHI: Committee for National Health Insurance

CNHM: Chicago Natural History Museum (Field Museum of Natural History)

CNIB: Canadian National Institute for the Blind

CNIPA: Committee of National Institutes of Patent Agents

CNJ: Central of New Jersey (railroad)

cnl: cancel; cancellation

CNL: Canadian National Library (Ottawa); Commonwealth National Library (Canberra)

CNLA: Council of National Library Associations

CNM: Cabrillo National Monument; Chief of Naval Material; Chiricahua National Monument; Colombo National Museum; Colorado National Monument

CNN: Campagnie de Navigation Nationale

CNNR: Caerlaverock National Nature Reserve (Scotland); Cairngorms National Nature Reserve (Scotland)

CNO: Chief of Naval Operations

CNOBO: Chief of Naval Operations Budget Office

C-note: $100 bill

CNP: Canyonlands National Park (Utah); Caramoan NP (Philippines); Cleveland NP (South Australia); Colonial NP (Virginia); Compagnie Navale des Petroles; Compagnie de Navigation Paquet; Corbett NP (India); Cyril Northcote Parkinson

cn/pnl: contractor's panel

CNPP: Centre National de Prévention et de Protection

CNPS: California Native Plant Society

cnr: carrier-to-noise ratio; composite noise rating; corner

CNR: Canadian National Railway; Civil Nursing Reserve; Coleford Nature Reserve (South Africa)

CNRA: Curecanti National Recreation Area (Colorado)

CNRN: Consiglio Nazionale delle Ricerche (National Research Council)

CNRS: Centre National de la Recherche Scientifique (National Center for Scientific Research)

cnrt: concrete

cns: central nervous system

c.n.s.: *cras nocte sumendus* (Latin —to be taken tomorrow night)

CNS: Congress of Neurological Surgeons

CNS: *Chubu Nippon Shimbun* (Central Japan Newspaper)

CNSA: Carl Nielsen Society of America

Cnst Pty: Constitution Party

cnstr: canister

CNT: celestial navigation trainer

CNT: *Confederación Nacional de Trabajo* (Spanish—National Confederation of Labor)—anarcho-syndicalist trades-union confederation; *Conselho Nacional de Telecommunicaoes* (Portuguese—National Telecommunications Council)—government-controlled radio and television for all Brazil

CNTB: Colombia National Tourist Board

CNTCA: Canadian National Railway—Transcanada Airlines

cntn: contain ontain

Cntr: Centaur (space vehicle)

cntr: container; contribute; contribution

Cnut: Canute

cnv: contingent negative variation

CNV: Cape Canaveral, Florida (tracking station)
CNVA: Committee for Non-Violent Action
cnvc: conveyance
cnvr: conveyor
cnvt: convict
C & NW: Chicago and North Western (railway)
CNWDI: Critical Nuclear Weapons Design Information
CNWR: Camas National Wildlife Refuge (Idaho); Chassahowitzka NWR (Florida); Chatauqua NWR (Illinois); Chincoteague NWR (Virginia); Columbia NWR (Washington)
CNYP: Central New York Power (corporation)
co: cleanout; conscientious objector; convenience outlet; cutoff; cutout
c-o: cutoff
c/o: care of; carried over; cash order
co: compagno (Italian—company)
Co: cobalt; Colombia; Colombian; Colombiano; Columbia; Columbian; Company; County
C/o: complained of
Co⁶⁰: radioactive cobalt
CO: carbon monoxide; Cleveland Orchestra; Commanding Officer; conscientious objector; Continental Airlines (2-letter code)
C/O: cash order
C & O: Chesapeake & Ohio (railroad)
C-d'O: Côte-d'Or
co 1mo: canto primo (Italian—first treble)
CO₂: carbon dioxide
COA: Change Order Account; Chattanooga Opera Association; Connecticut Opera Association; Cordova Airlines
CO(A): Change Order (Aircraft)
coac: clutter-operated anti-clutter receiver
coag: coagulant; coagulate; coagulation
Coah: Coahuila (inhabitants— Coahuileños or Coahuilenses)
Coal.: Coalition
coalit govt: coalition government
coam: coaming
CO-AMP: Cost Optimization-Analysis of Maintenance Policy
coas: crewman optical alignment sight
Coast Line: Atlantic Coast Line Railroad
coax: coaxial
c-o-b: close of business
COB: Change Order Board
C & O-B & O: Chesapeake and Ohio-Baltimore & Ohio (merged railroads)
cobol: common business-oriented language
COBSI: Committee on Biological Sciences Information
coc: cocaine; cathodal opening contraction
COC: Canadian Opera Company; Combat Operations Center
coca: cocaina (Spanish—cocaine)
COCAST: Council for Overseas Colleges of Art, Science, and Technology
cocb: crossed olivochochlear bundles
cocc: coccyx
coccy: coccidioidomycosis
coch.: cochleare (Latin—spoonful)
coch. ampl.: cochleare amplum (Latin—tablespoonful)
coch. infant.: cochleare infantis (Latin—teaspoonful)
coch. mag.: cochleare magnum (Latin—tablespoonful)
coch. med.: cochleare medium (Latin—dessertspoonful)
coch. parv.: cochleare parvum (Latin—teaspoonful)
COCI: Council on Consumer Information
cocl: cathodal opening clonus
C & OC NM: Chesapeake and Ohio Canal National Monument
Coco: (French—Little Pet)
Coco Chanel: Gabrielle Bonheur Chanel
COCOM: Coordinating Committee for Export to Communist Area(s)
cocp: closed olivocochlear potential
coct.: coctio (Latin—boiling)
COCU: Churches of Christ Uniting
cod.: chemical oxygen demand; cleanout door; codeine
c-o-d: cargo-on-deck
c.o.d.: cash-on-delivery
Co D: Costume Designer
COD: coding
CODA: Committee on Drugs and Alcohol
codac: coordination of operating data by automatic computer
CODAC: Community Organization for Drug Abuse Control
CODAF: Commission on Border Development and Friendship (U.S.–Mexican)
codag: combined diesel and gas (turbine machinery)
codan: carrier-operated device anti-noise
CODASYL: Conference on Data Systems Languages
CODC: Canadian Oceanographic Data Center
codd: codices
CODE: Committee on Donor Enlistment
coded.: computer-oriented design of electronic devices
codel(s): congressional delegation(s)
Code N: Code Napoléon
codic: computer-directed communication(s)
codog: combined diesel or gas
CODOT: Classification of Occupations and Directory of Occupational Titles (UK)
CODSIA: Council of Defense Space Industries Association
coe: cab over engine (truck); close of escrow (realty)
COE: Corps of Engineers
CO(E): Change Order (Electronic)
coed: coeducation(al); girl or woman student
COEDS: Char Oil Energy Development Systems
COEES: Central Office Equipment Engineering System (Bell)
coef: coefficient
Coel: Coelenterata
COESA: Committee on Extension of the Standard Atmosphere (United States)
coexsec: coexsecant
cof: cause of failure
coff: cofferdam
C of F: Chief of Finance
COFI: Committee on Fisheries (FAO)
COFO: Council of Federated Organizations (CORE, NAACP, SCLC, SNCC)
COFRC: Chevron Oil Field Research Company
cofron: copper iron (patent medicine mixture)
cog.: cognate
COG: Change Our Gender; Change Our Goal; Council of Governments
cogag: combined gas and gas
CoGARD: Coast Guard
cogita: computerized general I.Q. test(ing)
cogn: cognomen
cogo: coordinate geometry
cog/prsl: cognizant personnel
coh: cash-on-hand; coefficient of haze
COH: carbohydrate (generalized formula)
COHATA: Compagnie Haitienne des Transports Aeriens
Co Hd: coral head
coho: coherent oscillator
COHO: Council of Health Organization
COI: Central Office of Information; Coordinator of Information

CoID: Council of Industrial Design
coif: coiffure
COIMS: Council for International Organizations of Medical Sciences
coin.: coinage; counterinsurgency—anti-guerrilla warfare
COIN: Counterinsurgency
coin gold: 90% gold, 10% copper
coin-op: coin-operated
COINS: Cooperative Intelligence Network System
coin silver: 50 to 92.5 % silver with balance of copper or other metals
COIR: Commission on Intergroup Relations (NYC)
COIT: Central Office of the Industrial Tribunal (UK)
COIU: Congress of Independent Unions
COJ: Court of Justic
coke: coca drink; cocaine
Coke: Coca Cola
col: colon; colonial; colonic; colonist; colonization; colonize; colony; color; coloring; colorist; colors; column
col: (French—pass)
col.: *colatus* (Latin—strained, as through a filter); *collum* (Latin—collar); *colon* (Latin—large intestine)
c-o-l (COL): cost of living
co-L: co-latitude
Col: Colima; College; Cologne; Colombia; Colombiano; Colón; Colonel; Colossians, Epistle to the; Columbia; Columbian; Coronel
COL: Computer Oriented Language
cola.: cost-of-living allowance
COLA: Committee on Library Automation (ALA)
Col Alb: College of the Albermarle
colat.: *colatus* (Latin—strained)
col bh: collision bulkhead
col C: *col canto* (Italian—follow the voice)
COLC: Cost of Living Council
Col$: Colombian peso
cold.: chronic obstructive lung disease
COLDEMAR: Compañía Colombiana de Navegación Maritima
Col Ency: Columbia Encyclopedia
coleop: coleoptera; coleopterist
Colette: Sidonie Gabrielle Claudine de Jouvenal
colidar: coherent light detection and ranging
colingo: compile online and go (data processing)
coll: collect(or); collection; colloid(al); colloquia(ism)

Coll: College; Collegiate
collab: collaboration; collaborator
coll agc: collection agency
collat: collateral
Coll Ency: Colliers' Encyclopedia
Coll L: Collection Letter
Collodi: (pseudonym—Carlo Lorenzini)
colloq: colloquial(ism); colloquium
collr: collector
collun.: *collunarium* (Latin—nose wash)
collut.: *collutorium* (Latin—mouthwash)
collyr.: *collyrium* (Latin—eyewash)
colm: column
colo: colophon (printer's or publisher's device, symbol, or trademark)
Colo: Colorado; Coloradan
colog: cologarithm
Colom: Colombia; Colombian
Col Sym: Columbia Symphony
COLT: Council on Library Technology
Columbus: Cristóbal Colón (Spanish); Cristoforo Colombo (Italian)
com: comedy; comma; command; commercial; commission; committee; common; complement; compliment
com (COM): computer-output microfilm(ing)
com.: *commemoratio* (Latin—commemoration)
Com: Comoro Islands
COM: Chief Operations Manager; Council of Ministers
COMAIRCENT: Commander, Allied Air Forces, Central Europe
COMAIRNORTH: Commander, Allied Air Forces, Northern Europe
COMAIRSOUTH: Commander, Allied Air Forces, Southern Europe
Comalco: Commonwealth Aluminum Company (Australia)
COMANSEC: Computation and Analysis Section (Canadian Defense Research Board)
COMANTDEFCOM: Commander, United States Antilles Defense Command
comat: computer-assisted training
COMATS: Commander Military Air Transport Service
comb.: combat; combination; combine; combustion
COMBALTAP: Allied Command Baltic Approaches (NATO)
combi: combination
combo: combination (of musicians, or of a safe)

COMBO: Combined Arts of San Diego
combu: combustion
ComCm: communications countermeasures and deception
COMCRUDESFLOT: Commander Cruiser-Destroyer Flotilla
COMCRUDESPAC: Commander Cruisers and Destroyers in the Pacific (USN)
comd: command
comdg: commanding
Comdr: Commander
Comdt: Commandant
comeas: countermeasures
COMECON: Council of Mutual Economic Assistance (of communist nations)
COMEINDORS: Composite Mechanized Mechanized and Document Retrieval System
Com Err: Comedy of Errors
comet.: computer operated management evaluation technique
COMIBOL: Corporación Minera de Bolivia (Bolivian Mining Corporation)
COMICEDEFOR: Commander, United States Iceland Defense Force
COMINCH: Commander-in-Chief, United States Fleet
Cominform: Communist Information Bureau (latter-day name for the Comintern)
comint: communications intelligence
Comintern: Communist International; Cominform
Com Int Sec: Committee on Internal Security (formerly House Committee on Un-American Activities—HUAC)
comisº: *comisario* (Spanish—commissary; delegate; deputy; manager; police inspector)
comkd: completely knocked down
coml: commercial
COMLANDCENT: Commander, Allied Land Forces; Central Europe
COMLANDEAST: Commander, Allied Land Forces, Southeastern Europe
COMLANDMARK: Commander, Allied Land Forces, Denmark
COMLANDNORWAY: Commander, Allied Land Forces, Norway
COMLANDSOUTH: Commander, Allied Land Forces, Southern Europe
COMLOGNET: Combat Logistics Network
comm: commerce; commercial; commission; committee; com-

monwealth; commune; com-
munication; commutator
comm.: *commune* (Latin—all the
people; the community)
Com Mat Cen: Communication
Materials Center (Columbia
University)
commdg: commanding
Commdr: Commander
Commdt: Commandant
Commerce: Department of Commerce
commfu: complete and utterly monumental foulup
commi: communism; communist
commie: commisary; communist
commies: communists
commod: commodity
Commr: Commissioner
commun: communication
commun dis: communicable disease
comn: commission; communica-
tion(s)
ComNAB: Commander, Naval Air
Bases
COMNAVCENT: Commander,
Allied Naval Forces, Central
Europe
COMNAVFORCESMARIANAS:
Commander, Naval Forces, Marianas Islands
COMNAVFORJAPAN: Com-
mander, Naval Forces, Japan
COMNAVNORTH: Commander,
Allied Naval Forces, Northern
Europe
COMNAVSUPPACT: Commander, Naval Support Activity
comnr: commissioner
Como: Commodore; Comodoro Ri-
vadavia (Argentine naval hero
and seaport name); Comoro
comp: compose(d); composer;
composition; composition roof
(ing); compression; compressor;
computation(al); computer; computerization, computerize; computerized
comp.: *compositus* (Latin—compound)
comp a: compressed air
COMPAC: Commonwealth Pacific
Telephone Cable (linking Australia, New Zealand, and Pacific
Ocean islands with the rest of the
world)
COMPACT: Computator Planning
and Control Technique
compand: compress + expand (radio communication term describing compression followed
by expansion)
compar: comparative
compare.: computerized performance and analysis response

evaluator; console for optical
measurement and precise analysis of radiation from electronics
COMPASS: Comprehensive Assembly System
Comp Curr: Comptroller of the
Currency
compd: compound
compdes: compensator design;
competitive design
compen: compensate; compensatory
Compendex: *Computerized Engineering Index*
compf: composition floor
Comp Gen: Comptroller General
compl: complete; compilation; compiled
Compl: *A Lover's Complaint*
comp mar: companionate marriage
COMPMR: Commander, Pacific
Missile Range
compo: compensation; component;
composer; composite; composition; compositor
compool: common pool
compos: components; composers;
composites; compositions; com-
positors
compr: compressor
compreg: compressed-impregnated
(wood)
compt: compartment
Compt: Comptroller
Comptes Rend.: *Comptes rendus
de l'Académie des Sciences*
(Proceedings of the Academy of
Science)
compu: computable; computability;
computation(al); computer; computerization; computerize
comput: computer
computes.: computers
COMRAC: Combat Radius Capability (DoD)
com rcn: command reconnaissance
comsat(s): communications satel-
lite(s)
Comsat: Communications Satellite
(corporation)
ComSeaFron: Commander Sea
Frontier (USN)
comsec: communications security
comsn: commission
comsoal: computer method of se-
quencing operations for assembly lines
COMSTRIKFLTLANT: Com-
mander, Striking Fleet Atlantic
(USN)
COMSTRIKFORSOUTH: Commander, Naval Striking and
Forces Support, Southern Europe

COMSTS: Commander Military
Sea Transport Service
COMSUBPAC: Commander, Sub-
marines, Pacific
comsy: commissary
comt: comptroller
comte: committee
com tech: communications techni-
cian
COMUSAFSO: Commander, Unit-
ed States Air Forces, Southern
Command
COMUSFORAZ: Commander,
U.S. Forces, Azores
COMUSJAPAN: Commander,
U.S. Forces, Japan
COMUSKOREA: Commander,
U.S. Forces, Korea
COMUSTDC: Commander, U.S.
Taiwan Defense Command
Com Ver: Common Version (of the
Bible)
com wc: command weapon carrier
Com Z: Communications Zone
con: confidence (game; man; men);
conned; conning; consolidated;
control; conversation; convict
con.: *contra* (Latin—against)
con8va.: *con ottava* (Italian—with
octaves)
Con: Concord; Conservative
CON: Conservative; Conservative
Party
CONAC: Continental Air Command
CONAD: Continental Air Defense
Command
ConArC: Continental Army Command
conc: concentrate; concentration;
concentric; concrete
conc b: concrete block
conc c: concrete ceiling
Concertg: *Concertgebouworkest*
(Dutch—Concertgebouw Or-
chestra)—Amsterdam's celebrated symphony orchestra
conc clg: concrete ceiling
conc f: concrete floor
conc fl: concrete floor
conch.: conchology
Concha: Maria de la Concepción
conchie: conscientious objector
Concorde: Anglo-French supersonic airplane attaining normal
cruising speeds of 1300 miles
per hour
concr: concrete
cond: condenser; condition; conductivity; conductor
condit: conditional
condiv: continental divide
condr: conductor
cond ref: conditioned reflex
cond resp: conditioned response
CONE: Collectors of Numismatic

Errors

CONEA: Confederation of National Educational Associations

Con Ed: Consolidated Edison (gas and electric light company)

conelrad: control of electromagnetic radiation

con esp: *con espressione* (Italian—with expression)

co-netic: high-permeability non-shock-sensitive (alloy developed for maximum attenuation at low flux density)

conex (CONEX): connection(s)

conf: confer; conference; confidential

conf.: *confer* (Latin—compare)

Conf: Confucian; Confucius

confab: confabulation; confabulate

Confed: Confederate

confer.: conference

confid: confidential

confr: confectioner

cong: congress(ional)

cong.: *congius* (Latin—gallon)

congal: *(cuarto) con gal* [(Mexican-American—(room) with girl)]—house of prostitution

Cong: Congress

Cong Christ: Congregational Christians

congen: congenital

Cong Fr: Congolese franc

Congl; Congregational

Congrats: congratulations

Cong Rec: *Congressional Record*

Congreg: Congregationalist

conics: conic sections

conj: conjunction

con man: confidence man; swindler

conn: connection; connective; connector

Conn: Connecticut; Connecticuter

CONN: Connellan Airways

Connie: Conrad; Constance; Cornelia; Cornelius

Conn Turn: Connecticut Turnpike

conobjtr: conscientious objector

CONOCO: Continental Oil Company

Conr: Conrad

con rod: connecting rod

cons: consider; consist

con(s): convict(s)

cons.: *conserva* (Latin—a preserve)

Cons: Conservative

CONSCIENCE: Committee on National Student Citizenship in Every National Case of Emergency

con sect: conic section

Cons Eng: Consulting Engineer

conserv: conservation; conservationist; conservatoire; conservatory

Conserv: Conservatoire; Conserva-

tory

Cons Gen: Consul General

conshelf: continental shelf

Consc°: *Consejo* (Spanish—Council)

consol: consolidated

consols: consolidated annuities

CONSORT: Conversation System with On-line Remote Terminals

consperg.: *consperge* (Latin—dust; sprinkle)

conspic: conspicuous

const: constitution; constitutional; construction; constructor

Const: Constable

constab: constabulary

Constan: Constantine; Constantinople (Istanbul)

Constantinian Century: the 300s—Roman emperor Constantine builds the city of Constantinople on the site of ancient Byzantium and proclaims it capital of the Eastern Empire— the 4th century

constn: construction

constr: construction; constructor

Const US: Constitution of the United States

consult.: consultant

consv: conservation; conserve

cont: contact; content(s); continent(al); continue(d); contract(or); control(ler)

Cont: Continent; Continental

contag: contagious

contam: contaminant; contaminate; contamination

contax: consumers and taxpayers

cont. bon. mor.: *contra bonos mores* (Latin—contrary to good manners)

contemp: contemporary

contempo: contemporary

Cont Eur: Continental Europe

Cont Eur & Br I: Continental Europe and British Isles

contg: containing

Cont HH: continental range of ports from Havre to Hamburg

cont hp: continental horsepower

contin: *continuo* (Italian—continuous); *continuetur* (Latin—let it be continued)

contl: continental

contr: contracted; contraction; contractor

contrail: condensation trail

contralat: contralateral

contran: control translator

contra(s): contraceptive(s)

cont. rem.: *continuetur remedia* (Latin—let the remedy be continued)

contrib: contribution; contributor

contus.: *contusus* (Latin—bruised;

contused)

cont w: continuous window

conurb(s): conurbation(s)

Con US (CONUS): Continental United States

CONUS Intel: Continental United States Intelligence (USA)

conv: convalescent; convention; conventional

Convair 600: Convair-Liner powered by Rolls-Royce turboprop engines

conv encl: convector enclosure

Convis Bur: Convention and Visitor's Bureau

convl: conventional

convn: convenient

convt: convert(ible)

conv^te: *conveniente* (Spanish—convenient)

CONWR: Crab Orchard National Wildlife Refuge (Illinois)

COO: Chief Ordnance Officer

COOH: (carboxyl group found in all organic acids)

cook.: cookery

Cooks: Cook's Tours (Thomas Cook and Son, Ltd)

cool.: coolant

coon(s): coonhound(s)—contraction of racoon hounds

'coon(s): racoon(s)

coop.: cooperation

co-op: cooperative

COOPLAN: Continuity of Operations Plan (USN)

COORS: Communications Outage Restoration Section

COOS: Chemical Orbit-to-Orbit Shuttle (NASA)

cop: capillary osmotic pressure; casing operating pressure; copper; copyright; customer owned property; policeman (slang)

Cop: Copernican; Coptic

COP: City of Prineville (railroad); Combat Outpost; Commissary Operating Program; Continuity of Operations Plan

COPA: Compañía Panameña de Aviación

COPARS: Contractor-Operated Parts Stores (DoD)

copd: chronic obstructive pulmonary disease; coppered

COPDAF: Continuity of Operations Plan—Department of the Air Force

cope: chronic obstructive pulmonary emphysema

COPE: Committee for Original People's Entitlement (Canadian Eskimo's claim to Canadian land); Committee on Political Education (AFL-CIO); Congress on Optimum Population and

Environment; Council on Population and Environment

COPEI: *Comité Organizador del Partido Electoral Independiente* (Spanish—Organization Committee of the Independent Electoral Party)—Venezuela's Social Christian Party

Copen: Copenhagen

COPH: Congress of Organizations of the Physically Handicapped

copo: copolymer

copp: cobaltiprotoporphyrin

COPP: Conservation Organization Protesting Pollution

copperas: ferrous sulfate; green vitriol

COPPS: Committee on Power Plant Siting (Nat Acad Engineering)

COPR: Critical Officer Personnel Requirement (USAF)

cops: coppers; policemen (slang)

Copt: Coptic

copter(s): helicopter(s)

copu: copulate; copulation; copulatory

copy.: copyright

coq.: *coque* (Latin—boil)

cor: contactor, running; corner; cornet; correction

Cor: Corinthians; Corona; Coronado; Coroner; Corsica; Coruña

cor bd: corner bead

corbfus: copy of reply to be furnished us

Corc: Cornell computing (language)

CORCO: Commonwealth Oil Refining Company (Puerto Rico)

cord.: *cordillera* (Spanish—mountain range)

Cord: Cordelia; Córdoba

C of Ord: Chief of Ordnance

cordpo: correlated radar data printout

CORDS: Civil Operations and Revolutionary Development Support

CORE: Competitive Operational Readiness Evaluation (Air Force); Congress of Racial Equality

corfam: (computer-devised word—not an acronym—microporous artificial leather)

corflu: correction fluid

CORG: Combat Operations Research Group

corin: corinthian

Coriol: *Coriolanus*

CORL: Canadian Operations Research Society

cormant: cormorant

Cor Mem: Corresponding Member

Corn: Cornelius; Cornish; Cornwall

Corner House: Central Mining and Finance Corporation (South Africa)

coroll: corollary

coron: coronary

Corp: Corporation

Corpl: Corporal

Corpn: Corporation

corppin: corporeal pin (tuberculin testing)

corr: correction; correspondence; corrosion; corrugate

corr: *corregido* (Spanish—corrected); *corriage* (French—corrected)

corr case: corrugated case

Correggio: Antonio Allegri

correl: correlative

correo: (Spanish—mail; post office

corres: correspondence; correspondent; corresponding

corrig: corrigenda

corros: corrosive

corrte: *corriente* (Spanish—current month)

corrupt.: corruption

CORS: Canadian Operational Research Society

cort: cortex; cortical

cort.: *cortex* (Latin—bark)

CORT: Council On Radio and Television

Cory: Cornelia

cos: cash-on-shipment; contactor, starting; cosine; cosmic; cosmogany; cosmography; cosmology; cosmopolitan

COS: Canadian Ophthalmological Society; Chief of Section; Colorado Springs, Colorado (airport); Czechoslovak Ocean Shipping

cosag: combined steam and gas (turbine machinery)

cosa nostra: (Italian—our thing) —nickname for international criminal syndicate network

COSA NOSTRA: Computer-Oriented System And Newly Organized Storage-To-Retrieval Apparatus

COSATI: Committee on Scientific and Technical Information (Federal Council for Science and Technology)

COSD: Council of Organizations Serving the Deaf

cosec: cosecant

COSEC: Coordinating Secretariat of National Unions of Students

cosh: hyperbolic cosine (symbol)

COSI: Committee on Scientific Information

COSINE: Committee on Computer Science in Electrical Engineering Education

COSIP: College Science Improvement Program

Co60: radioactive cobalt

cosm: cosmetic; cosmetics; cosmetologist; cosmetology

COSMIC: Computer Programmes Information Center (Univ of Georgia)

cosmo: cosmoline; cosmopolitan

cosmograph(s): composite photograph(s)

COSPAR: Committee on Space Research (International Council of Scientific Unions)

COSPUP: Committee on Science and Public Policy (National Academy of Sciences)

cosr: cutoff shear

COSR: Committee on Space Research

cost.: contaminated oil settling tank; costume

COST: Cost-Oriented Systems Technique

costa: (Italian, Portuguese, Spanish—coast)

coster: costermonger

COSTS: Committee on Sane Telephone Service

COSY: Checkout Operating System

cot.: cathodal opening tetanus; cotangent; cotter; cotton

COT: Consecutive Overseas Tour

COTA: confirming telephone or message authority

COTAL: Confederación de Organizaciones Turísticas de la América Latina (Confederation of Touristic Organizations of Latin America)

COTC: Canadian Officers' Training Corps

côte: (French—coast)

coth: hyperbolic cotangent (symbol)

cotics: narcotics

cots.: cottages

'cot(s): apricot(s)

couldn't: could not

COUP: Congress of Unrepresented People

cov: cutout valve; cover

covers.: coversed sine

couch: couchant

covff: coverings, facing, or floor (cargo)

cov pl: coverplate

COWAR: Committee on Water Research

Cowboy Philosopher: Will Rogers

cowl.: cowling

COWRR: Committee on Water Resources Research

cox'n: coxswain (pronounced as contracted)

Coy: Company

Coyle: Coyle Lines

coz: cousin (colloquial contraction)

cozi: communication zone (indicator(s)

cp: camp; candlepower; center of pressure; cesspool; claw plate; cold-punched; command post (CP); concrete-piercing

c/p: change package; control panel

c & p: carriage and packing

cP: polar continental air

CP: Caminhos de ferro Portuguese (Portuguese Railways); Canadian Press (news agency); cerebral palsy; charter party; chemically pure; Communist Party; Conservative Party; Constitution Party; copilot; Country Party

C-P: Colgate-Palmolive

C of P: Captain of the Port

cpa: closest point of approach; cost planning and appraisal

CPA: Canadian Pacific Airlines; Canaveral Port Authority; Cathay Pacific Airways; Certified Public Accountant; Civilian Production Administration

CPAA: *Current Physics Advance Abstracts*

CPAB: California Prune Advisory Board

cpaf: cost plus award fee

CP Air: Canadian Pacific Air

CPAO: Country Public Affairs Office(r)

cpap: continuous positive airway pressure

Cpb: Campbelltown

CPB: Centraal Plan Bureau (Netherlands' Central Planning Bureau); Corporation for Public Broadcasting (U.S.A.)

cpba: competitive protein-binding analysis

cpbl: capability; capable

CPBMP: Committee on Purchases of Blind-Made Products

cpc: computer production control

CPC: California Polytechnic College; City Planning Commission; City Projects Council; Cogswell Polytechnical College; Communist Party of China; Consumers Power Company; Creole Petroleum Corporation

CPCC: Central Piedmont Community College

CPCGN: Canadian Permanent Committee on Geographical Names (Ottawa)

CPCU: Chartered Property and Casualty Underwriter

cpd: charterer pays dues; compound

cpe: circular probable error

CPE: Certified Property Exchanger

CPEA: Cooperative Program for Educational Administration

CPEG: Contractor Performance Evaluation Group

c pen: *code penal* (French—penal code)

CPEP: Contractor Performance Evaluation Plan

cpf: conditional peak flow

cpff (CPFF): cost plus fixed fee

cpg: controlled-pore glass; cotton piece goods

CPG: College Publishers Group

C_pge: course per gyro compass

cph: cycles per hour

CPH: Copenhagen, Denmark (airport)

CPHA: Canadian Public Health Association

CP & HA: Canadian Port and Harbour Association

cpi: characters per inch; commercial performance index; constitutional psychopathic inferior; consumer price index; crash position indicator

CPI: California Psychological Inventory; Chemical Processing Industries; Communist Party of India; Consumer Price Index

cpia: close-pair interstitial atom

CPIA: Chemical Propulsion Information Agency

cpiaf (CPIAF): cost-plus-incentive-award fee

cpif (CPIF): cost plus incentive fee

CPILS: Correlation-Protected Integrated Landing System

CPIM: Curaçaosche Petroleum Industrie Maatschappij

cpin: crankpin

cpl: cement plaster; common program language

Cpl: Corporal

CPL: Calgary Public Library; Certified Parts List; Certified Products List; Charleston Public Library; Charlotte Public Library; Chattanooga Public Library; Chicago Public Library; Cinicinnati Public Library; Civilian Personnel Letter; Cleveland Public Library; Columbus Public Library; Coronado Public Library

CPLA: California Palace of the Legion of Honor

cplg: coupling

cplmt: complement

cplr: center of pillar

cpm: cards per minute; commutative principle of multiplication; critical path method; cycles per minute

CPMA: Computer Peripheral Manufacturers Association

CPMC: Columbia-Presbyterian Medical Center

CPMS: Computer Performance Monitoring System

cpn: coupon

Cpn: Copenhagen

CPN: *Communistische Partij van Nederland* (Dutch—Netherlands Communist Party)

CPNP: Cape Perth National Park (Western Australia)

CPNZ: Communist Party of New Zealand

cpo: cost proposal outline

CPO: Calgary Philharmonic Orchestra; Chief Petty Officer; Civilian Personnel Office(r); Czech Philharmonic Orchestra

cpp: critical path plan

CPP: *Civilian Personnel Pamphlet*

CPPA: Canadian Pulp and Paper Association

CPPCA: California Probation, Parole, and Correctional Association

CPPL: Canadian Pacific Princess Lines (Vancouver-Nanaimo run)

cpps: critical path planning and scheduling

cpr: cardiopulmonary resuscitation; copper

CPR: Canadian Pacific Railway; Carlos Peña Romulo; Cobourg Peninsula Reserve (Australian Northern Territory); Committee on Polar Research; Council for Public Responsibility

CPRA: Council for the Preservation of Rural America

CP Rail: Canadian Pacific Rail

CPRE: Council for the Preservation of Rural England

CPRF: Cancer and Polio Research Fund

CPRSA: Cape Peninsula Road Safety Association

cps: constitutional psychopathic state; coupons; critical path scheduling; cycles per second

CP's: Command Posts

CPS: California Physicians' Service; California Production Service; Canadian Pacific Steamships; Catholic Pamphlet Society; Center for Population Studies (Harvard); College Placement Council; Commission on Presidential Scholars; Congregational Publishing Society; Conseil Permanent de Sécurité (Permanent Security Council); Current Population Survey

C.P.S.: *Custos Privati Sigilli* (Latin—Keeper of the Privy Seal—Great Britain)

CPSA: Canadian Political Science Association; Civil and Public

Services Association (UK); Clay Pigeon Shooting Association

cpsac: cycles-per-second alternating current

cpsd: cross-power spectral density

C_pse: course per standard compass

cpse: counterpoise

cpsi: casing pressure shut in

CPSL: Canadian Pacific Steamship Line

CPSP: Cove Palisade State Park (Oregon)

C_p stg c: course per steering compass

CPSU: Communist Party of the Soviet Union

cpt: casement projected transom; cockpit procedure trainer; counterpoint

Cpt: Capitaine (French—Captain)

CPT: Cape Town, South Africa (Malan Airport); Civilian Pilot Training

CPT: *Current Physics Titles*

cptr: capture; carpenter; carpentry

cpu: central processing unit

CPU: Commonwealth Press Union

CPUSA: Communist Party USA

CPV: Combination Pump Valve; Compañía Peruana de Vapores (Peruvian Steamship Line)

CPVPL: Charles Patterson Van Pelt Library (University of Pennsylvania)

cpw: commercial projected window

cPw: polar continental air warmer than underlying surface

CPW: California Press Women

CPWH: Committee for the Preservation of the White House

CPX: Command Post Exercise

CPY: Communist Party of Yugoslavia

cq: come quick; conceptual quotient; copy correct; copy spelled correctly

CQ: Charge of Quarters; Conditionally Qualified; radio inquiry call signal

CQ: *Caribbean Quarterly; Congressional Quarterly*

CQC: Citizens for a Quiet City

CQCs: Citizens for Quieter Cities

CQD: wireless distress signal

CQR: Customer Quality Representative

CQT: College Qualification Test

CQU: College Qualification Test(s)

cr: cathode ray; center; center of resistance; cold-rolled; complete round; compression ratio; credit; creek; crew; cruise

c/r: company risk

cr.: *crux* (Latin—cross)

c/r: *cuenta y riesgo* (Spanish—for account and risk of)

cr (CR): critical ratio

c & r: cops and robbers

Cr: creditor; chromium

Cr.: *Credo* (Latin—I believe; the creed); *Ceskoslovensky rozhlas* (Czechoslovak Radio)

CR: Ceskoslovenska Republika (Czechoslovakian Republic); Change Recommendation; Combat Ready; Commonwealth Railways (Australia); Costa Rica; Costa Rican; cost reimbursement

C R: *comptes rendus* (French—proceedings; report)

C/R: Chicago Rawhide (manufacturing company)

C & R: convoy and routing

cra: central retinal artery

Cra: *Carretera* (Spanish—highway)

CRA: California Redwood Association; California Republican Assembly; Canadian Rheumatism Association; Cave Research Associates; Centres de la Recherche Appliqué (Applied Research Centers); Colorado River Aqueduct; Colorado River Authority; Community Redevelopment Agency; Continuing Resolution Authority; Convair Recreation Association

C.R.A.: Conzinc Riotinto of Australia (their periods as shown)

CRAC: Careers Research and Advisory Center

CRAF: Civil Reserve Air Fleet

cram.: card random access memory

CRAM: Contractual Requirements Recording, Analysis, and Management

cran: cranial; craniology; cranium

cranapple: cranberry-and-apple juice

craniol: craniology

craniom: craniometry

cran(s): cranberries; cranberry

CRAR: Critical Reliability Action Request

cras: coder and random access switch

CRASH: Citizens to Reduce Airline Smoking Hazards; Community Resource and Self Help

crast.: *crastinus* (Latin—of tomorrow)

C-rat(s): C-ration(s)

CRAW: Combat Readiness Air Wing (USN)

CRB: Civilian Review Board; Commission for Relief in Belgium; Cooper River Bridge (Charleston, South Carolina)

cr & br: crown and bridge (dental)

crc: complete round chart; cyclic

redundancy check

CrC: control and reporting center; Crew Chief

CRC: Chemical Rubber Company; Civil Rights Commission; Consolidated Railroads of Cuba; Control and Reporting Center; Coordinating Research Council

CRCC: Consolidated Record Communications Center (USA)

CRCE: Centaur Reliability Control Engineering

CRCNJ: Central Railroad Company of New Jersey

crcp: continuously reinforced concrete paving

CRCRS: Civil Rights Community Relations Service

CRCS: Canadian Red Cross Society

crd: chronic respiratory disease; complete reaction of degeneration

CRD: Crop Research Division

crdf: cathode ray direction finding

CRDL: Chemical Research and Development Laboratories; Contractor Data Requirements List

Cr$: cruzeiro (Brazilian monetary unit)

CR & DP: Cooperative Research and Development Program

CRDSD: *Current Research and Development in Scientific Documentation*

cre: corrosion resistant

Cre: Crescent

CRE: Congress of Racial Equality

CREA: California Real Estate Association

C Real: Ciudad Real

cream of tartar: potassium acid tartrate ($KHC_4H_4O_6$)

CREATE: Computational Requirements for Engineering, Simulation, Training, and Education (USAF time-sharing computer complex)

cred: credit; creditor

CREFAL: Centro Regional de Educación Fundamental para la America Latina (Regional Center of Fundamental Education for Latin America—United Nations organization)

CREI: Capitol Radio Engineering Institute

crem: cremation

cremains: cremation remains

cremo: crematorium

crep.: *crepitus* (Latin—crepitation)

cres: corrosion-resistant stainless steel; crescent; crescentic

cres: *crescendo* (Italian—expanding, swelling)

CRES: Center for Research in Engineering Science (University of Kansas); Corrosion Resistant Stainless Steel

CRESS: Combined Reentry Effort in Small Systems

crest.: crew-escape and rescue techniques (USAF)

CREST: Committee on Reactor Safety Technology

Cret: Cretaceous

CrewTAF: Crew Training Air Force

crf: capital recovery factor; continuous reinforcements; cross-reference file

CRF: Citizens Research Foundation

CRFA: Czechoslovak Rationalist Federation of America

crg: carriage

cri: chemical rust inhibitor; cold running intelligibility; criminal

CRI: Caribbean Research Institute; Coconut Research Institute; Committee for Reciprocity Information; Communications Research Institute; Composers Recordings Incorporated

CR & I: Chicago River and Indiana (railroad)

crim: criminal; criminalism; criminalist; criminologist; criminology

crim con: criminal conversation (British euphemism—adultery)

criminotic: criminal neurotic

crip: cripple

CRI & P: Chicago, Rock Island and Pacific (railroad)

CR & IR: Chicago River and Indiana (railroad)

Cris: Cristóbal

CRIS: Command Retrieval Information System

crisco: cream received in separating cottonseed oil

CRISP: Cosmic Radiation Ionization Spectrographic Program (NASA)

crit: critic; critical; criticality; criticism

CRITICOMM: Critical Intelligence Communications System

crits: critical reactor experiments

Crk: Cork

crkc: crankcase

CRL: California Republican Leadgue Cambridge Research Laboratory; Center for Research Libraries

C.R.L.: Certified Record Librarian; Certified Reference Librarian

CRLA: California Rural Legal Assistance

CRLLB: Center for Research on Language and Language Behav-

ior (Univ Mich)

crm: counter radar missile; count rate meter

cr/m: crew member

CRM: Combat Readiness Medal; Communications/Research/Machines (publisher); Counter Radar Missile

crmch: cruise Mach change

CRMD: Children with Retarded Mental Development

crmn: crewman

crmnls: criminalism; criminalist; criminalistics; criminals

crmoly: chrome molybdenum

CRMWD: Colorado River Municipal Water District

crn: crane

Crn: (The) Crown (The Monarchy)

CRNL: Chalk River Nuclear Laboratories (Canada)

CRNM: Capitol Reef National Monument

CRNP: Cape Range National Park (Western Australia)

CRNWR: Cape Romain National Wildlife Refuge (South Carolina); Clarence Rhode National Wildlife Range (Alaska)

cro: cathode-ray oscilloscope

CRO: Carnarvon, Australia (tracking station); Contractor's Resident Office; County Recorder's Office

Croat.: Croatia; Croatian

croc(s): crocodile(s)

CROC: Committee for the Rejection of Obnoxious (tv) Commercials

crock.: crockery; crocks (English slang—broken-down animals or athletes)

cro'jack: crossjack

cross.: crossing

CROSS: Committee to Retain Our Segregated Schools (Arkansas)

Crp: C-reactive protein

CRP: Control and Reporting Post; Corpus Christi, Texas (airport); Cost Reduction Program

CRPD: Chicago Regional Port District

cr pl: chromium plate

CRPL: Central Radio Propagation Laboratory

CrR: Croix-Rouge (French—Red Cross)

CRR: Cost Reduction Representative

CRRA: Component Release Reliability Analysis

CRRB: Centaur Reliability Review Board

CRRC: Costa Rica Railway Company

CRREL: Cold Regions Research

and Engineering Laboratory (USA)

crrl: contour roller

CRRS: Combat-Readiness Rating System (USAF)

crs: cold-rolled steel; crew reserve status

cr's: character reactions

Crs: Cristóbal, CZ

CRS: Career Service Status (USAF); Child Rearing Study; Congressional Research Service; Conseil de la Recherche Scientifique (Quebec)

crsp: criminally receiving stolen property

CRSP: Colorado River Storage Program

CRSR: Center for Radiophysics and Space Research (Cornell University)

CRSS: Collectors of Religion on Stamps Society

crt: cathode-ray tube; cold-rolled and tempered

CRT: Combat Readiness Training

cr tan lthr: chrome-tanned leather

CRTC: Canadian Radio-Television Commission; Cavalry Replacement Training Center

crtgc: cartographer

crtn: correction

crtog: cartographer; cartographic; cartography

cr tp: contour template

crt's: cathode-ray tubes

cru: combined rotating unit

CRU: Cecil Rhodes University

CRUBATFOR: cruisers, battle force

CRUDIV: cruiser division

CRUEL: Commission on Reform of Undergraduate Education and Living (Univ Ill)

cruis: cruiser; cruising

CRUSK: Center for Research on Utilization of Scientific Knowledge (Univ Mich)

Crust: Crustacea

crustas: ice-encrusted cocktails

CRUZEIRO: Servicos Aéreos Cruzeiro do Sul (Southern Cross Air Service—Brazil)

crvan: chrome vanadium

crypt.: cryptography

crypta: cryptanalysis; cryptanalyst

crypto: cryptographer; cryptographic; cryptography

cryptos: cryptograms

crys: crystal; crystalline; crystallization; crystallize; crystallography; crystalloids

cs: capital stock; carbon steel; cast steel; cast stone; center section; cirrostratus; close support; color stabilizer; common steel (projectile); crucible steel; cryptographic system; current series; cutting specification(s); single cotton single silk

c/s: cases; cycles per second

c & s: clean and sober

c/s: *con safos* (Spanish-American slang—impervious to attack; the same to you; you're stuck with it)

Cs: cesium; cirrostratus

Cs^{137}: radioactive cesium

CS: Communications Station; Communications System; contract surgeon; Cryptographic System; current series; current strength; cutting specifications

C/S: call signal; certificate of service

C & S: Chicago & Southern (Delta Airlines); Colorado & Southern (railroad)

C *del* S: *Corriere della Sera* (Evening Courier—Milan)

C *of* S: Chief of Staff; Chief of Service

CSA: Canadian Standards Association; Ceskoslovenske Aerolinie (Czechoslovakian Airline); Chief of Staff, United States Army; Commercial Service Authorization; Communication Service Authorization; Confederate States of America; Confederate States Army

C & SA: Counterinsurgency and Special Activities (Joint Chiefs of Staff)

CSAA: Child Study Association of America

CSAC: Cameron State Agricultural College; Conners State Agricultural College

CSAE: Canadian Society of Agricultural Engineering

CSAF: Chief of Staff, United States Air Force

CSAL: Central Scientific Agricultural Library (Moscow)

CSAV: Compañía Sud America de Vapores (Chilean Line)

csb: chemical stimulation (of the brain); concrete splash block

Csb: Casablanca

CSB: Central Statistical Board; Christian Service Brigade; Committee for Safe Bicycling; Copra Stabilization Board

C.S.B.: Bachelor of Christian Science

CSBE: California State Board of Education

csc: cartridge storage case; change schedule chart; cosecant

c & sc: capital and small capital letters

CSC: Central Security Control; Child Safety Council; Citizens Service Corps; Civil Service Commission; Civilian Screening Center; Colorado State College; Combat Support Company; Command and Staff College (USAF); Communications Satellite Corporation; Computer Science Corporation; Consolidated Coal Company (stock exchange symbol); Conspicuous Service Cross; Continuous Service Certificate

CSCC: Civil Service Commission of Canada

CSCFE: Civil Service Council for Further Education (UK)

csch: hyperbolic constant

CSCJ: Center for Studies in Criminal Justice

CScO: Chief Scientific Officer

CSCP: Christian Science Committee on Publications

CSCS: Cost, Schedule, and Control System

cscu: countersink cutter

csd: constant-speed drive; controlled-slip differentials; cortical spreading depression

CSD: Civil Service Department; Convair San Diego (Division of General Dynamics Corporation)

CSD: *Ceskolovenske Statne Draphy* (Czechoslovak State Railway)

CSDI: Center for the Study of Democratic Institutions

CSDP: Coordinated Ship Development Plan (USN)

CSDS: chicago Sewage Disposal System

CSE: Calcutta Stock Exchange; Certificate of Secondary Education

CSEIP: Center for the Study of the Evaluation of Instructional Programs

CSEPA: Central Station Electrical Protection Association

CSEU: Confederation of Shipbuilding and Engineering Unions

csf: cerebrospinal fluid

CSF: Compagnie Générale de Télégraphie Sans Fil

CSFAC: Colorado Springs Fine Arts Center

CSFPA: Central Station Fire Protection Association

csg: casing

CSG: Centre Spatial Guyanais (French Guiana Space Center)

CSGBI: Cardiac Society of Great Britain and Ireland

CSGUS: Clinical Society of Genito-Urinary Surgeons

cshaft: crankshaft

csi: contractor standard item

CSI: Campus Studies Institute; Construction Specification Institute

C.S.I.: Companion of the Order of the Star of India

CSigO: Chief Signal Officer

csink: countersink

CSIR: Council for Scientific and Industrial Research (South Africa); Council of Scientific and Industrial Research (India)

CSIRO: Commonwealth Scientific and Industrial Research Organization (Australia)

CSISRS: Cross-Section Information Storage and Retrieval System (AEC)

CSJ: *Christian Science Journal*

csk: cask; countersink; countersunk

CSK: Cooperative Study of the Kuroshio (UNESCO)

csko: countersink other side

csl: computer-sensitive language; console

CSL: Canada Steamship Lines; Chicago Short Line (railroad)

CSLEA: Center for the Study of Liberal Education for Adults

CSLS: Civil Service Legal Society (UK)

csm: combustion stabilization monitor; command and service module

CSM: Colorado School of Mines; Command and Service Module; Cosmopolitan School of Music

CSM: *Christian Science Monitor*

CSMA: Chemical Specialities Manufacturers Association

csmith: coppersmith

CSM-LM: Command Service Module—Lunar Module (Apollo spacecraft)

CSMMG: Chartered Society of Massage and Medical Gymnastics

CSMPS: Computerized Scientific Management Planning System

CSMSW: Carver School of Missions and Social Work

CSN: Companhia Siderurgica Nacional (National Steel Company); Confederate States Navy; Contract Serial Number; Control Symbol Number

CSNAR: Charles Sheldon National Antelope Refuge (Nevada)

CSNH: Cincinnati Society of Natural History

CSNWR: Carolina Sandhills National Wildlife Refuge (South Carolina)

CSO: Cairo Symphony Orchestra; Central Statistical Office; Charlotte Symphony Orchestra;

Chattanooga Symphony Orchestra; Chicago Symphony Orchestra; Cincinnati Summer Opera; Cincinnati Symphony Orchestra; Clothing Supply Office(r); Columbia Symphony Orchestra; Columbus Symphony Orchestra; Montevideo, Uruguay (Carrasco airport)

CSOP: Commission to Study the Organization of Peace (UN)

CSOs: Community Service Officers; Community Service Organizations

csp: concurrent spare parts

Csp: Caspar; Caspian

CSP: Charles Stewart Parnell; Chartered Society of Physiotherapists; Christian Science Practitioner; Corporation Standard Practice; Custer State Park (South Dakota)

C.S.P.: Congregation of St Paul

CSPA: California State Psychological Association

CSPB: California State Personnel Board

CSPC: California State Polytechnic College

CSPCA: Canadian Society for the Prevention of Cruelty to Animals

C/SPCS: Cost-Schedule Planning Control Specification

CSPI: Center for Science in the Public Interest

CSPM: Communications Security Publications Memorandum

CSPP: Community Shelter Planning Program

CSPR(s): Christian Science Practioner(s)

csr: compulsive security ritual; corrected sedimentation rate

CSR: Certified Shorthand Reporter; Chartered Stenographic Reporter; Civil Service Requirement; Colonial Sugar Refining; Commonwealth Strategic Reserve

CSRA: Central Savannah River Area (Planning and Development Commission)

CSRC: Communication Science Research Center (Batelle Memorial Institute—Columbus, Ohio)

CSRL: Center for the Study of Responsive Law

CSRO: Consolidated Standing Route Order (USA)

CSRP: Congnitive Systems Research Program

CSS: Calcutta School Society; Coded Switch System (to arm nuclear weapons); Combat Service Support (USA); Commit Sequence Summary; Confederate

States Ship (C.S.S.); Contractor Storage Site

CSSA: Cactus and Succulent Society of America

cssb: compatible single sideband

C S-S Co: Cunard Steam-Ship Company

CSSDA: Council of Social Science Data Archives

CSSDC: Canadian Society for the Study of Diseases in Children

CSSM: Council of State Supervisors of Music

CSSO: Consolidated Surplus Sales Office

CSSP: Center for Studies of Suicide Prevention

CSSRC: Canadian Social Science Research Council

CSSS: Canadian Soil Science Society

cst: convulsive shock therapy

CST: Cargo Ships and Tankers; Celeban Standard Time; Central Standard Time

CSta: consolidating station

cs & tae: combat surveillance and target acquisition equipment (DoD)

CSTC: Coppin State Teachers College

C'sted: Christiansted, St Croix

cstg: casting

CSTI: Chattanooga State Technical Institute

cstol: combined short takeoff and landing; controlled short takeoff and landing

cstr: canister

csts: combined systems test stand

CSTS: Combined Systems Test Stand

csu: catheter specimen of urine; central statistical unit; circuit switching unit(s)

CSU: Casualty Staging Unit; Colorado State University

CSU: Christlich-Soziale Union (German—Christian Social Union)—political party

CSUC: California California State University at Chico

CSUCA: Consejo Superior Universitaria Centroamericano (Superior Council of Central American Universities)

CSUF: California State University at Fresno

CSUH: California State University at Humboldt

CSULA: California State University at Los Angeles

CSULB: California State University at Long Beach

CSUS: California State University at Sacramento

CSUSA: Copyright Society of the U.S.A.

CSUSB: California State University at San Bernardino

CSUSD: California State University at San Diego

CSUSF: California State University at San Francisco

CSUSJ: California State University at San Jose

CSWI: Commission for Synoptic Weather Information

Cswy: Causeway

csz: copper, steel, or zinc (freight)

ct: cent; center tap; ceramic tile; coffee table; current transformer

c/t: conference terms

c & t: classification and testing

ct: (underground slang—colored time; cock teaser; cunt teaser)—respectively, a person who is late and therefore on colored time, a female flirt without serious sexual intentions, a male flirt without serious sexual intentions

Ct: celtium; Court

CT: chronometer time; Ciudad Trujillo; Combat Team

cta: call time adjustor; catamenia (menstruation)

cta: communiquer à toutes adresses (French—circulate to all addresses); *cuenta* (Spanish—account)

c.t.a.: cum testamento annexo (Latin—with the will annexed)

CTA: California Teachers Association; Canadian Tuberculosis Association; Caribbean Tourist Association; Chemical Toilet Association; Chicago Transit Authority; Compañía Transatlántica Española (Spanish Line); Council for Technical Advancement; Covered Threads Association

cta corrte: cuenta corriente (Spanish—current account)

cta cte: cuenta corriente (Spanish—current account)

CTAF: Crew Training Air Force

ctb: ceramic-tile base

CTB: Commercial Traffic Bulletin; Commonwealth Telecommunications Board; Corporation for Television Broadcasts

CTBA: California Toll Bridge Authority

ctbore: counterbore

ctc: carbon tetrachloride

CTC: California Tankers Company; Canadian Tire Corporation; Catholic Teachers College; Central Test Control; Chicago Teachers College; Chicago

Technical College; Citizens Training Camp; Citizens Training Corps; Concordia Teachers College; Curaçao Trading Company; Cyclists Touring Club

CTCP: Contract Task Change Proposal

ctd: coated

ctdc: control track direction computer

CTDC: Chemical Thermodynamics Data Center (NBS)

ctdh: command and telemetry data handling

cte: coefficient of thermal expansion

CTE: Car Tours in Europe; Compañía Transatlántica Española (Spanish Line)

CTEB: Council of Technical Examining Bodies

Cten: Ctenophora

CTES: Computer Telex Exchange System (RCA)

ctf: certificate; correction to follow; cytotoxic factor

CTF: Canadian Teachers Federation; Commander Task Force

CTFA: Cosmetics, Toiletry, and Fragrance Association

ctfm: continuous-transmission frequency-modulated (sonar)

ctg: cartage; cartridge; cutting

Ctg: Cartagena

CTG: Commander Task Group

CTGI: Canadian Test of General Information

C3S: College Chemistry Consultants Service

CTH: Chalmers Tekniska Högskola (Swedish—Chalmers Institute of Technology); Corporation of Trinity House

Cthse: Courthouse

cti: Container Transport International (trademark)

CTI: Central Technical Institute; Cooling Tower Institute

CTIC: Cable Television Information Center

cTk: tropical continental air colder than underlying surface

CTK: *Ceskoslovenska Tiskova Kancelar* (Czechoslovak Press Bureau)

ctl: castellate; cental; central; control

CTL: Cincinnati Testing Laboratories

ctlo: constructive total loss only

ctm: communications terminal modules

ctmdr: clamptop metal drum

ctn: carton; cotangent

C Tn: Cape Town (British maritime contraction)

CTN: Canton Island (tracking station)

CTNE: Compañía Telefónica Nacional de España (National Telephone Company of Spain)

CTNS: Chicago Tribune News Service

cto: concerto

CTO: Central Treaty Organization; Cognizant Transportation Office; Courier Transfer Officer

CTOA: Creative Tour Operators Association

c-to-c: center-to-center

ctol: conventional takeoff and landing

ct ord: court order

ctr: center; contour; controlled thermonuclear reactor; counter; cutter

Ctr: Center

CTR: Controlled Thermonuclear Reactor

CTRA: Coal Tar Research Association

CTRP: Controlled Thermonuclear Research Program

cts: cents; contralateral threshold shift (audiometry)

cts: *centavos* (Spanish—cents); *centimes* (French—cents); *centimos* (Spanish—cents)

Cts: courts

CTS: Centralized Title Service; Chicago Theological Seminary; Combined Test Stand; Concordia Theological Seminary; Contract Technical Services; cosmic top secret; Courier Transfer Station

ctsp: contract technical services personnel

CTSS: Compatible Time-Shared System

CTT: Columbia Technical Translations

Cttee: Committee

ctu: centigrade thermal unit

CTU: Commander Task Unit

CTU (AFL-CIO): Commercial Telegraphers' Union

C-tube: C-shaped tube

CTV: Canadian Television

ctvo: *centavo* (Spanish—cent)

ctw: counterweight

cTw: tropical continental air warmer than underlying surface

CTW: Children's Television Workshop

C₁₂H₂₂O₁₁: cane sugar

$C_{12}H_{22}O_{11}$: cane sugar

ctwt: counterweight

ctx: computer telex exchange (RCA system)

CTZ: Corps Tactical Zone

cu: cleanup; clinical unit; closeup; container unit (CU); cube; cubic; cumulus

c-u: see you

c/u: *cada uno* (Spanish—each one)

Cu: Cuba; Cuban; cumulus; *cuprum* (Latin—copper)

CU: Cambridge University; Capital University; Carleton University; Clafkin University; Clark University; Colgate University; Columbia University; Cooper Union; copper Cornell University; Creighton University; Cumberland University

CUA: Canadian Underwriters Association; Catholic University of America; Council on Urban Affairs

cuad: *cuadrado* (Spanish—square)

CUB: advanced unit base

CUBANA: Compañía Cubana de Aviacion

CUC: Canberra University College; Canadian Unitarian Council

cu cm: cubic centimeter

'cuda(s): barracuda(s)

Cuddy: Cuthbert

CUE: Center for Urban Education

CUEBS: Commission on Undergraduate Education in the Biological Sciences

Cuen: Cuenca

CUF: Canadian Universities Foundation

'cuffs: handcuffs

cu ft min: cubic feet per minute

cu ft sec: cubic feet per second

cu in: cubic inch

cuis: *cuisine* (French—cookery; kitchen)

cuj.: *cujus* (Latin—of which)

CUK: São Paulo, Brazil (Combica Airport)

cukes: cucumbers

cul: culinary

c-u-l: see you later

CUL: Cambridge University Libraries; China Union Lines; Columbia University Library; Cooper Union Library; Cornell University Library

cull.: cullage; cullboard; culling; cullion

cult.: cultural; culture

culv: culvert

cum: central-unit memory

cu m: cubic meter

Cumb: Cumberland

cu mm: cubic millimeter

cu mu: cubic micron

cun: cuneiform

cuni: cupro-nickel (coin alloy)

cu-nim: cumulo-nimbus (clouds)

CUNY: City University of New York

cup.: cupboard

CUP: Cambridge University Press; Columbia University Press

cuppa': cup of tea (Cockney contraction)
CUPR: Catholic University of Puerto Rico
CUPS: Consolidated Unit Personnel Section
cur.: curiosa; curiosity; currency; current
Cur: Curaçao (maritime abbreviation)
CUR: Curaçao, Netherlands West Indies (Plesman Airport)
CURE: Citizens United for Racial Equality
CURLS: College, University, and Research Libraries Section (California Library Association)
CURMCO: City Urban Renewal Management Corporation (NYC)
curr: currency; current
Currer Bell: Charlotte Bronte
curt.: curtain
Curt: Curtis
CURTS: Common-User Radio Transmission System
curv: cable-operated unmanned recovery vehicle
CURV: Cable-controlled Underwater Research Vehicle
Curzio Malaparte: pseudonym —Curzio Suckert)
CUS: Cambridge Union Society
CUSA: Conservative United Synagogue of America
cusecs: cubic feet per second
Cus Ho: Custom House
CUSM: Columbia University School of Medicine
CUSO: Canadian University Service Overseas
CUSP: Central Unit for Scientific Photography
CUSRPC: Canada-United States Regional Planning Committee
CUSRPG: Canada-United States Regional Planning Group
CUSS: Continental, Union, Shell, Superior (oil companies' deep-sea oil-drilling ship)
cust: custard; custodian; custody; custom(s)
CUSW/NAS: Committee on Undersea Warfare—National Academy of Sciences
cut.: cutler; cutlery; cutter; cutting
CUTS: Computer-Utilized Turning System
Cu₂SO₄: copper sulfate
CUUS: Consumers Union of the United States
CUW: Committee on Undersea Warfare (DoD)
cu yd: cubic yard
cv: cardiovascular; check valve; coefficient of variation; collec-

tion voucher; concave; convertible; culture vulture
cv: *cheval-vapeur* (French—horsepower)
Cv: molecular heat (symbol)
CV: aircraft carrier (2-letter naval symbol); Central Vermont (railroad); Chula Vista; collection voucher; combat vehicle; Convair
CV: *cheval-vapeur* (French—horsepower)
C-V: Convair (Division of General Dynamics)
cva: cerebrovascular accident (medical euphemism for a stroke)
CVA: attack aircraft carrier (naval symbol); Columbia Valley Authority
CVA: Civilian Voluntary Agency
CVAA: Centre de Vulgarisation Aero-Astronautique
CVAC: Consolidated Vultee Aircraft (now Convair)
CVAN: nuclear-powered aircraft carrier (naval symbol)
cvb: combined very-high-frequency band
CVB: large aircraft carrier (naval symbol)
c-v-c: consonant-vowel-consonant
CVC: Clinch Valley College; Consolidated Vacuum Corporation
cvcc: compound vortex-controlled combustion (Japanese automotive engine designed by Honda to reduce air pollution by reducing pollutant emissions)
cvd: cardiovascular disease; cash versus documents; coordination of valve development; coupled vibration dissociation; current-voltage diagram
CVDE: *Columbia-Viking Desk Encyclopedia*
cve (**CVE**): customer-vended equipment
CVE: aircraft carrier, escort (naval symbol)
CVF: Caravelle fan jet airplane; Corporation Venezolano de Fomento (Venezuelan Promotion Corporation)
CVG: Cincinnati, Ohio (Greater Cincinnati Airport)
CVG: Corporacion Venezolana de Guayana
CVHS: Chelsea Vocational High School
cvi: cerebrovascular insufficiency
CVI: Cape Verde Islands; College of the Virgin Islands
CVIS: Computerized Vocational Information System
cvk: centerline vertical keel
CVL: Caravelle jet airplaine; small

aircraft carrier (naval symbol)
CVMA: Canadian Veterinary Medical Association
cvn: convene
c.v.o.: *conjugata vera obstetrica* (Latin—conjugate obstetric diameter)
CVO: Chief Veterinary Office(r)
C.V.O.: Commander of the Royal Victorian Order
cvp: central venous pressure
CVP: Corporación Venezolano del Petróleo (Venezuelan Petroleum Corporation)
cvr: cardiovascular renal; cardiovascular-respiratory; cerebrovascular resistance; continuous video recorder
CVS: antisubmarine warfare support aircraft carrier (3-letter symbol)
cvt: convertible
CVT: training aircraft carrier (naval symbol)
c/vta: *cuenta de venta* (Spanish —bill of sale)
CVW: attack carrier air wing (naval symbol)
cw: clockwise; cold water; continuous wave; copperweld (copper-covered steel); cubic weight
c-w: chronometer time minus watch time
c/w: counterweight
c & w: country and western (music)
CW: Channel Airways; chemical warfare; continuous wave
C-W: Curtiss-Wright
C of W: College of Wooster (Ohio)
CWA: Civil Works Administration; Communication Workers of America; County Water Authority
cwar: continuous-wave acquisition radar
cwas: contractor-weighted average share
CWB: Child Welfare Bureau
cw-bw: chemical warfare—biological warfare
CWC: Canadian Welfare Council; Central Wesleyan College
CWCC: Civil War Centennial Commission
cwe: current working estimate
CWE: Commonwealth Edison
cwg: corrugated wire glass
CWGC: Commonwealth War Graves Commission
cwi: clear word identifier
cwik: cutting with intent to kill
CWIS: Chaim Weizmann Institute of Science
cwit: concordance words in title
CWLA: Child Welfare League of America

CWMTU: Cold Weather Matériel Test Unit
cwo: cash with order
CWO: Chief Warrant Officer
cwp: circulating water pump
CWPEA: Childbirth Without Pain Education Association
CWR: California Western Railroad
CWRA: California Water Resources Association
cws: clockwise; cold-water soluble; countersunk wood screw
Cws: Cowes
CWS: Canadian Welding Society; Canadian Wildlife Service; Chandraprabha Wildlife Sanctuary (India); Child Welfare Services; Cooperative Wholesale Society; Cunard-White Star (steamship line)
C-WS: Crop-Weather Service
CWSC: Central Washington State College
cw sig gen: continuous wave signal generator
CWSP: College Work-Study Program
cwt: hundredweight
CWT: Cooperative Wind Tunnel
CWTC: California World Trade Center
cwu: composite weighted work unit
CWU: California Western University
cwv: continuous-wave video
cx: complex; connection; convex
cxr: carrier
cy: calendar year; capacity; currency; current year; cycle
Cy: cyanogen; Cyprus; Cyrus

cya: cover your anatomy; cover your ass
CYA: California Youth Authority; Carded Yarn Association; Catholic Youth Adoration (Society); Covenant Youth of America
cyan: cyanamid; cyanic; cyanide; cyanogen; cyanotype
cyath.: cyathus (Latin—cup, ladle, glass)
cyath. vin.: cyathus vinarius (Latin—wineglassful)
cyb: cybernetic; cyberneticist; cybernetics
CYB: Canada Year Book
cyborg: cybernetic organism
cyc: cycle; cycling; cyclist; cyclone
Cycl: Cyclostomata
cyclams: cyclamates
cyclecade: bicycle or motorcycle parade
cyclo: cyclopedia; cyclopedic; cyclotron
cyclon: cyclonometer
CYEE: Central Youth Employment Executive (UK)
CYFA: Club for Young Friends of Animals
CYHA: Canadian Youth Hostels Association
cyk: consider yourself kissed
cyke: cyclorama
cyl: cylinder; cylindrical; cylindroid
cyl l: cylinder lock
cyls: cylinders
cym: cymbal(s)
Cym: Cymric
CYMA: Catholic Young Men's Association
Cymb: Cymbeline

cyn: cyanide
Cyn: Canyon; Cynthia
CYO: Catholic Youth Organization; Civic Youth Orchestra
Cyp: Cyprian; Cypriote; Cyprus
CYP: Cyprus Airways
cys: cysteine; cystoscopy
cys (CYS): cystine (amino acid)
CYS: Cheyenne, Wyoming (airport)
CYSA: Combed Yarn Spinners Association
cysto: cystoscope; cystoscopic examination
cyt: cytology
cytac: control of tactical aircraft
Cz: Czech; Czechoslovakia; Czechoslovakian
CZ: Canal Zone; combat zone; communications zone
C.Z.: Canal Zone
C-Z: Crown-Zellerbach
Cza: Constanza
CZA: Coastal Zone Authority
CZBA: Canal Zone Biological Area
CZC: Canal Zone College
CZC: Canal Zone Code (legal)
Czech: Czechoslovakia; Czechoslovakian
Czech Phil: Czech Philharmonic
CZG: Canal Zone Government
CZJC: Canal Zone Junior College
Cz kr: Czechoslovakian kronen (monetary unit)
CZm: compass azimuth
C-Zone: commercial zone
CZP: Chicago Zoological Park (Brookfield Park)
czy: crazy

D

d: angular deformation (symbol); date; daughter; day; declination; degree; depth; dextrorotatory; died; differentiation; dime; dinar; diopter; divorced; dorsal; drizzling; dyne; grating space in calcite (symbol); liter (symbol); pence (symbol); penny (symbol)
d: decimus (Latin—tenth); *der* (German—the); *denarii* (Latin—pennies); *danarius* (Latin—penny); *dexter* (Latin—right)
D: December; degree of curve (symbol); Delta—code for letter D; democracy; Democrat(ic);

density; Denver; department; derivation; Detroit; deuterium; diameter; dielectric flux density (symbol); Dietzgen; dioptric power (symbol); director aircraft; disaster; disaster broadcasting; dollar; dose; Douglas; down; drag (symbol); drone-control version (symbol); Dublin; Dutch; Fraunhofer lines caused by sodium (symbol); propeller diameter (symbol)
D: Damen (German—ladies); *damas* (Spanish—ladies); *darin* (German—in); *Dauer* (German—bulb-type camera shutter

stop); *dehors* (French—out); *depart* (French—departure); *derecha* (Spanish—right); *Deus* (Latin—God); *dexter* (Latin—right *dun* (Danish—down)
D.: Don (Spanish—Sir)—Mr
D3: Douglas DC-3 airplane
D4: Douglas DC-4 airplane
D6: Douglas DC-6 airplane
D7: Douglas DC-7 airplane
D8F: Douglas D8F fan jet airplane
D8S: Douglas super DC-8 fan jet airplane
D9S: Douglas super DC-9 fan jet airplane
D'66: Democrats 1966 (Dutch poli-

tical party)

D-150: Dimension 150 (150-degree field of vision achieved by deeply curved motion-picture screen)

da: daughter; days after acceptance; delayed action; delayed arming; density altitude; deposit account; direct action; discharge afloat; district attorney; documents against acceptance; documents attached; do not answer; double acting; double aged; drift angle

d-a: direct-action (adjective)

d/a (D/A): deposit account

da: *dette ar* (Norwegian—this year)

dA: *dette Aar* (Danish—this year)

dÄ: *der Ältere* (German—senior)

Da: Denmark; Danish

Dª: *Doña* (Spanish—lady; woman of rank)

DA: Daughters of America; Defense Aid; Dental Apprentice; Department of Agriculture; Department of the Army; direct action (DA as a noun; d-a as an adjective); District Attorney; Division Artillery; does not affect; Dominion Atlantic (railroad); Dragon Airways; drift angle (symbol)

DA: *Dissertation Abstracts*

D of A: Department of Agriculture

DAB: *Deutsches Aporthekerbuch* (German Pharmacopoeia); *Dictionary of American Biography*

DABPN: Diplomate American Board of Psychiatry and Neurology

DABS: Discrete Address Beacon System

dac: direct air cycle

DAC: Daughters of the American Colonists; Defenders of the American Constitution; Douglas Aircraft Company; Durex Abrasives Corporation

DACAN: Douglas Aircraft Company of Canada

D.Acc.: Doctor of Accountancy

DACCC: Defense Area Communications Control Center

dachs: dachshund

dacks: slacks (sport pants) made of dacron

DACO: Douglas Aircraft Corporation Overseas

dacon: digital to analog converter

dacor: data correction

dacr: dacron (synthetic fiber)

DACRP: Department of the Army Communication Resources Plan

DACS: Data Acquisition and Correction System

dacty: dactylography; dactyloscopy

dactygram: dactylogram (finger-print)

dad: daddy (father)

dad.: double-acting door

DAD: Directorate of Armament Development

D.Adm.: Doctor of Administration

DADS: Director Army Dental Service

D.Ae.: Doctor of Aeronautics

DAE: *Dictionary of American English*

daea: dimethyl aminoethyl acetate

DAEC: Danish Atomic Energy Commission

D.Ae.Eng.: Doctor of Aeronautical Engineering

D.Ae.Sc.: Doctor of Aeronautical Science

daf: described as follows

DAF: Department of the Air Force; *van Doorne Auto Fabriek* (Dutch autos and trucks made by van Doorne's auto factory)

dafa: data accounting flow assessment

dafc: digital automatic frequency control

DAFCCS: Department of the Air Force Command and Control System

DAFFO: *Dansk Forening til Fremme af Opfindelser* (Danish Society for Encouraging Inventions)

daffs: daffodils

DAFIE: Directorate for Armed Forces Information and Education

dafm: discard-at-failure maintenance

DAFO: Division Accounting and Finance Office

DAFS: Department of Agriculture and Fisheries (Scotland); Duty Air Force Specialty

DAFSC: Duty Air Force Specialty Code

DAFSO: Department of the Air Force Special Order

Dag: Dagestan(i); Dag Hammarskjöld; Dagmar; Dagna

Dag: *Dagbladet* (Oslo's Daily Blade)

D.Ag.: Doctor of Agriculture

dag(h): (Turkish—mountain)

daglari: (Turkish—mountain range)

dagmar: drift-and-ground-speed-measuring radar

Dag Nyh: *Dagens Nyheter* (Sweden's Daily News)

Dago: (navalese for San Diego, California)

D.Agr.: Doctor of Agriculture

D.Agr.Eng.: Doctor of Agricultural Engineering

D.Agr.Sc.: Doctor of Agricultural Science

Dah: Dahomey

DAH: disordered action of the heart

dai (DAI): death from accidental injuries

DAI: Drug Abuse Information

DAIR: Driver Aid Information and Routing (System)

DAIS: Defense Automatic Integrated Switching System

daisy.: data acquisition and interpretation system

Dak: Dakota; Dakotan

dal: decaliter

dal: (Dano-Norwegian, Dutch, Swedish—dale; valley)

d'AL: d'Amico Line

Dal: Dallas; Dalmatia; Dalmatian

DAL: Dallas, Texas (Love Field); Delta Air Lines; Department of Agriculture Library; Deutsche Afrika Linien (German Africa Line)

DALE: Drug Abuse Law Enforcement

Dalh: Dalhousie

Dall: *Dallas' Reports—U.S. Supreme Court*

Dal Sym Orch: Dallas Symphony Orchestra

dalvp: delay enroute authorized chargeable as ordinary leave provided it does not interfere with reporting on date specified and provided individual has sufficient accrued leave

dam.: damage

DAM: Damascus, Syria (airport); Dayton Art Museum; Denver Art Museum

dame.: data acquisition and monitoring equipment

DAMIS: Department of the Army Management Information System

DAMWO: Department of the Army Modification Work Order

dan: dekanewton

Dan: Daniel (name); Daniel, Book of; Danish; Danmark (Denmark)

DAN: Dan-Air Services

DANBIF: *Danske Boghandleres Importrfrening* (Danish Booksellers Importation Association)

Danl: Daniel

Danl W: Daniel Webster

Danm: Danmark (Denmark)

d'Annunzio: (Gabriel) Gaetano Rapagnetta

Danny: Daniel

Dansker: Dane; Danish sailor

Dante: Dante (Durante) Alighieri

dao: duly-authorized officer, paldao (Philippine wood)

DAO: District Accounting

Office(r); District Aviation Office(r); Division Air Office(r); Division Ammunition Office(r); Dominion Astrophysical Observatory (Victoria, British Columbia)

dap: data automation proposal; do anything possible

d-a-p: draw-a-person (psychological test)

DAP: Division of Air Pollution (US Public Health)

dapon: diallyl phthalate resin

dapr: digital automatic pattern recognition

DAPS: Direct-Access Programming System

dar: (Arabic—land)

Dar: Dar-es-Salaam

Dar: Dar-es-Salaam (Arabic—There is the Peace)—capital and seaport of Tanzania; nickname for Dar-es-Salaam

DAR: Daughters of the American Revolution; Dominion Atlantic Railway

DARAS: Direction and Range Acquisition System

DARCEE: Demonstration and Research Center for Early Education (Peabody College)

D.Arch.: Doctor of Architecture

D.Arch.E.: Doctor of Architectural Engineering

DARE: Drug Abuse Research and Education (UCLAs neuropsychiatric institute); Drug Assistance, Rehabilitation, and Education

daren't: dare not

DARES: Data Analysis and Reduction System

DARF: Defense Atomic Research Facility

DARR: Department of the Army Regional Representative

DARs: Design Assist Reports; Development Appraisal Reports

DARS: Digital Adaptive Recording System

DARTS: Dynamically-Actuated Road Transit System

Darwin's Bulldog: Thomas Henry Huxley

darya: (Persian—salt lake)

das: delivered alongside ship

DAs: Design Assist Reports

DAS: Director of Administrative Services

DAS: *Dictionary of American Slang*

DASA: Defense Atomic Support Agency

DASC: Defense Automotive Supply Center; Direct Air Support Center

dasd: direct access storage device

dash.: drone antisubmarine helicopter

DASH: Delta Airlines Special Handling (of small packages)

dasht: (Persian—desert; plain)

daso (DASO): development and shakedown operations

DASS: Direct Air Support Squadron (USAF)

dat: dative; datum; delayed-action tablet; differential agglutination titer

DAT: Differential Aptitude Test; Docking Alignment Target (NASA)

DATA: Defense Air Transportation Administration; Development and Technical Assistance (international organization)

datacom: data communications

datacor: data correction; data correlator

datan: data analysis

datar: digital automatic tracking and ranging

datico: digital automatic tape intelligence checkout

datin: data inserter

DATO: Disbursing and Transportation Office; Discover America Travel Organizations

dator: digital (data), auxiliary (storage), track (display), outputs (and) radar (display)

datran: data transmission

datrix: direct access to reference information

DATSC: Department of the Army Training and Support Committee

dau(s): daughter(s)

D.Au.Eng.: Doctor of Automobile Engineering

Dav: David

DAV: Disabled American Veterans

davc: delayed automatic-volume control

Dave: David

DAVI: Department of Audio-Visual Instruction (National Education Association)

Davy: David

DAW: Directorate of Atomic Warfare

dawid: device for automatic word identification and discrimination

Day: Dayton

DAY: Dayton, Ohio (airport)

db: day book; dead body; decibel; distribution box; double bayonet-base (lamp); double-biased (relay); double braid; double-breasted; dry bulb

d & b: dead and buried

dB: decibel

DB: Deutsche Bundesbahn (Ger-

man State Railways); Disciplinary Barracks; Dispersal Base; Dodge Brothers

D-B: Daimler-Benz

D & B: Dun & Bradstreet

D of B: Daughters of Bilitis

d b a: doing business as

DBA: Duke Bar Association

D.B.A.: Doctor of Business Administration

dbb: detector back bias

db & b: deals, boards, and battens

dbc: diameter bolt circle

DBC: Demerara Bauxite Company; Detective Book Club

D.B.C.: Doctor of Beauty Culture

DBCA: Du Bois Clubs of America

DBCM: De Beers Consolidated Mines

dbe: double-bell euphonium (marching band tuba)

D.B.E.: Dame Commander of the Order of the British Empire

dbed (DBED): dibenzyl-ethylene-diamine (penicillin)

D.B.Ed.: Doctor of Business Education

dbh: diameter breast high

dbhp: drawbar horsepower

DBib: Douay Bible

D.Bi.Chem.: Doctor of Biological Chemistry

D.Bi.Eng.: Doctor of Biological Engineering

D.Bi.Phy.: Doctor of Biological Physics

D.Bi.Sc.: Doctor of Biological Sciences

DBJC: Daytona Beach Junior College

dbk: debark; drawback

DBK: Daiichi Bussan Kaisha (Japanese steamship line); Dobeckmun (company)

dbkn: debarkation

dbl: double; doubler

DBL: Displaced Business Loan (SBA)

dbl act.: double acting

dbl eleph fol.: double elephant folio—books about 50 inches high

dblr: doubler

dbm: decibels per milliwatt; diabetic management

dBm: decibel referred to one milliwatt

DBM: Division of Biology and Medicine (Atomic Energy Commission)

DBMS: Director of Base Medical Services

dbo: dead blackout

D-box: distribution box

dbp: drawbar pull

DBP: Division of Beaches and

Parks

db part: double-beaded partition

DBPO: Data Buoy Project Office

dbr: double book rack

DBR: Division of Building Research

dbre: diciembre (Spanish—December)

dbrn: decibels above reference noise

db rts: debenture rights

dbs (DBS): direct broadcast satellite

db's: dirty books

DBS: Division of Biological Standards

DBST: Double British Summer Time

dbt: dry-bulb temperature

dbtt: ductile-brittle transmission temperature

dbv: decibel referred to 1 volt

DBV: Deutscher Bund für Vogelschutz (German Birdshooters Bund)

dbw: differential ballistic wind

dc: deck cargo; deposited carbon; deviation clause; digital computer; direct cycle; directional coupler; disorderly conduct; double cap; double column; double contact; down center

d-c: direct-chill (casting); direct-current (adjective)

d/c: deviation clause; double-column (bookkeeping)

d & c: dilation and curettage

dc: da capo (Italian—again)

d/c: dinero contante (Spanish—cash)

dC: dopo Cristo (Italian—after the birth of Christ)

DC: Dana College; Dartmouth College; Davidson College; decimal classification; Defiance College; Dental Corps; Department of Commerce; Dickinson College; Diners Club; direct current (when used as a noun); District of Columbia (D.C.); Doane College; Doctor of Chiropractic; Dominican College; Donnelly College; Dordt College; Drury College; Duchesne College, Dumbarton College; Dyke College; D'Youville College

D-C: Denver-Chicago (truck line); Dow-Corning (chemical products)

D/C: drift correction

D & C: Detroit and Cleveland (steamship line)

DC: Democrazia Christiana (Italian—Christian Democracy)—political party; *Distrito Capital* (Spanish—Capital District)

D C: da capo (Italian—from the beginning)

D of C: Daughters of the Confederacy; Department of Commerce

DC-8: Douglas DC8 jet airplane

DC-9: Douglas twin-jet short-range airplane

DC-10: McDonnel-Douglas jumbo jetliner

DCA: Dachshund Club of America; Dalmatian Club of America; Damage Control Assistant; Defense Communications Agency; desoxycorticosterone acetate; Diamond Council of America; Diapulse Corporation of America; Digital Computers Association; Disassembly Compliance and Analysis; Disc Company of America; Distribution Contractors Association; Drug Control Agency; Dynamics Coproration of America; Washington, D.C. (national airport)

DCA: Défense Contre Aéronefs (French—anti-aircraft defense)

DCAA: Defense Contract Audit Agency

DCA/A: Disassembly Compliance and Analysis/Abbreviated

DCADA: District of Columbia Alley Dwelling Authority

DCAOC: Defense Communications Agency Operations Center

d cap: double foolscap (paper)

DCAR: Disassembly Compliance and Analysis Report

DCAS: Data Collection and Analysis System; Defense Contract Administration Services; Deputy Chief of Air Staff

DCASR: Defense Contract Administrative Service Region

DCATA: Drug, Chemical, and Allied Trades Association

DCB: Decimal Currency Board (British)

DCBRE: Defense Chemical, Biological, and Radiation Establishment

dcc: double concave; double cotton covered

DCC: Defense Concessions Committee; Dutchess Community College

DCCA: Design Change Cost Analysis

DCCB: Defense Center Control Building (USA)

d & c color: drug and cosmetic color (synthetic dye)

DCCS: Digital Command Communications System

dcd: differential current density

DCD: Daitch Crystal Dairies; Directorate of Civil Disturbance

DCDMA: Diamond Core Drill

Manufacturers Association

DCDPO: Directorate for Civil Disturbance Planning and Operations (USA)

dcdr: decoder

dcds: double cotton double silk

DCE: Division of Compensatory Education

D.C.E.: Doctor of Civil Engineering

dcf: deal-cased frame; direct centrifugal flotation; discounted cash flow

dcg: dancing; decigram

dch: dicyclohexyl

DCH: Diploma in Child Health

D.Ch.E.: Doctor of Chemical Engineering

DCHCL: Dropsie College for Hebrew and Cognate Learning

dci: driving car intoxicated

DCI: Department of Citizenship and Immigration; Des Moines and Central Iowa (railway); Director of Central Intelligence

DCJ: District Court Judge

DCL: Detroit College of Law; Deuterium of Canada, Limited; Distillers Company Limited

D.C.L.: Doctor of Civil Law

DCM: Director of Civilian Marksmanship; Directorate of Classified Management; Distinguished Conduct Medal; District Court Martial; Dominican Campaign Medal

D.C.M.: Doctor of Comparative Medicine

DCMA: Dry Color Manufacturers Association

dcmi: disclosure of classified military information

DCMs: Deputy Chiefs of Missions

DCN: Design Change Notice

D.Cn.L.: Doctor of Canon Law

DCNO: Deputy Chief of Naval Operations

DCNS: Deputy Chief of Naval Staff

DCO: Dallas Civic Opera; Dominion, Colonial, and Overseas (Department of Barclays Bank)

D. Com.: Doctor of Commerce

D. Comp. L.: Doctor of Comparative Law

DCOR: Defense Committee on Research (USAF)

dcp: discrete component parts

DCP: Diploma in Clinical Pathology; Disaster Control Plan

DCPL: District of Columbia Public Library

dcr: decrease; decreasing

DCR: Design Characteristic Review; Design Change Request; Drawing Change Request

DCRLA: District of Columbia Re-

development Land Agency
dcs: double cotton single silk
DCS: Damage Control School (USN); Defense Communications System; Deputy Chief of Staff; Digital Command System; Direct Coupler System; Distillers Corporation—Seagrams
D.C.S.: Doctor of Christian Science; Doctor of Commercial Science
DCSAB: Distinguished Civilian Service Awards Board
DCSC: Defense Construction Supply Center
DCS/P: Deputy Chief of Staff for Personnel
DCS/P&O: Deputy Chief of Staff for Plans and Operations
DCS/P&R: Deputy Chief of Staff for Programs and Resources
DCS/R&D: Deputy Chief of Staff for Research and Development
DCS/S&L: Deputy Chief of Staff for Systems and Logistics
dct: depth-charge thrower; document
DCTC: District of Columbia Teachers College; Dodge County Teachers College
dctl: direct-coupled transistor logic
DCTSC: Defense Clothing and Textile Supply Center
dcu: dynamic checkout unit
dcutl: direct-coupled unipolar transistor logic
dcv: double cotton varnish
DCW: Detroit Chemical Works
dcx: double convex
dd: days after date; day's date; deadline date; deep-drawn; deferred delivery; delayed delivery; delivered; development directive; differential diagnosis; digital display; discharged dead; double draft; drydock; due date; dutch door
d-d: dumb-dumb
d'd: deceased
d/d: dated; delivered at dock(s); demand draft; detergent dispersant; domicile to domicile; due date
d & d: drunk and disorderly
d.d.: *dono dedit* (Latin—he gave as a gift)
Dd: David
DD: Deputy Director; destroyer (naval symbol); Development Directive; Dishonorable Discharge; E.I. du Pont de Nemours & Company (stock exchange symbol)
D.D.: Doctor of Divinity
D en D: *Docteur en Droit* (French —Doctor of Law)

dda (DDA): digital differential analyzer
DDA: da; dangerous Drug Act
ddalv: days delay enroute authorized chargeable as leave
DDAS: Digital Data Acquisition System
D-Day: day of attack
ddc: direct digital control
DDC: corvette (naval symbol); Defense Documentation Center; Dewey Decimal Classification; Diamond Dealers Club
ddc's: deck decompression chambers
DDCs: Desk and Derrick Club members (petroleum professionals)
DDD: direct distance dialing
d.d. in d.: *de die in diem* (Latin—from day to day)
ddda: decimal digital differential analyzer
DDE: Dwight David Eisenhower
DDEM: Dwight D. Eisenhower Museum
DDEP: Defense Development Exchange Program
ddf: design disclosure format
DDF: Dental Documentary Foundation
DDG: guided missile destroyer (naval symbol)
ddi: depth deviation indicator
DDI: Deputy Director, Intelligence (CIA)
ddl: digital data link
DDL: Det Danske Luftfartsselskab (The Danish Airways)
ddm: data demand module
DDM: Diploma in Dermatological Medicine
DDN: nuclear-powered destroyer (naval symbol)
DDNI: Deputy Director of Naval Intelligence
DDO: David Dunlap Observatory (Ontario)
DDP: Deputy Director, Plans (CIA)
DDPS: Discrimination Data Processing System
DDr: Doktor, Doktor (Austrian-German—person with two doctor's degrees)
DDR: Deutsche Demokratische Republik (German Democratic Republic); radar picket destroyer (3-letter naval symbol)
DD R & D: Department of Defense Research and Development
DDR&E: Defense Development Research and Engineering
dds: diaminodiphenylsulfone; digital dynamics simulator
DDS: Deep-Diving System; Deployable Defense System

D.D.S.: Doctor of Dental Science; Doctor of Dental Surgery
D.D.Sc.: Doctor of Dental Science
DDSG: Donau-Dampfschiffahrts-Gesellschaft (Danube Steamship Travel Service)
DDST: Double Daylight Saving Time (two hours ahead)
ddt: deduct
DDT: dichlorodiphenyl-trichloro-ethane (insecticide)
ddt & e: design, development, test, and evaluation
DDTV: Dry Diver Transport Vehicle (naval)
ddv: deck drain valve
de: diesel-electric; double end; double entry
de: det er (Norwegian—that is)
DE: Deere (stock exchange symbol); Department of Education; Department of Employment; Department of the Environment; destroyer escort (naval symbol); District Engineer
D of E: Department of the Environment (UK)
Dea: Deacon
DEA: Dance Educators of America; Department of External Affairs
deac: deacon
DEACONS: Direct English Access and Control System
DEADS: Detroit Air Defense Sector
deal: decision evaluation and logic
DEAN: Deputy Educators Against Narcotics
dear.: diamonds, emeralds, amethysts, rubies
DEB: Dental Examining Board
Deb(by): Deborah
de Bc: Honoré de Balzac
debk: debark; debarkation
deb(s): debenture(s); debutante(s)
dec: decimal; decimeter; decision; declination; decorate; decoration; decorator
dec.: *décembre* (French—December); *décor* (French—decoration; stage scenery); *decubitus* (Latin—lying down)
Dec: Decca; December
DEC: Detroit Edison Company
deca-: 10
decaf: decaffeinated
decal: decalcomania
DECAL: detection and classification of an acoustic lens
deccan: (Indian—south)
DECCO: Defense Commercial Communications Office
decd: deceased
deci: 10^{-1}
decid: deciduous
decim: decimeter

decis: decision
decl: declension
declon: declaration
DECMD: Detroit Contract Management District
decn: decision; decontamination
deco: direct energy conversion operation
decoct: decoction
decomp: decomposition
decon: decontaminate; decontamination
D. Econ.: Doctor of Economics
decor: decorate; decoration; decorative
decr: decrease
decres: *decrescendo* (Italin—contracting; subsiding)
DECS: Direct Evacuation Control System (air filtration)
Decuary: December and January
decub.: *decubitus* (Latin—lying down)
DECUS: Digital Equipment Users Society
ded: dedendum; dedicate; dedicated; deduct; deducted; deduction
D. Ed.: Doctor of Education
de d. in d.: *de die in diem* (Latin—from day to day)
deduct.: deduction
dee: digital events recorder
Dee Cee: Washington, D.C.
dee-dee: deaf and dumb
Dee High: Doctor of Hygiene
dee jay: disc jockey
deeks: duck decoys
deel: (Dutch—volume)
Dee Pee: Doctor of Pharmacy
deep 6: burial at sea; disposing of anything unwanted in at least six fathoms of water
Dee R: doctor
def: defecate; defecation; defect; defection; defective; defector; defendant; defense; defensive; defer; deferred; deficiency; deficient; define; definite; definition; deflagrate; deflagrating; deflagration; deflect; deflecting; deflection; defoliate; defoliating; defoliation; defrost; defroster; defrosting; defunct; defunction; defunctive
def art.: definite article
defcon: defense condition
defec: defective
Defense: Department of Defense
defi: deficiency
defl: deflate; deflation; deflect; deflection
deform.: deformity
DEFREPNAMA: Defense Representative North Atlantic and Mediterranean
defs: definitions

DEFSIP: Defense Scientists Immigration Program
deft.: defendant; dynamic error free transmission (DEFT)
DEFY: Drug Education For Youth
deg: degenerate; degeneration; degree(s)
DEG: guided-missile escort ship (naval symbol)
de ga: depth gage
degen: degeneration
deglut.: *deglutiatur* (Latin—let it be swallowed)
dei: double electrically isolated
dej: dento-enamel junction
Dek: *Dekabr* (Russian—December)
deka: 10
dekag: dekagram
del: delegate; delegation; delete; deletion; deliberate; deliberation; delineate; delineated; delineation
del.: *delineavit* (Latin—he or she drew it)
Del: Delaware; Delawarean; Delhi; Delphinus
del acct: delinquent account
deld: delivered
dele: delete
deleg: delegation
deli(s): delicatessen(s)
delib: deliberate; deliberation
delinq: delinquent
deliq: deliquescent
De L Isls: De Long Islands
Del-Mar-Va: Delaware-Maryland-Virginia (Eastern Shore peninsula)
D. Elo.: Doctor of Elocution
delphi: declaiming eclectic liberalism possessively, hotly, instantaneously
delpho: deliver by telephone
delt: delete; deletion
de lt: deck edge light
delta.: detailed labor and time analysis
Delta: code for letter D
deltic: delay line time compression
delu: delusion
Delv: Delvalle
delvd: delivered
dely: delivery
dem: demand; democracy; democrat; democratic; demodulate; demodulator; demonstrate; demonstration; demonstrative; demote; demotion; demur; demurrage; demy
Dem: Demerera (British Guiana); democracy; Democrat; democratic; Democratic Party
DEMA: Diesel Engine Manufacturers Association
dem adj: demonstrative adjective
Demba: Demarara bauxite

demij: demijohn
demo: demolition; demonstration (model)
demob: demobilization; demobilize
demod: demodulator
demogr: demographer; demographic(al); demography
demon.: demonology; demonstrate demonstration; demonstrator
demos: demonstrators (usually led by misguided clericals or by radical communist and fascist anti-liberal elements who would not dare demonstrate in any of many totalitarian countries of the type they seek to establish)
demo(s): demonstration(s); demonstrator(s)
Demos: Democrats
dem pro: demonstrative pronoun
dems: defensively-equipped merchant ship
demur: demurrage
den: denotation; dental; dentist; dentistry
den: *Denier* (German—denier)
Den: Denbighshire; Deniz; Denmark; Denver
Den: *Denizi* (Turkish—lake; sea)
D. En.: Doctor of English
DEN: Denver, Colorado (airport)
denat: denatured
Denb: Denbighshire
dend: dendrology
dendro: dendrometer
dendrol: dendrology
D. Eng.: Doctor of Engineering
D.Eng.Sc.: Doctor of Engineering Science
deniz: (Turkish—sea)
Denny: Denis; Dennis
denom: denomination
dens: density
dent.: dental; dentist; dentistry; denture
D. Ent.: Doctor of Entomology
Dent Corps: Dental Corps
Dent Hyg: Dental Hygienist
dent. tal. dos.: *dentur tales doses* (Latin—give of such doses)
DEO: District Engineering Office; District Engineers Office; Divisional Education Office(r); Divisional Entertainment Office (r)—British Army
DEOR: Duke of Edinburgh's Own Rifles
dep: depart; department; departure; dependency; dependent; depilate; depilatory; depose; deposit; depositor; depot; deputize; deputy; do everything possible
dep.: *depuratus* (Latin—purify)
DEP: Defense Electronic Products (RCA); Department of Employment and Productivity

Dep: Deputy
Dep: Département (French —Department); *Député* (French —Deputy)
DEPA: Defense Electric Power Administration
depart.: department; departure
dep ctf: deposit certificate
depend.: dependent; dependency
dep inst: depot installed
depn: dependency; dependent
depos: depositary
deposn: deposition
depr: depreciation; depreciative; depression
DEPS: Diploma in Economics and Political Science
DepSO: Departmental Standardization Office
dept: depart; department; departure; deponent; depot; deputy
DePU: De Paul University; De Pauw University
deputn: deputation
der: derivation; derivative; derived; dermatine
der: derecha (Spanish—right); *dernier* (French—last)
Der: Derringer
DeR: reaction of degeneration
DER: Development Engineering Review; radar picket escort ship (naval symbol)
Derb(s): Derby; Derbyshire
Derby.: Derbyshire
DERBY: Derby Aviation
Derbys: Derbyshire
Der Führer: (German—The Leader)—sobriquet of Adolf Hitler —dictator of Germany before and during World War II
deriv: derivation
derm: dermatitis; dermatology; dermatophyte
dermat: dermatology
Der Meister: (German—The Master)—Johann Wolfgang von Goethe
dernier(e): (French—last)
deros: date eligible for return from overseas; date of estimated return from overseas service
Derry: Londonderry
derv: disel-engine road vehicle
des: desert; design; designate; designation; designator; designer; desire; dessert
des (Des): diethylstilbestrol (morning-after contraceptive)
Des: Desierto (Spanish—desert); (German—D-flat)
DES: Department of Education and Science; destroyer (naval symbol); Director of Educational Services; Director of Engineering Stores

desat: desaturated
desc: descendant
DESC: Defense Electronics Supply Center
descron: description
descto: descuento (Spanish—discount)
desg: designate; designation
desid: desiderata; desideratum
desider: desiderative
desig: designate; designer
desp: despatch
DESP: Department of Elementary School Principals
DESRON: destroyer squadron
dess: dessiatine
dest: destination; destroy; destroyer; destruction
DEST: Diplômé de l'École Supèrieure Technique (Diploma of the Technical Institute)
destil.: destilla (Latin—distill)
destn: destination
destr: destructor
destr fir: destructive firing
det: detach; detachment; detail; detective; detector; determine; detonator; double end trimmed
det (DET): diethyltryptamine (quick-acting hallucinogen drug)
det.: detur (Latin—let it be given)
det. in dup.: detur in duplo (Latin—let twice as much be given)
Det: Detroit
DET: Design Evaluation Testing; Detroit, Michigan (Detroit City Airport)
DETA: Direcção de Exploração dos Transportes Aéreos (Mozambique airline)
detd: determined
determin: determination
detm: determine
detn: detention
detoxcen: detoxification center (for alcoholics and others addicted to imbibing, inhaling, injecting, or otherwise putting poisons into their bodies)
détroit: (French—strait)
Det Sgt: Detective Sergeant
Det Sym Orch: Detroit Symphony Orchestra
deu: data exchange unit
DEUA: Diesel Engines and Users Association
deuce.: digital electronic universal computing engine
Deut: Deuteronomy
dev: develop; developer; development; deviate; deviation; deviator
Dev: Devon; Devonian; Devonshire; Eamon De Valera's nickname

De V: De Vilbiss
devel: developer; development
Devon: Devonshire
DEW: Distant Early Warning
DEWIZ: Distant Early Warning Identification Zone
DEW Line: Distant Early Warning Line
dex.: dexter (Latin—right)
Dex: Dexter
D. Ex.: Doctor of Expression
dexan: digital experimental airborne navigator
dexe: dexedrine
dexies: dexedrine tablets (stimulant drugs)
d. ex m.: deus ex machina (Latin—god from a machine)—introduction of a godlike device to resolve a play or problem
dext.: dexter (Latin—right)
dextrose: glucose ($C_6H_{12}O_6H_2O$)
dez: dezembro (Portuguese —December)
Dez: Dezember (German—December)
df: decontamination factor; defensive fire; defogging; degree(s) of freedom; dense film; direction finder; double feeder; double fronted; drinking fountain; drive fit; drop forge
d & f: determination and finding
d/f: días fecha (Spanish—days from date)
Df: Douglas fir
DF: Dean of the Faculty; Defender of the Faith; Destroyer Flotilla
D-F: Dansk-Franske; deflection factor (symbol)
DF: Distrito Federal (Spanish—Federal District)
D of F: Department of Fisheries
DFA: Dairy Farmers Association; Department of Foreign Afffairs; Drop Forging Association
D.F.A.: Doctor of Fine Arts
DFAC: Dried Fruit Association of California
dfb: distribution fuse board
dfc: dry-filled capsules
DFC: Distinguished Flying Cross
DFD: Dogs For Defense
DFDS: Det Forende Dampskibs-Selskab (United Steamship Company, Limited, Denmark)
dfg: diode function generator
DFGJPC: Daniel and Florence Guggenheim Jet Propulsion Center
DFH: Danmarks Fiskeri og Havundersøgelser
DFISA: Dairy and Food Industries Supply Association
DFL: Deutsche Forschungsanstalt

für Luft und Raumfahrt
DFM: Distinguished Flying Medal
DFMR: Dazian Foundation for Medical Research
DFMS: Domestic and Foreign Missionary Society
DFMSR: Directorate of Flight and Missile Safety Research
dfn: distance from nose
dfndt: defendant
DFNWR: Deer Flat National Wildlife Refuge (Idaho)
d forg: drop forging
DFP: Detroit Free Press
DFPA: Douglas Fir Plywood Association
dfr: decreasing failure rate; dropped from rolls
D fr: Djibouti franc
DFRA: Drop Forging Research Association
dfs: distance finding station
DFSC: Defense Fuel Supply Center
dfsr: diffuser
dft: deaerating feed tank; defendant; draft
dftmn: draftsman
dg: decigram; disk grind; double glass; double groove (insulators)
d/g: decomposed granite; displacement gyroscope
DG: Director General
DGA: Directors Guild of America
DGAA: Distressed Gentlefolk's Aid Association
DGC: Dangerous Goods Classification; Duty Group Captain
DGG: Deutsche Grammophon Gesellschaft (German Gramophone Record Company)
DGI: Date Growers Institute
Dgls: Douglas
DGMS: Director General of Medical Services
dgnast (DGNAST): design assist
Dgo: Durango
DGO: Diploma in Gynecology and Obstetrics
d Gr: der Grosse (German—the Great)
DGR: Dirección General de Radiocomunicaciones (Spanish—General Administration of Radio Communications) —Bolivian broadcasting control
DGRR: Deutsche Gesellschaft für Raketentechnik und Raumfahrt (German Society for Rocket Technique and Space Flight)
dgs: double green silk
DGSC: Defense General Supply Center
DGSS: Director General Secret Service
DGT: Dirección General de Turismo (Spanish—Administra-

tion of Tourism)
dgz: designated ground zero
dh: deadhead; dead heat; double hung
d & h: dressed and headed
dh: das heisst (German—that is to say)
Dh: Moroccan dirham(s)
DH: Declaration of Homestead; De Havilland (aircraft); Department of Health
D.H.: Doctor of Humanities
D & H: Delaware & Hudson (railroad)
dha: dicha (Spanish—good luck; happiness)
DHA: Dhahran, Saudi Arabia (airport)
DHAC: De Havilland Aircraft of Canada Limited
DH Canada: De Havilland Aircraft of Canada Limited
dhd: distillate hydrosulfurization
dh di: drophammer die
DHEW: Department of Health, Education, and Welfare
DHF: Dag Hammarskjöld Foundation
D. Hg.: Doctor of Hygiene
D.H.L.: Doctor of Hebrew Letters; Doctor of Hebrew Literature
DHM: Detroit Historical Museum
dho: dicho (Spanish—said)
D.Hor.: Doctor of Horticulture
dhp: developed horsepower
dhq: mean diurnal high water inequality
DHQ: Division Headquarters
DHR: Division of Housing Research
dhs: dry heat sterilization
DHSS: Department of Health and Social Security
dht: distillate hydrotreating
DHUD: Department of Housing and Urban Development
dhw: double-hung windows
D. Hy.: Doctor of Hygiene
di: daily inspection; de-ice; diameter; diametral; diplomatic immunity; document identifier
d i: das ist (German—that is)
Di: didymium
DI: Denizyollari Isletmesi (Turkish Maritime Lines); Department of the Interior; Director of Intelligence; District Inspector; Division Instruction; Drill Instructor
D of I: Daughters of Isabella; Declaration of Independence; Department of Insurance; Department of the Interior
DI-5: Defense Intelligence (British agency)
dia: date of initial appointment; diagram; diameter; diathermy;

due in assets
DIA: Defense Intelligence Agency; Design and Industries Association; Dulles International Airport (Washington, D.C.)
diab: diabetic
DIAC: Defense Industry Advisory Council
di ad: die adapter
diag: diagnose; diagnosis; diagnostic; diagnostician; diagonal; diagram
dial.: dialect; dialectical; dialectician; dialectics
DIAL: Disc Interrogation and Loading (system)
dial-a-mation: dial-a-cremation (telephone service offering low-cost cadaver disposal)
dialgol: dialect of algol (*q.v.*)
diam: diameter
dian: digital analog
DIAND: Department of Indian Affairs and Northern Development (Canada)
diap.: diapason (Greek—consonant harmony; octave)
diaph: diaphragm
dias.: defense-integrated automatic switch
DIAS: Dublin Institute for Advanced Studies
diath: diathermy
diat: diathermy
DIAT: Dundee Institute of Art and Technology
DIB: Department of Information and Broadcasting
DIB: Dictionary of International Biography
dibas: dibasic
dic: dictionary
dic: dicembre (Italian—December); *diciembre* (Spanish—December)
DiC: diesel cargo vessel
DIC: Diplomate of the Imperial College (London)
DICASS: Directional Command Active Sonobuoy System
dicautom: automatic dictionary look-up
Dick: Richard
dicot(s): dicotyledon(s)
dict: dictated; dictation; diction; dictionary
dicta: dictaphone
Dict Amer Slang: Dictionary of American Slang
did.: didactic
DID: Daily Intelligence Digest
didad: digital data display
didn't: did not
di/do: data input/data output
DIDS: Digital Information Display System
dieb. alt.: diebus alternus (Lat-

in—on alternate days)
dieb. tert.: *diebus tertius* (Latin —every third day)
Diedrich Knickerbocker: (pseudonym—Washington Irving)
Dief the Chief: John George Diefenbaker
diel: dielectrics
di el: diesel electric
DIEPO: Dieterich-Post
diet.: dietary; dietetic(s); dietician
dif: difference; differential
dif-amps: differential amplifiers
difce: difference
diff: difference; differential
diff calc: differential calculus
diff diag: differential diagnosis
diffr: diffraction
diffu: diffusion
DiFr: diesel fruit vessel
dig.: digest; digestion; digestive
dig.: *digeratur* (Latin—let it be digested)
DIG: Deputy Inspector General
digas: digastric
digicom: digital communications (system)
dig r-o: digital readout
di-H: hydrogen
DIH: Diploma of Industrial Health; Division of Indian Health
Dij: Dijon
dil: dilute; dissolve
dilat: dilatation; dilate
dild: diluted
diln: dilution
diluc.: *diluculo* (Latin—at daybreak)
dilut.: *dilutus* (Latin—dilute)
dim: *dimanche* (French—Sunday); *dimidius* (Latin—one half); *diminuendo* (Italian—diminishing gradually)
dim.: dimension; dimensional; diminutive
DIMA: Detroit Institute of Musical Art
dime.: dual independent map encoding
DIME: Division of International Medical Education (Assn Amer Med Colleges)
dimorph: dimorphous
dimple: deuterium-moderated pile low energy
din.: do it now
din: *dinar* (Yugoslavian monetary unit)
Din: *Dinsdag* (Dutch—Tuesday)
DIN: Data Identification Number; Deutsche Industrie-Norm (German Industrial Standard)
DIN: *das ist norm* (German—this is standard)
d in a: (found) dead in automobile (or) airplane

d in b: (found) dead in bed
diner: dining car
Ding: J.N. Darling
d. in p. aeq.: *divide in partes aequales* (Latin—divide into equal parts)
DINP: Dunk Island National Park (Queensland)
dio: diode
DIO: Directorate of Intelligence; Duty Intelligence Officer
dioc: dioceasan; diocese
diop: diopter; dioptrics
dior: diorama
diox: dioxygen
dip.: diploma; diplomat; diphtheria; (slang for pickpocket)
DIP: Document Improvement Program (DoD)
Dip Agr: Diploma in Agriculture
DIPEC: Defense Industrial Plant Equipment Center
Dip Ed: Diploma in Education
Dip Eng: Diploma in Engineering
diph: diphtheria
diph tet: diptheria tetanus
diph tox: diptheria toxin
dipl: diplomacy; diplomat; diplomatic
Dipl: *Diplom* (German—diploma)
diplo: diploma; diplomacy; diplomat; diplomatic; diplomatics; diplomatism; diplomatist
dipsey: deep-sea lead (line for measuring depths)
dipso: dipsomania(c); drunkard
Dip T: Teachers Diploma
dipth: diphthong (single sound as ae in aeolian)
dir: direct; direction; director
dir.: *directione* (Latin—directions); *direxit* (Latin—directed by)
Dirceu: Tomaz Antonio Gonzaga
dir conn: direct-connect
dir coup: directional coupler
direct.: directory
D.Ir.Eng.: Doctor of Irrigation Engineering
Dir Gen: Director General
Dirk: Derek; Everett McKinley Dirksen
diron: direction
dir. prop.: *directione propria* (Latin—with proper directions)
dis: disciple; discipline; disconnect; discontinued; discount; distance; distant; distribute; distribution
Dis: Disney (Walt Disney); Disneyland; Disraeli (Benjamin Disraeli); Pluto
Dis: (German—D-sharp)
DIs: Department(al) Instructions
DIS: Dairy Industry Society; Defense Intelligence School; Department of Industrial Services;

Disney Productions (stock exchange symbol); Ductile Iron Society
disable: disable; disability
disac: digital simulator and computer
disap: disapprove
disassy: disassembly
disb: disburse; disbursement
disbmt: disbursement
disc.: discography; disconnect; discontinue; discophile
DISC: Defense Industrial Supply Center
disch: discharge; discharging
disco: discotheque
DISCO: Defense Industrial Security Clearance Office
discol: discolored
discon: disconnect; disorderly conduct
discontd: discontinued
discr: discriminator
discron: discretion
DISCs: Domestic International Sales Corporations
disct: discount
discus: (*see* DSSCS)
DISD: Data and Information System Division
disg: disagreeable
DISI: Dairy Industries Society International
disk: *diskonto* (Norwegian—discount)
dissem: disseminate
disemb: disembark
disin: disinfectant; disinfection
dism: dismiss; dismissal
diso: die shoe
disod: disodium
disord: disorder
disp: dispensary; dispensatory; dispenser; disposition
disp.: *dispensa* (Latin—dispense)
dispen: dispensatories; dispensatory
displ: displacement
dispr: dispatcher
disr: disrated
diss: disassembly; dissent; dissenter; dissertation
dissd: dissolved
dissec: dissection
dissert: dissertation(s)
dissyl: dissyllable
dist: distance; distant; distribute; distribution; distributor; district
dist.: *distilla* (Latin—distill)
Dist: District
Dist Ad: District Administrator
Dist Atty: District Attorney
distb: distillable
Dist Ct: District Court
distil: distillation; distilled; distilling

Dist J: District Judge
distn: distillation
distng: distinguish; distinguishing
distr: distribute; distribution
distran: diagnostic fortran
DISUM: Daily Intelligence Summary (USAF)
disy: disyllabic
dit: domestic independent tour; dual input transponder
DIT: Detroit Institute of Technology; Drexel Institute of Technology; Durham Institute of Technology
DiTa: diesel tanker vessel
diu: data interface unit
div: divergence; diverse; divide; divided; dividend; divisibility; division; divisor; divorce; divorced
Div Arty: Division Artillery
divd: dividend
Divine Poet: John Donne
Div E: Division Engineer
divear: diving instrumentation vehicle for environmental and acoustic research
divs: dividends
diw: dead in the water
Dixie: southern United States; the South
diy: do it yourself
Dizzy: Benjamin Disraeli—British Prime Minister
dj: disc jockey; dust jacket
d J: der Jüngere (German—junior); *dieses Jahres* (German—of this year)
DJ: David Jones (Austrilian department store chain); Department of Justice; District Judge; Divorce Judge
D-J: Dow-Jones (average)
DJ: Divehi Jumhuriyya (Divehi Arabic—Republic of Maldives)—Maldive Islands
D.J.: Doctor Juris (Latin—Doctor of Law)
D of J: Department of Justice
Dja: Djakarta
djd: degenerative joint disease
djeziret: (Arabic or Turkish—island)
DJI: Dow-Jones Industrial (average)
DJIA: Dow-Jones Industrial Average
Djkta: Djakarta (Batavia), Java
Djl: Djalan (Malay—road or street)
Djokja: Djokjakarta, Java, Indonesia
D.Journ.: Doctor of Journalism
D.J.S.: Doctor of Juridical Science
D.Jur.: Doctor of Jurisprudence
dk: dark; deck; dock; duck
DKB: Det Kongelige Bibliotek

(The Royal Library—Copenhagen)
DKC: De Kalb College
dk di: dinking die
dkg: decking; dekagram(s)
dk hse: deck house
dkl: dekaliter
dkm: dekameter
dkm^2: square dekameter
dkm^3: cubic dekameter
DKP: Danmarks Kommunistiske Parti (Danish Communist Party); *Deutsche Kommunistische Partei* (German Communist Party)
DKr: Danish krone(r)
DKR: Dakar, Senegal (airport)
dks: dekastere
dkt: docket
DKTC: Door-Kewaunee Teachers College
DKW: Deutsche Kraftfahrt Werks (German—German Power-drive Works)
DKW: Dampf Kraft Wagen (German—steam power vehicle); *Das Kleine Wunder* German —The Little Wonder—automobile)
dkyd: dockyard
dl: data link; day letter; deadlight; dead load; deciliter; delay line; demand loan; difference limen (threshold); dog license; double acetate; drawing list; driver's license
d-l: -dextro-levo
d/l: data link; demand loan
Dl: Daniel
DL: Danger List; Delta Air Lines (2-letter symbol); Department of Labor; difference of latitude; Drawing List; frigate (naval symbol)
DL: Danske Lov (Danish Law)
D en L: Docteur en Leyes (French —Doctor of Law)
D of L: Department of Labor
DLA: Divisional Land Agent (UK)
D.Lang.: Doctor of Languages
d lat: difference in latitude
DLAT: Defense Language Aptitude Test (USA)
dlb's: dead-letter boxes
dlc: direct lift control; down left center
DLC: Disaster Loan Corporation; Duquesne Light Company
dld: deadline date; delivered
dle: data link escape
dlea: double leg elbow amplifier
DLG: David Lloyd George; guided-missile frigate (naval symbol)
DLGA: Decorative Lighting Guild of America
DLGN: nuclear-powered guided-

missile frigate (naval symbol)
DLI: Defense Language Institute
DLIA: Dental Laboratories Institute of America
dlir: depot-level inspection and repair
D. Litt.: Doctor Litterarum (Latin- —Doctor of Letters; Doctor of Literature)
dll: dial long line
DLL: Deutsche Levante-Linie (Levant Line); Donaldson Line Limited
dllf: design limit load factor
DLM: Daily List of Mails
DLNWR: Des Lacs National Wildlife Refuge (North Dakota)
dlo: difference in longitude; dispatch loading only
D'Lo: The Lord (town in Mississippi)
DLO: Dead Letter Office; Difference of Longitude; District Legal Office(r)
DLOC: Division Logistical Operation Center
d lock: dial-lock
DLP: Director of Laboratory Programs (USN)
dlq: deliquescent; mean diurnal low water inequality
dlr: dealers; dollar; double-lens reflex (camera)
DLR: Distrito de la Luz Roja (Spanish—Red Light District)
DLRO: District Labor Relations Office(r)
dls: debt liquidation schedule; dollars
dls: dólares (Spanish—dollars)
DLS: Debt Liquidation Schedule
D.L.S.: Doctor of Library Science; Doctor of Library Service
D.L.Sc.: Doctor of Library Science
DLSC: Defense Logistics Service Center
dls/shr: dollars per share
dlt: deck landing training
dlt: dans le texte (French—in the text)
DLTS: Deck Landing Training School
dlu: digitizer logic unit
dlvr: deliver; delivery
dlvry: delivery
DLW: Diesel Locomotive Works
DL & W: Delaware, Lackawanna and Western (railroad)
dly: delay; dolly
dlyd: delayed
dm: decimeter; demand meter; diesel-mechanical; draftsman
d/m: density/moisture
dm^2: square decimeter
dm^3: cubic decimeter
d & m: dressed and matched

d M: dieses Monats (German—this month)

DM: Des Moines; Deutsche Mark (German mark—currency unit); Du Mont (television network); light minelayer, high-speed (naval symbol)

D & M: Detroit and Mackinac (railroad)

D en M: Docteur en Médecine (French—Doctor of Medicine)

DMA: Dance Masters of America

DMAA: Direct Mail Advertising Association

DMAC: Des Moines Art Center

D.Ma.Eng.: Doctor of Marine Engineering

Dmb: Dumbarton

dmbl: demobilization; demobilize; demobilized

DMC: Del Mar College

dmd: diamond

D.M.D.: *Dentariae Medicinae Doctor* (Latin—Doctor of Dental Medicine)

dme: distance measuring equipment

DME: Director of Medical Education

DMEA: Defense Minerals Exploration Administration

D.Mech.: Doctor of Mechanics

D.M.Ed.: Doctor of Musical Education

D.Mec.E.: Doctor of Mechanical Engineering

dmet: distance-measuring equipment and tacan

D.Met.: Doctor of Metallurgy

D.Met.Eng.: Doctor of Metallurgical Engineering

dmf: decayed, missing, or filled (teeth)

dmg: damage; damaged; damaging

dmh: drop manhole

DMHS: Director of Medical and Health Services; Dolley Madison High School

dmi: defense mechanisms inventory

DMI: Director of Military Intelligence

DMIAAI: Diamond Manufacturers and Importers Association of America, Incorporated

DMIC: Defense Metals Information Center (Batelle Memorial Institute)

D.Mi.Eng.: Doctor of Mining Engineering

D.Mil.S.: Doctor of Military Science

DMIR: Duluth Mesabi and Iron Range (railroad)

dml: demolish; demolition

D.M.L.: Doctor of Modern Languages

d mld: depth moulded

DMM: Directorate of Materiel Management

dmn: dimension; dimensional

Dmn: Drammen

Dmn Fst: Damnation of Faust

DMNH: Denver Museum of Natural History

dmnstr: demonstrator

DMPL: Des Moines Public Library

DMPP: Duck Mountain Provincial Park (Manitoba and Saskatchewan)

dmpr: damper

DMPS: Deepwater Motion Picture System

DMR: Diploma in Medical Radiology

DMRC: Deering Milliken Research Corporation

DMRD: Diploma in Medical Radio-Diagnosis

DMRE: Diploma in Medical Radiology and Electrology

DMRT: Diploma in Medical Radio-Therapy

DMS: Data Management System; Decision Making System; Director of Medical Services; Disk Monitoring System; Display Management System

D.M.S.: Doctor of Medical Science

D.M.Sc.: Doctor of Medical Science

DMSC: Defense Medical Supply Center

DMSDS: Direct Mail Shelter Development System

DMSGR: Dowd's Morass State Game Reserve (Victoria, Australia)

DMSI: Directorate of Management and Support of Intelligence

dmso: dimethyl sulfoxide

DMSS: Director of Medical and Sanitary Services

dmst: demonstrate; demonstration

dmstn: demonstration

dmt: dimethyltryptamine—DMT (dangerous hallucinogen)

DM & TS: Department of Mines and Technical Surveys

dmu: dual maneuvering unit

DMU: Des Moines Union (railway)

D.Mus.: Doctor of Music

D.Mus.A.: Doctor of Musical Arts

D.Mus.Ed.: Doctor of Musical Education

DMV: Department of Motor Vehicles

D.M.V.: Doctor of Veterinary Medicine

DmZ: demilitarized zone

dn: debit note; delta amplitude (symbol); died near; down; downward

d/n (D/N): debit note

D^{n}: Don (Spanish—title equivalent to "SIR")

DN: Department of the Navy

D of N: Daughters of the Nile

dna: does not answer

dna(s): *docena(s)* [Spanish —dozen(s)]

Dña: Doña (Spanish—Lady)—Mrs

DNA: desoxyribonucleic acid (chromosome and gene component); Deutscher Normenausschusz (German Committee of Standards)

DNANR: Department of Northern Affairs and National Resources

D.N.Arch.: Doctor of Naval Architecture

DNB: Distribution Number Bank

DNB: Dictionary of National Biography

DNC: Democratic National Committee; Domestic National Committee; Director of Naval Construction

DNCCC: Defense National Communications Control Center

DNCMD: Dayton Contract Management Office

Dnd: Dunedin

DND: Department of National Defense

dne: douane (French—customs)

DNE: Director of Nursing Education

D.N.Ed.: Doctor of Nursing Education

D.N.Eng.: Doctor of Naval Engineering

DNHW: Department of National Health and Welfare (United Kingdom)

DNI: Director of Naval Intelligence

D of '98: Daughters of '98

DNJ: Det Norske Justervesen (Norwegian Bureau of Weights and Measures)

Dnk: Dunkirk

dnl: do not load

DNL: Det Norske Luftfartselkap (Norwegian Airlines)

DNM: Dinosaur National Monument

DNMS: Division of Nuclear Materials Safeguards (AEC)

D-Note: $500 bill

DNP: Dinder National Park (Sudan)

D.N.P.P.: Dominus Noster Papa Pontifex (Latin—Our Lord the Pope)

dnr: does not run

DNR: Department of National Revenue

D.N.Sc.: Doctor of Nursing Science

DNSS: Defense Navigation Satellite System

dnt: dinitrotoluene
DNTO: Danish National Travel Office
Dnus.: *Dominus* (Latin—Lord)
DNV: Det Norske Veritas (Norwegian ship classifier)
DNWR: Darling National Wildlife Refuge (Florida); Delta NWR (Louisiana); Desert NWR (Nevada)
do: first tone in diatonic scale; *C* in fixed-do system
do.: day(s) off; diesel oil; dissolved oxygen
d-o: dropout
d/o: delivery order
do: (Korean—island)
do.: *ditto* (Italian—the same)
d:o:dito (Swedish—ditto)
d O: *der (die, das) Obige* (German—the aforementioned)
Do: Dominican; Dominican Republic; Dominican or Santo Domingan; Dornier
DO: Defense Order; Department of Oceanography; Director of Operations; Disbursing Office(r); District Office(r); Dominion Observatory; Dominion Office(r); Duty Officer
D.O.: Doctor of Osteopathy
D/O: Disbursing Officer
D2O: deuterium oxide (heavy water)
doa: date of availability; dead on arrival
DOA: Dead on Arrival
DOAE: Defence Operational Analysis Establishment (UK)
DOAL: Deutsche Ost Afrika Linie (German East Africa Line)
DOARS: Donnelley Official Airline Reservations System
dob: date of birth; disbursed operating base
DoB: Daughters of Bilitis
DOB: Date of Birth; doctor's order book
DOB: *Deutsche Oper Berlin* (German Opera of Berlin)
Dob(bin): Robert
'dobe: adobe
doc: doctor; document
Doc: doctor
doca: data of current appointment; deoxycorticosterone acetate
DOCA: Deoxycorticosterone Acetate
doce: date of current enlistment
Doct.: Doctor (Latin—Doctor)
docu: document(ary)
docum: document; documentary; documentation; documented
docum^to: *documento* (Spanish—document)
DOCUS: Display-Oriented Computer Usage System

dod: date of death; died of disease
Dod: Dodecanese
Dod(dy): Dorothy
DoD: Department of Defense
DOD: Department of Defense; date of death; died of disease
DODAS: Digital Oceanographic Data Acquisition System
DoDCI: Department of Defense Computer Institute
DoDDAC: Department of Defense Damage Assessment Center
dodprt: date of departure
doe.: date of enlistment
DOES: Disk-Oriented Engineering System
doesn't: does not
dofab: damned old fool about books
dofic: domain-originated functional integrated circuit
DOFL: Diamond Ordnance Fuze Laboratories
dog.: disgruntled old graduate
dohc: double overhead cam; dual overhead cam
doi: dead of injuries; descent orbit insertion
doi: (Thai—mountain)
D Ø K: Det Østasiaatiske Kompagni (Royal Danish East Asiatic Company)
dol: dear old lady; dollar
dol: *dolce* (Italian—sweet)
Dol: Dolph (Adolf); dolph9n; Dorothea; Dorothy
dolciss: *dolcissimo* (Italian—very sweetly)
dolichocephs: dolichocephalics (long-skulled people)
Dolf: Adolph; Adolphus; Rudolph
Doll: Dorothy
Dolley (Dolly): Mrs. Doreathea (Dolley) Payne Madison (wife of President James Madison); Dorothea; Dorothy
dollies: dolophine pills
dolo: dolophine (methadone hydrochloride used as a morphine substitute in withdrawing addicts from heroin)
dom: date of marriage; dirty old man; domestic; domicile; dominion; drawn over mandrel
dom: *domenica* (Italian—Sunday); *domingo* (Spanish—Sunday)
Dom: Domenico; Dominic; Dominican; Dominican Republic; Dominion
Dom.: *Dominicus* (Latin—of the Lord, as in *Dies Dominica*—the Lord's Day)
DOM: Date of Marriage; dimethoxyalpha methyl phenethylmine (dangerous psychedelic drug also called STP)

D.O.M.: *Deo Optimo Maximo* (Latin—to God the Best and the Greatest— inscription found on some cemetery cornerstones and on labels of some benedictine bottles
DOMAINS: Deep-Ocean Manned Instrument Station(s)
Dom Can: Dominion of Canada
dom econ: domestic economy (home economics)
dom ex: domestic exchange
dom^o: *domingo* (Spanish—Sunday)
Dom^o: *Domingo* (man's name)
Dom Rep: Dominican Republic
DOMS: Diploma in Opthalmic Medicine and Surgery
Don: Donald; Donegal
Don: Donderdag (Dutch—Thursday); *Donnerstag* (German —Thursday); (Spanish—Lord and Master; from the Latin —dominus)
Doña: (Spanish—dame; woman of rank; from the Latin—*domina*)
donec alv. sol. fuerit: *donec alvus soluta fuerit* (Latin—until the bowels move)
Doneg: Donegal (sometimes Don)
Don Francisco: Francisco I. Madero—Mexican president
Don Pepe: José Figueres Ferrer— democratic leader of Costa Rica
Don Porfirio: Don Porfirio Díaz —Mexican dictator-president
Don Q: Don Quixote
Don Romulo: Romulo Betancourt— democratic leader and recent president of Venezuela
don't: do not
do-nut: doughnut
Don Venus: Don Venustiano Carranza—Mexican general-president
doo: diesel oil odor
doom.: deep ocean optical measurement
dop: dermo-optical perception; developing-out paper
D. Oph.: Doctor of Ophthalmology
dopl: *doplene* (Czech—enlarged)
D.Opt.: Doctor of Optometry
D.Opth.: Doctor of Opthalmology
dor: date of rank; dental operating room; doric; dormitory
Dor: Dorado; Doric; Dorothy
D. Or.: Doctor of Oratory
Dora: Dorothea; Dorothy; Eudora; Theodora
DORA: Defence of the Realm Act
doran: Doppler range and navigation
Dord: Dordogne
Doric(k): Theodoric(k)
Dorie: Doris
Doris: Doreen; Dorothea; Dorothy;

Eudora; Theodora
DORIS: Direct Order Recording and Invoicing System
DORL: Developmental Orbital Research Laboratory
dorm: dormitories; dormitory
dorp: (Dutch—village)
Dors: Dorset; Dorsetshire
Dorset: Dorsethshire
dos: date of separation; dosage; dose; dosimetric; dosimetry; dosiology
DoS: Department of State
DOS: Date of Separation; Department of State; Digital Operation System; Digital Operating System
D.O.S.: Doctor of Ocular Science; Doctor of Optical Science; Doctor of Optometric Science
dosim: dosimetry (measurement of radiation doses)
dot.: deep-ocean technology; deep-oceanic turbulence
Dot: Dorothy; Dotty
Do T: Department of Transportation
DOT: Deep Oil Technology (company)
DOT: Dictionary of Occupational Titles
DOTIPOS: Deep Ocean Test-in-Place and Observation System
Dott: Dottore (Italian—Doctor)
Dotty: Doreen; Dorothea; Dorothy; Eudora
double-B: double-backed; double-banked; double-barreled; double-bass; double-bedded; double-benched; double-bonded; double-bottomed; double-breasted; double-brooded
double-X: doublecross; double quality; double quantity; double thickness; doubleweight; two-X; XX
doubt.: doubtful
Doug: Douglas(s)
Doug fir: Douglas fir
dov: double oil of vitriol (sulphuric acid)
Dov: Dover
dovap: Doppler velocity and position
dow: died of wounds; dowager; dowel; dowelled
Dow: Dowager
DOW: Died of Wounds; Dow Chemical Company; Dow Chemicals
dowb: deep ocean work boat
doz: dozen
dozer: bulldozer
dp: damp proof(ing); dash pot (relay); deck piercing; deep penetration; deflection plate; departure point; dewpoint; diame-

tral pitch; displaced person; distribution point; double paper; double pole; drip-proof; drop point; dump; potential difference (symbol)
d & p: developing and printing
d.p.: directione propria (Latin —with proper direction)
d. in p.: divide in partes (Latin—divide)
DP: by direction of the President; Democratic Party; Department of the Pacific; Detrucking Point; Director of the Port; Displaced Person
D-P: Data-Phone
D.P.: dementia praecox
D & P: Deberny and Peignot
D of P: Daughters of Pennsylvania; Daughters of Pocahontas
dpa: deferred payment account
DPA: Deutsche Presse-Agentur (German Press Agency); Doulat i Padshahi ye Afghanistan (Kingdom of Afghanistan)
D.P.A.: Doctor of Public Administration
DPA: Deutsche Press Agentur (German news agency)
dpb: deposit passbook
dpbc: double pole both connected
dpc: data processing control; double paper single cotton
DPC: Daniel Payne College; Defense Plant Corporation; Defense Procurement Circular; Defense Production Chief; Desert Protective Council; Displaced Persons Commission; Duke Power Company
dpcm: differential pulse-code modulation
dpd: data project directive
DPD: Data Products Division (Stromberg-Carlson); Department of Public Dispensary; Diploma in Public Dentistry
dpdc: double paper double cotton
dp di: dimple die
dp dt: double pole, double throw
dpe: data processing equipment
Dpe: Dieppe
dpf: deferred pay fund
DPf: Deutsche Pfennig (German —pfennig)
dpfc: double pole front connected
dpft: double-pedestal flat-top (desk)
DPG: Dugway Proving Ground
dph: diamond pyramid hardness; (DPH) diphenylhydantoin
D. Ph.: *Doctor Philosophiae* (Latin—Doctor of Philosophy)
DPH: Department of Public Health; Diploma in Public Health
D.P.H.: Doctor of Public Health
D.Pharm.: Doctor of Pharmacy

D.Ph.Sc.: Doctor of Physical Science
dpi: data processing installation
DPI: Department of Public Information; Distillation Products Industries
DPII: Dairy Products Improvement Institute
dpl: diploma; diplomat; dual propellant loading; duplex
DPL: Dallas Public Library; Dayton Power and Light; Dayton Public Library; Denver Public Library; Detroit Public Library; diplomatic corps (license plate)
DP & L: Dallas Power and Light
DPL: Den Polytekniske Laeranstalt (Danish—The Polytechnic Institute)—Copenhagen
DP & LC: Dundee, Perth & London (shipping) Company
dplx: duplex
DPM: Diploma in Psychological Medicine
DPMA: Data Processing Management Association
dpn: diamond pyramid number
d pnl: distribution panel
DPNM: Devil's Postpile National Monument
dpo: depot
DPO: Dayton Philharmonic Orchestra; Distributing Post Office
dpob: date and place of birth
DPP: Director of Public Prosecutions
DPPS: Department of Public Printing and Stationery
dpr: day press rates; double lapping of pure rubber
DPRI: Disaster Prevention Research Institute
DPRK: Democratic People's Republic of Korea (North Korea)
dps: double-pole snap switch
DP's: displaced persons
DPS: Data Processing Station; Defense Printing Service; Division of Primary Standards
DPSA: Data Processing Supplies Association
DPSC: Defense Personnel Support Center; Defense Petroleum Supply Center
dpst: deposit
dp st: double pole, single throw
D. Psych.: Doctor of Psychology
dpt: department; deponent; deposition; depth
dpt (DPT): dipropylphytamine
DPT: Design Proof Test(ing)
dptw: double-pedestal typewriter (desk)
dpty: deputy
D.Pub.Adm.: Doctor of Public

Administration
dpv: dry pipe valve
dp/w: drawbar pull/weight (ratio)
DPW: Department of Public Works
DPWO: District Public Works Office
dq: definite quantity; deterioration quotient; direct question(s)
DQU: Deganawidah-Quetzalcoatl University (University of California at Davis)
dr: debit; differential rate; door; double-reduction; drachma; dram; draw; drawn; drill; drive; drum
Dr: debtor; doctor; Drive; drachma (Greek monetary unit)
DR: Data Report; Date of Rank; Dead Reckoning; Deficiency Report; Dental Recruit; Design Requirements; Despatch Rider; Detailed Report; Development Report; Document Report; National Distillers and Chemical Corporation (stock exchange symbol); reaction of degeneration (symbol)
D/R: date of rank; dead reckoning
DR: *Deutsche Reischbahn* (German State Railway)
dra: dead-reckoning analyzer
dra: *derecha* (Spanish—right)
dr & a: data reporting and accounting
Dra: *Doctora* (Spanish—woman doctor)
dr ad: drill adaptor
Dr.Ae.Sc.: Doctor of Aeronautical Science
Dr. Agr.: Doctor of Agriculture
drai: dead-reckoning analog indicator
drain.: drainage
dram.: drama; dramatic; dramatist
dram. pers.: *dramatis personae* (Latin—cast of characters)
dr ap: dram, apothecaries'
drapes: draperies
dr av: dram avoirdupois
Drav: Dravidian
draw.: drawing
Drb: Durban
DRB: Defense Research Board (Canada); Druggists' Research Bureau
DRBC: Delaware River Basin Commission
dr bg: drill bushing
Dr.Bi.Chem.: Doctor of Biological Chemistry
drc: damage-risk criteria (noise-exposure limits); down right center (driving, lighting, or seating)
DRC: Dutch Reformed Church; Dynamics Research Corporation

drch: drachma
Dr. Chem.: Doctor of Chemistry
dr ck: drill chuck
Dr.Com.: Doctor of Commerce
DR & D: Defense Research and Development
DRDT: Division of Reactor Development and Technology (AEC)
drdto: detection-radar data takeoff
dre: dead reckoning equipment
DRE: Defense Research Establishment (Canada)
D.R.E.: Doctor of Religious Education
DR & E: Defense Research and Engineering
DREA: Defense Research Establishment, Atlantic
Dream King: Ludwig II of Bavaria
drec: detection-radar electronic component
Dr.Ec.: Doctor of Economics
dred.: dredging
DREE: Department of Regional Economic Expansion (Canada)
Dr.Eng.: Doctor of Engineering
Dr.Ent.: Doctor of Entomology
DREP: Defense Research Establishment, Pacific
DRES: Defense Research Establishment, Suffield
DRET: Defense Research Establishment, Toronto
drews (DREWS): direct readout equatorial satellite
drf: differential reinforcement
DRF: Deafness Research Foundation
Dr Franklin: Benjamin Franklin
drftmn: draftsman
dr fx: drill fixture
drg: drawing(s)
DRGM: Deutsches Reichgebrauchsmuster (German registered design)
D & RGW: Denver and Rio Grande Western (railroad)
dr hd: drill head
Dr.Hor.: Doctor of Horticulture
Dr.Hy.: Doctor of Hygiene
DRI: Defense Research Institute; Denver Research Institute
drill.: drilling
DRINC: Dairy Research Incorporated
D-ring: capital-D-shaped ring
Dr. Ing.: *Doktor-Ingenieur* (German—Doctor of Engineering)
drip.: digital ray and intensity projector
dr jg: drill jig
Dr Jinnah: Mohammed 'Ali Jinnah—president of All-India Moslem League and first governor-general of Pakistan

Dr.J.Sc.: Doctor of Judicial Science
Dr. Jur.: *Doctor Juris* (Latin—Doctor of Law)
DRK: Deutsches Rotes Kreuz (German Red Cross)
drl: data retrieval language
DRL: Design Report Letter; Diamond Research Laboratory
Dr. és L.: *Docteur és Lettres* (French—Doctor of Letters)
Dr.Lit.: Doctor of Literature
drm: direction of relative movement
DRM: Drafting Room Manual
Dr Med: *Doktor der Medizin* (German—Doctor of Medicine)
Dr. Med.: *Doctor Medicinae* (Latin—Doctor of Medicine)
Dr.Mus.: Doctor of Music
drn: drawn
Drn: Darien
DRN: Daily Reports Notice; Detroit River Navigation
dro: destructive readout
dro: *derecho* (Spanish—custom duty; right)
DRO: Disablement Resettlement Office(r)
drod: delayed readout detector
DRO-LA: Defense Research Office—Latin America (USA)
dron: data reduction
dros: date returned from overseas
drp: dead reckoning position
DRP: Deutsches Reichspatent (German—patent); Diebold Research Program
DRP: *Deutsche Reichspartei* (German Reich Party)
DRPA: Delaware River Port Authority
Dr. Phil.: *Doktor der Philosophie* (German—Doctor of Philosophy)
DRPL: Del Rio Public Library
Dr.Pol.Sc.: Doctor of Political Science(s)
drps: drapes
drq: discomfort relief quotient
Dr.Ra.Eng.: Doctor of Radio Engineering
DRRB: Data Requirements Review Board (DoD)
Dr.Rec.: Doctor of Recreation
Dr.Re.Eng.: Doctor of Refrigeration Engineering
DRRI: Defense Race Relations Institute (DoD)
drs: data reduction system; drawers
DRs: Discrepancy Reports
DRS: Data Reduction System
Dr. és S.: *Docteur és Sciences* (French—Doctor of Sciences)
Dr Salazar: Antonio de Oliveira Salazar—dictator and prime

minister of Portugal from 1932 to 1969

Dr.Sc.: Doctor of Science

Dr.Sci.: Doctor of Science

D.Sc.Jur.: Doctor of the Science of Jurisprudence

DRSCS: Digital Range-Safety Command System

Dr Seuss: Theodor Seuss Geisel

dr sh: drill shell

drsmkr: dressmaker

DRSO: Danish Radio Symphony Orchestra

drsr: dresser

drt: dead reckoning tracer

Drt: Dartmouth

DRT: Diagnostic Rhyme Test

DRTC: Documentation Research and Training Center

DRTE: Defence Research Telecommunications Establishment (Canada)

Dr.Tech.: Doctor of Technology

Dr.Theol.: Doctor of Theology

Dr. Theol.: *Doktor der Theologie* (German—Doctor of Theology)

dr tp: drill template

dru: digital remote unit

drub: digital remote unit buffer

D.Ru.Eng.: Doctor of Rural Engineering

Dr und Vrl: *Druck und Verlag* (German—printed and published by)

DRV: Democratic Republic of Vietnam (North Vietnam)

DRVN: Democratic Republic of Vietnam

dr vs: drill vise

DRW: Darwin, Australia (airport)

DRWW: Distillery, Rectifying, Wine Workers (union)

drx: drachma (Greek monetary unit)

dry.: drying

dry ice: solidified carbon dioxide

ds: days after sight; day's sight; decanning scuttle; detached service; direct support; discarding sabot; document signed; domestic service; double-screened; double silk; doublestitch(ed); douwnspout; draft stop

d.s.: document signed

d/s: dextrose in saline

d & s: demand and supply

d. et s.: *detur et signatur* (Latin—let it be given and labelled)

Ds: dysprosium (symbol)

Ds.: *Deus* (Latin—God)

DS: Date of Service; Delphian Society; Delta Society; Department of Sanitation; Department of State; Design Standard(s); Detached Service; Direct Support; Directing Staff; Director of

Services; Drug Store; Durham & Southern (railroad)

D-S: Deux-Sèvres; Ditlev-Simonsen Lines

D S: *dal segno* (Italian—return to the sign :S:)

D/S: *Dampskip* (Norwegian—steamer; steamship)

D & S: Durham & Southern Railway

D es S: Dar es Salaam

D of S: Daughters of Scotia; Department of State

dsa: dial service assistance; dimensionally-stabilized anode; discrete sample anaylzer

DSA: Danish Sisterhood of America; Dante Society of America; Defense Shipping Authority; Defense Supply Agency; Defense Supply Association; Design Schedule Analysis; Division Service Area; Drum Seiners Association; Duluth, South Shore and Atlantic (railroad); Duodecimal Society of America

DSAB: *Dictionary of South African Biography*

dsabl: disable; disability

DSAM: *Defense Supply Agency Manual*

DSAP: Data Systems Automation Program

D/S A/S: *Dampskipaksjeselskap* (Norwegian—joint stock steamship company, limited)

dsasbl: disassemble

dsb: double sideband

DSB: Danske Stats Baner (Danish State Railways); Drug Supervisory Body (UN)

dsbg: disbursing

dsbn: disband

D. Sc.: Doctor of Science

DSC: Defense Supply Corporation; Delaware State College; Depot Supply Center; Die Casters' Conference; Distinguished Service Cross; Document Service Center

D.S.C.: Doctor of Christian Science; Doctor of Commercial Science; Doctor of Surgical Chiropody

D & SC: Defense and Space Center (Westinghouse)

DSCC: Deep Space Communications Complex

D.Sc.Com.: Doctor of Science in Commerce

D.Sc.Eco.: Doctor of Science in Economics

D.Sc.Eng.: Doctor of Science in Engineering

D.Sch.Mus.: Doctor of School Music

D.Sc.Hyg.: Doctor of Science in Hygiene

DSC (I): Die Sinkers' Conference (International)

D.Sc.I.: Doctor of Science in Industry

D.Sc.L.: Doctor of the Science of Law

DSCMD: Dallas Contract Management District

D. Sc. Os.: Doctor of the Science of Osteopathy

D.Sc.Pol.: Doctor of Political Science(s)

DSCS: Defense Satellite Communications System(s)

dsd: dry surgical dressing

DSD: Daily Staff Digest; Director of Signals Division

DSDP: Deep Sea Diving Project; Deep Sea Drilling Program; Deep Sea Drilling Project

DSDS: Deep Sea Diving School (USN)

DSEA: Delaware State Education Association

dsf: day-second-feet (or foot)

Dsf: Düsseldorf

DSF: Dainippon Silk Foundation; Division of Sea Fisheries

dsg: designate; designation

DSG: *Deutsche Schlaf- und Speisewagen Gesellschaft* (German Sleeping-and-Dining-Car Company)

dsgl: *desgleichen* (German—ditto)

dsgn: design; designed; designer

DSI: Dairy Society International; Dalcroze Society Incorporated; Distilled Spirits Institute; Drinking Straw Institute

DSIA: Diaper Service Institute of America

DSIATP: Defense Sensor Interpretation and Application Training Program

DSIF: Deep-Space Instrumentation Facility

DSIR: Department of Scientific and Industrial Research

DSIs: Directorate of Service Intelligence members or operatives

DSIS: Directorate of Scientific Information Services

dsj: differential space justifier

dsl: deep scattering layer; diesel

DSL: Delta Steamship Lines; Dickinson School of Law; Dominican Steamship Line

DSL: *Directory of Special Libraries and Information Centers*

D & SL: Denver and Salt Lake (railroad)

DSLC: Defense Logistics Services Center

dsl elec: diesel electric

ds lt: deck surface light

d & sm: dressed and standard matched (lumber)

DSM: Des Moines, Iowa (airport); Distinguished Service Medal

dsmd: dismissed

D.S. Met. Eng.: Doctor of Science in Metallurgical Engineering

DSM Project: Development of Substitute Materials (Manhattan Engineer District secret project from 1942 to 1947; responsible for development of A-bomb)

DSN: Deep Space Network

DSNWR: De Soto National Wildlife Refuge (Iowa)

D.So.: Doctor of Sociology

DSO: Dallas Symphony Orchestra; Denver Symphony Orchestra; Detroit Symphony Orchestra; Distinguished Service Order; District Security Office(r); District Service Office(r); District Supply Office(r); Division Signal Officer; Duluth Symphony Orchestra

D.S.O.: Doctor of the Science of Oratory

D.So.Sc.: Doctor of Social Science

D.So.Se: Doctor of Social Service

d.s.p.: *decessit sine prole* (Latin—died without issue)

DSP: Detroit Steel Products; Division Standard Practice

DS & P: Duell, Sloan & Pearce

dspch: dispatch; dispatcher

d spec(s): design specification(s)

dspl: disposal

dspln: disciplinary; discipline

dspn: disposition

dspo: disposal; dispose; disposition

DSPS: Dynamic Ship-Positioning System

DSR: Danmarks Radio (Danish radio and tv); Detroit Street Railways

ds & r: document search and retrieval

DSRC: David Sarnoff Research Center (RCA)

d's & r's: dailies and rushes (motion-picture film editing)

dsrv (DSRV): deep-submergence rescue vehicle

dss: documents signed

DSS: Defense Supply Service; Directorate of Statistical Services

D.S.S.: Doctor of Social Science

DS & S: Data Systems and Statistics

D S S & A: Duluth, South Shore & Atlantic (railroad)

DSSc: Diploma in Sanitary Science

DSSC: Defense Subsistence Supply Center

DSSCS: Defense Special Security Communications System (spoken of as *discus*)

DSSN: Disbursing Station Symbol Number

DSSO: Defense Surplus Sales Office; Duty Space Surveillance Officer

dssp: deep-sea submergence project

DSSRG: Deep Submergence System Review Group

DSSV: Deep Submergence Search Vehicle

dst: door stop; drop survival time

DST: Daylight Saving Time; Defense et Sécurité du Territoire (French equivalent of FBI); Dermatology and Syphilology Technician; Desensitization Test (for allergies); Director of Supplies and Transport; Double Summer Time

D.S.T.: Doctor of Sacred Theology

D.St.Eng.: Doctor of Structural Engineering

dstl: distill

dstn: destination

DSTP: Director, Strategic Target Planning

dstpn: dessert spoon

dstr: distribution; distributor

dsu: drum storage unit

dsuh: direct suggestion under hypnosis

dsuphtr: desuperheater

D. Sur.: Doctor of Surgery

D.Surg.: Dental Surgeon

dsv: double silk varnish

dsw: door switch

DSW: Department of Social Welfare

D.S.W.: Doctor of Social Welfare

D Sz: Diego Suarez

dt: dead time; delirum tremens; dinette; diphtheria tetanus; double throw; double time; drain tile; dual tires

d-t: double-throw

d/t: deaths (total ratio)

dt: *doit* (French—debit)

Dt: duration tetanus

DT: Daylight Time; Detroit Terminal (railroad); Department of Transportation; Department of the Treasury; Distance Test; Dylan Thomas

D.T.: Dental Technician; Doctor of Theology

DT: *Daily Telegraph* (London); *Danmarks Turistrad* (Danish Tourist Board)

D of T: deed of trust; Department of Transport

dta: development test article; differential thermal analysis; distributing terminal assembly; double tape armored cable

DTA: Defense Transportation Administration; Development Test Article; Differential Thermal Analysis; Diploma in Tropical Agriculture; Divisão de Exploração dos Transportes Aéreos

dtas: diffuse thalamic activating system

dtc: direct-to-consumer

DTC: Department of Trade and Commerce

DTCD: Diploma in Tuberculosis and Chest Diseases

D.T.Chem.: Doctor of Technical Chemistry

DTCS: Digital Test Command System

dt c sk: don't countersink

dtd: dated

d.t.d.: *detur talis dosis* (Latin—let such a dose be given)

D.T.Eng.: Doctor of Textile Engineering

dtf: daily transaction file

dtg: date time group

Dtg: Dienstag (German—Tuesday)

DThPT: Diploma in Theory and Practice of Teaching

dti: dial test indicator

DTI: Department of Trade and Industry (UK)

DT & I: Detroit, Toledo and Ironton (railroad)

dtl: detail; detailed; diode transistor logic

DTL: Detroit Testing Laboratory

dtm: duration time modulation

Dtm: Dortmund

D.T.M.: Doctor of Tropical Medicine

DTMB: David Taylor Model Basin

DTMBAL: David Taylor Model Basin Aerodynamics Laboratory

DTMH: Diplomate of Tropical Medicine and Hygiene

DTMI: Dairy Training and Merchandising Institute

dt mld: draft moulded

DTMS: Defense Traffic Management Service

dtn: detain

DTN: *Drug Trade News*

DTNM: Devil's Tower National Monument

d-to-a: digital-to-analog

d-to-d: dawn-to-dusk (daylight patrol); dusk-to-dawn (night patrol)—"when in doubt—spell it out"

dtp: diphtheria, tetanus, pertussis (whooping cough)—combined vaccination

DTP: distal tingling on pressure

dtps: diffuse thalamic projection system

dtr: deep tendon reflexes
DTRA: Defense Technical Review Agency (USA)
Dtrt: Detroit
dt's: delirium tremens; dementia tremors
DTS: Defense Telephone Service; Defense Transportation System
D & TS: Detroit and Toledo Short Line (railroad)
Dtsch: *Deutsch* (German—German)
dtt: diptheria tetanus toxin; duplicate title transferred
D of TT: Dominion of Trinidad and Tobago
dtu: data transformation unit
DTV: *Deutsche Taschenbuch Verlag* (German Pocketbook Publisher)
DTVM: Diploma in Tropical Veterinary Medicine
DTW: Detroit, Michigan (Detroit Metropolitan Airport)
d2s & cm: dressed two sides and center matched (lumber)
d2s & m: dressed two sides and matched (lumber)
d2s & sm: dressed two sides and standard matched (lumber)
Dtz: Dutzend (German—dozen)
DTZ: Division Tactical Zone (USA)
Dtzd: Dutzend (German—dozen)
du: died unmarried; digital unit
Du: Ducal; Duchy; Duke; Dutch
DU: Dalhousie University; Denison University; diagnosis undetermined; Dillard University; Drake University; Drew University; Duke University; Duquesne University
dua: digital uplink assembly
DUA: Digitronics Users Association
DUADS: Duluth Air Defense Sector
DUAH: Department of Urban Affairs and Housing
DUAL: Data Use and Access Laboratories
dub.: double; dubious
Dub: Dublin
DUB: Dublin, Eire (airport)
duc: demonstration unity capsule
DUC: Distinguished Unit Citation; Durban University College
DUCS: Deep Underground Communications System
duct.: ductile
dudat: due date
dui: driving under the influence (of alcohol and/or drugs)
Duke: Marmaduke
Duke Ellington: Edward Kennedy Ellington

DUKW: amphibious truck
Dul: Duluth
DUL: Duke University Library
Dumas the Elder: Alexandre Davy de la Pailleterie Dumas (father of the latter; 1802–1870)
Dumas the Younger: Alexandre Dumas (son of the former; 1824–1895)
Dumb: Dumbarton
DUMBO: seaplane used for rescue work (naval symbol)
DUMC: Duke University Medical Center
Dumf: Dumfries
dums: deep unmanned submersibles
dun.: dunnage
Dun: Dundee
Dunb: Dunbarton
dunc: deep underwater nuclear counter
Dunc: Duncan
Dunk: Dunkerque (Dunkirk)
DUNS: Data Universal Numbering System
duo.: duodecimo
duod: duodenum
dup: duplicate; duplicating; duplication
DUP: Diplomate of the University of Paris
dup^do: duplicado (Spanish—duplicate)
dupe.: duplicate; duplicate copy
dupl: duplicate; duplication
dupli: duplicate; duplicated; duplication
DUPONT: E.I. du Pont de Nemours & Company
dur: duration
Dur: Durango; Durban; Durham
Dur: (German—major musical key)
dur. dolor.: durante dolore (Latin—as long as the pain lasts)
Durf: Durfee's Reports
Durh: Durham
Dur Mus: Durban Museum
DUS: Düsseldorf, Germany (airport)
DUSA: Defense Union of South Africa
DUSA: Dispensatory of the United States of America
du 26 ct: du 26 mois courant (French—the 26th of this month)
Dutch Century: the 17th century marked by Dutch exploration and settlement of what is now New York, Capetown, and Indonesia; after sea battles arranged a mutual defense pact with their British rivals—the 1600s
Dutch William: William III of Orange—Dutch-born British

king
Dutz: Dutzend (German—dozen)
dv: dependent variable; device; dilute volume; direct vision; distemper virus; distinguished visitor; dive; double vibrations
DV: Douay Version
D/V: Discovery Vessel
D.V.: Deo volente (Latin—God willing)
dva: dynamic visual acuity
DVA: Distribuidora Venezolana de Azucareros (Venezuelan Sugar Growers Distributing Organization)
DVC: Daiblo Valley College
DVCSA: Delaware Valley College of Science and Agriculture
dvd: direct-view device
d Verf: der Verfasser (German—the author)
DVES: Defense Value Engineering Services
dvfr: defense visual flight rules
DVH: Diploma in Veterinary Hygiene
dvm: digital voltmeter
d.v.m.: decessit vita matris (Latin—he died during his mother's lifetime)
D.V.M.: Doctor of Veterinary Medicine
D.V.M.S.: Doctor of Veterinary Medicine and Surgery
DvN: D. Van Nostrand
DVNM: Death Valley National Monument
DVO: Divisional Veterinary Office(r)
d.v.p.: decessit vita patris (Latin—he died during his father's lifetime)
dvr: driver
DVR: Division of Vocational Rehabilitation
dvs: det vill säga (Swedish—that is); *det vil si* (Norwegian—that is); *det vil sige* (Danish—that is)
D.V.S.: Doctor of Veterinary Surgery
D.V.Sc.: Doctor of Veterinary Science
DVSM: Diploma of Veterinary State Medicine
dvst: direct-view storage tube
DVTI: De Vry Technical Institute
dvtl: dovetail
dynam: dynamic; dynamics; dynamo
dw: deadweight; dishwasher; distilled water; double weight; dumbwaiter; dust wrapper
d/w: dextrose in water; dock warrant
dwa: double wire armor(ed)
DWA: Deadly Weapon Act

dwb: double with bath
dwc: deadweight capacity
DWCHS: De Witt Clinton High School
DWCP: Detroit-Wayne County Port
dwd: driving while drunk; dumb-waiter door
dw di: draw die
DWDL: Donald W. Douglas Laboratory
dwel: dwelling
dwg: drawing
DWG: Diamond Walnut Growers
dwg-ho: dwelling house
DWGNRA: Delaware Water Gap National Recreation Area (New Jersey and Pennsylvania)
dwi: driving while intoxicated
DWI: Descriptive Word Index; Durable Woods Institute; Durham Wheat Institute; Dutch West Indies (Netherlands Antilles)
dwl: designed waterline; dowel
DWM: Deutsche Waffen und Munitionsfabriken
dwn: down
DWOP: Denver War On Poverty
DWP: Department of Water and Power
D W & P: Duluth, Winnipeg & Pacific (railroad)
dwr: drawer
dws: drop wood siding; double white silk
DWS: Department of Water Supply
DWSG & E: Department of Water Supply, Gas, and Electricity
DWSO: Drainage and Water Supply Office(r)

dwt: deadweight tons; pennyweight (denarius weight)
dwv: drain, waste, and vent (pipe)
dwz: dat wil zeggen (Dutch—that is to say)
dx: distance (radio); double cash ruled; duplex; static (symbol)
Dx: diagnosis (medical)
DX: distance radio reception or transmission; Sunray Mid-Continent Oil
DXC: Penn-Dixie Cement (stock exchange symbol)
dxr: deep X-ray
dxrt: deep X-ray therapy
dy: delivery; dockyard; duty; penny (nails)
Dy: Dylan; dysprosium
DY: De Young Memorial Museum; Druk-Yul (Kingdom of Bhutan)
dyb: dynamic braking
dy bf hl: day before holiday
dyd: dockyard
dye.: dyeing
dy fl hl: day following holiday
dyk: (Dutch—dam; dike)
dyke: bulldike
dykes: diagonal wire cutters
dymaxion: dynamic maximum
DYMM: M.H. De Young Memorial Museum
DYMM: (Malay—His Highness the Ruler or Her Highness the Ruler)
dyn: dynamic; dynamics; dynamo; dynamometer; dyne
dyna: dynamite
dynam: dynamic; dynamics; dynamite; dynamo
dynamo.: dynamic model
DYNAMO: Dynamic Action Management Operation

dynasoar: dynamic soaring (space flight)
Dynastic Century: the 32nd century before the Christian era when the first and second Egyptian dynasties ruled—the 3100s
dynmt: dynamite
dyno: dynamometer
dypso: dypsomania(c)
dysen: dysentary
dysp: dyspepsia
dystac: dynamic storage analog computer
dystal: dynamic storage allocation language
DX: Aerotaxi (Colombia); distance radio reception or transmission; Sun Ray Mid-Continent Oil (stock exchange symbol)
dz: dozen
dz: deppelzentner (German—100 kilograms); ***distance zénithale*** (French—zenith distance)
d Z: der Zeit (German—of the time)
Dz: Deniz (Turkish—sea)
DZ: Department of Zoology; Drop Zone
D.Z.: Doctor of Zoology
DZA: Drop Zone Area
DZF: Deutsche Zentrale für Fremdenverhkehr (German National Tourist Association)
dzg: dizygotic
Dzl: Delfzijl (Dutch port)
dzne: douzaine (French—dozen)
D. Zool.: Doctor of Zoology
D-Zug: Durchgangszug (German—express train; through train)

E

e: coefficient of impact (symbol); electron; emulsifier; emulsion; error; errors; longitudinal strain per unit length (symbol); numerical value of electron charge in an electron or proton (symbol)
e: angle of downwash (symbol); natural logarithmic (Napierian) base
E: American Export-Isbrandtsen Lines; Eagle Airways; Earth; east; eccentricity of a curve (symbol); Echo—code for letter E; Edinburgh; efficiency; ein-

steinium; emmetropia; engineer; engineering; England; English; Equator; equatorial; erbium; estimated weight (symbol); excellent; exempt; eye; Fraunhofer line caused by iron (symbol); instantaneous value alternating current (symbol); modulus of elasticity (symbol)
E¹: Lhotse I (27,890-ft adjoining peak of Mount Everest, world's highest mountain—29,028 ft)
E²: Lhotse II (27,560-ft adjoining peak of Mount Everest)

E$: Eurodollar (American dollar deposited in Europe)
E: east; Einstein unit of energy (symbol); electromotive force (symbol); ***en*** (Dutch, Portuguese, Spanish—in); Envoy Extraordinary and Minister Plenipotentiary; ***est*** (French or Italian—east); ***este*** (Portuguese or Spanish—east); ***etelä*** (Finnish—south); experiment (symbol); voltage (symbol)
E = mc²: Einstein's equation where energy (E) equals the

atomic mass *(m)* and the speed of light *(c)* squared; the speed of light being 186,000 miles per second

ea: each; ends annealed; enemy aircraft; enlistment allowance

EA: East Africa(n); Eastern Air Lines; educational age; Egyptian Army; Electronic Associates; experimental aircraft

E/A: Ecology Action; enemy aircraft

EAA: Engineers and Architects Association; Equipment Approval Authority; Experimental Aircraft Association; Export Advertising Association

E.A.A.: Engineer in Aeronautics and Astronautics

EAA: Encyclopedia of American Associations

EAAC: East African Airways Corporation

EAAP: European Association for Animal Production

EABn: Engineer Aviation Battalion

eabrd: electrically-actuated band-release device

EAC: East Asiatic Company; Eastern Air Command

EACSO: East African Common Services Organization

ead: equipment allowance document; estimated availability date; extended active duty

ead.: eadem (Latin—the same)

EADF: Eastern Air Defense Force

EAEC: East African Economic Community; European Atomic Energy Community

EAEG: European Association of Exploration Geophysicists

EAEI: Ecology Action Educational Institute

EAES: European Atomic Energy Society

eaf: emergency action file

EAFC: Eastern Association of Fire Chiefs

EAG: Edmonton Art Gallery

Eagle: (see *Columbia*)

Eagle and Serpent: (see *Aguila y Serpiente*)

eahf: eczema, asthma, and hay fever

EAI: East Asian Institute (Columbia University); Education Audit Institute

EAIC: East African Industrial Council

EAID: Equipment Authorization Inventory Data

EAJC: Eastern Arizona Junior College

EAL: East Asiatic Line; Eastern Air Lines; Ethiopian Airlines

eam (EAM): electrical accounting machine

EAM: Eastern Atlantic and Mediterranean

EAM: Ethniko Apelevtherotiko Metopo (Greek—National Liberation Front)

EAME: European, African, Middle Eastern

EAMECM: European-African-Middle Eastern Campaign Medal

EAMF: European Association of Music Festivals

EAMFRO: East African Marine Fisheries Research Organization

EAN: Emergency Action Notification

EANA: Esperanto Association of North America

EANDC: Edgewood Arsenal Nuclear Defense Center; European-American Nuclear Data Center

EANS: Emergency Action Notification System (radio broadcasting)

eaon: except as otherwise noted

eap: eye artifact potential

EAP: Edgar Allan Poe

EAPA: Employment Aptitude Placement Association

EAPD: Eastern Air Procurement District

ear.: electronic analog resolver

Ea-R: Entartungs-Reaktion (German—degeneration reaction)

EAR: East African Railways; Edwin Arlington Robinson

EARC: Eastern Air Rescue Center

EAR & H: East African Railways and Harbours

EARS: Emergency Airborne Reaction System

eas: equivalent airspeed

EAs: East African shilling

EAS: Early American Society

EASA: Electrical Apparatus Service Association

EASE: Emigrant's Assured Savings Estate

easemt: easement

EASEP: Early Apollo Scientific Experiments Payload

EA sh: East African shilling

easl: engineering analysis and simulation language

EAST: Eastern Australian Standard Time

EASTAF: Eastern Transport Air Force

Eastcommrgn: Eastern Communications Region

easter: storm from the east

EASTLANT: Eastern Atlantic Area

East Phil: Eastman Philharmonia

EASY: Early Acquisition System (USA); Engine Analyzer System

eat.: earliest arrival time; estimated arrival time (both shown as EAT on some timetables)

EAT: earliest arriving time; Experiments in Art and Technology

EATS: Equipment Accuracy Test Station

EATTA: East Africa Tourist Travel Association

eau: (French—water)

eaw: equivalent average words

EAWS: East African Wildlife Society

eax: electronic automatic exchange

eb: electron beam; elementary body

e-b: estate-bottled

eb: point d'ébullition (French —boiling point)

Eb: Ebenezer; erbium (symbol)

EB: Avitour Airlines; Eesti Vabariik (Estonian Republic)

E-B: Electric Boat (Division of General Dynamics)

E & B: Ellerman and Bucknall (Ellerman Lines)

EB: Engineering Bulletin

EBA: English Bowling Association

EBAA: Eye-Bank Association of America

ebar: edited beyond all recognition

EBAR: E.B. Aabys Rederi (Norwegian freight line)

EBB: Elias Baseball Bureau; Elizabeth Barrett Browning

ebc: enamel bonded single cotton

EBC: Educational Broadcasting Corporation; European Bibliographical Center (Oxford, England)

ebcdic: extended binary-coded decimal interchange code

ebd: effective biological dose

ebd: ebenda (German—in the same place)

ebds: enamel bonded double silk

EBEC: Encyclopedia Britannica Educational Corporation

Eben: Ebenezer

EBF: Encyclopedia Britannica Films

EBI: Emerson Books, Incorporated

eb i s: edge bead one side (lumber)

ebk: embryonic bovine kidney

EBL: Eastern Basketball League

ebm: expressed breast milk

EBM: Empresa Bacaladera Mexicana (Mexican Codfishing Enterprise)

EBNI: Electricity Board for Northern Ireland

E-boat: enemy boat

ebp: enamel single paper bonded

ebr: electron-beam recorder

EBR: Emu Bay Railway

EBRD: Export Business Division (U.S. Department of Commerce)

ebs: enamel single cotton

EBS: Emergency Bed Service; Emergency Broadcast System; English Bookplate Society; Ethiopian Broadcasting Service

EBSR: Eye-Bank for Sight Restoration

ebt: earth-based tug (NASA); electron-beam technique

eb 2 s: edge bead two sides (lumber)

EBU: European Broadcasting Union

ebul: ebullition

ebw: exploding bridge wire

ebwr (EBWR): experimental boiling-water reactor

ec: economics; electric(al) coding; emergency capability; enamel coated; enteric coated; entering complaint; error correcting; expansive classification; expiratory center; extended coverage; extension and conversion; extension course

ec: en cuento (Spanish—on account)

e.c.: exempli causa (Latin—for example)

Ec: Ecuador; Ecuadorian

EC: Earlham College; East African Airways; East Carolina (railroad); East Central; Eastern College; Eastern Command; Edgewood College; Elizabethtown College; Elmhurst College; Elmira College; Elon College; Emergency Coordinator; Emerson College; Emmanuel College; Engineer Captain; Engineering Change; Engineering Construction; Episcopal Church; Erskine College; Essex College; Established Church; Eureka College; Evangel College; Evansville College; Explorers Club

E-C: Erckmann-Chatrian (combined name for two friendly collaborators: Emile Erckmann and Alexandre Chatrian)

E & C: Engineering and Construction

EC: Encyclopedia Canadiana

eca: electronics control assembly

ECA: Economic Commission for Africa (UN); Economic Control Agency; Economic Cooperation Administration; European Confederation of Agriculture

ECAC: Eastern College Athletic Conference; Electromagnetic Compatibility Analysis Center

ECAFE: Economic Commission for Asia and the Far East (UN)

ecan: excitation, calibration, and normalization

ECAP: Electronic Circuit Analysis Program; Environmental Compatability Assurance Program (USN)

e & cb 1 s: edge and center bead one side (lumber)

e & cb 2 s: edge and center bead two sides (lumber)

ecc: eccentric; electrically-continuous cloth; emergency combat capability

ecc: eccetera (Italian—et cetera)

ECC: Electronics Capital Corporation; Emergency Conservation Committee; Employees Compensation Commission; European Coordinating Committee; European Cultural Center

ECCA: Empresa Consolidada Cubana de Aviación

ECCAA: Executive Chefs de Cuisine Association of America

ECCC: English Country Cheese Council

ECCDA: Eastern Connecticut Clam Diggers Association

eccen: eccentric; eccentrics

ECCI: Executive Committee Communist International

Eccl: Ecclesiastes

eccles: ecclesiastic; ecclesiastical

eccm: electronic counter-countermeasures

ECCP: East Coast Coal Port

ECCS: Emergency Core Cooling Systems (AEC)

eccsl: emitter-coupled-current steered logic

ecd: endocardial cushion defect; estimated completion date

EC & D: Electronic Components and Devices

ecdn: electrical cables down

ece: extended coverage endorsement

ECE: Economic Commission for Europe (UN)

ecf: extracellular fluid

ECF: European Cultural Foundation

ECFMG: Educational Council for Foreign Medical Graduates

ecg: electrocardiogram; electrocardiography

ECG: electrocardiogram

ECGD: Export Credit Guarantee Department

ech: echelon

echo.: enteric cytopathogenic human orphan (virus)

Echo: code for letter E

ECHO: Experimental Contract Highlight Operation

ECHS: Evander Childs High School

ECI: Electronic Communications Incorporated; Extension Course Institute (Air University)

ECIC: Export Credits Insurance Corporation (Canada)

ECITO: European Central Inland Transport Organization

ECIUSAF: Extension Course Institute, USAF

eck: embryonic chicken kidney

ecl: eclipse; electrocardiograph log; electronic crash locator (aircraft)

écl: éclairage (French—lighting)

ECL: Equipment Component List; Europe-Canada Line

ECLA: Economic Commission for Latin America (UN)

eclec: eclectic; eclecticism

ecli: eclipse; ecliptic

ecm: electric coding machine; electrochemical machining; electronic countermeasure(s); ends matched, center (lumber)

ECM: Engineering Change Management; European Common Market

EC & M: Electric Controller and Manufacturing (company)

ECMA: Engineering College Magazines Associated; European Computer Manufacturers Association

Ecmalgol: European Computer Manufacturers Association Algorithmic Language

ECME: Economic Commission for the Middle East (UN)

e-c mix.: ether-chloroform mixture

ECMR: Eastern Contract Management Region

ECMSA: Electronics Command Meteorological Support Agency (USA)

ECN: Engineering Change Notice

eco: electron-coupled oscillator; exempted by commanding officer

ECO: East Coast Overseas; Economic Corporation Organization; Effective Citizens Organization; Engineering Change Order; Environmental Control Organization; European Coal Organization

ECOA: Equipment Company of America

ecol: ecology

Ecol Soc Am: Ecological Society of America

ECOM: Electronics Command (USA)

econ: economic; economics; economist; economy

e con.: e contrario (Latin—on the contrary)

economan: effective control of manpower

economet: econometric

EcoSoc: Economic and Social (Council)
ecp(s): external casing packer(s)
ECP: Engineering Change Proposal
ECPD: Engineers Council for Professional Development
ecpog: electrochemical potential gradient
ECPS: European Center for Population Studies
ECPTA: European Conference of Postal and Telecommunication Administrations
ecr: external channels ratio
ECR: Engineering Change Request
ECRB: Export Control Review Board
ECRC: Electronic Component Reliability Center; Engineering College Research Council
ecs: emperor's clothes syndrome; extended core storage
ECS: Electrochemical Society; Environmental Control Systems; Etched Circuit Society
ECSA: East Coast of South America; European Communication Security Agency; Expanded Clay and Shale Association
ECSC: European Coal and Steel Community
ECSIL: Experimental Cross-Section Information Library (University of California—Livermore)
ECSTC: Elizabeth City State Teachers College
ect: electroconvulsive therapy; engine cutoff time; enteric coated tablet
ectl: emitter-coupled transistor logic
ecu: environmental control unit
Ecu: Ecuador; Ecuadorean
ECU: English Church Union
Ecua: Ecuador; Ecuadorean
ecuador: (Spanish—equator)
ECUK: East Coast of United Kingdom
ecumen: ecumenical
e & cV 1 s: edge and center-V one side (lumber)
e & cV 2 s: edge and center-V two sides (lumber)
ecw: extracellular water
ed: edge distance; edit; edited; edition; editor; editorial; educate; educated; education; educational; educator; effective dose; enemy dead; error detecting; erythema dose; excused from duty; existence doubtful; extra duty
ed: edición (Spanish—edition), *edition* (French—edition); *edizione* (Italian—edition)
ed₅₀: median effective dose

Ed: Edgar; Editor; Edmond; Edmund; Edson; Edward; Edwin
Ed.: Editor
ED: Consolidated Edison Company (stock exchange symbol); Eastern District; Economics Division; Efficiency Decoration; Elder Dempster Line; Electric Dynamic; Engineering Data; Engineering Depot; Engineering Design; Engineering Draftsman
E-D: Electro Dynamics (Division of General Dynamics)
E.D.: Doctor of Engineering
eda: early departure authorized
EDA: Economic Development Administration (Puerto Rico); Environmental Development Agency
EDARR: Engineering Drawing and Assembly Release Record
Ed.B.: Bachelor of Education
edc: electronic digital computer; engine-driven compressor; estimated date of completion; estimated date of confinement
EDC: Eastern Defense Command; European Defense Community
edcn: education
EDCPF: Environmental Data Collection and Processing Facility (USA)
EDCs: Economic Development Committees
edcsa: effective date of change of strength accountability
edcv: enamel double cotton varnish
edd: electronic data display; expected date of delivery
edd: ediderunt (Latin—published by)
edd.: editiones (Latin—editions)
Ed. D.: Doctor of Education
EDD: Eastman Dental Dispensary
eddf: error detection and decision feedback
EDDS: Electronic Devices Data Service
ede: electronic defense evaluator
EDF: European Development Fund
Edg: Edgar
EDI: Economic Development Institute; Edinburgh, Scotland (airport); Engineering Department Instruction
edict.: engineering document information collection technique
Edin: Edinburgh
Ed-in-Ch: Editor-in-Chief
EDIS: Engineering Data Information Service; Engineering Data Information System
edit.: editing; edition; editor; editorial
EDITS: Experimental Digital Television System

EDL: Elder Dempster Lines
EDLNA: Exotique Dancers League of North America
edm: electrical-discharge machining
Edm: Edmund
Ed. M.: Master of Education
EDMICS: Engineering Data Mangement Information Control System
Edmn: Edmonton
edn: electrodesiccation
Edn: Edwin
edo: effective diameter of objective; error demodulator output; error detector output
EDO: Employee Development Officer; Engineering Duty Officer; Engineering Duty Only
edoc: effective date of change
EDOPAC: Enlisted Personnel Distribution Office Pacific Fleet
edp (EDP): electronic data processing
edpe: electronic data processing equipment
edpm: electronic data processing machine(s)
edr: electrodermal response; equivalent direct radiation
EDPS: Electronic Data Processing System
EDPT: Electronic Data Processing Test
edrl: effective damage risk level
EDRS: Education Document Reproduction Service
edrt: effective date of release from training
eds: editors; enamel double silk; estimated date of separation
EDs: Explosive Disposal specialists
EDS: English Dialect Society; Environmental Data Service
Ed. Spec.: Educational Specialist
edst: elastic diaphragm switch technology
EDST: Eastern Daylight Saving Time
edsv: enamel double silk varnish
edt: effective date of training
EDT: Eastern Daylight Time
edta: ethylene diamine tetra-acetic (acid)
edtr: experimental, developmental, test, and research
edu: experimental diving unit
educ: education; educational
edv: end-diastolic volume
Edw: Edward
eDx: electrodiagnosis
ee: eased edges (lumber); embryo extract; equine encephalitis; errors excepted; expriation of enlistment; eye and ear
e & e: evacuation and evasion;

evasion and escape; eye and ear
e-to-e: end-to-end
EE: Early English; Electrical Engineer(ing); Electronics Engineer(ing); Envoy Extraordinary; Estado Español (The Spanish State)
E.E.: Electrical Engineer
EEA: Electronic Engineering Association; Ethical Education Association
EEC: East Erie Commercial (railroad); European Economic Community
EECA: Engineering Economic Cost Analysis
eecom: electrical, environmental, and communications
eed: electrical explosive device
eee: eastern equine encephalitis
EEF: Egyptian Expeditionary Force
eefi: essential elements of friendly information
eeg: electroencephalogram
EEI: Edison Electric Institute; Environmental Equipment Institute; Essential Elements of Information
EEL: Ecology and Epidemiology Laboratory; English Electric Limited; Evans Electroselenium Limited
eem: *Electronic Engineers Master* (catalog)
EE & MP: Envoy Extraordinary and Minister Plenipotentiary
e'en: even; evening
E Eng: Early English
EENT: end, evening nautical twilight; eye, ear, nose, and throat
EENWR: Exe Estuary National Wildlife Refuge (England)
eeo: equal employment opportunity
EEOC: Equal Employment Opportunity Commission
eep: electronic evaluation and procurement; electronic event programmer(s); emergency essential personnel
eepnl: estimated effective-perceived noise level
e'er: ever
EERI: Earthquake Engineering Research Institute
EERL: Electrical Engineering Research Laboratory (University of Texas)
ees: electronic environment simulator
EES: Engineering Experiment Station; Enlisted Evaluation System; European Exchange System
EESS: *Encyclopedia of Engineering Signs and Symbols*
EET: Eames Eye Test; Eastern

European Time; Education Equivalency Test
EETS: Early English Text Society
EEUA: Engineering Equipment Users Association
EEV: English Electric Valve (company)
eex: electronic egg exchange (computer program)
ef: each face; elevation finder; equivalent focal length; expectant father; experimental flight; extra fine
EF: Educational Foundation; Emergency Fleet; Expeditionary Force
E & F: Elders and Fyffes (steamship line)
efa: essential fatty acids
EFA: Environmental Financing Authority
efc: earth fixed coordinate; Evergreen Fir Corporation (initials)
EFCX: Evergreen Freight Car Express
efd: excused from duty
EFEA: Empresa Ferrocarriles del Estado Argentino (Argentine State Railways)
eff: effect; effective; efficiency
effcy: efficiency
effect.: effective; effectivity
effer: efferent
Effie: Euphemia
effl: efflorescent
eff wd: effective wind
EFG: Edward FitzGerald
ef & i: engineer, furnish, and install
EFINS: Enrico Fermi Institute for Nuclear Studies (Univ of Chicago)
efl: effective focal length
EFLA: Educational Film Library Association
EFLC: Engineers Foreign Language Circle
EFMG: Electric Fuse Manufacturers Guild
EFNS: Educational Foundation for Nuclear Science
efp: effective filtration pressure; electric(al) fuel propulsion
EFPA: Educational Film Producers Association
EFPW: European Federation for the Protection of Waters
efr: effective filtration rate
E Fris: East Frisian
EFS: Edinburgh Festival Society; Emergency Feeding Service
eft: earliest finish time
EFT: Embedded Figures Test; Engineering Flight Test
EFTA: European Free Trade Association
eftf: *efterfolger* (Dano-Norwegian

—successor)
Eftf(lg): *Efterfölgere* (Dano-Norwegian —successor)
EFTI: Engineering Flight Test Instrumentation
eftm: *eftermiddag* (Norwegian —after noon)—p.m.
efto: encrypt for transmission only
e.g.: *exempli gratia* (Latin—for example)
Eg: Egypt; Egyptian
EG: Equatorial Guinea (formerly Spanish Guinea); grid voltage (symbol)
egad.: electronegative gas detector
egads: electronic ground automatic destruct sequencer (system for destroying malfunctioning missiles)
Egb: Egbert
egcr: experimental gas-cooled reactor
EGCRNR: Eilat Gulf Coral Reef Nature Reserve (Israel)
egd: electrogasdynamics
egdg: electrogasdynamic generator
ege: *eau, gaz, électricité* (French —water, gas, electricity)
E Ger: East Germany
egg.: electrogastrogram
EG & G: Edgerton, Germeshausen & Grier
eggler: egg + dealer (an egg dealer)
eggwich: egg sandwich
EGIFO: Edward Grey Institute of Field Ornithology
EGL: Eglin, Florida (tracking station)
EGmc: East Germanic
EGMRSA: Edible Gelatin Manufacturers Research Society of America
EGNR: Ein Gedi Nature Reserve (Israel's Dead Sea oasis)
EGO: Ankara Elektrik, Havagazi ve Otobüs Isletme Müessesesi (Ankara Electricity, City-Gas, and Bus Traffic Department); Eccentric-Orbiting Geophysical Observatory
egp: embezzlement of government property; exhaust gas pressure
EGPC: Egyptian General Petroleum Corporation
egr: egress; exhaust gas recirculation
egt: exhaust gas temperature
Egyp: Egypt; Egyptian; egyptology
Egyptian Century: the 15th century before the Christian era when the kingdom of Egypt extended from the Sahara to beyond the Euphrates—the 1400s
egyptol: egyptology
e & h: environment and heredity
EH: *Enciclopedia Hoepli* (Italian

—Hoepli's Encyclopedia)
EHA: Economic History Association
ehbf: extrahepatic blood flow
E & HC: Emory and Henry College
ehd: electrohydrodynamics
ehf: extreme high-frequency—30,000-300,000 mc
EHF: Experimental Husbandry Farm
EHG: Edvard Hagerup Grieg
EHH: Ernst Heinrich Haeckel
EHHS: Erasmus Hall High School
EHI: Emergency Homes, Incorporated
ehl: effective half life
EHL: Eastern Hockey League
e/h/m: eggs per hen per month
EHMA: Electric Hoist Manufacturers Association
ehp: effective horsepower; electric horsepower; extra-high potency
EHS: Emergency Health Service; Experimental Horticultural Station (UK)
eht: extra-high tension
EHTRC: Emergency Highway Traffic Regulation Center
ehv: extra-high voltage
EHV: Empresa Hondureña de Vapores (Honduran Steamship Line)
ehw: extreme high water
e/h/yr: eggs per hen per year
e-i: extraversion-introversion
e/i: endorsement irregular
Ei: Eire (Irish Free State)
Ei: *encéphale isolé* (French—isolated intellectual)
EI: East Indies; Electro Institute; Essex Institute; Eunice Institute
EI: *Engineering Index*
EIA: East Indian Association; Electronic Industries Association; Empire Industries Association; Engineering Institute of America
EIB: Ernst Ingmar Bergman; European Investments Bank; Export-Import Bank
EIBW: Export-Import Bank of Washington
eic: emotional inertia concept
EIC: Engineering Institute of Canada
EICF: European Investment Casters' Federation
eid: end item description
EID: End Item Delivery; End Item Description; Engineering Item Description
Eidg: *Eidgenössisch* (Swiss—federal)
eid lt: emergency identification light
eiff: enemy identification—friend or foe
eiii: Electrical Industry Information

Institute
eil: electron injection laser
Eimac: Eitel-McCullough
EIMO: Electronic Interface Management Office
EIN: Empresa Insulana de Navegação (Island Navigation Line)
EINP: Elk Island National Park (Alberta)
einschl: *einschliesslich* (German—including)
Einw: *Einwohner* (German—inhabitants; population)
EIO: Emergency Information Office(r)
EIP: Environmental Improvement Program; Experiment Implementation Plan
EIR: East Indian Railway; Emergency Information Readiness
eirnv: extra incidence rate in non-vaccinated groups
eirv: extra incidence rate in vaccinated groups
eis: electrical intersection splice
Eis: (German—E-sharp)
EIS: Economic Information Systems; Epidemic Intelligence Service (HEW)
Eisted: (Welsh—Eisteddfod—annual meeting of Welsh bards)
eit: engineer in training
ei & t: emplacement, installation, and test(ing)
EIT: Electrical Information Test
EITA: Electric Industrial Truck Association
EITB: Engineering Industry Training Board
EITS: Educational and Industrial Testing Service
ej: elbow-jerk
ej: *ejemplo* (Spanish—example)
EJC: Edison Junior College; Engineers Joint Council; Engineers Junior College; Everett Junior College
eject.: ejector
EJ & E RY: Elgin, Joliet & Eastern Railway
EJMA: Educational Jewelry Manufacturers Association; Expansion Joint Manufacturers Association
EJN: Endicott Johnson (stock exchange symbol)
EJT: Engineering Job Ticket
ek: single enamel single cellophane (insulation symbol)
eK: *etter Kristi* (Norwegian—after Christ)
EK: Eastman Kodak
EK: *Eisernes Kreuz* (German—Iron Cross)—military decoration
EKCO: E.K. Cole (Limited)
Eken: (Swedish slang—Stockholm)

ekg: electrokardiogram (electrocardiogram); electrocardiography
EKG: Electrokardiogram
eks: *eksempel* (Danish—example)
EKSC: Eastern Kentucky State College
ekv: electron kilovolt
el: each layer; educational level; elastic level; elevation; elongation
El: Elbert; Elevated Railroad; Elias; Elvie; Elvira
EL: Eastern League; Electrical Laboratory; Electronics Laboratory; Empresa do Limpopo (Limpopo Line); Engineer Lieutenant; Epworth League; Erie-Lackawanna (railroad)
E-L: Erie-Lackawanna (railroad)
E-et-L: Eure-et-Loire
ELAC: East Los Angeles College
e lact.: *e lacte* (Latin—with milk)
EL AL: El Al Israel Airlines
elas: elastic; elasticity; emergency logistical air support
ELAS: *Ethnikos Laikos Apelephterotikos Stratos* (Greek—Hellenic Peoples' Army of Liberation)
Elasm: Elasmobranchia
E.L.B.: Bachelor of English Literature
elc: extra-low carbon (electrodes)
ELC: Electronic Location Center
El Caudillo: (Spanish—The Chief)—sobriquet of General Francisco Franco-Bahamonde—Spanish dictator and soldier who earned title of El Caudillo while subduing Riffs in Morocco under Abd-el-Krim
El Cid: *El Cid Campeador* (Spanish—The Lord Champion)—Rodrigo Díaz de Bivar
elct: electronics
eld: eldest
Eldercare: plan providing medical care for the elderly
ELDO: European Launcher Development Organization
ELDS: Editorial Layout Display System
Eleanor: Mrs Anna Eleanor Roosevelt—wife of President Franklin Delano Roosevelt
elec: electric; electrical; electrician; electricity; electro-; electuary
ELEC: European League for Economic Cooperation
elect.: election; elector; electoral; electrolyte; electrolytic
electn: electrician
electraac: electronic auto analysis clinic
electrochem: electrochemistry
electroenceph: electroencephalog-

raphy
electrol: electrolysis
electron.: electronic(s)
electrophys: electrophysics
electro(s): electrotype(s)
electrum: 50% gold, 50% silver
Elekt: *Elektrizität* (German—electricity)
elem: element; elementary
eleph fol: elephant folio—books about 23 inches high
El Español: (Spanish—The Spaniard)—Giuseppe Maria Crespi—Italian painter's nickname
elev: elevated; elevation; elevator
elf.: early lunar flare; extra low frequency
elf: (Swedish—river)
ELF: Early Lunar Flare
ELFA: Electric Light Fittings Association
El G: El Paso Natural Gas Company
ELG: European Liaison Group (USA)
elgas: electricity and gas
El Gran Libertador: (Spanish—The Great Liberator)—Simón Bolívar—liberated Venezuela, Colombia, Ecuador, Peru, and Bolivia from Spanish rule
El Greco: (Spanish—The Greek)—Kryiakos Theotokopoulos (Domingo Theotocopuli)
elhi: elementary and high school (textbooks)
Eli: Elias; Elijah
ELI: Environmental Law Institute
Elia: Charles Lamb
elig: eligible
Elij: Elijah
elim: eliminate; eliminated; elimination
El Inca: (Spanish—The Inca)—Garcilaso de la Vega
elint: electronic intelligence
elints: electronic intelligence-gathering vessels
elip: electrostatic latent image photography
Elis: Elisabeth
Elise: Elizabeth
elix: elixir
Eliz: Elizabeth(an)
Elizabethan Age: England before and after 1600 when Shakespeare, Milton, Locke, and Newton were adding luster to the literate and the scientific world
ell.: elbow; ellipsoid(al); elliptic(al)
ell: *eller* (Swedish—or)
ELLA: European Long Lines Agency
El Libertador: (Spanish—The Liberator)—Simón Bolívar

ellip: elliptic; elliptical; elliptically
ELLIS: Ellis Air Lines
el lt: electric light; electric lighting
elm.: element
ELM: Eastern Atlantic and Mediterranean; Edgar Lee Masters
ELMA: Empresa Lineas Maritimas Argentinas (Argentine Lines)
elmint: electromagnetic intelligence
ELMS: Experimental Library Management System
EL Mus: East London Museum
E Ln: East London
ELNA: Esperanto League of North America
El Niño: El Niño Current
ELNM: Edison Laboratory National Monument (West Orange, New Jersey)
elo: elocution; eloquence
Elo: Eloheimo
ELOI: Emergency Letter of Instruction
elong: elongate; elongation
E long: east longitude
E Loth: East Lothian
elox: electrical spark erosion
ELP: El Paso, Texas (airport)
elpc: electroluminescence photo conductor
El Precursor: (Spanish—the Precursor)—Francisco Miranda—fighter for Venezuelan freedom from Spanish rule; Antonio Nariño—fighter for Colombian freedom from Spanish rule
ELR: Engineering Laboratory Report
elra: electronic radar
ELRO: Electronics Logistics Research Office (USA)
Elroy: American country-boy name derived from the French for king—*Le Roi* or the Spanish equivalent—*El Rey*—or their combination
Els: Elsinore (Helsingör)
ELS: Escanaba and Lake Superior (railroad)
El Sal: El Salvador
elsec: electronic intelligence
elsie: emergency life-saving instant exit
Elsie: Elizabeth
ELSS: Emplaced Lunar Scientific Station
ELT: *English Language Teaching*
el2: elongation in 2 inches
elv: extra-low voltage
elv: (Dano-Norwegian—river)
elw: extreme low water
El Wld: *Electrical World*
Ely: easterly
Elz: Elzevir
em: emanation; emergency mobilization; enlisted man; expanded

metal
e/m: specific electronic mass
e & m: endocrine and metabolism; erection and maintenance
em: *eftermiddag* (Danish—afternoon)—p.m.
Em: Emily; Emma; Emmanuel; Emy
EM: Earl Marshal; Education Manual; Electrician's Mate; electromagnetic (symbol); Engineer Manager; Engineering Memorandum; Enlisted Man (Men); Etna & Montrose (railroad); European Movement; External Memorandum
E-M: Electric Machinery (company); Electro-Motive (corporation)
E.M.: Engineer of Mines; Engineer of Mining
E-M: *État-Major* (French—Headquarters)
EM 1 C: Electrician's Mate First Class (USN)
EMA: Electronics Manufacturers Association; Envelope Manufacturers Association; European Monetary Agreement; Evaporated Milk Association; Exposition Management Association; Extended Mission Apollo
E MacD: Edward MacDowell
EMAD: Engine Maintenance Assembly and Disassembly
Emancipator of the Serfs: Czar Alexander II of Russia
EMAS: Emergency Message Authentication System; Employment Medical Advisory Service (UK)
EMATS: Emergency Message Automatic Transmission System
emb: embankment; embargo; embark; embarkation; embassy; embroidered; embroidery; embryo; embryology
emball: *emballasje* (Norwegian—packing)
Emb: Embassy
embk: embark
embkn: embarkation
EMBL: Eniwetok Marine Biological Laboratory
EMBO: European Molecular Biology Organization
embry: embryology
embryol: embryology
emc: engineered military circuit; equilibrium moisture content
EMC: Education Media Council; Einstein Medical Center; Electronic Material Change; End Mollycoddling in America; Engineering Maintenance Center; Engineer(ing) Maintenance Con-

trol; Engineering Manpower Commission

EMCCC: European Military Communications Coordinating Committee

EMCE: Eastern Montana College of Education

emcee: master of ceremonies

emcees: masters of ceremony

emcon: emission control

emcv: encephalomyocarditis virus

emd: electric-motor-driven

Emd: Emden

E-MD: Electro-Motive Division (General Motors)

emdp: electromotive difference of potential

EMEA: Electrical Manufacturers Export Association

EMEC: Electronics Maintenance Engineering Center

emend.: emendatis (Latin—corrected; edited; emended)

emer: emergency

Emer: Emeritus

emerg: emergency

emergcons: emergency conditions

emerit.: emeritus (Latin—retired with honor)

emery: aluminum oxide (Al_2O_3)

E.Met.: Engineer of Metallurgy

EMETF: Electromagnetic Environment Test Facility (USA)

emf: electromotive force; erythrocyte maturing factor; every morning fix (your old automobile)

EMF: European Motel Federation; Excerpta Medica Foundation

emg: electromyogram; electromyography

emi: electromagnetic intereference

emi: (Berber—mountain)

EMI: Electrical and Musical Industries; Equipment Manufacturing Incorporated

emic: emergency maternity and infant care

emig: emigrant; emigration

Emil Ludwig: Emil Cohn

emis: emission

EMJC: East Mississippi Junior College

Emjo: Emmanuel Jobe

Eml: Emily

EML: Equipment Modification List

em log: electromagnetic log

emm: electromagnetic measurement

Emm: Emmanuel

emma: electron microscopy and microanalysis

Emmy: award given for outstanding television performances in the United States; statuette named after tv entertainer Faye Emerson

EMNM: El Morro National Monument

Emos: Earth's mean orbital speed

emot: emotion(al)

emp: electromagnetic pulses; empennage

emp.: emplastrum (Latin—adhesive; a plaster)

e.m.p.: ex modo prescripto (Latin—in the manner prescribed)

Emp: Emperor; Empire; Empress

emp agcy: employment agency

empath: empathetic; empathy

empd: employed

emph: emphasis

EMPI: European Motor Products Incorporated

EMPIRE: Early Manned Planetary-Interplanetary Round-Trip Experiment

empl: emplace; emplacement; employ; employee; employer; employment

EMPOCOL: Empresa Puertos de Colombia (Colombian Port Works)

EMPPO: European and Mediterranean Plant Protection Organization

Empress of India: Queen Victoria

emp. vesic.: emplastrum vesicatorium (Latin—a blistering plaster)

emq: electromagnetic quiet

emr: educable mentally retarded; electromagnetic resonance

EMR: Emerson Electric (stock exchange symbol); Engineering Master Report; Enlisted Manning Report

EM & R: Equipment Maintenance and Readiness

EMRIC: Educational Media Research Information Center

Ems: Bad Ems

EMS: Econometric Society; Emergency Medical Service

EMSA: Electron Microscope Society of America

EMSC: Educational Media Selection Center

emt: electrical metallic tubing

EM 2 C: Electrician's Mate Second Class (USN)

EM 3 C: Electrician's Mate Third Class (USN)

emu.: electromagnetic unit

EMU: Eastern Michigan University

EMU: Europese Monetaire et Economische Unie (Dutch—European Monetary and Economic Union

emul: emulsion

EMSO: European Mobility Service Office (USA)

EMSU: Environmental Meteoro-

logical Support Unit

emuls.: emulsio (Latin—emulsion)

emv: electron megavolt

en: enema; exceptions noted

En: English

ENA: English Newspaper Association

enam: enamel; enameled; enamels

ENAP: Empresa Nacional del Petroleo (Chile)

enc: enclosed

encap: encapsulate(d); encapsulation

Enc Can: Encyclopedia Canadiana

encl: enclose; enclosed; enclosure

enclit: enclitic

ENCO: Energy Company (Humble Oil & Refining)

ency: encyclopedia

Ency Assn: Encyclopedia of Associations

Ency Brit: Encyclopaedia Britanica

end.: endorsement

END: Environment Near Death

endo: endocrine; endocrinology

EndocSoc: Endocrine Society

endor: electron nuclear double resonance

endow.: endowment

ENE: east northeast

ENEA: European Nuclear Energy Association

ENEL: Ente Nazionale per l'Energia Elettrica (National Electric-Power Company of Italy)

enem.: enema (Greek—injection)

ener: energize

energe: energicamente (Italian—energetically)

en fav de: en faveur de (French—in favor of)

En1c: Engineman, first class

eng: engine

Eng: England; English

Eng: Engineering (British periodical)

Eng. D.: Doctor of Engineering

eng fnd: engine foundation

engin: engineering

engitist: engineer + scientist

English American: Thomas Gage—adventurer-explorer who helped establish English rule around the Caribbean

English Lit: English Literature

Eng Lit: English Literature

Eng News-Rec: Engineering News-Record

engr: engineer

eng rm: engine room

engrv: engraver; engraving

Eng. Sc. D.: Doctor of Engineering Science

ENI: Ente Nazionale Idrocarburi (National Fuel Agency)

eniac: electronic numerical integrator and computer

ENIT: Ente Nazionale Industrie Turistiche (Italian—National Tourist Industry)

enl: enlist

enlgd: enlarged

Enlightenment: *(see* The Enlightenment)

en ml: end mill

ENMU: Eastern New Mexico University

ENNWR: Eastern Neck National Wildlife Refuge (Maryland)

eno: enero (Spanish—January)

en°: enero (Spanish —January)

E/no: estacionamiento no (Spanish —no parking)

enol: enology

En1c: Engineman, first class

ENP: Egmont National Park (North Island, New Zealand); Etosha NP (South-West Africa); Everglades NP (Florida)

ENPA: Ente Nazionale Protezione Animali (National Society for the Protection of Animals—Italy)

enr: en route; equivalent noise resistance

ENR: Emissora Nacional de Radiodifusão (Radio Portugal)

E & NR: Esquimalt and Nanaimo Railway

enrt: enroute

Ens: Ensign

ENSA: Entertainments National Service Association

Ensen: Ensenada

ensi: equivalent—noise-sideband input

ENSIDESA: Empresa Nacional Siderurgica SA (Spanish—National Steel Works)

ent: ear, nose, and throat; enter; entrance

ENT: Aerolineas Argentinas (Argentine Airlines); Ear, Nose, and Throat (clinic or hospital department)

entd: entered

ENTE: Ente Nazionale per l'Energia Elettrica (National Electric Energy Enterprise)

entl: entitle

entom: entomology

entr: entrance

entspr: entsprechend (German —corresponding)

Ent Sta Hall: Entered at Stationers' Hall

ent-vio: entero-vioform (antidiarrhetic)

env: envelop; envelope; environ; envoy

Env: Envoy

Env Ext: Envoy Extraordinary

ENWR: Erie National Wildlife Refuge (Pennsylvania); Eufaula National Wildlife Refuge (Alabama)

enz: enzovoort(s) (Dutch—and so on)

eo: engine oil

e-o: even-odd

e.o.: ex officio (Latin—by virtue of office)

Eo: Ecuadorian escudo(s); escudo(s) (Portuguese currency)

EO: Eastern Orthodox; Education Officer; Engineering Order; Entertainments Office(r); Executive Office(r); Executive Order

E & O: Eastern and Oriental

eoa: effective on or about; examination, opinion, advice (medical)

EOA: Economic Oil Association; Essential Oil Association

EOB: Executive Office Building

eoc: electric overhead crane; emotional-organic combination

Eoc: Eocene

EOC: Economic Opportunity Commission; Electronic Operations Center; Enemy Oil Committee; Executive Officers Council

EOCI: Electric Overhead Crane Institute

eod: entry on duty; every other day; explosive ordnance disposal

EODP: Engineering Order Delayed for Parts

eoe: earth orbit ejection

e & oe: errors and omissions excepted

EOE: Enemy-Occupied Europe

eof (EOF): end of file

EOF: Earth Orbital Flight

eog: effect on guarantees; electrooculogram

EOGs: Educational Opportunity Grants

EOH: Emergency Operation Headquarters

eohp: except otherwise herein provided

Eol: Eolic

EOL: Ex Oriente Lux (The Light of the Orient—The Oriental Society)

eom: end of month; extra-ocular movements

eooe: error or omission excepted

eop: earth orbit plane; end of part

EOP: Equipment Operations Procedure; Excutive Office of the President

eoq: economical ordering quantity; end of quarter

EOQC: European Organization for Quality Control

eor: earth orbital rendezvous; explosive ordnance reconnaissance

EOR: Earth Orbit Rendezvous

EORSA: Episcopalians and Others for Responsible Social Action

eos: eligible for overseas service

EO's: Engineering Orders

EOS: Earth Orbiting Shuttle (NASA); European Orthodontic Society

eosins: eosinophils

eosp: economic order and stocking procedure

EOSS: Earth Orbital Space Station

eot: end of transmission; enemy-occupied territory

EOT: Eagle Ocean Transport

ep: electrically polarized; electric primer; electroplate; electroplated; electroplating; electropneumatic; endpaper(s); estimated position; exit pupil; experienced playgoer; explosion-proof; external publication; extreme pressure

e/p: endpaper

e & p: exploration and production (area)

e p: en passant (French—in passing)

e.p.: editio princeps (Latin—first edition)

Ep.: Episcopus (Latin—Bishop or overseer)

EP: Eagle-Picher; École Polytechnique (Polytechnic School); engineering personnel; Engineering Publications; entrucking point; estimated position; exceptions passed

E-P: European Plan (no meals)

E & P: Extraordinary and Plenipotentiary

E & P: Editor & Publisher

epa: estimated profile analysis

EPA: Emergency Powers Act; Empire Parliamentary Association; Empire Press Agency; Environmental Protection Agency; European Productivity Agency; Evangelical Press Association

EPAA: Educational Press Association of America; Employing Printers Association of America

epam (EPAM): elementary perceiver and memorizer

epc: electroplate on copper

EPC: Esso Petroleum Company

EPCOT: Experimental Prototype Community of Tomorrow (Orlando, Florida)

EPCS: Equitable Pioneers Cooperative Society

epd: earliest practicable date; excess profits duty

epd: en paz descanse (Spanish —may he rest in peace)

EPDA: Exhibit Producers and Designers Association

epdm: epidemiological; epidemiologist; epidemiology

EPE: Editorial Projects for Education

epedemiol: epedemiology

epf: exopthalmos-producing factor

EPF: European Packaging Federation

EPFL: Enoch Pratt Free Library (Baltimore)

epg: eggs per gram (parasitology)

EPG: Electronic Proving Ground (US Army)

Eph: Ephraim; Epistle to the Ephesians

ephmer: ephemeral; ephemerides; ephemeris

epi: electronic position indicator; emotional-physiologic illness

EPI: Emergency Public Information

EPIC: Electronic Properties Information Center; End Poverty in California

epid: epidemic

epil: epilogue

Epiph: Epiphania; Epiphany

epis: episiotomy

Epis: Episcopal(ian)

Epist.: *Epistola* (Latin—epistle or letter)

epistom.: *epistomium* (Latin—stopper)

epit: epitaph; epitome

epith: epithelial; epithelium

epivag: epivaginitis

epl: extreme pressure lubricant

EPL: Erie Public Library; Evansville Public Library

EPL: *École Polytechnique de Lausanne* (French—Polytechnic School of Lausanne)

epm: explosions per minute

EPMS: Engine Performance Monitoring System; Engineering Project Management System

epn: effective-perceived noise

epnd: effective-perceived noise decibels

epndbl: effective-perceived noise-decibel level

EPNG: El Paso Natural Gas

epns: electroplated nickel silver

epo: experimental processing operation

epp: end plate potential

epp: *edellä puolenpäiven* (Finnish —before noon)

Epp.: *Episcopi* (Latin—Bishops or overseers)

EPP: Earth Physics Program; European Pallet Pool

EPPL: El Paso Public Library

EPPO: European and Mediterranean Plant Protection Organization

epr: electron paramagnetic resonance

EPRA: Eastern Psychiatric Research Association

ep's: epithelial cells

eps (EPS): energetic particles satellites

EPS: El Paso Southern (railroad); Emergency Procurement Service; Engineering Purchase Specification; Escape Propulsion System

epsom salt: magnesium sulfate ($MgSO_4 \cdot 7H_2O$)

epsp: excitatory postsynaptic potential

ept: ethylene-propylene terpolymer; excess profits tax; external pipe thread

EPT: Excess Profits Tax

EPTA: Expanded Program of Technical Assistance (UN)

epte: existed prior to entry

epts: existed prior to service

EPU: Empire Press Union; European Payment Union

EPUL: École Polytechnique de l'Université de Lausanne (Polytechnic School of the University of Lausanne)

eput: events-per-unit-time

epw: enemy prisoner of war

epwm: electroplated white metal

EPZ: École Polytechnique de Zürich (Polytechnic School of Zurich)

eq: equal; equation; equivalent

Eq: Equator

EQ: educational quotient; enthusiasm quotient; ethnic quotient

EQA: Environmental Quality Act (California)

EQAA: Environmental Quality Advisory Agency

EQC: Environmental Quality Council

eqi: environmental quality index

eqp: equip; equipment

eqpt: equipment

eqq: electric quadripole-quadripole

EQSC: Environmental Quality Study Council

Eq T: equation of time

eq tr: equipment trust

Equa: Equator; Equatorial

Equa C Cur: Equatorial Countercurrent

equat: equator; equatorial

equin: equinox

equip.: equipment

equipt: equipment

Equity: Actors' Equity Association

equiv: equivalent

er: echo ranging; electronic reconnaissance; emergency rescue; external resistance

e/r: en route

Er: erbium; Eritrea; Eritrean

ER: East Riding; East River; Edwardus Rex (King Edward); Effectiveness Report; Elizabeth Regina (Queen Elizabeth); Emergency Request; Emergency Rescue; Emergency Reserve; Emergency Room; Engine Room; Engineering Report; Equipment Requirement; Evaluation Report; Expert Rifleman; Explosives Report; External Report; Express Route

E.R.: *Elizabeth Regina* (Queen Elizabeth)

ERA: Electrical Research Association; Electronic Representatives Association; Engineering Research Associates; Engineering Research Association; Equitable Reserve Association

ERA: *Equal Rights Amendment*

ERAA: Equipment Review and Authorization Activity

Era of Good Feeling: (administration of James Monroe—fifth President of the United States)

ERAI: Embry-Riddle Aeronautical Institute

ERAP: *Entreprise de Recherches et d'Activites Petrolienes* (Petroleum Research and Development Enterprise)—French

Eras: Erasmus

eraser. (ERASER): elevated radiation seeker rocket

ERB: Educational Records Bureau; Equipment Review Board

er bh: engine room bulkhead

erbm (ERBM): extended-range ballistic missile

erc: en-route chart; equatorial ring current

ERC: Economic Resources Corporation; Electronics Research Center (NASA); Enlisted Reserve Corps

Erckmann-Chatrian: Emile Erckmann + Alexandre Chatrian

ERCS: Emergency Rocket Communications System

erd: equivalent residual dose

ERDA: Electronics Research and Development Agency; Energy Research and Development Administration

ERDE: Explosives Research and Development Establishment

erect.: erection

erf: error function

ERF: Eye Research Foundation

ERFA: European Radio-Frequency Agency

erg: unit of mechanical energy or work (derived from the word *energy*)

erg.: electroretinogram

erg: (Arabic—desert; sand dune)

ERI: Erie, Pennsylvania (airport)

eric: electronic remote and independent control

ERIC: Educational Resources Information Center (US Office of Education)

ERIC/AE: Educational Resources Information Center / Adult Education

ERIC/CEA: Educational Resources Information Center / Clearinghouse on Educational Administration

ERIC/CLIS: Educational Resources Information Center / Clearinghouse for Library and Information Sciences

ERIC/CRIER: Educational Resources Information Center / Clearinghouse on Retrieval Information and Evaluation on Reading

Erich Maria Remarque: Erich Maria Kramer

ERIC/IRCD: Educational Resources Information Center / Information Retrieval Center on the Disadvantaged

Ericofon: Ericsson telephone

Erie: Erie-Lackawanna (railroad)

ERiEI: Eastern Regional Institute for Education

Erit: Eritrea

Erl: *Erläuterung* (German—explanatory note)

ERL: Environmental Research Laboratories

erm: ermine

erma: electronic recording machine accounting

Ern: Ernest; Ernst

Ernie: Ernest

ERNIE: Electronic Random Number Indicator Equipment

ERO: Eastman-Rochester Orchestra

eroduction(s): erotic production(s)

EROS: Earth Resources Observation Satellite; Eliminate Zero Range System (for collision avoidance); Experimental Reflector Orbital Shot (space probe)

erp: effective radiated power; electrorust proofing

ERP: Easy Revolving Plan; Emerson Radio & Phonograph (stock exchange symbol); European Recovery Program

ERPC: Eastern Railroads Presidents Conference

erpf: effective renal plasma flow

err.: error; erroneous

ERR: Engineering Release Record

err & app: error and appeals (legal)

errc: expandability, recoverability, repairability cost

erron: erroneous(ly)

ers (ERS): environmental research satellite

ERS: Economic Research Service; Edwards Rocket Site; Emergency Relocation Site; Experimental Research Society

E-R S O: Eastman-Rochester Symphony Orchestra

ERSR: Equipment Reliability Status Report

ERTS: Earth Resources Technology Satellite; European Rapid Train System

ERU: English Rugby Union

erv: expiratory reserve volume

ERV: English Revised Version

erw: *erweiterte* (German—enlarged; extended)

ER Yorks: East Riding, Yorkshire

es: echo sounding; eldest son; electrostatic; enamel single silk (insulation); engine-sized (paper); equal section

es: *esempio* (Italian—example)

Es: einsteinium; Essen

Es: (German—E-flat)

ES: Econometric Society; Educational Specialist; Electrochemical Society; Ellis Air Lines; El Salvador; Endocrine Society; Engineering Study; Espirito Santo; Experiment(al) Station

ESA: Ecological Society of America; Economic Stabilization Agency; Electrolysis Society of America; Engineers and Scientists of America; Entomological Society of America; Epiphyllum Society of America; Euthanasia Society of America; Exceptional Service Award; Export Screw Association

ESAC: Environmental Systems Applications Center

esar: electronically-steered array radar

ESAWC: Evaluation Staff, Air War College

esb: electrical stimulation (of the) brain; electric storage battery

ESB: Economic Stabilization Board; Electric Storage Battery (company); Empire State Building

esc: escadrille; escape; escort; escrow; escutcheon

Esc: escudo (Portuguese currency)

ESC: Economic and Social Council (UN); Electronics Systems Center; Electronic Systems Command (USN); Executive Service Corps

eschat: eschatology

ES/CIP: Employee Suggestion-/Cost Improvement Proposal

ESCL: Evans Signal Corps Laboratory

esc^o: *escudo* (Spanish —coat of arms; gold coin; gold crown)

Escom: Electrical Supply Commission

ESCORTDIV: escort division

escr: escrow

escrit^a: *escritura* (Spanish—deed; document; handwriting)

escr^{no}: *escribano* (Spanish—court clerk; notary; scribe)

esd: estimated shipping date; extended school day

ESD: Electronic Systems Division (USAF)

ESDAC: European Space Data Analysis Center (Darmstdat)

ESE: east southest

ESEA: Elementary and Secondary Education Act

esf: electrostatic focusing; erythropoietic stimulating factor

ESF: Eastern Sea Frontier; Engineering Specification Files

Esg: English standard gage

esh: equivalent solar hour(s)

ESH: European Society of Haematology

eshp: equivalent shaft horsepower

ESIS: Executive Selection Inventory System

E 605: parathion (deadly insecticide)

Esk: Eskimo

eski: (Turkish—old, as in Eskisehir)

esl: expected significance level

ESL: Eastern Steamship Lines; Engineering Societies Library

ESLAB: European Space Laboratory (Delft)

ESLO: European Satellite Launching Organization

esm: ends standard matched (lumber)

ESM: Eastman School of Music; Engineering Services Memo; Engineering Shop Memo

ESMA: Electronic Sales-Marketing Association; Engraved Stationery Manufacturers Association

ESMRI: Engraved Stationery Manufacturers Research Institute

esn: essential

ESN: Elastic Stop Nut (corporation); English-Speaking Nations (NATO)

ESNA: Elastic Stop Nut Corporation of America; Empire State

Numismatic Association
ESNE: Engineering Societies of New England
esntl: essential
ESO: Educational Services Office(r); Electronic Supply Office(r); Embarkation Staff Office(r)
ESOC: European Space Operations Center
ESOMAR: European Society for Opinion Surveys and Market Research
esp: especially; extrasensory perception
e & sp: equipment and spare parts
Esp: Esperanto
Esp: Espagne (French—Spain); *España* (Spanish—Spain); *Español* (Spanish—Spanish)
ESP: École des Sciences Politiques (School of Political Science); Extrasensory Perception
ESPA: Evening Student Personnel Association
espec: especial(ly)
Esper: Esperanto
espg: espionage
espress: espressivo (Italian—espressive)
Esq: Esquire
esr: effective signal radiated; electrical skin resistance; electronically-scanned radar; electron skin resonance; equivalent series resistance; erythrocyte sedimentation rate
ESR: Engineering Summary Report
ESRANGE: European Space Research (northern rocket range) —Kiruna
ESRIN: European Space Research Institute
ESRO: European Space Research Organization
ess: essence; essences; essential
Ess: Essex
ESS: Educational Services Section; Electronic Switching System; Employment Security System; Evaluation SAGE Sector; Experimental SAGE Sector
ESS: Encyclopedia of the Social Sciences
essa: environmental survey satellite (weather satellite)
ESSA: Environmental Science Services Administration—Central Radio Propagation Laboratory, Coast and Geodetic Survey, Weather Bureau (Department of Commerce); environmental survey satellite
Essandess: Simon and Schuster
ESSO: Esso Shipping; Standard Oil
ESSPO: Electronic Support System

Project Office
ESSR: Estonian Soviet Socialist Republic
est: establish; established; establishment; estimate; estimated; estimation; estimator; estuary
est: estación (Spanish—station)
Est: The Book of Esther; Estonia(n)
Est: (French—east)
EST: Eastern Standard Time; Eastern Summer Time; Enlistment Screening Test; Enroute Support Team; Epidemiology and Sanitation Technician
estab: established
estab tip: establecimiento tipografico (Spanish—publishing company)
estar: estimated arrival
estb: establish
estbl: establishment
este: (Italian, Portuguese, Spanish —east)
ESTEC: European Space Technology Center
estero: (Spanish—estuary)
estg: estimating
esth: esthetics
Esth: Esthonia; Esthonian
Esthr: Apocryphal Book of Esther
estn: estimation
ESTRACK: European Space Satellite Tracking and Telemetry Network
estrecho: (Spanish—strait)
est wt: estimated weight
esu: electrostatic unit
ESU: English-Speaking Union
E Suffolk: East Suffolk
E Sussex: East Sussex
esv: earth satellite vehicle; enamel single varnish (insulation code)
ESV: Earth Satellite Vehicle; Experimental Safety Vehicle
et: edge thickness; educational therapy; educational training; effective temperature; electrical time; electric telegraph; electrical transcription; electronic tests; engineering test; engineering testing
Et: ethyl
ET: Eastern Time; East Texas (Pulp & Paper Company); Electronics Technician; English translation; Ethiopian Airlines; European Theater (of war)
eta: estimated time of arrival; expect to arrive
Etab: Établissement (French—business establishment or factory)
ETAB: Environmental Testing Advisory Board (Dow)
et al.: et alibi (Latin—and elsewhere); *et alii* (Latin—and others)

étang: (French—lake; pond)
ETAP: Expanded Technical Assistance Program
état: (French—state)
etc: estimated time of completion
etc.: *et cetera* (Latin—and so forth)
ETC: Electro Tech Corporation; Emergency Training Center; Engine Technical Committee; European Translations Center; European Travel Commission
ETC.: A Review of General Semantics (Official Organ of the International Society for General Semantics)
etd: estimated time of departure
ete: estimated time enroute
etf: electron-transferring flavorprotein
eth: ether; ethical; ethics; ethmoid; ethmoidal
Eth: Ethiopia; Ethiopian; Ethiopic
ETH: Eidgenössiche Technische Hochschule (Swiss Federal Institute of Technology)
ethanol: ethyl alcohol or grain alcohol (C_2H_5OH)
eth dat: ethic dative
Eth$: Ethiopian dollar
ether: ethyl ether ($(C_2H_5)_2O$)
Ethiop: Ethiopia; Ethiopian
ethno: ethnology
ethnog: ethnography
ethnol: ethnology
etho: ethylene oxide
eti: elasped-time indicator; estimated time of interception
ETI: Electric Tool Institute; Electronic Technical Institute; Equipment and Tool Institute
etiol: etiology
etkm: every test known to man
etl: ending tape label
ETL: Essex Terminal (railroad)
ETM: Electronic Technician's Mate
etn: equipment table nomenclature
ETN: Eastern Technical Net (USAF)
eto: estimated time off
ETO: European Theater of Operations; European Transport Organization
Et OH: ethyl alcohol
etp: estimated turnaround point; estimated turning point
ETP: Effluent Treatment Plant
et-pnl: engine test panel
ETPS: Empire Test Pilots School
etr: estimated time of return
Etr: Etruscan
Etr: entrada (Spanish—entrance)
ETR: Eastern Test Range; Engineering Test Reactor; Export Traffic Release; External Technical Report

etra: estimated time to reach altitude

ETRC: Educational Television and Radio Center; Engineering Test Reactor Critical Facility

etro: estimated time of return to operation

ets: electronic telegraph system; expiration term of service

Ets: *Établissements* (French— establishments)

ETS: Educational Television Stations; Educational Testing Service; Engineering Task Summary; Engine Test Stand

ETSC: East Tennessee State College; East Texas State College

et seq.: *et sequens* (Latin—and following)

etsp: entitled to severance pay

etsq: electrical time superquick

Etta: Henrietta

et to: extractor tool

etu: electron tube

ETU: Electrical Trades Union

et ux.: *et uxor* (Latin—and wife)

etv: educational television; engine test vehicle

ETV: Educational Television; Electrotechnischer Verein (Electrotechnical Society); Engine Test Vehicle

etw: *etwas* (German—something)

ETWN: East Tennessee & Western North Carolina (railroad)

etym: etymology

Eu: entropy unit (symbol); Euler unit; Europe; European; europium; Eustace; Eustatia

EU: Emory University; Estados Unidos (Spanish—United States); Evacuation Unit

E-U: États-Unis (French—United States)

EU: *Europa Unie* (French—United Europe)

eua: examination under anesthetic

EUA: Eastern Underwriters Association; Estados Unidos de América (Spanish—United States of America); États-Unis Amérique (French—United States of America)

EUB: Estados Unidos do Brasil (Brazil)

EUC: Euclid (railroad)

Eucl: Euclid

EUCOM: European Command

euc(s): eucalyptus tree(s)

EUF: European Union of Federalists

Eug: Eugene; Eugenia

eugen: eugenics

Eug⁰: Eugenio

EUI: *Enciclopedia Universal Ilustrada* (Spanish—Universal Illustrated Encyclopedia)

EUM: Estados Unidos Mexicanos (Spanish—Mexican United States—Mexico); European-Mediterranean

EUM-AFTN: European-Mediterranean Aeronautical Fixed Telecommunications Network

Euni: Eunice

EUP: English Universities Press

euphem: euphemism; euphemistic(al)

euphon: euphonic; euphonically; euphony

Eur: Europe; European

Eurafrica: Europe and Africa

Eurailpass: European tourist railroad pass

Eurasafrica: Europe, Asia, and Africa

Eurasia: Europe and Asia

Eurasian(s): person(s) of European and Asian parents such as Euro-Chinese, Euro-Indian, Euro-Japanese, etc.

Euratom: six-nation atomic energy pool consisting of France, Germany, Italy, and the three Benelux countries: Belgium, Netherlands, and Luxembourg

eurex: enriched uranium extraction

EUROCAE: European Organization of Civil Aviation Electronics

Eurodol(s): European dollar(s)

Eurofima: European Company for the Financing of Rolling Stock

Eurofinance: Union International d'Analyse Economique et Financière

Euromart: European Common Market

Europe's Liberator: Duke of Wellington

Eurosat: European application satellite systems

Eurotox: European Committee on Toxicity Hazards

Eurovision: European Television

EUS: Eastern United States

EUSIDIC: European Association of Scientific Information Dissemination Centers

euv: energetic ultraviolet; equivalent ultraviolet; extreme ultraviolet

eutec: eutectic; eutectoid

euvsh: equivalent ultraviolet solar hour

EUW: European Union of Women

ev: electron volt; enclosed and ventilated; escort vessel; evangelical; exposure value

eV: electronvolt

eV: *eingetragener Verein* (German—registered society)

Ev: Evenkian; Everest; Everett

Ev: *Eingang vorbehalten* (German—rights reserved)

Ev.: *Evangelium* (Latin—the Gospel)

EV: Elivie (Italian Heliways); English Version; Erne Valley; Everett (railroad)

eva: ethyl-vinyl acetate; extravehicular activity

EVA: Electrical Vehicle Association; Engineer Vice Admiral

evac: evacuate; evacuation

eval: evaluate; evaluation

Evan: Evangelical; Evangelist

evap: evaporate; evaporation; evaporator; evaporize

evapd: evaporated

EVC: Educational Video Corporation

evce: evidence

EVDF: Eugene V. Debs Foundation

eve: evening

evea: extravehicular engineering activities

event.: *eventuell* (German—possibly)

evg: evening

EVG: Europäische Verteidigungsgemeinschaft (European Defense Community)

e viv. disc.: *e vivis discessit* (Latin—departed from life)

EVL: E(dward) V(errall) Lucas

evln: evolution

evmu: extra-vehicular material unit

evng: evening

evol: evolution; evolutionary; evolutionist

evop: evolutionary operation

eV 1 s: edge-V one side (lumber)

eV 2s: edge-V two sides

evr: electronic video recording

evs (EVS): extravehicular system

evss: extravehicular space suit

evstc (EVSTC): extravehicular suit telemetry and communications

EVV: Evansville, Indiana (airport)

ew: effective warmth; electronic warfare; extensive wound

EW: early warning; electronic warfare; enlisted woman; enlisted women

EWA: East-West Airlines; East and West Association; Education Writers Association

EWAS: Economic Warfare Analysis Section

ewc: electric water cooler

EWC: East-West Center (University of Hawaii)

EWCRP: Early Warning Control and Reporting Post

EWD: Economic Warfare Division

EWES: Engineering Waterways

Experiment Station
ewf: equivalent weight factor
EWF: Electrical Wholsealers Federation
EWG: *Europaische Wirtschaftsgemeinschaft* (German—European Common Market)
EWHS: Eli Whitney High School
ewi: education with industry; entered without inspection
EWL: Ellerman's Wilson Line
EWMC: Eli Whitney Metrology Center
EWO: Electrical and Wireless Operators; Electronic Warfare Officer; Emergency War Order; Engineering Work Order; Essential Work Order
EWOS: Electronic Warfare Operational System (USAF)
EWP: Emergency War Plan
ewr: early-warning radar
EWR: Newark, New Jersey (airport)
EWRC: European Weed Research Council
EWS: Emergency Water Supply; Emergency Welfare Service; European Wars Survey
EWSC: Eastern Washington State College; Electric Water Systems Council
EWT: Eastern War Time (advanced time)
EWWS: Electronic Warfare Warning System
ex: examination; examine; examined; examiner; example; excess; exercise; experiment (al; s)
Ex: Excelsior; Exchange; Exchequer; Exeter; Exmoor; Exmouth; Extremadura; Exuma
EX: experimental broadcasting
exacct: expense account
ex af.: *ex affinis* (Latin—of affinity)
exag: exaggerate; exaggerated; exaggeration
Ex Agt: Executive Agent
exam: examination; examine; examiner
exametnet: experimental meteorological sounding rocket network
examg: examining
exams: examinations
ex aq.: *ex aqua* (Latin—out of water)
exbedcap: expanded bed capacity
Ex B/L: exchange bill of lading
exc: excavate; excellent; exciter
exc.: *excudit* (Latin—he engraved it)
Exc: Excelencia (Spanish—Excellency)
Exc: *Excelsior* (Mexico City)
Excª: Excelencia (Spanish—Excel-

lency)
ex cath.: *ex cathedra* (Latin—from the seat of authority)
ex champ: ex-champion; former champion
Excheq: exchequer
excl: exclude(d); excluding; exclusive
Excmo: Excelentísimo (Spanish—Most Excellent)
Excᵐᵒ: Excelentísimo (Spanish—Most Excellent)
Ex Com: Executive Committee
ex-con(s): ex convict(s); former convict(s)
ex cp: ex coupon
EXDAMS: Extendable Debugging and Monitoring System
Ex Doc: Executive Document
ex div: ex dividend
Ex Div: Experimental Division
Exe: Exeter
Exec: execute; executed; execution; executive; executive officer; executor
Exec Dir: Executive Director
execs: executives
Exec Sec: Executive Secretary
exer: exercise
ex f: extremely fine
ex fy: extra fancy
ex ga: external gage
ex gr.: *exempli gratia* (Latin—for example)
exh: exhaust
exhib: exhibit; exhibition; exhibitor
exhib.: *exhibeatur* (Latin—let it be shown)
exh t: exhaust turbine
exh v: exhaust vent
ex hy: extra heavy
EXIMBANK: Export-Import Bank
ex int: ex interest
exist.: existing
exkl: *exklusiv* (German—excepted; not included)
ex lib.: *ex libris* (Latin—from the library of)
exmr: examiner
ExO: executive officer; executive order
Ex O: Experimental Office(r)
Exod: *Exodus*
ex off.: *ex officio* (Latin—by authority of his office)
Exon: Exeter (Exonia)
exot: exotic
exp: expansion; expense; experiment(al); exponential; export; express; expulsion
exp: *expreso* (Spanish—express)
ex p.: *ex parte* (Latin—on one side only)
expdivun: experimental diving unit
exped: expedite; expedition

exper: experiment; experimental
Expert: Expanded Pert (program evaluation and review technique)
expir: expiratory; expiration
expl: *exemple* (French—example)
explo: explosion; explosive
explor: exploration
explos: explosive
expnd: expenditure
expo: exposé; exposition
exp o: experimental order(s)
expol: expanded polysterene (lightweight packing moulding)
Expo 70: 1970 exposition at Tokyo
Expo 67: 1967 exposition in Montreal
expr: expiration; expire
EXPRESO: Expreso Aéreo Interamericano
expt: experiment
exptl: experimental
exptr: exporter
expul: expulsion
expur: expurgate(d)
Expy: Expressway
ex-quay: free on quay
exr: executor
exrx: executrix
exs: expenses; expropriations
exsec: exsecant
Ex Sta: Experimental Station
ext: extend; extension; exterior; external; extinguish; extinguisher; extra
Ext: Extended; Extension
extal: extra time allowance
extd: extracted
ext d & cc: external drug and cosmetic color
Extel: Exchange Telegraph (press agency)
EXTEL: Exchange Telegraph (British news agency)
extemp: extemporaneous(ly)
exten: extension
extend.: *extensus* (Latin—spread)
extern: external; externally
EXTERRA: Extraterrestrial Research Agency (USA)
extg: extinguish(er)
exting: extinguished
ex tm.: *ex testamento* (Latin—in accord with the testament)
extn: extraction
extr: extract; extrude; extruded; extrusion
Extr: Extremadura
extra: extraordinary
extrad: extradition
extradop: extended range doppler
extrap: extrapolate; extrapolated; extrapolation
extra sess: extra session (legislature)
extrd: extruded

extrem: extremity
extro: extroversion; extrovert
extrx: executrix
exurb: exurban; exurbanite; exurbia; exurbian
exx: examples; executrix
Exz: Exzellenz (German—Excellency)

eyawtkas: everything you always wanted to know about sex
EYOA: Economic and Youth Opportunites Agency
EYW: Key West, Florida (airport)
ez: easy; electrical zero
e-z: easy
Ez: Ezekiel; Ezra; The Book of

Ezra
EZ: Eastern Zone; Emile Zola; Extraction Zone
EZ Duzit: Easy Does It
Ezek: The Book of Ezekiel
Ezi: Ezias; Eziel; Eziongaber
EZU: Europäische Zahlungsunion (European Payment Union)

F

f: farthing; fast; father (capitalized in religious orders); fathom; female; feminine; filment; final target; fine; flat; focal length; fog; folio; following; following page; force; forecastle; franc(s); frequency; freshwater; fugacity; function; latitude factor (symbol); relative humidity (symbol)
f⁰: folio
f/: relative aperture of a lens (also shown as f:)
f: *fecit* (Latin—he did); *filius* (Latin—son); *forte* (Italian—loud); für (German—for)
F: Fahrenheit; Fairchild; farad; Faraday; Faraday constant (symbol); Farrell Lines; fathom(s); February; Fellow; field of vision (symbol); fighter; fire; fixed; fixed broadcast; fixed broadcasting; flagship; florin; fluorine; formal(ity); formula; Foxtrot—code for letter F; French; franc(s); Fraunhofer line (caused by hydrogen); freedom; freedom, degree of (symbol); free energy (symbol); French; Friday; fuel; furlong(s); Furness Lines; Grumman; longitude factor
F.: fats (dietary symbol)
F: *feria* (Latin, Portuguese, Spanish—fair or market); *fora* (Portuguese—out); *framkomst* (Swedish—arrival); *Frauen* (German—women); *freddo* (Italian—cold); *frio* (Portuguese, Spanish—cold); *froid* (French—cold); *fuera* (Spanish—out); *fuori* (Italian—out)
⁰F: degree Fahrenheit
F₁: first filial generation
F-1: Fury single-engine jet fighter-bomber flown from aircraft carriers
F1S: finish one side
F²: prostaglandin alpha (abortion-

producing hormone)
F₂: second filial generation
F2S: finish two sides
F-3: Demon single-engine supersonic all-weather jet fighter
F-4: Phantom II twin-engine all-weather supersonic jet fighter-bomber
F-6: Skyray single-engine supersonic all-weather jet fighter
F-8: Crusader single-engine all-weather supersonic jet fighter
F₁₀: decimetric solar flux (symbol)
F-11: Tiger single-engine supersonic jet fighter
f-12: freon (refrigerant)
F-89: Scorpion all-weather interceptor with twin turbojet engines
F-100: Super Sabre supersonic turbojet fighter
F-101: Voodoo supersonic twin-engine turbojet aircraft
F-102: Delta Dagger single-engine supersonic turbojet interceptor
F-104: Starfighter supersonic single-engine turbojet fighter
F-105: Thunderchief supersonic single-engine turbojet tactical fighter
F-106: Delta Dart supersonic single-engine turbojet interceptor aircraft
F-111: twin-engine turbojet tactical fighter-bomber all-weather interceptor aircraft (TFX)
F-111A: variable-geometry supersonic fighter-bomber (TFX)
fa: family allowance; fatty acid; filterable agent; fire alarm; first aid; first attack; folic acid; fortified aqueous; free aperture; frequency agility; friendly aircraft; field activities; fuel-air (ratio)
f/a: fuel-air ratio
f & a: fore and aft
fa: (Italian—fourth tone; D in diatonic scale; F in fixed-do

system)
fA: *forrige Aar* (Danish—last year)
Fa: Faeroes
Fa: *Firma* (German—firm; business)
FA: Farm Advisor; Field Ambulance; Field Artillery; Fireman Apprentice; Flota Argentina (de Navegación Fluvial)—Argentine River Navigation Line; Football Association; Frankford Arsenal
F/A: friendly aircraft
F & A: Finance and Accounting
F of A: Foresters of America; Freethinkers of America
faa: field artillery airborne; formalin, acetic acid, alcohol (mixture); free of all average
FAA: Federal Aviation Administration; Fifth Avenue Association; Finska Angpartygys (Finnish Steamship Line); Fleet Air Arm; Foreman's Association of America; Foundation for American Agriculture; Fraternal Actuarial Association
FAAAS: Fellow of the American Academy of Arts and Sciences; Fellow of the American Association for the Advancement of Science
FAABMS: Forward Army Anti-Ballistic Missile System
FAAG: First Advertising Agency Group
FAAN: First Advertising Agency Network
FAAO: Finance and Accounts Office (US Army)
FAAP: Federal Aid to Airports Program
faar: forward area alerting radar
fab: fabric(ate); first-aid box
fab: *fabrique* (French—factory); *franco à bord* (French—free on board); *frei an bord* (German —free on board)
FAB: Fleet Air Base; Força Aérea

Brasileira (Brazilian Air Force); Frédéric Auguste Bartholdi

FABI: Fédération Royale des Associations Belges d'Ingénieurs (Royal Federation of Belgian Engineering Associations)

fabl: fire alarm bell

FABMDS: Field Army Ballistic Missile Defense System

FABMIDS: Field Army Ballistic Missile Defense System

fabr: fabricate; fabrication

Fab Soc: Fabian Society

FABU: Fleet Air Base Unit

fabx: fire alarm box

faç: façade; facial; facility; facsimile; factor; factory; faculty; fast as can; field accelerator

fac: facade

fac.: factum similie (Latin—facsimile)

Fac: Faculty

FAC: Factor (Max; stock exchange symbol); Federal Advisory Council; Federal Aviation Commission; Financial Administrative Control; Fleet Air Control; Forward Air Controller; Frequency Allocation Committee

FACA: Fellow of the American College of Anaesthetists; Fellow of the American College of Angiology

FACAl: Fellow of the American College of Allergists

FACAn: Fellow of the American College of Anesthesiologists

FACC: Fellow of the American College of Cardiology

FACCA: Fellow of the Association of Certified and Corporate Accountants

FACD: Fellow of the American College of Dentistry

face.: field artillery computer equipment

FACE: Facilities and Communications Evaluation (USA)

FACFO: Fellow of the American College of Foot Orthopedics

FACG: Fellow of the American College of Gastroenterology

FACI: First Article Configuration Inspection

facil: facility

FACMTA: Federal Advisory Council on Medical Training Aids

FACOG: Fellow of the American College of Obstetricians and Gynecologists

facp: forward air control point

FACP: Fellow of the American College of Physicians

FACPM: Fellow of the American College of Preventive Medicine

fac pwr ctl: facility power control

fac pwr mon: facility power monitor

fac pwr pnl: facility power panel

FACR: Fellow of the American College of Radiology

FACS: Fellow of the American College of Surgeons

FACSFAC: Fleet Air Control and Surveillance Facility

facsim(s): facsimile(s)

fact: factura (Spanish—bill of lading; invoice)

fact.: factory; fully-automatic compiler translator

FACT: Flanagan Aptitude Classification Test; Flight Acceptance Composite Test(ing); Fully-Automatic Compiler Translator; Fully-Automatic Compiling Technique

factª: factura (Spanish—invoice)

facty: fact filled; factory

fad. (FAD): flavine adenine dinucleotide

FAD: Fleet Air Defense

fadac: field artillery digital automatic computer

F Adm: Fleet Admiral

FAE: Federación de Amigos de la Enseñanza (Federation of the Friends of Teaching); Fund for the Advancement of Education

Faer: Faeroe Islands

FAETUA: Fleet Airborne Electronic Training Unit, Atalantic

FAETUP: Fleet Airborne Electronic Training Unit, Pacific

faf: forage acre factor; flyaway factory

FAF: Fafnir Bearings (stock exchange symbol); Financial Analysts Federation; Fine Arts Foundation

fag(s): faggot(s)

fag: fagotto (Italian—basson)

FAG: Failure Analysis Group; Fine Arts Gallery

fagms (FAGMS): field artillery guided missiles

fags: fagottos (Italian—bassoons)

FAGS: Federation of Astronomical and Geophysical Permanent Services; Fellow of the American Geographical Society

fagt: first available government transportation

fagtrans: first available government transportation

FAGU: Fleet Air Gunnery Unit

fah: failed to attend hearing

FAHA: Finnish-American Historical Archives

fahqmt: fully automatic high-quality machine translation

Fahr: Fahrenheit

fai: frequency-azimuth intensity; fresh air intake

FAI: Fairbanks Alaska (airport); Fédération Aéronautique Internationale

FAI: Federación Anarquista Iberica (Spanish—Iberian Anarchist Federation)

FAIA: Fellow of the American Institute of Architects

FAIAS: Fellow of the Australian Institute of Agricultural Science

FAIME: Foreign Affairs Information Management Effort (Dept State)

FAIO: Field Army Issuing Office(r)

fair.: fairing; fast-access information retrieval

FAir: fleet air

FAIR: Fleet Air (Wing); Friends in America for Independence of Rhodesia

Fair Deal: (administration of Harry S. Truman—thirty-third President of the United States)

FAIRS: Fair and Impartial Random Selection System (military draft)

fairships: fleet airships

FAK: Federasie van Afrikaanse Kultuurvereniginge (Afrikaans—Federation of Afrikaans Cultural Societies)

fak-pak: freight all kinds (in a box on wheels)

faks: faksimile (Dano-Norwegian—fascsimile)

Fakt: Faktura (German—invoice)

Fal: Falmouth

F a L: Fathers-at-Large

FAL: Frequency Allocation List; Frontier Airlines

'falfa: alfalfa

Falk Cur: Falkland Current

Falk Isl: Falkland Islands (Islas Maldivas)

fallwarn: fallout warning

FALN: Fuerzas Armadas de Liberación Nacional (Armed Forces of National Liberation—Communist paramilitary organization)

FALS: Ford Authorized Leasing System

fam: familiar; family

FAM: foreign airmail; Free and Accepted Masons

F & AM: Free and Accepted Masons

FAMA: Fellow of the American Medical Association; Fire Apparatus Manufacturers Association

fame.: fatty-acid methyl ester(s)

FAME: Farmers Allied Meat Enterprises Cooperative; Future American Magical Entertainers

FAMOS: Fleet Applications of Meteorological Observations from Satellites

fam phys: family physician

fan.: fanatic (usually in sense of enthusiast); fantasia; fantasy

Fan(ny): Frances; Francisca; Frasquita

Fannie Mae: Federal National Mortgage Association

fant: fantasia; fantasy

fantabulous: fantastic + fabulous

fantac: fighter analysis tactical air combat

FANU: Flota Argentina de Navegación de Ultramar (Argentine High Seas Navigation Line)

FANY: First-Aid Nursing Yoemanry

fanzines: fan + magazines

fao: finish all over

FAO: Field Audit Office(r); Finance and Accounts Office(r); Fleet Accountant Officer; Fleet Administration Office(r); Food and Agriculture Organization (UN); Free Albania Organization

F & AO: Finance and Accounts Office (US Army)

fap: final approach; floating arithmetic pakage

FAP: Family Assistance Plan; Family Assistance Program(ming); First Aid Post; Frequency Allocation Panel

FAPA: Filipino-American Political Association

FAPHA: Fellow of the American Public Health Association

FAPI: First Article Production Inspection

FAPIG: First Atomic Power Industry Group

FAPR: Federal Aviation Procurement Regulations

FAPS: Fellow of the American Physical Society

faq: fair average quality; free at quay

FAQ: Free at Quay

far.: false alarm rate; farad; Faraday; faradic; farthing; finned air rocket; forward-acquisition radar

Far: Faraday

FAR: Failure Analysis Report; Federal Aviation Regulations; finned air rocket; flight aptitude rating

FARA: Foreign Agents Registration Act

FARADA: Failure Rate Data (BuWeps Program)

FARC: Federal Addiction Research Center

faret: fast reactor test

farmobile: farm automobile

faro.: flow (ed; ing) at rate of

Fars: Faristan

fas: first and seconds; free alongside ship

FAS: Federal Agricultural Service; Federal Air Surgeon; Federation of American Scientists; Fellow of the Society of Arts; Food Advice Service; Foreign Agricultural Service; Free Alongside Ship; Frequency Assignment Subcommittee

FASA: Fellow of the Acoustical Society of America

fasc: *fascicule* (French—part); *fasciculus* (Latin—little bundle)

fase: fundamentally-analyzable simplified English

FASEB: Federation of American Societies of Experimental Biology

FASL: Florida Association of School Librarians

FASPM: Flotte Administrative des Iles Saint Pierre et Miquelon

FAST: First Atomic Ship Transport

fastnr: fastener

fat.: final assembly test(ing); fixed asset transfer; full annual toll

FAT: Fresno, California (airport)

Fatah: *Harakat-Tahrir Falastin* (Arabic—Palestinian terrorist underground organization) — Arabic acronyms such as this have inverted initials

fatdog: fatty hotdog (fat-filled frankfurter)

Fate: American nickname for Lafayette and one adorning many country boys

fatfurters: fat-filled frankfurters

fath: fathom

Father Abraham: Abraham Lincoln

Father of America: Sam(uel) Adams

Father of Angling: Izaak Walton

Father Christmas: Santa Claus

Father of Comedy: Aristophanes

Father of Confederation: John A. Macdonald—Canada's first prime minister

Father of the Constitution: James Madison—fourth President of the United States

Father of the Continental Congress: Benjamin Franklin

Father of English Poetry: Geoffrey Chaucer

Father of English Printing: William Caxton

Father of Epic Poetry: Homer

Father of Greek Tragedy: Aeschylus

Father of His Country: Cicero and

several Roman caesars; George Washington — Commander - in - Chief of the Continental Army and first President of the United States

Father of History: Herodotus

Father of Medicine: Hippocrates

Father of Mexican Independence: Miguel Hidalgo y Costilla

Father of the Potteries: Josiah Wedgwood

Father of Ridicule: Rabelais

Father of Spanish Drama: Lope de Vega

Father of the Tariff: Alexander Hamilton—first Secretary of the Treasury of the United States

Father of the Telephone: Alexander Graham Bell

Father of Texas: Stephen F. Austin

Father of the University of Virginia: Thomas Jefferson—third President of the United States

Father of the U.S. Navy: John Adams—second President of the United States

Father of the U.S. Post Office: Benjamin Franklin—author, inventor, patriot, printer, philosopher, scientist, statesman

Father of the Waters: Mississippi River

fau: faucet; field action units; forced air unit

FAU: Florida Atlantic University

FAUSST: French-Anglo-U.S. Supersonic Transport

fav: favor; favorable; favorite

FAVO: Fleet Aviation Officer

FAWA: Factory Assist Work Authorization; Federation of Asian Women's Associations

FAWS: Flight Advisory Weather Service

fax: facsimile; facts

FAX: fixed aeronautical station

Fay: Fagele; Faith; Fanny

FAZ: *Frankfurter Allgemeine Zeitung* (Frankfurt's Universal Newspaper)

fb: film bulletin; flat bar; fog bell; freight bill; fullback

f & b: fire and bilge; fumigation and bath

FB: Fenian Brotherhood; Film Bulletin; Fire Brigade; Fisheries Board; Flying Boat; Forth Bridge; Free Baptist

FBA: Federal Bar Association; Fellow of the British Academy; Fibre Box Association; Fur Brokers Association

FBAA: Fellow of the British Association of Accountants and Auditors

FBC: Federal Broadcasting Corporation

fbd: freeboard

FB & D: Ford, Bacon and Davis

fbfm: frequency feedback frequency modulation

FBI: Federal Bureau of Investigation; Federation of British Industries; Food Business Institute

FBIs: Forgotten Boys of Iceland (American armed forces personnel stationed in Iceland)

fbk: flat back (lumber); fast buck

fbl: forged billet

FBL: Federal Barge Lines; Furness Bermuda Line

FBLA: Future Business Leaders of America

fbm: feet board measure; fleet ballistic missile

FBM: Fleet Ballistic Missile

FBN: Federal Bureau of Narcotics

fbo: fixed-base operation; foreign building office

FBOA: Fellow of the British Optical Association

FBOU: Fellow of the British Ornithologists' Union

fbp: final boiling point

FBP: Federal Bureau of Prisons; Federation of Podiatry Boards

FBPS: Fellow of the British Psychological Society

fbr: fast burst reactor; fiber

fbrk: firebrick

fbrl: final bomb release line

fbro: *febrero* (Spanish—February)

fbs: fasting blood sugar

FBS: Fellow of the Botanical Society; Fighter Bomber Squadron

FBu: Burundi franc(s)

FBU: Oslo, Norway (Fornebu Airport)

FBUI: Federation of British Umbrella Industries

fbw: full bandwidth

FBW System: Fly-by-Wire System

fby: future budget year

fc: file cabinet; filter center; fire clay; fire-control; follow copy; foot-candle; franc; front-connected; functional code; fund code

f/c: flight control; for cash; free and clear

Fc: fractocumulus

FC: Fairbury College; Fenn College; Finch College; Findlay College; fire control; Fontbonne College; Foothill College; Franconia College; Frederic Chopin; Frederick College; Free Church (Scotland)

FC: *Ferrocarril(es)* [Spanish railroad(s)]

fca: frequency control and analysis

FCA: Farm Credit Administration;

Fellow (of the Institute) of Chartered Accountants

FCAA: Federal Clean Air Act; Florence Crittenton Association of America

FCACS: Federal Civil Agencies Communications System

f cant.: forward cant frames

fcap: foolscap

FCAP: Fellow of the College of American Pathologists

fcb: free-cutting brass

FCB: Facility Clearance Board; Flight Certification Board; Foundation for Commercial Banks; Freight Container Bureau

FCBA: Federal Communications Bar Association

fcc (FCC): first-class certificate

FCC: Federal Communications Commission; Federal Council of Churches; First-Class Certificate; Flight Coordination Center; Florida Citrus Commission

FCCA: Four Cylinder Club of America

FCCCA: Federal Council of Churches of Christ in America

FCCP: Fellow of the College of Chest Physicians

FCCS: Fellow of the Corporation of Certified Secretaries

fcd: failure-correction coding

FCDA: Federal Civil Defense Administration

F & CD—IR: Failure and Consumption Data—Inspector's Report

FCE: Florida Citrus Exchange; Foreign Currency Exchange; French-Canadian Enterprises

FCEX: Fruit Growers Express

fcg: facing

FCG: Foreign Clearance Guide

FCGI: Fellow of the City and Guilds of London Institute

FCGP: Fellow of the College of General Practitioners

FChS: Fellow of the Society of Chiropodists

FCI: Fellow of the Clothing Institute; Fluid Controls Institute; Franklin College of Indiana

FCIA: Foreign Credit Insurance Association

FCIC: Fairchild Camera and Instrument Corporation; Farm Crop Insurance Corporation; Fellow of the Chemical Institute of Canada

FCIF: Flight Crew Information File

FCII: Fellow of the Chartered Insurance Institute

fcim: farm, construction, and industrial machinery

FCIS: Fellow of the Chartered

Institute of Secretaries

FCJC: Flint Community Junior College

fclty: facility

fcly: face lying

FCM: Ferrocarril Mexicano (Mexican Railway)

FCMA: Finch College Museum of Art

FCMI: Federation of Coated Macadam Industries

FCMSBR: Federal Coal Mine Safety Board of Review

fco: cleanout flush with finished floor; fair copy; franking privilege; free postage

fco: *franco* (Italian—delivered free)

Fco: Francisco (Spanish—Francis)

Fco: Francisco (Spanish—Francis)

FCO: Fire Control Officer; Fleet Constuctor Officer; Rome, Italy (Leonardo da Vinci airport, formerly Fiumicino—hence FCO)

fcos: *francos* (Spanish—francs)

fcp: final common pathway; foolscap

FCP: Ferrocarril de Chihuahua al Pacifico (Chihuahua Pacific Railroad)

FCPC: Federal Committee on Pest Control

fc pl: face plate

FCPS: Fellow of the College of Physicians and Surgeons

fcr: forward contactor; full cold rolled (steel sheeting)

FCR: Fire Control Room; First City Regiment; Flinders Chase Reserve (South Australia)

FCRLS: Flight-Congrol Ready Light System

fcs: francs

fc & s: free of capture and seizure (insurance)

FCS: Farmer Cooperative Service; Fellow of the Chemical Society; Fire Control School; Fire Control Station; Fire Control System

F/CS: Flight-Control System

fcsad: free of capture, seizure, arrest, or detainment (shipping insurance)

FCSBC: Ferrocarril Sonora-Baja California (Sonora-Baja California Railroad)

FCSC: Foreign Claims Settlement Commission

FCSCUS: Federal Claims Settlement Commission of the United States

fcsle: forecastle

fcsrcc: free of capture, seizure, riots, and civil commotion (shipping insurance)

fc & s and r & cc: free of capture,

seizure, riots, and civil commotion

fcst: forecast

FCST: Federal Council for Science and Technology (Executive Office of the President)

fct: filament center tap; fraction thereof; function

FCT: Federal Capital Territory

fcty: factory

FCU: Federal Credit Union(s)

FCUS: Federal Credit Union System

FCWA: Fellow of the Chartered Institute of Cost and Works Accountants

fcy: fancy

fcy pks: fancy packs

FCZ: Ferrocarril de Coahuila y Zacatecas (Coahuila and Zacatecas Railroad)

fd: field; flight deck; floor drain; focal distance; forced draft; framed; free discharge; free dispatch; front of dash; fund

f/d: father and daughter

f & d: faced and drilled; fill and drain; findings and determination; fire and flushing; freight and demurrage

fdso: median fatal dose

Fd: Ferdinand; Fiord (Fjord)

FD: field drum; Finance Department; Fire Department

fda: flight-direction attitude; frontodextra anterior

FDA: Food and Drug Administration

FDATC: Flying Division, Air Training Command

fdb: field dynamic braking; forced-draft blower

fdc: fire-direction center (FDC)

fdc: *fleur de coin* (French—mint condition)

FDC: Fire-Direction Center; Forsyth Dental Center (Harvard)

FDCC: Fort Dodge Community College

F D & C-color: Food, Drug, and Cosmetic (Act) color

fdd: *franc de droits* (French—free of charge)

FDD: Fondation Documentaire Dentaire (Dental Documentation Foundation)

fddl: frequency division data link

fddlp.: frequency division data link printout

fde: field decelerator

F del P: Ferrocarril del Pacífico (Pacific Railroad)

FDFU: Federation of Documentary Film Units

fdg: funding

fdi: field discharge

FDI: Federal Department of Information (Malaysia); Fédération Dentaire Internationale (International Dental Federation); Fir Door Institute

FDIC: Federal Deposit Insurance Corporation

FDJ: *Freie Deutsche Jugend* (Free German Youth)—communist youth organization in East Germany

FDL: Fast Deployment Logistic(s)—naval Logistic(s) —naval cargo carrier(s); fleet deployment logistic ship (naval symbol); Flight Dynamics Laboratory; Foremost Defended Localities

F & DL: Food and Drug Laboratory

fd ldg: forced landing

FDLI: Food and Drug Law Institute

FDLS: Fast Deployment Logistics Ship

fdm: frequency division multiplexing

FDMA: Fibre Drum Manufacturers Association

FDMHA: Frederick Douglass Memorial and Historical Association

fdn: foundation

FDN: Field Designator Number

FDO: Fleet Dental Officer

F do I: *Foz do Iguaçu* (Portuguese—Mouth of the Iguazu)—three miles above the gigantic Iguazu Waterfalls shared by Argentina, Brazil, and Paraguay at their juncture

fdp: foreign duty pay

FDP: foreign duty pay; fronto-dextra posterior

FDP: *Freie Demokratische Partei* (German—Free Democratic Party)

FDPA: Fogg Dam Protected Area (Australian Northern Territory)

Fd PO: Field Post Office

fdr: feeder

f dr: fire door

FDR: Franklin Delano Roosevelt —thirty-second President of the United States

FDRHS: Franklin Delano Roosevelt High School

FDRL: Franklin D. Roosevelt Library (Hyde Park, New York)

FDRMC: Franklin Delano Roosevelt Memorial Commission

fdry: foundry

FDS: Fellow in Dental Surgery; fighter-director ship

fdt: first destination transportation; fronto-dextra transverse

FDU: Fairleigh Dickinson University

f/d vlv: fill-and-drain valve

fdw: feed water

FD-Zug: *Fernschnellzug* (German —long-distance express train)

fe: fighter escort; fire extinguisher; first edition; flanged ends

f & e: facilities and equipment

Fe: *ferrum* (Latin—iron)

Fe⁵²/₃: radioactive iron

FE: Far East; Fighter Escort; Flight Engineer

FE: *Fonetic English* (for spelling words as they sound)

F & E: Fearnley & Eger (FernVille [steamship] Lines)

FEA: Failure Modes and Effects Analysis; French Equatorial Africa

FEAF: Far East Air Force

FEA(I): Federal Employees Association (Independent)

FEANI: Federation Européenne d'Associations Nationales d'Ingénieurs (Federation of European National Associations of Engineers)

feath: feather(ed; r(ed; ing)

feb: functional electronic block

Feb: February

FEB: Flying Evaluation Board

feba (FEBA): forward edge of battle area

Febarch: February and March

febb: *febbraio* (Italian—February)

feb. dur.: *febre durante* (Latin—as long as fever lasts)

febᵒ: *febrero* (Spanish—February)

FEBs: Federal Executive Boards

FEBS: Federation of European Biochemical Societies

fec: feckless; forward error correction

fec: *foi, espérance, charité* (French —faith, hope, charity)

fec.: *fecit* (Latin—he made)

FEC: Facilities Engineering Command; Far East Command; Federal Electric Corporation; Florida East Coast (railway); Free Europe Committee

FECA: Facilities Engineering and Construction Agency

FECB: Foreign Exchange Control Board

feck((Scottish abbreviation—effect; efficacy; value)

fed.: federal; federated; federation

Fed: Federal; Federalist (Party); Federation

FEDC: Federation of Engineering Design Consultants

fedja: (Arabic—pass)

Fed Mal: Federation of Malaya; Federation of Malay States; Malaysia

Fed Mal Sta: Federated Malay States

fedn: federation

fed narc: federal narcotics agent

Fed Reg: *Federal Register*

Fed Rep: *Federal Reporter*

Feds: federal excise tax collectors; federal law-enforcement officers

Feds: Federales (Spanish—federal police; federal troops)

FEDS: Foreign Economic Development Service

Fed-Spec: Federal Specification(s)

Fed-Std: Federal Standard

FEE: Foundation for Economic Education

feeb: feeble; feebleminded

FEEB: Fleet Electronic Effectiveness Branch (USN)

FEER: *Far Eastern Economic Review*

FEF: Foundry Educational Foundation

FEGLI: Federal Employees Group Life Insurance

FEHB: Federal Employees Health Benefit

FEI: Farm Equipment Institute; Financial Executives Institute; Flight Engineers International (association)

FEIA: Flight Engineers International Association

FEIS: Fellow of the Educational Institution of Scotland

f eks: *for eksempel* (Dano-Norwegian—for example)

fel: fellow

Fel: Felicita; Felix

Fels: (German—rock)

fem: female; feminine; femoral; femur

f.e.m. (fem or FEM): fuerza electromotriz (Spanish—electromotive force)

FEMA: Farm Equipment Manufacturers Association; Fire Equipment Manufacturers Association; Foundry Equipment Manufacturers Association

fem. ext.: femur externum (Latin—external thigh)

FEMIC: Fire Equipment Manufacturers Institute of Canada

fem.int.: femur internum (Latin—inner thigh)

femo: femoral

fem-sem: feminine seminary (woman's college)

femto: 10^{-15}

F/Eng: Flight Engineer

FENSA: Film Entertainment National Service Association

Fen-Scan: Fenno-Scandia; Fenno-Scandinavian

FEO: Federal Executive Office;

Fleet Engineer(ing) Officer

fep: fore edges painted

FE al P: Ferrocarril Eléctrico al Pacífico (Costa Rican electric railway)

FEPC: Fair Employment Practices Commission

FEPE: Fédération Européenne pour la Protection des Eaux (European Federation for the Protection of Waters)

fer: forward engine room

Fer: Ferdinand; Fermanagh; Ferris

FERA: Federal Emergency Relief Administration

FERC: Franco-Ethiopian Railway Company

fer con: ferrule-contact

Ferd: Ferdinand

Ferm: Fermanagh

fermentol: fermentology

Fern^{do}: Fernando (Spanish—Ferdinand)

Fernspr: Fernsprecher (German—telephone)

FERPC: Far Eastern Research and Publications Center

ferr: ferrovia (Italian—railroad)

fert: fertility; fertilization; fertilizer

fertd: fertilized

fertz: fertilizer

ferv.: fervens (Latin—boiling)

fes: festival(s); fundamental electrical standards

Fes: (German—F-flat)

FES: Fellow of the Entomological Society; Fellow of the Ethnological Society; Fisheries Experiment Station; Florida Engineering Society

FESA: Fonetic English Spelling Association

FESO: Federal Employment Stabilization Office

fest: festival; festive; festivities; festivity

fest.: festivus (Latin—festive or gay)

FEST: Federation of Engineering and Shipbuilding Trades (British)

fet: field-effect transistor

FET: Federal Excise Tax

FETF: Flight Engine Test Facility (National Reactor Test Station, Idaho)

fetol: fetological; fetologist; fetology

fets: field-effect transistors

Fe₂O₃ • H₂O: rust

FEU: Federated Engineering Union

feud.: feudal; feudalism; feudalistic

fev: fever(ish); forced expiratory volume

fev: fevereiro (Portuguese—February)

fév: février (French—February)

fev₁: forced expiratory volume in one second

FEVA: Federal Employees Veterans Association

Fevr: Fevral' (Russian—February)

FEW: Federally-Employed Women

fey: forever yours

ff: fat-free; file finish; fixed focus; folded flat; following folios; fortissimo; french fried; front focal (length); front focus; full fashioned; full field

f/f: flip-flop

f & f: fire and flushing; furniture and fixtures

f to f: face to face

ff: følgende (Danish—following); *folgende Seiten* (German—following pages); *fortissimo* (Italian—very loud)

Ff: Fortsetzung folgt (German—to be continued)

FF: Field Foundation; fleet flagship (naval symbol); Ford Foundation

FF: Faith and Freedom; Fianna Fail (Irish—Republican Party); *fratres* (Latin—brothers); *frères* (French—brothers)

F of F: field of fire; Firth of Forth

ffa: for further assignment; free of fatty acid; free from alongside

FFA: Fellow of the Faculty of Actuaries; Foriegn Freight Agent; Foundation for Foreign Affairs; Future Farmers of America

ffar: folding-fin aircraft rocket; forward-fighting aircraft rocket

FFARCS: Fellow of the Faculty of Anaesthetics—Royal College of Surgeons

ffb: fat-free body

ffc: free from chlorine

FFC: Farmers Federation Cooperative; Federal Facilities Corporation; Federal Fire Council

FFCC Nales: Ferrocarriles Nacionales (Colombian National Railways)

FFCDPA: Federal Field Committee for Development Planning in Alaska

FFCSA: Florida Fresh Citrus Shippers Association

ffd: focus film distance; fuel failure detection

FFDA: Flying Funeral Directors of America

FFE: Fight for Free Enterprise

fff.: forte fortissimo (Italian—very, very loud)

FFF: Frozen Food Foundation

ffff: forte forte fortissimo (Italian—very, very, very loud)

ffgt: firefighter; firefighting

ffh: formerly-fat housewife; formerly-fat husband

FFHMA: Full-Fashioned Hosiery Manufacturers of America

FFHom: Fellow of the Faculty of Homeopathy

ffi: free from infection

FFI: Flanders Filters Incorporated; Freight Forwarders Institute; Frozen Food Institute

ffl: field failure; fixed and flashing

F Fl: fixed and flashing (light)

FFL: Forces Françaises Libres (Free French Forces)

FFLA: Federal Farm Loan Association

FFLI: Frozen Food Locker Institute

ffly: faithfully

FFMC: Federal Farm Mortgage Corporation

FFNM: Fort Frederica National Monument (Georgia)

ffp: firm fixed price

FFP: Forest Fires Prevention

F & FP: Force and Financial Program

FFPS: Fellow of the Faculty of Physicians and Surgeons

FFR: Fellow of the Faculty of Radiologists; Fleay's Fauna Reserve (Queensland)

ffrr: full frequency range recording

ffs: fat-free solids

FFs: first families

FFS: Ferrovie Federali Svizzere (Swiss Federal Railways); Fruit-Frost Service

fft: for further transfer

FFTF: Fast Flux Test Facility

fftr: firefighter

FFV: First Families of Virginia

Ffy: Faithfully

FFZ: Free Fire Zone (USA)

fg: fine grain; fire glaze; flat grain; friction glaze; frog; fuel gas; fully good

fg: *faubourg* (French—suburb)

FG: Fitzroy Gardens

FG: *Fine Gael* (Irish—United Ireland Party)

fga: foreign general average; free of general average

FGA: Freer Gallery of Art

FGAA: Federal Government Accountants Association

fgc: facility group control

FGC: Fish and Game Code

FGCSSWA: Federation of Glass, Ceramic, and Silica Sand Workers of America

FGDS: *Federation de la Gauche Démocrate et Socialiste* (French—Federation of the Democratic and Socialist Left)

FGEX: Fruit Growers Express

FGMD: Fairchild Guided Missile Division

fgn: foreign; foreigner

FGNRA: Flaming Gorge National Recreation Area (Utah and Wyoming

FGO: Fleet Gunnery Officer

FGR: Franklin Game Reserve

FGS: Fellow of the Geological Society

FGSA: Fellow of the Geological Society of America

FGSM: Fellow of the Guildhall School of Music

fgt: freight

FGTO: French Government Tourist Office

fh: firehose; flathead; forehatch

f.h.: *fiat haustus* (Latin—make a draft)

FH: Fair Haven; Family History; Far Hills; Fashion Hills

fha: *fecha* (Spanish—date)

FHA: Farmers Home Administration; Federal Housing Administration; Fine Hardwoods Association; Friends Historical Association; Future Homemakers of America

FHAA: Field Hockey Association of America

FHASA: Forces Hydroelectriques de l'Andorre (Andorra Hydroelectric Power)

fhb: family hold back

fhc: fire-hose cabinet

FHC: Freed-Hardeman College

fhdo: *fechado* (Spanish—dated)

FH5: Firehouse Five

FHI: Fraser-Hickson Institute; Fuji-Hakone-Izu (national park on Honshu, Japan)

FHIP: Family Health Insurance Plan

FHKSC: Fort Hays Kansas State College

FHLB: Federal Home Loan Bank

FHLBB: Federal Home Loan Bank Board

FHLBS: Federal Home Loan Bank System

fhld: freehold

FHNWR: Flint Hills National Wildlife Refuge (Kansas)

f-holes: f-shaped sound holes in tops of stringed instruments such as violins, violas, cellos, double basses

fhp: fractional horsepower

FHPRP: Family Housing Program Review Panel

fhr: fire-hose rack

FHR: Federal House of Representatives (Australian)

fhs: fetal heart sounds

FHS: Forest History Society

fhsg: family housing

fht: fetal heart tone

FHWA: Federal Highway Administration

fhws: flat-headed wood screw

fhy: fire-hydrant

fi: fixed interval; for instance

Fi: Finland; Finnish

FI: Falkland Islands; Faeroe Islands; Fiji Islands; Franco-Iberian; Franklin Institute

F of I: Fruit of Islam (Black Muslim storm-troop disciplinary corps)

fia: financial inventory accounting; full interest admitted

FIA: Factory Insurance Association; Federal Intelligence Agency; Fellow of the Institute of Actuaries; Flatware Importers Association; Flight Information Area

FIAB: Fédération Internationale des Associations de Bibliothécaires (International Federation of Librarian Associations)

FIAJY: Fellowship in Israel for Arab-Jewish Youth

FIAL: Fellow of the Institute of Arts and Letters

FIAMS: Fellow of the Indian Academy of Medical Sciences

FIAP: Fédération Internationale de l'Art Photographique (International Federation of the Photographic Art)

FIAR: Fabbrica Italiana Apparecchi Radio (Italian Radio Apparatus Factory)

FIAT: Fabrica Italiana Automobili, Torino (Italian Automobile Factory—Turin)

FIAV: Fédération Internationale des Agences de Voyage (International Federation of Travel Agencies)

fib.: fibula; free into barge; free into bond; free into bunkers

FIB: Fédération des Industries Belges (Federation of Belgian Industries); Franklin Institute of Boston

FIBM: Fellow of the British Institute of Management

fibril: fibrillation

fic: fiction; freight, insurance, carriage; frequency interference control

FIC: Federal Insurance Corporation; Fellow of the Institute of Chemistry; Flight Information Center; Forest Industries Council

F 1 C: Fireman 1st Class (USN)

FICA: Federal Insurance Contributions Act; Ferrocarriles Internacionales de Centro America (International Railways of Central America); Food Industries Credit Association

FICCI: Federation of Indian Chambers of Commerce and Industry

FICD: Fellow of the International College of Dentists

FICeram: Fellow of the Institute of Ceramics

FICO: Ford Instrument Company

fic(s): *aficionado(s)* [Spanish —devotee(s)]

FICS: Fellow of the International College of Surgeons

fict: fiction; fictitious

fid: fiduciary

FID: Falkland Island Dependencies; Federation of International Documentation; Fellow of the Institute of Directors

FIDA: Federal Industrial Development Authority

fidal: fixed-wing insecticide-dispersal apparatus, liquid (USNs defoliant spraying system)

FIDE: Federation Internationale des Echecs (International Chess Federation)

Fidel: Fidel Castro

FIDEL: *Frente Izquierda de Liberación* (Spanish—Leftist Liberation Front)

fido: fog investigation dispersal operation

FIDO: Flight Dynamics Officer

FIDS: Foolproof Identification System

FIER: Foundation for Instrumentation Education and Research

fif: ferric ion free

FIF: First Investment Fund

fi. fa.: *fieri facias* (Latin—see it done)

Fife: Fifeshire

fifo: first in, first out (inventory)

FIFO: Flight Inspection Field Office(r)

FIFRA: Federal Insecticide, Fungicide, and Rodenticide Act

fig(s).: figure(s); finger-sized banana(s)

Fig: *Figur(en)* [German—figure(s)]; *Le Figaro* (Paris' oldest daily newspaper)

FIG: Farmers Insurance Group

FIGA: Fretted Instrument Guild of America

FIH: Fédération Internationale des Hôpitaux (International Federation of Hospitals)

FII: Fellow of the Imperial Institute

FIIAL: Fellow of the International Institute of Arts and Letters

fiigmo: forget it, I've got my orders

FIIN: Federal Item Identification Number

fil: filament; fillet; fillister; filter; filtrate

f-i-l: father-in-law

FIL: Fellow of the Institute of Linguists

file 13: trashcan; wastebasket

fil h: fillister head

fill.: filling

filo: first in, last out

filt: filter; filtrate; filtration

filt.: *filtra* (Latin—filter)

fim: field ion microscope

FIM: Fellow of the Institute of Metallurgists; Flight Information Manual

FIMLT: Fellow of the Institute of Medical Laboratory Technology

fin.: finance; financial; financier; finish

fin.: *finis* (Latin—the end)

Fin: Finistère; Finland; Finnic; Finnish

fina: following items not available

FINAST: First National Stores

fin dec: final decree

FINEBEL: France, Italy, Netherlands, Belgium, and Luxembourg (economic agreement)

fines.: fine particulates

fin fl: finished floor

F-ing: fucking (slang—copulating)

Finn: Finnish

FINNAIR: Aero O/Y (*q.v.*; Finnish Airlines)

FINS: Fire Island National Seashore

FINSINDER: Societa Finanziaria Siderurgica (Steel Financing Society)

F Inst F: Fellow of the Institute of Fuel

F Inst P: Fellow of the Institute of Physics

F Inst Pet: Fellow of the Institute of Petroleum

F Inst SP: Fellow of the Institute of Sewage Purification

Fin-Ug: Finno-Ugric

fio: for information only; free in and out

FIO: Fleet Information Office

fip: fi'pence (fivepence); fi'penny (fivepenny); fire insurance policy

FIP: Flight Instruction Program

FIPA: Fellow of the Institute of Practitioners in Advertising

FiPo: Fire and Police (Research Association)

FIPS: Federal Information Processing Standards

fir.: firkin; flight information region; floating in rate(s); fuel indicator reading

FIRAA: Fire Insurance Research and Actuarial Association

FIRB: Fire Insurance Rating Bu-

reau; Florida Inspection and Rating Bureau

FIRE: Fellow of the Institution of Radio Engineers

FIREBRICK: Federal Inter-Agency River Basin Committee

Firestreak: air-to-air missile

FIRI: Fellow of the Institute of the Rubber Industry; Fishing Industry Research Institute

FIRST: Financial Information Reporting System

Fis: (German—F-sharp)

FIS: Fighter Interceptor Squadron; Flight Information Service

FISAR: Federal Institute for Snow and Avalanche Research

fisc irre: fiscal irresponsiblity

fish.: fishery; fishes; fishing

FISH: Friends in Service Here

fishwich: fish sandwich

fit.: foreign independent traveler; foreign independent trip; free of income tax; free in truck

FIT: Fashion Institute of Technology; Federal Income Tax; Fédération Internationale des Traducteurs (International Federation of Translators)

fitw: federal income tax withholding

Fitzw: Fitzwilliam Library (Cambridge)

FIU: Forward Interpretation Unit (US Army)

fiume: (Italian—flood; river)

fiw: free in wagon

fix.: fixture

Fj: Fjord

FJ: Fiji Airways

FJA: Future Journalists of America

fjäll: (Swedish—mountain)

fjärd: (Swedish—bay; inlet)

FJC: Fullerton Junior College

Fjd: Fjord

FJH: Franz Josef Haydn

FJI: Fellow of the Institute of Journalists

FJIC: Federal Job Information Center

FJNM: Fort Jefferson National Monument

fjord: (Dano-Norwegian—inlet of the sea)

fjördur: (Icelandic—fjord)

FJS: Fulton J. Sheen

fk: flat keel; fork

Fk: Frank

FK: Fluid Kinetics; Fujita Airways

FK: *Frankfurt Kassenverien* (German—Frankfurt Clearinghouse)

FKBD: Fort Knox Bullion Depository

FKBI: Fourdrinier Kraft Board Institute

FKC: Fellow of King's College

Fkd: Frankford
FKJC: Florida Keys Junior College
FKL: Frauen Konzentration Lager (German—Women's Concentration Camp)
Fkn: Franklin; Frederikshavn
Fks: Fredrikstad
FKSNS: Fort Kent State Normal School
FKWR: Florida Keys Wildlife Refuges
fl: flash(ing); flight level; flood(ing); floor(ing); flow(ing); flow line; fluid(s); flush(ing); follow(ing); foot-lambert
fl: flauto; flauti (Italian—flute, flutes); *flores* (Latin—flowers); *floruit* (Latin—he flourished)
f.l.: falsa lectio (Latin—false reading)
fL: foot-lambert
Fl: Flemish; fluorine
FL: Flag Lieutenant; Flight Lieutenant; focal length; foreign language; Frontier Airlines (2-letter code)
F.L.: Franz Liszt
FL: Fürstentum Liechtenstein (Principality of Liechtenstein)
fla: fronto-laeva anterior
f.l.a.: fiat lege artis (Latin—according to the rules of art)
Fla: Florida; Floridian
FLA: Federal Loan Administration; Federal Loan Agency; Fellow of the Library Association; Florida; Florida East Coast Railway (symbol); Foam Laminators Association
fl abwth: flush armor balanced watertight hatch
Fla Cur: Florida Current
flag.: flageolet
Flagellum Dei: (Latin—Scourge of God)—Attila the king of the Huns
FLAIR: Floating Airport
flak: fliegerabwehrkanone (German—anti-aircraft cannon; anti-aircraft shrapnel)
flam(s): flamenco (songs); flaming(s);); flammable(s)
FLAME: Facility Laboratory for Ablative Materials Evaluation
flar: forward-looking airborne radar
flav: flavor(ing)
flav.: flavus (Latin—yellow)
FLB: Federal Land Bank
FLC: Foundation Library Center
fld: field; flowered; fluid
fldec: floating-point decimal
fl di: flare die
FL & DI: Food Law and Drug Institute
fldo: final limit, down
fldop: field operations

fl dr: fluid dram
fldxt: fluid extract
Fl e: Flemish ell (unit of measure)
Flem: Flemish
FLES: Foreign Languages in Elementary Schools (linguistic teaching program)
FLETC: Federal Law Enforcement Training Center
FLETRABASE: Fleet Training Base (USN)
flex.: flexible
flf: final limit, forward
flg: flagging; flange; flooring; flying
flgd: flanged
flgstn: flagstone
flh: final limit, hoist
fl hd: flathead
flhls: flashless
FLIC: Film Library Information Council
flick(s): flicker(s; motion picture[s])
flicon: flight control
flicr: fluid-logic industrial control relay
Flint: Flintshire
Flints: Flintshire
FLIP: Flight Information Publication; Floated Lightweight Inertial Platform; Floating Instrument Platform
flir: forward-look infrared
FLIRT: Federal Librarians Round Table
fliv: flivver
Flivver King: Henry Ford
fll: final limit, lower
FLL: Fort Lauderdale, Florida (airport); Friends Library, London
fllar: forward-looking light attack radar
fl ld: floor load
Flli: fratelli (Italian—brothers)
FLMI: Fellow of the Life Management Institute
fl/mtr: flow meter
Fln: Flensburg
FLN: Front de Liberation Nationale (French—National Liberation Front)—official Algerian political party
FLNM: Fort Laramie National Monument
Flo: Florence
Fl O: Flight Officer
floc: floccule; flocculent; floccus
FLOC: For Love of Children
flod: (Danish or Swedish—river)
Fl Offr: Flying Officer
FLOG: Fleet Logistics Air Wing
flor: floriculture
flor: flores (Latin—flowers); *floruit* (Latin—he flourished)
Flor: Floréal (month of calendar of French Revolution)
Floribbean: Floridian-Caribbean (resort area)

flot: flotation; flotilla; flotsam
fl ovth: flush oiltight ventilation hole
flox: fluorine + liquid oxygen
fl oz: fluid ounce
flp: fault location panel; fronto-laeva posterior
fl pl.: flore pleno (Latin—in full bloom)
fl prf: flameproof
fl pt: flashpoint
FLQ: Front de Liberation Quebecois (French—Front for the Liberation of the people of Quebec)—radical terrorist separatists
flr: final limit, reverse; floor; florin
FLR: Florence, Italy (Firenze Airport)
flrg: flooring
flrng: flash ranging
flrs: flowers
fl/rt: flow rate
Fls: Flushing
FLS: Fellow of the Linnaean Society
flsc: flight shape charge
FLSEP: Family Life and Sex Education Program
FLSO: Fort Lauderdale Symphony Orchestra
FLSP: Fort Lincoln State Park (North Dakota)
flt: filter; fleet; flight; float; flotation; flotation; fronto-laeva transverse
Flt: Fleetwood
Flt Adm: Fleet Admiral
Fltchr C: Fletcher College
fltg: floating
fltl: flight line
Flt Lt: Flight Lieutenant
flt/pg: flight programmer
flt pln: flight plan
fltr: floater
Flt Sgt Nav: Flight Sergeant Navigator
flu: final limit, up; influenza
fluc: fluctuant; fluctuate; fluctuating; fluctuation
FLUG: Flugfelag Islands (Iceland Airways)
flummery: foolish humbuggery (named after British custard made of flour or oatmeal boiled with water until almost too thick to swallow)
fluor: fluoresce; fluorescence; fluorescent; fluoric; fluoridation; fluoride; fluorine; fluorite; fluoroscope; fluoroscopy; fluorspar
fluorspar: calcium fluoride (CaF_2)
fluss: (German—river)
flüss: flüssig (German—fluid)
FLW: Frank Lloyd Wright
flx: flexible

fly.: flinty; flying; flyweight
FLY: Flying Tiger Line
FlyTAF: Flying Training Air Force
FLZO: Farband-Labor Zionist Order
fm: face measurement; facial measurement; fan marker; farm; farmer; fathom; fathometer; fine measurement; form; frequency modulation; from; fumigation
fm: *formiddag* (Dano-Norwegian —before noon)—a.m.; *formiddagen (Swedish—before noon)—a.m.*
f.m.: *fiat mistura* (Latin—make a mixture)
Fm: fermium
FM: Fed Mart; Ferrocarril Mexicano (Mexican Railroad); Field Manual; Field Marshal; Flight Mechanic; Foreign Minister; frequency modulation
F-am-M: Frankfurt-am-Main (Frankfurt-on-Main)
F & M: Franklin and Marshall College
FMA: Felt Manufacturers Association; File Manufacturers Association; Flour Mills of America; Forging Manufacturers Association
FMACC: Foreign Military Assistance Coordinating Committee
FMAI: Financial Management for Administrators Institute
fman: foreman
FMB: Federal Maritime Board; Felix Mendelssohn Bartholdi
FMBSA: Farmers and Manufacturers Beet Sugar Association
FMC: Failure Mode Center (Reliability Laboratory); Federal Maritime Commission; Felt Manufacturers Council; Food Machinery Corporation; Ford Motor Company
FMCC: Fulton-Montgomery Community College
F McH NM: Fort McHenry National Monument
FMCS: Federal Mediation and Conciliation Service
fm cu: form cutter
fmd: foot-and-mouth disease
FMD: Federated Metals Division—American Smelting and Refining; Fixtures Manufacturers and Dealers; Flota Mercante Dominicana (Dominican Steamship Line); Forward Metro Denver
fm di: form die
FMEA (FEA): Failure Modes and Effects Analysis
FMECA: Failure Mode, Effects, and Criticality Analysis

FMF: Fleet Marine Force
FMF-A: Fleet Marine Force—Atlantic
fmfb: frequency-modulation feedback
FMFIC: Federation of Mutual Fire Insurance Companies
FMF-P: Fleet Marine Force—Pacific
fmg: foreign medical graduate
FMG: Flota Mercante Grancolombiana (Colombian national steamship lines); franc(s) Malagasy
FMGJ: Federation of Master Goldsmiths and Jewelers
FMI: FM Intercity (relay broadcasting); Fonds Monétaries Internationals (International Monetary Fund)
Fmk: Finnmark; Finnish markka (currency unit)
FML: Factory Mutual Laboratories
fmly k a: formerly known as
FMMA: Floor Machinery Manufacturers Association
fmn: formation
FMN: Ferrocarril Mexicano del Norte (Northern Mexican Railroad)
FMNH: Field Museum of Natural History
FMNM: Fort Matanzas National Monument
FMO: Fleet Mail Office; Fleet Medical Officer; Flight Medical Officer
FMP: Fairbanks Morse Pump
FMPE: Federation of Master Process Engravers
fm prot: fine-mesh (cover) protected
FMPS: Fairbanks Morse Power Systems
fmr: former
fm rl: form roll
fmrly: formerly
FMRS: Federal Mediation and Reconciliation Service
fms: fathoms; flush metal saddle; free-machining steel
fm's: formerly-married persons
FMS: Federal Mining and Smelting (company); Federated Malay States; Field Music School; Financial Management System; Floating Machine Shop; Fort Myers Southern (railroad); Friends Mission Society
fmsa: frequency measuring spectrum analyzer
FMSI: Friction Materials Standards Institute
FMSL: Fort Monmouth Signal Laboratory
FMSM: Fédération Mondiale pour

la Santé Mentale (World Mental Health Federation)
fmt: flush metal threshold
fm to.: form tool
FMTS: Field Maintenance Test Station
F & MTVHS: Food and Maritime Trades Vocational High School
fmu: force measurement unit
FMVSS: Federal Motor Vehicle Safety Standard
FMWS: Fairbanks Morse Weighing Systems
fmk: full-mouth radiograph
fn: flatnose (projectile); footnote; fusion
fn: *fête nationale* (French—national holiday)
Fn: fractonimbus
FN: Flight Nurse; Fridtjof Nansen
F N: Fabrique Nationale (French —National Factory)
FNA: following named airmen; French North Africa
FNB: Food and Nutrition Board
FNC: Federación Nacional de Cafeteros (National Federation of Coffee Growers—Colombia); Ferrocarriles Nacionales de Colombia (National Railroads of Colombia)
FNCB: First National City Bank
FNCR: Ferrocarril del Norte de Costa Rica (Northern Railway of Costa Rica)
fnd: found; foundered
fndd: founded
fndg: founding
fndn: foundation
fndr: founder
fndry: foundry
fne: fine
fnh: flashless nonhygroscopic (gunpowder)
FNH: Ferrocarril Nacional de Honduras (National Railway of Honduras)
FNIMC: Florida Normal and Industrial Memorial College
FNL: Friends of the National Libraries
FNLA: *Frente Nacional de Libertacão de Angola* (Portuguese—Angolan National Liberation Front)
FNM: Ferrocarriles Nacionales de México (National Railroads of Mexico)
FNMA: Federal National Mortgage Association
FNNWR: Fort Niobrara National Wildlife Refuge (Nebraska)
FNO: following-named officers
FNOA: following-named officers and airmen
fnp: fusion point

FNP: Fiordland National Park (South Island, New Zealand); Fundy National Park (New Brunswick, Canada)

FNRJ: Federationa Narodna Republika Jugoslavija (Yugoslavia)

FNS: Frontier Nursing Service

fnshr: finisher

FNTO: Finnish National Travel Office

fnu: first name unknown

FNU: Forces des Nations Unies (United Nations Forces)

FNWF: Fleet Numerical Weather Facility

fo: faced only; fast operating; firm offer; flat oval; folio; for orders; free overside; fuel oil; full out terms

FO: Field Order; Finance Officer; Foreign Office; Forward Observer

F.O.: Foreign Office

F/O: Flight Officer; Flying Officer

fo⁰: *folio* (Spanish—folio)

FOA: Football Officials Association; Foreign Operations Administration; Foresters of America; Friends of Animals

fob: feet out of bed

f.o.b.: free on board; fuel on board

fo & b: fuel oil and ballast

FOB: Federal Office Building; Forward Operating Base; Free on Board

FOBS: Fractional-Orbit Bombardment System

foc: final operational capability; focal; focus; focusing

f.o.c.: free of charge; free on car

FOC: Ferrocarriles Occidentales de Cuba (Western Railroads of Cuba); Flight Operations Center

FOCI: Farrand Optical Company, Incorporated

FOCSL: Fleet-Oriented Consolidated Stock List

fo'c's'le: forecastle

fod: fodder; foreign object damage; free of damage

f.o.d.: free of damage

FOE: Fraternal Order of Eagles; Friends of the Earth

FOF: *Facts On File*

fog.: flow of gold

FOG: Florida Orange Growers

FOGA: Fashion Originators Guild of America

Fog Sig: fog signal (station)

foh: front of house

foi: freedom of information

FOI: (station) Operations Intelligence; Fighter Officer Interceptors; Fruit of Islam (Black Nationalists)

FOIC: Flag Officer In Charge

FOIR: Field-of-Interest Register

f.o.k.: free of knots

fol: folio; folios; follow; following; follows

fol.: *folium* (Latin—leaf); *folia* (Latin—leaves)

FOL: Foreign Office Library; Friends of the Land

fold.: folding

folg: *folgend* (German—follwing)

foll: followed by

folnoaval: following (items) not available

fonecon: telephone conversation

fono: photograph

fonoff: foreign office

fopt: fiber-optics photon transfer

f.o.q.: free on quay

for.: foreign; foreigner; forensic; forest; forester; forestry; forint (Hungarian monetary unit); free on rail; free on road

f.o.r.: free on rail

For: Formosa; Formosan

FOR: Fellowship of Reconciliation

forac: for action

FORACS: Fleet Operational Readiness Accuracy Check Site

for. bal: forensic ballistics

forbloc: fortran-compiled block-oriented (simulation programme)

for. bod: foreign body

for'd: forward

FORD: Families Opposed to Revolutionary Destruction

FORDS: Floating Ocean Research and Development Station

fores'l: foresail

forf: forfeit; forfeiture

forf: *forfatter* (Dano-Norwegian—author)

förf: *författare, författarinna* (Swedish—author, authoress)

forg: forger; forgery; forging

fork: *forkortning* (Swedish—abbreviation)

fork.: *forkortelse* (Danish—abbreviation)

form.: format; formation; former-(ly)

form: *formiddag* (Norwegian —before noon)—a.m.

forma: fortran matrix analysis

formac: formula manipulation compiler

formal.: formaldehyde; formalin

formalin: HCHO

format.: fortran matrix abstraction technique(s)

for med: forensic medicine

For Min: Foreign Minister; Minister of Foreign Affairs

formn: foreman

for'm'st: foremast

formul: formulary

forpac: forecasting passengers and cargo

for'rd: forward

for. rts: foreign rights

fors: (Swedish—waterfall)

Forsch: *Forschung* (German —research)

for's'l: foresail

Forst: (German—forest)

fort.: fortification; fortify; fortress; full-out rye terms (grain trade)

for. tox: forensic toxicology

fortran: formula translation

Forts: *Fortsetzung* (German—continuation)

forwn: forewoman

fos: fossil; fuel-oxygen scrap

fos: (Dano-Norwegian—waterfall)

f.o.s.: free on steamer

FOS: Fisheries Organization Society; Fuel Oil Supply (company)

fosdic: film optical sensing device for input to computers

fos fls: fossil fuels (coal, natural gas, oil, etc.)

FOSH: Foshing (airlines)

foss: (Norwegian—waterfall)

fot: frequency optimum traffic; fuel-oil transfer

f.o.t.: free on truck

FOT: Fraternal Order of Police

FOTM: Friends of Old-Time Music

foto: photograph(ic)

found.: foundation; founding; foundling; foundry

fount: fountain

FOUO: For Official Use Only

Fourth Estate: (communications: press radio, tv, etc.)

FOUSA: Finance Office(r), United States Army

f.o.w.: first open water (shipping term); free on wagon

Foxtrot: code for letter F

Foy: Fowey

fp: fireplace; fixed price; flame-proof; flat point; flight pay; flower people; foot pound; forward perpendicular; freezing point

f/p: flat pattern

f.p.: *fiat potio* (Latin—make a potion)

FP: Ferrocarril del Pacífico (Pacific Railroad); Franklin Pierce

FP: *Freiheitliche Partei* (German —Freedom Party)—Austrian party with neo-Nazi orientation

F del P: Ferrocarril del Pacífico (formerly Southern Pacific of Mexico)

fpa: free of particular average

FPA: Family Planning Association; Flying Physicians Association; Foreign Policy Association; Franklin Pierce Adams; Freethought Press Association

fpaAc: free of particular average, American conditions

FPAD: Fund for Peaceful Atomic Development

fpaEc: free of particular average, English conditions

fpaf: fixed-price award fee

FPBA: Folding Paper Box Association

fpc: fish protein concentrate; fixed-price call; for private circulation

FPC: Family Planning Center; Federal Pacific Electric (stock exchange symbol); Federal Power Commission; Food Packaging Council; Friends Peace Committee; Frozen Pea Council

FPCC: Fair Play for Cuba Committee

FPCE: Fission Products Conversion and Encapsulation (AEC plant)

fpdi: flight path deviation indicator

fpe: fixed price with escalation

FPE: Foundation for Personality Expression; Full Personality Expression

FPEBT: Fire Prevention and Engineering Bureau of Texas

FPED: Farm Production Economics Division (USDA)

FPF: French Protestant Federation

FPHA: Federal Public Housing Authority

fphs: fallout protection in homes

fpi: faded prior to interception; family pitch in; fixed price incentive

FPI: Federal Prison Industries

fpif: fixed-price-incentive firm

fpil: full premium if lost

f. pil.: *fiat pilulae* (Latin—make pills)

fpis: fixed-price incentive successive

fpl: final protective line; fire plug

FPL: Forest Products Laboratory

fpm: feet per minute

FPML: Forest Products Marketing Laboratory

FPNM: Fort Pulaski National Monument

fpo: fixed price open

FPO: Field Post Office; Field Project Office; Fleet Post Office; Fleet Postal Organization

FPP: Family Planning Program

FPPS: Flight Plan Processing System

fpr: fixed price redeterminable

FPR: Factory Problem Report; Field Personnel Record

FPRC: Fair Play for Rhodesia Committee

fprf: fireproof

FPRI: Foreign Policy Research Institute (University of Pennsylvania)

FPRL: Forest Products Research Laboratory

FPRS: Forest Products Research Society

fps: feet per second; foot per second; foot-pound-second; frames per second

f'ps: former priests

FPS: Farm Placement Service; Fauna Preservation Society; Fellow of the Philharmonic Society; Fellow of the Philological Society; Fellow of the Philosophical Society; Fluid Power Society

FPSA: Fellow of the Photographic Society of America

fpsps: feet per second per second

fpt: female pipe thread; full power trial

FPTU: Federation of Progressive Trade Unions

fq: fiscal quarter

fqawt: flush quick-acting watertight

fqcy: frequency

FQL: Food Quality Laboratory

FQS: Federal Quarantine Service

fr: fast release (relay); field relay; frame; front

f/r: freight release

f & r: feed and return (plumbing); force and rhythm (pulse)

fr.: *folio recto* (Latin—front of the sheet)

Fr: France; Franco-; francium; Frau (German—Missus); French; Froude number

Fr: *Frau* (German—Missus); *Fredag* (Danish—Friday)

FR: Feather River (railroad); Federal Register; Federal Reserve; Field Report; fighter reconnaissance (aircraft); Final Report; Fireman Recruit; flash red—enemy aircraft nearby; Fleet Reserve; Friden (stock exchange symbol)

fra: *factura* (Spanish—invoice)

Fra: Francis

Fra.: *frater* (Latin—brother; monk)

FRA: Fleet Reserve Association; Footwear Research Association; Frankfurt-am-Main, Germany (airport)

FRACP: Fellow of the Royal Australian College of Physicians

FRACS: Fellow of the Royal Australian College of Surgeons

fract. dos.: *fracta dosi* (Latin—in divided doses)

FRAeS: Fellow of the Royal Aeronautical Society

frag: fragile; fragment; fragmentary; fragmentation; fragmented

FRAI: Fellow of the Royal Anthropological Institute

FRAIA: Fellow of the Royal Australian Institute of Architects

FRAIC: Fellow of the Royal Architectural Institute of Canada

FRAM: Fellow of the Royal Academy of Music; Fleet Rehabilitation and Maintenance (USN)

FRAME: Fund for the Replacement of Animals in Medical Research

fran: framed-structure analysis

Fran: Frances; Francis; Franciscan

Franco: Francisco (Spanish—Francis)

Franco: Francisco Paulino Hermenegildo Teodulo Franco-Bahamonde—Spanish dictator

Françoise Sagan((pseudonym—Françoise Quoirez)

Fra Angelico: Giovanni da Fiesole

frank(s): frankfurter(s)

Frank: Francis; Franklin

Frank Richard: (pen name—Charles Hamilton)

FRAS: Fellow of the Royal Asiatic Society; Fellow of the Royal Astronomical Society

Frasca: Francesca

Frasco: Francisco

frat: fraternity

frat: *fratello* (Italian—brother)

frater: fraternity brother

fraud.: fraudulent

FRB: Federal Reserve Bank; Federal Reserve Board

FRBC: Fisheries Research Board of Canada

fr bel: from below

FRBk: Federal Reserve Bank

FRBS: Fellow of the Royal Botanic Society

frc: functional residual capacity

FRC: Facility Review Committee; Fasteners Research Council; Federal Radiation Council; Federal Radio Commission; Federal Records Center; Federal Republic of Cameroon; Filipino Rehabilitation Commission; Flight Research Center; Foreign Relations Committee; Foreign Relations Council; Fuels Research Council

Fr-Can: French-Canadian

fr & cc: free of riots and civil commotion

FRCI: Fellow of the Royal Colonial Institute

FRCM: Fellow of the Royal College of Music

FRCO: Fellow of the Royal College of Organists

FRCOG: Fellow of the Royal College of Obstetricians and Gynaecologists

FRCP: Fellow of the Royal College of Physicians
FRCP(C): Fellow of the Royal College of Physicians of Canada
FRCPE: Fellow of the Royal College of Physicians of Edinburgh
FRCPI: Fellow of the Royal College of Physicians of Ireland
FRCS: Fellow of the Royal College of Surgeons
FRCSc: Fellow of the Royal College of Science
FRCS(C): Fellow of the Royal College of Surgeons of Canada
FRCSE: Fellow of the Royal College of Surgeons of Edinburgh
FRCSI: Fellow of the Royal College of Surgeons of Ireland
FRCTS: Fast Reactor Core Test Facility
FRCVS: Fellow of the Royal College of Veterinary Surgeons
frd: formerly restricted data; friend; friendly
FR Dist: Federal Reserve District
Frdn: Friedenau
fre: *fracture* (French—invoice)
Fre: Freemantle; French
Fre: *Freitag* (German—Friday)
FREB: Federal Real Estate Board
FR Econ Soc: Fellow of the Royal Economic Society
Fred: Alfred; Alfredo; Freddie; Frederic; Frederick; Fredric; Fredrick; Wilfred
Fred(die): Frederica; Fredrica
Fred(dy): Alfred; Frederick; Wilfred
Fredk: Frederick
Fredk D: Frederick Douglass
Free: Freeway
freebd: freeboard
freeway: toll-free express highway
Freib: Freiburg (Germany)
FRELIMO: *Frente de Libertação de Moçambique* (Portuguese—Mozambique Liberation Front)
French Century: the 18th century of kings and courtesans, of vast territories acquired and lost, of the French Revolution and an end to Louis XVI and Marie Antoinette who were guillotined only to be succeeded by Napoleon—the 1700s
french fries: french fried potatoes
French West Africa: *Afrique Occidentale Française*—AOF
freon tf: trifluorotrichloroethane (solvent)
freq: frequency; frequent
FrEqAfr: French Equatorial Africa
freq m: frequency meter
fres: fire-resistant
fres: *frères* (French—brothers)
FRES: Fellow of the Royal En-

tomological Society
frescanar: frequency scan radar
fresh.: freshman; freshmen
Freud.: Freudian
frf: flight-readiness firing; frequency response function
fr-f: french-fried (potatoes)
FRFPS: Fellow of the Royal Faculty of Physicians and Surgeons
FrG: French Guiana
FRG: Federal Republic of Germany (West Germany)
FRGS: Fellow of the Royal Geographical Society
frgt: freight
frhgt: free height
FR Hist S: Fellow of the Royal Historical Society
FR Hort S: Fellow of the Royal Horticultural Society
Fr hr: French horn
Frhr: *Freiherr* (German—Baron)
FRHS: Fellow of the Royal Horticultural Society
fri: feeling rough inside
Fri: Friday
FRI: Fels Research Institute; Food Research Institute; Friends of Rhodesian Independence
Frib: Fribourg (Switzerland)
FRIBA: Fellow of the Royal Institute of British Architects
fric: frication; fricative; fricatrice; fricatrix; friction; frictional
FRIC: Fellow of the Royal Institute of Chemistry
frict: friction
fridge(s): refrigerator(s)
Friedrh: Friedrichshafen
Friends: Society of Friends (Quakers)
Friends Meet: Friends Meeting
Fries: Friesic
frig: refrigerator
Frim: *Frimaire* (month in calendar of French Revolution)
FRIPHH: Fellow of the Royal Institute of Public Health and Hygiene
Fris: Friesland; Frisia; Frisian
frisco: fast-reaction integrated submarine control
FRISCO: St. Louis-San Francisco Railway
Fritalux: France, Italy, and Benelux nations
frits: fritters
Fritz: Friedrich
frjm: full-range joint movement
frk: *fröken* (Swedish—Miss)
Frk: Frankfort
Frk: *Frøken* (Dano-Norwegian—Miss)
frl: fractional
Frl: El Ferrol
Frl: *Fräulein* (German—Miss)

frm: fireroom; framing
FR Met Soc: Fellow of the Royal Meteorological Society
frmn: formation
frmr: former
FRMS: Fellow of the Royal Microscopical Society
FRN: Federal Republic of Nigeria
FRNHS: Fort Raleigh National Historic Site
FRNS: Fellow of the Royal Numismatic Society
Frnz: Fernández
frof: fire risk on freight
frog.: free rocket over ground
fron: frontal; frontalis
FRONAPE: Frota Naccional de Petroleiros (National Petroleum Fleet—Brazil)
front.: frontispiece
frosh: freshman; freshmen
frp: fiberglass reinforced plastic
FRPS: Fellow of the Royal Photographic Society
frs: francs
Frs: Frisian
FRS: Federal Reserve System; Fellow of the Royal Society; Fisheries Research Society
FRSA: Fellow of the Royal Society of Arts
FRSC: Fellow of the Royal Society of Canada
FRSE: Fellow of the Royal Society of Edinburgh
FRSGS: Fellow of the Royal Scottish Geographical Society
FRSH: Fellow of the Royal Society of Health
FRSI: Fellow of the Royal Sanitary Institute
FRSL: Fellow of the Royal Society of Literature; Fellow of the Royal Society—London
FRSM: Fellow of the Royal Society of Medicine
Fr Som: French Somaliland
FRSS: Fellow of the Royal Statistical Society
frt: free return trajectory; freight; fruit
Fr To: French Togoland
frt ppd: freight prepaid
fru: fructose; fruit sugar
Fruc: *Fructidor* (month in calendar of French Revolution)
frugal: fortran rules used as general applications language
frust.: *frustillatim* (Latin—in small portions)
frwk: framework
Frwy: Freeway
frx: firex
Fry: Freeway
fs: factor of safety; far side; film strip; fin stabilized; fire station;

flight service; flying status; foot second; foreign service; foresight; freight supply; front spar; sulfur trioxide chlorsulfonic acid (commercial short form or symbol)

f/s: first-stage

fs: *faites suivre* (French—please forward)

Fs: fractostratus

FS: Faraday Society; Feasibility Study; Federal Specification(s); Field Security; Field Service; Fighter Squadron; Fire Station; Flight Sergeant; Fog Signal (station); Foreign Service; Forest Service; Franz Schubert; Freedom School; Free State; freight supply (vessel); small freighter (naval symbol)

F-S: Fenno-Shipping

F/S: Financial Statement

FS: *Filharmonisk Selskap* (Norwegian—Philharmonic Orchestra); *Forente Staterna* (Swedish—United States)

F de S: Ferrovie dello Stato (Italian State Railways)

F del S: Ferrocarril del Sureste (Southeast Railway—Tabasco, Campeche, Veracruz, Yucatan)

fsa: family separation allowance; fuel storage area

FSA: Farm Security Administration; Federal Security Administration; Federal Security Agency; Federal Supply Classification; Federation of South Arabia; Fellow of the Society of Antiquaries; Fellow of the Society of Arts; Finance Service—Army; Fire Support Area; Fraternal Scholastic Association; Free Society Association; Freethinkers Society of America; Future Scientists of America

FSAA: Family Service Association of America

fsaga: first sortie after ground alert

FSAICU: Federation of State Associations of Independent Colleges and Universities

FSB: Federal Specifications Board; Field Selection Board

FSBC: Ferrocarril Sonora—Baja California (Sonora—Baja California Railway)

fsc: foreign service credit

FSC: Family Services Bureau; Federal Safety Council; Federal Stock Catalog; Federal Supply Classification; Federal Supply Code; Flight Service Center; Flying Status Code; Foreign Service Credits; Foundation for the Study of Cycles

FSC: *Federal Supply Catalog*

FSCC: Federal Surplus Commodities Corporation; Fire-Support Coordination Center; Food Surplus Commodities Corporation

fscl: fire-support coordination line

fscp: foolscap

FSCS: Fire Support Coordination Section; Flight Service Communications System

fsd: flying spot digitizer; foreign sea duty

FSD: Federal Systems Division; Fuel Supply Depot; Sioux Falls, South Dakota (airport)

fse: field-support equipment

FSE: Federation of Stock Exchanges

FSEA: Food Service Executives Association

FSES: Federal-State Employment Service

FSF: Flight Safety Foundation

FSG: Federal Supply Group

FSGB: Foreign Service Grievance Board

fsh (FSH): follicle-stimulating hormone

fsh stk: fish steak

FSI: Federal Stock Item; Fellow of the Sanitary Institute; Fellow of the Surveyors' Institution; Foreign Service Institute; Free Sons of Israel

FSIA: Fellow of the Society of Industrial Artists

FSIC: Foreign Service Inspection Corps (US Department of State)

FSJC: Fort Smith Junior College

fsk: frequency shift keying

fsl: formal semantic language

FSL: Folger Shakespeare Library

FSLIC: Federal Savings and Loan Insurance Corporation

FSM: Federation Syndicale Mondiale (World Federation of Trade Unions); Fort Smith, Arkansas (airport); Free Speech Movement

FSMC: Flora Stone Mather College

FSMWO: Field Service Modification Work Order

FSN: Federal Stock Number

FSNC: Federal Steam Navigation Company

FSNM: Fort Sumter National Monument

FSNP: Fuyot Spring National Park (Philippines)

FSNWR: Fish Springs National Wildlife Refuge (Utah)

FSNY: Free Synagogue of New York

FSO: Flint Symphony Orchestra; Florida Symphony Orchestra; Flying Safety Officer; Floreign

Safely Officer; Fuel Supply Office(r)

FSOs: Foreign Service Officers

FSOTS: Foreign Service Officers Training School

fsp: foreign service pay

FSP: Field Security Police; Food Stamp Program

FSPT: Federation of Societies for Paint Technology

fsr: flight safety research

FSR: Fellow of the Society of Radiographers; Field Service Representative; Foreign Service Reserve

FSRA: Federal Sewage Research Association

FSRJ: Federativna Socijalisticka Republika Jugoslavija (Republic of Yugoslavia)

FSS: Federal Supply Schedule; Federal Supply Service; Flight Service Station; Flight Standard Service

FSSC: Federal Standard Stock Catalog

fssd: foreign service selection date

fst: forged steel; full-scale tunnel

Fst: *Funkstelle* (German—radio station)

FSTC: Farmington State Teachers College; Fayetteville State Teachers College

FS & TC: Foreign Science and Technology Center (US Army)

F'sted: Frederiksted, St. Croix

FSTWP: Fellow of the Society of Technical Writers and Publishers

fsu: freak student union

FSU: Florida State University; Friends of the Soviet Union

fsv: final-stage vehicle

FSWA: Federation of Sewage Works Associations

F & SWMA: Fine and Specialty Wire Manufacturers Association

fswt: free-surface water tunnel

ft: feet; flush threshold; firing table; formal training; fumetight

ft²: square feet; square foot

ft³: cubic feet; cubic foot

f-t: follow through

f & t: fire and theft

ft.: *fiat* (Latin—let it be made)

Ft: Fort; forint (Hungarian currency unit)

Ft: *Folyoirat* (Hungarian—journal; review)

FT: Flying Tiger Lines (2-letter coding)

FT: *Financial Times* (London)

F de T: *Fulano de Tal* (Spanish—So-and-So)

fta: fluorescent treponemal antibody

FTA: Finnish Travel Association;

Free Trade Association; Future Teachers of America

FTAF: Flying Training Air Force

ftb: fails to break

ftbrg: footbridge

ftc: fast time constant; final turn collision

ft c: foot-candle

FTC: Federal Telecommunications Laboratories; Federal Trade Commission; Flight Test Center; Flying Training Command

FTCA: Federal Tort Claims Act

ft. catap.: fiat cataplasma (Latin —make a poultice)

FTCC: Flight Test Coordinating Committee

ft. cerat.: fiat ceratum (Latin —make a cerate)

ft. colly.: fiat collyrium (Latin —make an eyewash)

ftd: fails to drain

FTD: Field Training Detachment; Florists' Telegraph Delivery; Foreign Technology Division

ft di: flattening die

ftdr: friction-top drum

ft. emuls.: fiat emulsio (Latin- —make an emulsion)

ft. enem.: fiat enema (Latin —make an enema)

FTF: Flygtekniska Forsoksantalten (Aeronautical Research Institute of Sweden)

ftfet: four-terminal field-effect transistor

ftg: fitting; footing

ft. garg.: fiat gargarisma (Latin —make a gargle)

fth(m): fathom

ft/hr: feet per hour

fti: federal tax included; frequency time indicator; frequency time intensity

FTI: Facing Tile Institute; Federal Tax Included; Fellow of the Textile Institute

FTIMA: Federal Tobacco Inspectors Mutual Association

ft. infus.: fiat infusum (Latin —make an infusion)

ft. injec.: fiat injectio (Latin—make an injection)

ftk: forward track kill

ftl: faster than light

ft l: foot-lambert

FTL: Federal Telecommunications Laboratory; Flying Tiger Line

ft lb: foot-pound

ft-lbf: foot-pound force

ft. linim.: fiat linimentum (Latin —make a liniment)

ft. mas.: fiat massa (Latin—make a mass)

ft. mas. div. in pil.: fiat massa dividenda in pilulas (Latin-

make a mass and divide into pills)

ft md: flattening mandrel

ft/min: feet (foot) per minute

ft³/min: cubic feet per minute

ft. mist.: fiat mistura (Latin—make a mixture)

ftn: fortification

Ftn: Freetown

FTN: Facsimile Transmission Network

FTO: Fleet Torpedo Officer

ftp: final-turn pursuit (aircraft); folded, trimmed, and packed (books); full-time personnel (civil service)

FTP: Fleet Training Publication; Flight Test Program

ft-pdl: foot poundal

ft. pil.: fiat pilulae (Latin—make pills)

FTPS: Fellow of the Technical Publishing Society

ft. pulv.: fiat pulvis (Latin—make a powder)

ftr: fighter; fixed-transom; flat-tile roof

F Tr: flag tower

FTR: Final Technical Report; flag tower (chart and map designation); Flight Test Report; Fruehauf (stock exchange symbol); Functional Test Report; Functional Test Request

ftrac: full-tracked (vehicle)

FTRF: Freedom-to-Read Foundation

ft/s: feet (foot) per second

ft/s²: foot per second squared

ft³/s: cubic feet per second

FTS: Federal Telecommunications System; Flying Traffic Specialist; Flying Training School; Forged Tool Society; Funeral Telegraph Service

ft sec: foot second

ft. sol.: fiat solutio (Latin—make a solution)

ft. suppos.: fiat suppositorium (Latin—make a suppository)

ftt: full-time temporary (civil-service employee)

FTT: Fever Therapy Technician

fttr: fitter

ft & tw: combination flat top and typewriter (desk)

ftu: fuel tanking unit

Ftu: Freeman time unit

FTU: Field Torpedo Unit; First Training Unit

ft. ung.: fiat unguentum (Latin- —make an ointment)

FTV: Flight Test Vehicle

Ft W: Fort Worth

FTZ: Foreign Trade Zone

FTZB: Foreign Trade Zones Board

fu: Farmers Union

F-u: fuck you (underground slang—very insulting epithet)

FU: Fairfield University; Fisk University; Fordham University; Franklin University; Freie Universität (Berlin Free University); Fridnds University; Furman University

FUB: Freie Universität Berlin (Free University, Berlin)

fubar: fouled up beyond all recongition

fubb: fouled up beyond belief

FUC: Ferrocarriles Unidos de Yucatan (United Railroads of Yucatan)

FUDR: Failure and Usage Data Report

FUIB: Fire Underwriters Inspection Bureau

FULICO: Fidelity Union Life Insurance Company

fum: fuming

fumi: fumigant; fumigate; fumigation

fumtu: fouled up more than usual

fun.: funeral; funerary

func: function(al)

fund.: fundador (Spanish—founder)

FUND: International Monetary Fund

Fundador de Nueva Granada: (Spanish—Founder of New Granada)—Francisco de Paula Santander—founder of Colombia (Nueva Granada)

Fundador de la República: (Spanish—Founder of the Republic)—José Nuñez Cáceres —founder and first president of the Dominican Republic (Spanish Haiti)

fungi.: fungicide

FUNM: Fort Union National Monument

FUNNs: For Your Nieces and Nephews

fuo: fever (of) unknown origin

fup: fusion point

fuposat: follow-up on supply action taken

fur.: furlong

furl.: furlough

furlong: furrow long (one eighth mile or 220 yards—201.17 meters), originally the average length of a plowman's furrow

furn: furnace; furnish(es; ed; ing; ings); furniture

furngs: furnishings

furnit: furniture

furt: (German—ford)

fus: fuselage

FuSf: Fortsetzung und Schluss folgen (German—to be concluded in the next issue)

fut: future

FUTC: Fidelity Union Trust Company

fv: flush valve; forward visibility; fire vent

fv.: *folio verso* (Latin—back of the sheet)

FV: Falck's Flyvetjeneste (Copenhagen); fishing vessel; Fruit and Vegetable (US Department of Agriculture)

fvc: forced vital capacity

FVMMA: Floor and Vaccum Machinery Manufacturers Association

FVNM: Fort Vancouver National Monument

FVPA: Flat Veneer Products Association

FVPRA: Fruit and Vegetable Preservation Research Association

FVRDE: Fighting Vehicles Research and Development Establishment

fv's: fashion victims

f. vs.: *fiat venaesectio* (Latin—perform a venesection)

FVSC: Fort Valley State College

fw: fire wall; fixed wing; formula weight; fresh water

f & w: feed and water; feeding and watering

fw: Funk & Wagnalls

FW: Fairbanks Whitney (stock exchange symbol); FockeWulf; Fog Whistle; Fort Worth; Foster Wheeler

fwa: first word address; fluorescent whitening agent

FWA: Family Welfare Association; Federal Works Agency; French West Africa; Future Weapons Agency

FWAA: Football Writers Association of America

FWAS: Fort Wayne Art School

fwb: four-wheel brake; four-wheel braking; free-wheel bicycle; front-wheel bicycle; furnished with bed

FWB: Fort Worth Belt (railroad); Free-Will Baptists

FWC: Foster Wheeler Corporation

FW & C: Furness, Withy & Company

fwd: forward; forwarding; four-wheel drive; freshwater damage

F W & D: Fort Worth & Denver (railroad)

FwdBL: forward bomb line

fwdct: fresh water drain collecting tank

fwdg: forwarding

fwdr: forwarder

fwe: finished with engines

FWGE: Fort Worth Grain Exchange

FWHF: Federation of World Health Foundations

FWI: Federation of the West Indies; French West Indies

FWL: Foundation for World Literacy

FWO: Facilities Work Order; Fleet Wireless Officer

FWOA: Fort Worth Opera Association

fwop: furloughed without pay

FWP: Federal Writers' Project

FWPCA: Federal Water Pollution Control Administration

FWPO: Fort Wayne Philharmonic Orchestra

FWQA: Federal Water Quality Administration; Federal Water Quality Association

fwr: full-wave rectifier; full-wave reflector

FWRC: Federal Water Resources Council

fws: filter wedge spectrometer

F & WS: Fish and Wildlife Service

FWSO: Forth Worth Symphony Orchestra

FWSSUSA: Federation of Worker's Singing Societies of the U.S.A.

FWT: fair wear and tear

fwth: flush watertight hatch

FWWS: Fire-Weather Warning Service

Fwy: Freeway

fx: fixed; foreign exchange; foxed; fractured

Fx: fracture (bone)

FX: Foreign Exchange

F.X.: Francis Xavier

fxd: fixed; foxed

fxle: forecastle

fy (FY): fiscal year

Fy: Ferry

FY: fiscal year; Ferdinand (e) Ysabella

fyi: for your information

fyig: for your information and guidance

FYP: Five-Year Plan; Four-Year Plan; etc.

FYPB: Five-Year Planning Base (USA)

FYPP: Five-Year Procurement Program (USA)

fz: fuze (ordnance explosive device)

fz: *forzando* (Italian—accented strongly)

Fz: Fernández; Franz

FZ: Franc Zone; Free Zone; French Zone

FZIA: First Zen Institute of America

FZS: Fellow of the Zoological Society

FZSL: Fellow of the Zoological Society, London

G

g: gage; gender; gilbert; gold; gram; gravitational acceleration (symbol); great; green; grey; gross; gyromagnetic ratio (symbol); Lande factor (symbol)

g: acceleration of gravity (symbol); gloom (gloomy weather symbol)

g/: *giro* (Spanish—bank check)

G: conductance (symbol); control grid (symbol); Fraunhofer line caused by iron (symbol); gap; gear; German(ic); Germany;

Gibbs function (free energy symbol); glider; go; God (on Masonic emblems); Golf—code for letter G; good; Goodyear; gourde (Haitian unit of currency); government (broadcasting); Grace (steamship line); Green Line; Greene Line; Greenwich; Greyhound (bus line); guineas; gulden (Netherlands guilder); gulf; Gulf Oil (stock exchange symbol); Newtonian gravitation-

al constant (symbol); specific gravity (symbol)

G: Gade (Danish—Street); *Gasse* (German—Street); *Gata* (Swedish—Street); *Gate* (Norwegian —Street)

G-1: Army or Marine Corps personnel section; personnel officer

G-2: military intelligence section of Army or Marine Corps; military intelligence officer

G-3: operations and training section

of Army or Marine Corps; operations and training officer

G-4: logistics section of Army or Marine Corps; logistics officer

G-5: civil affairs section of Army; civil affairs officer

G₁₁: hexachlorophene (antibacterial agent)

ga: gage; gas amplification; gastric analysis; general average; glide angle; go ahead; ground to air

g/a: general average; ground-to-air

Ga: gallium; Georgia; Georgian; Ghana (tribe)

GA: Gage Man; Garrison Adjutant; General Agent; General Assembly (UN); Georgia (railroad); Glen Alden (stock exchange symbol); Gypsum Association

G-A: General Atomic (Division of General Dynamics)

GAA: Gaelic Athletic Association; Gay Activists Alliance

GAAC: Graphic Arts Advertisers Council

GAATV: Gemini-Atlas-Agena Target Vehicle

gab: gabardine; gabbing; gabble; gable

Gab: Gabon Republic (République Gabonaise); Gabriel

GABA: gamma-aminobutyric acid

Gabl: Gabriel

Gabriela Mistral: Lucila Godoy de Alcayaga

gac: grilled American cheese (sandwich)

GAC: General Acceptance Corporation; Geological Association of Canada; Goodyear Aircraft Corporation; Gustavus Adolphus College

g/a con: general average contribution

g/a dep: general average deposit

GADS: Goose Air Defense Sector

Gae: Gaelic

GAE: General American English

GAEC: Goodyear Aircraft and Engineering Corporation; Grumman Aircraft Engineering Corporation

Gael: Gaelic

gaf: General Aniline & Film Corporation (trademark)

GAFB: Goodfellow Air Force Base

GAFD: Guild of American Funeral Directors

gag.: gaging

g/a/g/: ground-air-ground

gai: guaranteed annual income

GAI: Government Affairs Institute

GAIA: Graphic Arts Information Association

gal: galileo (unit of acceleration); gallon (unit of capacity)

Gal: Epistle to the Galatians; Galicia; Galway

Gal: *General* (French—General)

GAL: Gdynia America Line; Guggenheim Aeronautical Laboratory; Guinea Airways

G A & L: General Aircraft and Leasing (Division of General Dynamics Corporation)

Galap: Galápagos Islands

gal cap: gallon capacity

GALCIT: Guggenheim Aeronautical Laboratory, California Institute of Technology

gall.: gallery

Gall: *Galleria* (Italian—gallery or tunnel)

Gallo-Rom: Gallo-Romance

gal per min: gallons per minute

gal(s): girl(s)

gals: gallons

galumphing: galloping and triumphing

galv: galvanic; galvanism; galvanize(d); galvanometer

Galv: Galveston

galv i: galvanized iron

galvnd: galvannealed

galvo(s): galvanometer(s)

Galw: Galway

gam: gammon (sailor's gossip; seamen's talkfest); gamut; guided-aircraft missile

Gam: Gamaliel; Gambia

GAM: Guest Aerovías México; Guided-Aircraft Missile

GAMA: Gas Appliance Manufacturers Association

GAMAA: Guitar and Accessories Manufacturers Association of America

Gamerco: (acronymic place-name —Gallup American Coal Company)—coal-mining town near Gallup in northwestern New Mexico .

GAMIS: Graphic Arts Marketing Information Service

GAMM: Gesellschaft für Angewante Mathematik und Mechanik

GAMMA: Guns and Magnetic Material Alarm (anti-hijacking device)

GAN: Generalized Activity Network

Gandhi: *Mahatma* (Hindustani—Great Souled)—Mohandas Karamchand Gandhi

gang.: ganglia; ganglion

Ganga: (Hindi or Sanskrit—Ganges)

ganzl: *gänzlich* (German—complete, entire)

GAO: General Accounting Office; General Administrative Order;

General American Oil (company); General American Overseas (corporation)

GAO: *Glavnaya Astronomicheskaya Observatoriya* (Russian —Main Astronomical Observatory)

gap.: guidance autopilot

GAP: Government Aircraft Plant; Great American Public; Great Atlantic & Pacific (Tea Company); Group for the Advancement of Psychiatry

gapa: ground-to-air pilotless aircraft

GAPL: Group Assembly Parts List

gar.: garage; garrison; guided aircraft rocket

GAR: Gioacchino Antonio Rossini; Grand Army of the Republic; Guided Aircraft Rocket; Gustavus Adolphus Rex (King Gustav II of Sweden)

garb.: garbage; green, amber, red, blue (airway priority color code)

garbd: garboard

garbz: *garbanzos* (Spanish—chickpeas)

GARC: Graphic Arts Research Center

G.Arch.: Graduate in Architecture

gard: gamma atomic radiation detector; garden; gardener; gardening; general address reading device; guard

GARD: Gamma Atomic Radiation Detector

gards: gardenias

garg.: *gargarisma* (Latin—gargle)

garioa: government and relief in occupied areas

GARP: Global Atmospheric Research Program

G.A.R.S.: Gustavus Adolphus Rex Sueciae (Gustavus Adolphus King of Sweden)

gar str: garboard strake

Gart: Garrett

GARUDA: Garuda Indonesian Airways

gas: gasoline

g-a s: general-adaptation syndrome

ga & s: general average and salvage

GAs: Gamblers Anonymous

GAS: Georgia Academy of Science; Ghana Academy of Sciences; Government of American Samoa

GASL: General Applied Science Laboratories

gaso: gasoline

gasp.: gravity-assisted space probe

GASP: Greater (Washington, D.C.) Alliance to Stop Pollution (air and water); Group Against Smog and Pollution

Gasparilla: (Spanish—Little Gaspar)—nickname of José Gaspar —pirate active along west coast of Florida around 1750

gast: gastric

Gast: Gaston

gastro: gastronomy

gastroc: gastrocnemius

gastroenterol: gastroenterology

gat: gatling gun; gun; revolver

gat: gata (Swedish—Street); (Dano-Norwegian—channel)

GAT: Georgetown Automatic Translation; Greenwich Apparent Time

gata: (Japanese—lake)

GATA: Graphic Arts Technical Association

gatac: general assessment tridimensional analog computer

GATB: General Aptitude Test Battery

GATE: Group to Advance Total Energy (American Gas Association)

GATF: Graphic Arts Technical Foundation

'gator(s): alligator(s)

GATT: General Agreement on Tariffs and Trade

GATX: General American Transportation Corporation (tank car marking)

gaw: guaranteed annual wage

gawa: (Japanese—river)

gawam: great American wife and mother

gawr: gross axle weight rating

Gay: Gaylord

gaz: gazette; gazetteer

GAZ: (Russian—*Gorki Avtomobilnii Zavod*)—Gorki Automobile Factory producing the Volga sedan-type auto

gb: gall bladder; glide bomb; goodbye; grid bearing; gun bed

g-b: goof-ball (barbiturate pill)

g/b: ground based

gB: greenish blue

Gb: gilbert

GB: General Board; General Bronze (corporation); Georges Bizet; Great Books; Great Britain; gunboat (naval symbol)

gba: give better address

GBBA: Glass Bottle Blowers Association

GBC: General Binding Corporation; Gibraltar Broadcasting Company; Greenland Base Command

GB & C: General Battery and Ceramic (corporation)

gb'd: goofballed (underground slang—drugged)

GBDC: Grand Bahama Development Company

gbe: gilt bevelled edge

GBF: Gakujitsu Bunken Fukyukai (Japanese Society of Scientific Documentation and Information); Great Books Foundation

GBG: General Baking (Stock exchange symbol)

gbh (GBH): gamma benzene hydrochloride

GBHC: Governor Bacon Health Center

GBI: Grand Bahama Island (tracking station)

GB & I: Great Britain and Ireland

g/bl: government bill of lading

GBL: Georgian Bay Line; government bill of lading

GBMA: Golf Ball Manufacturers Association

GBNE: Guild of British Newspaper Editors

GBNM: Glacier Bay National Monument

G-bomb: gravitational bomb

GBPA: Grand Bahama Port Authority

gbr: give better reference; gun, bomb, rocket

gbs: gall-bladder series

gb's: goofballs (barbiturates)

GBS: George Bernard Shaw; Guyana Broadcasting Service

GBSM: Guild of Better Shoe Manufacturers

GBSTC: General Beadle State Teachers College

GBV: Gusstahlwerk Bochumer Verrein (Krupp Steel)

GB & W: Green Bay & Western (railroad)

gc: gas check; gigacycle; glucocorticoid; gonorrhea case; great circle; grid course; ground control; guidance control; gun control

Gc: great tropic range

GC: Gallaudet College; Gannon College; Gaston College; Geneva College; Georgetown College; Gettysburg College; Glendale College; Glucocorticoid; Goddard College; Gordon College; Goshen College; Goucher College; Graceland College; Grambling College; Greensboro College; Greenville College; grid course (symbol); Grinnell College; Grover Cleveland; Guilford College; Gustave Charpentier

G.C.: gonorrhea case

gca (GCA): ground-controlled approach

GCA: Girls' Clubs of America; Green Coffee Association; Greet-

ing Card Association; Government Contract Committee; Ground Control Center

GCAHS: Guggenheim Center for Aviation Health and Safety

g cal: gram calorie

G-Cass: Gomes-Cásseres; Gomez-Cásseres

GCB: Glen Canyon Bridge

GCC: Grand Canyon College; Gulf Coast College

GCCC: Goshen County Community College

gcd: greatest common divisor

GCD: Grand Coulee Dam

GCE: Gas City Empire; General Certificate of Education; General College Entrance (diploma or examination)

gcf: greatest common factor

GCFI: Gulf and Caribbean Fisheries Institute

gcfr: gas-cooled fast reactor

GCGR: Giant's Castle Game Reserve (South Africa)

gci: gray cast iron; ground-controlled interception

GCI: Grand Canary Island (tracking station); ground-controlled interception

GCIA: Granite Cutters' International Association

GCIS: Ground Control Interception Squadron

GCJC: Gulf Coast Junior College

gcl (GCL): ground-controlled landing

GCL: Gulf Caribbean Lines

gcm: greatest common measure

GCM: General Court-Martial; Gian Carlo Menotti; Good Conduct Medal; Grand Cayman, Cayman Islands (airport)

GCMI: Glass Container Manufacturers Institute

GCNA: Guild of Carillonneurs in North America

GCNM: Grand Canyon National Monument

GCNP: Grand Canyon National Park (Arizona)

GCNRA: Glen Canyon National Recreation Area (Arizona and Utah)

GCO: Guidance Control Officer

GCPL: Glasgow Corporation Public Libraries

gcr (GCR): ground-controlled radar

g crg: gun carriage

GCRI: Gilette Company Research Institute

gcs: gate-controlled switch; gram-centimeter-second

gc/s: gigacycles per second

gc's: genetic girls (real girls)

Gc/s: gigacycle per second

GCS: Game Conservation Society
GCSCO: Göta Canal Steamship Company
gct: ground-control unit
GCT: General Classification Test; Glamorgan College of Technology; Greenwich Civil Time
GCTC: Green County Teachers College
GCTS: Ground Communication Tracking System
gcw: gross combination weight (of tractor and loaded trailer)
gd: good; good delivery; granddaughter; gravimetric density; ground; guard; guardian
g-d: god-damned
g/d: gallons per day
g & d: galvanized and dipped
gd: *gade* (Danish—street)
Gd: gadolinium
GD: General Discharge; General Dispensary; General Dynamics (corporation); George Dewey; Grand Duchy; Gudermannian or hyperbolic amplitude (symbol)
G-D: General Dynamics Corporation
G & D: Garcia & Diaz (steamship line)
GD: *Globe-Democrat*
gda: gun-defended area
GDA: General Dynamics Ardmore
GD/A: General Dynamics/Astronautics
gdc: geocentric dust cloud
GDC: General Dynamics Convair; Gesellschaft Deutscher Chemiker (Society of German Chemists)
GDCL: General Dynamics Canadair Limited
GD/Convair: General Dynamics/Convair
GD/D: General Dynamics/Daingerfield
gde: gilt deckle edging
Gde: gourde (Haitian monetary unit)
GDE: General Dynamics Electronics
GD/EB: General Dynamics/Electric Boat
GDED: General Dynamics Electro Dynamic
GD Fort Worth: General Dynamics Fort Worth
GDFW: General Dynamics Fort Worth
GDGA: General Dynamics General Atomic
gdh: growth and development hormone
GDHS: Ground Data Handling System
GDIFS: Gray and Ductile Iron Founders' Society

Gdk: Gdansk (Danzig)
Gdl: Guadalajara; Guadalajareños (inhabitants)
GDL: Grand-Duche de Luxembourg (Grand Duchy of Luxemburg); Guadalajara, Mexico (airport)
GDLC: General Dynamics Liquid Carbonic
gdling: good looking
GDMO: General Duty Medical Officer
GDMS: General Dynamics Material Service
GDNA: Gesellschaft Deutscher Naturforscher und Ärzte (Society of German Naturalists and Physicians)
gdnce: guidance
gdnr: gardener
Gdns: Gardens
gdp: gross domestic product; guanosine diphosphate; gun director pointer
GDP: General Dynamics Pomona; Guanosine diphosphate
GDP(D): General Dynamics Pomona (Daingerfield)
gdr: guard rail
GDR: German Democratic Republic
gds: goods
Gdsk: Gdansk (Danzig)
gdu: graphic display unit
Gdy: Gdynia
ge: gas ejection; gastroenterology; gilt edge(s); good evening; gyroscope error
Ge: German; Germanic; germanium; Germany
GE: General Electric; Great Exuma; Group Engineer
GEA: Gravure Engravers Association; Greater East Asia
GE-ANPD: General Electric Aircraft Nuclear Propulsion Development
gear.: gearing
geb: *geboren* (German—born); *gebunden* (German—bound)
GEB: General Education Board; Gerber Products (stock exchange symbol); Guiding Eyes for the Blind
GEBECOMA: Groupement Belge des Constructeurs de Matériel Aérospatial
gebel: (Arabic—mountain)
gebergte: (Dutch—mountain ranges)
Gebirge: (German—mountain range)
Gebr: *Gebroeders* (Dutch—brothers); *Gebrüder* (German—brothers)
gec: *gecartonneerd* (Dutch—bound

in boards)
GEC: General Electric Company
GED: General Educational Development (testing service)
GEDP: General Educational Development Program (USA)
gedr: *gedrukt* (Dutch—printed)
GEDT: General Educational Development Test
GEEIA: Ground Electronics Engineering Installation Agency
geek: geomagnetic electrokinetograph
Ge.Eng.: Geological Engineer
GEG: Spokane, Washington (airport)
gegr: *gegründet* (German—founded)
GEIA: Ground Equipment Electronics Installations Agency
geistl: *geistlich* (German—spiritual)
gek: geomagnetic electrokinetograph
gek: *gekürtz* (German—abbreviated)
gel: gelatine; gelatinous
GEL: General Electric Laboratory; Great Eastern Line
gelat: gelatinous
gel. quav.: *gelatina quavis* (Latin—in some jelly)
gem.: ground-effect machine; guidance evaluation missile
Gem: Gemini
GEM: Gas Equipment Manufacturers
Gemini: two-man spacecraft
gem's: ground-effect machines
Gemy: General Motors Corporation
gen: gender; genealogy; genera; general; generator; generic; genetic(s); genital; genitive; gentian; genus
Gen: General; Genoa; Genoese
Gen: *Genesis*
GEN: Oslo, Norway (Gardermoen Airport)
gen av: general average
genda: general data analysis and simulation
Gene: Eugene; Eugenia
geneal: genealogy
genet: genetic; geneticist; genetics
Genet: Janet Flanner's pen name
gen. et sp. nov.: *genus et species nova* (Latin—new genus and species)
Gen Hosp: General Hospital
genit: genitive
genl: general
Genl: General (Spanish—General)
Gen Mgr: General Manager
genn: *gennaio* (Italian—January)
gen. nov.: *genus novum* (Latin—new genus)
gen prac: general practice

gen proc: general procedure
gen pub: general public
genr: generate; generation; generator
genrl: general
Gensek: Generalnyi Sekretar (Russian—Secretary General)—leader of the secretariat of the Central Committee of the Communist Party—post held by Stalin
Gen Supt: General Superintendent
gent: gentleman
gents: gentlemen; gentlemen's
Geo: George
GEO: Georgetown, Guyana (Atkinson Field)
GEOC: General Estate and Orphan Chamber (trust company)
geod: geodesic; geodesist; geodesy; geodetic; geodynamic(s)
Geod. E.: Geodetic Engineer
geog: geographer; geographical; geography
geol: geologic; geological; geologist
Geol.E.: Geological Engineer
Geol Surv: Geological Survey
geom: gemoetry
geon (GEON): gyro-erected optical navigation
geoph: geophysics
geopol: geopolitical; geopolitics
Geor: Georgian
Georef: World Geographic Reference System
George Eliot: Mary Ann Evans Cross
George Orwell: Eric Blair
George Sand: Amandine Aurore Lucie Dupin (Baroness Dudevant)
Georges Simenon: (pen name—Georges Sim)
geos: generator, earth orbital scene; geodetic orbiting satellite
GEOS: Geodetic Orbiting Satellite
Geph: Gephyra
GEPI: Gestioni e Partecipazioni Industriali (Italian—Industrial Management and Participation)
ger: gerund; gerundial; gerundival; gerundive
Ger: German; Germanic; Germany
GER: Great Eastern Railway
Gerard de Nerval: (pseudonym —Gerard Labrunie)
ger grndng: gerund grinding (pedagogic pedantry)
geriat: geriatrics
Germ: Germinal (month in calendar of French Revolution)
german silver: 50% copper, 30% nickel, 20% zinc
germi: germicide
gerontol: gerontology

Gerry: Gerald; Gerard; Gerhard
Gersis: General Electric range safety instrumentation system
gert: graphical evaluation and review technique
Gert: Gertie; Gertrude
ges: gesetzlich (German—registered)
Ges: (German—G-flat); ***Gesellschaft*** (German—association; company; society)
GES: Great Eastern Shipping
GESCO: General Electric Supply Corporation
gest: gestorben (German—dead; deceased)
Gestapo: Geheime Staatspolizei (German—State Secret Police)
get.: ground-elapsed time
GET: Getty Oil (stock exchange symbol)
getlo: get locally
getma: get from local manufacturer; purchase for local manufacturer
getol: ground-effect takeoff and landing
gev: giga electron volt (10^9 electron volts)
gez: gezeichnet (German—signed)
GEZ: Gosudarstvennoe knigoisdatelstvo (Russian—State Publishing House)
gf: gap filler; generator field; girl friend; globular fibrous; glomerular filtrate; goldfield; ground fog; growth fraction; guiltfree
GF: General Fireproofing; General Foods; Georgia & Florida (railroad)
G & F: Georgia & Florida (railroad)
gfa: good fair average; gunfire area
GFA: Generale Française (de Construction) Automobile
gfae: government-furnished aerospace equipment
gfci: ground fault circuit interrupter
GFDL: Geophysical Fluid Dynamics Laboratory
gfe: government-furnished equipment
gff: granolithic finish floor
GFH: George Frideric Handel
Gfk: Gustafsvik
gfm: government-furnished materiel
GFMVT: General Foods Moisture Vapor Test
gfp: government-furnished property
gfr: gap-filled radar; glomerular filtration rate
GFR: German Federal Republic
gfrp: glass-fiber reinforced plastic
GFS: Girls Friendly Society
gfst: ground fuel start tank
gfu: glazed facing units

gfut: ground fuel ullage tank
GFWC: General Federation of Women's Clubs
gg: gamma globulin; gas generator; great gross
g-g: ground-to-ground
Gg: Georgian
G-G: Goodrich-Gulf (chemicals)
GGA: Girl Guides Association; Gulf General Atomic
GGAC: Gulf General Atomic Company (formerly General Atomic division of General Dynamics)
GGB: Golden Gate Bridge
GGB & HD: Golden Gate Bridge and Highway District
ggc: ground guidance computer
GGC: Golden Gate College
ggd: great granddaughter
gge: generalized glandular enlargement
g.g.g.: gummi guttae gambiae (Latin—gamboge)—cathartic
GGHNP: Golden Gate Highlands National Park (South Africa)
g gl: ground-glass
ggm (GGM): ground-to-ground missile
GGNRA: Golden Gate National Recreation Area (San Francisco)
Ggo: Gallego
GGOC: Goldovsky Grand Opera Company
g gr: great gross
GGR: Gambill Goose Refuge (Texas); Ground Gunnery Range
g-g's: go-go girls
GGS: Ground Guidance System
ggts: gravity-gradient test satellite
gh: grid heading; growth hormone; guardhouse
Gh: Ghana, Commonwealth of
GH: General Hospital; Grosvenor House
GH: Good Housekeeping
GHA: Greenwich Hour Angle
GHAA: Group Health Association of America
GhAF: Ghanian Air Force
GHANA: Ghana Airways
ghat: (Indian—mountain pass; river course)
ghats: (Indian—mountain ranges)
GHC: Grays Harbor College
GHDVHS: Grace H Dodge Vocational High School
ghe: ground handling equipment
G H & H: Galveston, Houston & Henderson (railroad)
Ghirlandaio: Domenico di Tommaso Bigordi
ghost.: global horizontal sounding technique
GHQ: General Headquarters
g/hr: gallons per hour
GHS: Galileo High School; Girls

High School
Ght: Ghent
ghubbet: (Arabic—bay)
GHz: gigahertz (gigacycle per second)
gi: galvanized iron; gastrointestinal; general issue; gill; globulin insulin; government issue; gross inventory
Gi: Giles; Guy
GI: Air Guinée; American Soldier (from *gi*—general issue or government issue); Gideons International; Gimbel Brothers (stock exchange symbol); Government of India; Gunner Instructor
gia: grant-in-aid (diplomatese—handout)
GIA: Garuda Indonesian Airways; Gemmological Institute of America; Goodwill Industries of America; Gregorian Institute of America; Gummed Industries Association
gib: guy in the back
Gib: Gibraltar; Gibraltarian
GIB: Gibraltar, British Crown Colony (airport)
GIBAIR: Gibraltar Airways
Gibfo: Gibraltar for orders
gibs: guy in the back seat
GIC: General Investment Corporation
GICA: Green Island Coral Atoll (Queensland)
gi'd: prepared for military-type inspection
Gid: Gideon
gidp: grounded into double plays
GIF: Rio de Janeiro, Brazil (Galeo Airport)
giga: 10^9
gigo: garbage in, garbage out (acronym describing a computer whose operation is suspect because input is suspect)
GIIS: Graduate Institute of International Studies (Geneva)
GIJ: Guild of Irish Journalists
Gil: Gilbert; Giles
Gilberts: Gilbert Islands
GIMPEX: Guyana Import-Export
GIMRADA: Geodesy, Intelligence and Mapping Research and Development Agency (US Army)
ging: gingival; gingivitis
gins: aborigine girls
gio: giovedi (Italian—Thursday)
GIO: Government Information Organization
g ion: gram ion
Giorgione: Giorgio Barbarelli
GIPR: Great Indian Peninsula Railway
giq: giant imperial quart (of beer)

gir: girder
GIRB: Georgia Inspection and Rating Bureau
GIRLS: Generalized Information Retrieval and Listing System
giro: autogiro
gis: gastrointestinal series
Gis: (German—G-sharp)
GI's: enlisted men; enlisted soldiers in the US Army
GIS: General Mills (stock exchange symbol)
Gisep: Giuseppe
GISS: Goddard Institute of Space Studies (NASA)
git: guitar
GIT: General Information Test; Georgia Institute of Technology
git (GIT): group insurance tour (travel plan)
Gita: Bhagavad-Gita
Gitmo: Guantánamo Naval Base (Guantánamo Bay, Cuba)
GIUK: Greenland, Iceland, United Kingdom
GIW: Gulf Intracoastal Waterway
gj: grapefruit juice
GJC: Gibbs Junior College
Gjn: Gijon
Gk: Greek
GKIAE: Gossurdarstveinny Komitet po Ispolzovaniyu Atomnoi Energi (Russian—State Committee for the Use of Atomic Energy)
GK & N: Guest, Keen & Nettleworth
gl: glass; glazed; gloss
g/l: grams per liter
Gl: Glagolitic; glucinium
Gl.: Gloria in excelsis Deo (Latin—Glory be to God in the highest)
GL: Germanischer Lloyd's (German ship classifier); Great Lakes (load line mark); Greek Line
G.L.: Graduate in Law
gla: gingiovolinguo—axial
GLA: General Laboratory Associates; Glasgow, Scotland (airport)
glac: glacial
Glad: Gladstone; Gladwin; Gladys
glads: gladiolas
Glam: Glamorganshire
Glamorgan: Glamorganshire
Glas: Glasgow; Glaswegian
GLASLA: Great Lakes—St. Lawrence Association
glasphalt: glass + asphalt (paving)
glass: silicon dioxide—SiO_2
glass.: glassware
glassie: glass playing marble
glauc: glaucoma
glb: glass block
GLB: Greater London Borough

(City of London)
GLBA: Great Lakes Booksellers' Association
glc: gas - liquid - chromatographic; global loran (navigation) chart(s)
GLC: Greater London Council; Great Lakes Carbon; Great Lakes Commission
GLCA: Great Lakes College Association
gld: guilder
Gld Cst: Gold Coast
GLe: Grand Larousse encyclopédie (French—Great Larousse Encyclopedia)
GLF: Gay Liberation Front
Glf Mex: Gulf of Mexico
Glf Str: Gulf Stream
GLHA: Great Lakes Harbor Association
gli: glider
GLI: General Time (stock exchange symbol); Great Lakes Institute (University of Toronto)
glina: (Russian—clay; mud)
glit: glittering
glitch: unexpected transient
GLLO: Great Lakes Licensed Officers' Organization
glm: graduated length method
glm: *grand livre du mois* (French —great book of the month)—best-seller
GLM: Gay Liberation Movement
GLMI: Great Lakes Maritime Institute
gln (GLN): glutamine (amino acid)
GLNTC: Great Lakes Naval Training Center
GLO: General Land Office; Goddard Launch Operations (NASA); Ground Liaison Office(r); Gunnery Liaison Office(r)
glob: globular; globule
globecomm: global communications
glock: glockenspiel
glomb: glide bomb
Glos: Gloucestershire
gloss.: glossary
Gloster: Gloucester
Glostr: Glostrup
glotrac: global tracking
glow.: gross liftoff weight
GLP: Great Lakes Pilot
GLPA: Great Lakes Pilotage Administration
glq: greater than lot quantities
Glr: Gloucester
Gls: Glasgow
GLS: Georgetown Law School; Graduate Library School (University of Chicago); Greene Line Steamers (Mississippi); Gypsy Lore Society
glt: gilt; guide light

glu: glutamic acid
Glubb Pasha: John Bagot Glubb
glv: globe valve
GLV: Gemini Launch Vehicle
GLW: Corning Glass Works (stock exchange symbol)
glwb: glazed wallboard
gly: glycerine; glycerol; glycogen
gly (GLY): glycine (amino acid)
glycerol: glycerine—$C_3H_5(OH)_3$
glyp: glyphography; glyptics; glyptography
GLZ: General Bronze Corporation (stock exchange symbol)
gm: general medicine; general mortgage; good morning; gram; guard mail; guided missile; mutual conductance (symbol)
g/m: gallons per minute
GM: General Manager; General Medicine; General Motors; Grand Master; Guided Missile; Gunner's Mate; Gustav Mahler
GM: metacentric height (symbol)
G & M: Globe and Mail (Toronto)
GMA: Gallery of Modern Art; Government Modification Authorization; Grocery Manufacturers of America
GMAA: Gold Mining Association of America
gmac: gaining major air command
GMAC: General Motors Acceptance Corporation
GMAIC: Guided Missile and Aerospace Intelligence Committee
GMAT: Greenwich Mean Astronomical Time
GMATS: General Motors Air Transport Section
gm-aw: gram atomic weight
gmb: good merchandise brand
GMB: Georg Morris Brandes (originally Cohen)
GMBE: Grand Master (of the Order of the) British Empire
GmbH: Gesellschaft mit beschränkter Haftung (German—incorporated, limited liability company)
gmbl: gimbal
gmc: gun motor carriage
Gmc: Germanic
GMC: General Medical Council; General Motors Corporation; George Mason College; Guggenheim Memorial Concerts; Guided Missile Command; Guided Missile Committee
g-m counter: Geiger-Müller counter for measuring cosmic rays and radioactivity
GMDRL: General Motors Defense Research Laboratories
G-men: FBI law-enforcement officers

g met: gun-metal
GMFC: General Mining and Finance Corporation
Gmh: Grangemouth
GM-H: General Motors-Holden (Australia)
GMI: General Motors Institute
GMIA: Gelatin Manufacturers Institute of America
gmk: grand master keyed
GML: Gold Mining Lease
gmldg: garnish molding
GMNNR: Glasson Moss National Nature Reserve (England)
GMNP: Guadalupe Mountains National Park (Texas)
Gmo: Guillermo (Spanish—William)
GM & O: Gulf, Mobile & Ohio (railroad)
g mol: g molecule
GMOO: Guided Missile Operations Office(r)
gmq: good merchantable quality
GMRD: Guided Missiles Range Division (Pan American World Airways)
gms: guidance monitor set
gm & s: general, medical, and surgical
Gms: Grimsby
GMST: General Military Subjects Test
GMT: General American Transportation (stock exchange symbol); Greenwich Mean Time; Greenwich Meridian Time
GMT: Geo Marine Technology
GMTC: General Motors Technical Center; Glutamate Manufacturers Technical Committee
GMTL: Goudy Memorial Typographic Laboratory (Newhouse Communications Center—Syracuse University)
gmts: guided missile test set
gmv: gram molecular volume
gn: general; green; golden number; good night; guinea (21 shillings); gun
g:n: glucose-nitrogen (ratio)
GN: Great Northern (railroad); great novel (in sense of great American novel as discussed in World-War-I days by e.e. cummings, John Dos Passos, Gilbert Seldes, and their generation of writers)
G.N.: Graduate Nurse
GN$_2$: gaseous nitrogen
GN$_2$ s/a: gaseous nitrogen storage area
GNAL: Georgia Nuclear Aircraft Laboratory
gn & c: guidance, navigation, and control

GNC: General Nursing Council
gnd: ground
gne: gross national effluent
gni (GNI): gross national income
gnl: general
GNL: Georgia Nuclear Laboratory
GNM: Ghana National Museum
GNN: Great Northern Nekoosa
g noz: grease nozzle
g np: gas, nonpersistent
gnp (GNP): gross national product
GNP: Glacier National Park (one in British Columbia and another in Montana); Gombe National Park (Tanzania); Gorongoza National Park (Mozambique); gross national product
GNP & BL: Great Northern Pacific & Burlington Lines (merger of Chicago, Burlington & Quincy; Great Northern; Northern Pacific; Pacific Coast Railroad; Spokane, Portland & Seattle Railway)
GNPC: Great Northern Paper Company
gnr: gunner; gunnery
GNR: Great Northern Railway
GNRA: Gateway National Recreation Area (New York City's designation by the Department of the Interior)
gnrl: general
gnry: gunnery
gns: guineas
Gns: Guernsey
gnte: gerente (Spanish—manager)
GNTO: Greek National Tourist Organization
Go: gadolinium; Gothic
G^o: Gonzalo (Spanish)
GO: General Office; general order(s); Gulf Oil (stock exchange symbol)
GO$_2$: gaseous oxygen
gob.: gobbledygook; good ordinary brand
GObC: Ground Observers Corps (Canada)
gobi: (Mongolian—desert)
gob^o: gobierno (Spanish—government)
Gob^r: Gobernador (Spanish—Governor)
GOC: General Officer Commanding; Ground Observer Corps; Gulf Oil Company
goco: government-owned contractor-operated
g.o.d.: good old days
goe: gas, oxygen, ether (mixture)
goe: (Japanese—pass)
gof: good old Friday
GOFAR: Global Ocean Floor Analysis and Research

gogo: government-operated government-owned

gogs: goggles

Goi: Goidelic

GoI: Government of Indonesia

GOI: Gallup Organization Incorporated

GOIN: *Gossudarstvienny Okeanograficheskiy Institut* (Russian—State Oceanography Institute)

gol: (Turkish—lake)

Golden Age: (see *Siglo de Oro*)

golf: (Dutch or German—bay; gulf)

Golf: code for letter G

golfe: (French—gulf)

golfo: (Italian, Portuguese, Spanish—gulf)

gölü: (Turkish—lake)

gom (GOM): government-owned material

Gom: God's own medicine (opiates)

G.O.M.: Grand Old Man (sobriquet for William Ewart Gladstone)

GOMA: Good Outdoor Manners Association

gon: *goniff* (Yiddish—thief)

gond(s): gondola[s; railroad car(s)] car[s])

gong: (Italian—village)

GONP: Gal Oya National Park (Ceylon)

Gonz: Gonzáles

Goo: Goole

GOO: Get Oil Out (of Santa Barbara, California)

Good Queen Bess: Queen Elizabeth I of England (1558 to 1603)

Good Richard: (pseudonym—Benjamin Franklin)

GOP: Grand Old Party (Republican)

GO & P: Griffith Observatory and Planetarium

Gor: Gorki

GOR: General Operational Requirements

gora: (Russian—mountain)

Gordie: Gordon

Gordon Pasha: Charles George Gordon

GORF: Goddard's Optical Research Facility

gorill(s): gorilla(s)

gorm: gormandize(r)

gorod: (Russian—town)

Gos: *Gossudarstvo* (Russian—State)

GOS: General Operating Specification(s); Global (weather) Observing Systems

GOSS: Ground Operational Support System

GOST: Goddard Satellite Tracking

goth.: gothic type

Goth.: Gothic

Got(h): Göteborg (Gothenburg)

Gött: Göttingen

Gouv: Gouverneur

gov: government

Gov: Governor

govg: governing

Gov Gen: Governor General

Gov Is: Governor's Island

govt: government

govtalk: government talk

gox: gaseous oxygen

gp: gas, persistent; general paralysis; general practice; general practitioner; general purpose; geographic position; grateful patient; gratitude patient; guinea pig; gun pointer

g-p: general purpose

GP: Gaspesian Park (Quebec); general public; Georgia-Pacific (stock-exchange symbol); Giacomo Puccini

G-P: Georgia-Pacific (forest products); Gunier-Preston zone

GP: *Generalpause* [German—general pause (musical term)]

gpa: grade-point average

gpad: gallons per acre per day

gpc: gallons per capita; general purpose computer; gypsum-plaster ceiling

GPC: Georgia Power Company; Gulf Park College

Gp Capt: Group Captain

gpcd: gallons per capita per day

GPCT: George Peabody College for Teachers

gpd: gallons per day

GPDS: General-Purpose Display System

GPE: General Precision Equipment

Gp.Eng.: Geophysical Engineer

gperf: ground passive electronic reconnaissance facility

GPES: Ground Proximity Extraction System

gpf: gasproof

Gp Fl: group flashing (light)

gpg: grains per gallon

gph: gallons per hour

G. Ph.: Graduate in Pharmacy

gpi: ground-position indicator

GPI: General Printing Ink

GPII: Geist Picture Interest Inventory

gpl : geographic position locator

GPL: General Precision Laboratory

gpm: gallons per minute

GPMS: Gross Performance Measuring System (USAF)

GPNITL: Great Plains National Instructional Television Library

GPO: General Post Office; Government Printing Office

Gp Occ: group occulting (light)

gps: gallons per second

g-p's: general practitioners (GPs)

Gps: general-parents motion pictures (for youngsters only with parent's consent)

GPU: General Postal Union

GPU: *Gosudarstvennoe Politicheskoe Upravlenie* (Russian—State Political Administration)—secret police—*Gay-Pay-Ooo*

gpw: gypsum-plaster wall

GPW: Geneva (Convention Relative to Treatment of) Prisoners of War

GPX: Greyhound Package Express

GQ: general quarters

GQNM: Gran Quivira National Monument

gr: gear; grab rod; grade; grain; gram; grammar; gross; group

Gr: Grashof number; Grecian; Greece; Greek

GR: B.F. Goodrich (stock exchange symbol); General Radio; General Reconnaissance; General Reserve; Georgius Rex (King George); Grand Recorder; Grasse River (railroad); Graves Registration; Group Report; Gunnery Range

GRA: Governmental Research Association; Grass Roots Association; W.R. Grace & Company (stock exchange symbol)

gr ab: grade ability

GRACE: Grace Agencies; Grace Chemicals; Grace Line; W.R. Grace and Company (stock exchange symbol); graphic arts composing equipment; group routing and exchange equipment (telephone)

grad: gradient; grading; graduate

grad: (Russian—town)

grad.: *graditim* (Latin—by degrees)

grad(s): gradient(s); graduate(s)

GRADS: Great Falls Air Defense Sector

gral: *general* (Spanish—general)

Gral: General (Spanish—General)

gram.: grammar; gramophone

'gram: cablegram; radiogram; telegram

gran: granite

Gran: Granada

Grandma Moses: Anne Mary Moses

grando: *grandioso* (Italian—grandiose)

Gran Libertador: (Spanish—Great Liberator—Simón Bolívar)

grape sugar: glucose ($C_6H_{12}O_6$)

graph.: graphology

gr ar: grinding arbor

gras: generally recognized as safe (beverage or food additives)

grat: graticule

grats: congratulations

grav: gravimetric; gravitation; gravity

grazo: *grazioso* (Italian—gracious)

grb: granolithic base

grbm (GRBM): global-range ballistic missile

Gr Br: Grande Bretagne (French —Great Britain); Great Britain

grd: grind; ground; ground detector; guard

Gr D: Grand Duchy

GRD: Geophysics Research Directorate

GRDC: Gulf Research and Development Company

Grdn: *The Guardian* (London and Manchester)

GRE: Graduate Record Examination; Guardian Royal Exchange

Great Compromiser: Henry Clay —U.S. Senator from Kentucky

Great Emancipator: Abraham Lincoln—sixteenth President of the United States and author of the *Emancipation Proclamation*

Great Engineer: Herbert Hoover— thirty-first President of the United States

Greatest Show on Earth: Barnum and Bailey—Ringling Brothers Circus

Great Society: (administration of Lyndon Baines Johnson—thirty-sixth President of the United States)

Great Stone Face: Daniel Webster

Green.: Greenland

green vitriol: copperas, ferrous sulfate (FeSO4 • 7H2O)

Grefco: General Refractories

Greg: Gregorian; Gregory

Greg⁰: Gregorio (Spanish—Gregory)

Gren: Grenada

Grepo: *Grenzpolizei* (German— border-control police)

GRF: Gerald R. Ford; Grassland Research Foundation; Gravity Research Foundation

GRFMA: Grand Rapids Furniture Market Association

gr fx: grinding fixture

GRI: Geothermal Resources International; Government of the Ryukyu Islands

GRIP: Grass Roots Improvement Program

grit.: gradual reduction in tensions

GRITS: Goddard Range Instrumentation Tracking System (NASA)

GRJC: Grand Rapids Junior College

Grk: Greenock

gr lp: ground lamp

grm: gram

grn: green

Gr.N.: Graduate Nurse

Grnld: Greenland

grnsh: greenish

grnt: guarantee

gro: gross

Gro: Guerrero

GRO: Greenwich Royal Observatory

groc: grocer(y)

grom: grommet

Gron: Groningen

groot: (Dutch—great)

gross: (German—great)

grosso: (Italian, Portuguese—big)

Grotius: Hugo de Groot

grp: ground relay panel

GRR: Grand Rapids, Michigan (airport)

grreg: graves registration

GrReg: graves registration

grs: grains; grass; greens

gr-s: government rubber plus styrene (buna-S synthetic rubber)

GRS: General Railway Signal; Graves Registration Service

grt: gross register(ed) tonnage (tons)

grtg: grating

GRU: *Glavnoye Razvedyvatelnoye Upravlenie* (Russian—Intelligence Directorate of the Red Army)—(*q.v.* VOT)

Grv: Grove

Grwd: Grunewald

gr wt: gross weight

gs: galvanized steel; gauss; german silver; glide slope; grandson; ground speed; guardship; guineas

g/s: gallons per second

Gs: general motion pictures (for the general public); Gomes

GS: General Schedule (civil service classification system); General Secretary; General Service; General Staff; General Support; Geochemical Society; Geological Survey; Gerontological Society; Gillette (stock exchange symbol); Girl Scouts; Grand Secretary; Gunnery School; Gunnery Sergeant

G-S: Gallard-Schlesinger

gsa: gross soluble antigen

GSA: Garden Seed Association; General Services Administration; Genetics Society of America; Geological Society of America; Girl Scouts of America; Gourd Society of America

G & SA: Gulf and South American (steamship line)

GSAI: General Services Administration Institute

gsb: gypsum sheathing board

GSBAA: General Service Board of Alcoholics Anonymous

gs bot: glass-stoppered bottle

gsbr: gravel-surface built-up roof

gsc: geodetic spacecraft

GSC: General Staff Corps; Geological Survey of Canada; Group Study Course

GSCBA: Georgia State College of Business Administration

GSCW: General Society of Colonial Wars

GSD: General Supply Depot

GSDFJ: Ground Self-Defense Force Japan

GSDNM: Great Sand Dunes National Monument

gse (GSE): ground-service equipment; ground-support equipment

GSE: Graduate School of Education (Harvard University)

GSED: Ground Support Equipment Division (USN)

GSF: General Support Force (USAF)

GSFC: Goddard Space Flight Center

GSFLT: Graduate School Foreign Language Test

gsfu: glazed structural facing units

gshr: grand-slam home run(s)

gshv: globe stop hose valve

gsi: ground speed indicator

GSI: General Safety Inspection; General Safety Inspector; General Service Infantry; General Steel Industries; Geological Survey of Israel; Geophysical Services International; Government Source Inspection

G & SI: Gulf and Ship Island (railroad)

g sil: german silver

gskt: gasket

GSL: Geological Society of London

GS & LA: Guam Savings and Loan Association

gslcv: globe stop lift check valve

GSM: Guildhall School of Music

GSMD: Guildhall School of Music and Drama

GSMNP: Great Smoky Mountains National Park (Tennessee and North Carolina)

GSNC: General Steam Navigation Company

GSNWR: Great Swamp National Wildlife Refuge (New Jersey)

GSO: General Staff Officer; Girls Service Organization; Greensboro, North Carolina (airport);

Ground Safety Officer
GSPA: Gulfport State Port Authority
gsr: galvanic skin reflex; galvanic skin response
GSRI: Gulf South Research Institute
gsrv: globe stop radiator valve
GSS: General Service School; General Supply Schedule; Geo-Stationary Satellite; Gilbert and Sullivan Society; Global Surveillance System
GSSF: General Supply Stock Fund
GSSH: Grand Street Settlement House
GST: Greenwich Sidereal Time; Guamanian Standard Time
GSTC: Gorham State Teachers College
G-string: capital-G-shaped string-like genital covering worn by exotic entertainers
gsu: glazed structural units
GSU: General Service Unit; Gulf States Untilities
gsub: glazed structural unit base
g-suit: antigravity suit worn during supersonic flight
GSUSA: Girl Scouts of the USA
gsv: globe stop valve
GSV: Guided Space Vehicle
gsw: gunshot wound
GSW: Fort Worth, Texas (Greater Southwest International Airport)
GSW 1812: General Society of the War of 1812
gt: gastight; gilt top; grease trap; great; gross tonnage; gross ton(s); ground transmit
g/t: granulation time; granulation tissue
gt: gate (Norwegian—street)
gt.: gutta (Latin—drop)
GT: Good Templar; Goodyear Tire & Rubber (stock exchange symbol); Grand Tiler; Gran Turismo; Grupo de Transportes (Transport Group)
GT: Gran Turismo (automobile)
gta: graphic training aid
gtc: gain time control; good till cancelled
GTC: Guam Territorial College; Gulf Transport Company (railroad)
GTCs: Government Training Centres (UK)
gtd: geometrical theory of diffraction; guaranteed
GTDS: Goddard Trajectory Determination System (NASA)
gte: gilt top edge
gte: gerente (Spanish—manager)
GT & E: General Telephone and Electronics (Corporation)

GT & EA: Georgia Teachers and Education Association
GT & EL: General Telephone and Electronics Laboratories
gtf: glucose tolerance factor
GTF: Great Falls, Montana (airport)
gth: go to hell
GTI: Grand Turk Island (tracking station)
GTIL: Government Technical Institute Library
GTIO: German Tourist Information Office
GTL: Glass Technology Laboratories
gtm: good this month
Gtmo: Guantanamo Bay
GTNP: Grand Teton National Park (Wyoming)
gto: gate turnoff
Gto: Gunajuato
GTO: Gran Turismo Omologato [hard-top type of high-performance Pontiac-Tempest auto certified (*omologato*) to enter Gran Turismo automobile race]
gtol: ground takeoff and landing
gtr: gantry test rack
GTR: Grand Trunk Railway
Gtr Ant: Greater Antilles
Gts: Gateshead
GTS: gas turbine vessel (3-letter code); General Telephone System
gtss: gas turbine self-contained starter
gtt.: guttae (Latin—drops)
gtT: gone to Texas (one jump ahead of the sheriff)
gtv: gate valve
gtw: good this week
GTW: Grand Trunk Western (railroad)
gty: gritty
Gtz: Galatz
gu: gastric ulcer; genitourinary; glycogenic unit
Gu: Gujarat; Gujarati
GU: genito-urinary; Georgetown University; Gonzaga University
GUA: Guatemala City, Guatemala (airport)
Guad: Guadeloupe
Guadal: Guadalajara
Guam ST: Guamanian Standard Time
'Guana: Iguana Island, British Virgin Islands
guar: guarantee
Guar: Guarani (Brazil)
GUARD: Government Employees United Against Discrimination
GUBC: Guyana United Broadcasting Company (Radio Demerara)
Guat: Guatemala; Guatemalan

Guay: Guayaquil
guba: (Russian—bay; gulf)
Gui: Guinea
Gui Cur: Guinea Current
guid: guidance
guide.: guidance for users of integrated data equipment
Guillo: Guillermo (Spanish—William)
Guip: Guipuzcoa
Guj: Gujarat; Gujarati
GULAG: Chief Administration of Corrective Labor Camps, Prisons, Labor, and Special Settlements of the Soviet Secret Police (*q.v.* VOT)
GULC: Georgetown University Law Center
GULF: Gays United for Liberty and Freedom (street-people subculture society)
GUM: Gosudarstvennoe Universalny Magasin (Russian—State Universal Store); Guam (airport)
gun.: guncotton; guncrete; gunnery; gunpowder
gun: gunung (Malay—mountain)
gun'l: gunwale
Gun Sgt: Gunnery Sergeant
gunto: (Japanese—archipelago)
gunung: (Malay—mountain)
gup: guppy
guppy.: greater underwater propulsive-powered (guppy-shaped) submarine
gups: guppies
GURC: Gulf Universities Research Corporation
Gus: August; Augustus; Gustaf; Gustave; Gustavus
GUS: Globe Universal Services; Great Universal Stores
Gussie: Augusta; Augustina; Augustine
Gussies: Great Universal Stores
gut.: gutter
Gutenberg: Johannes Gensfleisch (German—John Gooseflesh)— the inventor of movable type was probably of Judaic origin as Teutonic princes liked to name their Jewish subjects as they seemed to see them
GUTS: Georgians Unwilling to Surrender
guttat.: guttatim (Latin—drop by drop)
GuV: Gerecht und Volkommen (German—correct and complete)
Guy: Guido
Guybau: Guyana Bauxite
gv: gate valve; gentian violet; gravimetric volume; grid variation; ground visibility

GV: Giuseppe Verdi; Göta Verken (steel company); grid variation
gva: general visceral afferent
GVA: Geneva, Switzerland (airport)
GVC: Grand View College
gve: general visceral efferent
GVF: Grazhodanskii Vozdushnyi Flot (Russian—Civil Air Fleet)
gvhd: graft versus host disease(s)
gvhr: graft versus host reaction(s)
GVI: Gas Vent Institute
GVL: Global Van Lines
GVP: General Vice President
GVP: Gereformeerd Politiek Verbond (Dutch—Reformed Political Union)
GVS: Government Vehicle Service
gvty: gingivectomy
gvw: gross vehicle weight
gw: guerrilla warfare
GW: George Washington; Great Western (savings)
G-W: Globe-Wernicke
GWA: Girl Watchers of America
GWB: George Washington Bridge
GWCHS: George Washington Carver High School
GWCM: George Washington Carver Museum
Gwen: Gwendolyn

GWHNWR: Great White Heron National Wildlife Refuge (Florida)
GWHS: George Washington High School; George Westinghouse High School
GWI: Grinding Wheel Institute; Ground Water Institute
G'wich Village: Greenwich Village
GWMNP: George Washington Memorial National Parkway
GWOA: Guerrilla Warfare Operational Area
gwp (GWP): gross world product
GWP: Government White Paper
GWR: General War Reserves; Great Western Railway
GWRI: Ground Water Resources Institute
GWS: Geneva (Convention for the Amelioration of the) Wounded and Sick (in Armed Forces in the Field); George Washington School; Gir Wildlife Sanctuary (India)
gwt: glazed wall tile
GWTA: Gift Wrappings and Tyings Association
GWU: George Washington University
GWVA: Great War Veterans As-

sociation
gxmtr: guidance transmitter
gy: gray; gunnery, gyro; gyrocar; gyrocompass; gyrodyne; gyroscope
gY: greenish yellow
GYE: Guayaquil, Ecuador (airport)
gym: gymnasium; gymnastics
GYM: General Yard Master; Guaymas, Mexico (tracking station)
gyn: gynecology
G.Y.N.: gynecologist
gynecol: gynecology
gyp: gypsum; gypsy; cheat or swindle (slang)
GYP: Guild of Young Printers
gypsum: calcium sulfate ($CaSO_4 \cdot 2H_2O$)
gyro: gyrocompass; gyroplane; gyroscope
gyrocop: gyrocopter
GYS Co: Great Yarmouth Shipping Company
gywp: gee you're wonderful, professor
gz: ground zero
Gz: Gomez
GZn: grid azimuth
GZT: Greenwich Zone Time

H

h: hard; hardening; hardness; hazy; hecto; height; hit(s); hour(s); hundred(s); husband; hydrant; hydrodynamic head (symbol); hydrolysis; Planck's constant (symbol); Planck's element of action (symbol)
h: altitude (symbol); atmospheric head (symbol)
(h): per hypodermic
H: amateur broadcasting (symbol); ceiling (symbol); Fraunhofer line produced by calcium (symbol); Hamiltonian function (symbol); hard; hardness; hatch; headlines; heat; heater; helicopter; henry; heroin (drug-user's abbreviation); Hindu; Hinduism; horizontal component of the earth's magnetism (symbol); hot; Hotel—code for letter H; humidity; hydrogen; hyperopia; intensity of magnetic field (symbol); maximum altitude (symbol); McDonnell Aviation; Min-

neapolis-Honeywell(trademark); very hazy (symbol)
H: hacienda (Spanish—customs service; treasury); *haut* (French —up); *heet* (Dutch—hot); *Herren* (German or Swedish—gentlemen); *herrer* (Norwegian—gentlemen); *het* (Norwegian—hot); *hinaus* (German—out); *hombres* (Spanish—men); *Hoyre* (Norwegian — Right) — Conservative Party
H¹: protium
H¹⁺: proton
H24: hard rolled and partially annealed (half hard)
H₂O: water
H₂O₂: hydrogen peroxide
H₂SO₄: sulfuric acid
H³: tritium
H₃BO₃: boric acid
ha: hectare; high altitude; high angle; home address; hour angle; hour aspect
h.a.: *hoc anno* (Latin—in this

year)
Ha: hahnium (element 105); Haiti(an)
Ha: (German—B-sharp)
HA: Hawaiian Airlines; Headquarters Administration; Heavy Artillery; Horse Artillery; Hospital Apprentice
H-A: Hautes-Alpes
H/A: Havre-Antwerp (range of ports)
haa: heavy antiaircraft artillery
HAA: Helicopter Association of America; Hotel Accountants Association
HAAC: Harper Adams Agricultural College
HAAFE: Hawaiian Army and Air Force Exchange
haandb: haandbog (Dano-Norwegian—handbook)
haatc: high altitude air traffic control
haaw: heavy anti-tank assault weapon

hab: high-altitude bombing; habitat; habitation
Hab: Habana (Spanish—Havana); The Book of Habakkuk
HAB: Hazards Analysis Board (USAF)
habit.: habitat (Latin—it inhabits)
HAC: Hines Administrative Center; Honourable Artillery Company; Hughes Aircraft Company
HACC: Harrisburg Area Community College
hack: hackney coach; hackney horse; taxicab
had.: heat-actuated device (thermostat); hereinafter described
HADA: Hawaiian Defense Area
HADC: Holloman Air Development Center
HADES: Hypersonic Air Data Entry System
HADIZ: Hawaiian Air Defense Identification Zone
hadn't: had not
hads: hypersonic air data sensor
Haeck: Ernst Heinrich Haeckel; Haeckelian; Haeckelism
haf: high-abrasion furnace; high-altitude fluorescence
haf: (Swedish—sea)
HAF: Hebrew Arts Foundation; Helms Athletic Foundation; Helvetia-America Federation
Hafen: (German—harbor; haven)
HAFMED: Headquarters—Allied Forces Mediterranean
HAFO: Home Accounting and Finance Office (USAF)
HAFTB: Holloman Air Force Test Base
Hag: The Book of Haggai; The Hague
HAG: Hardware Analysis Group
hagiol: hagiology
HAI: Hospital Audiences Incorporated
HAIL: Hague Academy of International Law
H&AIns: Health and Accident Insurance
hairdrsr: hairdresser
hairies: long-haired hippies
HAJ: Hanover, Germany (airport)
Hak: Hakka
HAKASH: Hayl Kashish (Hebrew-Army of Elders)—Israel's senior-citizen corps
Hak Soc: Hakluyt Society
hal: halogen
Hal: Halensee; Harold
HAL: Hamburg-Amerika Linie (Hamburg-America Line); Hamburg-Atlantic Line; Hawaiian Airlines
Halbinsel: (German—half island; peninsula)

Halifax: (named for the second Earl of Halifax)
halluc: hallucination
halo.: high-altitude low opening
Hal Orch: Hallé Orchestra
ham.: hardware-associated memory
Ham: Hamburg; Hamilton; Hamitic; Hamlet; Hammerfest
HAM: Hamburg, Germany (airport)
Hamb: Hamburg
Haml: Hamlet, Prince of Denmark
hamlet: ham omelet
hamletom: ham, lettuce, and tomato (sandwich)
hammada: (Arabic—rocky plateau)
hamn: (Swedish—harbor)
Hamp: Hampton Roads
HAMTC: Hanford Atomic Metal Trades Council
hamwich: ham sandwich
Han: Handel Society
hand.: handling
Handl: Handlingar (Swedish—transactions)
hane: high-altitude nuclear effects
Hank: Henry
hanki: handkerchief
Hans: Johann(es)
Hans Fallada: (pseudonym—Rudolf Ditzen)
han't: has not; have not (British contraction)
hanto: (Japanese—peninsula)
Hants: Hampshire
Hanuk: Hanukkah (Hebrew—Feast of Lights)
HAO: High Altitude Observatory
hap: happening
HAPAG: Hamburg-American Line
hapdar: hardpoint demonstration array radar
ha'penny: halfpenny
ha'p'orth: halfpennyworth
har: harbor; harmonic
Har: Harbin; Harold
HAR: Harrisburg, Pennsylvania (airport)
HARAO: Hartford Aircraft Reactor Area Office
harb: harbor
Harbrace: Harcourt Brace Jovanovich
harcft: harbor craft
hard.: hardware
harm.: harmonic; harmony
harn: harness
harn lthr: harness leather
harp.: harpoon; harpsichord; harpsichordist; high-altitude relay point
Harp: Halpern's anti-radar point
HARP: Honeywell Acoustic Research Program
harps.: harpsichord
Harry: Harold; Henry

Harry Golden: Herschel Goldhirsch
Hart: Hartford
Hart Sym Orch: Hartford Symphony Orchestra
Harv: Harvard; Harvey
has.: high-altitude sample
Has: Haselhorst
HAS: Helicopter Air Service
HASC: House (of Representatives) Armed Services Committee
HASCO: Haitian-American Sugar Company
hash.: hashish
Hashbury: Haight-Ashbury (district of San Francisco)
Hasid: Hasidim (Hebrew—godly pious people)
HASL: Health and Safety Laboratory (Atomic Energy Commission)
hasn't: has not
HASP: Hawaiian Armed Services Police
hasr: high-altitude sounding rocket
hast: high-altitude supersonic target
hasvr: high-altitude space-velocity radar
hato: handling tool
Hattie: Harriet
Hau: Hausa
haus(en): [German—house(s) as in Oberhausen, Rheinhausen, Schaffhausen]
haust.: haustus (Latin—a draught)
haut: (French—high; upper)
hav: haversine
HAV: Havana, Cuba (airport)
HAVEN: Help Addicts Voluntarily End Narcotics
haven't: have not
havn: (Dano-Norwegian—harbor; port)
havoc.: histogram average ogive calculator
havre: (French—harbor; port)
Haw: Hawaii; Hawaiian (unauthorized abbreviations)
HAW: Kauai, Hawaii (tracking station)
HAWE: Honorary Association for Women in Education
hawk. (HAWK): homing-all-the-way kill (missile)
Haw'n: Hawaiian
hax: hrir/apt interface (high-resolution infrared radiometer/ automatic picture transmission)
haystaq: have you stored answers to questions?
haz: hazard; hazardous
hb: halfback; halfbound; hard black; heavy barrel; heavy bombardment; heavy bombing; hemoglobin; homing beacon; horizontal bands; horizontal bombing; hose bib; human being

h/b: handbook
Hb: Hemoglobin
HB: Hawthorn Books; Hector Berlioz; High Bridge
HB: Hindi Bharat (Hindustani—Republic of India)
Hba: Habana (Spanish—Havana)
HBA: Hoist Builders Association; Hollywood Bowl Association; Honest Ballot Association
H-bar: capital-H-shaped bar
HBAVS: Human Betterment Association for Voluntary Sterilization
HBC: Hudson's Bay Company
hbd: has been drinking; hereinbefore described
hbe: hard-boiled egg (s)
H-beam: capital H-shaped beam
Hbf: Hauptbahnhof (German—depot; main station)
Hbg: Hamburg; Harrisburg
HBG: Huntington Botanical Gardens
HBJ: Harcourt Brace Jovanovich
hbk: hollow back (lumber)
Hbk: Hoboken
HB & K: Humboldt, Bonpland, and Kunth (botanists)
HBM: His (Her) Britannic Majesty
HBNNR: Hickling Broad National Nature Reserve (England)
HBNWR: Holla Bend National Wildlife Refuge (Arkansas)
H-bomb: hydrogen bomb
hbp: high blood pressure; hit by pitcher (baseball)
Hbr: Harbor
HBR: Hudson Bay Railway
HBR: Harvard Business Review
HBS: Harvard Business School; Hawaiian Botanical Society; Hope Botanic Gardens
Hbt: Hobart
HB & T: Houston Belt and Terminal (railroad)
H&BV: Houston and Brazos Valley (railroad)
hc: hand control; heating cabinet; hexachlorethane; high-capacity; high carbon; screening smoke
h/c: held covered
h & c: heroin + cocaine; hot and cold; (running water)
h.c.: hac nocte (Latin—tonight); *honoris causa* (Latin—out of respect for); *hors commerce* (French—not for sale; privately printed)
Hc: computed altitude
HC: Hagerstown College; Hamilton College; Hamline College; Hanover College; Harding College; Harpur College; Hartford College; Hartnell College; Hartwick College; Hastings College; Ha-

verford College; Heidelberg College; Helicopter Council; Hendrix College; Hershey College; Hesston College; Hillsdale College; Hiram College; Hood College; Hope College; Hospital Corps; House of Commons; Howard College; Humphreys College; Hunter College; Huntingdon College; Huntington College; Huron College; Hussan College; Hutchinson College
H.C.: High Commission
H-C: Harbison-Carborundum
HC: Hartford Courant
H of C: House of Commons
hca: held by civil authorities
HCA: High Conductivity Association; Hobby Clubs of America; Hotel Corporation of America; Hunting-Clan Air Transport
hcap: handicap
H-caps: heroin capsules
hcc: hydraulic cement concrete
HCC: Hebrew Culture Council; Holyoke Community College
hcd: high current density
hce: human-caused error
hcf: height-correction factor; highest common factor; hundred cubic feet
HCF: Hungarian Cultural Foundation
hcg: horizontal location of center of gravity; human chorionic gonadotropin pregnancy test
HCH: Herbert Clark Hoover
HCHI: Hand Chain Hoist Institute
HCIL: Hague Conference on International Law
HCJ: High Court of Justice
HCJC: Howard County Junior College
hcl: high cost of living; horizontal center line
h cl: hanging closet
HCl: hydrochloric acid (muriatic acid)
HCL: Hod Carriers, Building and Common Laborers (union)
HCM: Ho Chi Minh (Chinese—He Who Shines)
HCMW: Hatters, Cap and Millinery Workers (union)
hcn: hydrocyanic acid
HCO: Harvard College Observatory
hcp: handicap; hexachlorophene
HCP: Honors Cooperative Program
HCPNI: Hardware Cloth and Poultry Netting Institute
hcptr: helicopter
HCRAO: Hat Creek Radio Astronomy Observatory (University of California)
hcrw: hot and cold running water

hcs: high-carbon steel
hc's: hard cover books
HCS: Hallé Concerts Society; Harvey Cushing Society; Home Civil Service
HCSA: House (of Representatives) Committee on Space and Astronautics
hcsht: high-carbon steel heat treated
hct: hematocrit
HCT: Huddersfield College of Technology
hcu: homing comparator unit; hydraulic cycling unit
hd: hard-drawn; head; hearing distance; high density; hourly difference; hurricane deck
h-d: high-density
h/d: holddown
h.d.: hora decubitus (Latin—at bedtime)
Hd: Head
HD: Hansen's Disease (leprosy); Harbor Defense; Harbor Drive; Historical Division; Home Defense; Honorable Discharge; Hoover Dam
H.D.: Hilda Doolittle
H/D: Havre-Dunkirk (range of ports)
H & D: Hurter & Driffield (photo emulsion speed)
HDA: High Duty Alloys
hdatz: high-density air traffic zone
hdbk: handbook
hdc: holder in due course
HDC: Housing Development Corporation
HD Clinic: Hansen's Disease Clinic (for lepers)
hd cr: hard chromium
hdd: heavy-duty detergent
HDD: Higher Dental Diploma
hddr: high-density digital recording
HDDS: High-Density Data System
hded: heavy-duty enzyme detergent
hdg: heading
HDHD: Hawaiian District Harbors Division
HDI: Humane Development Institute
hdk: husbands don't know
h dk: hurricane deck
hdkf: handkerchief
hdl: handle
HDL: Harry Diamond Laboratory (US Army Diamond Ordnance Fuze Laboratory)
hdlg: handling
hdls: headless
hdlw: hearing distance, watch at left ear
hdm: high-duty metal
hdmr: high-density moderated reactor

hdn: harden
H Doc: House Document
hdpe: high-density polyethylene
hdqrs: headquarters
hdr: handrail
HDRSS: High-Data-Rate Storage System(s)
hdrw: hearing distance, watch at right ear
hds: hydrodesulfurization
HDS: Hospital Discharge Survey
hdsp: hardship
HDST: Hawaiian Daylight Saving Time
HDT: Henry David Thoreau
HDTMA: Heavy-Duty Truck Manufacturers Association
HDTS: Harbor Drive Test Site (Convair Ramp)
hdw: hardware
hdw c: hardware cloth (wire screen)
hdwd: hardwood
hdwe: hardware
hd whl: hand wheel
he.: heat engine; heavy enamel; height of eye; high explosive; hub end; human enteric
h&e: hemotoxylin and eosin; heredity and environment
h.e.: *hic est* (Latin—this is)
He: Hebraic; Hebrew; helium; Hertz
HE: high explosive; His Eminence; His Excellency; Hollis & Eastern (railroad); Human Engineering; Hydraulics Engineer(ing)
H.E.: His Eminence; His Excellency
heaa: high-explosive anti-aircraft (shell)
heaf: heavy end aviation fuel
HEAO: High-Energy Astronomical Observatory
heap.: high-explosive armor-piercing (shell)
heat.: heating; high-explosive anti-tank (projectile)
Heb: Epistle of Paul the Apostle to the Hebrews; Hebraic; Hebrew
hebc: heavy enamel bonded single cotton
hebd: hebdomadal (weekly)
hebdom.: *hebdomas* (Latin—week)
hebdp: heavy enamel bonded double paper
hebds: heavy enamel bonded double silk
Hebr: Hebrides
hec: heavy-enamel single-cotton (insulation)
HECO: Hydro-Electric Commission of Ontario
hect: hectare; hectoliter
Hect: Hector
hecto: 10^2
hectog: hectogram

hectol: hectoliter
hectom: hectometer
hed: horizontal electric dipole
he'd: he had; he would
HED: *Haut-Einheits Dosis* (German—unit skin dose)—X-rays
HEDCOM: Headquarters Command
hed sked: headline schedule
hedsv: heavy-enamel double-silk varnish (insulation)
heent: head, ears, eyes, nose, throat
hef: heifer; high-energy fuel
HEF: High-Energy Fuel
heg: heavy-enamel single-glass (insulation)
HEH: Her (His) Exalted Highness
HEHF: Hanford Environmental Health Foundation (AEC)
HEHL: Henry E. Huntington Library
hei: high-explosive incendiary
HEI: *H/F Eimiskipafelag Islands* (Icelandic Steamship Company)
HEIAS: Human Engineering Information and Analysis Service (Tufts U)
Heide: Adelaide
Heidel: Heidelberg
Hein: Heinersdorf
heit: high-explosive incendiary with tracer
hek: heavy-enamel single-cellophane (insulation)
hel: helicopter
Hel: Helen; Helena; Helvetia (Switzerland)
HEL: Hartford Electric Light; Helsinki, Finland (airport)
heli: helicopter; heliport
helio: heliochrome; heliodon; heliodor; helioelectric; helioengraving; heliogram; heliograph; heliogravure; heliology; heliostat; heliotherapy; heliotrope; heliotype
helipad: helicopter landing pad
Hell: Hellerup
HELL: Higher Education Learning Laboratory
he'll: he will
Hellen: Hellenic; Hellenism; Hellenistic
helminthol: helminthology
helo: heliport
HELP: Helicopter Electronic Landing Path; Help Establish Lasting Peace; Highway Emergency Locating Plan
HELPR: Handbook of Electronic Parts Reliability
hel rec: health record
Hel San: *Helsingin Sanomat* (Helsinki's News)
hem.: hemoglobin; hemorrhage; hemorrhoid

hem: (Swedish—hamlet)
Hem: Ernest Hemingway
hematol: hematology
hemi engine: hemispherical combustion chamber engine
hemolysis: hemocytolysis
Hen: Henrietta; Henry
Hence: Henderson
Hen V: *King Henry V*
Hen VIII: *King Henry VIII*
Henk: Hendrik
Henriqz: Henriquez
Henry the K: Henry Kissinger
heos (HEOS): high eccentric orbiting satellite
hep: high-energy phosphate; high-explosive plastic
HEP: Have Error-free Product
HEPC: Hydro-Electric Power Commission
her.: heraldry
hera: high explosive rocket assisted
herb.: herbarium
Herb: Herbert
Herblock: Herbert Lawrence Block
Herdez: (Spanish contraction—Hernandez)
herdr: *herdruk(ken)* [Dutch—reprint(s)]
hered: heredity
hereds: *herederos* (Spanish—heirs)
Heref: Herefordshire
Herefs: Herefordshire
here's: here is
herf: high-energy rate forging
herfs: high-energy-rate forging systems
herj: high explosive ramjet
herm: hermetically
Hermit of Slabsides: John Burroughs
Hero: *heroina* (Spanish-American slang shortcut—heroin)
HERO: Historical Evaluation and Research Organization
Hero of a Hundred Fights: Admiral Horatio Nelson
Hero of Appomatox: General U.S. Grant
herp: herpetologist; herpetology
HERPOCO: Hercules Powder Company
herps: herpetologists
HERS: Home Economics Reading Service
Herts: Hertfordshire
hes: heavy-enamel single-silk (insulation)
he's: he has; he is
HES: Hawaiian Entomological Society
Hesperus: the evening star—Venus (see Lucifer)
hest: heavy-end aviation fuel emergency service tanks
HEST: High-Explosive Simulation

Test
hesv: heavy-enamel single-silk varnish (insulation)
heterocl: heteroclite
heterog: heterogeneous
HETS: Hyper-Environmental Test System
heu: hydroelectric units
HEW: Health, Education, and Welfare (US department)
hex: hexagon(al); uranium hexafluoride
hexag: hexagon(al)
hex hd: hexagonal head
hf: hageman factor; half; hard firm; height finding; high frequency (3000 to 30,000 kc); hold fire; hook fast; horse and foot (calvalry and infantry); hyperfocal
h/f: held for
Hf: hafnium
HF: Handwriting Foundation; Home Fleet; Home Forces
H/F: *Hlutafjelagid* (Icelandic—limited company)
H of F: Hall of Fame
Hfa: Haifa
HFAA: Holstein-Friesian Association of America
hf bd: half-bound
hfbr: high flux beam reactor
hfc: hard-filled capsules; high-frequency current
HFC: Household Finance Corporation
HFCC: Henry Ford Community College
hf cf: half-calf
hf cl: half-cloth (binding)
hf-df: high-frequency direction finder
hfe: human factors (in) electronics; human factors engineering
HFFF: Hungarian Freedom Fighters Federation
hfg: heavy free gas
HFGA: Hall of Fame for Great Americans
hfh: half-hard (steel)
HFIA: Heat and Frost Insulators and Asbestos Workers Union
hfim: high-frequency instruments and measurements
hfir: high flux isotope reactor
HFL: Human Factors Laboratory (NBS)
hfm: hold for money
HFM: Henry Ford Museum
hfmf: home-finish monolithic floor
hf mor: half-morocco
hfo: high-frequency oscillator; hole full of oil
HFORL: Human Factors Operations Research Laboratory
hfp: hostile fire pay
h&f pool: heated and filtered (swimming) pool

HFPS: Home Fallout Protection Survey
HFR: (Sir Edward) Hallstrom Faunal Reserve (New South Wales)
HFRB: Hawaii Fire Rating Bureau
hfs: hyperfine structure
Hfs: Helsinki (Helsingfors)
HFS: Human Factors Society
hft: *hefte* (Dano-Norwegian—part)
Hft: *Heft* (German—part)
HFT: Human Factors Team
HFTS: Human Factors Trade Studies (USN)
hfw: hole full of water
Hfx: Halifax
hg: hand generator; hectogram; heliogram
Hg: *hydrargyrum* (Latin—mercury)
h & g: harden and grind
HG: Haute-Garonne; Her (His) Grace; H(erbert) G(eorge) (Wells); High German; Home Guard; Horse Guards
H-G: Haute-Garonne
HGA: Heptagonal Games Association; Hobby Guild of America; Hop Growers of America; Hotel Greeters of America; Hungarian Gypsy Association
h-galv: hot-galvanize
hgb: hemoglobin
HgCl₂: bichloride of mercury; mercuric chloride
HGD: Hourglass Device
HGF: Human Growth Foundation
hg ga: height gage
HGH: human growth hormone
hgo: hepatic glucose output
Hgo: Hidalgo
HGOA: Houston Grand Opera Association
hgor: high gas-oil ratio
hgps: high-grade plow steel
hgr: hangar; hanger
HGR: Hluhluwe *(shloosh-loo-way)* Game Reserve (northern Zululand)
hgs: hangars; hangers
Hgs: Haugesund
hgsw: horn gap switch
hgt: height
HGTAC: Home Grown Timber Advisory Committee
HGTB: Haiti Government Tourist Bureau
HGW: Herbert George Wells
Hgy: Highway
hh: half-hard; handhole; heavy hydrogen
h/h: hard of hearing
hh: *hojas* (Spanish—leaves)
h to h: heel-to-heel
hH: heavy hydrogen
HH: Harry Hansen; Helen Hunt Jackson; Her (His) Highness;

His Holiness; Howard Hanson; Huntington Hartford
H/H: Havre-Hamburg (range of ports)
H & H: Handy & Harman; Holland & Holland
HH: *Herren* (German—Gentlemen)
hhd: hogshead
HH. D.: *Humanitatis Doctor* (Latin—Doctor of Humanities)
hhf: household furniture
HHFA: Housing and Home Finance Agency
hhg: household goods
hhh: triple hard
HHHC: Hunt the Hunters Hunt Club (Amory Foundation funded)
HHI: Hellenic Hydrobiological Institute
H-hinge: capital-H-shaped hinge
hhld: household
HHMS: His Hellenic Majesty's Ship
hhmu: hand-held maneuvering unit
H-hour: hostile operations commencement hour
HHPL: Herbert Hoover Presidential Library
HHS: Haaren High School; Hunter High School
HHSP: Highland Hammock State Park (Florida)
HHUMC: Hadassah-Hebrew University Medical Center
HHW: higher high water
HHWI: higher high water interval
hi: contracted form of "hail"; high; high intensity; humidity index
h & i: harassing and interdictory (artillery fire)
Hi: Hering illusion; Hindi; Hiram
HI: Harris Intertype; Hat Institute; Hawaiian Islands; Heat Index; Henrik Ibsen; Humidity Index; Hydraulic Institute
hia: hold in abeyance
HIA: Handkerchief Industry Association; Horological Institute of America; Hospital Industries Association; Hungarian Imperial Association
HIAA: Health Insurance Association of America
hi-ac: high accuracy
HIAD: *Handbook of Instructions for Airplane Designers*
HIAG: *Hilfsorganisation auf Gengenseitigkeit* (German—Mutual Aid Organization)
HIAGSED: *Handbook of Instruction for Aircraft Ground Support Equipment Designers*
HIAS: Hebrew Immigrant Aid Society

Hib: Hibernia (Ireland); Hibernian (Irish)

HIB: Herring Industry Board

Hibbd: *Halbband* (German—half binding)

hibex: high-acceleration booster experiment

HIC: Herring Industries Council

hicapcom: high-capacity communications

hicat: high-altitude clear-air turbulence

hic jac: *hic jacet* (Latin—here lies)

hiclass: hierarchical classification

Hi Com: High Command; High Commission; High Commissioner

hid.: headache, insomnia, depression (syndrome)

Hid: Hidalgo

hidal: helicopter insecticide-dispersal apparatus, liquid

hidalgo: *hijo de algo* (Spanish—son of someone)

Hidalgo: Miguel Hidalgo y Costilla (Padre Hidalgo)

hier: hieroglyphics

HIES: Hadassah Israel Education Services

HIF: Health Information Foundation

hi-fi: high-fidelity

hifor: high-level forecast

hig: hermetically sealed integrating gyroscope

HIG: Hartford Insurance Group

higashi: (Japanese—east)

HIGED: *Handbook of Instruction for Ground Equipment Designers*

high-Q: high quality

HIH: Her (His) Imperial Highness

HII: Health Insurance Institute

hijack: hijacked; hijacker; hijacking

hik: hiking

hil: high intensity lighting

Hil: Hilary

hi-lo: high-low

Hil-Vis: Hiligaynon-Visayan

HIM: Her (His) Imperial Majesty

hi mi: high mileage

HIMS: Heavy Interdiction Missile System

Hind: Hindi; Hindu; Hindustani

HINP: Hundred Islands National Park (Philippines)

HINWR: Hawaiian Islands National Wildlife Refuge

H-ion: hydrogen ion

hip.: high-impact pressure

HIP: Health Insurance Plan

hipar: high-power acquisition radar

hipot: high potential

hippo(s): hippopotamus(es)

hips.: hippies

HIR: Heron Island Resort (Queensland)

hiran: high-precision shoran

HIRB: Health Insurance Registration Board

hirel: high reliability

HIRS: High-Impulse Retrorocket System

HIRS/smrd: High-Impulse Retrorocket System/spin-motor rotation detector

his. (HIS): histidine (amino acid); history

Hi-S: Hi-Standard (firearms)

HIS: Health Interview Survey; Hospital Information System

HISC: House Internal Security Committee (formerly House Un-American Activities Committee—HUAC)

Hisp: Hispaniola

Hispan: Hispanic

Hispano: Hispanoamericano (Spanish American); Hispano-Suiza (automobile)

hist: historical; history

Histadrut: (Hebrew—General Federation of Labor)

histo: histoplasmosis

histol: histology

Hit: Holtzman inkblot technique

hi-T: high torque

HIT: Health Indication Test

hi-temp: high temperature

Hitler: Adolf Schicklgruber

Hitt: Hittite

HIUS: Hispanic Institute of the United States

hiv: *hiver* (French—winter)

hi wat: high water

Hiwi: *Hilfsfreiwilliger* (German—auxiliary volunteer)

HIWRP: The Hoover Institution on War, Revolution and Peace

HJ: Hitler Jugend (German—Hitler Youth); Honest John (short-range unguided missile); Howard Johnson (stock exchange symbol)

H. J.: *hic jacet* (Latin —here lies)

HJBS: Hashemite Jordan Broadcasting Service

HJC: Hershey Junior College

HJPA: Holmes Junge Protected Area (Australian Northern Territory)

H J Res: House Joint Resolution

H.J.S.: *hic jacet sepultus* (Latin —here lies buried)

h-k: hand to knee

HK: Hong Kong

HK: *Helsingin Kaupunginorkesteri* (Finnish—Helsinki City Symphony Orchestra)

HKA: Hong Kong Airways

hk cells: human kidney cells

HK$: Hong Kong dollar

hkf: handkerchief

H Kg: Hong Kong

HKG: Hong Kong, British Crown Colony (airport)

HKJ: Hashemite Kingdom of Jordan

HKL: Halldor Kilyan Laxness

hkm: high-velocity kill mechanism

HKPO: Hong Kong Philharmonic Orchestra

HKTA: Hong Kong Tourist Association

HKTDC: Hong Kong Trade Development Council

hl: hand lantern; hectoliter; hinge line; holiday

h&l: door hinge resembling ligature of capital H and capital L

h.l.: *hoc loco* (Latin—in this place)

Hl.: latent hypermetropia (symbol)

HL: Haute-Loire; Herpetologists League; Home Lines; Honours List; House of Lords; Hygienic Laboratories; Hygienic Laboratory

H-L: Haute-Loire

H of L: House of Lords

HL&AG: Henry E. Huntington Library and Art Gallery

HLBB: Home Loan Bank Board

HLC: Hospital Library Council (Dublin)

hl di: hole die

hlg: halogen

HLL: Hellenic Lines Limited

HLNP: Hattah Lakes National Park (Victoria, Australia)

HLNWR: Havasu Lake National Wildlife Refuge (California); Hutton Lake National Wildlife Refuge (Wyoming)

hlpr: helper

HLRS: Homosexual Law Reform Society

hls: heavy logistics support; hills

HLS: Harvard Law School; Heavy Logistics Support

hl sa: hole saw

hlv: herpes-like virus

hlw: higher low water; high-level waste

HLW: higher low water

HLWI: higher low water interval

HLWRP: Hoover Library on War, Revolution, and Peace (Stanford University)

hm: hallmark; harmonic mean; hectometer; hollow metal

h & m: hit and miss; hull and machinery

hm²: square hectometer

hm³: cubic hectometer

Hm: manifest hypermetropia

HM: Harbour Master; Haute-Marne; Head Master; Head Mistress; Her (His) Majesty; Herman Melville; Home Missions

H-M: Haute-Marne

Hma: Hiroshima

HMA: Her (His) Majesty's Airship; Hoist Manufacturers Association; Home Manufacturers Association

H & MA: Hotel and Motel Association

HMAA: Horse and Mule Association of America

HMAS: Her (His) Majesty's Australian Ship

HMB: Hops Marketing Board

hmc: howitzer motor carriage

HMC: Harvey Mudd College; Her (His) Majesty's Customs

HMC & H: Hahnemann Medical College and Hospital

HMCN: Her (His) Majesty's Canadian Navy

HMCS: Her (His) Majesty's Canadian Ship

HMCyS: Her (His) Majesty's Ceylonese Ship

hmd: hollow metal door; humid; hyaline membrane disease; hydraulic mean depth

HMDBA: Hollow Metal Door and Buck Association

hmdf: hollow metal door and frame

hmf: hollow metal frame

HMFI: Her (His) Majesty's Factory Inspectorate

HMG: heavy machine gun; Her (His) Majesty's Government

HMHS: Horace Mann High School

HMI: Her (His) Majesty's Inspector; Hughes Medical Institute

HML: Harper Memorial Library (University of Chicago)

HMLI: Horace Mann—Lincoln Institute

hmlt: hamlet

HMM: Her (His) Majesty's Minister

HMNAO: Her (His) Majesty's Nautical Almanac Office

HMNAR: Hart Mountain National Antelope Refuge (Oregon)

hmo: heart minute output

HMO: Health Maintenance Organization

hmp: handmade paper

H.M.P.: *hoc monumentum posuit* (Latin—he erected this monument)

HMPMA: Historical Motion Picture Milestones Association

HMRC: Heineman Medical Research Center

HMRCS: (Her) (His) Majesty's Royal Canadian Ship

hms: hours, minutes, seconds

HMS: Harvard Medical School;

Her (His) Majesty's Service, Ship, or Steamer

HMSO: Her (His) Majesty's Stationery Office

hmstd: homestead

HMV: His Master's Voice (phonograph records)

hmy: too little

h.n.: *hac nocte* (Latin—tonight)

HN: Head Nurse

Hna: Habana

HNBI: Hellenic National Broadcasting Institute

HNC: Harbors and Navigation Code

Hnd: *The Hindu* (Madras)

hndbk: handbook

hndlr: handler

hn fm: hand form

HNL: Honolulu, Hawaii (airport)

HNNNR: Herma Ness National Nature Reserve (Scotland)

Hno: Hanover

HNO₃: nitric acid

Hnos: *Hermanos* (Spanish—brothers)

hnp: high needle position

HNP: Haleakala National Park (Maui, Hawaii)

hnrs: honors

HNWR: Hagerman National Wildlife Refuge (Texas); Horicon National Wildlife Refuge (Wisconsin)

ho: hoist

ho: (Chinese—river)

'ho': whore

Ho: Ho Chi Minh

Ho: holmium; Honduran; Honduras; Hondureño

HO: Hydrographic Office (USN)

HO: *Handelsorganisation* (German—trade organization)

hoa: hands off—automatic

HOA: Home Owners Association

hoax: (Contraction—hocus pocus)

hob.: height of burst

Hob: Anthony van Hoboken (Dutch chronologist-enumerator of Haydn's music); Hoboken (Belgian seaport near Antwerp; place near Waycross, Georgia; port city in New Jersey opposite lower Manhattan)

Hoban: Holborn

hobe: honeycomb before expansion

hobgob(s): hobgoblin(s)

Hob-Job: Hobson-Jobson (similar-sounding words to those of other languages with some or complete loss of meaning; e.g., Hobson—Jobson supposedly equivalent to Arabic cry of mourning for grandsons of Mohammed—*ya Hasan!—o Hu-*

sain!; Key West believed same as *Cayo Hueso* (Spanish—Bone Key); Leghorn invented by British sailors who thought it equivalent to *Livorno*; Coromuel—beach in Baja California —named after English pirate —*Cromwell*; white rhino really the Dutch *weid rhino*—a wide-mouthed rhinoceros and really not white)

Hobo: Hoboken

hoc: heavy organic chemical(s)

HOC: House of Commons

hoch: (German—high)

Ho Chi Minh: Nguygen That Tan

hock.: hockheimer (Rhine wine)

hoc vesp.: *hoc vespere* (Latin—this evening)

Hodge: (nickname for the typical English farmer)

HOD Test: Hoffer, Osmond, and Desmond Test (for schizophrenia)

hoek: (Dutch—cape)

HoF: Hall of Fame

HO-gage: ⅝-inch track gage (model railroads)

ho & gcm: heavy oil and gas-cut mud

HOI: Headquarters Operating Instruction

HoJo: Howard Johnson (roadside restuarants)

hoke: hokum

hoku: (Japanese—north)

hol: holiday; hollow; holly

HOL: House of Lords

Holl: Holland; Hollander

Hollyw'd: Hollywood

holm: (Dano-Norwegian or Swedish—island)

holo: holograph

hol-ry: whole rye

hom: homonym

Hom: Homer

Hom.: *Homilia* (Latin—homily; sermon)

HOME: Home Ownership Made Easy

home ec: home economics

homeo: homeopath; homeopathic; homeopathy

Homer.: Homeric

Homer Wilbur: (pseudonym— James Russell Lowell)

HOMES: mnemonic for remembering the five Great Lakes—Huron, Ontario, Michigan, Erie, Superior

homo: homeopath; homeopathic; homeopathy; homosexual; homosexuality

homolat: homolateral

hon: honey; honor; honorable; honorarium; honorary; honored

Hon: Honduran; Honduras; Hondureño; Honorable
Hon'ble: Honourable
Hon Consul: Honorary Consul
Hond: Honduran; Honduras
Honest Abe: Abraham Lincoln
Honest John: solid-sustainer motor surface-to-surface ballistic missile produced by Douglas Aircraft
Hono: Honolulu
hons: honors
hood.: hoodlum
Hoosier Poet: James Whitcomb Riley
hop.: high oxygen pressure; holding procedures
HOPE: Health Opportunity for People Everywhere
hoppers: grasshoppers
hor: home of record; horizon; horizontal
Hor: Horace; Horatio
hora decub.: hora decubitus (Latin —at bedtime)
hora interm.: hora intermedius (Latin—at the intermediate hours)
hora som.: hora somni (Latin —at bedtime)
HO & RC: Humble Oil and Refining Company
horiz: horizontal
horn: (German—peak)
horo: horoscope
horol: horology
hort: horticulture
'ho's: whores
Hos: The Book of Hosea
HOS: Hawaiian Orchid Society
hose.: hosiery
Hosea Biglow: (pseudonym—James Russell Lowell)
hosp: hospital
hosp ins: hospital insurance
hot.: human old tuberculin
HOT: Hot Springs, Arkansas (airport)
Hotel: code for letter H
HOTLIPS: Honorary Order of Trumpeters Living in Possible Sin
Hou: Houston
HOU: Houston, Texas (ai port)
Hous: Houston
House: The House—House of Commons in England; House of Representatives in the United States; London's Stock Exchange; Oxford University's Christ College
House of D: (Women's) House of Detention
Hou Sym Orch: Houston Symphony Orchestra
houv: houvere (Finnish—charity)

hoved: (Dano-Norwegian—cape)
how.: howitzer
How: Howard (U.S. Supreme Court Reports)
HoW: Happiness of Womanhood
howtar: howitzer-mortar
HOW-TO: Housing Operation with Training Opportunity (OEO)
hp: high pass; high pressure; hollowpoint; horizontal parallax; horizontally polarized; horsepower; hot press(ed)
h & p: history and physical (examination)
HP: Haute-Pyrénées; House Physician; Houses of Parliament
H-P: Handley-Page; Haute-Pyrénées; Hewlett-Packard
HP: Homeopathic Pharmacopoeia
HPA: Hospital Physicists Association
HPAAS: High-Performance Aerial Attack System
hpac: hydropress accessor
HPAL: Holland Pan-American Line
hpb: hinged plotting board
HPC: Hercules Powder Company; Highland Park College
HPCC: High-Performance Control Center
hp cyl: high-pressure cylinder
hpf: highest possible frequency; hydropress form
H_{pge}: heading per gyro compass
hp hd: high-pressure high-density
hp hr: horsepower hour
hpi: history of present illness
Hpl: Hartlepool
HPL: Halifax Public Library; Hamilton Public Library; Hartford Public Library; Houston Pipe Line; Houston Public Library
hplr: hinge pillar
HPM: Human Potential Movement
HPMA: Hardwood Plywood Manufacturers Association
hpn: horsepower nominal
hpo: high-pressure oxygenation
HPO: Hamilton Philharmonic Orchestra; Highway Post Office
H-pole: H-shaped telegraph or telephone pole
hpox: high-pressure oxygen
HPPA: Horses and Ponies Protection Association
h-p plan: hire-purchase plan (British equivalent of American installment-plan purchasing)
HPR: House of Pacific Relations
HPRF: Hypersonic Propulsion Research Facility
hps: high-pressure steam; high protein supplement; hot-pressed sheet
HPS: Harlem Preparatory School;

Health Physics Society
H_{psc}: heading per standard compass
H_{pstgc}: heading per steering compass
hpt: high point; high-pressure test
hptn: hypertension
hpu: hydraulic pumping unit
hpv: high-passage virus
hpv-de: high-passage virus (grown in) duck embryo
hpv-dk: high-passage virus (grown in) dog kidney
hq: headquarters
h.q.: hoc quaere (Latin—see this)
H-Q: Hydro-Quebec
hqc: hydroxyquinoline citrate
HQ COMD USAF: Headquarters Command, USAF
HQ USAF: Headquarters, USAF
hr: hairspace; handling room; heat resisting; height range; home run; hook rail; hoserack; hour; relative humidity (symbol)
hr: herr (Swedish—Sir)—Mr
Hr: Herr (Danish or German—Mr; Sir)
HR: Hospital Recruit; House of Representatives; International Harvester (stock exchange symbol)
H-R: Haut-Rhin
H & R: Harper & Row; Harrington & Richardson; Herweg & Romine
Hra: Herra (Finnish —Mister)
HRA: Human Resources Administration
HRAG: Helena Rubinstein Art Gallery
HRB: Highway Research Board; Highway Research Bureau; Housing and Redevelopment Board
hrc: high rupturing capacity
HRC: Humacao Regional College; Humanities Research Council
hrd: hard
HRD: Human Resources Development
HRDA: Human Resources Development Agency
HRDL: Hudson River Day Line
hrdwd: hardwood
hrdwr: hardware
hre: hypersonic research engine
HRE: Holy Roman Empire
H Rept: House Report
HRes: House Resolution (US House of Representatives)
HREU: Hotel and Restaurant Employees Union
HRF: Hat Research Foundation
HRFA: Hudson River Fishermen's Association
HRG: Halford, Robins, and God-

frey
HRH: His (Her) Royal Highness
hri: height-range indicator
HRIP: Highway Research in Progress
H.R.I.P.: *hic requiescit in pace* (Latin—here rests in peace)
hrir: high-resolution infrared radiometer
HRIS: Highway Research Information Service
hrl: horizontal reference line
Hrl: Harlingen
HRL: Hughes Research Laboratories; Human Resources Laboratory
Hrm: Herman
HRMA: Hampton Roads Maritime Association
Hr Ms: Haar Majesteits Schip (Dutch —Her Majesty's Ship)
Hrn: Herren (German—gentlemen)
HRO: Housing Referral Office (USAF)
HRP: Hampton Roads Ports; Human Reliability Program; Huntsville Research Park
HRRC: Human Resources Research Center
HRRL: Human Resources Research Laboratory
HRRO: Human Resources Research Office
hrs: hot-rolled steel; hours
HRS: Hydraulics Research Station
hrsg: *herausgegeben* (German—edited)
Hrsg: *Herausgeber* (German—editor)
HRSRS: Hartbeestehoek Radio Space Research Station
HRT: Honolulu Rapid Transit
hrts: high risk test site
hrtwd: heartwood
Hrtz: *Ha'aretz* (Hebrew—The Land)—Israel's leading newspaper
HRU: Hydrological Research Unit
hrv: hypersonic research vehicle
HRWMC: House of Representatives Ways and Means Committee
Hry: Henry
HRZ: Hertz Corporation (stock exchange symbol)
hs: half strength; hardstand; highspeed; hinged seat; horizontal shear; horizontal stripe(s); hot stuff; hypersonic
h.s.: *hoc sensu* (Latin—in this sense)
Hs: Henriques
HS: Hakluyt Society; Haute-Saône; Haute-Savoie; High School; Home Secretary; House Surgeon; Hunterian Society; hy-

drofoil ship (naval symbol)
H-S: Haute-Saône; Haute-Savoie
hsa: human serum albumin; hypersonic aircraft (HSA)
HSA: Herb Society of America; Hispanic Society of America; Holly Society of America; Hospital Savings Association; Hunt Saboteurs Association
HSAA: Health Sciences Advancement Award
HSAC: House (of Representatives) Science and Astronautics Committee
HSA & D: High School of Art and Design
HSC: Health and Safety Code
Hschonhsn: Hohenschonhausen
hscp: high-speed card punch
hscr: high-speed card reader
HSD: Hawker Siddeley Dynamics
hsda: high-speed data acquisition
HSDG: Hamburg-Südamerika Dampfschiffahrts Gesellschaft (Columbus Line)
hse: house
HSFI: High School of Fashion Industries
hsg: housing
Hsg: Helsingör (Elsinore)
HSG: Hawker Siddeley Group
hsgt: high-speed ground transport
HSGTP: High-Speed Ground Transportation Program
HSH: Her (His) Serene Highness
hsien: (Chinese—district; district capital)
Hsinhua: New China News Agency
HSK: Honorary Surgeon to the King
hskpg: housekeeping
hskpr: housekeeper
HSLA: Home and School Library Association
HSLWI: Helical Spring Lock Washer Institute
hsm: high-speed memory
HSM: Historical Society of Montana
HSMB: Hydronautics Ship Model Basin
HSNP: Hot Springs National Park
HSNR: Huleh Swamp Nature Reserve (Israel)
HSO: Haifa Symphony Orchestra; Hamburg Symphony Orchestra; Hartford Symphony Orchestra; Honolulu Symphony Orchestra; Houston Symphony Orchestra
hsp: high-speed printer
HSP: Historical Society of Pennsylvania
HSPA: Hawaiian Sugar Planters' Association; High School of the Performing Arts

HSPG: Hansard Society for Parliamentary Government
HSPH: Harvard School of Public Health
hsptp: high-speed paper-tape punch
HSQ: Honorary Surgeon to the Queen
hsr: high-speed reader
HSRI: Highway Safety Research Institute
hss: high-speed steel
HSS: History of Science Society; Hungarian State Symphony
HSSA: History of Science Society of America
HSSO: Hungarian State Symphony Orchestra
hst: hoist; hypersonic transport
H St: Hugo Stinnes (steamship line)
HST: Harry S. Truman; Hawaiian Standard Time; hypersonic transport
HSTC: Henderson State Teachers College
HSTS: House Subcommittee on Traffic Safety
HSTI: Hartford State Technical Institute
HSTL: Harry S. Truman Library
hsts: horizontal stabilizer trim setting(s)
HSU: Hardin-Simmons University
HSUNA: Humanist Student Union of North America
HSUS: Humane Society of the United States
hsv: heat-suppression valve
HSV: Huntsville, Alabama (airport)
hswf: housewife
hszd: hermetically-sealed zener diode
ht: halftime; halftone; heat; heat treat; heat-treated; heat treatment; heavy formex; heavy tank; height; height telling; high temperature; high tension; hollow tile; hydrotherapy; hypertropia; hypodermic tablet
h & t: harden(ed) and temper(ed); hospitalization and treatment; hospitalize and treat
h.t.: *hoc tempore* (Latin—at this time); *hoc titulo* (Latin—under this title)
Ht: total hypermetropia
HT: Hawaiian Telephone; Hawaiian Territory; Hawaiian Theater; Hawaiian Time; Height Technician; Horsed Transport; Hospital Train
hta: heavier than air
htb: high-tension battery
HTB: Horserace Totalisator Board
htc: hydraulic temperature control
htd: heated
htd pl: heated pool

htd rm: heated room
ht eye: height of eye
htfc: high-temperature fuel cell
ht fx: heat treat fixture
htg: heating
htgr (HTGR): high-temperature gas-cooled reactor
Htg & Vent: Heating & Ventilating
htk: headline to come
htm: high-temperature metallography
HTMC: High Temperature Materials Corporation
Htn: Hamilton, Bermuda
hto: high-temperature oxidation; horizontal takeoff
htofore: heretofore
htol (HTOL): horizontal-take-off-and-landing
htp: high-test peroxide
h-t-p: house-tree-person (psychological drawing test)
HTP: House-Tree-Person (test)
htr: heater
htr (HTR): high-temperature reactor
HTR: Highway Traffic Regulation(s)
htrac: half-track
HTRDA: High-Temperature Reactor Development Associates
hts: half-time survey; heights; high-tensile steel
Hts: Heights
HTS: Huntington, West Virginia (airport)
htst: high-temperature short-time (pasteurization)
htt (HTT): heavy tactical transport
htu: heat transfer unit
htv (HTV): hypersonic test vehicle
htvt: heating and ventilating
htw: high-temperature water
HT&W: Hoosac Tunnel & Wilmington (railroad)
hu: hyperemia unit
Hu: Hungarian; Hungary
HU: Harvard University; Hebrew University; Howard University
HUA: Housing and Urban Affairs
HUC: Hebrew Union College
HUCJIR: Hebrew Union College Jewish Institute of Religion
hucks: huckleberries
hucr: highest useful compression ratio
hud: head-up display
HUD: Housing and Urban Development
Huel: Huelva
Hues: Huesca
huff-duff: high-frequency direction finder
HUFSM: Highway Users Federation for Safety and Mobility
HUGHES: Hughes Aircraft Company

hugo: highly unusual geophysical operations
HUJ: Hebrew University of Jerusalem
huk (HUK): hunter-killer
huk: (Dano-Norwegian or Swedish —point)
HUL: Harvard University Library; Helsinki University Library
Hull: Kingston-upon-Hull
hum: human; humane; humanism; humanities
human eng: human engineering
HUMBLE: Humble Oil (Company)
humer: humerus
humi: humidity
Humph: Humphrey
HUMRRO: Human Resources Research Office
hums: humanitarian reasons
hun: hundred
Hun: Hungarian; Hungary
hund: hundred
Hung: Hungaria; Hungarian; Hungarica; Hungary
hunth: hundred thousand
Hunts: Huntingdonshire
HUP: Harvard University Press
HUPAS: Hofstra University Pro Arte Symphony
hur: hurricane
HURRAH: Help Us Reach and Rehabilitate America's Handicapped (HEW program)
hus: (Dano-Norwegian or Swedish—house) as in Aarhus
husb: husbandry
hv: heavy; high velocity; high voltage
h-v: high-voltage
h & v: heating and ventilating
HV: Health Visitor
Hva: Huelva
hvac: heating, ventilating, and air conditioning
hvar (HVAR): high-velocity aircraft rocket
HVB: Hawaii Visitors Bureau
hv & c: heating, ventilating, and cooling
HVCA: Heating and Ventilating Contractors' Association
HVCC: Hudson Valley Community College
hvd: high-velocity detonation; hypertensive vascular disease
hvdc: high-voltage direct current
HVEC: High Voltage Engineering Corporation
hvem: high-voltage transmission electron microscopy
hvh: herpesvirus hominis
HVI: Home Ventilating Institute
hvl: half-value layer
HVL: Hanseatic Vaasa Line; Heitor Villa-Lobos

HVNP: Hawaii Volcanoes National Park
HVO: Hawaiian Volcano Observatory
HVP: Hudson Vitamin Products
HVPO: Hudson Valley Philharmonic Orchestra
hvps: high-voltage power supply
hvr: high-vacuum rectifier
HVRA: Hawaiian Volcano Research Association
hvsa: high-voltage slow activity
hvss: horizontal volute spring suspension
hvtp: high-velocity target-practice
HVWS: Hebrew Veterans of the War with Spain
hvy: heavy
hw: headwaiter; headwind; herewith; high water; hot water
h/w: husband and wife
H-W: Harbison-Walker (refractories)
H & W: Harland and Wolff (Belfast shipbuilders)
hwang: (Chinese—yellow, as in Hwang Ho)
hwc: hot-water circulating
HWC: Heriot-Watt College
hwctr: heavy-water components test reactor
H'w'd: Hollywood
hwf & c: high water full and change
hwi: high water interval
HWI: Helical Washer Institute
hwl: high-water line
HWL: Henry Wadsworth Longfellow
hwm: high-water mark
HWMC: House Ways and Means Committee
HWO: Homosexual World Organization
hwocr (HWOCR): heavy-water (moderated) organic-cooled reactor
hwost: high-water ordinary spring tides
hwq: high-water quadrature; tropic high-water inequality
hwr (HWR): heavy water reactor (AEC)
hws: hot-water soluble
HWS: Hurricane Warning Service
H & WSC: Hobart and William Smith Colleges
HWWW: Hochschule für Welthandel, Wien (School for World Trade—Vienna)
Hwy: Highway
hx: hexode; history
Hx: history (medical case)
Hxd: Hardinxveld
hy: henry
Hy: Highway; Hiram; Hyman
HY: Helsingin Yliopisto (Universi-

ty of Helsinki)
hyball: hydraulic ball
hycol: hybrid computer link
hycon: hydraulic control
hycotran: hybrid computer translator
hyd: hydrate; hydraulic(s); hydrostatics
Hyd: Hyderabad
hydapt: hybrid digital-analog pulse time
hydraul: hydraulic(s)
hydraweld: hydraulic-drawn welded (steel tubing)
hydro: hydrodynamic group or hydrodynamics (slang); hydroelectric; hydroelectrical; hydrographic; hydrology; hydrostatic
HYDRO: Hydrographic Office
hydrodyn: hydrodynamics
hydroelec: hydroelectric
hydrog: hydrography
hydrol: hydrology

hydrom: hydromechanics
hydromagnetics: magnetohydrodynamics
hydros: hydrostatics
hydrot: hydrotherapy
HYDRSS: High Data Rate Storage System (NASA)
hydx: hydroxide(s)
hyfes: hypersonic flight environmental simulator
hyg: hygiene; hygienic; hygroscopic
hygas: hydrogen gasification
hyla: hybrid language assembler
HYMA: Hebrew Young Men's Association
hymnol: hymnologist; hymnology
hyp: hyperbola; hyperbolic; hyphen; hyphenate; hyphenation; hypochondria(c); hypothesis; hypothetical
HYP: Harvard, Yale, and Princeton
hype: hypodermic (underground slang—person who injects drugs

with a hypodermic syringe)
hyper: hypercritical
hyperdop: hyperbolic doppler
hypn: hypertension
hypno: hypnotism
hypo: hypochondria; hypochondriac; hypochondriacal; hypodermic (injection or needle); hyposulfite of soda (sodium thiosulfate—$NaS_2O_3 + 5H_2O$)
hypoth: hypothesis
hyst: hysteresis; hysteria
hystad: hydrofoil stabilizing device
HYSURCH: Hydrographic Survey and Charting System
hytemco: high-temperature coefficient nickel-iron alloy
hy tr: heat treat
hz (Hz): hertz (one cycle per second); hertzian
Hz: Henriquez; hertz (cycles per second)
Hzk: Hezekiah
hzy: hazy

I

i: angle of incidence (symbol); incisor; indigo; infant; instantaneous current (symbol); interest; intransitive; isotopic fine structure (symbol); moment of photographic plate (symbol); optically inactive (symbol); rate of interest (symbol); Van't Hoff factor (symbol); vapor pressure constant (symbol)
i': in
i: Imperial Savings
I: acoustic intensity (symbol); candlepower or intensity of luminosity (symbol); conduction current (symbol); convection current (symbol); Ido (artificial language); in; inclination; India—code for letter I; Indian; industrial broadcasting; inertia; infantry; iodine; ionic strength (symbol); Ireland; Irish; Island; Isthmian Line; Italian Line; Italy—auto plaque; izzard
I: in (German or Italian—in); *inde* (Danish—in); *Isle* (French—island); *itä* (Finnish—east); *izquierda* (Spanish—left)
I: Ile (French—Island; Isle)
I¹³¹: radioactive iodine
ia: immediately available; impedance angle; indicated altitude;

infra-audible; initial appearance; international angstrom; intra-arterial; intra-articular
i A: im Auftrage (German—by order; for; under instruction)
Ia: Iowa (no official abbreviation)
IA: Indian Army; Industrial Arts; Inspection Administration; International Angstrom; Iraqi Airways
I/A: Isle of Anglesey
IAA: Independent Airlines Association; Indian Association of America; Inspector Army Aircraft; Insurance Accountants Association; Interment Association of America; International Academy of Astronautics; International Acetylene Association; International Advertising Association; International Apple Association; International Association of Allergology; Intimate Apparel Associates
IAA: International Aerospace Abstracts
IAAA: Institute of Air Age Activities
IAAAA: Intercollegiate Association of Amateur Athletes of America
IAAB: Inter-American Association of Broadcasters

IAAC: International Agriculture Aviation Center
IAAE: Institution of Automotive and Aeronautical Engineers
IAAF: International Amateur Athletic Federation
IAAFA: Inter-American Air Force Academy
IAAI: Int ernational Association of Arson Investigators
IAALD: International Association of Agricultural Librarians and Documentalists
IAAM: International Association of Auditorium Managers; International Association of Automotive Modelers
IAAO: Interlochen Arts Academy Orchestra; International Association of Assessing Officers
IAAP: International Association of Applied Psychology
IAAS: Institute of Advanced Arab Studies
IAASE: Inter-American Association of Sanitary Engineering
IAASS: International Association of Applied Social Science
IAB: Inter-American Bank; International Air Bahama
IABA: Inter-American Bar Association

IABG: International Association of Botanic Gardens

IAB-ICSU: International Abstracting Board—International Council of Scientific Unions

IABLA: Inter-American Bank for Latin America; Inter-American Bibliographical and Library Association

IABO: International Association of Biological Oceanography

IABPAI: International Association of Blue Print & Allied Industries

IABPC: International Association of Book Publishing Consultants

IABSE: International Association for Bridge and Structural Engineering

iac: intergration, assembly, check-out; interview after combat

IAC: Indian Airlines Corporation; Industry Advisory Commission; Information Analysis Center; Insurance Advertising Conference; Intermediate Air Command; Interview After Combat; Irish Air Corps

IACA: Independent Air Carriers Association; Inter-American College Association

IACB: Indian Arts and Crafts Board; International Advisory Committee on Bibliography (UNESCO); International Association of Convention Bureaus

IACD: International Association of Clothing Designers

IACE: International Air Cadet Exchange

IACHR: Inter-American Commission on Human Rights

IACI: Irish-American Cultural Institute

IACID: Inter-American Center for Integral Development

IACM: International Association of Concert Managers

IACP: International Association of Chiefs of Police

IACP & AP: International Association for Child Psychiatry and Allied Professions

IACRL: Italian-American Civil Rights League

IACS: International Annealed Copper Standard

IACT: Illinois Association of Classroom Teachers

iad: intergrated automatic documentation

IAD: International Astrophysical Decade—1965–1975

IADB: Inter-American Defense Board; Inter-American Development Bank

IADC: Inter-American Defense College

IADR: International Association for Dental Research

iae: integral absolute error

IAE: Institution of Automobile Engineers

IAeA: Institution of Aeronautical Engineers

IAEA: International Atomic Energy Agency

IAEC: Israel Atomic Energy Commission

IAECOSOC: Inter-American Economic and Social Council

IAEI: International Association of Electrical Inspectors

IAEL: International Association of Electrical Leagues

IAES: International Association of Electrotypers and Stereotypers

IAESTE: International Association for the Exchange of Students for Technical Experience

iaf: interview after flight

IAF: Industrial Areas Foundation; International Abolitionist Federation (for abolition of prostitution); International Astronautical Federation; Israeli Air Force

IAFAE: Inter-American Federation for Adult Education

IAFC: International Association of Fire Chiefs

IAFE: International Association of Fairs and Expositions

IAFF: International Association of Fire Fighters

iafi: infantile amaurotic family idiocy

IAG: Interagency Advisory Group; International Association of Geodesy; International Association of Gerontology

IAGA: International Association of Geomagnetism and Aeronomy

iagc: instantaneous automatic gain control

IAGC: International Association for Geochemistry and Cosmochemistry

IAGFCC: International Association of Game, Fish, and Conservation Commissioners

IAGM: International Association of Garment Manufacturers

IAGS: Inter-American Geodetic Survey

IAH: Inter-American Highway; International Asian Highways; International Association of Hydrology

IAHA: Inter-American Hotel Association

IAHF: International Aerospace Hall of Fame

IAHP: Institutes for the Achievement of Human Potential; International Association of Horticultural Producers

IAHR: International Association for Hydraulic Research

IAI: Icelandic Airlines Incorporated; International African Institute; International Association for Identification

IAIAS: Inter-American Institute of Agricultural Sciences

IAICM: International Association of Ice Cream Manufacturers

IAIE: Inter-American Institute of Ecology

IAIs: Israel Aircraft Industries

IAL: Icelandic Airlines; Imperial Airways Limited; International Algebraic Language; International Arbitration League; International Association of Limnology; Irish Academy of Letters

IAL: *Icelandic Airlines-Loftleider*

IALA: International Association of Lighthouse Authorities

IALC: International Association of Lyceum Clubs

IALL: International Association of Law Libraries

i allg: *im allgemeinen* (German—generally; in general)

IAM: Institute of Appliance Manufacturers; Institute of Aviation Medicine; International Academy of Medicine; International Association of Machinists; International Association of Meteorology

IAMAM: International Association of Museums of Arms and Military History

IAMAP: International Association of Meteorology and Atmospheric Physics

IAMAT: International Association for Medical Assistance to Travelers

IAMB: International Association of Microbiologists

IAMC: Institute for Advancement of Medical Communication; Inter-American Music Council

IAMCA: International Association of Milk Control Agencies

IAMFS: International Association of Milk and Food Sanitarians

IAML: International Association of Music Libraries

IAMLT: International Association of Medical Laboratory Technologists

IAMM: International Association of Medical Museums

IAMO: Inter-American Municipal Organization

IAMP: Inter-Agency Motor Pool

IAMR: Institute of Arctic Mineral Resources

IAMS: International Association of Microbiological Societies

IAMTCT: Institute of Advanced Machine Tool and Control Technology

IAMTF: Inter-Agency Maritime Task Force

IAN: Instituto Agrario Nacional (National Agrarian Institute —Venezuela)

IANA: Inter-African News Agency

IANAP: Interagency Noise Abatement Program

IANC: International Airline Navigators Council

IANEC: Inter-American Nuclear Energy Commission

iao: intermittent aortic occlusion

IAOL: International Association of Orientalist Libraries

IAOR: *International Abstracts in Operations Research*

IAP: Institute of Agricultural Parasitology; International Academy of Pathology; International Academy of Proctology

IAPA: Inter-American Parliamentary Organization; Inter-American Police Academy; Inter-American Press Association

IAPB: International Association for the Prevention of Blindness

IAPC: International Association for Public Cleansing

IAPG: Interagency Advanced Power Group; International Association of Physical Geography

IAPH: International Association of Paper Historians; International Association of Ports and Harbors

IAPHC: International Association of Printing House Craftsmen

IAPI: Institute of American Poultry Industries; Instituto Argentino de Producción Industrial (Argentine Industrial Production Institute)

IAPN: International Association of Professional Numismatists

IAPO: International Association of Physical Oceanography

IAPP: International Association of Police Professors

IAPR: Indian Air Patrol Reserve

IAPSC: Inter-African Phytosanitary Commission

IAPSO: International Association of Physical Sciences of the Oceans

IAPT: International Association for Plant Taxonomy

IAPTA: International Allied Printing Trades Association

IAR: Institute for Air Research

IARF: International Association for Liberal Christianity and Religious Freedom

IARI: Industrial Advertising Research Institute

IARIGAI: International Association of Research Institutes for the Graphic Arts Industry

IARS: International Anesthesia Research Society

IARU: International Amateur Radio Union

ias: immediate access storage; indicated airspeed; instrument approach system

IAS: Institute for Advanced Study; Institute of the Aeronautical Sciences; Institute of Aerospace Sciences; Institute of American Strategy; Institute of Andean Studies; Instrument Approach System; International Accountants Society; International Association of Siderographers; International Aviation Service

IASA: International Air Safety Association

IASC: Inter-American Safety Council

IASCH: Institute for Advanced Studies in Contemporary History (formerly Wiener Library)

IASDI: Inter-American Social Development Institute

IASH: International Association of Scientific Hydrology

IASI: Inter-American Statistical Institute

IASLIC: Indian Association of Special Libraries and Information Centers

iasor: ice and snow on runway

IASP: International Association for Social Progress; International Association for Suicide Prevention

IASPEI: International Association of Seismology and Physics of the Earth's Interior

IASPO: International Association of Senior Police Officers

IASS: International Association for Shell Structures

iat: inside air temperature

IAT: Individual Acceptance Test(ing); Institute for Applied Technology; Institute of Atomic Physics (Peking); International Academy of Tourism

IATA: International Air Transport Association

IATC: International Association of Tool Craftsmen

iatd: is amended to delete

IATM: International Association for Testing Materials

IATME: International Association of Terrestrial Magnetism and Electricity

iatr: is amended to read

IATSE: International Alliance of Theatrical Stage Employees (and Moving Picture Machine Operators)

IATTC: Inter-American Tropical Tuna Commission

IATUL: International Association of Technical University Libraries

iau: intrusion alarm unit

IAU: International Association of Universities; International Astronomical Union

IAUPL: International Association of University Professors and Lecturers

IAUPR: Inter-American University of Puerto Rico

IAV: International Association of Volcanology

IAVA: Industrial Audio-Visual Association

iaw: in accordance with

IAWA: International Association of Wood Anatomists

IAZ: Inner Artillery Zone

ib: incendiary bomb; inclusion body; index of body build; infectious bronchitis; inner bottom; instruction book; instructional brochure

i b: im besonderen (German—in particular)

ib.: ibidem (Latin—in the same place)

Ib: Ibadan

IB: Iberia Líneas Aéreas de España (Iberian Airlines of Spain); incendiary bomb; Infantry Battalion; Information Bulletin; Intelligence Branch; international broadcast(ing)

I of B: Institute of Bankers

IBA: Independent Bankers Association; Independent Bar Association; Institute for Bioenergetic Analysis; Institute of British Architects; International Bar Association; International Briquetting Association; Investment Bankers Association; Investing Builders Association

IBAA: Investment Bankers Association of America; Italian Baptist Association of America

IBAHP: Inter-African Bureau for Animal Health and Protection

I-bar: capital-I-shaped metal bar

IBAU: Institute of British-American Understanding

ibb: intentional bases on balls

(baseball)

IBB: Illinois Inspection Bureau; International Bowling Board; International Brotherhood of Bookbinders

ibbm: iron body bronze (or brass) mounted

IBBY: International Board on Books for Young People

IBC: International Broadcasting Corporation

IBCS: Integrated Battlefield Control System (USA)

IBD: Institute of British Decorators

IBE: Institute of British Engineers; International Bureau of Education

I-beam: capital-I-shaped metal beam

IBEC: International Bank for Economic Cooperation; International Basic Economy Corporation

IBECC: Instituto Brasileiro de Educacao Ciencia e Cultura

IBERIA: Líneas Aéreas de España (Iberian Airlines of Spain)

IBEW: International Brotherhood of Electrical Workers

IBF: Institute of British Foundrymen

IBFD: International Bureau of Fiscal Documentation

IBFO: International Brotherhood of Firemen and Oilers

IBhd: initial beachhead

ibi: invoice book, inward

IBI: Illinois Bureau of Investigation; Indiana Bureau of Investigation; Insulation Board Institute

ibid.: *ibidem* (Latin—in the same place)

IBiol: Institute of Biology

IBK: Institute of Bookkeepers

IBM: International Business Machines

ibo: invoice book, outward

IBOP: International Brotherhood of Operative Potters

ibp: initial boiling point

IBP: Institute of British Photographers; International Biological Program

IBPOEW: Improved Benevolent and Protective Order of Elks of the World

ibr: integral boiling reactor

IBR: Institute of Behavioral Research

IBRD: International Bank for Reconstruction and Development (World Bank)

ibrl: initial bomb-release line

IBRM: Institute of Boiler and Radiator Manufacturers

IBS: Indian Boy Scouts; Institute of

Basic Standards; International Bach Society; Israel Broadcasting Service

IBSA: International Barber Schools Association

IBSGR: Isiolo Buffalo Spring Game Reserve (Kenya)

IBSS: Imperial Bureau of Soil Science

IBSTP: International Bureau for the Suppression of Traffic in Persons

IBT: International Brotherhood of Teamsters

IBTCWH: International Brotherhood of Teamsters, Chauffeurs, Warehousemen, and Helpers

ib test: inkblot test (Rorschach test)

IBTS: International Bicycle Touring Society

IBTTA: International Bridge, Tunnel, and Turnpike Association

ibu: imperial bushel

IBU: International Broadcasting Union

ibv: infectious bronchitis vaccine

ibw: information bandwidth

IBW: International Boiler Works

IBWM: International Bureau of Weights and Measures

IBWS: International Bureau of Whaling Statistics

ibx (IBX): intermediate branch exchange

IBY: International Book Year (1972)

ic: ice crystals; in charge of; index correction; informal communication; inspected and condemned; inspiratory capacity; inspiratory center; instruction counter; instrument correction; integrated circuit; intermediate language; internal combustion; internal connection; international control; interstitial cells; intracerebral; intracutaneous

i-c: integrated circuit

i/c: in charge; in command

i & c: installation and construction

i.c.: *inter cibos* (Latin—between meals)

Ic: Iceland; Icelander; Icelandic

IC: Idaho College; Ignatius College; Illinois Central (railroad); Illinois College; Immaculata College; Information Center; Interchemical Corporation; International Control; Iola College; Iona College; Itaska College; Itawamba College; Ithaca College

I-C: Indo-China; Indo-Chine; Indo-Chinese

I & C: Ictinus and Callicrates (designers of the Parthenon)

I de C: Islas del Cisne (Spanish—

Swan Islands)

ica: Institute of Contemporary Arts

ICA: Industrial Communication Association; Institute of Contemporary Arts; Intermuseum Conservation Association; International Chefs' Association; International Chiropractors Association; International Claims Association; International Cooperative Administration; International Cooperative Alliance; International Council on Archives

I of CA: Institute of Chartered Accountants

ICAA: Invalid Children's Aid Association; Investment Counsel Association of America

ICAAAA: Intercollegiate Association of Amateur Athletes of America

ICAB: International Council Against Bullfighting

ICAE: International Commission on Agricultural Engineering

ICAF: Industrial College of the Armed Forces; International Committee on Aeronautical Fatigue

ICAI: International Commission of Agricultural Industries

ICAITI: Instituto Centroamericano de Investigación y Technológica Industrial (Central American Institute of Investigation and Industrial Technology)

ICAN: International Commission for Air Navigation

ICAO: International Civil Aviation Organization

icas: intermittent commercial and amateur service

ICAS: Interdepartmental Committee for Atmospheric Sciences; Intermittent Commercial and Amateur Service; International Council of the Aeronautical Sciences; International Council of Aerospace Sciences

ICASALS: International Center for Arid and Semi-Arid Land Studies

ICB: Indian Coffee Board; Institute of Comparative Biology; International Container Bureau

ICBA: International Community of Booksellers Associations

icbm (ICBM): intercontinental ballistic missile

ICBO: Interracial Council for Business Opportunities

ICBP: International Council for Bird Preservation

icbt: intercontinental ballistic transport

icc: integrated circuit computer

ic & c: invoice cost and charges
ICC: Indian Claims Commission; International Chamber of Commerce; International Control Commission; International Correspondence Course(s); Interstate Commerce Commission
icca: initial cash clothing allowance
ICCA: Infants' and Children's Coat Association; International Corrugated Case Association; International Consumer Credit Association
ICCAT: International Commission for the Conservation of Atlantic Tunas
ICCR: Indian Council for Cultural Relations
ICCSL: International Commission of the Cape Spartel Light
icd: immune complex disease
ICD: Industrial Cooperation Division; Industry Cooperation Division; Institute for the Crippled and Disabled; International College of Dentists; International Cooperative Distributors
ice.: increased combat effectiveness; internal combustion engine
Ice: Iceland; Icelander; Icelandic
ICE: Institution of Civil Engineers; Instituto Costarricense de Electricidad Costa Rican Electric Institute); International Cultural Exchange
ICEF: International Children's Emergency Fund; International Council for Educational Films
ICEI: International Combustion Engine Institute
Icel: Icelandic
ICEM: International Commission for European Migration
ICES: Integrated Civil Engineering Systems; International Council for the Exploration of the Sea
ICESC: Industry Crew Escape Systems Committee
ICET: Institute for the Certification of Engineering Technicians; International Center of Economy and Technology
ICEWATER: Inter-Agency Committee on Water Resources
icf: intracellular fluid; intermediate care facilities
ICF: Ingénieur Civil de France (Civil Engineer of France); Inter-bureau Citation of Funds; International Canoe Federation
ICFC: Industrial and Commercial Finance Corporation
IC 4-A: Intercollegiate Amateur Athletic Association of America
ICFR: Intercollegiate Conference of Faculty Representatives (Big Ten)
ICFTU: International Confederation of Free Trade Unions
icg: icing
ICG: International Commission on Glass; International Congress of Genetics; Interviewers Classification Guide
ich: ichthyology
ICHAM: Institute of Cooking and Heating Appliance Manufacturers
ICHCA: International Cargo Handling Coordination Association
IChemE: Institute of Chemical Engineers
ICHEO: Inter-University Council for Higher Education Overseas
ichnol: ichnolite; ichnologist; ichnology
ichs: ichthyologists
ichth: ichthyology
ichthyol: ichthyology
ICI: Imperial Chemical Industries; Institution of Chemistry in Ireland; International Commission on Illumination; Investment Casting Institute; Investment Company Institue
ICIA: Interagency Committee on International Athletics; International Credit Insurance Association; International Crop Improvement Association
ICIANZ: Imperial Chemical Industries of Australia and New Zealand
ICIAP: Interagency Committee on International Aviation Policy
ICID: International Commission on Irrigation and Drainage
ICIE: International Council of Industrial Editors
ICIECA: Interagency Council on International Educational and Cultural Affairs
ICIMP: Interagency Committee for International Meteorological Programs
ICIPE: International Center for Insect Physiology and Ecology
ICITO: Interim Commission for the International Trade Organization
ICJ: Institute of Criminal Justice; International Commission of Jurists; International Court of Justice
icky: sticky
ICL: Institut de Chimie de Lyon; International Computers Limited
ICLA: International Committee on Laboratory Animals
Iclnd: Iceland
ICLP: Institute of Criminal Law and Procedure (Georgetown University)

icm: increased capability missile; intercostal margin
ICM: Increased Capability Missile; Indian Campaign Medal; Institute of Computer Management
ICMA: International City Manager's Association
ICMPH: International Center of Medical and Psychological Hypnosis
ICMREF: Interagency Committee on Marine Science, Research, Engineering, and Facilities
ICMS: International Commission on Mushroom Science
ICN: International Chemical and Nuclear (corporation); International Council of Nurses
ICNAF: International Commission for the Northwest Atlantic Fisheries
ICNV: International Committee on Nomenclature of Viruses
ico: iconology
ICO: Immediate Commanding Officer; Interagency Committee on Oceanography; International Coffee Organization; International Commission for Optics
ICOA: International Castor Oil Association
ICOGRADA: International Council of Graphic Design Associations
ICOM: International Council of Museums
icon.: iconic; iconoclasm; iconoclast; iconography
ICONS: Information Center on Nuclear Standards; Isotopes of Carbon, Oxygen, Nitrogen, and Sulfur (AEC)
ICOPA: International Conference of Police Associations
icp: inventory control point
ICP: Institut de Chimie de Paris (Chemical Institute of Paris); International Council of Psychologists
ICPC: International Criminal Police Commission (Interpol)
ICPHS: International Council for Philosophical and Humanistic Studies
ICPI: Insurance Crime Prevention Institute
i/c/pm/m: incisors, canines, premolars, molars (dentition formula, *e.g.*, i 4/4 means 4 upper and 4 lower incisors, c 2/2 means 2 upper and 2 lower canines, etc.)
ICPO: International Criminal Police Organization (Interpol)
ICPP: Idaho Chemical Processing Plant (AEC)

icr: increase; increment; instrumentation control rack

ICR: Independent Congo Republic; Institute of Cancer Research; Institute for Cooperative Research

ICRA: International Copper Research Association

ICRC: International Committee of the Red Cross

ICRF: Imperial Cancer Research Fund

ICRH: Institute for Computer Research in the Humanities (NYU)

icrm: intercontinental reconnaissance missile (ICRM)

ICRP: International Commission on Radiological Protection

ICRU: International Commission on Radiological Units and Measurements

ics: intercostal space

ic's: immediate constituents; integrated circuits

ICS: Indian Civil Service; Integrated Command System; Interagency Communications System; International Chamber of Shipping; International College of Surgeons; International Correspondence Schools

ICSAC: International Confederation of Societies of Authors and Composers

ICSC: Independent Colleges of Southern California; Interoceanic Canal Study Commission

ICSDW: International Council of Social Democratic Women

icsh (ICSH): interstitial cell-stimulating hormone

ICSLS: International Convention for Safety of Life at Sea

ICSOM: International Conference of Symphony and Opera Musicians

ICS & T: Imperial College of Science and Technology

ICSTS: Intermediate Combined System Test Stand

ICSU: International Council of Scientific Unions

ICSW: Interdepartmental Committee on the Status of Women

ICT: International Computers and Tabulators; Wichita, Kansas (airport)

ICT: *International Critical Tables*

ICTA: Imperial College of Tropical Agriculture; International Center for the Typographic Arts

ICTP: International Center for Theoretical Physics

ICTR: International Center of Theatre Research

ic tv: integrated-circuit television

icu: intensive care unit (medical)

ICU: International Code Use

ICUMSA: International Commission for Uniform Methods of Sugar Analysis

ICUS: inside continental United States

icw: interrupted continuous wave; intracellular water

ICW: India-China Wing (World War II); Institute of Child Welfare; Inter-American Commission of Women; International Chemical Workers; International Commission on Whaling; International Council of Women

ICWA: Institute of Current World Affairs

ICWM: International Committee on Weights and Measures

ICY: International Cooperation Year (1965)

ICZN: International Commission on Zoological Nomenclature

id: idea; identification; induced draft; infectious disease; infective dose; inside diameter; intradermal; island; islander

id.: *idem* (Latin—the same)

id₅₀: median infective dose

i & d: incision and drainage

Id: Iraqi dinar (monetary unit of Iraq)

I'd: I could; I had; I should; I would

ID: Interior (US department); Institute of Distribution; Intelligence Department; Iraqi dinar (currency unit)

IDA: Industrial Diamond Association; Institute for Defense Analyses; Institute for Design Analysis; Intercollegiate Dramatic Association; International Development Association; International Dredging Association

IDAA: International Doctors in Alcoholics Anonymous

id. ac: *idem ac* (Latin—the same as)

idast: interpolated data and speech transmission

idb: illicit diamond buyer; illicit diamond buying; intercept during burning

IDB: Industrial Development Board; Inter-American Development Bank

idc: interest during construction

IDC: Imperial Defense College; Industrial Development Corporation; Intercontinental Dynamics Corporation; Interdepartmental Committee; Interdepartmental Communication; International Danube Commission; Iowa Development Commission

ID-card: identification card

IDC(orp): International Disposal Corporation

IDCSP: Initial Defense Communications Satellite Program

IDD: Island Development Department

IDDD: International Direct Distance Dialing

IDEA: Institute for the Development of Educational Activities

idef: intercept during exo-atmospheric fall

iden: identification; identify

ident: identification; identify; identity

IDEP: Interagency Data Exchange Program; Interservice Data Exchange Program

idex: initial defense experiment

idf: intermediate distribution frame; international distress frequency

IDF: International Dairy Federation; International Democratic Fellowship; International Diabetes Federation

ID grinding: internal grinding

id he.: index head

IDHS: Intelligence Data Handling System

idi: improved data interchange

IDI: Industrial Designers' Institute

idiot.: instrumentation digital on-line transcriber

IDL: New York, New York (Kennedy International Airport—Idlewild); International Date Line

IDLIS: International Desert Locust Information Service

id lt: identification light

idm: illicit diamond mining

IDMA: Isaac Delgado Museum of Art

IDNL: Indiana Dunes National Lakeshore (Indiana)

IDO: Intelligence Division Office; International Disarmament Organization

idoc: inner diameter of outer conductor

idon. vehic.: *idoneo vehiculo* (Latin—in a suitable vehicle)

idp: integrated data processing

IDP: Independent Development Project; Integrated Data Processing; International Driving Permit

idr: intercept during reentry

IDR: Infantry Drill Regulations; Institute for Dream Research

ids: illicit diamond smuggling; inadvertent destruct

IDS: International Development Services; International Documents Service; Investigative Dermatological Society

IDSA: Industrial Designers Society of America

IDSCS: Initial Defense Satellite Communication System

IDSO: International Diamond Security Organization

idt: in de text (Dutch—in the text)

IDTS: Instrumentation Data Transmission System

idu: intermittent drive unit; iododeoxyuridine

IDU: idoxuridine; International Dendrology Union

idur: intercept during unpowered rise

i Durchshn: im Durchschnitt (German—on an average)

IDX: Index to Dental Literature

ie: index error; initial equipment; inside edge

i/e: ingress/egress

i & e: identification and exposition (lines)

i.e.: id est (Latin—that is)

IE: Indo-European; Industrial Engineering; Industrial Espionage; Information and Education

I.E.: Industrial Engineer

I & E: Information and Education

IE: Immunitats Einheit (German—immunizing unit)

I o E: Isle of Ely

IEA: Institute of Economic Affairs; International Economic Association

IEAF: Imperial Ethiopian Air Force

IEC: Institut d'Études Centrafricaines (Institute of Central African Studies); International Education Center; International Electrochemical Commission; International Electrotechnical Commission

iec's: integrated electronic components

ied: individual effective dose

IED: Institution of Engineering Designers; Integrated Electronics Division (USA Electronics Command)

iee: inner enamel epithelium

IEE: Institute of Environmental Engineers; Institution of Electrical Engineers

Ieee: I expect everything eventually

IEEE: Institute of Electrical and Electronics Engineers

IEETE: Institution of Electrical and Electronics Technician Engineers

IEF: International Eye Foundation

IEG: Information Exchange Group

IEHA: International Economic History Association

iei: indeterminate engineering items

IEI: Industrial Education Institute; Industrial Engineering Institute

IEIC: Iowa Educational Information Center

IEN: Imperial Ethiopian Navy

IEO: Instituto Español de Oceanografía (Spanish Oceanographic Institute)

iep: iso-electric point

IEP: Institut d'Études Politiques (Institute of Political Studies); Institute of Experimental Psychology

IEPA: International Economic Policy Association

IER: Industrial Equipment Reserve; Institue of Educational Research; Institute of Engineering Research; Interim Engineering Report

IERC: International Electronic Research Corporation

IERE: Institution of Electronic and Radio Engineers

IERT: Institute for Education by Radio-Television

IES: Illuminating Engineering Society; Indian Educational Service; Information Exchange Service; Institute of Environmental Sciences; Institution of Engineers and Shipbuilders

IESC: International Executive Service Corps

IESS: Institution of Engineers and Shipbuilders in Scotland

IET: Initial Engine Test

if.: ice fog; interstitial fluid

i-f: in-flight; intermediate frequency

if: iflge (Danish—according to)

i.f.: ipse fecit (Latin—he did it himself)

If: Ifni; Sidi Ifni (Spanish West Africa)

IF: grid current (symbol)

I-F: Isotta-Fraschini

I de F: Institut de France (Institute of France)

I f A: Institutt for Atomenergi (Norwegian—Atomic Energy Institute)

IFA: Industrial Forestry Association; Industry Film Association; Intercollegiate Fencing Association; International Federation of Actors; International Fertility Association; International Fiscal Association; International Footprints Association; International Franchise Association

IFA: Institut Fiziki Atmosfery (Russian—Atmospheric Physics Institute)

IFAC: International Federation of Automatic Control

IFALPA: International Federation of Air-Line Pilots' Associations

IFAN: Institut Français d'Afrique Noire (Dakar, Ivory Coast)

IFAP: International Federation of Agricultural Producers

IFAPA: International Federation of Airline Pilots Association

IFAS: Institute for American Strategy; International Federation of Aquarium Societies

IFATCA: International Federation of Air Traffic Controllers Associations

IFATCC: International Federation of Associations of Textile Chemists and Colourists

IFB: Invitation for Bid(s)

ifc: integrated fire control

IFC: International Finance Corporation; International Fisheries Commission; International Freighting Corporation

IFC-ALA: Intellectual Freedom Committee—American Library Association

IFCL: International Fixed Calendar League

IFCO: Interreligious Foundation for Community Organization

IFCS: International Federation of Computer Sciences

IFD: International Federation of Documentation

IFDA: Institutional Food Distributors of America

IFE: Industrial Foundation on Education

IFEMS: International Federation of Electron Microscope Societies

iff (IFF): identification friend or foe

IFF: Institute for the Future; International Flavors and Fragrances (corporation)

IFFJ: Independent Federation of Free Journalists

IFFJP: International Federation of Fruit Juice Producers

IFGO: International Federation of Gynecology and Obstetrics

IFHE: International Federation of Home Economics

IFHP: International Federation for Housing and Planning

IFI: Industrial Fasteners Institute

IFIP: Iguazu Falls International Park (shared by Argentina, Brazil, and Paraguay)—Argentinians spell it Iguazu, Brazilians —Iguaçu, Paraguayans—Iguassu; International Federation of Information Processing

IFIPS: International Federation of Information Processing Societies

I Fire E: Institution of Fire Engineers

IFIS: Integrated Flight Instrument System

IFJ: International Federation of Journalists

IfL: *Institut für Landeskunde* (German—Geographical Institute)—at Bad Godesberg

IFL: Imperial Fascist League

IFLA: International Federation of Landscape Architects; International Federation of Library Associations

IFLWU: International Fur and Leather Workers Union

IFM: Institute for Forensic Medicine

IFMA: International Federation of Margarine Associations

IFME: International Federation of Medical Electronics

IFMEO: International Fish Meal Exporters Organization

IFMP: International Federation of Medical Psychotherapy

IFNE: International Federation for Narcotic Education

if nec: if necessary

IFOFSAG: International Fellowship of Former Scouts and Guides

IFORS: International Federation of Operational Research Societies

ifp: international fixed public broadcast band

IFP: Imperial and Foreign Post; Institut Français du Pétrole (French Petroleum Institute)

IFPA: Industrial Film Producers Association

IFPCW: International Federation of Petroleum and Chemical Workers

IFPM: International Federation of Physical Medicine

IFPP: Imperial and Foreign Parcel Post

ifr: infrared; inflight refueling

i-f-r: image-to-frame ratio

IFR: Instrument Flight Rules

IFRA: International Foundation for Research in the Field of Advertising

IFRB: International Frequency Registration Board

IFRF: International Flame Research Foundation

IFS: International Federation of Surveyors; Irish Free State

IFSA: International Federation of Sound Archives

IFSPS: International Federation of Students in Political Sciences

IFSS: Instrumentation Flight Safety System

IFSSO: Irish Free State Stationery Office

IFSTA: International Fire Service Training Association

ift: inflight text

IFT: Institute of Food Technologists; International Federation of Translators; International Foundation for Telemetering; International Frequency Tables

IFTA: International Federation of Travel Agencies

IFTC: International Film and Television Council

IFTF: Inter-Faith Task Force

IFTR: International Federation for Theatre Research

IFUW: International Federation of University Women

IFVME: Inspectorate of Fighting Vehicles and Mechanical Equipment

IFWL: International Federation of Women Lawyers

ig: inertial guidance

IG: Indo-Germanic; Inspector General

IG: *Interessengemeinschaft* (German—pool; trust)

IGA: Independent Grocers' Alliance; International Geneva Association; International Geographical Association; International Golf Association; International Graduate Achievement

i gal: imperial gallon

IGAS: International Graphic Arts Society

IGB: *International Geophysics Bulletin*

igc: intellectually gifted children

IGC: Intergovernmental Copyright Committee; International Geophysical Cooperation

IGCI: Industrial Gas Cleaning Institute

i/g/d: illicit gold dealer

IGD: Inspector General's Department

ige: instrumentation ground equipment

IGE: International General Electric

IGF: International Grieg Festival

IGFA: International Game Fish Association

I.G. Farben: Interessengemeinschaft der Farbenindustrie (German Dye Trust)

ig. fat.: *ignis fatuus* (Latin—foolish fire)—will-o'-the-wisp; marsh gas

igfet: insulated gate field-effect transistor

IGIA: Interagency Group on International Aviation

igl: information grouping logic

igl: *iglesia* (Spanish—church)

igla: *iglesia* (Spanish—church)

iglª: *iglesia* (Spanish—church)

ign: ignite; ignition

ign.: *ignotus* (Latin—unknown)

Ign: Ignacio; Ignatius; Ignatz; Ignazio

IGN: International Great Northern (railroad)

Ignatius Loyola: Iñigo López de Recalde

Ignazio Silone: (pseudonym —Secondo Tranquilli)

Ignº: Ignacio (Spanish—Ignatius)

IGO: Independent Garage Owners; Intergovernmental Organization

igor: injection gas-oil ratio

IGOSS: Integrated Global Ocean Station System

IGP: Industrial Government Party

IGPP: Institute of Geophysics and Planetary Physics (UCLA)

igrf: international geomagnetic reference field

IGS: Imperial General Staff; Inertial Guidance System; Institute of General Semantics; International Geranium Society

IGSESS: International Graduate School for English-Speaking Students

IGT: Institute of Gas Technology

IGTO: India Government Tourist Office; Israel Government Tourist Office; Italian Government Tourist Office

IGU: International Gas Union; International Geographical Union

IGWF: International Garment Workers Federation

IGWUA: International Glove Workers Union of America

IGY: International Geophysical Year (July 1957 through December 1958)

ih: inside height

ih (IH): infectious hepatitis

IH: International Harvester

IHA: International Hahnemannian Association; International Hotel Association; International House Association

IHAR: Institute for Human-Animal Relationships

IHAS: Integrated Helicopter Avionics System

IHB: International Hydrographic Bureau (Monaco)

IHBR: Indiana Harbor Belt Railroad

ihc: interstate highway capability

IHC: Intercontinental Hotels Corporation

IHD: Institute of Human Development; International Health Division (Rockefeller Institute for Medical Research); International Hydrological Decade (1965

—1974)

IHE: Institute of Highway Engineers; Institute of Home Economics

I-head: capital-I-shaped head (gasoline engine)

IHEU: International Humanist and Ethical Union

IHF: Industrial Hygiene Foundation; Institute of High Fidelity; International Hockey Federation; International Hospital Federation

IHFA: Industrial Hygiene Foundation of America

IHFAS: Integrated High-Frequency Antenna System

IHI: Ishikawajima-Harima Heavy Industries

IHL: International Homeopathic League

iho: in-house operation

ihp: indicated horsepower; ischemic heart disease

IHPA: Imported Hardwood Plywood Association

ihph: indicated horsepower hour

IHR: Institute of Human Relations

ihrd: international rubber hardness degree(s)

ihs: independent hemopathic syndrome

IHS: Irish Hospitals Sweepstakes

I.H.S.: *Iesus Hominum Salvator* (Latin—Jesus Savior of Men); *In Hoc Signo* (Latin—In This Sign)

IHSA: Italian Historical Society of America

ihx: intermediate heat exchanger

ii: ingot iron; initial issue; inventory and inspection

II: Ikebana International; Instituto Interamericano (Interamerican Institute); Irish Institute

I/I: Inventory and Inspection (Report)

I & I: instruction and inspection

iia: if incorrect advise

IIA: Aerlinte Eireann (3-letter symbol for Irish Airlines); Incinerator Institute of America; Institute of Internal Auditors; Insurance Institute of America; International Information Administration; Invention Industry Association

IIAA: Independent Insurance Agents Association

IIAF: Imperial Iranian Air Force

IIAPCO: Independent Indonesian-American Petroleum Company

IIAS: International Institute of Administrative Services

IIASA: International Institute of Applied Systems Analysis

IIB: Institut International de Bibliographie

IIC: International Institute for the Conservation of Historic and Artistic Works

IID: Internal Investigation Division

IIDA: Irish Industrial Development Authority

IIE: Institute for International Education; International Institute of Embryology

IIEA: International Institute for Environmental Affairs

IIF: Institute of International Finance; Institut International du Froid (International Institute of Refrigeration)

IIHS: Insurance Institute for Highway Safety

III: International Institute of Interpreters (UN); International Isostatic Institute

IIJR: Illinois Institute of Juvenile Research

IILC: International Instituut voor Landaanwinning en Cultuurtechniek (International Institute of Land Reclamation and Cultivation)

IILS: International Institute for Labour Studies

IIM: Indian Institute of Management

IIMSD: International Institute for Music Studies and Documentation

IIN: Item Identification Number

IInfSc: Institute of Information Scientists

IIOE: International Indian Ocean Expedition

IIOOF: International Independent Order of Odd Fellows

iip: index of industrial production

IIP: Institute International de la Presse (International Institute of the Press); International Ice Patrol; International Institute of Philosophy

IIR: International Institute of Refrigeration

IIRA: International Industrial Relations Association

IIRS: Institute for Industrial Research and Standards (Erie)

ii's: illegal immigrants

IIS: Institut International de la Soudure (International Institute of Welding); Institut International de la Statistique (International Institute of Statistics)

IIS & EE: International Institute of Seismology and Earthquake Engineering

IISL: International Institute of Space Law

IISO: Institution of Industrial Safety Officers

IISR: International Institute for Submarine Research

IISS: International Institute of Strategic Studies

IIT: Illinois Institute of Technology; Israel Institute of Technology

IITB: Indian Institute of Technology—Bombay

IITM: Indian Institute of Technology—Madras

IITRAN: Illinois Institute of Technology Translators

IITRI: Illinois Institute of Technology Research Institute

IITYWYBAD?: If I tell you will you buy a drink?

IIW: International Institute of Welding

iiwfm: if it weren't for me

iiwfy: if it weren't for you

i J: im Jahre (German—in the year)

IJ: Institute of Journalists

I of J: Institute of Jamaica

IJA: Institute of Jewish Affairs; International Judiciary Association

IJC: Itawamba Junior College

IJF: International Judo Federation

I-J FC: Iselin-Jefferson Financial Company

ik: inner keel

ik: ikke (Danish—not)

Ik: Ichabod

IK: Immune Korper (German—immune bodies)

ike: iconoscope

Ike: Dwight David Eisenhower (nickname)—thirty-fourth President of the United States; Isaac

IKPK: Internationale Kriminal-Polizei-Kommission (International Criminal Police Commission)

I kr: Icelandic krona (monetary unit)

ik unit: infusoria killing unit

il: illustrate; illustrated; illustration; illustrator; including loading; incoming letter; inside layer; inside left; inside length; instrument landing; interline; interlinearly

Il: illinium

IL: Incres Line; Interocean Line; Israel (auto plaque)

IL: *Institut Littéraire*

I & L: Installations and Logistics

I-et-L: Indre-et-Loire

ila (ILA): instrument landing approach

ILA: International Laundry Association; International Law Association; International Leprosy

Association; International Long-shoremen's Association

ILAAS: Integrated Light Aircraft Avionics System; Integrated Light Attack Avionics System

ILAB: International League of Antiquarian Booksellers

ILAFA: Instituto Latinamericano del Fierro y del Acero (Latin American Institute of Iron and Steel)

ILAR: Institute of Laboratory Animal Resources

ilas: interrelated logic accumulating scanner

ilc: irrevocable letter of credit

ILC: International Law Commission (UN)

Il Cieco: (Italian—The Blind One)—Italy's blind poet—Luigi Groto who lived and wrote in the mid-sixteenth century

Ildef⁰: Ildefonso (Spanish)

Il Duce: (Italian—The Leader)—sobriquet of Benito Mussolini—dictator of Italy before and during World War II

Il^e: Illustre (Spanish—Illustrious)

Il^{mo}: Illustrísimo (Spanish—Most Illustrious)

île: (French—island)

ile (ILE): isoleucine (amino acid)

ilf: inductive loss factor

ILFO: International Logistics Field Office (USA)

Il Furioso: (Italian—the Furious One)—nickname of Tintoretto who painted at a furious rate

ILGWU: International Ladies' Garment Workers' Union

ILH: Imperial Light Horse

ilha: (Portuguese—island)

ILI: Indiana Limestone Institute; Institute of Life Insurance

ILIC: International Library Information Center

Ill: Illinois; Illinoisan

I'll: I shall; I will

illit: illiterate; illiteracy

ILLRI: Industrial Lift and Loading Ramp Institute

illum: illuminant; illuminate; illumination

illus: illustrated; illustration; illustrator

Illustrious Infidel: Colonel Robert G. Ingersoll

ILMA: Incandescent Lamp Manufacturers Association

Ilmo: Illustrissimo (Italian—Most Illustrious)

ILMP: International Literary Market Place

ILN: Illustrated London News

ilo: in lieu of

Ilo: Iloilo

ILO: International Labour Office (UN); International Labor Organization

iloue: in lieu of until exhausted

ILP: Independent Labour Party

ILPA: Independent Labor Press Association

ILR: International Luggage Registry

ILS: Instrument Landing System; International Latitude Service; International Lunar Society

ILSA: Insured Locksmiths and Safemen of America

ILSC: International Learning Systems Corporation

ilt: in lieu thereof

ILT: Illinois Terminal (railroad)

ILTF: International Lawn Tennis Federation

ILU: Institute of Life Insurance

ilw: intermediate-level wastes

ILWU: International Longshoremen's and Warehousemen's Union

ILZ: Illinois Zinc (company)

im: immature; imperial measure; impulse modulation; infectious mononucleosis; inner marker; intensity modulation; intermodulation; intramuscular

I'm: I am

IM: impulse modulation; intermediate modulation; Inventory Manager

IM: Index Medicus

I o M: Isle of Man

IMA: Ignition Manufacturers Institute; Indian Military Academy; Industrial Marketing Association; Industrial Medical Association; Institute for Mediterranean Affairs; Instituto Mobiliare Italiano; International Management Association; International Mineralogical Association; Islamic Mission of America

imag: imaginary

IMAR: Inner Mongolia Autonomous Region (of the People's Republic of China)

IMarE: Institute of Marine Engineers

IMB: Institute of Marine Biology

IMBE: Institute for Minority Business Education

IMBO: Institutt for Marin Biologi (Oslo)

imc: image motion compensation; instrument meteorological condition

IMC: Industrial Management Center; International Maritime Committee; International Meteorological Committee; International Minerals & Chemical; International Mining Corporation; International Missionary Council; International Music Council

IMCC: Integrated Mission Control Center

IMCI: Interracial Music Council, Incorporated

imco: improved combustion

IMCO: Inter-Governmental Maritime Consultative Organization

IMCOV: Iron Mines Company of Venezuela

imdtty: it's my duty to tell you

IME: Institute of Makers of Explosives; Institution of Mechanical Engineers

I&ME: Indiana and Michigan Electric Company

I of ME: Institution of Mining Engineers

imep: indicated mean effective pressure

IMER: Institute for Marine Environmental Research

IMF: International Metalworkers Federation; International Monetary Fund; International Motorcycle Federation; Interstate Motor Freight (stock exchange symbol); Israel Music Foundation

IM FI: International Mineral Fiber Institute

img: informational media guarantee

IMH: Institute of Materials Handling

IMHT: Institute for Material Handling Teachers

imi: improved manned interceptor

IMI: Ignition Manufacturers Institute; Irish Management Institute; Israel Military Industries

IMIB: Inland Marine Insurance Bureau

imieo: initial mass in earth orbit

IMIMI: Industrial Mineral Insulation Manufacturers Institute

IMinE: Institute of Mining Engineers

imit: imitate; imitation

imit lea: imitation leather

iml: inside mold line

Iml: Imanuel

IML: International Music League; Irradiated Materials Laboratory

imm: immune; immunization; immunologist; immunology

Imm: Immingham

IMM: Institute of Mining and Metallurgy; Integrated Maintenance Management; International Mercantile Marine

immat: immature; immaturity

immed: immediate

immie: immitation marble; low-grade playing marble

immig: immigrant; immigration

immob: immobilization; immobilize

Immortal Dreamer: John Bunyan

Immortal Four: Italian poets Dante Alighieri, Ludovico Ariosto, Francesco Petrarca (Petrarch), Bernardo Tasso

IMMS: International Material Management Society

immun: immunity; immunization

immunol: immunology

immy: immediately

IMNS: Imperial Military Nursing Service

imo: imitation (slang short form)

IMO: Inter-American Municipal Organization; International Meteorological Organization (World Meteorological Organization)

imp.: imperative; imperfect; imperial; implement; implementation; import; imprint; improve; improvement

imp.: imprenta (Spanish—printing office; printing press); *imprimatur* [Latin—let it be printed (R.C. Church)]; *imprimé* (French—printed); *imprimis* (Latin—especially; particularly)

Imp.: Imperator (Latin—Emperor); *Imperatrix* (Latin—Empress)

IMP: Instrumented Mobile Platform (oceanographic drone boat); International Monitoring Probe (space instrument); Interplanetary Monitoring Platform (space vehicle)

Imp B: Imperial Beach

imper: imperative

imperf: imperfect

impers: impersonal

impf: imperfect

impg: impregnate

imp. gal: imperial gallon

IMPI: International Microwave Power Institute

impig: impignorate; impignorated; impignorating; impignoration

impl: imperial; implement

impr: improvement

impr: impresión; imprenta (Spanish—edition; printing office)

Impr Nat: Imprimerie Nationale (French—National Printing Office of France)

improv: improvement

imptr: importer

impv: imperative

impx: impaction

IMR: Individual Medical Report; Institute of Marine Resources; Institute of Masonry Research; Institute for Materials Research; Institute for Medical Research; Institute for Mortuary Research; Institute for Motivational Research; Institute for Muscle Research; International Medical Research

IMS: Indian Medical Service; Industrial Management Society; Industrial Mathematics Society; Institute of Management Sciences; Institute of Marine Science; Institute of Mathematical Statistics; International Musicological Society; International Mythological Society

IMSA: International Municipal Signal Association

IMSR: Isle of Man Steam Railway

IMSS: Integrated Manned Systems Simulator

IMT: International Military Tribunal

IMTFE: International Military Tribunal for the Far East

IMTP: Industrial Mobilization Training Program

imu: inertial measurement unit

IMU: International Mailers Union; International Maritime Union

IMUA: Inland Marine Underwriters Association

imv: imperative; improve

imw: international map of the world

Im Yem: Imamate of Yemen

in.: inch(es)

in.²: square inch(es)

in.³: cubic inch(es)

In: India; Indian; indium; Indus

IN: Institute of Neurobiology (Göteborg); Interested Negroes

I & N: Immigration and Naturalization

ina: international normal atmosphere

INA: Indian National Army; Inspector Naval Aircraft; Institution of Naval Architects; Insurance Company of North America; Iraqi News Agency; Israeli News Agency

inacdutra: inactive duty training

inactv: inactivate; inactivation; inactive

INAEA: International Newspaper Advertising Executives Association

InAF: Indian Air Force

INAH: Instituto Nacional de Antropologia e Historia (National Institute of Anthropology and History)—Mexico

inanim: inanimate; inanimative

INAS: Inertial Navigation and Attack System(s)

inaug diss: inaugural dissertation (thesis for doctor's degree)

in bal.: in ballast

inbd: inboard

inc: inclosure; include; increase

Inc: Incorporated

INC: Indian National Congress; Island Navigation Company (tankers)

Inca: Incahuasi

INCA: Information Council of the Americas

incair: including air

incan: incandescent

Incan and Aztec Century: the 1000s—great monuments standing in the highlands of Peru and Mexico attest to these astounding American cultures—the 11th century

INCAP: Institute of Nutrition of Central America and Panama

incaps: incapacitating agents

incb: inclusion body

incd: incendiary; incident

incdt: incident

ince: insurance

inch.: inchoative

In-Ch: Indo-China

inchoat: inchoative

incid: incidence; incident; incidental

incl: inclose; inclosure; include; including; inclusive

incln: inclusion

inclr: intercooler

INCMD: Indianapolis Contract Management District

INCO: International Nickel Company

incog: incognito

incomp: incomplete

incompat: incompatible; incompatibility

incompl: incomplete

incor: incorrect

Incorp: Incorporated

inco(s): incorrigible(s)

incpt: intercept

incr: increase; increased; increasing; increasingly; increment; incremental

INCRA: International Copper Research Association

incun: incunabula

incur.: incurable

ind: independent; index; indicate; indicative; indicator; indigo; indorse; indorsement; industrial; industry

in d.: in diem (Latin—daily)

Ind: India; Indian; Indiana; Indianapolis; Indianian; Indo-

Ind.: Indulgentia (Latin—indulgence)

IND: India (auto plaque); Indianapolis, Indiana (airport)

Ind Dem: Independent Democrat

Ind.E.: Industrial Engineer

indef: indefinite

indef art.: indefinite article

indem: indemnify; indemnity
inden: indenture; indentured; indenturing
Ind Eng: Industrial Engineer(ing)
Ind & Eng Chem: *Industrial and Engineering Chemistry*
indep: independent
Independence Days: July Fourth
Index: *Index Librorum Prohibitorum* [Latin—Index of Forbidden Books (R.C. Church)]
India: code for letter I
Indian Princess: Pocahontas
indic: indicative; indicator
indiv: individual
indiv psychol: individual psychology
Ind et L: Indre-et-Loire
indm: indemnity
Ind Med: *Index Medicus*
Ind Mgr: Industrial Manager
Indo: Indonesia; Indonesian
Ind O: Indian Ocean
Indo-Afr: Indo-African
Indo-Austral: Indo-Australasian
indoc: indoctrinate; indoctrination
Indoc: Indochina; Indochinese
Indo-Eur: Indo-European
Indon: Indonesia
indre: indenture
indre: (Dano-Norwegian—inner)
ind reg: induction regulator
Ind Rep: Independent Republican
Ind Res: Indian Reservation
indsö: (Dano-Norwegian—lake)
Ind Ter: Indian Territory (now Oklahoma)
induc: inductance; induction
indus: industrial; industry
Indy: Indianapolis; Indianapolis Speedway
ined.: *ineditus* (Latin—unpublished)
INEOA: International Narcotic Enforcement Officers Association
Iness: Inverness-shire
in ex.: *in extenso* (Latin—at length)
inf: infantry; infectious; infinitive
inf.: *infra* (Latin—below; beneath); *infunde* (Latin—pour into)
Inf: Infirmary
infect.: infection; infectious
infl: inflammable
inflam: inflammable
influ: influence; influential
infmry: infirmary
INFN: Istituto Nazionale di Fisica Nucleare (National Institute of Nuclear Physics)—Italy
info: inform; information
Informbureau: Communist Information Bureau (Cominform)
Informex: *Informaciones Mexicanas* (Mexican Information Service)
info theory: information theory

infra: below
infra dig.: *infra dignitatem* (Latin—beneath one's dignity; undignified)
infral: information retrieval automatic language
infraptum.: *infrascriptum* (Latin—written below)
infric.: *infricetur* (Latin—let it be rubbed in)
inft: infant
infus: infusible
infx: inspection fixture
ing: inguinal
Ing: Ingmar
Ing: *Ingénieur* (French—engineer); *Ingenieur* (German—engineer)
inga: inspection gage
Ingl: Inglaterra (Spanish—England)
Ingm Berg: Ingmar Bergman
INGO: International Non-Governmental Organization
Ingria: Ingermanland
Inh: *Inhaber* (German—proprietor)
inhal: inhalation
in. Hg: inch of mercury
inhib: inhibition; inhibitory
INHP: Independence National Historical Park
INHS: Indian Naval Hospital Ship
INI: Indianapolis Newspapers Incorporated; Industrial Nurses Institute; Institut National De l'Industrie (National Institute of Industry)
INI: *International Nursing Index*
INIBP: Instituto Nacional de Investigaciones Biológico-Pesqueras
in./in.: inch per inch
INIS: International Nuclear Information System
init: initial
inj: inject; injection; injections; injure; injury
inj. enema: *injiciatur enema* (Latin —inject an enema)
inj. hyp.: *injectio hypodermica* (Latin—hypodermic injection)
inkl: *inklusiv* (German—inclusive)
inl: initial
in.-lb: inch-pound
in lim.: *in limine* (Latin—at the outset)
in litt.: *in litteris* (Latin—in correspondence)
in loc.: *in loco* (Latin—in the place)
in. loc. cit.: *in loco citato* (Latin—in the place cited)
in mem.: *in memoriam* (Latin—in memory of)
i n mi: international nautical mile(s)
inn.: inning
Inn.: Innoshima
innerv: innervated; innervation
Innis: Inniskilling

inns.: innings
inoc: inoculation; inoculate
inop: inoperative
inorg: inorganic
INOS: Instituto Nacional de Obras Sanitarias (National Institute of Sanitation—Venezuela)
in-out: input-output
inp: inert nitrogen protection
INP: Inyanga National Park (Rhodesia)
INPFC: International North Pacific Fisheries Commission
inph: interphone
in p. inf.: *in partibus infidelium* (Latin—in the region of the unbelievers)
in pr.: *in principio* (Latin—in the first place)
Inprecorr: *International Press Correspondence*
in prep: in preparation
inprons: information processing in the central nervous system
in pulm.: *in pulmento* (Latin—in gruel)
inq: inquiry
Inq: *Inquisidor* (Spanish—inquisitor; investigator)
INQUA: International Association on Quaternary Research
inr: impact noise rating
INR: Institut National de la Radio (National Radio Institute); Intelligence and Research
INRA: Instituto Nacional de la Reforma Agraria (National Institute of Agrarian Reform)—exercises economic control of Cuba
I.N.R.I.: *Iesus Nazarenus Rex Iudaeorum* (Latin—Jesus of Nazareth, King of the Jews)
ins: insulate; insulated; insulation; insurance; insure; insured
in./s: inch(es) per second
Ins: Insecta
INS: Indian Naval Ship; Institute of Naval Studies; Institute of Nutritional Sciences; Integrated Navigation System; International News Service
I & NS: Immigration and Naturalization Service
InsACS: Interstate Airway Communication Station
INSAIR: Inspector of Naval Aircraft
insce: insurance
INSCO: Intercontinental Shipping Corporation
inscr: inscribed; inscription
INSDC: Indian National Scientific Documentation Center
INSDOC: Indian National Scientific Documentation Center
insd val: insured value

INS & E: Institute of Nuclear Science and Engineering
in./sec: inches per second
Insel: (German—island)
INSEL: International Nickel Southern Exploration Limited
INSENG: Inspector of Naval Engineering Material
insep: inseparable
Ins Gen: Inspector General
insh: inspection shell
insinuendo: insinuate + innuendo
insjö: (Swedish—lake)
INSMACH: Inspector of Naval Machinery
INSMAT: Inspector of Naval Material
INSNAVMAT: Inspector of Navigational Material (USN)
insol: insoluble
insolv: insolvent
INSORD: Inspector of Naval Ordnance
insp: inspect; inspected; inspection; inspector; inspiration; inspire; inspired
Insp: Inspector
in-spec: within specifications
INSPEL: *International Journal of Special Libraries*
INSPETRES: Inspector of Petroleum Resources
inspir.: *inspiretur* (Latin—let it be inspired)
INSPIRE: Institute for Public Interest Representation
INSRADMET: Inspector of Radio Materials
inst: instant; instantaneous; institute; institution; instruct; instruction; instructor; instrument; instrumentation; instrumented
inst.: instant; this month
Inst: Institute; Institution
INSTAAR: Institute of Arctic and Alpine Research
instar: inertialess scanning, tracking, and ranging
INSTARS: Information Storage and Retrieval System
Inst CE: Institute of Civil Engineers
Inst Ceram: Institution of Ceramics
Inst Dirs: Institute of Directors
Inst EE: Institute of Electrical Engineers
Inst F: Institute of Fuel
Inst Gas Eng: Institute of Gas Engineers
Inst HE: Institute of Highway Engineers
instl: install; installation; installment
instm: instrument; instrumentation; instrumented
Inst ME: Institute of Mechanical

Engineers
Inst Met: Institute of Metals
instn: institution(al)
INSTN: Institut National des Sciences et Techniques Nucléaires (National Institute of Science and Nuclear Techniques)
instns: instructions
Inst P: Institute of Physics
Inst Pat: Institute of Patentees
Inst Pckg: Institute of Packing
Inst Pet: Institute of Petroleum
instr: instruct; instruction; instructor; instrument(s)
instru: instrumentation
instruct.: instruction; instructor
Inst W: Institute of Welding
Inst WE: Institute of Water Engineers
insuf: insufficient
INSURV: Board of Inspection and Survey
int: intake; integer; integral; interest; interior; interjection; internal; international; intersection
INT: Air Inter (Lignes Aériennes Intérieures)
int. al.: *inter alia* (Latin—among other things)
int. cib.: *inter cibos* (Latin—between meals)
intcl: intercoastal
Int Com Illum: International Commission on Illumination
intcp: intercept; interception; interceptor
int dec: interior decorator
INTECOM: International Council for Technical Communication
intel: intelligence
intelsat: international telecommunications satellite
Intend: *Intendente* (Spanish—manager; police commissioner; provincial governor; superintendent; supervisor)
intens: intensive
inter: intermediate; interrogation; intercalation
Interarmco: International Armament Corporation
INTERASMA: Association Internationale d'Asthmologie (International Association for the Study of Asthma)
Interavia: *World Review of Aviation and Astronautica*
Interchem: Interchemical Corporation
intercom: intercommunication system
interdict.: intelligence detection and interdiction countermeasures
interf: interference

Interior: US Department of the Interior
interj: interjection
InterMilPol: International Military Police (NATO)
intern.: internal
internat: international; internationalism; internationalist
interp: interpolation
Interpace: International Pipe and Ceramics
Interpol: International Criminal Police Commission
interr: interrogative
Intertel: International Television
inter/w: intersection with
INTEXT: International Textbook Company
intfc: interference
intg: interrogate; interrogator
intip: integrated information processing
intl: international
intmed: intermediate
int med (Int Med): internal medicine
intmt: intermittent
int. noct.: *inter noctem* (Latin—during the night)
intns: intransit
Intourist: Soviet Tourist Office
intpr: interpret; interpretation; interpreter
intr: intransitive; intruder; intrusion
in trans.: *in transitu* (Latin—in transit)
Int Rep: Intelligence Report
Int Rev: Internal Revenue
intrex: information transfer complex
intrmt: interment
intro: introduce; introduced; introducing; introduction; introductory; introversion; introvert
introd: introduction
introd: *introduzione* (Italian—introduction)
intropta.: *introscripta* (Latin—written within)
intro(s): introduction(s)
intrvlmtr: intervalometer
Int Sum: Intelligence Summary
INTUC: Indian National Trades Union Congress
intvw: interview
I Nuc E: Institute of Nuclear Engineering
InUS: inside the United States
in ut.: *in utero* (Latin—within the uterus)
inv: invent; inventor; invert; inverter; invoice
inv.: *invenit* (Latin—he devised it)
Inv: Inverness
invert.: invertebrate
inves: investigate; investigation; in-

vestigator
invest(s): investigation(s)
in vit.: in vitro (Latin—within glass; within a test tube or other laboratory glass vessel)
in viv.: in vivo (Latin—within a living body)
invol: involuntary
invt: inventory
INWATS: Inward Wide Area Telephone Service
INWR: Imperial National Wildlife Refuge (Arizona); Iroquois National Wildlife Refuge (New York)
INX: Inexco Oil (stock-exchange symbol)
io: ion engine; intraocular
i/o: inboard-outboard (motorboat engine); input/output
i & o: input and output
Io: ionium
IO: India Office; Information Officer; Intelligence Office(r); Intercept Office(r); Irish Office; Issuing Office(r)
IOAM: Institute Of Appliance Manufacturers
IOAT: International Organization Against Trachoma
IOB: Institute of Brewing
IOBB: Independent Order of B'nai B'rith
IOBC: Indian Ocean Biological Center
ioc: initial operational capability; in our culture
IOC: Institute of Chemistry; Intergovernmental Oceanographic Commission; International Olympic Committee; Interstate Oil Compact
IOCA: Interstate Oil Compounders Association
IOCC: Interstate Oil Compact Commission
IOCS: Input-Output Control System
IOCU: International Office of Consumer Unions; International Organization of Consumer Unions
IOCV: International Organization of Citrus Virologists
IOD: Imperial Order of the Dragon
IOE: International Office of Epizootics; International Organization of Employers
IOF: Independent Order of Foresters; International Oceanographic Foundation
IOFC: Indian Ocean Fishery Commission
ioga: industry-organized government-approved
IOGP: Independent Oil and Gas Producers

ioh: item(s) on hand
IOH: Institute of Heraldry
IOI: Israel Office of Information
I o J: Institute of Journalists
IO Ltd: Imperial Oil Limited
IOM: Institute of Metals; Institute of Metallurgists; Institute for Organization Management
IOME: Institute of Marine Engineers
IOMM & P: International Organization of Masters, Mates and Pilots
IOM SPC: Isle of Man Steam Packet Company
IOMTR: International Office for Motor Trades and Repairs
Ion: Ionic
ION: (pseudonymic initials—George Jacob Holyoake); Institute of Navigation
IOOC: International Olive Oil Council
IOOF: Independent Order of Odd Fellows
iop: input-output processor; intraocular power
i & op: in-and-out processing
IOP: Institute of Petroleum
IOPC: Interagency Oil Policy Committee
IOP & LOA: Independent Oil Producers and Land Owners Association
IOQ: Institute of Quarrying
IORM: Improved Order of Red Men
IOS: International Organization for Standardization; Investors Overseas Services
iota.: information overload testing aid
IOTC: International Originating Toll Center
iou: immediate operation use
I.O.U.: I owe you
IO UBC: Institute of Oceanography—University of British Columbia
IOUSP: Instituto Oceanográfico da Universidade de São Paulo (Oceanographic Institute of the University of São Paulo)
IOV: Instituto Oceanográfico de Valparaíso (Oceanographic Institute of Valparaiso)
IOVST: International Organization for Vacuum Science and Technology
iow: in other words
ip: incentive pay; identification point; industrial photographer; industrial photography; initial point; intermediate pressure; iron pipe; plate current (symbol)
i & p: indexed and paged

iP: in Preussen (German—in Prussia)
Ip: Ipanema
IP: Institut Pasteur; Instructor Pilot; Insular Police; Isla de Pinos (Isle of Pines); plate current (symbol)
I & P: Izvestia and *Pravda (Russian—News* and *Truth)*
I£: Israeli pound
ipa: including particular average; internal power amplifier; international phonetic alphabet (IPA)
IPA: Institute of Public Administration; Institute of Public Affairs; International Phonetic Association; International Police Archives (Manchester Central Library); International Police Academy; International Police Association; International Psychoanalytical Association; International Publishers Association
IPA: Information Please Almanac
IPAA: Independent Petroleum Association of America
IPAT: Institute for Personality and Ability Testing
ipb: illustrated parts breakdown
ipbm (IPBM): interplanetary ballistic missile
ipc: industrial process control; isopropyl carbanilate
IPC: Illinois Power Company; Industrial Process Control; Industrial Property Committee; Institute of Paper Chemistry; Institute of Pastoral Care; Institute of Printed Circuits; Inter-African Phytosanitary Commission; International Packings Corporation; International Paper Chemists; International Petroleum Company; International Polar Commission; International Poplar Commission; Iraq Petroleum Company; Isopropyl Carbanilate
IPCA: Industrial Pest Control Association
IPCEA: Insulated Power Cable Engineers Association
IPCI: International Potato Chip Institute
IPCS: International Peace Corps Secretariat
ip cyl: intermediate-pressure cylinder
ipd: insertion phase delay
IPD: Institute for Professional Development
IPE: International Petroleum Encyclopedia
IPEC: International Petroleum Exploration Company
ipecac: ipecacuanha
IPEU: International Photo Engrav-

ers' Union
IPFC: Indo-Pacific Fisheries Council
ipfm: integral pulse frequency modulation
iph: impressions per hour; inches per hour; interphalangeal
IPHC: International Pacific Halibut Commission
IPHE: Institute of Public Health Engineers
i.p.i.: in partibus infidelium (Latin —in the region of unbelievers)
IPI: Institute of Poultry Industries; International Press Institute
IPIP: Information Processing Improvement Program
IPIR: Initial Photographic Interpretation Report (USAF); Institute for Public Interest Representation
ipl (IPL): information processing language
IPL: Italian Pacific Line
ipm: inches per minute; inches per month; interruptions per minute
IPM: Institute of Personnel Management; Institute for Police Management
ipmin: inches per minute
IPMP: Industrial Plant Modernization Program
IPMS: International Polar Motion Service
IPO: Israel Philharmonic Orchestra
IPOEE: Institution of Post Office Electrical Engineers
IPOT: Imperial Philharmonic Orchestra of Tokyo
ipp: imaging photopolarimeter; impact prediction point; india paper proof(s); intrapleural pressure
IPP: Ivan Petrovich Pavlov
ippa: inspection, palpitation, percussion, auscultation
IPPA: International Planned Parenthood Association
IPPAU: International Printing Pressmen and Assistants' Union
ippb: intermittent positive-pressure breathing
IPPF: International Planned Parenthood Federation
ippr: intermittent positive pressure respiration
ipq: intimacy potential quotient
ipr: inches per revolution
IPR: Individual Pay Record; Institute of Pacific Relations; Institute of Philosophical Research
IPR: *International Public Relations*
IPRA: International Public Relations Association
IPRC: Institute of Puerto Rican

Culture
IPRO: International Patent Research Office
I Prod Eng: Institute of Production Engineers
ips: inches per second; interruptions per second; iron pipe size
Ips: Ipswich
IPS: Incremental Purchasing System; Industrial Planning Specification; Institute of Population Studies (Japan); Institute of Public Safety; International Phenomenological Society; International Pipe Standard; Interpretive Programming System
IPSA: Independent Postal System of America
IPSF: International Pharmacy Students Federation; International Piano Symphony Foundation
IPSSB: International Processing Systems Standards Board
ipt: indexed, paged, titled; internal pipe thread
IPT: Initial Production Test (USA)
ipth (IPTH): immunoreactive parathyroid hormone
ipts: international practical temperature scale
IPTS: Improved Programmer Test Section; International Practical Temperature Scale
IPU: International Paleontological Union; Inter-Parliamentary Union
IPW: interrogation prisoner of war
ipy: inches penetration per year; inches per year
IPY: International Polar Year
i.q.: idem quod (Latin—the same as)
Iq: Iraq
IQ: intelligence quotient
I.Q.; I Quit (smoking)
IQCT: Institute for Quality Control Training
I Qk: interrupted quick (light)
I Qk: Fl: interrupted quick flashing (light)
iq & s: iron, quinine, and strychnine
IQSY: International Quiet Sun Year (1964–1965)
Iqu: Iquique
ir: information retrieval; infrared; inland revenue; inside radius; inside right; instantaneous relay; instrument reading; insulation resistance; internal resistance; interrogator-responder
i-r: infra-red
i/r: interchangeability and replaceability
i & r: information and retrieval; intelligence and reconnaissance;

interchangeability and replaceability
i R: im Ruhestand (German—in retirement)
Ir: Iran; Irania; Ireland; iridium; Irish
IR: Industrial Relations; Information Request; Inspection Rejection; Inspector's Report; Intelligence Report; Internal Revenue; Invention Report; Investigation Record
I-R: Ingersoll-Rand
I & R: Initiative and Referendum; Intelligence and Reconnaissance
Ira: Iraq
IRA: Indian Rights Association; Intercollegiate Rowing Association; International Reading Association; International Recreation Association; Iranian Airways; Irish Republican Army; Israel Railway Administration
IRAA: Independent Refiners Association of America
IRAB: Institute for Research in Animal Behavior
IRAC: Industrial Relations Advisory Committee; Interdepartmental Radio Advisory Committee; Interfraternity Research and Administrative Council
IRAD: Institute for Research on Animal Diseases
iran: inspect and repair as necessary
IR/AR: Inspector's Report/Action Request
iraser: infrared amplification by stimulated emission of radiation
IRB: Indiana Rating Bureau; Irish Republican Brotherhood
IRBDC: Insurance Rating Bureau of the District of Columbia
irbm (IRBM): intermediate range ballistic missile
irc: infrared countermeasures; item responsibility code
IRC: Industrial Recreation Council; Industrial Relations Committee; Industrial Relations Council; Institutional Research Council; Internal Revenue Code; International Railways of Central America (stock exchange symbol); International Rainwear Council; International Red Cross; International Rescue Committee; International Resistance Company; International Rice Commission
IRCA: International Railways of Central America
IRCO: Industrial Rustproof Company
IRCP: International Commission on Radiological Protection
ird (IRD): internal research and

development
IRD: Instituto Rubén Darío
IR & D: International Research and Development
Ire: Ireland
IRE: Institute of Radio Engineers
IREE: Institute of Radio and Electronic Engineers
IREF: International Real Estate Federation
IRF: International Road Federation
IRFC: Ingersoll-Rand Finance Corporation
IRFM: *Industrias Reunidas Francisco Matarazzo* (Francisco Matarazzo's Reunited Industries)
IRG: Interdepartmental Regional Group
Ir Gael: Irish Gaelic
IRGRD: International Research Group on Refuse Disposal
irhd: international rubber hardness degrees
IRI: Industrial Research Institute; Institute of the Rubber Industry
IRIA: Infrared Information and Analysis
IRICA: Industrial Research Institute for Central America
irid: iridescent
IRIG: Inter-Range Instrumentation Group
iris.: infrared interferometer spectrometer
IRIS: Integrated Reconnaissance Intelligence System
IRJC: Indian River Junior College
irl: information retrieval language
IRL: Immigration Restriction League; Institute for Rational Living
Irlande: (French—Ireland)
IRLS: Interrogation, Recording, and Location Subsystem
irm: infrared measurement; innate release mechanism; intermediate range monitor
IRM: Improved Risk Mutuals; Islamic Republic of Mauritania
irma: information revision and manuscript assembly
irmak: (Turkish—river)
IRNP: Isle Royale National Park (Michigan)
IRO: Industrial Relations Office(r); Inland Revenue Office(r); Internal Revenue Office(r); International Refugee Organization; International Relief Organization
irod: instantaneous readout detector
Iron Chancellor: Prince Otto Eduard Leopold von Bismarck-Schönhausen—first chancellor of German Empire
Iron Duke: Arthur Wellesley—1st Duke of Wellington who

crushed Napoleon at Waterloo
IRP: Individualized Reading Program; Information Resources Press
IRPA: International Radiation Protection Association
IRPS: International Religious Press Service (Vatican City)
irr: irregular
IRR: Institute of Race Relations
IRRA: Industrial Relations Research Association
irrd: international road research documentation
irreg: irregular
irrig: irrigation
IRs: Inspector's Reports
IRS: Ineligible Reserve Section; Internal Revenue Service; International Recruiting Service; International Rorschach Society
I & RS: Information and Research Services
IRSG: International Rubber Study Group
IRSID: Institut des Recherches de la Sidérurgie Française (French Steel Research Institute)
IRSNB: Institut Royal des Sciences Naturelles de Belgique (Royal Belgian Institute of Natural Sciences)
IRSS: Instrumentation Range Safety System
irt: infrared tracker
IRT: Institute for Rapid Transit; Institute of Reprographic Technology; Interborough Rapid Transit (subway system)
IRTA: Illinois Retired Teachers Association
IRTE: Institute of Road Transport Engineers
IRTS: International Radio and Television Society
iru: international radium unit; international rat unit
IRU: International Road Transport Union
Irv: Irvin; Irving; Irwin
is.: ingot sheet; integrally stiffened; intercoastal space; internal shield; island; isle
i & s: inspection and security; inspection and survey
Is: Islam; Islamic; Island; Isle; Israel; Israeli
IS: Igor Stravinsky; Indian Summer (freeboard marking); Irish Society
I of S: Institute of Sound; Isle of Skye
isa: international standard atmosphere
Isa: Isaiah, The Book of the Prophet
ISA: Independent Showmen of

America; Instrument Society of America; Insulating Siding Association; International Schools Association; International Scientific Affairs; International Security Affairs; International Sign Association; International Silk Association; International Sociological Association; International Standards Association
Isab: Isabella
ISAB: Institute for the Study of Animal Behavior
ISAC: International Security Affairs Committee
ISACP: Italian Society of Authors, Composers, and Publishers
ISAD: Information Science and Automation Division (ALA)
IsAF: Israeli Air Force
Isak Dinesen: Baroness Karen Blixen-Finecke
isar: information storage and retrieval
ISAS: Isotopic Source Assay System
ISAW: International Society of Aviation Writers
ISB: International Society of Biometeorology
ISBN: International Standard Book Number
ISBS: Icelandic State Broadcasting Service
isc: interstate commerce
ISC: Icelandic Steamship Company; Idaho State College; Imperial Service College; Imperial Staff College; Indiana State College; Indian Staff Corps; Indoor Sports Club; Industrial Security Commission; Inter-American Society of Cardiology; International Science Center; International Sericultural Commission; International Society of Cardiology; International Softball Congress; International Statistical Classification; International Sugar Council; International Supreme Council (World Masons); Interseas Shipping Corporation; Interservice Sports Council; Interstate Sanitation Commission
ISCA: International Senior Citizens Association
iscan: inertialess steerable communication antenna
ISCB: International Society for Cell Biology
ISCC: Inter-Society Color Council
ISCE: International Society for Christian Endeavor
ISCEH: International Society for Clinical and Experimental Hypnosis

ISCET: International Society of Certified Electronics Technicians

ISCM: International Society for Contemporary Music

ISCOR: Iron and Steel Industrial Corporation (South Africa)

ISCP: International Society of Clinical Pathology

ISD: Internal Security Division (U.S. Dept of Justice)

ISDI: International Social Development Institute

ISDRA: International Sled Dog Racing Association

ISDS: Inadvertent Separation Destruct System

ise: integral square error

ISE: Institute of Social Ethics; Institution of Structural Engineers

ISEA: Industrial Safety Equipment Association

ISEEP: Infrared-Sensitive Element Evaluation Program

ISES: International Society of Explosives Specialists

ISEU: International Stereotypers' and Electrotypers' Union

isf: interstitial fluid

ISF: International Science Foundation; International Shipping Federation; International Society for Fat Research; International Softball Federation

ISFA: Intercoastal Steamship Freight Association; International Scientific Film Association

ISFR: Institute for the Study of Fatigue and Reliability

isg: imperial standard gallon

ISGM: Isabella Stewart Gardner Museum

ISGS: International Society for General Semantics

ISGW: International Society of Girl Watchers

Ish: Ishmael

ISH: International Society of Hematology

ISHAM: International Society for Human and Animal Mycology

ISHL: Illinois Social Hygiene League

ISHS: International Society for Horticultural Science

ISI: Institute for Scientific Information; Intercollegiate Society of Individualists; International Statistical Institute; Iron and Steel Institute

ISIC: International Standard Industrial Classification

ISIM: International Society of Internal Medicine

isis (ISIS): ionospheric studies

ISIS: Institute of Scrap Iron and Steel; International Science Information Service

ISKC: International Society for Krishna Consciousness

isl: island

ISL: Iceland Steamship Company; Interseas Shipping Lines; Iranian Shipping Lines; Irish Shipping Limited

isla: (Spanish—island, as in Isla de Cuba)

Islamic Century: the 600s—Mohammed flees from Mecca to Medina and dies in 632; Islam begins expanding throughout the Middle East and Africa—the 7th century

ISLIC: Israel Society of Special Libraries and Information Centers

isln: isolation

ISLRS: Inactive Status List Reserve Section

isls L: islands of Langerhans

ism: industrial, scientific, medical wave length

ISM: International Society for Musicology

ISMA: International Superphosphate Manufacturers Association

ISME: International Society of Musical Education

ISMI: Institute for the Study of Mental Images

Is N: (Sir) Isaac Newton

ISN: International Society for Neurochemistry

ISNP: International Society of Naturopathic Physicians

isn't: is not

iso: isolate; isolation; isolator (Soviet penal colony specializing in solitary confinement of political prisoners); isotope; isotopic

ISO: Imperial Service Order; Indianapolis Symphony Orchestra; Information Services Office(r); International Standardization Organization

isobu: isobutyl

is/oc: individual system/organization cost

isochr: isochronal

isom: isometric(s)

ISOMATA: Idyllwild School of Music and the Arts

isordil: isosrbide dinitrate + propranolol

isot: isotropic

iso wd: isolation ward

Isp: specific impulse (symbol)

ISP: Industrial Security Program; Institute of Social Psychiatry; Institute of Store Planners; Interamerican Society of Psychology

ISPA: International Screen Publicity Association; International Sporting Press Association

ISPO: Instrumentation Ships' Project Office

isr: information storage and retrieval

Isr: Israel; Israeli

ISR: Indian State Railways; Institute for Sex Research; Institute for Social Research; International Society of Radiology

IS & R: Information Storage and Retrieval (system)

ISRAD: Institute for Social Research and Development

Israelian Century: the 10th century before the Christian era when King Solomon reigned over the Israelites who defeated all their enemies and built the great temple of Jerusalem—the 900s

ISRB: Idaho Surveying and Rating Bureau

ISRU: International Scientific Radio Union

iss: ideal solidus structures; issue

ISS: Industry Standard Specifications; Inspection Surveillance Sheet; Institute of Space Sciences; Institute of Space Studies; Integrated Start System; International Schools Service; International Shoe Company (stock exchange symbol); International Social Service; International Students Society; International Sunshine Society

ISSA: International Social Security Association

ISSB: Inter-Services Security Board

ISSCT: International Society of Sugar Cane Technologists

issr: information storage, selection, and retrieval

ISSS: International Society of Soil Science; International Society for the Study of Symbols

ISST: International Society of Skilled Trades

ist: insulin shock therapy; interstellar travel

IST: Indian Standard Time; International Society of Toxicology; Istanbul, Turkey (airport); Institute of Science and Technology (University of Michigan)

IST: *International Steam Table*

IS & T: *International Science and Technology*

ISTA: International Seed Testing Association

istar: information storage translation and reproduction

ISTD: Inter-Services Topographical

Department

IS 201: Intermediate School 201 (for example)

isth: isthmian; isthmus

ISTI: Iowa State Technical Institute

ISTM: International Society for Testing Materials

istmo: (Italian or Spanish—isthmus, as in Istmo de Panamá)

ISTO: Italian State Tourist Office

I Struct E: Institute of Structural Engineers

istse: integral square time square error

ISU: Idaho State University; International Seamen's Union; International Skating Union; Iowa Southern Utilities; Iowa State University; Italian Service Unit; Southern Iowa Railway (railroad coding)

I-sub: inhibitor substance

ISUM: Intelligence Summary

ISUST: Iowa State University of Science and Technology

ISV: Institute for the Study of Violence (Brandeis U); International Scientific Vocabulary

ISVR: Institute of Sound and Vibration Research

isw: interstitial water

ISW: Institute for Solid Wastes

ISWG: Imperial Standard Wire Gauge

it: slang term for sex appeal

it.: inspection tag; internal thread; international tolerance; inventory transfer; item; itemization (s); itemize(d)

ft: item (Spanish—item)

i.t.: in transitu (Latin—in transit)

i/t: intensity duration

It: Italy

IT: Immunity Test; Imperial Territory; Imperial Typewriter; Income Tax; Indian Territory; Inner Temple; Institute of Technology; International Telephone and Telegraph (Wall Street slang)

ita: initial teaching alphabet

ITA: Independent Television Authority; Industrial Truck Association; Institut du Transport Aérien (Air Transport Institute); International Temperance Association; International Touring Alliance; International Twins Association

ITACS: Integrated Tactical Air Control System

ital: italic; italics

Ital: Italian

Italian Century: the 15th century when great Italian families such as the Borgias and the de Medicis bring about the renewal of art and architecture in Italy —the Italian Renaissance—the 1400s

ITAR: Interstate and Foreign Travel (or Transportation) in Aid of Racketeering Enterprises

ITB: International Time Bureau; Irish Tourist Board

itbh: internal broach

IT & BL: Island Tug & Barge, Ltd.

itc: installation time and cost

ITC: Illinois Terminal Company (railroad); Imperial Tobacco Company; Infantry Training Center; International Tin Council; International Toastmistress Clubs; International Traders Clubs; Island Trading Company

ITCA: International Typographic Composition Association

itcan: inspect, test, and correct as necessary

ITCP: Integrated Test and Checkout Procedures

ITCV: Inter-Tropical Convergence Zone

it'd: it had; it would

ITD: International Telephone Directory

ITE: Institute of Traffic Engineers

itf: inland transit floater (insurance)

ITF: International Television Federation

ITFCS: Institute for Twenty-First Century Studies

itfs: instructional television fixed service

ITFS: International Television Fixed Service

itga: internal gauge

ithy: I'm only trying to help you

ITI: Inagua Transports Incorporated; Integrated Task Indices; International Technical Institute; International Theatre Institute; International Thrift Institute

ITIB: Iceland Tourist Information Bureau

ITIC: International Tsunami Information Center

itin: itinerary

itl: integrate-transfer-launch

Itl: Italian

it'll: it will

itlx: italics (used for items from Latin or other languages, titles of books and periodicals, physical symbols)

itm: inch trim moment

ITN: Independent Television News

ITN: Independent Television News

ITO: Interim Technical Order; International Trade Organization (UN); Invitational Travel Orders

ITOA: Independent Taxi Owners Association

ITOFCA: Industrial Trailer-on-Flatcar Associates

itom: interstate transportation of obscene matter

ITR: Indiana Toll Road

ITRC: International Tin Research Council

it's: it has; it is

ITS: Idaho Test Station; Integrated Trajectory System; International Technogeographical Society; International Trade Secretariat; International Transportation Service

itsa: interstate transportation of stolen aircraft

ITSA: Institute for Telecommunication Sciences and Aeronomy

itsb: interstate transportation of strikebreakers

itsc: interstate transportation of stolen cattle

ITSC: International Telecommunications Satellite Consortium

itse: integral time square error

itsp: interstate transportation of stolen property

itt: instant-touch tuning

ITT: Institute of Textile Technology; Insulin Tolerance Test

IT & T: International Telephone and Telegraph

ITTA: International Table Tennis Association

ITTCS: International Telephone and Telegraph Communications System

ITTE: Institute of Transportation and Traffic Engineering

ITTF: International Table Tennis Federation

ITTTA: International Technical Tropical Timber Association

ITU: Income Tax Unit; International Telecommunications Union; International Typographical Union

ITUA: Industrial Trades Union of America

ITURM: International Typographical Union Ruling Machine

itv: instructional television

ITV: Independent Television

ITVA: Instructional Television Authority

ITW: Illinois Tool Works

ITWF: International Transport Workers Federation

iu: immunizing unit(s); international unit(s)

IU: Indiana University; Indianapolis Union (railroad); International Utilities

IÜ: Istanbul Üniversitesi (University of Instanbul)

IUA: International Union of Architects
IUAES: International Union of Anthropological and Ethnological Sciences
IUAI: International Union of Aviation Insurers
IUAPPA: International Union of Air Pollution Prevention Associations
IUAT: International Union Against Tuberculosis
IUB: International Union of Biochemistry; Interstate Underwriters Board
IUBS: International Union of Biological Sciences
IUC: International Union of Chemistry
IUCc: International Union of Crystallography
iucd: intrauterine contraceptive device
IUCN: International Union for Conservation of Nature and Natural Resources
IUCNNR: International Union for Conservation of Nature and Natural Resources
IUCr: International Union of Crystallography
IUCSTP: Inter-Union Commission on Solar -Terrestrial Physics
iud: intrauterine device; intrauterine diaphragm
IUD: Institute for Urban Development
iudr: idoxuridine
IUDZG: International Union of Directors of Zoological Gardens
IUE: International Union for Electroheat
IUEC: International Union of Elevator Constructors
IUER & MW: International Union of Electrical, Radio & Machine Workers
IUFA: International Union of Family Organizations
IUFRO: International Union of Forest Research Organizations
IUGG: International Union of Geodesy and Geophysics
IUGS: International Union of Geological Sciences
IUHA: Industrial Unit Heater Association
IUHS: International Union of the History of Science
IUL: Indiana University Library
IULIA: International Union of Life Insurance Agents
IUMC: Indiana University Medical Center
IUMM & SW: International Union of Mine, Mill and Smelter

Workers
IUMSWA: Industrial Union of Marine and Shipbuilding Workers of America
IUNS: International Union of Nutritional Sciences
IUOE: International Union of Operating Engineers
IUOT: Indiana University Opera Theater
IUOTO: International Union of Official Travel Organizations
IUP: Israel Universities Press
IUPAC: International Union of Pure and Applied Chemistry
IUPAP: International Union of Pure and Applied Physics
IUPLAW: International Union for the Protection of Literary and Artistic Works
IUPM: International Union for Protecting Public Morality
IUPN: International Union for the Protection of Nature
IUPS: International Union of Physiological Sciences
IUPW: International Union of Petroleum Workers
IUR: International Union of Railways
IUS: International Union of Students
IUSSI: International Union for the Study of Social Insects
IUSSP: International Union for the Scientific Study of Population
IUT: Instituts Universitaires de Technologie (University Institutes of Technology)
IUTAM: International Union of Theoretical and Applied Mechanics
IUUCLGW: International Union, United Cement, Lime & Gypsum Workers
IUVDT: International Union against the Venereal Diseases and the Treponematoses
IUVSTA: International Union for Vacuum Science Techniques and Applications
IUWWML: International Union of Wood, Wire, and Metal Lathers
iv: initial velocity; intravenous(ly); intravertebral; inverted vertical (engine)
i/v: increased value
i.v.: in verbo (Latin—under the word)
i V: in Vertretung (German—as a substitute; by proxy)
Iv: Ivan; Ivy
I-et-V: Ille-et-Vilaine
Iva: Godiva
IVA: Independent Voters Association

Ivan: (nickname for the typical Russian)
IVC: Imperial Valley College
ivcd: intraventricular conduction defect
Iv Cst: Ivory Coast
ivd: interpolated voice data
ivds: independent variable depth sonar
Ive: Ivan; Iven
I've: I have
I've had it: (popular American contraction—I have had enough of it)—corruption of the environment, higher taxation plus inflation and unemployment, long-haired dropouts and other public parasites, smelly street people, racists and racism, student unrest, hijacking, mugging, the dope racket, Watergate, etc.
IVFZ: International Veterinary Federation of Zootechnics
IVGMMA: International Violin, Guitar Makers, and Musicians Association
IVIS: International Visitors Information Service
ivjc: intervertebral joint complex
IVK: Institutet för Vaxtforskning och Kyllagring (Institute for Foodstuff Research and Refrigeration—Sweden)
ivmu: inertial velocity measurement unit
ivp: initial vapor pressure; inspected variety purity (certified seeds); intravenous pyelogram
IVP: Instituto Venezolano de la Petroquimica (Venezuelan Petrochemical Institute)
IVS: International Voluntary Service
ivsd: interventricular septal defect
ivt: intravenous transfusion
IVU: International Vegetarian Union
iw: indirect waste; inside width; isotopic weight; ivory woodpecker
i/w: in work
IW: Aero Trasporti Italiani (2-letter coding, Italian Air Transport)
I o W: Isle of Wight
IWA: Institute of World Affairs; Insurance Workers of America; International Woodworkers of America
IWAHMA: Industrial Warm Air Heater Manufacturers Association
IWC: Inland Waterways Corporation; International Whaling Commission; International Wheat Council
IWCA: International World Calen-

dar Association
IWCCA: Inland Waterways Common Carriers Association
IWCI: Industrial Wire Cloth Institute
IWCS: Integrated Wideband Communications System
IWCT: International War Crimes Tribunal
IWE: Institution of Water Engineers
IWG: Imperial Wire Gauge
IWGC: Imperial War Graves Commission
iwistk: issue while in stock
IWIU: Insurance Workers International Union
IWLA: Izaak Walton League of America
IWM: Imperial War Museum; Institute of Works Managers
IWMA: International Working Men's Association
IWO: International Wine Office; International Workers Order
IWRI: International Wildfowl Research Institute
IWRMA: Independent Wire Rope Manufacturers Association

IWS: Inland Waterway Service; International Wool Secretariat
IWSA: International Water Supply Association
IWSB: Insect Wire Screening Bureau
IWSc: Institute of Wood Science
IWSG: International Wool Study Group
IWSP: Institute of Work Study Practitioners
IWST: Integrated Weapon System Training
IWT: Indus Water Treaty; Inland Water Transport
IWTA: Inland Water Transport Authority
IWTO: International Wool Textile Organization
iwu: illegal wearing of uniform
IWU: Illinois Wesleyan University
IWW: Industrial Workers of the World; Intracoastal Waterway
IWWP: *International Who's Who in Poetry*
IWVA: International War Veterans Alliance
IX: unclassified vessel (2-letter naval code)

I.X.: *Iesous Christos* (Greek —Jesus Christ)
iy: ionized yeast
IY: Imperial Yeomanry; International Petroleum (stock exchange symbol)
IYHF: International Youth Hostel Federation
IYRU: International Yacht Racing Union
iyswim: if you see what I mean
Iyul: (Russian—July)
Iyun: (Russian—June)
i y v: *ida y vuelta* (Spanish—round trip)
iz: izzard; zed
Iz: Izar; Izmir (Smyrna)
Izd: *izdatl'* (Russian—publisher)
IZL: *Irgun Z'vai Leumi* (Hebrew—National Army Organization)
izqᵃ: *'izquierda* (Spanish—left)
izqᵒ: *izquierdo* (Spanish—left)
izs: insulin zinc suspension
Izv: *Izvestia* (Russian—news) —official newspaper of the Presidium of the Supreme Soviet- —published in Moscow

J

j: inner quantum number (symbol); jack; junior; square of minus 1 (symbol); unit vector in y direction (symbol)
J: action variable (symbol); advance ratio (symbol); electric current density (symbol); gramequivalent weight (symbol); heat transfer factor (symbol); Jacob; Jacobean; Jacobian; Jaen; January; jet; Jew; Jewish; joint; joule; Judaic; Judaism; Juliett —code for letter J; Julliard; July; June; North American Aviation (symbol); polar movement of inertia (symbol); radiant intensity (symbol)
J: *Jejunium* (Latin—fast; hunger); *Journal* (French—journal)
J-1: personnel section of joint military staff
J-2: intelligence section of joint military staff
J-3: operations and training section of joint military staff
J-4: logistics section of joint military staff
J-5: Plans and Policy (Joint Chiefs

of Staff)
J-6: Communications, Electronics (Joint Chiefs of Staff)
ja: jack adapter; job analysis
j/a (J/A): joint account
j & a: junk and abandon; junked and abandoned
Ja: Jacob; Jacque(s); James; Japan; Japanese
JA: Jewish Agency; John Adams; Judge Advocate; Junior Achievement
JAA: Japan Aeronautic Association
JAAF: Joint Army-Air Force
JAAFU: Joint Anglo-American Foulup
jaarg: *jaargang* (Dutch—annual volume)
JAARS: Jungle Aviation and Radio Service
JAAS: Jewish Academy of Arts and Sciences
Jab: Jabal; Jabalpur; Jabez; Jabneel
JAB: Joint Amphibious Board
jac: jet aircraft coating
Jac: Jacobean; Jacobite; Jacobus
JAC: Joint Advisory Committee;

Joint Apprenticeship Council
JAC: *Journal of Applied Chemistry*
Jace: Jason
jack: jackass
Jack: Jackson; Jacob; John
Jackie: Jack(son); Jacob; Jacqueline; John
JACKPOT: Joint Airborne Communications Center and Command Post
JACOB: Junior Achievement Corporation of Business
JACS: *Journal of the American Chemical Society*
Jad: Jadavpur, India
JAD: Julian astronomical day
JADB: Joint Air Defense Board
JADE: Japanese Air Defense Environment
JADF: Japan Air Defense Force
jaditbhkycc: just a drop in the basket helps keep your city clean (anti-litter-civic-responsibility campaign)
J Adv: Judge Advocate
J Adv Gen: Judge Advocate General
JAEC: Japan Atomic Energy Com-

mission
JAERI: Japan Atomic Energy Research Institute
JAF: Jordanian Air Force; Judge Advocate of the Fleet
JAFC: Japan Atomic Fuel Corporation
Jaffna: Jaffnapatam
Jag: Jaguar
JAG: James Abram Garfield; Judge Advocate General
JAG-A: Judge Advocate General—Army
JAGC: Judge Advocate General's Corps
JAGD: Judge Advocate General's Department
JAG-N: Judge Advocate General—Navy
JAGS: Judge Advocate General's School
JAH: John Adams House
Jahrb: Jahrbuch (German—yearbook)
Jahrg: Jahrgang (German—annual publication; year's growth; vintage of the year)
jai: juvenile amaurotic idiocy
JAIEG: Joint Atomic Information Exchange Group
JAIF: Japan Atomic Industrial Forum
Jak: Jakarta (Batavia)
Jake: Jacob; Jacobus
Jal: Jalisco
JAL: Japan Air Lines; Jet Approach and Landing Chart
Jam: Jamaica
JAM: James A. Michener; Joslyn Art Museum
JAMA: Journal of the American Medical Association
JAMAG: Joint American Military Advisory Group
James: James, The General Epistle of
JAMMAT: Joint Military Mission for Aid to Turkey
jamtrac: jammers tracked by azimuth crossings
JAMTS: Japan Association of Motor Trade and Service
jamwich: jam sandwich
jan: janitor; janitorial
Jan: January; John
JAN: Jackson, Mississippi (airport); Joint Army-Navy
JANAF: Joint Army-Navy Air Force
JANAIR: Joint Army-Navy Aircraft Instrument Research
JANAP: Joint Army-Navy-Air Force Publication
JANAST: Joint Army-Navy-Air Force Sea Transport
JanFeb: January and February

JANS: Jet Aircraft Noise Survey; Joint Army-Navy Specification
JANSRP: Jet Aircraft Noise Survey Research Program
janv: janvier (French—January)
Jap: Japan; Japanese; Jasper
JAP: Joint Apprenticeship Program
JA£: Jamaican pound
JAPAC: Japan Atomic Power Company; Joint Air Photo Center
Japanese Century: the 2000s—the 21st century (providing productivity, standard of living, and other growth factors are not disturbed by large-scale earthquakes or world wars)
JAPC: Joint Air Photo Center
JAPCO: Japan Atomic Power Company
Jap Cur: Japan Current
Japdic: Japanese dictionary
Japex: Japan Petroleum Exploitation Company
JAPIA: Japan Auto Parts Industries Association
jarg: jargon; jargonese; jargonist; jargonistic; jargonize
Jas: James
JAS: Jamaica Agricultural Society; Jewish Agricultural Society
JASA: Journal of the Acoustical Society of America
JASDF: Japan Air Self-Defense Force
JASG: Joint Advanced Study Group
jasp: jasper; jasperoid
Jasp: Jasper
jastop: jet-assisted stop
jasu: jet aircraft starting unit
JAT: Jugoslovenski Aero-Transport (Yugoslav Airlines)
JATMA: Japan Automobile Tire Manufacturers Association
jato: jet-assisted takeoff
JATS: Joint Air Transportation Service
jaund: jaundice
Jav: Java; Javanese
JAVA: Jamaica Association of Villas and Apartments
javelle water: sodium hypochlorite solution (NaOCl)
JAVHS: Jane Addams Vocational High School
JAWA: Jane's All the World Aircraft
Jax: Jacksonville
JAX: Jacksonville, Florida (airport)
jaycee (JC): Junior Chamber of Commerce
jb: jet bomb (JB); junction box
Jb: Jacob
Jb: Jahrbuch (German—annual; yearbook)

JB: James Buchanan; Jodrell Bank; John Bull (British Empire personified); Joint Board; Stetson hat (after its original maker, J.B. Stetson)
J.B.: *Jurum Baccalaureus* (Latin—Bachelor of Laws)
J-B: Jacques Barzun; Jean-Baptiste; Johannes Brahms
JBA: Japan Binoculars Association; Junior Bluejackets of America
J-bar: capital-J-shaped bar (as used in ski tow lifts)
JBC: Jamaica Broadcasting Corporation; Japan Broadcasting Corporation (*q.v.* NHK)
JBCA: Jewish Book Council of America
JB & Co: John Brown and Company (shipbuilders)
Jber: Jahresbericht (German—annual report)
JBES: Jodrell Bank Experimental Station (Cheshire, England)
JBHS: John Bartram High School
JBIA: Jewish Braille Institute of America
J-bird: jailbird (underground slang—convict)
JBMA: John Burroughs Memorial Association
J-boat: large yacht, often 76 feet or longer; small racing boat sailed by youngsters
J-bolt: capital-J-shaped bolt
J-box: J-shaped bleaching box; junction box
JBPS: Jamaica Banana Producers Steamship
JBS: John Birch Society
JBSW: Joseph Bulova School of Watchmaking
JBT: Jewelers Board of Trade
JBUSDC: Joint Brazil-United States Defense Commission
JBUSMC: Joint Brazil-US Military Commission
jc: joint compound
Jc: Junction
JC: Jackson College; Jacksonville College; Jamestown College; Jefferson City; Jefferson College; Jersey City; Jet Club; Job Corps; Jockey Club; Johnstown College; Joliet College; Judson College; Juniata College; Junior Chamber (of Commerce; members called Jaycees)
J.C.: Jesus Christ; Julius Caesar
J.C.: *Juris Consultus* (Latin—Juris Consult)
JCA: Jewelry Crafts Association; Joint Commission on Accreditation (of colleges and universities); Joint Communication Ac-

tivity; Joint Communications Agency; Joint Construction Agency; Junior College of Albany

JCAE: Joint Committee on Atomic Energy

JCAH: Joint Committee on Accreditation of Hospitals

JCAM: Joint Commission on Atomic Masses

JCAR: Joint Commission of Applied Radioactivity

J.C.B.: *Juris Canoni Baccalaureus* (Latin—Bachelor of Canon Law); *Juris Civilis Baccalaureus* (Latin —Bachelor of Civil Law)

JCBC: Junior College of Broward County

JCC: Jamestown Community College; Jefferson Community College; Jewish Community Center; Job Corps Center; John C. Calhoun; Joint Communications Center; Junior Chamber of Commerce

JC of C: Junior Chamber of Commerce

JCCA: Joint Conex Control Agency

JCCRG: Joint Command Control Requirements Group

J.C.D.: *Juris Canonici Doctor* (Latin—Doctor of Canon Law); *Juris Civilis Doctor* (Latin —Doctor of Civil Law)

JCE: Johannesburg College of Education; Junior Certificate Examination

JCENS: Joint Communication Electronic Nomenclature System

JCFA: Japan Chemical Fibres Association

JCI: Junior Chamber International

JCIC: Johannesburg Consolidated Investment Company

JCIEABJ: Joint Commission for the Investigation of the Effects of the Atomic Bomb in Japan

JCII: Japan Camera Inspection Institute

JCJC: Jasper County Junior College; Jefferson County Junior College

Jck: Jacksonville

Jcl: Johnny come lately

JCL: Job Control Language; John Crerar Library

J.C.L.: *Juris Canonici Licentiatus* (Latin—Licentiate in Canon Law)

JCLS: Junior College Libraries Section

JCM: Joint Committee on Microcards

JCNAAF: Joint Canadian Navy-Army-Air Force

JCNM: Jewel Cave National Monument

JCO: José Clemente Orozco

jcp: jungle canopy penetration

JCP: J.C. Penney; Joint Committee on Printing (Congress); Junior Collegiate Players; Justice of the Common Pleas

JCPCI: Junior College of Packer Collegiate Institute

JCs: Job Corpsmen

JCS: Jewish Community Center(s); Joint Chiefs of Staff

jct: junction

JCTC: Japanese Cultural and Trade Center; Juneau County Teachers College

jct pt: junction point

JCU: John Carroll University

JCUS: Joint Center for Urban Studies (MIT and Harvard)

jd: joined; joint dictionary; junior debutante; jury duty; juvenile deliquent

jd: *jemand* (German—someone; somebody)

Jd: Jordanian dinar (monetary unit of Jordan)

JD: Julian day; Junior Deacon; Junior Dean; Justice Department

J.D.: Doctor of Jurisprudence; *Juris* or *Jurum Doctor* (Latin—Doctor of Law or Laws)

JDA: Japan Defense Agency; Japan Domestic Airline; Jefferson Davis Association

JDC: Joint Distribution Committee; Juvenile Delinquency Control

JDCC: Juneau-Douglas Community College

J/deg: joule per degree

JDHS: Jefferson Davis High School

JDL: Jewish Defense League

JDP: John Dos Passos

jds: job data sheet

jd's: juvenile delinquents

JDS: John Dewey Society

JDSRF: Jim Dandy's Still and Refreshment Factory (Australian definition for the Joint Defense Space Research Facility near Alice Springs)

jé: *jésus* (French—paper of superroyal size)

JEA: Jesuit Educational Association; Joint Engineering Agency

Jean-Jacques: Jean-Jacques Rousseau

Jean l'Oiseleur: (French—Jean the bird tamer)—pseudonym of Jean Cocteau

Jean Moreas: (pseudonym—Jannis Papadiamantopoulos)

Jeanne d'Arc: Joan of Arc

Jean Paul: Johann Paul Friedrich Richter's pseudonym

jebel: (Arabic—mountain, as in Jebel Druse)

jebm: jet engine base maintenance

JECC: Japan Electronic Computer Company

Jed: Jedediah

JEDS: Japanese Expeditions to the Deep Sea

JEE: Japan Electronics Engineering

jeep: (from GP meaning general purpose) 4-wheel-drive quarterton utility vehicle

JEEP: Joint Emergency Evacuation Plan

Jef(f): Geoffrey; Geoffroy; Jefferson; Jeffery; Jeffry

Jeff D: Jefferson Davis

jefm (JEFM): jet engine field maintenance

JEI: Japan Electronics Industry

JEIA: Japanese Electronic Industries Association

JEIDA: Japan Electronic Industry Development Association

JEIPAC: Japan Electronic Information Processing Automatic Computer

jejun: jejunectomy; jejunitis; jejunostomy

Jem: Jemima

JEN: Junta de la Energia Nuclear (Atomic Energy Board)

Jen Jih: Jen-min Jih-pao (People's Daily)—published in Peking by Communist Party of China

jentac.: *jentaculum* (Latin—breakfast)

JEOCN: Joint European Operations Communications Network

JEOL: Japan Electron Optics Laboratory

JEPIA: Japan Electronic Parts Industry Association

Jer: Jersey

Jer.: Jeremiah, The Book of the Prophet

Jere: Jeremiah; Jerry

jerob: jeroboam (4-bottle capacity)

Jeronº: Jerónimo (Spanish —Jerome)

Jerry: Gerald; Gerard; Gerome; Jerald; Jeramy; Jeremiah; Jerome

Jersey Lily: Lily Langtry—English actress born on the island of Jersey where her original name was Emily Charlotte Le Breton

JES: James Ewing Society; John Ericsson Society

JESA: Japanese Engineering Standards Association

Jessie: Jess; Jessica

jet: jet-engine aircraft

jet.: jetsam

JETDS: Joint Electronics Type Des-

ignation System
JETEC: Joint Electron Tube Engineering Council
jet fag: jet flight fatigue
jetma: jet mechanic
jet-p: jet-propelled; jet propulsion
JETP: *Journal of Experimental and Theoretical Physics* (Academy of Sciences, USSR)
JETRO: Japan Exterior Trade Research Organization
JETS: Junior Engineers Technical Society
jett: jettison
jeu: jeudi (French—Thursday)
Jev: Japanese encephalitis virus
Jew.: Jewish
JEZ: Johannes Enschede en Zonen
JFACT: Joint Flight-Acceptance Composite Test
JFK: John Fitzgerald Kennedy
JFKCAS: John F. Kennedy College of Arts and Sciences (Trinidad)
JFKCPA: John F. Kennedy Center for the Performing Arts
JFKMF: John F. Kennedy Memorial Forest (near Jerusalem, Israel)
JFKMH: John F. Kennedy Memorial Highway (Baltimore, Maryland to Wilmington, Delaware)
JFKML: John F. Kennedy Memorial Library
JFKSC: John F. Kennedy Space Center
jfl: joint frequency list
JFMAMJJASOND: January, February, March, April, May, June, July, August, September, October, November, December (as abbreviated to conserve space on charts and graphs)
JFNP: John Forrest National Park (Western Australia)
JFO: San Francisco, California (heliport)
jfp: joint frequency panel
JFPS: Japan Fire Prevention Society
jfr: jevnfr (Dano-Norwegian—compare)
JFRC: James Forrestal Research Center
JFRO: Joint Fire Research Organisation (UK)
JFS: Japan Fishery Society
JFS: Jane's Fighting Ships
JFSOC: Junior Foreign Service Officers Club
JG: junior grade
jga: juxtaglomerular apparatus
JGC: Japan Gasoline Company
jg di: joggle die
JGE: Journal of General Education
J-girl: joy girl (prostitute)

jgn: junction gate number
JGNP: Japanese Gross National Product
JGR: Jaldapara Game Reserve (India)
JGSA: John G. Shedd Aquarium
jg sm: joggle shims
JGWTC: Jungle and Guerrilla Warfare Training Center (USA)
jh: juvenile hormone
Jh: Jahresheft (German—yearly publication)
JH: Jugendherberge (German—youth hostel)
J & H: Jack & Heintz
JHAI: John Herron Art Institute
JHC: John Hancock Center
JHI: Jacob Hiatt Institute
JHMO: Junior Hospital Medical Officer
JHO: Jam Handy Organization; Japan Hydrographic Office
JHOS: Johns Hopkins Oceanographic Studies
JHS: John Howard Society; Junior High School
J.H.S.: Jesus Hominum Salvator (Latin—Jesus Saviour of Men)
JHU: Johns Hopkins University
JHUL: Johns Hopkins University Library
JHVH: Jehovah (transliteration of Hebrew tetragrammaton Yhwh, Yahwah, or Jahvah [he was, he is, he will be], used by Hebrew tribes in 3rd century BCE because they thought "Jehovah" was too sacred to pronounce; perhaps the world's oldest abbreviation
JI: Aerovias Sudamericanos (symbol)
JIC: Joint Industrial Council; Joint Industry Council; Joint Intelligence Center; Joint Intelligence Committee
JICA: Joint Intelligence Collecting Agency
JICST: Japan Information Center of Science and Technology
JIDC: Jamaica Industrial Development Corporation
JIG: Joint Intelligence Group
JIE: Junior Institution of Engineers
JIIST: Japan Institute for International Studies and Training
JILA: Joint Institute for Laboratory Astrophysics
Jim: James
JIM: Japan Institute of Metals
jima: (Japanese—island, as in Iwo Jima)
JIMA: Japan Industrial Management Association
Jimmu: Jimmu Tenno—first emperor of Japan who began his

reign in 660 BCE
Jimmy: James
JINR: Joint Institute for Nuclear Research
JIOA: Joint Intelligence Objectives Agency
JIR: Jewish Institute of Religion
JIS: Jail Inspection Service; Japan Industrial Standard; Jewish Information Society; Joint Intelligence Staff
JISA: Japan Industrial Safety Association
JISC: Japanese Industrial Standards Committee
JISP: Jack Island State Park (Florida)
jit: jitney bus
jj: jaw jerk
JJ: Judges, Justices
J-J: Jean-Jacques
J & J: Johnson & Johnson
JJA: John James Audubon
JJCCJ: John Jay College of Criminal Justice
JJHL: John Jay Hopkins Laboratory for Pure and Applied Science (General Atomic Division of General Dynamics Corporation)
JJHS: John Jay High School
JJS: James Joyce Society
J-J S-S: Jean-Jacques Servan-Schreiber
JK: Jack Kerouac
J & K: Jammu and Kashmir (University)
J/°K: joule(s) per degree Kelvin (unit of entropy)
jkg: joules per kilogram
JKP: James Knox Polk
JKS: Julius Kayser (stock-exchange symbol)
JKT: Jakarta, Indonesia (airport); Job Knowledge Test
jl: just looking (pseudo customer)
Jl: Joel
JL: J. Lauritzen (steamship line); Johnson Line; Jones and Laughlin; Joseph Lewis
Jla: Julia
JLA: Jewish Librarians Association
JLB: Jewish Lads' Brigade; John Logie Baird (tv's inventor)
JLC: Jewish Labor Committee
JLCU: Johnson Line container unit
Jlem: Jerusalem
JLMIC: Japan Light Machinery Information Center
JLP: Jamaica Labour Party
JLPPG: Joint Logistics and Personnel Policy Guidance
JLRSS: Joint Long-Range Strategic Study
Jlt: Juliet
JM: James Madison; James Monroe; Jewish Museum; José

Martí
J-M: Johns-Manville
J-M: *Jiyu-Minshuto* (Japanese—Liberal Democratic Party)
JMA: Japan Medical Association; Japan Meteorological Agency; Jewish Music Alliance
JMB: J(ames) M(atthew) Barrie
JMC: Jefferson Medical College
JMDC: Japan Machinery Design Center
jmed: jungle message encoder decoder
JMF: Jewish Music Forum; Juilliard Musical Foundation
JMHS: James Madison High School; James Monroe High School; John Muir High School
JMI: John Muir Institute
JMJ: Jesus, Mary, and Joseph
JMMC: James Madison Memorial Commission
JMMF: James Monroe Memorial Foundation
JMP: *Jen Men Piao* (Chinese—People's Bank Dollar)
JMPTC: Joint Military Packaging Training Center
JMRMA: John and Mable Ringling Museum of Art
JMS: Johannesburg Musical Society
JMSDF: Japanese Maritime Self-Defense Force
JMTBA: Japan Machine Tool Builders Association
JMUSDC: Joint Mexico-United States Defense Commission
jn: join; junction
j-n: jet navigation
Jn: John
JNA: *Jena Nomina Anatomica*
JNB: Johannesburg, South Africa (airport)
jnd: just noticeable difference
JNDNWR: J.N. (Ding) Darling National Wildlife Refuge (Florida)
jne: *ja niin edespäin* (Finnish—and so on)
JNF: Jewish National Fund
Jnl: Journal
JNL: Japanese National Laboratory
jnls: journals
jnlst: journalist
Jno: John
JNODC: Japanese National Oceanographic Data Center
JNP: Jasper National Park (Alberta)
JNPGC: Japan Nuclear Power Generation Corporation
jnr: junior
Jnr: Jesurun
JNR: Japanese National Railways
JNS: Jet Noise Survey
JNSDA: Japan Nuclear Ship

Development Agency
jnt: joint; junction; juncture
JNTA: Japan National Tourist Association
JNTO: Japan National Tourist Organization
jnt stk: joint stock
JNU: Juneau, Alaska (airport)
jnwpu: joint numerical weather-prediction unit
jo: journalist
Jo: Joel; Joseph; Josephine
JO: Job Order
JO: *Justie Ombudsman* (Swedish—representative of justice)
JOA: Joint Operating Agreement
Jo Bapt: John the Baptist (Saul of Tarsus)
jo block(s): johannson block(s)
JOBS: Job Opportunities in the Business Sector
Jo'burg: Johannesburg
joc: jocose; jocular
JOC: Joint Operations Center
jock: jockey; jockstrap
Jock: John
joco: jocose
jod: joint occupancy date
Jo Div: John the Divine
Joe: Joel; Joseph; Josephine
Joe Zilch: (the average American; successor to Joe Blow and Joe Doakes)
J-off: jack off (underground slang—masturbate
jog.: joggle
JOG: Joint Operations Group; Junior Ocean Group (*jay-oh-gees*—smallest sailing cruisers)
Jogja: Jogjakarta
Johan: Johannesburg
John: The Gospel According to John
John B: John B. Stetson (hat)
John Bull: Great Britain
John D: John D. Rockefeller, Sr
Johnny: John
Johnny Appleseed: John Chapman
Johns H: Johns Hopkins University
John I: John the First (John Adams—second President of the United States)
John II: John the Second (John Quincy Adams—sixth President of the United States)
John XXIII: Angelo Giuseppe Roncalli—the Pope
JOIDES: Joint Oceanographic Institutions for Deep Earth Sampling
JOIDESP: Joint Oceanographic Institutions Deep Earth Sampling Program
join.: joinery
JOIN: Job Orientation in Neighborhoods

JOK: Oakland, California (heliport)
jökel: (Norwegian—glacier)
joki: (Finnish—river)
jökull: (Icelandic—ice-covered mountain, as in Hofs-Jökul or Vatna-Jökul)
Jolly Roger: black flag flown by pirates, sometimes emblazoned with a white hourglass or a white skull and crossbones
JOMO: Junta of Militant Organization (Black Nationalists)
Jon.: The Book of Jonah
Jona: Jonathan
Jonathan Oldstyle: (pseudonym—Washington Irving)
JONS: Juntas de Ofensiva Nacional Sindicalista (Spanish fascist organization)
JOOD: Junior Officer of the Deck
JOR: Jet Operations Requirements
Jord: Jordan
Jos: Joseph; Joshua; Josiah; Jossie
Josa: Josepha; Josephine
Joseph: a Guarneri violin (short form for Giuseppe Guarneri)
Joseph Conrad: Teodor Jozef Konrad Korzeniowski
Josh: Joshua; pseudonym—Samuel L. Clemens)
Josh.: The Book of Joshua
Josh Billings: (pseudonym—Henry Wheeler Shaw)
Josie: Josephina; Josephine
jot.: jump-oriented terminal
JOTS: Job-Oriented Training Standards
jour: journal; journalese; journalism; journalist; journalistic; journey
JOVE: Jupiter Orbiting Vehicle for Exploration
jp: jet penetration; jet pilot; jet power; jet propulsion; junior partner; precipitation in sight but not at weather station reporting (symbol)
j & p: joists and planks
Jp: Japan(ese)
JP: Japan Press (news agency); Jet Pilot; Justice of the Peace
J£: Jamaican pound (currency unit)
jpa: jack panel assembly
JPA: Japan Procurement Agency; Joint Passover Association
JPB: Joint Planning Board; Joint Production Board; Joint Purchasing Board
JPBHS: Judah P. Benjamin High School
jpbs: jettison pushbutton switch
JPC: Jan Pieterszoon Coen
JPCRSP: John Pennekamp Coral Reef State Park (Florida)

JPF: Jewish Peace Fellowship
JP-4: jet propellant 4
JPG: Job Proficiency Guide
JPGM: J. Paul Getty Museum
JPJ: John Paul Jones
JPL: Jacksonville Public Library; Java Pacific Line; Jet Propulsion Laboratory (California Institute of Technology)
Jpn: Japan(ese)
JPO: Joint Petroleum Office
jpp: jälkeen puolenpäiven (Finnish —afternoon; P.M.)
JPPS: Japan Pearl Promoting Society
J Prob: Judge of Probate
JPRS: Joint Publications Research Service
JPS: Jet Propulsion Systems; Jewish Publications Society; Johannesburg Philharmonic Society
JPSA: Jewish Publication Society of America
JPSO: Jamaica Philharmonic Symphony Orchestra
jpt: jet pipe temperature
JPTDS: Joint Photographic Type Designation System
jpto: jet-propelled takeoff
JP-X: jet-propellant rocket fuel
jq: job questionnaire
JQA: John Quincy Adams
JQAH: John Quincy Adams House
Jr: Journal; Junior
JR: Joint Resolution
J.R.: Jacobus Rex (Latin—King James)
JRA: Japan Ryokan Association
JRATA: Joint Research and Test Acvitity
JRB: New York, New York (Wall Street Heliport)
JRC: Jamaica Railway Corporation
JRCA: Junior Ruritan Clubs of America
JRCS: Jet Reaction Control System
JRD: Riverside, California (heliport, 3-letter code)
JRDB: Joint Research and Development Board
JRDC: Japan Research and Development Corporation
JRF: Judicial Research Foundation
jrg: jaargang (Dutch—year)
Jr HS: Junior High School
JRHS: Julia Richman High School
jri: jail release information
JRIA: Japan Radioisotope Association
Jro: Jerome
JRS: Jerusalem, Jordan (airpot)
JRTUR: Jugoslovenska Radio-Televisija Udruzenja Radio-stancia (Yugoslav Association of Radio and Television Sta-

tions)
Jrw: Jarrow-on-Tyne
j/s: jamming-to-signal ration
Js: Jesuits
JS: Al-Jamhourya as-Souriya (Syria); Jan Sibelius; Japan Society; Johnson Society; Judeo-Spanish
JSA: Jewelers Security Alliance; Journeymen Stone Cutters Association
jsact: jetstream anti-countermeasure trainer
JSACT: Joint Strategic Air Control Team
JSB: Jewish Society for the Blind; Jewish Statistical Bureau; Johann Sebastian Bach
JSC: Jackson State College; Joint Standing Committee; Joint Stock Company
JSCA: Journeyman Stone Cutters Association
J. Sc. D.: Doctor of Juristic Science
JSCM: Joint Service Commendation Medal
JSCP: Joint Strategic Capabilities Plan
JSCR: Job Schedule Change Request
J.S.D.: Jurum Scientiae Doctor (Latin—Doctor of the Science of Laws)
JSDFs: Japan Self-Defense Forces
JSDTI: John S. Donaldson Technical Institute (Trinidad)
JSE: Johannesburg Stock Exchange
JSEM: Japan Society for Electron Microscopy
JSESPO: Joint Surface Effect Ships Program
JSF: Japan Scholarship Foundation; Junior Statesmen Foundation
JSGMF: John Simon Guggenheim Memorial Foundation
JSGMRAM: Joint Study Group for Material Resource Allocation Methodology
jsi: job satisfaction inventory
JSLB: Joint Stock Land Bank(s)
JSM: Juilliard School of Music
JSMA: Joint Sealers Manufacturers Association
JSME: Japan Society of Mechanical Engineers
J-smoke: (underground slang —marijuana cigarette)
JSO: Jackson Symphony Orchestra; Jacksonville Symphony Orchestra
JSOP: Joint Strategic Objectives Plan
JSPC: Joint Strategic Plans Committee
jspf: jet shots per foot
JSPG: Joint Strategic Plans Group

JSSC: Joint Services Staff College; Joint Strategic Service Committee
JST: Japan Standard Time; Javanese Standard Time
J-stick: joystick (underground slang —marijuana cigarette)
JSTPB: Joint Strategic Target Planning Board
JSTPS: Joint Strategic Target Planning Staff
JSW: Japan Steel Works
JSWPB: Joint Special Weapons Publications Board
JSY: Jersey Airlines
jt: joint; joint tenancy; junction
JT: Jamaica Air Service (symbol); John Tyler; joint tenancy; Juvenile Templar
JT: Japan Times
JTA: Jewish Telegraphic Agency (news service)
JTAC: Joint Technical Advisory Committee
jt agt: joint agent
jtb: joint bar
JTB: Jamaica Tourist Board; Japan Travel Bureau; Jute Trade Board
JTBI: Japan Travel Bureau International
JTC: Joint Telecommunications Committee; Junior Training Corps
J-teacher: journalism teacher
JTF: Joint Task Forces
Jth.: Apocryphal Book of Judith
JTI: Jydsk Teknologisk Institut (Danish—Jutland Technological Institute)
JTII: Japan Telescopes Inspection Institute
jtly: jointly
jtms: jamb-template machine screws
JTNM: Joshua Tree National Monument
jto: jump takeoff
JTO: Jordan Tourist Office
jt r: joint rate
JTR: Joint Termination Regulation; Joint Travel Regulation; Jordan Travel Research
JTRE: Joint Tsunami Research Effort
JTS: Job Training Standards
JTSA: Jewish Theological Seminary of America
ju: joint use
JU: Jacksonville University; Jadavpore University
juana: marijuana
Juan Gris: José Victoriano Gonzalez
Juanita: Juana (Jane; Joan)
juco: junior college
jud: judgment; judicial; judo
Jud: Judah; Judaic; Judaism; Ju-

dean; Judson
J.U.D.: *Juris Utriusque Doctor* (Latin—Doctor of Civil and Canon Law)
Jude: The General Epistle of Jude
Judg.: The Book of Judges
Judge Adv Gen: Judge Advocate General
judgt: judgment
Judy: Judith
juev: jueves (Spanish—Thursday)
JUG: Joint Users Group
juil: juillet (French—July)
jul: julho (Portuguese—July); *juilo* (Spanish—July)
Jul: July
Jul Caes: Julius Caesar
Jules Romains: (pseudonym—Louis Farigoule)
Julians: Julián Alps (northwestern Yugoslavia)
Juliett: code for letter J
Jul^n: Julian (Spanish—Julius)
Julio Diniz: Joaquim Guilherme Coelho
Julust: July and August
JUMPS: Joint Uniform Military Pay System
jun: junio (Spanish—June; *juniore* (Italian—junior)
Jun: Juneau
Junc: Junction
Junuly: June and July

Jup: Jupiter
Jur: Jurassic
juris: jurisdiction
jurisp: jurisprudence
jus: justice(s)
jusc.: jusculum (Latin—broth)
JUSE: Japanese Union of Scientists and Engineers
Jusepe: José de Ribera
JUSMAG: Joint United States Military Advisory Group; Joint United States Military Aid Group to Greece
JUSMAP: Joint United States Military Advisory and Planning Group
JUSMG: Joint United States Military Group
JUSMMAT: Joint United States Military Mission for Aid to Turkey
JUSPAO: Joint United States Public Affairs Office
just.: justification
juv: juvenile
Juv: Juvenal
juve: juvenile
jux: juxtapose; juxtaposition
jv: japanese vellum
Jv: Java; Javanese
JV: Jules Verne; Junior Varsity
JVA: Jordan Valley Authority
JVC: Japan Victor Company

jvp: japanese vellum proofs
JVS: Joint Vocational School
jw: jacket water; jugwell (hydrocarbon storage well); junior wolf (a young philanderer)
JW: Jehovah's Witnesses
JWA: Japan Whaling Association
J-walker: jaywalker
JWB: Jewish Welfare Board
jwc: junction wire connector
JWGA: Joint War Games Agency
jwl: jewel; jeweler
JWL: Johnston Warren Lines
jwlr: jeweler
jwlry: jewelry
j & wo: jettison and washing overboard
JWO: Jardine Waugh Organisation
JWR: *Jane's World Railways*
JWR: Joint War Room
JWS: Japan Welding Society
JWT: J. Walter Thompson (advertising agency)
JWTC: Jungle Warfare Training Center
JWU: Jewelry Workers' Union
JWV: Jewish War Veterans (of the United States)
JY: British United Channel Islands Airways (2-letter coding)
JYL: Jugolinja-Yugoslav Line
Jyll: Jylland (Danish—Jutland)

K

k: Boltzman constant; carat (karat); cathode or vacuum tube; coefficient of alienation; compressibility factor; force constant; keel; kilo; knot(s); reaction velocity constant; reproduction factor; thermal conductivity; torsion constant; unit vector in Z-direction
K: capacity (symbol); centuple calorie (symbol); curvature (symbol); equilibrium constant (symbol); Fraunhofer line produced in part by calcium (symbol); Karman constant (symbol); Kelvin; Kerr constant; Kidde Fire Protection; Kilo—code word for letter K; kip; Kiwanis International; Knabe; Köchel, cataloger of Mozart's music; kopec(s); kosher; krone; kroner; luminous efficiency (symbol); modulus of cubic compressibility (symbol);

pilotless aircraft (symbol); potassium (kalium); proportionality constant (symbol); radius of gyration (symbol); tanker (naval symbol)
K: kade (Dutch—embankment; quay); *kald* (Norwegian—cold); *kall* (Swedish—cold); *kalt* (German—cold); *koel* (Dutch—cold); *kold* (Danish—cold); *Köln* (German—Cologne); *krinda* (Danish—women); *kvinne* (Norwegian—women); *kvinnor* (Swedish—women); *kylmä* (Finnish—cold)
^{0}K: degree Kelvin
K^2: Mount Godwin Austen, Kashmir (28,250-ft. mountain, second highest in the world)
K-9 Corps: Canine Corps (staffed by police dogs)
ka: cathode(s); kiloampere(s)
Ka: Komppania (Finnish—compa-

ny)
k/a: ketogenic to antiketogenic (diet ratio)
KA: Kapok Association; Karhumaki Airlines (Finland)
kaa: keep-alive anode
kaad: kerosene, alcohol, acetic acid, dioxane (insect larva killer)
kaap: (Dutch—cape)
KAB: Keep America Beautiful
KACC: Kaiser Aluminum Chemical Corporation
KACF: Korean American Cultural Foundation
KACIA: Korean-American Commerce and Industry Association
Kae: Katherine
kaf: kaffir
KAF: Kenya Air Force
Kaffir King: Barney Barnato
kafr: (Arabic—village)
KAH: Kahului Railroad
kaikyo: (Japanese—strait)

kal: kalamein

kal.: *kalendae* (Latin—calends, the first day of the month)

Kal: Kalgoorlie

KAL: Korean Air Lines

kald: kalamein door

Kamenev, Lev Borisovich: Lev Rosenfeld

kamk: keyed alike and master keyed

Kan: Kansas; Kanpur

kanaal: (Dutch—canal)

kang: (Chinese—village)

kang(s): kangaroo(s)

Kans: Kansas; Kansan

KANU: Kenya African National Union (party)

kao: kaolin

kaocon: kaopectate concentrate

kaolin: aluminum silicate ($Al_2O_3 \cdot 2SiO_2 \cdot 2H_2O$)

kap: knowledge, attitude, practice

kap: *kapitel* (Swedish—chapter)

Kap: (German—cape); *Kapital* [German—capital (money)]; *Kapitel* (Danish and German —chapter)

KAP: initials stand for Chinese Ministry of Public Security—external counterintelligence and internal secret police force of the People's Republic of China—mainland communist-controlled China

KAPL: Knolls Atomic Power Laboratory

Kar: Karachi; Karafuto

KAR: King's African Rifles

kara: (Turkish—black, as in Kara Kum)

KARAI: Karhumaki Airways (Finland)

Karel: Karelia; Karelian

Kas: Kansas

KAS: Kentucky Academy of Science; Kroeber Anthropological Society

KASC: Knowledge Availability Systems Center

Kash: Kashmir

KASSR: Karakalpak Autonomous Soviet Socialist Republic

Kat: Katowice

KAT: Kenosha Auto Transport

Kate: Catherine

Kath: Katherine

Katherine Mansfield: (pseudonym —Kathleen Beauchamp Murry)

Kathy: Katharine; Kathleen; Kathryn

KATUSA: Korean (soldier) attached to (the) United States Army

Katy: Missouri-Kansas-Texas Railroad

kaupunki: (Finnish—city; town)

kay: knockout (*kayo*—spelled abbreviation of ko); okay (truncated slang)

Kay: Catherine

Kaz: Kazak(stan)

kb: kilobit(s); kitchen and bathroom; kite ballon; knee brace

KB: Koninkrijk Belgie (Flemish—Kingdom of Belgium)

K.B.: Knight of the Order of the Bath

kba: killed by air

K-band: 10,900–36,000 mc

kbar: kilobar(s); 1 kbar equals approx 14,500 lbs per square inch

KBART: Kings Bay Army Terminal

KBASSR: Kabardian-Balkar Autonomous Soviet Socialist Republic

kbe: keyboard encoder; keyboard entry

K.B.E.: Knight Commander of the Order of the British Empire

Kbhvn: København (Copenhagen)

KBI: Keyboard Immortals (record label)

KBL: Kabul, Afghanistan (airport)

KBNWR: Klamath Basin National Wildlife Refuges (California and Oregon)

K Bon: Klein Bonaire (Netherlands Antilles)

KBP: Koala Bear Park (Adelaide)

kbps: kilo bits per second

kbs: kilobits per second

KB & TS: Kuwait Broadcasting and Television Service

kbtu: kilo british thermal unit (1,000 btu's)

kc: kilocycle(s); koruna (Czechoslovakian monetary unit)

KC: Kalamazoo College; Kansas City; Kendall College; Kenyon College; Keuka College; Keystone College; Keystone Shipping Company (flag code); Kilgore College; King College; King's College; Kirksville College (of osteopathy and surgery); Knox College; Knoxville College

K.C.: King's Counsel

K of C: Knights of Columbus

KC-50: tactical aerial tanker for refueling aircraft in flight

KC-97: Stratofreighter strategic tanker-freighter equipped for inflight refueling

KC-135: Stratotanker multipurpose aerial tanker-transport

KCA: *Keesings Contemporary Archives*

kcal: kilocalorie(s)

K.C.B.: Knight Commander of the Order of the Bath

kcc: kathodic closure contraction

KCC: Kellogg Community College; Kenai Community College; Kennedy Cultural Center; Ketchikan Community College; Kingsborough Community College; King's College, Cambridge

KCDMA: Kiln, Cooler, and Dryer Manufacturers Association

KCH: King's College Hospital

kCi: kiloCurie(s)

KCL: King's College, London

KCM: Kansas City Museum

KCM & O: Kansas City, Mexico & Orient (railroad)

KCNP: Kings Canyon National Park (California); Ku-ring-gai Chase National Park (New South Wales)

KCNS: King's College, Nova Scotia

KCPA: Kaolin Clay Producers Association; Kennedy Center for the Performing Arts

KCPL: Kansas City Public Library

KCPO: Kansas City Philharmonic Orchestra

kcps: kilocycles per second

KCR: Kowloon-Canton Railway

kcs: Czechoslovakian KORUNA(s); kilocycles per second

kc/s: kilocycles per second

KCS: Kansas City Southern (railroad)

KCS: *Kansas City Star*

KCSI: Knight Commander of the Star of India

KCSO: Kansas City Symphony Orchestra

KCT: Kansas City Terminal (railroad)

kcte: kathodic closure tetanus

K Cur: Klein Curaçao (Netherlands Antilles)

KCVO: Knight Commander of the Victorian Order

kd: killed; kiln dried; knocked down; pilotless aerial target (code)

Kd: Kuwait dinar(s)

KD: Kidderpore Docks (Calcutta); Kongeriget Danmark (Kingdom of Denmark)

KDA: Kongelik Dansk Aeroklub (Royal Danish Aero Club)

K-day: basic date for introduction of convoy system or lane; carrier aircraft assault day

kdcl: knocked down in carload lots

KDD: Kokusai Denshin Denwa (Japan's Overseas Radio and Cable System)

kdf: knocked-down flat

KDHNM: Kill Devil Hill National

Memorial

kdlcl: knocked down in less than carload lots

kdm: kingdom

KDM: Kongelige Danske Marine (Royal Danish Navy)

Kdo: Kasado

K-do: *Kamarado* (Esperanto—comrade)

KDP: potassium dihydrogen phosphate

ke: kinetic energy

K + E: Keuffel & Esser

KEA: Kentucky Education Association

keas: knots estimated airspeed

kebir: (Arabic—great, as in Mersel-Kebir)

Kech: Kechua (Quechua)

KEF: Keflavik Airport, Iceland

Kem: *Kemi* (German—chemistry)

KEMA: Kitchen Equipment Manufacturers Association

Ken: Kendall; Kenilworth; Kenneth; Kennit; Kent(on); Kentuckian; Kentucky; Kenya; Kenyan

Kent: Kentucky

KEPZ: Kaohsiung Export Processing Zone

kern: kernan

kero: kerosene

keto: ketonaemia; ketogenic; ketone; ketonuria; ketoses; ketosis

ketol: ketone alcohol (compound)

kev: kilo electron volt; 1,000 electron volts

keV: kiloelectronvolt(s)

Kev: Kelvin; Kevin

kf: kitchen facilities; koff

KF: Kaiser-Frazer; Kellogg Foundation; Kent Foundation; Kooperative Förbunded (Federation of Cooperatives-Sweden); Kresge Foundation

KF: *Konservative Folkeparti* (Danish—Conservative Party)

KFASSR: Karelo-Finnish Autonomous Soviet Socialist Republic (formerly the Karelia of Finland)

Kfc: Kentucky fried chicken

KFC: Kropp Forge Company

KFEA: Korean Federation of Education Associations

KFL: Kenya Federation of Labour

kfm: *kaufmännisch* (German—commercial)

Kfm: *Kaufmann* (German—merchant)

KFNP: Kaieteur Falls National Park (Guyana)

kfo: killing federal officer

KFP: *Kristelig Folkeparti* (Norwegian—Christian People's Party)

KFSR: Karakul Fur Sheep Registry

Kfz: *Kraftfahrzeug* (German—motor vehicle)

kg: keg; kilogram; known gambler

kG: kilogauss

Kg: Kirghiz(ian)

KG: Kelly Girl

KG: *Kommanditgesellschaft* (German—limited partnership)

K.G.: Knight of the Order of the Garter

KGA: Kitchen Guild of America

KGB: Komitet Gossudarrstvennoi Bezopastnosti (Russian—Committee of State Security; Soviet Secret Police)

KGBW: Kewaunee, Green Bay, and Western (railroad)

kg cal: kilogram calorie

kg-cal: kilogram calorie

kg cum: kilograms per cubic meter

kgf: kilogram-force

Kgf: *Kriegsgefangener* (German—prisoner of war)

KGK: Kabushiki Goshi Kaisha (Japanese—joint stock limited partnership of members with unlimited liability and shareholders with limited liability)

kgl: *kongelig* (Danish—royal)

Kgl: *Königlich* (German—royal)

kgm: kilogram meter

kg/m^2: kilograms per square meter

kg/m^3: kilograms per cubic meter

Kgn: Kingston, Jamaica

KGNP: Kalahari Gemsbok National Park (South Africa); Katherine Gorge National Park) Australian Northern Territory)

kgps: kilograms per second

kgs: kegs

kg/s: kilograms per second

KGS: Kate Greenaway Society; Kigezi Gorilla Sanctuary (Uganda)

KGWS: Keoladeo Ghana Wildlife Sanctuary (India)

Kh: Khmer (Cambodia)

KH: *Karen Hayesod* (Hebrew—United Israel Appeal); *Kupat Holim* (Hebrew—Health Insurance Fund)

K-H: Kelsey-Hayes

Khar: Kharkov

KHC: Karen Horney Clinic

KHI: Karachi, Pakistan (airport)

Khn: Knoop hardness number

KHPC: Karen Horney Psychoanalytic Clinic

KHS: Kennedy High School

khz (kHz): kilohertz(es), formerly kilocycle(s) per second

kHz: kilohertz (kilocycles per second)

ki: kilo; kitchen

KI: Kiwanis International; Kommunisticheskii Internatsional (Russian—Communist International; Komunisticna Internacijonala (Yugoslav—Communist International)

KI: *Kol Israel* (Hebrew—Voice of Israel)—broadcasting service

K-I: Kaiser-Illin

kia (KIA): killed in action

kias: knots indicated airspeed

KIB: Kansas Inspection Bureau; Kentucky Inspection Bureau

kid.: kidney

kidult: kid adult (older person who enjoys juvenile entertainment)

kieselguhr: silica (SiO_2)

Kifis: Kollsman integrated flight instrument system

KIICC: *Kommunisticheskaya Partiya Sovetskogo Soyuza* (Russian—Communist Party of the Soviet Union)

Kikdl: *Krokodil*

kil: (Celtic—church, as in Kilkenny or Kilbride)

kild: kilderkin(s)

Kild: Kildare

Kilk: Kilkenny

kilo: kilogram; 10^3

Kilo: code for K

kilohm: kilo-ohm

kilovar: kilovolt-ampere (reactive)

Kim: Kimball; Kimballton; Kimberley; Kimberly; Kimble; Kimbolton; Kimborough; Kimbrough; Kimiwan; Kimmell; Kimmins; Kimmswick; Kimsquit

Kin: Kingston, Ontario (maritime contraction)

KIN: Kingston, Jamaica (airport); Kinross

Kinc: Kincardinel

kind.: kindergarten

kine: kinema (variation of cinema)

King: Kingston

kingd: kingdom

King of Bath: Richard (Beau) Nash

King of Beasts: the lion

King of Birds: the eagle

King of Roads: John Loudon Macadam

King's College: Columbia University in colonial times

King Who Lost America: Great Britain's George III

Kinross: Kinross-shire

KINTEL: K Laboratories (instruments and television)

Kintetsu: Kinki Nippon Railway Company, Ltd.

kip: thousand pounds (from contraction of kilo and pound)

kip ft: thousand foot pounds

Kir: Kirghiz; Kirghizia; Kirghizian

Kircud: Kircudbrightshire

Kirk: Kirkcudbright

KISA: Korean International Steel

Associates

kisc: knowledge industry system concept

kismif: keep it simple—make it fun

KI smog: potassium-iodide smog (automobile induced)

KISO: Kol Israel Symphony Orchestra

kiss: keep it simple, Stupid

KIST: Korean Institute for Science and Technology

kit.: kitchen(ette)

Kit: Catherine; Christopher; Kitty

KIT: Kentucky and Indiana Terminal (railroad)

kita: (Japanese—north)

Kit Carson: Christopher Carson

KITCO: Kwajalein Import and exporting Company

kiteoon: kite + balloon

kitsch: kitschen (German—thrown together)—commercial art or art objects cheapened by vulgarity; e.g., miniature reproduction of the Venus de Milo with an alarm clock set in her belly

Kitty: Catherine

kizil: (Turkish—red, as in Kizil Arvat, Kizil Kum, Kizil Uzen)

kj: kilojoule; kimberly joint (plumbing); knee jerk

k-j: knee-jerk(s)

kJ: kilojoule

KJ: Kahil Jibran (Gibran)   ˏ

KJC: Kaiser Jeep Corporation; Keystone Junior College

K John: Life and Death of King John

KJV: King James Version

kk: killer karate

k-k: knee-kicks (knee-jerks)

KK: Kabushiki Kaisha (Japanese—joint stock company of shareholders with limited liability)

K.K.: Kahal Kadosh (Hebrew—Holy Congregation)

K of K: Kitchener of Khartoum

KKI: Keren Kayemeth le Israel (Hebrew—National Fund of Israel)

KKK: Ku Klux Klan (secret organization antagonistic to certain racial & religious groups)

KKK: Kinder, Kirche, Kuche (German—Children, Church, Kitchen)—traditional three K's of Teutonic womanhood

KKKK: Kansai Kisen Kabushiki Kaisha; Kawasaki Kisen Kabushiki Kaisha (steamship lines)

KKKK: Køenhavns Kul og Koks Kompagne (Copenhagen Coal and Coke Company)

KKKKs: Knights of the Ku Klux Klan

KKMKI: Kungliga Karolinska Me-

diko-Kirurgiska Institutet (Caroline Medico-Surgical Institute-Stockholm)

Kkr: Karlskrona

kl: kiloliter

kl: klockan (Swedish—o'clock); *klokken* (Dano-Norwegian—o'-clock)

Kl: Klasse (German—class)

KL: Key Largo; Klebs-Loeffler; Knutsen Line; Kwik Lok

kla: klystron amplifier

Klan: Ku Klux Klan (*q.v.* KKK)

klax: klaxon

klein: (Dutch or German—small)

klepto: kleptomania (c; al)

Klg: Keelung

klim: (milk spelled backwards) dried milk

K Line: Kawasaki Kisen Kaisha

KLM: Koninklijke Luchtvaart Maatschappij (Royal Dutch Airlines)

Klmpb: Klampenborg

Kln: Köln (Cologne)

klo: klystron oscillator

k-lo: kello (Finnish—hour; o'clock)

KLPA: Knuckeys Lagoon Protected Area (Australian Northern Territory)

kls: key lock switch

klt: kiloton (nuclear equivalent, 1,000 tons of high explosives)

klto: knurling tool

Kluxer: member of the Ku Klux Klan (*q.v.* KKK)

km: kilometer

km²: square kilometer

km³: cubic kilometer

KM: Kaffrarian Museum; Kearny Mesa; Khedivial Mail (steamship line)

KMAG: United States Military Advisory Group to the Republic of Korea

kmc: kilomegacycle

kmef: keratin, myosin, epidermin, fibrin (proteins)

km/h: kilometers per hour

KMI: Kentucky Military Institute

KMMA: Korean Merchant Marine Academy

KMP: Kaiser Metal Products; Kearny Mesa Plant (Convair)

kmph: kilometers per hour

kmps: kilometers per second

Kmr: Khorramshahr

KMR: Kwajalein Missile Range

KMT: Kuomintang

KMUL: Karl Marx Universität Leipzig (University of Leipzig)

kmw: kilomegawatt

KMW: Karlstads Mekaniska Werkstad (Swedish iron foundry)

kmwhr: kilomegawatt-hour

Kn: Knight

kn: kilonewton; knot; krone; kronen

KN: Koninkrijk der Nederlanden (Kingdom of the Netherlands); Kongeriket Norge (Kingdom of Norway)

K-N: Know-Nothing (political party)

KNA: Kenya News Agency; Korean National Airlines

KNAN: Koninklijke Nederlandse Akademie voor Naturwetenschappen (Royal Netherlands Academy of Sciences)

KNGR: Kruger National Game Reserve

Knick: Knickerbocker

knickers: knickerbockers

Knight of the Rueful Countenance: Don Quixote

Knight of the Swan: Lohengrin

KNK: Kita Nippon Koku (Northern Japan Airlines)

KNM: Katmai National Monument; Kongelige Norske Marine (Royal Norwegian Navy)

KNMI: Koninkliji Nederlands Meteorologisch Instituut (Royal Netherlands Meteorological Institute)

KNMR: Kenai National Moose Range (Alaska)

KNO: Kano, Nigeria (tracking station)

KNP: Kafue National Park (Zambia); Kalahari NP (South Africa); Kalbarri NP (Western Australia); Kanha NP (India); Kejimkujik NP (Nova Scotia); Kinabalu NP (Sabah); Kinchega NP (New South Wales); Kootenay NP (British Columbia); Kosciusko NP (New South Wales); Kruger NP (South Africa)

KNR: Kinki Nippon Railway

KNSM: Koninklijke Nederlandsche Stoomboot Maatschappij (Royal Netherlands Steamship Company)

kn sw: knife switch

KNT: Knight-Knott Hotels (stock-exchange symbol)

knu: knuckle

KNUST: Kwame Nkrumah University of Science and Technology

Knut Hamsun: Knut Pedersen

KNVL: Koninklijke Nederlandse Vereniging voor Luchtvaart (Royal Netherlands Aero Club)

KNWR: Kirwin National Wildlife Refuge (Kansas)

KNX: Kinney Company (stock-exchange symbol)

Knxv: Knoxville

ko: kilohm; knockout (KO)

k-o: knockout
Ko: Korea; Korean
KO: knockout; Kodiak Airways (2-letter coding)
Kob: Kobe (British Maritime contraction)
köbstad: (Danish—city)
KOC: Kollmorgen Optical Corporation; Kuwait Oil Company
ko'd: knocked out
KODAK: trade name for Eastman Kodak photographic products
k-o drops: knockout drops (chloral hydrate sedative)
kOe: kiloOersted(s)
kog: kindly old gentleman
KOG: Kansas, Oklahoma & Gulf (railroad)
KOH: potassium hydroxide
kohm: kilohm
Kok: Cochrane
KOKS: *Kul og Koks Selskab* (Danish—Coal and Coke Company)
kol: (Mongolian—lake)
Kol: Kolonia, Ponape (Trust Territory of the Pacific)
KOM: Knight of the Order of Malta
Komei: (Japanese—Komeito)—Buddhist party
Komp: Kompanie (German—company)
Komsomol: (Russian—Young Communist League)
Kon Dan: Kongeriget Danmark (Kingdom of Denmark)
kong: (Chinese—river, as in Mekong)
Kon Nor: Kongeriket Norge (Kingdom of Norway)
Konr: Konrad
KONR: Komitet Osvobozhdyeniya Narodov Rossii (Committee for the Liberation of the Peoples of Russia)
Kon Sver: Konungariket Sverige (Kingdom of Sweden)
konz: konzentriert (German—concentrated)
kop: kopeck(s)
KOP: Koppers (company)
kopf: (German—head; peak; summit)
köping: (Swedish—borough, as in Malmköping; market)
kopje: (Afrikaans—hill)
kops: keep off pounds sensibly
Kor: Korea; Korean; The Koran
kos: kilos
kosui: (Japanese—lake)
kov: key-operated valve
kp: key personnel; kick plate; kill probability; kilopond; king post; kitchen police (KP); knotty pine
Kp: Kochpunkt (German—boiling

point)
KP: Kommunistische Partei (German—Communist Party); *Komsomolskaya Pravda* (Russian —Young Communist League Truth)—Moscow newspaper claiming circulation of three million; *Kuvendi Popullore* (Albanian People's Assembly)
K of P: Knights of Pythias
KPA: Kraft Paper Association
kpc: keypunch cabinet
kp & d: kick plate and drip
KPD: Kommunistische Partei Deutschland (Communist Party of Germany)
kph: kilometers per hour
kpi: kips per inch
kpic: key phrase in context
KPL: Knoxville Public Library
kpm: kathode pulse modulation
Kpmtr: Kapellmeister (German—conductor)
KPNO: Kitt Peak National Observatory
KPNWR: Kern-Pixley National Wildlife Refuge (California)
kpo: keypunch operator
kpos: keep pounds off sensibly (scientific weight-reduction program)
KPP: Keeper of the Privy Purse
kpps: kilopulses per second
kpr: keeper
Kpr: Kodak photo resist
KPR: Korean Presidential Ribbon
kps: kips (thousnad pounds) per square foot
kpsi: kips (thousand pounds) per square inch
KPSS: Kommunisticheskaya Partiya Sovetskovo Soyuza (Russian—Communist Party of the Soviet Union)—CPSU
Kpt: Kaptajn (Danish—captain)
KPU: Kenya People's Union (party)
kq: line squall
kr: keel rider; kiloroentgen
Kr: krypton
KR: krona (Icelandic or Swedish monetary unit); krone (Danish or Norwegian monetary unit)
kraal: (Dutch—native village)
Krag: Krag-Jörggensen rifle
krasnaya: (Russian—beautiful; fair; red)
K-ration: Calorie ration (lightweight emergency meal)
KREEP: acronym describing lunarcrust material collected by astronauts—K (potassium), Rare -Earth Elements, Phosphorus— *KREEP*
Kreuzb: Kreuzberg
KRF: Kentucky Research Founda-

tion
Krh: Karachi
Kripo: Kriminalpolizei (German —Criminal Investigation Department)
krs: korus (Turkish—piastre)
Krs: Kristiansand
krt: cathode-ray tube
KRT: Khartoum, Sudan (airport)
KRU: Krueger Brewing (stock-exchange symbol)
ks: drifting snowstorm (symbol); keep (type) standing
Ks: kyats (Burmese money)
K-s: King-size (doughnuts, frankfurters, hamburgers, steaks, etc.)
KS: King's Scholar; Kipling Society; Konungariket Sverige (Kingdom of Sweden)
ksa: kite-supported antenna
KSAA: Keats-Shelley Association of America
KSC: Kansas State College; Kennedy Space Center; Kentucky State College; Korean Shipping Corporation; Kutztown State College
KSC: Komunisticka Strana Ceskoslovenska (Communist Party of Czechoslovakia)
ksf: kips (thousand pounds) per square foot
KSF: Kulkyne State Forest (Victoria, Australia)
KSFUS: Korean Student Federation of the United States
K sh: Kenya shilling(s)
ksi: kips (1000 pounds) per square inch
KSI: Keshvare Shahanshahiye Iran (Iran—Persia)
ksia: thousnad square inches absolute
KSK: ethyl iodoacetate (tear gas)
ksl: kidney, spleen, liver
KSL: Kinsel Drug (stock-exchange symbol)
KSM: Korean Service Medal; Kungliga Svenska Marinen (Royal Swedish Navy)
KSM: Kommunisticheskii Soyuz Molodozhi (Russian—All-Union League of Communist Youth)— Komsomol or Young Communist League—YCL
KSN: Kit Shortage Notice
KSNP: Khao Salob National Park (Thailand)
KSO: Kalamazoo Symphony Orchestra; Knoxville Symphony Orchestra
ksr: keyboard send-receive (set)
KSS: Komunisticka Strana Slovenska (Communist Party of Slovakia)

KSSR: Kazakh Soviet Socialist Republic
KSSU: Kiev I.G. Shevchenko State University (University of Kiev)
kst: keyseat
KST: King-Seeley Thermos (company)
KSTC: Kansas State Teachers College
ksu: key service unit
KSU: Kansas State University; Kent State University
KSUAAS: Kansas State University of Agriculture and Applied Science
KSY: King Seeley (stock-exchange symbol)
kt: karet (caret); kiloton (nuclear equivalent, 1000 tons of high explosives); knot
K$_t$: stress concentration factor
Kt: Knight
KT: Kentucky & Tennessee (railway); Knight of the Order of the Thistle; Knight Templar; Missouri-Kansas-Texas (Katy Route Railroad)
KTA: Knitted Textile Association
Ktb: Kriegstagebuch (German—war diary)
KTC: Keystone Tankship Corporation; Key Telephone System; Kodiak Tracking Station
KTH: Kungliga Tekniska Högskolan (Royal Institute of Technology, Stockholm)
ktl: kai ta loipa (Greek—et cetera)
KTN: Ketchikan, Alaska (Annette Island airport)
Kto: Konto (German—account)
K-truss: K-shaped truss
kts: knots
k through 12: kindergarten through high school
KTS: Key Telephone Systems; Kwajalein Test Site
KTTC: Kingston-upon-Thames Technical College
ktu: kill the umpire
KTX: Keith Railway Equipment (railway code)
KU: Kalmar Union; Kansas University; Københavns Universitet (University of Copenhagen); Kuwait Airways
kub: kidney(s)-ureter(s)-bladder
ku'd: knocked up (made pregnant)

K u H: Kingston upon Hull (official name for Hull)
KUK: Kollege of Universal Knowledge
kul: (Turkish—lake)
KUL: Kabul University Library (Kabul, Afghanistan)
kum: (Turkish—desert, as in Kara Kum)
Kur: (British maritime contraction of Kure); Kurile Islands
Kuril Cur: Kurile Current (Oyashio)
kutd: keep up to date
KUU: Kungliga Universitet i Uppsala (Royal University of Uppsala)
Kuw: Kuwait
Kuyb: Kuybyshev
kv: kilovolt
kva: kilovolt ampere
KVA: Kungliga Vetenskaps Akademien (Royal Swedish Academy of Sciences)
kvah: kilovolt-ampere-hour
kvam: kilovolt ampere meter
kvar: kilovar; kilovolt ampere reactive
kvarh: kilovar hour
kvcp: kilovolt constant potential
K-Vets: Korean War Veterans of the United States
kvg: keyed video generator
kvist: (Swedish—branch)
kvm: kilovolt meter
KVNP: Kidepo Valley National Park (Uganda)
kvp: kilovolt peak
KVP: Katholieke Volkspartij (Dutch—Catholic People's Party)
KVW: Kansas City Kaw Valley (railroad)
kw: kilowatt
kw: Zambian kwacha(s)—monetary unit(s)
KW: Key West
Kwaj: Kwajalein
Kwan: Kwantung
kwat: key well allowable transfer
KWC: Kentucky Wesleyan College
kwe: kilowatts electrical
KWest: Key West
K-W findings: Keith-Wagener (opthalmoscopic findings)
kwh: kilowatt hour
kwhr: kilowatt hour

kwic: key word in context
kwit: key word in text; key word in title
kwm: kilowatt meter
KWMA: Kirtland's Warbler Management Areas (Michigan)
KWNWR: Key West National Wildlife Refuge (Florida)
kwoc: key word out of context
kwot: key word out of title
KWPL: Kitchener-Waterloo Public Library
kwr: kilowatts reactive
KWS: Kaziranga Wildlife Sanctuary (India)
KWSM: Korean War Service Medal
kwt: kilowatts thermal
KWT: King William's Town
KWU: Kansas Wesleyan University
KWVZAB: Ko-operative Wijnbouwers Vereeniging van Zuid Afrika Beperkt (Dutch—Cooperative Wine Farmers Association of South Africa, Limited)
kwy: keyway
kxu: kilo-x-unit
ky: cocoa; keyer
Ky: Kentuckian; Kentucky
KY: Kentucky (zip code); (underground slang—federal hospital in Lexington, Kentucky where drug addicts are treated); Kol Yisrael (Israel Broadcasting Service)
kybd: keyboard
kyd: kilo yard
kyeri: know your endorsers —require identification (advice to all who cash checks)
kymo: kymograph; kymography
KYNP: Khao Yai National Park (Thailand)
kyo: (Japanese—capital, as in Kyogami or Kyoto)
Kyo: Kyoto
Kyr.: Kyrie eleison (Greek—Lord, have mercey upon us)
kytoon: kite balloon
kz: duststorm or sandstorm
Kz: Kazakh(stan)
KZ: Konzentrationslager (German—concentration camp)
K z S: Kapitan zur See (German—Sea Captain)—naval rating

L

l: azimuthal or orbital quantum number (symbol); elbow (plumbing); land; late; latent heat per unit mass (symbol); lateral; latitude; law; leaf; league; left or port (L or P); length; levorotatory; liaison; lignite; line; link; lire; liter; locus
l*: lumen
l/: *letra* (Spanish—letter)
l: *lectio* (Latin—reading)
L: Bell Aircraft (symbol); center line (symbol); elevated railroad (EL); inductance (symbol); kinetic potential (symbol); lactobacillus; lago; Lagrange function; lake; loch; lough; lake vessel; Lamar State College of Technology; lambert; Latin; launching; left (port side); lempira (Honduran currency unit); Leo; Leon; Liberal; lift (symbol); lift force; light; Lima—code for L; Linnaeus; Lions International; London; longitude; loran; Lorentz unit; Luckenbach Lines; Luxembourg (auto plaque); Lykes Lines; rolling moment (symbol)
L: *lähteä* (Finnish—departure); *lämmin* (Finnish—warm); *länsi* (Finnish—weat); Latin; *laudes* (Latin—praises); *levato* (Italian —raised); *Life Magazine; links* (German—left); *llegada* (Spanish—arrival)
l/3: lower third
L7: Hollywood slang for old-fashioned person or *square* as capital-letter L and figure 7 may be combined to form a square
L-1011: Lockheed's jumbo jetliner
la: lava; left angle; left atrium; left auricle; lighter than air; lightning arrestor; long-acting; low altitude; landing account
l/a: landing account; letter of advice; letter of authority; lighter than air
l & a: left and above; light and accommodation
la: (Italian—the); sixth tone in diatonic scale; *A* in fixed-do system
La: Lane; lanthanum; Lao; Laos; Laotian; Louisiana; Louisianian
LA: Latin America(n); Legislative

Assembly; Leschetizky Association; Letter of Activation; Library Association; Lieutenant-at-Arms; Local Authority; Los Angeles; Louisiana & Arkansas (railroad); Louvain Association
L-A: Loire-Atlantique (formerly Loire-Inférieure)
L & A: Louisiana & Arkansas (railroad)
LAA: League of Advertising Agencies; Life Insurance Advertisers; Los Angeles Airways
LAADS: Los Angeles Air Defense Sector
laag: (Dutch—low)
laar: liquid-air accumulator rocket
LAAS: Los Angeles Air Service
lab: label; labeling; labor; laboratory
Lab: Laboratory; Labour(ite); Labrador
LAB: Labour; Labour Party; Lloyd Aéreo Boliviano (Bolivian airline); low-altitude bombing
LABA: Laboratory Animal Breeders Association
Lab Cur: L'Abrador Current—cold Arctic current flowing southward along Atlantic coast of Canada and northern New England.
LABEN: Laboratori Elettronici e Nucleari (Electronic and Nuclear Laboratories—Milan)
Labor: US Department of Labor
lab proc: laboratory procedure(s)
labs: laboratories
Lab(s): Labrador retriever(s)
LABS: Low-Altitude Bombing System
lac: lacquer; lacrimal; lactation; shellac
lac: (French—lake, as in Lac des Mille Lacs)
Lac: Lacerta; Lacertilia
LAC: Leading Aircraftsman; Líneas Aéreas Chaqueñas (Aero Chaco); Lockheed Aircraft Corporation
LACATA: Laundry and Cleaners Allied Trades Association
lacc: lathe chuck
LACC: Los Angeles City College
LACE: liquid-air cycle engine
LACM: Los Angeles County Museum
LACMA: Los Angeles Conservato-

ry of Music and Arts; Los Angeles County Museum of Art
LACP: London Association of Correctors of the Press
lacr: low-altitude coverage radar
LACSA: Líneas Aéreas Costarricenses (Costa Rican Airlines)
LACW: Leading Aircraftswoman
lad.: ladder
Lad: Ladino
ladar: laser detection and ranging
LADE: Líneas Aéreas del Estado (State Airlines, Argentina)
LADO: Latin American Defense Organization; Latin American Development Organization
ladp: ladyship
LADWP: Los Angeles Department of Water and Power
Lady Bird: Mrs Claudia Alta Taylor Johnson—wife of President Lyndon Johnson
Lady of the Lamp: Florence Nightingale who nursed so many victims of the Crimean War
laev.: *laevus* (Latin—left)
LaF: Louisiana French
LAF: L'Académie Française (The French Academy); Living Arts Foundation
LAFB: Lincoln Air Force Base
LAFC: Latin-American Forestry Commission
Lafe: Lafayette
LAFS: Los Angeles Funeral Society
LAFTA: Latin American Free Trade Area; Latin American Free Trade Association
lag.: lagan
lag.: *lagena* (Latin—bottle; flask)
Lag: Lagoon; Laguna
La G: La Guaira
LAG: Layton Art Gallery
LAGB: Linguistics Association of Great Britain
LAGE: Los Angeles Grain Exchange
lago: (Italian or Spanish—lake, as in Lago Maggiore or Lago Titicaca)
lagoa: (Portuguese—lagoon, as in Lagoa dos Patos)
laguna: (Italian, Portuguese, Spanish —lagoon; lake, as in Laguna Salada)
Lah: Lahore

LAH: Licentiate Apothecaries Hall
LAHC: Los Angeles Harbor College; Los Angeles Harbor Commission
lahti: (Finnish—bay; gulf)
LAI: Linee Aeree Italiane (Italian Air Lines)
LAIC: Lithuanian-American Information Center
LAINS: Low-Altitude Inertial Navigation System
LAIS: Loan Accounting Information System (AID)
LAJ: Los Angeles Junction (railroad)
laks: lakrids (Danish—licorice)
Laksha Divi: (Sanskrit—Hundred Thousand Isles)—the Laccadives
LAL: Langley Aeronautical Laboratory (Langley Research Center)
LA-LB: Los Angeles-Long Beach (ports)
lali: lonely aged of low income
La Lollo: Gina Lollobrigida
lam: laminate
Lam: The Book of Lamentations; Lamarck; Lambretta
LAM: Lamarck; Lambert; Latin American Mission; London Academy of Music
L.A.M.: *Liberalium Artium Magister* (Latin—Master of Liberal Arts)
LAMA: Lead Air Materiel Area
lambwich: lamb sandwich
LAMC: Los Angeles Metropolitan College; Los Angeles Music Center
LAMDA: London Academy of Music and Dramatic Art
Lamia: P. L. Tyraud de Vosjoli (French underground fighter and chief of intelligence)
LAMP: Library Additions and Maintenance Program; Low-Altitude Manned Penetration; Lunar Analysis and Mapping Program
LAMPP: Los Alamos Molten Plutonium Program (AEC)
LAMPS: Light Airborne Multipurpose System
LAMS: Launch Acoustic Measuring System
län: (Swedish—county)
Lan: Lansing
L An: Los Angeles
LAN: Línea Aérea Nacional de Chile; Local Apparent Noon
lanac: laminair air navigation and anti-collision
Lanarks: Lanarkshire
Lanc: Lancaster
Lance: Lancelot

Lancs: Lancashire
land.: landscaping
LandCent: Allied Land Forces, Central Europe
LandCraB: landing craft and bases
Lands: Landsmaal (Norwegian national language)
landsby: (Dano-Norwegian—village)
lang: language
Lang: Languedoc
LANICA: Líneas Aéreas de Nicaragua (Air Lines of Nicaragua)
Lanny: Lawrence
LANSA: Líneas Aéreas Nacionales
Lant: Atlantic (naval short form)
LANWR: Laguna Atascosa National Wildlife Refuge (Texas); Lake Andes National Wildlife Refuge (South Dakota)
LANY: Linseed Association of New York
LAO: Licentiate of the Art of Obstetrics
LAOD: Los Angeles Ordnance District (USA)
lap.: laparotomy; launch analyst's panel
Lap: Lapland
La P: La Paz
LAP: Laboratory of Aviation Psychology (Ohio State University); Líneas Aéreas Paraguayas (Paraguayan Air Lines)
LAPC: Los Angeles Pacific College; Los Angeles Pierce College
LAPD: Los Angeles Police Department
LAPDis: Los Angeles Procurement District (US Army)
LAPES: Low-Altitude Parachute Extraction System
LAPL: Los Angeles Public Library
LAPO: Los Angeles Philharmonic Orchestra
La Pucelle: (French—The Maid) —Joan of Arc, Maid of Orleans
laq: lacquer
lar: left arm reclining; local-acquisition radar
lara (LARA): light armed reconnaissance aircraft
larc: lighter, amphibious, resupply, cargo (vehicle)
LARC: Langley Research Center; League Against Religious Coercion; Library Automation and Consulting
Larry: Laura; Laurence; Lawrence
Lars: Lawrence
LART: Los Angeles Rapid Transit
larva (LARVA): low-altitude research vehicle
laryng: laryngological; laryngolo-

gist; laryngology
laryngol: laryngology
las: low-alloy steel; large astronomical satellite
las: lassú (Hugarian—slow introductory passages leading to fast section, *friss,* of a csárdás or rhapsody)
LAS: Las Vegas, Nevada (airport); League of Arab States; Lebanese-American Society; Legal Aid Society; large astronomical satellite
LA & S: Liberal Arts and Sciences
LASAIL: Land-Sea Interaction Laboratory
LASC: Los Angeles State College
La Scala: Milan's opera house
laser: light amplification by stimulated emission of radiation; lucrative approach to support expensive research
LASH: Legislative Action on Smoking and Health; Lighter Aboard Ship (cargo system)
LASL: Los Alamos Scientific Laboratory
LASMCO: Liberian American-Swedish Minerals Company
lasrm (LASRM): low-altitude short-range missile
lass.: lighter-than-air submarine simulator (LASS)
LASSCO: Los Angeles Steamship Company
Last of the Incas: Atahualpa, Indian sovereign
LASUSSR: Library of the Academy of Science of the USSR (Leningrad)
lasv (LASV): low-altitude surface vehicle; low-altitude supersonic vehicle
lat: lateral; latitude
Lat: Latin; Latvia; Latvian
LAT: Local Apparent Time, Taxader (Bogotá)
LAT: Los Angeles Times
lat. admov.: *lateri admoveatum* (Latin—apply to the side)
lat. dol.: *lateri dolenti* (Latin—to the painful side)
LATH: Laos and Thailand Military Assistance
lats: long-acting thyroid stimulator
LATTC: Los Angeles Trade-Technical College
Latter-Day Saints: the Mormons
Latv: Latvia; Latvian
LATWPNS: Los Angeles Times-Washington Post News Service
lau: laundry
laughing gas: nitrous oxide (N_2O)
LAUK: Library Association of the United Kingdom
Lau Lib: Laurentian Library (Flo-

rence)
laun: launched
laund: launder; laundry
Laur: Laurence
Laura: World War II code name for Majuro, still in use by Americans and Marshallese islanders
LAUSC: Linguistic Atlas of the United States and Canada
lav: lavatory
LAV: Línea Aeropostal Venezolana (Venezuelan Airmail Line)
LAVC: Los Angeles Valley College
law.: lawyer; light assault weapon; low-altitude weapon
Law: Lawrence
LAW: League of American Wheelmen; League of American Writers; Legal Aid Warranty; Local Air Warning
Lawr: Lawrence; Lawrencian
Lawrence of Arabia: T.E. Lawrence
Law Rept: Law Report(s)
LAWS: Leadership and World Society
LAX: Los Angeles, California (International Airport)
Laz: Lazarus
lb: landing barge; letter box; lifeboat; linoleum base; local battery; lumen band; pound
l & b: left and below
lb: libra (Latin—pound)
LB: landing barge; Leonard Bernstein; Lloyd Brasileiro (Brazilian Steamship Line); Longview Bridge (Columbia River, Washington); Luther Burbank
L-B: Link-Belt
L v B: Ludwig van Beethoven
L-band: 390–1550 mc
lb ap: apothecaries' pound
L-bar: capital-L-shaped bar
lb av: avoirdupois pound
LBB: Lubbock, Texas (airport)
Lbc: Lübeck
LBC: Liberian Broadcasting Corporation
lb cal: pound calorie
LBCC: Long Beach City College
lbcd: left border of cardiac dullness
lb chu: pound centigrade heat unit
lbd: little black dress; lower-back disorder
LBD: League of British Dramatists
L-beam: capital-L-shaped beam
lbf: pound-force
LBF: Louis Braille Foundation (for blind musicians)
lbf-ft: pound-force foot
lbf/in.^{2}: pound-force per square inch
lb ft: pound foot
lb ft^2: pound per square foot

lb ft^3: pound per cubic foot
LBG: Paris, France (Le Bourget Airport)
lbh: length, breadth, height
LBHD: Long Beach Harbor Department
LBHS: Luther Burbank High School
LBI: Library Binding Institute; Licensed Beverage Industries
lb in.: pound inch
lb in.^{2}: pound per square inch
lb in.^{3}: pound per cubic inch
LBJ: Lyndon Baines Johnson—thirty-sixth President of the United States
LBJSHP: Lyndon B. Johnson State Historic Park (Texas)
LBJTMC: Lyndon B. Johnson Tropical Medical Center (American Samoa)
LBK: landing barge, kitchen
lb m: pound mass
lb/m: pounds per minute
lb-mol: pound-mole (mass)
LBO: Lima, Peru (Limatambo Airport)
lboe: lime-base oil emulsified
lbp: length between perpendiculars; low back pain; low blood pressure
LBP: London Borough Polytechnic
LBPL: Long Beach Public Library
lbr: labor; lumber
Lbr: Labrador; Librarian
lbs: pounds (from the Latin—*Librae*)
LBS: landing barge support; Libyan Broadcasting Service; Lifeboat Station; London Botanical Society
LBSC: Long Beach State College
LB & SCR: London, Brighton and South Coast Railway
lbs sq ft: pounds per square foot
lb t: pound(s) thrust; pound(s) troy
L v Bthvn: Ludwig van Beethoven
LBV: landing barge, vehicle
lc: inductance-capacitance; laundry chute; lead-covered; left center; light case; line-carrying; load carrier; locked-closed; low carbon; lower case; single acetate single cotton
l-c: launch control; low calorie; low carbohydrate
l/c: letter of credit; lower center
Lc: corrected middle latitude
LC: Lackawanna College; Ladycliff College; Lafayette College; Lake Central Airlines; Lakehead College; Lakeland College; Lambuth College; Lance Corporal; Lander College; landing craft; Lane College; Laredo College; Lassen College; L'As-

sumption College; Lawrence College; Lee College; Legal Committee; Lesley College; Lewis College; Library of Congress; Limestone College; Lincoln College; Lindenwood College; line of communication; Linfield College; Livingstone College; Longwood College; Loras College; Louisburg College; Louisiana College; Loyola College; Luther College; Lycoming College; Lynchburg College
L-C: Liquid-Carbonic (Division of General Dynamics)
L-et-C: Loir-et-Cher
LCA: Lake Carriers Association; Lake Central Airlines; landing craft—assault; Launcher Control Area; Library Club of America
lcal: lowercase alphabet length
L & C ATA: Laundry and Cleaners Allied Trades Association
lcb: longitudinal position of center of buoyancy
LCB: Liquor Control Board
LCBO: Liquor Control Board of Ontario
lcc: lateral center of gravity
LCC: landing craft, control (3-letter symbol); Lansing Community College; Launch Control Center; London County Council; Lower Columbia College
L & C C: Lewis and Clark College
LCCC: Lorain County Community College
lcd: lowest common denominator
LCDHWIU: Laundry, Cleaning, and Dye House Workers International Union
lcdo: licenciado (Spanish—licensed)
Lcdo: Licenciado (Spanish—lawyer)
lcdtl: load-compensated diode-transistor logic
lce: lance; left center entrance
lces: least-cost estimating and scheduling
lcf: least common factor; longitudinal position of center of flotation
LCF: landing craft, flak; launch control facility
LCFA: Lower California Fisheries Association
lcg: liquid-cooled (under) garment; longitudinal position of center of gravity
L Ch: Licentiate in Surgery
lchr: launcher
lci: locus of control interview
LCI: landing craft, infantry; Liquid Crystal Institute (Kent State University); Livestock Conservation

Incorporated
LCJ: Lord Chief Justice
LCJ: Louisville Courier-Journal
LCJC: Lake City Junior College
lcl: less than carload lot; lifting condensation level; local(izer)
LCLA: Lutheran Church Library Association
lcm: lead-coated metal; least common multiple; left costal margin; limit-cycle monitor; lowest common multiple
LCM: landing craft, mechanized; London College of Music
LCMS: Launch Control and Monitoring System
lcn: local civil noon
Lcn: Lincoln
LCN: *La Cosa Nostra* (Italian—Our Thing)—The Mafia
LCNM: Lehman Caves National Monument (Nevada)
LCNY: Linguistic Circle of New York
LCO: Launch Control Officer
lcoc: launch control officer's console
LCP: landing craft, personnel
LCPA: Lincoln Center for the Performing Arts
L Cpl: Lance Corporal
LCPS: Licentiate of the College of Physicians and Surgeons
l/cr: letter of credit
LCR: landing craft, rubber
LCRA: Lower Colorado River Authority
LCRT: Lincoln Center Repertory Theater
lcs: launch-control simulator
LCS: landing craft, support
LCSA: Lewis and Clark Society of America
lct: less than truckload lot
LCT: Laboratoire Central de Télécommunications (Central Telecommunications Laboratory); landing craft, tank; latest closing time; Local Civil Time; Loughsborough College of Technology
LCTC: Langlade County Teachers College; Leicester College of Technology and Commerce; Lewis and Clark Trail Commission
lcty: locality
lcu: launch-control unit; lower control unit
LCU: landing craft, utility
LCV: landing craft, vehicle
LCVP: landing craft, vehicle, personnel
lcx: launch complex
LCY: League of Communists of Yugoslavia
LC zone: land conservation zone
ld: ladies day; land; lead; lethal

dose; lid; lifeboat deck; light difference; line of departure; line of duty; load; load draft; low door; lower deck
l-d: low-density
l/d: length to diameter (ratio); life to drag (ratio)
l & d: loans and discounts; loss(es) and damage(s)
LD: Labor (US department); line of departure; line of duty; Low Dutch; lower berth (double occupancy)
ld₅₀: median lethal dose
lda: left dorso-anterior
ldb: light distribution box
LDBHS: Louis D. Brandeis High School
ldc: long-distance call; lower dead center
LDC: Laundry and Dry Cleaning (union); Less Developed Countries; Light Direction Center; Local Defense Center
LD & C: Louis Dreyfus & Compagnie
LDCMMA: Laundry and Dry Cleaners Machinery Manufacturers Association
ldc's: less-developed countries
LDF: Local Defense Force(s)
ldg: landing; loading; lodging
ldg & dly: landing and delivery
ldgs: lodgings
ldh: lactic-acid dehydrogenase
LDH: Ligue des Droits de l'Homme (League for the Rights of Man)
ldk: lower deck
ld lmt: load limit
ld mk: landmark
Ldn: London; Londoner
Lᵈᵒ: Licenciado (Spanish—lawyer; licentiate holding master's degree)
L-dopa: levodihydroxyphenylalanine (Parkinson's disease treatment drug)
ldp: left dorso-posterior
Ldp: Ladyship; Lordship
ldr: launder; laundry; leader; ledger; lodger
l/d ratio: length to diameter ratio
LDRC: Lumber Dealers Research Council
L-drivers: learner-drivers
ldry: laundry
lds: loads
Lds: Leeds
LDS: Latter Day Saints (Church of Jesus Christ of); Licentiate in Dental Surgery
LDSc: Licentiate in Dental Science
LDSR: League of Distilled Spirits Rectifiers
LDV: Local Defense Volunteer
ldx: long-distance xerography

Ldy: Londonderry
le: leading edge; left eye
l.e.: lupus erythematosus (skin disease)
Le: Lebanese; Lebanon
LE: light equipment; low explosive
lea: leather
LEA: Local Education Authority; Loss Executives Association; Lutheran Education Association
LEAA: Lace and Embroidery Association of America; Law Enforcement Assistance Administration
LEAD: Law Students Exposing Advertising Deception
LEADER: Lehigh Automatic Device for Efficient Retrieval
leaf(s): leaflet(s)
LEAJ: Law Enforcement and Administration of Justice (President's Commission on)
Lear: The Tragedy of King Lear
leaverats: leave rations
Leb: Lebanese; Lebanon
lec: lunar equipment conveyor
LEC: Livestock Equipment Council
Le Corbu: Le Corbusier
Le Corbusier: Charles Édouard Jeanneret-Gris
lect: lecture
lectr: lecturer
led.: light-emitting diodes
L Ed: Lawyer's Edition (US Supreme Court Reports)
LED: Library Education Division (American Library Association)
LEDC: League for Emotionally Disturbed Children
led's: light-emitting diodes
Lee: Leroy
Lee I: Leeward Islands
LEEP: Law Enforcement Education Program
LEF: Life Extension Foundation; Lincoln Educational Foundation
LEF: Liberté, Égalité, Fraternité (Liberty, Equality, Fraternity—slogan of the French Revolution)
leg.: legal; legislative; legislature
leg.: legato (Italian—smoothly flowing)
Leg: Leghorn
LEG: Law Enforcement Group
leg com: legally committed
legis: legislative; legislature
legit: legitimate
Le Grand Siècle: (French—The Great Century)—the 1600s when France was founding her academies and Molière was writing his comedies
LEG (UN): Legal Affairs)department of United Nations)
Leic: Leicester

Leics: Leicestershire
Leip: Lepzig
Leit: Leitrim
LEIU: Law Enforcement Intelligence Unit
lej: longitudinal expansion joint
lel: lower explosive limit
lem: lemon(ade)
lem (LEM): lunar excursion module
Lem: Lemuel
LeM:*LeMonde*(The World)—Paris
LEM: Lunar Excursion Module
lemac: leading edge mean aerodynamic chord
lemo: lemonade
LEMSIP: Laboratory for Experimental Medicine and Surgery in Primates
Len: Leningrad, formerly Petrograd, formerly St. Petersburg
Lenin: Vladimir Ilich Ulyanov
Lena: Magdalen(a)
LENA: Lower Eastside Neighborhoods Association
Leninpor: Lenin Port (Leningrad Harbor)
Len Lib: Lenin Library (Moscow)
Lenny: Leonard
Leo: Leonard; Leonese; Leonidas; Leonine; Leopold; Leopoldville
LEO: Leopoldville, Congo (airport)
Leonard Q. Ross: (pseudonym—Leo Rosten)
leopon: leopard + lioness (hybrid offspring of male leopard and lioness)
lep: lepton (collective term embracing anti-neutrino, electron, neutrino, photon, positron); lowest effective power
LEP: Library of Exact Philosophy
lep. dict.: *lepide dictum* (Latin —well said)
LEPMA: Lithographic Engravers and Plate Makers Association
LEPRA: Leprosy Relief Association (British)
Ler: Lerida
LeRC: Lewis Research Center (NASA)
Le Roi Soleil: (French—The Sun King)—Louis XIV
les: lesbian; local excitatory state
Les: Lester
LES: Launch Escape System; Lincoln Experimental Satellite
LESA: Lunar Exploration System—Apollo
Le Sage: (French—The Wise)— Charles V
lesb: lesbian(ism)
lesbo: lesbian (Lesbos-type woman); lesbianism
Les L: *Licensie es Lettres:* (French —Licentiate in Letters)

LESS: Least-cost Estimating and Scheduling Survey
Les Sc: *Licensie es Sciences:* (French—Licentiate in Science)
Lester: Leicester
let.: letter; linear energy transfer
Let: Lettish (Latvian)
letch: slang shortcut—lecher; lecheress; lecherous; lecherous feeling for; lechery
let's: let us
Letts: Lettish peoples (Latvians)
Letty: Leticia
Letz: Letzeburgesch (Flemish dialect of Luxembourg)
leu (LEU): leucine (amino acid)
lev: lever
lev: *levert* (Norwegian—delivered)
lev.: *levis* (Latin—light)
Lev: The Book of Leviticus
levis: Levi Strauss' reinforced denim workclothes but particulary dungaree trousers with heavily-stitched-and-riveted pockets
Lew: Lewis; Llewellyn
le'ward: leeward
Lewis Carroll: Charles Lutwidge Dodgson
lex: lexical; lexicographer; lexicography; lexicon
Lex: Lexington
LEX: Lexington, Kentucky (airport)
lexicog: lexicographer; lexicography
l/ext: lower extremity
Ley: Leyden
LEY: Liberal European Youth
lf: lawn faucet; life float; light face type; linoleum floor; low frequency (30–300 kc)
LF: Lindbergh Field
lfa: left fronto-anterior
lfc: laminar flow control
l-fc: low-frequency current
LFC: Lutheran Free Church
lfd: least fatal dose; low fat diet
lfd: *laufend* (German—current; consecutive)
LFE: Laboratory For Electronics
Lfg (Lfrg): *Lieferung* (German—installment; part delivery)
lfl: lower flammable limit
lf/mf: low-frequency medium-frequency
lfo: low-frequency oscillator
lfp: left fronto-posterior
LFP: Lindbergh Field Plant (Convair)
LFPS: Licentiate of the Faculty of Physicians and Surgeons
LFR: inshore fire-support ship (naval symbol)
LFRC: League for Fighting Religious Coercion

LFS: amphibious fire-support ship (naval symbol)
lft: left fronto-transverse
lg: landing; landing gear; language(s); length; long
l/g: locked gate
LG: Leipzig Gewandhaus; Low German
L-et-G: Lot-et-Garonne
LGA: New York, New York (La Guardia Airport)
LGB: Long Beach, California (airport)
L-G C: Lockheed-Georgia Company
lgd: leaderless group discussion
lge: large
L Ger: Low German
LGk: Late Greek
LGM: Lloyd's Gold Medal
Lgn: Leghorn
LGO: Lamont Geological Observatory (Columbia University)
LGOC: London General Omnibus Company
lgr: ligroin
Lgs: Lagos
lgth: length
lg tn: long ton
lg tpr: long taper
lg-type ed: large-type edition
lgv: lymphogranuloma venereum
LGW: London, England (Gatwick Airport); Longines-Wittnauer (watches)
lh: left hand; lower half
lh (LH): left hand; luteinizing hormone
LH: lighthouse; Lufthansa (airline)
L.H.: left hand
L + H: Lamport & Holt (Line)
L d'H: Légion d'Honneur — [French—Legion of Honor (decoration)]
L o H: Library of Hawaii (Honolulu)
LH2: liquid hydrogen
L-w-H: Lewis-with-Harris (Outer Hebrides)
lha: lower-half assembly
LHA: landing ship, helicopter, assault; local hour angle
LHAR: London-Hamburg-Antwerp -Rotterdam (range of ports)
LHAs: multipurpose amphibious-warfare ships (naval symbol)
LHC: Lord High Chancellor
LHCJEA: London and Home Counties Joint Electric Authority
L.H.D.: *Litterarum Humanorum Doctor* (Latin—Doctor of Human Letters); *In Litteris Humanioribus Doctor* (Latin—Doctor in Humane Letters)
lh dr: lefthand drive
LHe: liquid helium

LHI: Ligue Homéopathique Internationale (International Homeopathic League)

L-hinge: capital-L-shaped hinge

lhr: lumen hour(s)

LHR: London, England (Heathrow Airport)

L & HR: Lehigh and Hudson River (railroad)

lhs: lefthand side

LHS: Lafayette High School

LHSC: Lock Haven State College

LHT: Lord High Treasurer

lh th: lefthand thread

LHW: lower high water

LHWI: lower high water interval

li: link; lithograph; lithographer; lithography

Li: lithium

LI: Leeward Islands; Liberia; Liberian; Lions International; Long Island (L.I.)

LI: *Lydveldid Island* (Icelandic—Republic of Iceland)

L-I: Loire-Inférieure

LIA: Lead Industries Association; Leather Industries of America; Lebanese International Airways; Ligue Internationale d'Arbitrage (International Arbitration League); Long Island Association

LIAMA: Life Insurance Agency Management Association

LIAT: Leeward Islands Air Transport

lib: liberal; liberalism; libertarian; liberty; librarian; library

lib.: *liber* (Latin—book); *libra* (Latin—pound)

Lib: Liberal; Liberal Party; Liberty Party; Libyan

LIB: Let's Ignite Bras

LIBBA: Long Island Beach Buggy Association

Libby: Elizabeth

libe: librarian; library

lib ed: library edition

Libertador de Chile: (Spanish—Liberator of Chile)—Bernardo O'Higgins

Lib-Lab: Liberal-Labour (Australian coalition)

libr: librarian; library

Lib(s): Liberal(s)

Lib UN: Library of the United Nations (New York headquarters)

Lic: *Licenciado* (Spanish—lawyer; licentiate holding master's degree)

licm: left intercostal margin

Lic Med: Licentiate in Medicine

LID: League for Industrial Democracy

L & ID: London and India Docks

lidar: laser-impulsed radar; light detection and ranging (laser-beam air pollution or smog measuring device)

lidoc: lidocaine (xylocain)

LIE: Liberal Intellectual Establishment (Philip Wylie's acronymic description of the befuddled and often nonsensical liberals of his time; the Old Left; the so-called New Left)

Liech: Liechtenstein

Lief: *Lieferung* (German—issue)

LIEMA: Long Island Electronics Manufacturers Association

Lieut: Lieutenant

Lieut Col: Lieutenant Colonel

Lieut Comdr: Lieutenant Commander

lif: left iliac fossa

LIFE: Ladies Involved For Education; League for International Food Education

Life Sta: Lifeboat Station (US Coast Guard)

lifo: last in, first out

lig: ligament; ligature

Lig: Limoges

Lige: Elijah

liger: offspring of lion and tigress

light.: lighting; lightning

LIHDC: Low Income Housing Development Corporation

lil: lilliputian; little

li'l: little

LIL: Lunar International Laboratory (proposed in 1961 by Dr Theodore von Karman)

LILCO: Long Island Lighting Company

lilla: (Swedish—small)

lille: (Dano-Norwegian—little, as in Lillehammer)

lilo: last in, last out

LILS: Lead-in-Light System (airport term)

lim: limber; limit(er)

Lim: Limerick

LIM: Lima, Peru (Callao International Airport)

Lima: code word for letter L

LIMAC: Linden Industrial Mutual Aid Council

liman: (Turkish—bay; port)

lim dat: limiting date

lime: calcium oxide (CaO)

Limejuicer: British sailor

limestone: calcium carbonate $(CaCO_3)$

limewater: calcium-hydroxide solution—$Ca(OH)_2$; limejuice and water mixture

limnol: limnology

limo: lemonade; limousine

limon: lime-and-lemon (hybrid citrus fruit)

lin: lineal; linear

lín: *línea* (Spanish—line)

LIN: Linjeflyg (Swedish airline); Milan, Italy (Linate Airport)

linac: linear accelerator

Linc: Lincoln

LINC: Learning Institute of North Carolina

Lincs: Lincolnshire

LINCS: Language Information Network and Clearinghouse System

LINDE: Linde Air Products

Lindy: Colonel Charles A. Lindbergh

linim: liniment

Linn: Linné; Linnaeus

Linnaeus: Carl von Linné

lino: linoleum; linotype; linotypist

linol: linoleum

LINWR: Lake Ilo National Wildlife Refuge (North Dakota)

LIO: Lionel Corporation (stock exchange symbol); Lions International Organization

lip.: life insurance policy

LIPM: Lister Institute of Preventive Medicine

liq: liquid; liquor

liq f rkt: liquid fuel rocket

liqn: *liquidación* (Spanish—liquidation)

liquid.: liquidation

LIR: Library of International Relations

lirbm: liver, iron, red bone marrow

LIRI: Leather Industries Research Institute

LIRR: Long Island Railroad

Lis: Lisbon

LIS: Liberian Information Service; Lisbon, Portugal (airport); Long Island Sound

LISA: *Library and Information Science Abstracts*

lisp.: list processor (computer language)

LISPA: Long Island Sound Pilots Association

LISS: London Institute of Strategic Studies

LIST: *Library and Information Science Today*

lit.: liter; literal; literally; literary; literature; litter; little

l it: lire italiane (Italian lire)

LIT: Light Intratheater Transport (aircraft); Little Rock, Arkansas (airport)

lite: light

lith: lithograph; lithography; lithology

Lith: Lithuania; Lithuanian

litharge: lead oxide (PbO)

litho: lithograph

lithol: lithology

Litt.D.: *Litterarum Doctor* (Latin

—Doctor of Letters)

Little Flower: Fiorello H. La Guardia

Little Joe: Apollo spacecraft booster designed and produced by General Dynamics, Convair

Little John: surface-to-surface rocket produced by Emerson Electric

Litt.M.: Master of Letters

Lits: Lithuanians; Litvaks

litur: liturgical; liturgy

litz: litzendraht (wire)

LIU: Long Island University

LIUNA: Laborers International Union of North America

liv: liver

Liv: Liverpool

Liver: Liverpool; Liverpudlian(s)

livr: livraison (French—issue of a journal; part of a book or serial)

lix: lixiviation

liz: lizard; lizzie (as in *tin lizzie,* an old Ford automobile)

Liz(a): Eliza(beth)

Lizzy: Elizabeth

lj: life jacket

LJ: Libby, McNeil & Libby (stock exchange symbol); Lord Justice; Sierra Leone Airways (2-letter coding)

LJ: Library Journal

LJC: Lackawanna Junior College; Laredo Junior College; Lincoln Junior College

LJ/SLJ: Library Journal/School Library Journal

LJT: Lear jet airplane

lk: link

LK: Lockheed Aircraft Corporation (stock exchange symbol)

LKAB: Luossavaara-Kiirunavaara Aktiebolag (iron-ore mines in Luossa-Kiiruna range of northern Sweden)

LKB: Link-Belt Company (stock exchange symbol)

lkd: locked

lkg: locking

lkg & bkg: leakage and breakage

LKGR: Lake Kyle Game Reserve (Rhodesia)

LK & PRR: Lahaina-Kaanapali and Pacific Railroad

lkr: locker

Lkr: Landskrona

lks: liver, kidney, spleen

lkt: lookout

Lkw: Lastkraftwagen (German—lorry; truck)

lkwash: lockwasher

ll: light lock; live load; lower lid

'll: (contraction of till and will)

ll: lectiones (Latin—readings); *llegada* (Spanish—arrival)

l/l: library labels; line-by-line; low-

er left; lower limit

l & l: leave and liberty

LL: Lebanese pound; Lending Library; Loftleidir (Icelandic Airlines); Lord Lieutenant; Low Latin

L/L: Lutlang (Norwegian—limited company)

LLA: Lend-Lease Administration; Luther League of America

Llanfairp: Llanfairpwllgwyngllgogershwyrndro-bwllabtysiliogogoch (Welsh place-name meaning the Church of St Mary near the Raging Whirlpool and the Church of St Tysilio by the Red Cave)—probably the longest word in any of the world's more than 2700 languages and well deserving of abbreviation

llano: (Spanish—plain; prairie, as in Llano Estacado)

L Lat: Late Latin; Low Latin

LLB: Little League Baseball

LL.B.: Legum Baccalaureus (Latin—Bachelor of Laws)

LLBA: Language and Language Behavior Abstracts

llc: lower left center

LL.D.: Legum Doctor (Latin—Doctor of Laws)

lle: left lower extremity

lle: llegada (Spanish—arrival)

LLEI: Lincoln Library of Essential Information

LLF: Laubach Literacy Fund

lli: latitude and longitude indicator

LLI: Lord Lieutenant of Ireland

LLJ: Leaf Library of Judaica

LLJJ: Lords Justices

lll: light load line; loose-leaf ledger; low-level logic

l/l l: line-by-line libretto

LLL: Lutheran Laymen's League

L L L: Love's Labour's Lost

llll: left lower lung lobe

LL. M.: *Legum Magister* (Latin—Master of Laws)

LLN: League for Less Noise

LLNNR: Loch Leven National Nature Reserve (Scotland)

LLNWR: Long Lake National Wildlife Refuge (North Dakota)

Lloyd's: Lloyd's Register of Shipping

L L & P of H: Life, Liberty, and the Pursuit of Happiness (original draft of the *Declaration of Independence* read: "Life, Liberty, and the Pursuit of Profit")—hence the abiding confusion created by the pusillanimous politicians who edited Thomas Jefferson's finest writing

LLPI: Linen and Lace Paper Institute

llq: left lower quadrant

llr: line of least resistance; load-limiting resistor

llrv (LLRV): lunar landing research vehicle

LLS: Lunar Logistics System

LLSS: Low-Level Sounding System

llsv (LLSV): lunar logistics system vehicle

llti: long lead time items

llltv: low-light-level television

llu: lending library unit

LLU: Loma Linda University

LLUU: Laymen's League—Unitarian Universalist

llv (LLV): lunar landing vehicle

llw: lower low water (LLW); low-level waste

LLWI: lower low water interval

llwl: light load water line

Lly: Llanelly

llyp: long-leaf yellow pine

lm: land mine; light metal(s); liquid metal(s); long meter; longitudinal muscle; lower motor; lumen(s)

l/m: lines per minute

Lm: middle latitude

LM: Legion of Merit; Liggett Myers Tobacco (stock exchange symbol); Lincoln Memorial; Lord Mayor; Lunar Module

L & M: Linotype and Machinery

lma: left mento-anterior

LMA: Last Manufacturers Association; League for Mutual Aid; Lingerie Manufacturers Association; London-Midlands Association

LMAC: Labor-Management Advisory Committee

LMBP: Lake Manyas Bird Paradise (Turkey)

lmc: liquid-metal cycle; low middling clause

LMC: Lake Michigan College; Liberia Mining Company; Lloyd's Machinery Certificate

LMCC: Licentiate of the Medical Council of Canada

lmd: local medical doctor

LMDC: Lawyers Military Defense Committee

lme: liquid-metal embrittlement

LME: London Metal Exchange

LMEC: Liquid Metal Engineering Center (AEC)

LMEE: Light Military Electronic Equipment (department of General Electric)

lmfr: liquid metal fuel reactor

lm/ft^2: lumen per square foot

LMG: light machine gun

lm-hr: lumen-hour
LMI: Lawn Mower Institute; Logistics Management Institute
LMIS: Labor Market Information System
LML: Lerner Marine Laboratory
LMLA: Lizzadro Museum of Lapidary Arts
LMLI: Liberty Mutual Life Insurance
lm/lrv: lunar module/lunar roving vehicle (LM/LRV)
lmm: locator at middle marker (compass)
l/mm: lines per millimeter
lm/m²: lumen per square meter
LMM: Library Microfilms and Materials
lmmi: like mamma made it
lmn: lineman
LMNP: Lake Manyara National Park (Tanzania)
LMNRA: Lake Mead National Recreation Area (Arizona and Nevada)
lmp: last menstrual period
LMP: *Literary Market Place* (Directory of American Book Publishers)
LMPA: Library and Museum of the Performing Arts (Lincoln Center, New York City)
L Mq: Lourenço Marques
LMRC: London Medical Research Council
lm's: lunar modules (LMs)
lm/s: lumen per second
LMS: Licentiate in Medicine and Surgery; London Mathematical Society
LMSC: Lockheed Missiles & Space Company
LMSD: Lockheed Missile and Space Division
lmt: left mento-transverse
LMT: Local Mean Time
lmtd: logarithmic mean temperature difference
LMUM: Ludwig-Maximilians-Universität München (University of Munich)
lm/w: lumen per watt
ln: liaison
Ln: Lane
LN: Air Liban (Lebanese Airlines); League of Nations; Napierian logarithm (symbol)
L & N: Leeds & Northrup; Louisville & Nashville (railroad)
L of N: League of Nations
LN₂: liquid nitrogen
LNA: Liberian National Airways; Libyan News Agency
LNC: Leith Nautical College
LNDC: Lesotho National Development Corporation

lndrs: laundress
lndry: laundry
L & NE: Lehigh & New England (railroad)
lng: lining; liquefied natural gas
LNG tanker: liquefied-natural-gas tanker
LNLA: Lithuanian National League of America
lnmp: last normal menstrual period
LNNP: Lake Nakuru National Park (Kenya)
LNNR: Lindisfarne National Nature Reserve (England)
LNOC: Libya National Oil Company
L-note: $50 bill
LNP: Lamington National Park (Queensland); Lincoln NP (South Australia); London Northern Polytechnic
LNR: Loteni Nature Reserve (South Africa)
Lnrk: Lanark
LNT: Leo Nicholas Tolstoy
lntl: lintel
lnu: last name unknown
LNU: League of Nations Union
LNWR: Lacassine National Wildlife Refuge (Louisiana); Lacreek NWR (South Dakota); London and North Western Railway; Lostwood NWR (North Dakota; Loxahatchee NWR (Florida)
lo: local; local oscillator; locked open; low; low(er) order; lubricating oil; lubrication order
Lo: low (gear)
Lo: *Lordag* (Danish—Lord's Day) —Saturday
LO: Launch Operator; Liaison Office(r); Lick Observatory (Mount Hamilton, California); Louisville Orchestra; Lowell Observatory (Flagstaff, Arizona); Lubrication Order
LO: *Landsorganisationen* (leading trade union in Norway and Sweden)
L/O: Letter of Offer
LO₂: liquid oxygen
loa: leave of absence; left occiput anterior; length overall
LOA: Light Observation Aircraft; Lithuanian Organists Alliance
loan/A: vessel(s) loaned to Army
loan/C: vessel(s) loaned to Coast Guard
loan/m: vessel(s) loaned to miscellaneous governmental activities (Maritime Academy)
loan/s: vessel(s) loaned to states
lob.: line of balance
LOB: Launch Operations Building; Loyal Order of the Boar; Loyal Order of Boors; Loyal Order of

Bores
lobal.: long base-line buoy
lobar: long baseline radar
loboto: lobotomy
lob(s): lobster(s)
loc: locate; location
LOC: Lyric Opera of Chicago
lo-cal: low calorie
locat: location; low-altitude clear-air turbulence
LOCATE: Library of Congress Automation Techniques Exchange
loc.cit.: *loco citato* (Latin—in the place cited)
loc. dol.: *loco dolenti* (Latin—to the painful spot)
loch: (Celtic—bay; lake as in Loch Lomond, Loch Ness, Loch Tay)
loco: locomotion; locomotive
loc. primo cit.: *loco primo citato* (Latin—in the place first cited)
locpuro: local purchase order
LOCS: Librascope Operations Control System
loc. supra cit.: *loco supra citato* (Latin—in the place cited above)
lod: line of duty
LOD: Launch Operations Directorate
lodestone: magnetic iron oxide; Fe₃O₄; magnetite
lodor: loaded (vessel) awaiting orders or assignment
LOEE: Loyal Order of Overtime Experts
lof: lecherous old fool; lowest operating frequency
L-O-F: Libbey-Owens-Ford
lofti: low-frequency trans-ionosphere (research satellite)
Loftleidir: Icelandic Airlines
log.: logarithm; logic; logical
LOG: Legion of Guardsmen
logair: logistics transport by air
logairnet: logistics air network
logan(s): loganberry; loganberries
Log Com: Logistical Command; Logistics Command
logel: logic-generating language
logg: loggerhead; loggia; logging; log glass
logie: killogie
loglan: logical language
logland: logistics transport by land
logo: logogram [initial letter, number, or symbol used as an abbreviation or as part of an abbreviation as in Q & A (question and answer) 3M (Minnesota Mining and Manufacturing Company), ¢ (cents)]; logotype (two or more type characters cast as one piece of type, as in *and*, *on*, *re*, *the*, or as shown in many trademarks and trade

names cast as one piece)
logol: logological; logologically; logologist; logology
logr: logistical ration; logistics ratio
Logr: Logroño
logsea: logistics transport by sea
logsup: logistical support; logistics support
loh (LOH): light observation helicopter
LOI: Lunar Orbit Insertion
loib: lunar orbit insertion burn
loid: celluloid (strip used by burglars to unlock doors)
lo-J: low inertia
loktal: locked octal tube
lol: length of lead (actual); little old lady
LOL: Lobitos Oilfields Limited
lola: lollapalooza (excellent or extraordinary person or thing)
Lola: Dolores
lolli: lollipop
lom: locater at outer marker (compass)
LOM: Loyal Order of Moose
LOMA: Life Office Management Association
Lomb: Lombard; Lombardian; Lombardy
lo mi: low mileage
Lon: Alonso; London
LON: London, England (London-Central Airport)
Lond: London; Londonderry; Londoner(s)
Lone Eagle: Charles A. Lindbergh
long: longeron; longitude
Long Tom: Thomas Jefferson —third President of the United States
longv: longevity
long vac: long vacation
LONRHO: London and Rhodesian Mining and Land Company Limited
loo: looker; looker-after; looker-on
looktr: lookout tower
LOOM: Loyal Order of Moose
lop.: launch operator's panel; left occiput posterior
l-o-p: line-of-position
LOP: lunar orbiting photographic (vehicle)
L O P & G: Live Oak, Perry & Gulf (railroad)
loq: loquitur (Latin—he speaks)
lor: lunar orbital rendezvous
Lor: Lorenzo
LOR: L'Osservatore Romano (Papal Roman Observer)
loran: long-range aid to navigation
lord.: lordosis
Lord Acton: John E.E. Dalberg-Acton
Lord Chesterfield: Philip Stanhope

Lord Dunsany: Edward John Moreton Drax Plunkett
Lord Palmerston: Henry John Temple
Lord Passfield: Sidney Webb
Lord Russell: Bertrand A. Russell
lorl (LORL): large orbital research laboratory
lorv (LORV): low orbital reentry vehicle
Lor^zo: Lorenzo
los: loss of signal
l-o-s: line-of-sight
LOS: Lagos, Nigeria (airport); Little Orchestra Society
Losa: Los Angeles
LOSS: Large Object Salvage System
los sys: landing observer's signal system
lot.: large orbiting telescope; lateral olfactory tract; left occipito-transverse; load on top
lot.: lotio (Latin—lotion)
LOT: Polish Air Lines (3-letter symbol)
LOTADS: Long-Term Air Defense Study (USA)
lo-temp: low temperature
lotw: loaded on trailers or wagons
Lou: Lewis; Louis; Louisa; Louisiana; Louisville
lough: (Gaelic—bay; lake, as in Lough Neagh, Lough Oughter)
Louis: Louisville
Lou Orc: Louisville Orchestra
Louv: Louvain
l'Ouverture: Toussaint l'Ouverture—founder and first president of Haiti after defeating Napoleon's troops numbering 25,000
lo wat: low water
Low L: Low Latin
lox: liquid oxygen; also the name for smoked salmon
lox-sox: liquid oxygen, solid oxygen
loxygen: liquid oxygen
loy: loyalty
loz: liquid ozone
Loz: Lozère
lp: landplane; last paid; latent period; light perception; linear programming; liquid propellant; liquefied petroleum; litter patient; local procurement; long-play; long-playing; low pass; low point; low power; low pressure; lumbar puncture
l/p: launch platform
LP: Aeralpi (2-letter symbol); Labor Party; Labour Party; Liberal Party; Library of Parliament; litter patient; long-play (record); Lower Peninsula
LP: lunga pausa (Italian—long

pause)
L-P: Lionel-Pacific
LPA: Labor Party Association; Labor Policy Association; Little People of America
LPB: La Paz, Bolivia (airport)
lpc: low-pressure chamber
LPC: Lockheed Propulsion Company
lp cyl: low-pressure cylinder
lpd: least perceptible difference; local procurement direct
LPD: amphibious transport dock ship (naval symbol); Local Procurement District; low performance drone
lpf: leukocytosis-promoting factor; low-power field
lpg: liquefied petroleum gas
LPGA: Ladies Professional Golf Association; Liquefied Petroleum Gas Association
lpi: lines per inch
LPI: Lightning Protection Institute; Louisiana Polytechnic Institute
lpicbm (LPICBM): liquid-propellant intercontinental ballistic missile
LPIU: Lithographers and Photoengravers International Union
LPKS: Lone Pine Koala Sanctuary (Queensland)
lpl: lightproof louver
LPL: Liverpool Public Libraries; London Public Library; Louisville Public Library; Lunar and Planetary Laboratory (University of Arizona)
LPL: Lembaga Penelitian Laut (Indonesian—Institute for Marine Research)—Jakarta
LP & L: Louisiana Power and Light
L-plane: US Army liaison aircraft
LP & LC: Louisiana Power & Light Company
lplr: lock pillar
LPLs: Liverpool Public Libraries
lpm: lines per millimeter; lines per minute
LPN: Licensed Practical Nurse
LPNA: Lithographers and Printers National Association
LPNI: Langley Porter Neuropsychiatric Institute
lpo: local purchase order
LPO: London Philharmonic Orchestra; London Post Office
Lpool: Liverpool
lpr (LPR): liquid-propellant rocket
LPRC: Library Public Relations Council
lps: lightproof shade
LPS: Lebanese Press Syndicate; Light Photo Squadron
LPSA: Liberal Party of South Africa

LPSS: amphibious transport submarine (naval symbol)

lptv (LPTV): large payload test vehicle

Lpud: Liverpudlian (native to or inhabitant of Liverpool)

lpv: lightproof vent

lpw: lumens per watt

LPZG: Lincoln Park Zoological Gardens

lq: last quarter; lowest quartile

l.q.: *lege quaeso* (Latin—please read)

lr: latency relaxation; leave rations; letter report; lire; long run; long range; lower

l/r: lower right

l-to-r: left-to-right (photo caption abbreviation)

Lr: lawrencium

LR: Laboratory Report; Lee Rubber (stock exchange symbol); Letter Report; Little Rock

LR: *Lloyd's Register*

lra: long-range aviation

LRA: Labor Research Association; Lithuanian Regeneration Association

LRAM: Licentiate of the Royal Academy of Music

LRB: Laboratory of Radiation Biology (University of Washington); Loyalty Review Board

LRBA: Laboratoire de Recherches Balistiques et Aérodynamiques (Laboratory for Ballistic and Aerodynamic Research)

lrbm: long-range ballistic missile

lrc: lower right center

LRC: Langley Research Center (NASA); Lewis Research Center (NASA)

LRCE: Little Rock Cotton Exchange

LRCM: Licentiate of the Royal College of Music

LRCP: Licentiate of the Royal College of Physicians

LRCS: Licentiate of the Royal College of Surgeons

LRCVS: Licentiate of the Royal College of Veterinary Surgeons

LRFI: League for Religious Freedom in Israel

LRFPB: Louisiana Rating and Fire Prevention Bureau

LRFPS: Licentiate of the Royal Faculty of Physicians and Surgeons

lrg: large

lri: left-right indicator; long-range interceptor

LRI: Library Resources Incorporated

LRJC: Lake Region Junior College

LRL: Lawrence Radiation Labora-

tory; Lunar Receiving Laboratory

LRN: *Landslaget for Reiselivet i Norge* (Norway Travel Association)

L R-P: La Rochelle-Pallice

LRPL: Liquid Rocket Propulsion Laboratory; Little Rock Public Library

lrrp: lowest required radiated power

l/r/s: library rubber stamps (used-book trade abbreviation indicating book may belong or may have belonged to a public library)

LRSS: Long-Range Survey System

LRTgt: last resort target

LRTS: *Library Resources and Technical Services*

lrv (LRV): lunar roving vehicle

LRY: Liberal Religious Youth

ls: landing ship; left side; lightship; light vessel; limestone; liminal sensitivity; limit switch; long shot; loudspeaker; low speed

l's: losers (gambling short form)

l-s: lumbo-sacral

l & s: launch(ing) and servicing

l/s: liters per second

l.s.: *locus sigilli* (Latin—place of the seal)

Ls: Lopes; Louis

LS: Lamson & Sessions; Linnaean Society

L-S: Lewis-Shepard

lsa: left sacro-anterior

LSA: Labor Services Agency; Land Service Assistant; Land Settlement Association; Leukemia Society of America; Licentiate of the Society of Apothecaries; Linguistic Society of America; Lithuanian Society of America

LSAA: Linen Supply Association of America

LSAT: Law School Admission Test

lsb: lower sideband

LSB: Launch Service Building

LSBR: Large Seed-Blanket Reactor (AEC)

LSC: Laser Systems Center

LSCA: Library Services and Construction Act

LSCC: Library of the Supreme Court of Canada

LSCT: Lamar State College of Technology

lsd: least significant difference

ls & d: liquor store and delicatessen

£ s d: *librae, solidi, denarii* (Latin—pounds, shillings, pence)

LSD: landing ship, dock (naval symbol); League for Spiritual Discovery; lysergic acid die-

thylamide—dangerous psychedelic drug nicknamed *acid*

LSD: *Lyserginsaure Diathylamid* (German—lysergic acid diethylamide)

L.S.D.: Doctor of Library Science

LSE: London School of Economics; Louisiana Sugar Exchange

LSDS: Low-Speed Digital System

LSE: London School of Economics; London Stock Exchange; Louisiana Sugar Exchange

LSECS: Life Support and Environmental Control System

LSEL: London School of Economics Library

LSE & PS: London School of Economics and Political Science

LSEU: La Salle Extension University

LSF: Literary Society Foundation; Lock Security Force (Panama Canal)

LSHTM: London School of Hygiene and Tropical Medicine

lsi: large-scale integration

LSI: Lake Superior & Ishpeming (railroad); Law-Science Institute (University of Texas); Law of the Sea Institute; Lear Siegler Incorporated

LS & I: Lake Superior & Ishpeming (Railroad)

LSIA: Lamp and Shade Institute of America

lsk: liver, spleen, kidney

LSL: landing ship, logistic; Lucy Stone League

lsm: lysergic acid morpholide

LSM: landing ship, medium

LS/mft: Leopold Stokowski/means fine tone; Lucky Strike/means fine tobacco

LSMI: Lake Superior Mining Institute

LSMR: rocket ship

LSMSC: Lake Superior Mines Safety Council

LSNR: League of Struggle for Negro Rights

LSNY: Linnean Society of New York

LSO: Landing Signal Officer; Leningrad Symphony Orchestra; London Symphony Orchestra

lsp: left sacro-posterior

LSPOJC: La Salle-Peru-Oglesby Junior College

L-square: capital-L-shaped square; carpenter's square

lsr: launch signal responder

Lsr: *Luftschutzraum* (German —air raid shelter)

Lsr Ant: Lesser Antilles (Leeward and Windward Islands)

LSS: Life Saving Service; Life

Saving Station; Life Support System; Lockheed Space Systems; Logistic Support Squadron

L.S.S.: Leopold-Sedar Senghor

lssm: local scientific surface module

LSSR: Latvian Soviet Socialist Republic (formerly Republic of Latvia); Lithuanian Soviet Socialist Republic (formerly Republic of Lithuania)

LSSS: London School of Slavonic Studies

lst: large space telescope; left sacrotraverse; liquid-oxygen start tank; liquid storage tank; living structures tank

LST: landing ship, tank; Local Sidereal Time

LSU: landing ship, utility; Louisiana State University

LSV: landing ship, vehicle

lsw: least significant word

lsw lt: landing signal wand light

LSWR: London and South Western Railway

lt: laundry tray; lid tank; light; light trap; long ton; low tension; low torque

lt: laut (German—according to)

l/t: loop test

Lt: Lieutenant

LT: landing team; large tug; London Transport; local time

lta: lighter-than-air

LTA: Lawn Tennis Association; lighter-than-air

ltb: laryngo-trachael bronchitis

Lt.B.: Bachelor of Literature

LTB: London Transport Board

LTBT: Limited Test Ban Treaty (prohibiting nuclear testing in certain environments)

LTC: Le Tourneau College

Lt. Cdr.: Lieutenant Commander

Lt. Cmdr.: Lieutenant Commander

Lt. Col.: Lieutenant Colonel

Ltd.: Limited

Ltda: Limitada (Spanish—limited)

ltd ed: limited edition

lte: large table electroplotter; linear threshold element

Lte: (French—Limite)—limited

LTE: London Transport Executive

ltf (LTF): lipotrophic factor

LTF: Lithographic Technical Foundation; tropical fresh water load line (Plimsoll mark)

ltfrd: lot tolerance fraction reliability deviation

ltg: lighting

ltgc: lithographic

ltge: lighterage

Lt. Gen.: Lieutenant General

ltgh: lightening hole

Lt. Gov.: Lieutenant Governor

lth: lath; lathing; luteotrophic hormone (LTH)

Lth: Leith

lthr: leather

lti (LTI): light transmission index

Lti: Laotian

LTI: Lowell Technological Institute

Lt. JG: Lieutenant Junior Grade

ltl (LTL): less than truckload

LTM: Licentiate of Tropical Medicine

ltng: lightning

lto: landing takeoff

Lto: lento (Italian—slowly)

ltof: low-temperature optical facility

LTon: long ton

ltp: limit on tax preferences

LTP: Library Technology Program

ltr: letter

LTR: Long Term Reserve

LTR: *Library Technology Reports*

LtrO: letter order

LTRS: Laser Target Recognition System

LTS: Landfall Technique School; London Transport System

ltta: long-tank thrust augmented

L-T-V: Long-Temco-Vought (corporation)

lu: logic unit; lumen

lu.: *lues* (Latin—contagious disease)—plague or syphilis

lu. I: *lues I*—primary syphilis

lu. II: *lues II*—secondary syphilis

lu. III: *lues III*—tertiary syphilis

Lu: Lugano; Lugo; lutetium

LU: Langston University; Laurentian University; Laval University; Lehigh University; Lethbridge University; Ligue Universelle (Universal Esperantist League); Lincoln University; Liverpool University; London University; Loyola University

LUA: London Underwriters Association

lub: lubricant; lubricate; lubrication

lube: lubricate; lubrication

lub oil: lubricating oil

lubs: large undisturbed bottom sampler

Luc: Lucretius

Luci: Lucifer

Lucifer: the devil; the morning star—Venus (see Hesperus)

Luck: Lucknow

Lucr: The Rape of Lucrece

Lucy: Lucia; Lucilla; Lucille

lud: liftup door

lue: left upper entrance; left upper extremity

luf: lowest useful high frequency

LUFTHANSA: Deutsche Lufthansa (West German Airline)

lug: luggage; lugger; lugging; lug-sail; lugworm

luhf: lowest usable high frequency

LUIP: London University Institute of Psychiatry

Luke: The Gospel according to St. Luke

lul: left upper lobe (lung)

LUL: London University Library

LULAC: League of United Latin-American Citizens

Lulu: Louise

lum: lumbago; lumbar; lumber; lumen; luminosity; luminous

Lum: Columbus

lumb: lumber; lumbering

Lumpen: Lumpenproletariat (German—unskilled city workers)

lun: lunar; lunette

lun: lundi (French—Monday); *lunedi* (Italian—Monday); *lunes* (Spanish—Monday)

lunada: (Spanish—moon-shaped)

lunar caustic: silver nitrate ($AgNO_3$)

Lunik: Soviet cosmic rocket landed on Moon September 14, 1959

lun int: lunitidal interval

lupa: lupanar (Latin—brothel)

luq: left upper quadrant (abdomen)

lust.: lustrous

lut: launcher umbilical tower (LUT)

lut.: luteum (Latin—yellow)

LUT: Launcher Umbilical Tower; Ludwig Universe Tankships

Luth: Luther(an)

luv: let us vote (popular teenage plea); lightweight utility vehicle (pickup truck)

Lux: Luxembourg; Luxembourger

LUXAIR: Luxembourg Airlines

Lux Fr: Luxembourger franc

Luz: Luzon

lv: launch vehicle (LV); leave; low voltage

Lv: Latvia; Latvian; lev (Bulgarian currency unit)

LV: Las Vegas; launch vehicle; Lehigh Valley (railroad); light vessel (light ship); Lindholmens Varv (Lindholmens Shipyard)

L da V: Leonardo da Vinci

LV-3: Atlas launch vehicle (Convair)

lvd: louvered door

lvda: launch vehicle data adapter

lvdc: launch vehicle digital computer

lvfa: low-voltage fast activity

lvh (LVH): landing vehicle hydrofoil

lvhv: low volume high velocity

LVI: Local Veterinary Inspector

lvl: level

LVL: La Verendrye Line (Hall Corporation)

LVNM: Lava Beds National Monu-

ment (California)
LVNP: Lassen Volcanic National Park (California); Luangwa Valley National Park (Zambia)
lvp: low-voltage protection
LVP: Launch Vehicle Program(s)
lvp dr: leverpak drum
lvr: low-voltage release
LVRB: Launch Vehicle Reliability Board
LVs: launch vehicles
LVT: landing vehicle, tracked
LVUSA: Legion of Valor of the USA
lw: low water
l & w: living and well
Lw: lawrencium (element 103)
LW: light warning; lower berth
lwb: long wheelbase
lwc: lightweight concrete
lwd: larger word
LWF: Lutheran World Federation
LWFB: Lake Washington Floating Bridge
lwf & c: low water full and change
lwic: lightweight insulating concrete
lwl: length at waterline; load waterline; low-water line (tidal marking)
LWL: Limited War Laboratory (US

Army)
lwm: low-water mark
LWMEL: Leonard Wood Memorial for the Eradication of Leprosy
LWNWR: Lake Woodruff National Wildlife Refuge (Florida)
lwop: leave without pay
lwos: low-water ordinary spring
lwost: low-water ordinary spring tide
lwp: leave with pay; load water plane
lwr: lower
lwr (LWR): light water reactor
l'wrd: leeward
Lwt: Lowestoft
LWT: amphibious warping tug (naval symbol)
LWU: Leather Workers Union
LWV: Lackawanna & Wyoming Valley (railroad); League of Women Voters
lww: launch window width
lwyr: lawyer
lx: lux
lx.: lux (Latin—light)
LX: Los Angeles Airways (2-letter coding)
LXX: Septuagint (70)
lxxx: love and kisses
ly: last year; last year's model

Ly: Lyman; Lyon
LY: Love Year
Lyd: Lydia; Lydian
lye: potassium hydroxide (KOH) or sodium hydroxide (NaOH)
LYK: Lykes Brothers Steamship company (stock exchange symbol)
lym: last year's model(s); lymph; lymphatic(s)
lympho(s): lymphocyte(s)
Lyo: Lyons (British maritime contraction)
lyr: lyric; lyrical; lyricism; lyricist; lyrics
lyric.: language for your remote instruction by computer
lys: lysine
Lyt: Lyttelton, New Zealand
Lz: Lopez
LZ: Landing Zone
LZOA: Labor Zionist Organization of America
LZSU: Leningrad A.A. Zhdanov State University (University of Leningrad)
LZT: Local Zone Time
L-Zug: Luxus-Zug (German—luxury railroad train)
lzy: lazy

M

m: difference of meriodional parts (symbol); magnetic dipole moment (symbol); main; male; manual; married; masculine; measure; megohm; member; meridian; mesh; meter; mile; mill; milli- (thousandth); minim; minute; minutes; modulus; molar; month; moon; morning; mother
m: mass (symbol); *Mazda* (Japanese auto with German Wankel rotary engine)
m²: square meter(s)
m³: cubic meter(s)
m/3: middle third (long bones)
M: bending moment (symbol); Mach (Austrian physicist); mach number; mach speed; magnaflux; magnetic inspection; maintainability; Malay; Malaya; Malaysia; March; mark; Martin; materiel; Matson Navigation Company; median; medium; mega- (million); megacycle; metal; metropolitan; Mike—

code for letter M; Min; missile; mixture; mobile; Mohammedan; Mohammedanism; molecular weight (symbol); moment; Monday; Monsieur (French—Mister); Montour (railroad); Moore-McCormack (steamship lines); Moslem; muscle; pitching moment (symbol); thousand (symbol)
M: Missa (Latin—Mass); *mujeres* (Spanish—women)
M': Mac (Gaelic—son of)
M-16: British Foreign Office Military Intelligence (Secret Intelligence Service)
ma: machine account; machine accountant; manufacturing assembly; map analysis; mechanical advantage; menstrual age; mental age mill annealed; milliampere
m/a: my account
mA: milliangstrom
Ma: Malayalam; Mama; Manchuria; Manchurian; María; ma-

surium (symbol)
Ma: Mandag (Danish—Monday)
Ma.: María
Mª: María
MA: Magma Arizona (railroad); Magnesium Association; Mahogany Association; Manpower Administration; Maritime Administration; Marshaling Area; May Department Stores (stock exchange symbol); Mediterranean Area; Menorah Association; Metric Association; Military Academy; Military Attaché
M.A.: *Magister Artium* (Latin —Master of Arts)
M & A: Missouri & Arkansas (railroad)
M es A: Maitre es Arts (French —Master of Arts)
maa: maximum authorized altitude
Maa: Maandag (Dutch—Monday)
MAA: Manufacturers Aircraft Association; Master Army Aviator; Master-at-Arms; Mas-

ter-of-Arms; Mathematical Association of America; Medieval Academy of America; Medical Assistance for the 'Aged; Mutual Aid Association; Mutual Assurance Association

MA of A: Motel Association of America

MAAC: Mutual Assistance Advisory Committee

MAAF: Mediterranean Allied Air Force; Mediterranean Army Air Force

MAAG: Military Assistance Advisory Group

MAAH: Museum of African-American History

ma'am: madam

ma'amselle: mademoiselle

MAAN: Mutual Advertising Agency Network

MAAP: Minority Association for Animal Protection

M.A.Arch.: Master of Arts in Architecture

MAATC Mobile Antiaircraft Training Center

Mab: Mabel

MAB: Magazine Advertising Bureau; Maracaibo Oil Exploration (stock exchange symbol); Marine Air Base; Medical Advisory Board; Missile Assembly Building; Munitions Assignment Board

MABO: Marianas-Bonin (islands)

mabp: mean arterial blood pressure

MABRON: Marine Air Base Squadron

MABS: Marine Air Base Squadron

mac: macerate; machine-aided cognition; maximum allowable concentration(s); mean aerodynamic chord; motion analysis camera; multiple-access computer

mac.: *macerare* (Latin—macerate)

Mac: Macao, Portuguese China; nickname of anyone whose surname begins with Mac

M.Ac.: Master of Accountancy

MAC: Maintenance Advisory Committee; Major Air Command; Marine Amphibious Corps; Maritime Advisory Committee; McDonnell Aircraft Corporation; Mediterranean Air Command; Miami Aviation Corporation; Middle Atlantic Conference; Military Airlift Command

MACAIR: Macao Air Transport

Macc: Maccabees

MACE: Missile and Control Equipment (North American Aviation)

M.A.C.E.: Master of Air Conditioning Engineering

Maced: Macedonia; Macedonian

MACG: Marine Air Control Group

mach: machine; machinery; machinist

Mach: *The Tragedy of Macbeth*

Mach: velocity unit equal to speed of sound at standard temperature and pressure (1115 fps); named in honor of Ernst Mach—Austrian physicist

mack: mackinaw; mackintosh; maststack (marine superstructure containing mast and smokestack)

MACR: Missing Air Crew Report

macrobop: macrobopper (underground slang—older teenager in sympathy with the modern scene including draft dodgers, drug addicts, and long-haired parasites as well as their approving and permissive parents and professors)

macrocephs: macrocephalics (large-headed people)

macroeco: macroeconomics

MACS: Marine Air Control Squadron

MACSS: Medium-Altitude Communication Satellite System

MACTU: Mines and Contermeasures Tactical Unit (USN)

MAC/V: Military Assistance Command, Vietnam

mad.: magnetic airborne detector; magnetic anomaly detector; midpoint air dose

Mad: Madeira; Madison; Madras

MAD: Madrid, Spain (airport); Manufacturing Assembly Drawing; Marine Air Detachment; Marine Aviation Detachment; Michigan alorithmetic decoder; Mine Assembly Depot; Mongolian Asiatic Development (plan)

MAD: *Militarischer Abschirmdienst* (German—Military Screening Service)—West German counterintelligence corps

MADAEC: Military Application Division of the Atomic Energy Commission

Madag: Madagascar

MADAIR: Societé Nationale Malgache des Transports Aériens (Madagascar Air Transport)

Mad Av: advertising and communications enterprises (many are located on Madison Avenue in New York City)

MADD: Manufacturers of Artificial Dog Dung (probably the ultimate acronymic absurdity)

maddam: macromodule and digital differential analyzer

madevac: medical evacuation

Madge: Margaret; Margarita

Mad Isl: Madeira Islands

madr: minimum adult daily requirement

Madr: Madrid; Madrileño

madrec: malfunction detection and recorder

mads: mind-altering drugs

MADs: Mothers Against Drugs

mae: mean absolute error

Mae: Mary

MAE: Medical Air Evacuation; Museum of Atomic Energy

M.A.E.: Master of Aeronautical Engineering; Master of Art Education; Master of Arts in Education; Master of Arts in Elocution

M.A.Ed.: Master of Arts in Education

MAEE: Marine Aircraft Experimental Establishment

MAELU: Mutual Atomic Energy Liability Underwriters

M.Aero.E.: Master of A eronautical Engineering

maesto: *maestoso* (Italian—majestically)

Maestro Crescendo: Rossini's nickname

maf: major academic field; manpower authorization file; minimum audible field; multiplanar angular forces

MAF: Marine Air Facility; Middle Atlantic Fisheries

MAFB: Mitchell Air Force Base

MAFCA: Model-A Ford Club of America

mafe: magnesium + iron (Ma + Fe)

MAFF: Ministry of Agriculture, Fisheries and Food

MAFI: Medic-Alert Foundation International

MAFIA: *Morte Alla Francia Italia Anela* (Italian—Death to France Is Italy's Cry), acronym devised when secret society was first organized in 1860's, to combat French forces of intervention

mafr: merged accountability and fund reporting

MAFS: Mobilization Air Force Specialty

mag: magazine; magnesia; magnesium; magnet; magnetic; magnetism; magneto; magnetron; magnum

Mag: Magallanes (Punta Arenas); Magellanic; Magyar; Margaret

Mag.: *Magnificat* [Latin—it magnifies (song of the Virgin Mary)]

MAG: Magnavox (stock eschange symbol); magnesium (machine shop style); Marine Aircraft Group; Marine Aviation Group;

Military Advisory Group
mag ampl: magnetic amplifier
mag card: magnetic card
magcheck: magneto check
mag ci: magnetic cast iron
mag cs: magnetic cast steel
Magda: Magdalen(a)
M.Ag.Ec.: Master of Agricultural Economics
M.Ag.Ed.: Master of Agricultural Education
magg: *maggio* (Italian—May); *maggiore* (Italian—major)
Maggie: Margaret; stock market nickname for Magnavox
MAGIC: Madison Avenue General Ideas Committee
maglev: magnetic levitation
magloc: magnetic logic computer
mag mod: magnetic modulator
magn: magnetism
Magna Charta Libertatum: (Latin —Great Charter of the Liberties) —Magna Carta sealed by King John at Runnymede on June 15 of the year 1215
magneform: magnetic forming (process)
magnesia: magnesium oxide (MgO)
magno: manganese-nickel alloy
magnox: magnesium oxide
magnum: high-powered cartridge or weapon for firing magnum ammunition; 2/5-gallon champagne bottle
mag. op.: *magnum opus* (Latin —major work)
M. Agr.: Master of Agriculture
mags: magazines; magnesium wheels
mag tape: magnetic tape
maha: [Indian—great, as in Mahanadi (Great River) southwest of Calcutta]
Mahatma: (Hindi—Great Souled) —sobriquet of India's greatest leader, Mohandas Karamchand Ghandi
MAHE: Michigan Association for Higher Educatiion
mahog: mahogany
mai: marriage adjustment inventory; minimum annual income
MAI: Military Assistance Institute; Museum of the American Indian
MAIBL: Midland and International Banks Limited
maid.: maintenance automatic integration detector
Maid of Orleans: Joan of Arc
Maimon: Maimonides
MAIN: Medical Automation Intelligence System
Maine Turn: Maine Turnpike
Mainichi: (Japanese—Daily)—

leading Japanese newspaper; one of the *Big Three*
maint: maintenance
maitre d': *maitre d'hotel* (French —head waiter)
maj: major; majority
Maj: Major
MAJ: Muhammad Ali Jinnah
Maj Com: Major Command
Maj Gen: Major General
MAKN: *Mongol Ardyn Khuv'sgalt Nam* (Kalkha Mongol—Mongolian People's Revolutionary Party)
maksutsub: make suitable substitutions
Mal: The Book of Malachi; Malaga; Malagueña(o); Malay; Malayan; Malaysia; Malta; Maltese
MAL: Malaysian Airways Limited; Material Allowance List
Mala: Malaya; Malayan; Malaysia; Malaysian
malac: malacology
malaprop: *mal à propos* (French —out of place; unappropriate)
Malbrook: (Louis XIV's mispronunciation of Marlborough —John Churchill—Duke of Marlborough—whose British soldiers drove the French from the field in battle after battle)—*see* Mambru
Mald: Maldive Islands
Mal $: Malaya dollar
M.A.L.D.: Master of Arts in Law and Diplomacy
MALEV: (Hungarian Airline)
Malg Rep: Malagasy Republic
MALI: Air Mali
malig: malignant
Mal Isl: Maldive Islands
mall.: malleable
Mall: Mallorca
Mal-Port: Malay-Portuguese (East African patois)
malprac(s): malpractice(s); malpractitioner(s)
M.A.L.S.: Master of Arts in Liberal Studies; Master of Arts in Library Science; Master of Arts in Library Service
Mal St: Malay States
malt.: malted milkshake
mam: medium automotive maintenance; milliampere minute(s)
mam: *mot a mot* (French—word for word)
ma'm: madam
m + am: (compound) myopic astigmatism
MAM: Military Assistance Manual; Montclair Art Museum
MAMA: Mobile Air Materiel Area; Middletown Air Materiel Area
MAMB: Military Advisory Mis-

sion—Brazil
MAMBO: Mediterranean Association of Marine Biology and Oceanography
Mambru: (Spanish mispronunciation of Marlborough—John Churchill—Duke of Marlborough—whose military exploits were much admired by the Spaniards during the War of the Spanish Succession)—*see* Małbrook
MAMENIC: Marina Mercante Nicaraguense (Nicaraguan Merchant Marine—Mamenic Line)
mamie: minimum automatic machine for interpolation and extrapolation
Mamie: Margaret
mammal.: mammalogy
mamos: marine automatic meteorological observing station
MAMS: Missile Assembly and Maintenance Shop
man.: manhold; manifest; manifold; manual; manufacture; manure
man.: *manipulus* (Latin—handful)
m A n: *meiner Ansicht nach* (German—in my opinion)
Man: (La) Mancha; Manchester; Manhattan; Manila; Manitoba
MAN: Managua, Nicaragua (airport); Motorcyclists Against Noise
M-A-N: Maschinefabrik-Augsburg-Nurnberg
Man Brdg: Manhattan Bridge (New York City)
Manc: Manchester; Mancunian— inhabitant of Manchester
Manch: Manchuria
mand: mandamus; mandate; mandatory; mandible; mandibular
Mand: Mandarin
MANDFHAB: Male and Female Homosexual Association of Great Britain
mandy: man day
Mandy: Amanda manda
manf: manifold; manufacture; manufacturer; manufacturing
MANFORCE: Manpower for a Clean Environment
manganin: manganese-copper-nickel alloy
manhr: manhour
MANI: Minister of Agriculture for Northern Ireland
maniac (MANIAC): mathematical analyzer, numerical integrator, and computer
manif: manifest
manit: man minute
Manit: Manitoba
Man¹: Manuel (Spanish—Emanu-

el)

Man Med Dept: *Manual of the Medical Department* (USN)

manmo: man month

Manny: Emanuel; Manuel

mano: manograph; mánometer

Manolete: Manuel Rodriguez

MANP: Masai Amboseli National Park (Kenya); Mount Apo NP (Mindanao, Philippines); Mount Arayat NP (Luzon, Philippines)

man(s) rep(s): manufacturer(s) representative(s)

MANS: Map Analysis System

mansat: manned satellite

mansec: man second

Manuel: Emanuel

manuv: maneuvering

manwich: man-sized sandwich

manwk: man week

manyr: man year

mao: monamine oxidase

mao: *med andra ord* (Swedish—in other words); *med andre ord* (Danish—in other words)

Mao: Mao Tse-tung

MAO: Master of the Art of Obstetrics; Musica Aeterna Orchestra

MAO: *Magyar Allami Operhaz* (Hungarian State Opera)

MAOT: Member of the Association of Occupational Therapists; Military Assistance Observer Team

map.: manifold absolute pressure; manifold air pressure; mapping; minimum audible pressure; missed approach procedure

MAP: Maghreb-Arabe Presse (Maghreh Arab Press Agency); Medical Aid Post; Military Aid Program; Military Assistance Program; Military Association of Podiatrists; Ministry of Aircraft Production; Mutual African Press (agency)

M-A-P: Modified American Plan (breakfast and dinner included)

MAPA: Mexican-American Political Association

MAPAG: Military Assistance Program Advisory Group

mapche: mobile automatic programmed checkout equipment

MAPCO: Mid-America Pipeline Company

MAPHILINDO: Malaysia, Philippines, Indonesia (proposed unification of these Malayan countries)

MAPI: Machinery and Allied Products Institute

MAPL: Manufacturing Assembly Parts List

MAPNY: Maritime Association of the Port of New York

MAPOM: MAP-owned materiel

mapp: methylacetylenepropadiene

mapros: maintain production schedule(s)

MAPS: Major Assembly Performance System; Management Analysis and Planning System; Middle Atlantic Planetarium Society; Military Products and Systems (RCA); Miniature Air Pilot System; Monetary and Payments System; Multiple Address Processing System

maq: monetary allowance in lieu of quarters

MAQ: Measures for Air Quality (NBS)

mar.: marine; maritime; married; marry; memory address register; minimal angle resolution; multiarray radar; multifunction array radar

mar.: *mardi* (French—Tuesday); *martedi* (Italian—Tuesday); *martes* (Spanish—Tuesday)

Mar: Marathi; March; Marseilles; Marshall Islands

M. Ar.: Master of Architecture

MAR: Manistee and Repton (railroad); Maracaibo, Venezuela (airport); Maritime Central Airways; Mars Excursion Module

MARAD: Maritime Administration (US Department of Commerce)

marb: marbling

marble: calcium carbonate ($CaCO_3$)

marc: monitoring and results computer

Marc: Marcus

MARC: Machine-Readable Cataloging (Library of Congress magnetic-tape catalog system); Manpower Authorization Request for Change; Matador Automatic Radar Command; Metropolitan Applied Research Center; Model-A Restorers Club (Model-A Ford autos)

MarCad: Marine Cadet

MARCEP: Maintainability and Cost-Effectiveness Program

M.Arch.: Master of Architecture

MARCOR: US Marine Corps

marg: margarine; margin; marginal; marginalia

Marg: Margrave; Margravine

marge: margarine (oleomargarine); margin

Marge: Margaret; Margery

Mar Gils Area: Marshalls-Gilberts (island) Area

Marg^(ta): Margarita (Spanish—Margaret)

MARI: Middle America Research Institute

Marichu: (Spanish-American nickname—María de Jesús)—see *Chuey*

mariculture: marine culture (growing food in the sea)

marifarm: maritime farm

mariholic: marijuanaholic (addict)

Mariner: Venus-Mars fly-by space vehicle

Mariol: Mariolatry; Mariology

marit: maritime

Marit Admin: Maritime Administration

Marit Com: Maritime Commission

Maritime Alps: *Alpes Maritimes* (French)—*AM*

Maritimes: Canadian provinces of New Brunswick, Nova Scotia, and Prince Edward Island

maritrain(s): maritime train(s)—articulated sea-going barges

mark.: market; marketing

Mark: The Gospel according to St. Mark

Mark Twain: Samuel Langhorne Clemens

Marlag: *Marinenlager* (German—sailor's camp for prisoners of war)

Marpril: March and April

Marq: Marquesas Islands

Marr: Marrano

mars: master attitude reference system; military affiliated radio system

Mars: Marseilles

MARS: Manned Astronautical Research Station; Military Affiliate Radio System; Miniature Accurate Ranging System; Mobile Atlantic Range Station

MARSAP: Mutual Assistance Rescue and Salvage Plan .

M. Ar. Sci.: Master of Arts and Sciences

Marse Robert: (southern American—Master Robert)—General Robert E. Lee

marsh gas: methane (CH_4)

mart.: mean active repair time

Mart: Martinique

Mart.: Martyrology

Mart: (Russian—March)

MART: Metropolitan Area Rapid Transit

MARTA: Metropolitan Atlanta Rapid Transit Authority

Marth: Martha

mart(s): market(s)

MARTS: Master Radar Tracking Station

Mart(y): Martin

Marv: Marvin

mas: masonry; metal anchor slots; military assistance sales

MAS: Marine Acoustical Services;

Maryland Academy of Sciences; Military Agency for Standardization

MAS: *Motoscafi Anti Sommergibili* (Italian—antisubmarine motor torpedo boat)

M & AS: Music and Art School

MASA: Member of the Acoustical Society of America; Military Automotive Supply Agency

Masaccio: Tommaso Guidi

masc: masculine

M.A. Sc.: Master of Applied Science

MASCOT: Meteorological Auxiliary Sea Current Observation Transmitter

maser: microwave amplification by stimulated emission of radiation

MASH: Medical Aid for Sick Hippies; Mobile Army Surgical Hospital; Multiple Accelerated Summary Hearing (for alien deportation)

MASIS: Management and Scientific Information Service

MASL: Military Assistance Articles and Services List

mas. pil.: *massa piluarum* (Latin —pill mass)

mass.: masseter

Mass: Massachusetts; Massachusettsan

MASS: Marine Air Support Squadron; Michigan Automatic Scanning System

MASSR: Mari Autonomous Soviet Socialist Republic

Mass Turn: Massachusetts Turnpike

mast.: missile automatic supply technique

MAST: Military Assistance to Safety and Traffic

MAST: *Minimum Abbreviations of Serial Titles*

MASTIF: Multiple Axes Space Test Inertia Facility

mat.: material; materiel; matins; microalloy transistor; mol-ankothane (molybdenum disulfide urethane)

Mat: Matanzas; Matthew

MAT: Mechanical Aptitude Test; Military Air Transport

M.A.T.: Master of Arts in Teaching

MATA: Motorcycle and Allied Trades Association

Mata Hari: Gertrud Margarete Zelle

Mata Soc: Mattachine Society

MATCH: Manpower and Talent Clearinghouse

MATCOMTELNET: MATS Command Teletype Network

Mat.E.: Materials Engineer

math: mathematics

Math. D.: Doctor of Mathematics

mathn: mathematician

matl: material; materiel

Mat Lab: Material Laboratory

mat. med.: materia medica

matnav: mathematics for navigators

mato: (Portuguese—jungle, as in Mato Grosso)

MATP: Military Assistance Training Program

matric: matriculate; matriculation

MATS: Military Air Transport Service

Matt: Matthew; Matthewtown, Great Inagua; The Gospel according to St. Matthew

MATTS: Multiple Airborne Target Trajectory System

Mattw: Matthew

Matty: Matthew

matut.: *matutinus* (Latin—in the morning)

matv: master antenna television

matw: metal awning-type window

Maud: Mathilda

Maude: Morse automatic decoder

M. Au. E.: Master of Automotive Engineering

mauka: (Hawaiian—inland; toward the mountain; upland)

Maur: Mauritius

M.A. Urb. Plan.: Master of Arts in Urban Planning

Maurit: Mauritania (Islamic Republic of)

mav: manpower authorization voucher

maw: medium assault weapon

maw: *met andere woorden* (Dutch —in other words)

MAW: Marine Aircraft Wing

MAWS: Marine Air Warning Squadron

max: maximal; maximum

m'ax: (American contraction—my ax)

Max: Maxim; Maximilian; Maxwell

maxi: maximum

maxibop: maxibopper (underground slang—fatter or older woman wearing miniskirts)

maxill: maxilla; maxillary

Maxim Gorki: (pseudonym—Alexei Maximovich Peshkov)

maxis: maximum-length garments (coats, skirts, etc.)

Max Nordau: (pseudonym—Max Simon Sudfeld)

May: Maybelle

May: (Russian—May)

MAYA: Maya Airways (British Honduras); Mexican-American

Youth Association

Mayan Century: the 900s—great American civilization leaving monumental ruins from Honduras to Yucatan—the 10th century

mayday: international distress call (from the French *m'aidez*—help me)

Mayjun: May and June

Maymo: *Mayordomo* (Spanish —butler; estate manager; steward)

mayo: mayonnaise

maz: mazda

Maz: Mazatlán

mazh: missile azimuth heading

mb: macrobiotic (MB); magnetic bearing; main battery; methyl bromide; methylene blue; midbody; millibar(s); motorboat

m.b.: *misce bene* (Latin—mix well)

m & b: matched and beaded; metes and bounds

MB: magnetic bearing; March-Bender (factor); Marine Barracks; Marine Base; Mechanized Battalion; Meridian & Bigbee (railroad); Munitions Board; Music for the Blind

M-B: Mercedes-Benz

M.B.: *Medicinae Baccalaureus* (Latin—Bachelor of Medicine)

M & B: metes and bounds

Mba: Mombasa

MBA: Make or Buy Authorization; Marine Biological Association; Military Benefit Association; Monument Builders of America; Mortgage Bankers of America

M.B.A.: Master of Business Administration

MBAA: Master Brewers Association of America

MBAC: Member of the British Association of Chemists

mbar: millibar

MBAUK: Marine Biological Association of the United Kingdom

MBAWS: Marine Base Warning System

mbc: maximum breathing capacity

MBC: Malawi Broadcasting Corporation; Mauritius Broadcasting Corporation; Mercantile Bank of Canada

MBCC: Massachusetts Bay Community College; Migratory Bird Conservation Commission

MBCMC: Milk Bottle Crate Manufacturers Council

mbd: macro-block design; minimum brain damage

mbe: missile-borne equipment

M.B.E.: Member of the Order of the British Empire

M. B. Ed.: Master of Business Education

MBF: Military Banking Facility; Milk Bottlers Federation

MBFR: Mutual Balanced-Forced Reduction

MBG: Missouri Botanical Garden

mbge: missileborne guidance equipment

mbh: manual bomb hoist

mbi: may be issued

MBIA: Malting Barley Improvement Association

M. Bi. Chem.: Master of Biological Chemistry

M. Bi. Eng.: Master of Biological Engineering

M. Bi. Phy.: Master of Biological Physics

M. Bi. S.: Master of Biological Science

MBJ: Montego Bay, Jamaica (airport)

mbl: mobile

Mbl: *Monatsblatt* German —monthly report)

MBL: Marine Biological Laboratory (Woods Hole, Massachusetts); Mobile, Alabama (airport)

MBLIC: Mutual Benefit Life Insurance Company

mbm: thousand feet board measure

MBM: Mac Bride Museum

MBMA: Master Boiler Makers' Association; Metal Building Manufacturers Association

MBNA: Moument Builders of North America

MBNBR: Mount Bruce Native Bird Reserve (North Island, New Zealand)

MBOU: Member British Ornithologists Union

mpb: mean blood pressure

MBPA: Military Blood Program Agency

MB & PR: MacMillan, Bloedel & Powell River

mbps: megabits per second; million bits per second

mbr: member

MBR: *Mineraçôes Brasileiras Reunidas* (Brazilian Mining Reunited)

MBRF: Mission Bay Research Foundation

Mbro: Middlesbrough

mbruu: may be retained until unserviceable

mbrv: maneuverable ballistic reentry vehicle (MBRV)

mbs: magnetron beam switching; main bang suppressor

MBS: Miami Beach Symphony; Motor Bus Society; Mutual Broadcasting System

MBSA: Modular Building Standards Association; Munitions Board Standards Agency

M. B. Sc.: Master of Business Science

MBSI: Musical Box Society International

MBSM: Mexican Border Service Medal

mbt: metal-base transistor

MBTA: Massachusetts Bay Transportation Authority; Metropolitan Boston Transit Authority; Midwest Book Travelers Association

MBTI: Manpower Business Training Institute

MBTS: Meteorological Balloon Tracking System

MBT-70: Main Battle Tank (designed for use in the 1970s)

MBUCV: Museo de Biología de la Universidad Central de Venezuela (Biology Museum of the Central University of Venezuela)

M. Bus. Ed.: Master of Business Education

MBV: Mexican Border Veterans

mc: magnetic center (MC); magnetic course (MC); marginal check megacycle(s); message composer; metal case; metric carat; miles on course; military characteristics; millicurie(s); momentary contact; monkey cells; multiple contact

m-c: medico-chirugical (surgical); mineralo-corticoid (hormones)

m/c: middle center

m & c: morphine and cocaine

Mc: Mac (Gaelic—son of)

MC: Macalester College; Machinery Certificate; Madison College; Madonna College; magnetic course; Mailet College; Maine Central (railroad); Malin College; Malone College; Manatee College; Manchester College; Manhattan College; Manhattanville College; Manpower Commission; Maria College; Marian College; Marietta College; Marine Corps; Marion College; Marist College; Maritime Commission; Marlboro College; Martin College; Mary College; Marycrest College; Maryglade College; Marygrove College; Marylhurst College; Marymount College; Maryville College; Marywood College; Master of Ceremonies; Materiel Center; Materiel Command; Maunaolu College; Medical Center; Medi-

cal College; Medical Corps; Member of Congress; Memorial Commission; Memphis College; Menlo College; Mesa College; Michigan Central (railroad); Microfilm Corporation; Microstat Corporation; Middlebury College; Midland College; Miles College; Military Committee; Military Cross; Milligan College; Mills College; Milsaps College; Milton College; Misericordia College; Mitchell College; Monmouth College; Monticello College; Moravian College; Morehouse College; Morris College; Morse College; Muhlenberg College; Multnomah College; Mundelein College; Munitions Command; Muskingum College; Muskogee College

M.C.: *Magister Chirurgiae* (Master of Surgery)

M de C: *Maître de Chapelle* (French—conductor)

mca: minimum crossing altitude

MCA: Malayan Chinese Association; Manufacturing Chemists Association; Maritime Central Airways; Maritime Control Area; Material Coordinating Agency; Maternity Center Association; Mechanical Contractors Association; Medical Correctional Association; Millinery Credit Association; Movers Conference of America; Muscat Control Agency; Music Corporation of America; Music Critics Association; Musicians Club of America

MCAA: Mason Contractors Association of America; Mechanical Contractors Association of America; Military Civil Affairs Administration

MCAB: Marine Corps Air Base

MCAD: Military Contracts Administration Department

MCADO: Micronesian Community Action Development Organization

MCAF: Marine Corps Air Facility; Marine Corps Air Field; Military Construction, Air Force

MCAIR: McDonnell Aircraft Company

MCAS: Marine Corps Air Station

MCAT: Medical College Admission Test; Midwest Council on Airborne Television

McB: McBurney's (point)

MCB: Marine Corps Base; Mobile Construction Battalion

MCBA: Master Car Builders' Association

mcc: maintenance of close contact; modified close control

MCC: Maintenance Control Center; Marylebone Cricket Club; Manual Combat center; Marine Corps Commandant; Mesta Machine Company (stock exchange symbol); Missile Control Center; Mission Control Center; Monroe Community College; Munitions Carriers Conference; Music Critics' Circle

MCCA: *Mercado Común Centro Americano* (Central American Common Market)

MCCC: Muskegon County Community College

mcd: mean corpuscular diameter; median control death; metal-covered door

McDA: McDonnell Aircraft

McDAC: McDonnell Aircraft Corporation

Mc D O: Mc Donald Observatory

MCDS: Management Control Data System

mcd/slv: minimum - cost - design/ space launch vehicle (MCD/ SLV)

mcdt: mean corrective down time

mce: military characteristics equipment

MCE: Memphis Cotton Exchange; Montgomery Cotton Exchange

M.C.E.: Master of Civil Engineering

MCEB: Military Communications Electronics Board

M.C.Eng.: Master of Civil Engineering

M. Cer. E.: Master of Ceramic Engineering

MCET: Mississippi Center for Educational Television

mcf: medium corpuscular fragility; thousand cubic feet

mcfd: 1000 cubic feet of gas per day

mcfh: 1000 cubic feet of gas per hour

mcflm: microfilm; microfilming

mcfm: 1000 cubic feet of gas per month

mcg: microgram

MCG: Mandalay Coral Gardens (Queensland)

McG-H: McGraw-Hill

McG U: McGill University

McGUL: McGill University Library

mch: mail chute; mean corpuscular hemoglobin (MCH)

Mch: Manchester

M. Ch.: *Magister Chirurgiae* (Latin—Master of Surgery)

mchc: mean corpuscular hemoglobin concentration

M.Ch.E.: Master of Chemical Engineering

M. Chem. E.: Master of Chemical Engineering

mc hr: millicurie hour(s)

MCHS: Maternal and Child Health Service

mci: malleable cast iron; mottled cast iron

MCI: Marine Corps Institute; Mexican Coffee Institute; Milk Can Institute

McINP: McIwaine National Park (Rhodesia)

M.C.J.: Master of Comparative Jurisprudence

MCJC: Mason City Junior College

McKS: (Sir Colin) McKenzie Sanctuary (Victoria, Australia)

McKVHS: McKee Vocational High School

mcl: midclavicular line; midcostal line

MCL: Manchester Central Library; Marine Corps League; Master Control Log; Metal Control Laboratories; Mid-Canada Line (radar warning fenceline); Moore-McCormack Lines; Mushroom Canners League

M.C.L.: Master of Civil Law

MCLA: Marine Corps League Auxiliary

MCLO: Medical Construction Liaison Office

mcm: military characteristics motor vehicles; missile-carrying missile; thousand circular mils

MCM: Manual for Courts-Martial; Marine Corps Manual; Monte Carlo Method

MCMA: Machine Chain Manufacturers Association; Marine Corps Memorial Commission; Metal Cookware Manufacturers Association

MCMC: Marine Corps Memorial Commission

MCM&T: Michigan College of Mining & Technology

McM U: McMaster University

MCN: Management Control Number; Manual Control Number

MCNP: Mammoth Cave National Park (Kentucky); Mount Cook NP (South Island, New Zealand)

MCNY: Museum of the City of New York

mco: main civilian occupation; mills culls out

mço: *março* (Portuguese—March)

MCOAG: Marine Corps Operations Analysis Group

MCOM: Mobility Command (US Army)

M. Com. Adm.: Master of Commercial Administration

M. Comp. Law: Master of Comparative Law

M. Com. Sc.: Master of Commercial Science

MCON: Military Construction —Navy

mcos: *marcos* (Spanish—marks), German coins

MCOW: Medical College of Wisconsin

mcp: male chauvinist pig; manual control panel; mode control panel; multi-component plasma; multiple chip package

MCP: Management Control Plan; Maritime Company of Philadelphia; Maritime Company of the Philippines; Massachusetts College of Pharmacy; Master Control Program; Military Construction Program; Minerals and Chemicals Philipp; Model Cities Program

M.C.P.: Master of City Planning

mcph: metacarpal-phalangeal

MCPO: Master Chief Petty Officer

mcps: megacycles per second

MCPS: Member of the College of Physicians and Surgeons

McQ-E: McQuaid-Ehn (grain size)

mcr: military compact reactor

MCR: Marine Corps Reserve; Master Change Record; Manufacturing Change Request

M.C.R.: Master of Comparative Religion

MCRC: Mass Communications Research Center (University of Wisconsin)

MCRD: Marine Corps Recruit Depot

MCROA: Marine Corps Reserve Officers Association

mcrt: multichannel rotary transformer

mcs: meridian control signal; meter-candle second; motor circuit switch

mc/s: megacycles per second

MCs: Military Characteristics

MCS: coastal minesweeper (naval symbol); Maintenance Control Section; Marine Cooks and Stewards (union); Marine Corps School; Marine Corps Station; mine countermeasures support ship (naval symbol); Missile Commit Sequence; Mobile Checkout Station; Mobile Coastal Service

M.C.S.: Master of Commercial Science

MCSC: Medical College of South

Carolina; Military College of South Carolina (The Citadel)

MCSH: Manhattan College of the Sacred Heart

MCSP: Member of the Chartered Society of Physiotherapy

MCSC: Military College of South Carolina (The Citadel)

MC S & T: Manchester College of Science and Technology

mct: multiple-compressed tablet

MCTA: Metropolitan Commuter Transportation Authority

MCTI: Metal Cutting Tool Institute

mcu: median control unit; medium closeup

m & cu: monitor and control unit

mcv: mean corpuscular volume

MCV: Medical College of Virginia

mcw: metal casement window; modulated continuous wave

MCW: Mallinckrodt Chemical Works

mcx: maximum-cost expediting

MCZ: Museum of Comparative Zoology

md: maximum design; mean deviation; memorandum of deposit; mental(ly) defective; mentally deficient; message dropping; minute difference(s); mitral disease; month's date; movement directive; muscular dystrophy

m-d: manic-depressive

m/d: memorandum of deposit(s); month(s) after date

m & d: medicine and duty

m d: *mano destra* (Italian—right hand)

Md: Maryland; Marylander; mendelevium

MD: Management Directive; Marine Detachment; Medical Department; Medical Discharge; Mess Deck; Middle Dutch; Mine Depot; Music Director; Musical Director

M$: Malaysia dollar (Singapore dollar)

M.D.: *Medicinae Doctor* (Latin —Doctor of Medicine)

M D: *mano destra* (Italian—right hand)

mda: maintenance depot assistance

Mda: Mérida (inhabitants —Meridanos)

MDA: Marking Device Association; Master Dyes Association; Material Disposal Authority; Mural Decorators Association; Muscular Dystrophy Association; Mutual Defense Agency; Mutual Defense Assistance

MDAA: Mutual Defense Assistance Act

MDAC: McDonnell Douglas Astro-

nautics Company; Mutual Defense Assistance—China area

MDAGT: Mutual Defense Assistance, Greece and Turkey

MDAIKP: Mutual Defense Assistance, Iran, Republic of Korea, and the Philippines

MDANAA: Mutual Defense Assistance, North Atlantic Area

MDAP: Mutual Defense Assistance Program

M-day: manufacturing day; mobilization day; moratorium day

M d B: *Mitglied des Bundestages* (German—member of the Bundestag)

MDB: *Movimento Democrático Brasileiro* (Portuguese—Brazilian Democratic Movement) —political party

MDBVHS: Mabel D. Bacon Vocational High School

mdc: maintenance data collection

MDC: McDonnell Douglas Corporation; Manhattan Drug Corporation; Metropolitan District Commission; Moncure Daniel Conway

MDCA: Master Diamond Cutters Association

MDC-W: McDonnell Douglas Corporation—West

mdd: milligrams per square decimeter per day

MDE: *Modern Drug Encyclopedia*

M. Des.: Master of Design

mdf: main distributing frame; manual direction finder

MDF: Modderfontein Dynamite Factory

MDFC: McDonnell Douglas Finance Corporation

MDHB: Mersey Docks and Harbour Board (Liverpool)

mdi: magnetic detection indicator

m. dict.: *more dictu* (Latin—in the manner directed)

M. Di. Eng.: Master of Diesel Engineering

M. Dip.: Master of Diplomacy

MDJC: Miami-Dade Junior College; Mississippi Delta Junior College

m dk: main deck

M d L: *Mitglied des Landtages* (German—member of the Landtag)

MDL: Mine Defense Laboratory

MDM: Movement (for a) Democratic Military (New Leftist device to destroy military morale)

Mdme: Madame (French—Missus)

m$n: *moneda (pesos) nacional* [Spanish—national monetary unit(s)—Argentinian peso(s)]

mdn: median

MDNA: Machinery Dealers National Association

MDNS: Modified Decimal Numbering System

M-dog: mine dog (trained to find buried mines)

mdr: minimum daily requirement

Mdr: Madras

mds: minimum discernible signal; mission design and series

MDS: mail distribution schedule; mail distribution scheme; Main Dressing Station; Manufacturing Data Series; Medical-Dental Service; meteoroid detection satellite

M.D.S.: Master of Dental Surgery

M$S: peso *(moneda nacional—*Argentine letter symbol)

mdse: merchandise

mdsg: merchandising

MDST: Mountain Daylight Saving Time

mdt: mean down time; moderate

MDT: Mutual Defense Treaty

MDTA: Manpower Development and Training Act

MDU: Mine Disposal Unit; Mobile Development Unit

mdw: measured day work

MDW: Chicago, Illinois (Midway Airport); Military District of Washington; Minnesota, Dakota & Western (railroad)

Mdx: Middlesex

mdy: magnetic deflection yoke

MDY: Midland Oil (stock exchange symbol)

me.: marbled edges; marbled edging; maximum effect; maximum effort; metabolizable energy; methyl; milligram equivalent; miter end; most excellent; multiengine; muzzle energy

m/e: mechanical/electrical; mobility equipment

m E: *meines Erachtens* (German—in my opinion)

Me: Maine; Mainers; Mexican(s); Mexico

ME: Managing Editor; Marine Engineer; Medical Examiner; Methodist Episcopal; Middle English; Military Engineer; Mining Engineer; Morristown and Erie (railroad); Mouvement Europeen (European Movement)

M.E.: Master of Education; Mechanical Engineer

mea: measure(s); measuring; minimum enroute altitude; monoethanolamine (MEA)

MEA: Medical Exhibitors Association; Michigan Education Association; Middle East Airlines; Minnesota Education Association; monoethanolamine; Montana Education Association; Music Educators Association; Musical Educators Association

M.E.A.: Master of Engineering Administration

meas: measure; measurement

Meas for M: *Measure for Measure*

meb: military early bird

MEB: Marine Expeditionary Brigade; Master Electronics Board; Medical Board; Melbourne, Australia (airport); Midlands Electricity Board (UK)

MEBA: Marine Engineers' Beneficial Association

mec: main engine cutoff

M. Ec.: Master of Economics

MEC: Maine Central (railroad); Marine Expeditionary Corps; Master Executive Council; Methodist Episcopal Church

meca: maintainable electronics component assembly; malfunctioned equipment corrective action; mercury evaporation and condensation; multi-element component array

mecano: mechanotherapy

MECAS: Middle Eastern College for Arabic Studies (Beirut, Lebanon)

MECCA: Minnesota Environmental Control Citizens Association

mech: mechanic; mechanical; mechanism

Mech Eng: *Mechanical Engineering*

meco: main engine cutoff

mecz: mechanized

med: medal; medalist; medallion; median; median erythrocyte diameter; medic; medical; medication; medicinal; medicine; medieval; medievalism; medievalist; medium; minimal effective dose; minimal erythema dose

Med: medieval; Mediterranean

Med: *Médico* (Italian, Portuguese, Spanish—Doctor)

M.Ed.: Master of Education

MED: Manhattan Engineer District (cover name used during World War II by the developers of the first atomic bomb); Metalworking Equipment Division (US Department of Commerce); Military Electronics Division (Motorola)

medal.: micromechanized engineering data for automated logistics

Med C: Medical Corps

Med CAP: Medical Civil Action Program

medcat: medium clear-air turbulence

MEDCOM: Mediterranean Communications System

medda: mechanized defense decision anticipation

MED-DENT: Medical-Dental Division (USAF)

medevac: medical evacuation

medex: medical expert

medex: *medecin extension* (French —doctor's aides; medics)

MEDIA: Manufacturers Educational Drug Information Association; Missile Era Data Integration Analysis; Move to End Deception in Advertising

medic: medical corpsman; medical doctor; medical student

medicaid: medicinal aid (free medicine for the needy)

medicare: medical care

MEDICO: Medical International Corporation

medio: (Spanish—middle)

MEDIUM: Missile Era Data Integration Ultimate Method

medivac: medical evacuation

medix: medical students

MEDLARS: Medical Literature Analysis and Retrieval System

M. Ed. L. Sc.: Master of Education in Library Science

MEDRECO: Mediterranean Refining Company

MEDSAC: Medical Service Activity (USA)

Med. Sc. D.: Doctor of Medical Science

med show: medicine show (carnival slang)

med tech: medical technology

Med Tech: Medical Technician; Medical Technologist

M.E.E.: Master of Electrical Engineering

M.E. Eng.: Master of Electrical Engineering

meer: (Dutch or German—lake; sea, as in IJsselmeer)

mef: maximal expiratory flow

MEF: Marine Expeditionary Force; Mesopotamian Expeditionary Force; Middle East Forces; Musicians Emergency Fund

mef's: morality enhancing factors

meg: megacycle; megaton; megawatt; megohm

Meg: Margaret

MEG: Management Evaluation Group

mega: 10^6

megabuck: one million bucks (dollars)

megacorpses: one million corpses (atomic bomb unit)

megacurie: one million curies

megacycle: one million cycles

megajoule: one million joules

megameter: one million meters

megamouse: one million mice (statistical unit—experimental biology)

megaton: one million tons

megawatt: one million watts

megger: megohmmeter

mego: megaphone; megohm(s);

megohm: one million ohms

megs: megacycles

megv: million volts

megw: megawatt

megwh: megawatt-hour

MEI: Manual of Engineering Instructions; Metals Engineering Institute; Middle East Institute

MEIC: Member of The Engineering Institute of Canada

MEIS: Military Entomology Information Service

Mej Mejuffrouw (Dutch—Miss)

mek: methyl ethyl ketone

Mel: Melanesia; Melanesian; Melanesian Pidjin English (Bêche de Mer); Melanie; Melba; Melbourne; Melvil; Melville; Melvin; Melvina; Melvyn

MEL: Music Education League

M.E.L.: Master of English Literature

Melan: Melanesia; Melanesian

Melanchthon: Philipp Schwarzert

Melb: Melbourne

Meld: melt + weld

melg: most European languages

melo: melodrama

M. Elo.: Master of Elocution

mem: member; memoirs; memorial

mem.: *memoria* (Latin—memory)

MEM: Mars Excursion Module; Member; memorial; Memphis, Tennessee (airport)

memb: membrane

MEMC: Marathon Electric Manufacturing Corporation

MEML: Master Equipment Management List

memo: memoranda; memorandum

MEMO: Medical Equipment Management Office

men.: menses; menstruation; mensuration

M. En.: Master of English

MEN: Manasco (stock-exchange symbol)

MENC: Music Educators National Conference

Mencius: Meng-tse

Menckonaclast: Henry L. Mencken

MEN: *Middle East News*

MEND: Medical Education for National Defense

Mendl Lib: Mendelssohn Library
Mendy: Mendelssohn
M.Eng.: Master of Engineering; Mining Engineer
M. Eng. P.A.: Master of Engineering and Public Administration
Menn: Menninger
Mennon: Mennonite
meno: menopausal; menopause; menorrhoea
MENP: Mount Elgon National Park (Kenya)
menst: menstrual; menstruation
ment: mental; mentalis
M. Ent.: Master of Entomology
Meo: Bartolomeo
mep: mean effective pressure
MEP: Management Engineering Program
M.E.P.: Master of Engineering Physics
MEP: *Movimiento Electoral del Pueblo* (Spanish—People's Electoral Movement)—Venezuelan political party
MEPC: Metropolitan Estate and Property Corporation
meq/l: millequivalents per liter
mer: meridian
mer: (French—sea); *mercoledi* (Italian—Wednesday); *mercredi* (French—Wednesday)
m & er: mechanical and electrical room
Mer: Mercury
MERB: Mechanical Engineering Research Board
merc: mercury
MERC: Music Education Research Council
merch: merchantable
Merch V: *Merchant of Venice*
MERDL: Medical Equipment Research and Development Laboratory (USA)
Meri: Merionethshire
merid: meridian
Merritt Pkwy: Merritt Parkway
Merry W: *Merry Wives of Windsor*
MERT: Milwaukee Electric Railway and Transit
Merv: Mervin
mes: main engine start
Mes: Mesozoic
Mes: *Mesdames* (French—ladies)
mesa.: modularized equipment storage assembly
mesa: (Spanish—table; plateau or tabletop mountain, as in Costa Mesa, Mesa Verde)
MESA: Malarial Eradication Special Account; Mechanics Educational Society of America
mesc: mescaline
M. E. Sc.: Master of Engineering Science

MESF: Mobile Earth Station Facility
mesh.: medical subject headings
MeSH: Medical Subject Headings
meson: meso + electron; mesotron
Mesop: Mesopotamia (Iraq)
MESP: More Effective Schools Program
Messrs: *Messieurs* (French—Gentlemen)
mest: mestizo
met.: metal; metallic; metallize; metaphor; metaphysics; meteorology; methionine (amino acid) (MET); metronome; metropolitan
Met: Metropolitan Opera; Metropolitan Museum of Art
META: Metropolitan Educational Television Association (Canadian)
metab: metabolism
metall: metallurgy
metallog: metallography
METALMA: Metalúrgica Matarazzo (Brazilian company)
metaph: metaphysic; metaphysical; metaphysician; metaphysics
metaphys: metaphysics
metb: metal base
metc: metal curb; mouse embryo tissue culture
METCO: Metropolitan Council for Educational Opportunity
metd: metal door
Met. E.: Metallurgical Engineer
METEI: Medical Expedition to Easter Island
meteor.: meteorology
meteorolo: meteorology
metf: metal flashing
metg: metal grille
meth: methadone; methamphetamine; methane; methedrine; methyl; methyprylon
Meth: Methodist
methanol: methyl alcohol or wood alcohol (CH_3OH)
Meth Epis: Methodist Episcopal
meth freak: methedrine freak (underground slang—habitual user of methedrine)
meth head: methedrine head (underground slang—methedrine addict)
metho: methodology; methyl alcohol
methu: methuselah (8-bottle capacity)
metj: metal jalousie
metm: metal mold
meto: maximum except takeoff
METO: Middle East Treaty Organization
metol: methyl-p-aminophenol (photographic developer)

meton: metonomy
metp: metal partition
metr: metal roof
metro: metropolitan
métro: *chemin de fer métropolitain* (Paris subway system)
Metro: Metropolitan Life Insurance Company
metroc: meteorological rocket
metrocenter: metropolitan center
metrocomplex: metropolitan complex
metrocore: metropolitan core
metroframe: metropolitan framework
metrol: metrology
mets: metal strip
metsats: meteorological satellites
Metternich: Prince Klemens Wenzel Nepomuk Lothar von Metternich-Winneburg—Austrian statesman convening Congress of Vienna at end of Napoleonic wars
METU: Middle East Technical University (Ankara)
Met-Vic: Metropolitan-Vickers (electrical company)
MEU: Marine Expeditionary Unit
mev: million electron volts
Mev: *Mevrouw* (Dutch—Missus)
MeV: megaelectronvolt; million electronvolt
Mevr: *Mevrouw* (Dutch—Missus)
MEW: Microwave Early Warning; Ministry of Economic Warfare
MEWA: Motor and Equipment Wholesalers Association
MEWS: Missile Early Warning Station
MEWTA: Missile Electronic Warfare Technical Area
Mex: Mexican; Mexico
MEX: Mexico City, Mexico (airport)
Mex C: Mexico City
Mex Cy: Mexican currency
Mex$: Mexican peso
MEXICANA: Compañía Mexicana de Aviación
MEXSM: Mexican Service Medal
Mex Sp: Mexican Spanish
mez: mezcal(ine)
MEZ: *mitteleuropäische Zeit* (German—Central European Time)
mezz: mezzanine; mezzotint
mf: machine finish; main feed; male-to-female (ratio); manufacture(d); manufacturing; mastic floor; medium frequency (300–3,000 kc); microfarad(s); mill finish; millifarad(s); motor field; motor freight; multiplying factor
m/f: marked for
m/f: *mi favor* (Spanish—my favor)

m & f: male and female
MF: Magazines for Friendship; Marshall Field (stock exchange symbol); Medal of Freedom; Middle Fork (railroad); Millard Fillmore; Ministry of Food
M-F: Massey-Ferguson
M.F.: Master of Forestry
mfa: malicious false alarm
MFA: Military Flying Area
M.F.A.: Master of Fine Arts; Museum of Fine Arts
MFAH: Museum of Fine Arts of Houston
MFAR: Michigan Foundation for Advanced Research
mfb: message from base
MFB: MFB Mutual Insurance (Manufacturers, Firemen's and Blackstone combined)
mfc: microfilm frame card
mfco: manual fuel cutoff
mfd: manufactured; microfarad; minimum fatal dose (MFD)
MFED: Manned Flight Engineering Division (NASA)
M. F. Eng.: Master of Forest Engineering
mfg: manufacturing; molded fiber glass
mfh: military family housing
MFI: Musicians Foundation Incorporated
MFIANE: Mutual Fire Insurance Association of New England
MFIBNE: Mutual Fire Inspection Bureau of New England
MFIC: Military Flight Information Center
MFIT: Manual Fault Isolation Test
MFL: Mobile Field Laboratory
mf(n): microfiche (negative)
MFNP: Mount Field National Park (Tasmania); Murchison Falls NP (Uganda)
M.For.: Master of Forestry
MFOWW: Marine Firemen, Oilers, Watertenders, and Wipers
mf(p): microfiche (positive)
MFPB: Mineral Fiber Products Bureau
mfr: manufacture; manufactured; manufacturer; missile firing range (MFR)
M Fr: Mali franc(s); Moroccan franc(s)
MFRP: Midwest Fuel Recovery Plant (AEC)
mf & s: magazine flooding and sprinkling
MFS: Malleable Founders' Society; Manned Flying System; Medal Field Service; Military Flight Service; Missile Firing Station; Mountain Fuel Supply; steel-hulled fleet minesweeper (3-let-

ter naval symbol)
M.F.S.: Master of Food Science; Master of Foreign Service; Master of Foreign Study
MFSA: Metal Finishing Suppliers' Association
mfso: main fuel shutoff
mfsov: main fuel shutoff valve
MFSS: Missile Flight Safety System(s)
mft: major fraction thereof; mechanized flamethrower
m. ft.: mistura fiat (Latin—make a mixture)
MFT: Muscle Function Test
M.F.T.: Master of Foreign Trade
MFTD: Mobile Field Training Detachment
MFURB: Maryland Fire Underwriters Rating Bureau
mfv: magnetic field vector; microfilm viewer
MFV: Mars Flyby Vehicle
MfVB: Museum für Volkerkunde, Berlin
MFW: Maritime Federation of the World
mg: machine gun; marginal; milligram; motor generator; multigauge
m-g: machine glazed
m & g: mapping and geodesy
Mg: magnesium
MG: machine gun; major general; Marine Gunner; Military Government; Minas Gerais; Morris Garage (M-G)
MG: *Maschinegewehr* (German —machine gun)
M-G: Morris-Garage (British sports car)
M & G: Mobile & Gulf
Mga: Malaga
MGA: Managua, Nicaragua (Las Mercedes airport); Military Government Association; Monongahela (railroad); Mushroom Growers Association
mgal: milligal
M-gauge: meter gauge (39.37-inch) railroad track
MGB: Soviet Ministry of State Security (*q.v.* VOT)
mgc: manual gain control
MGC: Machinery of Government (committee); Marriage Guidance Council
mgcr: maritime gas-cooled reactor
mg/cu m: milligrams (dust, fume, or mist) per cubic meter of air
mgd: magnetogasdynamics; million gallons per day
Mgd: Magdeburg
MGD: Military Geographic Documentation
mge (MGE): maintenance ground

equipment
M.G.E.: Master of Geological Engineering
M. Geol. Eng.: Master of Geological Engineering
MGF: Myasthenia Gravis Foundation
mgg: mouse gamma globulin
mgh: milligram hour(s)
MGH: Massachusetts General Hospital
MGI: Mining and Geological Institute of India
MGID: Military Geographic Information and Documentation
MGk: Medieval Greek
MGM: Metro-Goldwyn-Mayer
mgmt: management
mgn: micrograin
mg %: milligrams percent
Mgr: Manager; Monseigneur (French—Monsignor); Monsignore (Italian—Monsignor)
Mgr: Monseigneur (French—Monsignor); Monsignore (Italian—Monsignor)
MGR: Matusadona Game Reserve (Rhodesia)
mgs: missile guidance set (system)
MGSA: Military General Supply Agency
mgt: management
MGTB: Mexican Government Tourist Bureau
MGTD: Mexican Government Tourist Delegation
MGU: *Moskovskiy Gosudarstvenny Universitet* (Moscow State University)
M Gun Sgt: Master Gunnery Sergeant
mgw: maximum gross weight
MGW: *Manchester Guardian Weekly*
mh: magentic heading; main hatch; manhole; marital history; materials handling; menstrual history; mental health; millihenries; millihenry; murine hepatitis
mH: millhenry
Mh: *Monatsheft* (German—monthly magazine)
MH: magnetic heading; Master Hosts; Medal of Honor; Ministry of Health; Mission Hills; Most Honorable; Most Honourable
MH: *Mo'etzet Hapo'alot* (Hebrew—Woman Workers Council)
M-H: Minneapolis-Honeywell (stock exchange symbol and trademark)
M & H: Mason and Hamlin
MHA: auxiliary minehunter (naval

symbol); Marine Historical Association; Medal for Humane Action; Member of the House of Assembly; Mental Health Administration; Mental Health Association

M.H.A.: Master of Hospital Administration

M-H B: Mid-Hudson Bridge

MHC: coastal minehunter (naval symbol)

MHCOA: Motor Hearse and Car Owners Association

mh cp: mean horizontal candlepower

mhcv (MHCV): manned hypersonic cruise vehicle

mhd: magnetohydrodynamics

mhd lt: masthead light

mhe: materials handling equipment

M.H.E.: Master of Home Economics

MHEDA: Material Handling Equipment Distributors Association

M.H.E.E.: Master of Home Economics Education

M. H. E. Ed.: Master of Home Economics Education

mhf: medium high frequency

M-H-F: Massey-Harris-Ferguson

MHG: Middle High German

mhhw: mean higher high water

MHI: Material Handling Institute; Metal Hydrides Incorporated; Mitsubishi Heavy Industry

M. Hi. E.: Master of Highway Engineering

M. Hi. Eng.: Master of Highway Industry Engineering

MHII: Material Handling Institute Incorporated

MHJC: Mary Holmes Junior College

MHL: Manaus Harbour Limited

M.H.L.: Master of Hebrew Literature

Mhm: Mannheim

MHMA: Mobile Homes Manufacturers Association

mho: unit of conductance or reciprocal ohm

M. Hor.: Master of Horticulture

M. Ho. Sc.: Master of Household Science

MHR: Member of the House of Representatives

MHRA: Modern Humanities Research Association

MHRI: Mental Health Research Institute (University of Michigan)

MHS: Massachusetts Historical Society; Morris High School; Musical Heritage Society

mht: mean high tide

MHT: Museum of History and Technology (Smithsonian Institution)

mhtl: mean high tide line

M. Hu.: Master of Humanities

mhv: mean horizontal velocity; murine hepatitis virus

mhw: mean high water

mhwli: mean high water lunitidal interval

mhwn: mean high water neaps

mhws: mean high water springs

M. Hy.: Master of Hygiene

MH y C: Miguel Hidalgo y Costilla

M. Hyg.: Master of Hygiene

mhz (MHz): megahertz(es), formerly megacycle(s) per second

mi: malleable iron; manual input; metabolic index; middle initial; mile(s); mill; minor; minute(s); mitral; mitral insufficiency; mutual inductance

mi: (Italian—third tone in diatonic scale; *E* in fixed-*do* system)

mi²: square mile(s)

mi³: cubic mile(s)

Mi: Mach indicated; Mach speed indicated; Miami; Mitte

MI: Mare Island; Marshall Islands; Match Institute; Mauritius Institute; Meat Inspection (US Department of Agriculture); Mellon Institute; Military Intelligence; Ministry of Information; Missouri-Illinois (railroad)

M-I: Missouri-Illinois (railroad)

mia (MIA): missing in action

MIA: Marble Institute of America; Miami, Florida (airport); Mica Industry Association; Millinery Institute of America; missing in action

M.I.A.: Master of International Affairs

MIAPD: Mid-Central Air Procurement District

MIASI: Moore Institute of Art, Science, and Industry

MIB: Management Improvement Board; Maritime Index Bureau; Meat Inspection Branch; Mental Information Bureau; Michigan Inspection Bureau; Missouri Inspection Bureau

mic: microphone; microwave integrated circuit; military-industrial complex

Mic: The Book of Micah

MIC: Malayan Indian Congress; Marshall Islands Congress; Monaco Information Centre; Motors Insurance Corporation; Music Industry Council

MICA: Moscow Institute for Complex Automation

micbm (MICBM): mobile inter-

continental ballistic missile

micc: miniature integrated circuit computer

MICE: Member of the Institution of Civil Engineers

Mich: Michael; Michigan; Michiganite; Michoacan; Mitchell

Michael Angelo Titmarsh: Thackeray's pseudonym adorning some of his earlier works

Michael Tilson Thomas: Mike Thomashefsky

Michelangelo: Michael Angelo Buonarroti

MI Chem E: Member of the Institution of Chemical Engineers

Michl: Michael

Mickey Mouse: Walt Disney Productions (Wall Street nickname)

Micky: Micaela; Michael; Michelle

MICMD: Milwaukee Contract Management District

micpac: molecular integrated circuit package

mic. pan.: mica panis (Latin— bread crumb)

micr: magnetic ink character recognition; microscope; microscopic; microscopy

micro: 10^{-6}

Micro: Micronesia (Trust Territory of the Pacific); Micronesian

microbiol: microbiology

microbop: microbopper (underground slang—very young person attuned to the modern scene)—*see* macrobop

microcephs: microcephalics (small-headed people)

micro-in.: micro-inch

micromation: microfilm + automation

micron: millionth of a meter

Micron: Micronesia; Micronesian

micropaleo: micropaleontology

micros: microscopy

microt: microtome

micr's: magnetic ink characters

MICRS: Magnetic Ink Character Recognition System

mic's: military-industrial complex executives; military-industrial complex salesmen

MICS: Museum of the International College of Surgeons

mid.: middle

mid. (MID): minimal inhibiting dose; minimum infective dose

Mid: Midshipman

MID: Merida, Yucatan (airport)

M.I.D.: Master of Industrial Design

MIDAS: Missile Defense Alarm System

midden: (Dutch—middle)

Middlx: Middlesex

MIDFL: Malayan Industrial Development Finance Limited
midis: mid-length (below-the-knee) skirts
Mid Loth: Midlothian
Midn: Midshipman
mid. sag.: midsagittal
Mids N D: A Midsummer-Night's Dream
midw: midwestern
mie: military-industrial establishment
mie: miércoles (Spanish—Wednesday)
M.I.E.: Master of Industrial Engineering
MIECO: Marshall Islands Import-Export Company
miérc: miércoles (Spanish—Wednesday)
mif: merthiolate-iodine-formaldehyde (fecal examination technique)
MIF: Milk Industry Foundation
MI 5: (British) Military Intelligence Security Service (somewhat equivalent to American FBI)
MIFCT: Moscow Institute of Fine Chemical Technology
mig: magnesium-inert gas
MIG: Mikhail Ivanovich Glinka (Soviet jet fighter aircraft named for designers Mikoyan and Gurevich)
mightn't: might not
Migl: Miguel (Spanish—Michael)
mi/h: mile(s) per hour
MIHS: Marshall Islands High School
MIIA: Medical Information and Intelligence Agency
MIIS: Marshall Islands Intermediate School
mij: maatschappij (Dutch—company; society)
MIJ: Muhammad Ali Jinnah
mike: micrometer; microphone
Mike: code letter for M; Michael
mil: mileage; military; militia; millieme; million; 1/1000 inch; 1/10 cent; 1/1000 Palestinian pound (currency formerly used in Israel)
m-i-l: mother-in-law
Mil: Milan
MIL: Malaya Indonesia Line; Milan, Italy (Malpensa Airport)
MILA: Merritt Island Launch Area
MilAdGru: Military Advisory Group
mile: mille passuum (Latin—1000 paces), a pace being a double step
Mil-Hndbk: Military Handbook
Mil Jrn: Milwaukee Journal
milk of magnesia: magnesium

hydroxide—$Mg(OH)_2$
mill.: millinery; milling
Mill: Million(en) [German—million(s)]
milli: 10^{-3}
Millie: Mildred; Millicent
milob: military observer
mil pers: military personnel
M.I.L.R.: Master of Industrial and Labor Relations
mils: missile impact locator system
milspec: military specification
Mil-Spec: Military Specification(s)
MILSTAMP: Military Standard Transportation and Movement Procedures
Mil-Std (MIL-STD): Military Standard
MILSTRAP: Military Standard Requisitioning and Accounting Procedures
MILSTRIP: Military Standard Requisitioning and Issue Procedures
Milt: Milton
Milw: Milwaukee
MILW: Milwaukee Route (Chicago, Milwaukee, St. Paul & Pacific Railroad)
mim: micro-impulse mosaic; mimeograph(ing; y)
MIM: Maintenance Instruction Manual (DoD); Mount Isa Mines (Queensland)
MI Mech E: Member of the Institution of Mechanical Engineers
mi/min: miles per minute
MIMR: May Institute of Medical Research
MIMS: Monthly Index of Medical Specialties
mimsy: miserable and flimsy
min: minim; minimum; minor; minority; minute
min: minore (Italian—minor)
Min: Minister; Ministry; Minoan
Mina: Wilhelmina
Min Agric: Ministry of Agriculture
minas: (Portuguese or Spanish—mines, as in Minas Gerais)
Mind: Mindanao
mindac: miniature inertial navigation digital automatic computer
mindd: minimum due date
Min. E.: Mining Engineer
Mineap: Minneapolis
minec: military necessity
minelco: miniature electronic component
mineral.: mineralogy
Mineral Soc: Minerological Society
mingy: mean and stingy
mini: minibop(per); minibra; minimum; miniskirt; miniswimsuit

minibop: minibopper (underground slang—older child attuned to the modern scene)—*see* macrobop
minibra(s): miniature brassiere(s)—(less concealing—more revealing)
minibus: miniature autobus
minicam: miniature camera
minimax: (selecting move to) minimize maximum possible losses
minis: minimum-length skirts
miniskirt(s): miniature skirt(s)—(barely covering the upper thighs)
Minn: Minnesota; Minnesotan
Minne: Minnesota
Minnie: Minerva; Minneapolis; Minnesota
Minn Trib: Minneapolis Tribune
Min⁰: Ministro (Spanish—Minister; Ministry)
Min P: Minister Plenipotentiary
MINP: Mallacoota Inlet National Park (Victoria, Australia)
MINRON: Mine Squadron
mins: minutes
MINTACTS: Mobile Integrated Telemetry and Tracking System
M. Int. Med.: Master of Internal Medicine
Minuteman: solid-fuel intercontinental ballistic missile produced by Boeing
MINWR: Merritt Island National Wildlife Refuge (Florida)
mio: meteoritic impact origin; minimum identifiable odor
MIO: Marine Inspection Office; Mobile Issuing Office; Movements Identification Order
Mioc: Miocene
MIOUDO: Museo del Instituto Oceanográfico de la Universidad de Oriente (Museum of the Oceanographic Institute of the University of Oriente)
mip: malleable iron pipe; marine insurance policy; mean indicated pressure; missile impact predictor; modulated interference plan; monthly investment plan; mortgage insurance premium(s)
MIP: Manufacturers of Illumination Products; Material Improvement Program; Methods Improvement Program; Military Improvement Program
mipir: missile precision instrumentation radar
MIPR: Military Interdepartmental Purchase Request
mir: mirror
M Ir: Middle Irish
MIRA: Monthly Index of Russian Accessions
mirad: monostatic infrared intru-

sion detector

MIRE: Member of the Institution of Radio Engineers

mirv: multiple independent reentry vehicle

mis: missing

Mis.: *Miserere* (Latin—have mercy)

MIS: Management Information System; Material Inspection Service; Military Intelligence Service; mine issuing ship (naval symbol); Minstrel Instruction Society

M.I.S.: Master of International Service

mis. accur.: *misce accuratissme* (Latin—mix very intimately)

misc: miscellaneous; miscible

Mischa: Michael

MI 6: (British) Military Intelligence Secret Service (somewhat like Covert Plans Division of American CIA)

mis. caute: *misce caute* (Latin—mix cautiously)

miscon: misconduct

miser.: microwave space relay

mis. et sig.: *misce et signa* (Latin—mix and write a label)

misg: missing

MISHAP: Missile High-Speed Assembly Program

mis. mei: *miserere mei* (Latin—have mercy on me)

misn: misnumbered

MISO: Military Intelligence Service Organization

MISP: Member of the Institution of Sewage Purification

mispo: mission summary printout

MISR: Macauley Institute for Soil Research; Major Item Status Report

miss.: mission; missionary

Miss.: Mississippi; Mississippian

Missie: Miss; Mississippi; Missus; Mrs.

Missini: Mussolini's neo-fascist followers

mist.: *mistura* (Latin—mixture)

Mist: Mistress

MIST: Medical Information Service (via) Telephone

MISTRAM: Missile Trajectory Measurement System

mit: master instruction tape; milled in transit; minimum individual training; mono-iodotyrosine

mit.: *mitte* (Latin—send)

Mit: *Mittwoch* (German—Wednesday)

MIT: Massachusetts Institute of Technology (M.I.T. preferred as periods set it apart from all other MITs); Massachusetts Investors

Trust; Military Intelligence Translator; Milwaukee Institute of Technology; Miracidial Immobilization Test

M.I.T.: Massachusetts Institute of Technology

MITC: Magdalen Island Transportation Company

Mitch: Mitchell

MITGS: Marine Institute of Technology and Graduate Studies

MITI: Ministry of International Trade and Industry (Japan)

mit insuf: mitral insufficiency

mito: minimum interval takeoff

mi tp: miniature template

Mitropa: Mitteleuropäische Schlaf- und Speisewagen Aktiengesellschaft (Middle-European Sleeping Car and Dining Car Company)

mit. sang.: *mitte sanguinem* (Latin—bleed)

Mitt: *Mitteilungen* (German—communications)

mit. tal.: *mitte tales* (Latin—send such)

mittel-: (German—middle, as in Mitteleuropa)

Mitya: (Russian diminutive— Dmitri)

mitz: *mitzvah* (Yiddish from Hebrew *miswah*—a good deed)

Mitzi: Margaret

MIV: Moody's Investor Service (stock exchange symbol)

MIWE: Member of the Institution of Water Engineers

mix.: mixture

mixt: mixture

mizzle: mist + drizzle

mj: marijuana

MJ: Mary Jane (underground slang —marijuana

M.J.: Master of Journalism

MJA: Manuel José Arce

MJC: Manatee Junior College; Metropolitan Junior College; Moberly Junior College

MJI: Member of the Journalists Institute

MJQ: Modern Jazz Quartet

MJS: Member of the Japan Society

MJV: Mojud Hosiery (stock exchange symbol)

mk: mark (British equivalent of type)

Mk: markka (Finnish monetary unit)

MK: Mackey Airlines; Member of Knesset

M/K: Member of the Knesset

MKC: Kansas City, Missouri (airport)

mkd: marked

MKE: Milwaukee, Wisconsin (air-

port)

mkg: meter kilogram

MKH: Mackintosh-Hemphill (stock-exchange symbol)

mkm: marksman

MKNP: Malawi Kasungu National Park (Malawi); Mount Kenya National Park (Kenya)

MKO: Muskogee Company (stock exchange symbol)

MKR: Mkuzi Game Reserve (South Africa)

mks: meter, kilogram, solar second system of fundamental standards

mksa: meter, kilogram, second, ampere system

mkt: market

MKT: Missouri-Kansas-Texas (railroad)

mk tp: mark template

MKY: McKee and Company (stock-exchange symbol)

ml: machine language; mean level; millilambert(s); milliliter(s); mine layer; mixed lengths; molder; mold line; money list; motor launch; muzzle-loading

ml: *moneda legal* (Spanish—legal tender)

m/l: middle left; missile lift

m/l: *mi letra* (Spanish—my letter)

m or l: more or less

mL: millilambert(s)

Ml: Malay; Malaya; Malayan; Malaysia; marl

ML: Manuel; Martin-Marietta (stock exchange symbol); Middle Latin; Military Liaison; Missile Launcher; motor launch; small minesweeper (naval symbol)

M/L: Maersk Line

M de L: Metropolitano de Lisboa (Lisbon subway system)

M-et-L: Maine-et-Loire; Meurthe-et-Loire

mla: magnetic lens assembly; man-pack loop antenna; microwave linear accelerator

MLA: Medical Library Association; Member of the Legislative Assembly; Minnesota Library Association; Modern Language Association; Music Library Association

M-LA: Mont-Laurier Aviation

M.L.A.: Master of Landscape Architecture

m'lady: my lady

ml ar: mill arbor

M. L. Arch. Master of Landscape Architecture

MLAT: Modern Language Aptitude Test

mlb: multilinear board

MLB: Maritime Labor Board

MLBPA: Major League Baseball Players Association

mlc: main lobe clutter; mesh level control; microelectric logic circuit; mixed leucocyte culture; motor load control; multilayer circuit; multilens camera; multiplanar chain link

MLC: Military Liaison Committee

MLCAEC: Military Liaison Committee to the Atomic Energy Commission

ml cu: mill cutter

mld: middle landing; minimum lethal dose; minimum line of detection; molded

mldso: minimum lethal (radioactive) dose

M. L. Des.: Master of Landscape Design

mldr: molder

M. L. Eng.: Master of Landscape Engineering

MLF: Multi-Lateral Force

ml fx: mill fixture

mlg: main landing gear; most languages

MLG: Middle Low German

mlg(s): mailing(s)

Ml'H: Musee de l'Homme, Paris

mli: minimum line of interception

M-Li: Müller-Lyer (illusion)

M. Lit.: Master of Letters; Master of Literature

MLL: Music Lovers League

Mlle: Mademoiselle (French —Miss)

Mlles: Mesdemoiselles (French— Misses)

mllw: mean lower low water

MLMA: Metal Lath Manufacturers Association

Mln: Milan

MLNP: Malawi Lengwe National Park

mlnr: milliner

MLNR: Ministry of Land and Natural Resources

MLNWR: Medicine Lake National Wildlife Refuge (Montana)

m'lord: my lord

Mloth: Midlothian

mlp: metal lath and plaster

MLQ: Modern Language Quarterly

mlr: main line of resistance

MLR: Marine Life Resources (program)

MLRB: Mutual Loss Research Bureau

MLRP: Marine Life Research Program

mls: machine literature search(ing)

MLS: Moon Landing Site (attained by two men from spacecraft Apollo XI on July 20, 1969);

Multiple Listing Service

M.L.S.: Master of Library Science

M & LS: Manistique & Lake Superior (railroad)

MLSU: Moscow M.V. Lomonosov State University (University of Moscow)

mlt: mean low tide; median lethal (radioactive) time (MLT)

Mlt: Malta

mltl: mean low tide line

mlv: murine leukemia virus

mlv(M): murine leukemia virus (Moloney)

mlv(R): murine leukemia virus (Rauscher)

ml vs: mill vise

mlw: mean low water; medium-level waste

MLW: Monrovia, Liberia (airport)

mlwli: mean low water lunitidal interval

mlwn: mean low water neaps

mlws: mean low water springs

mlx: millilux

mm: made merchantable; megameter(s); merchant marine; middle marker; millimeter(s); mismated; mucous membrane

mm: med mera (Swedish—and so forth; etc.)

mm²: square millimeter(s)

mm³: cubic millimeter(s)

m & m: make and mend

mM: millimole

Mm.: Martyres (Greek—witnesses; martyrs)

MM: Machinist's Mate; Maintenance Manual; Majesties; Marilyn Monroe; Marine Midland (stock exchange symbol); Martyres (martyrs); Master Mason; maximum misfit; Medal of Merit; mercantile marine; merchant marine; Messageries Maritimes; Messieurs (French—gentlemen); Metropolitan Museum; Military Medal; Minister of Munitions

M.M.: Master of Music

M.M.: Maelzel's Metronome (e.g., M.M. 75 means that composer indicated composition be performed at 75 half-notes per minute as measured by Maelzel's Metronome)

M de M: Metropolitano de Madrid (Madrid subway system)

M-et-M: Meurthe-et-Moselle

M of M: Ministry of Munitions; Museum of Man

mma: major maladjustment

MMA: Maine Maritime Academy; Massachusetts Maritime Academy; Metropolitan Museum of Art; Monorail Manufacturers

Association; Museum of Modern Art

MMB: Milk Marketing Board

mm bat: main missile battery

MMC: Marine Moisture Control; Materiel Management Code; Meharry Medical College

MMcKNP: Mount McKinley National Park (Alaska)

MMCT: maritime mobile coastal telegraphy

MMD: minelayer, fast (naval ship symbol)

mme: maximum maintenance effort

Mme: Madame (French—Missus)

MME: Manned Mars Expedition

M.M.E.: Master of Mechanical Engineering; Master of Music Education

M. Mech. Eng.: Master of Mechanical Engineering

M. Med.: Master of Medicine

Mmes: Mesdames (French—ladies)

M. Met.: Master of Metallurgy

M. Met. E.: Master of Metallurgical Engineering

mmf: magnetomotive force

MMF: fleet mine layer (naval symbol); Maggio Musicale Fiorentino (Florence May Festival); Milbank Memorial Fund

MMFA: Montreal Museum of Fine Arts

mmfds: microfarads

MMFI: Moravian Music Foundation, Incorporated

MMFPI: Man-Made Fiber Producers Institute

MMGR: Masai Mara Game Reserve (Kenya)

MMGS: Mount Muhavura Gorilla Sanctuary (Uganda)

M.Mgt.Eng.: Master of Management Engineering

mmHg: millimeter of mercury

MMI: Micro-Magnetic Industries; Moslem Mosque Incorporated (formerly American Mohammedan Society)

M. Mic.: Master of Microbiology

M. Mi. Eng.: Master of Mining Engineering

MMJC: Meridian Municipal Junior College

mmm: military medical mobilization; millimicron(s)

MMM: Modern Music Masters

MMMS: Modern Music Masters Society

MMNP: Mount McKinley National Park (Alaska)

Mmo: Malmö

MMO: Music Minus One

mmp (MMP): maritime mobile phone

MMP: Masters, Mates and Pilots

(union)

MM & P: Masters, Mates and Pilots

MMPC: maritime mobile phone coastal

MMPDC: maritime mobile phone distress and calling

MMPI: Minnesota Multiphase Personality Inventory

MMPNC: Medical Materiel Program for Nuclear Casualities

mmpp: millimeters partial pressure

MMPP: Moose Mountain Provincial Park (Saskatchewan)

mmrbm (MMRBM): mobile medium-range ballistic missile

MMS: Manpower Management System; Mass Memory System; Metabolic Monitoring System; Mobile Monitoring System; Modulation Measuring System; Multiplex Modulation System

MMSA: Mining and Metallurgical Society of America

mmscfd: million standard cubic feet per day

MMSW: Mine, Mill and Smelter Workers (union)

MMT: maritime mobile telegraphy

MMTC: maritime mobile telegraphy calling

MMTDC: maritime mobile telegraphy distress and calling

mmtv: mouse mammary tumor virus; murine mammary tumor virus

mmu: millimass unit(s)

M.Mus.: Master of Music

MMY: *Mental Measurements Yearbook*

m(n): microfilm negative

m. et n.: *mane et nocte* (Latin —morning and night)

m/n: *moneda nacional* (Spanish —national currency)

Mn: manganese

MN: magnetic north

MN: *Magyar Nepkoztarsasag* (Hungarian People's Republic)

M.N.: Master of Nursing

MNA: Matematikmaskinnämnden (Swedish Computing Machinery Board)

M.N.A.: Master of Nursing Administration

MNAG: Museo Nacional de Antropología, Guatemala

Mnais: Mnasidika

MNAM: Museo Nacional de Antropología, Mexico

M. N. Arch.: Master of Naval Architecture

MNC: Major NATO Commanders; Multinational Corporation

mnd: minimum necrosing dose

M.N.E.: Master of Nuclear Engineering

MNEA: Merchant Navy Establishment Administration

mnem: mnemonic

M. N. Eng.: Master of Naval Engineering

MNF: Menagasha National Forest (Ethiopia); Multilateral Nuclear Force (NATO navy)

mnfrs: manufacturers

mng: managing

MNH: Museum of Natural History (Smithsonian)

mnl: marine navigating light

Mnl: Manuel

MNL: Manila, Philippines (airport)

MNLS: Marine Navigating Light System

MNM: Museum of New Mexico

MNNP: Malawi Nyika National Park

M-note: $1000 bill

MNP: Marsabit National Park (Kenya); Meru National Park (equatorial Kenya); Mikumi National Park (Tanzania); Mushandike National Park (Rhodesia)

MNPL: Machinist Non-Partisan Political League

mnr: massive nuclear retaliation; mean neap rise

Mnr: Manor

MNRU: Medical Neuropsychiatric Research Unit

mns: metal-nitride-semiconductor (transistor)

M.N.S.: Master of Nutritional Science

M. N. Sc.: Master of Nursing Science

m'ns'l: mainsail

MNT: Minnesota and Ontario Paper (stock exchange symbol)

MNTO: Moroccan National Tourist Office

MNU: Maniti Sugar (stock exchange symbol)

M.Nurs.: Master of Nursing

MNV: Marion Power Shovel (stock-exchange symbol)

MNWEB: Merseyside and North Wales Electricity Board

MNWR: Malheur National Wildlife Refuge (Oregon); Mattamuskeet NWR (North Carolina); Merced NWR (California); Mingo NWR (Missouri); Minidoka NWR (Idaho); Mississiquoi NWR (Vermont); Modoc NWR (California); Montezuma NWR (New York); Moosehorn NWR (Maine)

mnx: (short-order slang contraction—ham and eggs)

mo: mail order; manual operation; manually operated; mass obser-

vation; method of operation; moment; money order(s); month(s); monthlies; monthly; mustered out

m.o.: *modus operandi* (Latin— manner, method, or mode of operating; way of working)

m/o: *mi orden* (Spanish—my order)

m & o: management and organization

Mo: Missouri; Missourian; molybdenum; Moselle; Mozelle

Mo: *Maestro* (Italian—master; title given any great artist, composer, conductor, or teacher)

MO: Mail Order; Medical Officer; Mobile Station; Mohawk Airlines (2-letter coding); Money Order; Monthly Order; Movement Order(s)

M-O: Morris-Oxford

M & O: Muscat and Oran

moa.: medium observation aircraft

MOA: Marine Office of America; Metropolitan Oakland Area; Metropolitan Opera Association; Ministry of Aviation; Music Operators of America

MOADS: Montgomery Air Defense Sector

MOAMA: Mobile Air Materiel Area

MOARS: Mobilization Assignment Reserve Section

mob.: mobilization; mobilize

mob.: *mobile vulgus* (Latin—disorderly group of people)

Mob: Mobile, Alabama (maritime abbreviation)

MOB: Mobile, Alabama (airport); Montreux - Oberland - Bernois (railway)

Mo' Bay: Mobile Bay, Alabama; Montego Bay, Jamaica

mobidic: mobile digital computer

mobil: mobility

mobl: macro-oriented business language

möbl: *möbliert* (German—furnished)

mob lt: man overboard and breakdown light

mobula: model-building language

moc: mission operations computer

MOC: Makapuu Oceanic Center (Hawaii); Mauna Olu College (Maui)

moca: minimum obstruction clearance altitude

MoCom: Mobile Command

MOCOM: Mobile Command (US Army)

mocp: missile out of commission for parts

mocr: mission operation control room

mod   **233**   **mopeds**

mod: manned orbital development (MOD); mesial-occlusal-distal (dental cavities); model; moderate; modern; modernize(d); modification; modify

m-o-d: mesial-occlusal-distal (inlay)

MOD: Medical Officer of the Day; Ministry of Defense; Miscellaneous Obligation Document

modasm: modular air-to-surface missile

m-o-d-b: mesial-occlusal-distal-buccal (inlay)

modcom: modernity commercialized (exploitation of addictive drugs, electronic amplifiers of pseudomusical noises, psychedelic poster art, unredeemed pornography)

ModE: Modern English

moderm: modulator-demodulator

ModGr: Modern Greek

ModHeb: Modern Hebrew

mod/iran: modification, inspection, and repair as necessary

modo.: *moderato* (Italian—moderately)

mod. pres.: *modo prescripto* (Latin—in the manner prescribed)

mods: mesial-occlusal-distal (dental cavities); models; moderates; moderators; moderns; modification; modifiers; modulators; modules

MODS: Manned Orbital Development Station (or System); Manned Orbiting Development Station (or System)

Moe: Moses

mof: maximum observed frequency; member of (the police) force; metal oxide film

MOF: Ministry of Food

MOG: Metropolitan Opera Guild

M.O.G.: Master of Obstetrics and Gynaecology

mogas: motor gasoline

MOH: Ministry of Health; Mohawk Airlines

Moham: Mohammedan

Mohammed Ali: Cassius Clay

MOHATS: Mobile Overland Hauling and Transport System (USAF)

mohms: milliohms

moho: Mohorovicic discontinuity

Mohole: a hole to the Mohorovicic discontinuity, the boundary between the earth's crust and mantle

moi: maximum obtainable irradiance; military occupational information; multiplicity of infection

MOI: Military Operations and Intelligence; Ministry of Information

MOIC: Medical Officer in Command

M.O.I.G.: Master of Occupational Information and Guidance

MOK: Mohawk Carpet Mills (stock-exchange symbol)

mol: machine-oriented language; molecular

mol.: *mollis* (Latin—soft)

Mol: Mollendo

MOL: Manned Orbiting Laboratory

MOLAB: Mobile Lunar Laboratory

Moldv: Moldavia; Moldavian

mole.: molecular; molecule

Molière: Jean-Baptiste Poquelin

Molink: Moscow link (teletype cable circuit linking Moscow's Kremlin with Washington, D.C.'s White House), The Hot Line

moll: metallo-organic liquid laser

Moll: Mary (slang); Molly

mollie: mollienisia (tropical fish)

Mollus: Mollusca

MOLOC: Ministry of Labour Occupational Classification

MOLS: Mirror Optical Landing System

mol wt: molecular weight

moly: molybdenum

mom: military ordinary mail

m-o-m: middle of month; milk of magnesia

m/ o m/: *más o menos* Spanish —more or less)

Mom: Momma

MOM: Musée Océanographique Monaco

momar: modern mobile army

moms: *mervaerdiomsaetningsskat* (Danish—value-added tax); *mervardesomsattningsskatt* (Swedish—value-added tax)

MOMS: Mothers for Moral Stability

MOM/WOW: Men Our Masters/Women Our Wonders (antifeminist acronym reading the same upside down as shown)

mon: monetary; monsoon; monument

Mon: Monaco; Monday; Monegasque; Monmouthshire; Monsieur (French—Mister)

Mon: *Montag* (German—Monday)

Mona: Ramona

Monag: Monaghan

monbas: monobasic

MONC: Metropolitan Opera National Council

Mong: Mongol; Mongolia(n)

Mongol Century: the 13th century dominated by the Mongol emperor Genghiz Khan whose

hordes conquered and overran China and Russia—the 1200s

mon-H: monohydrogen

Monitor: *Christian Science Monitor*

Monkey Ward: Montgomery-Ward

mono: mononucleosis; monophonic; monopropellant; monorail- (road); monotype; monotyper

monob (MONOB): mobile noise barge

monocl: monoclinic

monocot(s): monocotyledon(s)

monog: monogram; monograph

Monon: Monon Railroad

monot: monotonous; monotony; monotype; monotypic

Mons: *Monsieur* (French—Mister)

Mons Cur: Monsoon Current

Monsig: *Monseigneur* (French —My Lord)

monsoons: seasonal storms of southern Aisa

monstro(s): monstrosity; monstrosities

mont: (French—mountain)

Mont: Montana; Montanan; Monterrey; Montevideo; Montgomery; Montpelier; Montreal

montagna: (Italian—mountain)

montagne: (French—mountain)

montagnes: (French—mountain range)

montaña: (Spanish—mountain)

monte: (Italian, Portuguese, Spanish—mountain as in Monte Carlo, Monte Cassino)

Monte: Montague; Montefiore

Montgom: Montgomeryshire

Montr: Montreal

montrg: monitoring

Mont S: *Montreal Star*

Mony: monastery

MONY: Music Operators of New York; Mutual Life Insurance Company of New York

MOOP: *Ministerstvo Okhranenia Obshehestvennogo Poriadka* (Russian—All-Union Ministry for the Preservation of Public Order)—latest of a long line of secret police agencies—(q.v.— VOT)

MOOSE: Move Out of Saigon Expeditiously (USA)

mop: mother-of-pearl; mustering-out pay

M o P: Minister of Power

MOP: *Ministerio de Obras Públicas* (Spanish—Ministry of Public Works)

mopa: master oscillator power amplifier

MoPac: Missouri Pacific — Texas & Pacific (railroad)

mopeds: motorized pedals (bicycles

containing auxiliary motors saving riders much pedalling)

mopr: manner of performance rating; mop rack

MOPS: Missile Operations System

M. Opt.: Master of Optometry

mor: morocco; mortar

mor: *morendo* (Italian—dying away; gradual softening of tone and slowing of tempo)

Mor: Morelia; Morelos; Morisco; Moroccan; Morocco

Morav: Moravia; Moravian

MORC: Medical Officers Reserve Corps; Midget Ocean Racing Club (*mor-sees*—smallest racing cruisers)

Mord: Mordehai

Mordhy: Mordehai

mor. dict.: *more dicto* (Latin—as directed)

Mordy: Mordehai

more: (Russian—sea, as in Aralskoe More)

mor fib: moral fiber

morg mar: morganatic marriage

MORL: Manned (or Medium) Orbital Research Laboratory

Morm: Mormon

Morm: *Mormon, Book of*

morn: morning

morph: morphine; morphology

morpha: hermaphrodite (mispronounced *morphadite*)

Morrie: Maurice; Morris

morro: (Portuguese or Spanish —hill; promontory, as in Morro Castle

mor. sol.: *more solito* (Latin—in the usual manner)

mort: mortal; mortality; mortar; mortgage; mortician; mortuary

mor t: Morse taper

Mort: Morton

mortal.: mortality

mos: metal-oxide semiconductor; metal-oxide-silicon (compound); missile on stand; months; mosaic

mos: *mitout sound* (Hollywood-American slang—without sound)

Mos: Moscow

MOs: Military Observers (UN)

MOS: Management Operating System; Manned Orbital Station; Ministry of Supply

MOSC: Midland-Odessa Symphony and Chorale

MOSES: Manned Open Sea Experimentation Station

mosfet: metal-oxide semiconductor field-effect transistor

mosic: metal-oxide-semiconductor integrated circuit(s)

mosm: milliosmol(s)

MOSS: Manned Orbital Space Station

most.: metal-oxide semiconductor transistor

mot: middle of target; motor; motorized

MOT: Military Ocean Terminal

mots: minitrack optical tracking system

mounties: mounted policemen (especially Royal Canadian Mounted Police)

MOUSE: minimum orbital unmanned satellite

mov: movement

movi: movie; moving pictures

movies: moving pictures

MOW: Moscow, USSR (Vnukovo Airport)

MOWW: Military Order of the World Wars

mox: oxidized metal explosive

moy: money

moyen: (French—middle, as in Moyen Atlas mountains)

Moz Cur: Mozambique Current (Natal)

mp: mail payment; manifold pressure; medium pressure; meeting point; melting point; milepost; motion picture; multipole

m(p): microfilm positive

mP: polar maritime air

MP: Member of Parliament; Metropolitan Police; Military Police; Minister Plenipotentiary; Missouri Pacific (railroad); Mounted Police

M & P: Maryland & Pennsylvania (railroad)

MPA: Magazine Publishers Association; Maryland & Pennsylvania (railroad); Mechanical Packing Association; Medical Procurement Agency; Metal Powder Association; Military Police Association; Mobile Press Association; Modern Poetry Association; Motion Picture Alliance; Music Publishers Association

M.P.A.: Master of Professional Accounting; Master of Public Administration; Master of Public Affairs

MPAA: Motion Picture Association of America; Musical Performing Arts Association

m part: movable partition

MPAUS: Music Publishers Association of the United States

m payl: maximum payload

MPB: Miniature Precision Bearings; Missing Persons Bureau; Montpelier & Barre (railroad)

mp br: multipunch bar

MPBW: Ministry of Public Buildings and Works

mpc: marine protein concentrate; material program code; maximum permissible concentration; military payment certificate; minimal planning chart

MPC: Manpower and Personnel Council; Manpower Priorities Committee; Manufacturing Plan Change; Member of Parliament of Canada; Military Payment Certificate; Military Pioneer Corps; Military Police Corps; Montana Power Company

MPCA: Magnetic Powder Core Association

MPCL: Movimiento Patriótico Cuba Libre (Free Cuba Patriotic Movement)

mpcp: missile power control panel

mpd: magnetoplasmadynamics; missile purchase description

M. Pd.: Master of Pedagogy

MPD: Military Pay Division

MPDFA: Master Photo Dealers' and Finishers' Association

mp di: multipunch die

MPDS: Message Processing Distribution System

mpe: maximum permissible exposure (to radiation)

M.P.E.: Master of Physical Education

MPEAUS: Master Printers and Engravers Association of the United States

M. Pe. Eng.: Master of Petroleum Engineering

MPers: Middle Persian

mpf: multipurpose food

MPF: Metropolitan Police Force (London)

mpg: miles per gallon

MPG: Magazine Promotion Group; Max Planck Gesellschaft

MPGR: Mana Pools Game Reserve (Rhodesia)

mph: miles per hour

M.Ph.: Master of Philosophy

MPH: Methodist Publishing House

M.P.H.: Master of Public Health

M. Phar.: Master of Pharmacy

M. Pharm.: Master of Pharmacy

M. Ph. Ed.: Master of Public Health Education

M. P.H. Eng.: Master of Public Health Engineering

M.Phil.: Master of Philosophy

M. Pho.: Master of Photography

mphps: miles per hour per second

M. Ph. Sc.: Master of Physical Science

M.P.H.T.M.: Master of Public Health and Tropical Medicine

M. Phy.: Master of Physics

mpi: magnetic particle inspection; mean point of impact

MPI: Max Planck Institute; Museum of the Plains Indians

M-pill: menstruation pill

mPk: polar maritime air colder than underlying surface

mpl: maximum payload; maximum permissible level

MPL: Maintenance Parts List; Memphis Public Library; Metropolitan Police Laboratory; Miami Public Library; Milwaukee Public Library; Minnesota Power and Light; Missouri Pacific Lines; Montreal Public Library

MPLA: Mountain Plains Library Association

MPLP: Marxist Progressive Labor Party

Mpls: Minneapolis

mpm: meters per minute; multipurpose meal

mpn: most probable number

MPNA: Midwest Professional Needlework Association

MPO: Miami Philharmonic Orchestra; Military Pay Order; Military Post Office

MPOIS: Military Police Operating Information System

mpp: most probable position

MPP: Member Provincial Parliament (Canada)

M & PP: Manitou & Pikes Peak (railroad)

MPPA: Music Publishers Protective Association

mppcf: millions of particles per cubic foot of air

mp pl: multipunch plate

MPPWCOM: Military Police Prisoner of War Command

MPR: Military Pay Record

MPRC: Military Personnel Records Center

M. Prof. Acc.: Master of Professional Accountancy

mps: marbled paper sides; megacycles per second; meters per second; motor parts stock

M.Ps.: Master of Psychology

MPS: Manufacturing Process Specification; Milwaukee Public Museum; Ministry of Public Security; Motor Products Corporation

MPSP: Military Personnel Security Program

mpt: male pipe thread

MPT: Minister of Posts and Telecommunications

MPTA: Machine Power Transmission Association

MPU: Medical Practitioners Union

M. Pub. Adm.: Master of Public Administration

mPw: polar martime air warmer than underlying surface

MPW: Minneapolis-Moline (stock exchange symbol)

mpx: multiplex

Mpy: *Maatschappij* (Dutch—company)

MPZ: Mid-Continent Petroleum (stock-exchange symbol)

mq: Metol-quinol (MQ); multiple quotient (register); multiplier quotient

Mq: mosque

MQ: merit quotient

MQA: Manufacturing Quality Assurance

mqf: mobile quarantine facility

mqil: miniature quartz incandescent lamp

mql: miniature quartz lamp

MQO: Marksmanship Qualification Order

MQS: Mobile Quality Services

MQT: Model Qualification Test

mr: machine record(s); machine rifle; map reference; medium range; metabolic rate; methyl red; milliroentgen; mill run; mineral rubber; mine run; motivational research (MR)

mr: *meester* (Dutch—master)—attorney-at-law; *mi remesa* (Spanish—my remittance)

m/r: middle right

m & r: maintainability and reliability; maintainability and repairs

Mr.: Mister

MR: Machinery Repairman; Marketing Research (division, US Department of Agriculture); Master of the Rolls; Memorandum for Record; Memorandum Report; Military Railroad; Military Requirement; Minister Residentiary; Ministry of Reconstruction; Miscellaneous Report; Mobilization Regulation; Monon Railroad; Monthly Report; Morning Report; Municipal Reform

M & R: maintenance and repairs

M/R: map reading

mra: medium-powered radio range (Adcock); minimum reception altitude

MRA: Moral Rearmament

mrad: millirad

M. Rad.: Master of Radiology

M. Ra. Eng.: Master of Radio Engineering

MRAM: Multimission Redeye Air-launched Missile

MRAS: Manpower Resources Accounting System (USAF)

mrb: marble base

MRB: Material Review Board; Mileage Rationing Board; Modification Review Board; Mutual Reinsurance Bureau

mrbm: medium-range ballistic missile (MRBM)

MRBP: Missouri River Basin Project

MRC: Marine Research Committee; Market Research Council; Marlin-Rockwell Corporation; Material Redistribution Center; Material Review Crib; Medical Research Center (Council); Medical Reserve Corps; Men's Republican Club; Metals Reserve Company; Methods Research Corporation; Mississippi River Commission; Movement Report Center

mrca: multi-rate combat aircraft (MRCA)

MRCC: Medical Research Council of Canada

MRCI: Medical Registration Council of Ireland; Medical Research Council of Ireland

MRCO: Member of the Royal College of Physicians

MRCOG: Member of the Royal College of Obstetricians and Gynaecologists

Mr Common Sense: Thomas Paine

MRCS: Member of the Royal College of Surgeons

MRCVS: Member of the Royal College of Veterinary Surgeons

MRCWA: Midland Railway Company of Western Australia

mrd: metal rolling door; minimum reacting dose (MRD)

MRDC: Military Research and Development Center

MR & DC: Medical Research and Development Command (US Army)

MRDF: maritime radio direction finding

Mr Dooley: (pseudonym—Finley Peter Dunne)

MRDTI: Metal Roof Deck Technical Institute

mre: mean radial error

MRE: Microbiological Research Establishment (UK)

M.R.E.: Master of Religious Education

M. Ref. Eng.: Master of Refrigeration Engineering

mrf: marble floor

MRF: Meteorological Rocket Facility; Music Research Foundation

mrg: magnetic radiation generator; margin; marginal; marginalia

MRG: Material Review Group; Minorities Research Group (aiding homosexuals)

mr/hr: millir oentgens per hour

MRHS: Midwest Railway Historical Society

mri: mean rise interval; medium-range interceptor; milstrip routing identifier

MRI: Mental Research Institute; Meteorological Research Institute; Midwest Research Institute

mrir: medium resolution infrared

MRIS: Maritime Research Information System; Market Research Information System; Material Readiness Index System; Medical Research Information System; Mobile Range Instrumentation System

mrkr: marker

mrl: medium-powered radio range (loop radiators); multiple rocket launcher (MRL)

MRL: Materiel Requirements List; Medical Records Librarian

MRLA: Malayan Races Liberation Army (Chinese-communist guerrillas)

mrm: mail readership measurement; miles of relative movement

Mrn: Martin

MRN: Meteorological Rocket Network

mrng: morning

MRNP: Mount Rainier National Park (Washington); Mount Revelstoke National Park (British Columbia)

Mrnz: Martínez

Mro: Maestro

MRO: Maintenance, Repair, and Operation(s); Materiel Release Order

M-roof: M-shaped roof

mrp: manned reusable payload; maximum resolving power

M.R.P.: Master in Regional Planning

M rps: Mauritius rupee(s)

Mr Q: Marquardt Corporation

MRQ: Marquardt Corporation (stock exchange symbol)

mrr: medical reasearch reactor

MRRC: Mechanical Reliability Research Center

Mr Republican: U.S. Senator Robert A. Taft

Mrs: Missus; Mistress

MRs: Maintenance Reports

MRS: Marseilles, France (airport); Military Railway Service

MR & S: Materials Research and Standards

Mrs Grundy: (nickname synonym for conventional morality)

MRSH: Member of the Royal Society of Health

MRSP: Myakka River State Park (Florida)

mrsss: manned revolving space systems simulator (MRSSS)

mrt: mildew-resistant thread

Mrt: Martinique

Mrt: *Maart* (Dutch—March)

mrtm: maritime

MRTS: Master Radar Tracking Station

mru: minimal reproductive units; mobile radio unit (MRU)

MRU: mobile radio unit

Mr UN: Carlos P. Romulo

mrv: missile re-entry vehicle (MRV); mixed respiratory vaccine; multiple re-entry vehicle (MRV)

MRV: missile recovery vessel(s)

mrw: morale, recreation, and welfare

MRWA: Midland Railway of Western Australia

ms: machine screw; machine steel; main switch; maintenance and service; major subject; manuscript; margin of safety; master switch; maximum stress; mean square; medium shot; medium steel; meters per second; metric system; mild steel; minimum stress; mint state; mitral stenosis; months after sight; multiple sclerosis; muscle strength

ms.: manuscript

m s: *mano sinistra* (Italian—left hand)

m/s: marking and stenciling

m/s: *motorskib* (Norwegian—motorship)

m & s: maintenance and supply

m³/s: cubic meter per second

mS: millisiemens (millimho)

Ms: mature motion pictures (for adults); Mendes; mesothorium; (pronounced *Miz*)—feminine title replacing Miss and Mrs and used with the original first and last name of the bearer to insure against loss of individual identity

MS: Machinery Survey; magnetic south; Mail Steamer; major subject; Manuscript Society; Master Sergeant; Material Specifications; Medical Survey; Metallurgical Society; Meteoritical Society; Michigan State University of Agriculture and Applied Science; Military Service; Military Standard; Ministry of Shipping; Ministry of Supply; Misair (Egyptian Airline); Motorship

MS: *Material Standard* (usually followed by a number)

M-S: Material Service (division of General Dynamics)

M-S: *Minshu-Shakaito* (Japanese—Democratic Socialist Party)

M.S.: Master of Science; Master of Surgery

M/S: Mannlicher-Schoenauer; motorship

M & S: Maintenance and Supply; Medicine and Surgery

M es Sc: *Maitre es Sciences* (French—Master of Sciences)

M o S: Ministry of Supply

msa: method of steepest ascent

MSA: Malaysia Singapore Airlines; Medical Statistics Agency (US Army); Mineralogical Society of America; Mine Safety Appliances (company); Mutual Security Agency

M-S-A: Mine Safety Appliances

mˢ aˢ: *muchos años* (Spanish—many years)

MSAUS: Masonic Service Association of the United States

MSB: Mackinac Straits Bridge (Michigan); Marine Safety Board; minesweeping boat (naval symbol)

M.S.B.A.: Master of Science in Business Administration

msc: millisecond; moved, seconded, and carried

M. Sc.: Master of Science

MSC: coastal minesweeper (3-letter naval symbol); Maine Sardine Council; Manned Spacecraft Center (NASA); Maple Syrup Council; Marine Science Center (Lehigh University); Medical Service Corps; Medical Specialist Corps; Mediterranean Sub-Commission; Melbourne Steamship Company; Missile and Space Council; Mississippi Central (railroad)

M & SC: Missile and Space Council

MSCA: Moore School of Automatic Computers; Mount Saint Agnes College; Murray State Agricultural College

M.S.C.E.: Master of Science in Civil Engineering

M.S.Ch.E.: Master of Science in Chemical Engineering

Mschr: *Monatsschrift* (German—monthly magazine)

M. Sc. L.: Master of the Science of Law

MSC(O): old coastal minesweeper (naval symbol)

M.S. Conv.: Master of Science in Conservation

M. Sc. Ost.: Master of Science in Osteopathy

mscp: mean spherical candlepower
MSCP: Master Shielding Computer Program
MSCRB: Margaret Sanger Clinical Research Bureau
mscrbl: manuscribble (handscribbled manuscript)
MSCW: Mississippi State College for Women
msd: missile system development
M & SD: Missile and Space Division (General Electric)
M.S. Dent.: Master of Science in Dentistry
M.S. Derm.: Master of Science in Dermatology
MSDF: Maritime Self-Defense Force (Japanese Navy)
M & SDI: Mayonnaise and Salad Dressing Institute
mse: mean square error; military stressful era(s)
MSE: Midwest Stock Exchange; Mississippi Export Railroad (stock exchange symbol); Montreal Stock Exchange
M.S.E.: Master of Sanitary Engineering; Master of Science in Education; Master of Science in Engineering
m sec: millisecond
M.S.E.E.: Master of Science in Electrical Engineering
M.S. Eng.: Master of Science in Engineering
msf: muscle shock factor
MSF: fleet minesweeper (naval symbol); mobile striking force
M.S.F.: Master of Science in Forestry
MSFC: Marshall Space Flight Center
ms fm: master form
msfn: manned space flight network
ms fx: master fixture
msg: message; monosodium glutamate
MSG: Madison Square Garden; Marine Systems Group (General Dynamics)
ms ga: master gauge
M.S.G.E.: Master of Science in Geological Engineering
msgfm: messageform
MSGp: Mobile Support Group
msgr: messenger
MSGR: Mobile Support Group
M Sgt: Master Sergeant
msh: melanocyte-stimulating hormone (MSH)
MSH: Music Society for the Handicapped
M.S.H.: Master of Science in Horticulture; Master of Science in Hygiene
M.S.H.A.: Master of Science in

Hospital Administration
M.S.H.E.: Master of Science in Home Economics
M.S. Hort.: Master of Science in Horticulture
M.S. Hyg.: Master of Science in Hygiene
msi: medium-scale integration
MSI: minesweeper, inshore (naval symbol); Museum of Science and Industry
MSI: *Movimento Sociale Italiano* (Italian Social Movement)—neo-fascist followers of Mussolini known as Missini
MSIB: Mountain States Inspection Bureau
M.S.J.: Master of Science in Journalism
msk: mission support kit
MS-KCC: Memorial Sloan-Kettering Cancer Center
MSKK: Mitsui Sempaku Kabushiki Kaisha (Mitsui Line)
Mskr: *Manuskript* (German—manuscript)
msl: mean sea level; missile
msl: *mesela* (Turkish—for example)
Msl: Marseilles
MSL: Marine Science Laboratories; minesweeping launch (naval symbol)
M.S.L.: Master of Science in Linguistics
MSLC: Manufacturing Specification Liaison Change
ms lo: master layout
MSM: Manhattan School of Music; Montana School of Mines
M.S.M.: Master of Science in Music
MSMM: Missouri School of Mines and Metallurgy
M.S. Mus.: Master of Science in Music
M.S. Mus. Ed.: Master of Science in Music Education
msn: mission
MSN: Madison, Wisconsin (airport)
M.S.N.: Master of Science in Nursing
MSNB: Machine Screw Nut Bureau
M.S.N. Ed.: Master of Science in Nursing Education
M.S.Nucl.Eng.: Master of Science in Nuclear Engineering
MSNY: Mattachine Society of New York
MSO: Manila Symphony Orchestra; Melbourne Symphony Orchestra; Memphis Symphony Orchestra; Milwaukee Symphony Orchestra; Minneapolis Symphony Orchestra (former name

of the Minnesota Symphony); Montreal Symphony Orchestra; ocean minesweeper (naval symbol)
M. Soc. Wk.: Master of Social Work
msp: metal splash pan
MSP: Maximum Security Prison; Minneapolis, Minnesota (airport); Mutual Security Program
MSpC: Medical Specialist Corps
MSPE: Master of Science in Physical Education
M.S. Pet. Eng.: Master of Science in Petroleum Engineering
M.S.P.H.: Master of Science in Public Health
M.S.Pharm.: Master of Science in Pharmacy
M.S.P.H.E.: Master of Science in Public Health Engineering
M.S.P.H.Ed.: Master of Science in Public Health Education
ms pl: master plate
msr: main supply route; mineral-surface roof; missile site radar
m & sr: missile and surface radar
MSR: Manufacturing Specification Request; mean spring tide
M.S. Rad.: Master of Science in Radiology
MSRB: Mississippi State Rating Bureau
M.S. Rec.: Master of Science in Recreation
M.S. Ret.: Master of Science in Retailing
MSRG: Member of the Society for Remedial Gymnasts
MSRN: Manufacturing Specification Revision Notice
msrpp: multidimensional scale for rating psychiatric patients
MSRS: Missile Strike Reporting System
msry: masonry
mss.: manuscripts
MSS: Manufacturers Standardization Society of the Valve and Fittings Industry; Medical Service School (USAF)
M.S.S.: Master of Social Science
M.S.Sc.: Master of Sanitary Science; Master of Social Science
M & SSD: Missile & Space System Division (Douglas Aircraft)
M.S.S.E.: Master of Science in Sanitary Engineering
M.S. S. Eng.: Master of Science in Sanitary Engineering
MSSH: Massachusetts Society for Social Hygiene
MSSMS: Munition Section Strategic Missile Squadron
M.S. St.Eng.: Master of Science in

Structural Engineering
MSSVD: Medical Society for the Study of Venereal Diseases
MSSVFI: Manufacturers Standardization Society of the Valve and Fittings Industry
mst: mean survival time; measurement
MST: Marconi Telecommunications Systems; Maximum Service Telecasters; Military Science Training; Mountain Standard Time
M.S.T.: Master of Science in Teaching
MSTA: Michigan State Teachers Association
mstb: 1000 stock tank barrels
mstc: mastic
MSTC: Maryland State Teachers College; Massachusetts State Teachers College
M.S. T.Ed.: Master of Science in Teacher Education
M & ST L: Minneapolis & St. Louis (railroad)
ms tp: master template
M ST P & SSM: Minneapolis, St. Paul & Sault Ste. Marie Railroad (Soo Line)
M.S. in Trans.E.: Master of Science in Transportation Engineering
mstr: master
msts (MSTS): missile static test site
MSTS: Military Sea Transport Service; Missile Static Test Site
msu (MSU): maximum security unit
MSU: Memphis State University; Michigan State University; Mississippi State University; Montana State University
MSUC: Middle South Utilities Company
MSUL: Memphis State University Library; Michigan State University Library; Mississippi State University Library; Montana State University Library
M. Surgery: Master of Surgery
msv (MSV): magnetically-supported vehicle; Martian surface vehicle; mean square velocity; miniature solenoid valve; molecular solution volume; murine sarcoma virus
MSVC: Mount Saint Vincent College
MSVD: Missile and Space-Vehicle Department (General Electric)
msv(M): murine sarcoma virus (Moloney)
M.S.W.: Master of Social Work
MSX: Seaboard Oil (stock exchange symbol)

MSY: New Orleans, Louisiana (airport)
mt: empty; machine translation; mail transfer; maximum torque; mean tide; measurement ton; mechanical translation; mechanical transport; megaton (MT); metric ton; missile test; motor transport
mT: tropical maritime air
m & t: maintenance and test
Mt: Mount; tympanic membrane
MT: Machine Translation; Mandated Territory; Masoretic Text; Mechanical Translation; Medical Technologist; Meteorological Aids; Military Training; Military Transport; Ministry of Transport; Motor Transport; Mountain Time; Muscat Transport
M de T: Mengano de Tal (Spanish—so and so)
MTA: Maine Teachers Association; Manpower Training Association; Metropolitan Transit Authority; Mississippi Teachers Association; Mississippi Test Area
mtac: mathematical tables and other aids to computation
MTACCS: Marine Tactical Command and Control System
mtb: maintenance of true bearing
MTB: Malayan Tin Bureau; Medium Tank Battalion; motor torpedo boat
MTBA: Machine Tool Builders' Association
mtbf: mean time before failure; mean time between failures
mtbff: mean time between first failure
mtbfl: mean time between function loss
mtbm: mean time between maintenance
MTBRON: Motor Torpedo Boat Squadron
mtbsf: mean time between system failure
MTC: Marine Technology Center (Electric Boat); Materiel Testing Command; Mechanical Transport Corps; Medical Training Center; Military Training Cadets; Missile Test Center; Montreal Trust Company; Monsanto Chemicals (stock exchange symbol); Morse Telegraph Club; Motor Transport Corps; Mystic Terminal (railroad)
M.T.C.: Master of Textile Chemistry
MTCA: Ministry of Transport and Civil Aviation

mtce: maintenance
mtd: midpoint tissue dose; mounted
m.t.d.: mitte tales doses (Latin —send such doses)
MTD: Mobile Training Detachment
MT$: Maria Theresa dollar (Yemeni currency unit)
MTDS: Marine Tactical Data System
mte: maximum temperature engine
MTE: Marine Technical Education
mtf: mechanical time fuze
MTF: Mississippi Test Facility
mtg: main turbogenerator(s); meeting; mortgage; mounting
mtgd: mortgaged
mtge: mortgage
mtgee: mortgagee
mtgor: mortgagor
M. Th.: Master of Theology
mti: moving target indicator; moving target information
MTI: Metal Treating Institute
MTIRA: Machine Tool Industry Research Association
mTk: tropical maritime air colder than underlying surface
mtl: material; materiel; mean tide level
mtl: monatlich (German—monthly)
Mtl: Montreal
MTL: mean tide level
mtlp: metabolic toxemia of late pregnancy
MTMC: Mother Teresa's Missionaries of Charity
Mt McK NP: Mount McKinley National Park
MTMTS: Military Traffic Management and Terminal Service
mtn: motion
MTNA: Music Teachers National Association
MTNWR: Mark Twain National Wildlife Refuge (Illinois)
MTO: Mississippi Test Operations
Mton: Moncton
Mt P: Mount Palomar (observatory)
MTP: Mobilization Training Program
Mt P O: Mount Palomar Observatory
mtr: materials testing reactor; mean time to restore; missile-tracking radar; moving target reactor; multiple track radar
Mtr: Montrose
MTr: meridian transit
MTR: Materials Testing Report; Montour (railroad)
mtrcl: motorcycle
mtre: missile test and readiness equipment
MTRF: Mark Twain Research Foundation
mtrg: metering

mtri: missile test range instrumentation

mtrl: material

Mt R NP: Mount Rainier National Park

mtr rdr: meter reader

mts: mountains

mt's: empties

MTS: Marine Technology Society; Mashinno-Traktornye Stantsii (Russian—Machine Tractor Stations); Middlebare Technical School; Missile Test Stand; Missile Test Station

MTSC: Middle Tennessee State College

mtt: mean transit time

MTTAGB: Machine Tool Trades Association of Great Britain

mttf: mean time to failure

mttff: mean time to first failure

mttr: mean time to repair

mtu: mobile tracking unit; mobile training unit

MTU: Michigan Technological University

MTUOP: mobile training unit out for parts

MtV: Mount Vernon

M.Tv.: Master of Television

MTV: Motor Test Vehicle

mtw: main trawl winch

mTw: tropical maritime air warmer than underlying surface

Mt W O: Mount Wilson Observatory

MTX: Morrell Tank Line (railway symbol)

Mty: Monterrey (inhabitants —Regiomontanos)

MTY: Monterrey, Mexico (airport)

mtz: motorize

mu: marijuana user; mouse unit

m μ: millimicron

m/u: mockup

MU: Marquette University; Marshall University; Mercer University; Mercy University; Mercyhurst University; Meredith University; Merrimack University; Mesa University; Messiah University; Methodist University; Miami University; Midwestern University; Millikin University

muc: mucilage

muc.: *mucilago* (Latin—mucilage)

MUC: Magee University College; Meritorious Unit Citation; Muchea, Australia (tracking station); Munich, Germany (Riem airport)

mu car: multiple-unit (railroad) car

MUCC: Michigan United Conservation Clubs

Much Ado: *Much Ado About*

Nothing

mudpie: Museum and University Data, Programs, and Information Exchange

muf: maximum usable frequency

Muh: *Muharram* (Arabic—first month of the Mohammedan year)

Muhammad: (Arabic—The Praised)—Mahomet

Muhammad Ali: Cassius Clay

Muk: Mukden

mulat: mulatto

mult: multiplication

multics: multiplexed information and computing service

multitran: multiple translation (translating one language into several target languages)

multr: multimeter

MUMMS: Marine Corps Unified Management System

mums: chrysanthemums

mun: munition

Mun: Munich

Mün: Münster

MUN: Memorial University of Newfoundland

Mund: Edmund

münde: (German—river mouth, as in Peenemunde)

muni: municipal; municipality

munit: munitions

Muñoz Marín: Luis Muñoz Marín—democratic leader and first governor of Puerto Rico

muo: myocardiopathy of unknown origin

MUO: Municipal University of Omaha

muon: mu meson

muong: (Siamese—town, as in Muong Boten, town on border of Laos and Thailand)

M.U.P.: Master of Urban Planning

mura: (Japanese—village, as in Nakamura on Shikoku Island)

MURA: Midwestern Universities Research Association

muriatic acid: hydrochloric acid (HCI)

mus: musculoskeletal; museum; music; musical; musician

Mus: Muscat; museum; music; Muslim

MUS: Magnetic Unloading System; Manned Underwater Station

Mus. Bac.: Bachelor of Music

musc: muscle; muscular

Mus. Doc.: Doctor of Music

Mus.Ed.B.: Bachelor of Music Education

Mus.Ed.D.: Doctor of Music Education

Mus.Ed.M.: Master of Music Education

museo: museography; museological; museologist; museology

MUSIC: Maryland University Sectored Isochronous Cyclotron

musicol: musicological; musicologist; musicology

muskie: muskellunge

Mus.M.: Master of Music

Musso: Mussolini

must.: manned undersea station

MUST: Medical Unit, Self-contained, Transportable

mustargen: mustard-nitrogen (poison compound)

mustn't: must not

mut: mutation

mutil: mutilate; mutilated; mutilation

mutt: muttonhead

muttnik: second Soviet satellite launched in 1957, so nicknamed because its astronaut was a mongrel dog used to test the vehicle

mutu: mutual; mutualism

muw: music wire

MUWS: Manned Underwater Station

mux: multiplex

mv: mean variation; millivolt; monochromatic vision; muzzle velocity

m v: *mezzo voce* (Italian—middle voice)

Mv: megavolt; mendelevium

MV: *Maria Vergine* (Italian—Virgin Mary)

M.V.: *Medicus Veterinarius* (Veterinary Physician)

M/V: motor vessel

mva: mean vertical acceleration; megavolt ampere; motor vehicle accident

MVA: Machinists Vise Association; Mississippi Valley Association; Missouri Valley Authority

MVAS: Milwaukee Vocational and Adult School

MVB: Martin Van Buren

MVBA: Mercado de Valores de Buenos Aires (Buenos Aires Stock Exchange)

mvbd: multiple V-belt drive

MVBL: Mississippi Valley Barge Line

mvc: manual volume control; manufacturing variation control

MVC: Military and Veterans Code

MVCC: Mount Vernon Community College

MVD: Montevideo, Uruguay (Carrasco Airport)

MVD: *Ministerstvo Vnutrenniy Delo* (Russian—Ministry of Internal Affairs)—(*q.v.—VOT*)

MVE: Metropolitan Vickers Electrical
M.V.E.: Master of Vocational Education
mvg: most valuable girl
MVHS: Mergenthaler Vocational High School
MVJC: mount Vernon Junior College
mvm: million vehicle miles
mvmt: movement
MVNP: Mesa Verde National Park
MVNWR: Monte Vista National Wildlife Refuge (Colorado)
Mvo: Montevideo
MVO: Member of the Victorian Order
mvp: most valuable player (sports)
MVP: Manpower Validation Program
MVPCB: Motor Vehicle Pollution Control Board
mvri: mixed vaccine—respiratory infections
M.V.Sc.: Master of Veterinary Science
MVSS: Motor Vehicle Safety Standard
mvt: moisture-vapor transmission
MV & THS: Manhattan Vocational and Technical High School
MVTI: Mohawk Valley Technical Institute
mvv: maximum voluntary ventilation
mw: milliwatt; molecular weight
m/w: manufacturing week
m W: *meines Wissens* (German—as far as I know)
Mw: megawatt
MW: Montgomery Ward
M-W: Merriam-Webster
MWA: Modern Woodmen of America
MWAA: Movers' and Warehousemen's Association of America
mwb: motor whale boat
MWAI: Mystery Writers of America, Incorporated
MWC: Ministry of War Communi-

cations; Motorola Western Center
MWD: Metropolitan Water District; Mutual Weapons Development
MWDP: Mutual Weapons Developemnt Program
mwg: music wire guage
MWHS: Martha Washington High School
MWIA: Medical Women's International Association
MWJC: Marjorie Webster Junior College
MWMCA: Michigan Women for Medical Control of Abortion
MWN: *Medical World News*
MWNM: Muir Woods National Monument
MWO: Marshallese Women's Organization; Midwest Oil; Modification Work Order; Mount Wilson Observatory
mwp: maximum working pressure; membrane waterproofing
mwr: mean width ratio
MWR: Morton Wildlife Refuge (New York)
MWS: Manas Wildlife Sanctuary (India); Mudamalai Wildlife Sanctuary (India)
MWSC: Midwestern Simulation Council
M.W.T.: Master of Wood Technology
mwv: maximum working voltage
mww: manual wire wrap; municipal waste water
MWZ: Manischewitz (stock exchange symbol)
mx: maxwell; multiplex
Mx: maxwell; Middlesex
MX: Mexicana de Aviación (2-letter code)
MXC: Minnesota Experimental City
mxd: mixed
Mxl: Mexicali (inhabitants—Cachanias)
mxm: maximum

MXP: Milan, Italy (Malpensa Airport)
mxr: mask index register
my.: myopia; myopic
My: Malayalam; Milo; Mylan
MY: Medinat Yisrael (State of Israel); motor yacht
Myc: Mycenaean
myco: mycobacterium
mycol: mycology
myel(s): myelocyte(s)
myg: myriagram
myl: myrialiter
mylo: mylohyoid
mym: myriameter
myo: *mayo* (Spanish—May)
myob: mind your own business
myodyn: myodynamics
myol: myology
myop: myopia
Myr: Myriopeda
mys: (Russian—cape)
Mys: Mysore
myst: mystagogue; mystagogy; mysteries; mysterious; mystery; mystic; mystical; mysticism; mystics
myth.: mythological; mythologist; mythology
mz: monozygotic
Mz: Méndez
MZ: Mail Zone; Museum of Zoology; R.H. Macy and Company (stock exchange symbol)
mzm: multiple-zone monitor
MZMA: (Russian—*Moskva Zavod Maloitrazhkaya Automobili*)—Moscow Small-Engine Car Factory producing the Moskvich auto
MZn: magnetic azimuth
MZNP: Mountain Zebra National Park (South Africa)
mzo: *marzo* (Spanish—March)
M-zone: manufacturing zone
Mzt: Mazatlán (inhabitants —Mazatlecos)
M.Z.Sc: Master of Zoological Science

N

n: nasal; national; nautical; naval; neap; negative; nerve; neuter; neutral; neutron; new; night; noon; norm; normal; noun; nuclear; number; refractive index (symbol); shear modulus of elasticity (symbol); transport num-

ber (code)
n: index of refraction (symbol); load factor (symbol); revolutions per second (symbol); rotative speed (symbol)
n/: and
n/: *nuestro* (Spanish—our)

N: International Nickel (stock exchange symbol); national; nautical; naval; Navy; Negro; neon; neutral; night; nimbus; Nippon; nitrogen; noon; normal; Norse; north; Norway (auto plaque); November—code for letter N;

nuclear-propelled vessel (naval symbol); nucleus

N: avogadro constant or number (symbol); *neer* (Dutch—down); *noord* (Dutch—north); *nord* (Danish, French, Italian, Norwegian, Swedish—north); *Nord* (German—north); *norre* (Danish—north); *norte* (Portuguese or Spanish—north); north; number of turns (symbol); rate of propeller rotation (symbol); revolutions per minute (symbol); yawing moment (symbol)

(N): nuclear-powered ship (naval symbol, as in CL[N]—nuclear-powered cruiser)

N^{14}: radioactive nitrogen

N_2: nitrogen

na: negative attitude; nicotinic acid; no account; not applicable; not appropriated; not authorized; not available; nucleic acid (NA); numerical aperture

na: *nestre ar* (Norwegian—next year)

n/a: next assembly; no account

Na: nadir; sodium (symbol)

Na^{24}: radioactive sodium

Na_2CO_3: sodium carbonate (sal soda)

NA: Narcotics Anonymous; National Academician; National Academy National Airlines; National Archives; National Association; Nautical Almanac; Naval Academy; Naval Architect; Naval Attaché; Naval Auxiliary; Naval Aviator; Netherlands Antilles (Aruba, Bonaire, Curaçao, Saba, Sint Eustatius, Sint Maarten); Neurotics Anonymous; North America; North American; Northrup Aircraft; Nurse's Aide

NA: *Nautical Almanac*

naa: neutron activation analysis; not always afloat

NAA: National Academy of Arbitrators; National Aeronautic Association; National Alumni Association; National Apple Association; National Arborist Association; National Archery Association; National Association of Accountants; National Auctioneers Association; Naval Attaché for Air; North American Aviation

NAAA: National Alliance of Athletic Associations; National Association of American Academicians; National Auto Auction Association

NAAB: National Architectural Accrediting Board

NAABI: National Association of Alcoholic Beverage Importers

NAAC: National Agricultural Advisory Commission

NAACC: National Association for American Composers and Conductors

NAACP: National Association for the Advancement of Colored People

NAADC: North American Area Defense Command

NAAFI: Navy, Army, and Air Force Institutes

NAAMM: National Association of Architectural Metal Manufacturers

NAAN: National Advertising Agency Network

NAANACM: National Association for the Advancement of Native American Composers and Musicians

NAAO: National Association of Amateur Oarsmen; Navy Area Audit Office

NAARI: National Aero- and Astronautical Research Institute

NAAS: National Agricultural Advisory Service; Naval Area Audit Service; Naval Auxiliary Air Station

NAASC: North American Aviation Science Center

NAA S & ID: North American Aviation Space and Information Division

NAAUS: National Archery Association of the United States

NAAW: National Association of Accordion Wholesalers

NAB: National Assistance Board; National Associated Businessmen; National Association of Broadcasters; Naval Advanced Base; Naval Air Base; Naval Amphibious Base

NABA: North American Benefit Association

NABACO: National Association for Bank Audit, Control, and Operation

NABC: National Association of Boys' Clubs

NABD: North American Band Directors

NABDC: National Association of Blueprint and Diazotype Coaters

NABE: National Association of Book Editors

NABET: National Association of Broadcast Employees and Technicians

NABIM: National Association of Band Instrument Manufacturers

NABISCO: National Biscuit Company

nabor: neighbor

Nabrico: Nashville Bridge Company

NABRT: National Association for Better Radio and Television

NABS: National Association of Barber Schools; National Association of Black Students; nuclear-armed bombardment satellite

NABSP: National Association of Blue Shield Plans

NABT: National Association of Biology Teachers

NABTE: National Association for Business Teacher Education

nabu: non-adjusting ballup (unsolvable confusion)

nac: nacelle

NAC: National Achievement Clubs; National Agency Check; National Airways Corporation (New Zealand); National Americanism Commission (American Legion); National Arts Club; National Association of Cemeteries; National Association of Chiropodists; National Association of Coroners; National Association of Counties; National Aviation Club; National Aviation Corporation; National Can Corporation (stock exchange symbol); Naval Academy; Naval Air Center; Naval Aircraftman; Non-Airline Carrier; North Atlantic Council; Northeast Air Command; Norwegian-American Council

NACA: National Advisory Committee for National Aeronautics; National Agricultural Chemicals Association; National Air Carrier Association; National Armored Car Association; National Association of Cost Accountants; National Association of County Administrators

NACATTS: North American Clear-Air Turbulence-Tracking System

NACB: National Association of Convention Bureaus

NACCAM: National Coordinating Committee for Aviation Meteorology

NACCD: National Advisory Commission on Civil Disorders

NACDR: National Association of College Deans and Registrars

NACE: National Association of Corrosion Engineers

NACEL: Naval Air Crew Equipment Laboratory

NACFI: North American Council

on Fishery Investigations

Nachf: *Nachfolger* (German— successor)

nachm: *nachmittags* (German—afternoon; p.m.)

NACHM: National Advisory Committee on Health Manpower

Nachr: *Nachrichten* (German— bulletin)

Nachtr: *Nachtrag* (German—appendix; supplement)

NACIMFP: National Advisory Council on International Monetary and Financial Problems

NaCl: sodium chloride (salt)

NACL: National Advisory Commission on Libraries

NACLIS: National Commission on Libraries and Information Science

NACM: National Association of Chain Manufacturers; National Association of Credit Management

naco: night-alarm cutoff

NACO: National Arts Centre Orchestra (Ottawa); National Association of Counties

NACOA: National Advisory Committee on Oceans and Atmosphere

NACOC: National Arts Centre Orchestra of Canada

NACOM: National Communications

NACS: National Association of College Stores; National Association of Cosmetology Schools

NACTA: National Association of Colleges and Teachers of Agriculture

NACUA: National Association of College and University Administrators; National Association of College and University Attorneys

NACUBO: National Association of College and University Business Office Associations

NACUFS: National Association of College and University Food Services

NACUSS: National Association of College and University Summer Sessions

NACWPI: National Association of College Wind and Percussion Instruments

nad: nadir (lowest point); no appreciable difference; no appreciable disease; nothing abnormal discovered; not on active duty

NAD: National Academy of Design; National Association of the Deaf; Naval Air Depot; Naval Air Division; Naval Ammuni-

tion Depot; North Atlantic Division

NADA: National Association of Dealers in Antiques; National Automobile Dealers Association

NADAR: North American Data Airborn Recorder

NADB: National Aerometric Data Bank

NADC: National Anti-Dumping Committee; Naval Air Development Center

NaDefCol: Nato Defense College

NADEM: National Association of Dairy Equipment Manufacturers

NaDevCen: Naval Air Development Center

NADGE: Nato Air Defense Ground Environment

NADGEMO: Nato Air Defense Ground Environment Management Office

nadi: (Indian—creek; river; stream, as in Mahanadi, southwest of Calcutta)

NADL: National Association of Dental Laboratories; Navy Authorized Data List

NADO: Navy Accounts Disbursing Office

NADSA: National Association of Dramatic and Speech Arts

NAE: National Academy of Education; National Academy of Engineering; National Association of Evangelicals

NAEA: National Art Education Association

NAEB: National Association of Educational Broadcasters

NAEBM: National Association of Engine and Boat Manufacturers

NAEC: National Aviation Education Council

NAEd: National Academy of Education

NAEF: Naval Air Engineering Facility

NAES: National Association of Educational Secretaries; National Association of Episcopal Schools

NAEYC: National Association for the Education of Young Children

naf: nonappropriated funds

NAF: National Amputation Foundation; National Arts Foundation; Naval Aircraft Factory; Naval Air Facility; Netherland-America Foundation; Northern Attack Force

NAFA: National Academy of Foreign Affairs; National Association of Fleet Administrators

NAFAG: NATO Air Force Arma-

ments Group

NAFB: National Association of Franchised Businessmen

NAFBRAT: National Association for Better Radio and Television

NAFC: National Association of Food Chains

NAFCA: North American Family Campers Association

NAFEC: National Aviation Facilities Experimental Center

NAFFBIA: National Association of Former FBI Agents

NAFI: Naval Avionics Facility

NAFM: National Armed Forces Museum

NAFMB: National Association of FM Broadcasters

N Afr: North Africa

NAFS: National Association of Foot Specialists

NAFSA: National Association of Foreign Student Advisers; National Association of Foreign Student Affairs

NAFTA: North Atlantic Free Trade Area (Canada, United Kingdom, United States)

Nag: Nagasaki; Nagoya

NAG: National Action Group; National Association of Gag Writers; National Association of Gardeners; Naval Advisory Group; Naval Applications Group (USN); Negro Actors Guild

NA & G: Norgulf Lines (North Atlantic & Gulf)

NAGC: National Association for Gifted Children

NAGE: National Association of Government Employees

NAGM: National Association of Glue Manufacturers

Nagp: Nagpur

NAGT: National Association of Geology Teachers

nagy: (Hungarian—big; great; large, as in Nagykörös)

Nah: The Book of Nahum

NAHA: National Association of Handwriting Analysts

Nahal: *Na'or Halutsi Lohem* (Hebrew—Fighting Pioneer Youth) —youngest section of the Israeli army

NAHB: National Association of Home Builders

NAHC: National Advisory Health Council

NAHSA: National Association of Hearing and Speech Agencies

NAHT: National Association of Head Teachers

nai: no action indicated; no address instruction

NAI: National Agricultural Institute

NAIA: National Association of Insurance Agents; National Association of Intercollegiate Athletics

NAIC: National Association of Insurance Commissioners

NAIEC: National Association for Industry-Education Cooperation

NAIL: Neurotics Anonymous International Liaison

NAILSC: Naval Air Integrated Logistics Support Center

naiop: navigational aids inoperative for parts

NAIRE: National Association of Internal Revenue Employees

Nairns: Nairnshire

NAIS: National Association of Independent Schools

NAJC: Northwest Alabama Junior College

NAJE: National Association of Jazz Education

nak: negative knowledge

náka: [Japanese—middle, as in Náka Iwo (Iwo Jima)]

nakl: naklad (Polish—edition; publisher), *nakladatel* (Czech—edition; publisher)

NAL: National Agricultural Library (US Department of Agriculture); National Airlines; Norwegian America Line

NALC: National Association of Letter Carriers; National Association of Litho Clubs

NALCO: Newfoundland and Labrador Corporation

NALDEF: Native American Legal Defense and Education Foundation

NALGO: National and Local Government Officers Association

NALS: National Association of Legal Secretaries

Nam: (military slang—Vietnam); Namibia (South-West Africa)

N Am: North America

NAM: National Air Museum (Smithsonian Institution); National Association of Manufacturers; Naval Aircraft Modification; Newspaper Association Managers; North America(n)

NAM: Nederlandsche Aluminium Maatschappij (Netherlands Aluminum Company)

NAMA: New Amsterdam Musical Association; North American Maritime Agencies

NAMBO: National Association of Motor Bus Operators

NAMC: Naval Air Materiel Center; Naval Air Materiel Command

NAMCC: National Association of Mutual Casualty Companies

NAMCO: Naval and Mechanical Company

NAMESU: National Association of Music Executives in State Universities

NAMF: National Association of Metal Finishers

NAMFI: NATO Missile Firing Installation

NAMH: National Association for Mental Health; Norwegian-American Historical Museum

NAMIA: National Association of Mutual Insurance Agents

Namib: Namibia or South-West Africa

Namibia: (Bantu—South-West Africa)

NAMIC: National Association of Mutual Insurance Companies

NAMilCom: North Atlantic Military Committee

naml: namligen (Swedish—namely)—viz.

NAMM: National Association of Music Merchants

NAMMW: National Association of Musical Merchandise Wholesalers

NAMOA: National Association of Miscellaneous Ornamental and Architectural Products Contractors

NAMOS: National Art Museum of Sport

NAMP: National Association of Married Priests

namppf: nautical air miles per pound of fuel

NAMT: National Association for Music Therapy

NAMTC: Naval Air Missile Test Center

NAMTRADET: Naval Air Maintenance Detachment

n.a.n.: nisi aliter notetur (Latin —unless it is otherwise noted)

Nan: Anna; Nancy; Nanking

NAN: Nandi, Fiji Islands (airport)

NANA: National Advertising News Association; North American Newspaper Alliance

NANAC: National Aviation Noise Abatement Council

NANE: National Association for Nursery Education

nano: 10^{-9}

NANWEP: Navy Numerical Weather Problems (USN)

NAO: Noise Abatement Office

NAOA: Navy Officers Accounts Office

NAOC: Nigerian Agip Oil Company

NaOH: sodium hydroxide (caustic soda)

NAOT: National Association of Organ Teachers

NAOTS: Naval Aviation Ordnance Test Station

nap.: knapsack; napalm (naphthalene and coconut oil—jellied gasoline incendiary mixture); naphtha; naval aviation pilot (NAP); non-agency purchase; not at present

Nap: Naples; Napoleon; Napoleonic

NAP: Naples, Italy (airport); Narragansett Pier (railroad); National Association of Parliamentarians; National Association of Postmasters; National Association of Publishers; Naval Aviation Pilot

NAP: Nomina Anatomica, Paris

NAPA: National Asphalt Paving Association; National Association of Performing Artists; National Association of Purchasing Agents

NAPAC: National Program for Acquisitions and Cataloging

napalm: naphthene palmitate (napththalene plus coconut oil —jellied gasoline used in flame-throwers)

NAPBL: National Association of Professional Baseball Leagues

NAPCA: National Air Pollution Control Administration

NAPE: National Alliance of Postal Employees; National Association of Port Employees; National Association of Power Engineers

NAPECW: National Association for Physical Education of College Women

NAPFE: National Alliance of Postal and Federal Employees

NAPH: National Association of Professors of Hebrew

NAPL: National Association of Photo Lithographers

NAPM: National Association of Punch Manufacturers

NAPNES: National Association for Practical Nurse Education and Service

Napoleon: Napoleon Bonaparte

na pr: na priklad (Czech—for example)

NAPR: National Association for Pastoral Renewal

NAPS: National Alliance of Postal Supervisors

NAPSAE: National Association for Public School Adult Education

NAPT: National Association of Physical Therapists; National Association for the Prevention of

Tuberculosis
NAPTC: Naval Air Propulsion Test Center
NAPVD: National Association for the Prevention of Venereal Disease
nar: narrow
Nar: Narragansett
NAR: North American Rockwell; North American Royalties; Northern Alberta Railway
NARAD: Navy Research and Development
NARAS: National Academy of Recording Arts and Sciences
NARB: National Advertising Review Board
narc: narcotic
NARC: National Agricultural Research Center; National Archives and Records Service; National Association for Retarded Children
narcos: narcotics; narcotics police officers
nard: spikenard
NARD: National Association of Regimental Drummers
NARDIC: Naval Research and Development Information Center
NAREB: National Association of Real Estate Boards; National Association of Real Estate Brokers
NARF: Naval Air Rework Facility; Nuclear Aircraft Research Facility
NARFE: National Association of Retired Federal Employees
NARI: National Atmospheric Research Institute
NARM: National Association of Relay Manufacturers
NARMCO: National Research and Manufacturing Company
NAROCTESTSTA: Naval Air Rocket Test Station
NARP: National Association of Railroad Passengers
NARS: National Archives and Records Service; Non-Affiliated Reserve Section
NARST: National Association for Research in Science Teaching
NARTB: National Association of Radio and Television Broadcasters
NARTS: Naval Air Rocket Test Station
NARTU: Naval Air Reserve Training Unit
NARVRE: National Association of Retired and Veteran Railroad Employees
nas: nasal; nasalis; nasology

n-a-s: no added salt
NAS: Nassau, Bahamas (airport); National Academy of Sciences; National Advocates Society; National Aerospace Standard(s); National Aircraft Standard(s); National Airspace System; National Association of Sanitarians; National Association of Stevedores; National Association of Supervisors; National Audubon Society; Naval Air Station; Nursing Auxiliary Service
N A S: Noise Abatement Society
NˢᵃSᵃ: Nuestra Señora (Spanish—Our Lady)
NASA: National Acoustical Suppliers Association; National Aeronautics and Space Administration; National Appliance Service Association; National Association of Securities Administrators; National Association of Schools of Art; National Automobile Salesmen's Association
NASAA: National Aeronautics and Space Administration Act
NASA-CF: NASA—Cocoa Beach, Florida
NASA-CO: NASA—Cleveland, Ohio
NASA-EC: NASA—Edwards, California
NASA-GM: NASA—Greenbelt, Maryland
NASA-HA: NASA—Huntsville, Alabama
NASA-HT: NASA—Houston, Texas
Nasakom: Nationalist-Communist
NASA-LV: NASA—Langley Field, Virginia
NASA-MC: NASA—Moffett Field, California
NASAO: National Association of State Aviation Officials
NASA-SC: NASA—Santa Monica, California
NASBE: National Association of State Boards of Education
NASC: National Aeronautics and Space Council; National Aircraft Standards Committee; National Association of Student Councils; NATO Supply Center; North American Supply Council
NASCAR: National Association of Sports Car Racing; National Association for Stock Car Advancement and Research
NASCom: Naval Air Systems Command
NASCOM: NASA's tracking network, also performing command and control functions

NASD: Naval Aviation Supply Depot
NASDAQS: National Association of Security Dealers Automated Quotation System
nase: neutral atom space engine (sputtering engine)
NASE: National Association of Steel Exporters
NASF: National Association of State Foresters
NASFAA: National Association of Student Financial Aid Administrators
NAS & FCA: National Automatic Sprinkler and Fire Control Association
NAS-GB: Noise Abatement Society of Great Britain
Nash: Nashville
NASIS: National Association for State Information Systems
NASL: North American Soccer League
NASM: National Air and Space Museum (Smithsonian); National Association of Schools of Music; Naval Aviation School of Medicine
NASM: *Nederlandsche-Amerikaansche Stoomvaart Maatschappij* (Holland-American Line)
NASN: National Air Sampling Network
NASNI: Naval Air Station, North Island (Halsey Field, San Diego, California)
NAS-NRC: National Academy of Science—National Research Council
NASP: National Airport Systems Plan; Negro Anglo-Saxon Protestant
Nas Par: *Nasionale Party* (Afrikaans—National Party)—South Africa's Apartheid party
Nas Pers: *Nasionale Pers* (Afrikaans—National Press)—publisher of apartheid books and periodicals
NASRC: National Association of State Racing Commissioners
NASS: National Association of School Superintendents; National Association of Summer Sessions
NASSC: National Alliance on Shaping Safer Cities
NASSCO: National Steel and Shipbuilding Company
NASSO: National Association of Socialist Students' Organizations
NASSP: National Association of Secondary-School Principals
NASSR: Nakhichevan Autonomous

Soviet Socialist Republic

NASTBD: National Association of State Text Book Directors

NASTI: Naval Air Station, Terminal Island

NASU: National Adult School Union

NASULGC: National Association of State Universities and Land-Grant Colleges

NASW: National Association of Science Writers; National Association of Social Workers

nat: nation; national; nationalist; native; natural; naturalist; naturalization; naturalize(d); nature

Nat: Nathan; National(ist); natural(ized)

NAT: National Air Transport

NATA: National Association of Tax Accountants; National Association of Tax Administrators; National Association of Transportation Advertisers; National Athletic Trainers Association; National Automated Transportation Association; National Aviation Trades Association; North Atlantic Treaty Alliance

NATAPROBU: National Association of Professional Bureaucrats

Nat Arc: National Archives

NATAS: National Academy of Television Arts and Sciences

Nat Assn: National Association

NATB: National Automobile Theft Bureau; Naval Air Training Base

NATC: National Air Transportation Conferences; Naval Air Training Command

natch: naturally (slang)

NATCO: National Automatic Tool Company; National Tank Company

Nate: Nathan(iel)

Nath B: Nathaniel Bowditch

nat hist: natural history

Nathl: Nathaniel

nation.: nationality

NATIONAL: National Cash Register

natl: national

N Atl Cur: North Atlantic Current

Nat Lib: National Library of Canada (Ottawa)

Nat Mon: National Monument

Nat Mus: Natal Museum; National Museum

nato: no action—talk only

NATO: National Association of Taxicab Owners; National Association of Trailer Owners; National Association of Travel Organizations; North Atlantic Treaty Organization (Belgium, Canada, Denmark, France, Greece, Iceland, Italy, Luxembourg, Netherlands, Norway, Portugal, Turkey, United Kingdom, United States, West Germany)

NATO-AGARD: North Atlantic Treaty Organization—Advisory Group for Aeronautical Research and Development

NATO-ELLA: North Atlantic Treaty Organization—European Long Lines Agency

NATO-LRSS: North Atlantic Treaty Organization—Long-Range Scientific Studies

NATO-RDPP: North Atlantic Treaty Organization—Research and Development Production Program

NATOs: National Association of Theatre Owners

NATPE: National Association of Television Program Executives

Nat Pk: National Park

Nat Rev: *National Review*

Nats: Nationalists; naturalized citizens

NATS: National Association of Teachers of Singing; Naval Air Test Station; Naval Air Transport Service

Nat Sci: Natural Science(s)

NATSOPA: National Society of Operative Printers and Assistants

NATTC: National Tank Truck Carriers

NATTS: Naval Air Turbine Test Station

Nat U: Nations Unies (French—United Nations)

natur: naturalist

NATUSA: North African Theater of Operations

NAU: Naval Administrative Unit

NAUA: National Aircraft Underwriters' Association

naut: nautical

nav: naval; navigable; navigate; navigation; navigational; navigator

Nav: Navaho; naval; Navarra; Navarre

NAVA: National Audio-Visual Association; North American Vexillological Association

NAVAERORECOVF: Naval Aerospace Recovery Facility

navaid(s): navigation aid(s)

NAVAIR: Naval Air (Systems Command)

NAVAIRLANT: Naval Air Forces, Atlantic

NAVAIRPAC: Naval Air Forces, Pacific

NAVAIRREWORKF: Naval Air Rework Facility

NAVAIRSYSCOM: Naval Air Systems Command

Nav.Arch.: Naval Architect

NAVBASE: Naval Base

nav brz: naval bronze

NavCad: Naval Cadet

NAVCENT: Allied Naval Forces, Central Europe

NavCm: navigation countermeasures and deception

Nav.Const.: Naval Constructor

navdac: navigation data assimilation computer

NAVDAC: Navigation Data Assimilation Center

Nav.E.: Naval Engineer

NAVELEX: Naval Electronic (Systems Command)

NAVEOFAC: Naval Explosive Ordnance Disposal Facility

NAVFE: Naval Forces Far East

NAVFEC: Naval Facilities

NAVFECENGCOM: Naval Facilities Engineering Command

NAVFOR: Naval Forces

NAVFORJAP: Naval Air Forces, Japan

NAVFORKOR: Naval Air Forces, Korea

NAVH: National Aid to Visually Handicapped

navicert(s): navigation certificate(s)

navig: navigation

NAVLIS: Navy Logistics Information System

NAVMAR: Naval Forces, Marianas

NAVMEDIS: Naval Medical Information System

NavMisCen: Naval Missile Center

NAVNORTH: Allied Naval Forces, Northern Europe

NavOceanO: Naval Oceanographic Office (USN)

NAVOCS: Naval Officer Candidate School

NAVORDSYSCOM: Naval Ordnance Systems Command

NAVPERSRANDLAB: Naval Personnel Research and Development Laboratory

NAVPORCO: Naval Port Control Officer

NAVPRO: Naval Plant Representative Office(r)

navsat: navigational satellite

NAVSEC: Naval Ship Engineering Center

NavShipyd: Naval Shipyard

NAVSMO: Navigation Satellite Management Office

NAVSPASUR: Naval Space Surveillance (USN)

NAVSTA: Naval Station

NAVSUPORANT: Naval Support Forces, Antarctica

NAVTRACEN: Naval Training Center

NAVTRADEVCEN: Naval Training Device Center

NAVUWSEC: Naval Underwater Weapons Systems Engineering Center

NAVWAG: Naval Warfare Analysis Group

NAW: National Association of Wholesalers; National Association for Women; North African Waters

NAWA: National Association of Women Artists

NAWAS: National Air Warning Service

NAWDC: National Association of Women Deans and Counselors

NAWF: North American Wildlife Foundation

NAWM: National Association of Wool Manufacturers

NAWPA: North American Water and Power Alliance

NAWS: National Aviation Weather System

Naxas: Naxalites (Maoist extremists)

Nay: Nayarit

NAYC: National Association of Youth Clubs

NAYRU: North American Yacht Racing Union

Nazi: adherent of the former National Socialist German Workers' Party *(Nationalsozialistische Partei)*

nb: narrow band; no bias (relay)

n.b.: *nota bene* (Latin—note well)

Nb: nimbus; niobium (formerly columbium)

Nb⁹⁴: radioactive niobium

NB: Navy Band; New Brunswick; North Borneo

NBA: National Band Association; National Bankers Association; National Banking Association; National Bar Association; National Basketball Association; National Boat Association; National Bowling Association; National Boxing Association; National Button Association

NBAA: National Business Aircraft Association

N balance: nitrogen balance

NBBB: National Better Business Bureau

NBBU: New Brunswick Board of Underwriters

NBC: National Ballet of Canada; National Baseball Congress; National Beagle Club; National

Beef Council; National Book Committee; National Bowling Council; National Braille Club; National Broadcasting Corporation; Navy Beach Commando; Nigerian Broadcasting Corporation

NB & C: Norfolk, Baltimore and Carolina Line

NBD: National Bank of Detroit

NBDA: National Bicycle Dealers Association

NB & DA: National Barrel & Drum Association

NBE: National Bank Examiner(s)

NBEA: National Business Education Association

NBER: National Bureau of Economic Research; National Bureau of Engineering Registration

NBET: National Business Entrance Test(s)

NBF: National Boating Federation

NB & FAA: National Burglar and Fire Alarm Association

nbfm: narrow-band frequency modulation

NBFU: National Board of Fire Underwriters; Newfoundland Board of Fire Underwriters

nbg: no bloody good

NBGC: National Ballet Guild of Canada

NBH: National Bellas Hess

NBHA: National Builders Hardware Association

nbi: no bone(y) injury

NBI: Nattianiel Branden Institute

NBI: Norges Byggforskninginstitutt (Norwegian Building Institute)

NBIT: New Bedford Institute of Technology

NBL: National Basketball League; National Book League

NBL & P: National Bureau for Lathing and Plastering

nbm: nothing by mouth

NBME: National Board of Medical Examiners

NBMG: Navigation Bombing and Missile Guidance System

NBMV & NSL: New Bedford, Martha's Vineyard, and Nantucket Steamship Line

NBO: Nairobi, Kenya (airport); Navy Bureau of Ordnance

n-bomb: neutron bomb

nbp: normal boiling point

NBP: National Business Publications

NBPI: National Board for Prices and Income

NBPRP: National Board for the Promotion of Rifle Practice

NBR: National Bison Range (Montana)

nbre: noviembre (Spanish—November)

NBRF: National Biomedical Research Foundation

NBRPC: New Brunswick Research and Productivity Council

NBS: National Bureau of Standards; New British Standard

NBSA: National Bank of South Africa; Netherlands Bank of South Africa

NBSBL: National Bureau of Standards Boulder Laboratory

NBT: National Book Trust (India)

NBTA: National Baton Twirlers Association; National Business Teachers Association

NBTC: New Brunswick Teachers College

NBTS: National Blood Transfusion Service

n butt: national buttress (thread)

nbw: noise bandwidth

Nby: Newbury

nc: national coarse (thread); nitrocellulose; no charge; no connection; noise criteria; normally closed; nuclear capability; numerical control(s)

nc: non chiffre (French—unnumbered)

n-c: numerical control (automation)

n/c: numerical control (automation)

nC: na Christus (Dutch—after Christ)

NC: Napa College; Nashville, Chattanooga & St. Louis (railroad); Nasson College; Natchez College; National Coarse (screw threads); National Cash Register (stock exchange symbol); Newark College; Newberry College; New Caledonia; Newcomb College; Nicholls College; Nichols College; Norfolk College; Norman College; North Carolina; North Carolinian; Northland College; Northwestern College; Nuclear Congress; Nurse Corps

nca: neurocirculatory asthenia

NCA: National Camping Association; National Canners Association; National Capital Award; National Cashmere Association; National Charcoal Association; National Cheerleaders Association; National Chiropractic Association; National Civic Association; National Club Association; National Coal Association; National Coffee Association; National Commission on Accrediting; National Confectioners Association; National Constructors Association; National Contesters Association; National Costumers Association; National Council on Alcoholism; National Council on the Arts; National Coursing Association; National Cranberry Association; National Creameries Association; National Credit Association; Naval Communications Annex; Navy Contract Administrator; Ngorongoro Conservation Area (Tanzania); North Central Airlines; Northern Consolidated Airlines

NCAA: National Collegiate Athletic Association

NCAAA: National Center of Afro-American Artists

NCAB: National Cancer Advisory Board

NCAB: *National Cyclopedia of American Biography*

NCAE: National Center for Audio Experimentation; National College of Agricultural Engineering

NCAI: National Congress of American Indians

NCANH: National Council for the Accreditation of Nursing Homes

NCAR: National Center for Atmospheric Research

NCASF: National Council of American-Soviet Friendship

NCAT: Northampton College of Advanced Technology

ncb: new crime buffer; nickel-cadmium battery

NCB: National Cargo Bureau; National Coal Board; National Conservation Bureau

NCBA: Northern California Booksellers Association

NCC: Nassau Community College; National Carloading Corporation; National Castings Council; National Computer Center; National Conference on Citizenship; National Container Committee; National Cotton Council; National Council of Churches of Christ in the USA; National Cultural Center; Newhouse Communications Center (University of Syracuse); Newspaper Comics Council; Noise Control Committee; NORAD Control Center; Northwest Community College

NCCA: National Coil Coaters Association

NCCAS: National Center of Communication Arts and Sciences

NCCC: Niagara County Community College

NCCCC: Navy Command, Control, and Communications Center

NCCCLC: Naval Command Control Communications Laboratory Center (formerly NEL—Navy Electronics Laboratory)

NCCCUSA: National Council of the Churches of Christ in the U.S.A.

NCCD: National Council on Crime and Delinquency

NCCF: National Committee to Combat Fascism (Black Panther front); National Commission on Consumer Finance

NCCJ: National Conference of Christians and Jews

NCCPA: National Council of College Publications Advisers

NCCPV: National Commission on the Causes and Prevention of Violence

NCCR: National Council for Civic Responsibility

NCCY: National Council of Catholic Youth

NCDA: National Center for Drug Analysis

NCDAI: National Clearinghouse for Drug Abuse Information

NCDC: National Communicable Disease Center

NCDS: National Center for Dispute Settlement (American Arbitration Association)

NCE: Newark College of Engineering; Nice, France (Côte d'Azur airport)

NCEA: National Catholic Educational Association; North Carolina Education Association

NCEC: National Committee for an Effective Congress

NCEI: National Commission on Emerging Institutions

NCEL: Naval Civil Engineering Laboratory

NCER: National Center for Earthquake Research

NCES: National Center for Educational Statistics

NCET: National Council for Educational Technology

ncf: nerve cell food

NCF: National Consumer Federation

NCFA: National Commission of Fine Arts

NCFDA: National Council on Federal Disaster Assistance

NCFIRB: North Carolina Fire Insurance Rating Bureau

NCFM: National Commission on Food Marketing

NCFPC: National Center for Fish Protein Concentrate

NCFR: National Council on Family Relations

NCFT: National College of Food Technology

NCG: National Council for the Gifted; National Cylinder Gas (division of Chemotron)

NCGE: National Council for Geographic Education

NCH: National Children's Home

NCHA: National Campers and Hikers Association; National Capital Housing Authority

n chg: normal charge

NCHMT: National Capitol Historical Museum of Transportation

NCHP: Nouvelle Compagnie Havraise Peninsulaire (de Navigation) (Havre Peninsula Navigation Line)

n Chr: *nach Christus* (German—after Christ; A.D.)

NCHS: National Center for Health Statistics

NCHSR & D: National Center for Health Services Research and Development (HEW)

NCHVRFE: National College for Heating, Ventilating, Refrigeration, and Fan Engineering

nci: napthalene-creosote-iodiform (lice-control powder); no-cost item

NCI: National Cancer Institute; National Casing Institute; National Cheese Institute; Naval Cost Inspection; Naval Cost Inspector

NCIC: National Crime Information Center

NCIO: National Council on Indian Opportunity

NCISC: Naval Counterintelligence Support Center

NCJSC: National Criminal Justice Statistics Center

NCL: National Central Library; National Chemical Laboratory; National Consumers League; National Culture League

NCLIS: National Commission on Libraries and Information Science

ncm: non-corrosive metal; non-crew member

NCMC: NORAD Cheyenne Mountain Complex

NCMDA: National Commission on Marijuana and Drug Abuse

NCME: National Council on Measurements in Education

NCMEA: National Catholic Music Educators Association

NCMH: National Committee on Maternal Health; National Committee for Mental Hygiene

NCMHE: National Clearinghouse

for Mental Health Education

NCMLB: National Council of Mailing List Brokers

NCN: New Caledonian Nickel

NCNA: National Council on Noise Abatement; New China News Agency (mainland China)

NCNC: National Council of Nigeria and the Cameroons

NCNP: National Conference for New Politics (coalition of communist, left socialist, and militant revolutionary elements comprising the New Left); North Cascades National Park (Washington)

NCO: Noncommissioned Officer

NCOA: National Council on the Aging

NCOIC: Noncommissioned Officer in Charge

N/COM: Navy/Chief of Naval Operations

NCOMP: National Catholic Office for Motion Pictures

NCOR: National Committee on Oceanographic Research

ncp: nitrogen charge panel

NCP: National Capital Parks; Naviera Chilena del Pacífico (Chilean Pacific Line)

NCPC: National Capital Planning Commission; Northern Canada Power Commission

NCPI: National Clay Pipe Institute; Navy Civilian Personnel Instructions

NCPRV: National Council of Puerto Rican Volunteers

NCPS: National Commission on Product Safety

NCPT: National Congress of Parents and Teachers

NCPTWA: National Clearinghouse for Periodical Title Word Abbreviations

NCQR: National Council for Quality and Reliability

ncr: natural circulation reactor; no calibration required

NCR: National Cash Register; National Council of Reconciliation (in Vietnam)

NCRE: Naval Construction Research Establishment

NCRFCL: National Commission on Reform of Federal Criminal Laws

NCRFP: National Council for a Responsible Firearms Policy

NCRL: National Chemical Research Laboratory

NCRP: National Committee on Radiation Protection

NCRS: National Committee for Rural Schools

NCRT: National College of Rubber Technology

NCS: National Cartoonists Society; National Cemetery System; National Chrysanthemum Society; National Communications System; Naval Communication Station; Net Control Station; Numerical Control Society

NCSA: National Carl Schurz Association; National Council of Seamen's Agencies; National Crushed Stone Association; National Customs Service Association; North Coast of South America

NCSBEE: National Council of State Boards of Engineering Examiners

NCSC: National Council of Senior Citizens

NCSE: National Commission on Safety Education

NCSF: National College Student Foundation

NCSGC: National Council of State Garden Clubs

NCSH: National Clearinghouse for Smoking and Health

NCSI: National Council for Stream Improvement

NCSL: National Civil Service League; National Conference of Standards Laboratories; Naval Code and Signal Laboratory

NCSO: Naval Control of Shipping Office(r); North Carolina Symphony Orchestra

NCSPA: North Carolina State Ports Authority

NCSPS: National Committee for the Support of Public Schools

NCSS: National Center for Social Statistics; National Council for Social Studies

NCSSA: Naval Command Systems Support Activity

NCSSC: Naval Command Systems Support Center

NCSSFL: National Council of State Supervisors of Foreign Languages

NCSTAS: National Council of Scientific and Technical Art Societies

NC & ST L: Nashville, Chattanooga & St. Louis (railroad)

NCSWCL: National Commission on State Workmen's Compensation Laws

NCSWD: National Center for Solid Waste Disposal

NCSWR: National Conference on Solid Waste Research

NCT: National Culture Trust (India)

NCRT: National College of Rubber Technology

n/cta: *nuestra cuenta* (Spanish —our account)

NCTA: National Capital Transport Agency

NCTAEP: National Committee on Technology, Automation, and Economic Progress

NCTC: National Collection of Type Cultures

NCTE: National Council of Teachers of English

NCTJ: National Council for the Training of Journalists

NCTM: National Council of Teachers of Mathematics

NCTR: National Center for Toxicological Research

NCTS: National Council of Technical Schools

ncu: nitrogen control unit

NCUA: National Credit Union Administration; National Credit Union Association

ncup: no commission until paid

NCUPUFUB: National Clean-Up, Paint-Up, Fix-Up Bureau

NCUSIF: National Credit Union Share Insurance Fund

NCUTLO: National Committee on Uniform Traffic Laws and Ordinances

ncv: no commercial value

NCVA: National Center(s) for Volunteer Action

NCWC: National Catholic Welfare Conference

NCWUS: National Council of Women of the U.S.

NCY: National Cylinder Gas (stock-exchange symbol)

NCYC: National Council of Yacht Clubs

nd: national debt; next day; no date; no decision; no deed; no delay; no drawing; not dated; not deeded; not drawn; nothing doing; nuclear detonation

n-d: non-drying

n/d: neutral density

Nd: neodymium; refractive index (symbol)

ND: National Dairy Products (stock exchange symbol); Naval District; Navy Department; New Drugs; North Dakota; Notre Dame

N.D.: Doctor of Naturopathy

nda: new drug application

NDA: National Dental Association

NDAA: National District Attorneys Association

NDAC: National Defense Advisory Commission

N Dak: North Dakota; North Dakotan

ndb: non-directional beacon

NDB: Navy Department Bulletin

NDBS: National Data Buoy System

NDC: National Dairy Council; National Defense Contribution; National Defense Corps; National Democratic Club; National Development Corporation; Naval Dental Clinic; Nuclear Development Corporation

NDD: National Diploma in Dairying

NDEA: National Defense Education Act

NDER: National Defense Executive Reserve

ndf: nacelle drag efficiency factor

NDG: National Dance Guild

NDH: Delhi, India (airport; National diploma in Health

NDHA: National District Heating Association

NDHS: New Dorp High School

ndi: numerical designation index

Ndl: *Nederland* (Dutch—The Netherlands)

NDL: Nuclear Defense Laboratory

NDLB: National Dock Labour Board

NDP: National Dairy Products; New Democratic Party (Canada)

NDP: *Nationaldemokratische Partei Deutschlands* (Germany's National-Democratic Party)—neo-Nazi oriented

NDPA: National Democratic Party of Alabama

NDPBC: National Duck Pin Bowling Congress

NDR: *Norddeutscher Rundfunk* (North German Radio)

NDRC: National Defense Research Committee

NDRI: Naval Dental Research Institute

ndro: nondestructive readout

nds (NDS): nuclear detection satellite

NDSF: North Dakota School of Forestry

NDSM: National Defense Security Medal

NDSSS: North Dakota State School of Science

ndt: nondestructive testing

NDT: Ferrocarril Nacional de Tehuantepec (National Railroad of Tehuantepec—symbol); National Drivers' Test; Newfoundland Daylight Time

NDTA: National Defense Transportation Association

NDTC: Nottingham and District Technical College

ne: new edition; not enlarged

ne: *non ebarbe* (French—untrimmed)

n/e: no effects

Ne: neon; Nepal; Nepalese; Netherlander; Netherlands

NE: National Emergency; Naval Engineer(ing); new edition; New England(er); northeast; Northeast Airlines (2-letter coding); Nuclear Engineer(ing)

N.E.: Nuclear Engineer

ne/6m: new edition in preparation, expected in 6 months (for example)

NEA: National Education Association; National Endowment for the Arts; New England Aquarium (Boston); Northeast Airlines

N.E.A.: Newspaper Enterprise Association

NEACSS: New England Association of Colleges and Secondary Schools

NEAFC: Northeast Atlantic Fisheries Commission

NEAP: National Assessment of Educational Progress

NEAR: National Emergency Alarm Repeater

NEARA: New England Antiquities Research Association

NEATE: New England Association of Teachers of English

neb: *nebbisch* (Yiddish—colorless; plain; retiring; socially ill at ease)

NEB: National Energy Board (Canada)

nebbie: (underground slang—nembutal)

NEBHE: New England Board of Higher Education

Nebr: Nebraska; Nebraskan

nebuchad: nebuchadnezzar (16-quart-capacity champagne bottle)

nebul.: *nebula* (Latin—spray) —nebulizer

nec: necessary; not elsewhere classified

NEC: National Economic Council; National Egg Council; National Electrical Code; National Exchange Club; New England Conservatory of Music; New England Council

NECA: National Electrical Contractors' Association; Near East College Association

NECCO: New England Confectionary Company

NECM: New England Conservatory of Music

NECMD: Newark Contract Management District

NECP: New England College of Pharmacy

necr: necrosis

necrol: necrology

NECS: National Electrical Code Standards

ned: normal equivalent deviation

Ned: Edmund; Edward; Edwin

NED: *New English Dictionary (Oxford English Dictionary)*

NEDA: National Economic Development Association

neder: (Dutch—low, as in Nederland)

NEDICO: Netherlands Engineering Consultants

Nedlloyd: Netherlands Line

NEDT: National Educational Development Tests

NEDU: Navy Experimental Diving Unit

NEEB: North Eastern Electricity Board (UK)

NEEC: National Export Expansion Council

need.: needlework

ne'er: never

NEES: Naval Engineering Experiment Station; New England Electric Service

nef: national extra fine (screw thread)

NEF: Naval Emergency Fund; Near East Foundation; New Education Fellowship

nefa: nonesterified fatty acid

NEFA: Northeast Frontier Agency

NEFC: Near East Forestry Commission

NEFEN: Near and Far East News

NEFIRA: New England Fire Insurance Rating Association

Nefos: New Emerging Forces

NEFSA: National Education Field Service Association

neg: negative; negritude

Neg: Negro; Negroid

negatron: negative electron

Negrasian(s): person(s) of African and Asian parents such as Afro-Chinese, Afro-Indian, Afro-Japanese, etc.

negro: (Portuguese, Spanish—black as in Rio Negro)

NEGRO: National Economic Growth and Reconstruction Organization

negtax: negative (income) tax

Neh: The Book of Nehemiah

NEH: National Endowment for the Humanities

NEHA: National Executives Housekeepers Association

nehi: knee-high

nei: not elsewhere indicated

n.e.i.: *non est inventus* (Latin—it is not found)

NEI: National Eye Institute; Netherlands East Indies

NEIC: National Earthquake Information Center
nek: nekton
NEK: *Norsk Electrotecnisk Komite* (Norwegian Electrotechnical Committee)
nekolim: neocolonialist-colonialist-imperialist (Indonesian acronym)
Nel: Eleanor(a); Ellen; Helen(a); Nelly
NEL: National Engineering Laboratory (Great Britain); Navy Electronics Laboratory (USN)
NELA: National Electric Light Association; New England Library Association
NELC: Naval Electronics Laboratory Center (formerly NEL)
NELIA: Nuclear Energy Liability Insurance Association
NELINT: New England Library Information Network
Nell: Eleanor(e)
Nelly: Eleanor(a) Ellen; Helen
NELMA: Northeastern Lumber Manufacturers Association
Nels: Nelson
NELS: National Environmental Laboratories
NEly: north-easterly
nem: not elsewhere mentioned
nema: nematode
NEMA: National Eclectic Medical Association; National Electrical Manufacturers Association
nemat: nematology
Nemat: Nemathelminthes
NEMI: National Elevator Manufacturing Industry
NEMLA: New England Modern Language Association
nemmies: nembutal capsules (dangerous sedative)
Nemo: Guillaume; Guillermo
NEMO: Naval Edreobenthic Manned Observatory (for sedentary sea bottom research); Naval Experimental Manned Observatory
NEMPS: National Environmental Monitoring and Prediction System
NEN: New England Nuclear (corporation)
ne/nd: new edition in preparation —no date can be given
NENP: New England National Park (New South Wales)
neo: near earth orbit
neo: (Latin—new)
NEOB: New Executive Office Building (D.C.)
neocolim: neocolonial-colonial-imperialist
NEODTC: Naval Explosive Ordinance Disposal Technical Center

Neo-Nor: Neo-Norwegian
Nep: Nepal; Neptune
NEP: New Economic Policy; New England Power (company); Nixon Economic Policy
nepa (NEPA): nuclear energy for the propulsion of aircraft
NEPA: National Environmental Policy Act
NEPCO: New England Provision Company
NEPEX: New England Power Exchange
neph: nephew
nepho: nephograph; nephological; nephologist; nephology
Nep Rs: Nepalese rupees
Nept: Neptune
N Equ Cur: North Equatorial Current
ner: nervous system
NER: National Educational Radio; National Elk Refuge (Wyoming); North Eastern Railway (England)
NERA: National Emergency Relief Administration
NERC: National Electronic Reliability Council; National Environmental Research Center; Natural Environment Research Council
nerv: nervous; nuclear emulsion recovery vehicle (NERV)
nerva: nuclear engine for rocket vehicle application
nes: not elsewhere specified
nes: (Dano-Norwegian or Swedish —cape, as in Lindesnes Cape projecting into North Sea from southern tip of Norway)
NESA: Near East and South Asia; New England School of Art
NESBIC: Netherlands Student's Bureau for International Cooperation
NESC: National Electric Safety Code; National Environmental Satellite Center
NESO: Naval Electronics Supply Office
NESS: National Environmental Satellite Service
nestor: neutron source thermal reactor
net.: network; not earlier than; nuclear electronic transistor
NET: National Educational Television
NETA: Northwest Electronic Technical Association
NETF: Nuclear Engineering Test Facility
Neth: Netherlands

Neth Ant: Netherlands Antilles
netic: nonretentive nonshocksensitive (alloy made for high-level attenuation)
netma: nobody ever tells me anything
NETRC: National Educational Television and Radio Center
Nettie: Henrietta
Netty: Henrietta
neu: neuter; neutral; neutrality
neu: (German—new, as in Neu-Hannover)
NEU: Northeastern University
neubarb: *neubearbeitet* (German—revised)
Neuk: Neuköln
neur: neuralgia; neurasthenia; neuritis; neurology
neuro: neurotic
neurol: neurological; neurologist; neurology
neuropath: neuropathology
neuropsychiat: neuropsychiatry
neurosurg: neurosurgeon; neurosurgery; neurosurgical
neurs: neurosis
NEUS: Northeastern United States
neut: neuter; neutral; neutralize; neutralizer
neutron: neutral ion
Nev: Nevada; Nevadan
Nevil Shute: Nevil Shute Norway
new: newton
Newc: Newcastle-upon-Tyne
New Cal: New Caledonia
New Deal: (administration of Franklin Delano Roosevelt —thirty-second President of the United States)
Newfie(s): Newfoundlander(s)
New Freedom: (administration of Woodrow Wilson–twenty-eighth President of the United States)
New Frontier: (administration of John F. Kennedy—thirty-fifth President of the United States)
New Hebr: New Hebrides
New Lib: Newberry Library
New Majority: (administration of Richard M. Nixon—thirty-seventh President of the United States)
NEWRADS: Nuclear Explosion Warning and Radiological Data System
news.: naval electronic warfare simulator
newscast(er): news broadcast(er)
New Sib: New Siberian Islands
Newt: Newton
New Test.: New Testament
NEWWA: New England Water Works Association
nez: (French—nose; cape; point)
nf: national fine; near face; no fool;

no funds; noise factor; non-ferrous; non-fundable; nose fuze; not fordable
n-f: nonfordable
n.f.: *ny foljd* (Swedish—new series)
n/f: no funds
n & f: near and far
n.F.: *neue Folge* (German—new series)
NF: National Fine (threads); National Formulary; National Foundation; Newfoundland; Norfolk, Virginia (airport); Norman French; nouveau franc (French—new franc, issued in 1960); Nutrition Foundation
NF: *Neue Folge* (German—new series)
N-F: Norman-French
NFA: National Federation of Anglers; National Food Administration; National Foundry Association; Nature Friends of America; Naval Fuel Annex; New Farmers of America; Night Fighters Association; Northwest Fisheries Association
NFAA: National Field Archery Association
NFAH: National Foundation for the Arts and the Humanities
nfb: no feedback
NFB: National Film Board (Canada)
NFBC: National Film Board of Canada; Newfoundland Base Command
NFBF: National Farm Bureau Federation
NFBPWC: National Federation of Business and Professional Women's Clubs
nfc: not favorably considered
NFC: National Foundry College; National Freight Corporation; Navy Finance Center
NFCC: National Foundation for Consumer Credit
nfcs: night fire-control sight
NFCSA: National Finance Corporation of South Africa
NFCTA: National Fibre Can and Tube Association
NFCU: Navy Federal Credit Union
NFD: National Federation of Doctors; Naval Fuel Depot
NFD: *National Faculty Directory*
nfd(m): non-fat dry (milk)
NFDA: National Food Distributors Association
nfe: nose-fairing exit; not fully equipped
NFEMC: National Federation of Export Management Companies
NFF: National Froebel Foundation;

Naval Fuel Facility
NFFE: National Federation of Federal Employees
NFFS: Non-Ferrous Founders' Society
NFI: National Fisheries Institute; Nature Friends of Israel
NFIC: National Foundation for Ileitis and Colitis
NFIP: National Foundation for Infantile Paralysis
NFIU: National Federation of Independent Unions
Nfl: *Nachfolger* (German—successor)
NFL: National Football League
Nfld: Newfoundland
NFMC: National Federation of Music Clubs; National Food Marketing Commission
NFME: National Fund for Medical Education
NFMLTA: National Federation of Modern Language Teachers Association
NFND: National Foundation for Neuromuscular Diseases
NFO: National Farmers Organization; Naval Flight Officer
NFPA: National Fire Protection Association; National Flaxseed Processors Association; National Flexible Packaging Association; National Fluid Power Association; National Forest Products Association; Niagara Frontier Port Authority
NFPC: Niagara Falls Power Company
NFPW: National Federation of Press Women
nfr: no further requirement
NFRC: National Forest Reservation Commission
nfs: not for sale
NFS: National Fire Service; National Forest Service
NFSA: National Fertilizer Solutions Association
NFSA & IS: National Federation of Science Abstracting and Indexing Services
NFSNC: National Federation of Settlements and Neighborhood Centers
NFSO: Navy Fuel Supply Office
NFTB: Nuclear Flight Test Base
NFTC: National Foreign Trade Council
nfu: not for us
NFU: National Farmers Union
NFWA: National Farm Workers Association; National Furniture Warehousemen's Association
NFWI: National Federation of Women's Institutes

ng: narrow gauge; new genus; nitroglycerin; no go; no good; not good; not ground; nut grounds
NG: National Gallery; National Guard; National Gypsum; New Guinea
Nga: Nagoya
NGA: National Gallery of Art; National Glider Association; Needlework Guild of America
NGAA: National Gift and Art Association; Natural Gasoline Association of America
N-gauge: narrow gauge (railroad track less than standard gauge: gauge: 4 feet 8-1/2 inches)
NGAUS: National Guard Association of the United States
NGB: National Garden Bureau; National Guard Bureau
NGC: National Gallery of Canada; National Gypsum Company
NGC: *New Galactic Catalog; New General Catalog* (astronomical)
NGCM: Navy Good Conduct Medal
NGCMS: National Guild of Community Music Schools
NGDA: National Glass Dealers Association
NGDC: National Geophysical Data Center
NGE: New York State Electric & Gas (stock exchange symbol)
ngf: naval gunfire
NGF: National Golf Foundation; Naval Gun Factory
NGFLO: Naval Gunfire Liaison Officer
NGFLT: Naval Gunfire Liaison Team
NGI: National Garden Institute
NGJC: North Greenville Junior College
N Gk: New Greek
NGK: Nihon Gakujutsu Kaigi (Japan Research Council)
ngl: natural gas liquids
NGL: North German Lloyd Line
ngo: national gas outlet (thread); nongovernmental organization
NGOs: Nongovernmental Organizations (UN)
NGPA: Natural Gas Processors Association
NGPT: National Guild of Piano Teachers
ngr: narrow gauze roll
NGr: New Greek
NGR: Ndumu Game Reserve (Zululand)
NGS: National Geographic Society
NGSA: National Gallery of South Africa
NGSR: Nizam's Guaranteed State

Railway

NGUS: National Guard of the United States

nh: no hurry (hospitalese); nonhygroscopic

NH: Naval Home; Naval Hospital; New Hampshire; New Hampshirite; New Haven, Connecticut; New York, New Haven & Hartford (railroad); New Hebrides

N & H: Nedlloyd & Hoegh (steamship lines)

nha: never has anything; next higher assembly; next higher authority

NHA: National Hay Association; National Health Association; National Hide Association; National Hockey Association; National Housing Act; National Housing Administration; National Housing Agency; New Homemakers of America; Nigerian Housing Administration

NHAIAC: National Highway Accident and Injury Analysis Center

NHAL: National Hellenic American Line

NHAS: National Hearing Aid Society

NHB: National Harbours Board (Canada)

NHBU: New Hampshire Board of Underwriters

NHC: National Health Council; National Hurricane Center

NHCA: National Hairdressers and Cosmetologists Association

NHDC: Naval Historical Display Center

nh di: notch die

nhe: nitrogen heat exchange

NHEA: National Higher Education Association; New Hampshire Education Association

N Heb: New Hebrew

NHEF: National Health Education Foundation

NHESA: National Higher Education Staff Association

NHF: National Heart Fund; Naval Historical Foundation

NH$_4$: ammonium radical

NH$_4$Cl: ammonium chloride; sal ammoniac

NH$_4$OH: ammonium hydroxide (ammonia)

NHFPL: New Haven Free Public Library

NHG: New High German

nhh: neither help nor hinder

NHHS: New Hampshire Historical Society

NHI: National Health Insurance; National Heart Institutes

NHK: *Nippon Hoso Kyokai* (Japanese—Japan Broadcasting Corporation)—as in NHK Symphony Orchestra

NHL: National Hockey League

NHLA: National Hardwood Lumber Association

NHO: Navy Hydrographic Office

NHOS: National Hellenic Oceanographic Society

nhp: nominal horsepower

NHPA: National Horsehoe Pitchers Association

NHPC: National Historical Publications Commission

NHPL: New Haven Public Library

NHPMA: Northern Hardwood and Pine Manufacturers Association

NHRA: National Hot Rod Association

NHRP: National Hurricane Research Project

NHRR: New Haven Railroad

NHS: National Health Service; National Honor Society; Newport Historical Society

NHSA: Negro Historical Society of America

NHSB: National Highway Safety Bureau

NHSC: National Home Study Council

NHSO: New Haven Symphony Orchestra

NHSR: National Hospital Service Reserve

NHTI: New Hampshire Technical Institute

NHTSA: National Highway Traffic Safety Administration

NH Turn: New Hampshire Turnpike

NHUC: National Highway Users Conference

Nhv: Newhaven

NHV: New Haven Clock and Watch (stock exchange symbol)

ni: night

Ni: Nica; Nicaragua; Nicaraguan; Nicaragüense; Nicas; nickel

NI: Naval Intelligence; Netherlands Indies; Northern Ireland

NI: ampere turns (symbol)

NIA: National Intelligence Authority; Neighborhood Improvement Association

NIAA: National Institute of Animal Agriculture

NIAAA: National Institute of Alcohol Abuse and Alcoholism

NIAB: National Institute of Agricultural Botany

NIAE: National Institute of Agricultural Engineering (UK); National Institute for Architectural Education

NIAID: National Institute of Allergies and Infectious Dieseases

NIAL: National Institute of Arts and Letters

NIAMD: National Institute of Arthritis and Metabolic Diseases

NIASA: National Insurance Actuarial and Statistical Association

nib: noninterference basis

NIB: National Information Bureau; Nebraska Inspection Bureau

nibo: nibonitschjo (ni boga ni tschjorta) (Russian—neither in god nor the devil)—materialist sceptics unaffected by Marxism—Leninism

nic: negative impedance converter; not in contact

Nic: Nicaragua; Nicolayev; Nicosia

NIC: Natick Industrial Centre; National Indications Center; National Industrial Council; National Institute of Credit; National Interfraternity Conference; National Inventors Council; National Investors Council; Niagara International Centre; Nicosia, Cyprus (airport)

Nica: Nicaragua(n)

nicad: nickel cadmium

NICAP: National Investigations Committee on Aerial Phenomena

Nicas: Nicaraguans

NICB: National Industrial Conference Board

NICE: National Institute of Ceramic Engineers

Nich: Nicholas

NICHHD: National Institute of Child Health and Human Development

nichrome: nickel-chromium alloy

NICJ: National Institute of Consumer Justice

Nick: Nicholas

Nickel Plate Road: New York, Chicago and St Louis Railroad Company

NICM: Nuffield Institute of Comparative Medicine

NICMA: National Ice Cream Mix Association

Nico: Nicobar Islands

NICO: Navy Inventory Control Office(r)

NICOP: Navy Industry Cooperation Plan

NICP: National Inventory Control Point

NICRA: Northern Ireland Civil Rights Association

NID: National Institute of Drycleaning; Naval Intelligence Department

NID: New International Dictionary (Webster's Third New International Dictionary of the English Language Unabridged)

NIDC: National Institute of Dry Cleaning

NIDH: National Institute of Dental Health

NIDM: National Institute for Disaster Mobilization

NIDR: National Institute of Dental Research

nie: not included elsewhere

NIE: National Institute of Education; National Intelligence Estimate

nieder: (German—lower)

NIESR: National Institute for Economic and Social Research

nieuw: (Dutch—new, as in Nieuw Amsterdam)

nif: nickel-iron film

nife: nickel + iron (Ni + Fe)

nig(s): renege(s); revoke(s)

Nig: Nigeria

NIGP: National Institute of Governmental Purchasing

nigyysob: now I've got you, you SOB

nih: not invented here

NIH: National Institutes of Health

NIHE: Northern Ireland Housing Executive

NII: Netherlands Industrial Institute

NIIP: National Institute of Industrial Psychology

NIIS: Niagara Institute for International Studies

NIJC: North Idaho Junior College

NIJFCM: National Institute of Jig and Fixture Component Manufacturers

Nikolaus Lenau: (pseudonym— Nikolaus Franz Niembsch von Strehlenau)

NIL: National Instrument Laboratories

NILA: National Industrial Leather Association

NILI: Netzach Israel Lo Ishakare (Hebrew—The eternity of Israel will not die)—acronymic password of the Nili spies who aided Britain by facilitating Turkish defeat in an effort to establish a homeland for Jews in Palestine

NILOJ: National Institute for Law/Order/Justice

NILP: Northern Ireland Labour Party

NIMA: National Insulation Manufacturers Association

NIMAC: National Interscholastic Music Activities Commission

NIMH: National Institute of Mental Health

nimm: nuclear-induced missile malfunction

nimphe: nuclear isotope monopropellant hydrazine engine

NIMR: National Institute for Medical Research

NINB: National Institute of Neurology and Blindness

NINDB: National Institute of Neurological Diseases and Blindness

NIO: National Institute of Oceanography; Naval Institute of Oceanology

NIOC: National Iranian Oil Company

NIOSH: National Institute of Occupational Safety and Health

nip.: nipple

Nip: Nipponese

NIP: Northern Ireland Parliament

NIPA: National Institute of Public Affairs

NIPCC: National Industrial Pollution Control Council

NIPH: National Institute of Public Health

NIPR: National Institute for Personnel Research

ni pri: nisi prius (Latin—unless before)

NIPS: National Information Processing System

NIPSSA: Naval Intelligence Processing Systems Support Activity

nipts: noise-induced permanent threshold shifts

NIR: Northern Ireland Railways

NIRA: National Industrial Recovery Administration

NIRC: National Industrial Relations Court

NIRD: National Institute of Research in Dairying

N Ire: Northern Ireland

NIRI: National Investor Relations Institute

NIRNS: National Institute for Research in Nuclear Science

NIROP: Naval Industrial Reserve Ordnance Plant (USN)

NIRR: National Institute for Road Research

n i s: not in stock

NIS: National Institute of Science; National Intelligence Survey

NISBS: National Institute of Social and Behavioral Science

NISP: National Information System for Psychology

NISS: National Institute of Social Sciences

NIST: National Institute of Science and Technology

nit.: negative income tax

nit: unit of luminance (symbol)

NIT: National Intelligence Test;

National Invitation Tournament; Northrop Institute of Technology

Nita: Juanita

NITA: National Industrial Television Association

NITC: National Iranian Tanker Company

NiteDevRon: Night Development Squadron

NITHC: Northern Ireland Transport Holding Company

NITL: National Industrial Traffic League

ni tp: nibbling template

NITR: National Institute for Telecommunications Research

nitrate of soda: sodium nitrate $(NaNO_3)$

nitro: nitrocellulose; nitroglycerine

nitros: nitrostarch

nitts: noise-induced temporary threshold shift

NITV: National Iranian Television

NIU: Northern Illinois University; Northern Interparliamentary Union

NIVE: Nederland Instituut voor Efficiency (Netherlands Institute for Efficiency)

NIW: National Industrial Workers Union

NIWR: National Institute for Water Research

nix: (from the German nichts) to ban; to cancel; to forbid; no one; nothing; to prohibit; to reject; to veto

NIYC: National Indian Youth Council

nizhni: (Russian—lower, as in Nizhni Novgorod, now known as Gorki)

n J: nächsten Jahres (German —next year)

NJ: New Jersey; New Jerseyite

NJA: National Jogging Association

njb: nice Jewish boy

NJC: Natchez Junior College; Navarro Junior College; Newton Junior College; Norfolk Junior College

NJCC: Northeastern Junior College of Colorado

NJEA: New Jersey Education Association

njg: nice Jewish girl

NJHS: New Jersey Historical Society

NJPBA: New Jersey Public Broadcasting Authority

NJROTC: Naval Junior Reserve Officers Training Corps

NJSO: New Jersey Symphony Orchestra

NJ Turn: New Jersey Turnpike

NJWB: National Jewish Welfare Board
NJZ: New Jersey Zinc
nk: neck; not known; not ours (publishing)
NK: Nippon Gakushiin (the Japanese Academy); Nomenklatur Kommission (Anatomical Nomenclature Commission); Nordiska Kompaniet (the Norse Company); North Korea(n)
NK: *Nihon Kyosanto* (Japanese Communist Party)
NKA: National Kindergarten Association
NKDR: National Key Deer Refuge (Florida)
NKF: National Kidney Foundation
NKGB: People's Commissariat for State Security (*q.v.* VOT)
NKK: Nippon Kokan Steel (Japan)
NKM: New Park Mining (stock exchange symbol)
NKP: Nickel Plate Railroad (stock exchange symbol for New York, Chicago & St. Louis Railroad) —locomotives on this line gleamed with nickel-plated ornaments
NKP: *Norges Kommunistiske Parti* (Norwegian Communist Party)
NKPA: National Kraut Packers Association
NKr: Norwegian krone(r)
NKS: *Norge Kjemisk Selskap* (Norwegian Chemical Society)
NKVD: *Narodnyi Kommissariat Vnutrennikh Del* (Russian —People's Commissariat for Internal Affairs, Soviet secret police; *q.v.* VOT)
nl: non-lubricant
NL: National League (of Professional Baseball Clubs); National Liberal; naval lighter (naval symbol); Navy League; Navy (US department) Library; Netherlands (auto plaque); New Latin; New London, Connecticut; Night Letter; North Latitude; Nuevo León
NL: Norddeutscher Lloyd (North German Lloyd Line)
NLA: National Lumbermen's Association
NL-A: Nationaal Luchtvaartlaboratorium-Amsterdam
NLAA: National Legal Aid Association
NLA & DA: National Legal Aid and Defender Association
NLAPW: National League of American Pen Women
N Lat: north latitude
NLC: National Lead Chemicals; National League for Cities; Na-

tional Leathersellers College; National Legislative Conference; National Legislative Council; National Liberal Club; National Library of Canada; New Location Code; New Orleans & Lower Coast (railroad)
NLD: National Legion of Decency
NLEC: National Lutheran Educational Council
nlf: nearest landing field
NLF: National Liberation Front; National Liberal Federation; nearest landing field
nlg: nose landing gear
NLGI: National Lubricating Grease Institute
NLI: National Library of Ireland
NLL: National Lending Library; Nedlloyd Lines
NLLST: National Lending Library for Science and Technology (UK)
nl lt: net-laying light
NLM: National Liberation Movement; National Library of Medicine
NLMA: National Lumber Manufacturers Association
NLN: National League for Nursing
NLNE: National League of Nursing Education
NLNP: Naujan Lake National Park (Philippines)
NLO: Naval Liaison Officer
NLP: National League of Postmasters
NLR: Nationaal Lucht- en Ruimtevaartlaboratorium (National Aero- and Astronautical Research Institute), Amsterdam
NLRB: National Labor Relations Board
NLs: New Leftists (subversives supporting enemies of the United States)
NLS: National Library of Scotland (Edinburgh); National Library Service (New Zealand and elsewhere); Non-Linear Systems
NLSB: National League Service Bureau
NLSCS: National League for Separation of Church and State
nlt: not later than; not less than
NLT: *Navigazione Libera Triestina* (Italian Line)
NLTA: National Lawn Tennis Association; National League of Teachers Associations
NLW: National Library Week
Nly: northerly
nm: nanometer; nautical mile(s); neuromuscular; nitrogen mustards; nomenclature; nonmetallic; non-motile (bacteria)

nm: *nachmittags* (German—afternoon; P.M.); *namiddag* (Dutch —afternoon; P.M.); nanometer; nautical . mile(s); nomenclature; nonmetallic
n/m: no mark
n/m²: newton per square meter
n. et m.: *nocte et mane* (Latin— night and early morning)
n M: *nächsten Monats* (German —next month)
Nm: newtonmeter
NM: Nigeria Museum
N de M: Nacional de México (railroad)
nma: negative mental attitude
NMA: National Management Association; National Medical Association; National Microfilm Association; Navy Mutual Aid (Association); Northwest Mining Association
NMAA: National Machine Accountants Association; Navy Mutual Aid Association
nmac: near mid-air collision
NMAF: National Medical Association Foundation
NMB: National Maritime Board; National Mediation Board
NMC: National Meteorological Center; National Museum of Canada; National Museums of Ceylon; National Music Council; Naval Material Command; Naval Medical Center; Naval Missile Center
NMCB: National Metric Conversion Board
NMCC: National Military Command Center
NMCDA: National Model Cities Directors Association
NMCO: Naval Material Catalog Office
NMCP: National Memorial Cemetery of the Pacific
NMCS: National Military Command System
NMCSSC: National Military Command System Support Center
NMDA: National Metal Decorators Association
NMDL: Navy Mine Defense Laboratory
NME: National Military Establishment
NMERI: National Mechanical Engineering Research Institute
N Mex: New Mexico; New Mexican
NMF: National Marine Fisheries
NMFMA: National Mutual Fund Managers Association
NMFRL: Naval Medical Field Research Laboratory

NMFS: National Marine Fisheries Service
NMFSL: National Marine Fisheries Service Laboratories
nmh: nautical miles per hour
NMHA: National Mental Health Association
nmi: no middle initial
n mi: nautical miles
NMI: New Mexico Military Institute
NMIM & T: New Mexico Institute of Mining and Technology
NMJ: Northern Masonic Jurisdiction
NML: National Music League; Northwestern Mutual Life (insurance)
NMMM: Navy Maintenance and Material Management
nmnc: nonmercuric noncorrosive
NMNH: National Museum of Natural History (D.C.)
NMO: Navy Management Office
nmoc: new man on campus
nmp: navigational microfilm projector
NMPA: National Music Publishers Association
NMPC: National Maintenance Publications Center (USA)
nmr: nuclear magnetic resonance
NMR: Natal Mounted Rifles
NMRA: National Model Railroad Association
NMRI: Naval Medical Research Institute
NMRL: Naval Medical Research Laboratory
NMRP: New Mexico Research Park
nms: nuclear materials safeguards
NMS: National Medal of Science; National Meteorological Service; Nobles of the Mystic Shrine
NMSE: Naval Material Support Establishment
NMSM: New Mexico School of Mines
NMSQT: National Merit Scholarships Qualifying Test
NMSSA: NATO Maintenance Supply Service Agency
NMSU: New Mexico State University
NMSWF: National Manufacturers of Soda Water Flavors
nmt: not more than
NMT: National Museum of Transport
NMTA: National Metal Trades Association
NMTBA: National Machine Tool Builders' Association
NMTS: National Milk Testing Ser-

vice
NMU: National Maritime Union
NMW: National Museum of Wales
NMWA: National Mineral Wool Association
nn: nouns
nn: *non numerato* (Italian—unnumbered)
n.n.: *nemini notus* (Latin—known to no one); *nescio nomen* (Latin—I do not know the name)
NN: Newport News
N/N: Northrop/Nortronics
NNA: National Neckwear Association; National Newspaper Association; National Notary Association
NNCR: North Norfolk Coast Reserves (England)
NND: New and Non-Official Drugs
NNE: north northeast
NNEB: National Nursery Examination Board
NN & EB: National Newark & Essex Bank
NNG: Netherlands New Guinea; Northern Natural Gas (company)
NNI: Norwegian Nobel Institute
nnk (NNK): notify next of kin
NNL: Nigerian National Line
NNN: Novy-Nicolle-McNeal (bacteriological culture)
NNNR: Noss National Nature Reserve (Shetlands)
nnp: net national product
NNP: Nairobi National Park (Kenya); Ngezi National Park (Rhodesia); Nimule National Park (Sudan)
NNPA: National Negro Press Association; National Newspaper Promotion Association
NNR: New and Nonofficial Remedies
NNRI: National Nutrition Research Institute
N Ns: Newport News
NNS & DDC: Newport News Shipbuilding and Dry Dock Company
NNSL: Nigerian National Shipping Line
NNSS: Navy Navigational Satellite System
NNTO: Netherlands National Tourist Office; Norwegian National Travel Office
NNW: north northwest
NNWR: Necedah National Wildlife Refuge (Wisconsin); Noxubee National Wildlife Refuge (Mississippi)
no.: normally open; number
nº: *número* (Spanish—number)
No: nobelium; Norskie (Norwegian-American); Norway; Nor-

wegian
NO: Naval Observatory; Naval Officer; New Orleans; North Central Airlines; Nuffield Observatory (Jordrell Bank, England)
NO: *Nordosten* (German—northeast)
No. 1: first; first quality; first rate; first person; most important; most important person; number one
No. 2: next in line; next in rank; number two; second; second person; second quality; second rate
noa: new obligational authority (NOA); not otherwise authorized
NOA: National Onion Association; National Opera Association; National Optical Association; National Orchestral Association
NOAA: National Oceanic and Atmospheric Administration
NO-AB: New Orleans-Algiers Bridge
nob.: *nobis* (Latin—to us)
NOB: Naval Operating Base
NOB: *Nationaal Orkest van Belgie* (Flemish—National Orchestra of Belgium)
Nobelst: *Nobelstiftelsen* (The Nobel Foundation)
noc: not otherwise classified
NOC: National Oceanographic Council
NOCHA: National Off-Campus Housing Association
NOCM: Nuclear Ordnance Commodity Manager
No Co: Northern Counties
noct.: *nocte* (Latin—by night; nocturnal)
noct. maneq.: *nocte maneque* (Latin—night and morning)
NOD: Navigation and Ocean Development
NODC: National Oceanographic Data Center
NODL: National Organization for Decent Literature (Catholic)
noe: not otherwise enumerated
NOE: Notice of Exception
NOF: National Oceanographic Foundation; National Osteopathic Foundation
NOFI: National Oil Fuel Institute
noforn: no foreign nationals; special handling—not to be released to foreign nationals
noft: notification of foreign travel
nohp: not otherwise herein provided
noibn: not otherwise identified by name; not otherwise indexed by name

NOIC: National Oceanographic Instrumentation Center; Naval Officer in Charge

NOISE: National Organization to Insure Sound-controlled Environment

NOJC: National Oil Jobbers Council

nok: next of kin

NOK: Norsk Aero Klub

NOL: Naval Ordnance Laboratory

NOLC: Naval Ordnance Laboratory, Corona

nol. con.: *nolo contendere* (Latin —I do not wish to contend)

Noll: Oliver

nolo: *nolo contendere*

nol. pros.: *nolle prosequi* (Latin —to be unwilling to prosecute)

NOLS: National Oceanographic Laboratory System

nol. vol.: *nolens volens* (Latin—unwilling or willing); willy-nilly

nom: nominal; nominate; nominated; nomination

NOMA: National Office Management Association

NOMAD: Navy Oceanographic and Meteorological Device (world's first nuclear-powered weather station)

nom. con.: *nomen conservandum* (Latin—generic or specific name to be preserved by special sanction)

nom dam: nominal damages

nom. dub.: *nomen dubium* (Latin —doubtful name)

nomen: nomenclature

nomin: nominative

nom. nov.: *nomen novum* (Latin —new name)

nom. nud.: *nomen nudem* (Latin —naked name); mere name for an animal or plant but lacking further description

NOMSS: National Operational Meteorological Satellite System

NOMTF: Naval Ordnance Missile Test Facilities

Non-Com: noncommissioned officer

none: no one; not one

non est: *non est inventus* (Latin—he was not found; it is wanting)

N/ONI: Navy/Office of Naval Intelligence

n-on-p: negative on positive

nonporno: not pornographic

non pos.: *non possumus* (Latin —we cannot)

N/ONR: Navy/Office of Naval Research

non repetat.: *non repetatur* (Latin —do not repeat)

non-res: nonresident

non seq.: *non sequitur* (Latin—it does not follow)

non-sked: non-scheduled (airplane, bus, train, etc.)

non std: nonstandard

non-U: not upper class

NOO: Navy Oceanographic Office (formerly Hydrographic Office, USN)

noong: (Siamese—lake; marsh, as in Noong Lahan)

no op: no opinion

noord: (Dutch—north)

nop: not our publication

NOP: National Oceanographic Program

NOPE: New Orleans Port of Embarkation

NOPHN: National Organization for Public Health Nursing

NOPL: New Orleans Public Library

NOPO: New Orleans Philharmonic Orchestra

NOQUIS: Nucleonic Oil Quantity Indication System

nor.: normal

nor: (Danish, French, German, Italian, Norwegian—north)

nor': norther (Middle English contraction); north

nør: *nørre* (Danish—north)

Nor: Norway; Norwegian

Nor: *Norr* (Swedish—north)

NOR: North Central Airlines

Nora: Eleanora

NORAD: North American Air Defense

Nor Ant: Norwegian Antarctica (Bouvet Island, Peter I Island, Queen Maud Land)

Nor Arc: Norwegian Arctic (Bear, Edge, and Hope islands in Barents Sea; Jan Mayen Island in Norwegian Sea; Svalbard or Spitsbergen in Arctic Ocean)

nor'ard: northward

norc: national ordnance research computer

NORC: National Opinion Research Center (University of Chicago); Naval Ordnance Research Computer

Nor Cur: Norwegian Current

nor'd: northward

NORD: Naval Ordnance

NORDITA: Nordic Institute for Theoretical Atomic Physics

nor'easter: northeaster (storm from the northeast)

Norelco: North American Philips Company

Norf: Norfolk

norm.: normal; normalize; normalizing; not operationally ready (because of) maintenance; nuclear operational readiness ma-

neuvers

Norm: Norman

Nor Pac: Northern Pacific

Nor Pol: Norsk Polarinstitutt (Norwegian Polar Institute)

nors: not operationally ready, supplies (supply)

norte: (Portuguese or Spanish—north, as in Norte America)

Northants: Northamptonshire

Northerns: Burlington, Great Northern, and Northern Pacific railroads

Northld: Northumberland

Northum: Northumberland

North Western Line: Chicago and North Western Railway

NORTLANT: North Atlantic

Nortraship: Norwegian Trade and Shipping Mission

Norw: Norwegian

NORWESTLANT: Northwest Atlantic (project)

nos: not otherwise specified; numbers

nos: (Russian—cape)

NOS: National Ocean Survey; Night Observation Sight

N OS: New Orleans

NOS: *Nederlandse Omroep Stichting* (Dutch—Netherlands Broadcasting Foundation)

NOSE: Neighbors Opposing Smelly Emissions

NOSG: Naval Operations Support Group

NOSOPEX: Northern Sumatra Offshore Petroleum Exploration

NOSTA: National Ocean Science and Technology Agency

notal: not to, nor needed by, all addressees

NOTAM: Notice to Airmen

NOTB: National Ophthalmic Treatment Board

noto: numbering tool

NOTP: *New Orleans Times-Picayune*

NOTS: Naval Ordnance Test Station

Not(t): Nottingham

Notts: Nottinghamshire

NOU: Noumea, New Caledonia (airport)

nouvelle: (French—new)

nov: novels; novelist; novels

Nov: November

novaya: (Russian—new, as in Novaya Zemlya [New Land] in Arctic Ocean)

Novdec: November and December

nove: noviembre (Spanish—November)

November: code for letter N

novo: (Portuguese—new)

Novo: Novosibirsk

NOVS: National Office of Vital Statistics

nov. sp.: *novum species* (Latin—new species)

NoW: News of the World

NOW: National Organization for Women; Negotiable Order of Withdrawal (interest-earning checking account)

NOWAPA: North American Water and Power Alliance

noxema: knocks eczema

noy: (unit of noisiness)

Noy: Noybr (Russian—November)

noz: nozzle

np: napalm (incendiary gasoline mixture); national pipe; neap; neap range; near point; net proceeds; neuropsychiatric; neuropsychiatry; new paragraph; nickel-plated; nonparticipating; nonpropelled; no paging; no place; no place of publication; no protest; normal pressure; nose plug; nursing procedure

n.p.: *nedsat pris* (Dano-Norwegian—reduced price)

Np: neap; neap range; neap tide; neper; neptunium (symbol)

N$_p$: neper

NP: Narragansett Pier; National Park; National Pipe; Naval Prison; Newport, Rhode Island; New Providence, Bahama Islands; no parking; Northern Pacific (railroad); Notary Public

NP: not published

N/P: nitrogen phosphorus ratio

NPA: National Paperboard Association; National Parenthood Association; National Parking Association; National Parks Association; National Particleboard Association; National Personnel Associates; National Pet Association; National Petroleum Association; National Pharmaceutical Association; National Pigeon Association; National Pilots Association; National Planning Association; National Preservers Association; National Proctologic Association; National Production Authority; Naval Procurement Account; Navy Postal Affairs; Nigerian Ports Authority

NPABC: National Public Affairs Broadcast Center

NPAC: National Program for Acquisitions and Cataloging (Library of Congress)

N Pac Cur: North Pacific Current

NPACT: National Public Affairs Center for Television

NPAP: National Psychological As-

sociation for Psychoanalysis

NPB: National Parole Board (Canada)

NPBI: National Pretzel Bakers Institute

npc: near point of convergence

NPC: National Patent Council; National Peach Council; National Peanut Council; National Personnel Consultants; National Petroleum Council; National Pharmaceutical Council; National Potato Council; National Press Club; Naval Photographic Center; Nigerian Population Commission

NPCA: National Parks and Conservation Association; National Pest Control Association

NPCI: National Potato Chip Institute

NPCP: National Press Club of the Philippines

npcr: no periodic calibration required

NPD: Nationaldemokratische Partei Deutschlands (National Democratic Party of Germany)

NPDC: National Patent Development Corporation

NPDEA: National Professional Driver Education Association

NPE: Navy Preliminary Evaluation

NPF: National Piano Foundation

NPFA: National Playing Fields Association

NPFC: Naval Publications and Forms Center

NPFI: National Plant Food Institute

NPFSC: North Pacific Fur Seal Commission

NPG: National Portrait Gallery

NP en G: Nederlandse Postcheque en Girodienst (Netherlands Postal Check and Transfer Service)

NPGS: Naval Postgraduate School

npH: neutral protamine Hegedorn (isoophane insulin)

NPI: Neuro-Psychiatric Institute

NPIA: Norfolk Port and Industrial Authority

NPIC: Naval Photographic Interpretation Center

npl: new program language; nipple

NPL: Nashville Public Library; National Physical Laboratory; Newark Public Library; Norfolk Public Library

NPMAA: National Piano Manufacturers Association of America

npn (NPN): nonprotein nitrogen

NPN: negative positive negative

N & PNWR: Ninepipe and Pablo National Wildlife Refuge (Montana)

n.p.o.: *ne per oris* (Latin—not by

mouth)

NPO: National Philharmonic Orchestra (Manila); Navy Post Office Navy Purchasing Office(r); New Philharmonia Orchestra (London)

NPOAA: National Police Officers Association of America

NP & OSR: Naval Petroleum and Oil Shale Reserve

NPP: Naval Propellant Plant

NPPA: National Press Photographers Association

NPPF: National Planned Parenthood Federation

NPPR: Nationalist Party of Puerto Rico

NPPS: Navy Publication Printing Service

NPQ: Naviera de Productos Químicos (Chemical Products Shipping Line)

npr: night press rates

NPR: National Public Radio; Nickel Plate Road (railroad)

NPRA: National Petroleum Refiners Association; Naval Personnel Research Activity

NPRL: National Physical Research Laboratory

NPRO: Navy Plant Representative Office(r)

nps: nominal pipe size; no prior service

NPS: National Park Service

npsh: net positive suction head

npt: normal pressure and temperature

Npt: Newport

NPT: national taper pipe thread

NPTA: National Passenger Traffic Association; National Piano Travelers Association

NPTC: National Postal and Travelers Censorship

NPTRL: Naval Personnel Training Research Laboratory

n.p.u.: *ne plus ultra* [Latin—nothing beyond (it); the summit; the ultimate]

NPU: National People's Union; National Police Union; National Postal Union

npv: net present value

NPVLA: National Paint, Varnish, and Lacquer Association

NPW: Naturpark Pfalzer Wald (German—Falls Forest Nature Park)—in western Germany near France

NPWS: National Parks and Wildlife Service (Australia)

NPX: National Phoenix Industries (stock-exchange symbol)

nq: notes and queries

nqa: net quick assets

NQD: Notice of Quality Discrepancy

nr: near; nonreactive (relay); number

nr: *non rogne* (French—untrimmed); *nummer* (Polish—issue; number); *nummer* (Dano-Norwegian or Swedish—number)

n/r: no record; not required; not responsible (for)

nR: *neue Reihe* (German—new series)

Nr: *Nummer* (German—number)

NR: Norsk Rikskringkasting (Norwegian Broadcasting)

NR: *National Review*

nra: never refuse anything; no repair action

nra: *nuestra* (Spanish—our, *f.*)

NRA: National Reclamation Association; National Recovery Act; National Recovery Administration; National Recreation Association; National Reform Association; National Rehabilitation Association; National Research Associates; National Restaurant Association; National Rifle Association (of America); Naval Reserve Association

NRAA: National Rifle Association of America

NRAC: National Resources Analysis Center

NRACCO: Navy Regional Air Cargo Control Office(r)

NRAF: Navy Recruiting Aids Facility

NRAO: National Radio Astronomy Observatory

NRAS: Navy Readiness Analysis Section; Navy Readiness Analysis System

Nra Sra: *Nuestra Señora* (Spanish—Our Lady)

NRB: Narodna Republika Blgariya (Bulgaria)

nrc: normal retinal correspondence

NRC: Nacozari Railroad Company; National Referral Center (Library of Congress); National Republican Club; National Research Corporation; National Research Council; National Resources Committee; National Resources Council; National Roofing Contractors; Naval Retraining Command; Netherlands Red Cross; Nuclear Research Council

NRC: *Nieuwe Rotterdamse Courant* (New Rotterdam Courant)

NRCA: National Retail Credit Association

NRCC: National Research Council of Canada

NRCI: National Red Cherry Institute

NRC-NAS: National Research Council—National Academy of Sciences

nrcp: nonreinforced concrete pipe

NRCR: Northern Railway of Costa Rica (Ferrocarril del Norte de Costa Rica)

NR Crit: Nuclear Rocket—Critical

NRD: National Range Division

NRDA: National Research and Development Authority (Israel)

NRDC: National Research Development Corporation

NRDC: Natural Resources Defense Council

NRDL: Naval Radiological Defense Laboratory

NRDS: Nuclear Rocket Development Station

NREB: Navy Reserve Evaluation Board

NRECA: National Rural Electric Cooperative Association

NRF: Naval Reactor Facility; Naval Repair Facility

NRFA: National Retail Furniture Association

NRFC: Navy Regional Finance Center

NRG: Naval Research Group

NRGA: National Rice Growers Association

NRh: Northern Rhodesia

NRHC: National Rural Housing Coalition

NRHS: National Railway Historical Society

NRIMS: National Research Institute for Mathematical Sciences

Nrk: Newark

NRK: Nikolai Rimsky-Korsakov

NRK: *Norsky Rikskringkasting* (Royal Norwegian Broadcasting)

nrl: normal rated load

NRL: National Research Library; Naval Research Laboratory

NRLCA: National Rural Letter Carriers' Association

NRLDA: National Retail Lumber Dealers Association

NRLSI: National Reference Library of Science and Invention

nrm: next to reading matter; normal rabbit serum

NRM: Naval Reserve Medal

NRMA: National Retail Merchants Association

NRMC: National Records Management Council; Naval Records Management Center

NRMCA: National Ready-Mixed

Concrete Association

nrml: normal

nro: *nuestro* (Spanish—our, *m.*)

NRO: Naval Research Objectives

NROO: Naval Reactors Operations Office

NROTC: Naval Reserve Officers Training Corps

NRPA: National Recreation and Park Association

NR & PA: National Recreation and Park Association

NRPB: National Research Planning Board

NRPC: National Railroad Passenger Corporation

NRRE: Netherlands Radar Research Establishment

N rs: Nepalese rupee(s)

NRS: Navy Relief Society

nrt: net register(ed) tonnage (tons)

NRTA: National Retired Teachers Association

NRTC: Naval Reserve Training Center

nrts: not reparable this station

NRTS: National Reactor Testing Station

nru: nuclear reactor—universal

NR-U: Nederlandsche Radio-Unie (Netherlands Union of Radio Broadcasters)

Nrvkrg: *Nervenkrieg* (German—nerve warfare)

NRVN: Navy of the Republic of Viet Nam

Nrw: Norwegian

NRWC: National Right to Work Committee

nrx: nuclear reactor—experimental

NR Yorks: North Riding, Yorkshire

nrz: non-return (to) zero

ns: nanosecond; near side; neuropsychiatric; new series; nickel steel; nonstandard; not specified

ns: *nouvelle serie* (French—new series)

n/s: not sufficient

nS: *neue Serie* (German—new series)

Ns: nimbostratus; Nunes; Nuñez

NS: National Society; National Special (screw threads); Naval Shipyard; Naval Station; New Style; Norfolk Southern (railroad); North Sea; Nova Scotia; Nuclear Ship; Nuclear Submarine; Numismatic Society

NS: *Nachschrift* (German—postscript); *Notre Seigneur* (French—Our Lord); *Nuestro Señor* (Spanish—Our Lord)

N.S.: New Style; Norfolk Southern (railroad)

N.S.: *Nuestro Señor* (Spanish

—Our Lord)

nsa (NSA): nonenyl succinic acid

NSA: National Secretaries Association; National Security Agency; National Service Acts; National Shellfisheries Association; National Sheriff's Association; National Shipping Authority; National Showmen's Association; National Silo Association; National Ski Association; National Slag Association; National Slate Association; National Society of Auctioneers; National Standards Association; National Students Association; Naval Stock Account; Naval Supply Account; Neurological Society of America; Norwegian Seamen's Association

NSA: Nuclear Science Abstracts

NSAA: Norwegian Singers' Association of America

NSAC: Nova Scotia Agricultural College

NSAD: National Society of Art Directors

NSAM: Naval School of Aviation Medicine

NSASAB: National Security Agency Scientific Advisory Board

NSB: National Science Board; Norske Stasbaner (Norwegian State Railways)

NSB: Norges Statsbaner (Norwegian State Railway)

NSBA: National Small Business Association

NSBC: National Student Book Club

NSBIU: Nova Scotia Board of Insurance Underwriters

NSBMA: National Small Business Men's Association

nsc: non-service connected

NSC: National Safety Council; National Security Council; National Steel Corporation; Naval Supply Center; Newark State College

NSCA: National Society for Clean Air; Nova Scotia College of Art

NSCC: National Society for Crippled Children

NSCCA: National Society for Crippled Children and Adults

NSCDRF: National Sickle Cell Disease Research Foundation

NSCID: National Security Council Intelligence Directive

NSCT: North Staffordshire College of Technology

nsd: noise-suppression device

NSD: Naval Supply Depot

NSDAP: Nationalsozialistische Deutsche Arbeiterpartei (German National Socialist [Nazi] Workers Party)

NSDF: National Sex and Drug Forum

NSDP: National Society of Dental Prosthetists

nsec: nanosecond

nsf: not sufficient funds

NSF: National Science Foundation

nsftd: normal spontaneous full-term delivery

NSG: Naval Security Group

nsh: not so hot

NSHEB: North of Scotland Hydro-Electric Board

nsi: nonstandard item

NSI: National Stock Exchange

NSIA: National Security Industrial Association

NSID: National Society of Interior Designers

NSIO: Nova Scotia Information Office

NSJC: Nuestro Señor Jesucristo (Spanish—Our Lord Jesus Christ)

nsk: not specified by kind

NSKK: Nito Shosen Kabushiki Kaisha (Japanese steamship line)

NSL: Northrop Space Laboratory

NSLI: National Service Life Insurance

NSLS: National Science Library System

nsm: noise source meter

NSM: National Security Medal; National Selected Morticians; Naval School of Music; Nevada State Museum

NSMA: National Scale Men's Association

NSMC: Naval Submarine Medical Center

NSMHC: National Society for Mentally Handicapped Children

NSMPA: National Screw Machine Products Association

NSMS: National Sheet Music Society

NSMSES: Naval Ship Missile Systems Engineering Station

NSNC: Nova Scotia Normal College

NSO: Nashville Symphony Orchestra; National Symphony Orchestra; Navy Subsistence Office(r); Norfolk Symphony Orchestra; Northern Sinfonia Orchestra

NSOA: National School Orchestra Association

n sp: new species

NSP: Navy Standard part; Northern States Power

NSPA: National Scholastic Press Association; National Society of Public Accountants; National Soybean Processors Association; National Split Pea Association; National Standard Part Association; Naval Shore Patrol Administration

NSPB: National Society for the Prevention of Blindness

NSPC: National Security Planning Commission; National Society of Painters in Casein; Northern States Power Company

NSPCA: National Society for the Prevention of Cruelty to Animals

NSPCC: National Society for the Prevention of Cruelty to Children

NSPD: Naval Shore Patrol Detachment

NSPE: National Society of Professional Engineers

nspf: not specifically provided for

NSPI: National Society for Programmed Instruction; National Swimming Pool Institute

NSPO: Navy Special Projects Office; Nuclear Systems Project Office

NSPWA: National Society of Patriotic Women of America

nsq: neuroticism scale questionnaire

nsr: natural sinus rhythm; normal sinus rhythm

NSR: National Scientific Register; Norfolk Southern Railway

NSRA: National Shoe Retailers Association; National Shorthand Reporters Association

NSRB: National Security Resources Board

NSRDC: National Standards Reference Data System

NSRDF: Naval Supply Research and Development Facility

NSRDL: Naval Ship Research and Development Laboratory

NSRDS: National Standard Reference Data System

NSRF: Nova Scotia Research Foundation

NSRP: National States Rights Party

nsrt: near-surface reference temperature

nss (NSS): normal saline solution

NSS: National Sculpture Society; National Serigraph Society; National Slovak Society; National Speleological Society; National Stockpile Site; Newburgh and South Shore (railroad)

NSSA: National Sanitary Supply Association; National Skeet Shooting Association

NSSC: National Society for the Study of Communication

NSSCC: National Space Surveillance Control Center

NSS Co: Northern Steam Ship Company (New Zealand)

NSSF: National Shooting Sports Foundation

NSSFC: National Severe Storm Forecast Center; National Society of Student Film Critics

NSSFNS: National Scholarship Service and Fund for Negro Students

NSSL: National Severe Storms Laboratory

NSSMA: National Spanish-Speaking Management Association

NSSP: National Severe Storms Project

NSSR: New School for Social Research

nst: nonslip thread

NST: Newfoundland Standard Time

NSTA: National Science Teachers Association

NSTAP: National Strategic Targeting and Attack Policy

NSTC: Nebraska State Teachers College

NSTI: Norwalk State Technical Institute

NSTL: National Strategic Target Line

NSTS: National Sea Training Schools

nsu: non-specific urethritis

NSU: Neckarsulmer Fahrzeugwerke (NSU Motorenwerke)

NSUC: North Staffordshire University College

nsurg: neurosurgeon; neurosurgery; neurosurgical

NSW: New South Wales

NSWC: New South Wales Centre

NSWGR: New South Wales Government Railways

NSWPP: National Socialist White People's Party (formerly American Nazi Party)

NSY: New Scotland Yard

nt: nit (unit of luminous intensity); nontight; no trace

n.t.: *nel testo* (Italian—in the text)

n/t: net tonnage

n & t: nose and throat

Nt: nitron

NT: New Testament; Northern Territory

N.T.: *Novum Testamentum* (Latin —New Testament)

NT$: New Taiwan dollar

nta: nitrilotriacetic (phosphate substitute for detergents); nuclear test aircraft (NTA)

NTA: National Tax Association; National Technical Association; National Tourist Association; National Travel Association;

National Tuberculosis Association; Northern Textile Association; Northern Trade Association

NTAA: National Travelers Aid Association

NTB: Norsk Telegrambyra (Norwegian news service)

NtBuStnds: National Bureau of Standards

ntc: negative temperature coefficient

NTC: National Teacher Corps; National Theatre Conference; National Travel Club; Naval Training Center

NTCC: Nimbus Technical Control Center

ntd: non-tight door

NTDC: Naval Tactical Data System; Naval Technical Data System; Naval Training Device Center

NTDPMA: National Tool, Die, and Precision Machining Association

NTDS: Naval Tactical Data System; Naval Technical Data System

NTE: National Teacher Examination

N-test: nuclear test(ing)

NTF: Navy Technological Forecast

ntfy: notify

NTGB: North Thames Gas Board

Nth: Netherlands

NTH: Norges Tekniske Hogskole (Norwegian Technical University, Trondheim)

Nth country: next country of a series accepting nuclear power

n/30: net (payment) in 30 days

NTIAC: Nondestructive Testing Information Analysis Center

NTID: National Technical Institute for the Deaf

NTIS: National Technical Information Service

ntl: no time lost

NTL: National Tennis League; National Training Laboratories

NTLS: National Truck Leasing System

ntm: net ton mile

Ntm: Nottingham

NTNP: Natchez Trace National Parkway

nto: not tried on

nto: *neto* (Spanish—net)

NTO: National Tenants Organization; National Theatre Organisation (South Africa)

ntp: normal temperature and pressure; no title page

NTPC: National Technical Processing Center; Navy Training

Publications Center

ntpl: nut plate

ntr: noise temperature ratio

NTR: National Tape Repository; Northern Test Range

Ntra Sra: *Nuestra Señora* (Spanish—Our Lady)

NTRB: Northern Territory Reserve Board (Australia)

NTRL: Naval Training Research Laboratory

nts: not to scale

Nts: Nantes

NTS: National Traffic System; Naval Transportation System; Nederlandse Televisie Stichting (Netherlands Television Foundation); Nevada Test Site

NTS: *Narodnyi Trudovoy Soyuz:* (Russian—National Labor Union)—anti-communist Russian exiles

NTSA: National Traffic Safety Agency

NT & SA: National Trust and Savings Association

NTSB: National Transportation Safety Board

NTSC: National Television Standards Committee; North Texas State College

NTTC: National Tank Truck Carriers

NTT & TTI: National Truck Tank and Trailer Tank Institute

NTU: National Taiwan University; Navy Toxicology Unit

NTV: Nippon Television

nt wt: net weight

NTX: Navy Teletype Exchange

nu: name unknown; new

nu: (Yiddish—so?; so what?); colloquial interrogative exclamation

Nu: Nusselt number

NU: Naciones Unidas (Spanish— United Nations); Nations Unies (French—United Nations); Niagara University; Northeastern University; Northwestern University; Norwich University

NUAAW: National Union of Agricultural and Allied Workers

NUB: National Union of Blastfurnacemen

nube(s): nubile(s)

NUC: National Urban Coalition; Naval Undersea Center

NUC: *National Union Catalog*

Nuc.E.: Nuclear Engineer

nuc(l): nuclear; nucleus

NUCS: National Union of Christian Schools

nud: nudism; nudist

nud: *nudnick* (Yiddish—nuisance; pest)

NUDET: Nuclear Detonation Report

NUDETS: Nuclear Detonation, Detection, and Reporting System

NUE: Nuremberg, Germany (airport)

NUEA: National University Extension Association

NUF: National Urban Fellows

nug: nuggar (cargo boat used on the Nile)

NUHS: New Utrecht High School

NUI: National University of Ireland (Ollscoil na h-Éireann)

NUJ: National Union of Journalists

nuke: nuclear (slang)

nukes: nuclear explosives

nul: no upper limit

NUL: National Urban League; Northwestern University Library

num: number; numbered; numbering; numeral(s); numeration(s); numerical; numerologist; numerology

num: *número(s)* [Portuguese or Spanish—number(s)]

Num: The Fourth Book of Moses, called Numbers

numb.: numbered

NUMEC: Nuclear Materials and Equipment Corporation

numis: numismatics

numism: numismatic(s); numismatist

nuna: not used on next assembly

NUOS: Naval Underwater Ordnance Station

nuovo: (Italian—new)

NUP: Negro Universities Press

NUPE: National Union of Public Employees

NUR: National Union of Railwaymen

NUS: National Union of Students; Nuclear Utility Service(s)

nusar: nuclear sweep and radar

NUSAS: National Union of South African Students

NUSC: Naval Underwater Systems Center

NUSL: Navy Underwater Sound Laboratory

NUSRL: Navy Underwater Sound Reference Laboratory

nusum: numerical summary

N u T: Newcastle-upon-Tyne

NUT: National Union of Teachers (Great Britain)

nu-tec: nuclear detection (radiation monitoring device)

nutr: nutrition

NUWC: Naval Undersea Warfare Center

nv: naked vision; needle valve; new version

nv.: *novicius* (Latin—new; recent)

n-v: non-vaccinated; non-veteran; non-voting

n & v: nausea and vomiting

NV: Nord-Viscount

NV: *Naamloze Vernootschap* (Dutch—corporation); *Naviera Vascongada* (Basque Navigation Company); *Norske Veritas* (Norwegian Register of Shipping)

nva: *nueva* (Spanish—new)

NVA: North Vietnamese Army

NVAiO: Norske Videnskaps-Akademi i Oslo (Norwegian Academy of Science and Letters in Oslo)

NVC: National Violence Commission

NVF: National Volunteer Force

NVFC: National Vulcanized Fibre Company

nvg: null voltage generator

NVGA: National Vocabulary Guidance Association

NVL: Night Vision Laboratory

NVNS: Naamloze Vernootschap Nederlandsche Spoorwagen (Netherlands Railway Corporation)

nvp: natural vegetable powder (powdered psyllium seed and dextrose laxative)

NVPA: National Visual Presentation Association

nvr: no voltage release

NVRS: National Vegetable Research Station

nvs: neutron velocity selector

NVS: Night Vision System

NVT: National Veld Trust

NVTS: National Vocational Training Service

nw: nanowatt; no wind

NW: Chicago & North Western Railway; Noah Webster; Norfolk & Western (railroad); Northern Wings Ltd; North Wales; Northwest; Northwest Airlines

NW: *Nordwesten* (German—northwest)

N & W: Norfolk & Western (railroad)

NWA: Northwest Airlines

NWAH & ACA: National Warm Air Heating and Air Conditioning Association

nwb: non-weight bearing

NWBA: National Wheelchair Basketball Association

nwc: nuclear war capability

Nwc: Newcastle-upon-Tyne

NWC: National War College; National Water Commission; National Writers Club

NWCC: Northern Wyoming Community College

NWCCL: Naval Weapons Center —Corona Laboratories

NWCTU: National Woman's Christian Temperance Union

NWD: *New World Dictionary*

NWDR: Nordwestdeutscher Rundfunk (North-West German Broadcasting System)

NWEB: Northwestern Electricity Board (UK)

NWF: National Wildlife Federation

NWF: *National War Formulary*

Nwfld: Newfoundland

NWFP: North-West Frontier Province

NWGA: National Wool Growers Association

nwh: normal working hours

NWI: Netherlands West Indies

NWIP: Naval Warfare Instruction Publication

NWIRP: Naval Weapons Industrial Reserve Plant

NWJA: National Wholesale Jewelers Association

NWL: Naval Weapons Laboratory

NWLB: National War Labor Board

NWly: northwesterly

NWMC: Northwest Michigan College

Nw Ned: Nieuw Nederland (Dutch —New Netherlands)

NWO: Nuclear Weapons Office(r)

nwoc: new woman on campus

n-word: nonce word (word coined for the nonce or the occasion)

NWP: Naval Weapons Plant

NWPFC: Northwest Pacific Fisheries Commission

NWPSC: Northwestern Public Service Company

NWQAO: Naval Weapons Quality Assurance Office

nwr: next word request

NWR: National Welfare Rights; National Wildlife Refuge; National Wildlife Reserve; Nuclear Weapon Report

NWRC: National Weather Records Center

NWRF: Naval Weather Research Facility

NWRO: National Welfare Rights Organization

NWRS: National Wildlife Refuge System

NWS: National Weather Service; Naval Weapons Station; Nimbus Weather Satellite

NWSA: National Welding Supply Association

NWSC: National Weather Satellite Center

NWSF: Nuclear Weapons Storage Facility (USA)

NWSO: Naval Weapons Services Office
NWSS: Nuclear Weapons Support Section (USA)
NWSY: Naval Weapons Station—Yorktown, Va
nwt: nonwatertight
NWT: Northwest Territories
nwu: nosewheel up
NWU: Nebraska Wesleyan University
NWUS: Northwestern United States
nx: nonexpendable
NXDO: Nike-X Development Office (USA)
NXMIS: Nike-X Management Information Office
NXPM: Nike-X Project Manager
NXPO: Nike-X Project Office
nxr: non-crossing rule
NXSO: Nike-X Support Office
ny: no year
Ny: Niles; Nylan
NY: New York; New York Airways (2-letter code); New Yorker
NY: *New Yorker* (magazine)
Nya: Nyasaland
NYA: Neighborhood Youth Association; New York Aquarium
NYAC: New York Athletic Club
NYADS: New York Air Defense Sector
NYAM: New York Academy of Medicine
NYANA: New York Association for New Americans
NYAO: New York Assay Office
Nyas: Nyasaland
NYAS: New York Academy of Science
nyasa: (Bantu—lake)
NYATI: New York Agricultural and Technical Institute
NYBFU: New York Board of Fire Underwriters
NYBG: New York Botanical Garden
NYBSBC: New York Bureau of State Building Codes
NYC: Neighborhood Youth Corps; New York Central (railroad); New York City
NYCC: New York Cultural Center
NYCCC: New York City Community College
NYCE: New York Cocoa Exchange; New York College of Education; New York Cotton Exchange
NYCHA: New York City Housing Authority
NYCMA: New York City Metropolitan Area
NYCMD: New York Contract Management District
NYCNHA: New York City Nursing Home Association

NYCOC: New York City Opera Company
NY Col: New York Coliseum
NYCS: New York Choral Society
NYC & ST L: New York, Chicago & St. Louis (Nickel Plate Line)
NYCT: New York Community Trust
NYCTA: New York City Transit Authority
nyd: not yet diagnosed
NYDMC: New York Downstate Medical Center
NYDR: New York Dock Railway
NYF: New York Foundation
NYFIRO: New York Fire Insurance Rating Organization
NYGC: New York Governor's Conference
NYHCMC: New York Hospital—Cornell Medical Center
NYHS: New York Historical Society
NYIAS: New York Institute of the Aerospace Sciences
NYIT: New York Institute of Technology
N Yk: New York
NYK: Nippon Yusen Kaisha Line
nyl: nylon
NYLA: New York Library Association
NY & LB: New York & Long Branch (railroad)
NYLS: New York Law School
NYMC: New York Maritime College
nympho: nymphomania; nymphomaniac; nymphomaniacal
N Y N H & H: New York, New Haven and Hartford (railroad)
NYOGB: National Youth Orchestra of Great Britain
NYOL: New York Opera Library
NYOSL: New York Oceans Science Laboratory
NYOTBC: New York Off-Track Betting Corporation
NYOW: National Youth Orchestra of Wales
NYO & W: New York, Ontario and Western (railroad)
nyp: not yet published
NYP: New York Philharmonic (orchestra)
NYPA: New York Port Authority
NYPD: New York Police Department
NYPDis: New York Procurement District (US Army)
NYPE: New York Port of Embarkation; New York Produce Exchange
NYPFO: New York Procurement Field Office (USAF)

NYPL: New York Public Library
NYPM: New York Pro Musica
NYPs: Neighborhood Youth Programs
NYPS: New York Psychiatric Society; New York Publishing Society
NYPSS: New York Philharmonic-Symphony Society
nyr: not yet returned
NYRA: New York Racing Association
NYRB: *New York Review of Books*
NYS: New York State
NYSA: New York Shipping Association
NYSAA: New York State Aviation Association
NYSAC: New York State Athletic Commission
NYSASDA: New York State Atomic and Space Development Authority
NYSAVC: New York State Audio-Visual Council
NYSBC: New York State Barge Canal (modern extension of Erie Canal)
NYSC: New York Shipbuilding Corporation
NYSCC: New York State Crime Commission
NYSE: New York Stock Exchange
NYSES: New York State Employment Service
NYSF: New York Shakespeare Festival
NYSM: New York State Museum
NYSP: New York School of Printing
NYSPA: New York State Power Authority
NYSSMA: New York State School Music Association
NYSTA: New York State Teachers Association; New York State Thruway Authority
NYS & W: New York, Susquehanna and Western (railroad)
NYT: *The New York Times*
NY Thru: New York Thruway
NYTNS: New York Times News Service
NYU: New York underworld (used in law-enforcement circles); New York University
NYUL: New York University Library
NYWASH: Navy Yard, Washington
NYZP: New York Zoological Park
NYZS: New York Zoological Society
Nz: Nuñez
NZ: New Zealand; New Zealand National Airways (2-letter cod-

ing); Novaya Zemlya
N-Z: Nike-Zeus
NZ £ : New Zealand pound
NZb: New Zealand black (mice hybrids)
NZB: New Zealand Ballet
NZBC: New Zealand Broadcasting Corporation
NZD: New Zealand Division
NZDE: New Zealand Department of Education
NZED: New Zealand Electricity Department
NZedder(s): [En-zed-der(s)]—New Zealander(s)
NZEF: New Zealand Expeditionary Force
nzf: near zero field

NZFS: New Zealand Forest Service
nzg: near zero gravity
NZGR: New Zealand Government Railways
NZGTC: New Zealand Government Travel Commissioner
NZHC: New Zealand High Commission
NZIS: New Zealand Information Service
NZLA: New Zealand Library Association
NZNAC: New Zealand National Airways Corporation
NZOC: New Zealand Opera Company
NZOI: New Zealand Oceanographic Institute

NZP: National Zoological Park; New Zealand Players
NZPA: New Zealand Press Association
NZR: New Zealand Railways
NZS: New Zealand Standards Institute
NZS Co: New Zealand Shipping Company
NZ Sea Fron: New Zealand Sea Frontier (NZSEAFRON)
NZTC: New Zealand Trade Commission
NZw: New Zealand white (mice hybrids)
NZZ: *Neue Zürcher Zeitung* (New Zurich Newspaper)

O

o: observer; occasional; occidental; octavo; ohm; oil; oiliness; Olivetti; opium; orange; oriental; overcast
o: (Japanese—big; great; large)
o.: *oculus* (Latin—eye); *oeste* (Portuguese or Spanish—west); *oost* (Dutch—east); *op* (Dano-Norwegian or Dutch up); *os* (Latin—bone); *ouest* (French—west); *ovest* (Italian—west)
ö: (Dano-Norwegian or Swedish —island); *öster* (Swedish—east)
ø: *øst* (Dano-Norwegian—east)
o/: *order* (Spanish—order)
O: absence of perception of sound (symbol); New Orleans Mint (coin symbol); observation; ocean; Oceanic Steamship Company; October; office; officer; Ohio; Olsen Line; Omaha; Ontario; order; Oregon; ortho; Oscar—code for letter O; oxygen; unofficial abbreviation for Ohio
O': (Gaelic prefix meaning of)
O: center of earth (symbol); observer (symbol); *Ost* (German— east)
Ö: *Österreich* (German—Eastern Empire)—Austria
Ø: shortage (symbol)
O1: organized seagoing naval reserve
O2: organized naval reserve aviation
O₃: ozone
oa: on account; on account of; on or

about; overall
o/a: on account; on or about
oa: *och andra* (Swedish—and others)
o/A: *oro Americano* (Spanish —American—gold; American money)
OA: Obligation Authority; Office of Applications; Olympic Airways; Operations Analysis; Osborne Association; overall noise level (symbol)
OaA: Office of Aging
OAA: Old Age Assistance; Organisation des Nations Unies pour l'Alimentation et l'Agriculture (United Nations Organization for Food and Agriculture)
OAAA: Outdoor Advertising Association of America
OAAU: Organization of Afro-American Unity
oac: on approved credit
OAC: Operating Agency Code; Ordnance Ammunition Command; Oregon Agriculture College
OACI: Organisation de l'Aviation Civile Internationale (International Civil Aviation Organization)
OACT: Ohio Association of Classroom Teachers
oad: overall depth
OAD: ordered, adjudged, and decreed
OAFIE: Office of Armed Forces Information and Education
OAG: Office of the Adjutant Gener-

al
OAG: Official Airline Guide
OAGB: Osteopathic Association of Great Britain
oah: overall height
OAH: Organization of American Historians
OAHE: Ohio Association for Higher Education
OAI: Office of Aeronautical Intelligence
oais: opinion, attitude, and interest survey
oak.: oakum
Oak: Oakland
OAK: Oakland, California (Metropolitan International Airport)
Oak Sym: Oakland Symphony
oal: overall length
OAL: Ordnance Aerophysics Laboratory
OALMA: Orthopedic Appliance and Limb Manufacturers Association
OAM: Office of Aviation Medicine
OAMA: Ogden Air Materiel Area
oame: orbital attitude and maneuvering electronics
OAMS: Orbital Attitude and Maneuvering System
oao: off and on
OAO: Orbiting Astronomical Observatory
OAP: Office of Aircraft Production; Old-Age Pension
OAPC: Office of the Alien Property Custodian
OAPs: Old-Age Pensioners
OAR: Office of Aerospace Re-

search; Organized Air Reserve

OART: Office of Advanced Research and Technology (NASA)

oas: old-age security; on active service

OAS: Office of Appalachian Studies; Old Age Security; Organization of American States

OAS: *Organisation de l'Armee Secrete* (French—Organization of the Secret Army)—General Salan's secret counter-revolutionary group attempting to crush Algerian independence

OASD-AE: Office Assistant Secretary of Defense, Application Engineering

OASDHI: Old-Age, Survivors, Disability, and Health Insurance Social Security

OASDI: Old Age, Survivors, and Disability Insurance

OASD-R & D: Office Assistant Secretary of Defense, Research and Development

OASD-S & L: Office Assistant Secretary of Defense, Supply and Logistics

OASI: Old-Age and Survivor's Insurance

oat.: outside air temperature

OAT: Office of Advanced Technology (USAF)

OATS: Office of Air Transportation Security

OAU: Organization for African Unity

oaw: old abandoned well; overall width

Oax: Oaxaca

OAYR: Outstanding Airman of the Year Ribbon

ob: oboe; oboes; obsolete; obstetric; obstetrical; obstetrician; obstetrics; old boy; on board; operational base (OB); ordered back; outboard buffer; output buffer; overboard (vent line)

o/b: opening of books

o B: ohne Befund (German—without findings)

Ob: object art (art accented with real objects, *e.g.*, a real watch chain dangling between two pockets of a man's vest in a painting)

OB: Old Bailey; Operating Base; Operational Base; Order of Battle; Ordnance Battalion; Ordnance Board; Ox Box (corporation)

OB: *Oranjeboom* (Dutch—orange tree)—Amsterdam-brewed beer

O.B.: obstetrical; obstetrician; obstetrics

O'B: O'Brien

OBAWS: On-Board Aircraft Weighing System

Obad: The Book of Obadiah

obb: obbligato

OBB: battleship, old (3-letter naval symbol)

ÖBB: Österreichische Bundesbahnen (Austrian Federal Railways)

obc: on-board checkout

OBC: Outboard Boating Club

obce: on-board checkout equipment

obd: omnibearing distance

ob dk: observation deck

obdt: obedient

OBE: Office of Business Economics; Officer of the British Empire; Order of the British Empire

Obediah Skinflint: (pseudonym—Joel Chandler Harris)

ober: (German—upper)

obfusc: obfuscated

Ob-G: Obstetrician-Gynaecologist

ob-gyn: obstetrical-gynecological; obstetrician-gynecologist

OBulg: Old Bulgarian

obi: omnibearing indicator

obit: obituary

obj: object; objective

obl: obligation; oblique; oblong; obloquy

ob/l: ocean bill of lading

OBL: Ohio Barge Line

oblg: obligate; obligation

oblig: obligation(s); obligatory

obln: obligation

obre: octubre (Spanish—October)

obro: outubro (Portuguese—October)

obs: observation; observe; observer; obsolete; obstacle; obstetrical; obstetrics; obstetrician

obsc: obscure(d)

obsd: observed

obsn: observation

obsol: obsolescent

obss: ocean bottom scanning sonar

obs spot: observation spot

obst: obstacle; obstruction

obstet: obstetrical; obstetrician; obstetrics

obstr: obstruction

obsv: observation; observatory; observer

obt.: obiit (Latin—he died)

OBU: One Big Union

obv: obverse; ocean boarding vessel

obw: observation window

oc: ocean; odor control; on center

o'c: o'clock (of the clock)

o-c: open-circuit

o/c: overcharge

o & c: onset and course (disease)

Oc: Ocean

OC: Oakland City; Oakwood College; Oberlin College; Oblate College; Occidental College;

Odessa College; Office of Censorship; Officer Candidate; Ohio College; Okolona College; Olivet College; Olympic College; Orlando College; Otero College; Overeseas Chinese; Overseas Commands

O-in-C: Officer-in-Charge

O of C: Order of the Coif

oca: ocarina (flutelike clay instrument nicnamed "sweet potato")

OCA: Office of Consumer Affairs (ombudsman function of the U.S. Postal Service)

OCAA: Oklahoma City-Ada-Atoka (railroad)

OCAC: Office of Chief of Air Corps

OCADS: Oklahoma City Air Defense Sector

OCAFF: Office Chief of Army Field Forces

OCAM: Organisation Commune Africaine et Malgache [Organization of the African and Malagasy Community (of former French colonies)]

OCAMA: Oklahoma City Air Materiel Area

OCAS: Organization of Central American States

OCAW: Oil, Chemical and Atomic Workers (union)

ocb: oil circuit breaker

OCB: Officer Career Brief (DoD résumé)

occ: occupation

Occ: occulting (light)

OCC: Olney Community College; Onondaga Community College; Orange Coast College

OCCA: Oil and Colour Chemists Association

occas: occasional(ly)

OCCC: Orange County Community College

Oc C Cm O: Office of the Chief Chemical Officer

OCC-E: Office of the Chief of Communications — Electronics (USA)

occip: occipital; occiput

OCCIS: Operational Command and Control Intelligence System (USA)

OCCM: Office of Commercial Communications Management

OCCO: Office of the Chief Chemical Officer

occ th: occupational therapy

occup: occupation(al)

OCD: Office of Civil Defense

OCDA: Ordnance Corps Detroit Arsenal

OCDM: Office of Civil and Defense Mobilization

OCDR: Office of Collateral Development Responsibility
OCE: Office of the Chief of Engineers; Ontario College of Education
OC & E: Oregon, California, and Eastern (railroad)
OCEAN: Oceanographic Coordination Evaluation Analysis Network
OCEANAV: Oceanographer of the U.S. Navy
oceaneer(ing): ocean engineer(ing)
Ocean Inst: Oceanografiska Institute (Oceanographic Institute in Göteborg, Sweden)
oceanog: oceanography
OCEE: Organisation de Coopération Économique Européene (European Economic Cooperation Organization)
ocf: originally cultured formulation
OC of F: Office of the Chief of Finance
ocg: omnicardiogram
OCHAMPUS: Office for the Civilian Health and Medical Program of the Uniformed Services
OCI: Office of the Coordinator of Information
OCL: Ocean Cargo Line
o'clock: of the clock
OCMH: Office of the Chief of Military History
OCNM: Oregon Caves National Monument (limestone caverns near Medford, Oregon)
oco: open-close-open
OCO: Office of the Chief of Ordnance; San José, Costa Rica (El Coco Airport)
o'coat: overcoat
OComS: Office of Community Services
OConUS: outside continental limits of the United States
OCORA: Office de Cooperation Radiophonique (French—Office of Radiophonic Cooperation) —French overseas radio help for former colonies
ocp: overland common points
OCP: Office of Cultural Presentations
OCPL: Oklahoma City Public Library
ocr: optical character recognition
OCR: Office of Civilian Requirements; Office of Coal Research; Office of Coordinating Responsibility; Office of the County Recorder; Organization Change Request; Organization for the Collaboration of Railways
OCRA: Organisation Clandestine de la Revolution Algerienne

(French—Secret Organization of the Algerian Revolution)
ocs: outer continental shelf
oc's: obscene (telephone) callers; obscene (telephone) calls
OCS: Office of Civilian Supply; Office of Commercial Services; Office of Contract Settlement; Officer Candidate School; Officers' Chief Steward; Organe du Controle des Stupefiants (Agency for the Control of Narcotics)
OCS': Overseas Civil Servants (members of the British Overseas Civil Service)
OC of SA: Office, Chief of Staff, Army
OCSIGO: Office of the Chief Signal Officer
ocst: overcast
oct: octagon; octane; octave; octet
Oct: October
OCT: Office of the Chief of Transportation
oct^e: octubre (Spanish—October)
Octember: October and November
octup.: octuplus (Latin—eightfold)
octv: open-circuit television
ocv: open-circuit voltage
od: olive-drab; optical density; outside diameter; overdose; overdrive
od: och dylika (Swedish—and the like)
o/d: on demand; overdraft
o & d: origin and destination
o.d.: oculus dexter (Latin—right eye)
OD: Aerocondor (Aerovias Condor de Colombia); external grinding; officer of the day; olive drab; Ordnance Department; original design; outside dimension
O.D.: Doctor of Optometry
oda: occipito-dextra anterior
Oda: Odessa
ODa: Old Danish
ODA: Office of Debt Analysis; Office of the District Administrator; Overseas Development Administration
ODALE: Office of Drug Abuse Law Enforcement
odb: opiate-directed behavior
ODC: Old Dominion College
ODCTI: Old Dominion College Technical Institute
od'd: overdosed
odde: (Dano-Norwegian—cape; point)
ODDRE: Office of the Director of Defense Research and Engineering
ODEC: Ocean Design Engineering Corporation

ODECA: Organización de Estados Centroamericanos (Organization of Central American States)
ODECO: Ocean Drilling and Exploration Company
ODESSA: Organisation Der Ehe maligen SS Angehoerigen (German—Organization of Former Members of the SS)—device for simulating suicides and arranging new names, occupations, and countries for war criminals who served Hitler
ODF: Old Dominion Foundation
ODFI: Open Die Forging Institute
ODGSO: Office of Domestic Gold and Silver Operations
o-d-ing: overdosing
o dk: orlop deck
ODL: Office of Defense Lending
ODM: Office of Defense Mobilization; Order of De Molay
odn: own doppler nullifier
Odn: Odense; Odin; Odinist (member of Nordic-supremacy sect)
odom: odometer
odont: odontology
odop: offset doppler
odoram.: odoramentum (Latin —perfume)
odorat.: odoratus (Latin—odorous; perfuming)
odorl: odorless
odp: occipito-dextra posterior
ODP: Orbit Determination Program
ODR: Office of Defense Resources
o'drive: overdrive
odsd: overseas duty selection date
ODSI: Ocean Data Systems Inc
odt: occipito-dextra transverse
od units: optical-density units
ODWIN: Opening Doors Wider in Nursing
ODWSA: Office of the Directorate of Weapon Systems Analysis (USA)
oe: oersted; omissions excepted
Oe: oersted
OE: Office of Education; Old English; Oregon Electric (railroad)
OEA: Organización de los Estados Americanos (Organization of American States); Outdoor Education Association; Overseas Education Association
OEB: Oregon Educational Broadcasting
ÖEC: Österreichischer Aero-Club; Ohio Edison Company
OECD: Organization for Economic Cooperation and Development
OECE: Organisation Européenne de Coopération Économique (Organization for European Economic Cooperation)
oeco: outboard engine cutoff

OECQ: Organisation Européenne pour la Contrôle de la Qualité (European Quality-Control Organization)
OED: *Oxford English Dictionary*
oedjoeng: (Malayan—cape)
oee: outer enamel epithelium
OEEC: Organization for European Economic Cooperation
OEEO: Office of Equal Educational Opportunities
OEG: Operations Evaluation Group
oegt: observable evidence of good teaching
OEIU: Office Employees International Union
OEL: Organization Equipment List
oem: original equipment manufacturer
OEM: Office of Executive Management
oen: oenanthic; oenanthyl; oenolyn; oenology; oenological; oenologist; oenomancy; oenomel (wine and honey); oenometer; oenophilist; oenophobist; oenopoetic
OEO: Office of Economic Opportunity
OEOB: Old Executive Office Building (D.C.)
OEP: Office of Emergency Planning; Office of Emergency Preparedness
OEPP: Organisation Européenne et Méditerranéenne pour la Protection des Plantes (European and Mediterranean Organization for the Protection of Plants)
oer: oersted (unit of magnetic force); original equipment replacement
o'er: over
OER: Office of Aerospace Research (USAF); Officer Effectiveness Report; Officer Efficiency Report; Officers Emergency Reserve; Officer Engineering Reserve; Organization for European Research
OES: Office of Economic Stabilization; Official Experimental Station; Order of the Eastern Star; Organization of European States
oesoph: oesophagus
OESP: *O Estado de São Paulo* (State of Sao Paulo)—Brazil's leading newspaper
OESS: Office of Engineering Standards Services
oeste: (Portuguese or Spanish —west)
OET: Office of Education and Training
OEW: Office of Economic Warfare
OEX: Office of Educational Exchange

OEZ: *osteuropäische Zeit* (German—East European Time)
of.: old face (type); optional form; outside face; oxidizing flame
OF: Oceanographic Facility; Odd Fellows; Old French; Operating Forces; Ophthalmological Foundation; Osteopathic Foundation; Oxbow Falls; Oxenstierna Foundation; Oxford Foundation
OFA: Office of Financial Analysis
ofc: office
OFCC: Office of Federal Contract Compliance
ofcl: official
OFDI: Office of Direct Investments
OFEMA: Office Français d'Exportation de Matériel Aéronautique
off.: office(r); official
offen: offensive (ammunition)
offer.: offertories; offertory
OFHA: Oil Field Haulers Association
ofhc: oxygen-free high-carbon (copper)
Oflag: *Offizierlager* (German —officer's prison camp)
OFlem: Old Flemish
OFM: Office of Flight Missions (NASA)
OFPA: Order of the Founders and Patriots of America
OFPM: Office of Fiscal Plans and Management
O Fr: Old French
OFR: Office of the Federal Register
OFris: Old Frisian
OFS: Orange Free State
OFST: Office of the Secretary of the Air Force
OFT: Ohio Federation of Teachers
og: oh gee; old girl; on ground; on guard; original gum
o-g: orange-green
OG: Old Gaelic; Olympic Games
OG: *O Globo* (Rio de Janeiro's Globe)
ÖG: *Österreichische Galerie* (Austrian Gallery)
O/G: Opto/Graphic
OGAMA: Ogden Air Materiel Area
O-gauge: 1-1/4-inch track gauge (model railroads)
OGCMD: Ogden Contract Management District
Ogd: Ogdensburg
oge (OGE): operational ground equipment
OGEM: Overzees Gas en Elektriciteit Maatschappij (Dutch —Overseas Gas and Electric Company)
O Ger: Old German
OGJ: *Oil and Gas Journal*
ogl: obscure glass
OGMC: Ordnance Guided Missile

Center
OGNR: Oribi Gorge Nature Reserve (South Africa)
OGO: Orbiting Geophysical Observatory
OGPU: *Obiedinennoye Gosudarstvennoye Politicheskoye Upravlenie* (Russian—United State Political Administration)—*q.v.m.* —*VOT*)
OGR: Ontario Government Railway (Ontario Northland)
ogse: operational ground-support equipment
OGSEL: Operational Ground-Support Equipment List
OGU: Occupational Guidance Unit
OGR: *Official Guide of the Railways*
oh.: office hours; on hand; open hearth; out home; oval head; overhead; over-the-horizon(communication)
o-H: on-Hudson
OH: hydroxyl radical (symbol); San Francisco and Oakland Helicopter Airlines (2-letter code)
oha: outside helix angle
OHBMS: On Her (His) Britannic Majesty's Service
ohc: overhead cam
OHC: Ottumwa Heights College; Overseas Hotel Corporation
ohd: organic hearing disease
OHD & W: Outer Harbor Dock and Wharf
O Henry: William Sydney Porter
OHG: Old High German
OHG: *offene Handelsgesellschaft* (German—ordinary partnership)
ohi: ocular hypertension indicator
OHI: Oil Heat Institute
OHIA: Oil Heat Institute of America
Ohio Turn: Ohio Turnpike
ohm.: ohmmeter
ohm-cm: ohm-centimeter
oho: out-of-house operation
ohp: oxygen at high pressure
OHRG: *Official Hotel and Resort Guide*
ohs: open-hearth steel
OHS: Office of Highway Safety; Oregon Historical Society
OHSIP: Ontario Health Services Insurance Plan
ohv: overhead valve; overhead vent
oi: oil-immersed; oil-immersion
o/i: opsonic index
OI: Office Instruction; Operating Instruction; Optimist International; Oriental Institute
OIA: Ocean Industries Association; Office of Industrial Associates; Office of International Administration; Oil Import Administra-

tion; Oil Insurance Association; Outboard Industry Associations

OIAA: Office of International Aviation Affairs

OIB: Ohio Inspection Bureau; Oklahoma Inspection Bureau

oic: oil cooler

OIC: Oceanographic Instrumentation Center; Officer in Charge; Ohio Improved Chester (white swine); Opportunities Industrialization Centers

OIcel: Old Icelandic

OICS: Office of Interoceanic Canal Studies

OIE: Office of International Epizootics

OIF: Office for Intellectual Freedom (ALA)

OIG: Office of the Inspector General

oih (OIH): ovulation-producing hormone

OIHP: *Office International d'Hygiene Publique* (French—International Office of Public Health) —UN

OII: Office of Invention and Innovation

OIL: Operation Inspection Log

oil of vitriol: concentrated sulfuric acid (H_2SO_4)

OIM: Oriental Institute Museum (University of Chicago)

OINA: Oyster Institute of North America

OINC: Officer in Charge

oint: ointment

OIPH: Office of International Public Health

OIr: Old Irish

OIR: Office of Inter-American Radio

OIRB: Oregon Insurance Rating Bureau

OIRT: Organisation Internationale de Radiodiffusion et Télévision (International Radio and Television Organization)

OIS: Overseas Investors Services

OISA: Office of International Scientific Affairs

OISE: Ontario Institute for Studies in Education

OIt: Old Italian

OITF: Office of International Trade Fairs

OIUC: Oriental Institute of the University of Chicago

OIVV: Office International de la Vigne et du Vin (International Office of Vines and Wines)

OIW: Oceanographic Institute, Wellington (New Zealand)

OĪWR: Office of Indian Water Rights

oj: open-joint; open-joist(ed) orange juice

oJ: *ohne Jahr* (German—without year)—no date

OJD: Office de Justification de la Diffusion

ojt: on-the-job-training

ok: all correct; okay; outer keel

ok: *ohne kosten* (German—without cost)

OK: all correct; okay; Old Kinderhook (birthplace and home of President Martin Van Buren; Democratic O.K. Club believed to have started practice of putting "O.K." on deals and documents they approved of); Old Kingdom (Egypt)

Ø K: *Østasiatiske Kompagni* (East Asiatic Company—Danish)

oka: otherwise known as

OKA: Okinawa, Ryukyu Islands (airport)

OKC: Oklahoma City, Oklahoma (airport)

OKd: okayed

OKH: *Oberkommando des Heeres* (German—Army High Command)

Okie: Oklahoman

Okin: Okinawa(n)

OKL: *Oberkommando der Luftwaffe* (German—Air Force High Command)

Okla: Oklahoma; Oklahoman

OklaC: Oklahoma City

OKM: *Oberkommando der Marine* (German—Naval High Command)

Okt: *Oktober* (German—October); *Oktyabr* (Russian—October)

OKT: Oslo Kommune Tunnelbanekontoret (Oslo subway system)

Oktronics: Oklahoma Electronics (corporation)

OKW: *Oberkommando der Wehrmacht (German—Armed Forces High Command*

ol: oil level; operating license; or less

ol.: *oleum* (Latin—oil)

o.l.: *oculus laevus* (Latin—left eye)

o/l: operations/logistics

Ol: olive

OL: Olsen Line; Oranje Line (Orange Line)

ola: occipito-laeva anterior

OLA: Osteopathic Libraries Association

OLAS: Organization of Latin American Solidarity; Organization of Latin American Students

olbm (OLBM): orbital-launched ballistic missile

OlBr: olive brown

olc: on-line computer

OLC: Oak Leaf Cluster

OLD: Office of Legislative Development

Old Abe: Abraham Lincoln

Old Buena Vista: General Zachary Taylor who attacked Mexicans at Buena Vista in February 1847; later was twelfth President of the United States

Old Chapultepec: General Winfield Scott whose victory at Chapultepec ended Mexican War in September 1847

old-fash: old-fashioned

Oldfos: Old Established Forces

Old Glory: the American flag

Old Guard: conservatives; Napoleon's imperial guard who made the last charge at Waterloo; the establishment

Old Harry: (the devil)—Satan

Old Hickory: General Andrew Jackson—seventh President of the United States

Old Ironsides: USS *Constitution*

Old Kinderhook: Martin Van Buren—eighth President of the United States

Old Lady of Threadneedle Street: Bank of England

Old Man Eloquent: Isocrates in the opinion of Milton; John Quincy Adams in the opinion of the Congress he served after being sixth President of the U.S.

Old Nick: (the devil)—Satan

Old Noll: Old Oliver Cromwell

Old Party: W(illiam) Somerset Maugham

old rep: old repertory; old reprobate

Old Rough-and-Ready: General Zachary Taylor—twelfth President of the United States

Olds: Oldsmobile

OLDS: On-Line Display System

Old Scratch: Satan

Old Test.: Old Testament

Old Tippecanoe: General William Henry Harrison—ninth President of the United States

Old Vic: repertory theater in London

OLEA: Office of Law Enforcement Assistance

oleo: oleomargarine; oleoresins; oleum

olericult: olericulture

'oleum: petroleum

olf: olfactory

OLF: Orbital Launch Facility

OlG: olive green

OLG: Old Low German

Olig: Oligocene

OLL: Office of Legislative Liaison

Ollie: Olive(r)

ol. oliv.: *oleum olivea* (Latin—olive oil)
olp: occipito-laeva posterior
OLPS: On-Line Programming System
olr: overload relay
ol res: oleoresin
olrt: on-line real time
OLS: Optical Landing System
olt: occipito-laeva transverse
ol & t: owners, landlords, and tenants
olv: olivaceous; olive
Olym: Olympia
Olympics: Olympic Games; Olympic Mountains, Washington
om: old measurement; old man; old men; outer marker
o.m.: *omni mane* (Latin—every morning)
o & m (O & M): operation and maintenance
Om: Omaha; Oman
OM: Old Man (colloquial)
OM: *Ostmark* (East German mark)
O.M.: Order of Merit
O & M: Organization and Methods
OMA: Office of Maritime Affairs; Oklahoma Military Academy; Omaha, Nebraska (airport); Ontario Medical Association
omarb: *omarbetad* (Swedish— revised)
OMARS: Outstanding Media Advertising by Restaurants
OMAT: Office of Manpower, Automation, and Training
Omb: Ombudsman
OMB: Office of Management and Budget; Ontario Municipal Board
OMC: Office of Munitions Control; Outboard Marine Corporation
OME: Office of Minerals Exploration
OMEL: Orient Mid-East Lines
omfp: obtaining money by false pretenses
OMGE: Organisation Mondiale de Gastro-Entérologie (World Gastro-Enterological Organization)
OMGUS: Office of Military Government, United States
OMI: Operation Move-In
omiom: original meaning is the only meaning
omkr: *omdring* (Norwegian— about)
oml: outside mold line
OML: Ontario Motor League; Orbiting Military Laboratory
OMM: Office of Minerals Mobilization; Organisation Météorologique Mondiale; Organisation Mondiale de la Santé (World Health Organization)

OMMA: Outboard Motor Manufacturers Association
OMMS: Office of Merchant Marine Safety (USCG)
omn. bih.: *omni bihora* (Latin— every two hours)
omn. hor.: *omni hora* (Latin— every hour)
omni: omnidirectional; omnirange; omnivisual
omn. man.: *omni mane* (Latin— every morning)
omn. noct.: *omni nocte* (Latin—every night)
omn. quad. hor.: *omni quadrante hora* (Latin—every quarter of an hour)
OMPER: Office of Manpower Policy Evaluation and Research
ompf: omphaloskepsis
OMR: Officer Master Record
oms: output per man shift
OMSA: Orders and Medals Society of America
OMSF: Office of Manned Space Flight (NASA)
OMSIP: Ontario Medical Surgical Insurance Plan
on.: octane number
on.: *onomastikon* (Greek—lexicon)
On: *Onorevole* (Italian—Honorable); *Onsdag* (Danish—Wednesday)
ON: Ogden Nash; Old Norse
ÖN: Österreichische National-bibliotek (Austrian National Library)
O.N.: Orthopedic Nurse
O & N: Oregon & Northeastern (railroad)
ONA: Overseas National Airways; Overseas News Agency
ONAC: Office of Noise Abatement and Control
ONAP: Orbit Navigation Analysis Program
onc: operational navigational chart(s)
ONC: Oficina Nacional del Café (National Coffee Administration—Honduras); Oregon-Nevada-California (fast freight truck line)
oncol: oncology
OND: Opthalmic Nursing Diploma
ONEO: Office of Navajo Economic Opportunity
ONERA: Office National des Études et des Recherches Aérospatiales (French space research agency)
ONF: Old Norman-French
ONI: Office of Naval Intelligence
ONM: Ocmulgee National Monument; Office of Naval Materiel
ONO: *Oesnoroeste* (Spanish—west northwest)

onomat: onomatopoeia
o noz: oil nozzle
ONP: Olympic National Park (Washington)
ONR: Office of Naval Research
ONRL: Office of Naval Records and Library
ONRRR: Office of Naval Research Resident Representative
ON Rwy: Ontario Northland Railway
ONSR: Ozark National Scenic Riverways (Missouri)
ont: ontology
Ont: Ontario
ONT: Our New Thread (Clark's trademark)
ONU: Organisation Nations Unies (French—United Nations Organization); Organizzazione Nazioni Unite (Italian—United Nations Organization)
ONUC: Operation des Nations Unies, Congo (United Nations Operation in the Congo)
ONUESC: Organisation des Nations Unies pour l'Education, la Science et la Culture Intellectuelle (UNESCO)
ONWR: Okefinokee National Wildlife Refuge (Florida and Georgia); Ottawa National Wildlife Refuge (Ohio); Ouray National Wildlife Refuge (Utah)
o-and-o: one-and-only
OO: Oceanic Operators; Oceanographic Office
O/O: Office of Oceanography (UNESCO)
O of O: Order of Owls
OOA: Office of Ocean Affairs
OOAA: Olive Oil Association of America
OOAMA: Ogden Air Materiel Area
oob: out of bed
oobe: out of body experience
OoC: Office of Censorship
OOD: Officer of the Deck
OO/Eng: out of stock but on order from England (for example)
OOG: Office of Oil and Gas
OOHA: Operation Oil Heat Associates
ooj: obstruction of justice
ool: oology; operator-oriented language
OOL: Orient Overseas Line
oolr: opthalmology, otology, laryngology, rhinology
OOM: Officers Open Mess
Oom Paul: (Afrikaans—Uncle Paul)—sobriquet of Stephanus Johannes Paulus Kruger—leader of Boer rebellion and president of Transvaal
OOO-gauge: +3/8-inch track

gauge (model railroads)

oop: out-of-print

OOP: Oceanographic Observations of the Pacific

oops: offshore oil-pollution sleeve

oos: orbit-to-orbit shuttle

OOSC: Olfactronics and Odor Sciences Center (IITRI)

oost: (Dutch—east)

oote: out-of-town executive

ootg: one of the greats

OOW: Officer On Watch

op: open policy; opera; operation; operational; operation plan(s); operational priority; operetta; opposite prompt (stage left); opus; other people's (possessions); outer panel; out of print; outside production; overproof; overprune; overpuff

op: (Dutch—on)

Op: optical art (art accented with or based on optical illusions); Oregon pine

OP: Observation Post; Office of Protocol (US Department of State); Oregon pine

O-P: Oppenheimer-Phillips (process)

OPA: Office of Population Affairs; Office of Price Administration; Office of Public Affairs

op amp: operational amplifier

op art: optical art (art involving optical illusion)

OPBMA: Ocean Pearl Button Manufacturers Association

opc: office percentage

OPC: Ohio Power Company; Out-Patient Clinic; Overseas Press Club

OPCA: Overseas Press Club of America

op. cit.: opus citato (Latin—in the work cited)

OPCNM: Organ Pipe Cactus National Monument

OPCS: Office of Population Censuses and Surveys

opd: optical path difference

OPD: Officer Personnel Directorate; Out Patient Department

opdar: optical direction and ranging

OPDD: Operational Plan Data Document

op dent: operative dentistry

OPDR: Oldenburg-Portugiesische-Dampfschiffs-Rederei (steamship company)

ope: open-point expanding

O P & E: Oregon, Pacific & Eastern (railroad)

OPEC: Organization of Petroleum Exporting Countries

op-ed: opinion-editorial (newspaper page combining readers' opin-

ions with editorials)

open.: open circuit; opening

opens.: open circuits (electrical parlance); openings

opep (OPEP): orbital plane experiment package

oper: operational

Opéra-Com: Opéra-Comique (Paris)

OPers: Old Persian

opex: operational (and) executive (personnel)

OPEX: Operational, Executive (and Administrative Personnel Program of the United Nations)

opg: opening

Oph.D.: Doctor of Ophthalmology

ophthal: ophthalmology; ophthalmoscope

opi: omnibus personality inventory

OPI: Office of Public Information; Offsite Production (Purchase) Inspection; Ordnance Procedure Instrumentation; Outside Production (Purchase) Inspection

opis: opisometer

opl: operational

OPL: Omaha Public Library; Orlando Public Library; Ottawa Public Library

OPLP: Office of Program and Legislative Planning

opm: operations per minute; operator programming method; optically-projected map; other people's money

opn: operation

OpNav: Office of the Chief of Naval Operations

opng: opening

opo: one price only

Opo: Oporto

OPO: Office of Personnel Operations (US Army)

OPOR: Office of Public Opinion Research

oporf: operation(s) order

opp: opportunity; opposed; opposite; opposition; out of print at present

OPP: Ontario Provincial Police

opplan: operating plan

oppor: opportunity

oppy: opportunity

opr: operate; operator

OPr: Old Provençal

OPR: Office of Primary Responsibility

OPruss: Old Prussian

ops: operations; opposite prompter's side (of stage)

op's: other people's (cigarettes or money)

OPS: Office of Price Stabilization; Oxygen Purge System

ops analysis: operations analysis

opt: optic; optical; optician; optics; optimal; optimum; option; optional

OPTA: Organ and Piano Teachers Association

Opt.D.: Doctor of Optometry

opti: optimist(ic); optimize; optimum

opticon: optical tactical converter

optmrst: optometrist

optn: optician

optoel: optoelectronics

optom: optometrist; optometry

optr: optryk (Dano-Norwegian —reprint)

OPUS: Older People United for Service

oq: oil quench; overmation quotient

OQ: Officers Quarters

oqe: objective quality evidence

OQMG: Office of the Quartermaster General

OQR: Officer's Qualification Record

or.: operationally ready; other ranks; out of range; outside radius; outside right; overseas replacement; owner's risk; oxidation-reduction

or.: oratio (Latin—speech; discourse)

o & r: ocean and rail; overhaul and repair

OR: Officer Records; omnidirectional radio range (symbol); Operating Room; Operational Requirement; Operations Requirement; Operations Research; Operations Room; Ordnance Report; Owasco River (railroad); Oyster River

OR: Operations Research

O.R.: Operating Room (hospital abbreviation)

ÖR: Österreichischer Rundfunk (Austrian Radio and Television)

ORA: Oil Refiners Association; Operations Research Analyst

ORAD: Office of Rural Areas Development

orang: orangutan (Malay—man of the forest), a reddish-haired arboreal anthropoid ape found in Borneo and Sumatra

orat: oration; orator; oratorio; oratory

ORAU: Oak Ridge Associated Universities

orbic: orbicular; orbicularis

Orbis: Polish Travel Office

ORBS: Orbital Rendezvous Base System

Orc: Orcadian (inhabitants of or pertaining to Orkney Islands)

ORC: Officers Reserve Corps; Opinion Research Corporation;

Ozarks Regional Commission
ORCB: Order of Railway Conductors and Brakemen
orch: orchestra; orchestral; orchestration
Orch Consv: Orchestre de la Société des Concerts du Conservatoire de Paris
orches: orchestration
Orch H: Orchestra Hall
Orch Nat: Orchestre National de la Radiodiffusion Française
Orch de l'Opéra: Orchestre du Théâtre National de l'Opéra de Paris
Orch Suisse Rom: Orchestre de la Suisse Romande
ORCMD: Orlando Contract Management District
orcon: organic control
ord: order(s); ordinal; ordnance
Ord: Orderly
ORD: Chicago, Illinois (O'Hare Airport); Office of Research and Development
ORDA: Oceanographic Research for Defense Application
OrdC: Ordnance Corps
Ordo: Ordovician
ORE: Ocean Research Equipment; Operational Research Establishment
OR & E: Office of Research and Engineering
Oreg: Oregon; Oregonian
Ore-Ida pots: Oregon-Idaho potatoes
o/r enema: oil-retention enema
orf: orifice
ORF: Norfolk, Virginia (airport)
ÖRF: *Österreichischer Rundfunk* (Austrian radio and TV network)
org: organ; organic; organization; organize; organizer
ORG: Operations Research Group
Orgburo: Organizational Bureau of the Central Committee (of the Communist Party)
orgl: organizational
orgn: organization
ori: orientation inventory
Ori: Oriente
ORI: Operation Readiness Inspection
orient.: oriental; orientation
Orient(al): Asia(tic)
ORIENT: Orient Airways
orig: origin; original; originator
O-ring: O-shaped ring
ORINS: Oak Ridge Institute of Nuclear Studies
oris: orismological; orismologist; orismology
ORIT: Operational Readiness Inspection Test
Ork: Orkney Islands

orl: orlon (synthetic fiber)
ORL: Orbital Research Laboratory; Ordnance Research Laboratory; Orlando, Florida (Harndon Airport)
orn: orange; ornament
Orn: Oran (British maritime contraction)
orn: *orne* (French—decorated; ornamented)
ORN: Operating Room Nurse
ornith: ornithology
ORNL: Oak Ridge National Laboratory
ORO: Operations Research Office (Johns Hopkins University)
orog: orographer; orographic; orographical; orography
ORP: Okret Rzecypospolitej Polskiej (Polish—Ship of the Polish Republic)
o-r pot.: oxidation-reduction potential
orr: operations research research (ORR)
o-r release: own-recognizance release (legal device freeing responsible citizens from need for going to jail or posting bail bond until case comes to court for hearing)
ORRRC: Outdoor Recreation Resources Review Commission
ors: owner's risk of shifting
ors.: *orationes* (Latin—speeches)
ORS: Old Red Sandstone; Operational Research Society
ORSA: Operations Research Society of America
ORSANCO: Ohio River Valley Water Sanitation Commission
ORSTOM: Office de la Recherche Scientifique et Technique d'Outre Mer (Overseas Office of Scientific and Technical Research)
ort: operational readiness training
ORT: Operational Readiness Test; Order of Railroad Telegraphers
ORTF: Office Radio-Télévision Française (French Radio-Television Office)
ortho: orthochromatic; orthographic; orthography; orthopedic(s)
Ortho: Greek Orthodox
orthog: orthography
orthop: orthopedics
orthor: orthorhombic
ORTO: Occupational Rehabilitation Training for Overseas
ORU: Oral Roberts University
ORuss: Old Russian
ORV: Ocean Range Vessel (naval symbol)
orw: owner's risk of wetting
ORY: Paris, France (Orly Airport)

os: oil switch; old series; old style; on station; out of stock; output secondary; outside; outsize; overseas; oversize
o/s: out of service
os: (Latin—bone; mouth)
o.s.: *oculus sinister* (Latin—left eye)
Os: osmium
OS: Ocean Station; Old Saxon; Old Series; Operation Sandstone; Operation Snapper; Ordinary Seaman; Ordnance Specifications; Optical Society
O.S.: Old Style
Osa: Osaka
OSA: Office of the Secretary of the Army; Official Secrets Act; Omnibus Society of America; Optical Society of America; Osaka, Japan (airport); Overseas Supply Agency; Oyster Shell Association
OSAF: Office of the Secretary of the Air Force
OSAS: Overseas Service Aid Scheme
OSBA: Ohio School Boards Association
OSBM: Office of Space Biology and Medicine
osc: oscillator
Osc: Oscan
OSC: On-Scene Commander; Ontario Securities Commission; Ordnance Systems Command (formerly Bureau of Weapons); Overseas Shipping Company
OSCA: Officine Specializzate Costruzione Automobili (Italian sports car)
Oscar: code for letter O
oscp: oscilloscope
o s & d: over, short, and damaged
OSD: Office of the Secretary of Defense; Operational Support Directive; Ordnance Supply Depot
osdp: on-site data processing
ose: operational support equipment
OS & E: Ocean Science and Engineering
OSerb: Old Serbian
OSFI: Open Steel Flooring Institute
OSG: Office of the Secretary General
OSG: *Official Steamship Guide*
Osh: Ossian
OSHA: Occupational Safety and Health Act; Occupational Safety and Health Administration
OSI: Office of Special Investigation (USAF)
OSIS: Office of Science Information Service
Osk: Oskarshamm

OSK: Osaka Syosen Kaisha (Osaka Mercantile Steamship Company)
Osl: Oslo
OSl: Old Slavonic
OSL: Oslo, Norway (airport)
osm: osmosis; osmotic
OSM: One of the Swinish Multitude (Philip Freneau, poet of the American Revolution, used this three-letter device after his name, thereby deriding similar-looking British titles); Overzees Scheepvaart Maatschappij(Overseas Shipping Company)
OSMM: Office of Safeguards and Materials Management (AEC)
OSN: Office of the Secretary of the Navy
OSN: Orquesta Sinfónica Nacional (Spanish—National Symphonic Orchestra)
OSNY: Oratorio Society of New York
oso (OSO): orbiting solar observatory
OSO: Omaha Symphony Orchestra; Oregon Symphony Orchestra
OSO: Oessudoeste (Spanish—west southwest); Orbiting Solar Observatory; Ordnance Supply Office
OSODS: Office of Strategic Offensive and Defensive Systems (USN)
osp: outside purchased
OSp: Old Spanish
OSQ: Orchestre Symphonique de Québec (French—Quebec Symphonic Orchestra)
OSR: Office of Scientific Research; Office of Security Review; Operational Support Requirement(s); Orchestre de la Suisse Romande (Orchestra of French Switzerland); Oversea Returnee
OSRD: Office of Scientific Research and Development; Office of Standard Reference Data
OSRO: Office of Scientific Research and Development
OSRTN: Office of the Special Representative for Trade Negotiations
oss (OSS): orbiting space station
OSS: Orbital Space Station; Office of Strategic Services; old submarine (3-letter code)
OSSA: Office of Space Sciences and Applications (NASA)
OSSS: Orbital Space Station Studies
ost: oldest
øst: (Danish or Norwegian—east)
Öst: Österreich (German—Austria)
OST: Office of Science and Tech-

nology; Old Spanish Trail (US 90); Operational Suitability Test
OS & T: Office of Science and Technology
osteo: osteopath(ic)
osteoart: osteoarthritic; osteoarthritis
osteol: osteology
osteomy: osteomyelitis
osteop: osteopath(ic); osteopathy
öster: (Swedish—east)
OSTF: Operational System Test Facility
OSTI: Office for Scientific and Technical Information
OSTIV: Organisation Scientifique et Technique Internationale du Vol à Voile
Ostpr: Ostpreussen (German—East Prussia)
OSU: Ohio State University; Oklahoma State University; Oregon State University
OSUK: Ophthalmological Society of the United Kingdom
OSUL: Ohio State University Library; Oklahoma State University Library; Oregon State University Library
osv: och sa vida (Swedish—and so forth); *og sa videre* (Dano-Norwegian—and so forth)—etc.
Osv: Osvald; Osvaldo
OSV: Ocean Station Vessel
Osv Rom: Osservatore Romano (Vatican newspaper)
Osw: Oswald
OSw: Old Swedish
OSW: Office of Saline Water
os & y: outside screw and yolk
ot: observer target; oiltight; old terms; old tuberculin; on time; on track; otitis; otology
ot (OT): occupational therapy; otolaryngology; overtime
o/t: overtime
o-T: on-Thames
OT: Occupational Therapist; Occupational Therapy; Ocean Transportation; Office of Territories; Old Testament; Operational Training; Oregon Trunk (railroad); Organization Table; Otis Elevator (stock exchange symbol); Overseas Tankship (Caltex Line)
OTAG: Office of the Adjutant General (USA)
OTAN: Organisation du Traité del l'Atlantique Nord (NATO)
OTASE: Organisation du Traité de l'Asie du Sud-Est (SEATO)
OTATO: One-Trip Air Travel Orders
otb: off-track betting
otbd: outboard

otc: over the counter
OTC: Officer in Tactical Command; Organization for Trade Cooperation; Ottawa Transit Commission
otd: organ tolerance dose
OTD & SP: Office of Technical Data and Standardization Policy
OTeut: Old Teutonic
OTF: Ontario Teachers Federation
Oth: Othello, The Moor of Venice
oti: official test insecticide
OTI: Oregon Technical Institute
OTIA: Ordnance Technical Intelligence Agency
OTIS: Occupational Training Information System; Oregon Total Information System
otj: on the job
otl: output transformerless; out to lunch
OTM: Office of Telecommunications Management
o-to-o: out-to-out
olol: otology
otolaryngol: otolaryngology
OTO/Neth: only to order from Netherlands (for example)
otorhinol: otorhinolaryngology
otp: obstacle to progress; oxygen tanking panel
OTP: Office of Telecommunications Policy
otr: on the rag (underground slang—on the menstrual cycle)
OTR: Registered Occupational Therapist
OTRACO: Office de l'Exploitation des Transports Coloniaux (Congolese railway and river transportation administration)
otran: ocean test range and instrumentation
OTS: Office of Technical Services; Officers Training School
OTSG: Office of the Surgeon General
ott: one-time tape; otter; out-going teletype
ott: ottobre (Italian—October)
Ott: Ottawa
otu (OTU): operational training unit
OTUS: Office of the Treasurer of the United States
o.u.: oculus uterque (Latin—either eye)
o & u: over and under
OU: Oglethorpe University; Ohio University; Ottawa University; Otterbein University; Owen University; Owosso University; Oxford University
OUA: Organisation de l'Unite Africaine (Organization of African Unity)

OUCC: Oxford University Cricket Club

ouest: (French—west)

oughtn't: ought not

Ouida: pseudonym of Marie Louise de la Ramée who as a child pronounced Louise as Ouida

OUN: Organizatsia Ukrainiskikh Nationalistiv (Russian—Ukrainian Nationalist Organization)—anti-communist

OUP: Oxford University Press

oupt: output

o/US: oro US (Spanish—American gold; American money)

out.: outlet

outbd: outboard

ouv: ouvrage (French—work)

ov: orbiting vehicle (OV); over

ov: oi vay (Yiddish—alas)

ov.: ovum (Latin—egg)

Ov: Ovid; Oviedo

OV: Oranje Vrystaat (Afrikaans—Orange Free State); Orbital Vehicle

ÖV: Österreichische Volkspartei (German—Austrian People's Party)

OVA: Office of Veterans' Affairs

OVAC: Overseas Visual Aids Center

ovbd: overboard

ovc: other valuable consideration(s); overcast

ovcst: overcast

ove: on vehicle equipment

over.: overture

overmation: over instrumentation

overs: overshoes

ovfl: overflow

ovhd: oval head; overhead

ovhl: overhaul

ovht: overheat

ovk: overkill

ovld: overload

ovm: on-vehicle material

ovm: oi vayz mir (Yiddish—woe unto me)

ovpd: overpaid

OVR: Office of Vocational Rehabilitation

OVRA: Opera Voluntaria per la Repressione dell' Anti-fascismo (Italian—Voluntary Work for the Repression of Anti-Fascism)— Fascist secret police

ovrd: override

ovsp: overspeed

OVSVA: Oranje Vrystaatse Veld Artillerie (Afrikaans—Orange Free State Field Artillery

ow: old woman (slang for wife); one way; ordinary warfare (OW); outer wing; out of wedlock (born of unmarried parents)

o-w: oil-in-water

OWAA: Outdoor Writers' Association of America

OWC: Outline of World Cultures

owf: optimum working frequency

owgl: obscure wire glass

OWH: Office of the War on Hunger

OWHA: Oliver Wendell Holmes Association

OWI: Office of War Information

OWL: Older Women's Liberation; Other Woman, Limited

OWM: Office of Weights and Measures

owp: outer wing panel

OWPP: Office of Welfare and Pension Plans

owpr: ocean wave profile recorder

OWR: Ouse Washes Reserve (England)

OWRR: Office of Water Resources Research

ows (OWS): operational weapon satellite

OWS: Ocean Weather Station

OWSS: Ocean Weather Ship Service

OWU: Ohio Wesleyan University

OWWS: Office of World Weather Systems

ow/ym: older woman/younger man

ox.: oxalic; oxide; oxygen

Ox.: Oxford

OX: oxygen (commercial symbol)

oxa: oxalic acid

oxalic acid: $(COOH)_2$

Oxbridge: Oxford + Cambridge (the ultimate in British formal education)

Oxf: Oxfordshire

OXOCO: Offshore Exploration Oil Company

Oxon: Oxfordshire

Oxon.: Oxonia (Latin—Oxford); *Oxoniensis* (Latin—Oxonian)

oxr: oxidizer

oxwld: oxyacetylene weld

oxy: oxygen

oxycephs: oxycephalics (pointed-skulled people)

OY: orange yellow

O/Y: Osakeytiö (Finnish—limited company)

OYA: Oy Yleisradio Ab (Finnish Broadcasting Company)

Oya Cur: Oyashio Current (Kurile or Okhotsk or Oyasiwo)

oys: oysters

oz: ounce

Oz: ooze

OZ: Ozark Airlines (two-letter designation)

OZA: Ozark Airlines

ozarc: ozone-atmosphere rocket

ozd: observed zenith distance

ozero: (Russian—lake)

oz-in.: ounce-inch

ozone: O_3

ozs: ounces

oz t: ounce troy

Ozzie: Osborn; Oscar; Oswald; Oswaldo

P

p: page; pamphlet; park; parking; part; participle; past; paste; pawn; pebbles; pectoral; pengü (Hungarian monetary unit); penny; percussion; perforate; perforated; perforation; perimeter; period; perishable; peseta; peso; piaster; piastre; picot; pie; pilaster; pint; pipe; pitch; pitcher; plaster; plate; plus; point; polar; pole; pond; population; port, or left side of an airplane of vessel when looking forward (P or L); position; post; postage; posterior; power; predicate; premolar; present; pressure; primary; principal; probability raito; proton; publication; pupil

p: fluid density (symbol); *piano* (Italian—softly); pitch; *per* (Latin—by)

p %: por ciento (Spanish—per hundred; percent)

P: Pacific; pamphlet; Panama Line; Papa—code letter for P; Paris; Parisian; passenger vessel (symbol); patrol; Pennzoil; Philadelphia Mint (symbol); phosphorus; Piasecki; plate; Pleyel; polar; polarization; pole; police; poor; Pope; port; Portugal (auto plaque); power; present value; President; Prince Line; principal; priority; project; propulsion; Protestant; protozoa; pulse

P: absolute humidity (symbol); amplitude of simple harmonic pressure (symbol); *pa* (Swedish—in); *partire* (Italian—departure); *piazza* (Italian—square); *pohjoinen* (Finnish—north); *pugillus* (Latin—a handful)

P.: protein(s) (dietary symbol)

P 1/C: Private First Class

P 1/C M: Private First Class Marine

P-2: Neptune twin-jet all-weather long-range land-based antisubmarine aircraft

P-3: Orion four-engine turboprop all-weather long-range land-based antisubmarine aircraft

P-5: Marlin twin-engine all-weather seaplane for long-range antisubmarine patrol and electronic reconnaissance

P³³: radioactive phosphorus

P-60: 60-minute parking

pa: intensity of atmospheric pressure (symbol); paper; paralysis agitans; participial adjective; particular average; patient; pattern analysis; pending availability; performance analysis; permanent appointment; pernicious anemia; personal appearance; piaster; piastre; point of aim; position approximate; power amplifier; power approach; power of attorney; press agent; pressure altitude; private account; provisional allowance; psychoanalyst; public address (system); public assistance; publication announcement; purchasing agent

p/a: power of attorney

p & a: percussion and auscultation; price and availability

p.a.: *per abdomen* (Latin—by the abdomen); *per annum* (Latin—by the year)

p A: *por autorización* (Spanish—by authority of)

pA: *per Adresse* (German—in care of)

Pa: Panama; Panameña; Panamanian; Panameño; Papa; Pará; Pennsylvania; Pennsylvanian; protactinium

PA: Passenger Agent; Pennsylvanian Railroad (stock exchange symbol); Philippine Army; Philippine Association; Piedmont Airlines; Port Agency; Post Adjutant; Prefect Apostolic; Press Agent; Press Association; Prince Albert (coal); Proprietary Association; Prosecuting Attorney; Prothonotary Apostolic; psycho-

logical age; Public Act; Puppeteers of America; Purchasing Agent

PA: *Psychological Abstracts*

P-A: Pacific-Atlantic Line; Pan-Atlantic Line

P/A: Picatinny Arsenal

P & A: Professional and Administrative

P of A: Port of Anchorage

paa: (Finnish—mountain)

PAA: Pacific Alaska Airways; Pan American World Airways System (3-letter designation); Potato Association of America; Purchasing Agents Association

PAAA: Premium Advertising Association of America

PAAC: Program Analysis Adaptable Control

PAAE: Pennsylvania Association for Adult Education

PAAO: Pan-American Association of Ophthalmology

pab: per acre bonus

PAB: Panair do Brasil (airline); Petroleum Administrative Board; Price Adjustment Board

paba: para-amino benzoic acid

pabla: problem analysis by logical approach

Pablo Neruda: Neftali Ricardo Reyes

pabx: private automatic branch telephone exchange

pac: phenacetin-aspirin-caffeine (all- purpose capsule); prearrival confirmation; production acceleration capacity; pursuant to authority contained (in); put and call (stock exchange jargon)

Pac: Pacific

PAC: Pacific Air Command; Pacific Automotive Corporation; Pacific Telephone & Telegraph (stock exchange symbol); Palo Alto Clinic; Pan-Africanist Congress; Pan-American Congress; Pharmaceutical Advertising Club; Philbrook Art Center; Political Action Committee; Public Affairs Committee; Public Assistance Cooperative

Paca: Francesca

PACAF: Pacific Air Force

PACB: Pan-American Coffee Bureau

PacD: Pacific Division

pace (PACE): package-crammed executive; performance and cost evaluation; precision analog computing equipment; prelaunch automatic checkout equipment; program to advance creativity in education; programmed automatic communica-

tions equipment; projects to advance creativity in education

PACE: Professional Association of Consulting Engineers

PACECO: Pacific Coast Engineering Company

PACED: Program for Advanced Concepts in Electronic Design

PACFLT: Pacific Fleet

pack.: packing

pacm: pulse amplification code modulation

PACMD: Philadelphia Contract Management District

Paco: Pancho (Francisco)

Pac O: Pacific Ocean

PACOM: Pacific Command

pacor: passive correlation and ranging

PACRNB: President's Advisory Commission on Recreation and Natural Beauty

PACS: Pacific Area Communications System

PACT: Production Analysis Control Technique; Project for the Advancement of Coding Techniques

Pac T & T: Pacific Telephone and Telegraph

pacv (PACV): personnel air-cushion vehicle

PACV: Patrol Air-Cushioned Vehicle (naval)

pad.: padding; padlock

PAD: Port of Aerial Debarkation; Public Administration Division

padal: pattern for analysis, decision, action, and learning

padang: (Malayan—plain)

padar: passive detection and ranging

Paddy: an Irishman; Patrick

PADL: Pilotless Aircraft Development Laboratory

padloc: passive detection and location of countermeasures

p Adr: *per Adresse* (German—in care of)

padre.: portable automatic data-recording equipment

Padre Hidalgo: (Spanish—Father Hidalgo)—revolutionary priest who proclaimed Mexican independence from Spanish rule —excommunicated, beheaded, and impaled but sanctified in modern times when Roman Catholic Church made peace with Mexican government

Padre de Independencia: (Spanish—Father of Independence) —José Martí—Cuban patriot, poet, and soldier

p. ae.: *partes aequales* (Latin—equal parts)

PAE: Peoria and Eastern (railroad); Port of Aerial Embarkation

pa & f: percussion, auscultation, and fermitus

PAF: Pacific Air Forces; Philippine Air Force

PAFA: Pennsylvania Academy of Fine Arts

PAFB: Patrick Air Force Base

PAFMECA: Pan-African Freedom Movement of East and Central Africa

PAFS: Primary Air Force Specialty

PAFSC: Primary Air Force Specialty Code

pág.: *página* (Spanish—page)

Pag: pagoda

PaG: Pennsylvania-German

PAG: Prince Albert's Guard

pageos (PAGEOS): passive geodetic satellite

pagg segg: *pagine seguenti* (Italian—following pages)

pág(s): *página(s)* [Spanish—page(s)]

PAGT: Port Authority Grain Terminal

pah: polynuclear aromatic hydrocarbon(s)—(photochemical smog ingredient)

Pah: Pahlavi

PAH: Pan-American Highway (also called Inter-American Highway)

PAHC: Pan American Highway Congress

PAHO: Pan-American Health Organization

PAI: Panama Airways Incorporated; Piedmont Airlines (3-letter coding)

PAIGCV: *Partido Africano da Independencia da Guine e Cabo Verde* (Portuguese—African Party for an Independent Guinea and Cape Verde)

PAIGH: Pan-American Institute of Geography and History

PAIN: Pan-American Institute of Neurology

paint.: painter; painting

PAIRC: Pacific Air Command

PAIS: Project Analysis Information System (AID); Public Affairs Information Service

PAIT: Program for the Advancement of Industrial Technology

PAJU: Pan-African Journalists Union

Pak: Pakistan

PAKISTAN: *Pak* (Persian—holy) plus *stan* (Urdu—land)—hence Pakistan means Holy Land; it is also an acronym made up of Punjab, Afghan Border States, Kashmir, Sind, and *tan* from Baluchistan

pal.: paleontology; permissive action link; phase-alteration line (color tv system); prescribed action link

Pal: Palace; Palencia; Paleozoic; Palestine

PAL: Pacific Aeronautical Library; phase-alternating (television) line; Phillipine Air Lines; Police Athletic League; prisoner-at-large; Public Archives Library

PALC: Point Arguello Launch Complex

paleo: paleography

paleob: paleobotany

paleon: paleontology

Palgrave: Francis Meyer Cohen

PALI: Pacific and Asian Linguistics Institute (University of Hawaii)

palp: palpable; palpitation

PALs: Parcel Air Lifts (U.S. Post Office parcel-post service for servicemen)

pam: pamphlet; pulse amplified modulation; pulse amplitude modulation

Pam: Lord Palmerston; Pamela

PAM: Palestine Archeological Museum; Pasadena Art Museum; Portland Art Museum

PAMA: Pan-American Medical Association

PAMIPAC: Personnel Accounting Machine Installation Pacific Fleet

PAML: Pan American Mail Line

PAMO: Port Air Materiel Office

PAMPA: Pacific Area Movement Priority Agency (DoD)

pampas: (Spanish—grasslands; grassy plains)

Pampas: grassland plains of Argentina, Paraguay, and Uruguay

pamph: pamphlet

PAMT: Port Authority Marine Terminal

pan (PAN): peroxyacetyl nitrate (smog ingredient)

pan.: panchromatic; panorama; panoramic; pantomime; pantry

Pan: Panama; Panamanian; Panameño

PAN: Pan American Navigation; Parents Against Narcotics; peroxyacetylnitrate (air-pollutant poison)

PAN: *Partido Acción Nacional* (Spanish—National Action Party)—Mexican; *Polska Akademia Nauk* (Polish Academy of Sciences)

PAN: Polska Akademia Nauk (Polish Academy of Sciences)

PANAGRA: Pan American-Grace Airways

PANAIR: Panair do Brasil (Brazil-

ian airline)

Pan-Am: Pan-American World Airways

PANANEWS: Pan-Asia Newspaper Alliance (Hong Kong)

pan b: panic bolt

panc: pancreas

Pan Can: Panama Canal

Pancho: Francisco

Pancho Villa: Doroteo Arango

pandex: *pan* (Greek—all) + *dex* (from index)—all-inclusive index

Pank: Pankow

panol: panology

panorams: panoramas

Pan Sea Fron (PANSEAFRON): Panama Sea Frontier

panto: pantograph(ic); pantomime; pantomimic

pants: pantaloons

PANY: Power Authority of the State of New York

PAO: Public Affairs Officer

pap.: papa; papacy; papal; paper; papyrus

PAP: Port-au-Prince, Haiti (airport); Polska Agencja Prasowa (Polish News Agency)

Papa: code for letter P

PAPI: Pacific Automation Products Incorporated

Pap Ter: Papua Territory

Pap Test: Papanicolaou Test (for cervical cancer)

Paquita: Francisca (Frances)

par.: paragraph; parallax; parallel; per acre rental; precision approach radar

Par: Parish

PAR: Paris, France (Orly airport); Program Appraisal and Review

para: parachute; paragraph; parallel; perceiving and recognition automation

parab: parabola

Paracelsus: Theophrastus Bombastus von Hohenheim

paradrop: parachute airdrop

par. aff.: *pars affecta* (Latin—to the part affected)

Parag: Paraguay; Paraguayan

paral: parallax; paralysis

Parami: Parsons active ring around miss indicator

parapsych: parapsychologist; parapsychology

paras: parasite(s); parasitic; parasitism; paratroopers

parasail: parachute sail (steerable parachute)

parasitol: parasitology

Parbo: Paramaribo

parc: progressive aircraft repair cycle

PARCA: Pan American Railway

Congress Association
pard: partner
pardop: passive-ranging doppler
paren: parenthesis
parens: parentheses
parent.: parental(ly)
par for: par for the course (golfer's term meaning average, typical, usual)
pari: parietal
paris green: copper acetoarsenite
parkade: parking arcade
Parl: Parliament
PARL: Palo Alto Research Laboratory (Lockheed)
Parl Const: Parliamentary Constituency
Parlour Panther: *New York Review of Books*
PARM: *Partido Autentico de la Revolución Mexicano* (Authentic Party of the Mexican Revolution)
Parmigianino: Francisco Massuoli
parochiaid: parochial-school aid (provided by tax monies)
paros: passive ranging on submarines
parot: parotid
parox: paroxysm(al)
pars: paragraphs
PARS: Passenger Airlines Reservation System; Programmed Airlines Reservation System
parsec: parallax second (3.26 light-years or 19.2 trillion miles)
parsq: pararescue
part.: partial; participate; particle; partition; partner; partnership
part. aeq.: *partes aequales* (Latin—equal parts)
partan: parallel tangents
parth: parthenogenesis
partic: participle; particular
partit: partitive
part. vic.: *partibus vicibus* (Latin—in divided doses)
paru: postanesthetic recovery unit
par uni: party unity (political utopia)
parv: paravane
parv.: *parvus* (Latin—small)
pas: passive
pas: [French—channel; pass; strait—as in Pas de Calais (Straits of Calais)]
PAs: Police Agents
PA's: purchasing agents
PAS: Percussive Arts Society; Pregnancy Advisory Service; Primary Alerting System; Professor of Air Science
pasar: psychological abstracts search and retrieval
PASB: Pan-American Sanitary Bureau

PASC: Pan American Standards Committee
PASCO: Pan American Sulfur Corporation
pasim: pasimological; pasimologically; pasimologist; pasimology (study of gestures as means of communication)
paso: (Spanish—mountain pass, as in El Paso)
PASO: Pan-American Sanitary Organization
pass.: passage; passenger; passivate
PASSIM: President's Advisory Staff on Scientific Information Management
passo: [Italian or Portuguese—mountain pass, as in Passo Brennero (Brenner Pass)]
p-a system: public-address system
pat.: patent(s); patrol(s)
Pat: Patricia; Patrick
PAT: Pacific Air Transport; Philippine Aerial Taxi
PATA: Pacific Area Travel Association
patam: (Hindustani—city; town)—as in Vizagapatam on Bay of Bengal
PATCA: Panama Air Traffic Control Area
PATCO: Professional Air Traffic Controllers Association
patd: patented
path.: pathological; pathologist; pathology; pituitary adrenotrophic hormone (PATH)
PATH: Port Authority Trans-Hudson (Hudson Tubes)
patho: pathological
pathogen: pathogenic
pathol: pathological; pathologist; pathology
Patk: Patrick
pat. med: patent medicine
Pat Off: Patent Office
Patronat: (French equivalent of National Association of Manufacturers in United States)
pats.: patents
patt: pattern
Patty: Martha; Patience; Patricia
PATWAS: Pilot's Automatic Telephone Weather Answering Service
Pau: Pablo
PAU: Pan American Union
Paul VI: Giovanni Batista Montini
P-au-P : Port-au-Prince
pav: paving
Pav: pavilion
PAV: Personnel Allotment Voucher
PAV: *Poste Avion* (French—air-mail)
pave.: position and velocity extraction

PAVE: Professional Audiovisual Education (study)
PAVN: Peoples Army of Viet Nam
paw.: portable auxiliary workroom
PAWA: Pan American World Airways
pax.: passenger(s); private automatic exchange
paye: pay as you enter; pay as you earn (paying for tax benefits while earning)—P.A.Y.E. in the United Kingdom
PAYS: Patriotic American Youth Society
pb: painted base; patrol bombing; pull box; push button
p/b: pass book; poor bastard
pB: purplish blue
Pb: *plumbum* (Latin—lead)
PB: Packard Bell; patrol bomber; patrol bombing; Publication Bulletin
P-B: Pitney-Bowes
PB: *Planta Baja* (Spanish—ground floor), elevator pushbutton designation
pba: pressure-breathing assister
PBA: Patrolmen's Benevolent Association; Port of Bristol Authority; Professional Bookmen of America
P-band: 225–390 mc
pbc: point of basal convergence
PBC: Philadelphia Blood Clinic; Provincial Bank of Canada
pbdndb: perceived barking dog noise decibels
PBEC: Pacific Basin Economic Council; Public Broadcasting Environment Center
P. B. Ed.: Bachelor of Philosophy in Education
Pbg: Pittsburgh
PBH: Paul B. Hoeber
pbhp: pounds per brake horsepower
pbi: protein-bound iodine
PBI: Paper Bag Institute; Paving Block Institute; Pitney-Bowes Incorporated; Plumbing Brass Institute; Projected Books Incorporated; West Palm Beach, Florida (airport)
PBiB: *Paperback Books in Print*
PBJC: Palm Beach Junior College
PBK: Phi Beta Kappa
PBL: Public Broadcast Laboratory
pbm (PBM): permanent bench mark
PBM: Mariner twin-engine Navy bomber built by Martin; Paramaribo, Surinam (airport)
PBMA: Peanut Butter Manufacturers Association
pbo: polite brushoff
PBOS: Planning Board for Ocean Shipping (USA)

pbp: pushbutton panel

pbr (PBR): power breeder reactor; precision bombing range

pb's: paperback books

PBS: Public Broadcasting Service; Public Buildings Service

PBSCMA: Peanut Butter Sandwich and Cookie Manufacturers Association

PBSE: Philadelphia-Baltimore Stock Exchange

pbt: performance-based teaching

pbte: performance-based teacher education

pbw: parts by weight; posterior bite wing

PBWSE: Philadelphia-Baltimore-Washington Stock Exchange

pbx: private branch exchange

pbz: phosphor bronze

pc: parent cells; paycheck; pay clerk; percent; percentage; percentile; personal correction; petty cash; pica(s); piece(s); pitch circle; point of curve; port of call; postcard; prices current; printed circuit; privileged character; pull chain; pulsating current; purchasing and contracting purified concentrate

p-c: phophlogistic-corticoid

p/c: percent; percentage; programmer-comparator

p & c: put and call

p.c.: *post cebum* (Latin—after a meal; after meals)

PC: Pace College; Pacific Airlines; Pacific Coast (railroad); Pacific College; Paine College; Palmer College; Palomar College; Panama Canal; Panola College; Paris College; Park College; Parsons College; Pasadena College; Peace Corps; Pembroke College; Pepperdine College; personnel carrier; Pfeiffer College; Pharmacy Corps; Philadelphia College; Philippine Constabulary; Phoenix College; Piedmont College; Pikeville College; Pilotage Chart(s); Pineland College; Plane Commander; Pomona College; Porterville College; Presbyterian College; Principia College; Privy Council; Privy Councillor(s); ProcurementCommand; Producers Council; Providence College; submarine chaser patrol vessel (naval symbol)

P-C: Penn-Central (railroad)

PC: *Partido Colorado* (Spanish—Colorado Party); *Partido Conservador* (Spanish—Conservative Party); *Poder Chicano* (Spanish—Chicano Power)

pca: permanent change of assignment

Pca: Pensacola

PCA: Parachute Club of America; Permanent Court of Arbitration (The Hague); Portland Cement Association; Production Credit Association

pcam: punchcard accounting machine

PCAPA: Pacific Coast Association of Port Authorities

PCAPK: President's Commission on the Assassination of President Kennedy

PCAs: Progressive Citizens of America

pcb: petty cash book; printed circuit board

PCB: Pest Control Bureau; Program Control Board

pcb's: polychlorinated biphenyls (industrial pollutants of lakes, reservoirs, and streams)

pcc: phosphate carrier compound

PCC: Pacific Coast Conference; Palmer Community College; Panama Canal Company; Port of Corpus Christi; Portland Community College

PCC: *Partido Comunista Cubano* (Spanish—Cuban Communist Party)

PCCEMRSP: Permanent Commission for the Conservation and Exploitation of the Maritime Resources of the South Pacific

PCCI: President's Committee on Consumer Interests

PCCU: President's Commission on Campus Unrest

pcd: pounds per capita per day

PCD: Panama Canal Department

pc di: pierce die

pce: pyrometric cone equivalent

PCE: patrol craft escort (3-letter coding)

PCE: *Partido Comunista Española* (Spanish Communist Party)

PCEA: Pacific Coast Electrical Association

PCEH: The President's Committee on Employment of the Handicapped

PCEQ: President's Council on Environmental Quality

PCER: rescue escort (naval symbol)

pcf: pounds per cubic foot; power per cubic foot

PCF: *Parti Communiste Français* (French Communist Party)

PCFAP: The President's Committee on the Foreign Aid Program

PCH: hydrofoil submarine chaser (3-letter coding)

pci: peripheral command indicator; perpetual cost index

PCI: Packer Collegiate Institute; Planning Card Index; Prestressed Concrete Institute

PCI: *Partito Comunista Italiano* (Italian Communist Party)

PCIB: Pacific Cargo Inspection Bureau

PCII: Potato Chip Institute International

PCIM: Presidential Commission on Income Maintenance

Pck: conditional probability of kill (armament)

pckt: printed circuit

pcl: printed-circuit lamp

pclk: pay clerk

pcm: phase-change material(s); pulse-code modulation; pulse-count modulation; punchcard machine(s)

PCM: Peabody Conservatory of Music; President's Certificate of Merit

PCM: *Partido Comunista Mexicano* (Mexican Communist Party)

PCMA: Professional Convention Management Association

pcmi: photographic micro-image(s)—microdot photos

PCMO: Principal Colonial Medical Officer

pcm/pl: pulse-code modulated/polarized light

PCMR: President's Committee on Mental Retardation

PCMSER: President's Commission on Marine Science, Engineering, and Resources

PCN: Part Control Number; Procurement Control Number

PCN: *Partido de Conciliación Nacional* (Spanish—National Conciliation Party)

PCNB: Permanent Control Narcotics Board

PCNG: President's Commission on National Goals

PCNR: Part Control Number Request

PCN's: Planning Change Notices

PCO: Printing Control Office(r); Procuring Contracting Office(r); Public Carriage Office(r)

PCOB: Permanent Central Opium Board (UN)

PCOP: President's Commission on Obscenity and Pornography

pcp: production change point

PCP: Postgraduate Center for Psychotherapy; Program Change Proposal; Progressive Conservative Party

PCP: *Partido Comunista Panameño*

(Spanish—Panamanian Communist Party); *Partido Comunista Paraguayo* (Spanish—Paraguayan Communist Party); *Partido Comunista Peruviano* (Spanish—Peruvian Communist Party); *Partido Communista Portugues* (Portuguese Communist Party)

PCPD: Portland Commission of Public Docks

PCPF: President's Council on Physical Fitness

PCPS: Philadelphia College of Pharmacy and Science

pcpt: perception

PCR: Program Change Request; Publication Contract Requirement

pcr: photoconductive relay

PCR: *Partidul Comunist Roman* (Romanian Communist Party)

PC R & D C: Pomona Colleges Research and Development Center

PCRC: Paraffined Carton Research Council

PCRI: Papanicolaou Cancer Research Institute

pcs: permanent change of station; picas; pieces

PCs: Police Constables

PCS: 136-foot submarine chaser (3-letter coding)

PCSE: Pacific Coast Stock Exchange; President's Council on Scientists and Engineers

pc sh: pierce shell

PCSW: President's Commission on the Status of Women

pct: percent

pct: *procent* (Norwegian—percent)

PCT: Portsmouth College of Technology

PCT: *Partido Conservador Tradicional* (Spanish—Traditional Conservative Party)—Nicaragua

pc tp: pierce template

PCTS: President's Committee for Traffic Safety

pcu: photocopy unit; power-control unit; pressurization-control unit

pcv: packed-cell volume; pollution-control valve; positive crankcase ventilation

PCV: *Partido Comunista Venezolana* (Spanish—Venezuelan Communist Party)

PCVs: Peace Corps Volunteers

PCY: coastal yacht (3-letter naval symbol); Pittsburgh, Chartiers & Youghiogheny (railroad)

PCZ: Panama Canal Zone

PCZST: Panama Canal Zone Standard Time

pd: interpupillary distance; paid; paralysing dose; passed; period;

pitch diameter; point detonating; poop deck; port dues; position doubtful; postage due; post date; post dated; potential difference; pound; pour depressant; preliminary design; prism diopter; procurement directive; property damage; public domain; pulse duration; purchase description

p-d: prism diopter

p & d: pickup and delivery

p.d.: *per diem* (Latin—by the day)

Pd: palladium

PD: Pharmacopoeia Dublin; Phelps-Dodge; Physics Department; Police Department; Port of Debarkation; Port Director; Port Dues; position doubtful (chart marking); Preliminary Design; Production Department

P-D: Parke-Davis

PD: *Partido Democratico* (Spanish—Democratic Party); *(Cleveland) Plain Dealer*

P.D.: *posdata* (Spanish—postscript)

P-de-D: Puy-de-Dôme

P of D: Port of Duluth

pda: predicted drift angle; public display of affection

PDAS: Police Department American Samoa

P-day: day when rate of production of an item for military consumption equals rate required by armed forces

pdb: paradichlorobenzine

Pdc: probability of detection and conversion

PDC: Prevention of Deterioration Center (National Academy of Sciences)

PDC: *Partido Democratico Cristiano* (Spanish—Christian Democratic Party)

PDD: Public Documents Department (GPO)

pdda: power-driven decontaminating apparatus

pde: paroxysmal dyspnea on exertion

PDE: Post-test Disassembly Examination

pdf: point detonating fuse

pdh: past dental history

pdi: powered-descent initiation

PDI: Printing Developments Incorporated

pdic: periodic

p dk: poop deck

pdl: poundal

pdm: pulse-delta modulation; pulse-duration modulation

Pd.M.: Master of Pedagogy

pdn: production

PDO: Publication Distribution

Office(r); Property Disposal Office(r)

p/doz: per dozen

pdp: project definition phase

PDP: Program Definition Phase; Program Development Plans

pd pt: production pattern

p d q: pretty damn (or darn) quick

pdr: pounder; powder; precision depth recorder (PDR)

PDR: People's Democratic Republic; Philippine Defense Ribbon

PDR: *Physicians' Desk Reference*

PDRK: People's Democratic Republic of Korea (North Korea)

PDRL: Permanent Disability Retirement List

PDRP: Power Distribution Reactor Program

PDRY: People's Democratic Republic of Yemen (capitals—Aden and Medina as-Shaab)

pds: point detonating self-destroying

pd's: parental delinquents (sires of juvenile delinquents)

PDS: Priority Distribution System

PDST: Pacific Daylight Saving Time

pdt: power distribution trailer

PDT: Pacific Daylight Saving Time

PDTC: Plymouth and Devonport Technical College

PDTLO: Pierre Dominique Toussaint L'Ouverture

pdu: power distribution unit

PDX: Portland, Oregon (airport)

pe: personnel equipment; probable error; program element; printer's error

p/e: porcelain enamel; price earning

pe: *par exemple* (French—for example); *per esempio* (Italian—for example); *por ejemplo* (Spanish—for example)

Pe: Pecltet number; Pernambuco

Pe: *Padre* (Spanish—father)

PE: Pacific Electric (railroad); patrol vessel (naval symbol); Petroleum Engineer(ing); Philadephia Electric; Pistol Expert; Plant Engineer(ing); Port of Embarkation; Port Everglades, Florida; Post Exchange; probable error; Production Engineer(ing); Professional Engineer; Protestant Episcopal

P & E: Peoria & Eastern (railroad)

pea. (PEA): primary expense account

PEA: Plastics Engineers Association; Potash Export Association; Publication Effectiveness Audit; Public Education Association

PEACE: People Emerging Against

Corrupt Establishments; Project Evaluation and Assistance in Civil Engineering (USAF)

Pearl: Pearl Harbor—Oahu, Hawaii

PEARL: (Committee for) Public Education and Religious Liberty

PEB: Physical Evaluation Board

pebd: pay entry base date

pec: photoelectric cell; program element code

PEC: Production Equipment Code; Protestant Episcopal Church

pecan.: pulse envelope correlation air navigator

PECE: President's Emergency Committee for Employment

'pecker: woodpecker

Peck's Bad Boy: (pseudonym —George W. Peck)

pecto: pectoral

ped: pedagogue; pedagogy; pedal; pedestal; pedestrian

Ped.: pedal (music)

pedag: pedagogue; pedaguese (patois of pedants)

Ped.B.: Bachelor of Pedagogy

Ped.D.: Doctor of Pedagogy

pediat: pediatrics

Ped.M.: Master of Pedagogy

Pedrarias: Pedro Arias

PED XING: Pedestrian crossing (America's most perplexing highway abbreviation)

P & EE: Proving and Experimental Establishment

Peeb: Peebles

Peebl: Peeblesshire

pees: South Vietnamese piasters

pef: peak expiratory flow

Peg: Peggy

Peggy: Margaret

PEI: Porcelain Enamel Institute; Preliminary Engineering Inspection; Prince Edward Island

pej: premolded expansion joint

p ej: *por ejemplo* (Spanish—for example)

Pek: Peking; Pekinese

peke: pekinese dog

pel: pelagic; pellet; pelvis

P EL: Port Elizabeth

PELNI: Pelajaran Nasional Indonesia (National Shipping Company of Indonesia)

pem: program element monitor

Pemb: Pembrokeshire

Pemex: Petróleos Mexicanos

PE Mus: Port Elizabeth Museum

pen.: penal; penetrate; penology; peninsula; penitentiary; penmanship

Pen: Penelope

PEN: Poets, Playwrights, Editors, Essayists, and Novelists (international organization often referred to as the P.E.N. Club)

peni: penicillin

penic: penicillin

penic.: *penicillum* (Latin—brush)

Penn: Pennsylvania; Pennsylvanian

Penna: Pennsylvania

Penn Central: Pennsylvania New York Central Transportation Company (merger of Pennsylvania, New York Central, New Haven, and Lehigh Valley railroads)

Pennsy: Pennsylvania; Pennsylvania Railroad

Penn Turn: Pennsylvania Turnpike

Penny: Penelope

Pen of the American Revolution: Thomas Paine

penrad: penetration radar

pent.: penetrate; penetration; pentode

Pent: Pentagon

pento: (sodium) pentothal

PEO: Protect Each Other (secret women's organization)

PEOC: Publishing Employees Organizing Committee

People's Daily: communist government gazette published in Peking

pep.: pepper; peppermint; peppy

P e P: *Partija e Punes:* (Albanian —Workers Party)

PEP: P.E.P. Deraniyagala; Pepsi-Cola (stock exchange symbol); Personalized Engineering Program; Petroleum Electric Power; Political and Economic Planning; Program Evaluation Procedure

PEPA: Petroleum Electric Power Association

Pepco: Potomac Electric Power Company

Pepe: José (Joseph)

pepg: piezo-electric power generator

pepr: precision encoder and pattern recognizer

peps.: pepsin

PEQC: President's Environmental Quality Council

pequeño(a): [Spanish—little, as in Angra Pequeña (Luderitz Bay)]

Per: Persia; Persian

Per: *Pericles, Prince of Tyre*

PER: Perth, Australia (airport)

per an.: *per annum* (Latin—by the year); *per anum* (Latin—by the anus)

perc: percussion

PERC: Peace on Earth Research Center

perco: percobarb (barbiturate synthetic morphine derivative); percodan (synthetic morphine derivative—both addictive and dangerous

PERCOS: Performance Coding System

Percy: Percival

perden.: *perdendosi* (Italian—dying away)

peresheyek: (Russian—peninsula)

perf: perfection; perforate; performance; perfume

perg: *pergamino* (Spanish—parchment)

peri: perigee; perimeter

PERI: Platemakers Educational and Research Institute

periap: periapical

Peric: Periclean

Perico: Pedro

PERINTREP: Periodic Intelligence Report

period.: periodical

periodontol: periodontology

peris: periscope

perk.: payroll earnings record keeping

perk(s): perquisite(s)

perla: pupils equal—react to light and accommodation

perm: permanent

Perm: Permian

permaflowers: permanent (plastic) flowers

permafrost: permanent frost

permafruit: permanent (plastic) fruit

permed: permanently waved

PERO: President's Emergency Relief Organization

peroxide: hydrogen peroxide (H_2O_2)

perp: perpendicular

per rec: *per rectum* (Latin —through the rectum)

pers: person; personal; personality; personnel; persons

Pers: Persia(n)

Persian Century: the 500s—Persia makes peace with the Byzantine Empire and extends Persian rule throughout the Middle East—the 6th century

pers n: personal noun

persp: perspective

pers pron: personal pronoun

pert.: pertaining

pert.: *pertussis* (Latin—whooping cough)

PERT: Program Evaluation Review Technique

Perths: Perthshire

Peru Cur: Peruvian Current

Perugino: Piero Vannucci

pes: photoelectric scanner

P es: *per esempio* (Italian—for example)—*e.g.*

PEs: Professional Engineers

PES: Philosophy of Education Society

PESA: Petroleum Equipment Suppliers Association
Pesh: Peshawar
pet.: petroleum; petrological; petrologist; petrology; point of equal time
PET: Pet Milk Company (stock exchange symbol); Production Environmental Test(ing, s); Production Evaluation Test (ing, s)
Pete: Peter
Peterhouse: Saint Peter's College, Cambridge
Peter Martyr: (pseudonym—Pietro Martire d'Anghiera)
peth: petroleum ether
petit(e): (French—little; small; tiny, as in Petit-Canal)
petr: petrifaction; petrified
PETR: Preliminary Flight Test Report
Petrarch: Francesco Petracco
petri: petroleum
petro: petrochemical; petroleum; petrology
petro-chem: petroleum-chemical
Petrofina: *Compagnie Financiere Belges des Petroles* (Belgian Financed Petroleum Company)
petrog: petrography
Petroleum Vesuvius Nasby: (pseudonym—David Ross Locke)
pets.: prior to expiration of term of service
peua: pelvic examination under anesthesia
PEVE: Prensa Venezolana (Venezuelan press service)
pewter: lead-tin alloy containing some antimony
p ex: *par exemple* (French—for example)
pf: perfect; performance factor; pfennig; picofarad; pneumatic float; power factor; preferred; preflight; profile; profiled; proximity fuse; public funding; public funds; pulse frequency
pf: *pro forma* (Latin—for the sake of the form), an advance declaration for a financial statement or overseas invoice
pf.: *piano e forte* (Italian—soft and then loud)
Pf: Pfennig (German—penny)
PF: frigate—patrol escort vessel (naval symbol); Physician's Forum; Pioneer & Fayette (railroad); Procurator Fiscal
P/F: Peace and Freedom (political party)
pfa: psychologic-flight avoidance; pulverized fuel ash
PFA: Private Fliers Association
PFBMF: Polaris Fleet Ballistic Missile Force

PFBrg: pneumatic float bridge
Pfc: Private first class
PFC: Pusan Fisheries College
pfce: performance
pfd: preferred; present for duty
Pfd: *Pfund* (German—pound)
pf di: progressive die
pfd s: preferred spelling
PFEFES: Pacific and Far East Federation of Engineering Societies
PFEL: Pacific Far East Line
pf fx: profiling fixture
PFGX: Pacific Fruit Growers Express
pfi: physical fitness index (PFI)
PFI: Pacific Forest Industries; Pet Food Institute; Photo Finishing Institute; Picture and Frame Institute; Pie Filling Institute; Pipe Fibrication Institute
pfl: pressed-for-life (dress materials)
PFL: Pacific Freight Lines
PFLP: Popular Front for the Liberation of Palestine
pfm: power factor meter; pulse frequency modulation
PFMA: Plumbing Fixture Manufacturers Association
PFNM: Petrified Forest National Monument
PFNP: Petrified Forest National Park
pfr: peak flow rate; peak flow reading; programmable film reader; prototype fast reactor (PFR)
PFRB: Pacific Fire Rating Bureau
PFRS: Programmed Film Reader System
PFRT: Performance Flight-Rating Test; Preliminary Flight-Rating Test
pft: portable flame thrower
PFTC: Pestalozzi Froebel Teachers College
pfu: pock-forming units
PFV: *Pestalozzi-Froebel Verband* (Pestalozzi-Froebel Association)
pfx: prefix
PFX: Pacific Fruit Express
pg: page; paregoric; paris granite; pay group; paying guest; permanent grade; pistol grip; postgraduate; pregnant (pronounced *pee-gee*); program guidance; proving ground; public gaol
p.g.: *persona grata* (Latin—an acceptable person)
Pg: Paraguay; Paraguayan
PG: gunboat patrol vessel (naval symbol); Pan American-Grace Airways; Pennsylvania-German; Post Graduate; Proctor & Gamble

PG: *Prisonnier de Guerre* (French —prisoner of war)
P & G: Procter & Gamble
P of G: Port of Galveston
pga: pressure garment assembly
PGA: Professional Golfers Association
PGAH: Pineapple Growers Association of Hawaii
pgc: per gyro compass
PGCOA: Pennsylvania Grade Crude Oil Association
pgd: paged; paradigm
pge: phenyl glycidyl ether
PGE: Pacific Great Eastern (railroad); Portland Grain Exchange
PG & E: Pacific Gas and Electric
PGEC: Professional Group on Electronic Computers
PGER: Pacific Great Eastern Railway
pgh (PGH): pituitary growth hormone
PGH: patrol gunboat—hydrofoil (naval)
P-girls: pub girls (waitresses in British barrooms)
PGIT: Professional Group on Information Theory (IEEE)
pgl: puppy beagle (pronounced *pee-gul*)
P Gl: Port Glasgow
pgm: program
PGM: motor gunboat (3-letter naval symbol)
pgn: pigeon
PGNP: Pagsanjan Gorge National Park (Philippines)
PGNS: Primary Guidance and Navigation System
PGOC: Philadelphia Grand Opera Company
pgr: population growth rate; psychogalvanic reaction; psychogalvanic response
pgs: predicted ground speed
PGS: Pennsylvania-German Society; Pidaung Game Sanctuary (Burma); Power Generation System; Primary Guidance System
pgt: per gross ton
PGT: Pacific Gas Transmission (company)
PGU: Pontifical Gregorian University
ph: pharmacopoeia; phase; phone; phosphor; phot; photon; power house; precipitation hardening; previous hardening
p/h: per hour
p & h: postage and handling
pH: hydrogen-ion concentration
Ph: Pahari; phenyl
PH: Pearl Harbor; Parachute Handler; Philharmonic Hall; Plane Handler; Power House; Public

Health; Purple Heart (military decoration awarded Americans wounded in action)

PHA: Public Housing Administration

PHADS: Phoenix Air Defense Sector

phal: phalange; phalanx

phar: pharmacy

Phar. B.: Bachelor of Pharmacy

Phar. C: Pharmaceutical Chemist

Phar. D.: Doctor of Pharmacy

pharm: pharmaceutical; pharmacist; pharmacology; pharmacopoeia(s); pharmacy

Phar. M.: *Pharmaciae Magister* (Master of Pharmacy)

pharmacol: pharmacology

Pharm.D.: *Pharmaciae Doctor* (Latin—Doctor of Pharmacy)

Ph.B.: *Philosophiae Baccalaureus* (Latin—Bachelor of Philosophy)

ph brz: phosphor bronze

Ph. C.: Pharmaceutical Chemist

PHC: Patrick Henry College

PHCC: Plumbing, Heating, Cooling Contracters

PHCIB: Plumbing-Heating-Cooling Information Bureau

ph const: phase Constant

Ph. D.: *Philosophiae Doctor* (Latin—Doctor of Philosophy)

PHD: Port Huron and Detroit (railroad)

PHE: phenylalanine (amino acid)

P.H.E.: Public Health Engineer

PHEAA: Pennsylvania Higher Education Assistance Agency

P-head: pinhead (underground slang—small-minded person; user of amphetamine)

pheno: phenobarbital; (underground slang—user of phenobarbital)—hypnotic drug

phenolp: phenolphthlein

phenom: phenomena; phenomenal; phenomenon

Ph. G.: Graduate in Pharmacy

PHHS: Patrick Henry High School

phi: philosophy

Ph I: *Pharmacopoea Internationalis*

phil: philosophy

Phil: Philadelphia; Philadelphian; Philbert; Philharmonia; Philharmonic; Philip; Philippa; Philippine; Philippines; Phillip; Philipa; The Epistle of Paul to the Philippians

Phila: Philadelphia; Philadelphian

Philada: Philadelphia (old-style abbrevation)

philat: philately

PHILDis: Philadelphia Procurement District (US Army)

Philem: The Epistle of Paul to Philemon

Phillies: Philadelphians

PHILLIPS: Phillips Petroleum Company

Philly: Philadelphia

Phil Mag: *Philosophical Magazine*

philol: philology

Phil Orch: Philadelphia Orchestra

philos: philosophy

philos educ: philosophy of education

phiz: physiognomy

Phl: (Port of) Philadelphia

Ph. L.: Licentiate in Philosphy

PHL: Philadelphia, Pennsylvania (airport)

phl h: phillips head

PHLS: Public Health Laboratory Service

phm: phase meter

Ph. M.: *Philosophiae Magister* (Latin—Master of Philosophy)

Phm. B.: Bachelor of Pharmacy

Phm. G.: Graduate in Pharmacy

PHN: Public Health Nurse; Public Health Nursing

PhOD: Philadelphia Ordnance Depot

Phoen: Phoenix

Phoenician Century: the 9th century before the Christian era when Carthage was founded by the Phoenicians who traded in all areas of the Mediterranean—the 800s

phofl: photoflash

phon: phonetics; phonology

phono: phonograph

phonovision: telephone television

Phor: Phoronida

phos: phosphate; phosphorescent

photac: photographic typesetting and composing (AT & T)

photint: photographic intelligence

photo: photograph; photographer; photography

photocomp: photocomposed; photocomposition

photog: photograph; photographer; photographic; photography

photogeog: photogeography

photog(s): photographer(s)

photom: photometry

p'house steak: porterhouse steak

php: pounds per horsepower; propeller horsepower

phr: pounds per hour; preheater

PHRA: *Poverty and Human Resources Abstracts*

Phrasemaker President: Woodrow Wilson—twenty-eighth President of the United States

phren: phrenic; phrenology

PHRI: Public Health Research Institute

Phronie: Sophronia

Ph S: Philosophical Society of

England

PHS: Public Health Service

pht: pitch, hit, and throw

Ph T: putting husband through (college or university)

PHTS: Psychiatric Home Treatment Service

ph v: phase velocity

phw: pressurized heavy water

PHX: Phoenix, Arizona (airport)

phy: physical; physics

phyce: photocopy-control electronics unit

phylo: phylogeny

phys: physic; physical; physician; physics

phys dis: physical disability

phys ed: physical education

physexam: physical examination

physiog: physiognomy

physiogr: physiography

physiol: physiology

physl: physiological

phys med: physical medicine

Phys S: Physical Society

phys ther: physical therapy

pi: personal income; photo interpreter; photo interpretation; pigeon trainer; pig iron; pilotless interceptor; pimp; point initiating; point insulating; point of interception; point interception; poison ivy; position indicating; position indicator; present illness; private investigator; production interval; programmed instruction; protamine insulin; protocol international (international protocol); public investigation

pi: Greek-letter symbol (π) indicating ratio of circumference of a circle to its diameter; the ratio itself; expressed as a number, *pi* is approximately 3.14159

p & i: principal and interest; protection and indemnity

Pi: piaster

PI: Packaging Institute; Paducah and Illinois (railroad); Paul Isnard (Mana River settlement, French Guiana); Perlite Institute; Philippine Islands; Piedmont Airlines; Plastics Institute; Popcorn Institute; Pratt Institute; Public Information

PI: *Printer's Ink*

P.I.: *Pharmacopoeia Internationalis*

P-I: *Seattle Post-Intelligencer*

PIA: Pakistan International Airlines; Plastics Institute of America; Printing Industries of America

PIAI: Printing Industry of America, Incorporated

pias: piaster
pib: power ionosphere beacon
PIB: Polytechnic Institute of Brooklyn; Prices and Incomes Board
pibal: pilot balloon
pic: piccolo; picture
pic: (French—peak)
PIC: Physics International Company; Poison Information Center (Cleveland Academy of Medicine)
PICA: Palestine Israel Colonization Association; Printing Industry Computer Associates
Pickle Works: nickname of building occupied by Central Intelligence Agency in Langley, Virginia
pico: 10^{-12}
pico: (Portuguese or Spanish—peak)
PICOE: Programmed Initiations, Commitments, Obligations, and Expenditures
PICOP: Philippine Industries Corporation of the Philippines
pics: pictures
PICS: Pacific Islands Central School
pict: pictorial; picture
pid: pelvic inflammatory disease; prolapsed intervertebral disk
PID: Procurement Information Digest
PIDA: Pet Industry Distributors Association
PIDC: Pakistan Industrial Development Corporation
Pid Eng: Pidgin English (hybrid dialect spoken throughout Far East)
pie.: pulmonary infiltration (with) eosinophilia
PIE: Pacific Intermountain Express (fast freight); St. Petersburg, Florida (airport)
PIEA: Petroleum Industry Electrical Association
piedras: (Spanish—rocks; stones, as in Piedras Negras)
Pierre Loti: (pseudonym—Louis-Marie Julien Viaud
Pierre Louÿs: Pierre (pseudonym —Pierre Louis)
Pieter Timmerman: (Dutch—Peter Carpenter)— pseudonym used by Peter the Great of Russia while working as a shipwright in Dutch shipyards
PIF: Pilot Information File
pig.: pigment; pigmentation
PIG: Pride, Integrity, Guts (acronym adopted by the Chicago police)
Pig Alley: Place Pigalle
Pig Islander: New Zealander (Aus-

tralian slang)
PIGS: Poles, Italians, Greeks, Slavs—(some of America's most talented minorities)
pig's ear: (Cockney English—beer)
pik: payment in kind
pik: (Russian—peak)
pil: percentage increase in loss
pil.: pilula (Latin—pill)
PIL: Pest Infestation Laboratory
pilc: paper-insulated lead covered
pilnav: piloting navigation
PILO: Public Information Liaison Officer
pilot.: printing industry language for operations of typesetting
PILOT: Piloted Low-speed Test
Pil Sta: Pilot Station
pim: penalties in minutes; pulse-interval modulation
PIMA: Paper Industry Management Association
pimola: pimento olive (pimento-stuffed olive)
pimpmobile: pimp's automobile (often custom-made with bedroom facilities)
pin.: position indicator
$p/in.^2$: parts per square inch
$p/in.^3$: parts per cubic inch
PIN: Police Information Network
ping.: pinguis (Latin—fat; grease)
PINS: Padre Island National Seashore (Texas)
Pinturicchio: Barnardino Betti
PINWR: Pungo National Wildlife Refuge (North Carolina)
pinx.: pinxit (Latin—he painted it)
PIO: Public Information Office(r)
pi-on: pi-meson; pioneer
Pioneer: deep-space probes designed for interplanetary investigation
PIOSA: Pan Indian Ocean Science Association
pip.: proximal interphalangeal
Pip: Philip
PIP: Product Improvement Program
PIPA: Pacific Industrial Property Association
PIPR: Polytechnic Institute of Puerto Rico
piq: property in question
Pir: Piraeus
PIR: Phillip Island Reserve (Victoria, Australia); Philippine Independence Ribbon
PIRG: Public Interest Research Group (Ralph Nader's)
PIRGs: Public Interest Groups
pi rm: pilot reamer
Pis: Pisces
PISC: Phoenix International Science Center
pit.: pitot static; progressive inspection tag

Pit: Pittsburgh
PIT: Pasadena Institute of Technology; Petr Ilich Tchaikovsky; Pittsburgh, Pennsylvania (airport)
Piter: (Russian nickname for Petrograd or St. Petersburg)
piti: principal, interest, taxes, insurance
pit. log: pitot-static log
PITO: Portuguese Information and Tourist Office
pitr: plasma iron turnover rate
PITS: Pacific Islands Training School
Pius XII: Eugenio Pacelli
piv: peak inverse voltage; post indicator valve
PIV: Positive Infinity Variable
pix: photographs; pictures
pix/sec: pictures per second
PIYA: Pacific International Yachting Association
pizz.: pizzicato (Italian—plucked)
Pizza (PIE): Pacific Intermountain Express (stock exchange nickname)
pj: prune juice
PJ: Police Judge; Presiding Judge; Probate Judge
P of J: Port of Jacksonville
PJBD: Permanent Joint Board on Defense (Canada-US)
PJC: Paducah Junior College; Paris Junior College
pjm: postjunctional membrane
pj's: peejays (pajamas)
Pjs: Pasajes
pk: pack; peak; peck; psychokinesis
pK: negative logarithm of the dissociation constant (symbol)
Pk: Park; Peak; pink
PK: probability of kill (symbol)
PK: Posta Kutusu (Turkish—post office box)
pkb: photoelectric keyboard
pkdom: pack(ed) for domestic use
pkg: package; packing
pkmr: packmaster
PKNP: Pu Kradeung National Park (Thailand)
pkp: pre-knock pulse
PKP: Partido Komunista Pilipinas (Pilipino—Communist Party of the Philippines)
pkr: packer
PKR: Parker Pen (stock exchange symbol)
Pk Rdg: Park Ridge
pks: packs; pecks
pksea: pack(ed) for overseas use
PKSRP: Possum Kingdom State Recreation Park (Texas)
pkt: packet
PKTF: Printing and Kindred Trades

Federation (UK)
pkts: packets
pku: phenylketonuria
Pkw: *Personenkraftwagen* (German
—automobile; passenger vehicle)
Pkwy: Parkway
pky: pecky
pl: parting line; phase line, pipeline, plate(d); plural
p/l: plain language
p & l: profit and loss
pl.: *plenarius* (Latin—complete;
fully attended)
Pl: Place
Pl: *Place* (French—place; plaza);
plantage (Dutch—plantation);
plass (Scandinavian—place;
plaza); *Platz* (German—place;
plaza); *plaza* (Spanish—place;
plaza); *plein* (Dutch—place;
plaza)
PL: perception of light (symbol);
Place; Pluto (usually not abbreviated but sometimes as
shown in honor of Percival
Lowell); Point Loma; Poland
(auto plaque); Port Line; Public
Law; Public Library
P.L.: Poet Laureate
PL: *Partido Liberal* (Spanish—Lib-
eral Party)
P des L: Parc des Laurentides
(Quebec)—Laurentian Moun-
tains Park
£L: pound Lebanese
PL 1: Programming Language
(version 1)
Pla: Pula (Pola)
PLA: Pedestrians League of Ameri-
ca; People's Liberation Army
(Chinese Communist); Philatelic
Literature Association; Port of
London Authority; Port of Los
Angeles; Public Library As-
sociation; Pulverized Limestone
Association
P of LA: Port of Los Angeles
place.: programming language for
automatic checkout equipment
PLADS: Parachute Low-Altitude
Delivery System
plame (PLAME): propulsive lift
aerodynamic maneuvering entry
plan.: planet; planetarium
PLAN: Paterson Looks Ahead Now
Plan A: North Atlantic Treaty Re-
ginal Planning Group
planalto: (Portuguese—plateau)
plane(s): airplane(s)
PLANNET: Planning Network
plantflex: plantar flexion
Plant Wizard: Luther Burbank
plas: plaster
plaster of paris: calcium sulfate
($CaSO_4)_2 \cdot H_2O$

plat.: plateau; platinum; platoon
platf: platform
PLATO: Port Lincoln Advancement Trust Organization; Programmed Logic for Automatic
Teaching Operations
platy: *Platypoecilus* (genus of tropical fishes); platysma
Platy: Platyhelminthes
playa: (Spanish—beach; shore, as
in Point Playa)
plb: plumber; plumbing; pull button
plc: power-line carrier
PLC: Probe Launch Complex; Products List Circular
P of LC: Port of Lake Charles
PLCA: Pipe Line Contractor's
Association
plcs: propellant-loading control system
plcu: propellant-level control unit
plcy: policy
pld: payload
Pld: Portland, Oregon
PLDG: Portuguese Language Development Group
PLDTC: Philippine Long Distance
Telephone Company
P & LE: Pittsburgh & Lake Erie
(railroad)
PLEA: Poverty Lawyers for Effective Advocacy
plebe: plebeian
PLEI: Public Law Education Institute
Pleis: Pleistocene
plenipo: plenipotentiary
pleon: pleonastical(ly)
plf: polyforming
plff: plaintiff
plg: piling
plgl: plateglass
pli: preload indicating
PLI: *Partido Liberal Independiente*
(Spanish—Independent Liberal
Party); *Partito Liberale Italiano*
(Italian Liberal Party); *Photo-
Lab-Index*
PLIDCO: Pipe Line Development
Company
Plioc: Pliocene
plis: propellant-level indicating system
plk: plank
PLK: Phi Lambda Kappa; Poin-
care-Lighthill-Kuo (mathematical method)
p lkr: peacoat locker
PLL: Prince Line Limited
P-L-M: Paris-Lyon-Méditerranée
(famous French railway)
plmb: plumber; plumbing
PLN: *Partido Liberación Nacional*
(Spanish—National Liberation
Party); *Partido Liberal Na-
cionalista* (Spanish—National

Liberal Party)
plng: planning
PLNP: Port Lincoln National Park
(South Australia)
PLO: Palestine Liberation Organi-
zation; Presidential Libraries
Office (Library of Congress)
PLO: *Pairti Lucht Oibre* (Irish
—Labour Party); *Polskie Linie
Oceaniezne* (Polish Ocean
Lines)
plot.: plotting
PLP: Parliamentary Labour Party;
Progressive Labor Party
pl & pd: personal loss and personal
damage
PLPP: Pennsylvania League for
Planned Parenthood
plr: pillar
PLR: Philippine Liberation Ribbon
PLR: *Partido Liberal Radical*
(Spanish—Radical Liberal Party)
P L & R: Postal Laws & Regulations
pls: plates; please
PLS: Purnell Library Service
plsd: promotion list service date
plshr: polisher
PLSS: Portable Life-Support System
plstc: plastic
plstr: plasterer
plt: pilot
pltc: political
pltf: plaintiff
pltry: poultry
PLTS: Point Loma Test Site (Convair)
plu: plural; plurality
plumb.: plumber; plumbing
plumb.: *plumbum* (Latin—lead)
plumcot: plum plus apricot (hybrid)
PLUNA: Primeras Líneas Uruguayas
de Navegación Aérea (First Uruguayan Aerial Navigation Lines)
pluperf: pluperfect
plute(s): plutocrat(s)
pluto (PLUTO): pipeline under the
ocean
plx: plexus; propellant-loading
transfer
Ply: Plymouth
plywd: plywood
Plz: Plaza
pm: post mortem; premium; premolar; presystolic murmur; preventive maintenance (PM); publicity man; pulse modulation; pum-
ice
p.m.: *post meridiem* (Latin—after
noon)
p-m: permanent magnet; phase
modulation
p/m: pounds per minute
Pm: promethium

PM: Past Master; Pattern Maker; Pay Master; Peabody Museum; Pere Marquette (railroad); Petróleos Mexicanos; Physical Medicine; Police Magistrate; Pontifex Maximus; Postmaster; Prime Minister; Provost Marshal (pronounced *provo marshal*); publicity man

P.M.: Prime Minister

P de M: Principauté de Monaco (Monte Carlo)

pma: positive mental attitude

PMA: Pacific Maritime Association; Parts Manufacturing Associates; Peat Moss Association; Pencil Makers Association; Pharmaceutical Manufacturers Association; Philadelphia Museum of Art; Philippine Mahogany Association; Phonograph Manufacturers Association; Precision Measurements Association; Primary Mental Abilities (test); Production and Marketing Administration

PMAE: Peabody Museum of Archeology and Ethnology

pmb: post-menopausal bleeding

PMB: Potato Marketing Board

pmbx: private manual branch exchange

PMC: Pennsylvania Military College; Princeton Microfilm Corporation

P Me: Portland, Maine

PMEA: Powder Metallurgy Equipment Association

PMEL: Precision Measuring Equipment Laboratory

pmet: painted metal

pmf: progressive massive fibrosis

PMF: Presidential Medal of Freedom

PMG: Provost Marshal General

pmh: past medical history

pmi: photographic micro-image

PMI: Palma de Mallorca, Balearic Islands, Spain (airport)

PMIS: Personnel Management Information System

PMJC: Pine Manor Junior College

pmk: pitch mark; postmark(ed)

PML: Pacific Micronesian Line; Pierpont Morgan Library

PMLA: Publications of the Modern Language Association of America

PMMI: Packaging Machinery Manufacturing Institute

pmn: polymorphonuclear neutrophil

PMNA: Parkers Marsh Natural Area (Virginia)

PMNH: Peabody Museum of Natural History

PMO: Palomar Mountain Observatory; Principal Medical Officer

pmp: precious metal plating; previous menstrual period

pm & r: physical medicine and rehabilitation

PMR: Pacific Missile Range

PMRL: Pulp Manufacturer's Research League

PMRS: Physical Medicine and Rehabilitation Service

pms: poor miserable soul; post-menopausal syndrome; pregnant mare's serum

pm's: push monies

PMST: Professor of Military Science and Tactics

pmt: payment; premenstrual tension

PMU: Pattern Makers Union

p mvr: prime mover

pmyob: please mind your own business

pn: partition; part number; percussion note; percussive note; please note; position; promissory note; psychiatry-neurology; psychoneurotic

p-n: positive-negative

p/n: part number; promissory note

p & n: psychiatry and neurology

Pn: North Pole; North Celestial Pole; perigean range

PN: Pacific Northern (airline); Pan-American World Airways (stock exchange symbol); part number; plasticity number; point of no return; Practical Nurse

P/N: Part Number

P & N: Piedmont and Northern (railroad)

PN: *Partido Nacional* (Spanish—National Party); *Partido Nacionalista* (Spanish—Nationalist Party)

Pna: Panama

PNA: Pacific Northern Airlines

PNAI: Provincial Newspapers Association of Ireland

PNBA: Pacific Northwest Booksellers Association

PNBB: *Parc National de la Boucle du Baoule* (French—Baoule River Bend National Park)—in the highlands of Mali

PNBP: *Parc National de la Boucle de la Pendjari* (French—Pendjari River Bend National Park)—in northwestern Dahomey

pnc: penicillin

PNC: Prohibition National Committee

PNC: *Parque Nacional Canaima* (Spanish—Canaima National Park)—encloses Venezuela's Angel Falls — world's tallest waterfall

Pncla: Pensacola

pnd: paroxysmal nocturnal dyspnoea; postnasal drip

pndb: perceived noise decibels

pndg: pending

P-N-D-L-R: parking-neutral-driving-low-gear-reverse (positions on automatic automotive transmission dial)

Pndo: Pinedo

pne: practical nurse's education

PNEA: *Parque Nacional El Avila* (Spanish—El Avila National Park)—between Caracas and the Caribbean where it encloses the Humboldt National Monument of Venezuela

pneu: pneumatic(s)

pnfd: present not for duty

p.n.g.: *persona non grata* (Latin—an unacceptable person)

Png: Penang

PNG: Papua New Guinea; Professional Numismatists Guild

PNG: *Parque Nacional Guatopo* (Spanish—Guatopo National Park)—near Caracas, Venezuela

PNH: Phnom-Penh, Cambodia (airport)

PNHP: *Parque Nacional Henri Pittier* (Spanish—Henri Pittier National Park)—near Maracay, Venezuela

PNI: *Parque Nacional Iguazu* (Spanish—Iguazu National Park) —international park surrounding the Iguazu Falls shared by Argentina, Brazil, and Paraguay

pnl: panel

PNL: Pacific Naval Laboratories; Pacific Northwest Laboratories; Philippine National Line

PNLA: Pacific Northwest Library Association; Pacific Northwest Loggers Association

PNM: Pinnacles National Monument (California)

pno: *pergamino* (Spanish—parchment)

PNO: Port of New Orleans

PNO: *Parque Nacional Ordesa* (Spanish—Ordesa National Park)—near Spain's French frontier

pnom: (Siamese—mountain)

pnp: positive negative positive

PNP: People's National Party; Platt National Park (Oklahoma)

pnpn: positive-negative positive-negative

pnpr: positive-negative pressure respiration

pnr: prior notice required

PNR: Passenger Name Record (airlines); Pulletop Nature Reserve

(New South Wales)

pns: parasympathetic nervous system; peripheral nervous system

PNS: Pacific Navigation Systems; Pakistan Naval Ship; Philadelphia Naval Shipyard; Philippine News Service; Professor of Naval Science

PNSN: *Parque Nacional Sierra Nevada* (Spanish—Sierra Nevada National Park)—encloses Venezuela's Mount Bolívar —highest peak in the republic

PNSY: Portsmouth Naval Shipyard

Pnt: Pentagon

PNT: *Parque Nacional Tijuca* (Portuguese—Tijuca National Park) —on the slopes of Mount Tijuca in the ring of mountains enclosing Rio de Janeiro, Brazil

Pnt Anx: Pentagon Annex

pntd: painted

pntr: painter

PNU: Pneumatic Scale Corporation (stock-exchange symbol)

p-nut butter: peanut butter

PNW: Parc National du W (W-shaped national park on the borders of Dahomey, Niger, and Upper Volta)

PNWL: Pacific Northwest Laboratory (AEC)

PNWR: Piedmont National Wildlife Refuge (Georgia); Presquile National Wildlife Refuge (Virginia); Pungo National Wildlife Refuge (North Carolina)

pnx: pneumothorax

PNYA: Port of New York Authority

PNYCTC: Pennsylvania New York Central Transportation Company (merger of Pennsylvania and New York Central railroads)

Pnz: Penzance

po: poetry; polarity; power-operated; power oscillator; previous orders

p-o: postoperative

p/o: part of

p & o: paints and oil; pickled and oiled

po: (Chinese—lake)

p.o.: *per os* (Latin—by mouth)

Po: polonium; Portugal; Portuguese

P⁰: Pedro

PO: Passport Office; Patent Office; Personnel Office(r); Petty Officer; Philadelphia Orchestra; Port Office(r); Post Office; Project Office; Province of Ontario; purchase order

P-O: Pyrénées-Orientales

P/O: Parole Officer; Pilot Officer; Probation Officer

P & O: Peninsular & Occidental Steamship Company; Peninsular

& Oriental Line

PO: *Portland Oregonian*

PO 1/C: Petty Officer First Class

PO 2/C: Petty Officer Second Class

PO 3/C: Petty Officer Third Class

poa: primary optical area; primary optic atrophy

POA: Portland Opera Association

POAC: Peace Officers Association of California

POADS: Portland Air Defense Sector

POAU: Protestants and Other Americans United for Separation of Church and State

pob: point of beginning

POB: post office box

po'-boy: poor-boy (sandwich)

pobra: pony + zebra (hybrid)

poc: privately-owned conveyance

POC: Pittsburgh Opera Company; port of call

Poca(loo): Pocatello, Idaho

pocill.: *pocillum* (Latin—small cup)

pock: pocket

POCS: Patent Office Classification System

pocul.: *poculum* (Latin—cup)

pod.: payable on (or upon) death; point-of-origin device; port of debarkation; port of departure

POD: Port of Debarkation; Post Office Department

POE: Pacific Orient Express; port of embarkation; port of entry

poe buoy: plank-on-edge buoy

p o'ed: put out

poet.: poetical(ly); poetry

POETS: Phooey On Everything—Tomorrow's Saturday

pof: please omit flowers

POFI: Pacific Oceanographic Fisheries Investigation

POG: Pacific Oceanographic Group (British Columbia)

POGO: Pennzoil Offshore Gas Operators; Polar Orbiting Geophysical Observatory

pOH: alkalinity factor

poi: poison; poisonous (on labels should be spelled out and symbolized with skull and crossbones)

POI: Personal Orientation Inventory; Program of Instruction

pointe: (French—point, as in Pointe à Pitre)

pois: poison

pol: petroleum-oil-and-lubricants (POL); polar; polarize(d); police; political; politician; problem-oriented language

Pol: Poland; Polish

POL: Pacific Oceanography Laboratories; petroleum-oil-and-lubricants; Polish Ocean Lines

p-ola: payola (remuneration for touting a so-called hit tune)—device of disreputable disc jockeys and record reviewers

Pol Ad: Political Adviser

polad(s): political adviser(s)

polar.: polarity; polarization; polarize(d)

polder: (Dutch—reclaimed marshland)

pol econ: political economy

pol ind: pollen index

polio: poliomyelitis

polit: political; politician; politics

Politburo: Politicheskoe Byuro (Russian—Political Bureau of the Central Committee)

poll.: pollution

Polly: Mary; Pauline; Pollyanna

pol(s): politician(s)

POLs: Problem-Oriented Languages (computer)

poluostrov: (Russian—peninsula)

polwar: political warfare

poly: polyethylene; polymer; polytechnic; polytechnical; polyvinyl

Poly: Polynesia; Polynesian; Polytechnic (institute or school)

poly bot: polyethylene bottle

polymorph: polymorphous

polysex: polysexual(ity)

polytech: polytechnic(al)

polywater: polymerized water

pom: pomeranian; pomological; pomology; pom-pom; preparation for overseas movement

POM: Port Moresby, New Guinea (airport)

POME: Prisoners of Mother England—Pommies; early convict immigrants (Australian slang)

POMFLANT: Polaris Missile Facility, Atlantic

POMPAC: Polaris Missile Facility, Pacific

pomsee: preparation, operation, maintenance, shipboard electronics equipment

POMSIP: Post Office Management Service Improvement Program

pon: pontoon

Pon: Ponce

Pon: *Ponedelnik* (Russian—Monday)

pona: paraffin, olefin, napthene, aromatic (test for petroleum octane rating)

PonBrg: pontoon bridge

pond.: *pondere* (Latin—by weight)

p-on-n: positive on negative

pont: (French—bridge, as in Pont-Aven)

Pont: Pontevedra

ponta: (Portuguese—headland; point, as in Ponta Delgada,

pont b

285

PPA

Azores)
pont b: pontoon bridge
ponte: (Italian or Portuguese—bridge)
Ponti: Pontiac
pood: poodle dog; (Russian—36-lb weight)
POOD: Provisioning Order Obligation Document
Poor Richard: Richard Saunders (pseudonym used by Benjamin Franklin in writing *Poor Richard's Almanack*)
pop: carbonated beverage; poppet; popular; population
pop.: perpendicular ocean platform
p-o-p: plaster of paris; printing-out-paper
Pop: Poppa
popex: population explosion
popf: prepared-on-premises flavor
popi: post office position indicator (navigation system developed by British post office)
poplit: popliteal
pops: popular concerts; popular tunes
POQ: Public Opinion Quarterly
por: porosity; porous; public opinion research
p-o-r: pay-on-receipt; payable-on-receipt
Por: Porifera
PORAC: Peace Officers Research Association of California
porc: porcelain
PORC: Peralta Oaks Research Center
porno: pornofilm; pornographer; pornographic; pornographically; pornographic bookshop; pornography (defined by Irvin S. Cobb as when the depth of the dirt exceeded the width of the wit)
pornofilm: pornographic motion picture
pornos: pornographic books, moving pictures, photographs, recordings, etc.
pornovel: pornographic + novel (usually what it sounds like—a poor novel)
porp(s): porpoise(s)
PORS: Post Office Research Station
port.: portable; portrait; portraiture
Port: Portland; Portugal; Portuguese
Port Chi: Port Chicago; Portuguese China
Port Ind: Portuguese India
porto: (Italian or Portuguese—harbor; port, as in Portofino; Oporto)
port side: *lefthand* side of an airplane, ship, or other craft when looking forward, symbol-

ized by a fixed *red* light—on the *lefthand* wingtip of an airplane or set against a *red* background on the *lefthand* side of a ship's bridge or pilothouse
Port Tim: Portuguese Timor
Portuguese Century: the 12th century when the first king of Portugal—Affonso I Henriques—rules over what was to become a great maritime empire—the 1100s
pos: position; positive
POs: Police Officers
POS: Port-of-Spain, Trinidad (airport)
POSB: Post Office Savings Bank
posdcorb: planning-organization-staffing- directing- coordinating-reporting-budgeting (mnemonic device for remembering the functions of management)
posh: port side out, starboard side home (British slang)
positron: positive electron
posn: position
POSNY: People of the State of New York
pos pron: possessive pronoun
poss: possession; possessive
POSS: Passive Optical Satellite Surveillance (System)
POSSUM: Polar Orbiting Satellite System
possum(s): opossum(s)
post.: postage; postal
POST: Frederick Post Drafting Equipment
poster.: posterior
postgangl: postganglionic
postgrad(s): postgraduate(s)
posth: posthumous
postl: postlude
post-mort: post mortem (autopsy)
post-op: post-operative
pot.: point of tangency; potash; potassa (potassium hydroxide); potassium; potential; potentiometer; (slang—marijuana)
pot.: potaguaya (Mexican Indian—marijuana); *potio* Latin—dose; draft; potion)
potash: potassium carbonate (K_2CO_3)
potass: potassium
potats: potatoes
POTC: PERT *(q.v.)* Orientation and Training Program
pots.: potentiometers
pott: pottery
pot w: potable water
poul: poultry
POUM: Partido Obrero de Unificación Marxista (Spanish—Workers Party of Marxist Unification)—political alliance of anar-

cho-syndicalists, left-wing socialists, and Trotskyite communists who were powerful at the beginning of the Spanish Civil War but were soon defeated by right-wing socialists, Stalinist communists, and fascists
POUR: President's Organization for Unemployment Relief
pov: privately owned vehicle
pow: power; prisoner of war (POW)
powd: powder; powdered
POWER: Professionals Organized for Women's Equal Rights
pows (POWS): prisoners of war
Poz: Poznan
pozn: poznamka (Czech—footnote)
pp: pages; panel point; parcel post; part paid; partial pay; partially paid; past participle; passive participle; pellagra preventive (factor); permanent party; petticoat peeping; physical profile; physical properties; pickpocket; postpaid; postage paid; present position; pressure-proof; privately printed; private property; professional paper; purchased part(s); push-pull
p-p: peak-to-peak; push-pull
p-to-p: peak-to-peak; point-to-point
pp: pianissimo (Italian—very softly)
p.p.: piena pelle (Italian—full leather)
Pp.: Papa (Latin—father or Pope)
PP: Pacific Petroleum; Parcel Post; Parish Priest; Past President; Power Plant; Proletarian Party (Communist)
P-P: pellagra-preventive factor
P-au-P: Port-au-Prince
PP: Patres (Latin—Fathers)
P.P.: Pater Patriae (Latin—Father of his Country)
ppa: palpitation, percussion, auscultation; photo-peak analysis
p. pa.: per procura (Latin—by proxy)
p.p.a.: phiala prius agitate (Latin—bottle having first been shaken)—shake well before using
PPA: Pakistan Press Association; Paper Pail Association; Paper Plate Association; Parcel Post Association; Periodical Publishers Association; Popcorn Processors Association; Poultry Publishers Association; President's Professional Association; Produce Packaging Association; Professional Photographers of America; Proletarian Party of America; Public Personnel Association; Purple Plum Association

PPATRA: Printing, Packaging, and Allied Trades Research Association

ppb: parts per billion

PPBS: Planning-Programming-Budgeting System

ppc: picture postcard

p p c: *pour prendre congé* (French —to take leave)

PPC: Policy Planning Council (US Department of State)

PPCD: Plant Pest Control Division

ppd: prepaid; purified protein derivative (tuberculin)

PPD: Portland Public Docks

p p^do: *próximo pasado* (Spanish —last month)

PPDP: Preprogram Definition Phase

PPDSE: Plate Printers, Die Stampers, and Engravers (union)

PPF: Plumbers and Pipefitters (union)

PPFA: Planned Parenthood Federation of America

p-p factor: pellagra-preventive factor

PPG: Pago Pago, Samoan Islands (airport); Pittsburgh Plate Glass

pph: post-partum hemorrhage; pounds per hour; pulses per hour

ppi: pages per inch; parcel post insured; plan position indicator

PPI: Plastic Pipe Institute; Project Public Information

pp/in.: pages per inch

pPk: purplish pink

ppl: pipeline

PPL: Philadelphia Public Library; Phoenix Public Library; Pittsburgh Public Library; Portland Public Library; Providence Public Library; Provisioning Parts List

PP&L: Pennsylvania Power and Light (company)

pplo: pleuropneumonia-like organism(s)

ppm: parts per million; pounds per minute; pulse position modulation

ppn: proportion(al)

PPNP: Point Pelee National Park (Ontario)

ppo: polyphenylene oxide; prior permission only

p-p-ola: political plugola (media plugging or touting of a candidate or an ideological issue) —propaganda device in disrepute

ppp: petty political pismire

p & pp: pull and push plate

ppp: *piu pianissimo* (Italian—very very softly)

PPP: Peoples Party of Pakistan; Petroleum Production Pioneers; Population Policy Panel (Hugh Moore Fund)

ppr: present particple; prior permission required

PPR: Permanent Pay Record; Permanent Personal Registration; Procurement Problem Report

pps: pictures per second; pounds per second; pulses per second

PPS: Paper Publications Society

PPS: *Partido Popular Salvadoreño* (Spanish—Salvadoran Popular Party)—of El Salvador, Central America; *Partido Popular Socialista* (Spanish—Popular Socialist Party)

P.P.S.: *post postscriptum* (Latin —additional postscript)

PPSAWA: Pan Pacific and Southeast Asia Women's Association

PPSB: Periodical Publishers' Service Bureau

PPT: Papeete, Society Islands (airport); Pre-Production Test(ing)

ppty: property

P & PU: Peoria and Pekin Union (railroad)

PPVT: Peabody Picture Vocabulary Test

PPWP: Planned Parenthood-World Population

pq: peculiar; personality quotient (PQ); previous question

PQ: personality quotient; Province of Quebec; South Pacific Airlines of New Zealand (2-letter code)

pqa: procurement quality assurance

PQAP: Procurement Quality Assurance Program

PQC: Production Quality Control

PQD: Plant Quarantine Division

PQIH: Plant Quarantine Inspection House

pr: pair; payroll; percentile rank; peripheral resistance

p & r: parallax and refraction

pR: purplish red

Pr: Parana; prandtl number; praseodymium; presbyopia; Press; Prince; propyl

Pr: *Praça* (Portuguese—plaza; square); *Presbyter* (Latin—elder or priest)

PR: Parachute Rigger; Performance Report; Photoreconnaissance; Pinar del Rio; Plant Report; Problem Report; Progress Report; Public Relations; Puerto Rican(s); Puerto Rico; river gunboat (2-letter naval symbol)

P-R: Pennsylvania-Reading (Seashore Lines)

P/R: payroll

PR: *Partido Republicano* (Spanish

—Republican Party); *Polskie Radio* (Polish Radio); *Puerto Rico*

pra: probation and rehabilitation of airmen

PRA: Pay Readjustment Act; Personnel Research Activity; Popular Rotocraft Association; Psoriasis Research Association; Psychological Research Association; Public Roads Administration; Puerto Rico Association

prac: practice; practitioner

prado: (Spanish—field; meadow)

praen: praenomen

prag: pragmatic; pragmatism

pral: principal (Spanish—principal)

pram: perambulator

prand.: *prandium* (Latin—dinner)

PRANG: Puerto Rico Air National Guard

PRAT: Prattsburgh (railroad)

PRAY: Paul Revere Associated Yeoman

PRB: Personnel Review Board; Population Reference Bureau; Pre-Raphaelite Brotherhood

prc: procedure

PRC: Pension Research Council; People's Republic of China (Red China); Picatinny Research Center (Picatinny Arsenal); Planning Research Corporation; Public Relations Club

PRCA: Puerto Rico Communications Authority

prchst: parachutist

prcht: parachute

prcs: process; processing

prcst: precast

prd: partial reaction of degeneration

PRD: Pesticides Regulation Division (USDA); Program Requirement Document

PRDC: Power Reactor Development Corporation

PRDL: Personnel Research and Development Laboratory (USN)

pre: progressive resistance exercise

preamp(s): preamplifier(s)

prec: precedence; precision

precip: precipitate; precipitation

PRECIS: Preserved Context Index System

PREDA: Puerto Rico Economic Development Administration

pre-design: preliminary design

pre-em: preeminence; preeminent; preempt; preemptible; preemption; preemptive; preemptor; preemptory

preemies: premature babies

preemy: premature baby

pref: preface; prefatory; prefecture;

preference; prefix
prefab: prefabricated
prefd: preferred
preg: pregnancy; pregnant
pregang: preganglionic
prehis: prehistoric
prej: prejudice
prel: prelude
prelim: preliminary
prem: premature; premium
pre-med: premedical
Prensa: La Prensa (Buenos Aires' Press)
Prenzl Bg: Prenzlauer Berg
pre-op: preoperation; preoperational
prep: preparation; preparatory; prepare; preposition
PREP: Personal Radio-Equipped Police; Preparation Rehabilitation Education Program; Pupil Record of Educational Progress
prepd: prepared
prep'ed: prepared
prepn: preparation
prepr: prepracovane (Czech—rewritten)
pres: present
Pres: President
PRES: Puerto Rico Employment Service
presby: presbyopia; presbyopic
Presby: Presbyterian
presc: prescription
President ships: American President Line vessels named after such statesmen as *President Lincoln, President Roosevelt, President Taft*
presq'ile: (French—peninsula, as in Presque Isle Park, Pennsylvania)
press.: pressure
Presse: Die Presse (Neue Freie Presse)—Vienna's Press
prestmo.: prestissimo (Italian—very quickly)
PRESTO: Program Reporting and Evaluation System for Total Operations
Preston K. Swinehart: (nickname—movie actor Alan Dinehart in villain roles)
presv: preservation; preserve
pret: preterit
Pret: Pretoria
prev: previous
preven: preventive
prevoc: prevocational
prex(y): president (usually college of university)
prf: proof; pulse recurrence frequency; pulse repetition frequency
prf.: praefatio (Latin—introduction; preface)

PRF: Petroleum Research Fund; Plywood Research Foundation; Public Relations Foundation; Puerto Rican Forum
prfnl: professional
prfr: proofreader
PRG: Prague, Czechoslovakia (airport); Provisional Revolutionary Government (of South Vietnam)
PRHS: Port Richmond High School
pri: primary; primer; primitive; priority; private
PRI: Paleontological Research Institute
PRI: Partido Revolucionario Institucional (Spanish—Institutional Revolutionary Party); *Partito Repubblicano Italiano* (Italian Republican Party)
PRIDCO: Puerto Rico Industrial Development Company
PRIDE: Personal Responsibility in Defect Elimination
prim.: primary
prime.: precision recovery including maneuvering entry
prin: principal
PRINAIR: Puerto Rico International Airlines
PRINCE: Parts, Reliability, and Information Center (NASA)
Prince of Gossips: Samuel Pepys
Prince of Orators: Demosthenes
Prince of the Oyster Pirates: Jack London
Prince of Philosophers: Plato
Prince of Poets: Edmund Spenser
Prince of Showmen: P.T. Barnum
Princess of Fruits: (Linnaeus' sobriquet for the pineapple)
Prince of Trees: (Linnaeus' nickname for the palm)
print.: printed; printing
PRINUL: Puerto Rico International Undersea Laboratory
PRIO: Peace Research Institute, Oslo (Norway)
prior.: priority
PRI & RB: Puerto Rico Inspection and Rating Bureau
pris: prison(er)
PRISE: Pennsylvania's Regional Instruction System for Education (intercollegiate network)
pris g: prisonnier de guerre (French—prisoner of war)
Prissy: Priscilla
pritac: primary tactical radio circuit
priv: private
privatdozent: university professor not belonging to a professorial staff
priv pr: privately printed
priv pub: privately published
PRJC: Puerto Rico Junior College

pr kassa: per kassa (Norwegian—for cash)
PRL: Personnel Research Laboratory; Polska Rzeczpospolita Ludowa (Polish Republic); Precision Reduction Laboratory
prm: prime
prmld: premolded
p.r.n.: pro re nata (Latin—as needed; for an emergency)
PRNC: Potomac River Naval Command
PRNL: Pictured Rocks National Lakeshore (Michigan)
PRNS: Point Reyes National Seashore
prntr: printer
PRNWR: Parker River National Wildlife Refuge (Massachusetts)
pro: procedure; proceed; procure; procurement; profession; professional; professionally; prophylactic
pro (PRO): proline (amino acid)
pro: (Latin—for)
PRO: Personnel Relations Office(r); Plant Representative's Office; Public Relations Office(r)
PROA: Public Record Office Archives
prob: probably
Prob Off: Probation Officer
proc: procedure; proceeding(s); procure; procurement
Proc: Proceedings
procd: procedure
Proc Roy Soc: Proceedings of the Royal Society
procto: proctocolitis; proctocolonoscopy; proctologist; proctology; proctosigmoidoscopy; proctosigmoidectomy; proctoplegia
prod: product; production
prof: profession; professional; professor
Prof: Professor
PROF: Peace Research Organization Fund
profac: propulsive fluid accumulator
Prof Eng: Professional Engineer
Professor Julius Ceasar Hannibal: (pseudonym—W.H. Levinson)
Profintern: Red International of Trade Unions
prog: progenitor; progeny; prognose; prognosis; prognostic; prognostication; prognosticator; program; programmer
progr: program(mer); programme
Prog(s): Progressive(s)
prohib: prohibit(ion)
proj: project; projectile; projection; projector
Prol: Prolongación (Spanish —pro-

longation as in the extension of Mexico City's Paseo de la Reforma—Prol Paseo de la Reforma)

prole(s): proletarian(s)

proliv: (Russian—strait)

PROLLAP: Professional Library Literature Acquisition Program

prolong.: prolongatus (Latin—prolonged)

ProLt: procurement lead time

prom: promenade (concert or dance); prominent; promontory; promote; promoter; promotion; promotional; prompter

proml: promulgate

pron: pronoun; pronounced; pronunciation; pronunciator(y)

prop: propaganda; propeller; property; proportion(al); proposed; proprietary

PROP: Portland Regional Opportunities Program

propay: proficiency pay

proph: prophetic; prophylactic; prophylaxis

propjet: propeller turned by jet engine (same as turboprop)

props: (theatrical) properties

prop wash: propeller wash

pro rect.: pro recto (Latin—by rectum)

pros: prosody; prostitute

Pros Atty: Prosecuting Attorney

prosc: proscenium

prosig: procedure signal

prosine: procedure sign

prosp: prospecting

prost: prostate; prosthetics; prostitution

prostie(s): prostitute(s)

prot: protective; protectorate; protozoa; protractor

Prot: Protectorate; Protestant; Protozoa

Protector de los Indios: (Spanish—Protector of the Indians)—people like Padre Bartolomeo de las Casas in Mexico

prothrom: prothrombin

Protoch: Protochorda

prov: provide; provision; provisional; proviso

Prov: Provençal; Provence; Proverbs, The (book of the Bible); Providence; Province

Prov: Provinz (German—province)

prover: procurement-value-economy-reliability

provn: provision

provos: provokers (Dutch—street people engaged in militant tactics to provoke the police)

Provos: Provisionals (Provisional Sinn Fein party members of Northern Ireland)

PROVOST: Priority Research and Development Objectives for Vietnam Operations Support

proword: procedure word

prox: proximal; proximity

prox.: proximo (Latin—next, *adv.*)

prox. luc.: proxima luce (Latin—the day before)

prp: pulse repetition period

PRP: Production Requirements Plan; Production Reserve Policy; Public Relations Personnel

PRPA: Puerto Rico Ports Authority

prpln: propulsion

PRPUC: Philippine Republic Presidential Unit Citation

prr: pulse repetition rate

PRR: Pennsylvania Railroad

PRRI: Puerto Rico Rum Institute

prs: pairs; printers

Prs: Preston

PRs: Pakistani rupees; Problem Reports; Puerto Ricans

PRS: Pennsylvania-Reading Seashore (railroad); Precision Ranging System

PRSA: Public Relations Society of America

prsd: pressed

prsd met: pressed metal

prsfdr: pressfeeder

prsmn: pressman

PRSS: Pennsylvania-Reading Seashore Lines

PRST: Puerto Rican Standard Time

PRSY: People's Republic of Southern Yemen

prt: parachute radio transmitter; personnel research test; publication requirement table(s); pulse repetition time

PRT: Personnel Research Test; Philadelphia Rapid Transit; Production Re-evaluation Testing

prtg: printing

PRTS: Personal Rapid Transit System

Pru: Prudence; Prudential Life Insurance Company

PRU: Polish-Russian Union (South African Jews who joined this were called Peruvians because of their abbreviation of their society seemingly alien to their Christian neighbors)

Prus: Prussia; Prussian

prussic acid: hydrocyanic acid

prv: pressure-reducing valve

Prv: Pravda (Russian—truth)—daily newspaper published in Moscow by Central Committee of the Communist Party

prx: pressure regulator exhaust

PRY: Pittsburgh Railways Corporation (stock exchange symbol)

ps: parlor snake; parts shipped;

parts shipper; passenger service; passing scuttle; patient's serum; penal servitude; pico-second; pieces; plastic surgery; point of switch; point of symmetry; proof shot; pseudo; pseudonym(s); pull switch; pulmonary stenosis

p-s: pressure-sensitive

p & s: paracentesis and suction; port and starboard

Ps: Psalms, The (book of the Bible); South Pole; South Celestial Pole; static pressure

PS: Paleontological Society; Palm Society; Paymaster Sergeant; Pennsylvania State University; Pharmaceutical Society; Philippine Scouts; Photo(graphic) Service; picket ship(s); Pistol Sharpshooter; Pittsburg & Shawmut (railroad); Plastic Surgery; Privy Seal; Public Safety; Public School; Puget Sound

P.S.: paddle steamer; public school

P-S: Pullman-Standard

P & S: Physicians and Surgeons; Pittsburg & Shawmut (railroad)

P of S: Port of Spain

PS: Pferdestärke (German—horsepower)

P.S.: post scriptum (Latin—written after)

PSA: Pacific Science Association; Pacific Southwest Airlines; Photographic Society of America; Poetry Society of America; Poultry Science Association; Program Study Authorization

PSAC: President's Science Advisory Committee

PSACPOO: President's Scientific Advisory Committee Panel On Oceanography

psad: prediction-simulation-adaptation-decision (data processing)

PSAL: Public School Athletic League

Psalt.: Psalterium (Latin—Book of Psalms)

PSAT: Palm Springs Aerial Tramway; Preliminary Scholastic Aptitude Test(ing)

psb: public service band (radio)

PSB: Psychological Strategy Board

P & SB: Portland & South Bend

PSBLS: Permanent Space-Based Logistics System

psc: per standard compass

PSC: Pacific Sea Council; Peralta Shipping Corporation; Pittsburgh Steel Company; Point Shipping Company; Porcelain-on-Steel Council; Potomac State

College; Program Structure Code; Public Service Commission

PSC: *Partido Social Cristiano* (Spanish—Social Christian Party)—Catholic actionists

PSCNI: Public Service Company of Northern Illinois

psd: power spectral density; promotion service date

P Sd: Port Said

PSD: Pittsburgh Steamship Division (United States Steel); Port of San Diego

psdo: pseudo

PSDUPD: Port of San Diego Unified Port District

pse: please; point of subjective equality

PSEA: Pennsylvania State Education Association; Physical Security Equipment Agency

PSE & GC: Public Service Electric and Gas

PSE & G: Public Service Electric and Gas Company

pseud: pseudonym

psf: payload-structure-fuel (ratio); pounds per square foot

PSF: Phelps-Stokes Fund

P & SF: Panhandle and Santa Fe (railroad)

P of SF: Port of San Francisco

PSFC: Pacific Salmon Fisheries Commission

PSFL: Puget Sound Freight Lines

PSFS: Philadelphia Savings Fund Society

PSGBI: Pathological Society of Great Britain and Ireland

psgr: passenger

psi: pounds per square inch

PSI: Pacific Semiconductors Incorporated; Physician's Services Incorporated; Population Services Incorporated

PSI: *Partito Socialista Italiano* (Italian Socialist Party)

psia: pounds per square inch absolute

PSIC: Pacific Scientific Information Center (Bernice Pauahi Bishop Museum, Honolulu)

psig: pounds per square inch gage

PSIUP: *Partito Socialista Italiano di Unita Proletaria* (Italian Socialist Party of Proletarian Unity)

psk: phase shift keying

p sl: pipe sleeve

PSL: Pacific Star Line; Peruvian State Line; Philharmonic Society of London

p-slips: old-fashioned postcard-size (3-×-5-inch) slips of paper used for filing

ps lt: port side light

psma: progressive spinal muscular atrophy

PSMA: Power Saw Manufacturers Association

PSMFC: Pacific States Marine Fisheries Commission

psmsl: permanent service for mean sea level

psn: position

PSN: *Partido Socialista de Nicaragua* (Spanish—Socialist Party of Nicaragua)—Moscow-oriented group

PSNA: Phytochemical Society of North America

PSNC: Pacific Steam Navigation Company

PSNS: Puget Sound Naval Shipyard

PSO: Pad Safety Officer; Pasadena Symphony Orchestra; Phoenix Symphony Orchestra; Pilot Systems Operator; Pittsburgh Symphony Orchestra; Portland Symphony Orchestra; Prague Symphony Orchestra

pson: person

PS 166: Public School 166 (for example)

psp: phenolsulfonphthalein (test); pierced-steel plank; positive screened print

PSP: Pocahontas State Park (Virginia); Program Support Plan

PSP: *Pacifistisch Socialistische Partij* (Dutch—Pacifist-Socialist Party)

PSP & L: Puget Sound Power and Light (company)

PSPMW: Pulp, Sulphite and Paper Mill Workers

PSPP: Proposed System Package Plan

PSPS: Paddle Steamer Preservation Society

p's & q's: expression about minding your p's & q's originated when printers instructed apprentices about similarity of lower-case p's and q's when handsetting type; also used in saloons to keep count of the number of pints and quarts of beer consumed

psr: plow-steel rope

PSR: Physicians for Social Responsibility

PSRF: Profit Sharing Research Foundation

pss: physiological saline solution

Pss: Princess

PSS: Pad Safety Supervisor

P.S.S.: *postscripta* (Latin—postscripts)

PSSC: Physical Science Study Committee (National Science Foundation)

pst: polished surface technique

PST: Pacific Standard Time

PSTBC: Puget Sound Tug and Boat Company

PSTC: Pressure Sensitive Tape Council

PSTD: Prison Service Training Depot (Pretoria)

p stg c: per steering compass

pstl: postal

P-strip: P-shaped strip

PSU: Pennsylvania State University

PSU: *Partito Socialista Unitario* (Italian—Unitary Socialist Party)

PSUC: Pennsylvania State University Center(s)

p surg: plastic surgeon; plastic surgery

PSW: Psychiatric Social Worker

psy: psychological

Psy: Paisley

psych: psychiatry; psychology; psychopathology

psychiat: psychiatric; psychiatry

psycho: dangerous lunatic; a psychiatric hospital or ward; a psychoneurotic personality; a psychotic individual (pseudoscientific slang)

psychoan: psychoanalytic; psychoanalysis; psychoanalyst

psychol: psychological; psychologist; psychology

psychomet: psychometric

psychopathol: psychopathological; psychopathologist; psychopathology

psychophys: psychophysical; psychophysics; psychophysicist

psychophysiol: psychophysiology (and derivatives)

psychot: psychotic

psychother: psychotherapist; psychotherapeutic(al, s); psychotherapy

psyop: psychological operation

psysom: psychosomatic

psywar: phychological warfare

pt: part; personal trade; physical therapy; physical training; pint(s); plenty tough; plenty trouble; pneumatic tube; point; point of tangency; point of turn; point of turning; primary target; private terms; prothrombin time

p & t: personnel and training; posts and timbers

pt: *partie* (French—part)

Pt: platinum; Point; Port; Porto; Puerto

PT: motor torpedo boat (naval symbol); Pacific Time; Peninsula Terminal (railroad); Philadelphia Transportation; Postal

Telegraph; primary trainer; Provincetown-Boston Airline (2-letter coding)

£T: pound Turkish

P & T: Pope & Talbot (steamship line)

pta: plasma thromboplastin antecedent; posttraumatic amnesia; primary target area; prior to admission; proposed technical approach; peseta (Spanish monetary unit, diminutive of peso)

Pta: *Punta* (Spanish—Point)

Pt A: Port Arthur, Ontario

PTA: Paper and Twine Association; Parent-Teacher Association; Pope and Talbot; Postal Transportation Association; Protestant Teachers Association

Pt Art: Port Arthur

ptas: pesetas

pta's: part-time alcoholics

PTAs: Passenger Transport Authorities

ptbl: portable

PT-boat: patrol torpedo boat

ptbr: punched-tape block reader

ptc: personnel transfer capsule; positive temperature coefficient

PTC: Pacific Tin Consolidated; Paisley Technical College; patrol vessel (naval symbol); Peoria Terminal (railroad); Philadelphia Transportation Company; Pine Tree Camp; Pipe and Tobacco Council; Power Transmission Council; Press Trust of Ceylon; Private Truck Council

PTCA: Private Truck Council of America

ptd: painted

P o TD: Port of The Dalles

PTDA: Power Transmission Distributors Association

PTDP: Preliminary Technical Development Plan

PTDR: Post- Test Disassembly Report

PTDS: Photo Target Detection System

pte: *parte* (Spanish—part)

Pte: *Pointe* (French—Point)

PTF: fast patrol boat (naval symbol); Propulsion Test Facilities

ptg: printing

Ptg: Portugal; Portuguese

PTG: Piano Technician's Guild

ptgt: primary target

PTI: Philips Telecommunicatie Industrie; Press Trust of India

PTIS: Piano Teachers Information Service

ptl: pintle; primary target line

PTL: Photographic Technology Laboratory

ptm: proof test model; pulse-time modulation

Ptm: Pietermaai

ptn: partition

pto: please turn over; power takeoff

Pto: Porto; Puerto; Punto

Pto Cab: Puerto Cabello

Ptol: Ptolemaic; Ptolemy

PTP: Pointe à Pitre, Guadeloupe (airport)

pt/pt: point-to-point

PTR: pool test reactor

pts: pesetas (Spanish—plural of peseta); pints

Pts: Portsmouth

PTS: Postal Transportation Service; Princeton Theological Seminary

pts/hr: parts per hour; pieces per hour

Pt Sp: Port of Spain

ptt: push to talk

PTT: Posta, Telgraf ve Telefon (Turkish—Post, Telegraph, and Telephone); Postes, Télégraphes, Téléphone (French—national postal, telegraph, and telephone system)

PTTA: Philippine Tourist and Travel Association

pt-tm: part-time

pttnmkr: patternmaker

ptv: public television

ptv (PTV): propulsion test vehicle

Pt W: Port Weller

Pty: Party; Proprietary

pu: pickup; plant unit; pregnancy urine; propellant utilization; propulsion unit; pump unit

p-u (pee-you): phew (what a stench)

pu: (Chinese—village)

p.u.: *plus ultra* (Latin—beyond the pinnacle; beyond the ultimate)

Pu: plutonium

PU: Pacific University; Phillips University; Princeton University; Purdue University

PUAS: Postal Union of the Americas and Spain

pub: public; publication; publicity; publish

pub aide: publication aide

Pub Doc: Public Document

pub ed: publication editor

pubinfo: public information

publ: publication; publicity, publisher; publishing

pub(s): public house(s) (British short form)

Pub Wks: Public Works

PUC: Peoples University of China; Presidential Unit Citation; Public Utilities Code; Public Utilities Commission; Public Utilities and Corporations

pud: puddle; pudding

Pue: Puebla

pueblo: (Spanish—town; village)

puerto: (Spanish—harbor; port)

PUF: Presses Universitaires de France (University Presses of France)

pufa: polyunsaturated fatty acid

pug.: puggy; pugilism; pugilist

PUHS: Phoenix Union High School

pul: pulley

pul: *pulau* [Malay— island, as in Pulau Pinang (Penang Island)]

PUL: Princeton University Library

pulm: pulmonary

pulmo: pulmonary

pulmotor: (pulmonary + motor)

pulsar: pulse + star (pulsed radio-wave-emitting star); pulsing astronomical signal (received from outer space)

pulv: pulverize(r)

pulv.: *pulvis* (Latin—powder)

pulv. gros.: *pulvis grossus* (Latin—coarse powder)

pulv. subtil.: *pulvis subtilis* (Latin—smooth powder)

pulv. tenu: *pulvis tenuis* (Latin—very fine)

PUM: Postal Union Mail

pump.: pumping

PUMP: Protesting Unfair Marketing Practices

pums: permanently unfit for military service

pun.: puncheon

PUN: *Partido Union Nacional* (Spanish—National Union Party)

punc: punctuation

pundonor: *punta de honor* (Spanish—point of honor)

Punj: Punjabi

Punkt: (German—point)

punt: (Dutch—point)

punta: (Italian or Spanish—point, as in Punta del Este)

puo: pyrexia of unknown origin

PUP: Princeton University Press

pur: purchase; purchaser; purchasing; purifier; purification; purify; purple; purplish; pursuant; pursuit

purch: purchasing

purg.: *purgativus* (Latin—purgative)

purp: purple

purv: powered underwater research vehicle

pus.: permanently unfit for service

Pus: Pusan

Push: Pushtu

PUSH: People United to Save Humanity

puta(s): *prostituta(s)*—[Spanish—prostitute(s)]

putty: linseed oil and powdered

chalk mixture

puvep: propellant-utilization vehicle- borne electronic package

pv: paravane; par value; plasma value; position value; prime vertical; public voucher

p/v: peak-to-valley

p v: *petite vitesse* (French—slow train); *piccola velocity* (Italian —slow train)

Pv: Peru; Peruvian

PV: Eastern Provincial Airways (2-letter coding); patrol vessel; Post Village; Priest Vicar; Puerto Vallarta

P.V.: *Procès verbaux* (French —official report); *Processi verbali* (Italian—official report)

pva: polyvinyl acetate

PVA: Paralyzed Veterans of America

pval: polyvinyl alcohol

pvb: potentiometer voltmeter bridge

PVB: Prison Visitors' Board

pvc: polyvinyl chloride (thermoplastic)

PVC: Precision Valve Corporation

PVD: Providence, Rhode Island (airport)

PvdA: *Partij van de Arbeid* (Dutch—Labor Party)

pvdc: plyyvinyl dichloride

pvem: pulse-vector emittance meter

pvf: polyvinyl fluoride

pvm: polyvinyl methyl

PVMNM: Perry's Victory Memorial National Monument

pvnt: prevent; preventive

PVO: Principal Veterinary Officer

pvpp: polyvinyl-polypyrrolidone

PVS: Pecos Valley Southern (railroad)

pvt: pressure volume temperature; private

p v t: *par voie telegraphique* (French—by telegraph)

Pvt: Private

Pvt 1/C: Private First Class

PVU: Prairie View University

pw: packed weight; passing window; pivoted window; postwar; prisoner of war; projected window; psychological warfare; public works; pulse width

p/w: parallel with

PW: Philadelphia & Western (railroad); Pittsburgh & West Virginia (railroad); prisoner of war; Public Works

PW: *Publishers' Weekly*

P & W: Pratt and Whitney Aircraft Division, United Aircraft Corporation

PWA: Pacific Western Airlines; Public Works Administration

p-wave: pressure wave

PWC: Public Works Center (USN)

pwd: powered

PWD: Public Works Department

PWE: Political Warfare Executive; Prisoner of War Enclosure

pwf: pregnancy without fear (pillow-simulated pregnancy); present-worth factor

PWFP: Prince William Forest Park (Virginia)

PWI: Physiological Workload Index

PWJC: Piney Woods Junior College

pwm: pulse width modulation

PWMS: Public Works Management System (USN)

PWNP: Parra Wirra National Park (South Australia)

PWO: Public Works Office(r)

pwr: power; pressurized water reactor (PWR)

PWRS: Pacific War Research Society

pwr sup: power supply

pws: paddlewheel steamer

pw's: prisoners of war

PWS: Periyar Wildlife Sanctuary (India); Private Wire System

pwt: pennyweight; propulsion wind tunnel

pwtr: pewter

P & WV: Pittsburgh & West Virginia (railroad)

px: past history; physical examination; please exchange; pneumothorax; prognosis

PX: Aspen Airways (2-letter code); Post Exchange

PXCMD: Phoenix Contract Management District

px in: time of arrival

px me: report my arrival and departure

px out: takeoff time

pxt.: *pinxit* (Latin—he painted it)

py: pitch and yaw

PY: commissioned and armed yacht (2-letter naval symbol); Surinam Airways (2-letter symbol); program year

pya: plan, year, age (insurance)

Pya: *Pyatnitsa* (Russian—Friday)

PYE: Protect Your Environment

pyph: polyphase

pyr: pyridine

p-y-r: pitch-yaw-roll

pyro: pyromaniac; pyrotechnic(s); pyroxylin

pyrom: pyrometer; pyrometry

pyrot: pyrotechnics

pyx.: *pyxis* (Latin—box; vessel)

PZ: Paolei Zion(ist); Pickup Zone; Police Zone

pza: *pieza* (Spanish—piece)

pzi: protamine zinc insulin

PZM: Polska Zegluga Morska (Polish Merchant Marine)

PZPR: *Polska Zjednoczona Partia Robotnicza* (Polish United Workers Party)

Q

q: coefficient of association (statistical symbol); dynamic pressure (symbol); electric charge (symbol); quality factor; quart; quarter; quartile; quarterly; quarto; quench; quenching; queries; query; question(s); quick; quintal; quire; semi-interquartile range (symbol); stagnation pressure (symbol)

q2h: *quaque secunda hora* (Latin

—every two hours)

q3h: *quaque tertia hora* (Latin— every three hours)

q4h: *quaque quarta hora* (Latin —every four hours)

Q: bankruptcy or receivership (stock exchange symbol); electric quadruple moment of atomic nucleus (symbol); Fairchild (symbol); Polaris correction (symbol); quadrillion; Quaker

Line; quarantine; Quartermaster; quartile variation (symbol); Quebec—code for letter Q; Queen; Queensland; quetzal (Guatemalan monetary unit named after this plume-tailed bird); radio inductive reactance to resistance (symbol); semi-interquartile range (symbol); target or drone (symbol); thermoelectric power (symbol)

Q1, Q2, Q3, Q4: first quartile, second quartile, third quartile, fourth quartile

Q: pseudonym for Sir Arthur Quiller-Couch; *Quai* (French—embankment or quay); *quetzal* (Guatemalan monetary unit); torque (symbol)

qa: quality assurance; quick-acting; quiescent aerial

QA: Quality Assurance; Quarters Allowance

Q & A: question and answer

QAA: Quality Assurance Assistant

QAB: Queen Anne's Bounty (for indigent clergymen)

qac: quaternary ammonium compound

QAC: Quality Assurance Code

qad: quick-attach-detach

QAD: Quality Assurance Directive; Quality Assurance Division

QADC: Queen's Aide-de-Camp

qadk: quick attach-detach kit

QADS: Quality Assurance Data System

QAE: Quality Assurance Engineer(ing)

qaf: quality-assurance firing

qafo: quality-assurance field operation(s)

QAG: Quaker Action Group

qagc: quiet automatic gain control

QAI: Quality Assurance Instruction

QAIMNS: Queen Alexandra's Imperial Military Nursing Service

QAIP: Quality Assurance Inspection Procedure

qak: quick-attach kit

qal: quartz aircraft lamp

qal: *quintal* (French—hundredweight)

QAL: Quality Assurance Laboratory; Quarterly Accession List; Quebec Airways Limited

qall: quartz aircraft landing lamp

QALTR: Quality Assurance Laboratory Test Request

qam: quadrature amplitude modulation

QAM: Quality Assurance Manager

QAM: *Quality Assurance Manual*

QANTAS: Queensland And Northern Territories Aerial Services

qao: quality assurance operation

QAO: Quality Assurance Office (USN)

QAOP: Quality Assurance Operating Procedure

qap: quinine, atebrin, plasmoquine (malaria treatment)

QAP: Quality Assurance Procedure(s); Quality Assurance Program

QA & P: Quanah, Acme & Pacific (railroad)

QAPL: Queensland Airlines Proprietary Limited

qar: quick-access recording

QAR: Quality Assurance Representative

QAR: *Quality Assurance Report*

QARAFNS: Queen Alexandra's Royal Air Force Nursing Service

QARANC: Queen Alexandra's Royal Army Nursing Service

QARNNS: Queen Alexandra's Royal Naval Nursing Service

qas: quick-acting scuttle

QAs: Queen Alexandra's

QAS: Quality Assurance Service

QASP: Quality Assurance Standard Practice

QAST: Quality Assurance Service Test(s)

Qat: Qatar

QATP: Quality Assurance Technical Publication(s); Quality Assurance Test Procedure(s)

qavc: quiet automatic volume control

qb: qualified bidders; quarterback; quick break

QB: Queensboro Bridge (New York City); Quiet Birdmen (glider enthusiasts)

Q.B.: Queen's Bench

QBA: Quebecair

QBAA: Quality Brands Associates of America

QBAC: Quality Bakers of America Cooperative

Q-band: 36,000–46,000 mc

Qbc: Quebec

QBD: Queen's Bench Division

qbi: quite bloody impossible

QBL: Qualified Bidder's List

Q-boats: mystery ships used in antisubmarine warfare by the British in World War I

QBSM: *que besa su mano* (Spanish—who kisses your hand)—used in closing personal letters

QBSP: *que besa sus pies* (Spanish—who kisses your feet)—used in closing personal letters

qc: qualification course; quality control; quantitative command; quantum counter; quartz crystal; quick connect; quit claim

QC: Quality Control; Quartermaster Corps; Quebec Central (railroad); Queens College; Queen's College; Quezon City; Quincy College; Quinnipiac College; Quit Claim

Q.C.: Queen's Counsel

QCA: Queen Charlotte Airlines

Q-card: qualification card

qcc: qualification correlation certification; quick-connect coupling(s)

QCC: Queensborough Community College; Quinsigamond Community College

QCCARS: Quality Control Collection Analysis and Reporting System

qcd: quality-control data; quit-claim deed

QCD: quit claim deed

QCDR: Quality Control Deficiency Report

QCE: Quality Control Engineering

qcf: quartz-crystal filter

qcfo: quartz-crystal frequency oscillator

qch: quick-connect handle

qci: quality-control information

QCI: Quota Club International

QCIM: *Quarterly Cumulative Index Medicus*

QC Isl: Queen Charlotte Islands

qck: quick-connect kit

qcl: quality-control level

QCM: Quality Control Manager

QCM: *Quality Control Manual*

qco: quartz-crystal oscillator

QCO: Quality Control Officer

QCOP: Quality Control Operating Procedure

QCP: Quality Control Procedure

QCPE: Quantum Chemistry Program Exchange

qcr: quick-change response

QCR: Quality Control Representative

QC & R: Quality Control and Reliability

QCRC: Quebec Central Railway Company

QC Rep: Quality-Control Representative

QC Rept: Quality-Control Report

Q C Ry: Quebec Central Railway

QCS: Quality Control System; Quality Cost System

QC Stand: Quality-Control Standard

qct: quiescent carrier telephony; questionable corrective task

Q C & T: Quality Control and Test

QCTR: Quality Control Test Report

qcu: quartz crystal unit; quick-change unit

qcus: quartz crystal unit set

qcvc: quick-connect valve coupler

qcw: quadrant continuous wave

QCWA: Quarter-Century Wireless Association

Qcy: Quincy

qd: quarterdeck

q-d: quick-disconnect

q & d: quick and dirty

q.d.: *quater in die* (Latin—four times a day)

QD: Sadios Transportes Aéreos

qda: quantity discount agreement

qdc: quick dependable communications; quick-disconnect cap; quick-disconnect connector; quick-disconnect coupling

qdcc: quick-disconnect circular connection

qdc's: quick, dependable, communications

qdd: qualified for deep diving; quantized decision detection

QD/GD: Quincy Division/General Dynamics

qdh: quick-disconnect handle

qdk: quick-disconnect kit

qdn: quick-disconnect nipple

Qd'O: Quai d'Orsay

qdp: quick-disconnect pivot

QDRI: Qualitative Development Requirements Information (program)

qds: quick-disconnect series; quick-disconnect swivel

qdta: quantitative differential thermal analysis

qdv: quick disconnect valve

qe: quadrant elevation

q.e.: quod est (Latin—which is)

QE: Quality Engineer(ing)

QEA: Qantas Empire Airways

qeav: quick-exhaust air valve

qec: quick engine change

qecu: quick engine-change unit

qed: quantitative evaluative device; quantum electrodynamics; quick-reaction dome

q.e.d.: quod erat demonstrandum (Latin—that which was to be proved)

q.e.f.: quod erat faciendum Latin—that which was to be done)

QEH: Queen Elizabeth Hall

q.e.i.: quod erat inveniendum (Latin—that which was to be discovered)

qel: quiet extended life

QEL: Quality Evaluation Laboratory

qem: quadrant electrometer

QEM: Qualified Export Manager

QENP: Queen Elizabeth National Park (Uganda)

qeo: quality engineering operations

QEONS: Queen Elizabeth's Overseas Nursing Service

QEOP: Quartermaster Emergency Operation Plan

QEP: Quality Examination Program

qer: qualititative equipment requirements

qescp: quality engineering significant control points

QEST: Quality Evaluation System Test(s)

QE2: Queen Elizabeth 2 (passenger vessel)

qev: quick exhaust valve

qf: quality factor; quick freeze

QF: quick-firing

Q-factor: quality rating

q-fastener(s): quick-fastener(s)

qfc: quantitative flight characteristics

qfcc: quantitative flight characteristics criteria

qff: quadruple flip-flop

QFI: Qualified Flight Instructor

qfirc: quick-fix interference-reduction capability

qfl: quasi-fermi level

qfm: quantized frequency modulation

qfo: quartz frequency oscillator

qfp: quartz fiber product

QFP: Quick-Fix Program

Q-fract: quick fraction (membrane potentials)

qft: quantized field theory

qg: quadrature grid

QG: Quartermaster General

qgb: searchlight sonar (symbol)

qgv: quantized gate video

qh: quartz helix

q.h.: quaque hora (Latin—every hour)

QH: Queen's Hall

QHDS: Queen's Honorary Dental Surgeon

QHM: Queen's Harbour Master

QHNS: Queen's Honorary Nursing Sister

QHP: Queen's Honorary Physician

QHS: Queen's Honorary Surgeon

QHV: Queen's Honorary Veterinarian

qi: quality indices

QI: Quota International

QI: Quality Index; Quarterly Index

qic: quality inspection criteria; quartz-iodine crystal

QIC: Quality Information Center

q.i.d.: quater in die (Latin—four times a day)

QIDN: Queen's Institute of District Nursing

QIE: Qualified International Executive

qil: quartz incandescent lamp; quartz iodine lamp

qip: quartz insulation part

Q.I.P.: Quiescat in Pace (Latin—Rest in Peace)

qit: qualification information and test (system)

QJC: Quincy Junior College

qk: quick

Qk Fl: quick flashing (light)

qkm: Quadratkilometer (German—square kilometers)

ql: quick look

ql: quilate (Portuguese—carat)

q.l.: quantum libet (Latin—as much as you like)

QL: Queen's Lancers

QLAP: Quick Look Analysis Program

QLCS: Quick Look and Checkout System

Qld: Queensland

qli: quality of life index

qlit: quick-look intermediate tape

qll: quartz landing lamp

qlm: quasi-laser machine

QLR: Quebec Law Reports

qlsm: quasi-laser sequential machine

qlt: quantitative leak test

qlty: quality

qm: Quadratmeter (German—square meter); *quintal métrico* (Spanish—metric quintal; 220 pounds)

q.m.: quaque mane (Latin—every morning); *quo modo* (Latin—in what manner)

QM: Decca navigation system; Quartermaster; Queen's Messenger

qma: quality material approach

QMA: Quartermasters Association

QMAAC: Queen Mary's Army Auxiliary Corps

qmao: qualified for mobilization ashore only

Q-max: quarantine maximum

QMC: Quartermaster Corps

QMC & SO: Quartermaster Cataloging and Standardization Office

QMDEP: Quartermaster Depot

qmdk: quick mechanical disconnect kit

QMDO: Qualitative Materiel Development Objective

QMDPC: Quartermaster Data Processing Center

QMEPCC: Quartermaster Equipment and Parts Commodity Center

QMFCI: Quartermaster Food and Container Institute

QMFCIAF: Quartermaster Food and Container Institute for the Armed Forces

QMG: Quartermaster General

QMGMC: Quartermaster General—Marine Corps

QMI: Qualification Maintainability Inspection

QMIMSO: Quartermaster Industrial Mobilization Services Offices

qmo: qualitative material objective

QMORC: Quartermaster Officers Reserve Corps

QMP: Quezon Memorial Park (Philippines)

QMPA: Quartermaster Purchasing

Agency
QMPCUSA: Quartermaster Petroleum Center US Army
qmqb: quick-make quick-break (connection)
qmr: qualitative materiel requirement
QMRC: Quartermaster Reserve Corps
QMR & E: Quartermaster Research and Engineering
QMRL: Quartermaster Radiation Laboratory
QMs: quartermasters
QMS: Quartermaster School (US Army)
Qm Sgt: Quartermaster Sergeant
QMSO: Quartermaster Supply Office(r)
qmsw: quartz metal sealed window
QMT: Queens-Midtown Tunnel
QMTOE: Quartermaster Table of Organization and Equipment
qmw: quartz metal window
qn: question; quotation
q.n.: quaque nocte (Latin—every night); *quid nunc* (Latin—what now?)—person eternally interested in getting the latest news
Qn: Queen
QNP: Quezon National Park (Philippines)
qns: quantity not sufficient
Qns: Queens
QNS & L: Quebec North Shore and Labrador Railway
Qnsld: Queensland
qnty: quantity
QNWR: Quivira National Wildlife Refuge (Kansas)
qo: quick opening; quick outlet
QO: Quaker Oats; Qualified in Ordnance; Quartermaster Operation; Queen's Own (regiment)
Q & O: Quebec and Ontario (transportation company)
QO2: oxygen consumption (or quota)
QOA: Quasi-Official Agencies
QOCH: Queen's Own Cameron Highlanders
qod: quick-opening device
QOF: Quaker Oats Foundation
QOIC: Quarantine Officer in Charge
qon: quarter ocean net
qor: qualitative operational requirement
QOR: Queen's Own Royal (regiment)
qp: queen post; quick process(ing)
q.p.: quantum placet (Latin—at discretion)
QP: Qualification Proposal; Queen's Printer
QPC: Quatar Petroleum Company

QPF: Quebec Police Force
qpi: quadratic performance index
QPIS: Quality Performance Instruction Sheet
QPL: Qualified Parts List; Queens Public Library
QPP: Quebec Provincial Police; Quetico Provincial Park (Ontario)
QPR: Quality Progress Report; Quantity Progress Report; Quarterly Progress Report
QPRI: Qualitative Personnel Requirements Information
qpsk: quad-phase shift key
qq: quartos; questionable questionnaires
qq: quelques (French—some); *quintales* (Spanish—quintals)
QQ: Celestial Equator
q.q.d.: quantum quatra die (Latin—every fourth day)
qqf: quelquefois (French—sometimes)
q.q.h.: quantum quatra hora (Latin—every four hours)
qq. hor.: quaque hora (Latin—every hour)
qqpr: quantitative and qualitative personnel requirements
q.q.v.: quae vide (Latin—which see)
qr: qualifications record; quick reaction; quire
q.r.: quantum rectus (Latin—quantity is correct)
QR: Queensland Railways; Quintana Roo
Q & R: Quality and Reliability
qra: quality reliability assurance; quick reaction alert
qrbm: quasi-random band model
qrc: quick reaction capability
QRDC: Quartermaster Research and Development Command
QRDEA: Quartermaster Research and Development Evaluation Agency
qrga: quadrupole residual gas analyzer
qri: qualitative requirements information
QRICC: Quick Reaction Inventory Control Center
qro: quick reaction operation
Qro: Querétaro
QRO: Quick Reaction Operation; Quick Reaction Organization
Q Roo: Quintana Roo
Q-room: cue room (billiard room)
QRPA: Quartermaster Radiation Planning Agency
QRPS: Quick Reaction Procurement System
QRRR: extreme emergency amateur radio call signal

QR's: Quality Reports
qrtg: quartering
qrtly: quarterly
qrtmstr: quartermaster
qrv: quick-release valve
qry: quality and reliability year
qs: quarter section; quarter sessions
q.s.: quantum satis (Latin—as much as is sufficient); *quantum sufficit* (Latin—as much as suffices)
QS: Quarantine Station; Quarter Section; Quarter Sessions; Quartermaster Sergeant; Queensland Society; Queen's Scholar
QSAL: Quadripartite Standardization Agreements List
qsbg: quasi-stellar blue galaxies
QSD: Quality Surveillance Division (USN); Quincy Shipbuilding Division—General Dynamics
qse: qualified scientists and engineers
qsf: quasi-static field; quasi-stationary front
qsg: quasi-stellar galaxy
Q-ship: disguised man-of-war used to decoy enemy vessels
qsi: quality salary increase
qsic: quality standard inspection criteria
qs & l: quarters, subsistence, and laundry
Q & SL: Qualifications and Standards Laboratory
qsm: quadruple-screw motorship; quarter-square multipliers
qso: quasibiennial stratospheric oscillation; quasistellar object
QSO: Quebec Symphony Orchestra
QSOP: Quadripartite Standing Operating Procedure(s)
qsp: quality search procedure
QSPP: Quebec Society for the Protection of Plants
QSR: Quarterly Status Report; Quarterly Summary Report
qsrs: quasi-stellar radio sources
qss: quasi-stellar source
QSS: quadruple-screw ship; Quota Sample Survey
qssa: quasi-stationary-state approximation
qssp: quasi-solid-state panel
QSSR: Quarterly Stock Status Report
QST: Quebec Standard Test
QSTAG: Quadripartite Standardization Agreement
Q-star: quiet observation aircraft
qstnr: questionnaire
qsy: quiet sun year
qt: quantity; quart; quick test; quiet (*see* q.t.)
q.t.: quiet (as "on the q.t.")
q & t: quenched and tempered

QT: Quick's Test (pregnancy or prothrombin)

qta: quadrant transformer assembly

qtam: queued telecommunication access method

qtaux: *quintaux* (French—quintals)

qtb: quarry-tile base

qtd: quartered

QTDGs: Quaker Theological Discussion Groups

qtf: quarry-tile floor

QTIB: Quebec Tourist Information Bureau

qtly: quarterly

qto: quarto

qtp: quantum theory of paramagnetism

QTP: Qualification Test Procedure

qtr: quarry-tile roof; quarter; quarterly

QTR: Quarterly Technical Report

qtrs: quarters

qts: quarts

qtte: quartette

qty: quantity

qtydesreq: quantity desired or requested

qtz: quartz

qtze: quartzose

qtzic: quartzitic

qtzt: quartzite

qu: question

Qu: Queen

QU: Queen's University

qua: quadrate; quadratus

quad: quadrangle; quadrangular; quadrant; quadruplet; quadruplicate; quadruplication

quad .50's: quadruple .50-caliber machine guns

quadradar: four-way radar (surveillance)

quadrup: quadruped(s); quadruple

quadrupl.: *quadruplicato* (Latin —four times as much)

quads: quadraphonic records; quadruplets

Quaker Poet: John Greenleaf Whittier

Quakers: members of the Society of Friends

quake(s): earthquake(s)

qual: qualification; qualify; quality

qual anal.: qualitative analysis

quals: qualifying examinations; qualifying tests

quam: quadrature-amplitude modulation

quant: quantity; quantum

quant anal.: quantitative analysis

quantras: question analysis transformation and search (data processing technique)

quar: quarantine

quarpel: quartermaster water-repellent (cloth or clothing)

quarr: quarries; quarry; quarrying

quart: quarter gallon; quarterly

quart.: quartet; quartette; quartile

Quart: Quarterly

QUART: Quality Assurance and Reliability Team

quartz: crystalline silica (SiO_2)

quasar: quasi-stellar radio (object)

quaser: quantum-amplification-by-stimulated-emission-of-radiation (acronym covering irasers, lasers, and masers varying only in operational frequency)

quat: quaternary; quaternary era

quat.: *quattuor* (Latin—four)

Quat: Quaternary

QUB: Queen's University of Belfast

Que: Quebec (inhabitants—Québecois); Quechua; Quechuan

QUE: Quebecair

Quebec: code for letter Q

Queenie: Regina

Queen of Queens: (Brutus' nickname for Cleopatra)

Queen's College: Rutgers University in colonial times

Quen: Quentin

ques: question

quest.: quality electrical system test; questioned

QUEST: Quality Electrical Systems Test; Queens Educational and Social Team

questal: quiet, experimental, short-takeoff-and-landing (program of NASA)

quester: quick and efficient system to enhance retrieval

QUI: Queen's University of Ireland; Quincy (railroad)

quicklime: calcium oxide—CaO

quicksilver: mercury (Hg)

quico: quality improvement through cost optimization

quin: quintet; quintette; quintuplet; quintuplicate; quintuplication

quinq.: quinque (Latin—five)

quins: quintuplets

quint.: *quintus* (Latin—fifth)

Quintilian: Marcus Fabius Quintilianus

quint(s): quintet(s); quintuplet(s); quintuplicate(s)

quintupl: quintuplicate

Quisquellano(s): Santo Domingan(s)

QUJ: true course to station

QUL: Queen's University Library

quo': quoth

quod.: *quodlibet* (Latin—as you please)

Quon Pt: Quonset Point, Rhode Island

quor: quorum

quot: quotation

quot.: *quotidie* (Latin—daily)

quotes: quotation marks

quote-unquote: quotation marks (slang shortcut—some phrase or word set between quotation marks to indicate an actual spoken or written quotation or even to imply a satiric meaning really not intended)

quotid.: *quotidie* (Latin—every day)

qup: quantity per unit pack

QUSA: "Q" Airways

q.v.: *quantum vis* (Latin—as much as is desired); *quod vide* (Latin—which see)

QVR: Queen Victoria's Rifles

qvt: quality verification test

qw: quarter wave

qwa: quarter-wave antenna

qwd: quarterly world day

q-wedge: quartz wedge

QWG: Quadripartite Working Group

qwl: quick weight loss

QWMP: Quadruped Walking Machine Program (US Army)

qwp: quarter-wave plate

qx: *quintaux* (French—hundredweights)

qy: quantum yield; query

qz: quartz

Qz: quartz

QZ: Zambia Airways (2-letter coding)

QZS: Quebec Zoological Society

R

r: angle of reflection (symbol); position vector (symbol); racemic; radius; rain; range; rare; rate of interest; received; recipe; reconnaissance; recto; red; redetermination; refraction; registered; relative; relative humidity; report; reprint; research; reserve; resistance; restricted; retard; retarded; right or starboard side of an airplane or vessel looking forward (R or S); ring; ringer; riser; rod; rook; rough; rule; rules; runs; rupee (Indian monetary unit); rupees; solubilizing agent (symbol)

r: angular yaw velocity (symbol); front of the sheet (recto)

R: acoustic resistance (symbol); annual rent; electrical resistance; gas constant; ohmic resistance; product moment coefficient of statistical correlation; Rabbi; radioactive range; radiolocation; Rankine; rare; ratio; Réaumur; received solid; reconnaissance; Regina (Queen); registered; Reiz; report(s); Representative; reprint; Republic; Republican; research; reserve; resistance; respiration; restricted; Rex (King); rial (Iranian monetary unit); Richfield Oil; right; ring; river; Road; Robin Line; rocket; Rocketdyne Division of North American Aviation; Roentgen; Roger—radio slang meaning all right or okay; Roma; Roman; Rome; Romeo—code for letter R; Rotary International; ruble (Russian monetary unit); rupee (Indian monetary unit); Rwanda; Rydberg; US Rubber Company

R: rechts (German—right); resultant force (symbol); *rett (Danish—right); rio* (Portuguese —river); *río* (Spanish— river); *rua* (Portuguese—street); *rubeus* (Latin—red); *rue* (French —street); The Book of Ruth

R.: rand (South African monetary unit)

R-1: residential zone with one residence per lot

R-2: residential zone with one or two-family homes

R-3: medium-high density residential area for three or more garden-type apartments

R-4: high-rise apartment area for four or more apartments per lot

R-5: dining, lodging, recreational zone

ra: radio; reduced area; right ascension; robbery committed while armed; rubber-activated; ruling action

r/a: radioactive; return to author

r & a: right and above

Ra: radium

RA: Argentina (auto plaque); Coast Radar Station (symbol); high-powered radio range (Adcock symbol); Rabbinical Assembly; Rdeca Armada (Yugoslav—Red Army); Rear Admiral; Reduction of Area; Regular Army; Rental Agreement; República Argentina; Republic Aviation; Resident Auditor; Right Arch; right ascension; Rotogravure Association; Royal Academician; Royal Academy; Royal Arcanum; Royal Artillery

R.A.: right ascension

R/A: Redstone Arsenal

RAA: Rabbinical Alliance of America; Royal Academic Association; Royal Academy of Arts

RAAA: Red Angus Association of America

RAAF: Royal Afghan Air Force; Royal Australian Air Force

Rab: Rabat; Rabbi; Rabbinic Hebrew

RAB: Radio Advertising Bureau

rabar: Raytheon advanced battery acquisition radar

rabb: rabbinate; rabbinic; rabbinical

RABDF: Royal Association of British Dairy Farmers

RABT: Rederiaktiebolaget Transatlantic (Swedish Transatlantic Line)

rac: raccommodage(s) [French —repair(s)]

RAC: Railway Association of Canada; Rear Admiral Commanding; Reliability Action Center; Republic Aviation Corporation; Research Advisory Council; Research Analysis Corporation; Royal Air Cambodge; Royal Arch Chapter; Royal Armoured Corps; Royal Automobile Club; Rubber Allocation Committee

racc: radiation and contamination control

race.: rapid automatic checkout equipment

RACE: Research on Automatic Computation Electronics

racep: random access and correlation for extended performance

races. (RACES): radio amateur civil emergency service

RACI: Royal Australian Chemical Institute

RACIC: Remote Area Conflict Information Center

racine: (French—root)

racon: radar beacon

RACS: Remote Access Computing System

rad: radar; radian; radiation; radiation-absorbed dose; radiator; radical; radicalism; radio; radioactive; radius; radix; released from active duty; return to active duty; roentgen-administered dosage; roentgen-administered dose

Rad: Radnor; Radnorshire

RAD: Royal Academy of Dancing; Royal Albert Docks; Rural Area Development

rada: radioactive

RADA: Royal Academy of Dramatic Arts

radac: rapid digital automatic computing

radal: radio detection and location (system)

radan: radar doppler automatic navigator

radar: radio detection and ranging

RADAS: Random Access Discrete Address System (battlefield communications system)

radat: radar data transmission and ranging; radiosonde observation data

radata: radar automatic data transmission assembly

RADC: Rome Air Development Center; Royal Army Dental Corps

RADCC: Rear Area Damage Control Center

rad-ch: radical-changing

RADCM: radar countermeasures and deception
radcon: radar data converter
raddef: radiological defense
radem (RADEM): random access data modulation
rad encl: radiator enclosure
radep: radar departure
radex: radiation exclusion plot (actual or predicted fallout)
radfac: radiating facility
radhaz: radiation hazard(s)
radi: radiological inspection
radiac: radioactivity-detection-indication-and-computation
RADIC: Research and Development Information Center
radiclib(s): radical liberal(s)
radint: radar intelligence
radiog: radiography
radiol: radiology
radir: random access document indexing and retrieval
radl: radiological
rad lab: radiation laboratory
radlfo: radiological fallout
radlic: radio link
radlop: radiological operations
RADLO: Radiological Defense Officer
radlsafe: radiological safety
radlwar: radiological warfare
R Adm: Rear Admiral
radmon: radiological monitor (ing)
radn: radiation
radnote: ratio note
radome: radar dome
rad op: radio operator
radose: radiation dosimeter satellite
RadPropCast: radio propagation forecast
rad rec: radiator recess
rad/s: radians per second
Rad(s): Radical(s)
RADS: Ryukyu Air Defense System
RadSo: Radiological Survey Officer
radsta: radio station
radu: radar analysis and detection unit
radvs: radar altimeter and doppler velocity sensor
radwar: radiological warfare
rae (RAE): radio astronomy explorer
Rae: Rachel; Raquelle
RAE: Royal Aircraft Establishment
RAEL: Real Academia Española de la Lengua (Royal Spanish Academy of Language)
RAeS: Royal Aeronautical Society
raet: range-azimuth-elevation-time
RAF: Regular Air Force; Royal Aircraft Factory; Royal Air Force
rafar: radio-automated facsimile

and reproduction
rafar: radar-automated facsimile reproduction
rafax: radar facsimile transmission
RAFB: Randolph Air Force Base
Rafe: Ralph
Rafl: Rafael
RAFMS: Royal Air Force Medical Services
rafos: long-range navigation system (sofar reversed)
RAFS: Royal Air Force Station
RAFT: Regional Accounting and Finance Test
RAFTC: Royal Air Force Technical College
RAG: River Assault Group; Royal and Ancient Game (of golf)
RAGE: Radio Amplification of Gamma Emissions
RAH: Royal Albert Hall
rai: radioactive interference; random access and inquiry
RAI: Radiotelevisione Italiana; Réseau Aérien Interinsulaire (Tahiti)
RAIC: Royal Architectural Institute of Canada
rail.: railroad; railway
rails.: runway alignment indicator lights
Railsplitter: Abraham Lincoln
railwayac: railway + maniac (railway fan)
RAIRS: Recordak Automated Information Retrieval System
RAI-TV: Radio Audizioni Italiane—TV (Italian Radio Audition—TV)
ra k: raised keel
ral: resorcylic acid lactone
Ral: Raleigh
RAL: Resort Airlines; Royal Air Laos
Ralegh: Sir Walter Raleigh (who spelled his name Ralegh)
rallo.: rallentando (Italian—slower by degrees)
ram.: radio attenuation measurement; random access memory; rapid area maintenance; right ascension of the meridian
ram. (RAM): research and applications module
Ram: Raman effect in spectrum analysis; Ramona
RAM: Royal Academy of Music; Royal Air Maroc; Royal Arch Masons
RAMA: Rome Air Materiel Area
ramac: random access memory accounting
RAMC: Royal Army Medical College; Royal Army Medical Corps
RAMIS: Rapid Automatic Mal-

function Isolation System
ramont: radiological monitoring
ramp.: rate-acceleration measuring pendulum
RAMP: Radar Mapping of Panama; Radiation Airborne Measurement Program
RAMPC: Raritan Arsenal Maintenance Publication Center
RAMPS: Resources Allocation and Multiproject Scheduling
rams.: right ascension of mean sun
Rams: Ramsgate
RAMS: right ascension mean sun
RAMSA: Radio Aeronáutica Mexicana S.A.
RAMSS: Royal Alfred Merchant Seamen's Society
ran.: reconnaissance-attack navigator; request for authority to negotiate
Ran: Rangoon
RAN: Royal Australian Navy
Ranally: Rand McNally
RANC: Royal Australian Naval College
Rance: Ransom(e)
Rand: Witwatersrand (Johannesburg)
randam: random-access nondestructive advanced memory
RAND Corporation: Research and Development Corporation (corporate style insists on use of capital letters as shown)
randid: rapid alphanumeric digital indicating device
Randy: Randolph
Ranger: American program for investigation of the moon and region between the moon and the earth; Texas state policeman
rann: (Indian—wasteland, as in Rann of Kutch)
RANN: Research Applied to National Needs
RANSA: Rutas Aéreas Nacionales
RANVR: Royal Australian Naval Volunteer Reserve
rao: radio astronomical observatory
RAO: Rudolf A. Oetker (steamship line)
RaOb: radiosonde observation
RAOC: Royal Army Ordnance Corps
raomp: report of accrued obligations—military pay
rap.: rapid; rapport; rupees, annas, pies
rap: rapido (Spanish—rapid)—fast train
RAP: Radiological Assistance Plan (AEC); Regimental Aid Post; Royal Army Post
rapcoe: random access programming and checkout equipment

rapcon: radar approach control
rapec: rocket-assisted personnel ejection catapult
Raph: Raphael
Raphael: Raffaello Sanzio
RAPM: Russian Association of Proletarian Musicians
rapp: rapport; rapporteur; rapprochement
RAPP: Registered Air Parcel Post
rapp's: radiologists, anesthesiologists, pathologists, and psychiatrists
RAPRA: Rubber and Plastics Research Association
rap's: rocket-assisted projectiles
RAPS: Risk Appraisal of Programs System
raptap: random access parallel tape
raptus.: rapid thorium-uranium-sodium (reactor)
rar: radio acoustic ranging; rapid-access recording; right arm reclining
RAR: Reliability Action Report; Royal Australian Regiment
rarad: radar advisory
RARDE: Royal Armament Research and Development Establishment
rare.: ram air rocket engine
RARE: Rehabilitation of Addicts by Relatives and Employers
rarep: radar report
ras: radome antenna structure; radula sinus; rapid audit summary; rectified air speed; requirements allocation sheet; rheumatoid arthritis serum
ras: (Arabic—cape; summit, as in Ras at Tannura, near Bahrein)
ras.: *rasurae* (Latin—shavings)
RAS: Report Audit Summary; Royal Aeronautical Society; Royal Asiatic Society; Royal Astronomical Society
RASA: Railway and Airline Supervisors Association
RASC: Royal Army Service Corps; Royal Astronomical Society of Canada
RASC/DC: Rear Area Security and Damage Control
RASE: Royal Agricultural Society of England
raser: range and sensitivity extending resonator
rastac: random access storage and control
rastad: random access storage and display
RASTAS: Radiating Site Target Acquisition System
rat.: ram air turbine; ratchet; rate; rating; ration(s); rocket-assisted torpedo (RAT)

RAT: Remote Associates Test
ratac: radar analog target acquisition computer
ratan: radio television aid to navigation
ratc: radar-aided tracking computer
RATCC: Radar Air Traffic Control Center
ratcon: radar terminal control
rate.: remote automatic telemetry equipment
ratel: radiotelephone
ratelo: radio telephone operator
ratepayer(s): [Canadian English —taxpayer(s)]
rat/epr: ram air temperature/engine pressure ratio
ratg: radiotelegraph
rato: rocket-assisted takeoff
RATP: Régie Autonome des Transports Parisiens (Le métro— Paris subway system)
RATR: *Reliability Abstracts and Technical Reviews*
rats.: repeat-action tablets
RATS: Ram Air Turbine Systems
ratscat: radar target scatter site
RATSEC: Robert A. Taft Sanitary Engineering Center
ratt: radioteletypewriter
'raus mit i'm: *heraus mit ihm* (German—out with him)
RAVA: Rochester Audiovisual Association
RAVC: Royal Army Veterinary Corps
rave.: radar acquisition vocal-tracking equipment
raven.: ranging and velocity navigation
rawarc: radar and warning coordination
RAWI: Radio American West Indies (Virgin Islands)
rawin: radar wind sounding
raws: radar altimeter warning set
rawx: returned account of weather (aviation)
rax: random access (computing system)
Ray: Rachel; Raymond
razel: range, azimuth, elevation
razon: range and azimuth only
razz: razzberry (slang for raspberry)
rb: relative bearing; rigid boat; road bend; rubber-base(d)
r & b: rhythm and blues; right and below
Rb: rubidium
RB: reconnaissance bomber; Regiment Botha; Renegotiation Board; Republica Boliviana (Bolivian Republic); Republic of Burma; Rifle Brigade; Ritzaus Bureau (Danish news agency); Royaume de Belgique (Kingdom

of Belgium)
R$_B$: Rockwell hardness (B-scale)
RBA: Rabat, Morocco (airport); Roadside Business Association
RBAF: Royal Belgian Air Force
rbc: red blood cell; red blood cell (count); red blood corpuscle
RBC: Richard Bland College; Roller Bearing Company; Royal Bank of Canada
rbcd: right border of cardiac dullness
rbe: relative biological effectiveness
RBEC: Roller Bearing Engineering Committee
rbelet: relative biological effectiveness linear energy transfer
rbf: renal blood flow
RBF: Rockefeller Brothers Fund
RBG: Royal Botanic Gardens (Kew Gardens)
RBH: Rutherford B. Hayes
rbi: reply by indorsement; request better information
rbí: *recibí* (Spanish—I received)
RBI: Reserve Bank of India; Rochester Business Institute
rb imp: rubber-base impression
rbl: ruble
R Bn: radio beacon
RBNA: Royal British Nurses' Association
RBNM: Rainbow Bridge National Monument (Utah)
RBO: Russian Brotherhood Organization
RBP: Raffinerie Belge de Petroles
rBr: reddish brown
RBR: Renegotiation Board Regulation
RBRF: Reproductive Biological Research Foundation
rbs: radar bomb scoring
RBS: Ranganthittoo Bird Sanctuary (India); Research for Better Schools; Royal Botanical Society
RBU: Rabindra Bharati University
rc: radio code; radio coding; rate of change; ready calendar; red cell; red corpuscle; reinforced concrete; resistance capacitance; resistor-capacitor; respiratory center; reverse course; right center; rigid center; rock-crushed; rubber-cushioned
RC: Radcliffe College; Radio City; Radio Code; Reception Center; Reconstruction Commission; Red China; Red Cross; Regina College; Regis College; Reinhardt College; Renison College; República de Chile; República de Colombia; República de Cuba; Ricker College; Ricks Col-

lege; Rider College; Río Colorado; Ripon College; Rivier College; Roanoke College; Rockefeller Center; Rockford College; Rockhurst College; Rockmount College; Rollins College; Roman Catholic; Rosary College; Rosemount College; Rosenwal College; Rust College

R, C: Cauchy constant

R$_c$: Rockwell hardness (C-scale)

R.C.: *Rendiconti* Italian—proceedings or reports)

R de C: *Radiodiffusion du Cameroun* (French—Radio Network of Cameroon)

RCA: Rabbinical Council of America; Radio Club of America; Radio Corporation of America; Rocket Cruising Association; Rodeo Cowboys Association; Roofing Contractors Association; Royal Canadian Academician; Royal Canadian Academy; Royal Canadian Artillery

RCA: *République Centrafricaine* (French—Central African Republic)

RCAA: Royal Cambrian Academy of Art; Royal Canadian Academy of Arts

RCAC: Radio Corporation of America Communications

RCAF: Royal Canadian Air Force

RCAMC: Royal Canadian Army Medical Corps

R Can: Rio Canario

RCAT: Royal College of Arts and Technology

RCA Vic: RCA Victor

RCB: Regiment Christiaan Beyers; Retail(ers) Credit Bureau

rcc: rough combustion cutoff

r & cc: riot and civil commotion

RCC: Radio-Chemical Center; Radiological Control Center; Rag Chewers Club; Reply Coupon Collector(s); Rescue Control Center; Rescue Coordination Center; Rockland Community College; Roman Catholic Church; Royal Crown Cola

RCCC: Republican County Central Committee

rcd: received; relative cardiac dullness

RCD: Regional Cooperation for Development (Pakistan, Iran, Turkey)

RCDA: Retail Coin Dealers Association

RCDC: Royal Canadian Dental Corps

RCDEP: Rural Civil Defense Education Program

RCDI: Reliability Control Depart-

mental Instruction

rce: right center entrance

RCE: Reliability Control Engineering

RCEEA: Radio Communications and Electronic Engineers Association

RCEME: Royal Canadian Electrical and Mechanical Engineers

RCEP: Royal Commission on Environmental Pollution

RCET: Royal College of Engineering Technology; Rugby College of Engineering Technology

rcf: relative centrifugal force

RCFA: Reliability Control Failure Analysis

RCFCA: Royal Canadian Flying Clubs Association

Rch: Rochester

rci: radar coverage indicator

RCI: Range Communications Instructions; Reichold Chemicals Incorporated; Research Council of Israel; Resident Cost Inspection; Resident Cost Inspector; Royal Canadian Institute

RCIA: Retail Clerks International Association; Retail Credit Institute of America

RCIC: Rumor Control and Information Center

rcirc: recirculate

RCIs: Recontres Culturelles International (International Cultural Meetings)

RCL: ramped cargo lighter (naval designation); Royal Canadian Legion

rclm: reclaim; reclamation

rcm: radar countermeasure(s); radio-controlled mine; radio countermeasure(s); right costal margin

RCM: Reliability Control Manual; Royal College of Music

RCMP: Royal Canadian Mounted Police

RCN: Reactor Centrum Nederland; Record Control Number; Republic of China Navy; Royal Canadian Navy

RCN: *Radio Cadena Nacional* (Spanish — National Radio Chain)—Mexican broadcasting system

RCNC: Royal Corps of Naval Constructors

RCNM: Russell Cave National Monument

RCNR: Royal Canadian Naval Reserve

rco: rendezvous compatible orbit

RCO: Radio Control Office; Royal College of Organists

RCOA: Radio Club of America;

Record Club of America

RCOG: Royal College of Obstetricians and Gynecologists

RCP: Royal College of Physicians

RCPL: Realtors Co-op Photo Listing

rcpt: receipt

rcr: reverse contactor

RCR: República de Costa Rica

RCRBSJ: Research Council on Riveted and Bolted Structural Joints

rcrd: record

RCS: Reaction Control System; Rearward Communications System; Reentry Control System; Reliability Control Standard; Report Control Symbol; Royal College of Science; Royal College of Surgeons

RCSE: Royal College of Surgeons —Edinburgh

RCSI: Royal College of Surgeons —Ireland

RCST: Royal College of Science and Technology

Rct: Recruit

RCT: Rorschach Content Test

rctl: resistor capacitor transistor logic

rcu: remote control unit

RCU: Road Construction Unit

RCUEP: Research Center for Urban and Environmental Planning (Princeton U)

rcv: receive

rcvr: receiver

RCVS: Royal College of Veterinary Surgeons

RCZ: Radiation Control Zone

rd: reaction of degeneration; readiness date; renal disease; required date; research and development (R & D); restricted data; retinal detachment; round; rutherford

r & d: reamed and drifted; research and development

Rd: Road

RD: Air Lift International; Radio Denmark; República Dominicana; Restricted Data; Royal Dragoons; Royal Dutch Petroleum (stock exchange symbol); Rural Delivery

R/D: Research/Development

RD$: República Dominicana peso (Dominican currency)

R & D: research and development (should be. in lowercase letters but scientists, engineers, and other recognize it as shown)

R of D: Report of Debate

rda: recommended dietary allowance; right dorso-anterior

rd a (Rd A): reading age

RDA: Reliability Design Analysis;

Respiratory Diseases Association; Royal Docks Association
RDA: *Reader's Digest Almanac*
R & D A: Research and Development Association
RDAF: Royal Danish Air Force
Rdam: Rotterdam
RDAR: Reliability Design Analysis Report
rdb (RDB): radar decoy balloon
RDB: Ramped Dump Barge; Research and Development Board; Royal Danish Ballet
rd bot: rubber diaphragm (stoppered) bottle
rdc: rail diesel car; running down clause
RDC: Rand Development Corporation
RDCO: Reliability Data Control Office
rdd: required delivery date
rde: receptor-destroying enzyme
r d & e: research, development, and engineering (usually R D & E)
rdf: radio direction finder
Rdg: Reading
RDG: Reading Railroad
rd hd: round head
RDL: Radiocarbon Dating Laboratory (Florida State University); Ritter Dental Laboratories
RDLI: Royal Durban Light Infantry
RdlR: Regiment de la Rey
rdm: root drum
RDM: *Rand Daily Mail* (Johannesburg)
Rdm3c: Radarman, third class
rdmu: range- drift measuring unit
RDN: Royal Danish Navy
rdo: research and development objectives
RDO: Radiological Defense Office(r)
rdp: right dorso-posterior
RDPC: Research Data Publication Center
rdpe: radar data-processing equipment
rd/q: reading quotient
rdr: radar
RDR: Reliability Diagnostic Report
rdr rel: radar relay
rdrsmtr: radar transmitter
rds: respiratory distress syndrome
Rds: Rixdollar; Roads; Roadstead
RDs: Revolutionary Development teams
RDS: Royal Dublin Society
RD/S: Royal Dutch/Shell
RD & S: Research, Development, and Studies (USMC)
rdt: reserve duty training
RDT: Regiment Danie Theron; Reliability Demonstration Test
rdt & e (RDT & E): research,

development, test, and evaluation
rdvu: rendezvous
RDW: Regiment De Wet
rdx: cyclonite (research department explosive)
rdy: ready
RDY: Royal Dock Yard
RDZ: *République Démocratique du Zaïre* (French—Democratic Republic of Zaire)—formerly the Belgian Congo
rdz(s) (RDZ or RDZs): radiation danger zone(s)
re: radium emanation; real estate; research and engineering (R & E); reticulo-endothelium; right eye
re: (Italian—second tone; *B* in diatonic scale, *D* in fixed-do system)
r/e: rate of exchange
Re: Reno; Reynold's Number; rhenium; rupee (Ceylon, India, Pakistan currency)
Ré: *récipe* (Spanish—recipe; prescription)
RE: Radio Eireann (Radio Ireland); Reformed Episcopal (church); Reliability Engineering; República de Ecuador; Rifle Expert; Right Excellent; Royal Engineers; Royal Exchange
r & e (R & E): research and engineering
REA: Railway Express Agency; Request for Engineering Authorization; Rice Export Association; Rubber Export Association; Rural Electrification Administration (US Department of Agriculture)
reac: reactor
REAC: Reeves electronic analog computer; Reliability Engineering Action Center
react: reactance; reaction; reactor; register-enforced automated-control technique
REACT: Radio Emergency Associated Citizens Team; Register-Enforced Automated Control Technique; Resource Allocation and Control Techniques
READ: Real-Time Electronic Access and Display
readi: rocket-engine-analyzer-and-decision-instrumentation
readm: readmission
READS: Reno Air Defense Sector
REAL: Real-Aerovias do Brasil
realcom: real-time communication(s)
real est: real estate
REAP: Rural Environmental Assistance Program

reapt: reappoint; reappointment
REAR: Reliability Engineering Analysis Report
Rear Adm: Rear Admiral
reasm: reassemble
REAT: Radiological Emergency Assistance Team
Reba: Rebecca
reb(s): rebel(s)
rec: receipt; receive; record; recreation
Rec: Recife
REC: Recife, Brazil (airport)
R & EC: Research and Engineering Council
recap: recapitulate; recapitulation
RECAP: Reliability Evaluation Continuous Analysis Program
rec chg: record change(r)
recco: reconnaissance
recd: received
recg: radioelectrocardiograph
rec hall: recreational hall
recid: recidivism; recidivist(ic); recidivous recidivous
recids: recidivists
recip: reciprocating
recip & lp turb: reciprocating steam engine and low-pressure turbine
recit.: *recitativo* (Italian—recitative)
reclam: reclamation
recm: recommend
RECMF: Radio and Electronic Component Manufacturers Federation
recog: recognition; recognize
recom: recommendation; recommend(ed)
recon: reconcentration; reconciliation; recondite; recondition; reconduction; reconnaissance; reconnoiter; reconsign; reconsigned; reconsignment; reconstruct; reconstructed; reconstruction; reconversion; reconvert; reconverted; reconvey; reconveyance; reconveyed
RECON: Retrospective Conversion of Bibliographic Records (Library of Congress)
record: recondition
R Econ S: Royal Economic Society
RECONS: Reliability and Configurational Accountability System
reconst: reconstruct
recov: recover; recovery
recp: receptacle; reciprocal; reciprocating
recpt: receptionist
rec room: receiving room; reception room; record room; recreation room
Rec S: Record of Survey
RECSTA: Receiving Station

recsys: recreational systems analysis

rect: rectified; rectifier; rectify

rect.: rectificatus (Latin—rectified)

recur.: recurrence; recurrent; recurring

red.: reduce; reduction

red: redaktör (Swedish—editor); *redige* (French—compiled; edited)

Red: Sinclair Lewis

Red: Rederi (Scandinavian—shipowners)

REDAR: R. E. Darling (Company)

redcape: readiness capability

redcat: readiness requirement

redcon: readiness condition

Redcraft: Red aircraft (communist-controlled aircraft)

redig: redigerat (Swedish—edited)

redig. in pulv.: redigatur in pulverem (Latin—reduce to powder)

red. in pulv.: reductus in pulverem (Latin—reduced to a powder)

REDLARS: Reading Literature Analysis and Retrieval Service

red lead: lead oxide—Pb_3O_4; minium

redondo: (Spanish—round)

redox: reduction oxidation

redsg: redesign; redesigned; redesigning

redsh: reddish

Red Skelton: Richard Bernard Skelton

ree: rare-earth elements

REECO: Reynolds Electrical and Engineering Company

Reed: Reederei (German—shipowners)

reefer(s): marijuana cigarette(s); refrigerated compartment(s) or hold(s) in a ship; refrigerator(s)

reeg: radioelectroencephalograph

reenl: reenlist

reep: range estimating and evaluation procedure

ref: refer; referee; reference; refraction; refresher

ref: refondue (French—reorganized)

Ref: Referate (German—abstract; compendium)

refd: refund

refl: reflection; reflective; reflector; reflex; reflexive

ref l: reference line

refl pron: reflexive pronoun

reforst: reforestation

ref phys: referring physician

ref press: reference pressure

refr: refraction; refractory; refrigerate; refrigerator

refrg: refrigerate; refrigeration; refrigerator

refrig: refrigeration; refrigerator

Refrig Eng: Refrigerating Engineering

ref temp: reference temperature

Ref Zhu: Referativnyi Zhurnal (Russian—Abstract Journal)

reg: region; regular; regulate; regulation

RegAF: Regular Air Force

regal.: range and elevation guidance for approach and landing

Reg Bez: Regierungsbezirk (German—administrative district)

reg bot: regular bottle (3/4-liter of wine)

regen: regenerate; regeneration

Reggie: Regina(ld)

regis: register; registered; registration; registry

regt: regiment

rehab: rehabilitate

rehob: rehoboam (6-bottle capacity)

REI: Régie Aérienne Interinsulaire

REIC: Radiation Effects Information Center; Rare Earth Information Center (Atomic Energy Commission, Ames Laboratory, Iowa State University)

reils: runway end identification lights

reimb: reimburse; reimbursement

reincorp: reincorporate(d)

reinf: reinforce(d); reinforcing

reins.: radio-equipped inertial navigation system

REIT: Real Estate Investment Trusts

rejase: re-using junk as something else (old bathtub as setee; ouija board as coffee table; radio cabinet as bookcase, etc.)

rejn: rejoin

REK: Reykjavik, Iceland (airport)

reka: (Russian—river)

rel: rate of energy loss; relation; relative; relay; release; relief; relieve; religion; religionist

rel: relie; reliure (French—bound; binding)

REL: Radio Engineering Laboratories

RELACS: Radar Emission Location Attack Control System

rel adv: relative adverb

RELCV: Regional Educational Laboratory for the Carolinas and Virginia

RELHS: Robert E. Lee High School

rel hum: relative humidity

relig: religion; religious

reliq.: reliquus (Latin—remainder)

reloc: relocate; relocated; relocation

rel pron: relative pronoun

Rel R: Reliability Report

rem: rapid eye movements; remission; remit; remittance; removable; remove; removed; roentgen equivalent, man

Rem: Remington; roentgen equivalent, man

REM: Registered Equipment Management

REMA: Refrigeration Equipment Manufacturers Association

remab: radiation equivalent manikin absorption

Rembrandt: Rembrandt Harmenszoon van Rijn—RvR

remc: resin-encapsulated mica capacitor

remcal: radiation equivalent manikin calibration

remd: rapid eye movement (sleep) deprivation

REME: Royal Electrical and Mechanical Engineers

REML: Radiation Effects Mobile Laboratory

REMS: Registered Equipment Management System

REMSA: Railway Engineering Maintenance Suppliers Association

REMT: Radiological Emergency Medical Teams

ren.: renovetur (Latin—renew)

Ren: Renaissance

rene: rocket-engine nozzle ejector

Rene: Irene

Renf: Renfrew

RENFE: Red Nacional de los Ferrocarriles Españoles (National Network of Spanish Railroads)

ren. sem.: renovetum semel (Latin—renew only once)

rent.: reentry nose tip

renv: renovate; renovation

reo: rare-earth oxide; regenerated electrical output

Reo: (early American automobile named after initials of its maker, Ransom E. Olds of Oldsmobile fame)

reoc: report when established on course (aviation)

reorg: reorganization; reorganize; reorganized

reorgn: reorganization

REOS: Reflective Electron Optical System

reo viruses: respiratory-enteric-orphan viruses

rep: repair; repertory; represent; reputation

r-ep: rational-emotive psychotherapy

rep.: repetatur (Latin—let it be repeated)

Rep: Representative; Republic; Republican; Republican Party; roentgen equivalent, physical

REP: Radical Education Project; Recovery and Evacuation Program; Republic Corporation (stock exchange symbol); Research Expenditure Proposal; Reserve Enlisted Program; River Engineering Program

REPA: Research and Engineers Professional Employees Association

repl: replace(d); replacement; replacing

REPM: Representatives of Electronic Products Manufacturers

repo: repossess; repossessed; repossession

reppac: repetitively-pulsed plasma accelerator

repr: repairman; representative; reprint; reprinted; reprinting

repro: reproduce; reproducing; reproduction

repro typ: reproduction typist; reproduction typing

reps: representatives

rept: report; reprint; reptile; reptilia(n)

Rept: Reptilia

REPUBLIC: Republic Aviation Corporation

Republocrat: Republican Democrat

Repubs: Republicans

req: request; require

reqafa: request advise as to further action

reqd: required

reqdi: request disposition instructions

reqfolinfo: request following information

reqid: request if desired

reqint: request interim (reply)

reqmad: request mailing address

reqn: requisition

reqssd: request supply status (and expected delivery) date

reqsupstafol: request supply status of following

reqt: requirement

reqtat: requested that

rer (RER): radar effects reactor

REREI: Redwood Empire Research and Education Institute

rerl: residual equivalent return loss

res: research; researcher; rescue; reservation; reserve; reservoir; resistant; respiratory; reticuloendothelial system (RES)

Res: Reservation

RES: República de El Salvador; Royal Economic Society; Royal Entomological Society

RESA: Research Society of America

ResAF: Reserve of the Air Force

Res Aud: Resident Auditor

resc: rescue

rescan: reflecting satellite communication antenna

rescu: rocket-ejection seat catapult upward

RESCU: Radio Emergency Search Communications Unit

rescue.: remote emergency salvage and cleanup equipment

reser: reentry system evaluation radar

resgnd: resigned

resig: resignation

RESIG: Research and Engineering System Integration Group

resist.: resistance

resojet: resonant pulse jet

resp: responsibility; responsible

Res Phys: Resident Physician

respir: respiration; respiratory

RESPO: Responsible Property Officer

RESS: Radar Echo-Simulation Study; Radar Echo-Simulation System

rest.: restrict; restricted; restriction

REST: Radar Electronic-Scan Technique; Reentry Environment and Systems Technology; Reentry System Test Program

resta: reconnaissance, surveillance, and target acquisition

restr: restaurant

ResTraCen: Reserve Training Center

resup: resupply

resvr: reservoir

ret: retainer; retire; retirement

r-et: rational-emotive psychotherapy

RET: Rotterdamse Elektrische Tram (Rotterdam electric tramway and subway system)

reta: retrieval of enriched textual abstracts

RETA: Refrigerating Engineers and Technicians Association

retain.: remote technical assistance and information network

retard.: retardation; retarded

retd: retired

retics: reticulocytes

retl: retail

RETL: Rocket Engine Test Laboratory

RETMA: Radio-Electronics-Television Manufacturers Association

retng: retraining

retnr: retainer

retr: retractable

retro: retroactive; retrofit; retrograde; retrorocket

retros: retrogrades; retrorockets

RETS: Renaissance English Text Society

RETTO: (Japanese—archipelago)

Reun: Reunion Island

rev: reverse; reversed; review; revise; revised; revision; revolute; revolution

rev: *revisado* (Spanish—revised)

Rev: Reverend; The Revelation of St. John the Divine

revel.: reverberation elimination

revid: *reviderad* (Swedish—revised)

revocon: remote volume control

revs: revolutions

REVS: Rotor-Entry Vehicle System

rew: reward

rewrc: report when established well to right of course

REWSON: Reconnaissance Electronic Warfare Special Operations and Naval Intelligence Processing System(s)

rex: real-time executive routine; reduced exoatmospheric cross-section

Rex: (Latin—King); Reginald

REX: Rexall Drug and Chemical (stock exchange symbol)

rf: radiofrequency; range finder; reception fair; reflight; relative flow; replacement factor; representative fraction; rheumatic fever; rheumatoid factor; right fullback; rim fire; rubber-free

r-f: radiofrequency

Rf: Reef; rutherfordium (element 104)

rfa: radiofrequency attenuator; request further airways; right fronto-anterior

RF: République Française; Reserve Force; Rockefeller Foundation; Rodeo Foundation; Royal Fusiliers

R de F: República de Filipinas

rfa: radiofrequency authorization(s)

RFA: République Fédérale Allemande (Federal Republic of Germany) West Germany; Royal Field Artillery; Royal Fleet Auxiliary

RFAC: Royal Federation of Aero-Clubs

rfad: release for active duty

rfa's: return(ed) for alterations (tailoring)

rfb: request for bid

RFB: Recording for the Blind

RFB: *República Federative do Brasil* (Portuguese—Federative Republic of Brazil)

rfc: radiofrequency choke

RFC: Reconstruction Finance Cor-

poration; Royal Flying Corps
RFCWA: Regional Fisheries Commission for Western Africa
rfd: raised foredeck; reentry flight demonstration; reporting for duty
RFD: Radio Frequency Devices; Rural Free Delivery
rfdr: rangefinder
RFDS: Royal Flying Doctor Service
RFE: Radio Free Europe
RFED: Research Facilities and Equipment Division (NASA)
RFFS: River and Flood Forecasting Service
rfg: roofing
RFH: Royal Festival Hall
rfi: radiofrequency interference; ready for issue
R Fix: running fix
rfl: refuel
RFL: Rugby Football League
RFMA: Reliability Figure of Merit Analysis
RFN: Registered Fever Nurse
rfna: red-fuming nitric acid
rfo: request for factory order
rfp: right frontoposterior
RFP: Request for Proposal
RF & P: Richmond, Fredericksburg and Potomac (railroad)
RFPS(G): Royal Faculty of Physicians and Surgeons of Glasgow
RFQ: Request for Quotation
rfr: refraction; reject failure rate; required freight rate
R fr: Ruanda franc(s)
RFR: Royal Fleet Reserve
RFRC: Reliability Flight Readiness Center
rfs: regardless of future size
rft: right frontotransverse
rfts: radiofrequency test set
rfz: *rinforzando* (Italian—with extra emphasis)
rg: real girl (not a birl)
RG: República de Guatemala; Reserve Grade
R te G: Rijksuniversiteit te Groningen (State University at Groningen)
Rga: Riga
RGA: Republican Governors Association
R-gauge: Russian gauge (5-foot) railroad track
rgd: reigned
R Gd: Rio Grande
rge: relative gas expansion
Rge: range
RGE: *República de Guinea Ecuatorial* (Spanish—Republic of Equatorial Guinea)
RGEB: Rockefeller General Education Board

rgf: range-gated filter
RGI: Robert G. Ingersoll
rgn: region
Rgn: (Port of) Rangoon
RGN: Rangoon, Burma (airport)
RGNR: Rugged Glen Nature Reserve (South Africa)
RGO: Royal Greenwich Observatory
RGP: Riegel Paper Company (stock-exchange symbol)
rgs: radar ground stabilization
RGS: Rio Grande do Sul; Royal Geographical Society
RG do S: Rio Grande do Sul
RGTC: Robert Gordon's Technical College
rg tp: rough template
RGV: Rio Grande Valley Gas Company (stock exchange symbol)
rgz: recommended ground zero
rh: righthand (RH); roundhead
rh.: *rhonchi* (Latin—rales)
r/h: relative humidity; roentgens per hour
Rh: Rhesus factor (symbol); rhodium
Rh−: Rhesus negative
Rh +: Rhesus positive
Rh: *Rhein* (German—Rhine)
RH: Air Rhodesia; Random House; República de Honduras; Round House; Royal Highlanders; Royal Highness
R d'H: République d'Haiti
RH106: radioactive rhodium
RHA: Road Haulage Association; Royal Hibernian Academy; Royal Humane Association; Rural Housing Alliance
RHAF: Royal Hellenic Air Force
rhap: rhapsody
RHAWS: Radar Homing and Warning System
RHB: Regional Hospital Board
rhbdr: rhombohedral
rhc: respirations have ceased; rubber hydrocarbon
RHC: Rosary Hill College
RHC: *Radio Habana Cuba* (Spanish—Havana, Cuba Radio)
RHCSA: Regional Hospitals Consultants' and Specialists' Association
rhd: radioactive health data; relative hepatic dullness; rheumatic heart disease
RHD: *Random House Dictionary*
RHDO: Robin Hood Dell Orchestra
rhe: reversible hydrogen electrode
RHE: Reliability Human Engineering
rheo: rheostat
rhet: rhetoric; rhetorical; rhetorician

rheu: rheumatic; rheumatism; rheumatoid
rheu fev: rheumatic fever
rhf: right heart failure
RHGPS: Rhodesian Hunters and Game Preservation Society
RHHI: Royal Hospital and Home for Incurables
rhi: range height indicator
rhino: range height indicator not operating
rhinol: rhinological; rhinologist; rhinology
rhino(s): rhinoceros(es)
rhip: rank has its privileges
rhir: rank has its responsibilities
RHK: Radio Hong Kong
RHL: Radiological Health Laboratory
rhm: roentgen per hour per meter
RHMS: Royal Hibernian Military School
RHN: Royal Hellenic Navy
RHOB: Rayburn House Office Building
Rhod: Rhodesia
RHOFLIGHT: Rhodesian Air Services
rhom: rhombic; rhomboid; rhombus
RHQ: Regimental Headquarters
rhr: roughness height reading
r/hr: roentgens per hour
rhs: righthand side; roundheaded screw
RHS: Radio Ham Shack (amateur radio operator's station); Royal Historical Society; Royal Horticultural Society
Rhumba: (stock exchange short form for Royal McBee Company whose symbol is RMB)
ri: random interval; reflective insulation; refractive index; reliability index; require identification; respiratory illness; retroactive inhibition; rubber-insulated; rubber insulation
RI: Recruit Instruction; Refractories Institute; Republic of India; Republik Indonesia; Rhode Island (R.I.); Rhode Islanders; Rice Institute; Rock Island (Chicago, Rock Island & Pacific Railroad); Rotary International; Royal Institute
RI: *Républicains Independants* (French—Independent Republicans); *Ring Index*
ria: (Spanish—river mouth)
RIA: Research Institute of America; Rock Island Arsenal; Royal Irish Academy
RIAA: Record Industry Association of America
RIAC: Research Information Anal-

ysis Corporation
RIAEC: Rhode Island Atomic Energy Commission
RIAF: Royal Indian Air Force; Royal Iranian Air Force; Royal Iraqui Air Force
RIAL: Rock Island Arsenal Laboratory
RIAS: Rundfunk im amerikanischen Sektor (Radio in the American Sector), Berlin
RIASLP: Rattlesnake Island Air Service Local Post
rib.: ribbon
RIB: Railway Information Bureau; Referee in Bankruptcy; Rural Industries Bureau
RIBA: Royal Institute of British Architects
ribeira or ribeiro: (Portuguese —river, as in Ribeira de Iguape)
ric: radar intercept calculator
RIC: Republic Industrial Corporation; Republic of the Ivory Coast; Richmond, Virginia (airport); Royal Institute of Chemistry
RICA: Research Institute on Communist Affairs (Columbia University)
RICASIP: Research Information Center and Advisory Service on Information Processing
RICE: Rhode Island College of Education
Rich: Richmond
Rich II: *King Richard II*
Rich III: *King Richard III*
Richd: Richard; Richmond
Rich-Pete Turn: Richmond-Petersburg Turnpike (Virginia)
Rick: Richard
ricksha(w): *jinrikisha* (Japanese—man-drawn two-wheeled carriage)
ricm: right intercostal margin
RICMD: Richmond Contract Management District
RICS: Royal Institute of Chartered Surveyors
RICU: Russian Institute, Columbia University
RID: Riddle Aviation
RIDA: Rural and Industrial Development Authority
RIDE: Research Institute for Diagnostic Engineering
ridp: radar-iff (if friend or foe) data processor
RIE: Royal Institute of Engineers
RIEC: Royal Indian Engineering College
RIEI: Republic Industrial Education Institute (Republic Steel)
RIEM: Research Institute for Environmental Medicine

rif: reduction in force; right iliac fossa
rif: *rifatto* (Italian—restored; repaired)
rifi: radio interference field intensity
rifma: roentgen-isotope-fluorescent method of analysis
rift. (RIFT): reactor-in-flight test
Rig: Riga
RIGB: Royal Institution of Great Britain
RIGHT: Rhodesian Independence Gung-Ho Troops
RIH: Royal Institute of Horticulture
RIHS: Rhode Island Historical Society
RIIA: Royal Institute of International Affairs
RIISOM: Research Institute for Iron, Steel, and Other Metals
RIL: Royal Interocean Lines
rim.: radar input mapper; receiving, inspection, and maintenance; rubber insulation material
RIM: Resident Industrial Manager
RIMB: Roche Institute of Molecular Biology
RINA: *Registro Italiano Navale* (Italian Shipping Register)
RIND: Research Institute of National Defense
RIMR: Rockefeller Institute for Medical Research
RIN: Registro Italiano Navale (Italian ship-classification agency)
rina: reinitiation
RINA: Royal Institution of Naval Architects
rinf: *rinforzando* (Italian—with additional emphasis)
RINM: Resident Inspector of Naval Material
RINS: Research Institute for the Natural Sciences
rio: (Italian or Portuguese—river)
río: (Spanish—river, as in Rio Grande)
RIO: Reporting In and Out; Rhodesian Information Office; Rio de Janeiro (Galeao Airport)
Rio Branco: José Mariá de Silva Paranhos—Baron of Rio Branco—Brazil's great statesman
Rioj: La Rioja
riometer: relative ionospheric opacity meter
RIOP: Royal Institute of Oil Painters
RIOPR: Rhode Island Open-Pool Reactor
riot.: real-time input-output transducer (translator)
rip.: radar identification point
RIP: Reduction in Implementation Panel; Reduction in Personnel

(layoffs); Reliability Improvement Program; Reserve Intelligence Program; Rockefeller Institute Press
R.I.P.: *requiesca[n]t in pace* (Latin—may he [they] rest in peace)
RIPHH: Royal Institute of Public Health and Hygiene
RIPO: Rhode Island Philharmonic Orchestra
RIPPR: Reliability Improvement Program Progress Report
RIPWC: Royal Institute of Painters in Water Colours
rir: reduction in requirement
RIS: Range Instrumentation Ship
RISCO: Rhodesian Iron and Steel Company
RISCOM: Rhodesian Iron and Steel Commission
RISD: Rhode Island School of Design
rise.: reusable inflatable salvage equipment
RISE: Research Information Services for Education
RISM: Research Institute for the Study of Man (USA)
risp: *rispettivamente* (Italian—respectively)
RIT: Radio Information Test; Radio Network for Inter-American Telecommunication; Rochester Institute of Technology; Rorschach Inkblot Test; Royal Institute of Technology
Rita: Margarita; Margarita
RITA: Rural Industrial Technical Assistance
ritard: *ritardando* (Italian—holding back; retarding)
RITE: Rapid Information Technique for Evaluation
riten: *ritenuto* (Italian—retaining the tempo)
RITU (Profintern): Red International of Trade Unions
riv: radio influence voltage; river; rivet(ed)
riv: *riveduto* (Italian—revised)
rivière: (French—river)
RIZ: Radio Industry Zagreb
rj (RJ): ramjet
RJ: Rio de Janeiro; Royal Jordanian (airlines)
R de J: Rio de Janeiro
RJA: Reform Jewish Appeal; Retail Jewelers of America
RJAF: Royal Jordanian Air Force
RJC: Rochester Junior College; Rosenwald Junior College; Roswell Junior College
Rjk: Reykjavik
rk: rock; run of kiln
Rk: rock
RK: Air Afrique (2-letter coding);

Radio Kabul
RK: *Rdeci Kriz* (Yugoslavian —Red Cross)
rkg: radiocardiogram
RKN: Republic of Korea Navy
RKO: Radio-Keith-Orpheum (theater circuit)
rkt: rocket
Rkt Sta: Rocket Station
RKU: Ruprecht-Karl-Universität (Heidelberg)
RKV: Rose Knot (tracking station vessel)
rkva: reactive volt-ampere
rky: rocky
rl: rail; rocket launcher (RL)
r/l: radio location
r & l: rail and lake
Rl: Raphael
RL: high-powered radio range loop radiator(s); Radiation Laboratory; Reading List; Regent's Line; Republic of Liberia; Research Laboratory; Richfield Oil (stock exchange symbol); River Lines (railroad); Roland Line
R te L: Rijksuniversiteit te Leiden (State University at Leyden)
rla: restricted landing area
RLA: Religious Liberty Association
rladd: radar low-angle drogue delivery
RLAF: Royal Laotian Air Force
rlbm (RLBM): rearward-launched ballistic missile(s)
RLC: Radio Liberty Committee
RLCA: Rural Letter Carriers' Association
RLCS: Radio-Launch Control System
rld: radar laydown delivery; rolled
rld's: retail liquor dealers
rle: right lower extremity
rl est: real estate
rletfl: report leaving each thousand-foot level
rlf: relief
RLF: Royal Literary Fund
rlg: railing
rlg: *rilegato* (Italian—bound)
RLG: Royal Laos Government
RLHTE: Research Laboratory of Heat Tranfer in Electronics (MIT)
rll: right lower lobe (lung)
RLM: Regional Library of Medicine (PAHO)
RLNWR: Rice Lake National Wildlife Refuge (Minnesota); Ruby Lake National Wildlife Refuge (Nevada)
RLO: Regional Liaison Office(r)
RLPO: Royal Liverpool Philharmonic Orchestra
rlq: right lower quadrant (abdomen)

Rls: rial (Iranian currency unit)
RLS: Robert Louis Stevenson; Royal Lancastrian Society
RLSS: Royal Life Saving Society
rltr: realtor
RLTS: Radio-Linked Telemetry System
rltv: relative
rlty: realty
rlv: relieve
rly: relay
rm: range mark(s); raw material; ream; receiving memorandum; respiratory movement; ring micrometer; room; rubber marker(s)
r/m: revolutions per minute
r & m: redistribution and marketing; reliability and maintainability; reports and memoranda
Rm: Romania (Rumania); Romanian (Rumanian)
RM: Radioman; Raybestos-Manhattan; Registered Mail; Reichsmark (German currency); Research Memorandum; Ringling Museum; Royal Mail; Royal Marine; Royal Marines
R & M: Robbins & Myers
R/M: Raybestos/Manhattan
rma: right mento-anterior
RMA: Radio Manufacturers Association; Rice Millers Association; Ringling Museum of Art; Robert Morris Associates (Bank Loan Officers and Credit Men's Association); Royal Marine Artillery; Royal Military Academy; Rubber Manufacturers Association
RMADB: Reactor Maintenance and Disassembly Building
RMAF: Royal Moroccan Air Force
rm ar: reaming arbor
RMAS: Rochester Museum of Arts and Sciences
r mast: radio mast
RMB: Royal McBee
RMBAA: Rocky Mountain Business Aircraft Association
rmc: rod memory computer
RMC: Radio Monte Carlo; Reynolds Metals Company; Rochester Manufacturing Company; Royal Military College
RMCC: Royal Military College of Canada
RMCM: Royal Manchester College of Music
RMCPA: Rocky Mountain College Placement Association
RMCS: Royal Military College of Science
rmd: ready money down
RMD: Reaction Motors Division (Thiokol Chemical Corporation)

R-meter: radiation meter
R Met S: Royal Meteorological Society
rmi: reliability maturity index
RMI: Rack Manufacturers Institute; Reaction Motors Incorporated; Reactive Metals Incorporated; Roll Manufacturers Institute
rmicbm (RMICBM): roadmobile intercontinental ballistic missile
r/min: revolutions per minute
RMJC: Robert Morris Junior College
RML: Rand Mines Limited; Royal Mail Lines
RMM & EA: Rolling Mill Machinery and Equipment Association
RMN: Richard Milhous Nixon
RMNP: Rhodes Matopos National Park (Rhodesia); Riding Mountain National Park (Manitoba); Rocky Mountain National Park (Colorado)
RMNS: Royal Merchant Navy School
RMO: Regional Medical Officer
RMOGA: Rocky Mountain Oil and Gas Association
RMP: Reentry Measurement Program; Regional Medical Program; Research Management Plan; Research and Microfilm Publications; Royal Marine Police; Royal Mounted Police
RMPA: Royal Medico-Psychological Association
rmpc: rubber-mold plaster casting
Rmrs: Ramirez
rms: root mean square
RMS: Royal Mail Service; Royal Mail Ship; Royal Microscopical Society
rmse: root mean square error
RMSM: Royal Marines School of Music; Royal Military School of Music
RMSP: Royal Mail Steam Packet (company)
rmte: remote
rmu: remote maneuvering unit
rmv: respiratory minute volume
RMWC: Randolph-Macon Woman's College
rn: reception nil; research note; running noose; running nose
Rn: radon; Rangoon
RN: radionavigation; Registered Nurse; República de Nicaragua; Reynold's number; Royal Navy
rna (RNA): ribonucleic acid
R/NAA: Rocketdyne/North American Aviation
RNAC: Royal Nepal Airline Corporation
RNADC: Royal Netherlands Air Defense Command

RNAFF: Royal Netherlands Aircraft Factories Fokker
RNAS: Royal Naval Air Station
rnb: received—not billed
RNB: Royal Naval Barracks
RNBT: Royal Naval Benevolent Trust
RNC: Republican National Committee
RN & CR: Ryde, Newport, and Cowes Railway
rnd: round
RNE: Radio Nacional de España (Spanish National Radio Broadcasting System)
RNEC: Royal Naval Engineering College
RNES: *Radiodifusora Nacional de El Salvador* (Spanish—National Radio Network of El Salvador)—in Central America
Rnf: Renfrew
rnfp: radar not functioning properly
rng: range
R ng P: *Republika ng Pilipinas* (Pilipino—Republic of the Philippines)
rngt: renegotiate
RNIB: Royal National Institute for the Blind
RNID: Royal National Institute for the Deaf
rnit: radio noise interference test
RNL: Raffles National Library (Singapore); Royal Netherlands Line
RNLAF: Royal Netherlands Air Force
RNLI: Royal National Lifeboat Institution
rnm (RNM): radionavigation mobile
RNMD: Registered Nurse for Mental Defectives
RNMS: Royal Naval Medical School
RNMWS: Royal Naval Minewatching Service
RNN: Royal Nigerian Navy
RNNP: Royal Natal National Park (South Africa)
RNoAF: Royal Norwegian Air Force
RNOC: Royal Naval Officers Club
R No N: Royal Norwegian Navy
RNP: Redwood National Park (California); Rondane National Park (Norway); Ruaha National Park (Tanzania); Ruhana National Park (Ceylon)
RNP: *Radio Nacional de Peru* (Spanish—National Radio of Peru)
RNPS: Royal Naval Patrol Service
RNR: Royal Naval Reserves
rns: radar netting station
RNS: Royal Naval School

RNSA: Royal Naval Sailing Association
RNSC: Royal Netherlands Steamship Company
RNSS: Royal Naval Scientific Service
rnth: raised non-tight hatch
rnu: radar netting unit; radio noise voltage
RNVR: Royal Naval Volunteer Reserve
RNW: Radio Navigational Warning
RNWMP: Royal Northwest Mounted Police
RNWR: Ravalli National Wildlife Refuge (Montana)
rnwy: runway
RNZ: Radio New Zealand
RNZAC: Royal New Zealand Aero Club
RNZAF: Royal New Zealand Air Force
RNZN: Royal New Zealand Navy
ro: receive only; right opening; right orifice; road oil; rough opening; runover
ro: recto (frontside of page)
ro.: *recto* (Latin—front of the page; right-hand page)
r⁰: *recto* (Portuguese—face of page; right-hand page; this side)
r/o: rollout (final turn of an interceptor); rule out
r & o: rail and ocean
rO: reddish orange
RO: Radar Observer; Radar Operator; Radio Observer; Radio Operator; Recorder's Office; Recruiting Officer; Reserve Order
RÖ: Republik Österreich (Republic of Austria)
R-O: *Residentie-Orkest* (Dutch —Residency Orchestra)—at The Hague where the Netherlands government resides
R de O: Rio de Oro (Spanish Sahara)
roa: received on account; right occiput anterior
ROA: Reserve Officers Association
ROA: *Russkaya Osvoboditelnaya Armiya* (Russian Liberation Army)
ROAD: Reorganization Objective Army Division; Re-Organize Army Division
roam.: return of assets managed (banking)
ROAMA: Rome Air Materiel Area
rob.: remaining on board (cargo)
Rob: Robert
robeps: radar operating below prescribed standards
robo: rocket orbital bomber
Rob Roy: (Gaelic—Red Rob) —Robert Macgregor the Scot-

tish freebooter
Robt: Robert
roc: required operational capabilities
R o C: Republic of Congo
ROC: Rochester, New York (airport); Royal Observer Corps
R o Cam: Republic of Cameroons
ROCAPPI: Research on Computer Applications in the Printing and Publishing Industries
rocas: (Spanish—rocks)
Roch: Rochester
R o Ch: Republic of Chad
Roch Phil: Rochester Philharmonic
rocid: reorganization of combat infantry divisions
Rock: Knute Kenneth Rockne
Rockie: Nelson A. Rockefeller
rockoon(s): balloon-supported rocket(s)
ROCMD: Rochester Contract Management District
rocp: radar (or radio) out of commission for parts
rod.: required operational data; required operational date
Rod: Roderick; Rodney
ROD: *Rosskoye Osvoboditelnoye Dvizheniye* (Russian Liberation Movement)
rodiac: rotary dual input for analog computation
roentgen: roentgenology
rof: reporting organizational file
ROFA: Radio of Free Asia
rofor: route forecast
roft: radar off target
rog: rise-off-ground
R o G: Republic of Guinea
roger: your message received and understood
roi: return on investment
ROI: Range Operating Instructions
Rois: Rodrigues
Roiz: Rodriguez
Rok: a South Korean
ROK: Republic of Korea
ROKA: Republic of Korea Army
ROKAF: Republic of Korea Air Force
ROKN: Republic of Korea Navy
ROKPUC: Republic of Korea Presidential Unit Citation
roksonde: rocket sounding
Rolf: Rudolf; Rudolph
rol k: rolling keel
Rolls: Rolls-Royce
ROLS: Recoverable Orbital Launch System
rom: roman type
Rom: The Letter of Paul to the Romans; Roman; Romance language
R o M: Republic of Malagasy
ROM: Rome, Italy (Fiumicino air-

port); Royal Ontario Museum

Roman Century: the 2nd century before the Christian era when the Punic wars resulted in the destruction of Carthage by the Romans—the 100s

Rom Ant: Roman Antiquities

Rom Cath: Roman Catholic

romemo: refer to our memorandum

Romeo: code for letter R

Rom Hist: Roman History

Rom & Jul: Romeo and Juliet

romom: receiving-only monitor

romv: return on market value

ron: remain overnight; research octane number

Ron: Ronald

RONDA: Royal Oriental Nut Date Association

Ronnie: Ronald; Ronda; Vernonica

Ronny: Ronald

ROO: Range Operations Office(r)

roo(s): kangaroo(s)

Roosevelt I: Theodore Roosevelt—26th President of the United States

Roosevelt II: Franklin D. Roosevelt—32nd President of the United States

root.: relaxation oscillator optically tuned

rop: right occiput posterior; run of press

ROP: Regional Occupational Program

ropp: receive-only page printer

ror: rocket-on-rotor (device for assisting helicopter takeoffs)

Ror: Rorschach (inkblot test)

RORA: Reserve Officer Recording Activity

RORC: Royal Ocean Racing Club

ro/ro: roll on/roll off

ros: reduced operational status

Ros: Roscommon; Rostock

R o S: Republic of Senegal

ROS: Royal Order of Scotland

rose.: rosewood

ROSPA: Royal Society for the Prevention of Accidents

Ross: Ross and Cromarty

rot.: remedial occupational therapy; right occipito-transverse; rotary; rotate; rotation; rotor

Rot: Rotterdam

ROTC: Reserve Officers Training Corps

rotcc: receiver-off-hook-tone connecting circuit

roti: recording optical tracking instrument

rotn: rotation

roto: rotary press; rotogravure

ROTS: Reusable Orbital Transport System

Rou: Rouen

ROU: República Oriental del Uruguay

rouge: (French—red)

Rough Rider: Theodore Roosevelt—26th President of the United States

Roum: Roumanian

rout: routine

row.: reverse-osmosis water; risk of war

RoW (ROW): Right of Way

Rox: Roxburgh; Roxburghshire; Roxbury

Roy: Royal

Roy Com Soc: Royal Commonwealth Society (formerly Royal Empire Society; formerly Royal Colonial Institute)

ROY G. BIV: (acronymic mnemonic for recalling spectral colors—red, orange, yellow, green, blue, indigo, violet)—*see* vibgyor

Roy Liv Phil Orch: Royal Liverpool Philharmonic Orchestra

Roy Opera: Royal Opera House Orchestra (Covent Garden)

Roy Phil: Royal Philharmonic Orchestra

Roz: Rodriguez; Rosalind(a)

rp: plate resistance (symbol); raid plotter; rally point; received pronunciation (RP); reception poor; release point; relay paid; reporting post; reprint; retained personnel; rhodium-plated; rhodium plating; rocket projectile (RP); rocket propellant; rust preventive

r-p: reprint; reprinting

rP: reddish purple

Rp: Rappen (Swiss—centime); rupiah (Indonesian currency unit)

RP: remote pickup (broadcast); República de Panamá; República del Paraguay; República del Peru; República Portuguesa (Portugal); rocket projectile; Rules of Procedure

RP: Radiotelevisão Portuguesa (Portuguese Radio-Television)

R-P: Rhône-Poulenc

R de P: República de Panamá; República del Paraguay; República Portuguesa

RP-1: rocket-propellant type-1 fuel (kerosine)

rpa: radar performance analyzer

RPA: Rationalist Press Association; Regional Planning Association

RPB: Regional Preparedness Board; Research to Prevent Blindness (fund)

rpc: radar planning chart; remote position control; reply postcard; request (the) pleasure (of your)

company; reversed phase column

RPC: Reliability Policy Committee

RPCC: Reactor Physics Constants Center

rpd: radar planning device

RPDL: Radioisotope Process Development Laboratory

rpe: related payroll expense

RPE: Radio Propagation Engineering; Rocket Propulsion Establishment

RPEA: Regional Planning and Evaluation Agency

rpf: radiometer performance factor; relaxed pelvic floor; renal plasma flow

rpfod: reported for duty

rpg: radiation protection guide; report program generator; rocket-propelled grenade; rounds per gun

RPHST: Research Participation for High School Teachers

RPI: Rensselaer Polytechnic Institute; Rose Polytechnic Institute

RPIA: Rocket Propellant Information Agency

rpie (RPIE): real property installed equipment

RPK: Regiment President Kruger

rpl: running program language

RPL: Radiation Physics Laboratory (NBS); Regina Public Library; Repair Parts List; Richmond Public Library; Roanoke Public Library; Rochester Public Library; Rocket Propulsion Laboratory; Rockhampton Public Library

rplca: replica

rpm: reliability performance measure; repairman; revolutions per minute; rotations per minute

RPM: Rustenburg Platinum Mines

RPMF: Radiation Pattern Measurement Facility

rpmi: revolutions-per-minute indicator

RPMI: Roswell Park Memorial Institute

rpo: revolutions per orbit

RPO: Rochester Philharmonic Orchestra; Rotterdam Philharmonic Orchestra; Royal Philharmonic Orchestra

RPO: Rotterdams Philharmonisch Orkest (Dutch—Rotterdam Philharmonic Orchestra)

rpoc: report proceeding on course

rpp: radar power programmer; reply paid postcard; request present position; return paid postal

RPP: Radio Propagation Physics

rppe: research, program, planning, evaluation

RPQ: Request for Price Quotation
rpr: read printer
RPR: Republica Populara Romana (Romania)
RPRAGB: Rubber and Plastics Research Association of Great Britain
rprt: report
rps: revolutions per second
RPS: Railway Progress Society; Rapid Processing System; Registered Publication Section; Reliability Problem Summary; Republika Popullore e Shqiperise (Albania); Royal Philharmonic Society; Royal Photographic Society
RPSM: Resources Planning and Scheduling Method
RPSs: Reliability Problem Summary Cards; Republic of the Philippines Ships
rpt: repeat
RPT: Registered Physical Therapist
RPU: Radio Propagation Unit (USA)
rpv: remotely-piloted vehicle
rq (RQ): respiratory quotient
R/Q: Request for Quotation
R & QA: reliability and Quality Assurance
rqdcz: request clearance to depart control zone
rqecz: request clearance to enter control zone
rqmt: requirement
rqr: require; requirement
rqs: ready qualified for standby
rqtao: request time and altitude over
rr: radiation response; radio range; radio ranging; railroad; rapid rectilinear; rear; rearward; respiratory rate; rifle range; rural route; rush release; rush and run
r & r: rate and rhythm (pulse); rest and recreation; rest and rotation (of military personnel); rock and roll; rock and rye (whiskey); rush and run
RR: Railroad; Raritan River (railroad); Recovery Room; Recruit Roll; Reliability Requirements; Remington Rand; Renegotiation Regulations; Research Report; Rifle Range; Right Reverend; Rolls-Royce; Rural Route
R-R: Rolls-Royce
R v R: Rembrandt van Rijn
rRA: specific acoustic resistance
RRA: Radiation Research Associates
R/RA: Repair/Rework Analysis
RRAF: Royal Rhodesian Air Force
RRB: Railroad Retirement Board
RRBC: R.R. Bowker Company

RRBS: Rapid-Response Bibliographic Service
rr & c: records, reports, and control
RRC: Recruit Reception Center; Requirements Review Committee; Rocket Research Corporation; Royal Red Cross; Rubber Reserve Committee; Rubber Reserve Company; Rubber Reserve Corporation
RRCC: Redwood Region Conservation Council
rr cells: radiation reaction cells
rrd: receive, record, display
rr & d: reparations, removal, and demolition
RRD: Reliability Requirements Directive
rrda: rendezvous retrieval, docking, and assembly (of orbital station or space vehicle)
rr & e: round, regular, and equal (eye pupils)
RRE: Railroad Enthusiasts; Royal Radar Establishment
R Rep: Records Repository (USAF)
RRF: Refrigeration Research Foundation
rri: range rate indicator
RRI: Radio Republik Indonesia; Rocket Research Institute; Rubber Research Institute
RRIM: Rubber Research Institute of Malaya
RRIS: Remote Radar Intergration Station
RRL: Regimental Reserve Line; Reserve Retired List; Road Reserve Laboratory
R.R.L.: Registered Record Librarian (hospital)
RRLNWR: Red Rock Lakes National Wildlife Refuge (Montana)
RRLs: Registered Record Librarians
RRP: Rotterdam-Rhine Pipeline
RRPS: Ready Reinforcement Personnel Section (USAF)
rrr: rebel, resist, riot (New Left student-activist program in abbreviated form)
RRS: Radiation Research Society; Reaction Research Society; Retired Reserve Section; Royal Research Ship
rrt: rendezvous radar transponder
RRU: Radio Research Unit (USA)
rs: radio station; reading of standard; ready service; rear spar; receiver station; receiving ship; receiving station; reception station; regulating station; reinforcing stimulus; response stimulus; right side; road space; rubble stone

r/s: range safety; revolutions per second
r & s: reenlistment and separation
Rs: restricted motion pictures (adults only); rupees
RS: Radio Station; Receiving Ship; Receiving Station; Reception Station; Reconnaissance Squadron; Reconnaissance Strike; Recording Secretary; Recruiting Station; Regular Station; Regulating Station; Regulation Station; Republic Steel; Research Summary; Revised Statutes; Ringer's Solution; Rio Grande do Sul; Roberval & Saguenay (railroad); Royal Scots; Royal Society
RS-70: reconnaissance-strike bomber (formerly B-70)
rsa: radar signature analysis; remote station alarm; right sacro-anterior
RSA: Railway Supervisors Association; Railway Supply Association; Redstone Arsenal; Regional Science Association; Renaissance Society of America; Rental Service Association; Republiek van Suid-Afrika; Royal Scottish Academy; Royal Society of Arts
RSA (AFL-CIO): Railway and Airline Supervisors Association
RSAF: Royal Swedish Air Force
rsalt: running, signal, and anchor lights
RSAM: Royal Scottish Academy of Music
rsb: range safety beacon
RSB: Regimental Stretcher Bearer
RSBA: Rail Steel Bar Association; Royal Society of British Artists
RSBS: Radar Safety Beacon System
rsc: range-safety command; range-safety control
RSC: Range Safety Command; Records Service Center; Richard Strauss Conservatory (Munich); Royal Society of Canada
rsch: research
RSCN: Registered Sick Children's Nurse
RSCS: Rate Stabilization and Control System
RSCT: Rhode Sentence Completion Test
rsd: rolling steel door
RSD: Riverside Drive; Royal Society of Dublin
rsdp: remote-site data processor
RSDS: Range Safety Destruct System
RSE: Royal Society of Edinburgh
rseu: remote scanner-encoder unit

RSF: Russell Sage Foundation

RSFPP: Retired Serviceman's Family Protection Plan

RSFSR: Russian Socialist Federated Soviet Republic(s)

rsg: reassign; receiver of stolen goods; receiving stolen goods; regional seat of government

RSGB: Radio Society of Great Britain

RSGS: Royal Scottish Geographical Society

rsh: radar status history

Rsh: Rosyth

RSH: Royal Society for the Promotion of Health

RSHA: Reichssicherheitshauptampt (Nazi German Secret Police headed by Heinrich Himmler)

RSHWC: Royal Society for the Health of Women and Children (New Zealand's Plunkett Society)

rsi: radarscope interpretation; reflected signal indication; replacement stream input

rs & i: rules, standards, and instructions

RSI: Research Studies Institute

RSIC: Radiation Standards Information Center; Redstone Scientific Information Center

rsj: rolled-steel joist

RSL: Radio Standards Laboratory; Red Star Line; Royal Society of London

rsla: range safety launch approval

rsm (RSM): reconnaissance strategic missile

RSM: Royal Society of Medicine; Royal Society of Musicians

RSMA: Railway Systems and Management Association; Repubblica di San Marino (San Marino—world's smallest republic); Royal School of Mines; Royal Society of Medicine

rsn: reason

RSN: Radiation Surveillance Network (USPHS)

RSNA: Radiological Society of North America

RSNP: Registered Student Nurse Program

RSNZ: Royal Society of New Zealand

rso: railway sorting office; railway suboffice; research ship of opportunity

RSO: Range Safety Officer; Research Ships of Opportunity; Richmond Symphony Orchestra

rsp: right sacro-posterior

RSPA: Royal Society for the Prevention of Accidents

RSPB: Royal Society for the Protection of Birds

RSPCA: Royal Society for the Prevention of Cruelty to Animals

RSPWC: Royal Society of Painters in Water Colours

rsq: rescue

rsr: regular sinus rhythm; required supply rate

RSR: Range Safety Report; Request for Scientific Research; Research Study Requests

R-SR B: Richmond-San Rafael Bridge

RSROAA: Roller Skating Rink Operators Association of America

RSRS: Radio and Space Research Station

rss: root-sum square

RSS: Range Safety System; Reactant Service System; Rehabilitation Support Schedule; Royal Security Service; Royal Statistical Society; Rural Sociological Society

RSSA: Royal Society of South Africa

RSSPCC: Royal Scottish Society for the Prevention of Cruelty to Children

RSST: Recruiter-Salesman Selection Test

rst: radius of safety trace; reinforcing steel; right sacro-transverse

r-s-t: readability—signal strength—tone (amateur radio signal)

RST: Royal Society of Teachers

RST: *Republica Socialista Romania* (Romanian Socialist Republic)

R Sta: radio station

RSTMH: Royal Society of Tropical Medicine and Hygiene

rstr: restricted

RSU: Radical Student Union

rsv: respiratory syncytial virus

Rsv: Rous sarcoma virus

RSV: Revised Standard Version (Bible)

rsvp: research-selected vote profile; restartable solid variable pulse

RSVP: Retired Senior Volunteer Persons; Retired Senior Volunteer Program

R.S.V.P.: *respondez s'il vous plait* (French—please reply)

rsvr: reservoir

rswc (RSWC): right side up with care

R Sw N: Royal Swedish Navy

rt: radio telephone; radio telephony; rate; reaction time; receive-transmit; reduction table(s); right; rocket target; room temperature; round table; round trip;

runup and taxi

r/t: radiotelephone

r & t (R & T): research and technology

RT: Radio Technician; Ranger Tab; Reading Test; Recreational Therapy; Registered Technician; Registered X-ray Technician; Republique Togolaise (Togo Republic); River Terminal (railroad); Rubber Technician

RT: *République Togolaise* (French —Togolese Republic)—Togo

R/T: Record of Trial

rta: road traffic accident

RTA: Rail Travel Authorization; Railway Tie Association; Refrigeration Trade Association; Royal Thai Army; Rubber Trade Association

RTA: *Radiodiffusion et Television Algerienne* (French—Algerian Radio and Television Network)

RTAC: Regional Technical Aids Center

rt ad: router adapter

RTAF: Royal Thai Air Force

rtb: return to base

RTB: Radiodiffusion Télévision Belge (Belgian Radio-Television Broadcasting)

RTB: *Radiodiffusion-Télévision Belge* (French—Belgian Radio-Television Network)

RTB/BRT: *Radifussion-Television Belge/Belgische Radio den Televisie* (French and Dutch—Belgian Radio and Television Network)

RTBL: Richard Thomas and Baldwins Limited

rtc: ratchet

RTC: Rail Travel Card; Real Time Command; Replacement Training Center; Reserve Training Corps; Revenue and Taxation Code; Rochester Telephone Corporation; Royal Trust Company

RTCA: Radio Technical Commission for Aeronautics

rtcu: real-time control unit

rt cu: router cutter

rtd: returned

RTD: Rapid Transit District (Southern California); Research and Technology Division

rtdd: real-time data distribution

RTDHS: Real-Time Data Handling System

rt dr: returnable-trip drum

RTDS: Real-Time Data System

rte: route

RTE: *Radio Telefís Eireann* (Irish Radio Television)

rtem: radar tracking error measurement

RTES: Radio and Television Executives Society
RTESO: Radio Telefís Eireann Symphony Orchestra (Irish Radio Television Symphony Orchestra)
rtf: rubber-tile floor
RTF: Radiodiffusion-Télévision Francaise (French tv network)
rt fm: router form
RTFR: Reliability Trouble and Failure Report
rtfv: radar target folder viewer
rtg: radioactive thermal generator; rare tube gas; reusable training grenade
RTG: Royal Thai Government
RTG: Radiodiffusion Télévision Gabonaise (French—Gabonese Radio-Television Network)
rtgd: room temperature gamma detector
rt gu: router guide
rtgv: real time generation of video
Rt Hon: Right Honourable
RTHPL: Radio Times Hulton Picture Library
rti: rise time indicator; rotor temperature indicator
RTI: Reliability Trend Indicator; Research Triangle Institute; Roanoke Technical institute
RTI: Radiodiffusion Télévision Ivoirienne (French—Ivorian Radio-Television Network)—Ivory Coast
rtip: radar target identification point
RTIR: Reliability Trend Indicator Report
RTK: Ras Tafari Makonnea (Haile Selassie)
rtl: reinforced tile lintel; resistor transistor logic
RTLO: Regional Training Liaison Office(r)
rtm: running time meter
RTM: Rotterdam, Netherlands (airport)
RTM: Radiodiffusion Télévision Marocaine (French—Moroccan Radio-Television Network)
RTMA: Radio and Television Manufacturers Association
RTMS: Radar Target Measuring System
rtn: retain; return
RTN: registered trade name; Royal Thai Navy
rto: radio-telephone operator
RTO: Railway Transport Office
rtp: reinforced thermoplastic
R Tp: radio telephone
RTP: Request for Technical Proposal (DoD)
rtqc: real-time quality control
rtr: returning to ramp

R Tr: radio tower
RTR: Reliability Test Requirement(s)
RTR: Radiodifuziunea Televisiunea Romana (Romanian Radio-Television Network)
rtrc: radio telemetry and remote control
RTRC: Regional Technical Report Centers
Rt. Rev.: Right Reverend
rts: radar target simulation; radar tracking station
RTS: Repair Technical Service (tractor stations—USSR)
RTSD: Resources and Technical Services Division (American Library Association)
RTSRS: Real-Time Simulation Research System
rtt: radiation tracking transducer
RTTDS: Real-Time Telemetry Data System
rt tp: router template
rttv: research target and test vehicle
r-ttv: real-time television
rtu: remote terminal unit
RTU: Railroad Telegraphers Union; Reinforcement Training Unit; Reserve Training Unit
rtv: reentry test vehicle (RTV); room-temperature vulcanizing
rtw: ready to wear
rtx: rapid-transit experimental (bus); report time crossing
rty: rarity; realty
rtz: return to zero
RTZ: Rio Tinto Zinc
ru: radium unit; rat unit; roentgen unit
Ru: Rumania (Romania); Rumanian (Romanian); Russia; Russian; ruthenium
RU: Rhodes University; Roosevelt University; Rugby Union; Rutgers University; Rumanian Union
R te U: Rijksuniversiteit te Utrecht (State University at Utrecht)
rub.: rubber
rub: rubato (Italian—with varying tempo); *ruber* (Latin—red)
RUB: Radio Ulan Bator
rubd: rubberized
Rube: Ruben
Rubén Darío: Félix Rubén García Sarmiento
Rubg: Rummelsburg
RUC: Royal Ulster Constabulary
Rucos: Russian Communists
rud: rudder
rud: (Persian—river)
Rud Kip: Rudyard Kipling
Rudy: Rudolf; Rudolph
rue.: right upper entrance; right upper extremity

RUE: Regional Urban Environment
rug.: red under gold
RUI: Royal University of Ireland
RUKBA: Royal United Kingdom Beneficent Association
rul: right upper lobe (lung)
RUL: Rutgers University Library
rum (RUM): remote underwater manipulator
Rum: Rumania (Romania); Rumanian (Romanian)
RUM: Royal University of Malta
RUN: Revolutaionary United Nations
rupt: rupture(d)
ruq: right upper quadrant (abdomen)
RUR: Rossum's Universal Robots (acronym-titled play by Karel Capek)
Rus: Russ; Russia; Russian
Rusdic: Russian dictionary
rush.: remote use of shared hardware
russ: russet; russian (leather)
rúst: rústico, a la (Spanish—paperback; paperbound)
Rut: Rutland Railroad; Rutlandshire
rv: rear view; reentry vehicle (RV); relief valve; residual volume; retroversion; right ventricle
r/v: reentry vehicle
RV: Rahway Valley (railroad); Reading and Vocabulary Test; República de Venezuela; Revised Version; Rifle Volunteer(s)
RV: Radikale Venstre (Danish—Radical Left)—Radical Liberal Party
R/V: rendezvous; research vessel
rva: reactive volt-ampere (meter)
Rva: Rouva (Finnish—Madam)
rvb: radar video buffer
rvbr: riveting bar
rvc: random vibration control; relative velocity computer
RVC: Rifle Volunteer Corps; Royal Veterinary College
rvd: radar video digitizer; right vertebral density
RVDA: Recreational Vehicle Dealers of America
rvdp: radar video data processor
rve: radar video extractor
RVFN: Report of Visit of Foreign Nationals
rv fx: riveting fixture
rvh: right ventricular hypertrophy
RVI: Recreational Vehicle Institute
RVLP: Rift Valley Lakes Park (Ethiopia)
rvm: reactive voltmeter
Rvn: Ravenna
RVN: Republic of Vietnam

RVNAF: Republic of Vietnam Air Force; Republic of Vietnam Armed Forces
rvo: relaxed vaginal outlet; runway visibility observer
R v O: Rijksinstituut voor Oorlogsdocumentatie (Netherlands State Institute for War Documentation)
RVO: Royal Victorial Order
Rvp: Reid vapor pressure
rvpa: rivet pattern
rvr: runway visual range
rv's: recreation vehicles
rvsc: reverse self check
R.V.S.V.P.: repondez vite, s'il vous plait (French—please reply at once)
rvsz: riveting squeezer
rvtol: rolling vertical takeoff and landing
rvu: relief valve unit
rvx: reentry vehicle—experimental
rw: radiological warfare; railwater (transport); random widths; raw water; recreation and welfare; recruiting warrant; rotary wing; runway
r/w: right-of-way
r & w: rail and water
Rw: Rwanda
RW: radiological war; radiological warfare; Recruiting Warrant; redwood; Richard Wagner; Right Worshipful; Right Worthy; Royal Welsh
rwa (RWA): rotary-wing aircraft
RWA: Railway Wheel Association
rwb: rear wheel brake
RWB: Rand Water Board; Royal

Winnipeg Ballet
rwbh: records will be handcarried
rwc: rainwater conductor; read, write, compute; read, write, continue; receive with code
RWC: Roberts Wesleyan College
RWEMA: Ralph Waldo Emerson Memorial Association
rwg: rigid waveguide
RWG: Radio Writers' Guild; Reliability Working Group; Roebling Wire Gage
rwgl: rough wire glass
rwh: radar warning and homing
rwi: read, write, initial; real world interval; remote weight indicator
RWJC: Roger Williams Junior College
rwk: rework
rwl: relative water level
rwlr: relative water-level recorder
rwm: rectangular wave modulation; resistance welding machine; roll wrapping machine
RWMA: Resistance Welding Manufacturers' Association
rwp: radio wave propagation
RWQCB: Regional Water Quality-Control Board(s)
RWR: rail-water-rail
rwrc: remain well to right of course
rws: range while search; reaction wheel scanner; reaction wheel system;
RWS: Royal Water-Colours Society
rwt: read-write-tape
rwth: raised watertight hatch
rwv: read-write-versify
rwy: railway; runway

rx: reverse; rix dollar; tens of rupees
Rx: recipe; prescription
rxb: roxburgh (binding)
rxp: radix point
rxs: radar cross-section
ry: railway; rydberg
Ry: railway; Ryukyu (islands)
RY: Royal Air Lao (coding)
RYA: Railroad Yardmasters of America; Royal Yachting Association
Ry Age: Railway Age
ryal: relay alarm
Ryan: Ryan Aeronautical Company (coding)
rym: refer to your message
RYM: Revolutionary Youth Movement
Rys: Railways
RYS: Royal Yacht Squadron
Ryu: Ryukyu; Ryukyuan
R y'u R: Republika y'u Rwanda (Kinyarwanda—Rwanda)
rz: return to zero
Rz: Rodriguez
RZA: Religious Zionists of America
RZMA: Rolled Zinc Manufacturers Association
RZn: relative azimuth
RZS: Royal Zoological Society
RZ Scot: Royal Zoological Society of Scotland
RZSI: Royal Zoological Society of Ireland
RZSS: Royal Zoological Society of Scotland
rzl: return to zero level
rzm: return to zero mark

S

s: displacement (symbol); sacral; sand; schilling (Austrian currency unit); scuttle; sea-air temperature difference correction (symbol); second(s); secret; section; sections; sen (Japanese monetary unit); sensation; separate; separation; share(s); shilling (British monetary unit); ship; sign; silver; simultaneous transmission of range signals and voice (symbol); single; singular; sinister (left); sister; slip; slope; slow; small; smooth; snow; sol (Peruvian monetary unit); son(s); sou (French monetary unit); spar; specific; specific factor; speed; steel; stere; stock;

string; subject; succeeded; sucre (Ecuadorian monetary unit); summary; summer; surface; symbol
s.: *sinister* (Latin—left)
s l s l e: surfaced on one side and one edge (lumber)
s 4 s: surfaced on four sides (lumber)
S: antisubmarine (symbol); sailing vessel (symbol); San; San Francisco (coin symbol denoting San Francisco mint); Santa; Santo; satisfactory; Saturday; Saturn; Saxon; Schilling (Austrian currency); school; Schweitzer; Schweizer Aircraft; Scotland; Seaman; seaplane; search and

rescue; Sears, Roebuck (stock exchange symbol); Seatrain Lines; secondary winding (symbol); secret; Section; See; sen (Japanese currency); Senate; Senate Bill; Senator; Shinto; Shintoism; Shintoist; ship; siemens (mho); Sierra—code for letter S; sign; Signor (Italian—mister); Sigma; Sikorsky; silver; Silver Lines; Sinclair; Sister; Socialist; sol (Peruvian monetary unit); solo; solubility; son; soprano; south; southern; spar buoy; specific factor; specification(s); Sperry; Staff; Statute; steamer; steamship; Steinway; stop; subject; sucre (Ecuadorian monetary unit); suite; sulfur; summer; sun; Sunday; Sweden (auto plaque); Sylvania; total entropy (symbol); wing plan area (symbol)

S: general area (symbol); *Sábado* (Spanish—Saturday); *San* or *Santo* (Italian, Spanish—saint, *m .); Santa* (Italian, Portuguese, Spanish—saint, *f.); São* (Portuguese—saint, *m.); semis* (Latin—half); *sinister* (Latin—left); *sisälle* (Finnish—in); *söder* (Swedish—south); *sør* (Norwegian—south); south; *strada* (Italian—street); *subir* (Spanish —to go up; mount); *sud* (French or Italian—south); *Süd* (German—south); *sul* (Portuguese—south); *sur* (Spanish —south); *syd* (Danish—south)

S/: sol (Peru); sucre (Ecuador)

S-1: military personnel; personnel officer

S1c: Seaman, first class

S-2: military intelligence; intelligence officer

S2F: Tracker twin-engine anti-submarine aircraft flown from carriers

S-3: military operations and training; military operations and training officer

S³: Systems, Science, and Software

S-4: military logistics; military logistics officer

S³⁵: radioactive sulfur

:/S/: sign (music)

sa: sail area; semiannual(ly); semiautomatic; sex appeal; shaft alley; sinoatrial; small arms; soluble in alkaline; special activities; spectrum analyzer; stone arch; subject to approval; subsistence allowance; sun-affected; superabnormal; supraabdominal; sustained action

sa: *siehe auch* (German—see also)

s.a.: *secundum artem* (Latin—according to the art)

s-a: sinoatrial

s/a: storage area

s & a: safety and arming (mechanism)

Sa: samarium; Sara; Sarah; Sarita; Serra; Sierra

Sa: *Summa* (German—total)

Sª: Señora (Spanish—Madam)

SA: Safeway Stores (stock exchange symbol); Salvation Army; Saudi Arabia; Saudi Arabian; Savannah & Atlanta (railroad); Seaman Apprentice; second attack (lacrosse); search amphibian; Secretary of the Army; sex appeal; Shipping Au-

thority; Society of Actuaries; South Africa; South African; South African Airways (2-letter coding); South America; South American; South Australia; South Australian; Southern Association; Special Agent; Special Artificer; State's Attorney; Sugar Association; Supplemental Agreement; Supplementary Agreement

SA: *Société Anonyme* (French—limited company)

S.A.: *Sociedad Anónima* (Spanish —corporation); *Sturmabteilung* (German—Stormtroopers, Adolf Hitler's brown-shirted Nazis); *Sucursales Asociados* (Spanish—associated branches)

S/A: *Societa Anonima* (Italian—limited company)

SA£: South African pound

S of A: Society of Actuaries

S por A: *Sociedad por Acciones* (Spanish—limited liability company)

saa: small arms ammunition

SAA: Saudi Arabian Airlines; Shakespeare Association of America; Signal Appliance Association; Society for Academic Achievement; Society for American Archeology; Society of American Archivists; Society for Applied Anthropology; Society for Asian Art; South African Airways; Southern Ash Association; Speech Association of America; Surety Association of America; Swedish-American Association

SAAA: Salvation Army Association of America

SAAARNG: Senior Army Advisor, Army National Guard

SAAAS: South African Association for the Advancement of Science

SAAASE: South African Association for the Administration and Settlement of Estates

SAAB: Svenska Aeroplan Aktiebolaget (Swedish Airplane Company)

SAAC: Sciences and Arts Camps; Seismic Array Analysis Center (IBM); Special Assistant for Arms Control (DoD)

SAAD: Sacramento Army Depot

SAAEB: South African Atomic Energy Board

SAAF: Saudi Arabian Air Force; South African Air Force

SAAL: Syrian Arab Airlines

SAAMA: San Antonio Air Materiel Area

SAAMI: Sporting Arms and Am-

munition Manufacturers Institute

SAAP: Saturn-Apollo Applications Program; South Atlantic Anomaly Probe (NASA)

sa ar: saw arbor

saari: (Finnish—island)

SAAS: Science Achievement Awards for Students; Society of African and Afro-American Students

SAAVS: Submarine Acceleration and Velocity System

SAAWK: *Suid Afrikaanse Akademie vir Wetnenskap en Kuns* (Afrikaans—South African Academy for Science and Art)

sab: sabbath; sabbatical; soprano, alto, baritone (SAB)

sáb: *sabado* (Spanish—Saturday); *sabato* (Italian—Saturday)

s-a b: steel-arch bridge

SAB: Sabena; Scientific Advisory Board; Society of American Bacteriologists

sabbat: sabbatical

SABC: South African Broadcasting Corporation

SABCO: Society for the Area of Biological and Chemical Overlap

SABCOA: Screw and Bolt Corporation of America

SABE: Society for Automation in Business Education

SABENA: Société Anonyme Belge d'Exploitation de la Navigation Aérienne (Belgian World Airlines)

saber (SABER): semiautomatic business environment research

sabh: simultaneous automatic-broadcast homer

sabir: semi-automatic bibliographic information retrieval

sable: (French—sand)

SABMIS: Seaborne Anti-Ballistic Missile Intercept System (USN)

SABMS: Safeguard Anti-Ballistic Missile System

sabo: sabotage

sabre.: self-aligning boost and reentry

SABS: South African Bureau of Standards

SABW: Society of American Business Writers

sac: sacral; sacrament; sacramental; sacred

Sac: Sacramento, California (nickname)

SAC: Sacramento, California (airport); San Angelo College; San Antonio College; Society of Analytical Chemistry; Southwest Automotive Company; Strategic Air Command; Sveriges Arbetares Centraloganisation (Swedish Workers Central Organization)

SACA: Steam Automobile Club of America

SACB: Subversive Activities Control Board

SACC: Supplemental Air Carrier Conference; Supporting Arms Coordination Center

SACCS: Strategic Air Command Control System

SACEM: Société des Auteurs, Compositeurs et Éditeurs de la Musique (Society of Authors, Composers, and Editors of Music)

SACEUR: Supreme Allied Command, Europe

Sacha: Alexander

Sacha Guitry: (pseudonym—Alexandre Pierre Georges)

SACI: South Atlantic Cooperative Investigations

SA & CL: South Atlantic & Caribbean Line

SACLant: Supreme Allied Commander, Atlantic

SACM: South African College of Music; South African Corps of Marines; South Arabian Common Market

SACMP: South African Corps of Military Policy

SACO: Sveriges Akademikers Centralorganisation (Swedish Professional Central Organization)

Sacr: Sacramento

SACS: South African College System; South African Corps of Signals; Southern Association of Colleges and Schools

SACSIR: South African Council for Scientific and Industrial Research

Sacto: Sacramento

SACU: Service for Admission to College and University

SACUBO: Southern Association of College and University Business Officers

sad.: safety, arming, destruct; safety and arming device; situation attention display

SAD: simple, average, or difficult; Social Affairs Department (Communist China's espionage agency)

SAD: *South African Digest*

S & AD: Science and Applications Directorate (NASA)

sadap: simplified automatic data plotter

SADE: *Sociedad Argentina de Escritores* (Argentine Writers' Society)

sadic: solid-state analog-to-digital computer

sadie: semi-automatic decentralized intercept environment

SADS: Swiss Air Defense System

sadsac: sampled data simulator and computer

sadsact: self-aligned descriptors from self and cited titles (automatic index)

sad sam (SAD SAM): sentence appraiser and diagrammer—semantic analyzer machine

SADTC: Shape Air Defense Technology Center

sad. test: sugar, acetone, diacetic acid test

sae: San Diego Aircraft Engineering (corporate symbol); self-addressed envelope; standard average European

SAE: Society of American Etchers; Society of Automotive Engineers

S.A.E.: Société Anonyme Egyptienne (Egyptian limited company)

SAEA: Southeastern Adult Education Association

saeb: self-adjusting electric brake

SAEC: South African Engineer Corps; Sumitomo Atomic Energy Commission (Japan)

SAEH: Society for Automation in English and the Humanities

SAEI: Sumitomo Atomic Energy Industries (Japan)

SAEL: South African Emergency League

SAEMR: Small Arms Expert Marksmanship Ribbon

SAET: Spiral Aftereffect Test

saf: Safety

SAF: Secretary of the Air Force; Society of American Foresters; Strategic Air Force

SAF: *Svenska Arbetsgivareforeningen* (Swedish Employers' Confederation)

SAF£: South African Pound

safa: solar-array failure analysis; soluble-antigen fluorescent antibody

SAFA: School Assistance in Federally Affected Areas; Society for Automation in the Fine Arts

SAFAA: South African Fine Arts Association

SAFB: Scott Air Force Base; Shaw Air Force Base

SAFC: South African Flying Corps

SAFCB: Secretary of the Air Force Correction Board

safe.: satellite alert force employment; system, area, function, equipment

SAFE: Braathens South American & Far East Air Transport; Survival and Flight Equipment Association

S.A.F.E.: Society of Aeronautic Flight Engineers

SAFE TRIP: Students Against Faulty Tires Ripping in Pieces

SAFI: Senior Air Force Instructor

SAFMARINE: South African Marine (corporation)

SAFO: Senior Air Force Officer (present)

SAFOH: Society of American Florists and Ornamental Horticulturists

SAFR: Senior Air Force Representative

S-Afr Du: South-African Dutch (Afrikaans)

SAFS: Secondary Air Force Specialty

SAFSL: Secretary of Air Force Space Liaison

SAFSO: Safeguard System Office(r)

SAFSR: Society for the Advancement of Food Service Research

sa fx: saw fixture

Sag: Sagittarius

SAG: Scientific Advisory Group; Screen Actors Guild; Society of Arthritic Gardeners; Systems Analysis Group

SAGE: semi-automatic ground environment (for continental defense against air attack)

SAGE/BUIC: Semi-Automatic Ground Environment and Back-Up Interceptor Control (systems)

Sage of Chelsea: Thomas Carlyle

Sage of Concord: Ralph Waldo Emerson—American philosopher-poet

Sage of Ebury Street: George Moore

Sage of Monticello: Thomas Jefferson—author of the *Declaration of Independence*, founder of the University of Virginia, third President of the United States

SAGP: Society for Ancient Greek Philosophy

SAGS: Semiactive Gravity Gradient System (NASA)

SAG & U: San Antonio, Gulf & Uvalde (railroad)

SAH: Society of American Historians

sahf: semiautomatic height finder

sahyb: simulation of analog and hybrid computers

sahra: (Arabic—desert)

sai: sell (sold) as is

Sai: Saigon

SAI: Schizophrenics Anonymous International; South African Irish (regiment)

said.: speech auto-instructional device

SAIF: South African Industrial Federation

SAIL: Sea-Air Interaction Laboratory

SAILS: Simplified Aircraft Instrument Landing System

SAIMR: South African Institute for Medical Research

SAIMS: Selected Acquisition Information and Management System

SAIRR: South African Institute of Race Relations

SAIS: School of Advanced International Studies

SAJ: Society for the Advancement of Judaism

SAJC: Southern Association of Junior Colleges

sa ji: saw jig

SAK: *Suomen Ammattilittojen Keskuslitto* (Finnish—Finnish Trade Union Confederation)

Saki: Hector Hugh Munro

sal: salt; salicylate; saloon

s.a.l.: *secundum artis leges* (Latin —according to the rules of art)

Sal: Salamanca; Salaverry; Salem; Salomon

Sal: *salida* (Spanish—departure; exit)

SAL: San Salvador, El Salvador (airport); Seaboard Airline Railroad; Svenska-Amerika Linien (Swedish-America Line)

SALA: Scientific Assistant Land Agent; Southwest Alliance for Latin America(ns)

salam: salamanzar (12-bottle capacity)

sal ammoniac: ammonium chloride (NH_4Cl)

sale.: simple algebraic language for engineers

sal gal: saloon girl

Sallie: Sarah

Sally: Sara(h); South Atlantic (baseball) League (nickname)

Sally Ann: Salvation Army (hobo abbreviation)

salm: salmonella

Salm: Salamon

SALM: Society of Airline Meteorologists

salmiak: sal ammoniac (ammonium chloride)

Salop(ian): Shrewsbury; Shropshire

salt: sodium chloride (NaCl)

SALT: Strategic Arms Limitation Talks (begun in Helsinki between US and USSR on Novem-

ber 17, 1969)

salut: salutation; sea-air-land-and-underwater targets (SALUT)

salv: salvage

Salv: Salvador

Salv Army: Salvation Army

sam: surface-to-air missile (SAM); synchronous amplitude modulation

sam: *samedi* (French—Saturday)

Sam: Samoa; Samoan; Samson; Samoyed; Samuel; Samuelito

Sam: *Samstag* (German—Saturday)

SAM: School of Aerospace Medicine; Society for the Advancement of Management; Society of American Magicians; Special Air Mission

SAMA: Sacramento Air Materiel Area; Scientific Apparatus Makers Association; Student American Medical Association

samar: (Mongolian—path; route)

SAMB: School of Aviation Medicine—Brooks AFB

SAMBA: Special Agents Mutual Benefit Association (FBI); Systems Approach to Managing Bureau of Ships Acquisitions (USN)

SAMC: South African Marine Corporation; South African Medical Corps

SAM/CAR: South America/Caribbean

SAME: Society of American Military Engineers

Saml: Samiel; Samuel

SAMLA: South Atlantic Modern Language Association

Samml: *Sammlung* (German—collection)

Sammy: American soldier (British slang); Samuel

SAMNS: South African Military Nursing Service

samos (SAMOS): satellite and missile observation system

SAMPE: Society of Aerospace Material and Process Engineers

SAM-SAC: Special Aircraft Modification for Strategic Air Command

SAM/SAT: South America/South Atlantic

SAMSO: Space and Missile Systems Organization (USAF)

SAM/SPAC: South America/South Pacific

SAMTEC: Space and Missile Test Center

SA Mus: South African Museum (Cape Town)

san: (Chinese or Japanese—hill; mountain, as in Fujisan); (Japanese—Miss; Mister; Missus)

SAN: San Diego, California (Lindbergh Field); South African Navy

SAN: *Space Age News*

SANA: State (Department), Army, Navy, Air (Force)

Sanc.: *Sanctus* (Latin—holy)

SANCAR: South African National Council for Antarctic Research

San Carlo: Teatro di San Carlo—Naples' opera house

SANCOB: South African Foundation for the Conservation of Birds

sand: silicon dioxide—SiO_2

Sand: *Sandford's New York Reports*

SAND: Sampling Aerospace Nuclear Debris

SANDA: Supplies and Accounts

Sandra: Alessandra

Sandro: Alessandro

Sandy: (nickname—San Diego, California; Sandra; Sandro; Saundra; a Scotsman)

sane.: severe acoustic noise environment

SANE: National Committee for a Sane Nuclear Policy

Sa Nev: Sierra Nevada(s)

San Fran: San Francisco

sanit: sanitary; sanitation; sanitize

sanka: sans kaffeine (coffee without caffeine)

San Martín: José de San Martín —patriot-soldier who fought to liberate Argentina, Chile, and Peru from Spanish rule

sanr: subject to approval—no risks

Sansan: San Diego to San Francisco (city complex)

Sansk: Sanskrit

Sant: Santander; Santiago

SANTA: South African National Tuberculosis Association; Souvenir and Novelty Trade Association

SANTAS: Send A Note To A Serviceman

Santa ships: Grace Line vessels —all names begin with Santa: *Santa Clara, Santa Magdalena, Santa Teresa,* etc.

SANWR: Santa Ana National Wildlife Refuge (Texas)

SAO: São Paulo, Brazil (airport); Smithsonian Astrophysical Observatory

sap: saphead

sap.: soon as possible

s ap: scruple, apothecaries'

SAP: San Pedro Sula, Honduras (airport); South African Police

SA y P: San Andres y Providencia (Spanish—San Andres and Providence Island Intendancy)

SAPA: South African Press Association

SAPAT: South African Picture Analysis Test

SAPE: Society for Automation in Professional Education

SAPF: South African Police Force

SAPL: San Antonio Public Library; South African Public Library

sapon: saponification; saponify

SAPRI: South African Pain Research Institute

sar: search and rescue; semiautomatic rifle; submarine advanced reactor

Sar: Saracen; Saracenic; Sardinia; Sardinian

SAR: Society of Authors' Representatives; Solar Aircraft (company); Sons of the American Revolution; South African Railways; South African Republic; South Australian Railways

SARAH: Search and Rescue and Homing (radio lifesaving beacon)

Saraw: Sarawak

SARB: South African Reserve Bank

sarcol: sarcological; sarcologist; sarcology

SARD: Special Airlift Requirement Directive

sare: self-addressed return envelope

sarge: sergeant

SAR & H: South African Railways and Harbours

SARHA: South African Railways, Harbours, and Airways

SARLANT: Search-and-Rescue, Atlantic

Sarmiento: Domingo Faustino Sarmiento—Argentinian educator and early president hostile to dictatorship

SARPAC: Search-and-Rescue, Pacific

SART: St Alban's Repertory Theater

sartac: search radar device

sartel: search and rescue telephone

Sarum: Salisbury

sas (SAS): supersonic attack seaplane

SAs: Special Agents (FBI)

SAS: Scandinavian Airlines System

SASBO: Southeastern Association of School Business Officials

SASC: South African Staff Corps

SASCOM: Special Ammunition Support Command (USA)

Sask: Saskatchewan

SASI: Society of Air Safety Investigators

SASIDS: Stochastic Adaptive Sequential Information Dissemina-

tion System

SASL: South American Saint Line

SASO: San Antonio Symphony Orchestra; South Australia Symphony Orchestra

SASOL: South African Coal, Oil, and Gas Corporation

SASS: San Antonio Symphony Society

SASSY: Supported Activity Supply System

SAST: Society for the Advancement of Space Travel

sat.: satisfactory; saturate

Sat: Satan; Satanic; Saturday; Saturn

SAT: San Antonio, Texas (airport); Scholastic Aptitude Test; School of Applied Tactics; Specific Aptitude Test

SATA: Sociedade Açoriana de Transportes Aéreos (Azores Air Transport Line)

SATAF: Site Activation Task Force

satan: satellite automatic tracking antenna; sensor for airborne terrain analysis

satanas: semi-automatic analog setting

satar (SATAR): satellite for aerospace research

satb (SATB): soprano, alto, tenor, bass

SATC: South African Tourist Corporation

Satchmo: Satchel-Mouth—Louis Armstrong's truncated nickname

satco: signal automatic air traffic control

satcom: satellite communication

SATCOM: Satellite Communications Agency (US Army)

satd: saturated

satel: satellite

SATENA: Servicio Aeronavegación a Territorios Nacionales (Bogotá)

SatEvePost: *Saturday Evening Post*

satfy: satisfactory

SATGA: Société Aérienne des Transports Guyane Antilles

SAtk: strike attack

S Atl Cur: South Atlantic Current

satn: saturation

SATO: South American Travel Organization; Southern Africa Treaty Organization

SATOUR: South African Tourist Corporation

Sat Rev: *Saturday Review*

sats (SATS): short airfield for tactical support

SATs: Scholastic Aptitude Tests

sat sol: saturated solution

SATU: South African Typographical Union

Sau: Saudi Arabia

SAUCERS: Saucer and Unexplained Celestial Events Research Society

sav: savings; stock at valuation

Sav: Savannah

SAV: Savannah, Georgia (airport)

SAVE: Service Activities of Volunteer Engineers; Society of American Value Engineers; Stop Addiction through Voluntary Effort; Student Action Voters for Ecology

savor: single-actuated voice recorder

SAW: Special Air Warfare

Sawbuck: Sears-Roebuck

SAWE: Society of Aeronautical Weight Engineers

SAWF: Special Air Warfare Force

SAWG: Special Air Warfare Center

Sawney: (nickname—a Scotsman)

SAWS: Small Arms Weapons Study

SAWTRI: South African Wool Textile Research Institute

sax: saxophone

Sax: Saxon

SAY: Salisbury, Rhodesia (airport)

Saybolt: viscosity number

SAZF: South African Zionist Federation

sb: simultaneous broadcast(ing); single-bayonet (lamp base); single-breasted (coat or jacket); small business; smooth bore; solid body; southbound; special bibliography; stove bolt; stretcher bearer; subbituminous; submarine (fog) bell; switchboard

sb: *styrbord* (Swedish—starboard); right side of an airplane or vessel looking forward, from Viking steering board or steering oar on right side of their long boats)

s/b: should be; surface based

Sb: *stibium* (Latin—antimony)

SB: Savings Bank; scouting-bombing (aircraft); Seaboard World Airlines (2-letter coding); Secondary Battery; Section Base; Selection Board; Senate Bill; Service Bulletin; shipbuilding; Signal Battalion; Signal Boatswain; South Buffalo (railroad); Standard Brands (stock exchange symbol); Stanford-Binet (intelligence test); Submarine Base

S.B.: *Scientiae Baccalaureus* (Latin—Bachelor of Science)

SB: *Sitzungsbericht* (German—proceeding)

S & B: sterilization and bath

SBA: School of Business Administration; Small Business Ad-

ministration
SBAC: Society of British Aerospace Companies
sbae: stabilized bombing approach equipment
S-bahn: *Stadt-Schnellbahn* (German—State Rapid Transit)—Berlin's electric railway system
SBAMA: San Bernardino Air Materiel Area
S-band: 1550–5200 mc
SBAW: Santa Barbara Academy of the West
SBAs: Sick Bay Attendants
Sbb.: *Sabbatum* (Latin—Sunday)
SBB: Schweizerische Bundesbahnen (Swiss Federal Railways)
SBC: Service Bureau Corporation; Surinam Bauxite Company
SBCC: Santa Barbara City College
SBCR: Stock Balance Consumption Report
sbdt: surface-barrier diffused transistor
sbe: soft-boiled egg(s); subacute bacterial endocarditis
SBE: State Board of Equalization
SBEA: Southern Business Education Association
sbfc: standby for further clearance
Sbg: Solvesborg
sbic's: small business investment companies
sbis (SBIS): satellite-based interceptor systems
SBL: Stephen B(utler) Leacock
sbm: submission; submit
SBM: Société Anonymes des Bains de Mer et du Cercle des Etrangers à Monaco (company managing gambling casino of Monte Carlo)
SBMA: Santa Barbara Museum of Art
SBME: Society of Business Magazine Editors; State Board of Medical Examiners
SBMI: School Bus Manufacturers Institute
sbn: standard book number(ing)
Sbn: Sebastián (Spanish—Sebastian)
SBN: South Bend, Indiana (airport)
SBNS: Society of British Neurological Surgeons
sbo: secure base of operations
Sbo: Sasebo
sbom: soy bean oil meal
sbp: slotted-blade propeller
sbr: styrene-butadiene rubber
SBRC: Santa Barbara Research Center
sbre: *septiembre* (Spanish—September)
SBRI: Simon Baruch Research Institute

sbs: surveyed before shipment
sb's: sonic booms
SBS: Swiss Broadcasting Society
SBSA: Standard Bank of South Africa
SBSUSA: Sport Balloon Society of the United States
sbtg: sabotage
SBW: Seaboard & Western (Airlines); single-engine scout bomber (3-letter naval symbol)
SBWR: Seal Beach Wildlife Refuge (near Long Beach, California); South Bay Wildlife Refuge (south end of San Francisco Bay)
sbx: S-band transponder
SBX: Student Book Exchange
sby: standby
sc: sad case (slang—unpopular person); same case; separate cover; shaped charge; single circuit; single contact; sized and calendered; slow cool; small caps (small capital letters); smooth contour; statistical control; supercycle; superimposed current
s & c: shipper and carrier; sized and calendered
s/c: short circuit (electrical); single-column (bookkeeping)
sc.: *scilicet* (Latin—mainly)
s/c: *su cuenta* (Spanish—your account)
Sc: scandium; stratocumulus
SC: Sacra Congregatio (Sacred Congregation); Sacramento City; Salem College; Sandia Corporation; Sanitary Corps; Scripps College; Seamen's Center; Security Council (United Nations); Service Club; Service Command; Shasta College; Shaw College; Shell Transport; Shelton College; Shenandoah College; Shepherd College; Sheridan College; Shimer College; Ship's Cook; Shorter College; Siena College; Sierra College; Signal Corps; Simmons College; Simpson College; Sinclair College; Skidmore College; Smith College; South Carolina; South Carolinian; Southern California; Southern Californian; Southern Conference; Southwestern College; Spelman College; Springfield College; Staff College; Staff Corps; Stephens College; Sterling College; Stockton College; Stonehill College; Stratford College; Strike Command; submarine chaser; Sullins College; Summary Court; Sumter & Choctaw (rail-

road); Suomi College; Supply Corps; Support Command; Supreme Court; Swarthmore College; Systems Command
S-C: Serbian-Croatian (people); Serbo-Croat (language); Stromberg-Carlson
S en C: *Sociedad en Comandita* (Spanish—limited partnership)—silent partnership
S/C: Star & Crescent (excursion steamer, ferry, towing, water-taxi service)
SCA: Schipperke Club of America; School and College Ability (test); Science Clubs of America; Screen Composers Association; Senior Citizens of America; Shipbuilders Council of America; Soybean Council of America; Stock Company Association; Sub-Contract Authorization; Suez Canal Authority; Svenska Cellulose AB; Switzerland Cheese Association; Synagogue Council of America
scad: schedule, capability, availability, dependability
SCAD: State Commission Against Discrimination (New York)
SCADS: Sioux City Air Defense Sector
SCAG: Southern California Association of Governments; Supplier Corrective Action Group
sc al: steel-cored aluminum
scama (SCAMA): switching, conferencing, and monitoring arrangement
scan.: self-correcting automatic navigation; switched-circuit automatic network
Scan: Scandinavia; Scandinavian
SCAN: Scheduling and Control by Automated Network; Selected Current Aerospace Notices (NASA-computerized dissemination of information); Self-Correcting Automatic Navigator; Switched-Circuit Automatic Network
SCANCAP: System for Comparative Analysis of Community Action Programs
Scand: Scandinavia; Scandinavian
ScanDoc: Scandinavian Documentation Center
SCANPED: System for Comparative Analysis of Programs of Educational Development
SCANs: Southern California Answering Networks (cooperative library information-retrieval system)
scap: scapula; scapular; scapuloid

SCAP: Supreme Commander, Allied Powers

SCAPA: Society for Checking the Abuses of Public Advertising

'scape: escape(ment); landscape; seascape; skyscape

scaphocephs: scaphocephalics (narrow-skulled people)

s caps: small capital letters

scar.: subcaliber aircraft rocket; submarine celestial altitude recorder

SCAR: Scandinavian Council for Applied Research; Scientific Committee for Antarctic Research

scard: signal conditioning and recording device

SCARF: Special Committee on the Adequacy of Range Facilities

scarp: escarpment

scat. (SCAT): speed-control attitude range; supersonic commercial air transport

scat.: scatula (Latin—box)

SCAT: School and College Ability Test; Service Command Air Transportation (USN)

scata: survival sited casualty treatment assemblage

SCATANA: Security Control of Air Traffic and Air Navigational Aids

SCATE: Stromberg-Carlson automatic test equipment

scat. orig.: scatula originalis (Latin—original box or package)

scat's: supersonic commercial air transports

SCATs: Southern California Acrobatic Teams

SCATS: Simulation, Checkout, and Training System

scav: scavenge

scb: strictly confined to bed (q.v. fob)

sc b: screw base (lamp)

Sc.B.: Scientia Baccalaureus (Latin—Bachelor of Science)

SCB: Sawyer College of Business

SCBA: Southern California Booksellers Association

SCC: Shoreline Community College; Sitka Community College; Society of Cosmetic Chemists; Spokane Community College; Standard Commodity Classification; Stromberg-Carlson Corporation

SCCA: Southeastern Cottonseed Crushers Association; Sports Car Club of America

SCCC: Suffolk County Community College; Sullivan County Community College

scert: sub-zero cooled, cold-rolled, and tempered

scd: screen door; screwed; service computation date; standard change dispenser

Sc.D.: Scientiae Doctor (Latin—Doctor of Science)

SCD: Specification Control Drawing

SCDL: Scientific Crime Detection Laboratory

sce: situationally caused error; standard calomel electrode

SCE: Schedule Compliance Evaluation; Southern California Edison

SCEI: Safe Car Educational Institute

SCEL: Signal Corps Engineering Laboratories

SCF: Save the Children Federation; Stephen Collins Foster

SCFA: Southern California Fishermen's Association

sc f & a: screw forward and aft

scfh: standard cubic feet per hour

scfm: standard cubic feet per minute

scfs: standard cubic feet per second

SCG: Society of the Classic Guitar

SCGC: Southern California Gas Company; Southern Counties Gas Company

SCGR: Sale Common Game Refuge (Victoria, Australia)

sch: school

Sch: Schiedam

SCHAVMED: School of Aviation Medicine (USN)

Schbg: Schönberg

sched: schedule

schem: schematic

Schen: Schenectady

scherz: scherzando (Italian—jesting; in a sportive manner)

schizo: schizoid; schizophasia; schizophrenia; schizophrenic

SCHLA: School of Latin America

schlem: schlemiel (Yiddish—person afflicted with bad luck)

schlemazl: (victim of a schlemiel)

Schloss: (German—castle; fortress)

schm: schematic

Sch M: School Master

Schmarg: Schmargendorf

Sch Mist: School Mistress

schmoo: space cargo handler and manipulator for orbital operations

Schnozzola: Jimmy Durante

schr: schooner

Schr: Schriften (German—publication; script; text; writing)

Schupo: Schutzpolizei (German—defense police used as a paramilitary force by Hitler)

sci: science; scientific; scientist

SCI: Seamen's Church Institute; Shipping Container Institute; Shipping Corporation of India; Simulation Councils Incorporated; Society of the Chemical Industry; Sponge and Chamois Institute; Supervisory Cost Inspector

SCI: Science Citation Index

SCIA: Signal Corps Intelligence Agency

Sci D: Doctor of Science

Sci D Com: Doctor of Science in Commerce

Sci D Met: Doctor of Science in Metallurgy

sci-fi: science-fiction

scim: standard cubic inches per minute

Sci M: Science Master

Sci Mist: Science Mistress

scinti: scintillate; scintillation

scioneer: scientist + engineer

SCIPA: Servicio Cooperativo Interamericano de Producción de Alimentos (Interamerican Cooperative Service for the Production of Food)

SCI & RB: South Carolina Inspection and Rating Bureau

SCITEC: Association of the Scientific, Engineering, and Technological Community of Canada

SCI(s): Success Motivation Institutes

SCISP: Servicio Cooperativo Interamericano de Salud Pública (Interamerican Cooperative Public Health Service)

scl: space charge limited

SCL: Santiago, Chile (airport); Scottish Central Library; Seaboard Coast Line; Southeastern Composers' League; Southern Composers' League; Springfield City Library

SCLC: Southern Christian Leadership Conference

SCM: Section Communication Manager; Smith-Corona-Marchant; Special Court-Martial; Summary Court-Martial

SCMA: Southern Cypress Manufacturers Association

Scn: Scunthorpe

SCNAWAF: Special Category Navy with Air Force

SCNM: Sunset Crater National Monument (Arizona)

SCNR: Scientific Committee of National Representatives (NATO)

scns: self-contained navigation system

SCNUL: Standing Conference of National and University Libraries (UK)

SCNVYO: Standing Conference of

National Voluntary Youth Organisations (UK)

SCNWR: Squaw Creek National Wildlife Refuge (Missouri)

sco: subcarrier oscillator; sustainer cutoff

ScO: Scientific Officer

SCO: Statistical Control Office(r)

scoda: scan coherent doppler attachment

scond: semiconductor

scoop.: scientific computation of optimum procurement

scop (SCOP): single copy order plan

scope: microscope; oscilloscope; telescope

SCOPE: Selected Contents of Periodicals for Educators; School-to-College Opportunity for Post high-school Education; Simple Checkout-Oriented Program Language; Special Committee on Problems of the Environment (ICSU); Student Council on Pollution and Environment

Scor: Scorpio

SCOR: Scientific Committee on Oceanographic Research

score.: signal communications by orbiting relay equipment

SCORE: Service Corps of Retired Executives

scot: steel car of tomorrow

Scot: Scotland; Scottish

ScotGael: Scots Gaelic

ScotNats: Scottish Nationalists

Scourge of God: Attila's nickname

scp: spherical candlepower

SCP: Social Credit Party; Survey Control Point

SCP (AFL-CIO): Sleeping Car Porters

SCPA: South Carolina Ports Authority

SCPE: State Committee on Public Education

SCPI: Structural Clay Products Institute

SCPL: Social Credit Political League (New Zealand party)

SCPN: Society of Certified Professional Numismatists

SCPO: Senior Chief Petty Officer

SCPR: Scottish Council of Physical Recreation

SCPt: security control point

SCQ: Coastal Sentry (tracking station vessel—naval symbol)

scr: screw; scruple; silicon-controlled rectifier

SCR: Signal Corps Radio; Standardized Casualty Rate

SCRA: Southern California Restaurant Association; Stanford Center for Radar Astronomy

scram: self-contained radiation monitor

scrap.: simple-complex reaction-time apparatus

SCRAP: Society for Completely Removing All Parking (Meters); Students Challenging Regulatory Agency Proceedings

scr bh: screen bulkhead

SCR brick: Structural Clay Research brick

SCRC: Southern California Research Council

SCREAMS: Society to Create Rapprochement among Electrical, Aeronautical, and Mechanical Engineers

SCRF: Scripps Clinic and Research Foundation

scrim: scrimmage

script: manuscript; prescription

Script: Scriptural; Scripture

SCRIS: Southern California Regional Information Study (Bureau of the Census)

scr's: silicon-controlled rectifiers

SCRTD: Southern California Rapid Transit District

Scrtrt: the Secretariat (UN)

scrum: scrummage

scs: satellite control system; secret cover sheet; space command station; stabilization control system

sc & s: strapped, corded, and sealed

SCS: Society of Civil Servants; Society of Clinical Surgery; Soil Conservation Service

SCSA: Soil Conservation Society of America; Southern California Symphony Association

SCSBM: Society for Computer Science in Biology and Medicine

SCSC: South Carolina State College

sct: structural clay tile; sub-zero cooled and tempered

SCTE: Society of Cable Television Engineers

sctl: short-circuited transmission line

sct's: sugar-coated tablets

SCTS: Sycamore Canyon Test Site (Convair)

Sctsmn: The Scotsman (Edinburgh)

scty: security

SCU: Special Care Unit

scuba: self-contained underwater breathing apparatus

scubasub: scuba-diver's submarine; scuba-diver's submersible

sculp: sculptor; sculpture

sculp.: sculpsit (Latin—he carved or engraved it)

SCUM: Society (for) Cutting Up Men

scup: scupper

S-curve: S-shaped curve

SCUS: Supreme Court of the United States

'scutcheon: escutcheon

scv: single concave

s-c-v: single-capsulated-virulent (bacteria)

SCV: Santa Città Vaticana (Italian—Holy Vatican City)—but Roman wiseacres insist SCV means Se Cristo Vedesse (If Christ could see!)

s & cv: stop and check valve

scvtr: scan-converting video tape recorder

SCW: State College of Washington

SCWC: Special Commission on Weather Modification

scwr (SCWR): supercritical water reactor

SCWS: Scottish Co-operative Wholesale Society

scx: single convex

S Cz: Salina Cruz

sd: second defense (lacrosse); self-destroying; semidiameter; shell-destroying; sight draft; single deck; sound; special duty; stage door; standard deviation; storm detection; system demonstration; systolic discharge

sd: siehe dies (German—see this)

s.d.: sine die (Latin—without date)

s-d: slow-drying

s/d: sea-damaged

s & d: search and destroy; song and dance

sD: samme Dato (Danish—same date)

Sd: Sound

Sd.£: Sudanese pound (currency unit)

SD: San Diegan; San Diego; Secretary of Defense; Senior Deacon; snare drum; Specification for Design; Spectacle Dispenser (oculist); Standard Oil Company of California (stock exchange symbol); State Department; Superintendent of Documents; Supply Depot

SD: Social(ist) Democrat(ic) (party); Stronnictwo Demokratyczne (Polish—Democratic Party)

sda: source data automation; specific dynamic action

SDA: Seventh Day Adventist; Soap and Detergent Association; Source Data Automation; Students for Democratic Action

SD & AE RR: San Diego & Arizona Eastern Railroad

S Dak: South Dakota; South Dako-

tan
SDAM: San Diego Aerospace Museum
sdbl: sight draft bill of lading
sd bl: sandblast
SDBRI: San Diego Biomedical Research Institute
sdc: shipment detail card; single drift connection; submersible decompression chamber
SDC: Southern Defense Command; Special Devices Center; State Defense Council; Strategic Defense Command; Support Design Change
SDCC: San Diego City College
SDCE: Society of Die Casting Engineers
SDCMD: San Diego Contract Management District
SD Co: San Diego County
SDCS: San Diego City Schools
sdd: store-door delivery
SDD: System Definition Directive
sde: self-disinfecting elastomer; simple designational expression
SDEA: South Dakota Education Association
SDEC: San Diego Ecology Center; San Diego Engineering Council; San Diego Evening College
SDECE: Service de la Documentation Extérieure et du Contre-Espionnage (French equivalent of American CIA)
SDEE: Société de la Diffusion d'Equipements Électroniques
sdf: single-degree-of-freedom (gyroscope)
SDF: Louisville, Kentucky (airport)
sdg: siding
SDG: Self-Development Group
SDG & E: San Diego Gas & Electric
sdi: selective dissemination of information
SDI: Saudi Arabian Airlines
S Diego: San Diego
SDJC: San Diego Junior Colleges
sdk: shelter deck
sdl: saddle
SDMC: San Diego Mesa College
SDMICC: State Defense Military Information Control Committee
sdml: seaward defense motor launch
SDMM: San Diego Museum of Man
SDMS: San Diego Memorial Society
SDN: System Designation Number
SDNHM: San Diego Natural History Museum
SDO: Santo Domingo
S Doc: Senate Document
SDOG: San Diego Opera Guild

SDP: *Sozialdemokratische Partei Deutschlands* (Germany's Social-Democratic Party)
SDPL: San Diego Public Library
SDQ: Santo Domingo, Dominican Republic (airport)
sdr: scientific data recorder; self-decoding readout; simple detection response; sodium deuterium reactor; sonar data recorder; splash-detection radar; strip domain resonance; successive discrimination reversal
SdRng: sound ranging
sds: speech discrimination score; sudden death syndrome
SDS: Scientific Data Systems; Samuel De Sola; Solomon De Sola; Sons and Daughters of the Soddies; Special District Services; Students for a Democratic Society (united front of communists and leftist socialists)
SDSC: San Diego State College; San Diego Steamship Company
SDSMT: South Dakota School of Mines and Technology
SDSNH: San Diego Society of Natural History
SDSO: San Diego Symphony Orchestra
SDSU: San Diego State University
sdt: scientific distribution technique; sea depth transducer; serial data transmission; source distribution technique; surveillance data transmission
SDTD: San Diego Transit District
sdtdl: saturating drift transistor diode logic
sdu: shelter decontamination unit; signal display unit; spectrum display unit; subcarrier display unit
SDU: Rio de Janeiro, Brazil (Santos Dumont Airport)
SDU: *San Diego Union*
SDUPD: San Diego Unified Port District
SDUSD: San Diego Unified School District
sdv: slowed-down video; swimmer delivery vehicle
sdw: swept delta wing
SDX: Stromberg DatagraphiX; Sunray Mid-Continent Oil Company
SDZ: San Diego Zoo
se: second entrance; semiannual; single end; single-ended; single engine; single entry; special equipment; spherical equivalent; standard error; straight edge
s/e: standardization/evaluation
Se: selenium
SE: Sanford & Eastern (railroad);

Sanitary Engineer(ing); Servel (stock exchange symbol); Southeast; Stock Exchange; Student Engineer
Sea: (Port of) Seattle
SEA: Safety Equipment Association; Seattle, Washington (Seattle-Tacoma Airport); Ships Editorial Association; Society for Education through Art; Southeast Airlines; Southeast Asia; Southern Economic Association; Special Equipment Authorization; Subterranean Exploration Agency
SEA: Students for Ecological Action
Seabees: Construction Battalion (USN)
seac: standards electronic automatic computer
seacel: silver-chloride/magnesium cell (battery)
SEACOM: South East Asia Commonwealth Cable
seacon: seafloor construction
SEADAG: Southeast Asia Development Advisory Group
Sea Devil: Felix Count von Luckner
SEADS: Seattle Air Defense Sector
Sea-green Incorruptible: Carlyle's nickname for Robespierre
sealab: sea laboratory (underwater research vessel)
SEALS: Sea-Air-Land Forces (counterinsurgents)
seamount: sea mountain
searam: semi-active radar missile
SEARS: Sears, Roebuck
seascarp: undersea escarpment
SEAT: *Sociedad Español de Automoviles de Turismo* (Spanish—Spanish Society of Touring Automobiles) — manufacturer's name
Seatac: Seattle-Tacoma (area)
seatainer(s): seagoing container(s) —theftproof steel containers for overseas cargo
Seatl: Seattle
SEATO: Southeast Asia Treaty Organization
sea water: 96.4% water plus 2.8% sodium chloride (common salt) and smaller quantities of magnesium chloride, magnesium sulfate, calcium sulfate, and potassium chloride; in inland seas such as the Dead Sea and the Salton Sea these percentages vary
seb: static error band
S & EBC: Ship and Engine Building Company
sebkha: (Arabic—marsh)
SEBM: Society of Experimental

Biology and Medicine
sec: secant; second; secondary; secret; section; security
Sec: Secretary
SEC: Section Emergency Coordinator; Securities and Exchange Commission; Supreme Economic Council (USSR)
SecA: Secretary of the Army
SECA: Southern Educational Communications Association
SECAM: *Séquentiel à Mémoire* (French—sequence and memory color television system)
secar: secondary radar
secd: second
SECDA: Southeastern Community Development Association
SECDEF: Secretary of Defense
secesh: secessionist
SECNAV: Secretary of the Navy
seco: second-stage engine cutoff; sustainer engine cutoff
secor (SECOR): sequential collation of range
secr: secret
secret³: *secretaria* (Spanish—secretariat)
secs: secants; seconds
sec's: soft elastic capsules
sect: section; sector
Section 8: mental case (military code)
Secty: Secretary
SECUS: Sex Education Council of the United States
sed: sedative
sed.: *sedes* (Latin—a chair; a stool)
SED: Scientific Equipment Division (Westinghouse)
SED: *Sozialistische Einheitspartei Deutschlands* (Germany's Socialist Unity Party)—Soviet-oriented East German Party
sedar: submerged electrode detection and ranging
SEDEIS: Société d'Études et de Documentation Économiques, Industrielles et Sociales (Paris)
sedi: sediment(ation)
sedi time: sedimentation time
see.: secondary electron emission; survival, evasion, and escape; systems efficiency expert(ise)
See: (German—lake; sea, as in Bodensee)
SEE: Society of Environmental Engineers
SEEB: Southeastern Electricity Board (UK)
SEED: Skills Escalation and Employment Development; Special Elementary Education (for the underdeveloped)
SEEJ: *Slavic and East European Journal*

SEEK: Search for Elevation and Educational Knowledge (NY State dropout program); Systems Evaluation and Exchange of Knowledge
Seekers: (truth-seeking Quakers)
seer.: submarine explosive echo ranging
SEER: System for Electronic Evaluation and Retrieval
seex: systems evaluation experiment
sef: small end first
SEF: Space Education Foundation
seg: segment; segmentation; segmented; segments; segregate; segrated; segregation; segregationist
seg.: *segno* (Italian—sign)
Seg: Segovia
SEG: Society of Economic Geologists; Systems Engineering Group
SEGB: South Eastern Gas Board
SEH: St. Elizabeth's Hospital
seha: specific emotional hazards of adulthood
sehc: specific emotional hazards of childhood
sei: (Japanese—west)
SEI: Scientific Engineering Institute
SEIC: Solar Energy Information Center; System Effectiveness Information Center
seis: seismograph; seismography; seismology; submarine emergency identification signal (SEIS)
SEISA: South Eastern Intercollegiate Sailing Association
Seiscor: Seismograph Service Corporation
seismol: seismology
sel: selectee; selector
SEL: Seoul, Korea (airport); Signal Engineering Laboratories; Stanford Electronics Laboratories
SELA: Southeastern Library Association
SELC: South Eastern Louisiana College
sel-cl: self-closing
selen: selenography; selenology
self-prop: self-propelled
Selk: Selkirk
SELMA: S.E.L. Maduro
sels: selsyn
selsyn: self-synchronous
SEly: southeasterly
sem: scanning electron microcope; semicolon; slow eye movements
sem.: *semen* (Latin—seed); *semper* (Latin—always; ever)
Sem: Seminary; Semitic
SEM: Society for Ethno-Musicology

seman: semantic(s)
semcor: semantic correlation
semicol: semicolon
semidr.: *semidrachma* (Latin—half drachma)
semidur: semiduration
semih.: *semihora* (Latin—half hour)
semipro: semiprofessional(ly)
semis: semifinished; semitrailers
sems: screw and washer assemblies
SEMT: Société d'Études des Machines Thermiques (Society for the Study of Thermal Machines)
sem ves: seminal vesicle
Sen: Senate; Senator
Sen Doc: Senate Document
Seneg: Senegal; Senegalese
Sen Rept: Senate Report
sensistor: semiconductor resistor
Sent: *Sentyabr* (Russian—September)
Seo: Seoul
SEO: Senior Experimental Officer
SEODSE: Special Explosive Ordnance Disposal Supplies and Equipment (USA)
seou: *salve error u omisión* (Spanish—except for error or omission)
sep: separate; separation
Sep: September
SEP: Selective Employment Payments (UK); Society of Engineering Psychologists; Society of Experimental Psychologists; Student Expense Program
SEPA: Southeastern Power Association
separ.: *separatum* (Latin—separately)
SEPE: Seattle Port of Embarkation
Seph: *Sephardi* (Hebrew—Jews from Portugal and Spain)
SEPO: Space Electric Power Office (AEC)
SEPR: Société pour l'Étude de la Propulsion par Réaction
SepRos: separation processing
SEPSA: Society of Educational Programmers and Systems Analysts
sept.: *septem* (Latin—seven)
Sept: September
SEPTA: Southeastern Pennsylvania Transportation Authority
septᵉ: *septiembre* (Spanish—September)
septel: separate telegram
Septober: September and October
seq: sequence
seq. luce: *sequenti luce* (Latin—the following day)
Seq NP: Sequoia National Park
S Equ Cur: South Equatorial Current

ser: serial; series

ser: *serie* (French—series)

ser (SER): serine (amino acid)

SER: Soil Erosion Service

SERA: Services, Education, Rehabilitation for Addiction

Serb: Serbia; Serbian

SEREB: Société pour l'Étude et la Réalisation d'Engins Balistiques

SERL: Services Electronics Research Laboratory

serm: sermon

SERM: Society of Early Recorded Music

serol: serology

SERPAC: Service Forces, Pacific (USN)

SERPLANT: Service Forces, Atlantic (USN)

serr: serrate

serra: (Italian—mountain range)

serranía: (Spanish—mountainous region)

sert: space electronic rocket test

serv: service

serv.: *serva* (Latin—keep; preserve)

Serv: Servia(n)

serv clg: service ceiling

SERVE: Serve and Enrich Retirement by Volunteer Experience

servo: anything using a servomechanism; servoamplifier, servocontrol, servodyne, servomotor, servosystem

serv^o: *servicio* (Spanish—service)

serv^{or}: *servidor* (Spanish—servant)

servos: servomechanisms

ses: secondary engine start; single-ended scotch boilers; socioeconomic strata; solar environment simulator

SES: Society of Engineering Science; Solar Energy Society; Standards Engineers Society; State Employment Service; Steam Engine Systems

SESA: Society for Experimental Stress Analysis

SESAC: Society of European Stage Authors and Composers

SESAME: Search for Excellence in Science and Mathematics Education

SESL: Space Environment Simulation Laboratory

sesoc: surface-effects ship for ocean commerce

sesquih.: *sesquihora* (Latin—an hour and a half)

sess: session

SESS: Space Environmental Support System; Summer Employment for Science Students

set.: settlement

set: *setembro* (Portuguese—September)

SET: Scientists, Engineers, Technicians; Security Escort Team; Senior Electronic Technician; Simplified Engineering Technique; Synchro Error Tester

SETAF: Southern European Task Force

set^e: *septiembre* (Spanish—September)

SETIL: Société de l'Équipment de Tahiti et des Iles (Equipment Company of Tahiti and the Islands)

seto: (Japanese—channel; strait)

SETP: Society of Experimental Test Pilots

sett: settling

sett: *settembre* (Italian—September)

settentrionale: (Italian—northern)

SEU: Southeastern University

SEUA: South Eastern Underwriters Association

SEUS: Southeastern United States

sev: sever

sev: *sever* (Russian—north)

Sev: Sevilla; Seville

Seven Deadly Sins: Anger, Covetousness, Envy, Gluttony, Lust, Pride, Sloth

severnaya: (Russian—north)

sevocom: secure voice communications

sew.: sewage; sewer; sewerage

SEWT: Simulator for Electronic Warfare Training

sex.: sextet; sexual

SExO: Senior Experimental Officer

sexpert: sex expert; sexual expert; sexpertise

sexploitation: sex(ual) exploitation

sext: sextant

sf: safety factor; salt free; science fiction; semifinished; single-feed; single feeder; sinking fund; sound and flash; special facilities; spinal fluid; spotface; standard form; stress formula; sulphation factor; sunkface

sf: *sans frais* (French—without expense); *sforzando* (Italian—accented strongly; forced; reinforced)

s.f.: *sub finem* (Latin—near the end)

SF: San Franciscan; San Francisco; Santa Fe, New Mexico; Santa Fe (Atchison, Topeka & Santa Fe Railway); Scouting Force; Security Force; Security Forces; Shipfitter; Special Facilities; Special Forces; Standard Frequency; Swedenborg Foundation; Swiss Federation (auto plate); Syrian Forces

SF: *Slovenska Filharmonica* (Serbo-Croat—Slovene Philharmonic—in Ljubljana, Yugoslavia; *Socialistisk Folkeparti* (Dano-Norwegian—Socialist People's Party); *Système français* (French system, of screw threads)

sfa: simulated flight automatic; slow flying aircraft; spatial frequency analyzer

s & fa: shipping and forwarding agent

SFA: Saks Fifth Avenue; Scandinavian Fraternity of America; Scientific Film Association; Show Folks of America; Slide Fastener Association; Société Française d'Astronautique (French Astronautical Society); Solid Fuels Administration; Soroptimist Federation of the Americas; Southeastern Fisheries Association; Symphony Foundation of America

SFAAW: Stove, Furnace, and Allied Appliance Workers (International Union of North America)

SFAC: Société des Forges et Ateliers du Creusot (Schneider-Creusot Forges and Factories)

SFAD: Society of Federal Artists and Designers

SFAO: San Francisco Assay Office

sfar: sound fixing and ranging

SFAR: System Failure Analysis Report

SFB: Sender Freies Berlin (Free Berlin Broadcasting Station); Spencer Fullerton Baird

SFBARTD: San Francisco Bay Area Rapid Transit District

sf bh: surface broach

SFBNS: San Francisco Bay Naval Shipyard

sfc: S-bank frequency converter; sight fire control; specific fuel consumption; supercritical fluid chromatography; switching filter connector; synchronized framing camera

Sfc: Sergeant First Class

SFC: Saint Francis College; Sioux Falls College; Space Flight Center

SFC: *San Francisco Chronicle*

SFCC: San Francisco City College

SFCM: San Francisco Conservatory of Music

SFCMD: San Francisco Contract Management District

SFCP: Shore Fire Control Party

SFCTA: San Francisco Classroom Teachers Association

sfcw: search for critical weakness

SFCW: San Francisco College for Women

sfe: stacking fault energy; surface-energy

SFE: Society of Fire Engineers

SFEA: Survival and Flight Equipment Association

SFEL: Standard Facility Equipment List

SFF: Solar Forecast Facility

sfff: salt-free fat-free (diet)

sfgd: safeguard

SFGGB: San Francisco Golden Gate Bridge

SFHS: Stephen Foster High School

SFIO: *Section Française de l'Internationale Ouvriere* (French section of the Worker's International)—communist organization

SFIT: Standard Family Interaction Test

SFL: Society of Federal Linguists

sfm: surface feed per minute; surface feet per minute

SFMA: San Francisco Museum of Art

SFMC: San Francisco Medical Center (University of California)

SFMR: San Francisco Municipal Railway (operates the cable cars)

SFMS: Shipwrecked Fishermen and Mariners (Royal Benevolent) Society

S F & N V: San Francisco & Napa Valley (railroad)

sfo: simulated flame out; submarine fog oscillator

S Fo: (Port of) San Francisco

SFO: San Francisco, California (airport); San Francisco-Oakland Airlines; San Francisco Opera; Service Fuel Oil; Space Flight Operations

SF-OBB: San Francisco-Oakland Bay Bridge (Transbay Bridge)

SFOD: San Francisco Ordnance District; Special Forces Operational Detachment

SFOF: Space Flight Operations Facility

SFP: Sherbrooke Forest Park (Victoria, Australia)

SFPDis: San Francisco Procurement District (US Army)

sf pe: surface plate

SFPE: San Francisco Port of Embarkation; Society of Fire Protection Engineers

SFPL: San Francisco Public Library

sfpm: surface feet per minute

SFPR: Society of Friends of Puerto Rico

sfprf: semifireproof

sfqa (SFQA): structurally fixed question-answering system

sfr (SFR): submarine fleet reactor

SFR: Safety of Flight Requirement

SFRA: Science Fiction Research Association

S Fran: San Francisco

SFRJ: Socijalisticka Federativna Republika Jugoslavija (Socialist Federated Republic of Yugoslavia)

SFRS: Sea Fisheries Research Station (Haifa)

sfs: surfaced four sides

SFs: Special Forces (Green Berets)

SFS: San Francisco Symphony

s 4 s: smooth 4 sides

SFSA: Steel Founders' Society of America

SFSC: San Francisco State College

SF & SC: Standard Fruit & Steamship Company

SFSE: San Francisco Stock Exchange

SFSO: San Francisco Symphony Orchestra

sft: soft; specified financial transactions; stop for tea; superfast train

SFTI: San Fernando Technical Institute (Trinidad)

SFU: Simon Fraser University

sfv: sight feed valve

SFVSC: San Fernando Valley State College

SFWA: Science Fiction Writers of America

sftwd: softwood

sftwr: software (officialese for paperwork as opposed to hardware)

sfxd: semifixed

sfxr: superflash X-ray

sfy: standard facility year(s)

sfz: *sforzando* (Italian—accented strongly; forced; reinforced)

sg: screen grid; single groove; singular; smoke generator; soluble gelatin; specific gravity; steel girder; structural glass; swamp glider

sg: *selon grandeur* (French—according to size); on menus, sg or SG indicates an item is priced according to the size of the serving

Sg: spring range of tide

SG: Aerotransporte Litoral Argentino (Argentine Coastal Air Transport); Scots Guards; Solicitor General; South Georgia (railroad); Standing Group; Sunset Gun; Surgeon General

S-G: Saint-Gobain, Space-General (Corporation)

SGA: Saskatchewan Government Airways; Society of the Graphic Arts; Southern Gas Association; Standards of Grade Authorization

S-gauge: standard gauge (4-foot 8½-inch) railroad track

SGB: Société Générale de Belgique

SGBIP: *Subject Guide to Books in Print*

sgc: screen grid current; simulated generation control; spartan guidance computer (SGC); spherical gear coupling; stabilizer gyro circuit

SGC: Saint Gregory College; South Georgia College

S-G C: Space-General Corporation

SGCA: *Secretariat General a l'Aviation Civil* (French—Secretariat General of Civil Aviation)

sgdg: *sans garantie du gouvernement* (French—patent issued without government guarantee)

sg di: swaging die

S Ge: South Georgia

sgg: sustainer gas generator

SGI: Spring Garden Institute

SGINDEX: System Generation Cross-Reference Index (NASA)

SGIO: State Government Insurance Office

sgl: signal

SGLS: Space-Ground Link Subsystem

sg md: swaging mandrel

SGMT: Société Générale des Transports Maritimes

Sgn: (Port of) Saigon

SGN: Saigon, Vietnam (airport); Surgeon General of the Navy

sgnr: signature

SGO: Surgeon General's Office

sgot: serum glutamic oxaloacetic transaminase

SGP: Shell Gasification Process; Society of General Physiologists

SGP: *Staatkundig Gereformeerde Partij* (Dutch—Political Reformed Party)

sgpt: serum glutamic pyruvic transaminase

SGR: Sumbu Game Reserve (Zambia)

SGS: Sunderbans Game Sanctuary (Bangladesh)

SGSB: Stanford Graduate School of Business

SGSR: Society for General Systems Research

Sgt: Sergeant

SGT: Society of Glass Technology

Sgt 1/C: Sergeant First Class

Sgt Maj: Sergeant Major

SGVHS: Samuel Gompers Vocational High School

SGX: Seeger Refrigerator Express (stock exchange symbol)

sh: scleroscope hardness; serum hepatitis; ship's heading; shop;

shopping; sick in hospital; social history; somatotrophic hormone; surgical hernia
s/h: shorthand
Sh: shells; shilling (British East Africa)
SH: Schenley Industries (stock exchange symbol); Soldier's Home; Station Hospital; Symphony Hall
S-H: Scripps-Howard
S & H: Sperry & Hutchinson (green stamps); Sundays and Holidays
sha (SHA): sidereal hour angle
SHA: Southern Historical Association
SHAA: Society of Hearing Aid Audiologists
shab: soft and hard acids and bases
sh abs: shock absorber
SHAC: Seale-Hayne Agricultural College
shaco: shorthand coding
SHAEF: Supreme Headquarters, Allied Expeditionary Forces
shags: shaggy carpets or rugs
shah: (Persian—King, as in Shah Mohammed Rena Pahlavi)
shahr: (Persian—town, as in Khorramshahr)
Shakaito: (Japanese—Socialist Party)
Shakes: Shakespeare
shamateur(s): sham amateur(s)
shamburger: sham hamburger (containing more additives and adulterants than meat)
SHAME: Save, Help Animals Man Expoits
shan: (Chinese—hill; mountain range)
Shang: Shanghai
shan't: shall not (colloquial)
SHAPE: Supreme Headquarters, Allied Powers, Europe
SHARP: Ships Analysis and Retrieval Project
SHAS: Shared Hospital Accounting System
SHAWCO: Students Health and Welfare Centers Organization
SHB: Svenska Handelsbanken (Swedish Bank of Commerce)
shbg: sex-hormone-binding globulin
SHC: Sacred Heart College; Seton Hall College; Siena Heights College; Spring Hill College; Streets and Highways Code; Surveillance Helicopter Company
sh con: shore connection
she.: signal handling equipment; standard hydrogen electrode
she'd: she had; she would
Sheff: Sheffield

shehr: (Turkish—town)
Sheila: Cecilia
she'll: she will
SHELL: Shell Oil Company
SHELREP: Shelling Report
Shelty: Shetland pony
Shen NP: Shenandoah National Park
Sher: Sherbrooke
she's: she has; she is
Shet: Shetland
shf: super high-frequency—300–30,000 mc
Shf: Sheffield
SHH: Sociedad Honoraria Hispánica
Shi: Shanghai
Shillelagh: anti-tank surface-to-surface guided missile produced by Aeronutronic
Shim: Shimonoseki
shima: (Japanese—island)
shimo: (Japnese—lower)
shinerium: shoe-shine stand
ship.: shipment; shipping
SHIP: Self-Help Improvement Program
ShipDTO: ship on depot transfer order
shipmt: shipment
shiu: (Chinese or Japanese—province)
SHJC: Sacred Heart Junior College
shk: shank
Shl: Shields; shoal
shld: shoulder
shl dk: shelter deck
shlp: shiplap
shm: simple harmonic motion
Shm: Shoreham
SHM: Service Hydrographique de la Marine (Naval Hydrographic Service)
SHMO: Senior Hospital Medical Officer
shmt: shock mount
SHNHS: Sagamore Hill National Historic Site
SHNNR: Studland Heath National Nature Reserve (England)
ShNP: Shenandoah National Park
SHO: Senior House Officer; Student Health Organization
SHOC: Self-Help Opportunity Center
SHOCK: Students Hot on Conserving Kilowatts
shocks.: shock absorbers
shoran: short-range navigation
short(s): short circuit(s)
shorted: short circuited (electrical parlance)
shoto: (Japanese—archipelago)
shouldn't : should not
show biz: show business
shp: shaft horsepower

SHPC: Scenic Hudson Preservation Conference
shpt: shipment
SHQ: Station Headquarters
shr: share(s)
shram (SHRAM): short-range air-to-surface missile
shrap: shrapnel
Shrops: Shropshire
shrtg: shortage
shs: ship's heading servo
SHS: Sacred Heart Seminary; Senior High School; Stuyvesant High School
SHSA: Steamship Historical Society of America
SHSLB: Street and Highway Safety Lighting Bureau
SHSN: Sod House Society of Nebraska
SHSP: Sam Houston State Park (Louisiana)
SHSS: Sanford Hypnotic Susceptibility Scale
SHSSI: Steamship Historical Society of Staten Island
sht: sheet
SHT: Society for the History of Technology
shtg: sheathing; shortage
sht mtl: sheet metal
sh tn: short ton
SHU: Seton Hall University
shv: solenoid hydraulic valve
s.h.v.: sub hoc voce (Latin—under this work)
SHW: Sherwin-Williams (stock exchange symbol)
S & H x: Sundays and Holidays excepted
si: salinity indicator; short interest; spark ignition; straight-in (aircraft landing approach); subicteric; subindex; subinguinal
si: (Chinese—west; western); (Italian—seventh tone; G in diatonic scale, B in fixed-do system)
s-i: semiconductor-integrated (circuits)
s/i: signal/intermodulation; subject issue
s & i: stocked and issued
Si: Silas; silicon (symbol); Simon; Simone
SI: Système International; Sandwich Islands; Saturday Inspection; Serra International; Sertoma International; Service Instruction; Shipping Instruction(s); Smithsonian Institution; Society of Illustrators; Spokane International (railroad); Staff Inspector; Staten Island; Stevens Institute; Sulfur Institute; Survey Instruction(s); Système International des Unités (Interna-

tional System of Units)

S-I: Seine-Inférieure; Spokane International (railroad)

sia: subminiature integrated antenna

SIA: Sanitary Institute of America; School of International Affairs (Columbia University); Self-Insurers Institute; Ski Industries of America; Society of Insurance Accountants; Soroptimist International Association; Sprinkler Irrigation Association; Standard Instrument Approach; Strategic Industries Association

SIAE: Società Italiano degli Autori ed Editori (Italian Society of Authors and Editors)

sial: silicon + aluminum (Si + Al)

siam: signal information and monitoring

SIAM: Society for Industrial and Applied Mathematics

SIAO: Smithsonian Institution Astrophysical Observatory

sib: satellite ionospheric beacon(s); sibilant; sibling; sibship

Sib: Siberia; Siberian

SIB: Shipbuilding Industry Board; Society of Insurance Brokers; Soviet Information Bureau

Sibr: Siberia

sibs: siblings

SIBS: Salk Institute for Biological Studies

sic: specific inductance capacity

sic.: siccus (Latin—dry)

Sic: Sicilian; Siciliana; Siciliano; Sicily

SIC: Scientific Information Center; Security Intelligence Corps; Société International de Cardiologie; Société Internationale de Chirurgie; Société Intercontinentale des Containers; Standard Industrial Classification; Survey Information Center

sicbm (SICBM): super-intercontinental ballistic missile

SICC: Staten Island Community College

SICR: Specific Intelligence Collection Requirement

sic transit: sic transit gloria mundi (Latin—so passes away the glory of the world)

sid: sidereal; standard instrument departure; sudden infant death; sudden ionospheric disturbance

Sid: Sidney; Sydney

SID: Security and Intelligence Department; Society for Information Display; Society for International Development; Society for Investigative Dermatology; Standard Instrument Departure; Sudden Ionospheric Disturbance

S & ID: Space and Information Division

sidase: significant data selection

Siddhartha: Gautama Buddha

SIDEC: Stanford International Development Education Center

SIDs: Sports Information Directors

SIE: Scientific Information Exchange; Society of Industrial Engineers; Southwestern Industrial Electronics

SIECUS: Sex Information and Educational Council of the United States

Siem: Siemensstadt

sierra: (Spanish—mountain range)

Sierra: code for letter S

sif: selective identification feature

SIFF: Suomen Illmailuliitto Finlands Flygforbund (Finnish Aeronautical Association)

sif/iff: selective identification feature/identification friend or foe

sig: signal; signaling; signature

sig.: signetur (Latin—mark with directions)

Sig: Siegfried; Sieglinde; Sigismund; Sigmund; Sigmunde

Sig: Signor (Italian—Mr; Sir)

SIG: Snowy Irrigation Scheme (Snowy Mountains Authority—Australia)

siga: sigatoka (banana leaf spot disease)

SigC: Signal Corps

Sigg: Signori (Italian—Messrs)

sigill.: sigillum (Latin—seal)

sigint: signals intelligence

Siglo de Oro: (Spanish—Golden Age)—the Spanish Century before and after 1600 when discovery and colonization were matched by great artistic and literary productions

sigmoido: sigmoidoscopy

sig. nom. pro.: signa nomine proprio (Latin—label with the proper name)

SIH: Samuel Ichiye Hayakawa

SIHS: Society for Italian Historical Studies

SII: Standards Institution of Israel

SIIA: Stevenson Institute of International Affairs

Sig Sta: signal station

SIIAS: Staten Island Institute of Arts and Sciences

SIIP: Systems Integration Implementation Plan

sil: silver; speech interference level

s-i-l: sister-in-law

Sil: Silesia; Silesian; Silurian

silcads: silver-cadmium batteries

Silent Cal: Calvin Coolidge—thirtieth President of the United States

silic: silicate; siliceous

silica: silicon dioxide (SiO$_2$)

silkool: silk + wool (Japanese synthetic textile combining qualities of silk and wool)

sils: silver solder

sil(s): speech interference level(s)

silv: silver; silvery

silvercel: silver-zinc cell (battery)

silvicult: silviculture

sim: similar; simile; simple; simulate; simulated approach

Sim: Simm(s); Simon(d); Sims; Syme(s); Symme; Syms; etc.

SIM: Society for Industrial Microbiology

sima: (Japanese—island)

SIMCA: Société Industrielle de Mécanique et Carosserie Automobile

simch: single mach change

simcon: simulated control

Simons: Simonstown

simp: simpleton

simp.: simplex (Latin—simple)

simula: simulation language

simulcast: simultaneous broadcast (am & fm)

sin.: sine; single

sin.: sinister (Latin—left)

Sin: Sinaloa (inhabitants—Sinaloens)

SIN: Singapore (airport); Société Industrielle et Navale

SIN: Scientific Information Notes (National Science Foundation)

SINB: Southern Interstate Nuclear Board

S Ind Cur: South Indian Current

sing.: singer; single; singing; singular

sing.: singulorum (Latin—of each)

Sing: Singapore

Singing Satellite: Red China's first satellite, launched in spring of 1970, broadcast rhymed song about Communist party chairman Mao Tse-tung

Sing U: Singapore University

Sinn Fein: (Gaelic—Ourselves Alone)

sinh: hyperbolic sine

Sinh: Sinhalese

Sink: Sinkiang

sins.: ship-inertial-navigation systems

sio: satellite in orbit; staged in orbit

SIO: Scripps Institution of Oceanography; Ship's Information Office(r)

sioh: supervision, inspection, and overhead

SIOP: Single Integrated Operations Plan

sip.: standard inspection procedure; step in place

SIP: Sociedad Interamericana de la Prensa (Inter-American Press Association—IAPA); Standard Inspection Procedure
SIPC: Securities Investor Protection Corporation
SIPI: Southwestern Indian Polytechnic Institute
Sipo: security police (Nazi)
SIPRE: Snow, Ice, and Permafrost Research Establishment
SIPRI: Stockholm International Peace Research Institute
siq: superior internal quality
sir. (SIR): submarine intermediate reactor
SIR: Society for Individual Responsibility; Society of Industrial Realtors; Staten Island Rapid Transit (railroad code)
SIRA: Scientific Instrument Research Association
SIRE: Small Investors Real Estate (plan); Society for the Investigation of Recurring Events
Sir Guatteral: (Hobson-Jobson —Sir Walter Raleigh)—as known to many Spaniards in colonial times
SIRR: Spokane International Railroad
SIRS: Student Information Record System
SIRT: Staten Island Rapid Transit
Sis: Cecilia; sister
SIS: Secret Intelligence Service; Shut-In Society; Strategic Intelligence School; Submarine-Integrated Sonar (system)
S & IS: Space and Information System(s)
sisi: short-increment sensitivity index
sisp: sudden increase of solar particles
siss: single-item single-source
SISS: Semiconductor-Insulation Semiconductor System; Submarine Improved Sonar System; System Integration Support Service
SISTER: Special Institution for Scientific and Technological Education and Research
SISUSA: Scotch-Irish Society of the United States of America
sit.: situation; statement of inventory transaction; stopping in transit
SIT: Society of Industrial Technology; Stevens Institute of Technology; Sugar Industry Technicians
SITA: Société Internationale de Télécommunications Aeronautiques; Students International Travel Association

SITC: Standard International Trade Classification
sitcom: situation comedy (tv)
SITES: Smithsonian Institution Traveling Exhibition Service
sitrep: situation report
SITS: Securities Instruction Transmission System; Société Internationale de Transfusion Sanguine (International Organization for Blood Transfusion)
SITU: Society for the Investigation of the Unexplained
SIU: Seafarers International Union; Société Internationale d'Urologie (International Urological Society); Southern Illinois University; Special Investigating Unit (NY Police Bureau of Narcotics)
SIUL: Southern Illinois University Library
SIUM: Southern Illinois University Museum
SIUP: Southern Illinois University Press
siv: survey of interpersonal values
siw (SIW): self-inflicted wounds
SIXPAC: System for Inertial Experiment Pointing and Attitude Control
SIZ: Security Identification Zone
SIZS: Staten Island Zoological Society
sj: slip joint; subject(s)
SJ: San Juan; Society of Jesus (S.J.—Jesuits); Statens Järnvägar (Swedish State Railways)
SJC: San Juan Carriers (ore and tankships); Snead Junior College; Spartanburg Junior College
S.J.D.: *Scientiae Juridicae Doctor* (Latin—Doctor of Juridical Science)
sje: swivelling jet engine
SJI: Steel Joist Institute
SJJC: Sheldon Jackson Junior College
sjø: (Norwegian—lake; sea)
sjö: (Swedish—lake)
SJO: San José, Costa Rica (La Sabana Airport)
SJPC: South Jersey Port Commission
SJPL: San Jose Public Library
SJSC: San Jose State College
SJSO: San Jose Symphony Orchestra
SJU: San Juan, Puerto Rico (airport); St. John's University
sk: sick; sketch
Sk: *Skizze* (German—sketch)
SK: end of transmission (telegraphic symbol); South Korea(n)
SK: *Stuttgarter Kammerochester* (German—Stuttgart Chamber Orchestra); *Suomen Kansal-*

lisoopera (Finnish National Opera)
s-ka: *spolka* (Polish—association; company)
SKA: Switchblade Knife Act
skamp: station keeping and mobile platform
skb: *skindbind* (Dano-Norwegian —leatherbound)
skc: sky clear
skd: skilled
sked: schedule
skel: skeletal; skeleton
SKF: Svenska Kullagerfabriken (Swedish ball-bearing factory)
SKI: Sloan-Kettering Institute
SKIP: Skimmer Investigation Platform
skiv: skiver
SKJ: *Savez Komunista Jugoslavije* (Yugoslavian Communist League)—political party
skl: spleen, kidney, liver
Skm: Stockholm
skmr (SKMR): hydroskimmer
skort: short skirt
skp: station-keeping position
skr: standardized kill rate; station-keeping radar
Skr: *Skrifter* (Swedish—publication)
SKr: Swedish krona (kronor)
SKR: South Korea Republic
sks: sacks
SKS: Søren Kierkegaard Society; station-keeping ship
SKS: *Savvezna Komisija za Standardizacija* (Serbo-Croatian— Federal Commission for Standardization)
Skt: Sanskrit
Skt: *Sankt* (German—saint)
SKY: Skyways Limited (aviation symbol)
skyjack: skyjacked; skyjacker; skyjacking (all indicate aircraft hijacking)
skys'l: skysail
sl: sales letter; sand-loaded; sea level; searchlight; shipowner's liability; slightly; sound locator; stock length; support line
s-l: short-long (flashlight or whistle signals); sound-locator sublease
s & l: savings and loan; supply and logistics
Sl: Slovak; Slovakian; small diurnal range
SL: San Luis Obispo; Savings and Loan (association or bank); Sea-Land (America's seagoing motor carrier); Sierra Leone; Solicitor-at-Law; Squadron Leader; Sub-Lieutenant; Support Line; Sydney & Louisburg (railroad)
S-L: short-long

S & L: Supply and Logistics
S-et-L: Saône-et-Loire
sla: single line approach
SLA: Showmen's League of America; Southeastern Library Association; Southwestern Library Association; Special Libraries Association; Standard Life Association; State Liquor Authority; Supply Loading Airfield; Supply Loading Airport
SLAB: Students for Labelling Alcoholic Beverages
SLAC: Stanford Linear Acceleration Center
slaked lime: calcium hydroxide ($Ca[OH]_2$)
slam. (SLAM): supersonic low-altitude (nuclear-powered) missile
s.l.a.m.: *sine loco, anno, nomine* (Latin—without place, year, or name)
SLANG: Systems Language
slanguage: slang (slum language)
SLANT: Student League Against Narcotic Traffic
slar: side-looking airborne radar
S Lat: south latitude
SLATE: Structured Learning and Teaching Environment; Systems for Learning by Applications of Technology to Education
Slav: Slavic; Slavonic
slbm (SLBM): submarine-launched ballistic missile
slc: searchlight control
SLC: Salt Lake City, Utah (airport); Scout Launch Complex; Space Launch Complex
slcm (SLCM): sea-launched cruise missile
SLCMD: St Louis Contract Management District
SLCPL: Salt Lake City Public Library
sld: sailed; solid; specific learning disability
Sld: Sunderland
sldf: solidification
sl di: slot die
sld's: specific learning disabilities
sle: systemic lupus erythematosus
S le: Sierra Leone leone(s)—monetary unit(s)
SLE: Society of Logistics Engineers
S-L Fl: short-long flashing (light)
Sli: Sligo
SLI: Slick Airways
SLICE: Southwestern Library Interstate Cooperative Endeavor
SLID: Student League for Industrial Democracy
slim. (SLIM): submarine-launched inertial missile

Slim Jannie: Jan Christian Smuts
SLIP: Skills Level Improvement Plan
slithy: lithe and slimy (Lewis Carroll's portmanteau word from *Through the Looking Glass*)
slm: *sul livello del mare* (Italian—at sea level)
SLMSU: Scientific Library of Moscow State University
SLMTA: St. Louis Municipal Theatre Association
sln: standard library number
slnd: *sans lieu ne date* (French —without place or date of publication)
SLNM: Statue of Liberty National Monument
SLNWR: Sand Lake National Wildlife Refuge (South Dakota); San Luis NWR (California); Swan Lake NWR (Missouri)
Slo: Saltillo (inhabitants—Saltilleños or Saltilleros); Slovak; Slovakia; Slovene(s)
SLOE: Special List of Equipment
slomar: space logistics, maintenance, and rescue
s/loss: salvage loss
Slov: Slovene; Slovenian
SLOWPOKE: Safe Low-Power Critical Experiment (AEC)
s.l.p.: *sine legitima prole* (Latin —without legitimate issue)
SLP: San Luís Potosí; Socialist Labor Party
SLPL: St. Louis Public Library
slr: side-looking radar; single-lens reflex (camera)
S & LR: Sydney and Louisburg Railway
SLRB: State Labor Relations Board
SLRC: San Luis Rey College
sl rd: searchlight radar
SLRP: *St. Lawrence River Pilot*
sls: sequential light switch
SLS: Sea-Land Service; St. Lawrence Seaway; St. Louis Symphony
sl sa: slotting saw
SLSA: Surf Life Saving Association
SLSC: Swedish Lloyd Steamship Company
SLSDC: Saint Lawrence Seaway Development Corporation
S L S F: St. Louis-San Francisco (railroad)
SLSFC: Severe Local Storm Forecast Center
slsmgr: salesmanager
slsmn: salesman; salesmen
SLST: Sierra Leone Selection Trust
SLS-UBC: School of Library Science—University of British Columbia

slt: searchlight
SLT: Solid-Logic Technology; Stress Limit Test(ing)
SLTAN: Società Lloyd Triestino per Azioni di Navigazione (Lloyd Triestino)
slto: sea-level takeoff
sl tr: silent treatment
Slu: slough
SLU: Saint Lawrence University; Saint Louis University; Southern Labor Union
slumlord: slum landlord
SLUSSR: State Library of the USSR (Lenin Library, Moscow)
slv: satellite launching vehicle; space launch vehicle; standard launch vehicle (SLV)
SLV-3: Atlas standard launch vehicle (Convair)
sly: slowly
Sly: southerly
slyp: short-leaf yellow pine
SLZG: St. Louis Zoological Gardens
sm: service module; servomechanism; sheet metal; small; statute mile; strategic missile (SM); streptomycin; sustained medication; systolic murmur; syzygy mathematical
s-m: sadist-masochist; sadomasochism
s/m: sensory-to-motor (ratio)
s & m: sadism and masochism; sausages and mashed potatoes; surface and matched
Sm: samarium
Sm: *Seemeile* (German—nautical mile)
s/M: *sur mer* (French—by the sea)
SM: mine-laying submarine; Salvage Mechanic; San Marino; Scientific Memorandum; Senior Magistrate; Sergeant-Major; Service Module; Shipment Memorandum; Signalman; Society of Mary; Society of Medalists; Soldier's Medal; Special Memorandum; Spiritual Mobilization; Staff Memorandum; State Militia; States Marine (steamship lines); Structures Memorandum; submarine; Summary Memorandum; Suomi Merivorma (Finnish Seapower); Supply Manual; Svenska Metallverken (Swedish Metal Works)
S.M.: *Scientiae Magister* (Latin —Master (Latin—Master of Science)
S-M: Seine-Maritime (formerly Seine-Inférieure)
S-et-M: Seine-et-Marne
SM-65: Atlas intercontinental ballistic missile (Convair)

SM-68: Titan intercontinental ballistic missile (Martin)
SM-75: Thor intermediate-range ballistic missile (Douglas)
SM-78: Jupiter intermediate-range ballistic missile (Chrysler)
SM-80: Minuteman intercontinental ballistic missile (Boeing)
sma: subject matter area
SMA: Safe Manufacturers Association; San Miguel Arizona (railroad); Santa María, Azores (airport); Scale Manufacturers Association; Screen Manufacturers Association; Senior Military Attaché; Service Merchandisers of America; Sheffield Metallurgical Association; Society of Makeup Artists; Solder Makers Association; Squadron Maintenance Area; Steatite Manufacturers Association; Steel Manufacturers Association; Stoker Manufacturers Association
SMAB: Solid Motor Assembly Building
SMAC: Scientific Machine Automation Corporation
SM & ACCNA: Sheet Metal and Air Conditioning Contractors National Association
s mach: sounding machine
smalgol: small computer algorithmic language
SMAMA: Sacramento Air Materiel Area
S Mar: San Marino
smarea (SMAREA): squadron maintenance area
SMART: Silent Majority Against Revolutionary Tactics; Supersonic Military Air Research Track; Supersonic Missile and Rocket Track
smartie: simple-minded artificial intelligence
SMASH: Students Mobilizing on Auto Safety Hazards
s-m-a showing: suggested-for-mature-adult showing (motion picture producers' code)
smat: see me about this
smaze: smoke + haze (*see* smog)
SMB: Straits of Mackinac Bridge
SMBA: Scottish Marine Biological Association
smbl: semimobile
smc: sperm (spore) mother cell; standard mean chord
Smc: Samic (Lapp)
SMC: Saugus Marine Corporation; Scientific Manpower Commission
S & MC: Supply and Maintenance Command (US Army)
SMCC: Saint Mary's College of

California; Santa Monica City College
SMCD: Saint Mary's Dominican College
smcln: semicolon
SMD: Submarine Mine Depot
SME: School of Military Engineering; Standard Medical Examination
SMEC: Strategic Missile Evaluation Committee
smel: single and multiengine license
smelt.: smelter; smelting
SMERSH: *Smert Shpionam* (Russian—Death to Spies)—Soviet organization for murdering political enemies
SMfVL: Stuttgart Museum für Volker und Landerkunde
smg: speed made good; submachine gun
Smg: Samarang
SMH: *Sydney Morning Herald*
s mi: statute mile(s)
SMI: Scale Manufacturers Institute; School Management Institute; Secondary Metal Institute; Spring Manufacturers Institute; Success Motivation Institute; Super Market Institute
SMIC: Study of Man's Impact on Climate
smicbm (SMICBM): semi-mobile intercontinental ballistic missile
S-mine: shrapnel-filled mine
smit: spin-motor interruption technique
Smithsonian: Smithsonian Institution (United States National Museum)
SMJ: Southern Masonic Jurisdiction
SMJC: Saint Mary's Junior College
smk: smoke
smk gen: smoke generator
smkls: smokeless
sml: simulate; simulation; simulator; small; symbolic machine language
sml: *sammenlign* (Danish—compare)
SML: States Marine Lines
smlm: simple-minded learning machine
smls: seamless
SMLS: Saint Mary of the Lake Seminary
smm: standard method of measurement
smmp: screw machine metal part
SMMT: Society of Motor Manufacturers and Traders
SMN: Société Maritime Nationale
SMNA: Safe Manufacturers National Association
SMNH: Saskatchewan Museum of

Natural History
SMNP: Simien Mountains National Park (Ethiopia)
SMNRA: Shadow Mountain National Recreation Area (Colorado)
SMNWR: Saint Marks National Wildlife Refuge (Florida)
SMO: Senior Medical Officer
smog: smoke + fog (*see* smaze); smoky air (with or without fog)
smogway: smog-polluted automobile freeway
SMOH: Society of Medical Officers of Health
smoker: smoking car
smokies: smoked haddocks
smon: subacute myelooptic neuropathy
smor: standard mean ocean water
smörgås: smörgåsbord (Swedish appetizers or delicatessen-style meal)
smorz: *smorzando* (Italian—dying away)
smp: scanning measuring projector; social marginal productivity; sound motion picture(s)
SMP: St Martin's Press
SMPC: Saint Mary of the Plains College
SMPTE: Society of Motion Picture and Television Engineers
smpx: smallpox
smr: somnolent metabolic rate; standard mortality rate; submucous resection
SMR: Student Master Record; South Manchurian Railway
SMRC: South Manchurian Railway Company
smrd: spin-motor rotation-detector
SMRE: Safety in Mines Research Establishment
SMRI: Sugar Milling Research Institute
SMRL: Submarine Medical Research Laboratory
sms: silico-manganese steel; subject matter specialist; synchronous meteorological satellite (SMS)
SMS: Sequence Milestone System
SMS: *Seine Majistäts Schiffe* (German—His Majesty's Ship)
smsa: standard metropolitan statistical area
SMSB: Strategic Missile Support Base
SMSG: School Mathematics Study Group
SMSgt: Senior Master Sergeant
SMSP: Spring Mill State Park (Indiana)
SMSSS: Sheet Metal Screw Statistical Society
smstrs: seamstress

smti: selective moving target indicator

SMU: Southern Methodist University

SMUSE: Socialist Movement for the United States of Europe

SMW: Society of Magazine Writers

s m w d sep: single; married; widowed; divorced; separated (vital statistic headings)

smx: submultiplexer unit

sn: sanitation; sanitary; service number; solid neutral; stock number

s-n: *sin número* (Spanish—unnumbered; without number)

s/n: serial number; service number; signal-to-noise ratio

Sn: *stannum* (Latin—tin)

S^n: San (Spanish—saint)

SN: Sacramento Northern (railroad); Scientific Note; Secretary of the Navy; Serial Number; Service Number; Standard Oil (stock exchange symbol)

S-N: stress versus number of cycles

S/N: Serial Number; Service Number

S/N: stress versus number of cycles (to failure); successes versus total number of trials

SNA: Society of Naval Architects

SNAC: Syndicat National des Auteurs et Compositeurs (National Union of Authors and Composers)

snafu: situation normal, all fouled up

SNAM: Società Nazionale Metanodotti

SNAME: Society of Naval Architects and Marine Engineers

SNAP: Society of National Association Publishers; Student Naval Aviation Pilot; Systems for Nuclear Auxiliary Power

Snapp: Servicos de Navegação· da Amazonia e de Administração do Porto do Pará

snap(s): snapshot(s)

snark: snake and shark (Lewis Carroll)

snc: severe noise environment; standard navigation computer

SNC: Société Navale Caennaise (Lamy et Cie)

SNCASCO: Société Nationale de Constructions Aeronautique de l'Ouest

SNCC: Student Nonviolent Coordinating Council (also called SNIC)

SNCFB: Societe Nationale des Chemins de Fer Belges (Belgian State Railways)

SNCFF: Société Nationale des Che-

mins de Fer Français (French State Railways)

snd: sound

SNDO: Standard Nomenclature of Diseases and Operations

sndp: *sin nota de precio* (Spanish—without indication of price)

SNEA: Student National Education Association

SNECMA: Société Nationale d'Etude et de Construction de Moteurs d'Aviation

SNEMSA: Southern New England Marine Sciences Association

snf: solids-non-fat

SNF: Serbian National Federation

sng: synthetic natural gas

sng: *sans notre garantie* (French—without our guarantee)

Sng: Singapore

SNHM: Stanford Natural History Museum

sni: sequence-number indicator

SNI: San Nicolas Island; Sports Network Incorporated

SNIC: Student Non-Violent Coordinating Committee (SNCC)

snirt: snort of laughter

SNL: Standard Nomenclature List

SNL: *Science News Letter*

snm: signal-to-noise merit

SNM: Saguaro National Monument (Arizona); Senior Naval Member; Sitka National Monument (Alaska); Society of Nuclear Medicine

SNMT: Society of Nuclear Medical Technologists

SNN: Shannon, Eire (airport)

sno: snow (used in combinations such as snocat, snomobile)

s no: serial number

SNO: Scottish National Orchestra; Singapore National Orchestra

snok: secondary next of kin

SNOOP: Students Naturally Opposed to Outrageous Prying

snoopervise: snoop and supervise

snop: standardized nomenclature of pathology

SNORT: Supersonic Naval Ordnance Research Track

snp: soluble nucleoprotein

SNP: Salorp National Park (Thailand); Scottish Nationalist Party; Sebakwe NP (Rhodesia); Sequoia NP (California); Serengeti NP (Tanzania); Shenandoah NP (Virginia); Sivpuri NP (India); Sitka NP (Alaska); Snowdonia NP (Wales); Swiss NP (Switzerland)

SNPO: Space Nuclear Propulsion Office

snr: signal-to-noise ratio

Snr: *Senhor* (Portuguese—Mister)

Snra: *Senhora* (Portuguese— Missus)

SNRA: Sanford National Recreation Area (Texas)

Snrta: *Senhorita* (Portuguese— Miss)

sns: sympathetic nervous system

SNSN: Standard Navy Stock Number

SNT: Society for Nondestructive Testing

snto: spinning tool

SNTO: Spanish National Tourist Office; Swedish National Tourist Office; Swiss National Tourist Office

SNWMA: Stillwater National Wildlife Management Area (Nevada)

SNWR: Sabine National Wildlife Refuge (Louisiana); Sacramento NWR (California); Santee NWR (South Carolina); Savannah NWR (South Carolina); Seedskadee NWR (Wyoming); Seney NWR (Michigan); Sherburne NWR (Minnesota); Shiawasse NWR (Michigan); Slade NWR (North Dakota)

so.: seller's option; senior officer; sex offender; shipping order; ship's option; shop order; show off; south(ern); special order; staff officer; standing order; strikeout; suboffice; supply office(r)

so.: *siehe oben* (German—see above)

sö: (Dano-Norwegian—lake; sea)

s-o: shutoff

s/o: shipping order

So.: Somali(a)

So: *Sondag* (Danish—Sunday)

SO: Scottish Office; Scouting-Observation (naval aircraft); Secretary's Office; Senior Officer; Shipment Order; Shipping Order; Shop Order; somalo (Somalian currency unit); Southern Airways (2-letter coding); Southern Company (stock exchange symbol); Special Order(s); Staff Officer; Standard Oil; Standing Order(s); Stationery Office; Supply Office(r)

SO: *sudoeste* (Spanish—southwest); *Südosten* (German—southeast)

S-et-O: Seine-et-Oise

SO2: sulfur dioxide

soa: speed of advance; speed of approach

SOA: Seattle Opera Association; Shoe Corporation of America (stock exchange symbol)

soap.: symbolic optimum assembly

programming
SOAP: Society of Airway Pioneers
SOAPD: Southern Air Procurement District
Soapy: G. Mennen Williams
SOAR: Society of Authors' Representatives
SOAS: School of Oriental and African Studies (University of London)
sob.: shortness of breath
s-o-b: son of a bitch (a dog; a no-good person)
sobe: sober; sobriety
sob's: silly old buggers; sons of bitches; souls on board (aircraft, ship, or other vehicle)
SOBs: Sons of Bosses
soc: social; society; sociology; socket
Soc: Socialist; Society
Soc: *Sociedad* (Spanish—society); *Sociedade* (Portuguese—society); *Società* (Italian—society); *Société* (French—society)
SOC: Southwestern Oregon College
Soc An: *Société Anonyme* (French —corporation)
Soc-Dem: Social-Democrat(ic) (Party)
Soc I: Society Islands
Society of Friends: the Quakers
sociol: sociological; sociologist; sociology
SOCMA: Synthetic Organic Chemical Manufacturers Association
Soc NC: *sociedad en nombre colectivo* (Spanish—general partnership under a collective name)
So Co: Southern Counties
SOCO: Standard Oil Company of California
socom: solar communication
SOCONY: Standard Oil Corporation of New York
SOCRATES: System for Organizing Content to Review and Teach Educational Subjects
socs: survey of clerical skills
soc sci: social science; social scientist
Soc Sec: Social Security
sod.: sodium; sodomite; sodomy
soda (SODA): source-oriented data acquisition
soda ash: sodium carbonate (Na_2CO_3)
sodar: sound-detecting and ranging
soda water: water charged with carbon dioxide (CO_2)
söder: (Swedish—south)
SODRE: Servicio Oficial de Difusión Radio Eléctrica (Uruguayan radio and tv network)

SOE: Special Operations Executive (World War II British intelligence operation for rescuing scientists and other useful citizens from Hitler)
SOE/F: SOE in France
soep (SOEP): solar-oriented experiment package
sof: sound on film
Sof: Sofia
SOFA: Student Overseas Flights for Americans
sofar: sound fixing and ranging
SOFINA: *Société Financière de Transports et d'Enterprises Industrielles* (Belgian investment syndicate)
sofnet: solar observing and forecasting network
SOFT: Status of Forces Treaty
softlenses: soft contact lenses
sog: speed over (the) ground
sog: *sogenannt* (German—so called)
SOG: Seat of Government (Washington, D.C.)
SOGAT: Society of Graphical and Allied Trades
SO & GC: Signal Oil and Gas Company
SoHo: South of Houston Street (New York City artist's colony in downtown Manhattan)
SOHO: Save Our Heritage Organization
soi: space object identification
SOI: Signal Operation Instruction(s); Southern Indiana (railroad); Specific Operating Instruction(s)
sok: *sokak* (Turkish—lane; street)
sol: solar; soldier; solenoid; soluble; solubility; solution; solvent(s)
sol: (Italian—fifth tone, *E* in diatonic scale, *G* in fixed-do system)
s-o-l: short of luck
Sol: Solomon; Solomon Islands
SOL: *Svenska Orient Line* (Swedish Orient Line)
sold.: solder; soldering
solder: 50% lead, 50% tin (common solder)
sol hgt: solid height
solidif: solidification
soln: solution
solion: solution of ions
SOLog: standardization of certain aspects of operations and logistics
sologs: standardization of operations and logistics
solr: solicitor
solrad: solar radiation
solut: solution
s l s l e: smooth 1 side 1 edge

solv: solvent
solv.: *solve* (Latin—dissolve)
som: somatology; start of message
Som: Somali(a); Somaliland(er); Somerset
somat: somatic
Son: Sonora
SON: Snijders-Oomen Non-verbal (intelligence scale)
Son: *Sonntag* (German—Sunday)
sonac: sonacelle (sonar nacelle)
sonar: sound navigation and ranging
Sonbrit: *Simfonischen orkestur na bulgarskoto radio i televiziya* (Bulgarian Radio and Television Symphony Orchestra)
Song of Songs: The Song of Solomon
Song Sol: The Song of Solomon
Sonia: Sophia
sonmc: sonar countermeasures and deception
Sonn: *Sonnets* of Shakespeare
sono: sonobuoy
sonoan: sonic noise analyzer
Son of Valladolid: José Zorilla
Sonya: Sophia
Soo: Sault Ste. Marie (canal and locks)
Soo Bridge: Sault Ste. Marie International Bridge
Soo Canals: Sault Ste. Marie Canals
Soo Line: Minneapolis, St. Paul & Sault Ste. Marie (railroad)
SOOP: Submarine Oceanographic Observation Program
s-o-p: standard operating procedure
SOP: Senior Officer Present; Standard Operating Procedure
SOPA: Senior Officer Present Afloat
Sopac: Southern Pacific Railroad (stock exchange nickname)
Soph: Sophocles
SOPHE: Society of Public Health Educators
soph(s): sophomore(s)
SOPLASCO: Southern Plastics Company
Soppnata: Sociedade Portuguesa de Navios Tanques (Portuguese Tankers)
sor: sorority; specific operating requirement
s-o-r: stimulus-organism-response
Sor: Señor (Spanish—Mister)
SOR: Special Order Request; Specific Operational Requirement
Sorbonne: University of Paris
Sores: Señores (Spanish—gentlemen)
SORI: Southern Research Institute
SORO: Special Operations Research Office

SORT: Slosson Oral Reading Test; Structured-Objective Rorschach Test

sos: same old stew; same only softer (musical direction); slag on a shingle (military description of creamed chicken or beef served on a slice of toast)

s.o.s.: *si opus sit* (Latin—if necessary)

SOS: (international distress signal—three dots, three dashes, three dots); Save Our Schools; Share Old Spectacles; Squadron Officer School; Stamp Out Smog; etc.

SOSC: Smithsonian Oceanographic Sorting Center

So sh: Somali shilling(s)

SOSS: Shipboard Oceanographic Survey System

sost: *sostenuto* (Italian—sustained)

Sost: *Sostavitel'* (Russian—compiler)

SOSUS: Sound and Surveillance System

sot.: shower over tub

sota: state of the the art

SOTAA: State-of-the-Art Association

sotd: stabilized optical tracking device

Soton: Southampton

Sou: Southampton

SOU: Southern Airways

soundamp: sound amplification; sound amplifier

SOUP: Students Opposed to Unfair Practices

Sou Pac: Southern Pacific

souther: storm from the south

Southern: Southern Railway

sov: shutoff valve; special orientation visit

Sov: Soviet; Sovietic; Soviets

s-o vlv: shutoff valve

Sov strike: attack by the Soviet Union

SOW: Sunflower Ordnance Works

sox: socks; solid oxygen; stockings

sp: self-propelled; selling price; shear plate; single-phase; single-pole; single-purpose; small paper; smokeless powder; solid-propellant; space; spare; spare part; special; special paper; special propellant(s); special-purpose; specie; species; specific; speed; starting point; starting price; static pressure; stop payment; summary plotter; summary programmed

sp: *sans prix* (French—without price)

s & p: systems and procedures

Sp: Spain; Spanish

Sp: *Spalten* (German—column; division)

SP: San Pedro, California; São Paulo, Brazil; Scientific Paper; Section Control; Security Publication; Shore Party; Shore Patrol; Shore Police; Socialist Party; Society of Protozoologists; Southern Pacific (railroad); Special Publication; Standard Practice(s); Strategic Plan(ning); subliminal perception; Submarine Patrol; subprofessional (civil service rating)

S-P: Studebaker-Packard

SP: *Senterpartiet* (Norwegian—Centrist Party); *Socialdemokratiet Parti* (Danish—Social Democratic Party); *Sozialistische Partei* (German—Socialist Party)

S.P.: *Sanctissimus Pater* (Latin—Most Holy Father); *Summus Pontifex* (Latin—Supreme Pontiff; the Pope)

S & P: Standard & Poor's Corporation

Sp/1: Specialist, 1st class

spa.: subject to particular average; sudden phase anomaly

SPA: Salt Producers Association; School of Performing Arts; Società per Azioni (Italian—joint stock company); Société Protectrice des Animaux (Society for the Protection of Animals); Society of Participating Artists; Society for Personnel Administration; Society of Philatelic Americans; Songwriters Protective Association; Southern Pine Association; South Pacific Area; Southwestern Power Administration; Standard Practice Amendment(s); Systems and Procedures Association

SPAAMFAA: Society for the Preservation and Appreciation of Antique Motor Fire Apparatus in America

SPAB: Society for the Protection of Ancient Buildings

spac: spatial computer

SPAC: Saratoga Performing Arts Center

S Pac Cur: South Pacific Current

spad (SPAD): space patrol air defense

SPAD: Space Patrol Air Defense; Support Planning and Design

SPADETS: Space Detection and Tracking System

SPAM: Society for the Publication of American Music

SPAMS: Ship Position and Altitude Measurement System

span.: space navigation

Span: Spanish

SPAN: Solar Particle Alert Network

Spanish Century: the 16th century when Spain's explorers and soldiers find and settle much of the New World as well as going around the globe; art and literature make this the Golden Age or *Siglo de Oro* but the British defeat the Spanish Armada—the 1500s

span(s): spaniel(s)

SPAR: Seagoing Platform for Acoustics Research; Selection Program for ADMIRAL Runs (*see* ADMIRAL)

sparc: steam power automation and results computer

SPARC: Space Program Analysis and Review Council

sparr: steerable paraboloid altazimuth radio reflector (Jordrell Bank Radio-Telescope, Cheshire, England)

SPARS: Women's Coast Guard Reserve (from the Coast Guard motto, *Semper Paratus*—Always Ready)

SPARTAN: Special Proficiency at Rugged Training and National Building (Green Beret training program); System for Personnel Automated Reports, Transactions, and Notices (NASA)

SPASM: Society for the Prevention of Asinine Student Movements

spasur: sapce surveillance

spat.: self-protective antitank (weapon); silicon precision alloy transistor

SPAT: Submarine Processing Action Team

spats: spatterdashes

S Pau: São Paulo

Spauld Turn: Spaulding Turnpike

spb: special boiling point

spc: salicylamide-phenacetin-caffeine; special fuel consumption; suspended plaster ceiling

SPC: Society for the Prevention of Crime; South Pacific Commission; Space Projects Center; Standard Products Committee; Subcontract Plans Committee

SPCA: Society for the Prevention of Cruelty to Animals

SPCC: Ships Parts Control Center; Society for the Prevention of Cruelty to Children

sp cd: spinal cord

SPCH: Society for the Prevention of Cruelty to Homosexuals

SPCK: Society for Promoting Christian Knowledge

SPCM: Special Court-Martial

SPCMO: Special Court-Martial Order

SPCO: St. Paul Civic Opera

spcr: spacer

SPCs: Suicide Prevention Centers; Suicide Prevention Clinics

Sp Cttee 24: Special Committee of 24 (United Nations' 24-member Special Committee concerning Granting Independence to Colonial Countries and Peoples)

spd: ship pays dues

Spd: Spandau

SPD: Sales Promotion Department; Sozialdemokratische Partei Deutschlands (Social Democratic Party of Germany); System Program Director

sp del: special delivery

spdl: spindle

spdltr: speedletter

sp dt: single pole, double throw

spe: special purpose equipment

SPE: Society of Petroleum Engineers; Society of Plastics Engineers; Society for Pure English

SPEBSQSA: Society for the Preservation and Encouragement of Barber Shop Quartet Singing in America

spec: specification; specimen; speculation

specat: special category

specif: specific; specifically

specl: specialist; specialize

specs: specifications; spectacles

SPECTRE: Special Executive for Counterintelligence, Terrorism, Revenge, and Extortion (fictional organization created by Ian Fleming for his James Bond books)

spectrog: spectrography

spectrophotom: spectrophotometry

spectros: spectroscopy

SPEDE: System for Processing Educational Data Electronically

S Pedro: San Pedro

speed: speed kills (nickname for killer-type psychedelic drugs of methamphetamine type)—nickname derived from automotive safety slogan—"speed kills"

SPEED: Systematic Plotting and Evaluation of Enumerated Data

speedo: speedometer

Spen: Spencer; Spencerian

Spence: Spencer

SPERT: simplified program evaluation and review task (technique)

S Pete: St. Petersburg

SPF: Society for the Propagation of the Faith

sp fl: spinal fluid

spg: spring

Spg: sponge

Spgfld: Springfield

spgg: solid-propellant gas generator

sp gr: specific gravity

sph: sphenoidal

sphd: special pay for hostile duty

sp hdlg: special handling

SPHE: Society of Packaging and Handling Engineers

SP & HE: Society of Packaging & Handling Engineers

sphen: sphenodon (tuatara lizard); sphenoid; sphenoidal

spher: spherical; spheroid

sp—hl: sun present—horizon lost

SPHS: Seward Park High School; Swedish Pioneer Historical Society

sp ht: specific heat

spi: scientific performance index

SPI: Secretariats Professionnels Internationaux (International Professional Secretariats); Service Pédagogique Interafricain (Inter-African Teaching Service); Society of Photographic Illustrators; Society of the Plastics Industry; Spanish Paprika Institute

SPIC: Society of the Plastics Industry of Canada; Society for the Promotion of Identity on Campus

spicbm (SPICBM): solid-propellant intercontinental ballistic missile

spid: submerged portable inflatable dwelling

spie: self-programmed individualized education

SPIE: Society of Photographic Instrumentation Engineers

sp. indet.: species indeterminata (Latin—species indeterminate)

sp. inquir.: species inquirendae (Latin—species of doubtful status)

s'pipe: standpipe

spir: spiral

spir.: spiritus (Latin—spirits)

SPIRES: Standard Personnel Information Retrieval System

SPIRGs: Student Public Interest Groups

spirits of hartshorn: ammonia water (NH_4OH)

spis: spissus (Latin—dried)

spit.: selective printing of items from tape

Spits: Spitsbergen Islands

spitze: (German—peak; point; summit, as in Zugspitze)

spiw: special-purpose infantry weapon

SPJC: Saint Petersburg Junior College

spk: speckled

Spk: Spokane

spkr: speaker

spl: simplex; sound pressure level; special

s.p.l.: sine prole legitima (Latin—without legitimate offspring)

Spl: Sevastopol

SPL: Sacramento Public Library; Saskatoon Public Library; Seattle Public Library; Space Programming Language; Spokane Public Library; Springfield Public Library; Syracuse Public Library

SPLAN: School Organization Budget-Planning System

SPLC: Standard Point Location Code

splf: simplification

spm: self-propelled mount; strokes per minute

Sp Mor: Spanish Morocco

SPMRL: Sulfite Pulp Manufacturers' Research League

SPMS: System Program Management Surveys

spn: sponsor

sp. n.: species nova (Latin—new species)

Spn: Spain; Spaniard; Spanish

SPNI: Society for the Protection of Nature in Israel

SPNR: Society for the Promotion of Nature Reserves

SPNWR: Salt Plains National Wildlife Refuge (Oklahoma)

S Po: São Paulo

SPO: Sea Post Office; Special Project(s) Office; System Program Office

SPOIE: Society of Photo-Optical Instrumentation Engineers

Spoke: Spokane, Washington

spont: spontaneous

Sport of Kings: (horseracing—a ruinous sport only kings can afford)

sportscast(er): sports broadcast(er)

spot.: spotlight

spp: species

SPP: System Package Program

SPPL: St Paul Public Library; St Petersburg Public Library

Sp Pt: Sparrows Point

S.P.Q.R.: Senatus Populusque Romanus (Latin—the Senate and People of Rome)

spr: solid-propellant rocket (SPR); spring

Spr: Springfield

SPR: Simplified Practice Recommendation(s); Society for Pediatric Research; Society for Psychical Research; solid-propellant rocket; Special Project Report; Supplementary Progress

Report

SPRDO: Service Parts Repairable Disposition Order

spre: siempre (Spanish—always)

SPRE: Society of Park and Recreation Educators

SPRI: Scott Polar Research Institute

spr's: small parcels and rolls

Sprs: Springs

sps (SPS): service propulsion system

SpS: Special Services

SPS: Society of Pelvic Surgeons; Southwestern Public Service; Special Services; Spokane, Portland & Seattle (railroad); Standard Pressed Steel; Symbolic Programming System; System of Procedure Specifications

SP & S: Spokane, Portland & Seattle (railroad)

SPSA: Senate Press Secretaries Association

SPSE: Society of Photographic Scientists and Engineers

SPSO: Senior Principal Scientific Officer

sp st: single pole, single throw

spt: seaport; support

Spt: Split (Yugoslavia)

sptc: specified period of time contract

Sp3c: Specialist, third class

SptL: support line

sptr: spectrum

spu: swimmer propulsion unit

SPUC: Society for the Protection of Unborn Children

spud.: solar power unit demonstrator

SPUD: St. Paul Union Depot

SPUR: Space Power Unit Reactor

spurv: self-propelled underwater research vehicle

sputnik: iskustvennyi sputnik zemli (Russian—artificial fellow-traveler around the earth, Soviet satellite launched October 4, 1957)

SPV: Society for the Prevention of Vice (prurient book burners in search of the putrid)

SpWAfr: Spanish West Africa

SPWLA: Society of Professional Well Log Analysts

sq: squadron; square; stereo-quadraphonic; superquick

sq.: sequens, sequentia (Latin— what follows; result; sequel)

Sq: Square

SQ: stereo-quadraphonic (discs and recordings)

sqa: stereo-quadraphonic amplifier

sqc: self-quenching control; statistical quality control

sq cm: square centimeter(s)

SQCP: Statistical Quality Control Procedure

sqd: squad

sqdc: special quick-disconnect coupling

Sqdn Ldr: Squadron Leader

sq ft: square foot (feet)

sq hd: square head

sq in.: square inch (inches)

Sqn Ldr: Squadron Leader

SqNP: Sequoia National Park

sq's: stereo-quadraphonic recordings; stereo-quadraphonic records

SQS: Stochastic Queuing System; Supplier Quality Services

sq3r: survey, question, read, review, recite (psychological sequence)

sqt: square rooter

SQT: Ship Qualification Test (USN)

squa: squamoid; squamous

squak: squall and squeal

square: symbol of four corners of the earth; four points of the compass; male symbol; quadrature; symbol of rigid uprightness as in, "Always honest, always fair, doing business on the square"; slang term for someone with unsophisticated tastes, "a square"

'squitoes: mosquitoes

sr: scientific research; sedimentation rate; selective ringing, sensitization response; separate rations; sex ratio; shipment request; short range; sigma reaction; single-reduction (geared turbine); sinus rhythm; slow release; sound ranging; spares requirement; split ring; standard range (aviation landing); steradian; stimulus response

sr: srovnej (Czech—compare)

sr (SR): saturable reactor; surveillance radar

Sr: Saudi Arabia; Saudi Arabian; Senior; strontium

Sr: Señor (Spanish—Mister)

Sr85: radioactive strontium

SR: saturable reactor; Scientific Report; Scottish Rifles; Seaman Recruit; seaplane reconnaissance (naval aircraft); Section Report; Senate Resolution; Senior Registrar; Service Record; Service Report; Shipping Receipt; Simulation Report; Society of Radiologists; Society of Rheology; Sons of the Revolution; Sound Report; Southern Railway; Special Regulation(s); Special Report; Specification

Requirement(s); Staff Report; Standardization Report; Star Route (rural postal delivery); Statsjanstemannens Riksforbund (National Association of Salaried Government Employees, Sweden); Status Report; Study Requirement; Summary Report; Supporting Research; surveillance radar; Sveriges Radio (Swedish radio broadcast network); Swissair

SR: Saudi Arabian riyal (currency unit)

S-R: stimulus-response

sra: sulforicinocleic acid

Sra: Señora (Spanish—Missus; Mistress)

SRA: Science Research Associates; Screw Research Association; Society of Residential Appraisers; Special Refractories Association; Station Representatives Association

SRAB: Sveriges Radio AB (Swedish Broadcasting Corporation)

sram (SRAM): short-range attack missile

Sras: Señoras (Spanish—ladies)

SRBC: Susquehanna River Basin Compact

Srb-Crt: Serbo-Croat (Yugoslavian)

srbm (SRMB): short-range ballistic missile

src: sample return container; solvent-refined coal

SRC: Science Research Council; Signal Reserve Corps; Southern Regional Council; Southwest Research Corporation; Standard Requirements Code; Sul Ross State College; Swiss Red Cross

srcc: strikes, riots, and civil commotions

srch: search (computer)

SRD: Secret Restricted Data

SRD: Standard Rate and Data

SRDC: Standard Reference Data Center

Sre: Sreda (Russian—Wednesday)

SRE: Society of Reproduction Engineers

SREB: Southern Regional Education Board

srem: sleep with rapid eye movements

srf: self-resonant frequency; semi-reinforced furnace; solar radiation flux; stable radio frequency; submarine range finder; supported ring frame; system recovery factor

SRGM: Solomon R. Guggenheim Museum

SRHL: Southwestern Radiological

Health Laboratory
Sr HS: Senior High School
sri: servo repeater indicator; silicone rubber insulation; spectrum resolver integrator; surface roughness indicator
SRI: Scientific Research Institute; Southern Research Institute; Southwestern Research Institute; Space Research Institute; Stanford Research Institute
Sría: Secretaría (Spanish—secretariat)
SRILTA: Stanford Research Institute Lead Time Analysis
Srio: Secretario (Spanish—Secretary)
SRIS: Safety Research Information Service; School Research Information Service
srj: self-restraint joint; static round jet
SRJC: Santa Rosa Junior College
SRL: Save-the-Redwoods League; Scientific Research Laboratory; Study Reference List
SRL: Saturday Review of Literature; sociedad de responsabilidad limitada (Spanish—limited liability company)
S rls: Saudi Arabian riyal(s)
srm: speed of relative movement
SRME: Society for Research in Music Education
Sr M Sgt: Senior Master Sergeant
SRN: State Registered Nurse
SR NC: Severn River Naval Command
SRNP: Stirling Range National Park (Western Australia)
SRO: standing room only; Superintendent of Range Operations
s rod: stove rod
SRP: Scientific Research Proposal
srr: survival, recovery, and reconstitution
SRRC: Sperry Rand Research Center
srs: slow reacting substance
SR's: Socialist Revolutionaries (moderates in czarist Russia)
SRS: Sight Restoration Society; Sperry Rail Service; Statistical Reporting Service; Structural Research Series
SRSA: Scientific Research Society of America
SRSC: Sul Ross State College
SRSM: Serenissima Repubblica di San Marino (Italian—Most Serene Republic of San Marino)—official name of San Marino
srt: speech reception threshold
SRT: Standard Radio och Telefon (Swedish Radio and Telephone)

Srta: Señorita (Spanish—Miss)
Srtª: Señorita (Spanish—Miss)
SRTC: Salford Royal Technical College
SRTN: Solar Radio Telescope Network
Srto: Señorito (Spanish—master; young gentleman)
sru: shop-replaceable unit
SRUBLUK: Society for the Reinvigoration of Unremunerative Branch Lines in the United Kingdom
srv (SRV): submarine research vehicle
srvlv: servovalve
SRW: Sherwin-Williams Company of Canada (stock exchange symbol)
ss: saline soak; semisteel; setscrew; single-seated; single signal; single strength; sparingly soluble; spin-stabilized; stainless steel; sterile solution; straight shank; superspeed; sword stick; sworn statement
ss.: *scilicet* (Latin—namely); *semis* (Latin—one-half); *supra scriptum* (Latin—written above; *ss.* usually printed to left of signature line in sworn statements)
s-s: solid-state
s/s: same size; suspended sentence
s & s: signs and symptoms
s/S: sur Seine (French—on the Seine)
SS: Science Service; Secret Service; Secretary for Scotland; Secretary of State; Selective Service; Sharpshooter; Ship Service; Ship's Stores; Silver Star; Social Security; Special Service; Special Staff; Specification(s) for Structure; Standard Score; steamship; Straits Settlements; submarine (naval symbol); Submarine Studies; Sunday School; supersonic; Support System; Surveillance Station; sworn statement
SS: *Saints; Schutzstaffel* (German—Nazi blackshirt elite corps)
ssa: smoke-suppressant additive
SSA: Seismological Society of America; Soaring Society of America; Social Security Administration; Southern Surgical Association
SSAFA: Soldiers', Sailors', and Airmen's Families Association
ss ar: spotface arbor
SSAR: Society for the Study of Amphibians and Reptiles
SSASA: Social Services Association of South Africa
ssb: single side band

SSB: fleet ballistic missile submarine (3-letter naval symbol); Security Screening Board; Selective Service Board; Society for the Study of Blood
SSBN: nuclear-powered fleet ballistic missile submarine (4-letter naval symbol)
s & sc: sized and supercalendered
SSC: Sacramento State College; Sarawak Shipping Company; Sculptors' Society of Canada; Ships Systems Command (formerly Bureau of Ships); Straits Steamship Company; Supply Systems Command (formerly Bureau of Supplies and Accounts)
sscc: spin-scan cloud camera
SSCC: Space Surveillance Control Center
S.Sc.D.: Doctor of Social Science
SSCDS: Small Ship Combat Data System
SSCI: Steel Service Center Institute
SSCNS: Ship's Self-Contained Navigation System
SSCQT: Selective Service College Qualification Test
ss cr: stainless-steel crown
SSCS: Shipboard Satellite Communications System
ssd (SSD): sentence-structure determination
SSD: Space Systems Division (USAF)
SSD: Staatssicherheitsdienst (German—State Security Service)—East German political police
ssdr: subsystem development requirement
SSE: south southeast
SSEB: South of Scotland Electricity Board
ssf: saybolt seconds furol; single-seated fighter; standard saybolt furol (viscosity)
SSF: Service Storage Facility; Ship's Service Force; Social Science Foundation (University of Denver); Special Service Force
SSFF: Solid Smokeless Fuels Federation
ss fx: spotface fixture
SSG: guided missile submarine (3-letter naval symbol)
SSGN: nuclear-powered guided-missile submarine (4-letter naval symbol)
SSgt: Staff Sergeant
SSH: Sailor's Snug Harbor
SSHA: Scottish Special Housing Association
Ssi: Sürekasi (Turkish—company)
SSIB: Seaway Skyway Internation-

al Bridge

SSIC: Southern States Industrial Council

SSIE: Smithsonian Science Information Exchange

ssk: soil stack

SSL: Saguenay Shipping Limited; Sapphire Steamship Lines; Seven Stars Line; Space Science Laboratory (Convair); Space Sciences Laboratory (GE)

SS loran: sky-wave synchronized loran

SSLS: Solid-State Laser System

ss lt: starboard side light

sslv (SSLV): standard space-launched vehicle

ssm (SSM): surface-to-surface missile

SSM: Singer Sewing Machine; System Support Management; System Support Manager

ssma: solid-state microwave amplifier

ssmm: space station mathematical model

SSMS: Submarine Safety Monitoring System

ssmt: supersonic magnetic (railroad) train

SSN: Space Surveillance Network

SS(N): nuclear-powered submarine (3-letter naval symbol)

SSNC: Scindia Steam Navigation Company

ssnd: solid-state neutral dosimeter

ssnf: source spot noise figure

***SS^{no}: escribano* (Spanish—court clerk; notary; scribe)**

SSO: Sacramento Symphony Orchestra; Savannah Symphony Orchestra; Seattle Symphony Orchestra; Shreveport Symphony Orchestra; Spokane Symphony Orchestra; Springfield Symphony Orchestra; Sydney Symphony Orchestra; Syracuse Symphony Orchestra; System Staff Office(r)

***SSO: sudsudoeste* (Spanish—south southwest)**

SSOFS: Smiling Sons of the Friendly Shillelaghs

ssp: seismic section profiler; ship's stores profit; single-shot probability; standby-status panel; steam service pressure; subspecies; sustained superior performance

SSP: scouting seaplane (3-letter naval symbol); Seashore State Park (Virginia); S.S. Pierce; Sunshine State Parkway

sspc: solid-state power controller

SSPC: Steel Structures Painting Council

SSPCA: Scottish Society for the Prevention of Cruelty to Animals

SSPFC: Stainless Steel Plumbing Fixture Council

SSPHS: Society for Spanish and Portuguese Historical Studies

SSPN: Satellite System for Precise Navigation

SSPP: Society for the Study of Process Philosophies

S-spring: S-shaped spring

ssq: simple sinusoidal quantity

SSQ: Station Sick Quarters

SSQT: Selective Service Qualification Test

ssr: secondary surveillance radar

SSR: Soviet Socialist Republic(s)

SSRC: Social Science Research Council

SSRL: Systems Simulation Research Laboratory

***sss (SSS): su seguro servidor* (Spanish—your sure servant; yours truly)**

***s.s.s.: stratum super stratum* (Latin—layer upon layer)**

SSS: Selective Service System

S-S-S: Schweiz-Suisse-Svizzera (Switzerland in the three languages of the country)

SSSA: Soil Science Society of America

S-S SA: Singapore-Soviet Shipping Agency

SSSB: System Source Selection Board

SSSC: Space Science Steering Committee (NASA)

sssd: second-stage separation device; solid-state solenoid driver

SSSJ: Student Struggle for Soviet Jewry

SSSL: Solid State Sciences Laboratory (USAF)

sssm: site space surveillance monitor

SSSP: Space Shuttle Synthesis Program

SSSS: Society for the Scientific Study of the Sea

sst: stainless steel; supersonic transport (airplane)

SST: Samoan Standard Time; Society of Silver Collectors; Space Systems Center (Douglas); Submarine Supply Center; supersonic transport (airplane); target and training submarine (naval symbol)

sstu: seamless steel tubing

ssu: saybolt seconds universal

SSU: Stanilaus State University

***s.s.v.: sub signa veneni* (Latin—under a poison label)**

SSV: ship-to-surface vessel

SSvc: Selective Service

SSV/GC & N: Space Shuttle Vehicle/Guidance, Control and Navigation

ssvs: slow-scan video simulator

ssw: safety switch

SSW: south southwest

SSX: South Coast Corporation (stock exchange symbol)

ssz: specified strike zone

SSZ: Society of Systematic Zoology

st: sedimentation time; service test; short ton; single-throw; single tire; slight trace; sounding tube; special text; special translation; statement(s); steel truss; stock transfer; stone; strata; surface tension; survival time; syncopated time

***st.: stet* (Latin—let it stand, usually referring to what has been mistakenly crossed out)**

s & t: sink and laundry tray

St: Stanton number; status; strontium

St.: Saint; Street

ST: Seaman Torpedoman; Service Test(ing); Shipping Ticket; Sons of Temperance; Standardized Test; Summer Time; Suomen Tasavalta (Finnish—Finland); Syrian Territory

S.T.: sidereal time

S & T: Supply and Transport

sta: station; stationary; stationery; stator

***Sta: Santa; Señorita* (Spanish—Miss); Station**

STA: Scottish Typographical Association; Society of Typographic Arts; Southern Textile Association; Supersonic Tunnel Association

STAA: Survey Test of Algebraic Aptitude

STAAS: Surveillance and Target Acquisition Aircraft System

***staat:* (German—state)**

stab.: stabilizer

***STAB: Svenska Tandsticks Aktiebolaget* [Swedish Match (stick) Company]**

sta'b'd: starboard

***stac: staccato* (Italian—separately and with great distinction)**

STAC: Science and Technology Advisory Committee (NASA)

***stad:* (Danish, Dutch, Norwegian, Swedish—town, as in Willemstad)**

stadan: space tracking and data acquisition network

***Stadt:* (German—town, as in Heiligenstadt)**

sta eng: stationary engineer

STAFF: Stellar Acquisition Flight Feasibility (guidance system)

Staffs: Staffordshire

staflo: stable-flow (free-boundary electrophoresis apparatus)

stag.: stagger; staggered

STAG: Special Task Air Group; Standards Technical Advisory Group; Strategy and Tactics Analysis Group

stagflation: stagnant (consumer demand) (price-wage) inflation

Stagirite: Aristotle the Stagirite —so named as he was born in Stagira, Macedonia

Stalag: *Stammlager* (German —base camp, for military prisoners)

Stalin: (Russian—steel)—Iosif Vissarionovich Dzhugashvili

sta mi: statute miles

STAMP: Systems Tape Addition and Maintenance Program

Stampa: *La Stampa* (Turin's Press—one of Italy's leading newspapers)

STAMPS: Structural Thermal and Meteorite Protection System

stan: stanchion; standard; standing

Stan: Standard; Stanford; Stanley; Stanleyville; Stanton

STANAG: Standardization Agreement (NATO)

St And: St. Andrews

standard.: standardization

STANDINAIR: Standing Instructions for Air Attachés

Stan Psychiat Nomen: Standard Psychiatric Nomenclature

STANVAC: Standard Vacuum (oil company)

staph: staphylococcus

star: symbol of perfection

STAR: Ship-Tended Acoustic Relay; Space Thermionic Auxiliary Reactor; submersible test and research (Electric Boat)

STAR: *Scientific and Technical Aerospace Reports*

staraya: (Russian—old)

starboard side: *righthand* side of an airplane, ship, or other craft when looking forward, symbolized by a fixed *green* light—on the *righthand* wingtip of an airplane or set against a *green* background on the *righthand* side of a ship's bridge or pilothouse

STARLAB: Space Technology Applications and Research Laboratory (NASA)

stars.: specialized training and reassignment students; stationary automotive road simulator (Toyota)

STARS: Satellite Telemetry Automatic Reduction System

START: Spacecraft Technology and Advance Reentry Test; Space Technology and Reentry Test(s); Space Transport and Reentry Test(s)

stas: staff-to-arm signal

STASH: Student Association for the Study of Hallucinogens

stat: electrostat; electrostatic; microstat; photostat; static; stationary; statistic(al); statuary; statue; statute

stat.: *statim* (Latin—immediately; right now)

Statesman's: *Statesman's Year Book*

STATIC: Student Taskforce Against Telecommunication Concealment

STATLIB: Statistical Computing Library (Bell System)

stato: (Italian—state)

Stats: statutes

Stat Off: Her (His) Majesty's Stationery Office

St AU: University of St. Andrew

s-t b: steel-truss bridge

STB: Surinam Tourist Bureau

S.T.B.: *Sacrae Theologiae Baccalaureus* (Latin—Bachelor of Sacred Theology)

stbd: starboard

st brz: statuary bronze

stc: security time control; sensitivity time control; short time constant; sound transmission class; stepchild

STC: Satellite Test Center; Satellite Tracking Committee; Scandinavian Travel Commission; Short Title Catalog; Southwestern Technical College; Standard Telephone and Cables; Standard Transmission Code; Sunderland Technical College

STCA: Stereo Tape Club of America

st cl: storage closet

std: salinity, temperature, depth; skin test dose; standard; standard test dose; state-of-the-technology design; subscriber trunk dialing

St D: Stage Director

STD: Society for Theological Discussion; Subscriber Trunk Dialing

S.T.D.: *Sacrae Theologiae Doctor* (Latin—Doctor of Sacred Theology)

std by: stand by

St DC: St. David's College

STDC: Society of Typographic Designers of Canada

stdcr: social introversion, thinking introversion, depression, cycloid tendencies, rhathymia (personality traits)

Stde: *Stunde* (German—hour)

stdn: standardization

std p: stand pipe

st dr: single-trip drum

Ste.: Sainte (French—saint, *f.*)

St E: St. Etienne

STE: Society of Tractor Engineers

steakwich steak sandwich

steamers: (slang nickname—steaming clams)

steelie: steel ball-bearing playing marble

STEFER: Società della Tranvia e Ferrovia Elettrica di Roma (Rome transportation system)

STEG: Supersonic Transport Evaluation Group

St E H: St. Elizabeth's Hospital

Stein: (German—stone, as in Arnstein, Einstein)

STEL: *Studenta Tutmonda Esperantista Liga* (Esperanto—Worldwide Esperanto Students League)

Stella: Estella; Estelle

stem.: storable tubular extendible member

STEM: stay time excursion module

sten: stencil

sten: (Danish, Norwegian, Swedish—stone)

Stendhal: (pseudonym—Marie-Henri Beyle)

steno: stenographer; stenography; stenotype; stenotypy

step: (Russian—steppe; treeless plain)

STEP: Safety Test Engineering Program; Scientific and Technical Exploitation Program; Secondary Teachers Education Program; Sequential Tests of Educational Progress; Solutions to Employment Problems

Steph: Stephen

STEPS: Solar Thermionic Electric Power System

ster: stereoscope; stereotype; sterilization; sterilize; sterilizer; sterling

stereo: stereophonic; stereoprojection; stereoprojector; stereoscope; stereoscopic

STERILE: System of Terminology for Retrieval of Information through Language Engineering

sterling silver: 92% silver, 8% copper

stet: let stand what has been crossed out

stev: stevedore; stevedoring

Steve: Stephan; Stephen; Steven

stew(s): steward(esses)

stf: staff

STF: Sycamore Test Facility

STF: *Svenska Turisforeningen* (Swedish Tourist Information)

st fm: stretcher form

stg: stage; staging

stg ar: staging area

stge: storage

St George: (patron saint of England

stgg: staging

Stgo: Santiago

Stgo de C: Santiago de Chile (Compostela, Cuba)

stgr: stringer

stgs: strings

STgt: secondary target

sth: somatotrophic hormone

Sth: Stockholm

Sthlm: Stockholm

sti: service and taxes included

s & ti: scientific and technical information

St I: St. Ives

STI: Service Tools Institute; Space Technology Institute; Steel Tank Institute

STIC: Scientific and Technical Intelligence Center

stiction: static friction

STID: Scientific and Technical Information Division (NASA)

STIF: Scientific and Technical Information Facility (NASA)

stiff.: stiffener

stillat.: *stillatim* (Latin—by drops; in small amounts)

stim: stimulant

stimn: stimulation

STIMS: Scientific and Technical Modular System

stinfo: scientific and technical information

STING: Stellar Inertial Guidance (System)

STINGS: Stellar Inertial Guidance System (USAF)

STIP: Science Teaching Improvement Program

STIPIS: Scientific, Technical, Intelligence, and Program Information Service (HEW)

Stir: Stirling

St J: St. John (New Brunswick)

STJC: South Texas Junior College; Southwest Texas Junior College

St John Perse: (pseudonym—Alexis Leger)

StJU: St. John's University

stjw: stretcher jaws

stk: sticky; stock

Stk: Stockton

stl: steel; studio transmitter link

St L: St. Louis

STL: Seatrain Lines; Space Tech-

nology Laboratories (Thompson-Ramo-Wooldridge); Speech Transmission Laboratory; Standard Telecommunication Laboratories; St. Louis, Missouri (airport); studio transmitter link (FM); Swedish Transatlantic Line

StLGR: Saint Lucia Game Reserve (South Africa)

St Lo: St. Louis

STLO: Scientific and Technical Liaison Office(r)

STLOs: Scientific/Technical Liaison Offices

STLOUISPDis: St. Louis Procurement District (US Army)

St L P-D: *St. Louis Post-Dispatch*

stlr: semi-trailer

ST L SW: St. Louis Southwestern (railroad)

STLT: studio transmitter link-TV

St LU: St. Lucia; St. Louis University

St L ZG: St. Louis Zoological Garden

stm: scientific, technical, and medical; shielded tunable magnatron; short-term memory; special test missile; surface-to-target missile; synthetic timing mode

St M: St. Malo

STM: Science Teaching Museum (Franklin Institute); System Training Mission

S.T.M.: *Sacrae Theologiae Magister* (Latin—Master of Sacred Theology)

Stmn: *The Statesman* (Calcutta)

stmt: statement

stn: stain

Stn: Station

St N: St. Nazaire

stnd: stained

Sto: *Santo* (Spanish—saint); *Señorito* (Spanish—master; young gentleman)

STO: Stockholm, Sweden (Arlanda Airport)

Stock: Stockholm

stol: short takeoff and landing

stol/vcd: short takeoff and landing/ vertical climb and descent

stom: stomach

stomat: stomatology

S'ton: Southampton

STon: short ton

Stonewall Jackson: General Thomas Jonathan Jackson of the Confederate Army

stop.: slight touch on pedal; spin tires on pavement

STOP: Strategic Orbit Point

stor: storage; stored

stor: (Danish, Norwegian, Swedish

—big; great; large)

STOR: Scripps Tuna Oceanographic Research

storet: storage and retrieval

Stormont: Stormont Castle—official Belfast resident of Northern Ireland's prime minister

stow.: stowage

stp: standard temperature and pressure; stop; stoppage

St P: St. Paul

STP: nickname of dangerous psychedelic drug—methylmethoxyamphetamine; Scientifically Treated Petroleum (gasoline additive); sodium tripolyphosphate (water softener); stop the police (dirty street people's slogan)

st part: steel partition

St Pete: St. Petersburg

STPL: Space Tracking Pty Ltd

St P & M: St. Pierre and Miquelon Islands

s tpr: short taper

stps: specific thalamic projection system

str: steamer; straight; strainer; strait; strength; structural; structure; submarine test reactor (STR)

str: *strana(y)* [Czech—page(s)]

Str: *Strasse* (German—street)

STR: section, township, range; Society for Theatre Research; Southern Test Range; Stuttgart, Germany (airport); submarine test reactor

STRA: State Teacher's Retirement System

straat: (Dutch—strait)

STRAC: Strategic Army Corps

strad: stradivarius (violin made by Antonio Stradivari or his sons Francesco and Omobono)

STRAF: Strategic Army Forces

strag: straggler

StragL: straggler line

strand: (Danish, Dutch, Norwegian, Swedish—beach; shore; strand, as in Tvedestrand)

Stras: Strasbourg

strat: strategic; strategist; strategy

strath: (Scottish—broad river valley)

stratig: stratigraphy

strato: stratosphere

straw: strawberry

STRC: Science and Technology Research Center; Scientific, Technical, and Research Commission

strep: streptococcus

stress. (STRESS): structural engineering system solver

STRESS: Stop the Robberies, Enjoy Safe Streets (program of the Detroit Police Department)

stret: *stretto* (Italian—squeezed together; more rapid [as musical notes]; strait)

STRICOM: Strike Command (US Army)

STRIKFORSOUTH: Striking and Forces Support, Southern Europe (USN)

string: *stringendo* (Italian—accelerate)

Strix: Peter Fleming

S-t-R L: Save-the-Redwoods League

strobo: stroboscope

strobotron: stroboscope + electron (tube)

ström: (Danish, Swedish—river; stream)

Strom: (German—river; stream)

stroom: (Dutch—river, stream)

struc: structure

struct: structural

sts: ship-to-shore (radio or radio telephone); special treatment steel; surfaced two sides

STS: Serological Test for Syphilis; Standard Test for Syphilis; Stockpile-to-Target Sequence

STSA: State Technical Services Act

STSC: Southwest Texas State College

St T: (Port of) St. Thomas

STT: Medical Stenographer (USN); St. Thomas, Virgin Islands (airport); Sensitization Test

ST T NHS: St. Thomas National Historic Site

stu: service trials unit; skin test unit; student; submersible test unit

Stu: Stewart; Stuart

STU: *Styrelsen foer Teknisk Utveckling* (Swedish—Board for Technical Development)

Stud: Studebaker

stude(s): student(s)

stud(s).: student(s)

stuns'l: studdingsail

stupidental(ly): stupidly accidental(ly)

stuvs: standard unit variance scale

stv (STV): subscription television

St V: St. Vincent

STV: Separation Test Vehicle

stvdr: stevedore

st w: storm water

STW: Society of Technical Writers

ST WAPNIACLE: (abbreviation mnemonic for U.S. departments in order of their creation before new ones were added and some were consolidated: State, Treasury, War, Attorney General (Justice), Post Office, Navy,

Interior, Agriculture, Commerce, Labor, Education

STWE: Society of Technical Writers and Editors

STWP: Society of Technical Writers and Publishers

stwy: stairway

stx: start of test (data processing)

STX: St. Croix, Virgin Islands (airport)

STZ: Sterling Drugs (stock exchange symbol)

su: sensation unit(s); service unit(s); setup; strontium unit(s); sulfur unit(s)

s u: *siehe unten* (German—see below)

Su: Sudan; Sudanese

SU: Saybolt Universal; Seattle University; Shaw University; Skinner Union; Southeastern University; Southwestern University; Soviet Union; Stanford University; Stetson University; Student Union; Suffolk University; Syracuse University

sua: shipped unassembled

SUA: Silver Users Association; State Universities Association

SUAB: *Svenska Utvecklinasaktiebolaget* (Swedish Development Corporation)

SUADPS: Shipboard Uniform Automatic Data Processing System (USN)

sub: submarine; submerse; subordinate; substitute; suburb; subway

Sub: *Subbota* (Russian—Saturday)

subac: subacute

subbase: submarine base

sub-bell: submarine fog bell

sub chap: subchapter

subcontr: subcontract(or)

subcrep: subcrepitant

subcut: subcutaneous(ly)

SUBDIZ: Submarine Defense Identification Zone

subgen.: *subgenus* (Latin)

subic (SUBIC): submarine integrated control program

subing: substituting

subj: subject; subjunctive

subl: sublimes

subling: sublingual

Sub Lt: Sub-Lieutenant

subm: submission; submit

submand: submandibular

submtl: submittal

subn: substitution

subor: subordinate

sub-osc: submarine oscillator

subot: submarine bottom

sub para: sub paragraph

subplane: submersible seaplane

sub-pro: subprofessional

subq: subsequent

subroc (SUBROC): submarine rocket

subrog: subrogation

subs: submarines; subscription(s); subsistence; substitutes

sub sec: subsection

subsis: subsistence

subsp.: *subspecies* (Latin)

subst: substantive

substa: substation

substd: substandard

subsys: subsystem

subtr: subtraction

suburb: suburban; suburbanite; suburbia; suburban

suc.: *succus* (Latin—juice)

SUC: Sussex University College

Sucr: *Sucursal* (Spanish—subsidiary; branch)

Sucre: Antonio José de Sucre —South American liberator fighting with Bolivar for freedom of Venezuela, Colombia, Ecuador, Peru, and Bolivia from Spanish rule

sud: (French or Spanish—south)

Sud: Sudan; Sudanese

Sud: (German—south)

SUD: Aerovias Sud Americanas (3-letter airline coding)

SUDAN: Sudan Airways

SUDS: Silhouetting Underwater Detecting System; Submarine Detecting System

Sue: Susan; Susannah; Suzanne

SUEL: Sperry Utah Engineering Laboratory

suf: sufficient; suffix

Suff: Suffolk

suffoc: suffocating

sug: suggest(ion)

SUG: Southern California Gas Company (stock exchange symbol)

SUGAR: Services, (to diabetics through) Understanding, Grants, Assistance, Recreation

SUI: State University of Iowa

suid: sudden unexplained infant death (crib death)

Suky: Susan; Suzanne

sul: (Portuguese—south)

SUL: Stanford University Libraries

sulcl: set up in less than carloads

sulf: sulfate; sulfur

sulfa: sulfanilamide

sulfd: sulfide(s)

sum.: summary; surface-to-underwater missile (SUM)

sum.: *sume* (Latin—take)

Sum: Sumatra; Sumatran; Sumer; Sumeria; Sumerian

SUMCMO: Summary Court-Martial Order

sumr: summer

Sun: Sunday

Sun: The Baltimore Sun
SUN: Symbols, Units, and Nomenclature Commission
sund: (Danish, Norwegian, Swedish —sound, as in Haugesund)
Sund: Sunda Islands; Sŭndanese
SUNFED: Special United Nations Fund for Economic Development
sungei: (Malayan—river)
SUNOCO: Sun Oil Company
SUNY: State University of New York
SUNYAB: State University of New York at Buffalo
sup: superfine; superior; superlative; supersede(s); supplement (ary); supplies; supply; support; supposition; supreme
SUP: Sailors Union of the Pacific; Socialist Unity Party
supchg: supercharger
supdel: superdelicious
supe (slang): superintendent; supernumerary
super: superficial; superfine; superheterodyne; superintendent; superior; supermarket; supernumerary; supersede; supersession
super: supermercado (Spanish —supermarket)
superaero: superaerodynamics
superhet: superheterodyne
supérieure: (French—upper)
superl: superlative
superstr: superstructure
Superte: Superintendente (Spanish —superintendent)
superv: supervisor
SUPIR: Supplementary Photographic Interpretation Report
supp: supplement; suppuration
suppl: supplement (French—supplement)
suppos: suppository
supps: supplements
SupPt: supply point
suppy: supplementary
supr: superior; supreme
supra cit.: supra citato (Latin— cited above)
supsd: supersede(d)
supt: superintend; superintendent
supv: supervise; supervisor
supvr: supervisor
supvry: supervisory
sur: surface; surfacing
sur: (French—on, as in Boulogne-Sur-Mer); (Spanish—south, as in América del Sur)
Sur: Surinam (Netherlands Guiana)
Suralco: Surinam Aluminum Company
Sur f: Surinam florin (guilder)
surg: surgeon; surgery; surgical
Sur Gen: Surgeon General

Surg Gen: Surgeon General
suric: surface ship integrated control
surpic: surface picture
surr: surrender
Surr: Surrogate
surv: survey; surveying; surveyor
Surveyor: American program for lunar surface and subsurface exploration
survll: surveillance
Sus: Saybolt universal second; Susanna, The (Apocryphal) History of; Sussex
SUS: Scottish Union of Students; Society of University Surgeons
Susie: Susan; Susannah; Suzanne
susp: suspend
susp b: suspension bridge
suspn: suspension
sust: sustainer
Suth: Sutherland
s'uth'ard: southward
SUV: Saybolt Universal Viscosity; Suva, Fiji Islands (Nandi Airport)
SUX: Sioux City, Iowa (airport)
suyu: (Turkish—river; water)
Suz: Suez
sv: sailing vessel (SV); selectavision (SV); (RCA patent); simian virus; single vibrations; sinus venosus; stroke volume; survey; surveyor
sv: svazek (Czech—volume)
s.v.: spiritus vini (Latin—alcohol); sub verbo or sub voce (Latin —under the word; under the voice)
s/v: survivability/vulnerability
SV: sailing vessel; Selective Volunteer; Sons of Veterans
S & V: Sinclair and Valentine
Sva: Suva
Sval: Svalbard (Spitsbergen)
SVB: Stephen Vincent Benét
svc: service; superior vena cava
SVC: Skagit Valley College; Society of Vacuum Coaters
SVCP: Special Virus Cancer Program
SVE: Society for Visual Education
Sven Akad: Svenska Akademien (Swedish Academy)
Sver: Sverdlovsk; Sverige (Swedish—Sweden)
s.v. gal.: spiritus vini gallici (Latin—brandy)
s.v.i.: spiritus vini industrialis (Latin—industrial alcohol)
svib: strong vocational interest blank
Svn Dag: Svenska Dagbladet (Swedish Daily Blade)
SVO: Moscow, USSR (Sheremetyevo Airport)

SVP: Society of Vertebrate Paleontology
S V P: s'il vous plaît (French—if you please)
s.v.r.: spiritus vini rectificatus (Latin—rectified spirit of wine)
SVR: Suomen Valtion Rautatiet (Finnish State Railways)
sv's: security violators
s.v.t.: spiritus vini tenuis (Latin —proof alcohol; proof spirit)
svtp: sound, velocity, temperature, pressure
s.v.v.: sit venia verbo (Latin—forgive the expression)
sw: salt water; sea water; sent wrong; shipper's weights; short wave; shotgun wedding; single weight; special weapon; spotweld; spotwelding; steelworker; stock width; switch; switchband wound
s-w: shortwave
Sw: Sweden; Swedish
SW: Secretary of War; Security Watch; Senior Warden; Shelter Warden; Ship's Warrant; South Wales; southwest; Southwest Airways (2-letter coding); Stone & Webster (stock exchange symbol)
S-W: Sherwin-Williams
S & W: Seaboard & Western (airlines); Smith & Wesson
swa: single-wire armored; superwide angle
Swa: Swahili
SWA: Seaboard World Airlines; South-West Africa; Southwest Airways
swabk: sealed with a big kiss
swac: special warhead arming control
SWAC: South-West Africa Company
SWAFAC: Southwest Atlantic Fisheries Advisory Commission
SWAI: South-West African Infantry
swak: sealed with a kiss
Swan of Avon: Ben Jonson's name for Shakespeare
SWANU: South-West Africa National Union
SWANUF: South-West Africa National United Front
SWAPO: South-West Africa People's Organization
swash: sea wash (scouring surf running up a beach after a wave breaks)
Swaz: Swaziland
swb: short wheelbase; single with bath; swing bridge
swbd: switchboard
swc: specific water content

SWC: Soil and Water Conservation (US Department of Agriculture); Special Weapons Command; Supreme War Council

SWCLR: Southwest Council of La Raza

SWD: South Wales Docks

SWE: Society of Women Engineers

sweat.: student work experience and training

Swed: Swede; Sweden; Swedish

Sw Fr: Swiss franc

sw fx: spotweld fixture

SWG: Society of Women Geographers; Standard Wire Gauge

Sw-Ger: Swiss-German (derived from Alemannic)

SWI: Spring Washer Institute

swife: sexual wife

swift.: selected words in full title

SWINE: Students Wildly Indignant (about) Nearly Everything (cartoonist Al Capp's contribution to contemporary acronyms)

SWIRS: Solid Waste Information Retrieval System

SWISSAIR: Swiss Air Transport

Switz: Switzerland

swives: sexual wives

Sw kr: Swedish krona (monetary unit)

swl: shortwave listener

SWL: safe working load (for cargo booms and derricks; SWL 5T 15 deg means the safe working load is 5 tons at 15 degrees off the horizontal); Swedish American Line

SWLA: Southwestern Library Association

SWLI: Southwestern Louisiana Institute

swlolak's: sealed with lots of love and kisses

SWly: south-westerly

SWM: Southwest Museum

SWO: Solid Waste Office (Environmental Protection Agency)

swoc: subject word out of context

swog: special weapons overflight guide

SWOPSI: Stanford Workshops on Political and Social Issues

swp: safe working pressure; sweep; sweeper; sweeping

SWP: Sherwin-Williams Paints; Socialist Workers Party; South Wales Ports; Southwest Pacific; Special Weapons Project

SWPA: Southwest Pacific Area; Southwestern Power Administration; Surplus War Property Administration

swr: serum wassermann reaction; standing-wave ratio; switch rails

S-W RI: Sterling-Winthrop Research Institute

swrj: split wing ramjet

sws: seam-welding system; service-wide supply; slow-wave sleep; solar-wind spectrometer; still water surface

Sws: Swansea

SWS: Sariska Wildlife Sanctuary (India); Space Weapons System; Special Weapons System

SWSC: Schlumberger Well Surveying Corporation

swt: short-wave transmitter; spiral-wrap tubing

SWT: Scottish Wildlife Trust

SWTC: Scottish Woolen Technical College

swtchmn: switchman

swtg: switching

SWUS: Southwestern United States

swv: swivel

swymmd: see what you made me do

sx: section

Sx: (medical) signs and symptoms

SX: Southern Pacific (stock exchange symbol)

sxa: stored index to address

SXC: Saint Xavier College

sxl: short-arc xenon lamp

SXM: St. Maarten, Netherlands Antilles (airport)

sxn: section

SXO: Senior Experimental Officer

sxr: soft X-ray region

sxrm: straight reamer

sxs: stellary X-ray spectra

SXS: Sigma Xi Society

sxt: stable X-ray transmitter

sy: shipyard; square yard; sticky; supply; sustainer yaw

Sy: Syria; Syrian

SY: (U.S. State Department) Security Office; steam yacht (naval symbol)

SYCATE: Symptom-Cause Test

sycom: synchronous communication(s)

syd: sum of the year's digits

syd: (Danish, Norwegian, Swedish —south)

Syd: Sydney

Syd: sydlig (Danish—southerly)

SYD: Scotland Yard; Sydney, Australia (airport)

syh: see you home

SYHA: Scottish Youth Hostels Association

syl: syllogism

syll: syllabication (syllabification)

sym: symbol; symbolic; symbolism; symmetric; symmetrical; symmetry; symphonic; symphony

sym.: symbolus (Latin—token; sign)

symb: symbol; symbolic; symbolism

symp: symposia; symposium

sympath: sympathetic; sympathy

sympt: symptom(s)

syn: synagogue; synesthesia; synonym; synonymous; synonymy; syntax; synthetic

Syn: synagogue

Synanon: anti-drug-addiction group (from the slurring of seminar by an addict attending one of the organization's daily seminars)

sync: synchronize; synchronous

synchro: synchronize; synchronous

synchros: synchronous devices

synco: syncopate(d); syncopation; syncopative; syncopator

syncom: synchronous communication (satellite)

synd: syndicalism; syndicate

syndet(s): synthetic detergent(s)

syndro: syndrome

SYNMAS: Synchronous Missile Alarm System

synop: synopsis; synoptic

syns: synopsis

synscp: synchroscope

synt: syntax

synth: synthesis; synthetic

syntol: syntagmatic organization of language

syph: syphilis; syphilitic

syphil: syphilology

syr: syrup

syr.: syrupus (Latin—syrup)

Syr: Syracusan; Syracuse; Syria; Syriac; Syrian

SYR: Syracuse, New York (airport)

Syrac: Syracusan; Syracuse

syrg: syringe

sys: system; systematic; systematization; systematize; systemic; systems

SYS: Sun Yat-sen

sysgen: systems generation

SYSP: Sixth-Year Specialist Program (library science)

syst: system; systematic; systemic; systems

systol: systolic

systran: systems analysis translator

syt: sweet young thing

syz: syzygetic; syzygial; syzygium; syzygy

sz: size

s Z: seinerzeit (German—at that time)

Sz: Swiss; Switzerland

SZA: Student Zionist Association

SZG: Salzburg, Austria (airport)

Szle: Szemle (Hungarian—journal; review)

SZO: Student Zionist Organization

szvr: silicon zener voltage regulator

T

t: airfoil temperature thickness (symbol); hour angle (symbol); meridian angle (symbol); table; tabulated (loran); tackle; tardy; tare; teaspoon; teeth; telephone; temperature; temporary; tenor; tense; tensor; tentative; tentative target; thunder; thunderstorm; tide; tide rips; time; title; ton; tonnage; tons; toward; town; trace of precipitation; transferred; transit; transitive; translation; tread; tropical; troy; true; tug; tugline

t ½: radioactive half life

t: *tome* (French—volume); *tomo* (Spanish—volume)

T: Northrup Aircraft (symbol); Pacific Transport Lines (1-letter symbol); propeller thrust (symbol); tablespoon; tactical; Tango—code for letter T; tanker; Taoism; Taoist; T-bar; tee; teletype; temperature; temple; temporary magnitude; tension of eyeball; Testla; Texaco; Texas; Texas Company; Thursday; torpedo; trainer; training; transport number; triangle; triple bond; true; truss; Tuesday; turboprop; Turk; Turkey; Turkish

T: tea (underground slang—marijuana or Texas tea as some users nickname this hallucinogen drug); *Teil* (German—division; part); thrust (symbol); *Time* (magazine); transformer (symbol); *tulo* (Finnish—arrival)

T$: Taiwan dollar(s)

T2: stabilized

T2g: Technician (second grade)

T3: triiodothyronine

T4: heat treated

T4: thyroxine

T6: heat treated and aged

T7: heat treated and stabilized

T51: specially aged

T-144: Tupelov 144 (Soviet supersonic transport)

ta: target area; temperature, axillary; test accessory; third attack (lacrosse); time and attendance; toxin-antitoxin; travel allowance; true altitude; tuberculin, alkaline

ta: transit authority (New York City Transit Authority—lower-case italic emblem on rolling stock)

t.a.: *testantibus actis* (Latin—as the records show)

t-a: toxin-antitoxin

t & a: taken and accepted; time and attendance; tonsillectomy and adenoidectomy; tonsils and adenoids

Ta: tantalum; Tasmania; Tasmanian

TA: Table of Allowances; Tax Amortization; Technical Assistance; Territorial Army; Trade Agreement(s); Trans-Air; Transamerica Corporation (stock exchange symbol)

taa: turbine-alternator assembly

TAA: Technical Assistance Administration; Trade Agreements Act; Trans-Australia Airlines; Transit Advertising Association; Transportation Association of America

TAAF: Terres Australes et Antarctiques Française (French Southern and Antarctic Territories)

TAALS: The American Association of Language Specialists

TAARS: The Army Ammunition Reporting Service

taas: three-axis attitude sensor

tab.: table; tablet; tabulate; tabulated; tabulation; tabulator

tab.: *tabella* (Latin—small board; tablet)

Tab: Tabascan; Tabasco

Tab: *Tabelle* (German—table; index)

TAB: Technical Assistance Board (UN); Tobago (airport)

TAB: *Technical Abstract Bulletin*

TABA: Transportes Aéreos Buenos Aires

tabel: *tabella* (Latin—tablet)

TABL: Tropical Atlantic Biological Laboratory

tabla(s): [Spanish—board(s); plank(s); table(s)]

tabl(s): tablet(s)

tab run: tabulator run

Tabs: Cantabrigians or Cantabs —Cambridge University undergraduates

TABS: Transatlantic Book Service

TABSO: Transport Aerien Civil Bulgare (Bulgarian Civil Air Transport)

tabsol: tabular systems-oriented language

TAB vaccine: typhoid plus paratyphoid A and B vaccine (triple vaccine)

tac: tactic; tactical; tactician; tactics; total automatic color (tv); try and collect

Tac: Tacitus; Tacoma

TAC: Tactical Air Command; Thai Airways Company; Trade Agreements Committee

TACA: Texas and Central American Airlines

tacan: tactical air navigation

Tac Brdg: Tacoma Bridge

TACC: Tactical Air Control Center

tacco: tactical coordinator

tacden: tactical data-entry device

TACG: Tactical Air Control Group

tach: tachometer

tachy: tachygraphy (shorthand)

tacit.: *tacitus* (Latin—unmentioned)

taclan: tactical landing system

tacmar: tactical malfunction-array radar

tacnav: tactical navigation

TACO: Tactical Coordinator

tacoda: target coordinate date

tacol: thinned-aperture computed lens

TACP: Tactical Air Control Party

TACRON: Tactical Air Control Squadron

TACs: Technical Assistance Committees (UN)

TACS: Tactical Air Control System

tacsatcom: tactical satellite communications

tact.: technological aids to creative thought

TACT: Truth About Civil Turmoil

TACTIC: Technical Advisory Committee to Influence Congress (Federation of American Scientists)

tacv: tracked air-cushion vehicle

Tad: Thaddeus; Theodore

TAD: Thrust-Augmented Delta

TADA: Teletypewriter Automatic-Dispatch System

TADARS: Tropo Automated Data Analysis Recorder System

TADC: Tactical Air Direction Center; Training and Distribution Center

tadic: telemetry analog-to-digital information computer

tad(s): tadpole(s)

Tadz: Tadzhik; Tadzhikistan; Tadzhikistanian

Tadzhik SSR: Tadzhik Soviet Socialist Republic (Tadzhikistan)

TAE: National Greek Airlines

TAEA: Texas Art Educators Association

TAEC: Turkish Atomic Energy Commission

TAEHS: Thomas A. Edison High School

TAERF: Texas Atomic Energy Research Foundation

taf: terminal aerodrome forecast

Taf: *Bildtafel* (German—list of illustrations)

TAF: Tactical Air Force

tafcsd: total active federal commissioned service date

Tafelland: (German—tableland)

Taffy: (nickname for a Welshman)

tafg: two-axis free gyro

TAFI: Technical Association of the Fur Industry

tafmsd: total active federal military service date

tafor: terminal aerodrome forecast

TAFSEA: Technical Applications for Southeast Asia

ta fx: tapping fixture

tag.: the acronym generator (RCA device)

Tag: Tagalog

TAG: The Adjutant General; Timken Art Gallery

T A & G: Tennessee, Alabama & Georgia (railroad)

TAGA: Technical Association of the Graphic Arts

tagawi: try and get away with it

tagh: (Mongolian or Turkish—mountain)

tägl: *täglich* (German—daily; per day)

TAGP: Transportes Aéreos do Guine Portuguesa (Air Transport of Portuguese Guinea)

tagw: takeoff gross weight

tah: temperature, altitude, humidity; total abdominal hysterectomy

TAHq: Theater Army Headquarters

tai: (Japanese—big; great; large)

Tai: Taipei; Taiwan (Formosa)

TAI: Thai Airways International; Transports Aériens Intercontinentaux

TA & IC: Texas Arts and Industries College

TAICH: Technical Assistance Information Clearinghouse

taid (TAID): thrust-augmented improved delta

TAJAG: The Assistant Judge Advocate General (USA)

take: (Japanese—peak; ridge)

take 5: take 5 minutes' rest

take 10: take 10 minutes' rest

Tal: *Talmud* (Hebrew canon and civil lawbook)

TAL: Transair Limited

talar: tactical landing-approach radar

talbe: talk and listen beacon

talc.: take a look see

TALC: Texas Association for the Advancement of Local Culture

TALIC: Tyneside Association of Libraries for Industry and Commerce

Talla: Tallahassee

'talpa(s): catalpa(s)

TALOA: Transocean Airlines

Talos: ship-to-air missile produced by Bendix and fired from destroyers and cruisers

tam: tambourine; tam-'o-shanter; tam-tam

Tam: Tamil; Tamaulipas (inhabitants—Tamualipecos); Tampa; Tampan; Tampico (inhabitants—Tampiqueños)

TAM: Tel Aviv Museum; Transporte Aéreo Militar (Paraguayan Military Air Transport)

tambo: tambourine

TAMC: Tripler Army Medical Center

TAME: Television Accessory Manufacturers Institute

Tamerlane's Century: the 14th century when the Mongol emperor Timur (Tamer the Lame) dominated the Middle East and western India from Iraq and Iran to Afghanistan—the 1300s

TAMIS: Technical Meetings Information Service

Tamp: Tampico

Tamps: Tamaulipas

TAMS: Token and Medal Society

Tam Shrew: *Taming of the Shrew*

tan.: tangent; tangential; tannery; tanning

Tan: Tanganyika; Tangier

TAN: Transportes Aéreos Nacionales

tan. bkt: tangency bracket

tandel: tandem + parallel

TANESCO: Tanzania Electric Supply Company

Tang: Tanganyika; Tangier

Tango: code for letter T

Tania: Tatiana

tanjong: (Malayan—cape)

TANS: Territorial Army Nursing Service

tanstaafl: there aint no such thing as a free lunch (abbreviated slogan of Young Americans for Freedom)

TANU: Tanganyika African National Union

TANY: Typographers Association of New York

Tanya: Tantiana

Tanzam: Tanzania-Zambia (railway)

tao: thromboangiitis obliterans

tao: (Chinese—island)

TAO: Taxi Aéreo Opita (Bogotá); The Athenaeum of Ohio

TAP: Total Action Against Poverty; Transportes Aéreos Portugueses (Portuguese Air Transport)

TAPE: Target Profile Examination (USAF); Transactional Analysis of Personality and Environment; Trust for Agricultural Political Education

TAPLINE: Trans-Arabian Pipeline

TAPPI: Technical Association of the Pulp and Paper Industry

taps: tapaderos (Mexican Border Spanish—leather hoods covering stirrups to protect the feet while riding through thorny cactus or mezquite); the last bugle call, the *taptoo*, meaning *lights out* or sounding the last honors at a military funeral

TAPS: Trajectory Accuracy Prediction System (USAF); Trans-Alaska Pipeline System

TAPSC: Trans-Atlantic Passenger Steamship Conference

tar.: tariff(s); terrain-avoidance radar

TAR: Technical Action Request (USA); Trans-Australian Railways

TARC: Tactical Air Reconnaissance Center

tarfu: things are really fouled up

targ: target

TARGET: Team to Advance Research for Gas Energy Transformation

tarmac: tar plus macadam (tarred road or runway)

tarn.: tarnish; tarnishes; tarnishing

TAROM: Transporturile Aeriene Romine (Romanian Air Transport)

TARP: Test and Repair Processor

tarp(s): tarpaulin(s)

Tarr: Tarragona

tart.: tartaric

TART: Test Analysis Reduction Technique (USN)

tart. a: tartaric acid

Tartar: shipborne surface-to-air guided missile (General Dynamics)

Tartu: Dorpat

tas: true airspeed

Tas: Tasmania

TAs: teaching assistants

TAS: Texas Academy of Science; Traveler's Aid Society; Turk Anonim Sirketi (Turkish Joint Stock Company)

TASAMS: The Army Supply and Maintenance System

tasc: terminal area sequence and control; treatment alternatives to street crimes

TASC: Test Anxiety Scale for Children

tascon: television automatic sequence control

TASES: Tactical Airborne Signal Exploitation System

TASF: Teachers Association of San Francisco

tash: (Turkish—rock; stone)

Tash: Tashkent

TASHAL: *Tseva Hagana LeIsrael* (Hebrew—Defense Army of Israel)

TASKFLOT: task flotilla

Tasm: Tasman; Tasmania; Tasmanian

TASO: Television Allocations Study Organization

TASS: Telegrafnoie Agenstvo Sovietskavo Soyuza (Soviet News Agency)

Tassie(s): Tasmanian(s)

TASSO: Tactical Special Security Office(r)

TASSq: Tactical Air Support Squadron (USAF)

TAST: Tactical Assault Supply Transport

tat. (TAT): tetanus antitoxin

Tat: Tatar (Turkestan)

TAT: tetanus antitoxin; Thematic Apperception Test; Thrust-Augmented Thor; Transportes Aéreos de Timor

Tat Aut Sov Soc Rep: Tatar Autonomous Soviet Socialist Republic

TATCO: Tactical Automatic Telephone Central Office

'tater(s): potato(es)

Tatts: Tattersalls

TATU: Tanganyika African Traders Union

tau: (Turkish—mountain range)

Tau: Taurus

TAU: Tel Aviv University

taurom: tauromachia

taut.: tautology

Tavia: Octavia

T & AVR: Territorial and Army Volunteer Reserve

TAVSS: Toward, Away, Versus Selection System

taw: twice a week

T A & W: Toledo, Angola & Western (railroad)

TAWC: Tactical Air Warfare Center

tax.: taxation; taxes; taxonomic; taxonomy

taxi: taxicab; taxiing

taxid: taxidermy

taxon: taxonomy

tb: temporary buoy; terminal board; thymol blue; tile base; total bouts; tractor biplane; trial balance; true bearing; tubercle bacillus; tuberculosis; turbine; turret-base; turret-based

t/b: title block

t & b: top and bottom; turned and bored

Tb: terbium

TB: Tank Battalion; temporary buoy; Troop Basis; Twin Branch (railroad); Tyburn (reports)

TB: *Technical Bulletin*

tba: tires-batteries-accessories; to be announced; to be assigned

TBA: Tables of Basic Allowance; Television Bureau of Advertising; Torrey Botanical Association

tban: to be announced

T-bar: T-shaped bar

tbawrba: travel by aircraft, military and/or naval water carrier, commercial rail and/or bus is authorized (USA)

TBB: tenor, baritone, base

TBC: The British Council; Trinidad Broadcasting Company

tbd: to be determined

TBDS: Test Base Dispatch Service

tbe: to be expended

T-beam: T-shaped beam

tb ex: tube expander

TBF: single-engine torpedo bomber (3-letter naval symbol)

tbfx: tube fixture

tbg: testosterone-binding globulin; thyroxine-binding globulin

t & bg: top and bottom grille

TBI: Texas Board of Insurance; The Business Institute

T-bird: Thunderbird

t-bk: talking-book

tb lc: term birth, living child

tbm (TBM): tired businessman

tb md: tube mandrel

TBMD: Terminal Ballistic Missile Defense (USA)

tbo: time between overhaul(s)

TBO: Test Base Office

T-bolt: bolt with T-shaped square head

T-bone: T-bone steak; T-shaped bone; trombone

T-bowl: toilet bowl

tbp: true boiling point

TBRI: *Technical Book Review Index*

tbs: tablespoon; talk-between-ships (radiotelephone)

tb & s: top, bottom, and sides

TBs: Torpedo Boats (World War I)

TBS: Tokyo Broadcasting System

tb sa: tube saw

TBSI: The Baker Street Irregulars

tbsn: tablespoon

tbsp: tablespoon

TBT: Terminal Ballistic Track

TB & TA: Triborough Bridge & Tunnel Authority

tbv: tubercle bacillus vaccine

TB & VD C: Tuberculosis and Venereal Diseases Clinic

tbw: total body water

tc: temperature controlled; terra cotta; tetracycline; thermocouple; thermocoupled; thermocoupling; thrust chamber; tierce(s); time check; time closing; top chord; trip coil; true course (TC); type certificate

tc: tre corde (Italian—three strings)

t/c: tabulating card; temperature coefficient; thermocouple; transformer rectifier; trim coil; type certificate

t & c: threads and couplings; turn and cough

Tc: technetium; tropic tides

TC: Air Canada (formerly TCA); Tabor College; Taft College; Talladega College; Tariff Commission; Tarkio College; Tax Court; Teachers College; Tea Council; Technical Circular; Technical Communication; Tennessee Central (railroad); Texarkana College; Texas College; The Citadel; Thiel College; Tift College; Training Center; Training Circular; Transaction Code; Transportation Corps; Transylvania College; Trial Counsel; Tri-State College; troop carrier; Trucial Coast (Arabian sheikdoms); True Course; Trusteeship Council; Turret Captain; Tusculum College

TC: *Technical Communications*

T & C: Turks and Caicos Islands

TC 1: Traffic Conference 1—North and South America, Greenland, Bermuda, West Indies, Hawaiian Islands

TC 2: Traffic Conference 2—Europe, adjacent islands, Ascension Island, Africa, and Asia west of and including Iran

TC 3: Traffic Conference 3—Asia, adjacent islands, East Indies, Australia, New Zealand, Pacific Islands except Hawaiian

tca: telemetering control assembly; track crossing angle; trichloro-acetate

TCA: Tanners Council of America; Technical Cooperation Administration; Temporary Change Authorization; Terminal Control Area; Textile Converters Association; Theater Commander's Approval; Thoroughbred Club of America; Tile Council of America; Tissue Culture Association; Trailer Coach Association; Trans-Canada Airlines

tcam: telecommunications access method

TCAS: The College of Advanced Science

tcb: take care of business

TCBI: Television Center for Business and Industry

tcc: tactical control computer; television control center; test conductor console

TCC: Telecommunications Coordinating Committee; Transcontinental Corps; Transport Control Center; Transportation Control Committee; Troop Carrier Command

T-C C: Tri-Continental Corporation

tcd: task completion date; tungsten carbide depositing

tce: total composite error

TCF: 20th-Century Fox; Twentieth Century Fund

TCG: Theatre Communications Group

T C & G B: Tucson, Cornelia & Gila Bend (railroad)

tch: travel counselor's handbook

TCH: Trans-Canada Highway

tchg: teaching

TcHHW: tropic higher high water

TcHHWI: tropic higher high water interval

TcHLW: tropic higher low water

tchr: teacher

TCI: The Combustion Institute; Theoretical Chemistry Institute

tcj: terminal coaxial junction

tcl: transistor-coupled logic

TCL: Transatlantic Carriers Limited; Turkish Cargo Lines

TcLHW: tropic lower high water

TcLLW: tropic lower low water

TcLLWI: tropic lower low water interval

TCM: Texas Citrus Mutual; Trinity College of Music

TCN: Transportation Control Number

TCNCO: Test Control Noncommissioned Officer

TCNM: Timpanagos Cave National Monument (Utah)

TCO: Termination Contracting Officer; Test Control Officer

tcp: traffic control post

TCP: Task Change Proposal; Task Control Proposal; Temporary Change Proposal

TCPL: Trans-Canada Pipe Lines

tcr: temperature coefficient of resistance

TCR: Tennessee Central Railway

TCRMG: Tripartite Commission for the Restitution of Monetary Gold (American-British-French commission, headquartered in Brussels)

TCS: Twin City Secularists

T & CS: Transportation and Communication Service

TCSO: Tri-City Symphony Orchestra

tctl: tactical

TCTO: Time Compliance Technical Order(s)

TCU: Texas Christian University

TCUS: Tax Court of the United States

T-cushion: T-shaped cushion

tcv: temperature-control valve

tcw: time code work

TCWH: Teamsters, Chauffeurs, Warehousemen and Helpers (union)

td: tank destroyer; technical data; test data; third defense (lacrosse); tile drain; time delay; time of departure; timed disintegration; tod (28 pounds of wool); tool design; tool disposition; touchdown (football); transmitter distributor; trust deed; turbine drive; 'tween deck

t/d: time deposit

t.d.: *ter die* (Latin—thrice daily)

t & d: taps and dies

TD: Table of Distribution; Tactical Division; tank destroyer; Teachers Diploma; Territorial Decoration; Testing and Development (USCG); Topographic Draftsman; Training Detachment; Treasury Decision; Treasury Department; Treasury Division; Trinidad and Tobago; Typographic Draftsman

TD: *Teachta Dala* (Gaelic—Member of the House of Commons)

tda: tunnel-diode amplifier

TDA: Timber Development Association; Train Dispatchers Association

T-day: day for time schedule testing

TDB: Toronto-Dominion Bank

tdc: top dead center

TDC: Telemetry Data Center

td cu: tinned copper

TDD: Tuberculous Diseases Diploma

tddl: time-division data link

tddlpo: time division data link printout

tdf: two-degree-of-freedom (gyroscope)

tdg: twist drill gauge

TDG: Transport Development Group

tdh: total dynamic head

Tdh: Trondheim

TDI: Target Data Inventory; Tool and Die Institute; Transportation Displays Incorporated

TDK: *Turk Dil Kurumu* (Turkish Language Association)

t dk(s): 'tween deck(s)

tdl: total damn loss

tdm: tandem; time division multiplexing

tdn: totally digestible nutrients

TDO: Technical Development Objective

TDOT: Thorndike Dimensions of Temperament

tdp: target director post; technical data package; technical development plans; thermal death point

TDP: Technical Development Plan

tdpfo: temporary duty pending further orders

tdr: time-delay relay; time domain reflectometry

TDR: Technical Documentary Report

TDRL: Temporary Disability Retired List

t/d rly: time-delay relay

tds: telemetering decommutation system

TDS: Tanami Desert Sanctuary (Northern Territory, Australia)

TDS: *Toronto Daily Star*

TDSTS: Tidbinbilla Deep-Space Tracking Station

TDT: Transport Department Tasmania

tdu: target detection unit

tdw: tons deadweight (tare of a ship)

tdwy: treadway

tdy: temporary duty; toady

te: table of equipment; task element; technical exchange; tenants; tenants by the entirety; thermal efficiency; tinted edge; trailing edge; transverse electric; transverse wave (symbol); trial and error; turbine electric; turboelectric; twin engine

t & e: testing and evaluation; trial and error

Te: tellurium

TE: Table of Equipment; Task Element; Technical Exchange;

Telefis Eireann (Television Ireland); Topographical Engineer

T & E: Toledo & Eastern (railroad)

TEA: Tennessee Education Association; Tucson Education Association

teach.: teacher; teaching

Teacher President: James Abram Garfield—twentieth President of the United States

Teague: (nickname for an Irishman)

TEAL: Tasman Empire Airways, Limited

TEAM: Technique for Evaluation and Analysis of Maintainability

TEAS: Threat Evaluation and Action Selection (program)

tease.: tracking errors and simulation evaluation (radar)

Teatro Colón: (Spanish—Columbus Theater)—Buenos Aires opera house

TEB: Tax Exemption Board; Textile Economics Bureau

tec: technic; technical; technician; technics; technological; technology

tech: technic; technical; technician; technics; technique(s); technological; technology

tech ed: technical editing; technical editor

tech memo: technical memorandum

techn: technician

technol: technological; technologist; technology

tech rep: technical representative

tech rept: technical report

tech writer: technical writer

TECOM: Test and Evaluation Command (US Army)

tecquinol: hydroquinone

Tec Sgt: Technical Sergeant

Ted(dy): Edward; Theodore; Theodosia

TEE: Trans Europe Express

teenybop: teenybopper (underground slang—young child attuned to the modern scene)—*see* macrobop

TEFL: teaching English as a foreign language

teflon: tetrafluoroethylene (polymerized synthetic plastic resin)

teg: top edge gilt

Teg: Tegel

te ga: taper gauge

TEGMA: Terminal Elevator Grain Merchants Association

Tegoose: Tegucigalpa (Honduras)

teg(s): thermoelectric generator(s)

Teh: Teheran

TEI: Texaco Experiment Incorporated

tel: telegraph; telegraphic; telegraphy; telephone; telephonic; tele-

phony; teletype; teletypewriter; television; tetraethyl lead

tel: (Arabic—hill, as in Tel Aviv, Tel el Amarna, Tel el Kebir)

Tel: Telefunken; Telugu

TELAM: Telenoticiosa Americana (Argentine press service)

telaut: telautograph; telautography

telecast(er): television broadcast-(er)

telecom: telecommunication

telecon: telephone communication

telecopy: telephonic copying process (developed by Xerox)

telecourse: television-constructed course

telef: *telefon* (Norwegian—telephone)

telefilm: television film

teleg: telegrapher; telegraphy

teleol: teleology

telepak: telemetering package

teleph: telephony

teleplay: televised play; television play

teleran: televised radar aerial navigation

telesurance: television insurance

telethon: television marathon

teletrial: television trial

telev (TV): television

telex (tex): teletype exchange

telly: television

tel no.: telephone number

telsim: teletypewriter simulator

tel sur: telephone survey

tem: temporal

tem.: *tempus* (Latin—time); *tempo* (Italian—time)

Tem: temple

TEM: Territorial Efficiency Medal

temar: thermoelectric marine application

temp: temper; temperature; tempered; tempering; template; temporary; temporize

Temp: *Tempest, The*

temp. dext.: *tempori dextro* (Latin —to the right temple)

temping: (office girl's jargon—temporary substituting)

TEMPO: Technical Military Planning Operation

tempos: temporary buildings, houses, offices, officials, workers, et cetera

temp sec: temporary secretary

temp. sin.: *tempori sinistro* (Latin —to the left temple)

ten.: tenant; tender; tenderize(d); tenement; tenor

ten.: *tenuto* (Italian—to hold, a chord or tone)

tend.: tendon

Tenn: Tennessee; Tennessean

tenna(s): antenna(s)

Tenneco: Tennessee Gas Companies

TENOC: ten years of oceanography (1961–1970)

tenot: tenotomy

tens: tensile; tension

tens str: tensile strength

tent.: tentative

Ten^te: *Teniente* (Spanish—Lieutenant)

TEOO: Territorial Economic Opportunity Office(r)

tepi: training equipment planning information

TEPS: Teacher Education and Professional Standards

ter: terminal; terminate; termination; terrace; terrazzo; territory; teritary

ter.: *tere* (Latin—rub)

Ter: Terrace; Territory; Teruel

tera: 10^{12}

TERA: The Electrical Research Association

terat: teratology

tercio: (Spanish—third)

t & e rec: time and events recorder

Teri: Theresa; Therese

therm.: terminal; terminate; terminology

te rm: taper reamer

TERPACIS: Trust Territory of the Pacific Islands

terps: (drug user's slang—elixir of terpin hydrate and codeine)— cough mixture and codeine combination

terr: terrace; terrotory

Terr: Terrace

terra: (Italian—earth; land)

TERRA: Terricide Escape by Rethinking, Research, Action

terre: (French—earth; land, as in Terrebonne, Terre Haute, Terres Mauvaises)

Terry: Terence; Teresa; Terrell; Terrill; Theresa; Therese

ter. sim.: *tere simul* (Latin—rub together)

Tert: Tertiary

TES: Telemetering Evaluation Station

TESO: *Texel's Eigen Stoomboot Onderneming* (Dutch—Texel's Own Steamship Society)

TESOL: Teachers of English to Speakers of Other Languages

Tess(ie): Theresa

TEST: *Thesaurus of Engineering and Scientific Terms*

test^mto: *testamento* (Spanish—testament)

test^o: *testigo* (Spanish—witness)

tet: test equipment tool; tetanus; tetrachloride

TET: Teacher of Electrotherapy

tetr: tetragonal
tetrah: tetrahedral
TEU: Test of Economic Understanding
Teut: Teuton; Teutonic
tew (TEW): tactical early warning
tex: telex (teletype exchange)
t ex: till exempel (Swedish—for example
Tex: Texan; Texas
TEX: Corpus Christi, Texas (tracking station)
TEXACO: The Texas Company
TEXAS: Trained Experienced Area Specialist
Texas RRC: Texas Railroad Commission
Tex Instr: Texas Instruments (Corporation)
text.: textile
textir: text indexing and retrieval
tf: tabulating form; tactile fremitus; temporary fix; thin film; tile floor; till forbidden (run ad until stopped by advertising client); transfer function; tuberculin filtrate
TF: Tallulah Falls (railroad); Task Force; Tax Foundation; Test Flight; Tolstoy Foundation; torpedo-fighter (airplane); trainer-fighter (airplane); training film; tropical freshwater (vessel loadline marking); Twentieth Century-Fox Films (stock exchange symbol)
T del F: Tierra del Fuego
tfa: total fatty acids; transfer function analyzer
TFA: Textile Fabrics Association; Tie Fabrics Association; Trout Farmers Association
TFAA: Track and Field Athletes of America
TFB: Thatcher Ferry Bridge (over Panama Canal)
tfc: traffic
TFCRI: Tropical Fish Culture Research Institute
tfcsd: total federal commissioned service date
tfd: target-to-film distance
tfe: tetrafluoroethylene (halon or teflon plastic)
TFF: Tropical Fish Farm
TFI: Table Fashion Institute; Tax Foundation Incorporated; Textile Foundation Incorporated
TFLA: Texas Foreign Language Association
TFNS: Territorial Force Nursing Service
TFP: Trees for People
tfr: terrain-following radar
TFr: Tunisian franc
tft: thin-film technology; thin-film transistor

TFX: variable geometry supersonic fighter-bomber
tg: tail gear; telegram; telegraph; tollgate; type genus; tongue and groove
t/g: tracking and guidance
t & g: tongue and groove
Tg: Tanjong (Malayan—cape)
TG: Task Group; Texas Gulf Sulphur (stock exchange symbol); Torpedo Group; Traffic Guidance
T & G: Traveres & Gulf (Florida railroad); Tremont & Gulf (Louisiana railroad)
T-et-G: Tarn-et-Garonne
tga: thermogravimetric analysis
TGA: Toilet Goods Association
t'gal'n't: topgallant (sail)
tgb: tongued, grooved, and beaded
TGC: Travel Group Charter(s)
tgca: transportable ground-control approach
tge: transmissible gastroenteritis
TGG: temporary geographic grid
tgl: toggle
TG loran: traffic guidance loran
TGM: Thomas G. Masaryk
tgn: tangent
TGP: Terminal Guidance Program
TGPLC: Transcontinental Gas Pipe Line Corporation
tgt: target
TGT: Tennessee Gas Transmission
TGU: Tegucigalpa, Honduras (airport)
TGWU: Transport and General Workers' Union
th: tee handle
t & h: transportation and handling
Th: Thai (Siamese); Thailand (Siam); Thomas; thorium
Th: Theil (German—part)
TH: true heading
T H: Technische Hochschule (German—technical college)
THA: Transvaal Horse Artillery
Thad: Thaddeus
THAI: Thai Airways International
Thal: (German—valley)
Thaler: (German abbreviation—Joachimsthaler)—Joachim's dollar—Bohemian coin struck in 16th century at Czech town of Jachymov (Joachimsthal)—its name has become *dollar*
thanat: thanatology
That Man: Franklin Delano Roosevelt
that's: that is
Th.B.: *Theologiae Baccalaureus* (Latin—Bachelor of Theology)
TH & B: Toronto, Hamilton and Buffalo (railroad)

TH & BA: Toll, Highways and Bridge Authority
thc: tetrahydrocannabinol (active ingredient in psychedelic drugs such as hashish, indian hemp, and marijuana)
THC: Toronto Harbour Commission; Toronto Harbour Commissioners
thd: thread; threaded; threads; total harmonic distortion
Th.D.: *Theologiae Doctor* (Latin—Doctor of Theology)
THD: Technisch Hogeschool te Delft (Technological University of Delft)
th di: thread die
thea: theater
T-head: Texas-tea head (underground slang—marijuana user)
theat: theater; theatrical
The Bank: The Bank of England
The Brothers: The Brothers Edmund and Jules de Goncourt; *The Brothers Karamazov*—Dostoevski
The Carthaginian Lion: General Hannibal
The Enlightenment: Europe's 18th century when encyclopedias appeared in France and England, when Voltaire and Lavoisier were matched across the Channel by Paine and Pries'ley
The Fuzz: [American underworld slang—detective(s); law-enforcement officer(s); police; etc.]
The Immortals: (jocular nickname—forty members of the French Academy)
The Invincible: Spanish Armada defeated by English vessels commanded by Sir Francis Drake
The Just Society: (nickname—Prime Minister Pierre Trudeau's administration of Canada)
THEN: Those Hags Encourage Neuterism
The Navigator: Prince Henrique of Portugal (1394 to 1460)
THEO: They Help Each Other
theod: theodolite
theol: theology
The Old: King Grom of Denmark (860–935)
The Old Party: W(illiam) Somerset Maugham
theor: theorem; theoretical
theos: theosophy
ther: therapy
therap: therapeutic; therapeutics; therapy
there's: there is
therm: thermometer; thermostat(ic)

thermistor: thermal resistor

thermoc: thermocouple

thermodyn: thermodynamics

thermonuc: thermonuclear

thesp(s): thespian(s)

The Sun King: Louis XVI

The Terrible: Ivan IV—Czar of Russia 1547 to 1584

The Tragic Queen: Marie Antoinette

The Tribune Man: (pseudonym —Henry Ten Eyck White)

they'd: they had; they would

they'll: they will

they're: they are

they've: they have

THF: West Berlin, Germany (Tempelhof Airport)

THG: Technische Hochschule Graz (Technical University of Graz)

th ga: thread gauge

THHS: Townsend Harris High School

thi: temperature-humidity index

THIWRP: The Hoover Institution on War, Revolution, and Peace

thixo: thixotropic

Th:J: Thomas Jefferson (initials written by him as shown)

thk: thick(ness)

THK: *Turk Hava Kurumu* (Turkish Air Association)

Th.M.: *Theologiae Magister* (Latin —Master of Theology)

Thomas Jefferson Snodgrass: (pseudonym—Samuel L. Clemens)

THOMIS: Total Hospital Operating and Medical Information System

thor: thorax; thoracic

Thor: medium-range ballistic missile

thoro: thorough

Thoro: thoroughfare

Thos: Thomas

Thos Jeff: Thomas Jefferson

thou.: thousand

thp: thrust horsepower; track history printout

THq: theater headquarters

thr: their; threonine (amino acid) (THR); through; thrust

THR: Teheran, Iran (airport)

three-R's: reading, writing, arithmetic (colloquially: readin', 'ritin', 'rithmetic)

thro': through

thrombo: thrombosis

throt: throttle

thru: through

Thru: Thruway

thruppence: threepence

THS: Technical High School; Tiwi Hot Springs (Philippines); Tottenville High School

THT: Teacher of Hydrotherapy

th ta: thread tap

thtr: theater

THTRA: Thorium High-Temperature Reactor Association

Thu: Thursday

THU: The Hebrew University (Jerusalem)

thud.: thorium-uranium-deuterium (mixture)

Thurs: Thursday

Thus: (nickname—Calcutta Steam Tug); Thursday

THW: Technische Hochschule Wien (Technical University of Vienna)

THY: Turk Hava Yollari (Turkish airline)

ti: target identification; temperature indication; temperature indicator; termination instruction; tricuspid insufficiency

ti: Texas Instruments (trademark); *tudni illik* (Hungarian—that is)

Ti: titanium

Ti: *Tirsdag* (Danish—Tuesday)

TI: Technical Inspection; Technical Institute; Technical Intelligence; Terminal Island; Termination Instruction; Texas Instruments; Textile Institute; Thread Institute; Title Insurance (and Trust Company); Toastmasters International; Tobacco Institute; Tonga Islands; Training Instruction; Treasure Island; Tungsten Institute; Tuskegee Institute

T of I: *Times of India*

TIA: Tax Institute of America; Trans International Airlines; Tricot Institute of America; Trouser Institute of America

TIAA: Teachers Insurance and Annuity Association of America

TIAS: Treaties and other International Acts Series (US Department of State)

tib: tibia(l); trimmed in bunkers

Tib: Isabel; Tibet; Tibetan

TIB: Technical Information Bulletin; Tennessee Inspection Bureau; Thousand Islands Bridge; Tourist Information Bureau

tibc: total iron-binding capacity

tibia: (Spanish—tepid, *f.*)

tibio: (Spanish—tepid, *m.*)

tic.: target intercept computer

TIC: Technical Information Center; Technical Institute Council; Technical Intelligence Center; Texas Industrial Commission

TICA: Technical Information Center Administration

tick.: tickler

Tico: Costa Rican; Ticonderoga; USS *Ticonderoga* (attack aircraft carrier)

Ticos: Costa Ricans (nickname given them by other Central Americans because of their frequent use of the Spanish diminutive *ico*)

TICUS: Tidal Current Survey System

tid: task initiation date

t.i.d.: *tres in die* (Latin—thrice a day)

tidskr: *tidskrift* (Swedish—periodical)

tie.: technical integration and evaluation

TIE: Truck Insurance Exchange

Tiempo: *El Tiempo* (Time—Bogotá's leading newspaper)

Tien: Tientsin

tier.: tierce

Tierg: Tiergarten

tierra: (Spanish—earth; land)

tif: telephone influence factor; telephone interference factor; tumor inducing factor

Tif: Tiflis

Tiff: *Tiffany's Reports*

TIFR: Tata Institute of Fundamental Research

tig: time in grade; tungsten-inert gas

TIG: The Inspector General

tigon: offspring of tiger and lioness

TII: Texas Instruments Incorporated; Toastmasters International Incorporated

TIJ: Tijuana, Mexico (airport)

'til: until

Tilda: Mathilda

Tilly: Mathilda

Tim: Timor; Timothy

Tim: *Timon of Athens*

timb: *timbales* (French—kettledrums)

TIMC: The Industrial Mangement Center

Times: *The New York Times* (leading American newspaper, published in New York City); *The Times* (leading British newspaper, published in London); local designation for all other newspapers containing *Times* in their title

timet: titanium metal(s)

timm: thermionic integrated micromodules

Timmy: Timothy

timp: *timpani* (Italian—kettledrums)

TIMS: The Institute of Management Sciences

TIN: Transaction Identification Number

Tina: Albertina; Christina; Clementina; Valentina

tinct: tincture

TINs: Temporary Instruction Notices

t$_{int}$: international practical temperature

Tintoretto: Jacopo Robusti

tio: time interval optimization

TIO: Target Indication Office(r); Television Information Office(r); Test Integration Office(r); Troop Information Office(r)

tip.: tax information plan; theory in practice

tip: tipografia; tipografico (Italian—printing firm; typographic); truly important person (TIP)

Tip: Tipperary

TIP: The Institute of Physics; Tripoli, Libya (airport); Troop Information Program(s); truly important person

TIPAC: Texas Instruments Programming and Control

tip. bkt: tipping bracket

Tipp: Tipperary

TIPRO: Texas Independent Producers and Royalty Owners

tips.: to insure prompt service (gratuities); truly important persons (TIPS)

TIPS: Technical Information Processing System; Total Integrated Pneumatic System; truly important persons

TIP & TPS: The Institute of Physics and The Physical Society

tir: total indicator reading

Tiradentes: (Portuguese—Tooth Puller)—nickname of José Joaquim da Silva Xavier—first Brazilian fighter for independence from Portuguese rule—a dentist

TIRB: Transportation Insurance Rating Bureau

Tiros: American meteorological satellite designed to observe cloud coverage and infrared heat radiation of the earth; television and infrared observation satellite

Tirso de Molina: (pseudonym —Gabriel Tellez)

tis: tissue(s)

TIS: Technical Information Service; Total Information System

Tish: Letitia

TISPM: Territorie des Îles St.-Pierre et Miquelon (French territory offshore Canada)

tit.: title; titular; titulary

tit: titre (French—title)

tit: título (Spanish—title)

Tit: Titus, The Epistle of Paul to

TIT: Tokyo Institute of Technology; Tustin Institute of Technology

Tit A: Titus Andronicus

Titan: intercontinental ballistic missile (Martin)

titanox: titanium dioxide

Titian: Tiziano Vecellio

tit^0: título (Spanish—title)

Tito: Josip Broz(ovich)

tiv: total indicator variation

tj: tomato juice; triceps jerk; turbojet (TJ)

tj: to jest (Polish—that is)

TJ: Thomas Jefferson

TJAG: The Judge Advocate General

tjc : trajectory

TjC: trajectory chart

TJC: The Jockey Club; Trenton Junior College; Tyler Junior College

TjD: trajectory diagram

TJHS: Thomas Jefferson High School

TJM: The Jewish Museum; Thomas Jefferson Memorial

tjp (TJP): turbojet propulsion

TJPOI: Twisted Jute Packing and Oakum Institute

TJSUSA: Thomas Jefferson Society of the United States of America

tk: track; truck; trunk

tk: to kum (printer's expression meaning material is *to come*)

Tk: Turkmenian; Turkmenistan

tkg: tanking

TKK: Teikoku Kaiji Kyokai (Imperial Japanese Marine Corporation, ship classifiers)

tko: technical knockout

tkr: tanker

tks: thanks

tkt: ticket

tl: terminal limen; test link; thrust line; time length; time limit; total load; transmission level; transmission line; truckload; truck loading

t-l: trade last (slang, a compliment)

t/l: total loss

Tl: thallium

TL: Technical Letter; Technical Library; Texas League; The Leprosarium (U.S. Public Health Service, Carville, Louisiana); Townland (UK); Turk lirasi (Turkish pound)

T-L: Time-Life (books, magazines, recordings)

TLA: Theatre Library Association; Trinidad Lake Asphalt

Tlax: Tlaxcala (inhabitants—Tlaxcaltecas)

TLB: temporary lighted buoy

tlc: tender loving care

TLCPA: Toledo-Lucas County Port Authority

tld: tooled

tle: theoretical line of escape

tlf: telefon (Norwegian—telephone)

tlg: tail landing gear; telegraph

TLH: Tallahassee, Florida (airport)

tli: translunar injection

tlm: telemeter; telemetry

Tln: Tallinn

tlo: total loss only

tlp: term-limit pricing; threshold learning process

tlr: trailer

TLR: Tool Liaison Request

tls: testing the limits for sex

TLS: Terminal Landing System; The Law Society; Trinity Lighthouse Service

TLS: Times Literary Supplement

tltr: translator

tlu: table look up

tlv: threshold limit value(s)

TLV: Tel Aviv, Israel (airport)

tlvsn: television

tlz: titanium, lead, zinc

tm: standard mean temperature; tactical missile (TM); team; temperature meter; time modulation; tractor monoplane (TM); trademark; transport mechanism; transverse magnetic; true mean; twisting moment

tm: tonelada métrica (Spanish —metric ton, 2,200 pounds)

t/m: test and maintenance

t & m: time and material

Tm: thulium

TM: tactical missile; Technical Manual; Technical Memoranda; Technical Memorandum; Technical Minutes; Technical Monograph; telemetering; Test Manual; Texas Mexican (railroad); The Maccabees; Toledo Museum; tractor monoplane; trademark; Training Manual; Training Mission(s); Trainmaster; Transcendental Meditation; Tropical Medicine

TM: Technical Manual; Turk Mali (Turkish—Made in Turkey)

T/M (t/m): trailmobile (automobile trailer)

T de M: Teléfonos de México (Telephone System of Mexico)

tma: total materiel assets; total military assets

TMA: Texas Maritime Academy; Theatrical Mutual Association; Tile Manufacturers Association; Tobacco Merchants Association; Toiletry Merchandisers Association; Toy Manufacturers Association

t mar: trial marriage

tmbr: timber

TMC: Technical Measurement Corporation; Texas Medical Center

(Houston); Trans Mar de Cortés (Mexican airline)

TMCA: Titanium Metals Corporation of America

tmcd: tetramethylcyclobutanediol

tmcp: trimethylenecyclopropane

TME: Teacher of Medical Electricity

T-men: Treasury Department law-enforcement officers

TMF: The Menninger Foundation

tmh: tons per manhour

TMI: Telemeter Magnetics Incorporated; Tool Manufacturing Instruction; Tube Methods Incorporated

TMIS: Technical Meetings Information Service

tmkpr: timekeeper

tml (TML): three-mile limit

TMNP: Tamborine Mountain National Parks (Queensland)

tmo (TMO): telegraph money order

TMO: telegraph money order; Traffic Management Officer

TMORN: Texaco Metropolitan Opera Radio Network

tmp: temperature; trimethyl phosphate (male contraceptive)

Tmp: Tampico

tmpry: temporary

tmp's: transcendental meditation practitioners

tmr: timer; total materiel requirement

tmrbm (TMRBM): transportable midrange ballistic missile

tms: type, model, and series

tms: tai muuta semmoista (Finnish—and so on)

TMS: Tactical Missile Squadron; Technical Museum, Stockholm

TMS: Tribunal Maritime Special (French—Special Maritime Court)—disciplinary prison court functioning in French Guiana

tmsd: total military service date

TMT: transonic model tunnel

TMTB: The Malayan Tin Bureau

TMUS: Toy Manufacturers of the United States

tmv: true mean value

TMV: Transportadora Maritima Venezolana (Venezuelan Line)

tmw: thermal megawatts; tomorrow

TMW: Textile Machine Works

tn: tariff number; telephone number; thermonuclear; train; true north

Tn: thoron

TN: Technical Note

T & N: Turner and Newhall

TNA: The National Archives

TNC: Thai Navigation Company

TNDC: Thai National Documenta-tion Center

tng: training

TNG: Tangier, Morocco (airport); The National Grange

tnge: tonnage

TNI: Tentara Nasional Indonesia (Indonesian National Army)

TNM: Telégrafos Nacionales de México; Texas-New Mexican; Texas-New Mexico; Tokyo National Museum; Tumacacori National Monument

TNNP: Taman Negara National Park (Malaysia); Terra Nova National Park (Newfoundland)

T & NO: Texas and New Orleans (railroad)

t no c: threads no couplings

TNP: Tarangire National Park (Tanzania); Taroba NP (India); Tonariro NP (North Island, New Zealand); Tsavo NP (Kenya)

tnpg: trinitrophloroglucinol

TNPG: The Nuclear Power Group

Tnpk: Turnpike

tnr: trainer

TNR: Tananarive, Malagasy (airport); Tucki Nature Reserve (New South Wales)

tns: toasted nutri-soy

Tns: Tunis

TNS: Transit Navigation System

tnt (TNT): trinitrotoluene

TNTC: Thames Nautical Training College

tntv: tentative

tn wep(s): thermonuclear weapon(s)

TNWR: Tamarac National Wildlife Refuge (Minnesota); Tewaukon NWR (North Dakota); Tishomingo NWR (Oklahoma)

tnx: thanks

to.: time opening; tool order (TO); turn over

t.o.: tinctura opii (Latin—tincture of opium)

tº: tomo (Spanish—volume)

t/o (TO): takeoff

t & o: taken and offered; technical and office (workers)

To: Togo

TO: Table of Organization; takeoff; Technical Observer; Technical Order(s); Theater of Operations; Tool Order; Transportation Office(r); Travel Order

To: Torsdag (Danish—Thursday)

TO: Technical Order

toa: total obligational authority

TOA: Theater Owners of America; Toledo Opera Association

toac: tool accessory

tob: tobacco

Tob: Tobago; The (Apocryphal) Book of Tobit

tobac: tobacco; tobacconist

TOBE: Test of Basic Education

TOBWE: Tactical Observing Weather Element (USAF)

Toby: Tobias

toc: top-blown oxygen converter

TOC: Tactical Operations Center; Technical Order Compliance; Television Operating Center

TOCCWE: Tactical Operations Control Center Weather Element (USAF)

tod: time of delivery

TOD: Technical Objective Document

toe.: term of enlistment; total operating expense

TOE: Table of Equipment

T O & E: Texas, Oklahoma & Eastern (railroad)

TOEFL: Test of English as a Foreign Language

TOES: Tradeoff Evaluation System

tof: time of flight

tofc: trailer on flatcar (or piggyback)

TOGA: Tests of General Ability

to'gal'nt: topgallant (mast or sail)

togw: takeoff gross weight

tog/wi: together with

tohp: takeoff horsepower

Tojo: General Hideki Tojo

Tok: Tokyo

tol: tolerance; toluene

Tol: Toledo; Toledan

TOL: Toledo, Ohio (airport)

Tol Orc: Toledo Orchestra

to lt: towing light

tom: tomo (Spanish—volume)

t-o-m: the old man (the boss; the captain; the chief; the father)

Tom: Thomas

TOM: Territoire d'Outre-Mer (Overseas Territory)

tomats: tomatoes

Tommie: Thomas

Tommy: nickname for a British soldier; Thomas

Tommy Atkins: (nickname for a British Army private)

tom thumb: (Cockney—rum)

Ton: Tonga or Friendly Islands

TONACS: Technical Order Notification and Completion System

Toni: Antonia

Ton Isl: Tonga Islands

tonn: tonnage

Tono: Tomuelo (Tony derived from Anthony)

Tony: Anthony; Antoinette Perry Awards (American Theatre Wing)

too.: time of origin

top.: temporarily out of print; topographical (three-dimensional) art; torque oil pressure

Top: Topeka

topa: tooling pattern

TOPICS: Tables of Periodical Indices Concerning Schools

topo: topographic; topography

TopoCom: Topographic Command (USA)

topog: topography

topol: topology

tops.: take off pounds sensibly (rational weight reduction program)

TOPS: Teen-age Opportunity Programs in Summer

TopSec: Top Secret

tops'l: topsail

tor: time of receipt; torque; torquing

Tor: Toronto

Toray: Tokyo Rayon Company (tradename)

torn.: tornado

torp: torpedo; torpedoman

torp: (Swedish—village)

torr: 1 mm of mercury

torre: (Italian, Portuguese, Spanish —tower, as in Torre del Greco)

tos: term of service

TOS: The Orton Society; Tiros Operational Satellite

tose: tooling samples

TOSS: Tiros Operation Satellite System

tot: time on (over) target; total; totalize; totalizer

t o t: tukus om tisch (Yiddish—put your cards on the table)

TOT: Tourist Organization of Thailand

TOTCO: Technical Oil Tool Corporation

TOTO: Tongue of the Ocean (deepwater channel in Great Bahama Bank)

totp: tooling template

Tou: Toulon

Tough Guy: (stock exchange nickname for Texas Gulf Sulphur company)

tour.: tourism; tourist

tourn: tournament

TOUS: Test on Understanding Science

townet: towing net

tox: toxemia; toxic; toxicant; toxicologist; toxicology

toxicol: toxicology

tp: target practice; teaching practice; technical paper; telephone; teleprinter; title page; total points; total protein; transport pilot; treaty port; turning point

t/p: test panel

t & p: theft and pilferage

Tp: Township; Troop

TP: Technical Pamphlet; Technical Paper; Technical Problem; Technical Publication; Technographic Publication; Texas & Pacific (railroad); Thompson Products; Torrey Pines (Institute); True Position

T.P.: Tempore Pachale (Latin —Easter time)

T & P: Texas and Pacific (railroad)

tpa: travel by privately owned conveyance authorized

TPA: Tampa, Florida (Tampa International Airport); Tampa Port Authority; Trans-Pacific Airlines (Aloha Airline); Travelers' Protective Association

TPC: The Peace Corps (US Department of State)

tpd: tons per day

tp'd: toilet papered (some teenager's idea of house-and-garden decoration)

TPE: Taipei, Formosa (airport)

TPEQ: Task of Public Education Questionnaire

TPF: Tactical Police Force; Thomas Paine Foundation

tpgh: tons per gang hour

tph: tons per hour

TPH: Theosophical Publishing House

TPH & PCA: Toy Pistol, Holster, and Paper Cap Association

TPHS: Thomas Paine High School

tpi: teeth (threads, tons, or turns) per inch; treponema pallidum immobilization (test)

TPI: Tennessee Polytechnic Institute; Torrey Pines Institute; Truss Plate Institute

Tpk: Turnpike

TPL: Tallahassee Public Library; Tampa Public Library; Toledo Public Library; Toronto Public Libraries; Tucson Public Library; Tulsa Public Library

tpm: tape preventive maintenance; tons per minute

TPN: Tatrzanskiego Parku Narodowego (Polish—High Tatra National Park)—in the Tatra Mountains of Poland

tyng: topping

TPNHS: Thomas Paine National Historical Society

tpnl: test panel

tpo: tiempo (Spanish—time)

TPO: Tulsa Philharmonic Orchestra

tpob: true point of beginning

TPP: Total Package Procurement

TPPC: Total Package Procurement Concept; Trans-Pacific Passenger Conference

tpqi: teacher-pupil question inventory

tpr: telescopic photographic recorder; temperature profile recorder; thermoplastic recording

TPRC: Thermophysical Properties Research Center

tpri: teacher-pupil relationship inventory

TPRI: Tropical Pesticides Research Institute

T & P Ry: Texas and Pacific Railway

tps: technical problem summary

tp's: taxpayers

TPS: Technical Publishing Society; The Physical Society

TPT: Toy Preference Test; Transonic Pressure Tunnel (NASA)

tptg: turned plate turned grid

tpw: title page wanting

TP & W: Toledo, Peoria & Western (railroad)

t.q.: tale quale (Latin—as is)

TQCA: Textile Quality Control Association

tr: temperature, rectal; test run; tons registered; toothed ring; trace; tracking radar; translation; transmit-receive; transmitter-receiver; tuberculin R

tr: trillo (Italian—rolled or shaken, as in drumming or when shaking a tambourine); *traduit* French—translated); *trykkeri* (Dano-Norwegian—printing office); *tryckt* (Swedish—printed); *trykt* (Dano-Norwegian—printed)

t-r: transmit-receive

Tr: Trieste

TR: Tasmanian Railway; Technical Regulation; Technical Report; Test Report; Texas Gulf Producing Company (stock exchange symbol); Theodore (Teddy) Roosevelt; Therapeutic Radiology; torpedo reconnaissance (naval aircraft); Training Regulations; Transportation Request; Travel Request; Trieste; Trip Report; Triumph (British auto or motorcycle); Turkey (auto plaque)

tra: transformer-reactor assembly

TRA: Technical Report Authorization; Textile Refinishers Association; Theodore Roosevelt Association; Thoroughbred Racing Associations; Tire and Rim Association; Trade Relations Association; Travel Research Association

trac: tracer; tractor

TRACALS: Traffic Control and Landing System

tracdr: tractor-drawn

TRACE: Task Reporting and Current Evaluation

tracon: terminal radar control

TRACS: Telescoping Rotor Aircraft System

Tracy: Theresa

trad: traducido (Spanish—translated)

Trader Horn: nickname of Alfred Aloysius Smith

tradic: transistor digital computer

traf: traffic

trag: tragedy

T-rail: T-shaped rail

TRAIN: Telerail Automated Information Network

TRAIS: Transportation Research Activity Information Service (Department of Transportation)

tram.: tracking radar automatic monitoring; tramcar; trammel; tramway

tran: transient

trans: transactions; transfer; transit; transport; transportation; transpose; transposition

Trans: Transactions

transac: transaction(s)

Transan: Transandean Railway

transatl: transatlantic

transc: transcription

Trans-Carib: Trans-Caribbean Airways

TRANSDEC: Transducer Electronic Center

transec: transmission security

transf: transfer; transference; transformer

transfax: facsimile transmission

transie(s): transvestite(s)

transistor: transfer resistor

Transj: Transjordan; Transjordanian

transl: translation; translator

translit: transliteration

translu: translucent

translun: translunar; translunarian; translunarite

transm: transmission

transp: transparent

transpac: transpacific

transpl: transplant(ation); transplanted

transport.: transportation

Transron: Transport Squadron

Trans-Sib: Trans-Siberian (railroad)

transv: transverse

Transv: Transvaal

transv sect: transverse section

trap.: trapdoor; trap drums; trapeze; trapezoid(al); trapezium

TRAP: Tracker Analysis Program

traps.: trap drums; trap drummer(s)

tratel: trailer motel

trau: traumatic

TRAUS: Thoroughbred Racing Association of the US

trav.: travel

Trav: Travancore; Travis

Traven: B. Traven (pseudonym used by Berick Traven Torsvan)

trc: total response to crisis

TRC: Trans-Caribbean Airways; Transportation Research Command

Tr & C: Troilus and Cressida

tr coil: tripping coil

TRCS: Trade Relations Council of the United States

Trd: Trinidad

TRD: Test Requirements Document

TRDCOM: Transportation Research and Development Command

TRE: Telecommunications Research Establishment

treas: treasure; treasurer; treasury

Treas: Treasurer

trec: tracking radar electronic components

TRECOM: Transportation Research and Engineeing Command

Tren: Trenton

treph: trephining (trepanning)

très sec: (French—extra-dry, almost tart champagne or wine)

trf: transfer; tuned radio frequency

TRF: Transportation Research Foundation; Turf Research Foundation

trg: training

trgt: target

TRH: Their Royal Highnesses

TRHS: Theodore Roosevelt High School

tri: total response index (TRI); triangle; triangulation; tricolor; tricycle; triode

Tri: Trieste

Tri: Tohtori (Finnish—doctor)

TRI: Technical Report Instruction; Textile Research Institute; The Rockefeller Institute; Tin Research Institute; Tire Retreading Institute; total response index

TRIAL: Technique for Retrieving Information from Abstracts of Literature

trian: triangle; triangulation

Trias Triassic

trib: tribade; tribadism; tribal; tribalism; tribalist; tribasic; tribunal; tribune; tributary

Tri B: Triborough Bridge

tribas: tribasic

TRIBE: Teaching and Research in Bicultural Education

trib^l: tribunal (Spanish—tribunal; court of justice)

tric: trichloroethylene

tricaphos: tricalcium phosphate

Tricia: Patricia

tricl: triclinic

trid.: triduum (Latin—three days)

tridundant: triple redundant

trig: trigonal; trigonometric; trigonometry

trihem: trihemeral; trihemirer

trike: tricycle

trim.: trimetric

TRIM: Targets, Receivers, Impacts, and Methods; Technical Requirements Identification Matrices

trimaran: three-hulled catamaran

Trin: Trinidad; Trinity

Trin Col: Trinity College

triol: triolism: triolist

trip.: triple; triplicate; triplication

triphib: triphibian; triphibious (land, sea, air)

triple-A S: AAAS (American Association for the Advancement of Science)

trishaw: tricycle rickshaw

trisk: triskelion

trisyll: trisyllable

trit: triturate

Trix(ie)(y): Beatrice; Beatrix

trk: track; truck; trunk

Trk: Turk; Turkey; Turkic; Turkish

trkdr: truck-drawn

trkg: tracking

trkhd: truckhead

trl: trailer

Trl: Trail

TRLB: temporarily replaced by lighted buoy

trlr: trailer

trm: task response module (engineer's desk area)

trml: terminal

trmn: trainman

trmr: trimmer

trmt: treatment

trnbkl: turnbuckle

trng: training

TRNMP: Theodore Roosevelt National Memorial Park

trnsp: transport; transportation

TRO: Technical Reviewing Office

troch: troche

Troch: Trochelminthes

troil: troilism; troilist

Troj: Trojan

Trojan Century: the 12th century before the Christian era when Troy fell to the Greeks after a ten-year siege described in Homer's *Iliad*—the 1100s

trom: tromba; trombone

trop: tropic; tropical; tropics

troparium: tropical aquarium

Trop Can: Tropic of Cancer—23½°N Lat

Trop Cap: Tropic of Capricorn—23½°S Lat

tropec: tropical experiment

TROPICS: Tour Operators Integrated Computer System

trop med: tropical medicine

troposcatter: beyond-the-horizon communication

Trotsky: Lev Davydovich Bronstein

trp: troop

trr: teaching and research reactor

TRRA: Terminal Railroad Association (of St. Louis)

TRRB: Test Readiness Review Board (NASA)

trs (TRS): tetrahedral research satellite

TRs: Technical Reports; Temporary Reserves

TRS: Ticket Reservation System; Transair Limited

trsd: total rated service date

tr sh: trim shell

TrSMS: triple-screw motor ship

trsp: transport

TRSP: Turtle River State Park (North Dakota)

TrSS: triple-screw steamer

trt: total response to trauma; treatment; turret

TRTC: Tropical Radio Telegraph Company

Tru: Trucial Sheikdoms; Truman

Tru: Truman's Railway Reports

TRU: The Rockefeller University

TRUB: temporarily replaced by unlighted buoy

Tru Cst 1: Trucial Coast Number 1

Tru Cst 2: Trucial Coast Number 2

trud: time remaining until dive (of satellite into Earth's atmosphere)

Trudy: Gertrude

TRUE: Teachers Resources for Urban Education

tru-fi: tru fidelity (sound reproduction)

trump.: trumpet

TRUMP: Target Radiation Measurement Program

trun: trunnion

tru(s): trustee(s)

trust.: trusteeship

trw: trawler

TRW: the corporation whose advertising states: "formerly Thompson-Ramo-Wooldridge"

trwov: transit without visa

trxrx: transmitter-receiver

Tryg: Trygve Lie

ts: taper shank; temperature switch; tensile strength; terminal sensation; test solution; time shack; too short; tool steel; tough situation; transit storage; transmitter station; triple strength; tubular sound; typescript; type specification(s)

t/s: test stand; third stage; transship(ed)(ment)

t/s: transship(ed)(ment)

t & s: toilet and shower

TS: Tasmanian Steamers; Tentative Specification; Terminal Service; Test Summary; Theosophical Society; Thoreau Society; Tidewater Southern (railroad); top secret; Training Ship; Transmittal Sheet; Type Specification

T S: tasto solo (Italian—play without accompaniment)

T de S: Teatro della Scala (La Scala)

tsa: two-step antenna

TSA: Transportation Standardization Agency; Tourist Savings Association; Track Suppply Association; Transportion Service, Army

tsac: title, subtitle, and caption

TSAC: Target Signature Analysis Center

TSBR: Thomas Stamford Bingley Raffles

TSC: Texas Southmost College; Transamerican Steamship Corporation

TSCA: Top Secret Control Agency

tscf: top secret cover folder

TSCO: Thomas Scherman's Concert Opera; Top Secret Control Officer

t-s curve: temperature-salinity curve

tsd: tactical simulator display

Tsd: Tausend (German—thousand)

TSd: Tay-Sachs disease (TSD)

TSD: Tay-Sachs Disease; towed submersible drydock

tsdd: temperature-salinity-density-depth

tse (TSE): test support equipment

TSE: Texas South-Eastern (railroad); T(homas) S(tearns) Eliot; Toronto Stock Exchange

tsf: tower shield facility

tsfr: transfer

TSgt: Technical Sergeant

tsh (TSH): thyroid stimulating hormone

T sh: Tanzanian shilling(s)

T-shirt: T-shaped shirt; T-shaped undershirt

tsi: tons per square inch

tsi: (Chinese—borough; village)

TSI: The Socialist International

tsiaj: this scherzo is a joke (abbreviation devised and used by composer Charles Ives)

TSID: Technical Service Intelligence Detachments

TSJC: Trinidad State Junior College

TSKK: Tsentralnya Kontrolnaya Komissiya (Russian—Central Control Commission)

TSL: Terrestrial Sciences Laboratory; Texas Short Line (railroad)

TSLNP: Tung Slang Luang National Park (Thailand)

tsms: twin-screw motor ship

Tsn: Tientsin

TSNHS: Touro Synagogue National Historic Site

TSO: Taiwan Symphony Orchestra; Teheran Symphony Orchestra: Toronto Symphony Orchestra; Tucson Symphony Orchestra

TSOR: Tentative Specific Operational Requirements

tsp: teaspoon; tracking station position

TSP: thyroid-stimulating (hormone of) prepituitary; trisodium phosphate (Na_3PO_4)

tspn: teaspoon

T-square: T-shaped ruler for making right angles

TSR: Test Schedule Request

T & SRC: Tubular and Split Rivet Council

tss: time-sharing system

TSS: turbine steamship; twinscrew ship

tssm: total ship simulation model

TSTA: Texas State Teachers Association

tstr: tester

tsu: this side up

tsu: (Japanese—port)

TSU: Texas Southern University; Tulsa-Sapulpa Union (railway)

TSUS: Tariff Schedule of the United States

tsvp: tournez s'il vous plaît (French—please turn over)

TSW: tropical summer winter (load line mark)

tt: tablet triturate; technical test(ing); teetotaler; telegraphic transfer; teletype; teletypewriter; tetanus toxoid; torpedo tube(s); transit time; tree top(s); tuberculin tested

tt.: tantum (Latin—fixed allowance; so much)

t.t.: totus tuus (Latin—all yours)

t-t: tube-in-tube

t/t: time to turn

TT: tam-tam (Chinese gong); target-towing (naval aircraft); Technical Test(ing); Tidningarnas Telegrambyra (Swedish news agency); Toledo Terminal (railroad); Trans-Texas (Airways); Troop Test

T/T: twin turbine (steamship)

T & T: Trinidad and Tobago

tta: test target array

TTA: Taiwan Telecommunication Administration; Trans-Texas Airways; Travel Time Authorization

TTAB: Trademark Trial and Appeal Board (US Patent Office)

TTAF: Technical Training Air Force

ttc: temperature test chamber; tetrazolium chloride; tight tape contact; tin telluride crystal; tow target cable; transient temperature control; tube temperature control

TTC: Technical Training Command; Teletypewriter Center; Texas Technological College; Tobacco Tax Council; Tokyo Tanker Company; Toronto Transit Commission

ttce: tooth-to-tooth composite error

ttci: transient temperature-control instrument

TTCS: Truck Transportable Communications Station

ttd: transponder transmitter detector

ttdr: tracking telemetry data receiver

tte: temporary test equipment; trailer test equipment

Tte: *Teniente* (Spanish—Lieutenant)

ttf: time to failure; tone telegraph filter; transistor text fixture

ttg: time to go

TT-gauge: Tiny Tim gauge—½-inch track gauge (model railroads)

ttgd: time-to-go engine dial

tth: thyrotropic hormone

tti: time-temperature indicator

TTI: The Technological Institute

T-time: takeoff time

TTIO: Turkish Tourism and Information Office

ttk: two-tone keying

ttl: to take leave; transitor-transistor logic

TTL: Tokaido Trunk Line (Japanese railroad running trains at 125 miles per hour)

TTMA: Truck-Trailer Manufacturers Association

tto: this transaction only

Tto: Toronto

TTO: Tanzania Tourist Office

T-town: Tijuana

ttp: total taxable pay

ttr (TTR): target-tracking radar; thermal test reactor

T & T RR: Tijuana and Tecate Railroad

tts: teletypesetter (TTS); teletypesetting; temporary threshold shift

ttt: telemetry time transposition; time to target; time to think; time to turn

TT & T: Texas Transport and Terminal

TTTB: Trinidad and Tobago Tourist Board

T & T TS: Trinidad and Tobago Television Service

ttu: timing terminal unit

ttvm: thermal transfer voltmeter

ttw: total temperature and weight

ttwl: twintandem wheel loading

tty: teletypewriter

tu: thermal unit; toxic unit; trade union (TU); traffic unit; transfer unit; transmission unit; turbidity unit

Tu: Turkey; Turkish

TU: Taylor University; Temple University; Tiffin University; Trade Union; transmission unit; Trinity University; Tufts University; Tulane University; Tunis Air; Typographical Union

TU: *Technische Universität* (German — technical university); *temps universel* (French—universal time)

T.U.: tuberculin unit(s)

TU-144: Tupolev supersonic transport

tu ar: turning arbor

tub.: tubing

TUB: temporary unlighted buoy

tube: television tube (contraction)

TUBE: Terminating Unfair Broadcasting Excesses

tuberc: tuberculosis

tuc: transportation, utilities, communications

Tuc: Tucson

TUC: Trades-Union Congress

tu ca: turning cam

TUCC: Temple University Community College; Triangle Universities Computation Center

TUCSA: Trade Union Council of South Africa

tudor: two-door

Tue: Tuesday

Tues: Tuesday

TUF: Tokyo University of Fisheries; Trade Union Federation (British)

tu fx: turning fixture

TUI: Trade Union International

Tul: Tulsa

TUL: Tokyo University Library; Tulane University of Louisiana; Tulsa; Oklahoma (airport)

tum: tummy (stomach); tumor

TUM: Panama City, Panama (Tocumen Airport)

tun: tuning

Tun: Tunis; Tunisia; Tunisian

tundra: (Russian—marshy plains)

tung: tungsten

tung: (Chinese—east; eastern, as in Shantung)

Tunic: Tunicata

tuppenny: twopenny

tur: transurethral resection (TUR); turbine; turret

Tur: Turin

turb: turbine

turbid.: turbidity

turboalt: turboalternator

turbo-elec: steam turbine connected to electric motor

turbogen: turbogenerator

turbojet: turbine-driven jet (airplane engine)

turboprop: turbine-driven jet engine (moving the) propeller

turbosuch: turbosupercharger

turbotrain: turbine-driven railroad train

turbpmp: turbopump

Turk.: Turkey; Turkish

Turkmen: Turkmenia; Turkmenian

Turkmen SSR: Turkmen Soviet Socialist Republic (Turkmenistan)

Turk-Tat: Turko-Tataric

turn.: turning

Turn: Turnpike

Turner Turn: Turner Turnpike

turp: turpentine

turps: turpentine

TURPS: Terrestrial Unattended Reactor Power System

tus.: *tussis* (Latin—cough)

TUs: Tenant's Unions

TUS: Tucson, Arizona (airport)

TUSAFG: The United States Air Force Group (American Mission for Aid to Turkey)

TUSC: Technology Use Studies Center

Tusitala: (Samoan—Teller of Tales)—Robert Louis Stevenson's nickname

TUSLOG: The United States Logistic Group

tut: tutor; tutorial

TUT: The University of Tokyo

Tutankhamen's Century: the 14th century before the Christian era when Egyptian Pharoah Tutankhamen ruled—the 1300s

TUTI: Temple University Technical Institute

tuwr: turning wrench

tux: tuxedo (dinner jacket)

tv (TV): television; terminal velocity; test vehicle; tetrazolium violet; total volume; transverse; trichomonas vaginalis; true view; tuberculin volution

t/v: thrust-to-weight

TV: television; test vehicle; Tidewater Oil (stock exchange symbol); transport vehicle

tva: thrust vector alignment

tva: *taxe a la valeur ajoutee* (French—value added tax)

TVA: Temporary Variation Authorization; Tennessee Valley Authority

tvac: time-varying adaptive correlation

TVA's: Temporary Variation Authorizations

TVBS: Television Broadcast Satellite

tvc: temperature valve control; thermal voltage converter; throttle valve control; thrust vector control; time-varying coefficient; timed vital capacity; torsional vibration characteristics

TVCC: Treasure Valley Community College

tvd: toxic vapor damper; toxic vapor detector; tuned viscoelastic damper

tvdc: test volts—direct current

TVDC: Tidewater Virginia Development Council

tvdp: thrust-vector display (unit)

tvdy: television deflection yoke

tve: test vehicle engine; thermal vacuum environment

TVE: Televisión Española (Spanish TV network)

tvel: track velocity

TVERS: Television Evaluation and Renewal Standards

tvft: television flyback transformer

tvg: threshold voltage generator; triggered vacuum gap

TVG: TV Guide

tvi: television interference

TVIC: Television Interference Committee

tvig: television and inertial guidance

tvist: television information-storage tube

tvk: terminal volume kill

T v K: Theodore von Karman

tvl: travel

Tvl: Transvaal

tvm: tachometer voltmeter; track via missile; trailer van mount; transistorized voltmeter

tvor: terminal visual omnirange; very high frequency terminal omnirange station

tvp: time-varying parameter

tvq: top visual quality

tvr: textured vegetable protein

TV-RI: TV-Republik Indonesia (Bahasa Indonesia—Republic Indonesia Television)

tvs: tactical vocoder system; telemetry video spectrum; television viewing system

tv's: television dinners; transvestites

tvsd: time-varying spectral display

tvsg: television signal generator

tvsm: time-varying sequential measuring (apparatus)

tvso: television space observatory

tvr's: television recordings

TVSTI: Thames Valley State Technical Institute

tvu: total volume urine

tw: tail water; tail wheel; tail wind; taxiway; tempered water; tile wainscot; traveling wave; twin(s)

Tw: Twaddell

TW: Trans World Airlines (2-letter coding)

twa: trailing wire antenna

TWA: Textile Waste Association; Tooling Work Authorization; Toy Wholesalers Association; Trans World Airlines

Twad: Twaddell

'twas: it was

twb: twin with bath

twbp: transcribed weather broadcast program

twcrt: travelling-wave cathode ray tube

twd: tail wags dog

twds: tradewinds

TWE: Textile Waste Exchange

TWEA: Trading With the Enemy Act

Twel N: Twelfth Night

twerl: tropical wind, energy conversion, and reference level

TW & FS: The Wine and Food Society

twh: typically wavy hair

twi: training within industry

TWI: The West Indies

twimc (TWIMC): to whom it may concern

twister: dustwhirl, sandspout, tornado, or waterspout wherein ascending and rotating movement of air column is especially apparent

twi zn: twilight zone

twk: typewriter keyboard

twl: top water level

twm: traveling-wave maser

Two Gent: Two Gentlemen of Verona

twot: travel without troops

Twp: Township

TWP: True Whig Party (Liberia)

twr: tower

TWR: Trans-World Radio

tws: timed wire service; track while scan

tw/s: twin-screw (ship)

twsr: track-while-scan radar

twsrs: track-while-scan radar simulator

twt: travelling-wave tube; travel with troops

t/wt: tare weight

TWT: Transonic Wind Tunnel

twta: travelling-wave-tube amplifier

TWU: Tata Workers Union; Transport Workers Union

TWUA: Textile Workers Union of America

twx: time-wire transmission

TWX: teletypewriter exchange (message)

twy: taxiway; twenty

twzo: trade-wind-zone oceanography (term of derision by experts or about armchair oceanographers)

tx: torque transmitter; radio transmitter

txe: telephone exchange electronic

txh: transfer on index high

txi: transfer on index incremented

txl: transfer on index low

txn: taxation

ty: type

Ty: Tyrone

tyc: tycoon

tydac: typical digital automatic computer

tymp: tympanic(ity); tympany

tymp memb: tympanic membrane

tyo: two-year-old (horse)

TYO: Tokyo, Japan (airport)

typ: typical; typing; typist; typographer; typography; typewriter

TYP: Ten-Year Plan; Twenty-Year Plan; etc.

type.: typewriter; typewriting

typh: typhoon

typo: typographical (error)

typog: typographer; typographical; typography

typr: typewritten

typw: typewriter

tyr (TYR): tyrosine (amino acid)

Tyr: Tyrol; Tyrolean; Tyrolese; Tyrone

tys: tensile yield strength

TYS: Knoxville, Tennessee (airport)

tysd: total years service date

Tyskl: Tyskland (Danish—Germany)

tz: tidal zone; time zero

TZ: Tactical Zone; Transair Limited, Canada (2-letter code)

tzd: true zenith distance

tze: transfer on zero

tzg: thermofit zap gun

TZIK: Tzentralny Ispolnitelny Kommitet (Russian—Central Executive Committee)

tzj: tubular zippered jacket

TZm: true azimuth

TZM: titanium-zirconium-molybdenum (alloy)

tzp: time zero pulse

tzt: te zijner tijd (Dutch—in due time)

tzv: tetrazolium violet

U

u: density of radiant energy (symbol); ugly threatening weather (symbol); unified atomic mass (symbol); unit(s); unknown; unoccupied; unsymmetrical; unwatched; upper; velocity (symbol); you (as in iou, IOU)

u: *und* (German—and); viscosity (symbol)

μ: micron (symbol)

μ^2: square micron

μ^3: cubic micron

u/3: upper third (long bones)

U: Chance Vought Aircraft (symbol); kilourane (1000 uranium units—symbol); overall coefficient of heat transfer (symbol); potential energy (symbol); total internal energy (symbol); unclassified; Uniform—code for letter U; University; up; uranium; Utah; Utahans; U Thant; utility; you

U: *ud* (Danish—out); *uit* Dutch—out); *ulos* (Finnish—out); *unter* (German—down); up; *upp* (Swedish—up); *ute* (Swedish—arrival); *violaceus* (Latin—violet-color)

U-2: high-altitude high-performance photo-reconnaissance airplane

U^{234}: trace component of natural uranium

U^{235}: 0.7 percent of natural uranium (atomic energy source)

U^{238}: 99.3 percent of natural uranium (atomic energy source)

ua: unauthorized absence; unauthorized absentee; uniform allowance; upper arm; urine aliquot

u a: *und andere(s)* (German—among other things; and others; inter alia)

ua: *uden ar* (Dano-Norwegian—without date)

u.a.: *usque ad* (Latin—as far as; up to)

u ä: *und ähnliche(s)* (German—and the like)

μa: microampere

u/a: unit of account

uA: *und andere* (German—and others)

UA: United Aircraft; United Air Lines (2-letter coding); United Artists; Universidad de las Americas

U-A: Universal-American

U de A: Universidad de Alcala; Universidad de Antioquia

U di A: Università di Arezzo

U of A: University of Aberdeen; University of Akron; University of Alabama; University of Alaska; University of Alberta; University of the Americans; University of Arizona; University of Arkansas

U van A: Universiteit van Amsterdam

UAA: United Arab Airlines; University Aviation Association

UAASUS: Ukrainian Academy of Arts and Sciences in the United States

UAB: Unemployment Assistance Board

UABS: Union of American Biological Societies

UAC: United Aircraft Corporation; Urban Affairs Council; Utility Aircraft Council

UACC: Upper Area Control Center

UACL: United Aircraft of Canada, Limited

uacte: universal automatic control and test equipment

UADPS: Uniform Automatic Data Processing System

UAE: United Arab Emirates (Trucial Sheikdoms of Trucial States)

uaf: unit authorization file

uafs/t: universal aircraft flight simulator/trainer

UAG: Universidad Autónoma de Guadalajara (University of Guadalajara)

UAHC: Union of American Hebrew Congregations

UAI: Urban America Incorporated (Action Council for Better Cities)

uaide: uses of automatic information display equipment

ual: upper acceptance limit

UAL: United Air Lines; University of Aberdeen Library; University of Akron Library; University of Alabama Library; University of Alaska Library; University of Alberta Library; University of

the Americas Library; University of Arizona Library; University of Arkansas Library

UALL: University of Arizona Lunar Laboratory

U of Alla: University of Allahabad

uam (UAM): underwater-to-air missile

UAM: Union Africaine et Malgache (African and Malagasy Union); United American Mechanics

UAMC: United Arab Maritime Company

UAMPT: *Union Africaine et Malagactie des Postes et Telecommunications* (French—Union of African and Malagasy Postal Service and Telecommunication)

uan: uric-acid nitrogen

uao: unexplained aerial object

UAOD: United Ancient Order of Druids

uap: unexplained atmospheric phenomenon

UAP: Union of Associated Professors

uar: underwater acoustic resistance; underwater angle receptacle; upper air route; upper atmosphere research

UAR: Uniform Airman Record; United Arab Republic

UARAEE: United Arab Republic Atomic Energy Establishment

UARL: United Aircraft Research Laboratories

UARTO: United Arab Republic Tourist Office

uas: unmanned aerial surveillance

UAS: Unit Approval System

UASCS: United States Army Signal Center and School

UASS: Unmanned Aerial Surveillance System

uat: ultraviolet acquisition technique

UAT: Union Aéromaritime de Transport

UATO: United Airlines Tour Order

UATP: Universal Air Travel Plan

UAW: United Automobile Workers

uAwg: *um Antwort wird gebeten* (German—reply requested)

uax (UAX): unit automatic exchange

Ub: Universiteitsbibliotheek (University Library, Amsterdam)

UB: Union of Burma; United Biscuit; Universität Basel; Universität Berne

U de B: Universidad de Barcelona: Université de Bâle (University of Basel)

U di B: Università di Bologna

U do B: Universidade do Brasil; Universidade do Brasilia

U i B: Universitet i Bergen

U of B: University of Baltimore; University of Birmingham; University of Bombay; University of Bridgeport; University of Bristol; University of Buffalo

U zu B: Universität zu Berlin

uba: undenatured bacterial antigen

UBA: Union of Burma Airways

U de BA: Universidad de Buenos Aires

U-bahn: *Untergrundbahn* (German —underground road)—subway system

UBAV: United Buddhist Association of Vietnam

ubc: universal buffer controller

UBC: United Baltic Corporation; University of British Columbia

UBC: *Uniform Building Code* (legal)

U of BC: University of British Columbia

UBC & J: United Brotherhood of Carpenters and Joiners

UBCL: University of British Columbia Library

UBCP: Union Bag-Camp Paper

ubd: utility binary dump

UBEA: United Business Education Association

U-beam: U-shaped beam

UBEM: Union Belge d'Entreprises Maritimes

übers: *übersetzt* (German—translated)

ubf: universal boss fitting

ubfc: underwater battery fire control

ubi: ultraviolet blood irradiation; universal battlefield identification

ubitron: undulating beam interaction electron tube

UBL: Union Barge Line; United Benefit Life

ubm: ultrasonic bonding machine; unit bill of material

U-boat: *Unterseeboot* (German —submarine)

U-bolt: capital-U-shaped bolt

U-bomb: uranium-cased atomic or hydrogen bomb

UBP: United Business Publications

UBS: United Business Service

UBSA: United Business Schools Association (formerly American

Association of Commercial Colleges)

UBSO: Uinta Basin Seismological Observatory

ubt: universal book tester

ubv: ultraviolet

uc: universal coarse (screw thread); upper case (capital letters)

u/c: upper center

UC: Umpqua College; Union Carbide; Union College; University of California; University of Ceylon; University of Colorado; University of Connecticut; Upland College; Upsala College; Ursinus College; Ursuline College; Utica College

UC: *una corda* (Italian—one string) —soft pedal

U de C: Universidad de Cartagena; Universidad de Cauca; Universidad de Chile; Universidad de Córdoba; Universidad de Cuzco; Universidade de Coímbra

U of C: University of Calcutta; University of California; University of Chattanooga; University of Chicago; University of Cincinnati; University of Colorado; University of Connecticut; University of Corpus Christi

UCAF: You See America First

UCAR: Union of Central African Republics; University Corporation for Atmospheric Research

UCAS: Uniform Cost Accounting Standards; Union of Central African States

ucb: unless caused by

UCB: United California Bank; University of California at Berkeley

ucc: unadjusted contractual changes; universal copyright convention

UCC: Uniform Commercial Code; Union Carbide and Carbon; Union de la Critique Cinématographique (Society of Cinema Criticism); United Cancer Council; United Community Campaign; United Electric Coal Companies (stock exchange symbol); University College (Cork)

U-CC: Upper Canada College

UCCA: United Citizens Concerned with America; Universities Central Council on Admissions

UCCC: Ulster County Community College

UCCELLO: Paolo di Dono

UCCS: Universal Camera Control System

ucd: usual childhood diseases

UCD: University of California at Davis; University College, Dublin

ucdp: uncorrect data processor

UCEA: University College of East Africa (Makerere College); University Council for Educational Administration

UCEMT: University Consortium in Education Media and Technology

U of Cey: University of Ceylon

UCF: United Community Funds

UCFE: Unemployment Compensation for Federal Employees

UCFH: University College of Fort Hare

UCG: University College, Galway; University College of Ghana

U-channel: U-shaped channel

U Chi: University of Chicago

U Chi Lib: University of Chicago Library

uci: unit construction index

UCI: Union Cycliste Internationale (Cyclists International Union)

UCIrv: University of California at Irvine

ucj: unsatisfied claim and judgement

ucl: upper control limit; urea clearance test

UCL: Union Castle Line; Union Central Life; Union Oil Company of California (symbol); University of California Library; University College, London

U c de L: Université catholique de Louvain

UCLA: University of California at Los Angeles

U-class: upperclass

UCMC: University of Colorado Medical Center

UCMJ: Uniform Code of Military Justice

U-C M S: Union-Castle Mail Steamship

UCN: University College of Nigeria

UCNW: University College of North Wales

UCP: Unified Command Plan

UCPA: United Cerebral Palsy Associations

ucr: unconditioned response

UCR: Uniform Crime Reports; University of California at Riverside; Utah Coal Route (railroad)

U de CR: Universidad de Costa Rica

UCRA: University Centers for Rational Alternatives

UCRI: Union Carbide Research Institute

UCRL: University of Califronia Radiation Laboratory

UCR & N: University College of Rhodesia and Nyasaland

ucs: unconditioned stimulus

UCs: Urban Coalitionists

UCS: United Community Service; Universal Classification System; Universal-Cyclops Steel; University Computer Systems (computerized real estate listings); Upper Clyde Shipbuilders

U-CS: Universal-Cyclops Steel

UCSB: University of California at Santa Barbara

UCSC: University of California at Santa Cruz; University City Science Center

UCSD: University of California at San Diego

UCSL: University College of Sierra Leone

UCSW: Univeristy College of South Wales

UCT: United Commercial Travelers; University of Cape Town

UC & U: Union College and University

UCUC: University College of the University of Cincinnati

ucv: uncontrolled variable

UCV: Universidad Central de Venezuela

UCVs: United Confederate Veterans

UCW: University College of Wales

UCWC: University College of the Western Cape

UCWI: University College of the West Indies

UCWP: University College of the Western Province

ucwr: upon completion will return

UCX: Unemployment Compensation for Ex-Servicemen

UCY: United Caribbean Youth

UCZ: University College of Zululand

ud: upper berth, double occupancy; upper deck

u.d.: *ut dictum* (Latin—as directed)

Ud: *Udjung* (Malay—point); *usted* (Spanish—you)

UD: Undesirable Discharge; United Dairies; University of Denver; University of Detroit; Urban District

UD: *Unlisted Drugs*

U of D: University of Dallas; University of Dayton; University of Delaware; University of Delhi; University of Denver; University of Detroit; University of Dublin; University of Dubuque; University of Durham

UDA: Ulster Defence Association (Protestant counterpart of the IRA)

udaa: unlawfully driving away auto

udarg: *udarbeidet* (Danish—pre-pared)

udc: universal decimal classification (UDC); upper dead center; usual diseases of childhood

UDC: United Daughters of the Confederacy; United Dye & Chemical; universal decimal classification; Urban District Council

udd(e): (Swedish—cape)

UDE: Union Douanière Équatoriale (Equatorial Customs Union)

UDEAO: *Union Douanière des Etats de l'Afrique de l'Ouest* (French—Customs Union of West African States)—former French colonies

udg: *udgave* (Danish—edition)

u dgl (m): *und dergleichen (mehr)* (German—and the like)

UDI: Unilateral Declaration of Independence

u dk: upper deck

udk: *udkom* (Dano-Norwegian —published)

udl: up-data link

udm: upright drilling machine

udM: *unter dem Meeresspiegel* (German—below sea level)

üdM: *über dem Meersspiegel* (German—above sea level)

UDM: United Merchants and Manufacturers (stock exchange symbol); Universal Drafting Machine (corporation)

Udm Aut Sov Soc Rep: Udmurt Autonomous Soviet Socialist Republic

UDN: Underwater Doppler Navigation

udo: unwilling drop-out

udom: udometer; udometric; udometrical

udr: universal data report(er); universal digital readout; usage data report; utility data reduction

UDR: Ulster Defence Regiment

UDR: *Union des Democrates pour la cinquième Republique* (French —Union of Democrats for the Fifth Republic)

udrc: utility data retrieval control

UDRI: University of Denver Research Institute

udro: utility data retrieval output

Uds: *ustedes* (Spanish—you, *pl.*)

UDS: Ultraviolet Detection System; Underwater Demolition School

udt: underdeck tonnage

UDT: Underwater Demolition Team

UDTC: University of Dublin Trinity College

UDU: Underwater Demolition Unit

udw: ultra-deep water

UDY: United Dye and Chemical

Corporation (stock exchange symbol)

ue: unit equipment

UE: University Extension

U of E: University of the East (Manila); University of Edinburgh; University of Exeter

UEA: University of East Africa; Utah Education Association

ueac: unit equipment aircraft

ueb: ultrasonic epoxy bonder

UEB: Union Économique Benelux

UEC: United Engineering Center

UECC: United Electric Coal Companies

UECM: Union Electric Company of Missouri

uee: unit essential equipment

uef: universal extra fine (screw thread)

uel: upper explosive limit

UEO: Union de l'Europe Occidentale (Western European Union)

uep: underwater electrical potential; uniform external pressure

UEP: Union Electric Power Company; Union Européenne des Payements (European Payments Union—EPU)

UEPA: Utility Electric Power Association

UERD: Underwater Explosives Research Division (USN)

UES: United Engineering Societies

uesk: unit essential spares kit

u/ext: upper extremity

uf: urea-formadehyde

uf: microfarad

UF: United Fruit

U-F: Ugro-Finnic

U de F: Université de Fribourg

U di F: Università di Firenze (University of Florence)

U of F: University of Florida

ufa: until further advised

UFA: Universum-Film-Aktiengesellschaft (Universe Film Company)

ufac: unlawful flight to avoid custody

ufaed: unit forecast authorization equipment data

ufap: unlawful flight to avoid prosecution

ufat: unlawful flight to avoid testimony

UFAW: Universities Federation for Animal Welfare

ufc: uniform freight classification

UFC: United Fruit Company

UFCc: United Free Churches

UFCS: Underwater Fire-Control System

UFCT: United Federation of College Teachers

uff: *und folgende* (German—and the

following)
UFF: University Film Foundation
UFI: Union des Foires Internationales (Union of International Fairs)
ufl: upper flammable limit
UfM: University for Man
ufn: until further notice
ufo: unidentified flying object
ufo's: unidentified flying objects
UFP: United Federal Party
UFPA: University Film Producers Association
U-frame: U-shaped frame
UFT: United Federation of Teachers
UFW: United Farm Workers; United Furniture Workers
ug: underground
ug: microgram
Ug: Uganda; Ugandan; Ugric; Ugus
UG: Underground Railroad—secret system set up before and during Civil War to aid Negro slaves seeking freedom in the northern United States and Canada; United Gas; Universität Graz
U de G: Universidad de Granada; Universidad de Guadalajara; Universidad de Guanajuato; Université de Genève; Université de Grenoble
U di G: Università di Genova
U i G: Universitet i Göteborg
U of G: University of Georgia; University of Glasgow; University of Guelph; University of Guyana
U zu G: Universität zu Göttingen
uga: unity gain amplifier
ugb: unity gain bandwidth
ugc: ultrasonic grating constant; unity grain crossover
UGC: United Gas Corporation; University Grants Committee
UG & CW: United Glass and Ceramic Workers
UGDP: University Group Diabetes Program
ugf: unidentified growth factor
ugmit: you got me into this
ugr: ultrasonic grain refinement; universal graphic recorder
UGR: Umfolozi Game Reserve (South Africa)
ugt: urgent
UGT: *Union General de Trabajadores* (Spanish—General Union of Workers)—Socialist trade union
UGW: United Garment Workers
uh: upper half
uh: microhenry
UH: Universidad de la Habana; Universität Hamburg
U d'H: Université d'Haiti

U de H: Universidad de la Habana
U of H: University of Hartford; University of Hawaii; University of Houston; University of Hull
uha: upper-half assembly
UHAA: United Horological Association of America
uhc: under honorable conditions
uhcs: ultra-high-capacity storage
uhf: ultra-high frequency—300-3000 mc
UHF: United Health Foundation
uhfdf: ultra-high-frequency direction finder
uhff: ultra-high-frequency filter
uhfg: ultra-high-frequency generator
uhfj: ultra-high-frequency jammer
uhfo: ultra-high-frequency oscillator
uhfr: ultra-high-frequency receiver
UHK: University of Hong Kong
uhmw: ultra-high molecular weight
uhp: ultra-high purity
UHP: University of Hawaii Press
uhr: ultra-high resistance; ultra-high resolution
uhs: ultra-high speed
UHS: Union High School
uht: ultrasonic hardness tester
uhv: ultra-high vacuum
uhtv: unmanned hypersonic test vehicle
uhvc: ultra-high vacuum chamber
UHVS: Ultra-High Vacuum System
ui: ultrasonic industries
u/i: unit of issue
u.i.: *ut infra* (Latin—as below)
UI: Ube Industries; Unemployment Insurance; Universität Innsbruck
U of I: University of Idaho; University of Illinois; University of Iowa; University of Israel; University of Istanbul
UIA: United Israel Appeal
UIAS: Union of Independent African States
uic: ultraviolet image converter
UIC: Unemployment Insurance Code; Unio Internationlis Contra Cancrum (International Union Against Cancer)
UICN: Union Internationale pour la Conservation de la Nature (International Union for the Conservation of Nature)
UICPS: Uniform Inventory Control Points System
UIE: UNESCO Institute for Education
UIEO: Union of International Engineering Organizations
uif: ultraviolet interference filter; unfavorable information file; universal intermolecular force
UIF: Unemployment Insurance

Fund
UIL: University of Idaho Library; University of Illinois Library; University of Indiana Library; University of Iowa Library
UIM: Union Industrielle & Maritime (Société Française de l'Armement)
UIMNH: University of Illinois Museum of Natural History
UIN: United States and International Securities (stock exchange symbol)
UIPC: Union Internationale de la Presse Catholique; Utah Industrial Promotion Commission
UIPD: *Ulrich's International Periodicals Directory*
UIR: University Industrial Research
UIS: Unemployment Insurance Service; Unit Identification System
uisc: unreported interstate shipment of cigarettes
uit: unit impulse train
uit: *uitgaaf* (Dutch—publication)
uitg: *uitgegeven* (Dutch—published)
UIU: Quito, Ecuador (airport)
UJ: Universidad Javeriana (Bogotá and Sucre)
UJA: United Jewish Appeal
U-joint(s): U-shaped joint(s)
uk (UK): urokinase
UK: United Kingdom; Universita Karlova (Karl University— University of Prague)
U of K: University of Kansas; University of Keele (formerly University College of North Staffordshire); University of Kentucky
UKAC: United Kingdom Automation Council
UKAEA: United Kingdom Atomic Energy Authority
ukb: universal keyboard
U of KC: University of Kansas City; University of King's College
UKCA: United Kingdom Citizens Association
uke: ukulele
UK fo: United Kingdom for orders
UKGBNI: United Kingdom of Great Britain and Northern Ireland
UKHH: United Kingdom-Havre-Hamburg (range of ports)
UKL: University of Kansas Library
UK£: United Kingdom pound
UKM: University of Kansas Museums
Ukr: Ukraine; Ukrainian
Ukrainian SSR: Ukrainian Soviet Socialist Repulic (Ukraine)
UKRAS: United Kingdom Railway

Advisory Service
UKSM: United Kingdom Scientific Mission
Ukulele (UK): stock exchange slang for Union Carbide
UKW: Ultra-Kurzwellen (German —ultra-short wave)
ul: up link; upper left; upper leg; upper lid
u/l: upper left; upper limit
UL: Underwriters Laboratories
UL: Union List
U de L: Universidad de Lérida; Universidad de Lima; Universidade de Lisboa (Lisbon); Université de Lausanne
U i L: Universitet i Lund
U of L: University of Laval; University of Leeds; University of Leicester; University of Liverpool; University of London; University of Louisville
U de LA: Universidad de Los Andes
ulan: (Mongolian—red)
ulb: universal logic bloc
ULB: Université Libre de Bruxelles (Free University of Brussels)
ulc: unsafe lane change (vehicular code); upper left center
u & lc: upper and lower case
ULC: Underwriters' Laboratories of Canada
ULCA: United Lutheran Church of America
uldest: ultimate destination
ulf: ultra-low frequency; unfair labor practice
ULI: Urban Land Institute
ull: ullage
ULL: Unitarian Laymen's League; University of Liverpool Library
ULMS: Underwater Long-range Missile System
ULO: Unmanned Launch Operations
ulpr: ultra low-pressure rocket
ULS: Universities Libraries Section (Association of College and Research Libraries)
ULS: Union List of Serials
ult: ultimate; ultimo
ult.: ultimo (Latin—at last)
ulto: ultimo
ultracom: ultraviolet communications system
ultrason: ultrasonic(s)
ultra-x: universal language for typographic reproduction applications
ult ts: ultimate tensile strength
U of Luck: University of Lucknow
um: umpire; unmarried
u/m: unit of measure
üM: über dem Meeresspiegel (German—above sea level)

UM: Universal Match; Univeral Mill; University of Malaysia (University of Malaya—Raffles Institute); University Museum
U de M: Universidad de Madrid; Universidad de México; Université de Montreal
U di M: Università di Milano
U of M: University of Maine; University of Malaysia; University of Manchester; University of Manitoba; University of Maryland; University of Massachusetts; University of Miami; University of Michigan; University of Minnesota; University of Mississippi; University of Missouri; University of Montreal
U Ma: Ursa Major (Big Bear)
UMA: Ultrasonic Manufacturers Association; Union de Mujeres Americanas (United Women of the Americas)
U-magnet: U-shaped magnet
U of Mand: University of Mandalay
UMAS: United Mexican-American Students
Umb: Umbrian
UMBIR: University of Michigan Bureau of Industrial Relations
umbl: umbilical
UMC: Universal Match Corporation
UMCA: Urabá, Medellín and Central Airways
UMD: Unit Manning Document
U of Mdrs: University of Madras
umf: ultramicrofiche
umgearb: umgearbeitete (German —revised)
UMHK: Union Miniére du Haut-Katanga (United Mines of Upper Katanga)
umi: (Japanese—gulf; sea)
U Mi: Ursa Minor (Little Bear)
UMI: University Microfilms Incorporated
U/min: Umdrehungen in der Minute (German—revolutions per minute)
UMIST: University of Manchester Institute of Science and Technology
UML: University of Michigan Library; University of Minnesota Library; University of Missouri Library
umler: universal machine language equipment register (railroads)
UM & M: United Merchants and Manufacturers
UMMZ: University of Michigan Museum of Zoology
UMNO: United Malay National Organization

umoc: ugly man on campus
U of Monc: University of Moncton
ump: umpire
UMP: Upper Mantle Project; Upper Merion and Plymouth (railroad); University of Massachusetts Press
UMR: Umvoti Mounted Rifles
UMREL: Upper Midwest Regional Educational Laboratory
UMRWFR: Upper Mississippi River Wildlife and Fish Refuge (Minnesota)
ums: unmanned machinery space
UMS: Undersea Medical Society; Universal Military Service
UMT: Universal Military Training
UMTA: Urban Mass Transportation Administration
umtd: using mails to defraud
UMTS: Universal Military Training and Service
UMW: United Mine Workers
U of Mys: University of Mysore
un (UN): unsatisfactory
UN: Union Twist Drill (trademark); United Nations; unsatisfactory
UN: União Nacional (Portuguese—National Union)
U di N: Università di Napoli
U of N: University of Natal; University of Nebraska; University of Nevada; University of Nottingham
UNA: United Nations Association; United Natives Association
UNAAF: Unified Action Armed Forces
unabr: unabridged
UNACC: United Nations Administrative Committee on Coordination
unalot: unallotted
UNAM: Universidad Nacional Autónoma de Mexico (National University of Mexico)
un-Amer: un-American (something contrary to democratic tradition and the principles of American government and way of life)
unan: unanimous
UNAPO: United National Association of Post Office (Craftsmen)
UNARCO: United Nations Narcotics Commission
unasgd: unassigned
unatt: unattached
UNAUS: United Nations Association of the United States
unauthd: unauthorized
UNB: United Nations Bookshop
U of NB: University of New Brunswick
UN Bank: International Bank for Reconstruction and Development

unbd: unbound
unc: unconcious; undercurrent; unified coarse (thread)
Unc: Uncle
UNC: United Nations Command; Universidad Nacional de Colombia; University of Northern Colorado
UNC: Union Nationale Camerounaise (French—Cameroon National Union)—party
U of NC: University of North Carolina
UNCC: United Nations Cartographic Commission
UNCF: United Negro College Fund
unch: unchanged
uncir: uncirculated
UNCL: University of North Carolina Library
unclas: unclassified
U.N.C.L.E.: United Network Command for Law Enforcement (fictional organization created for television)
Uncle Remus: (pseudonym—Joel Chandler Harris)
Uncle Robert: General Robert E. Lee, CSA
UNCMAC: United Nations Command Military Armistice Commission
unco: uncouth; (Scottish—extraordinary; foreign; strange; weird)
uncol: universal computer-oriented language
uncomp: uncompensated
uncond: unconditioned
UNCOPUOS: United Nations Committee on the Peaceful Uses of Outer Space
uncor: uncorrected
uncov: uncover; uncovered; uncovers
unct.: unctus (Latin—smeared)
UNCTAD: United Nations Conference on Trade and Development
UNCURK: United Nations Commission for the Unification and Rehabilitation of Korea
und: under
U of ND: University of North Dakota; University of Notre Dame
unded: underdeduction
Under Sec Nav: Under Secretary of the Navy
Undex: United Nations Index
UNDI: United Nations Document Index
undies: underthings (underwear)
UNDP: United Nations Development Program
undtkr: undertaker
undw: underwater
undwrtr: underwriter

unef: unified national extra fine (screw thread)
UNEF: United Nations Emergency Forces
UNESCO: United Nations Educational, Scientific, and Cultural Organization
unex: unexecuted
unexpur: unexpurgated
UNEXSO: Underwater Explorers Society
unf: unified fin thread; unfuzed
UNF: United National Front
unfav: unfavorable
unfd: unfurnished
UNFDAC: United Nations Fund for Drug Abuse Control
unfin: unfinished
UN Fund: International Monetary Fund
ung: unguent
ung: ungarische (German—Hungarian)
Ung: Ungava; Ungavan
U of NH: University of New Hampshire
UNHCR: United Nations High Commissioner for Refugees
UNI: United News of India
UNIA: Universal Negro Improvement Association (Garveyites)
UNICCAP: Universal Cable Circuit Analysis Program
UNICE: Union des Industries de la Communauté Européenne (Industrial Union of the European Community)
UNICEF: United Nations International Children's Emergency Fund
unicike: unicycle
unicom: universal communication
UNICOM: aeronautical advisory station operating on 122.8 mc
UNIDO: United Nations Industrial Development Organization
unif: uniform; uniformity
unif coef: uniformity coefficient
Uniform: code for letter U
unilat: unilateral
UNINCO: Union Internationale des Corps Consulaires (International Consular Corps Union)
unincorp: unincorporate(d)
UNIP: United Independence Party
unipol: universal procedure-oriented language
unis: unisoni (Italian—unison)
UNISOMI: Universal Symphony Orchestra and Music Institute
Unit: Unitarian
UNIT: Union Nationale des Ingénieurs Techniciens
UNITAR: United Nations Institute for Training and Research
UNITS: United Nations Informa-

tion for Teachers
univ: universal
Univ: Universal; Universalist; University
univac: universal automatic computer
Univ-Buchdr: Universitats-Buchdrukerie (German—university press)
Univ. D.: Doctor of the University (degree)
unk: unknown
Unk: Uncle
unkn: unknown
UNLL: United Nations League of Lawyers
UNKRA: United Nations Korean Reconstruction Agency
unldh: underloading
unliq: unliquidated
unlk: unlock
UNM: Ukrainian National Museum (Chicago)
U of NM: University of New Mexico
UNMC: University of Nebraska Medical Center
UNMEM: United Nations Middle East Mission
UNMSC: United Nations Military Staff Committee
UNMSM de L: Universidad Nacional de San Marcos de Lima (University of Lima)
UNO: United Nations Organization
UNO: Union Nacional Odría (Spanish—Odria National Union)—Peruvian-general's party
UNOC: United Nations Operations in the Congo
unodir: unless otherwise directed
unof: unofficial
UNOID: United Nations Organization for Industrial Development
unoindc: unless otherwise indicated
UNOLS: University-National Oceanographic Laboratory System
unp: unpaged
UNP: University of Nebraska Press; Urewara National Park (North Island, New Zealand)
unpd: unpaid
unpleas: unpleasant
unpub: unpublished
unqual: unqualified
UNR & EC: United Nuclear Research and Engineering Center
unrep: unreported; unrepresented
UNRRA: United Nations Relief and Rehabilitation Administration
UNRWA: United Nations Relief and Works Agency
uns: unified special (thread); unsymmetrical
UNSA: United Nations Specialized

Agencies; University of Nottingham School of Agriculture
unsat: unsatisfactory
unsatfy: unsatisfactory
unsatis: unsatisfactory
UNSC: United Nations Security Council
UNSCC: United Nations Standards Coordinating Committee
UNSCOB: United Nations Special Commission on the Balkans
UNSCOP: United Nations Special Commission on Palestine
unscv: unserviceable
UNSDRI: United Nations Social Defense Research Institute
UNSG: United Nations Secretary General
unsgd: unsigned
unskd: unskilled
UNSM: United Nations Service Medal; University of Nebraska State Museum
unst: unstable
unsvc: unserviceable
UNSvM: United Nations Service Medal
unsym: unsymmetrical
unter: (German—beneath; lower; under)
unthd: unthreaded
UNTSO: United Nations Truce Supervision Organization
UNTT: United Nations Trust Territory
UNTTA: United Nations Trust Territory Administration
UNWCC: United Nations War Crimes Commission
unwmk: unwatermarked
u & o: use and occupancy
UO: Ulster Orchestra (Belfast)
U de O: Universidad de Oviedo
U i O: Universitet i Oslo
U of O: University of Ohio; University of Oklahoma; University of Omaha; University of Oregon; University of Ottawa; University of Oxford
uoc: ultimate operational capability
UOCO: Union Oil Company
UOFS: University of the Orange Free State
uohc: under other than honorable conditions
uohm: microhm
uol: underwater object locator
uoo: undelivered orders outstanding
UOP: Universal Oil Products
UOPWA: United Office and Professional Workers of America
UOR: Uniform Officer Record
UORI: University of Oklahoma Research Institute
U or non-U: upperclass or not upperclass

uo's: undelivered orders
uos: Underwater Ordnance Station (USN)
uot: uncontrolled overtime
UOT: United Ocean Transport (Daido Line)
uov: unit of variance
up.: underproof; underproofed; underproofing; unpaged; upper
u & p: uttering and publishing
UP: Union Pacific (railroad); Union Postale (Postal Union); United Press; United Province; University of Paris; University of Pennsylvania; University of Pittsburgh; Uttar Pradesh
U di P: Università di Padova; Università di Perugia; Università di Piacenza; Università di Pisa
U do P: Universidade do Pôrto (University of Oporto)
U of P: University of the Pacific; University of Pennsylvania; University of Pittsburgh; University of Portland; University of Pretoria; University of Puget Sound
UPA: Union Postale Arabe (Arab Postal Union); Unions Professionnelles Agricoles (Professional Agricultural Unions); United Productions of America; University Photographers Association
UPADI: Unión Panamericana de Asociaciones de Ingenieros (Pan-American Union of Engineers Associations)
U de Pan: Universidad de Panamá
UPC: Unesco Publications Center; United Power Company
upd: unpaid
UPD: Unified Port District
UPDW: United Piece Dye Works
UPE: Union Parlementaire Européenne (European Parliamentary Union)
U of PE: University of Port Elizabeth
uphol: upholsterer; upholstery
UPI: United Press International (merger of United Press and International News Service)
UPL: United Philippine Line; University of Pennsylvania Library; University of Pittsburgh Library; University of Portland Library
UPNE: University Press of New England
UPNG: University of Papua and New Guinea
upo: undistorted power output
UPO: Unit Personnel Office(r)
upp: upplaga (Swedish—edition)
UPPC: Union Pacific Petroleum Corporation

upr: upper
UPR: Union Pacific Railroad; University of Puerto Rico
UPREAL: Unit Property Record and Equipment Authorization List
ups: uninterrupted power supply; United Parcel Service (trademark in lowercase)
UPS: Underground Press Syndicate; Underground Publication Society; Underwater Production System(s)
UPSG: universal polar stereographic grid
up tor: upper torso
UPU: Universal Postal Union
UPW: Union of Postal Service Workers
UPWA: United Public Workers of America
uq: upper quartile
U de Q: Universidad de Quito (Universidad Central)
ur: unconditioned response; up right (stage direction); upper right; urinal; urinary; urine; utility rectifier
u/r: upper right
Ur: Urania; Uranus; Urdu; Uruguay; Uruguayan
UR: Uniform Regulations; Universidad de la República (University of Uruguay); Unsatisfactory Report; Urban Renewal
U-R: Universal-Rundle
U di R: Università di Roma
U of R: University of Reading; University of Redlands; University of Richmond; University of Rochester
ura: (Japanese—bay; creek; shore)
Ura: Uranus
URA: United Republicans of America; Urban Renewal Adminstration
U-rail: U-shaped rail
Uran: Uranus
U of Rang: University of Rangoon
uranog: uranographer; uranographic; uranography
urb: urban; urbanism; urbanist; urbanistic; urbanite; urbanization; urbanize; urbicultural; urbiculture
urbol: urbanologist; urbanology
urbm (URBM): ultimate-range ballistic missile
urc: upper right center
URC: Universal Resources Corporation; Urban Renewal Commission
urd: upper respiratory disease (head cold)
Urd: Urdu (literary language of Pakistan)

Ur$: Uruguayan peso

URESA: Uniform Reciprocal Enforcement of the Support Act (for the collection and enforcement of child support)

uret: urethra(l)

urg: urgent

uri: upper respiratory illness (head cold)

URI: Union Research Institute (Hong Kong)

U of RI: University of Rhode Island

URISA: Urban and Regional Information System Association

urltr: your letter

urmsg: your message

urogen: urogenital

urol: urological; urology

URR: Union for the Resurrection of Russia

UR's: Unsatisfactory Reports

URS: Universal Reporting System; Universal Reference System

URSI: Union Radio Scientifique Internationale (International Scientific Radio Union)

urspr: ursprünglich (German—originally)

urt: utility radio transmitter

URT: United Republic of Tanzania (Tanganyika and Zanzibar)

urtel: your telegram

Uru: Uruguay; Uruguayan

urv: underseas research vehicle

URWA: United Rubber Workers of America

us.: under seal; undersize; uniform sales

u-s: upper-stage

u/s: unserviceable

u.s.: ubi supra (Latin—where mentioned above); *ut supra* (Latin—as above)

U de S: Universidad de Salamanca; Universidad de San Andrés (La Paz); Universidad de San Augustín (Arequipa); Universidad de San Javier (Panama); Universidad de San Marcos (Lima); Universidad de Santiago; Universidad de Santo Tomás (Bogotá or Santo Domingo)

U di S: Università di Siena

U i S: Universitet i Stockholm

U of S: University of Saskatchewan; University of Scranton; University of Sheffield; University of the South (Sewanee, Tennessee); University of Southampton; University of Sudbury

USA: Underwriters Service Association; Union of South Africa; United States of America (more correctly U.S.A., to distinguish the country from USA,

United States Army); United States Army

U.S.A.: United States of America

U of SA: University of South Africa

U.S. of A.: United States of America (as abbreviated a century ago)

USAAA: US Army Audit Agency

USAABMDA: United States Army Advance Ballistic Missile Defense Agency

USAAD: US Army Airmobile Division

USAADC: United States Army Air Defense Center

USAADEA: US Army Air Defense Engineering Agency

USAAF: United States Army Air Forces

USAAFINO: United States Army Aviation Flight Information and Navigation Aids Office

USAAFO: US Army Avionics Field Office

USAAMR & DL: United States Army Air Mobility Research and Development Laboratory

USAASO: United States Army Aeronautical Services Office

USAAVSCOM: United States Army Aviation Systems Command

USABRL: US Army Ballistic Research Laboratories

USAC: United States Aircraft Carriers (air cargo line); United States Auto Club; US Air Conditioning Corporation

USACDA: United States Arms Control and Disarmament Agency

USACDC: US Army Combat Developments Command

USACDCCA: United States Army Combat Development Command Combined Arms Agency

USACDCEC: United States Army Combat Development Command Experimentation Command

USACDCFAA: United States Army Combat Developments Command Field Artillery Agency

USACDCNG: United States Army Combat Developments Command Nuclear Group

USACDCOA: United States Army Combat Developments Command Ordnance Agency

USACDCQA: United States Army Combat Developments Command Quartermaster Agency

USACDCSWCAG: United States Army Combat Developments Command Special Warfare and Civil Affairs Group

USACE: US Army Corps of Engi-

neers

USACENDCDSA: United States Army Corps of Engineers National Civil Defense Computer Support Agency

USACPEB: United States Army Central Physical Evaluation Board

USACSA: US Army Combat Surveillance Agency

USAD: US Army Dispensary

USADSC: US Army Data Services and Administrative Systems Command

USAE: United States Army Engineer

USAEC: US Army Electronics Command; United States Atomic Energy Commission

USAECBDE: United States Army Engineer Center Brigade

USAECLRA: United States Army Electronics Command Logistics Research Agency

USAED: United States Army Engineer Division

USAEDC: United States Army Engineer Division—Caribbean

USAEDH: United States Army Engineer Division—Huntsville, Alabama

USAEDLMV: United States Army Engineer Division—Lower Mississippi Valley

USAEDM: United States Army Engineer Division—Mediterranean

USAEDMR: United States Army Engineer Division—Missouri River

USAEDNA: United States Army Engineer Division—North Atlantic

USAEDNC: United States Army Engineer Division—North Central

USAEDNE: United States Army Engineer Division—New England

USAEDNP: United States Army Engineer Division—North Pacific

USAEDOR: United States Army Engineer Division—Ohio River

USAEDPO: United States Army Engineer Division—Pacific Ocean

USAEDSA: United States Army Engineer Division—South Atlantic

USAEDSP: United States Army Engineer Division—South Pacific

USAEDSW: United States Army Engineer Division—Southwest

USAEEA: United States Army Enlistment Eligibility Activity

USAEL: US Army Electronic Laboratories

USAEMA: US Army Electronics Materiel Support Agency

USAEMCA: United States Army Engineer Mathematical Computation Agency

USAENGCOM: United States Army Engineer Command

USAEPG: US Army Electronic Proving Ground

USAERA: United States Army Electronic Command Research Agency

USAERDAA: United States Army Electronics Research and Development Activity (Fort Huachuca, Arizona)

USAERDL: US Army Electronics Research and Development Laboratory

USAERG: United States Army Engineer Reactor Group

USAES: United States Association of Evening Students

USAETDC: U.S. Army Engineer Topographic Data Center (D.C.)

USAEUR: United States Army Europe

U S Af: Union of South Africa

USAF: United States Air Force

USofAF: Under Secretary of the Air Force

USAFA: US Air Force Academy

USAFABD: United States Army Field Artillery Board

USAFACS: US Air Force Aircrew School

USAFAGOS: US Air Force Air Ground Operations School

USAFAPS: US Air Force Air Police School

USAFAS: United States Army Field Artillery School

USAFB: United States Army Field Bank

USAFBMS: US Air Force Basic Military School

USAFBS: US Air Force Bandsman School

USAFD: United States Air Force Dictionary

USAFE: US Air Forces in Europe

USAFECI: United States Air Force Extension Course Institute

USAFEURPCR: United States Air Force European Postal and Courier Region

USAFFGS: US Air Force Flexible Gunnery School

USAFFSR: US Air Force Flight Safety Research

USAFI: United States Armed Forces Institute

USAFIGED: United States Armed Forces Institute Tests of General Educational Development

USAFIT: US Air Force Institute of Technology

USAFLANT: US Air Force, Atlantic

USAFMPCR: United States Air Force Mideast Postal and Courier Region

USAFNS: US Air Force Navigation School

USAFOCS: US Air Force Officer Candidate School

USAFOF: United States Army Flight Operations Facility

USAFPACPCR: United States Air Force Pacific Postal and Courier Region

USAFPS: US Air Force Pilot School

USAFSAB: US Air Force Scientific Advisory Board

USAFSAM: US Air Force School of Aerospace Medicine

USAFSAWC: US Air Force Special Air Warfare Center

USAFSC: US Air Force Systems Command; United States Army Food Service Center

USAFSE: US Air Force Supervisory Examination

USAFSG: United States Air Field Support Group

USAFSO: US Air Forces, Southern Command

USAFSOC: United States Air Force Special Operations Center

USAFSOF: United States Air Force Special Operations Force

USAFSOS: United States Air Force Special Operations School

USAFSS: US Air Force Security Service

USAFSTDS: US Army-Air Force Standards

USAFSTRIKE: US Air Force Strike Command

USAFTS: US Air Force Technical School

USAGETA: United States Army General Equipment Test Activity

USAIC: US Army Infantry Center; US Army Intelligence Corps

USAICA: US Army Interagency Communications Agency

USAID: United States Aid for International Development

USAIG: United States Aircraft Insurance Group

USAIIG: United States Army Imagery Interpretation Group

USAILG: United States Army International Logistics Group

USAIMS: United States Army Institute for Military Systems

USAINTS: US Army Intelligence School

USAIPSG: US Army Industrial and Personnel Security Group

USAirA: United States Air Attaché

USAirMilComUN: US Air Force Representative, UN Military Staff Committee

USAIS: US Army Infantry School; US Army Intelligence School

USAJFKCMA: United States Army John Fitzgerald Kennedy Center for Military Assistance

USALAPA: United States Army Los Angeles Procurement Agency

USALDSRA: United States Army Logistics Doctrine, Systems and Readiness Agency

USAMBRL: United States Army Medical Biomechanical Research Laboratory

USAMC: US Army Materiel Command; US Army Medical Corps; US Army Missile Command; US Army Mobility Command; US Army Munitions Command

USAMD: United States Army Missile Detachment

USAMEDS: United States Army Medical Services

USAMERDC: United States Army Mobility Equipment Research and Development Center

USAMMCS: United States Army Missile and Munitions Center School

USAMOCOM: United States Army Mobility Command

USAMU: United States Army Medical Unit

USAN: United States adopted name (nonproprietary drug name)

USANAA: Upper Sixth Avenue Noise Abatement Association

USANAFBA: United States Army, Navy, and Air Force Bandsmen's Association

USANCG: United States Army Nuclear Cratering Group

USANDL: United States Army Nuclear Defense Laboratory

USAPA: US Army Photographic Agency

USAPC: US Army Petroleum Center

USAPDC: United States Army Petroleum Distribution Command

USAPEB: United States Army Physical Evaluation Board

USAPHC: United States Army Primary Helicopter Center

USAPO: United States Antarctic Projects Office

USAPRO: US Army Personnel Research Office

USAR: US Army Reserve

USARA: United States Army Reserve Affairs

USARADCEN: US Army Air Defense Center

USARADCOM: US Army Air Defense Command

USARAE: United States Army Reserve Affairs—Europe

USARAL: US Army, Alaska

USAREUR: US Army, Europe

USARIEM: US Army Research Institute of Environmental Medicine

USARJ: US Army, Japan

USARP: United States Antarctic Research Program

USARPA: US Army Radio Propagation Agency

USARPAC: US Army, Pacific

USARPACINTS: United States Army Pacific Intelligence School

USARSA: United States Amateur Roller Skating Association

USARSO: US Army, Southern Command

USARV: US Army, Vietnam

USAS: United States of America Standard

USASA: US Army School of the Americas; US Army Security Agency

USASAE: United States Army Security Agency—Europe

USASC: US Army, Southern Command—Caribbean; United States Army Support Center

USASCAF: US Army Service Center for Army Forces

USASCC: US Army Strategic Communications Command

USASCSA: US Army Signal Communications Security Agency

USASG: United States Army Standardization Group

USASI: United States of America Standards Institute

USASMC: US Army Supply and Maintenance Command

USASSG: United States Army Special Security Group

USATA: US Army Transportation Aviation

USATC: United States Army Traffic Command

USATEA: US Army Transportation Engineering Agency

USATECOM: US Army Test and Evaluation Command

USATIA: US Army Transportation Intelligence Agency

USATISU: US Army Troop Information Support Unit

USATMACE: United States Army Traffic Management Agency—Central Europe

USATopoCom: United States Army Topographic Command

USATRATCOM: United States Army Strategic Communications Command

USATSC: United States Army Terrestrial Sciences Center

USATTC: US Army Tropic Test Center

USATTU: United States Army Transportation Terminal Unit

USAU: United States Aviation Underwriters

usaw (USAW): underwater security advance warning

USAWES: United States Army Waterways Experiment Station

usb: unified S-band

USB: United States Borax (company)

USBA: United States Brewers Association

USBC: United States Bureau of the Census

USB & C: United States Borax and Chemical (company)

USBCSC: United Society of Believers in Christ's Second Coming (Shakers)

USBE: United States Book Exchange (company)

USBG: United States Botanic Garden

USBGN: United States Board on Geographical Names

USBH: United States Bureau of Highways

USBLS: United States Bureau of Labor Statistics

USBM: United States Bureau of Mines

USBP: United States Board of Paroles

USBPA: United States Bicycle Polo Association

USBR: United States Bureau of Reclamation

USBS: United States Border Station

USBTA: United States Board of Tax Appeals

usc: under separate cover

USC: United Shipping Company; United States Congress; United Steamship Company; University of South Carolina; University of Southern California

USC: *United States Code* (legal)

USCA: United States Copper Association

USCA: *United States Code Annotated*

USCAC: US Continental Army Command

USCANS: Unified S-band Communication and Navigation System

USCB: United States Customs Bonded

USCC: United States Chamber of Commerce; United States Commercial Company; United States Customs Court

USCCPA: United States Court of Customs and Patent Appeals

USCF: United States Chess Federation; United States Churchill Foundation

USCG: United States Coast Guard

U de SC de G: Universidad de San Carlos de Guatemala

USCGA: US Coast Guard Academy

USCG Aux: United States Coast Guard Auxiliary

USCGI: United States Coast Guard Institute

USCGR: US Coast Guard Reserve

USC & GS: United States Coast and Geodetic Survey

USCHS: United States Capitol Historical Society; United States Catholic Historical Society

USCIIC: United States Civilian Internee Information Center (USA)

USCINCEUR: United States Commander-in-Chief, Europe

USCINSO: United States Commander-in-Chief, Southern Command

USCMA: United States Coal Mines Administration; United States Court of Military Appeals

USCO: Union Steel Corporation (South Africa)

USCONARC: US Continental Army Command

US Const: *Constitution of the United States*

USCRS: United States Cotton Research Station

USCS: United States Civil Service; United States Claims Service; United States Conciliation Service; Universal Ship Cancellation Society

USCSC: United States Civil Service Commission

USCP: *United States Coast Pilot*

USCT: United States Colored Troops (1862–1865)

USCUN: United States Committee for the United Nations

US Cy: United States currency

usd: ultimate strength design

USD: Unified School District; University of San Diego; University of South Dakota

USD: *United States Dispensatory*

US$: United States dollar

U de SD: Universidad de Santo Domingo

USDA: United States Department of Agriculture

USDB: United States Disciplinary Barracks

USDC: United States Department of Commerce; United States District of Columbia; United States District Court

USDHUD: United States Department of Housing and Urban Development

USDJ: United States District Judge

USDL: United States Department of Labor

USDLGI: United States Defense Liaison Group—Indonesia

USDOCO: United States Document Officer

USDoD: United States Department of Defense

USDSA: United States Deaf Skiers Association

USDSEA: United States Dependent School—European Area

USDT: United States Department of Transportation

USE: United States Envelope (corporation)

usea: undersea

usec: microsecond

USELMCENTO: United States Element Central Treaty Organization

USEP: United States Escapee Program

USES: United States Employment Service

USEUCOM: United States European Command

USFA: United States Food Administration (World War I)

U of SF: University of South Florida

USFAA: United States Fronton Athletic Association

USFC: United States Foil Company

USFET: United States Forces —European Theater

USFF: United States Flag Foundation

USF & G: United States Fidelity & Guaranty (insurance underwriters)

USFIS: United States Foundation for International Scouting

USForAz: US Forces in the Azores

USFPL: United States Forest Products Laboratory

USfs: United States frequency standard

USFS: United States Forest Service

USFSA: United States Figure Skating Association

USFWS: United States Fish and Wildlife Service

USG: Ulysses S. Grant; United States Gypsum (company)

U.S.G.: United States Government (railroad)

USGA: United States Golf Association

USGLI: United States Government Life Insurance

USGOM: *United States Government Organization Manual*

USGPO: United States Government Printing Office

USGRS: United States Graves Registration Service

USGS: United States Geological Survey

ush: usher

U sh: Ugandan shilling(s)

USHA: United States Handball Association

USHDA: United States Highland Dancing Association

U of Sherb: University of Sherbrooke

USHL: United States Hygienic Laboratory

USHR: United States Highway Research

USHS: United States Hospital Ship

USI: United States of Indonesia; United States Industries

USIA: United States Information Agency

USIAS: Union Syndicale des Industries Aéronautiques et Spatiales

USIB: United States Intelligence Board

USIBR: United States Institute of Behavioral Research

USIC: United States Industrial Chemicals; United States Instrument Corporation

USIF: United States Investment Fund

USILA: United States Intercollegiate Lacrosse Association

USI & NS: United States Immigration and Naturalization Service

USIOSLCC: United States Inter-Oceanic Sea-Level Canal Commission

USIP: University of Stockholm Institute of Physics

USIS: United States Information Service

USISL: United States Information Service Library

USITA: United States Independent Telephone Association

USITT: United States Institute for Theater Technology

USIU: United States International University

USJC: United States Job Corps

USJCC: United States Junior Chamber of Commerce

USJF: United States Judo Federation

USJPRS: United States Joint Publications Research Service

USL: United States Legation; United States Lines; Union Steamships Limited

U-slang: upperclass slang

USLant: United States Atlantic Subarea

USLO: United States Liaison Office(r); University Students for Law and Order

USLSA: United States Livestock Sanitary Association

USLTA: United States Lawn Tennis Association

usm (USM): underwater-to-surface missile

USM: United Shoe Machinery; United States Mail (U.S.M.); United States Mint

U de SM: Universidad de San Marcos (Lima, Peru)

USMA: United States Military Academy

USMBPHA: United States-Mexico Border Public Health Association (of American and Mexican Public health officials)

USMC: United States Marine Corps; United States Microfilm Corporation (company)

USMCR: United States Marine Corps Reserves

USMeMilComUN: United States military members, UN Military Staff Committee

USMH: United States Marine Hospital

USMICC: United States Military Information Control Committee

USMilComUN: United States delegation, UN Military Staff Committee

USMilLias: United States Military Liaison Office

USMILTAG: United States Military Technical Advisory Group

USMM: United States Merchant Marine

USMMA: United States Merchant Marine Academy

USMMCC: United States Merchant Marine Cadet Corps

USMO: United States Marshal's Office

USMS: United States Maritime Service

USMSMI: United States Military Supply Mission to India

USMUN: United States Mission to the United Nations

USN: United States Navy

USNA: United States Naval Academy

USNAM: US Naval Academy Museum

USNAS: US Naval Amphibious School

USNB: United States National Bank

USNC: United States Navigation Company (North German Lloyd —Hamburg-American Line); United States Nuclear Corporation

USNCB: US Naval Construction Battalion (Seabees)

USND: United States Navy Department

USNEL: US Naval Electronics Laboratory

USNFEC: United States National Fruit Export Council

USNG: United States National Guard

USNH: United States Naval Harbor; United States Naval Hospital

USNHO: US Naval Hydrographic Office

USNI: United States Naval Institute

USNII: United States National Indian Institute

USNLM: United States National Library of Medicine

USNM: United States National Museum (Smithsonian Institution)

USNMR: United States National Military Representative

USNO: US Naval Observatory

USNOO: US Naval Oceanographic Office

USNPC: US Naval Photographic Center

USNPS: US Naval Postgraduate School

USNR: US Naval Reserve

USNRDL: US Naval Radiological Defense Laboratory

USNS: US Naval Ship (Military Sea Transport Service); United States Nuclear Ship

USNSA: United States National Student Association

USNSMC: United States Naval Submarine Medical Center

USNTAF: US Navy Training Aids Facility

USNWR: Union Slough National Wildlife Refuge (Iowa); Upper Souris NWR (North Dakota)

USN & WR: U.S. News & World Report

uso: unmanned seismological observatory

USO: United Service Organizations; Utah Symphony Orchestra

U-soc: upperclass society

USOC: United States Olympic Committee

USOE: United States Office of Education

USOEO: United States Office of Economic Opportunity

USOICP: United States Oil Import Control Program

USOID: United States Oversea Internal Defense (USA)

USOM: United States Operations Mission

USP: United States Plywood (company)

USP: United States Pharmacopeia

U de SP: Universidade de São Paulo

USPA: United States Philatelic Agency; United States Polo Association

USPC: United States Peace Corps

USPDO: United States Property and Disbursing Office(r)

U-speech: upperclass speech

USP & F: United States Pipe and Foundry (company)

USPFO: United States Property and Fiscal Officer

USPHS: United States Public Health Service

USPO (U.S.P.O.): United States Post Office

USPS: United States Postal Service; United States Power Squadron

USPWIC: United States Prisoner of War Information Center

USR: United States Reserves; United States Rubber

USR: United States Supreme Court Reports

USRB: United States Renegotiation Board

USRD: Underwater Sound Reference Division (USN)

USRepMilComUN: United States Representative, UN Military Staff Committee

USRL: Underwater Sound Reference Laboratory

USRS: United States Rocket Society

USRS: United States Revised Statutes

USS: Under-Secretary of State; Union Switch and Signal; United States Senate; United States Ship (U.S.S.); United States Shoe (company); United States Standard; United States Steel (company)

US & S: Union Switch and Signal

U of SS: University of the Seven Seas (Chapman College's classes held aboard motorship *Seven Seas*)

USSA: United States Salvage Association; United States Ski Association

USSB: United States Savings Bond(s); United States Shipping Board (World War I)

USSBD: United States Savings Bonds Division

USSC: United States Strike Command; United States Supreme Court

USS Co: Ulster Steam Ship Company; Union Steam Ship Company (New Zealand)

USSDP: Uniformed Services Savings Deposit Program

USSEI: United States Society of Esperanto Instructors

USSF: US Special Forces (Green Berets); United States Steel Foundation

USSFA: United States Soccer Football Association

USSG: United States Standard Gauge

USSIC: United States Sex Information Council

USS & LL: United States Savings & Loan League

USSPA: United States Student Press Association

USSR: Union of Soviet Socialist Republics

USSRA: United States Squash Rackets Association

USSS: United States Secret Service; United States Steamship

USSSA: United States Social Security Administration

USSTRICOM: US Strike Command

ust: undersea technology

ust: (Russian—river mouth)

ust.: ustus (Latin—burnt)

UST: United States Treaties

UST: UnderSea Technology: The Magazine of Oceanography, Marine Sciences, and Underwater Defense

U de ST: Universidad de Santo Tomás (Manila)

USTA: United States Trademark Association; United States Trotting Association

U of St A: University of St. Andrews

USTC: United States Tariff Commission

USTEMC: United States Territorial Expansion Memorial Commission

USTES: United States Training and Employment Service

USTFF: United States Track and Field Federation

USTMA: United States Trade Mark Association

ustol: ultra short takeoff and landing

USTS: United States Travel Service

USTTA: United States Table Tennis Association

usu: usual; usually

USU: Utah State University

USUN: United States Mission to the United Nations

usurp.: *usurpandus* (Latin—to be used)

USV: US Volunteers

USVA: United States Veterans Administration; United States Volleyball Association

USVH: United States Veterans Hospital

USVI: United States Virgin Islands (St. Croix, St. John, St. Thomas)

USVMS: Urine Sample Volume Measurement System

usw: ultra short wave; underwater submarine warfare (USW); unisex (hippie-culture delusion achieved through addictive drugs, transvestite garments, uncut hair, unwashed underwear); unsexed

usw: *und so weiter* (German—and so forth)

USW: United Show Workers

USWA: United Steel Workers of America

USWAC: United States Women's Army Corps

USWACC: United States Women's Army Corps Center

USWACS: United States Women's Army Corps School

USWB: United States Weather Bureau

USWGA: United States Wholesale Grocers' Association

USWI: United States West Indies (Virgin Islands—St. Thomas, St. John, St. Croix, and smaller islands in that group)

USWLS: United States Wild Life Service

USWV: United Spanish War Veterans

USYSF: United States Youth Symphony Federation

ut: universal trainer; urinary tract; user test; utilitarian; utility

u/t: untrained

UT: Union Terminal (railroad); United Territories; United Territory; United Utilities (stock exchange symbol); Universal Time (Greenwich Mean Time); Universal Tubes; Utilities Man

U.T.: U Thant

U de T: Universidad de Toledó; Universidad de Trujillo (Peru)

U di T: Università di Torino

U of T: University of Tampa; University of Tennessee; University of Texas; University of Toledo; University of Toronto;

University of Tulsa

UTA: Ulster Transport Authority; Union des Transports Aeriens; United Typothetae of America; Urban Transportation Administration

UTAD: Utah Army Depot

utarb: *utarb eidet* (Norwegian—prepared)

UTB: Universal Technological Bureau

UTC: United Tank Car; United Technology Center (United Aircraft); United Transformer Corporation Universe Tankships Corporation (National Bulk Carriers)

ut dict.: *ut dictum* (Latin—as ordered)

ute: underwater tracking equipment

uten: utensil(s)

utend.: *utendus* (Latin—to be used)

utend. mor. sol.: *utendus more solito* (Latin—use in the usual way)

utg: *utgave* (Norwegian—edition)

uti: urinary tract infection

UTI: Union Title Insurance

UTIAS: University of Toronto Institute for Aerospace Studies

util: utility; utilization

ut inf.: *ut infra* (Latin—as below)

utl: universal transport(er) loader

UTL: University of Tampa Library; University of Tennessee Library; University of Texas Library; University of Toronto Library; University of Tulsa Library

utm: universal transverse mercator

U of Tok: University of Tokyo

UTP: Unified Test Plan; University of Toronto Press

utr (UTR): university training reactor

uts: ultimate tensile strength; unit training standard

UTS: Underwater Telephone System; Uniform Thread Standard; Union Theological Seminary

uttc: universal tape-to-tape converter

UTU: United Transportation Union

U-tube: U-shaped tube

U-turn: U-shaped turn

utv (UTV): underwater television

UTV: Universal Test Vehicle

UTWA: United Textile Workers of America

UTX: 4-engine jet utility transport

uu: micromicron

u U: *unter Umständen* (German—circumstances permitting)

UU: Union University

UU: *ustedes* (Spanish—you, *pl.*)

U & U : Underwood and Under-

wood

U i U: Universitet i Uppsala

U of U: University of Uppsala; University of Utah

UUA: Unitarian Universalist Association

uue: use until exhausted

uuf: micromicrofarad

UUI: United Utilities Incorporated

UUIP: Uppsala University Institute of Physics

uum (UUM): underwater-to-underwater missile

UUP: Ulster Unionist Party

uut: unit under test

UUWF: Unitarian Universalist Women's Federation

uv: ultraviolet; under voltage

uv: microvolt

u-v: ultraviolet

U V: Unadilla Valley (railroad); Upper Volta

U de V: Universidad de Valencia; Universidad de Valladolid

U di V: Università di Venezia; Universersità de Vicenza

U of V: University of Vermont; University of Virginia

uvaser: ultraviolet amplification by stimulated emission of radiation

UVCT: University of Vermont College of Technology

uvd: undervoltage device

UVDC: Urban Vehicle Design Competition

uviol: ultraviolet

UVL: University of Virginia Library

U-vocab: upperclass vocabulary

UVSA: Unie van Suid Afrika (Union of South Africa)

uvsc: ultraviolet solar constant

uw: unconventional warfare; underwater; underwing; underwriter; unwound

uw: microwatt

u/w: underwriter; used with

UW: Universität Wien (University of Vienna)

U of W: University of Wales; University of Washington; University of Wichita; University of Wisconsin; University of Witwatersrand; University of Wyoming

UWA: University of Western Australia

UWaTU: Underwater Training Unit

U-wear: underwear

UWF: United World Federalists

UWFL: University of Washington Fisheries Laboratory

UWGB: University of Wisconsin at Green Bay

UWI: University of the West Indies (Jamaica)

UWL: University of Wales Library; University of Washington Library; University of Wichita Library; University of Wisconsin Library; University of Witwatersand Library; University of Wyoming Library
UWM: United World Mission; University of Wisconsin at Milwaukee
UWMI: University of Wisconsin Management Institute
UWO: University of Western Ontario
uwoa: unclassified without attachments
uwtr: underwater
UWW: University Without Walls (Antioch College)
ux.: *uxor* (Latin—wife)
uxb (UXB): unexploded bomb
uxgb: unexploded gas bomb
uxib: unexploded incendiary bomb
UY: Universal Youth
UYL: United Yugoslav Lines
Uz: Uzbek; Uzbekistan; Uzbekistanian
Uz: *Uhrzuender* (German—clockwork fuze)
UZ: Universität Zürich
U de Z: Universidad de Zaragoza
Uzbek SSR: Uzbek Soviet Socialist Republic (Uzbekistan)
UZM: Universitet Zoologiske Museum (Copenhagen)
UZRA: United Zionist Revisionists of America

V

v: vacuum; vacuum tube; vagabond; vagrant; value; valve; van; vapor; variable; variation; vector; vein; velocity; vent; ventilator; ventral; verb; verbal; verse; version; vertex; vertical; very; vice; vincinal; violet; violin; virus; viscosity; vise; visibility; vision; visual acuity; voice; volt; voltage; voltmeter; volume; volunteer; vowel
v.: *verso* (Latin—back of page or sheet; lefthand page); *versus* (Latin—against); vibrational quantum number; *voltare* (Italian—turn; turn the page); *von* (German—of; from; used in titles)
v/: *vostra (Italian—your)*
v-1 p: vernier engine 1 pitch
v-1 y: vernier engine 1 yaw
v 26 d M: *vom 26 dieses Monats* (German—of the 26th instant; of the 26th of this month)
V: coefficient of vibration (symbol); five-dollar bill; Lockheed (symbol); potential (symbol); relative wind velocity (symbol); stalling velocity (symbol); Standard Fruit & Steamship Company (Vaccaro Line); vanadium; Venerable; Ventzke; Venus; Verdet constant; Vicar; Vice (as in Vice-President); Victor—code for letter V; Victory—Winston Churchill's symbol in World War II; Village; volume (symbol)
V: airspeed, forward velocity (symbol); speed (symbol); vacuum tube (symbol); *varm* (Dano-Norwegian or Swedish—hot); *väst* (Swedish—west); *vertrek* (Dutch—departure); *vest* (Dano-Norwegian—west); *Via* (Italian—highway road; way); *Villa* (Spanish—village); *violaceus* (Latin—violet color); *viridis* (Latin—green); *vrouw* (Dutch—woman)
V: *Venstre* (Danish or Norwegian—Left)—Liberal Party
V-1, V-2: rockets launched by the Germans in World War II
V₁: decision speed (go-no-go) for aircraft to continue takeoff run or abort flight; valve-current voltage
V₂: aircraft takeoff speed or position where nose is lifted so plane becomes airborne
V-4: four-cylinder engine with two cylinders in each side of V-shaped engine block
V-6: six-cylinder engine with three cylinders in each side of V-shaped engine block
V-8: eight-cylinder engine with four cylinders in each side of V-shaped engine block
V-10: Viscount 10 jet airplane
va: variable; variance; verb active; verbal adjective; viola; voltampere(s)
v-a: volt-ampere(s)
v/a: verbal auxiliary
v.a.: *vixit—annas* (Latin—he lived —years)
Va: Virginia; Virginian
VA: Veterans Administration; Voice of America; voltaic alternative (symbol); Volunteers of America
V-A: Vickers-Armstrong Limited
V & A: Victoria and Albert (Museum)
V of A: Volunteers of America
VAA: Vaccination Assistance Act; Vietnamese-American Association
V-AA: Vietnamese-American Association
VAACR: Vietnamese Association for Asian Cultural Relations
Vaart: (Dutch—canal)
vab: voice answer back
VAb: Van Allen belt (zone of high-intensity radiation surrounding the earth at altitudes of about 500 miles)
VAB: Vandenberg Air Force Base; Vertical Assembly Building (world's largest all-steel structure of its type; used for assembling missiles and space exploration vehicles on Merritt Island at Cape Kennedy, Florida)
VABM: vertical angle bench mark (capitalized on topographic maps)
vac: vacant; vacate; vacation; vacuum; volts alternating current (*volts AC* preferable)
VAC: Volunteer Advisor Corps
vaca(s): [Spanish—cow(s)]
vacc: vaccination; vaccine
Vaccaro: Standard Fruit & Steamship Company
vacci: vaccinate; vaccination; vaccine
vache(s): [French—cow(s)]
vac pmp: vacuum pump
vacs: vacuum cleaners
v/act.: verb active
VAD: Voluntary Aid Detachment
vada: versatile automatic data exchange
V Adm: Vice Admiral
VAEA: Virginia Adult Education Association
VAF: Vendor Approval Form; Vincent Astor Foundation
VAFB: Vandenberg Air Force Base

vag: vagabond; vagina; vaginal; vaginitis; vagrant; vagrancy

VAG: Vancouver Art Gallery

vags: vagabonds; vagrants

VAH: Veterans Administration Hospital

vakt: visual-auditory-kinesthetic-and tactual (imagery applied to teaching reading)

val: valance; valence; valenciennes (lace); valentine; valise; valley; valuation; value; valued; valve; valvular

val (VAL): valine (amino acid)

Val: Valencia; Valentina; Valentine; Valentino

VAL: Vehicle Authorization List; Veterans Administration Library

VALB: Veterans of the Abraham Lincoln Brigade

Vald: Valdivia

valid.: validate; validation

vall: (Swedish—coast)

Vall: Valladolid

valle: (Spanish—valley)

vallée: (French—valley)

Valpo: Valparaiso

valsas: variable-length word symbolic assembly system

VALUE: Visible Achievement Liberates Unemployment (Air Force program for disadvantaged youth)

vam: volt ammeter

VAMCO: Village and Marketing Corporation

vamp: vampire; vampirism

van.: caravan; vanguard; vanilla; vanillin

Vanc: Vancouver

Vancoo: Vancouver, British Columbia

Vancoram: Vanadium Corporation of America

Vang Esp: *Vanguardia Española* (Barcelona's Spanish Vanguard)

vapi: visual approach path indicator

vapor.: vaporization

vap prf: vaporproof

var: variable; variant; variation; variety; variometer; visualaural range; volt-ampere reactive

var: variazione (Italian—variation)

VAR: Volunteer Air Reserve

varactor: variable capacitor

varad: varying radiation

var con: variable condenser

vari: VariType(r)

VARIG: Empresa de Viação Aérea Rio Grandense (airline in southern Brazil)

varistors: variable resistors

varizistor: variable resistor

varn: varnish

varr: variable-range reflector

vars: varieties

varsity: university

vas: vasectomy

VAs: Voluntary Aids

VAS: Virginia Academy of Science

VASA: Virginia Association of School Administrators

vasc: vascular

vascar: visual average-speed computer recorder

VASCO: Vanadium-Alloys Steel Company

vasi: visual approach slope indicator

VASP: Viação São Paulo (São Paulo airline)

VASSS: Van Allen Symplified Scoring System

vat.: value-added taxes (VAT); ventricular activation time

Vat: Vatican

VAT: Vertical Assembly Tower; Visual Apperception Test

vate: versatile automatic test equipment

VATI: Vermont Agricultural and Technical Institute

Vat Lib: Vatican Library (Rome)

VATLS: Visual Airborne Target Location System

vaud: vaudeville

vav: variable air volume

vavbd: vavband (Swedish—clothing)

v/a v/e: value-analyst value-engineer

vb: verb; verbal; vertical bomb (VB); vibration

v /b: vehicle-borne

VB: Navy bomber (2-letter naval symbol); very bad

Vᵒ Bᵒ: *visto bueno* (Spanish—okay)

vba: verbal adjective

VBA: Veterans Benevolent Association

V-band: 46,000–56,000 mc

VBEC: Venezuelan Basic Economy Corporation

V-belt: V-shaped belt (cross-section of belt is V-shaped)

VBI: Venetian Blind Institute

vbl: verbal

V-block: V-shaped block

vbn: verbal noun

V-bomb: German long-range missile-type bomb used during World War II; designated as V-1 and V-2

V-bottom: V-shaped bottom

V B R: Virginia Blue Ridge (highway)

VBS: Vedanthangal Bird Sanctuary (India); Vocabulary Building System

vc: valuation clause; venereal case, violoncello; visual communica-

tion

vc: *vuelta de correo* (Spanish—by return mail)

v/c: *vuelta de correo* (Spanish —return mail)

vC: *voor Christus* (Dutch—Before Christ)

VC: acuity of color vision (symbol); Vassar College; Vatican City; Vennard College; Ventura College; Vermont College; Veterinary Corps; Vice Consul; Victoria College; Victoria Cross; Viterbo College; Volusia College

VCA: Volunteer Civic Association

VCAR: Vendor Corrective Action Request

vcc: vasoconstrictor center

Vcc: supply voltage

VCC: Value Control Coordinator

vc card index (or reader): visual coincidence index (or reader)

VCE: Venice, Italy (airport)

vcg: vertical line through center of gravity

v Chr: *vor Christis* (German—before Christ)

vci: visual communication instructor; volatile corrosion inhibitor

VCI: Vision Conservation Institute

vcl: vertical center line

VCL: Vancouver Public Library

vcm: vacuum

VCN: Vendor Contact Notice

VCNS: Vice-Chief of Naval Staff

vcnty: vicinity

vco: voltage-controlled oscillator

v coul: volt coulomb

VCP: Vendor Change Proposal; São Paulo, Brazil (Viracopos Airport)

vcr: variable compression ratio

Vcr: Vancouver

VCR: Victor Comptometer (stock exchange symbol)

vcs: voices

VCs: Viet Congs

VCS: Vice Chief of Staff

V & C S: Virginia & Carolina Southern (railroad)

vctv: vocative

VCU: Virginia Commonwealth University

V Cz: Vera Cruz

vd: vapor density; various dates; venereal disease (VD); void

v/d: vandyke reproduction

Vd: vanadium

Vd: *usted* (Spanish—you; derived from *vuestra merced*—your grace)

vda: venereal disease awareness; visual discriminatory acuity

Vda: Viuda (Spanish—widow)

VDA: Vermont Department of

Agriculture
V-day: day of victory
VDB: Venereal Disease Branch (US Public Health Service); Verband Deutscher Biologen (Association of German Biologists)
VDBC: Vertol Division, Boeing Company (helicopter design and manufacturing)
vdc: volts direct current (*volts DC* preferable)
VDE: Verband Deutscher Elektrotechniker (Association of German Electrical Engineers)
VDEH: Verein Deutscher Eisenhüttenleute (German Foundry Society)
VDEL: Venereal Disease Experimental Laboratory
vdfg: variable diode function
vd-g: venereal disease—gonorrhea
vdh (VDH): valvular disease of the heart
VDI: Verein Deutscher Ingenieure (Association of German Engineers)
V-dies: V-shaped dies
VdK: Verband der Kriegsbeschadigten (German—League of War Invalids)
vdl: ventilation deadlight
vdm: vector-drawn map
Vdm: Veendam
VDN: Varudeklarationsnamnden (Swedish—Institute for Informative Labelling); *Vin Doux Naturel* (French—fortified wine; natural sweet wine)
vdp: vehicle deadlined for parts
VDRL: Venereal Disease Research Laboratory
vds: variable depth sonar
vd-s: venereal disease—syphilis
vdt: variable density wind tunnel
ve: vernier engine
ve: veuve (French—widow)
Ve: Venezuela; Venezuelan
VE: Value Engineer(ing); Vasileion tis Ellados (Kingdom of Hellas—Greece)
ve/a: value engineering/analysis (program)
VEA: Virginia Education Association
veb: variable elevation beam
vec: vector
vecchio: (Italian—old)
veco: vernier engine cutoff
VECP: Value Engineering Change Proposal
VECR: Vendor's Engineering Change Request
vecto: vectograph; vectographic; vectographical
ved: vedova (Italian—widow)
Ved: Vedic

VED: Vickers Electric Division
V-E Day: May 8, 1945, German surrender in World War II
vedr: vedrorende (Danish—concerning)
Vee: Venezuelan equine encephalomyelitis
Veecees: Vietcongs
vee dee: venereal disease; visiting dignitary
VEENAF: (South) Vietnamese Air Force
Veenees: Vietnamese
Veep: Vice-President
veg: vegetable; vegetarian; vegetarianism; vegetation
vegans: vegetarians
veh: vehicle; vehicular
vehic.: vehiculum (Latin—vehicle)
VEIS: Vocational Education Information System
vel: vellum; velocity; velvet
veld: (Dutch—field; plain)
velho: (Portuguese—old)
velin: velin (French—vellum)
vem: vasoexciter material
ven: veneer; veneering; venerable; venereal; venery; venetian; venetian blind(s); venison; venom; venomous; ventral; ventricle
ven: vendredi (French—Friday); *venerdi* (Italian—Friday)
Ven: Venetian; Venice; Venus
vend: vending; vending machine; vendor(s)
vend. mach: vending machine
Venerable Nestor of Massachusetts: John Quincy Adams —sixth President of the United States who served it from his 14th to his 80th year when he dropped dead during a debate on the floor of the House of Representatives in Washington, D.C.
venetian red: ferric oxide (Fe_2O_3)
Venez: Venezuela; Venezuelan
V-engine: V-shaped engine
vent.: ventilate; ventilating; ventilation; ventilator; venting; ventral; ventricle; venture
vent. fib.: ventricular fibrillation
ventric: ventricular
VEP: Voter Education Project
VEPCO: Virginia Electric and Power Company
ver: verification; verify; verse(s); versine; vertex (Ver)
Ver: Vera Cruz
Ver: Verband; Verein (German—association)
VERA: Vision Electronic Recording Apparatus (videotape)
verand: verandert (German—revised)
verb: *verbesserte* (Dutch or Ger-

man—improved)
verb. sap.: *verbum satis sapienti* (Latin—a word to the wise is sufficient)
Vercors: (pseudonym—Jean Bruller)
Verf: Verfasser (German—author)
Verh: Verhandlungen (German—proceedings)
verkhnyaya: (Russian—higher; upper)
Verl: Verlag (German—publisher)
Verlagshdlg: Verlagshandlung (German—book-publishing house)
verlort: very-long-range tracking (radar)
verm: vermiculite
verm: vermehrte (German—enlarged)
Vermeer: Jan van der Meer van Delft
Vern: Vernon's Law Reports
Veronese: Paolo Cagliari
Verrocchio: Andrea di Michele Cione
vers: versed sine; verses; versification; versine (versed sine)
versine: versed sine
Ver St: Vereinigte Staaten (German—United States)
vert: vertebra; vertebrate; vertical; vertigo
verticam: vertical camera
ves: vessel
ves: (Czech—village)
ves.: vesica (Latin—bladder)
Ves: Sylvester
VESC: Vehicle Equipment Safety Commission
vesca(s): vessel(s) and cargo
VESIAC: Vela Seismic Information Analysis Center
vesic.: vesicula (Latin—blister)
VESO: Value Engineering Services Office
vesp.: vesper (Latin—evening)
vest: vestibule
vest: (Dano-Norwegian or Swedish—west)
VEST: Volunteer Engineers, Scientists, and Technicians (organization)
ves. ur.: vesica urinaria (Latin—urinary bladder)
Vesuvian Century: the year 79 of the Christian era witnessed destruction of Pompeii, Herculaneaum, and nearby Neapolitan places by the volcano Vesuvius—the 1st century
vet: veteran; veterinarian; veterinary
v. et.: vide etiam (Latin—also see)
VET: Verbal Test
vet med: veterinary medicine

vet reg: veterans' regulations
vets: veterans; veterinaries
vet sci: veterinary science
vev: voice-excited vocoder
vexdex: vexation index
vexil: vexillogical; vexillologist; vexillology
vf: vertical file; very fair; very fine; video frequency; visual field; voice frequency; vulcanized fiber
Vf: *Verfasser* (German—author)
VF: fixed-wing fighter airplane (2-letter naval symbol); Valley Forge
VFA: Video Free America; Voluntary Foreign Aid
V-FA: Vietnamese-France Association
V-factor: verbal (comprehension) factor
v-f band: voice-frequency band
vfc: voice frequency carrier
VFHS: Valley Forge Historical Society
VFI: Vocational Foundation Incorporated
VFMJC: Valley Forge Military Junior College
vfn: very-flowery no
VFNP: Victoria Falls National Park (Rhodesia)
vfo: variable-frequency oscillator
VFR: Visual Flight Rules
VFSTC: Valley Forge Space Technology Center (General Electric)
vftg: voice frequency telegraph
VFW: Vereinigte Flugtechnische Werke; Veterans of Foreign Wars
vfy: verify
vg: velocity gravity; very good (VG)
vg: *verbigracia* (Spanish—for example); *virgen* (Spanish—virgin)
v.g.: *verbi gratia* (Latin—for example)
Vg.: *Virgo* (Latin—virgin)
VG: *Vaisseau de Guerre* (French—warship)
vga: variable gain amplifier
VGA: Victor Gruen Associates
VGAA: Vegetable Growers Association of America
VGB: Vandenberg Air Force Base
vgc: viscosity gravity constant
vge: visual gross error
V-girl: vice girl (equivalent to B-girl or C-girl)
vgl: *vergelijken* (Dutch—compare); *vergleiche* (German—compare)
Vgm: Vizagapatam
vgo: vacuum gas oil
vgpi: visual glide path indicator(s)
V-groove: V-shaped groove

VGSA: Viola da Gamba Society of America
vgu: *vorgelesen-genehmigt-unterschrieben* (German—read, confirmed, signed)
vh: very high
v/h: vulnerability/hardness
v/h: *vorheen* (Dutch—formerly)
v H: *vom Hundert* (German—percent; per hundred)
VH: Veterans Hospital
vhb: very heavy bombardment
vhf: very high frequency (30,000 kc–300 mc)
vhf/df: very high frequency direction finding
VHIS: Vaal-Hartz Irrigation Scheme
VHMCP: Voluntary Home Mortgage Credit Program
Vhn: Vickers hardness number
vho: very high output
vhocm: very-heavy oil-cut mud
vhp: very high performance
VHS: Vocational High School
V-hut: inverted V-shaped hut (sometimes called A-hut)
vi: variable interval; viscosity index; volume index
v/i: verb intransitive
v.i.: *vide infra* (Latin—see below)
Vi: Viola; Violet; Virginia; Vivian
VI: Vermiculite Institute; Virgin Islander(s); Virgin Islands (V.I.)
Via: Viaduct
VIA: Vancouver, British Columbia (Vancouver International Airport)
viad: viaduct
VIAR: Volcani Institute of Agricultural Research (Israel)
VIAs: Vocational Information Agencies
VIASA: Venezolana Internacional de Aviación SA
vib: vibrate; vibration; vibratory
VIB: Vertical Integration Building
vibes: vibraphones; vibrations
vibgyor: (mnemonic for remembering the spectral colors—violet, indigo, blue, green, yellow, orange, red)—*see* ROY G. BIV
vibra: vibraphone
vibs: vocabulary-information-block-design similarities
VIBS: Virgin Islands Broadcasting System
vic: vicinal; vicinity; victor; victorious; victory (V)
vic: *vices* (Latin—times)
Vic: RCA Victor; Vicar; Victor; Victoria; Victorine
VIC: Virginia Intermont College; Virgin Islands Corporation
VICA: Vocational Industrial Clubs of America

Vic Adm: Vice Admiral
Vicky: Victoria
vicoed: visual communications education
vicom: visual communication management
VICORP: Virgin Islands Corporation
vic(s): convict(s)
Vict: Victor(ia)
Vict^a: Victoria (Spanish)
Vic^{te}: Vincente (Spanish—Vincent)
Victor: code for letter V
Victor-Charlie: VC; Vietcong
Victor Serge: Victor Lvovich Kibalchich
vid.: *vide* (Latin—see); *Viuda* (Spanish—widow)
VID: Volunteers for International Development
vidat: visual data acquisition
VIDC: Virgin Islands Department of Commerce
VIDD: Virgin Islands Development Department
videocomp: videocomposition (highspeed phototypesetting controlled by programmed digital-control unit)
videot(s): video (television) idiot(s)
vie: *viernes* (Spanish—Friday)
VIE: Vienna, Austria (airport)
vieja(o): (Spanish—old, as in Castilla la Vieja)
vier: *viernes* (Spanish—Friday)
Viet: Vietnam
Viet Cong: *Vietnam Congsan* (Vietnamese—Vietnamese Communists)
Vietminh: Vietnam Doc Lap Dong Ming (League for the Independence of Vietnam)
vieux: (French—old)
vig: video image generator
VIG: Virgin Islands Government
VIGIC: Virgin Islands Government Information Center
vign: vignette
VIGOPRI: Virgin Islands Government Office of Public Relations and Information
vii: viscosity index improver
vik: (Swedish—bay, as in Larvik, Narvik, Västervik)
Viki: Victoria; Victorine
vil: village
Vil: Las Villas (Santa Clara)
villa: (Spanish—small town or village)
ville: (French—city; town, as in Hahnville, Iberville, Villefranche)
VIM: Vertical Improved Mail (conveyorized mail handling in tall buildings); Virgin Islands Mu-

seum; Visible Impact Management

VIMS: Vertical Improved Mail Service; Virginia Institute of Marine Science

vin: vehicle identification number; vinegar

vin.: *vinum* (Latin—wine)

Vin: Vincent

VIN: Vehicle Identification Number

VINB: Virgin Islands National Bank

Vince: Vincent

vinegar: acetic acid (CH_3COOH)

Vinegar Joe: U.S. General Joseph Stilwell

VINHS: Virgin Islands National Historic Site

vini: viniculture

VINP: Virgin Islands National Park (West Indies)

VIO: Veterinary Investigation Office(r)

vip: value improving products; variable information processing; very important passenger; very important people; very important person (VIP); visual identification point

vip: Virgil I. Partch

VIP: Value Improvement Project(s); Variable Information Processing; Very Important Person; Very Important Program; Vías Internacionales de Panamá (Panamanian airline); Virgin Islands Police

VIPAC: Virgin Islands Public Affairs Council

VIPI: Volunteers in Probation, Incorporated

vips: voice interruption priority system

VIP-VIP: Value in Performance through Very Important People (motivational program)

Vir: Virgil; Virgo

VIR: Vendor Information Request

VIRB: Virginia Insurance Rating Bureau

Virgin Queen: Elizabeth I

virol: virology

virr: verb irregular

v/irr: verb irregular

vis: viscera; visible; visibility; visual

Vis: Visayan

VIS: Veterinary Investigation Service; Visual Instrumentation Subsystem

visc: viscosity

Visc: Viscount(ess)

vishni: (Russian—high)

vissr: visible infrared spin-scan radiometer

VISTA: Volunteers in Service to America

vit: vital; vitamin; vitreous

vit A: carotene vitamin

VITA: Volunteers for International Technical Assistance

vit A$_1$: nutritive vitamin found in egg yolk, milk, and milk products such as butter

vit A$_2$: freshwater fish-liver-oil vitamin

vit B: nutritive vitamin essential to digestive and nervous systems; found in breads, egg yolk, lean meats, fruits, nuts, green vegetables

vit Bc: folic-acid vitamin

vit B cx: vitamin B complex (water-soluble vitamins B$_1$, B$_2$, etc.)

vit B$_1$: thiamine vitamin

vit B$_2$: riboflavin vitamin

vit B$_3$: nicotinamide vitamin

vit B$_6$: pyridoxine vitamin

vit B$_{12}$: cobalmine-cyancobalmine vitamin

vit B$_{12}$b: hydroxycobalmine vitamin

vit C: ascorbic acid vitamin

vit D: antirachitic vitamin

vit D$_1$: calciferol and lumisterol vitamin

vit D$_2$: calciferol vitamin

vit D$_3$: cholecalciferol (natural vitamin D)

vit E: antisterility vitamin; tocopherol vitamin

vitel.: *vitellus* (Latin—egg yolk)

vit G: riboflavin vitamin

vit H: biotin vitamin

viti: viticulture

vit K: coagulant vitamin

vit K$_1$: blood-clotting vitamin

vit M: folic-acid vitamin

vit. ov. sol.: *vitello ovi solutus* (Latin—dissolved in egg yolk)

vit P: permeability vitamin (bioflavonoid found in paprika)

vit PP: pellagra-preventive vitamin (nicotinamide nicotinic acid)

vitr: vitreous

vitr.: *vitreum* (Latin—glass)

vit rec: vital records

vitriol: concentrated sulfuric acid (oil of vitriol); copper sulfate (blue vitriol); ferrous sulfate (green vitriol); zinc sulfate (white vitriol)

vit stat: vital statistics

vit U: cabagin (anti-ulcer) vitamin

VIUS: Virgin Islands of the United States

viv: vivace

Viv: Vivian; Vivien; Vivienne; Vivyan; Vivyanne

VIV: *Virgin Islands View*

VIVA: Virgin Islands Visitors Association; Voices in Vital America (organization)

VIVB: Virgin Islands Visitors Bureau

vivi: vivisection

viz.: *videlicet* (Latin—namely)

Viz: Vizcaya (Biscay); Vizcayan (Biscayan)

Vizc: Vizcaya

vj: jet velocity

v J: *vorigen Jahres* (German—last year)

VJC: Vallejo Junior College

V-J Day: August 15, 1945, Japanese surrender in World War II

V-joint: angular V-shaped masonry joint

Vjschr: *Vierteljahrschrift* (German—quarterly)

vk: vertical keel; volume kill

V of K: Voice of Kenya (radio-television network)

VKC: Von Karman Center

VKIFD: Von Karman Institute for Fluid Dynamics

VKO: Moscow, USSR (Vnukovo Airport)

VKR: *Vodennaya Kontr Rozvedka* (Russion—Counter-Infiltration Organization)

v-1: vernier engine 1

v/l: vapor-to-liquid

V/l: vapor-liquid ratio

VL: Vaasa Line; Vaasan Laiva; Venezuelan Line; Viking Line; Volcano Line; Vulgar Latin

vla: very low altitude

Vlad: Vladimir; Vladivostok

vladd: visual low-angle drogue delivery

Vladimir Sirin: Vladimir Nabokov's pseudonym

v-l b: vertical-lift bridge

VLCC: very large cargo carrier (bulk freighter or tanker)

vld: visual laydown delivery

vlf: very low frequency (to 30 kc)

vllo: *violoncello* (Italian—cello)

vlnt: *van links naar rechts* (Dutch—from left to right)

vlr: very long range

vlrc: very long range commuter

vlt: violet

vltg: voltage

vlv: valve; valvular

vm: voltmeter

vm: *voormiddag* (Dutch—forenoon; A.M.); *vormittags* (German—forenoon; A.M.)

v/m: various marks; volts per meter

v M: *vorigen Monats* (German—last month)

VM: Viet Minh; Vulcan Materials

V & M: Virgin and Martyr

vma: vanillymandelic acid

VMA: Valve Manufacturers Association

VMAG: Vanderpoel Memorial Art Gallery

V-Mann: *Vertrauensmann* (German—Trusted Man)—idealistically motivated and especially trustworthy intelligence agent

vmap: video map equipment

V max: maximum flight velocity

vmc: visual meteorological conditions

VMCCA: Veteran Motor Car Club of America

V.M.D.: *Veterinariae Medicinae Doctor* (Latin—Doctor of Veterinary Medicine)

VMI: Virginia Military Institute

v/mil: volts per mil

V min: minimum flight velocity

v & mm: vandalism and malicious mischief

vm & p: varnish makers and painters

vmt: very many thanks

vn: *vellón* (Spanish—copper-silver alloy)

v/n: verb neuter

VN: Vietnam; Vietnamese

Vna: Vienna

VNA: Air Vietnam; Visiting Nurses Association

VNAF: Vietnamese Air Force

VNB: Valley National Bank

V-N B: Verrazano-Narrows Bridge

VN$: Vietnamese dollar

V-neck: V-shaped neck (line)

VNM: Victoria National Museum (Ottawa)

VNMC: Vietnam Marine Corps

VNN: Vietnam Navy

VNNBS: Vietnamese National Broadcasting Service

VNO: Vital National Objective

V-note: $5 bill

VNP: Vietnamese piastre; Voyageurs National Park (Minnesota)

VNR: Van Nostrand Reinhold

VNs: Vietnamese

VNS: Vereenigde Nederlands Scheepvaartmaatschappij (United Netherlands Navigation Company)

VNWR: Valentine National Wildlife Refuge (Nebraska)

vo.: *verso* (Latin—back of the page; lefthand page); *violino* (Italian—violin)

vᵒ: *verso* (Portuguese—lefthand page; other side; over; reverse)

v/o: *vossa ordem* (Portuguese—your order)

VO: verbal order(s); very old

VOA: Vasa Order of America; Voice of America

vo-ag: vocational agriculture (educators' jargon)

vob: vacuum optical bench

VᵒBᵒ: *visto bueno* (Spanish—approved; okay)

voc: vocal; vocalist; vocation; vocational

VOC: Very Old Company (Dutch East India Company)

VOC: *Vereenigde Oostindische Compagnie* (Dutch—United East India Company)—often called the Very Old Company as that it was

vocab: vocabulary

vocat: vocative

vocg: verbal orders—commanding general

voco: verbal order—commanding officer

vocoder: voice coder

vocs: verbal orders—chief of staff

voctl: vocational

vod: vision of right eye (d standing for *dexter*—Latin for right)

vodacom: voice data communication(s)

vodactor: voice data compactor

vodaro: vertical ozone distribution (from) absorption and radiation of ozone

voder: voice-operated demonstrator

VÖEST: Vereinigte Österreichische Eisen und Stahlwerke (United Austrian Iron and Steel Works)

VOG: Vanguard Operations Group

VOICE: Voice of Informed Community Expression

Voice of the American Revolution: Patrick Henry

VOIS: Visual Observation Instrumentation Subsystem

voit: *voiture* (French—railroad coach, truck, wagon, etc.)

vol: volume; volunteer

Vol: Volcán; Volcano

vol ash: volcanic ash

volat: volatile; volatizes

volc: volcanic; volcano; volcanology

Vol Isl: Volcano Islands (south of Japan and Bonin Islands)

Volks: Volkswagen

vollst: *vollstandige* (German—complete)

vol %: volume percent

vols: volumes

Voltaire: (assumed name—François-Marie Arouet)

volts AC: volts alternating current

volts DC: volts direct current

volum: volumetric

Volvo: (Latin—I roll)—Swedish automobile

vom: volt milliammeter; volt-ohm microammeter; vomer; vomer-

ine; vomit; vomitory; vomitus

vom.: *vomitus* (Latin—vomit)

vom neg: *vomito negro* (Spanish—black vomit)—last stage of yellow fever

von Reuter: Israel Beer Josphat (founder of Reuter's news agency)

vop: valued as in original policy

VOP: very oldest procurable

Vo-Po: *Volks Polizei* (East German Police)

VOQ: Visiting Officer's Quarters

vor: very high frequency omnidirectional range (VOR); visual omnirange

vorm: *vormals* (German—formerly); *vormittags* (Germans—forenoon; A.M.)

Vor Mus: Voortrekker Museum (Pietermaritzburg)

Vors: *Vorsitzender* (German—chairman)

vort: vortex; vortices

vortac: visual omnirange and tacan

vos: vision of left eye (s standing for *sinister*—Latin for left)

vo('s): verbal order(s)

vos: *vostok* (Russian—east, as in Vladivostok)

Vos: *Voskresene (Russian—Sunday)*

VOS: Victims of Superstition; visual observation airplane (naval symbol)

vot: voice on set time

vot.: *votivus* (Latin—promissory or votive)

VOT: Foreign Operational Center of Soviet Intelligence forces (formerly called MGB, MVD, NKGB, NKVD, OGPU, GPU, VECHEKA, and originally CHEKA—founded in December 1917, six weeks after Bolshevik seizure of power in October Revolution)

VOTE: Voters Organized to Think Environment

vou: voucher

vox: voice-operated transmission

vox pop.: *vox populi* (Latin—voice of the people)

voy: voyage

Voyager: American spacecraft destined for landings on Mars and Venus

vp: vanishing point; variable pitch; vertically polarized; vistaphone

v/p: verb passive

Vₚ: valve-position voltage

VP: British United Air Ferries (2-letter code); fixed-wing fighter airplane (2-letter naval symbol); Ville de Paris; Vice-President

VP: *Vigilancia de la Pesca* (Spanish—Fishery Patrol)
VPA: Vancouver Public Aquarium; Videotape Production Association
v pag: various paging
vpc: volume-packed cells
vpd: vapor-phase degrease; variation per day; vehicles per day
vph: variation per hour; vehicles per hour; vertical photography
VPI: Virginia Polytechnic Institute
vpm: vehicles per mile; versatile packaging machine; vertical panel mount; vibrations per minute volts per meter; volts per mile
VPM: Vendor Part Modification
Vpn: Vickers pyramid number
V P/N: vendor('s) part number
Vpo: Valparaiso
VPO: Vienna Philharmonic Orchestra
vps: vibrations per second; volume pressure setting
vq: virtual quantum; visual quotient
vqa: vendor quality assurance
vqc: vendor quality certification
vqd: vendor quality defect
vqzd: vendor quality zero defects
vr: variable ratio; voltage regulator; vulcanized rubber
v/r: verb reflexive
VR: fixed-wing transport airplane (2-letter naval symbol); Victoria Railways (Australia)
V-R: Veeder-Root
V f R: Verein für Raumschiffahrt (German—Society for Space Travel)
vra: *vuestra* (Spanish—your, *f.*)
VRA: Vocational Rehabilitation Administration
vras: *vuestras* (Spanish—your, *pl.*)
vrb: voice rotating beacon
vrbl: variable
VRC: Vehicle Research Corporation
vre: voltage-regulator exciter
V Rev: Very Reverend
VRF: Vehicular Research Foundation
vrg: veering
vri (VRI): visual rule instrument landing
Vri: *Vrijdag* (Dutch—Friday)
VRI: Vehicle Research Institute
VR et I: Victoria Regina et Imperatrix (Victoria, Queen and Empress)
V-ring: V-shaped ring
VRIS: Vietnam Refugee and Information Services
v rms: volt(s) root mean square
vro: (Spanish—your, *m*)
vros: *vuestros* (Spanish—your, *pl*)
vrp: very reliable product

VRP: Volta River Project
vrps: voltage-regulated power supply
vrr: visual radio range
VRR: Veterans Reemployment Rights
VRS: Vanguard Recording Society; Van Riebeeck Society
V & RS: Vocational and Rehabilitation Service
vrt: visual recognition threshold
vru: voltage readout unit
Vry: Viceroy
vs: venesection; ventricles; volumetric solution
v.s.: very soluble
vs.: *ve soire* (Turkish—and so forth); *versus* (Latin—against)
v.s.: *vide supra* (Latin—see above)
VS: scouting airplane (2-letter symbol); Vancouver Symphony; Victoria Symphony
VS: *Vereinigte Staaten* (German—United States); *Vostra Signoría* (Italian—Your Honor)
V S: *volti subito* [Italian—turn (music page) swiftly]
V.S.: Veterinary Surgeon
V & S: Valley & Siletz (railroad)
vsb: vestigial sideband
VSBA: Virginia School Boards Association
vsby: visibility
VSC: Vocations for Social Change
vscf: variable-speed constant-frequency
VSD: Vendor's Shipping Document
VSGLS: Vehicle Space Ground Link Subsystem
V-shape: V-shaped
vshps: vernier solo hydraulic power supply
vsi: variable-speed indicator; very seriously ill
V-sign: victory sign (raised index and middle fingers)
vs jw: vise jaws
vsm: vibrating-sample magnetometer
VSMF: *Vendor Spec Microfilm File*
vsn: vision
V S/N: vendor('s) serial number
vso: very special old; very superior old
VSO: Vancouver Symphony Orchestra; Victor Symphony Orchestra; Victoria Symphony Orchestra
vsop: very superior old pale (cognac)
Vsp.: *Vespertina* (Latin—Vespers)
VSPA: Virginia State Port Authority
V-spot: $5 bill
vsr: very short range

vss: versions
VSS: Vermont State Symphony
V St A: *Vereinigte Staaten von Amerika* (German — United States of America)
vstol: vertical and/or short takeoff and landing
vsw: vitrified stoneware
vswr: voltage standing wave ratio
VSX: heavier-than-air antisubmarine warfare carrier-based aircraft (naval symbol)
vt: vacuum technology; vacuum tube; variable time; velocity; verb transitive; voice tube
vt: *vaart* (Dutch—canal); *viz tez* (Czech—see also)
v-t: vacuum technology; variabletime (fuze); velocity-time (diagram)
v/t: verb transitive
v & t: volume and tension (of the pulse)
v T: *vom Tausend* (German—per thousand)
Vt: Vermont; Vermonter
VT: fixed-wing trainer-type airplane (2-letter naval symbol); Reseau Aérien Interinsulaire (Tahiti)
V.T.: *Vetus Testamentum* (Latin —Old Testament)
vᵗᵃ: *vuelta* (Spanish—turn)
VTA: Virginia Teachers Association
VTC: Vermont Technical College
vte: vertical-tube evaporator (for producing freshwater from the sea); vicarious trial and error
Vte: Vicomte
Vtesse: Vicomtesse
vtf: vertical test fixture
vt fuse: variable-fuse
vtg: voting
vti: volume thickness index
VTI: Valparaiso Technical Institute
vtl: variable threshold logic; vertical turret lathe
VTM: Victorian Tourist Ministry (Australia)
vto: vertical takeoff
vᵗᵒ: *vuelto* [Spanish—change (money)]
Vto: *Vtornik* (Russian—Tuesday)
vtohl: vertical takeoff and horizontal landing
vtol: vertical takeoff and landing
vtovl: vertical takeoff vertical landing
vtpr: vertical temperature profile radiometer
vtr: video tape recorder; video tape recording
VTRS: Video Tape Recorder System
VTU: Volunteer Training Unit
vtvm: vacuum-tube voltmeter

vu: volume unit

vu: *von untem* (German—from the bottom)

VU: Air Ivoire (2-letter code); fixed-wing utility airplane (2-letter naval symbol); Valparaiso University; Vanderbilt University; Victoria University; Villanova University; Vincennes University

VUA: Valorous Unit Award

Vul: Vulgate

vulc: vulcanize(d; r)

vulcan: vulcanization; vulcanize; vulcanizer; vulcanizing

vulg: vulgar; vulgar fraction; vulgarian; vulgarism; vulgarist; vulgarization

Vulg: Vulgar Era (Christian Era); Vulgar Latin; Vulgate

VUNC: Voice of United Nations Command

v u p (VUP): very unimportant person

vuv: vacuum ultraviolet

vv: vagina and vulva; verbs; verses;

vice versa

v/v: volume for volume:

v.v.: *vice versa* (Latin—conversely); *violini* (Italian—violins)

Vv.: *Virgines* (Latin—Virgins)

VV: Villa Viscaya (Dade County Art Museum, Miami, Florida); Voice of Vietnam (Hanoi)

VV: *ustedes* (Spanish—you, *pl.*)

VVAW: Vietnam Veterans Against the War

VVD: *Volkspartij voor Vrijheid en Democratie* (Dutch—People's Party for Freedom and Democracy)—Liberal Party

Vve: *Veuve* (French—widow)

vv hr: vibration velocity per hour

vv. ll.: *variae lectiones* (Latin—variant readings)

VVN: Verein der Verfolgten des Naziregimes (League of Victims of Naziism)

VVO: very, very old

vvr: variable-voltage rectifier

vvrm: vortex valve rocket motor

vvs: very, very superior

VVT: Visual-Verbal Test

v.v.v.: *veni, vidi, vici* (Latin—I came, I saw, I conquered)

vw: vessel wall

VW: Very Worshipful; Volkswagen (People's Car)

VWD: *Vereinigte Wirtschafte Dienst* (German News Agency)

vwl: variable word length

vwp: variable width pulse

VWPI: Vacuum Wood Preservers Institute

VX: Experimental Squadron (symbol)

vxo: variable crystal oscillator

Vxtmps: Vieuxtemps

vy: various years; very

VY: Air Cameroun

vyd: *vydani* (Czech—edition)

Vy Rev: Very Reverend

vyt: *vytah* (Czech—abstract)

vz: virtual zero

vzd: vendor zero defect(s)

VZP: Venezuelan Petroleum Company (stock exchange symbol)

W

w: transverse acoustical displacement (symbol); wall; war; warm; waste; water; water vapor constant; watt; weather; week; weight; wet; white; wide; widow; widowed; width; wife; win; wind; wine; with; won; wood; word; work; wrong

w: loading (symbol); work (symbol)

W: Canadian Car & Foundry (naval designator symbol); College of Wooster; gross weight (symbol); irradiance (symbol); tungsten (Wolfram); very wide (symbol); Wales; Ward Line; warning; Washington; water; Waterman Steamship Line; weather reconnaissance; Wednesday; Welsh; west; Westinghouse; Weyerhaeuser; Whiskey—code for letter W; Willys-Overland; Woolworth; Wu

W: *warm* (Dutch or German—hot); west; *west* (Dutch—west; *West* (German—west); Wilhelmsen (steamship line); women

wa: warm air; wire armored; with average; work energy

WA: Wabash Railroad (stock exchange symbol); Watchmen's

Association; Welfare Administration; West Africa; West African; Western Airlines; Western Approaches (to British Isles); Western Australia; Wheeler Airlines; Wire Association; Workshop Assembly

W A: *World Almanac and Book of Facts*

W of A: Western of Alabama (railroad)

waa: wartime aircraft activity; welded aluminum alloy

WAA: War Assets Administration; Warden's Association of America; Western Amateur Astronomers; Women's Auxiliary Association

WAAC: West African Airways Corporation

WAADS: Washington Air Defense Sector

WAAFB: Walker Air Force Base

waaj: water-augmented air jet

waapm: wide-area anti-personnel mine

WAAS: Women's Auxiliary Army Service; World Academy of Art and Science

wab: water-activated battery; when authorized by

WAB : Wabash (railroad); Wage Adjustment Board; Western Actuarial Bureau; Westinghouse Air Brake; Wine Advisory Board

WABCO: Westinghouse Air Brake Company

wac: wage analysis and control; weapon assignment console; write address counter

WAC: Women's Army Corps (USA); Worked All Continents; World Aeronautical Chart

WACB: Women's Army Classification Battery

WACM: Western Association of Circuit Manufacturers

waco: written advice of contracting officer

WACRI: West African Cocoa Research Institute

WACSM: Women's Army Corps Service Medal

WAD: Wright Aeronautical Division (Curtiss-Wright Corporation)

WADC: Western Air Defense Command; Wright Air Development Center

WADD: Westinghouse Air Arm Division; Wright Air Develop-

ment Division (USAF)
wadex: word and author index
WADF: Western Air Defense Force
wadi: (Arabic—intermittent river or stream)
WADS: Wide Area Data Service
wae: when actually employed
WAED: Westinghouse Aerospace Electrical Division
waf: with all faults
WAF: Women in the Air Force
WAFB: Warren Air Force Base
WAFC: West African Fisheries Commission
WAFF: West African Frontier Force
waf(s): waffle(s)
WAG: Walters Art Gallery; Winnipeg Art Gallery
W A & G: Wellsville, Addison & Galeton (railroad)
wagr: windscale advanced gas-cooled reactor
WAGR: Western Australian Government Railways
WAGRO: Warsaw Ghetto Resistance Organization
wags.: weighted agreement scores
wai: walk-around inspection
WAIF: World Adoption International Fund
WAIS: Wechsler Adult Intelligence Scale
waj: water-augmented jet
WAJ: World Association of Judges
wak: water analyzer kit
wal: walnut; wide-angle lens
Wal: Wallace; Wallach; Wallachian; Wallsend-on-Tyne
WA£: West African pound
WAL: Western Airlines; Westinghouse Astronuclear Laboratory; Westland Aircraft Limited
W-AL: Westinghouse-Astronuclear Laboratory
wald: (German—forest; woods; as in Schwarzwald)
Wal I: Wallops Island
Wall: Walloon
Wall: *Wallace* (US Supreme Court Reports)
walopt: weapons allocation optimizer
WALST: Western Alaska Standard Time
Wal Sta: Wallops Station
Walt: Walter; Walton
wam: walk-around money; wife and mother; words a minute
WAM: Wolfgang Amadeus Mozart; Women Against Men; Worcester Art Museum
WAML: Watertown Arsenal Medical Laboratory
wamoscope: wave-modulated oscilloscope

wampum.: wage and manpower process utilizing machines
wan: (Chinese or Japanese—bay; gulf)
WAN: West Africa Navigation (steamship line)
WANA: We Are Not Alone
WANAP: Washington National Airport
WANL: Westinghouse Astronuclear Laboratories
WANR: Wadi Amud Nature Reserve (Israel)
WANS: Women's Australian Nursing Society
WAO: Weapons Assignment Office(r)
WAOS: Wide-Angle Optical System
wap: wide-angle panorama
WAP: Work Assignment Plan; Work Assignment Procedure
WAPD: Westinghouse Atomic Power Division (AEC)
WAPET: Western Australia Petroleum Pty Ltd
WAPOR: World Association for Public Opinion Research
WAP's: Work Assignment Plans
WAPS: World Association of Pathology Societies
WAPT: Wild Animal Propagation Trust
WAPV: gunboat (4-letter USCG symbol)
war.: with all risks
War: War Department; Warsaw; Warwickshire
WARC: Western Air Rescue Center
WARES: Workload and Resources Evaluation System
WARF: Wisconsin Alumni Research Foundation
WARFI: Western Alumni Research Foundation Institute; Wisconsin Alumni Research Foundation Institute
warhd: warhead
Warks: Warwickshire
warla: wide-aperture radio location array
warn.: warning
warr: warranty
was.: wide-angle sensor; wideband antenna system
WAS: Worked All States
WASAL: Wisconsin Academy of Sciences, Arts, and Letters
WASC: Western Association of Schools and Colleges
WASCO: War Safety Council
Wash: Washington; Washingtonian
Wash DC: Washington, D.C.
washing soda: sodium carbonate crystals ($Na_2CO_3 \cdot 10H_2O$)

Washmic: Washington, (D.C.) military-industrial complex
WASHO: Western Association of State Highway Officials
Wash Post: *The Washington Post*
wasn't: was not
wasp.: weightless analysis sounding probe; window atmosphere sounding projectile
WASP: White Anglo-Saxon Protestant; Women Against Soaring Prices
WASP(S): White Anglo-Saxon Protestant(s)
Wass: Wasserman
WAST: Western Australian Standard Time
wat: weight, altitude, temperature
Wat: Waterford
WAT: Word Association Test
WATA: World Association of Travel Agencies
watashi: *watakushi* (Japanese—I; me; myself)
water: H_2O
Watergate: Potomac River waterfront of Washington, D.C. including Kennedy Center for the Performing Arts, Watergate Amphitheater for outdoor concerts, Watergate apartment-hotel-office-shopping center; synonym for a national scandal first detected here at the Watergate office building
waterglass: sodium silicate (Na_2SiO_3)
wats: wide-area telephone service
WATS: Wide Area Telephone Service
watt's: wire-area telephone transmission lines
W Aust Cur: West Australian Current
WAVES: Women Accepted for Volunteer Emergency Service (USN)
WAVFH: World Association of Veterinary Food Hygienists
WAW: Warsaw, Poland (airport)
WAwa: West Africa wins again
wax.: weapon assignment and target extermination
'ways: always
wb: warehouse book; water ballast; waybill; weber; wheelbase
w/b: will be
Wb: weber
WB: Wage Board; Weather Bureau; World Bank for Reconstruction and Development (UN)
W-B: Wilkes-Barre
wba: wideband amplifier
WBA: Washington Booksellers Association; Wisconsin Booksellers Association; World Boxing

Association
WBAFC: Weather Bureau Area Forecast Center
WBAN: Weather Bureau, Air Force-Navy
wbat: wideband adapter transformer
WBAWS: Weather, Briefing, Advisory, and Warning Service
wbc: white blood cell; white blood cell (count); white blood corpuscle
WBC: World Boxing Commission
wbco: waveguide below cutoff
wbct: wideband circuit transformer
wbd: wideband data
wbdl: wideband data link
WBEA: Western Business Education Association
WBF: World Bridge Federation
wbgt: wet-bulb globe temperature; wet-bulb globe thermometer
wbi: will be issued
WBI: Wooden Box Institute
WBINA: Wreck and Bone Islands Natural Area (Virginia)
WBIT: Wechsler-Bellevue Intelligence Test
wbl: wideband laser; wood blocking
Wbl: *Wochenblatt* (German —weekly publication)
WBL: Western Biological Laboratories
wblc: waterborne logistics craft
WBMA: Wirebound Box Manufacturers Association
wbn: well-behaved net
wbnl: wideband noise limiting
WBNM: Wright Brothers National Monument
WBNP: Wood Buffalo National Park (Northwest Territories, Canada)
WBNR: Wadi Bezet Nature Reserve (Israel)
wbns: water boiler neutron source
wbnv: wideband noise voltage
wbo: wideband oscilloscope; wideband overlap; wide bridge oscillator
wbp: weather and boilproof
WBP: Wartime Basic Plan
WBPA: Western Book Publishers Association
wbr: water boiler reactor; whole body radiation; wideband receiver
W Branch: Wireless Branch (British intelligence)
wbrbn: will be reported by notam (Notice to Airmen)
wbs: without benefit of salvage
WBSI: Western Behavioral Sciences Institute
WB Sig Sta: Weather Bureau Signal Station

wbt: wet-bulb temperature; wet-bulb thermometer; wideband transformer; wideband transmitter
WBTA: Webb-Pomerene Trade Association
W B T & S: Waco, Beaumont, Trinity & Sabine (railroad)
wbtv: weather briefing television
wbv: wideband voltage
wbvco: wideband voltage-controlled oscillator
W By: Walvis Bay
wc: wadcutter; wage change; water closet (English euphemism for *lavatory*); weapon carrier; wheelchair; will call; without charge; wood casing; working capital; working circle; workmen's compensation
w/c: wave change
WC: Wabash College; Wagner College; Waldorf College; Walker College; Walsh College; Wartburg College; Washington College; Waynesburg College; Weatherford College; Webber College; Weber College; Webster College; Wellesley College; Wells College; Wesley College; West African Airlines (2-letter code); West Coast Airlines (2-letter code); Westmar College; Westminster College; Westmont College; Wheaton College; Wheeling College; Wheelock College; Whitman College; Whittier College; Whitworth College; Wiley College; Wilkes College; Williams College; Wilmington College; Wilson College; Windham College; Winthrop College; Wofford College; Woodbury College; Woodstock College; World Court; Wycliffe College
W/C: Wing Commander
wca: wideband cassegrain antenna; worst case analysis
WCA: Washingtonian Center for Addiction; World Calendar Association
WCAA: West Coast Athletic Association
w cab: wall cabinet
WCAFS: Wideband Cassegrain Antenna Feed System
WCAP: Westinghouse Commercial Atomic Power
WCAT: Welsh College of Advanced Technology
WCBA: West Coast Bookmen's Association
WCBHS: William Cullen Bryant High School

wcc: water-cooled copper; wilson cloud chamber
WCC: Wayne County Community College; Westchester Community College; White Citizens Council (southern segregationist organization); World Council of Churches
wcca: worst-case circuit analysis
WCCE: West Coast Commodity Exchange
wcdb: wing control during boost
wcdo: war consumable distribution objective
wce: weapon control equipment
WCEMA: West Coast Electronic Manufacturers' Association
wcf: white cathode follower
WCF: Winchester Center Fire (rifle shell designation)
WCFPR: Washington Center of Foreign Policy Research
WCFST: Weigl Color-Form Sorting Test
wci: white cast iron; wind chill index
WCJE: World Council on Jewish Education
WCK: West Virginia Coal and Coke (stock exchange symbol)
wcl: watercooler
WCL: West Coast Line
wcld: watercooled
WCLIB: West Coast Lumber Inspection Bureau
wcm: welded cordwood module; wired-core matrix; wired-core memory; word combine and multiplexer
WCMA: Wisconsin Cheese Makers' Association
WCMR: Western Contract Management Region
WCNM: Walnut Canyon National Monument
WCNP: Wind Cave National Park (South Dakota)
WCOTP: World Confederation of Organizations of the Teaching Profession
wcp: welder control panel; white combination potentiometer
WCP: Weapon Control Plan; Work Control Panel; Work Control Plan
WCPA: Western College Placement Association; World Constitution and Parliament Association
WCPT: World Confederation for Physical Therapy
wcr: water-cooled reactor; water-cooled rod; watercooler; wire contact relay; word-control register
WCR: Western Communication Region (USAF)

WCRA: Weather Control Research Association

wcs: wing center section

WCS: Weapon(s) Control System

WCSA: West Coast of South America

WCSI: World Center for Scientific Information

WC & S's S & EBC: William Cramp & Son's Ship and Engine Building Company

WCT : World Championship Tennis

WCTL: Western Center Telecommunications Laboratory

WCU: West Coast University

WCTU: Woman's Christian Temperance Union

WCUK: West Coast of United Kingdom

wcv: water check valve

WCW: William Carlos Williams

wd: weed; well deck; whole depth; wind; window; withdrawn; wood; word; would; wound

w/d: weight-displacement ratio; wind direction

Wd: weeds

WD: War Department; Water Department; Waterworks Department; Western Division

wda: wheeldrive assembly; withdrawal of availability

WDC: World Data Center

WDC-A: World Data Center-A (Washington, D.C.)

WDC-B: World Data Center-B (Moscow, USSR)

wdd; western Development Division (USAF Air Research and Development Command)

wdf: wood door and frame

wdg: winding; wording

wdk: wives don't know

WDL: Western Defense Laboratories (Philco subsidiary of Ford Motor Company)

WDNR: Wadi Dishon Nature Reserve (Israel)

wdo: willing drop-out

wdp: wood door panel

WDPC: Western Data Processing Center

wdr: write drum

wds: wood-dye stain; word discrimination score; words; wounds

wd sc: wood screw

wdt: width

wdtahtm (wahm, for short): why does this always happen to me?

WDTC: Western Defense Tactical Command

wdu: window de-icing unit

we.: watch error; weekend

w & e: windage and elevation

We: Welsh

WE: Western Electric

W E: *Wärmeeinheit* (German—thermal unit)

wea: weapon(s); weather

WEA: Washington Education Association; Wisconsin Education Association; Workers Educational Association

WEAL: Women's Equity Action League

WeAPD: Western Air Procurement District

weat: weathertight

Web: *Webster's Third New International Dictionary of the English Language Unabridged*

WEBDEC: W.E.B. Du Bois Club(s)

webrock: weather buoy rocket

WEBS: Weapons Effectiveness Buoy System

WEC: Westinghouse Electric Corporation

WeCen: Weather Center (USAF)

WECO: Western Electric Company

WECOM: Weapons Command (USA)

we'd: we had; we would

Wed: Wednesday

Wed: *Weduwe* (Dutch—widow)

Wedd: Wedding (Berlin borough)

Wee: Western equine encephalitis

wef: with effect from

WEF: World Education Fellowship

wefax: weather facsimile

weg(s): wild-eyed guess(es)

WEHS: Wadleigh Evening High School

WEI: World Education Incorporated

Weiss: Weissensee

Wel: Welsh

Wel Adm: Welfare Administration

Wel Can: Welland Canal

weld: welding

Wel Dept: Welfare Department

we'll : we shall; we will

Well: Wellington

Welt: *Die Welt* (Hamburg's World)

WEMA: Western Electronic Manufacturers Association

Wen: Wendel; Wendell; Wendy

WEN: Wien-Alaska Airlines

Wend: *Wendell's Reports*

WENOA: *Weekly Notice to Airmen* (CAA)

WEP: Wisconsin Electric Power Company

WEPA: Welded Electronic Packaging Association

WEPCO: Weather-Proof Company

we're: we are

weren't: were not

Wes: Wesley; Weston

WES: Water Electrolysis System; Waterways Experiment Station;

Weather Editing Section (FAA); Women's Engineering Society

WESCON: Western Electronics Show and Convention

wesentl: *wesentlich* (German—essential; main)

WESO: Weapons Engineering Service Office

Wes Pac: Western Pacific

WESRAC: Western Research Application Center

WEST: Western Energy Supply and Transmission (Association); Women's Enlistment Screening Test

WESTAF: Western Transport, Air Force

WESTCOMMRGN: Western Communications Region

wester: storm from the west

westersch: (Dutch—western)

WestLant: Western Atlantic Area

Westm: Westminister; Westmorland

Westmld: Westmorland

West Pac: Western Pacific (ocean or railroad)

WESTPAC: Western Pacific

Westralia: Western Australia

WET: Weapon(s) Effectiveness Test(ing)

Wet Mary: Western Maryland Railway (stock exchange slang)

WEU: Western European Union (Belgium, France, Italy, Luxembourg, Netherlands, United Kingdom, West Germany)

we've: we have

Wex: Wexford

WEX: Westinghouse Electric Company (stock exchange nickname)

Wey: Weymouth

WEZ: *westeuropäische Zeit* (German—West European Time); Greenwich Mean Time

wf: wrong font

w/f: white female

w & f: water and feed

WF: Wake Forest; Wake Forest College; Wells Fargo & Company

W & F: Wallis and Futuna Islands

WFA: War Food Administration (World War II); White Fish Authority; World Friendship Association

w factor: will factor

WFB: Wells Fargo Bank

WFBI: Wood Fiber Blanket Institute

WFBMA: Woven Fabric Belting Manufacturers Association

WFC: Wake Forest College

WFD: World Federation of the Deaf

WFDY: World Federation of Dem-

ocratic Youth (communist)
wfe: with food element
WFEA: World Federation of Educational Associations
WFEB: Worcester Foundation for Experimental Biology
WFEO: World Federation of Engineering Organizations
WFEX: Western Fruit Express
WFF: World Friendship Federation
wfg: waveform generator
WFI: Wheat Flour Institute
WFL: Women's Freedom League
W Flem: West Flemish
WFM: Western Federation of Miners
WFMH: World Federation for Mental Health
wfn: well-formed net
WFN: World Federation of Neurology
wfna: white-fuming nitric acid
WFNS: World Federation of Neurosurgical Societies
wfo: wide-field optics
wfof: wide-field optical filter
WFOT: World Federation of Occupational Therapists
wfp: warm frontal passage
WFP: World Food Program (UN)
WFP: *Winnipeg Free Press*
WFPA: World Federation for the Protection of Animals
WFPT: World Federation for Physical Therapy
W Fris: West Frisian
WFS: World Future Society
WFSPL: Wright Field Special Projects Laboratory
WFTU: World Federation of Trade Unions
WFUNA: World Federation of United Nations Associations
WFY: World Federalist Youth
wg: water gauge; wing; wire gauge
WG: Western Gear (company)
wga: wheat-germ agglutinin
WGA: Writers Guild of America
W-gauge: wide-gauge railroad track (exceeding the standard gauge of 4 feet 8½ inches)
wgbc: waveguide operating below cutoff
WGC: West Georgia College
WGDS: Warm Gas Distribution System
W Ger: West Germany
WGER: Working Group on Extraterrestrial Resources
wgf: waveguide filter; wound glass filter
WGH: Warren G. Harding
WGI: Work Glove Institute
WGIPP: Waterton-Glacier International Peace Park (Alberta, Canada and Montana, U.S.A.)

wgj: wormgear jack
w gl: wireglass
WGL: Weapons Guidance Laboratory
WGMA: Wet Ground Mica Association
WGmc: West Germanic
WGP: Western Gas Processors
WGPMS: Warehousing Gross Performance Measurement System
wgr: wide gauze roll
WGR: War Guidance Requirements
Wg & Rgn Comdr: Wing and Regional Commander
W Grnld Cur: West Greenland Current
wgs: waveguide glide slope; web guide system
WGs: Welsh Guards
wgsj: wormgear screw jack
wgw: waveguide window
wh: water heater; watt hour; white; withholding
w/h: withholding
Wh: Whig Party
WH: White House
WHA: Western History Association
whap: when or where applicable
WHASA: White House Army Signal Agency
what's: what has; what is
WHCA: White House Communications Agency
WHCOA: White House Conference on Aging
WHCT: West Ham College of Technology
whd: warhead
whdm: watt-hour demand meter
whe: water hammer eliminator
Wheat: *Wheaton's* (US Supreme Court Reports)
wheats: wheatcakes
whecon: wheel control
where'er: wherever
whf: wharf
WHFAM: William Hayes Fogg Art Museum
whfg: wharfage
WHH: William H. Harrison
WHHA: White House Historical Association
WHI: Western Highway Institute
whis: whistle (fog)
Whiskey: code for letter W; Western Kentucky (coal company; stock exchange slang)
Whit: Whitcomb; Whitfield; Whitlock; Whittaker
Whitaker's: *Whitaker's Almanac*
white lead: lead carbonate
WHL: Western Hockey League
wh lt: white light
whmstr: weighmaster
WHMV & NSA: Woods Hole,

Martha's Vineyard and Nantucket Steamship Authority
Whn: Whitehaven
WHO: White House Office; World Health Organization (UN)
who'd: who had
WHOI: Woods Hole Oceanographic Institution
whol: wholesale(r)
who'll: who will
who's: who is
whp: water horsepower
W & H & PC: Wage and Hour and Public Contracts
whr: watt hour
WHRC: World Health Research Center
whrlp: whirlpool
whs: warehouse
WHS: Walton High School; White Sands, New Mexico (tracking station)
whse: warehouse
whsl: wholesale
whsmn: warehouseman
whsng: warehousing
whs rec: warehouse receipt
WHT: William H. Taft
WHTHS: William Howard Taft High School
whvs: wharves
wi: wrought iron
w & i: weighing and inspection
WI: Wake Island; West India; West Indian; West Indies; Windward Islands; Wine Institute; Wire Institute
wia (WIA): wounded in action
WIAB: Wistar Institute of Anatomy and Biology
Wib: Wibbert; Wilbert
WIBC: Women's International Bowling Congress
WIC: Welfare and Institutions Code; Women in Construction
WICHE: Western Interstate Commission for Higher Education
Wick: Wicklow
WICS: Women's Institute for Continuing Study
wid: widow; widower
WID: West India Docks
Widm: *Widmung* (German—dedication) ·
WIF: West India Fruit and Steamship Company; West Indies Federation
Wig: Wigtown
wigo: what is going on?
wih: went in hole
WIHS: Washington Irving High School
Wil: Wilber; Wilbert; Wilbur; Wilburn; Wiley; Wilford; Wilfred; Wylie
WIL: West India Lines

Wil Blvd: Wilshire Boulevard
wilco: will comply
Will: Willard; William; Willis
William Bolitho: William Bolitho Ryall
Will Rogers Turn: Will Rogers Turnpike
Willy: William
Wilm: Wilmersdorf; Wilmington
Wilts: Wiltshire
W I & M: Washington, Idaho & Montana (railroad)
WIMA: Western Industrial Medical Association; Writing Instrument Manufacturers Association
Wimb: Wimborne
w i m c: whom it may concern
WIN: Work Incentive Program
WINA: Webb Institute of Naval Architecture
win'ard: windward
WINBAN(GA): Windward Islands Banana Growers Association
wind.: windlass
WINE: Webb Institute of Naval Engineering
Wing Cdr: wing Commander
winkle(s): periwinkle(s)
Winn: Winnipeg; Winnipegger
Winnie: Sir Winston Churchill—British Prime Minister
wino: alcoholic addicted to wine
win'rd: windward (pronounced *win-urd* by sailors)
WINS: Western Integrated Navigation System
Wint Gard: Winter Garden
Wint T: *The Winter's Tale*
wip: work in process; work in progress
WIP: West Indian Process (for sorting ripe from unripe coffee berries); Work Incentive Program
WIPO: World Intellectual Property Organization
WIR: *Weekly Intelligence Report*
WIRA: Wool Industry Research Association
WIRDS: Weather Information Reporting and Display System
Wis: Wisconsin; Wisconsinite
WIS: Weizmann Institute of Science; West Indies Shipping
WISA: West Indian Sugar Association; West Indies Students Association
WISC: Wechsler's Intelligence Scale for Children
Wisd of Sol: Wisdom of Solomon (apocryphal book of the Bible)
Wiss: *Wissenschaft* (German—science)
wit.: witness
WIT: West India Tankers
WITCH: Women's International Terrorist Conspiracy (from) Hell
witned: witnessed
witneth: witnesseth
Wits U: Witwatersrand University
wiz: wizard
Wizard of Menlo Park: Thomas Alva Edison
WIZO: Women's International Zionist Organization
WJC: Westbrook Junior College
W & JC: Washington and Jefferson College
wk: week; work; wreck
Wk: wreck
WK: Western Alaska Airlines
wkd: worked
wkds: weekdays
wkg: working
wkly: weekly
WKNR: Wadi Kziv Nature Reserve (Israel)
wkr: workers; wrecker
wks: weeks; works; workshop(s)
Wks: wreckage
WKSC: Western Kentucky State College
wkt: wicket
WKY: Western Kentucky (coal company); Wall Street slang for this company is *Whiskey*
W Ky Pkwy: Western Kentucky Parkway
wl: wall lavatory; waterline; waterplane coefficient; wavelength
WL: *Wagon Lits* (French—sleeping cars)
W-L: Westfal-Larsen Line
W & L: Washington and Lee University
WLA: Washington Library Association; Western Literature Association; Wisconsin Library Association
wlb: wallboard
WLB: War Labor Board; Women's Liberation Party
WLC: World Liberty Corporation (Niarchos)
WL & Co: Westfal-Larsen & Company (steamship line)
wl coef: waterline coefficient
wld: west longitude date; would
wldr: welder
WLF: Women's Liberation Front; World Law Fund
WLFNWR: William L. Finley National Wildlife Refuge (Oregon)
WLG: Wellington, New Zealand (airport)
WLM: Women's Liberation Movement
Wlmsbrg Brdg: Williamsburgh Bridge
Wln: Wellington
W Long: west longitude
W Loth: West Lothian
WLP: Wallops Island, Virginia (tracking station)
WLPS: Wild Life Protection Society
WLRI: World Life Research Institute
WLS: Wild Life Sanctuary
WLSC: West Liberty State College
WLSR: Wild Life Society of Rhodesia
WLU: World Liberal Union
W & LU: Washington and Lee University
Wly: westerly
wlz: waltz
wm: wattmeter; wavemeter; white metal; wire mesh
w/m: weight or measure; white male
Wm: William
WM: Western Maryland (railroad); William McKinley
W & M: College of William and Mary; Washburn & Moen (wire gauge)
WMA: Wildlife Management Area; World Medical Association
WMAA: Whitney Museum of American Art
WMATC: Washington Metropolitan Area Transit Commission
WMB: War Mobilization Board
WMBL: Wrightsville Marine Biomedical Laboratory
WMC: Ways and Means Committee; Western Maryland College
WMCE: Western Montana College of Education
WMCL: William Mitchell College of Law
WMCP: Women's Medical College of Pennsylvania
wmd: wind measuring device
Wmd: Willemstad
WMD: Weights and Measures Division
WMECO: Western Massachusetts Electric Company
Wmg, Cal: Wilmington, California
Wmg, Del: Wilmington, Delaware
WMI: Webbing Manufacturers Institute; Wildlife Management Institute
wmk: watermark
Wmn: Wilmington, North Carolina
WMO: World Meteorological Organization
wmp: with much pleasure (the invitation is accepted)
WMR: Wasatch Mountain Railway
WMS: Webster Memory Scale; Women in Medical Service; Women's Medical Specialist; Work Measurement System; World Magnetic Survey
W & MS: Wisconsin & Michigan

Steamship (company)

WMSC: Women's Medical Specialist Corps

W & M SS Co: Wisconsin & Michigan Steamship Company

wmt: weighing more than

WMT: Wilson Marine Transit

WMU: Western Michigan University

W M W & NW: Weatherford, Mineral Wells & Northwestern (railroad)

WMWR: Wichita Mountains Wildlife Refuge (Oklahoma)

w/n: well-nourished

WNA: Washington, D.C. National Airport; winter North Atlantic (loadline marking for ships voyaging across the North Atlantic in winter)

WNAP: Washington National Airport

wnb: will not be

WNBA: Women's National Book Association

WnBanc: Western Bancorporation

wndml: windmill

wndp: with no down payment

wng: warning

wnl: within normal limits

wnm: white noise making

WNM: Washington National Monument

WNNP: Walpole-Nornalup National Park (Western Australia)

WNP: Wankie National Park (Rhodesia); Warrumbungle NP (New South Wales); Welsh National Party; Westland NP (South Island, New Zealand); Wilpattu NP (Ceylon); Wyperfeld NP (Victoria, Australia)

WNRE: Whiteshell Nuclear Research Establishment

WNS: Washington National Symphony (District of Columbia)

wintr: winter

WNW: west northwest

WNWR: Wapanocca National Wildlife Refuge (Arkansas); Washita NWR (Oklahoma); Wheeler NWR (Alabama); Willapa NWR (Washington)

WNYNRC: Western New York Nuclear Research Center

WNYNSC: Western New York Nuclear Service Center

wo: wait order; work order; write out; written order

w-o: water-in-oil (emulsion); without

w/o: without

wo: *wie oben* (German—as previously mentioned)

WO: Warrant Officer; Welsh Office

WOA: Wharf Owners' Association

wob: washed overboard

Wobblies: International Workers of the World (so named because Chinese members pronounced IWW as *I Wobbly Wobbly*)

woc: without compensation

W & O D: Washington & Old Dominion (railroad)

WODECO: Western Offshore Drilling and Exploration Company

woe.: without equipment

Woe: *Woensdag* (Dutch—Wednesday)

wog: golliwog; polliwog; water or gas (valve); with other goods

'wog: golliwog; polliwog

WOG: Wily Oriental Gentleman (nickname applied to Farouk I of Egypt and similar monarchs of the area)

WOGA: Western Oil and Gas Association

wogs: (British slang—wily oriental gentlemen; wily oriental peoples)

WOHC: Warrant Officer, Hospital Corps

WOJG: Warrant Officer, Junior Grade

wol: wharf owners' liability

WOM: Woomera, Australia (tracking station)

WOMAN: World Organization of Mothers of All Nations

Women's Lib: Women's Liberation Movement

womlib: women's liberation

WOO: Western Operations Office (NASA); World Oceanographic Organization

wood alcohol: methyl alcohol (CH_3OH)

Woodie: Woodmansee; Woodrow

Woody: Woodrow

woof: (cartoonist's language—dog's bark)

woof(s): woofer(s)

Wool: *Woolworth's* (Circuit Court Reports)

wop.: with other property; without personnel

wope: without personnel or equipment

WOQT: Warrant Officer Qualification Test

Worc: Worcester

WORC: Washington Operations Research Council

Worcs: Worcestershire

WORK: Wanted Older Residents (with) Knowhow

World: *World Almanac*

WOS: Washington Opera Society; Wilson Ornithological Society

wosac: worldwide synchronization of atomic clocks

wot: wide-open throttle

wouldn't: would not

W & O V: Washington & Ouachita Valley (railroad)

wow: waiting on weather

WOW: Woodmen of the World

w/o wn: without winch

wp: waste pipe; water repellency; water repellent; way point; weather permitting; white phosphorus; will proceed; working paper; working party; working point; working pressure

w-p: waterproofed

w/p: without prejudice

WP: War Plan(s); Warsaw Pact; Western Pacific (railroad); West Point; West Virginia Pulp and Paper (stock exchange symbol); Worthington Pump; Worthy Patriarch

WP: *Wiener Philharmoniker* (German—Vienna Philharmonic Orchestra); *Winkler Prins Encyclopedieen* (Dutch—Winkler Prins Encyclopedia)

wpa: with particular average

WPA: Western Pine Association; Works Progress Administration; World Parliament Association

WPAFB: Wright-Patterson Air Force Base

wpb: wastepaper basket

WPB: War Plan Basic; War Production Board (World War II)

wpc: water pollution control; watts per candle; wood plastic combination; world planning chart

WPC: Washington Press Club; William Penn College

WPCA: Water Pollution Control Act

WPCC: Western Pharmaceutical and Chemical Corporation

WPCF: Water Pollution Control Federation

WPF: World Peace Foundation

wpg: waterproofing

WPg: West Point graduate

WPG: gunboat (3-letter USCG symbol)

WPGR: Willem Pretorius Game Reserve (South Africa)

WPHC: Western Pacific High Commissioner

WPHI: Western Pennsylvania Horological Institute

wpi: wholesale price index

WPI: Wall Paper Institute; Waxed Paper Institute; Worcester Polytechnic Institute; World Press Institute

wpl: warning point level

WPL: Wichita Public Library; Winnipeg Public Library; Worcester Public Library

WPLO: Water Port Liaison Office(r)

wpm: words per minute

wpn: weapon

WPN: West Penn Traction (stock-exchange symbol)

WPO: Water Programs Office (Environmental Protection Agency); Wiener Philharmonic Orchester (Vienna Philharmonic Orchestra); World Ploughing Organization

WPOD: Water Port of Debarkation

WPOE: Water Port of Embarkation

wpp: waterproof paper packing

WPP: West Penn Power Company

WPPC: West Penn Power Company

WPPSS: Washington Public Power Supply System

wp & r: work-planning-and-review (discussions)

wps: with prior service; words per second

WPs: Warsaw Pact members; Warsaw Pact nations

WPSA: World's Poultry Science Association

WPSL: Western Primary Standard Laboratory

wpu: write punch

wpwod: will proceed without delay

WPY: World Population Year (1974)

WP & Y: White Pass & Yukon (railroad)

WP & YR: White Pass & Yukon Route

WPZ: Woodland Park Zoo (Seattle)

wq: water quench

WQF: Wider Quaker Fellowship

wr: war risk

w/r: water and rail

w & r: water and rail; welfare and recreation

WR: Wassermann reaction

WRA: Western Railway of Alabama

WRAC: Women's Royal Army Corps

wraceld: wounds received in action combat with enemy or in line of duty

WRAF: Women's Royal Air Force

WRAIN: Walter Reed Army Institute of Nursing

WRAIR: Walter Reed Army Institute of Research

WRAMA: Warner-Robins Air Material Area

WRAMC: Walter Reed Army Medical Center

WRAT: Wide-Range Achievement Test

WRB: War Refugee Board

WRBC: Weather Relay Broadcast System

wrc: water-retention coefficient

WRC: Weather Relay Center; Welding Research Council

WRDC: Westinghouse Research and Development Center

WRE: Weapons Research Establishment (Woomera, Australia)

WREN: Women's Royal Naval Service

wresat: weapons research establishment satellite

W-response: whole response

WRF: World Rehabilitation Fund

wrfg: wharfage

WRGH: Walter Reed General Hospital

WRH: Walter Reed Hospital

WRHS: Western Reserve Historical Society

wri: war risk insurance

WRI: War Resisters' International; Weatherstrip Research Institute; Wellcome Research Institute; Wire Reinforcement Institute; Wire Rope Institute

WRIR: Walter Reed Institute of Research

wrl: wing reference line

WRL: Wantage Research Laboratory; War Readiness Materiel; War Resisters League; Westinghouse Research Laboratories; Willow Run Laboratories (University of Michigan)

WRLC: World Role of Law Center (Duke University)

wrm: war readiness materiel

WRM: Wasatch Railway Museum

WRNS: Women's Royal Naval Service

wrnt: warrant

WRNWR: White River National Wildlife Refuge (Arkansas)

wro: war risk only

WRPA: Water Resources Planning Act

WRPC: Weather Records Processing Center(s)

WRRC: Willow Run Research Center

WRRR: Walter Reed Research Reactor

WRRS: Wire Relay Radio System

WRSIC: Water Resources Scientific Information Center

wrsk: war-readiness spares kit

WRSP: *World Register of Scientific Periodicals*

wrt: wrought

wrtd: warranted

wrtr: writer

wru: who are you?

WRU: Western Reserve University

wrv: water relief valve

wr(w): war reserve (weapon)

WRX: Western Refrigerator Express (railroad code)

WRY: World Refugee Year

WR Yorks: West Riding, Yorkshire

W Ry A: Western Railway of Alabama

ws: water supply; weather station

w & s: whiskey and soda

WS: Ware Shoals; wind speed

W S: *Washington Star*

wsa: weapons system analysis

WSA: Weed Society of America; Worker-Student Alliance

WSAC: West of Scotland Agricultural College

WSAD: Weapon System Analysis Division (USN)

WSAG: Washington Special Action Group (personnel in Situation Room in White House basement)

W Sam: Western Samoa

WSAO: Weapons System Analysis Office

wsb: will send boat

WSB: Wharton School of Business

wsc: weapon system contractor

WSC: Western Simulation Council; Winona State College; Wisconsin State College; Writing Services Center

WSCC: Western State College of Colorado

Wschr: *Wochenschrift* (German —weekly magazine)

WSCS: Woman's Society for Christian Service

wsd: working stress design

WSDL: Weapons System Development Laboratory

WSECL: Weapon System Equipment Component List

WSED: Weapon Systems Evaluation Division

WSEG: Weapons Systems Evaluation Group

WSEL: Weapons System Engineering Laboratory

WSEP: Waste Solidification Engineering Prototype Plant (AEC); Weapon System Evaluation Program

WSF: Washington State Ferries; Western Sea Frontier; Women's Strike for Peace; World Sephardic Federation

WSFI: Water Softener and Filter Institute

wsg: worthiest soldier in the group

WSG: Wesleyan Service Guild

WSGE: Western Society of Gear Engineers

WSHS: Wisconsin State Historical Society

WSJ: *Wall Street Journal*

WSL: Warren Spring Laboratory
WSLO: Weapon System Logistics Office(r)
WSM: Weapon System Manager; W. Somerset Maugham
WSMAC: Weapon System Maintenance Action Center
WSMO: Weapon System Materiel Office(r)
WSMR: White Sands Missile Range
WSNM: White Sands National Monument
WSO: Western Support Office (NASA); Wichita Symphony Orchestra
WSO: *Wiener Symphonisches Orchester* (German—Vienna Symphony Orchestra)
wsp: water supply point
WSP: Wyoming State Parks
WSPACS: Weapon System Program and Control System
WSPG: White Sands Proving Ground
WSPL: Winston-Salem Public Library
WSPO: Weapon System Project Officer
WSPOP: Weapon System Phase-Out Procedure
WSPU: Women's Social and Political Union
wsr (WSR): weapon system reliability
w/sr: watt(s) per steradian
Wsr: Wesermünde
W & S R: Warren & Saline River (railroad)
WS & RB: Washington Surveying and Rating Bureau
WSRI: World Safety Research Institute
w/srm²: watt(s) per steradian square meter
WSS: Warfare Systems School; Winston-Salem Southbound (railroad); World Ship Society
WSSA: Weapon System Support Activities; World Secret Service Association
WSSC: Weapon System Support Center
WSSCA: White Sands Signal Corps Agency
WSSO: Winston-Salem Symphony Orchestra
WSSS: Weapon System Storage Site
WSS & YP: White Sulphur Springs & Yellowstone Park (railroad)
WST: Whitworth Standard Thread
WSTA: White Slave Traffic Act
WSTC: Winston-Salem Teachers College
WSTF: White Sands Test Facility

(NASA)
WSTI: Waterbury State Technical Institute; Welded Steel Tube Institute
WSTNRA: Whiskeytown-Shasta-Trinity National Recreation Area (California)
WSU: Washington State University; Wayne State University; Western State University
w sup: water supply
W Sus: West Sussex
WSV: Wiener Stadtwerke Verkehrsbetriebe (Vienna transportation system)
wsw: white sidewall (tires)
WSW: west southwest
WSWL: Warheads and Special Weapons Laboratory
WSWMA: Western States Weights and Measures Association
WSWS: Wexford Slobs Wildfowl Sanctuary (Ireland)
wt: watch time; watertight; weight; withholding tax (WT)
w/t: wireless telegraph(y)
WT: war time; withholding tax; winterization test
W & T: Wrightsville & Tennille (railroad)
WTA: Washington Technological Associates
w/tax: withholding tax
Wtb: Whitby
WTBA: Washington Toll Bridge Authority
WTB & TS: Watchtower Bible and Tract Society (Jehovah's Witnesses)
WTC: World Tanker Corporation (Niarchos); World Trade Center
wtchmn: watchman
wtd: watertight door
WTD: *World Trade Directory*
WTE: World Tapes for Education
wtf: will to fire
Wtf: Waterford
WTFDA: Worldwide TV-FM-DX Association
WTFP: Wolf Trap Farm Park (Virginia)
wthr: weather
WTIS: World Trade Information Service
WTL: Wyle Test Laboratories
WTNR: Wadi Tabor Nature Reserve (Israel)
WTO: Warsaw Treaty Organization
WTP: Weapons Testing Program
wtqad: watertight quick-acting door
wtr: waiter; winter; writer
WTR: Western Test Range (formerly Pacific Missile Range)
wtrz: winterize
wtrzn: winterization
WTS: Watchtower Society

WTSC: West Texas State College
wu: work unit
WU: Washington University; Wesleyan University; Western Union; Wilberforce University; Wittenberg University
W/U: Western Union
WUA: Western Underwriters Association
wuaa: wartime unit aircraft activity
WUAA: Wartime Unit Aircraft Activity
wuc: work unit code
WUCM: Work Unit Code Manual
WUF: World Underwater Federation; World Union of Free Thinkers
WUI: Western Union International
WUIS: Work Unit Information System
WUM: Women's Universal Movement
WUMP(S): White Urban Middle-class Protestant(s)
WUNS: World Union of National Socialists
WUS: Western United States; World University Service
wut: warmup time
WUT: Washburn University of Topeka
wuts: work-unit time standard
WUX: Western Union (teleprinter) Exchange
wv: wall vent; wind velocity
w/v: weight in volume
WV: West Virginia Pulp and Paper Company
W Va: West Virginia; West Virginian
WVA: World Veterinary Association; Wyoming Vocational Association
W Va Turn: West Virginia Turnpike
WVAWRD: West Virginia Water Resources Division
WVC: Wenatchee Valley College
wvd: waived
wvdc: working voltage—direct current
WVEA: West Virginia Educational Association
WVF: World Veterans' Federation
WVIT: West Virginia Institute of Technology
WVL: Warfare Vision Laboratory (USA)
WVMA: Women's Veterinary Medical Association
W V N: West Virginia Northern (railroad)
WVPA: World Veterinary Poultry Association
WVRB: West Virginia Rating Bureau

WVS: Women's Voluntary Service
WVSC: West Virginia State College
wvt: water vapor transfer; water vapor transmission
WVT: Watervliet Arsenal
wvtr: water vapor transmission rate
WVU: West Virginia University
WVWC: West Virginia Wesleyan College
ww: warehouse warrant; water white; waterworks; wirewound
w/w: wall-to-wall (carpet, floor covering, linoleum, tile); weight for weight
WW: Walworth; Woodrow Wilson; world war; world wide
Ww: *Witwe* (German—widow)
W & W: Waynesburg & Western (railroad); Winchester & Western (railroad)
WW I: World War I (1914–1918)
WW II: World War II (1939–1945)
WWIVM: World War I Victory Medal
WWIIHSLB: World War II Honorable Service Lapel Button (often called the Ruptured Duck)
WWIIVM: World War II Victory Medal
wwa: with the will annexed
WWA: Western Writers of America
WWB: Walt Whitman Bridge
WWBA: Walt Whitman Birthplace Association; Western Wooden Box Association
WWC: Walla Walla College; Warren Wilson College; William Woods College; World Weather Centers (Melbourne; Moscow; Washington, D.C.)
wwd: weather working days
WWD: *Women's Wear Daily*
WWDC: World War Debt Commission
Wwe: *Weduwe* (Dutch—widow); *Witwe* (German—widow)
WWF: Welder Wildlife Foundation; Woodrow Wilson Foundation; World Wildlife Fund
WWG: *World Wildlife Guide*
WWHS: Wilbur Wright High School; Woodrow Wilson High School
wwi: whirlwind computer
WWICS: Woodrow Wilson International Center for Scholars
wwio: worldwide inventory objective
WWJC: Western Wyoming Junior College
WWMB: Woodrow Wilson Memorial Bridge
WWMC: Woodrow Wilson Memorial Commission
WWMCCS: Worldwide Military Command and Control System
w/wn: with winch
W Wnd Drft: West Wind Drift (Antarctic)
WWNFF: Woodrow Wilson National Fellowship Foundation
WWNSSS: World-Wide Network of Standard Seismograph Stations
WWNT: West Wales Naturalists Trust
wwp: water wall peripheral; working water pressure; write without program
WWP: Washington Water Power Company
WWPA: Western Wood Products Association
WWSA: Walt Whitman Society of America
WWSC: Western Washington State College
WWSN: World-wide Seismology Net (NBS)
WWSPIA: Woodrow Wilson School of Public and International Affairs (Princeton University)
wwss: water wall side skegs
WWTP: Waste Water Treating Process
W W V: call letters of United States Bureau of Standards worldwide radio time signal; Walla Walla Valley (railroad)
WWVH: World Wide Time (US Bureau of Standards, Hawaii)
WWW: World Weather Watch
WWWF: Worldwide Wrestling Federation
WWWV: Women World War Veterans
wwwwwh: who, what, when, where, why, how (many or much)—reporters' mnemonic for encompassing elements of a news story
wx: waxy
Wx: weather; Wilcox (formation)
wxb: wax bite
WXD: meteorological radar station
wxg: warning
wxp: wax pattern
wy: wey (14 pounds of wool)
Wy: Wyatt; Wycliffe
wyaio: will you accept (the position) if offered?
wye: Y (as in wye circuit)
Wyo: Wyoming; Wyomingite
WZ: *Welt Zeit* (German—world time)
WZO: World Zionist Organization
WZOA: Women's Zionist Organization of America

X

x: an abscissa (symbol); an unknown quantity (symbol); any point on a great circle; by (used between dimensional figures as in 3 × 5 file card); cross; cross reactance (symbol); exchange; extra; frost; mole ratio; no-wind distance; parallactic angle
x̄: specific acoustic reactance
x or X: Christ; Christian; Christianity; cross; experiment; experimental (symbol); explosive (symbol); extra; extract(ed); Kienbock unit (symbol); magnification power; reactance (symbol); research aircraft (symbol); single strength; $10 bill; times (multiplied by); univalent negative (symbol); unknown quantity; U.S. Steel Corporation (stock exchange symbol); Xavier; X ray; Xray—code for letter X
X: longitudinal axis
X-2: counterintelligence
X-15: rocket-propelled research aircraft
xa: chiasma; transmission adapter
XA: Crucible Steel (stock exchange symbol)
xaam: experimental air-to-air missile
xact: exact(ly); X (in any computer) automatic code translation
XAE: merchant ammunition ship (3-letter naval symbol)
xafh: X-band antenna feed horn
XAK: merchant cargo ship (3-letter naval symbol)

XAKc: merchant coastal cargo ship, small (3-letter naval symbol)

xal: xenon arc lamp

XAM: merchant ship converted to minesweeper (3-letter naval symbol)

x-a mix.: xylene-alcohol mixture (insect larva killer)

xan: xanthic; xanthine; yellow

Xan: Xanthe; Xanthian; Xanthippe; Xanthus

xanth: xanthoma(tosis)

XAP: merchant transport (3-letter naval symbol)

XAPc: merchant coastal transport, small (3-letter naval symbol)

x arm: cross arm

XAS: X-band Antenna System

xasm: experimental air-to-surface missile (XASM)

xat: X-ray analysis trial

XAV: auxiliary seaplane tender (3-letter naval symbol)

X-axis: horizontal axis on a chart, graph, or map

xb: crossbar; exploding bridgewire

XB: experimental bomber

X-band: 5,200–10,900 mc

xbar: crossbar

X bear: grizzly bear (abbreviation appearing on many American frontier epitaphs: "killed by an X bear")

Xber: December

xbr: experimental breeder reactor

Xᵇʳᵉ: *décembre* (French—December)

xbt: expendable bathythermograph

xbts: exhibits

xc: cross country; ex coupon; X-chromosome

X-c: X-chromosome (sex factor)

XC: experimental cargo aircraft (naval symbol); Xaverian College

xcar: from the railroad car

XCG: experimental cargo glider (naval symbol)

xch: exchange

X-chromosome: female-producing gene found in male sperm

xcit: excitation

xcl: excess current liabilities

XCL: armed merchant cruiser (naval symbol)

xconn: cross connection

xcp: without coupon

xcpt: except

xcs: cross-country skiing

xct: X-band communications transponder

xc & uc: exclusive of covering and uncovering

xcut: crosscut

xcvr: transceiver

x cy: cross country

xd: ex dividend

X'd: crossed out

X-day: launching day

xdcr: transducer

xder: transducer

xdh: xanthine dehydrogenase

xdis: ex distribution (without distribution)

xdiv: without dividend

xdp: X-ray density probe; X-ray diffraction powder

xdpc: X-ray diffraction powder camera

xdps: X-band diode phase shifter

xdr: transducer

Xdr: Crusader

XDS: Xerox Data Systems; X-ray Diffraction System

xdt: xenon discharge tube

Xe: experimental engine; xenon

xeg: X-ray emission gage

XEG: Xerox Education Group

Xen: Xenia; Xenocratic

xer: Xerox reproduction

xes: X-ray emission spectra

xf: extra fine

XF: experimental fighter (naval symbol)

xfa: crossed-field acceleration; X-ray fluoresence absorption

xfc: X-band frequency converter

xfd: X-band flow detection

xfer: transfer

xfh: X-band feed horn

Xfher: Christopher

xflt: expanded flight-line tester

xfm: X-band ferrite modulator

xfmr: transformer

xformer: transformer

xfqh: xenon-filled quartz helix

xft: xenon flash tube

xg: crossing

xgam: experimental guided air missile (XGAM)

xh: extra hard; extra heavy; extra high

XH: experimental helicopter (naval symbol)

x heavy: extra heavy

X-height: height of central portion of lowercase letters exclusive of ascenders and descenders

x-high: of a height equal to a lowercase x of the same face and size

xhil: xenon high-intensity light

xhm: X-ray hazard meter

xhmo: extended huckel molecular orbit

xhr: extra-high reliability

Xhs: Xhosa

xhst: exhaust

xhv: extremely high vacuum

x hvy: extra heavy

xi: ex interest

xia: X-band interferometer antenna

xic: transmission interface converter

xil: xilography; xilogravure (woodcuts)

xim: X-ray intensity meter

xin: without interest

Xina: Christina

XING: crossing (highway or railroad)

xio: execute input-output

xiph: xiphoid; xiphoidal

Xipho: Xiphosura

xirs: xenon infrared searchlight

xis: xenon infrared searchlight

xist: xistoma; xistomiasis

xk: X-band klystron

xl: crystal; crystalline; extra large; extra long

Xl: inductive reactance

xla: X-band limiter anntenuator

xlam: cross-laminate(d)

xlc: xenon lamp collimator

xldt: xenon laser discharge tube

xli: extra-low interstitial

xlnt: excellent

XLO: Ex-Cell-O (precision products; trade name)

xlps: xenon lamp power supply

xlr: experimental liquid rocket

xls: xenon light source

XLSS: Xenon Light-Source System

xlt: cross-linked polyethylene; excellent; xenon laser tube

xl & ul: exclusive of loading and unloading

xlwb: extra-long wheelbase

xm (XM): experimental missile

XM: experimental missile

Xmas: Christmas

X-matching: —cross matching

xmfr: transformer

xmit: transmit

xmitter: transmitter

x mod: experimental module

xms: X-band microwave source

xmsn: transmission

xmt: transmit; X-band microwave transmitter

xmtg: transmitting

xmtr: transmitter

xmt-rec: transmit-receive

xn: ex new

Xn: Christian

XN: experimental (USN)

X-note: $10 bill

xo: crystal oscillator

XO: Executive Office(r); Experimental Office(r)

xob: xenon optical beacon

xor: exclusive or (data processing)

xos: extra outside clothing; extra outsize (clothing)

X-O test: cross-out test

X-out: cross out; delete; strike out

xover: cross over

X-over: cross over

xp: express paid

Xp: fire-resistive protected cabinet, safe, or vault

xpa: X-band parametric amplifier; X-band passive array; X-band planar array; X-band power amplifier

xpaa: X-band planar-array antenna

XPARS: External Research Publication and Retrieval System

xpd: expedite

xper: without privileges

XPG: converted merchant ship (naval symbol)

xpl: explosive

xplo: explosion

xplt: exploit

xpn: expansion

Xpo: *Cristo* (Spanish—Christ)

xpond: transponder

xppa: X-band pseudo-passive array; X-band pulsed-power amplifier

xpr: ex privileges; without privileges

xprs: express

xps: X-band phase shifter

xpt: express paid telegram; X-band pulse transmitter

Xpto: *Cristóbal* (Spanish—Christopher)

X-punch: punch in X row (11th row) of an 80-column punchcard

xq: cross-question

XQ: Experimental Target Drone

xqh: xenon quartz helix

xr: ex rights; Xerox radiography

XR: External Relations (UNESCO)

Xray: code word for letter X

X ray: photograph or photography made by X rays; radiograph; radiography; roentgenograph; roentgenography; roentgen ray

xrb: X-band radar beacon

XRC: Extraterrestrial Research Center

xrcd: X-ray crystal density

xrd: X-ray diffraction

xref: cross-reference

xrep: auxiliary report

xrf: X-ray fluorescence

xrii: X-ray image intensifier

xrl: extended-range lance (missile)

xrm: X-ray microanalyzer

X-roads: crossroads

xrpm: X-ray projection microscope

xrpt: X-ray and photofluorography technician

xrspec: X-ray spectrograph

xrt: ex-rights; without rights; X-ray technician

Xrx: Xerox (corporation or copying process)

xs: cross-section; excess; extra strength; extra strong

Xs: atmospherics

xsa: X-band satellite antenna

xsal: xenon short arc lamp

XSB: Xavier Society for the Blind

X-scale: scale of a line parallel to the horizon

x sec: extra sec *(très sec)*—dry champagne

xsect: cross-section

xsf: X-ray scattering facility

xsistor: transistor

XSL: Experimental Space Laboratory

xsm: experimental strategic missile; experimental surface missile

X-sonad: experimental sonic azimuth detector

X-spot: $10 bill

xspv: experimental solid-propellant vehicle

xsr: X-band scatterometer radar

XSS: Experimental Space Station

xsta: X-band satellite-tracking antenna

xstd: X-band stripline tunnel diode

xstda: X-band stripline tunnel diode amplifier

xstr: transistor

x str: extra strong

xstrat: cross-stratified

xt: crosstalk; X-ray tube

Xt: Christ

xta: chiasmata; X-band tracking antenna

xtal: crystal

Xtet: (Swedish—the X)—Sven Erixson

Xtian: Christian

xtlo: crystal oscillator

xtnd: extend

xto: X-band triode oscillator

xtra: extra

xtran: experimental language

xtrm: extreme

xtry: extraordinary

xtwa: X-band traveling-wave amplifier

xtwm: X-band traveling-wave maser

Xty: Christianity

xu: x-unit

Xu: fire-resistive unprotected cabinet, safe, or vault

XU: Xavier University

xuv: extreme ultraviolet

xva: X-ray videcon analysis

xvers: transverse

XVP: Executive Vice President

xvtr: transverter

xw: experimental warhead; ex warrants; without warrants

XWS: Experimental Weapon System

xx: without securities or warrants

XX: doublecross; double strength

XX: *Dos Equis* (Spanish—Two X)—Mexican beer

XXer: doublecrosser

xxh: double extra hard; double extra heavy

XX-note (double-X note): $20 bill

xxs: extra-extra strength

xxx: international urgency signal

XXX: triple strength

XXXX: quadruple strength

XXXXX: quintuple strength

xya: x-y axis

xyat: x-y axis table

xyl: ex young lady (former sweetheart); xylene; xylography

xylo: xylophone

xyloc: xylocain (lidocaine)

xylog: xylography

xyp: x-y plotter

xyr: x-y recorder

x yr dev: ten-year device (US Army service badge)

xyt: x-y table

xyv: x-y vector

Y

y: altitude (symbol); depth or height (symbol); an ordinate (symbol); an unknown quantity (symbol); yard; year; yellow; yen (Japanese monetary unit)

Y: Convair (symbol); service test (symbol); yacht; Yankee—code for letter Y; yen (Japanese money unit); YMCA; YMHA; YWCA; YWHA

Y: admittance (symbol); lateral axis (symbol); *ylös* (Finnish—up)

Y1C: Yeoman First Class

Y2C: Yeoman Second Class

Y3C: Yeoman Third Class

Y62: Ilyushin Il-Y62 jet airplane
ya: yaw axis
YA: Youth Aliyah; Youth Authority
Y/A: York-Antwerp Rules
YAA: Yachtsmen's Association of America
YAAP: Young Americans Against Pollution
YABA: Yacht Architects and Brokers Association
YACH: Yugoslav-American Cooperative Home
YAEC: Yankee Atomic Electric Company
YAF: Young Americans for Freedom
YAF-PAC: Young Americans for Freedom—Political Action Committee
yag: yttrium aluminum garnet
YAG: district auxiliary miscellaneous (3-letter naval symbol)
yagl: yttrium-aluminum garnet laser
YAIC: Young American Indian Council
YAK: Yakolev aircraft (named for its designer)
yal: yttrium-aluminum laser
Yale LJ: *Yale Law Journal*
YAM: Yates American Machine (company)
yama: (Japanese—mountain, as in Fujiyama)
YAN: Yancey (railroad); Young American Nazis
YANCON: Yankee Conference (intercollegiate sports)
YANK: Youth of America Needs to Know
Yankee: code for letter Y
yap.: yaw and pitch
Yar: Yarmouth
YAR: Yemen Arab Republic (Sana—capital); York-Antwerp Rules (insurance)
YARA: Young Americans for Responsible Action
yarden: yard + garden
yas: yaw-attitude sensor
YA's: Young Adults (young people)
YASD: Young Adult Services Division (ALA)
YASSR: Yakut Autonomous Soviet Socialist Republic
yavis: young, attractive, verbal, intelligent, and successful
YAWF: Youth Against War and Fascism
Y-axis: vertical axis on a chart, graph, or map
Yb: ytterbium
YB: year book
YBA: Young Buddhist Association
YBC: Yerba Buena Center

yBr: yellowish brown
YBR: sludge-removal barge (3-letter naval symbol)
YBRA: Yellowstone-Bighorn Research Association
Y-branch: Y-shaped pipe fitting
yc: yaw channel; yaw coupling; yellow chrome
YC: open lighter (2-letter naval symbol); Yacht Club; Yankton College; York College; Yuba College
YCA: Yachting Club of America
YCC: Youth Conservation Corps
YCCA: Youth Council on Civic Affairs
YCCC: Yui Chui Chan Club
YCD: feuling barge (naval symbol); Youth Correction Division (US Dept Justice)
YCF: car float (naval symbol); Young Calvinist Federation
Y-chromosome: male-producing gene found in male sperm
YCI: Young Communist International
YCia: Ybarra Compañía (steamship line)
YCK: open cargo lighter (3-letter naval symbol)
YCL: Yarmouth Cruise Lines; York City Library; Young Communist League
YCNM: Yucca House National Monument
ycp: yaw-coupling parameter
yct: yacht
YCTF: Younger Chemists Task Force
YCU: aircraft transportation lighter (naval symbol)
YCV: aircraft transportation lighter 3-letter naval symbol)
yd: yard
yd^2: square yard(s)
yd^3: cubic yard(s)
YD: floating derrick (2-letter naval symbol); Yugoslav dinar
Y & D: Yards and Docks (USN)
YDA: Dawson City, Yukon Territory (airport)
yday: yesterday
ydb: yield-diffusion bonding
ydc: yaw-damping computer
YDCA: Youth Democratic Clubs of America
ydg: yarding
YDG: degaussing vessel (naval symbol)
ydi: yard drain inlet
YDI: Youth Development Incorporated
YDL: Young Development Laboratories
ydmn: yardman
ydmstr: yardmaster

yds: yards
YDS: Yale Divinity School
YDSD: Yards and Docks Supply Depot (USN)
YDSO: Yards and Docks Supply Office
YDT: diving tender (naval symbol)
Y-duct: Y-shaped duct
ye: yellow-edged; yellow edges; yellow edging
YE: aircraft homing system
yea.: yaw-error amplifier
YEA: Yale Engineering Association
yearb: yearbook
YEB: Yorkshire Electricity Board
yeg: yeast extract—glucose
YEG: Edmonton, Alberta (International Airport)
yel: yellow
Yel NP: Yellowstone National Park
yelsh: yellowish
yem: yeast extract—malt
Yem: Yemen; Yemenite
yeni: (Turkish—new)
Yeo: Yeoman
Yeoman F: Yeoman Female (naval rating)
yeomn: yeomanry
yep: your educational plans
yepd: yeast extract—peptone, dextrose
YES: Youth Educational Services; Youth Employment Service
yesty: yesterday
yf: wife (simplified orthographic contraction proposed by Benjamin Franklin)
YF: covered lighters (naval symbol)
YF-16: air-superiority single-engine lightweight-fighter aircraft (USAF)
YFB: ferryboat or launch (naval symbol)
YFC: car float (3-letter naval symbol); Young Farmers' Club
YFD: floating drydock (naval symbol)
YFFP: Yarrawonga Flora and Fauna Park (Australian Northern Territory)
YFN: covered lighter, nonself-propelled (naval symbol)
YFNB: large covered lighter (naval symbol)
YFND: drydock companion craft (naval symbol)
YFNX: special-purpose lighter (naval symbol)
YFP: floating power barge (naval symbol)
YFR: self-propelled refrigerated covered lighter (naval symbol)
YFRN: refrigerated covered lighter, nonself-propelled (naval symbol)

YFRT: covered lighter, range tender (naval symbol)
YFT: torpedo transportation lighter (naval symbol)
yfu: yard freight unit
YfU: Youth for Understanding (teenage exchange program)
YFU: harbor utility craft (naval symbol)
yG: yellowish green
YG: garbage lighter (naval symbol); yellow green
ygl: yttrium-garnet laser
YGN: garbage lighter, nonself-propelled (naval symbol)
YGR: Yankari Game Reserve (Nigeria)
YGS: Young Guard Society
YH: Youth Hostel
YHA: Youth Hostels Association
YHB: houseboat (naval symbol)
YHLC: salvage lift craft, heavy (naval ship symbol)
YHt: Young-Helmholtz theory
YHT: heating scow (naval symbol)
Yi: Yiddish
YIC: Yardney International Corporation
Yid: Yiddish; Yiddish-speaking person
Yie: Young interference experiment
yig: yttrium iron garnet (ferrite)
yigib: your improved group insurance benefits
YIJS: Young Israel Institute for Jewish Studies
yil: yellow indicator lamp
Yinglish: Yiddish-English
YIP: Detroit, Michigan (Willow Run Airport); Youth International Party (members, including narcotic-addicted hippies, called yippies)
YI & S: Yawata Iron and Steel
yj: radar homing beacon (map symbol)
YJC: York Junior College
Y-joint: Y-shaped joint
yk: radar beacon (map symbol)
yl: yellow; young lady
Yk: Yakut; York
YK: Yankee Airlines (2-letter code)
Yka: Yokohama
YKF: Yiddisher Kulture Farband (Yiddish Culture Club)
YKKK: Yamashita Kisen Kabushiki Kaisha (steamship line)
Yks: Yorkshire
Ykt: Yakut
yl: yellow
Y & L: York and Lancaster
YLA: open landing lighter (naval symbol)
YLI: Young Ladies Institute; Yorkshire Light Infantry
YLJ: *Yale Law Journal*

YLLC: salvage lift crane, light (naval ship symbol)
yl's: young ladies
ym: yacht measurement; yellow metal; your message
YM: dredge (naval symbol); Yehudi Menuhin
YMA: Yarn Merchants Association
ymb: yeast malt broth
YMBA: Yacht and Motor Boat Association
YMCA: Young Men's Christian Association
YM Cath A: Young Men's Catholic Association
ymd: your message date
Yme: Young's modulus of elasticity
YMF: Young Musicians Foundation
YMFS: Young Men's Friendly Society
YMHA: Young Men's Hebrew Association
YMHAL: Young Men's Hebrew Association Library
YMI: Young Men's Institute
YMLC: salvage lift craft, medium (naval ship symbol)
YMP: motor mine planter (naval symbol)
yms: yield measurement system
YMS: motor minesweepers (naval symbol)
YMT: motor tug (naval symbol)
YMV: Yazoo and Mississippi Valley (railroad)
YM & YWHA: Young Men's and Young Women's Hebrew Association
yn: yen
y-n: yes-no
YN: net tender (naval symbol)
yng: young
YNG: gate vessel (naval symbol)
YNHA: Yosemite Natural History Association
YNP: Yellowstone National Park (Idaho, Montana, Wyoming); Yoho NP (British Columbia); Yosemite NP (California)
YNT: net tender, tug (naval symbol)
Ynv: *Ynvar* (Russian—January)
YNWR: Yazoo National Wildlife Refuge (Mississippi)
yo: year old
y/o: years old
YO: fuel-oil barge (naval symbol); Yerkes Observatory
YOAN: Youth Of All Nations
yob: year of birth
YOC: Youth Opportunity Campaign; Youth Opportunity Center(s); Youth Opportunity Corps
yod: year of death
YOG: gasoline barge, self-

propelled (naval symbol)
YOGN: gasoline barge, nonself-propelled (naval symbol)
Yok: Yokohama
yokara: (Turkish—upper)
Yoko: Yokohama
yom: year of marriage
Yomiuri: (Japanese—Reading for Sale)—leading newspaper of Japan
yon: yonder
YON: fuel-oil barge, nonself-propelled (naval symbol)
yood: (slang pronunciation—iud)—intrauterine device; intrauterine diaphragm
YOP: Youth Opportunity Program
York: *Yorkshire Post*
Yorks: Yorkshire
YOS: oil storage barge (naval symbol)
Yos NP: Yosemite National Park
YOU: Youth Organizations United
you'd: you had; you would
you know: you know, you know (repetitive phrase most often used by those who don't know)
you'll: you shall; you will
Youngs: Youngstown
you're: you are
you've: you have
YOW: Ottawa, Ontario (airport)
yp: yield limit; yield point (psi)
YP: patrol craft (2-letter naval symbol); yellow peril; young people; young person(s)
ypa: yaw-precession amplifier
YPA: Young Pioneers of America
ypd: yaw-phase detector
YPD: floating pile driver (naval symbol)
YPEC: Young Printing Executives Club
YPF: Yacimientos Petroliferos Fiscales
YPG: Yuma Proving Ground
yPk: yellowish pink
YPK: pontoon stowage barge (naval symbol)
YPM: Yale Peabody Museum
YPO: Young Presidents' Organization; Youth Programs Office (Bureau of Indian Affairs)
Yps: Ypsilanti
YPSCE: Young People's Society of Christian Endeavor
YPSL: Young People's Socialist League
Y-punch: punch in Y row (12th row) of an 80-column punchcard
YQX: Gander, Newfoundland (airport)
yr: year; younger; your
y-r: yaw roll
YR: district patrol vessel (naval symbol); floating workshop (2-

letter naval symbol)
YRA: Yacht Racing Association
YRB: submarine repair and berthing barge (naval symbol)
YRBM: submarine repair—berthing and messing barge (naval symbol)
YRC: submarine rescue chamber (naval symbol)
YRD: submarine repair and berthing vessel (3-letter naval symbol)
YRDH: floating drydock hull workshop (naval symbol)
YRDM: floating drydock machinery workshop (naval symbol)
YRL: covered repair lighter (naval symbol)
yrly: yearly
YRNF: Young Republican National Federation
YRR: radiological repair barge (3-letter naval symbol)
yrs: years; yours
Yrs: Yours
YRs: Young Republicans
YRST: salvage craft tender (naval ship symbol)
yrs ty: yours truly
ys: yellow spot (on retina); yield strength
Ys: Yugoslavia; Yugoslavian
YS: Yard Superintendent
Y & S: Youngstown & Southern (railroad)
YSA: Young Socialist Alliance
ysb: yield-stress bonding
YSB: Yacht Safety Bureau
YSC: Yugoslav Seamen's Club
YSD: seaplane wrecking derrick (naval symbol)
ysdb: yield-stress diffusion bonding
yse: yaw-steering error
ysh: yellowish
Ysl: Ysrael
YSO: Youngstown Symphony Or-

chestra
ysp: years service for severance pay purposes
YSP: pontoon salvage vessel (naval symbol)
ysr: you're so right
YSR: sludge-removal barge (naval symbol)
YSS: Young Scots Society
yst: youngest
YST: Yukon Standard Time
YS & T: Youngstown Sheet & Tube
YSTO: Yugoslav State Tourist Office
YSU: Youngstown State University
yt: yoke top
Yt: yttrium
YT: harbor tug (naval symbol); Yukon Territory
Y & T: Yale & Towne
YTA: Yiddish Theatrical Alliance
ytb: yarn to back
YTB: large-harbor tug (naval symbol)
ytf: yarn to front
YTL: small-harbor tug (naval symbol)
YTM: medium-harbor tug (naval symbol)
YTPM: Yuma Territorial Prison Museum
YTS: Yuma Test Station
YTT: torpedo-testing barge (naval symbol)
Y-tube: Y-shaped tube
Yu: Yugoslav; Yugoslavian
YU: Yale University; Yeshiva University; York University; Youngstown University; Yugoslavia (auto plaque)
YUAG: Yale University Art Gallery
Yuc: Yucatán
yug: (Russian—south)
Yugo: Yugoslav; Yugoslavia; Yu-

goslavian
Yuk: Yukon
YUK: Youth Uncovering Krud (antipollution society)
YUL: Montreal, Quebec (airport); Yale University Library
YUO: Yale University Observatory
yup: you're uncommonly perceptive
YUP: Yale University Press
Yv: Yvette; Yvonne
YV: Young's Version
yvc: yellow-varnish cambric
YVC: Yakima Valley College
YVHS: Yorkville Vocational High School
YVJC: Yakima Valley Junior College
YVP: Youth Voter Participation
YVR: Vancouver, British Columbia (airport)
YVT: Yakima Valley Transportation (railro ad)
y v v: *y viaje vuelta* (Spanish—and return trip)
YW: water barge (naval symbol)
YWCA: Young Women's Christian Association
YWCTU: Young Women's Christian Temperance Union
YWF: Young World Federalists
YWG: Winnipeg, Manitoba (airport)
YWHA: Young Women's Hebrew Association
YWHS: Young Women's Help Society
YWLL: Young Workers Liberation League
YWN: nonself-propelled barge (naval symbol)
YWS: Young Wales Society
YWU: Yiddish Writers Union
y-y: yaw axis
YYC: Calgary, Alberta (airport)
YYZ: Toronto, Ontario (airport)

Z

z: complex variable (symbol); z-bar; zee (American usage); zed (British usage); zero; zinc; zone
z: *zu* (German—closed; shut)
Z: atomic number (symbol); azimuth (symbol); gram equivalent weight (symbol); impedance (symbol); lighter-than-air aircraft (symbol); obsolete (symbol); radius of circle of least confusion (symbol); zenith; ze-

nith distance; zero meridian time; Zionism; Zionist; Zoroaster; Zoroastrian; Zoroastrianism; Zulu—code for letter Z
Z: normal axis (symbol); *Zeit* (German—time); *Zeitschrift* (German—periodical publication); *zuid* (Dutch—south)
Z^1, Z^2, Z^3: first degree of contraction, second degree of contraction, third degree of contraction

za: zero absolute; zero and add
zaap: zero antiaircraft potential
zab: zabaglione; zinc-air battery
za: *zirka* (German—about; approximately)
Zab: *Zabriskie's Reports*
Zac: Zacatecas
Zach: Zachary
Zack: Zachariah; Zacharias; Zachary
ZADCA: Zinc Alloy Die Casters'

Association
ZAED: *Zentralstelle für Atomker-nenergie Dokumentation* (German—Atomic Energy Documentation Center)
zag: *zaguán* (Spanish—passageway from street door to central patio of homes in Mexico and American Southwest)
Zag: Zagreb
ZAG: Zagreb, Yugoslavia (airport)
Zahal: *Zva Hagana Leyisrael* (Hebrew—Israel Defense Forces)
Zahlentaf: *Zahlentafeln* (German—table of illustrations)
zai: zero address instruction
zaki: (Japanese—cape)
zal: *zaliv* (Russian—bay)
ZALIS: Zinc and Lead International Service
zam: Z-axis modulation
Zam: Zamora
Zamb: Zambia
ZAMPA: Zanzibar and Madagascar Peoples Airway
zam(s): examination(s)
Zan: Zanzibar
ZANU: Zimbabwe African National Union
zap: zero and add packed; zero antiaircraft potential
zap: *zapad* (Russian—west)
Zap: Zapotec; Zapotecan
zapb: zinc-air primary battery
ZAPU: Zimbabwe Africa People's Union
zar: zeus acquisition radar
Zar: Zaragoza
Zara: Zarathustra (Zoroaster)
ZARPS: *Zuid-Afrikaansche Republiek Polisie* (Afrikaans—South African Republic Police)
zas: zero-access storage
ZASM: *Zuid Afrikaansche Spoorweg Maatschappij* (South African Railway serving the Transvaal at the turn of the century)
zat: zinc atomspheric tracer
Zat: *Zaterdag* (Dutch—Saturday)
ZAW: *Zuid-Afrikaansche Weehuis* (Afrikaans—South African Orphan Asylum)
zb: zero beat
z B: *zum Beispiel* (German—for instance)
ZB: Zen Buddhist
Z-bar: Z-shaped bar
zbe: zinc battery electrode
zbl: zero-based linearity
Zbl: *Zentralblatt* (German—central publication)
zbr: zero-beat reception; zero-bend radius
ZBS: Zambia Broadcasting Services

zc: zone capacity
z of c: zones of communication
ZC: Zionist Congress
ZCA: Zirconium Corporation of America
ZCL: *Zona di Commercio Libero* (Italian—Free Trade Zone)
Z-clip: Z-shaped clip
ZCMI: Zion's Cooperative Mercantile Institution
zcn: zinc-coated nut
zcs: zinc-coated screw
zcw: zinc-coated washer
zd: zener diode; zero defects
Zd: zenith distance
ZD: zenith description; zero defects (quality-control goal)
ZDA: Zero Defects Association; Zinc Development Association
zdc: zinc die casting
ZDC: Zero Defects Council
zdg: zinc-doped germanium
Zdm: Zaandam
ZDP: Zero Defects Program; Zero Defects Proposal
zdpa: zero defects program audit
zdpg: zero defects program guideline
zdpo: zero defects program objective
zdpr: zero defects program responsibility
zdr: zeus discrimination radar
ZDR: *Zentraldeutsche Rundfunk* (Central German Radio)
ZDS: Zinc Detection System
zdt: zero-ductility transition
ze: zero effusion; zone effect
z E: *zum Exempel* (German—for example)
zea: zero-energy assembly
Zeb: Zebedee
zebra.: zero-energy breeder reactor assembly
zebrass: zebra + ass—hybrid of zebra and jenny ass or zebress and jackass
Zebrule: zebra + horse—hybrid of male zebra and domestic mare
zec: zero-energy coefficient
zecc: zinc electrochemical cell
Zech.: Zechariah (book of the Bible)
zed: (obsolete phonetic word—z; zero)
Zed: Zedekiah
zee: (Dutch—sea, as in Zeeland)
Zee: Zellerbach
zeep: zero energy experimental pile
zei: zero environmental impact
Zeichn: *Zeichnung(en)* [German—drawing(s)]
Zeke: Ezekiel
zel (ZEL): zero-length launcher
Zelda: Griselda
zell: zero-length launching

zemlya: (Russian—land, as in Novaya Zemlya)
zen: zenith (highest point)
zenith: zero-energy nitrogen-heated thermal reactor
Zentr: *Zentralblatt* (German—journal)
zeony: zebra + pony (hybrid)
Zep: Giuseppe
Zeph.: Zephaniah (book of the Bible)
zephyr: warm westerly breeze
zepp: zeppelin
zer: zero-energy reflection
zerc: zero-energy reflection coefficient
zero-g: zero gravity (weightlessness)
zert: zero-reaction tool
ZES: Zero Energy System
zet: zetetic(s)
zeta.: zero energy thermonuclear assembly
zetr: zero-energy thermal reactor
zeug: zeugma; zeugmatic; zeugmatically
ZEUS: Zero-Energy Uranium System
zf: zero frequency
z/f: zone of fire
ZF: *Zagrebacka Filharmonija* (Croatian—Zagreb Philharmonic)
ZFGBI: Zionist Federation of Great Britain and Ireland
zfp: zyglo-fluorescent penetrant
zfpt: zyglo-fluorescent penetrant testing
zfs: zero field splitting
ZG: Zoological Gardens
Z-gas: Zyklon-B gas (deadly)
zge: zero-gravity effect; zero-gravity environment; zero-gravity expulsion
zget: zero-gravity expulsion technique
ZGF: Zero Gravity Facility
zgg: zero gravity generator
zgh: zero-gravity harmonic
Z-grams: Admiral Zumwalt's policy statements
zgs: zero-gravity simulator
zgs (ZGS): zero gradient synchrotron
zh: zinc heads (freight)
z H: *zu Händen* (German—care of; deliver to)
ZH: lighter-than-air search and rescue aircraft (2-letter naval symbol)
zhr: zirconium hydride reactor
Z hr: zero hour
ZHRC: Zinsmaster Hol-Ry Company
zhs: zero hoop stress
Zi: Zollner illusion

ZI: Zim Israel (steamship line); Zone of the Interior; Zonta International

ZIA: Zone of the Interior Armies

ZID: Zionist Immigration Depot

Zier: Ziervogel process

zig: zero immune globulin

zigzag line: symbol of water

zil: zillion (a number beyond belief)

ZIL: (Russian—*Zavod Imieni Likhatov*)—Likhatov Auto Factory producing a Packard-like luxury car formerly named for Stalin—the ZIS *(Zavod Imieni Stalin)*

zim: zonal interdiction missile

Zim: Zimmerman(n)

Zim: *Zi Mischari* (Hebrew—merchant fleet) as in Zim Israel Line

Zimbabwe: (Bantu—Rhodesia)

ZINC: Zim Israel Navigation Company (Zim Israel Line)

zinco: zincograph

ZINCO: Zim Israel Navigation Company

zincog: zincography

zinc white: zinc oxide (ZnO)

zineb: zinc ethylenebis (fungicide)

zine(s): magazine(s)

Zinj: Zinjanthropus

Zinoviev, Grigori Evseevich: Hirsch Apfelbaum

zip: zero (slang); zinc impurity photodetector; zipper (slide fastener or similar device)

ZIP: Zone Improvement Plan (US Post Office Zip Code)

zir: zero internal resistance

ZIR: Zug Island Road (Delray Connecting Railroad)

ziram: zinc dimethyldithiocarbamate (fungicide)

ZIRCOA: Zirconium Corporation of America

zircon: zirconium silicate ($ZrSiO_4$)

zirox: zirconium oxide (ZrO_2)

ZISS: Zebulon Israel Seafaring Society

zith: zither

zix: zinc isopropyl xanthate

zj: zipper(ed) jacket

zj: *zonder jaartel* (Dutch—without date of publication)

zkrat: *zkratka(y)* [Czech—abbreviation(s)]

Zl: zloty (Polish ruble)

ZL: freezing drizzle (symbol)

zld: zero level drift; zero lift drag; zodiacal light device

zlg: zero line gap

zll: zero length launch

zm: zoom; zoomar (variable focus lens)

ZM: Zubin Mehta

ZM: Zeevaart Maatschappij (Dutch—navigation company)

Z-M: Zuckerman-Moloff (sewage treatment)

zmar: zeus malfunction array radar

ZMC: Zion Mule Corps

Zmd: Zung measurement of depression

zmkr: zone marker

ZMMD: Zurich, Mainz, Munich, Darmstadt (algol processor joint effort of universities in those cities)

ZMRI: Zinc Metals Research Institute

ZMT: Zip (Zone Improvement Plan) Mail Translator (post office sorting device)

zn: zenith

Zn: true azimuth (symbol); zinc

Znak: (Polish—Sign)—Roman Catholic pro-government party

ZnO: zinc oxide

Znpgc: azimuth per gyro compass

ZNP: Zimbawe National Park (Rhodesia); Zion National Park (Utah)

ZNPP: Zanzibar and Pemba People's Party

znr: zinc resistor

ZNZ: Zanatska Nabarnoproajna Zadruga (Yugoslavian—Procurement Sales Cooperative)

zo: zero output

ZO: Zionist Organization

ZO: *Zone Occupee* (French—Occupied Zone)

ZOA: Zionist Organization of America

zoba: bull + yak—hybrid offspring of common bull and yak cow

zobo: cow + yak—hybrid of yak bull and common cow

zóc: *zócalo* (Mexican Spanish—public square)

zod: zodiac; zodiacal

zoe: zero energy; zinc-oxide eugenol

zof: zone of fire

Zog: Ahmed Zogu

zoo: zoological (garden); zoology

zoochem: zoochemistry

zoogeog: zoogeography

zool: zoologic; zoological; zoologist; zoology

zoopal: zoopaleontology

zoopar: zooparasitology

zoopath: zoopathology

zooph: zoophytology

zoopharm: zoopharmacology

zop: zinc-oxide pigment

zor: zone of reconnaissance

Zor: Zoroastrian

ZOS: Zapata Corporation (stock exchange symbol)

zot: (slang—zero)

zounds: God's wounds (archaic oath)

zox: zirconium oxide

zoz: *zie ommezijde* (Dutch—the other side)—please turn over (to the other side of the page)

ZP: lighter-than-air patrol and escort aircraft (naval symbol); Zellerbach Paper

Z & P: Zanzibar and Pemba

zpa: zeus program analysis

ZPA: Zeus Program Analysis; Zoological Parks and Aquariums

zpar: zeus-phased array (radar)

zpb: zinc primary battery

zpe: zero-point energy

zpg: zero population growth

ZPG: Zero Population Growth

zp & j: *zonder plaats en jaar* (Dutch—without place of publication or date)

zpl: *zonder plaats* (Dutch—without place of publication)

zpo: zinc peroxide

ZPO: Zeus Project Office

Zpp: Zeiss projection planetarium

zppr: zero-power plutonium reactor

zpr: zero-power reactor

zprf: zero-power reactor facility

ZPRSN: Zurich Provisional Relative Sunspot Number

ZPT: Zero Power Test

Zr: zirconium

Zr^{95}: radioactive zirconium

ZR: freezing rain (symbol); Zenith Radio

zrc: zircorium carbide

ZRC: Zenith Radio Corporation

ZRH: Zurich, Switzerland (airport)

zrn: zirconium nitride

zrp: zero radial play

zrt: zero-reaction tool

zs: zero shift; zero and subtract; zero surpress; zero suppression (of non-significant zeros in computer-printed numerals)

z S: *zur See* (German—of the navy)

Zs: *Zeitschrift* (German—periodical)

ZS: Zoological Society

zsb: zinc storage battery

zsc: zero subcarrier; chromaticity; zinc silicate coat(ing)

Z-scale: height determination scale

zsd: zebra-stripe display; zinc sulfide detector

ZSDS: Zinc Sulfide Detection System

ZSE: Zagreb Soloists Ensemble (Solisti di Zagreb)

zsf: zero skip frequency

zsg: zero-speed generator

zsi: zero-size image

ZSI: Zoological Society of Ireland

ZSL: *Zjednoczone Stronnictwo Ludowe* (Polish—United Peasant Party)

ZSN: Zoological Station of Naples

ZSP: Zoological Society of Phila-

delphia
zspg: zero-speed pulse generator
ZSS: Zinc Sulfide System
ZSSD: Zoological Society of San Diego
Zssg(n): *Zusammensetzung(en)* [German—compound word(s)]
zst: zero strength time (measurement)
ZST: Zone Standard Time
z T: *zum Teil* (German—partly)
Zt: *Zeit* (German—time)
ZT: lighter-than-air training aircraft (naval symbol); Zachary Taylor; zone time
ZT: *Zone Torride* (French—torrid zone)
Z de T: *Zulano de Tal* (Spanish —so and so)
ZTA: Zulu Territorial Authority
Ztg: *Zeitung* (German—newspaper)
Z-time: zebra time or zulu time (jargon for Greenwich Mean Time)
ZTO: Zone Transportation Office(r); Zürich Tonhalle Orchester (Zurich Concert Hall Orchestra)
ztp: zero temperature plasma
Ztr: *Zentner* (German—hundredweight)
Ztschr: *Zeitschrift* (German—peri-
odical)
Z-twist: Z-shaped open-band twist
ZU: lighter-than-air utility aircraft (2-letter naval symbol)
zuid: (Dutch—south)
Zulu: code word for Greenwich mean time (Zulu time); code word for letter Z
Zür: Zürich
zus: *zusammen* (German—together)
Zus: *Zusammenfassung* (German— summary)
Zuschr: *Zuschrift(en)* [German— communication(s)]
zuverl: *zuverlassig* (German—authentic)
zv: *zu verfugung* (German—at disposal)
Zv: *Zollverein* (German—customs union)
ZVEI: *Zentralverband der Elektrotechnische Industrie* (Central Union of the Electrotechnical Industry)
zvrd: zener voltage regulator diode
zw: zero wear
zw: *zwart* (Dutch—black); *zwischen* (German—between; within)
zwc: zone wind computer
zwitt: zwitterion (diplole ion)
zwl: zero wave length

zwp: zone wind plotter
zwv: zero wave velocity
ZYA: Zionist Youth Association
zyg: zygote
zygo: zygomatic; zygomaticus
zym: zymurgy
zymol: zymology
Zyr: Zyrian (Finno-Ugric language spoken by Zyrians in Komi SSR)
zyz: zyzzyva
zz: increasing degrees of contraction (symbol); zigzag
zz.: *zingiber* (Latin—ginger)
z-z: longitudinal axis/roll axis
z Z: *zur Zeit* (German—at present; for the time being)
ZZ: Ariana Afghan Airlines; zz-approach; zed-zed
ZZ: longitudinal or roll axis (symbol)
zza: zamack zinc alloy
ZZB: Zanzibar (tracking station)
zzc: zero-zero condition
zzd: zig-zag diagram
zzr: zig-zag rectifier
z Zt: *zur Zeit* (German—at present; for the time being)
zzv: zero-zero visibility
ZZV: Zanesville, Ohio (airport)
zzz-zzz-zzz: sawing or snoring (cartoonist symbol)

AIRLINES OF THE WORLD

AA: American Airlines
AB: Keystone Commuter
AC: Air Canada
AD: Antilles Air Boats
AE: Air Ceylon
Aeronaves: Aeronaves de México (Mexico's largest air system)
AF: Air France
AG: AAT Airlines
AH: Air Algerie
AI: Air India
Air Canada: Canadian international airline
Air France: "the world's largest airline"
Air India: international Indian airline service
Air NZ: Air New Zealand
Air West: "serving 100 cities in the Western United States, Canada and Mexico"
AK: Altair Airlines
AL: Allegheny Airlines
Alaska: Alaska Airlines
Alitalia: international Italian airline
AM: Aeronaves de México
American: American Airlines
AN: Ansett Airlines of Australia
AO: Aviaco
AP: Apache Airlines
AQ: Air Paris
AR: Aerolineas Argentinas
AS: Alaska Airlines
AT: Royal Air Maroc
AU: Austral
AV: Avianca
AVENSA: Aerovias Venezolanas (Spanish—Venezuelan Airlines)
AVIANCA: Aerovias Nacionales de Colombia (Spanish—National Airlines of Colombia)
AW: Air Niger
AX: Air Togo
AY: Finnair
AZ: Alitalia
BA: BOAC (British Overseas Airways Corporation)
BD: British Midland Airways
BE: BEA (British European Airways)
BG: Guyana Airways
BH: Bahamas Airways
BI: Braniff International
BJ: Bakhtar Afghan Airlines
BK: BKS Air Transport
BL: Brothers Air Services
BM: Aero Transporti Italiana
BN: Braniff International Airways
BOAC: British Overseas Airways Corporation
BP: Botswana Airways
BR: British United Airways
Braniff: Braniff International

British European: British European Airways
BU: Braathens Air Transport
BV: BEA Helicopters
BW: BWIA (British West Indian Airways)
CB: Caribair
CC: Aerocosta
CD: Cardinal Airlines
CF: Faucett
CH: Chicago Helicopter Airways
CI: China Airlines
CK: Connair
CM: COPA (Compañía Panameña de Aviación—Panamanian Aviation Company)
CN: Craft Airlines
CO: Continental Airlines (Air Micronesia)
Continental: Continental Airlines
CP: CP Air (Canadian Pacific Airlines)
CP Air: Canadian Pacific Airlines
CQ: Aero-Chaco
CR: Commuter Airlnes
CS: Cambrian Airways
CT: Air Commuter Airlines
CU: Cubana Airlines
CW: Channel Airways
CX: Cathay Pacific Airways
CY: Cyprus Airways
CZ: Air Champagne Ardennes
DA: Dan-Air Services
DD: Command Airways
Delta: Delta Air Lines
DJ: Air Djibouti
DL: Delta Air Lines
DM: Maersk Air
DQ: Colony Airlines
DS: Air Senegal
DT: DTA (Divisão de Exploracão dos Transportes Aereos—Exploration Division of Air Transport)
DU: Del Air—Air Cargo
DW: Cross Sound Commuter Airlines
DX: Aerotaxi de Colombia
DY: Florence Airlines
EA: Eastern Airlines
Eastern: Eastern Airlines
EB: Metro-Aire Commuter Airlines
EC: East African Airways
EG: GCS Air Service
EI: Aer Lingus (Irish)
EK: Masling Airlines
El Al: El Al Israel Airlines
EO: Davey Air Services
EP: Aerolineas Peruanas
ER: Caribbean Executive Airlines
ES: Seagreen Air Transport—Air Cargo
ET: Ethiopian Airlines

EU: Compañia Ecuatoriana de Aviación (Ecuadorean Aviation Company)
EV: Elivie
EW: East-West Airlines
EX: Executive Airlines
EY: Europe Aero Service
FA: Florida Airlines
FC: Manufacturers Air Transport Service
FG: Ariana Afghan Airlines
FI: Flugfelag—Icelandair
Finnair: Finnish Airlines
FJ: Fiji Airways
FL: Frontier Airlines
FO: Fjellfly
FS: Key Airlines
FT: Flying Tiger Line—Air Cargo
FW: Wright Airlines
GA: Garuda Indonesian Airways
GB: Air Gabon
GC: Linacongo
GD: Air Antilles
GF: Gulf Aviation
GG: Golden Pacific Airlines
GH: Ghana Airways
GI: Air Guinee
GJ: Airlines of South Australia
GL: Greenlandair
GM: Great Northern Airways
GGN: Transgabon
GQ: Golden West Airlines
GR: General Air
GS: Air Vosges
GT: Gibraltar Airways
GU: Aviateca
GV: Territory Airlines
GX: Great Lakes Air Services
GY: Aurigny Air Services
HA: Hawaiian Air Lines
HB: Air Melanesiae
HD: Aero Servicios
HH: Somali Airlines
HJ: Toa Airways
HK: Cogeair
HL: Holiday Airlines
HN: NLM-Dutch Airlines
HP: Apollo Airways
HQ: Valley Airlines
HR: Pennsylvania Commuter
HS: Scenic Airlines
HT: Air Chad
HU: Cascade Airways
Hughes: Hughes Air West
HX: Virginia Air Cargo
HY: Houston Metro Airlines
IA: Iraqi Airways
IB: Iberia
Iberia: Iberia Air Lines of Spain
IC: Indian Airlines
IE: Solomon Islands Airways
IF: Interflug
IG: Alisarda

IH: Itavia
II: Imperial Airlines
IL: LANSA (Lineas Aereas Nacionales, SA—National Air Lines Corporation)
IM: Massachusetts Air Industries
Imperial: Imperial Airlines
IN: Aerlinte (Irish)
IO: Out Island Airways
IR: Iran National Airlines
Irish: Irish International Airlines
IT: Air Inter
IT: Air Inter
IU: Midstate Air Commuter
IV: Lineas Aereas Guinea Ecuatorial (Equatorial Guinea Airlines)
IW: International Air Bahama
IX: INAIR (Internacional de Aviación)
IY: Swift Airlines
IZ: Arkia-Israel Inland Airlines
JAL: Japan Air Lines
Japan: Japan Air Lines
JB: Aeronaves del Norte
JC: Rocky Mountain Airways
JD: Japan Domestic Airlines
jetliner: jet airliner
JH: Smyer Aircraft
JI: Aeronaves del Este
JL: Japan Air Lines
JM: Air Jamaica
JN: Sun Valley Air
JO: Aeronaves del Oeste
JQ: TAA (Trans-Australia Airlines)
JR: ACSA Airlines
JS: Air Champagne Ardennes
JT: Jamaica Air Service
JU: Jugoslavian Air Transport
JY: Air Caicos
JZ: Aeronaves del Centro
KAL: Korean Air Lines
KB: Kitsap Aviation
KE: Korean Air Lines
KF: Catskill Airways
KH: Time Airways
KK: Shawnee Air
KL: KLM (Koninklijke Luchtvaart Maatschappij—Royal Dutch Airlines)
KLM: Royal Dutch Airlines
KO: Kodiak Airways
Korean Air Lines: KAL
KP: Air Cape
KQ: King Airlines
KR: Dar-Air
KW: Dorado Wings
KX: Cayman Airways
KU: Kuwait Airways
KX: Cayman Airways
KX: Century Airlines
LA: LAN (Linea Aerea Nacional de Chile—National Air Line of Chile)

LB: Lloyd Aereo Boliviano
LC: Loganair Limited
LD: LADE (Lineas Aereas del Estade—State Air Lines)
LE: Lake Geneva Airways
LF: Linjeflyg
LG: Luxair—Luxembourg Airlines
LH: Lufthansa German Airlines
LI: Leeward Islands Air Transport
LJ: Sierra Leone Airways
LK: Alag-Alpine Lift-Trans
LL: Icelandic Airlines
LM: ALM—Dutch Antillean Airlines
LN: Libyan Arab Airlines
LO: Polish Airlines
LP: Air Alpes
LR: LACSA (Lineas Aereas Costarricenses—Costa Rican Airlines)
Lufthansa: Lufthansa German Airlines
LV: LAV (Lineas Aeropostal Venezolana—Venezuelan Aeropostal Lines
LY: El Al Israel Airlines
LZ: Bulgarian Airlines—Balkan
MA: Malev (Hungarian Air Transport)
MD: Air Madagascar
ME: Middle East Airlines
MG: Malta Airlines
MH: Air Manila
MI: Mackey International Air Commuter
MJ: SMB State Lines
MK: Air Mauritius
ML: Malaysia-Singapore Airlines
MM: Sociedad Aeronautica Medellín
MN: Commercial Airways
MO: Mohawk Airlines
MR: Air Mauritanie
MS: United Arab Airlines
MU: Misair
MV: Macrobertson Miller Airlines
MW: Maya Airways
MY: Air Mali
MZ: Merpati Nusantara Airlines
NA: National Airlines
NAC: National Airways Corporation (New Zealand)
National: National Airlines
NB: Newport Air Park
NC: North Central Airlines
ND: Nordair
NE: Northeast Airlines
NH: All Nippon Airways
NI: LANICA (Lineas Aereas de Nicaragua—Air Lines of Nicaragua)
NJ: Air South
NK: Namakwaland Lugdiens

NL: Liberian National Airlines
NM: Mt Cook Airlines
Northwest: Northwest Orient Airlines
NR: Northward Aviation Limited
NS: Northeast Airlines
NU: Southwest Airlines
NV: Combs Airways
NW: Northwest Orient Airlines
NY: New York Airways
NZ: New Zealand National Airways
OA: Olympic Airways
OB: Opal Air Services
OD: Aerocondor
OE: North-Air
OG: Chalk's Flying Service
OH: San Francisco and Oakland —Helicopter
OJ: Stol Commuters
OK: Czechoslovak Airlines
OM: Air Mongol
ON: North American Airlines
ONA: Overseas National Airlines
OO: Borrego Springs Airlines
OP: Air Panama International
OQ: Royale Airlines
OR: Air Comores
OS: Austrian Airlines
OT: Transportes Aereos de São Tome
OX: American Courier
OY: Air North
OZ: Ozark Air Lines
PA: Pan American World Airways
Pan Am: Pan American World Airways
PC: Pacair
PD: Pem Air Limited
PE: Papuan Airlines
PH: Polynesian Airlines
Philippine: Philippine Airlines
PI: Piedmont Aviation
PK: Pakistan International
PM: Pilgrim Airlines
PN: Ansett Airlines of Papua, New Guinea
PP: Phillips Michigan City Flying Service
PQ: Puerto Rico International Airlines
PR: Philipine Airlines
PS: Pacific Southwest Airlines
PSA: Pacific Southwest Airlines
PT: Provincetown-Boston Airline and Naples Airline Division
PU: PLUNA (Primeras Lineas Uruguayas de Navegación Aerea (First Uruguayan Air Navigation Lines)
PV: Eastern Provincial Airways
PW: Pacific Western Airlines
PX: Aspen Airlines
PY: Surinam Airways

PZ: LAP (Lineas Aereas Para-guayas—Paraguayan Air Lines)
QA: Dixie Airlines
QB: Quebecair
QC: Air Congo (Kinshāsa)
QD: Sadia
QE: Air Indies
QF: Quantas Airways
QH: St Thomas Tax-Air
QI: Comber Air
QJ: Mel Air Limited
QK: Aroostook Airways
QL: Lesotho Airways
QM: Air Malawi
QN: Bush Pilots Airway
QO: Bar Harbor Airlines
QP: Caspair
QQ: Aerovias Quisqueyana
QS: Air Michigan
QU: Mississippi Valley Airways
Quantas: Quantas Airways (Aus-tralian)—originally Queensland and Northern Territory Airways
QV: Monarch Airline
QZ: Zambia Airways
RA: Royal Nepal Airlines
RB: Syrian Arab Airlines
RC: Air Cambodge
RD: Airlift International (Air Cargo)
RG: Varig
RH: Air Rhodesia
RI: Tricon International Airlines
RH: Royal Jordanian Airlines
RK: Air Afrique
RO: TAROM (Transporturile Aeriene Romine—Roumanian Air Transport)
Route of the Red Baron: Lufthansa German Airlines
RU: Rousseau Aviation
RV: Reeve Aleutian Airways
RW:A Hughes Air West
RX: Capitol Air Services
RY: Royal Air Lao
RZ: Aero Mech
SA: South African Airways
SABENA: Societe Anonyme Belge d'Exploitation de la Navigation Aerienne (French—Belgian Corporation for the Exploitation of Aerial Navigation)—Sabena Belgian Airlines
SAS: Scandinavian Airlines System
SB: Seaboard World Airways
SC: Cruzeiro
SD: Sudan Airways
Seaboard: Seaboard World Airways
SG: Aerotransportes Litoral Argentino (Argentine Coastal Air Transport)
SH: Sahsa

SK: SAS (Scandinavian Airlines System)
SL: Southeast Airlines
SN: Sabena (Belgian Airlines)
SO: Southern Airways
SP: SATA (Sociedade Açoriana de Transportes Aeros—Azores Air Transport)
SQ: Norcanair
SR: Swissair
SU: Aeroflot (Soviet Airlines)
SV: Saudi Arabian Airlines
SW: Suidwes Lugdiens
Swissair: Swiss Airlines
SX: Skyways Coach
TA: Taca International
TAP: Transportes Aereos Portugueses (Portuguese—Portuguese Air Transport—Portuguese Airways
TC: Trans Caribbean Airways
TD: Transcarga
TE: Air New Zealand
TG: Thai Airways International
TH: Thai Airways
TJ: Transportes Aereos Buenos Aires
TK: Turk Hava Yollari
TL: Trans-Mediterranean Airways
TM: Direccao de Exploracao dos Transportes Aereos (Mozambique Air Transport)
TN: Trans-Australia Airlines
TP: TAP (Transportes Aereos Portugueses—Portuguese Air Transport)
TQ: Trans Central Airlines
TS: Aloha Airlines
TT: Texas International Airlines
TU: Tunis Air
TV: Trans International Airlines
TW: TWA (Trans World Airlines)
TWA: Trans World Airlines
TX: Transportes Aereos Nacionales (National Air Transport)
TY: Air Caledonie
TZ: Transair Limited
UA: United Air Lines
UB: Union of Burma Airways
UC: LADECO (Linea Aerea del Cobre)
UD: Brower Flight Service
UE: Trans Magic Airlines
UI: Star Airlines
UJ: Air Ulster
UK: British Island Airways
UL: Lansa Airlines of Honduras
UM: Morris Air Transport
United: United Air Lines
UQ: Suburban Airlines
UT: UTA (Union de Transports Aerien)
UU: Touraine Air Transport

UW: Midwest Airlines
UX: Air Illinois
UY: Buckeye Air Service
VA: Viasa
VB: Air Bangui
VD: Port Augusta Air Services
VE: AVENSA (Aerovias Venezolanas—Venezuelan Airlines)
VF: British Air Ferries
VG: Air Siam
VH: Air Volta
VI: STA (Société de Travail Aerien)
VJ: Allen Aviation
VK: Trans Michigan Airlines
VM: Monmouth Airlines
VN: Air Vietnam
VO: BC Airliens
VP: VASP (Viacão Sao Paulo)
VQ: International Dky Cab (Volusia Aviation Services)
VT: RAI (Reseau Aerien Interinsulaire—Tahiti)
VU: Air Ivoire
VV: Viking International Airfreight
VW: Civil Flying Services
VY: Air Cameroun
W: Western Airlines
WA: WAL (Western Air Lines)
WB: Shawnee Airlines
WC: Sien Consolidated Airlines
Western: Western Airlines
WF: Wideroes Flyveselskap
WG: ALAG (Alpine Luft Transport AG)
WJ: Jet Air
WK: Western Alaska
WL: Lao Airlines
WM: Windward Islands Airways
WQ: Georgia Air
WR: Altus Airlines
WS: Northern Wings Limited
WT: Waac-Nigeria-Limited
WU: Avna
WV: West Pacific Airlines
WX: Airlines of New South Wales
WY: Azgec Airways
WZ: Swazi Air Limited
XC: Compañia Chiterena de Aviación
XE: Hub Airlines
XF: Murchison Air Services
XK: Air California
XO: Rio Airways
XQ: Air New England
XT: Southern Airlines
XU: Trans Mo Airlines
XV: Ambassador Airlines
XX: Chicago and Southern Airlines
XY: Downeast Airlines
YE: Yemen Airlines
YH: Amistad Airlines
ZB: Midwest Commuter Airways

395

ZD: Aztec Airways
ZF: Village Airways
ZH: Royal Hawaiian Airways
ZJ: Aeronaves del Sureste
ZK: Davis Airlines

ZM: Winnipesaukee Aviation
ZN: Cherokee Airways
ZS: Sizer Airways
ZT: SATENA (Servicio Aeronave-
gacion a Territorios Nacionales

—Bogota
ZV: Air Midwest
ZW: Air Wisconsin
ZX: Aeronaves del Mayab
ZY: Skyway Aviation

ASTRONOMICAL CONSTELLATIONS, STARS, AND SYMBOLS

And: Andromeda (Princess En-
chained), also called Mirach
Ant: Antlia (Bilge Pump)
Aps: Apus (Bird of Paradise)
Aql: Aquila (Eagle); contains
Altair
Aqr: Aquarius (Water Carrier)
Ara (Altar)
Arg: Argo or Argo Navis (Ship
Argo or Ship of the Argo-
nauts); contains Carina (Keel),
Malus (Mast), Puppis (Stern),
Pyxis (Mariner's Compass),
Vela (Sails)
Ari: Aries (Ram); contains Ha-
mal
Aur: Auriga (Charioteer); con-
tains Capella
Boö: Boötes (Herdsman); con-
tains Arcturus
Cae: Caelum (Chisel)
Cam: Camelopardalis (Giraffe)
Cap: Capricornus (Horned Goat)
Car: Carina (Keel), in Argo;
contains Canopus
Cas: Cassiopeia (Queen En-
throned); contains supernova
1572
Cen: Centaurus (Centaur); con-
tains Alpha Centauri, Proxima
Centauri
Cep: Cepheus (Monarch)
Cet: Cetus (Whale); contains
Mira
Cha: Chamaeleon (Chameleon)
Cir: Circinus (Compasses)
CMa: Canis Major (Great Dog);
contains Sirius
CMi: Canis Minor (Little Dog);
contains Procyon
Cnc: Cancer (Crab); contains
Praesepe
Col: Columba (Dove)
Com: Coma Berenices (Berenice's
Hair)
CrA: Corona Australis (Southern
Crown)
CrB: Corona Borealis (Northern
Crown), also called Gemma
Crt: Crater (Cup)

Cru: Crux (Southern Cross);
Black Magellanic Cloud
nearby
Crv: Corvus (Crow)
CVn: Canes Venatici (Hunting
Dogs); contains Cor Caroli
Cyg: Cygnus (Swan); contains
Deneb, Northern Cross
Del: Delphinus (Dolphin)
Dor: Dorado, also called Xiphies
(Swordfish); Large Magel-
lanic Cloud
Dra: Draco (Dragon)
Equ: Equuleus (Colt)
Eri: Eridanus (Great River);
contains Achernar
For: Fornax (Furnace)
Gem: Gemini (The Twins);
contains Castor, Pollux
Gru: Grus (Crane)
Her: Hercules; contains Ras Al-
gethi
Hor: Horologium (Clock)
Hya: Hydra (Marine Monster);
contains Alphard
Hyd: Hydrus (Water Snake)
Ind: Indus (Indian)
Kif Aus: Kiffa Australis (South-
ern Breadbasket); contains
Zuben el Genubi
Kif Bor: Kiffa Borealis (Northern
Breadbasket); contains Zuben-
eschamali
Lac: Lacerta (Lizard)
Leo (Lion): contains Regulus,
Denebola
Lep: Lepus (Hare)
Lib: Libra (Balance or Scales)
LMi: Leo Minor (Little Lion)
Lup: Lupus (Wolf)
Lyn: Lynx
Lyr: Lyra (Lyre); contains Vega
Mal: Malus (Mast), in Argo
Men: Mensa (Table), also called
Mons Mensae (Table Moun-
tain)
Mic: Microscopium (Micro-
scope)
Mon: Monoceros (Unicorn)
Mus: Musca (Fly)

Nor: Norma (Rule)
Oct: Octans (Octant)
Oph: Ophiuchus (Serpent
Bearer); contains supernova
1604
Ori: Orion (Hunter); contains
Betelgeuse, Rigel
Pav: Pavo (Peacock)
Peg: Pegasus (Winged Horse)
Per: Perseus (Rescuer or Cham-
pion); contains Algol
Phe: Phoenix
Pic: Pictor (Painter's Easel)
PsA: Piscis Australis or Austrinus
(Southern Fish); contains For-
malhaut
Psc: Pisces (Fishes)
Pup: Puppis (Stern), in Argo
Pyx: Pyxis (Mariner's Compass
Chest or Binnacle), in Argo
Ret: Reticulum (Net)
Scl: Sculptor (Sculptor's Work-
shop)
Sco: Scorpio (Scorpion); con-
tains Antares
Sct: Scutum (Shield)
Ser: Serpens (Serpent)
Sex: Sextant
Sge: Sagitta (Arrow)
Sgr: Sagittarius (Archer), Center
of Galaxy
Tau: Taurus (Bull); contains Hy-
ades—Aldebaran; Pleiades
Tel: Telescopium (Telescope)
TrA: Triangulum Australe
(Southern Triangle)
Tri: Triangulum (Triangle)
Tuc: Tucana (Toucan); Small
Magellanic Cloud
UMa: Ursa Major (Great Bear);
contains Dubhe, Mizar
UMi: Ursa Minor (Little Bear);
contains Polaris (Pole Star)
Vel: Vela (Sails), in Argo
Vir: Virgo (Virgin)
Vol: Volans (Flying Fish)
Vul: Vulpecula (Little Fox),
also called Vulpecula cum An-
sere (Little Fox with Goose)

ASTRONOMICAL SYMBOLS

⊖☾ : center

☄ : comet

◑ : crescent moon (first quarter)

◐ : crescent moon (last quarter)

⊕ : Earth (symbol shows globe bisected by meridian lines into four quarters)

○ : full moon

◐ : gibbous moon (first quarter)

◑ : gibbous moon (last quarter)

◑ : half moon (first quarter)

◐ : half moon (last quarter)

♃ : Jupiter (symbol said to represent a hieroglyph of the eagle, Jove's bird, or to be the initial letter of Zeus with a line drawn through it to indicate its abbreviation)

☉☾ : lower limb

♂ : Mars (symbol represents shield and spear of the god of war, Mars; it is also the male or masculine symbol)

☿ : Mercury (symbol represents head and winged cap of Mercury, god of commerce and communication, surmounting his caduceus)

♆ : Neptune (symbolized by the trident of Neptune, god of the sea)

● : new moon

☽ : moon (symbol depicts crescent moon in last quarter)

♇ : Pluto (symbol is monogram made up of P and L in Pluto, also initials of the astronomer Percival Lowell, who predicted its discovery)

♄ : Saturn (symbol thought to represent an ancient scythe or sickle, as Saturn was the god of seed sowing and hence also of time)

☆ : star

☆-P : star-planet altitude correction

☉ : sun (symbolized by a shield with its boss; some believe this boss represents a central sunspot)

☉̄☾ : upper limb

♅ : Uranus (symbolized by combined devices indicating the sun plus the spear of Mars, as Uranus was the personification of heaven in the Greek mythology, dominated by the light of the sun and the power of Mars)

♀ : Venus (designated by the female symbol, thought to be the stylized representation of the hand mirror of this goddess of love)

AUTOMATIC DATA PROCESSING ABBREVIATIONS
FOR ZIP-CODED MAIL

AK: Alaska
AL: Alabama
AR: Arkansas
AZ: Arizona
CA: California
CO: Colorado
CT: Connecticut
CZ: Canal Zone
DC: District of Columbia
DE: Delaware
FL: Florida
GA: Georgia
GU: Guam
HI: Hawaii
IA: Iowa
ID: Idaho
IL: Illinois
IN: Indiana
KS: Kansas

KY: Kentucky
LA: Louisiana
MA: Massachusetts
MD: Maryland
ME: Maine
MI: Michigan
MN: Minnesota
MO: Missouri
MS: Mississippi
MT: Montana
NB: Nebraska
NC: North Carolina
ND: North Dakota
NH: New Hampshire
NJ: New Jersey
NM: New Mexico
NV: Nevada
NY: New York
OH: Ohio

OK: Oklahoma
OR: Oregon
PA: Pennsylvania
PR: Puerto Rico
RI: Rhode Island
SC: South Carolina
SD: South Dakota
TN: Tennessee
TX: Texas
UT: Utah
VA: Virginia
VI: Virgin Islands
VT: Vermont
WA: Washington
WI: Wisconsin
WV: West Virginia
WY: Wyoming

CHEMICAL ELEMENT SYMBOLS, ATOMIC NUMBERS,
AND DISCOVERY DATA

Symbol	Element	Atomic Number	Discovered
Ac	actinium	89	1899 by Debierne
Ag	silver (*argentum*)	47	Before the Christian Era
Al	aluminum	13	1825 by Oersted
Am	americium	95	1944 by Seborg and others
Ar or A	argon	18	1894 by Raleigh and Ramsay
As	arsenic	33	13th century by Magnus
As	astatine	85	1940 by Corson and others
Au	gold (*aurum*)	79	Before the Christian Era
B	boron	5	1808 by Davy
Ba	barium	56	1808 by Davy
Be	beryllium	4	1798 by Vauquelin
Bi	bismuth	83	15th century by Valentine
Bk	berkelium	97	1949 by Thompson, Ghiorso, and Seborg
Br	bromine	35	1826 by Balard
C	carbon	6	Before the Christian Era
Ca	calcium	20	1808 by Davy
Cd	cadmium	48	1817 by Stromeyer
Ce	cerium	58	1803 by Klaproth
Cf	californium	98	1950 by Thompson and others
Cl	chlorine	17	1774 by Scheele
Cm	curium	96	1944 by Seborg and others
Co	cobalt	27	1735 by Brandt
Cr	chromium	24	1797 by Vauquelin
Cs	cesium	55	1861 by Bunsen and Kirchoff
Cu	copper (*cuprum*)	29	Before the Christian Era
Dy	dysprosium	66	1886 by Boisbaudran
Er	erbium	68	1843 by Mosander
Es	einsteinium	99	1952 by Ghiorso and others
Eu	europium	63	1901 by Demarcay
F	fluorine	9	1771 by Scheele
Fe	iron (*ferrum*)	26	Before the Christian Era
Fm	fermium	100	1953 by Ghiorso and others
Fr	francium	87	1939 by Perey
Ga	gallium	31	1875 by Boisbaudran
Gd	gadolinium	64	1886 by Marignac
Ge	germanium	32	1886 by Winkler
H	hydrogen	1	1766 by Cavendish
Ha	hahnium	105	1970 by Ghiorso and others
He	helium	2	1895 by Ramsay
Hf	hafnium	72	1923 by Coster and Hevesy
Hg	mercury (*hydrargyrum*)	80	Before the Christian Era
Ho	holmium	67	1879 by Cleve
I	iodine	53	1811 by Courtois

Symbol	Element	Atomic Number	Discovered
In	indium	49	1863 by Reich and Richter
Ir	iridium	77	1804 by Tennant
K	potassium (*kalium*)	19	1807 by Davy
Kr	krypton	36	1898 by Ramsay and Travers
La	lanthanum	57	1839 by Mosander
Li	lithium	3	1817 by Arfvedson
Lu	lutetium	71	1907 by Welsbach and Urbain
Lw	lawrencium	103	1961 by Ghiorso and others
Md	mendelevium	101	1955 by Ghiorso and others
Mg	magnesium	12	1830 by Bussy and Liebig
Mn	manganese	25	1774 by Gahn
Mo	molybdenum	42	1782 by Hjelm
N	nitrogen	7	1772 by Rutherford
Na	sodium	11	1807 by Davy
Nb	niobium (formerly columbium)	41	1801 by Hatchett
Nd	neodymium	60	1885 by Welsbach
Ne	neon	10	1898 by Ramsay and Travers
Ni	nickel	28	1751 by Cronstedt
No	nobelium	102	1958 by Ghiorso and others
Np	neptunium	93	1940 by Abelson and McMillan
O	oxygen	8	1774 by Priestley and Scheele
Os	osmium	76	1804 by Tennant
P	phosphorus	15	1669 by Brandt
Pa	protactinium	91	1917 by Hahn and Meitner
Pb	lead (*plumbum*)	82	Before the Christian Era
Pd	palladium	46	1803 by Wollaston
Pm	promethium	61	1945 by Glendenin and Marinsky
Po	polonium	84	1898 by P. and M. Curie
Pr	praseodymium	59	1885 by Welsbach
Pt	platinum	78	1735 by Ulloa
Pu	plutonium	94	1940 by Seborg and others
Ra	radium	88	1898 by P. and M. Curie
Rb	rubidium	37	1861 by Bunsen and Kirchoff
Re	rhenium	75	1925 by Noddack and Tacke
Rf	rutherfordium	104	1969 by Ghiorso and others
Rh	rhodium	45	1803 by Wollaston
Rn	radon	86	1900 by Dorn
Ru	ruthenium	44	1845 by Claus
S	sulfur	16	Before the Christian Era
Sb	antimony (*stibium*)	51	1450 by Valentine
Sc	scandium	21	1879 by Nilson
Se	selenium	34	1817 by Berzelius
Si	silicon	14	1823 by Berzelius
Sm	samarium	62	1879 by Boisbaudran
Sn	tin (*stannum*)	50	Before the Christian Era
Sr	strontium	38	1790 by Crawford
Ta	tantalum	73	1802 by Eckeberg

Symbol	Element	Atomic Number	Discovered
Tb	terbium	65	1843 by Mosander
Tc	technetium	43	1937 by Perrier and Segre
Te	tellurium	52	1782 by von Reichenstein
Th	thorium	90	1828 by Berzelius
Ti	titanium	22	1789 by Gregor
Tl	thallium	81	1861 by Crookes
Tm	thulium	69	1879 by Cleve
U	uranium	92	1789 by Klaproth
V	vanadium	23	1830 by Sefström
W	tungsten (wolfram)	74	1783 by d'Elhuyar brothers
Xe	xenon	54	1898 by Ramsay and Travers
Y	yttrium	39	1794 by Gadolin
Yb	ytterbium	70	1878 by Marignac
Zn	zinc	30	Before the Christian Era
Zr	zirconium	40	1789 by Klaproth

CIVIL AND MILITARY TIME SYSTEMS COMPARED

Civil	Military	Civil	Military
12.01 A.M.	= 0001	12.01 P.M.	= 1201
12.02 A.M.	= 0002	12.02 P.M.	= 1202
12.03 A.M.	= 0003	12.03 P.M.	= 1203
12.04 A.M.	= 0004	12.04 P.M.	= 1204
12.05 A.M.	= 0005	12.05 P.M.	= 1205
12.15 A.M.	= 0015	12.15 P.M.	= 1215
12.30 A.M.	= 0030	12.30 P.M.	= 1230
12.45 A.M.	= 0045	12.45 P.M.	= 1245
1.00 A.M.	= 0100	1.00 P.M.	= 1300
1.15 A.M.	= 0115	1.15 P.M.	= 1315
1.30 A.M.	= 0130	1.30 P.M.	= 1330
1.45 A.M.	= 0145	1.45 P.M.	= 1345
2.00 A.M.	= 0200	2.00 P.M.	= 1400
3.00 A.M.	= 0300	3.00 P.M.	= 1500
4.00 A.M.	= 0400	4.00 P.M.	= 1600
5.00 A.M.	= 0500	5.00 P.M.	= 1700
6.00 A.M.	= 0600	6.00 P.M.	= 1800
7.00 A.M.	= 0700	7.00 P.M.	= 1900
8.00 A.M.	= 0800	8.00 P.M.	= 2000
9.00 A.M.	= 0900	9.00 P.M.	= 2100
10.00 A.M.	= 1000	10.00 P.M.	= 2200
11.00 A.M.	= 1100	11.00 P.M.	= 2300
12.00 noon	= 1200	12.00 midnight	= 2400

DIACRITICAL AND PUNCTUATION MARKS

´	acute accent (as in Bogotá)
'	apostrophe; single quotation mark
[ ]	brackets
˘	breve
¸	cedilla (as in Curaçao)
ˆ	circumflex (as in *rôle*)
:	colon
)	close parenthesis
,	comma
¨	diaeresis (as in München)
... or	ellipsis; leaders
!	exclamation point
`	grave accent (as in *funèbre*)
-	hyphen
?	interrogation or question mark
–	macron (dictionary pronunciation symbol indicating long vowel, as in dāme)
(	open parenthesis
( )	parentheses
.	period
" "	quotation marks; quotes
' '	quotation marks, single
;	semicolon
˜	tilde (as in São Paulo)
—	vinculum (mathematics: placed above letters)

GREEK ALPHABET

ALPHA	A	α	NU	N	ν
BETA	B	β	XI	Ξ	ξ
GAMMA	Γ	γ	OMICRON	O	o
DELTA	Δ	δ	PI	Π	π
EPSILON	E	ϵ	RHO	P	ρ
ZETA	Z	ζ	SIGMA	Σ	$\sigma\varsigma$
ETA	H	η	TAU	T	τ
THETA	Θ	θ	UPSILON	Y	υ
IOTA	I	ι	PHI	Φ	ϕ
KAPPA	K	κ	CHI	X	χ
LAMBDA	Λ	λ	PSI	Ψ	ψ
MU	M	μ	OMEGA	Ω	ω

INTERNATIONAL CIVIL AIRCRAFT MARKINGS

AN: Nicaragua
AP: Pakistan
B: Formosa
CB: Bolivia
CC: Chile
CCCP: Soviet Union (USSR)
CF: Canada
CR and CS: Portugal and colonies
CU: Cuba
CX: Uruguay
CZ: Principality of Monaco
D: Western Germany
EC: Spain
EI and EJ: Ireland
EL: Liberia
EP: Iran
ET: Ethiopia
F: France and French Union
G: United Kingdom
HA: Hungary
HB: Switzerland
HC: Ecuador
HH: Haiti
HI: Dominican Republic
HK: Colombia
HL: Korea
HS: Thailand
HZ: Saudi Arabia

I: Italy
JA: Japan
JY: Jordan
LN: Norway
LV: Argentine Republic
LX: Luxembourg
LZ: Bulgaria
MC: Monte Carlo
N: United States of America
OB: Peru
OD: Lebanon
OE: Austria
OH: Finland
OK: Czechoslovakia
OO: Belgium
OY: Denmark
PH: Netherlands
PI: Philippine Republic
PJ: Curaçao (Netherlands Antilles)
PK: Indonesia
PP and PT: Brazil
PZ: Surinam (Netherlands Guiana)
RX: Republic of Panama
SE: Sweden
SN: Sudan
SP: Poland
SU: Egypt

SX: Greece
TC: Turkey
TF: Iceland
TG: Guatemala
TI: Costa Rica
VH: Australia
VP; VQ; VR: British Colonies and Protectorates
VT: India
XA; XB; XC: Mexico
XH: Honduras
XT: China (Nationalist)
XY; XZ: Burma
YA: Afghanistan
YE: Yemen
YI: Iraq
YK: Syria
YR: Rumania
YS: El Salvador
YU: Yugoslavia
YV: Venezuela
ZA: Albania
ZK; ZL; ZM: New Zealand
ZP: Paraguay
ZS; ZT; ZU: Union of South Africa
4R: Ceylon
4X: Israel
5A: Libya
9G: Ghana

INTERNATIONAL RADIO ALPHABET AND CODE

A: Alpha ·—
B: Bravo —···
C: Charlie —·—·
D: Delta —··
E: Echo ·
F: Foxtrot ··—·
G: Golf ——·
H: Hotel ····
I: India ··

J: Juliet ·———
K: Kilo —·—
L: Lima (leema) ·—··
M: Mike ——
N: November —·
O: Oscar ———
P: Papa ·——·
Q: Quebec (kaybeck) ——·—
R: Romeo ·—·

S: Sierra ···
T: Tango —
U: Uniform ··—
V: Victor ···—
W: Whiskey ·——
X: Xray —··—
Y: Yankee —·——
Z: Zulu ——··

RADIO NUMERALS

0: (zee-ro) —————
1: (wun) ·————
2: (too) ··———
3: (thuh-ree) ···——

4: (fo-wer) ····—
5: (fi-yiv) ·····
6: (siks) —····
7: (sev-ven) ——···

8: (ate) ———··
9: (ni-yen) ————·

NUMBERED ABBREVIATIONS

o deg lat: zero degrees latitude—the Equator, encircling widest part of the earth

O²: both eyes

¼d: farthing (fourth of an English penny); a fourthling

¼ h: quarter-hard

¼ ly: quarterly

¼ ph: quarter-phase

¼ rd: quarter-round

½ can: narcotics equal to a half can of pipe tobacco

½d: halfpenny (half of an English penny); ha'penny

½ gr: half-gross

½ h: half-hard

½ rd: half-round

½ sovereign: 10 shillings

1b: first base(man)

1/: shilling; also called a *bob*

1/c: single-conductor

1d: an English penny

1s: shilling, also called a *bob*

1º: primero(a) (Spanish—first)

1: Year 1; in the beginning (slang)

1A: available for military service

1-BCE: first century before the Christian era (Caesar's Century)—Julius Caesar conquered Britain and Egypt before he was assassinated in the Roman senate in the year 44

1-C: first century (the Vesuvian Century)—destruction of Pompeii, Herculaneum, and nearby Neapolitan places by the volcano Vesuvius in the year 79 of the Christian era

1C: member or former member of US armed forces with honorable discharge

1 cent: 1 penny (10 mills)

1 Chron: The First Book of the Chronicles

1 Cor: The First Epistle of Paul the Apostle to the Corinthians

1 crown: 5 shillings

1 dime: 10 cents

1 double eagle: $20 (gold)

1 eagle: $10 (gold)

1er(e): premier(e) (French—first)

1 Esd: The First (Apocryphal) Book of Esdras

1 florin: 2 shillings

1 frogskin: $1 bill

1 guinea: 21 shillings

1G, 2G, 3G, etc.: slang for one, two, or three thousand dollars, etc.

1 half crown: 2 shillings, 6 pence

1 half dime: 5 cents

1 half dollar: 50 cents

1 half eagle: $5 (gold)

1 halfpenny: 2 farthings

1 Hen IV: First part of *King Henry IV*

1 Hen VI: First part of *King Henry VI*

1 John: The First Epistle General of John

1 Kings: The First Book of the Kings

1 Macc: The First (Apocryphal) Book of Maccabees

1mo: primo (Italian—first)

1-p: single pole

1 penny: 4 farthings

1 Pet: The First Epistle General of Peter

1 ph: single-phase

1 pound: 20 shillings

1Q: first quarter

1Q66: first quarter 1966

1 quarter dollar: 25 cents

1 quarter eagle: $2.50 (gold)

1 Sam: The First Book of Samuel

1 shilling: 12 pence

1 sixpence: 6 pence

1 sovereign: 1 pound sterling; 20 shillings

1-spot: $1 bill

1st: first

1st cl hon: first-class honors (in academic degrees)

1st Lieut: First Lieutenant

1st Naval District: Boston, Massachusetts

1-striper: ensign (USN); third assistant engineer or third mate (merchant marine); private first class (US Army)

1st Sgt: First Sergeant

1 threepence: 3 pence

1 Thess: The First Epistle of Paul the Apostle to the Thessalonians

1 Tim: The First Epistle of Paul the Apostle to Timothy

1½ striper: naval lieutenant, junior grade

1s & 2s: mixed first and second quality lumber

1-wd: one-wheel drive

1-A: available for military service

I-A-O: conscientious objector available only for noncombatant military service

I-C: member of the armed forces, Coast and Geodetic Survey, or Public Health Service

I-D: member of reserve component or student taking military training

I-O: conscientious objector available only for civilian work contributing to national health, safety, or interest

I-S: student deferred by statute until end of current school year

1st State: Delaware

I-W: conscientious objector performing civilian work contributing to national health, safety, or interest, or who has completed such work

I-Y: registrant does not meet present standards; available for military service only in event of war or national emergency

2/: two shillings; also the coin called a florin

2º: segundo(a) (Spanish—second)

II-A: registrant deferred because of civilian occupation (except agriculture and activity in study) or an apprentice deferred by statute

II-B: registrant deferred because necessary to war production

II-BCE: second century before the Christian era (Roman Century)—Punic wars result in destruction of Carthage by the Roman Legions—the 100s

2b: second base(man)

2 bits: 25 cents

2/c: two-conductor

II-C: registrant deferred because of agricultural occupation

II-C: second century (the Aurelian Century)—reign of the Roman emperor-philosopher Marcus Aurelius—the 100s

II Chron: The Second Book of the Chronicles

2d: second

2do: secondo (Italian—second)

IIe: deuxième, second, seconde (French—second)

II Esd: The Second (Apocryphal) Book of Esdras

2-F: two-seater fighter aircraft (naval symbol)

2g, 3g, 4g, etc.: multiples of acceleration of gravity which at the surface of the earth is 32.2 feet per second

2 Hen IV: Second part of *King Henry IV*

2 Hen VI: Second part of *King Henry VI*

2 i/c: second in command

II John: The Second Epistle of John

II Kings: The Second Book of Kings

II Macc: The Second (Apocryphal) Book of Maccabees

2n: diploid number

2nd: second

2nd Lieut: Second Lieutenant

403

2-p: double pole

II Pet: The Second Epistle General of Peter

2 ph: two-phase

2Q: second quarter

2Q66: 2nd quarter 1966

2s: two shillings; also the coin called a florin

II-S: registrant deferred because of activity in study

II Sam: The Second Book of Samuel

2-spot: S2 bill

2-striper: corporal (US Army); lieutenant (USN); second assistant engineer or second mate (merchant marine)

2/10–30: 2% discount if paid in 10 days, net in 30 days

2T: double throw

II Thess: The Second Epistle of Paul the Apostle to the Thessalonians

II Tim: Second Epistle of Paul the Apostle to Timothy

2-way: two-way

2-wd: 2-wheel drive

2½-striper: naval lieutenant commander

2-4-D: dichlorophenoxy-acetic acid (weed killer)

2/6: two-and-six (two shillings and sixpence); also called half a crown

2-13: drug addict

2244s: prisoners' petitions for judicial reviews of their cases

2-4-5-T: trichlorophenoxy-acetic acid (antiplant agent and defoliant)

2WW: Second Weather Wing (Air Force—New York)

III-A: registrant with child or children or registrant deferred by reason of extreme hardship to dependents

3b: third base(man)

III-BCE: third century before the Christian era (the Carthaginian Century)—Hannibal crossed the Alps to defeat the Romans—the 200s

3-Bs: Bach, Beethoven, Berlioz; Bach, Beethoven, Bernstein; Bach, Beethoven, Brahms; Bach, Beethoven, Bruckner; etc. (depending on one's favorite composers)

3/c: three-conductor

3C: Computer Control Company

III-C: third century (the Chinese Century)—Chin dynasty rules a reunited China—the 200s

3d: English threepenny; thruppence; third

3-d: dizzy, dopey, and dumb; three dimensional

3d 10h 40m: 3 days 10 hours 40 minutes (Atlantic crossing of SS *United States* in July 1952)

3-Ds: discouragement, disillusionment, disappointment (including frustration and loss)—often leads to suicide, experts insist

IIIe: *troisième* (French—third)

3 Hen VI: Third part of *King Henry VI*

3-I voters: Irish, Israeli, Italian

III John: The Third Epistle of John

3 K's: *Kinder, Küche, Kirche* (German—children, kitchen, church)

3M: Minnesota Mining and Manufacturing Company

3-M: Maintenance and Material Management (USN)

3⁰: *tercero(a)* (Spanish—third)

3-p: triple pole

3ph: three-phase

3Q: third quarter

3Q66: third quarter 1966

3rd: third

3rd degree: prolonged interrogation designed to produce a confession of guilt

3rd Naval District: New York, New York

3-R's: reading, writing, arithmetic (colloquially, readin', 'ritin' 'rithmetic)

3-star: admiral or general of three-star rank

3-striper: commander (USN); first assistant engineer or first mate (merchant marine); sergeant (US Army)

3T: triple throw

3-way: three-way

3WW: Third Weather Wing (Air Force—Nebraska)

4a: man 38 years or over and deferred from military service by reason of age

IV-A: registrant who has completed service or a sole surviving son

IV-B: government official deferred by statute

IV-BCE: fourth century before the Christian era (the Alexandrian Century)—Alexander the Great of Macedonia defeated the Egyptians, the Persians, and the Indians; encouraged the Greek philosophers and poets—the 300s

4 bits: 50 cents

4/c: four-conductor

4C: Community-Coordinated Child Care Program

IV-C: alien

IV-C: fourth century (the Constantinian Century)—Roman emperor Constantine builds the city of Constantinople on the site of ancient Byzantium and proclaims it capital of the Eastern Empire—the 300s

4-d meat: meat of dead, disabled, diseased, or dying animals

IV-D: minister of religion or divinity student

IVe: *quatrième* (French—fourth)

IV-E: conscientious objector available for, assigned to, or released for work of national importance

4-F: find, feel, fornicate, and forget—code of conduct of certain men in search of casual sexual relationships

IV-F: registrant not qualified for any military service

4-H: 4-H Clubs

4⁰: quarto (a book about 9 × 12 inches)

4⁰: *cuarto(a)* (Spanish—fourth)

4-p: quadruple pole

4Q: fourth quarter

4Q66: fourth quarter 1966

4R: Ceylon aircraft

4-star: admiral or general of four-star rank

4-striper: captain (merchant marine or USN); chief engineer (merchant marine)

4th: fourth

4th Naval District: Philadelphia, Pennsylvania

4-way: four-way

4-wd: four-wheel drive

4WW: Fourth Weather Wing (Air Force—Colorado)

4X: Israeli aircraft

5A: Libyan aircraft

V-A: registrant over the age liability for military service

5-and-10: variety store selling articles formerly costing not more than five or ten cents

V-BCE: fifth century before the Christian era (Athenian Century)—Athenians destroy Persian fleet at Salamis; complete the Parthenon in Athens—the 400s

5b: bald man with baywindow, bifocals, bridgework, and bunions (humorous Selective Service rating)

5-B's: Boston baked beans and

brownbread

5BX: five basic exercises (Royal Canadian Air Force physical fitness program)

V^e: *cinquième* (French—fifth)

V-C: fifth century (the Christian Century)—Christianity affirmed as the official faith by two Roman emperors—the 400s

5'er: $5 bill; 5-pound note

5°: *quinto(a)* (Spanish—fifth)

5-percenter: person who for 5 percent arranges introductions leading to valuable orders

5-Ps: (nickname of William Oxberry—British player, poet, publican, publisher, and printer)

5-spot: $5 bill

5th: fifth

5th Naval District: Norfolk, Virginia

5 w's: the *who, what, when, where,* and *why* reporters attempt to include in writing summary paragraphs

6 bits: 75 cents

VI-BCE: sixth century before the Christian era (Babylonian Century)—Babylonians defeat Israelites and make them captive after destroying the temple of Solomon in Jerusalem—the 500s

6/c: six-conductor

VI-C: sixth century (the Persian Century)—Khosru Nushirwan makes peace with the Byzantine Empire and extends Persian rule throughout the Middle East—the 500s

6d: English sixpenny; sixpence

6-dW: Six-day War between Arab countries of Egypt, Jordan, Lebanon, and Syria versus Israel; June 5 to 10, 1967

VIe: *sixième* (French—sixth)

6'er: leader of a pack of six scouts

6°: *sesto(a)*; *sexto(a)* Spanish —sixth)

6-pack: carton containing six of a kind (6 containers of beer, soda, etc.)

6-R's: remedial readin', remedial 'ritin', remedial 'rithmetic

6-shooter: revolver holding six cartridges

6th: sixth

6th Naval District: Charleston, South Carolina

6WW: Sixth Weather Wing (Air Force—Washington, D.C.)

7A: Seven Arts Society

VII-BCE: seventh century before the Christian era (Assyrian Cen-

tury) when Assyria rules Middle East and conquers Egypt—the 600s

7ber: September

7bre: *Septembre* (French—September); *septiembre* (Spanish—September

7/c: seven-conductor

VII-C: seventh century (the Islamic Century)—marked by Mohammed's flight from Mecca to Medina and his death in 632; Islam began expanding throughout the Middle East and North Africa as well as moving toward France and Spain—the 600s

7 Dec: Pearl Harbor Day (1941)

7ds: seven deadly sins—anger, covetousness, envy, gluttony, lechery, pride, sloth

7e: *septiembre* (Spanish—September)

7°: *septimo(a)* (Spanish—seventh)

VIIe: *septième* (French—seventh)

7th: seventh

7-Up: a carbonated beverage

7WW: Seventh Weather Wing (Air Force—Illinois)

8: numerical symbol for heroin as H is the eighth of the alphabet

VIII-BCE: eighth century before the Christian era (Chou Century)—eastern Chou dynasty begins ruling China for the next five centuries—the 700s

8 bits: one dollar

8bre: *octobre* (French—October); *octubre* (Spanish—October)

VIII-C: eighth century (the Carolingian Century)—Charlemagne or Charles the Great reigns as King of the Franks and Emperor of the West as well as being chief patron of learning—the 700s

8e: *octubre* (Spanish—October)

VIIIe: *huitième* (French—eighth)

8N: American National 8-thread series

8°: octavo (a book about 9¾ inches high)

8°: *octavo(a)* (Spanish—eighth)

8th: eighth

8th Naval District: New Orleans, Louisiana

8UN: Unified 8-thread series

8va bass.: *ottava bassa* (Italian—octave lower)

IX-BCE: ninth century before the Christian era (Phoenician Century)—Carthage founded by the Phoenicians who trade in all areas of the Mediterranean—the 800s

9ber: November

9bre: *novembre* (French—November); *noviembre* (Spanish—November)

IX-C: ninth century (the Century of Confusion)—Carolingian Empire of Charlemagne disintegrates; European unity dismembered and divided—the 800s

9e: *noviembre* (Spanish—November)

IXe: *neuvième* (French—ninth)

9th: ninth

9th Naval District: Great Lakes, Illinois

9°: *nono(a)*; *noveno(a)* (Spanish—ninth)

9 to 5: everyday job

'10: 1810 (Bolvarian-type Spanish-American Revolutions and wars of liberation, 1810–1826)

10^-1: deci (d)

10^-2: centi (c)

10^-3: milli (m)

10^-6: micro (μ)

10^-9: nano (n)

10^-12: pico (p)

10^-15: femto (f)

10^-18: atto (a)

10: deka (da)

10°: *decimo(a)* (Spanish—tenth)

10^2: hecto (h)

10^3: kilo (k)

10^6: mega (M)

10^9: giga (G)

10^12: tera (T)

10 Aug: Ecuadorian Independence Day

X-BCE: tenth century before the Christian era (Israelian Century)—King Solomon reigns and Israelites defeat all enemies and build the great temple of Jerusalem—the 900s

10bre: *décembre* (French—December); *diciembre* (Spanish—December)

Xber: December

X-C: tenth century (the Mayan Century)—great American civilization leaving monumental ruins strewn from Honduras to Yucatan—the 900s

10 Dec: Human Rights Day (Liberia)

10e: *diciembre* (Spanish—December)

X^e: *dixième* (French—tenth)

10 Downing Street: British prime minister's home in west central London

10-gallon hat: cowboy hat

10-spot: $10 bill

10th: tenth
10th Naval District: San Juan, Puerto Rico
10-V: the lowest; the opposite of A-1; the worst
XI-BCE: eleventh century before the Christian era (Century of Saul and David)—King Saul followed by King David as ruler of Israel—the 1000s
XI-C: eleventh century (the Aztecan and Incan Century)—vast monuments in the highlands of Mexico and Peru stand as mute witnesses to these great American civilizations—the 1000s
11th: eleventh
11th Naval District: San Diego, California
11-11-11: eleventh hour, eleventh day, eleventh month of 1918 when Armistice ended World War I
XII-BCE: twelfth century before the Christian era (Trojan Century)—Troy falls to the Greeks after a ten-year siege celebrated in Homer's epic poem the *Iliad*—the 1100s
XII-C: twelfth century (the Portuguese Century when Alfonso I Henriques reigns as king of Portugal soon to emerge as a great maritime power—the 1100s
12N: American National 12-thread series
12⁰: twelvemo (a book about 7¾ inches high)
12th: twelfth
12th Naval District: San Francisco, California
12UN: Unified 12-thread series
13: numerical symbol for marijuana as M is the thirteenth letter of the alphabet; police radio signal call 13 indicates an officer needs help—this is the highest priority radio call and all units respond
XIII-BCE: thirteenth century before the Christian era (Century of the Exodus)—Moses leads the Israelites out of Egypt—the 1200s
XIII-C: thirteenth century (the Mongol Century) dominated by the reign of the Mongol emperor Genghiz Khan whose hordes conquer China and Russia—the 1200s
13th: thirteenth
13th Naval District: Seattle, Washington

14: numerical symbol for narcotics as N is the fourteenth letter of the alphabet
XIV-BCE: fourteenth century before the Christian era (Century of the Pharoah Tutankhamen)
XIV-C: fourteenth century (Tamerlane's Century)—Mongol emperor Timur (Tamer the Lame) dominates Middle East and western India—the 1300s
14th: fourteenth
14th Naval District: Pearl Harbor, Oahu, Hawaii
15th: fifteenth
15th Naval District: Balboa, Canal Zone
XV-BCE: fifteenth century before the Christian era (Egyptian Century)—Egyptian kingdom extended from the Sahara to beyond the Euphrates—the 1400s
XV-C: fifteenth century (the Italian Century)—powerful families such as the Borgias and the de Medicis bring about the renewal of art and architecture in Italy—the Italian Renaissance—the 1400s
XVI to XXXII BCE: (*see* XXXII-BCE
XXXII-BCE: thirty-second century before the Christian era (Dynastic Century) when the first and second of many Egyptian dynasties began a rule lasting for at least seventeen centuries before the power of the pharoahs began to wane—the 3100s
XVI-C: sixteenth century (the Spanish Century) marked by discoveries and colonizations of much of the New World, circumnavigation of the globe, flowering of art and literature—the Golden Age or *Siglo de Oro*, as well as the defeat of the Spanish Armada by the British—the 1500s
16N: American National 16-thread series
16⁰: sixteenmo (a book about 6¾ inches high)
16's: 16 rpm phonograph records
16th: sixteenth
16UN: Unified 16-thread series
XVII-C: seventeenth century (the Dutch Century) sees the discovery and settlement of what is now New York as well as South Africa and the East Indies by the Dutch who after a war at sea arrange a mutual defense pact

with their British rivals—the 1600s (*see* the Elizabethan Age, *Le Grand Siecle, El Siglo de Oro*)
17-D: modified yellow-fever virus
17th: seventeenth
17th Naval District: Kodiak, Alaska
XVIII-C: eighteenth century (the French Century) of courtesans and kings, poets and playrights, of great territories acquired and lost, of Louis XVI and Marie Antoinette beheaded by the guillotine only to be replaced by Napoleon—the turbulent 1700s (*see* The Enlightenment)
18th: eighteenth
18–19 Sept: Chilean Independence Days
XIX-C: nineteenth century (the British Century) from Napoleon's defeat by Wellington at Waterloo to the defeat of the Boers in South Africa this century is marked by British advances in invention, in the success of its industrial revolution, in its colonization in all parts of the world, and its maritime supremacy on all the oceans—the 1800s
19th: nineteenth
XX-C: twentieth century (The American Century) characterized by industrial advances, victory in two world wars, as well as the development of inventions, the discovery of the North Pole, the placing of men on the moon, the elevation of living standards, the devotion to democratic ideals—the 1900s
20-spot: $20 bill
20th: twentieth; Twentieth Century Limited (New York Central Railroad)
XXI-C: twenty-first century (the Japanese Century)—providing productivity, standard of living, and other growth factors are not disturbed by large-scale earthquakes and world wars—the 2000s
21st: twenty-first
.22: .22-caliber ammunition, pistol, or rifle
22d: twenty-second
22nd: twenty-second
23½ deg N lat: Tropic of Cancer
23½ deg S lat: Tropic of Capricorn
23rd: twenty-third
24⁰: twenty-fourmo (a book about 5¾ inches high)

24th: twenty-fourth
25: LSD as 25 is part of the chemical name—d-lysergic acid diethylamide tartrate 25
25th: twenty-fifth
26th: twenty-sixth
27th: twenty-seventh
28th: twenty-eighth
29th: twenty-ninth
30: finis symbol used by newspapermen at end of article or story
30 days, etc.: (calendar mnemonic—30 days hath September, April, June, and November; all the rest have 31 save February; 28 are all its score, but in leap year one day more)
30th: thirtieth
.30-'06: 30-caliber American cartridge introduced in 1906; used by US Armed Forces in World Wars I and II for rifles and machine guns
32°: thirty-twomo (a book about 5 inches high)
33's: 33⅓ rpm phonograph records
.38: .38-caliber ammunition or pistol
40: 40 acres
40th: fortieth
40 winks: a nap or short sleep
42nd cousin: a distant relative
.44: .44-caliber ammunition or pistol
.45: .45-caliber ammunition, pistol, or submachine gun
45's: 45 rpm phonograph records
47th State: New Mexico
48: 48-hour weekend liberty pass
48°: forty-eightmo (a book about 4 inches high)
48er: emigrant who came to America in 1848; participant in German revolution of 1848
48th State: Arizona
49er: gold-rush settler who came to California in 1849
49th State: Alaska

.50: .50-caliber ammunition or machine gun
50-spot: $50 bill
50th: fiftieth
50th State: Hawaii
60th: sixtieth
64°: sixty-fourmo (a book about 3 inches high)
66: Phillips Petroleum Company
66 deg 17 min N lat: Arctic Circle
66 deg 17 min S lat: Antarctic Circle
69: pictorial numerical symbol for oral-genital copulation
70th: seventieth
73: best regards (amateur radio)
75's: 75mm cannon
76: Union Oil
'76: 1776
78's: 78 rpm phonograph records
80th: eightieth
88: love and kisses (amateur radio)
89d: 89 days (New York to San Francisco run of American clipper ship *Flying Cloud* in 1854)
89er: Oklahoman who settled in 1889 when the territory was opened
90-day wonder: officer commissioned after only 90 days of training
90 deg N lat: North Pole (zero degrees longitude)
90 deg S lat: South Pole (zero degrees longitude)
90th: ninetieth
93-score: best grade of butter (USDA grade AA)
'96: 1796 (Napoleonic Wars, 1796–1815)
100th: one-hundredth
111: One-Eleven (British Aircraft Corporation short-take-off-and-landing fan-jet aircraft)
240: Convair two-engine transport airplane; trotting horse speed—1 mile in 2 minutes and 40 seconds; synonym for high speed

280: copper alloy (Muntz metal); yellow metal
400: the four hundred; the socially elite (originally designated by Ward McAllister, who drew up a list containing the top 400 in New York society)
415 PC: Section 415 Penal code—disturbing the peace
502: drunken driving (police code)
606: arsphenamine compound sold as Salvarsan; 606th compound developed and tested by Paul Ehrlich for treatment of relapsing fevers and syphilis
707: Boeing Stratoliner jet-transport airplane
720: Boeing medium-range jet-transport airplane
727: Boeing jet-transport with three empennage-mounted engines
737: Boeing short-range twin-jet airplane
747: Boeing jumbo jet-liner (built to transport from 490 to 1000 passengers, depending on the model)
880: Convair 880 jet airplane
911: (police telephone number in many U.S. cities)
990: Convair 990 fan-engine jet airplane
1600 Pennsylvania Avenue: (Washington, D.C., address of the White House)
"1919": *Nineteen nineteen* (novel by John Dos Passos depicting World War I era of American life in series of camera-eye closeups)—1919 often used to symbolize this period
"1984": *Nineteen eighty-four* (novel of George Orwell describing totalitarian terror in the year 1984)—1984 has become a symbol for anti-libertarian trends
23102a V(ehicle) C(ode): driving under the influence of any intoxicating liquor or drug
2707: Boeing supersonic transport

NUMERATION

power		prefix	abbreviation	name
1,000,000,000,000	10^{12}	tera	t	one trillion*
100,000,000,000	10^{11}			one-hundred billion
10,000,000,000	10^{10}			ten billion
1,000,000,000	10^{9}	giga	g	one billion
100,000,000	10^{8}			one-hundred million
10,000,000	10^{7}			ten million
1,000,000	10^{6}	mega	m	one million
100,000	10^{5}			one-hundred thousand
10,000	10^{4}			ten thousand
1000	10^{3}	kilo	k	one thousand
100	10^{2}			one hundred
10	10^{1}			ten
1	10^{0}			one
0.1	10^{-1}	deci	d	one-tenth
0.01	10^{-2}	centi	c	one-hundredth
0.001	10^{-3}	milli	m	one-thousandth
0.0001	10^{-4}			one ten-thousandth
0.00001	10^{-5}			one hundred-thousandth
0.000001	10^{-6}	micro	$(u - mu)$	one millionth
0.0000001	10^{-7}			one ten-millionth
0.00000001	10^{-8}			one hundred-millionth
0.000000001	10^{-9}	nano	n	one billionth
0.0000000001	10^{-10}			one ten-billionth
0.00000000001	10^{-11}			one hundred-billionth
0.000000000001	10^{-12}	pico	p	one trillionth
0.0000000000001	10^{-13}			one ten-trillionth
0.00000000000001	10^{-14}			one hundred-trillionth
0.000000000000001	10^{-15}	femto	f	one quadrillionth
0.0000000000000001	10^{-16}			one ten-quadrillionth
0.00000000000000001	10^{-17}			one hundred-quadrillionth
0.000000000000000001	10^{-18}	atto	a	one quintillionth

* - trillions are followed by quadrillions, quintillions, sextillions, septillions, octillions, nonillions, decillions, undecillions, duodecillions, tredecillions, quattuordecillions, quinquedecillions, sexdecillions, septendecillions, octodecillions, novemdecillions, vigintillions (a thousand novemdecillions)

PROOFREADER'S MARKS

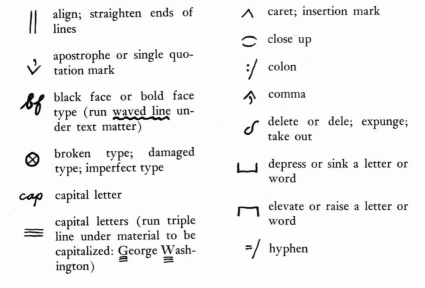

|| align; straighten ends of lines

∨ apostrophe or single quotation mark

𝒷𝒻 black face or bold face type (run waved line under text matter)

⊗ broken type; damaged type; imperfect type

𝒸𝒶𝓅 capital letter

≡ capital letters (run triple line under material to be capitalized: George Washington)

∧ caret; insertion mark

◯ close up

:/ colon

∧ comma

𝒹 delete or dele; expunge; take out

⊔ depress or sink a letter or word

⊓ elevate or raise a letter or word

=/ hyphen

ital set in *italics* (material to be italicized is <u>underlined</u>)

lc lower case (run / through letter or letters to be set in Lower Case)

lead insert lead spacing between lines

⌐ move to the left

⌐ move to the right

¶ paragraph

⊙ period

⊥ push down space which prints as a mark

⌄" quotation marks

rom set in roman type

;/ semicolon

sc small caps (run **double** line under material: a.d.)

space; # # double space; etc.

(sp) spell out (material to be spelled out is encircled: (U.S.))

stet let stand that which has been deleted; restore crossed out material (indicate by running dots under the letters of the words to be restored)

tr transpose (indicate in text by ~ or ⌣)

@ turn letter right side up

wf wrong font

RAILROADS OF THE WORLD
—abbreviations and nicknames
—reporting marks

AA: Ann Arbor Railroad

AAR: Association of American Railroads

A & B: Antofagasta and Bolivia

A y B: *Antofagasta y Bolivia* (Spanish—Antofagasta and Bolivia)—Chilean Railway linking Pacific port with highlands of landlocked Bolivia

ABB: Akron and Barberton Belt Railroad

ABL: Alameda Belt Line

AC: Algoma Central Railway

ACL: Atlantic Coast Line (Seaboard Coast Line Raliroad)

ACY: Akron, Canton and Youngstown Railroad

AD: Atlantic and Danville Railway

ADN: Ashley, Drew and Northern Railway (also AD & N)

AEC: Atlantic and East Carolina

AFE: *Administracion de los Ferrocarriles del Estado* (Spanish—State Railway Administration)—Uruguay

AFL: *Administracion de los Ferrocarriles del Estado* (Spanish—State Railways Administration)—Venezuela

AGS: Alabama Great Southern (Southern Railway)

AF: Alma and Jonquieres Railway

AL: Almanor Railroad

ALM: Arkansas and Louisiana Missouri Railway (also A & LM)

ALN: Albany and Northern Railroad

ALQS: Aliquippa and Southern

ALS: Alton and Southern Railroad

AL & S: Alton and Southern Railroad

Alton Route: Gulf, Mobile and Ohio Railroad

AMC: Amador Central Railroad

AMR: Arcata and Mad River

Amtrac: American (railroad) tracks —(government-sponsored program for reviving city-to-city passenger service)

AN: Apalachicola Northern Railroad

Ann Arbor: Detroit, Toledo and Ironton Railroad

Annie & Mary: (nickname—Arcata and Mad River Railroad) —originally the Union Wharf and Plank Walk Company

ANR: Angelina and Neches River Railroad

APA: Apache Railway Company

APD: Albany Port District

AR: Aberdeen and Rockfish

ARA: Arcade and Attica Railroad

ARC: Alexander Railroad (Southern)

ARR: Alaska Railroad

ART: American Refrigerator Transit

ARW: Arkansas Western Railway (Kansas City Southern)

A & S: Abilene and Southern

ASAB: Atlanta and Saint Andrews Bay Railway

ASDA: Asbestos and Danville

ASLRA: American Short Line Railroad Association

ASR: Association of Southeastern Railroads

ATC: Arnold Transit Company

ATN: Alabama, Tennessee and Northern Railroad

ATSF: Atchison, Topeka and Santa Fe Railway (also AT & SF)

ATW: Atlantic and Western

AUG: Augusta Railroad

AUS: Augusta and Summerville

AVL: Aroostook Valley Railroad

AW: Ahnapee and Western Railway

AWP: Atlanta and West Point Rail Road (includes Western Railway of Alabama and Georgia Railroad)—also A & WP

AWW: Algers, Winslow and Western Railway

AYSS: Allegheny and South Side

B & A: Boston and Albany (Penn Central)

BAP: Butte, Anaconda and Pacific Railway (also BA & P)

BAR: Bangor and Aroostook Railroad

BARC: Baltimore and Annapolis Railroad Company

B & ARR: Boston and Albany Railroad

BART: Bay Area Rapid Transit (San Francisco Bay Area mass transportation system)

Bay Line: Atlanta and Saint Andrews Bay Railway

BB: Birmingham Belt Railroad

BCE Route: British Columbia Electric Route

BCH: British Columbia Hydro and Power Authority

BCK: Buffalo Creek Railroad

BCK: Bas-Congo au Katanga (French—Lower Congo—Katanga)—railway of Zaire

BCRR: Boyne City Railroad

BCYR: British Columbia Yukon Railway

BDZ: (Cyrillic transliteration—Bulgarian State Railways)

BE: Baltimore and Eastern Railroad (Penn Central)

BEDT: Brooklyn Eastern District Terminal Railroad

BEEM: Beech Mountain Railroad

BEM: Beaufort and Morehead Railroad

Bessemer: Bessemer and Lake Erie

BFC: Bellefonte Central Railroad

BH: Bath and Hammondsport Railroad

BHS: Bonhomie and Hattiesburg Southern Railroad

Big Four: Cleveland, Cincinnati, Chicago and St Louis Railway (Penn Central)

Birmingham Southern: Birmingham Southern Railraod

BLA: Baltimore and Annapolis

B & LE: Bessemer and Lake Erie Railroad

BM: Boston and Maine Corporation

BME: Beaver, Meade and Englewood Railroad

BML: Belfast and Moosehead Lake

BMT: Brooklyn-Manhattan Transit (subway system)

BMRR: Beech Mountain Railroad

B & MRR: Beaufort and Morehead Railroad

BN: Burlington Northern (combining former Great Northern; Northern Pacific; Chicago, Burlington and Quincy; Spokane, Portland and Seattle; and Pacific Coast railroads)

B & N: Bauxite and Northern Railway

BNT: Buffalo Niagara Transit

B & O: Baltimore and Ohio Railroad (Chessie System)

BOCT: Baltimore and Ohio Chicago Terminal Railroad

BOYC: Boyne City Railroad

BR: British Railways; Burma Railways

BRC: Belt Railway Company of Chicago

BR & W: Black River and Western

BS: Birmingham Southern Railroad

B & S: Bevier and Southern

BTA: Boston Transportation Authority

BTC: Baltimore Transit Company

BTN: Belton Railroad

BU: Budapest Underground (subway system

Burlington Northern: combining Great Northern; Northern Pacific; Chicago, Burlington and Quincy; Spokane, Portland and Seattle; and Pacific Coast railroads)

Burlington Route: Chicago, Burlington and Quincy Railroad

BUSH: Bush Terminal Railroad

BVG: Berliner Verkehrs Betriebe (German—Berlin Traffic Management)—Berlin's subway system

BV & S: Bevier and Southern

BWC: Pennsylvania New York Central Transportation Company

BYR: British Yukon Railway

CAD: Cadiz Railroad

CAR: Central Australia Railway

CARR: Carrollton Railroad

CARW: Carolina Western Railroad

CASO: Canada Southern Railway

(Penn Central)

CBC: Carbon County Railway

CBL: Conemaugh and Black Lick

CB & Q: Chicago, Burlington and Quincy Railroad

CCCSL: Cleveland, Cincinnati, Chicago and St Louis Railway (Penn Central)

CCFPCS: Cie des Chemins de Fer de la Plaine du Cul-de-Sac (French—Cul-de-Sac Plaine Railroad Company)—Tahiti

CC & O: Carolina, Clinchfield and Ohio Railway

CC & ORSC: Carolina, Clinchfield and Ohio Railroad of South Carolina

CCR: Corinth and Counce Railroad

CCT: Central California Traction

C & EI: Chicago and Eastern Illinois Railroad

Central: (nickname—New York Central Railroad)—now part of the Penn Central

Central of Ga: Central of Georgia

CF: Cape Fear Railways

CF C-O: Chemin de Fer Congo-Ocean (French—Congo-Ocean Railroad)—Congo People's Republic (Brazzaville)

C de F D-N: Chemins de Fer Dakar-Niger (French—Dakar-Niger Railways)—Mali

CFF/SFF/FFS: Chemins de fer Federaux Suisses/Schweizerische Bundesbahnen/Ferrovie Dederali Svizzere (French, German, Italian—Swiss Federal Railways)

CFL: Societe Nationale des Chemins de fer Luxembourgeois (French—Luxembourg National Railways)

CFM: Caminho de Ferro de Moçambique (Portuguese—Mozambique Railroad); *Chemin de Fer Madagascar* (French—Madagascar Railroad)

CFR: Caile Ferate Ramane (Romanian—General Direction of the Romanian Railroads)

CFRC: Chemins de Fer Royaux du Cambodge (French—Royal Cambodian Railways)

CG: Central of Georgia Railway

C & G: Columbus and Greenville

C of G: Central of Georgia Railway

CGR: Ceylon Government Railway; Cyrenaica Government Railway (Libya)

C & GTR: Canada and Gulf Terminal Railway

CGW: Chicago Great Western

C & H: Cheswick and Harmer Railroad

Chessie System: Chesapeake & Ohio/Baltimore & Ohio

Chicago Outer Belt: Elgin, Joliet and Eastern Railway

Chihuahua-Pacific Railway: *Ferrocarril del Chihuahua al Pacific*—from the border of Texas at Presidio to the Pacific coast at Los Mochis via Chihuahua over route of the Kansas City, Mexico, and Orient

CH-P: Ferrocarril Chihuahua al Pacific. (Chihuahua-Pacific Railway formerly Mexico Northwestern Railway and Kansas City, Mexico and Orient Railway)

CHR: Chestnut Ridge Railway

CHTT: Chicago Heights Terminal Transfer Railroad

CHV: Chattahoochee Valley

CHW: Chesapeake Western

C & I : Cambria and Indiana Railroad

CIC: Cedar Rapids and Iowa City Railway

CIE: Coras Iompair Eireann (Gaelic—Irish State Railways)

CI & L: Chicago, Indianapolis, and Louisville Railway (Monon Railroad)

CIM: Chicago and Illinois Midland Railway (also C & IM)

CIND: Central Indiana Railway

CIRR: Chattahoochee Industrial Railroad

C & IRR: Cambria and Indiana Railroad

CIW: Chicago and Illinois Western Railroad

CIWL: Compangie Internationale des Wagon-Lits (French—International Sleeping Car Company)

CKSO: Condon, Kinzua and Southern Railroad

CLC: Columbia and Cowlitz

CLCO: Claremont and Concord

Clinchfield: Clinchfield Railroad (Carolina, Clinchfield and Ohio Railway)

CLK: Cadillac and Lake City Railway

CLP: Clarendon and Pittsford Railroad

CLRR: Camp Lejeune Railroad

CMO: Chicago, St Paul, Minneapolis and Omaha (Chicago North Western)

C M StP & P: Chicago, Milwaukee, St Paul and Pacific

CN: Canadian National (includes Canadian National Railways; Central Vermont Railway; Duluth, Winnipeg and Pacific Railway; Grand Trunk Lines in U.S.A.)

C & N: Carolina and Northwestern Railway

CNJ: Central Railroad of New Jersey

CN & L: Columbia, Newberry and Laurens Railroad

CNTP: Cincinnati, New Orleans and Texas Pacific

CNO & TPR: Cincinnati, New Orleans and Texas Pacific Railway

CNR: Chiriqui National Railroad (Panama)

CNW: Chicago and North Western Railway (includes Chicago, St Paul, Minneapolis and Omaha; Litchfield and Madison Railway; Minneapolis and St Louis)

C & NW: Chicago and North Western Railway

C & O: Chesapeake and Ohio (Chessie System)

Coahuila-Zacatecas Railway: Ferrocarril Coahuila-Zacatecas—Mexico

Cog Wheel Route: Manitou and Pike's Peak Railway

COP: City of Prineville Railway

COPR: Copper Range Railroad

Corn Belt Route: St Louis Southwestern Railway

Cotton Belt: Cotton Belt Route (St Louis Southwestern Railway—SSW)

CP: Canadian Pacific Railway (Dominion Atlantic Railway, Esquimalt and Nanaimo Railway, Grand River Railway, Lake Erie and Northern Railway, Quebec Central Railway, Vancouver and Lulu Island Branch)

CP: Companhia des Caminhos de ferro Portuguese (Portuguese—Portuguese Railways)

CPA: Coudersport and Port Allegany Railroad

CPF: Cotton Plant—Fargo Railway

CP & LT: Camino, Placerville and Lake Tahoe Railroad

CPR: Canadian Racific Railroad

CP Rail: Canadian Pacific Railroad

CPT: Chicago Produce Terminal

CR: Commonwealth Railways (Australia and Tasmania); Copper Range Railroad (Michigan, Wisconsin, Illinois)

CRANDIC Route: Cedar Rapids and Iowa City Railway

CRC: Cameroon Railways Corporation (West Africa); Cumberland Railway Company (Nova Scotia)

CRI: Chicago River and Indiana

CR & IC: Cedar Rapids and Iowa City Railway

CR & IR: Chicago River and Indiana Railroad

CRN: Carolina and Northwestern (Southern Railway)

CRP: Central Railway of Peru

CRR: Clinchfield Railroad

CRRNJ: Central Railroad of New Jersey

C & S: Colorado and Southern Railway

CSAR: Central South African Railways

CSD: Ceskoslovenske Statni Drahy (Czechoslovakian—Czechoslova State Railways)

CSL: Chicago Short Line Railway

CSP: Camas Prairie Railroad

CSS: Chicago South Shore and South Bend Railroad

CSS & SBR: Chicago South Shore and South Bend Railroad

C St P M & O: Chicago, St Paul, Minneapolis and Omaha (Chicago North Western)

CTA: Chicago Transit Authority (elevated and subway railroads)

CTC: Canadian Transport Commission; Cincinnati Transit Company

CTN: Canton Railroad

CTS: Cleveland Transit System

CUTC: Cincinnati Union Terminal Company

CUVA: Cuyahoga Valley Railroad

CV: Central Vermont Railway

CVRy: Cuyahoga Valley Railway

C & W: Colorado and Wyoming Railway

C & WC: Charleston and Western Carolina Railway (Seaboard Coast Line Railroad)

CWI: Chicago and Western Indiana

CWP: Chicago, West Pullman and Southern Railroad (also CWP & S)

CWR: California Western Railroad

DA: Dominion Atlantic Railway (Canadian Pacific)

DB: Deutsche Bundesbahn (German—German Railways)

DC: Delray Connecting Railroad

DCI: Des Moines and Central Iowa

DCR: Delray Connecting Railroad (Zug Island Road)

DCT: Washington, D.C. Transit

D & E: De Queen and Eastern

Delay Long and Wait: nickname for the Delaware, Lackawanna and Western Railroad (derived from the initials DL & W)

D & H: Delaware and Hudson

DHR: Darjeeling Himalayan Railway

diner: dining car

DKS: Doniphan, Kensett and Searcy Railway

DL & W: Delaware, Lackawanna and Western Railroad (Erie Lackawanna)

D & M: Detroit and Mackinac

DM & IRR: Duluth, Missabe and Iron Range Railway

DMM: Dansville and Mount Morris

DMU: Des Moines Union Railway

DMWR: Des Moines Western Railway

DNE: Duluth and Northeastern Railroad

DO: Direct Orient (Orient Express)

DORR: Delaware Otsego Railroad

DQ & ERR: De Queen and Eastern Railroad

D & R: Dardanelle and Russellville

D & RGW: Denver and Rio Grande Western Railroad

DRI: Davenport, Rock Island and North Western Railway

DRy: Devco Railway

DS: Durham and Southern Railway

D & S: Durham and Southern Railway

DSB: *Danske Statsbaner* (Danish—Danish State Railways)

DSR: Detroit Street Railways

DT: Detroit Terminal Railroad

D of T: Department of Transportation

DTC: Dallas Transit Company

DTI: Detroit, Toledo and Ironton Railroad (also DT & I)

D & TS: Detroit and Toledo Shore Line Railroad

DVS: Delta Valley and Southern Railway

DWP: Duluth, Winnipeg and Pacific Railway

E: Erie Lackawanna

EAR: East African Railways

EARC: East African Railways Corporation

EAR & H: East African Railways and Harbours

EBR: Emu Bay Railway (Tasmania)

EBRy: Eastern Bengal Railway (East Pakistan)

EDLR: Egyptian Delta Light Railways

EDW: El Dorado and Wesson

EEC: East Erie Commercial Railroad

EFA: *Empresa Ferrocarriles Argentinos* (Spanish—Argentine Railways Enterprise)

EFE: *Empresa de los Ferrocarriles del Estado* (Spanish—State Railways Enterprise)—Chile

EFEE: *Empresa de los Ferrocarriles del Estado Ecuatoriano* (Spanish—Ecuadorian State Railways Enterprise)

EJ & ERy: Elgin, Joliet and Eastern Railway

EJR: East Jersey Railroad

El: Elevated Railroad

EL: Erie Lackawanna Railway (merger of Erie with Delaware, Lackawanna and Western)

ELS: Escanaba and Lake Superior Railroad (also E & LSRR)

E & M: Edgmoor and Manetta

EN: Esquimalt and Nanaimo Railway (Canadian Pacific)

ENF: *Empresa Nacional de Ferrocarriles* (Spanish—National Railways Enterprise)—Bolivia

ER: Egyptian Railways

ERBR: Eastern Region of British Railways

Erie: Erie Railroad (Erie Lackawanna)

ESLJ: East St Louis Junction Railroad

ETL: Essex Terminal Railway

ET & WNC: East Tennessee and Western North Carolina Railroad

Eurailpass: European railroad pass (ticket system valid on almost all European railroads)

EW: East Washington Railway

EYB: *Europa Year Book*

F & C: Frankfort and Cincinnati Railroad

F de C: *Ferrocarriles de Cuba* (Spanish—Cuban Railroads)—Unidad Habana (western Cuba) and Unidad Camaguey (eastern Cuba)

FCAB: *Ferrocarril Antofagasta-Bolivia* (Spanish—Antofagasta and Bolivia Railway)

FCDN: *Ferrocarril del Nacozari* (Spanish—Nacozari Railroad)—Mexico

FCG: Fernwood, Columbia and Gulf Railroad

FCIN: Frankfort and Cincinnati

FCM: *Ferrocarriles Nacionales de México* (Spanish—Mexican National Railways)—includes Nacional de México and Nacional

de Tehuantepec

FCP: *Ferrocarril del Pacifico* (Spanish—Pacific Railroad)—links Arizona border with Mazatlan on west coast of Mexico

FC del P: *Ferrocarril Central del Perú* (Spanish—Central Railway of Peru)

FCZ: *Ferrocarril Coahuila-Zacatecas* (Spanish—Coahuila-Zacatecas Railway)—Mexico

FDDM: Fort Dodge, Des Moines and Southern Railway

Feather River Route: Western Pacific Railroad

FEC: Florida East Coast Railway

FEGUA: *Ferrocarriles de Guatemala* (Spanish—Railroads of Guatemala)

FEP: *Ferrocarril Electrico al Pacifico* (Spanish—Pacific Electric Railway)—Costa Rican line linking Pacific port of Puntarenas with mountain capital of San José

FER: Franco-Ethiopian Railway

FES: *Ferrocarril de El Salvador* (Spanish—El Salvador Railway)

F de G a LP: *Ferrocarril de Guayaquil–La Paz* (Spanish—Guayaquil–La Paz Railway)—Peru

FICA: *Ferrocarriles Internacionales de Centro America* (Spanish—International Railways of Central America)

FIPC: *Ferrocarril Industrial del Potosí y Chihuahua* (Spanish—Industrial Railroad of Potosi and Chihuahua)—Mexico

FJG: Fonda, Johnstown and Gloversville Railroad

FLR: Fayum Light Railways (Egypt)

FMS: Fort Myers Southern Railroad

FN: *Ferrocarriles Nacionales* (Spanish—National Railways—Argentina, Chile, Colombia, Cuba, Ecuador, Honduras, Mexico, Panama, Venezuela, etc.)

F del N: *Ferrocarriles del Norte* (Spanish—Northern Railways)—Paraguay

FNC: *Ferrocarriles Nacionales de Cuba* (National Railroads of Cuba nationalized by Castro government and consisting of Consolidated Railroads of Cuba—The Cuba Railroad—Cuba Northern Railways—Guantanamo and Western Railroad—Guantanamo Railroad—Hershey

Cuban Railway—et cetera)

FN de H: *Ferrocarriles Nacionales de Honduras* (Spanish—National Railways of Honduras)

FNM: *Ferrocarriles Nacionales de México* (Spanish—National Railways of Mexico)

FOM: *Ferrocarril Occidental de México* (Spanish—Western Railway of Mexico

FOR: Fore River Railroad

F del P: *Ferrocarril del Pacifico* (Spanish—Pacific Railroad)—Mexico

FPCAL: *Ferrocarriles President Carlos Antonio López* (Spanish—President Carlos Antonio Lopez Railways)—Paraguay

FPE: Fairport, Painesville and Eastern Railroad

FP & ER: Fairport, Painesville and Eastern Railway

FPN: *Ferrocarril del Pacifico de Nicaragua* (Spanish—Pacific Railway of Nicaragua)

FR: Feather River Railway

FRDN: Ferdinand Railroad

Frisco: St Louis-San Francisco Railway

FS: *Ferrovie dello Stato* (Italian—State Railway)

FSBC: Ferrocarril Sonora-Baja California (Sonora-Baja California Railroad)

FS del P: *Ferrocarril del Sur del Perú* (Spanish—Southern Railway of Peru)

FSVB: Fort Smith and Van Buren Railway (Kansas City Southern)

FtD DM & S: Fort Dodge, Des Moines and Southern Railway

FUD: *Ferrocarriles Unidos Dominicanos* (Spanish—United Dominican Railways)—Dominican Republic

FUS: Ferrocarriles Unidos del Sureste (United Railways of the Southeast)

FUY: *Ferrocarriles Unidos de Yucatan* (Spanish—United Railways of Yucatan)—Mexico

FWB: Fort Worth Belt Railway

FW & D: Fort Worth and Denver

GA: Georgia Railroad

GANO: Georgia Northern Railway

GASC: Georgia, Ashburn, Sylvester and Camilla Railway

GB & W: Green Bay and Western Lines (includes Kewaunee, Green Bay and Western Railroad)

GC: Graham County Railroad

GCW: Garden City Western Railway

George Washington's Railroad: Chesapeake and Ohio

Georgia: Georgia Railroad

G & F: Georgia and Florida Railway

GFS: Grand Falls Central Railway

GH & H: Galveston, Houston and Henderson Railroad

GJ: Greenwich and Johnsonville Railway

G & J: Greenwich and Johnsonville Railway

GM: Gainesville Midland Railroad

GM & O: Gulf, Mobile and Ohio Railroad

GMRC: Green Mountain Railroad Corporation

GN: Great Northern Railway

GNA: Graysonia, Nashville and Ashdown Railroad

GNW: Genessee and Wyoming Railroad

GNWR: Genesee and Wyoming Railroad

GO Transit: Government of Ontario Transit

G & Q: Guayaquil and Quito

Grand Trunk: Grand Trunk Railway System (Canadian National) and Grand Trunk Western Railroad

Green Bay Route: Green Bay and Western Railroad

GRN: Greenville and Northern Railway

GRNR: Grand River Railway (Canadian Pacific)

GR & PA: Ghana Railway and Port Authority

GRR: Georgetown Railroad

GRSS: Guyana Railways and Shipping Services

GSF: Georgia Southern and Florida (Southern)

GSW: Great Southwest Railroad

GTW: Grand Trunk Western Railroad (Canadian National)

G&U: Grafton and Upton Railroad

GWF: Galveston Wharves

GWR: Great Western Railway

GWWDR: Great Winnipeg Water District Railway

HB: Hampton and Branchville

HBLRR: Harbor Belt Line Railroad

HBS: Hoboken Shore Railroad

HBT: Houston Belt and Terminal

HE: Hollis and Eastern Railroad

HER: Hellenic Electric Railway (Athens-Piraeus subway system linking capital with its seaport)

HH: *Hamburger Hochbahn* (German—Hamburg Elevated Railway)—includes subway system

HI: Holton Inter-Urban Railway

HJR: Hedjaz Jordan Railway

HLNE: Hillsboro and Northeastern

HN: Hutchinson and Northern Railway

HNE: Harriman and Northeastern (Southern)

hovertrain: railroad train supported by an air cushion instead of wheels

HPTD: High Point, Thomasville and Denton Railroad

HRT: Hartwell Railway

HS: Hartford and Slocomb Railroad

HSW: Helena Southwestern Railroad

HTW: Hoosac Tunnel and Wilmington Railroad

i: Illinois Central Gulf Railroad

IAT: Iowa Terminal Railroad

IB&TC: International Bridge and Terminal Company

IC: Illinois Central Gulf (includes Mississippi Central)

ICC: Interstate Commerce Commission

IGA: Indian Government Administration (Railway Board of India)

IHB: Indiana Harbor Belt Railroad

IN: Illinois Northern Railway

IND: Independent (New York subway system)

Indiana Harbor Belt: "connects with all Chicago railroads"

Industrial Railway of Potosí and Chihuahua: (Ferrocarril Industrial del Potosí y Chihuahua)—Mexico

INT: Interstate Railroad

Interstate: Interstate Railroad

IPE: Indian-Pacific Express [Perth to Sydney—2461 miles (3960 kilometers) in 65 hours]

IR: Israel Railways

IRCA: International Railways of Central America (El Salvador, Guatemala, and Honduras)

IRN: Ironton Railroad

IRRys: Iraqi Republic Railways

IRT: Interborough Rapid Transit (New York City subway system)

IRS: Iranian State Railway

ITC: Illinois Terminal Company

ITRC: Iowa Transfer Railway Company

IU: Indiana Union Railway

JE: Jerseyville and Eastern

Jersey Central Lines: Central Railroad of New Jersey and Lehigh and New England

JHSC: Johnstown and Stony Creek Railroad

JNR: Japanese National Railways (world's fastest)
JRC: Jamaica Railway Corporation
JTC: Jacksonville Terminal Company
JWR: Jane's World Railways
Katy: Missouri-Kansas-Texas Railroad (MKT)
KBR: Kankakee Belt Route
KCC: Kansas City Connecting Railroad
KCMO: Kansas City, Mexico and Orient Railway (Ferrocarril Chihuahua al Pacifico)
KCNW: Kelley's Creek and Northwestern Railroad
KCPSFO: Kansas City Public Service Freight Operation
KCR: Kanawha Central Railway
K-C Ry: Kowloon-Canton Railway (Hong Kong)
KCS: Kansas City Southern Railway (includes Arkansas Western, Fort Smith and Van Buren, Louisiana and Arkansas railways)
KCT: Kansas City Terminal Railway
KGB: Kewaunee, Green Bay and Western Railroad (Green Bay and Western Lines)—also KGB&W
KIT: Kentucky and Indiana Terminal Railroad
K&M: Kansas and Missouri Railway and Terminal Company
KMRT: Kansas and Missouri Railway and Terminal Company
KNR: Klamath Northern Railway; Korean National Railways
KO&G: Kansas, Oklahoma and Gulf Railway
K&T: Kentucky and Tennessee
L&A: Louisiana and Arkansas Railway (Kansas City Southern)—also LA
LAJ: Los Angeles Junction Railway
LA&LR: Livonia, Avon and Lakeville Railroad
LAMCO: Liberian America Swedish Minerals Company (Liberian Railways)
Land of Evangeline Route: Dominion Atlantic Railway
LART: Los Angeles Rapid Transit
LAWV: Lorain and West Virginia Railway (Norfolk and Western)
LBR: Lowville and Beaver River Railroad
L&C: Lancaster and Chester Railway
LEE: Lake Erie and Eastern Railroad

LEF: Lake Erie, Franklin and Clarion Railroad
LE&FW: Lake Erie and Fort Wayne
LEN: Lake Erie and Northern Railway (Canadian Pacific)
LHR: Lehigh and Hudson River
LI: Long Island Railroad (Metropolitan Transportation Authority)—M
Lickenpurr: (Hawaiian nickname—Lahaina-Kaanapal and Pacific Rail Road)—nickname derived from abbreviation—LK&PRR
LK&PRR: Lahaina-Kaanapal and Pacific Rail Road (Maui, Hawaii)
LM: Litchfield and Madison Railway (Chicago North Western)—also L&M
LM: Leningrad Metro (Russian—Leningrad subway)
LMC: Liberia Mining Company
LMRBR: London Midland Region of British Railways
L&N: Louisville and Nashville Railroad
LNAC: Louisville, New Albany and Corydon Railroad
LNE: Lehigh and New England Railway (Central Railroad of New Jersey)
L&NR: Ludington and Northern Railway
L&NRY: Laona and Northern Railway
L&NW: Louisiana and North West Rail Road
LOPG: Live Oak, Perry and Gulf (Southern)
LPB: Louisiana and Pine Bluff Railway
LPN: Longview, Portland and Northern Railway
lrc (LRC): light, rapid, comfortable (high-speed railroad trans)
LRI: Lawndale Transportation Company
LRS: Laurinburg and Southern
L&S: Laurinburg and Southern
LS&BC: La Salle and Bureau County Railroad
LS&I: Lake Superior and Ishpeming Railroad
LSO: Louisiana Southern Railway (Southern)
LSR: Lebanese State Railroads
LST&TRC: Lake Superior Terminal and Transfer Railway Company
LT: Lake Terminal Railroad (also LTRR)

LRB: London Transport Board
LV: Lehigh Valley Railroad
LW: Louisville and Wadley Railway
L&W: Louisville and Wadley Railway
LWV: Lackawanna and Wyoming Valley Railway
M: Metropolitan Transit Authority (New York City's rapid-transit system); Metropolitan Transportation Authority (Long Island Railroad); Monon Railroad
MA: Magyan Allamvasutak (Hungarian—Hungarian State Railways)
MACR: Minneapolis, Anoka and Guyana Range Railroad
Main Line of Mid-America: Illinois Central Railroad
MARR: Magma Arizona Railroad
M-A Ry: Massawa-Agordad Railway (Ethiopia)
M&B: Meridan and Bigbee Railroad
MBI: Marianna and Bloustown Railroad
MBT: Marianna and Blountstown
MBTA: Massachusetts Bay Transportation Authority (Boston's Subway system)
MC: Michigan Central Railroad (Penn Central)
McR: McCloud River Railroad
MCRR: Maine Central Road; Monongahela Connecting Railroad
MCSA: Moscow, Camden and San Augustine Railroad
MD: Municipal Docks Railway of the Jacksonville Port Authority
MD&W: Minnesota, Dakota and Western Railway
M&E: Morristown and Erie Railroad
MEC: Maine Central Railroad
METC: Medesto and Empire Traction Company
Metro: (French short form—*Chemin de fer Metropolitain*)—Paris subway system
Metropolitano: Rome's subway system
Mexican Pacific Railroad: Ferrocarril Mexicano del Pacifico—Los Mochis to Camp
MF: Middle Fork Railroad
MGA: Monongahela Railway
MGU: Mobile and Gulf Railroad
MHM: Mount Hope Mineral Railroad
M&HMRR: Marquette and Huron Mountain Railroad
MI: Missouri-Illinois Railroad

MICO: Midland Continental Railroad

MID: Midway Railroad

MILW: Chicago, Milwaukee, St Paul and Pacific Railroad (Milwaukee Road)

Milwaukee Road: Chicago, Milwaukee, St Paul and Pacific Railroad

MINE: Minneapolis Eastern Railway

MIR: Minneapolis Industrial Railway

Mitropa: *Mitteleuropaische Schlaf und Speiswagen* (German—Middle-European Sleeping Car and Dining Car)

MJ: Manufacturers' Junction Railway

MKC: McKeesport Connecting Railroad

MKT: Missouri-Kansas-Texas Railroad (Katy)

MLD: Midland Railway of Manitoba

MLS: Manistique and Lake Superior Railroad

MMR: Moscow Metro Railway (Moscow's radiating subway system famed for its beautiful stations)

MNF: Morehead North Fork Railroad

MNJ: Middletown and New Jersey Railway

MNS: Minneapolis, Northfield and Southern Railway

MOB: Montreux-Oberland-Bernois (railway)

MON: Monon Railroad

Monon: Monon Railroad (formerly Chicago, Indianapolis and Louisville Railway)

Mon Rys: Mongolian Railways

Montour: Montour Railroad (Youngstown and Southern Railway)

MOP: Missouri-Pacific Lines

Mo-Pac: Missouri-Pacific Lines

MOV: Moshassuck Valley Railroad

MOW: Montana Western Railway

MP: Missouri Pacific Railroad

M del P: Méxicano del Pacifico (Mexican Pacific Railroad formerly Southern Pacific of Mexico)

MPA: Maryland and Pennsylvania

MPB: Montpelier and Barre Railroad

MPPR: Manitou and Pike's Peak Railway

MR: McCloud River Railroad (also McRRR)

M of R: Ministry of Railways

(mainland China)

MRA: Malayan Railway Administration

MRL: Malawi Railways Limited

MRR: Mattagami Railroad (Ontario); Mossi Railroad (Upper Volta)

MRS: Manufacturers Railway

MRy: Malayan Railway

MSC: Mississippi Central (Illinois Central)

MSE: Mississippi Export Railroad

M St L: Minneapolis and St. Louis (Chicago North Western)

M&StL: Minneapolis-St Louis (Chicago North Western)

MSTL: Minneapolis-St Louis (Chicago North Western)

MSTR: Massena Terminal Railroad

MSV: Mississippi and Skuna Valley Railroad

MT: Ministry of Transport (USSRs administration of twenty-six railway lines including the de-luxe Leningrad-Moscow and the transcontinental Trans-Siberian linking Moscow with Vladivostok)

MTC: Milwaukee Transport Company; Montreal Transportation Commission (subway and surface railways); Mystic Terminal Company (Boston and Maine)

MTFR: Minnesota Transfer Railroad

MTH: Mount Hood Railway

MTR: Montour Railroad

MTW: Marinette, Tomahawk and Western Railroad

MTWCR: Mt Washington Cog Railway

MWR: Muncie and Western Railroad

NAJ: Napierville Junction Railway

NAP: Narragansett Pier Railroad

NAR: Northern Alberta Railways; Northern Australia Railway

National Railroads of Cuba: Ferrocarriles Nacionales de Cuba (includes nationalized lines of the Cuba Railroad, Cuba Northern Railways, Guantanamo Railroad, Guantanamo Western, Hershey Cuban Railway, etc.)

National Railways of Mexico: Ferrocarriles de México

NB: Northampton and Bath Railroad

NC & StL: Nashville, Chattanooga and St Louis Railway (L&N)

New Haven: New York, New Haven and Hartford Railroad

NEZP: Nezperce Railroad

NFD: Norfolk, Franklin and Dan-

ville Railway

NGR: Nepalese Government Railway

NH: New York, New Haven and Hartford Railroad (Penn Central)

NHIR: New Hope and Ivyland Railroad

Nickel Plate: New York, Chicago and St Louis Railroad (merged with Norfolk and Western)

NJ: Niagara Junction Railway

NJI&I: New Jersey, Indiana and Illinois Railroad

NKP: Nickel Plate (New York, Chicago and St Louis Railroad) —merged with Norfolk and Western

NLC: New Orleans and Lower Coast Railroad

NLG: North Louisiana and Gulf Railroad

NM: Nagoya Municipality (subway system)

N de M: Nacional de México (National of Mexico)

NN: Nevada Northern Railway

NNC: Northern Navigation Company

NODM: Ferrocarril Noroeste de México (Northwest Railway of Mexico—Ferrocarril Chihuahua al Pacífico)

NO de M: Noroeste de México (Northwestern of Mexico)

NONE: New Orleans and Northeastern Railroad (Southern)

NOPB: New Orleans Public Belt Railroad

NOPS: New Orleans Public Service

NP: Northern Pacific Railway

N&PB: Norfolk and Portsmouth Belt Line Railroad

NR: Newfoundland Railway (Canadian National); Northern Railway of Costa Rica (from mountain capital of San José to Caribbean seaport of Limón)

NRC: Nigerian Railway Corporation

NRPC: National Railroad Passenger Corporation (Amtrak)

NRRC: National Railroad Company (of Haiti)

NS: Norfolk Southern Railway

NS: *Nederlandsche Spoorwagen* (Dutch—Netherlands Railway Carriage)—Netherlands Railways

NSB: *Norges Statsbaner* (Norwegian—Norwegian State Railways)

NSL: Norwood and St Lawrence Railroad

NSS: Newburgh and South Shore Railway

NSWGR: New South Wales Government Railways

N de T: Nacional de Tehuantepec (Tehuantepec National)

NUR: Natchez, Urania and Ruston Railway

NW: Norfolk and Western

N&W: Norfolk and Western Railway

NWP: Northwestern Pacific Railroad

NWRy: North Western Railway (West Pakistan)

NYC: New York Central Railroad (Penn Central)

NYCTA: New York City Transit Authority (subway systems include BMT, IRT, INDependent)

NYD: New York Dock Railway

NYLB: New York and Long Branch Railroad

NYNH&H: New York, New Haven and Hartford Railroad

NYS: Nepal Yatayat Samsthan (Nepali—Transport Corporation of Nepal)

NYSW: New York, Susquehanna and Western Railroad (NYS&W)

NZGR: New Zealand Government Railways

NZR: New Zealand Railways

ÖOB: Österreichischen Bundesbahnen (German—Austrian State Railways)

OE: Oregon Electric Railway (Spokane, Portland, and Seattle Railway)

OCE: Oregon, California and Eastern Railway

OGR: Official Guide of the Railways

OKT: Oakland Terminal Railway

OL&BR: Omaha, Lincoln and Beatrice Railway

OMTB: Osaka Metropolitan Transportation Bureau (subway system)

ONCF: Office National des Chemins de Fer (French—National Railways Office)—Morocco

ONRY: Ogdensburg and Norwood Railway

O&NW: Oregon and Northwestern

ONT: Ontario Northland Railway

ONW: Oregon and Northwestern

OPE: Oregon, Pacific and Eastern

ORER: Official Railway Equipment Register

OT: Oregon Trunk Railway (Spokane, Portland, and Seattle Railway)

OUR&D: Ogden Union Railway and Depot

Overland Route: Union Pacific Railroad

PA: Pittsburgh Authority (rapid transit)

PAA: Pennsylvania and Atlantic Railroad

PACC: Pacific Coast Railroad

Pacific Railroad: Ferrocarril del Pacifico (linking American border at Nogales with Mazatlan on Pacific coast of Mexico)

Pacific Railway of Costa Rica: from Pacific port of Puntarenas to San José)

Pacific Railways of Nicaragua: Ferrocarril del Pacifico de Nicaragua—from Corinto on the Pacific to Granada on Lake Nicaragua

PA&M: Pittsburgh, Allegheny and McKees Rocks Railroad

Panama Railroad: Division of the Panama Canal linking Cristóbal and Colón on the Atlantic with Balboa and Panama City on the Pacific and running parallel to the Panama Canal

P&AR: Pacific and Arctic Railway

PATCO: (transportation system linking Camden, New Jersey and Philadelphia, Pennsylvania)

PATH: Port Authority Trans-Hudson Corporation (operates Hudson Tubes between New Jersey and New York)

PBNE: Philadelphia, Bethlehem and New England Railroad

PBR: Patapsco and Back Rivers

PC: Penn Central (Pennsylvania New York Central Transportation Company: Pennsylvania Railroad; New York Central Railroad; New York, New Haven, and Hartford Railroad; Baltimore and Eastern Railroad; Canada Southern Railway; Cleveland, Cincinnati, Chicago and St Louis Railway; Michigan Central Railroad; Peoria and Eastern Railway; Waynesburg and Washington Railroad)

PCL: Peruvian Corporation Limited

PCN: Point Comfort and Northern

PCR: Paraguayan Central Railway

PCY: Pittsburgh, Chartiers and Youghiogheny Railway

PE: Pacific Electric (interurban railway system serving entire Los Angeles area before replacement by smog-producing buses); Pacific Electric Railway of Costa Rica (links Pacific seaport of

Puntarenas with mountain capital of San José)—also called FEP

P&E: Peoria and Eastern Railway (Penn Central)

Pennsy: (nickname—Pennsylvania Railroad)—now part of the Penn Central

Peoria: Peoria and Pekin Union Railway

P&F: Pioneer and Fayette Railroad

PGE: Pacific Great Eastern Railway

PH&D: Port Huron and Detroit Railroad

P&I: Paducah and Illinois Railroad

PIC: Pickens Railroad

Pick: Pickens Railroad

Pickens: Pickens Railroad

PKP: Polskie Koleje Panstwowe (Polish—Polish State Railways)

P&LE: Pittsburgh and Lake Erie Railroad

PLM: Paris-Lyon-Mediterranée

P&N: Piedmont and Northern Railway

PNKA: Perusahaan Negara Kereta Api (Indonesian—Indonesian State Railways)

PNR: Philippine National Railways

PNW: Prescott and Northwestern Railroad

Port St Joe Route: Apalachicola Northern Railroad

'Possum Trot Line: Reader Railroad

P&OV: Pittsburgh and Ohio Valley

P&PU: Peoria and Pekin Union

PR: Panama Railroad

P-R: Pennsylvania-Reading Seashore Lines

PRC: Philippine Railway Company

PRCR: Pacific Railway Costa Rica

PRR: Pennsylvania Railroad (Penn Central)

PRS: Pennsylvania-Reading Seashore Lines

PRTD: Portland Railroad and Terminal Division of the Portland Traction Company

PRV: Pearl River Valley Railroad

P y RV: Potosí y Rio Verde (Spanish—Potosi and Green River Railroad of Chihuahua)

PS: Pittsburg and Shawmut Railroad

P&SR: Petaluma and Santa Rosa

PTC: Peoria Terminal Company; Philadelphia Transportation Company (also called PATCO includes elevated and subway lines of Philadelphia area)

PTM: Portland Terminal Company

PTR: Parr Terminal Railroad

PTS: Port Townsend Railroad

Pullman: de-luxe railroad cars providing lounging, observation, and sleeping facilities aboard first-class express trains

PVS: Pecos Valley Southern

P&WV: Pittsburgh and West Virginia Railway (Norfolk and Western)

QAP: Quanah, Acme and Pacific

QC: Quebec Central Railway (Canadian Pacific)

QNS&LRC: Quebec North Shore and Labrador Railway Company

QR: Queensland Railways

Quanah Route: Quanah, Acme and Pacific Railway

QUI: Quincy Railroad

RC: Railway Corporation (Nigeria)

RCFA-N: *Regie du Chemin de Fer Abidjan-Niger* (French—Abidjan-Niger Railway Administration)—Ivory Coast

RD: Railway Directorate (Albania)

RDG: Reading Company (formerly Philadelphia and Reading Railroad)

REA: Railway Express Agency; Reader Railroad

Reading Lines: Reading Railway System (formerly Philadelphia and Reading Railroad)

Rebel Route: Gulf, Mobile and Ohio Railroad

RENFE: *Red Nacional de los Ferrocarriles Españoles* (Spanish—Spanish National Railway System)

RFFSA: *Rede Ferroviária Federal SA* (Portuguese—Federal Railway System Corporation— Brazil

RFP: Richmond, Fredericksburg and Potomac Railroad (RF&P)

RF&PRR: Richmond, Fredericksburg and Potomac Railroad

RI: Chicago, Rock Island and Pacific Railroad

Rio Grande: Denver and Rio Grande Western

RKG: Rockingham Railroad

RM: *Rotterdam Metro* (Dutch—Rotterdam Subway)

RNCF: *Reseau National des Chemins de Fer* (French—National Railway System)—Madagascar

Rock Island: Chicago, Rock Island and Pacific Railroad

RR: (abbreviation—Railroad or Rail Road); (reporting mark —Raritan River Rail Road); Rhodesian Railways

RRRR: Raritan River Railroad

RRys: Rhodesian Railways

RS: Roberval and Seguenay Railway

RSP: Roscoe, Snyder and Pacific

R-S Pacific Route: Roscoe, Snyder and Pacific Railway

RSS: Rockdale, Sandow and Southern Railroad

RT: River Terminal Railway

RTM: Railway Transfer Company of Minneapolis

RV: Rahway Valley Railway

Ry: Railway

S&A: Savannah and Atlanta Railway

SAL: Seaboard Airline Railroad (Seaboard Coast Line Railroad is official name adopted to avoid confusion with an airline)

SAN: Sandersville Railroad

Santa Fe: Atchison, Topeka and Santa Fe Railway

SAR: South African Railways; South Australian Railways

SAR&H: South African Railways and Harbours

SATS: San Antonio Transit System

SAVE: Swiss-Alberg-Vienna Express

SB: South Buffalo Railway

SBA: *Subterraneos de Buenos Aires* (Spanish—Buenos Aires Subways)

SBC: Ferrocarril Sonora Baja California (Sonora—Baja California Railway)

SBK: South Brooklyn Railway

SC: Sumter and Choctaw Railway

SCE: Shanghai-Canton Express

SCL: Seaboard Coast Line Railroad (Atlantic Coast Line Railroad, Charleston and Western Carolina Railway, Seaboard Air Line Railroad—former name of the Seaboard Coast Line Railroad)

SC&MR: Strouds Creek and Muddlety Railroad

SCT: Sioux City Terminal Railway

SDAE: San Diego and Arizona Eastern Railway

SD&AE: San Diego and Arizona Eastern Railway

SDTS: San Diego Transit System

SE: Ferrocarril del Sureste (Southeast Railroad)

Seashore Lines: Pennsylvania-Reading Seashore Lines

SERA: Sierra Railroad

SFBRR: San Francisco Belt Railroad

SFMR: San Francisco Municipal Railway (operates the cable cars)

SG: South Georgia Railway (Southern Railway)

SGR: Sa'udi Government Railroad (Saudi Arabia); Surinam Government Railway (Netherlands Guiana)

SH: Steelton and Highspire Railroad

Shawmut: The Pittsburg and Shawmut Railroad

SHK: *Sidirodromi Hellinikou Kratous* (Greek—Hellenic State Railways)—Greece

SI: Spokane International Railroad

SIR: Staten Island Rapid Transit Railway

SIRRI: Southern Industrial Railroad Incorporated

SJ: *Statens Jarnvargar* (Swedish—State Railways)

SJB: St Joseph Belt Railway

SJL: St Johnsbury and Lamoille County Railroad

SJ&LC: St Johnsbury and Lamoille County Railroad

SJTR: St Joseph Terminal Railroad

SKSL: Skaneateles Short Line Railroad

SLC: San Luis Central Railroad

SLGW: Salt Lake, Garfield and Western Railway

SLR: Sierra Leone Railway

SLSF: St Louis-San Francisco Railway

SM: St Marys Railroad

SMA: San Manuel Arizona Railroad

SMR: South Manchurian Railway

SMV: Santa Maria Valley Railroad

SN: Sacramento Northern Railway (also SNRy)

SNCB: *Societe Nationale des Chemins de fer Belges* (French —Belgian National Railways)

SNCF: *Societe Nationale des Chemins de fer Français* (French —French National Railways)

SNCFA: *Societe Nationale des Chemins de Fer Algeriens* (French —Algerian National Railways)

SNY: Southern New York Railway

SOE: Simplon-Orient Express

SOI: Southern Indiana Railway

Sonora—Baja California Railway: Ferrocarril Sonora—Baja California—Mexicali to Benjamin Hill

SOO: Soo Line Railroad

$oo Line: Soo Line Railroad

SOT: South Omaha Terminal Railway

Southern: Southern Railway System (Alabama Great Southern Railroad; Carolina and North-

417

western Railway; Cincinnati, New Orleans and Texas Pacific Railway; Georgia Southern and Florida Railway; Harriman and Northeastern Railroad; Live Oak, Perry and Gulf Railroad; Louisiana Southern Railway; New Orleans and Northeastern Railroad; South Georgia Railway)

Southern Pacific: SP

South Shore Line: Chicago South Shore and South Bend Railroad

SP: Southern Pacific (includes Southern Pacific Lines, Sunset Railway, Texas and Louisiana Lines, Texas and New Orleans, etc.)—in fact many school children once said the United States was bounded on the north by Canada and the Great Lakes, on the east by the Atlantic Ocean, and on the south and southwest by the Southern Pacific

SPGT: Springfield Terminal Railway

SPS: Spokane, Portland and Seattle Railway (includes Oregon Electric and Oregon Trunk railways)

SR: Southern Railway

SRBR: Southern Region of British Railways

SRC: Salvador Railway Company (El Salvador)

SRN: Sabine River and Northern

SRRC: Sierra Railroad Company; Strasburg Rail Road Company

SRRCO: Sandersville Railroad Company

SRT: State Railways of Thailand (Siam)

SSDK: Savannah State Docks Railroad

SSLVRR: Southern San Luis Valley Railroad

SSRy: Sand Springs Railway

SSW: St Louis Southwestern Railway (Cotton Belt Route)

STE: Stockton Terminal and Eastern Railroad

STRT: Stewartstown Railroad

STS: Seattle Transit System

SU: Stockholm Underground (subway system)

Sub: Suburban; Subway

Sud Rys: Sudan Railways

SUR: Soviet Union Railways (managed by Ministry of Communications and comprising some twenty-six lines including the Trans-Mongolian and the Trans-Siberian as well as the plush Leningrad-Moscow express)

Susquehanna: New York, Susquehanna and Western Railroad

Syr Rys: Syrian Railways

TAAA: Travelers Aid Association of America

TA&G: Tennessee, Alabama and Georgia Railway

TAG Route: Tennessee, Alabama and Georgia Railway

Tan-Zam: Tanzania-Zambia Railroad

TAR: Trans-Australian Railways

TAS: Tampa Southern Railroad

TASD: Terminal Railway Alabama State Docks

TA&W: Toledo, Angola and Western Railway

TB: Twin Branch Railroad

TBTMG: Transportation Bureau of the Tokyo Metropolitan Government (subway)

TC: Tennessee Central Railway

TCDD: *Turkiye Cumhuriyeti Deviet Demiryollari Isletmesi* (Turkish—Turkish State Railways)

TCG: Tucson, Cornelia and Gila Bend Railroad

TCT: Texas City Terminal Railway

TEBRCL: The Emu Bay Railway Company Limited

TEE: Trans-Europe Express

TENN: Tennessee Railroad

TEXC: Texas Central Railroad

THB: Toronto, Hamilton and Buffalo Railway

The Q: CB&Q (Chicago, Burlington and Quincy)

TM: Texas Mexican Railway; Transport Ministry (USSRs administration of twenty-six railway lines)—TM sometimes used on engines

TMR: Trans-Mongolian Railway

TN: Texas and Northern Railway

T-NM: Texas-New Mexico Railway

T&NO: Texas and New Orleans (Southern Pacific)—also TNO

TOC: Pennsylvania New York Central Transportation Company (Penn Central)

TOE: Texas, Oklahoma and Eastern Railroad

TOV: Tooele Valley Railway

T&P: Texas and Pacific Railway (also TP)

TPMP: Texas-Pacific-Missouri Pacific Terminal Railroad of New Orleans

TPT: Trenton-Princeton Traction Company

TP&W: Toledo, Peoria and Western Railroad

TR: Tasmanian Railways

TRA: Taiwan Railway Administration

Trans-Sib: Trans-Siberian Railway

TRC: Tela Railway Company (Honduras); Trona Railway Company (California)

TRRA: Terminal Railroad Association of St Louis

TS: Tidewater Southern Railway

TS-E: Texas South-Eastern

TSR: Trans-Siberian Railway

TSU: Tulsa-Sapulpa Union Railway

TT: Toledo Terminal Railroad

T&T: Tijuana and Tecate Railway (freight cars marked TITE)

TTC: Toronto Transit Commission (subway and surface railway systems)

TVG: Tavares and Gulf Railroad

TVRy: Tooele Valley Railway

Tweetsie: (nickname—East Tennessee and Western North Carolina Railroad)—believed to be derived from high-pitched whistles of its engines

T-Z RA: Tanzania-Zambia Railway Authority

U: Underground (London's subway system)

UBR: Ulan Bator Railway

UCR: Utah Coal Route

UFC: United Fruit Company (railroads in Costa Rica and Panama)

UMP: Upper Merion and Plymouth Railroad

UNF: Union Freight Railroad

UNI: Unity Railways

UO: Union Railroad—Oregon

UP: Union Pacific Railroad (includes Oregon Short Line and Oregon-Washington Railroad and Navigation Company)

URR: Union Railroad—Pittsburgh

USSR: (Ministry of Railways administers operation of twenty-six railway boards throughout the USSR)

UT: Union Terminal Railway

UTA: Ulster Transport Authority (railways of six counties in Northern Ireland)

UTAH: Utah Railway

Utah Coal Route: Utah Railway

UTR: Union Transportation Company

U de Y: *Unidos de Yucatan* (Spanish—United Railways of Yucatan, Mexico)

V: *Valtionrautatiet* (Finnish—State Railways)

VBR: Virginia Blue Ridge Railway

VC: Virginia Central Railway

VCS: Virginia and Carolina Southern Railroad
VCY: Ventura County Railway
VE: Visalia Electric Railroad
VGN: Virginian Railway (Norfolk and Western)
Virginian: Virginian Railway (Norfolk and Western)
V&LI: Vancouver and Lulu Island (branch of Canadian Pacific)
V-MNR: Viet-Minh National Railways (North Vietnam)
V-NR: Viet-Nam Railways (South Vietnam)
VR: Victorian Railways (Australia)
V Ry: Verapaz Railway (Guatemala)
VSL: Valley and Siletz Railroad
VSO: Valdosta Southern Railroad
VTR: Vermont Railway
W of A: Western Railway of Alabama
WAB: Wabash Railroad (Norfolk and Western)
Wabash: Wabash Railroad (Norfolk and Western)
WAG: Wellsville, Addison and Galeton Railroad
WAGR: Western Australian Government Railways
WATC: Washington Terminal Company
WAW: Waynesburg and Washington Railroad (Penn Central)
WBCRR: Wilkes-Barre Connecting Railroad
WBT&SRC: Waco, Beaumont, Trinity and Sabine Railway Company
Western Railway of Mexico: Ferrocarril Occidental de México—Culiacan to Limoncito
West Point Route: Atlanta and West Point Rail Road

WHBR: Western Region of British Railways
White Pass: British Columbia Yukon Railway, British Yukon Railway, Pacific and Arctic Railway
White Pass and Yukon Route: British Columbia Yukon Railway, British Yukon Navigation, British Yukon Railway, Pacific and Arctic Railway and Navigation Company
WIM: Washington, Idaho and Montana Railway
WL: *Wagon Lits* (French—sleeping cars)
WLO: Waterloo Railroad
WM: Western Maryland Railway
WMTA: Washington Metropolitan Transit Authority (subway system)
WMWN: Weatherford, Mineral Wells and Northwestern Railway
WMR: Wasatch Mountain Railway
WNF: Winfield Railroad
W&NO: Wharton and Northern Railroad
WOD: Washington and Old Dominion Railroad
W&OV: Warren and Ouachita Valley Railway
WP: Western Pacific Railroad
WPER: West Pittston-Exeter Railroad
WP&Y: White Pass and Yukon Railway
WRA: Western Railroad Association
WRNT: Warrenton Railroad
WRWK: Warwick Railway
WS: Ware Shoals Railroad
WSR: Warren and Saline River
WSS: Winston-Salem Southbound

Railway
WSYP: White Sulphur Springs and Yellowstone Park Railway
WTR: Wrightsville and Tennille Railroad
WVN: West Virginia Northern Railroad
WW: Winchester and Western Railroad
WWV: Walla Walla Valley Railway
WYS: Wyandotte Southern Railroad
WYT: Wyandotte Terminal Railroad
X: express; transport; transportation (as in many private bulk carriers' names such as GATX—General American Transportation)
Xing: crossing (highway or railroad)—also XING
Y&N: Youngstown and Northern Railroad
YAN: Yancey Railroad
YR: Yucatan Railways (*Ferrocarriles Unidos del Sureste* —United Railways of the Southeast) —along the Gulf of Mexico from Coatzacoalcos to Merida
YS: Youngstown and Southern Railway (Montour)
Y&S: Yakutat and Southern Railway
YVT: Yakima Valley Transportation Company
YW: Yreka Western Railroad
ZJZ: *Zajednica Jugoslovenskih Zalesnicca* (Yugoslavian—Community of Yugoslav Railways)
ZR: Zambia Railways
Zug Island Road: Delray Connecting Railroad (DC)

ROMAN NUMERALS

I: 1	LV: 55	DCCC: 800
II: 2	LIX: 59	CM: 900
III: 3	LX: 60	M: 1000
IV: 4	LXV: 65	MD: 1500
V: 5	LXIX: 69	MDC: 1600
VI: 6	LXX: 70	MDCC: 1700
VII: 7	LXXV: 75	MDCCC: 1800
VIII: 8	LXXIX: 79	MCM or MDCCCC: 1900
IX: 9	LXXX: 80	MCMX: 1910
X: 10	LXXXV: 85	MCMXX: 1920
XV: 15	LXXXIX: 89	MCMXXX: 1930
XIX: 19	XC: 90	MCMXL: 1940
XX: 20	XCV: 95	MCML: 1950

XXV: 25	XCIX: 99	MCMLX: 1960
XXIX: 29	C: 100	MCMLXX: 1970
XXX: 30	CL: 150	MCMLXXX: 1980
XXV: 35	CC: 200	MCMXC: 1990
XXXIX: 39	CCC: 300	MM: 2000
XL: 40	CD: 400	MMM: 3000
XLV: 45	D: 500	MMMM or $\overline{MV}$: 4000
XLIX: 49	DC: 600	$\overline{V}$: 5000
L: 50	DCC: 700	$\overline{M}$: 1,000,000

RUSSIAN ALPHABET TRANSLITERATED

Russian Capital Letters	English Capital Letters	Russian Small Letters	English Small Letters	Russian Alphabet Letter Names	Nearest English Equivalent Sounds
А	A	а	a	*ah*	*a* as in *a*rch
Б	B	б	b	*beh*	*b* as in *b*it
В	V	в	v	*veh*	*v* as in *v*est
Г	G	г	g	*geh*	*g* as in *g*et
Д	D	д	d	*deh*	*d* as in *d*ay
Е	Ye	е	ye	*yeh*	*y* as in *y*es
Ж	Zh	ж	zh	*zheh*	*zh* sound as in mea*s*ure
З	Z	з	z	*zeh*	*z* as in *z*ero
И	I	и	i	*ee*	*i* as in p*ee*l
Й	Y	й	y	*ee s krátkoi*	(short *i* after vowels
К	K	к	k	*kah*	*k* as in *k*ite
Л	L	л	l	*el*	*l* as in woo*l*
М	M	м	m	*em*	*m* as in *m*an
Н	N	н	n	*en*	*n* as in *n*ow
О	O	о	o	*oh*	*o* as in h*o*ax
П	P	п	p	*peh*	*p* as in *p*encil
Р	R	р	r	*err*	*r* as in *r*ye
С	S	с	s	*ess*	*s* as in *s*ay
Т	T	т	t	*teh*	*t* as in *t*ent
У	Oo	у	oo	*ooh*	*oo* as in l*oo*se
Ф	F	ф	f	*eff*	*f* as in *f*ancy
Х	Kh	х	kh	*khan*	*kh* as in lo*ch*
Ц	Ts	ц	ts	*tseh*	*ts* as in ha*ts*
Ч	Ch	ч	ch	*cheh*	*ch* as in *ch*air
Ш	Sh	ш	sh	*shah*	*sh* as in *sh*ave
Щ	Shch	ш	shch	*shchah*	*shch* as in Iri*sh* *ch*uck
Ъ		ъ		*tvyórdy znak*	(silent-hard sound)
Ы	Y	ы	y	*yery*	*y* as *i* in h*i*t
Ь		ь		*myakhki znak*	(silent)
Э	Eh	э	eh	*eh oborótnoye*	*eh* sound as in d*e*bt
Ю	Yu	ю	yu	*yoo*	*yu* as in *yo*u
Я	Ya	я	ya	*yah*	*ya* as in *ya*m

SHIP'S BELL TIME SIGNALS

1 bell —12:30 or 4:30 or 8:30 a.m. or p.m.

2 bells—	1:00	5:00	9:00
3 bells—	1:30	5:30	9:30
4 bells—	2:00	6:00	10:00
5 bells—	2:30	6:30	10:30
6 bells—	3:00	7:00	11:00
7 bells—	3:30	7:30	11:30
8 bells—	4:00	8:00	12:00

On many vessels the ship's whistle is blown at noon. On some ships a lightly struck 1 bell announces 15 minutes before the change of watch, usually at 4, 8, and 12 o'clock.

The ship's day starts at noon. The *afternoon watch* is from noon to 4 p.m. The 4 to 8 work period is called the *dogwatch*. From 8 p.m. to midnight is the *first watch*. From midnight to 4 a.m. is the *middle watch*. From 8 a.m. to noon is the *forenoon watch*.

SIGNS AND SYMBOLS FREQUENTLY USED

+ add; addition sign; north; plus
& and (ampersand)
&c et cetera (and so forth)
* asterisk
@ at
∴ because
¢ centavo; centime; cent(s)
© copyright
° degree(s)
÷ divide; divided by; division sign
$ dollar sign—used universally for monetary units as diverse as Nicaraguan cordobas; Brazilian cruzeiros; Australian, Bahamian, Barbadian, British Honduran, Canadian, Ethiopian, Guyanian, Hong Kongese, Levantine, Liberian, Malaysian, New Zealand, Taiwan, trade, Trinidadian-Tobagonian, U.S., Viet Namese, West Indian, yuan dollars; Portuguese escudos; Honduran lempiras; Brazilian milreis; Chilean, Colombian, Cuban, Dominican, Mexican, Philippine, Uruguayan pesos; Peruvian soles (often with a lower-case dollar sign, $); Chinese yuans
$A Australian dollar(s)
$b Bolivian peso(s)
$B Bahamian, Barbadian, British dollar(s)
$BH British Honduran dollar(s)
$C Brazilian cruzeiro(s); Canadian dollar(s)
$Col Colombian peso(s)

$E Ethiopian dollar(s)
$Eth Ethiopian dollar(s)
$G Guyanian dollar(s)
$HK Hong Kong dollar(s)
$K $1000 (e.g. $13K = $13,000)
$L Levant(ine) dollar(s)—Maria Theresa thaler(s); Liberian dollar(s)
$M Malay(sian) dollar(s)
$Mal Malay(sian) dollar(s)
$Mex Mexican peso(s)
$NT New Taiwan dollar(s)
$NZ New Zealand dollar(s)
$RD Republica Dominicana peso(s)—Dominican Republic monetary unit(s)
$S Singapore dollar(s)
$T Taiwan dollar(s); trade dollar(s); Trinidad(ian) and Tobago(nian) dollar(s)
$TT Trinidad(ian) and Tobago(nian) dollar(s)
$Ur Uruguayan peso(s)
$US United States dollar(s) [also shown as US$, as are other monetary units where national designations often precede dollar sign: C$—Canadian dollar(s), HK$— Hong Kong dollar(s)]
$VN Viet Namese dollar(s)
$WI West Indian dollar(s); West Indies dollar(s)
$Y yuan dollar(s)
= equality; equals; equal to
G Paraguayan guarani(s)
K certified kosher
LC Cyrian pound(s)

LR Rhodesian pound(s)
− minus; south; subtract; subtraction sign
× multiplication sign; multiplied by; multiply
≥ equal to or greater than
≤ equal to or less than
> greater than
< less than
>> much greater than
<< much less than
fracture(s) (medical); number(s) or pound(s) (commercial); sharp(s) (musical); space(s) (typographical); tic-tac-toe (game symbol); zinc (alchemical)
p Philippine peso(s)
% percent
+ plus; north
± plus or minus
£ pound (*libra*) sign—used universally for monetary units such as the Australian, British, Egyptian, Gambian, Ghanian, Irish, Israeli, Jamaican, Lebanese, Libyan, Malawi, New Zealand, Nigerian, South African, Sudanese, Syrian, Turkish, Western Samoan, Zambian pound
£A pound Australian
£E pound Egyptian (United Arab Republic)
£G pound Gambian; pound Ghanian
£I pound Irish; pound Israeli (also shown as I£)
£J pound Jamaican

£L   pound Lebanese; pound Lib-
     yan
£M   pound Malawi
£N   pound Nigerian
£NZ pound New Zealand (also
     shown as NZ£)
£S   pound sterling; pound Suda-
     nese; pound Syrian
£SAf pound South African (also

     shown as SAf)
£/s/d pounds, shillings, and pence
£T   pound Turkish
£WS pound Western Samoan
£Z   pound Zambian
R̂   registered
℞   prescription; receipt; recipe; re-
     sponse; reverse
     shilling mark; slash; solidus;

     virgule
∴   therefore
U   Union of Orthodox Jewish Con-
     gregations of America (symbol
     for kosher product approved for
     detergent or dietary use)
XMA$ (symbol—commercialized
     Christmas)
Y   Japanese yen

STEAMSHIP LINES

A: Ahearn Shipping Ltd; Alaska Steamship Company; Alcoa Steamship Company; American Export Isbrandtsen Lines; American Mail Line; American Oil Company; American Steamships; Tidewater Oil (capital A between red wings); et cetera

ABRT: A/B Rederi Transatlantic (Pacific Australia Direct Line)

AC: African Coasters

ACL: Atlantic Container Line

ACS: American Coal Shipping

ACSC: Australian Coastal Shipping Commission

AD: Armement Dieppe

AE: African Enterprises

AH: Afred Holt (Blue Funnel Line)

AHB: Great Eastern Line

AHL: Associated Humber Lines

Alcoa: Alcoa Steamship Company

ALL: Anchor Line Limited

All America Cables: All America Cables and Radio

AML: American Mail Line

AMOCO: American Oil Company

ANCAP: *Administracion Nacional de Combustibles Alcohol y Portland* (Spanish—National Administration of Flammable Alcohol and Portland Cement) —Uruguay

ANL: Australian National Line

AP: American Pioneer Lines

AP: *Atlantska Plovidba* (Yugoslavian—Atlantic Line)

APL: American President Lines

ASFS: Alaska State Ferry System

ASN: Atlantic Steam Navigation

ASOK: *Angfartigas Svenska Östasiatiske Kompaniet* (Swedish—Swedish East Asiatic Steamship Company)

ATLANTIC: Atlantic Refining Company

Atlantic Container Line: ACL

AUT: American Union Transport

B: Barber Lines; Booth Line; Branch Lines; Bull Steamship Lines; etc.

BAF: Belgian African Line

BCF: British Columbia Ferries

BCL: Bristol City Line

BCSC: British and Continental Steamship Company

BDS: *Bergenske Dampskibsselskab* (Norwegian—Bergen Steamship Line)—connecting Norway and United Kingdom ports

BFL: Belgian Fruit Lines

BHP: Broken Hill Proprietary

BISNC: British India Steam Navigation Company

B&I SPC: British and Irish Steam Packet Company

BL: Bergen Line; Bibby Line; Booth Line; etc.

B&L: Burns and Laird Lines

BLS: Ben Line Steamers

Blue Star: Blue Star Line

BM: British Methane Limited

BMM: Belfast, Mersey and Manchester Steamship Company

BOC: Burmah Oil Company

BOS: British Oil Shipping

BP: British Petroleum

BPC: British Phosphate Commissioners

BP&Co: Burns, Philp and Company

BR: British Railways (operates many ferry steamers linking England and Scotland with Belgium, France, Ireland, and Holland)

BSC: Baltic Steamship Company

BSL: Black Star Line; Blue Sea Line; Blue Star Line; Etc.

BSNC: Bristol Steam Navigation Company

BTC: Bethlehem Transportation Corporation

B&W: Brocklebank and Well Lines

C: Calmar Line (Bethlehem Steel); Caribbean Steamships Company; Clarke Line; Clyde Line; Etc.

"C": Costa Line

CA: *Carregadores Açoreanos* (Portuguese—Azorean Cargo Carri-

ers)

CAVN: *Compañía Anonima Venezolana de Navegación* (Spanish —Venezuelan Navigation Company)—Venezuela Line

CCAL: Christensen Canadian African Line

CC Co: Commercial Cable Company

CCN: *Companhia Colonial de Navegacão* (Portuguese—Colonial Navigation Company)

CEA: Central Electricity Authority

CF: Compagnie de Navigation Fraissinet

CFPO: *Compagnie Française des Phosphates de l'Oceanie* (French —French Phosphate Company of Oceania)

CGL: Canadian Gulf Line

CGS: Central Gulf Steamships

CGT: *Compagnie Générale Transatlantique* (French—General Transatlantic Company— CⁱᵉGˡᵉ Trᵃⁿˢ—the French Line

Chilean Line: (see *CSAV*)

China Merchants Steam Navigation Company: CMSNC

CI: Catalina Island Steamship Line; Christmas Island Phosphate Commission

Cⁱᵉ Gˡᵉ Trᵃⁿˢ: *Compagnie Générale Transatlantique* (French— General Transatlantic Company)—the French Line

Cities Service: Cities Service Oil Company

CL: Ceylon Lines; Coast Lines

Clipper Line: Wisconsin and Michigan Steamship Company

CM: *Compañía Maritima* (Spanish —Maritime Company)

CMB: *Compagnie Maritime Belge* (French—Belgian Maritime Company)—Royal Belgian Lloyd

CMSNC: China Merchants Steam Navigation Company

CMZ: Compagnie Maritime du Zaire

CNC: China Navigation Company

CNP: Compagnie Navigation Paquet (French—Paquet Navigation Company)—Paquet Line

CNS: Canadian National Steamships

COLDEMAR: Compañía Colombiana de Navegación Maritima (Spanish—Colombian Maritime Navigation Company)

Columbus Line: HSDG

CP Ships: Canadian Pacific Steamships (*Empress* vessels)

CPV: Corporación Peruana de Vapores (Spanish—Peruvian Steamship Corporation)

Crusader: Crusader Line

CSAV: Compañía Sud-Americana de Vapores (Spanish—South American Steamship Company)—Chile

CSC: Clyde Shipping Company

CSL: Canada Steamship Lines

CSO: Cities Service Oil

CSSCo: Cunard Steamship Company

CT: Cleveland Tankers

CT: Compania Transmediterranea (Spanish—Transmediterranean Company)

CTE: Compañía Transatlantica Española (Spanish—Spanish Transatlantic Line)—The Spanish Line

CTL: Coastal Transport Limited

Cunard: Cunard Steam-Ship Company, Limited (includes White Star Line)

D: Delta Line; Donaldson Line; Red 'D' Line; etc.

'D': Red 'D' Line (merged with Grace Line)

DAL: Deutsche-Afrika Linien (German—German Affica Line)

d'Amico: d'Amico Line

Day Line: Hudson River Day Line

DBK: Daiichi Bussan Kaisha

D-F: Dansk-Franske (Danish-French Line)

Djakarta Line: DL

DL: Djakarta Line

DPLC: Dundee, Perth and London Shipping Company

DS: Dominion Shipping

D-S: Ditlev-Simonsen, Halfdan and Company

E: American Export Isbrandtsen Lines; Eastern Steamship Line; Exxon Tankers; Hellenic Lines and many Greek lines where the letter E stands for Ellas or Hellas—Greece, or for the last name of an owner as in other lands

EAC: East Asiatic Company

E&B: Ellerman and Bucknall Steamship Company

E&F: Elders and Fyffes Ltd

ELMA: Empresa Lineas Maritimas Argentinas (Spanish—Argentine Maritime Lines)—formerly *FANU* and uses *FANU* house flag

Empress liners: Canadian Pacific ships

Esso: Esso Petroleum Company

F: Fabre Line; Falcon Tankers; Falkland Islands Trading Company; Farrell Lines; Finnlines; etc.

FAA: Finska Angfartygs Aktiebolaget (Finnish—Finnish Steamship Company)—Finland Line

Falline: Federal Atlantic-Lakes Line

FANF: Flota Argentina de Navegación Fluvial (Spanish—Argentine River Navigation Fleet)

FANU: Flota Argentina de Navegación de Ultramar (Spanish—Argentine High-Sea Navigation Fleet)

Far East Steamship Company: FESCO

FCNCo: Federal Commerce and Navigation Company

Fedpac: Federal Pacific Lakes Line

Fedsea: Federal South East Asia Line

FESCO: Far East Steamship Company

Finald Line: (see *FAA*)

FL: Fesco Pacific Line

FMC: Federal Maritime Commission

FMD: Flota Mercante Dominicana (Spanish—Dominican Merchant Fleet)

FMG: Flota Mercante Grancolombiana (Spanish—Great Colombian Merchant Fleet)

French Line: (see *CGT*)

FW: Furness, Withy and Company

FWL: Furness Warren Line

G: Glynafon Shipping; Graig Shipping; Arthur Guiness (the brewer); etc.

GAL: German Atlantic Line

GG: Guinea Gulf Line

GL: Greek Line

GO: Gulf Oil

GPRL: Gulf Puerto Rico Lines

GRACE: Grace Line (Prudential-Grace Lines)

Gran Flota Blanca: (Spanish—Great White Fleet)—United Fruit Company (fleet of white steamships)—United Brands

GSA: Gulf and South American Steamship Company

GULF: Gulf Oil Corporation

GYSCo: Great Yarmouth Shipping Company

H: Hansa Line; Heering Line; Horn Line; etc.

HAL: Holland Amerika Lijn (NASM—Nederlandsch-Amerikaasche Stoomvaart Maatschappij)—NASM appears on house flag

HANSA: Hansa Line

Hanseatic-Vaasa Line: VL

HAPAG: Hamburg-Amerika Paket Aktiengesellschaft (German—Hamburg-America Packet Company)—Hamburg-America Line

Hapag-Lloyd: Hamburg-Amerika—North German Lloyd Lines

HB C: Hudson's Bay Company

HCL: Hamburg-Chicago Line

HFL: Hawaii Freight Lines

HH: H. Hogarth and Sons

HHA: H.H. Andersen Line

HL: Home Lines

HMS: Her (His) Majesty's Ship (as in HMS *Dreadnought*)

hovercraft: marine craft supported by an air cushion instead of a conventional hull

HSAL: Hamburg South American Line

HSDG: Hamburg-Sudamerikanische Dampfs Gesell (Columbus Line)

H&W: Holm and Wonsild

HWAL: Holland West-Afrika Line

I: Incres Line; Interocean Steamship Lines; Isthmian Lines (U.S. Steel); Ivaran Lines; etc.

ICI: Imperial Chemical Industries

ICSN: Indo-China Steam Navigation Company

IFI: Inter-Freight International

INSCO: Intercontinental Shipping Corporation

Inter-Freight International: IFI

IO Ltd: Imperial Oil Ltd

IOM SPC: Isle of Man Steam Packet Company

IOT: Iron Ore Transport

IPL: Ital Pacific Line

Italia: Italian Line

ITI: Inagua Transports Incorporated

J: Japan Line; John I. Jacobs and Company; Johnson Line; etc.

JBPS: Jamaica Banana Producers' Steamship Co

K: Kavolines; Kawasaki Kisen Kaisha; Kerr Lines; Keystone Shipping (Chas Kurz); Kingsport

Shipping; Kirkconnel; Klaveness Line; Knutsen Line; etc.

KG: Koctug Line

KK: Karlander Kangaroo Line

K Line: Kawasaki Kisen Kaisha

KNC: Kingcome Navigation Company

KNSM: Koninklijke Nederlandsche Stoomboot Maatschappij (Dutch —Royal Netherlands Steamship Company)

Koctug Line: KL

KSN: Karachi Steam Navigation Line

L: Lauritzen Line; Luckenbach Line; Lykes Line; etc.

LASH: Lighter Aboard Ship Handling

LB: Lloyd Brasileiro

L + H: Lamport and Holt Line

LL: Lauro Line; Link Line

Lloyd's: Lloyd's Register of Shipping (LRS)

LRS: Lloyd's Register of Shipping

LT: Lloyd Triestino (Italian- —Trieste Line)

M: Maersk Line; Marine Transport Lines; Matson Line; Meyer Line; Montship Lines; Moore-McCormack Lines; Munson Line; etc.

Maersk: Maersk Line

MAMENIC: Marina Mercante Nicaraguense (Spanish—Nicaraguan Merchant Marine)

Maritime Fruit Carriers: MFC

MCP: Maritime Company of the Philippines

MFC: Maritime Fruit Carriers

MILI: Micronesia Interocean Line Incorporated

Milwaukee Clipper: Wisconsin and Michigan Steamship Company

Mitsui: Mitsui OSK Lines

ML: Manchester Liners

M. M: Messageries Maritimes (French—Maritime Mail, Parcel, and Passenger Service)

M/S: Motorship

MS Co: Melbourne Steamship Company

MSTS: Military Sea Transportation Service

MTL: Marine Transport Lines

MV: Motor Vessel

N: Naess Shipping Company; Niarchos Tankers; Nigerian National Line; etc.

NA&G: North Atlantic and Gulf Steamship Company

N-A-L: Norwegian America Line

NASM: (*see* HAL)

NB: Navibel (Belgian Maritime Navigation Company)

NB&C: Norfolk, Baltimore and Carolina Line

NCP : Naviera Chilena del Pacifico (Spanish—Chilean Shipping of the Pacific)

Nedlloyd: Nedlloyd and Hoegh Lines

NEE: New England Express

New England Express: NEE

NMB: Navigation Maritime Bulgare (Bulgarian Maritime Navigation)

NNC: Northern Navigation Company

NOL: Norse Oriental Lines

NPCL: North Pacific Coast Line

NTGB: North Thames Gas Board

NYK Line: Nippon Yusen Kaisha

NZSCo: New Zealand Shipping Company

O: Ocean Carriers; Olsen Line; M.J. Osorio; etc.

Official Steamship Guide International: OSGI

OG: O. Gross and Sons Ltd.

ØK: Østasiatiske Kompagni (Danish—East Asiatic Company) —EAL

Olympic: Olympic Steamship Company

OO: Orient Overseas Line

OSGI: Official Steamship Guide International

OSK: Osaka Syosen Kaisha (Osaka Mercantile Steamship Company)—Mitsui Lines

OW: Olof Wallenius Line

P: Panama Line (Panama Canal Company); Pocahontas Steamships; Prudential-Grace Lines; Pure Oil; etc.

P-A: Pan-Atlantic Steamship Corporation

PACE: Pacific America Container Express

Pacific America Container Express: PACE

Pacific Australia Direct Line: (*see* ABRT)

Petrobras: Petroleo Brasileiro (Portuguese—Brazilian Petroleum)

PFEL: Pacific Far East Line

P-G: Prudential Grace Lines

PITL: Pacific Islands Transport Line (Thor Dahls Hvalfangerselskap)

PL: Polynesia Line; Port Line; Poseidon Lines; Prince Line

PLA: Port of London Authority

PLL: Prince Line Limited

PLO: Polskie Linie Oceaniczne

(Polish—Polish Line)

PM: Petroleos Mexicanos (Spanish —Mexican Petroleum)

PNL: Philippine National Lines

P&O: Penisular and Occidental Steamship Company; Peninsular and Oriental Line

POE: Pacific Orient Express Line

PPL: Philippine President Lines

Princess Line: Gothenburg-Frederikshavn Line

PSC: Point Shipping Company

PSFL: Puget Sound Freight Lines

PSNC: Pacific Steam Navigation Company

PT: Pope and Talbot

PURE: Pure Oil Company

Q: Qatar Petroleum; Quaker Line; Queensland; Quintessence Navigation; etc.

Q&O: Quebec and Ontario Transportation

R: Rasmussen; Richfield Oil; Ringdal; Robbert; etc.

RIL: Royal Interocean Lines [(*Koninklijke Java-China-Paketvaart Lijnen*—(Dutch—Royal Java-China-Packet Line)]

RL: Regent's Line (Grand Union Shipping)

RLR: Royal Rotterdam Lloyd

RML: Royal Mail Lines

Royal Netherlands Steamship Line: (see *KNSM*)

S: Saguenay Terminals Ltd; Salen; Seatrain Lines; Sinclair Refining; Socony Mobil Oil; Standard Oil of California; States Marine Lines; States Line (seahorse-shaped red-letter S); Sun Oil; Svea Line; etc.

SA&CL: South Atlantic and Caribbean Line

Safmarine: South African Marine Corporation

SAL: Svenska Amerika Linien (Swedish-America Line)

Santa ships: Prudential-Grace Line vessels

SC: Submarine Cables Ltd

S&C: Star and Crescent

SCC: Shipping and Coal Company

SCI: Sea Containers Incorporated; Shipping Corporation of India

Scindia: Scindia Steam Navigation

SEGB: South Eastern Gas Board

Shell: Shell Tankers

Shipping Corporation of India: SCI

SL: Southern Lines

SLS: Sea-Land Service

SML: States Marine Lines

SOPONATA: Sociedade Portuguesa de Navios Tanques Limitada (Portuguese—Portuguese Tankships Limited)

Sovtorgflot: Soviet Merchant Marine Fleet

Spanish Line: Compañía Transatlantica Española

SS: Steamship (as in SS *Santa Clara*)

STANVAC: Standard-Vacuum Oil Company

STL: Seatrain Lines

SUNOCO: Sun Oil Company

T: Tankers Limited; Texaco (The Texas Company); Thai Mercantile Marine; Thompson Shipping; Thoren Line; Tirrenia; Transatlantic Line; etc.

TCL: Transatlantic Carriers Limited

TCR: Texas City Refining

Texaco: The Texas Company

TH: Thorvald Hansen

Thor Dahls Havalfangerselskap: Pacific Islands Transport Line

TMM: Transportación Maritima Méxicana

Transamerica Trailer Transport: TTT

TS: Tasmanian Steamers

TTT: Transamerica Trailer Transport

U: Union Oil; United Oriental Steamship Company; Universe Tankships; etc.

UA: United Africa Company, Ltd

UBC: United Baltic Corporation

UBL: Union Barge Line

UCMS: Union-Castle Mail Steamship

UFC: United Fruit Company

UIL: Ulster Imperial Line

U.O. Co.: Union Oil Company of California

UPL: United Philippine Lines

USC: Union Steamship Company

USL: United States Lines

USMSTS: U.S. Military Sea Transport Service

USS: United States Ship (as in USS *Constitution*)

USSCo: Ulster Steam Ship Company; Union Steam Ship Company

UT: United Transports

UYL: United Yugoslav Lines

V: Vaccaro Line (Standard Fruit); Valentine Chemical Carriers; Vinke Tankers; Von Sydow; Vulcan Shipping; etc.

VA: *Compañía de Navegación Vasco-Asturiana* (Spanish—Basque -Asturian Navigation Company)

VC: Victory Carriers

VL: Vaasa Line (Hanseatic-Vaasa Line)

VLC: Valley Line Company

VNGC: Van Niervelt, Goudriaan and Company (Rotterdam —South American Line)

VW: Volkswagen (auto-carrier ships)

W: Waterman Steamship Lines; West Line; Westriver Ore Transports; Weyerhaeuser Line; etc.

W&A: Wiel and Amundsen

Wallenius Line: OW (Olof Wallenius)

WHMV & NSSA: Woods Hole,

Martha's Vineyard and Natucket Steamship Authority

WIL: West India Lines

WIT: West India Tankers

WL: Westfal-Larsen Line

W&L: Westcott and Laurance Line (Ellerman's)

WL&Co: Westfal-Larsen and Company

W&M SS Co: Wisonsin and Michigan Steamship Company (The Clipper Line)

WSFS: Washington State Ferry System

WTC: Western Transportation Company

X: (funnel marking—Chandris America Lines; Southern Cross Steamship Line); Xenophon Navigation Company; etc.

X: (funnel marking—Chandris America Lines; Southern Cross Steamship Line); etc.

Y: Yamashita-Shinnihon Kisen Line; Ybarra Lines; Yukiteru Kaiun; Yung Yang Shipping; etc.

YPF: *Yacimientos Petroliferos Fiscales* (Spanish—Fiscal Petroleum Deposits)—Argentine tanker fleet

Y-S Line: Yamashita-Shinnihon Line

Z: Zacharissen; Zante Navegación; Zillah Shipping; Zim Israel Navigation; Zurga Shipping Company; Etc.

Zim: Zim Israel Line

ZPL: Zim Passenger Line

ZSC: Zeeland Steamship Company

U.S. NAVAL SHIP SYMBOLS

AD: Destroyer Tender

ADG: Degaussing Ship

AE: Ammunition Ship

AF: Store Ship

AFDB: Large Auxiliary Floating Dry Dock (non-self-propelled)

AFDL: Small Auxiliary Floating Dry Dock (non-self-propelled)

AFDM: Medium Auxiliary Floating Dry Dock (non-self-propelled)

AFS: Combat Store Ship

AG: Miscellaneous

AGDE: Escort Research Ship

AGEH: Hydrofoil Research Ship

AGER: Environmental Research Ship

AGF: Miscellaneous Command Ship

AGM: Missile Range Instrumenta-tion Ship

AGMR: Major Communications Relay Ship

AGOR: Oceanographic Research Ship

AGP: Patrol Craft Tender

AGR: Radar Picket Ship

AGS: Surveying Ship

AGSS: Auxiliary Submarine

AGTR: Technical Research Ship

AH: Hospital Ship

AK: Cargo Ship

AKD: Cargo Ship, Dock

AKL: Light Cargo Ship

AKR: Vehicle Cargo Ship

AKS: Stores Issue Ship

AKV: Cargo Ship and Aircraft Ferry

ANL: Net Laying Ship

AO: Oiler

AOE: Fast Combat Support Ship

AOG: Gasoline Tanker

AOR: Replenishment Oiler

AP: Transport

APB: Self-propelled Barracks Ship

APL: Barracks Craft (non-self-propelled)

AR: Repair Ship

ARB: Battle Damage Repair Ship

ARC: Cable Repairing Ship

ARD: Auxiliary Repair Dry Dock (non-self-propelled)

ARDM: Medium Auxiliary Repair Dry Dock (non-self-propelled)

ARG: Internal Combustion Engine Repair Ship

ARL: Landing Craft Repair Ship

ARS: Salvage Ship

ARSD: Salvage Lifting Ship
ARST: Salvage Craft Tender
ARVA: Aircraft Repair Ship (aircraft)
ARVE: Aircraft Repair Ship (engine)
ARVH: Aircraft Repair Ship (helicopter)
AS: Submarine Tender
ASPB: Assault Support Patrol Boat
ASR: Submarine Rescue Ship
ATA: Auxiliary Ocean Tug
ATC: Armored Troop Carrier
ATF: Fleet Ocean Tug
ATS: Salvage Tug
ATSS: Auxiliary Training Submarine
AV: Seaplane Tender
AVM: Guided Missile Ship
AVS: Aviation Supply Ship
AVT: Auxiliary Aircraft Transport
AW: Distilling Ship
BB: Battleship
CA: Heavy Cruiser
CC: Command Ship
CCB: Command and Control Boat
CG: Guided Missile Cruiser
CGN: Guided Missile Cruiser (nuclear propulsion)
CL: Light Cruiser
CLG: Guided Missile Light Cruiser
CVA: Attack Aircraft Carrier
CVAN: Attack Aircraft Carrier (nuclear propulsion)
CVS: ASW Support Aircraft Carrier
CVT: Training Aircraft Carrier
DD: Destroyer
DDG: Guided Missile Destroyer
DE: Escort Ship
DEG: Guided Missile Escort Ship
DER: Radar Picket Escort Ship
DL: Frigate
DLG: Guided Missile Frigate
DLGN: Guided Missile Frigate (nuclear propulsion)
DSRV: Deep Submergence Rescue Vessel
DSV: Deep Submergence Vehicle
E: (Prefix) Experimental Ship
F: (Prefix) Ship being built by U.S. for a foreign nation
FDL: Fast Deployment Logistics Ship
IX: Unclassified Miscellaneous
LCA: Landing Craft, Assault
LCC: Amphibious Command Ship
LCM: Landing Craft, Mechanized
LCPL: Landing Craft, Personnel, Large
LCPR: Landing Craft, Personnel, Ramped
LCSR: Landing Craft Swimmer Reconnaissance

LCU: Landing Craft, Utility
LCVP: Landing Craft, Vehicle, Personnel
LFR: Inshore Fire Support Ship
LFS: Amphibious Fire Support Ship
LHA: Amphibious Assault Ship (general purpose)
LKA: Amphibious Cargo Ship
LPA: Amphibious Transport
LPD: Amphibious Transport Dock
LPH: Amphibious Assault Ship
LPR: Amphibious Transport (small)
LPSS: Amphibious Transport Submarine
LSD: Dock Landing Ship
LSSC: Light SEAL Support Craft
LST: Tank Landing Ship
LWT: Amphibious Warping Tug
MAC: MIUW Attack Craft
MCS: Mine Countermeasures Ship
MON: Monitor
MSB: Minesweeping Boat
MSC: Minesweeper, Coastal (nonmagnetic)
MSD: Minesweeper, Drone
MSF: Minesweeper, Fleet (steel hull)
MSI: Minesweeper, Inshore
MSL: Minesweeping Launch
MSM: Minesweeper, River (Converted LCM-6)
MSO: Minesweeper, Ocean (nonmagnetic)
MSR: Minesweeper, Patrol
MSS: Minesweeper, Special (device)
MSSC: Medium SEAL Support Craft
NR: Submersible Research Vehicle (nuclear propulsion)
PBR: River Patrol Boat
PCE: Patrol Escort
PCER: Patrol Rescue Escort
PCF: Patrol Craft, Inshore
PCH: Patrol Craft (hydrofoil)
PG: Patrol Gunboat
PGH: Patrol Gunboat (hydrofoil)
PTF: Fast Patrol Craft
QFB: Quiet Fast Boat
RUC: Riverine Utility Craft
SDV: Swimmer Delivery Vehicle
SES: Surface-Effect Ship
SS: Submarine
SSBN: Fleet Ballistic Missile Submarine (nuclear propulsion)
SSG: Guided Missile Submarine
SSN: Submarine (nuclear propulsion)
SST: Target and Training Submarine (self-propelled)
STAB: Strike Assault Boat
T: (Prefix) Military Sealift Command Ship
W: (Prefix) U.S. Coast Guard Ship
X: Submersible Craft (self-propelled)
YAG: Miscellaneous Auxiliary (self-propelled)
YC: Open Lighter (non-self-propelled)
YCF: Car Float (non-self-propelled)
YCV: Aircraft Transportation Lighter (non-self-propelled)
YD: Floating Crane (non-self-propelled)
YDT: Diving Tender (non-self-propelled)
YF: Covered Lighter (self-propelled)
YFB: Ferryboat or Launch (self-propelled)
YFD: Yard Floating Dry Dock (non-self-propelled)
YFN: Covered Lighter (non-self-propelled)
YFNB: Large Covered Lighter (non-self-propelled)
YFND: Dry Dock Companion Craft (non-self-propelled)
YFNX: Lighter (special purpose) (non-self-propelled)
YFP: Floating Power Barge (non-self-propelled)
YFR: Refrigerated Covered Lighter (self-propelled)
YFRN: Refrigerated Covered Lighter (non-self-propelled)
YFRT: Covered Lighter (range-tender) (self-propelled)
YFU: Harbor Utility Craft (self-propelled)
YG: Garbage Lighter (self-propelled)
YGN: Garbage Lighter (non-self-propelled)
YHLC: Salvage Lift Craft, Heavy (non-self-propelled)
YLLC: Salvage Lift Craft, Light (self-propelled)
YM: Dredge (self-propelled)
YMLC: Salvage Lift Craft, Medium (non-self-propelled)
YNG: Gate Craft (non-self-propelled)
YO: Fuel Oil Barge (self-propelled)
YOG: Gasoline Barge (self-propelled)
YOGN: Gasoline Barge (non-self-propelled)
YON: Fuel Oil Barge (non-self-propelled)
YOS: Oil Storage Barge (non-self-propelled)
YP: Patrol Craft (self-propelled)
YPD: Floating Pile Driver (non-

self-propelled)

YR: Floating Workshop (non-self-propelled)

YRB: Repair and Berthing Barge (non-self-propelled)

YRBM: Repair, Berthing and Messing Barge (non-self-propelled)

YRDH: Floating Dry Dock Workshop (hull) (non-self-propelled)

YRDM: Floating Dry Dock Workshop (machine) (non-self-propelled)

YRR: Radiological Repair Barge (non-self-propelled)

YRST: Salvage Craft Tender (non-self-propelled)

YSD: Seaplane Wrecking Derrick (self-propelled)

YSR: Sludge Removal Barge (non-self-propelled)

YTB: Large Harbor Tug (self-propelled)

YTL: Small Harbor Tug (self-propelled)

YTM: Medium Harbor Tug (self-propelled)

YW: Water Barge (self-propelled)

YWDN: Water Distilling Barge (non-self-propelled)

YWN: Water Barge (non-self-propelled)

WEATHER SYMBOLS: BEAUFORT SCALE

WITH CORRESPONDING SEA STATE CODES

Beaufort number	Wind speed — knots	mph	meters per second	km per hour	Seaman's term	U.S. Weather Bureau term	Estimating wind speed — Effects observed at sea	Effects observed on land	Hydrographic Office — Term and height of waves, in feet	Code	International — Term and height of waves, in feet	Code
0	under 1	under 1	0.0–0.2	under 1	Calm		Sea like mirror.	Calm; smoke rises vertically.	Calm, 0	0	Calm, glassy, 0	0
1	1–3	1–3	0.3–1.5	1–5	Light air	Light	Ripples with appearance of scales; no foam crests.	Smoke drift indicates wind direction; vanes do not move.	Smooth, less than 1	1	Rippled, 0–1	1
2	4–6	4–7	1.6–3.3	6–11	Light breeze	Light	Small wavelets; crests of glassy appearance, not breaking.	Wind felt on face; leaves rustle; vanes begin to move.	Slight, 1–3	2	Smooth, 1–2	2
3	7–10	8–12	3.4–5.4	12–19	Gentle breeze	Gentle	Large wavelets; crests begin to break; scattered whitecaps.	Leaves, small twigs in constant motion; light flags extended.	Moderate, 3–5	3	Slight, 2–4	3
4	11–16	13–18	5.5–7.9	20–28	Moderate breeze	Moderate	Small waves, becoming longer; numerous whitecaps.	Dust, leaves, and loose paper raised up; small branches move.	Rough, 5–8	4	Moderate, 4–8	4
5	17–21	19–24	8.0–10.7	29–38	Fresh breeze	Fresh	Moderate waves, taking longer form; many whitecaps; some spray.	Small trees in leaf begin to sway.			Rough, 8–13	5
6	22–27	25–31	10.8–13.8	39–49	Strong breeze	Strong	Larger waves forming; whitecaps everywhere; more spray.	Larger branches of trees in motion; whistling heard in wires.	Very rough, 8–12	5	Very rough, 13–20	6
7	28–33	32–38	13.9–17.1	50–61	Moderate gale	Strong	Sea heaps up; white foam from breaking waves begins to be blown in streaks.	Whole trees in motion; resistance felt in walking against wind.				
8	34–40	39–46	17.2–20.7	62–74	Fresh gale	Gale	Moderately high waves of greater length; edges of crests begin to break into spindrift; foam is blown in well-marked streaks.	Twigs and small branches broken off trees; progress generally impeded.	High, 12–20	6	High, 20–30	7
9	41–47	47–54	20.8–24.4	75–88	Strong gale	Gale	High waves; sea begins to roll; dense streaks of foam; spray may reduce visibility.	Slight structural damage occurs; slate blown from roofs.				
10	48–55	55–63	24.5–28.4	89–102	Whole gale	Whole gale	Very high waves with overhanging crests; sea takes white appearance as foam is blown in very dense streaks; rolling is heavy and visibility reduced.	Seldom experienced on land; trees broken or uprooted; considerable structural damage occurs.	Very high, 20–40	7	Very high, 30–45	8
11	56–63	64–72	28.5–32.6	103–117	Storm	Whole gale	Exceptionally high waves; sea covered with white foam patches; visibility still more reduced.	Very rarely experienced on land; usually accompanied by widespread damage.	Mountainous, 40 and higher	8		
12	64–71	73–82	32.7–36.9	118–133	Hurricane	Hurricane	Air filled with foam; sea completely white with driving spray; visibility greatly reduced.		Confused	9	Phenomenal, over 45	9
13	72–80	83–92	37.0–41.4	134–149								
14	81–89	93–103	41.5–46.1	150–166								
15	90–99	104–114	46.2–50.9	167–183								
16	100–108	115–125	51.0–56.0	184–201								
17	109–118	126–136	56.1–61.2	202–220								

Note: Since January 1, 1955, weather map symbols have been based upon wind speed in knots, at five-knot intervals, rather than upon Beaufort number.

ZODIACAL SIGNS

♒ : Aquarius (The Water Carrier), eleventh sign of the zodiac, symbolized by two parallel water waves; sun enters this period on January 20

♈ : Aries (The Ram), first sign of the zodiac, symbolized by the ram's horns; the sun enters this period on March 21, marking the spring or vernal equinox

♋ : Cancer (The Crab), fourth sign of the zodiac, symbolized by overlapping crab claws; sun enters this period June 22, marking the summer solstice, the longest day in the year

♑ : Capricornus (The Goat), tenth sign of the zodiac; symbol taken from *tr* of *tragos*, Greek for goat; sun enters Capricorn on December 22, marking the winter solstice, the shortest day in the year

♊ : Gemini (The Twins), third sign of the zodiac, symbolized by wooden statues of Castor and Pollux coupled by horizontal lintels; sun enters this period May 21

♌ : Leo (The Lion), fifth sign of the zodiac, symbolized by stylized figure representing the lion's tufted tail; sun enters this period on July 23

♎ : Libra (The Balance), seventh sign of the zodiac, symbolized by a stylized balance; sun enters this period on September 23, marking the autumnal equinox

♓ : Pisces (The Fishes), twelfth sign of the zodiac; symbolized by two fishes tied by a thong; sun enters this period on February 19

♐ : Sagittarius (The Archer), ninth sign of the zodiac; symbolized by archer's bow and arrow; sun enters this period on November 22

♏ : Scorpio (The Scorpion), eighth sign of the zodiac, symbolized by stylized representation of legs and stinger tail of the scorpion; sun enters this period on October 24

♉ : Taurus (The Bull), second sign of the zodiac, symbolized by the bull's head and horns; sun enters this period April 20

♍ : Virgo (The Virgin), sixth sign of the zodiac; symbol taken from *par* in *parthenos*, Greek for virgin; sun enters Virgo on August 23